"This is the most comprehensive, up-to-date compendium in the psychology of sport and exercise. Covering an array of topics from emotional experience to motor control, this volume is more than a just a reference, it's a source of inspiration to researchers and practitioners."
– *Richard M. Ryan, Institute for Positive Psychology and Education, Australian Catholic University, North Sydney, Australia*

"*The Routledge International Encyclopedia of Sport and Exercise Psychology* is a much-needed encyclopedia in the field of sport and exercise psychology. Most importantly, it has the hallmark of global authorities in this field. Their scholarly description of over 90 key topics will provide enormous assistance to lecturers and newcomers in the fields of psychology and sport sciences all over the world. Another monumental contribution to the field of sport and exercise psychology by Dieter Hackfort, Robert Schinke, and the International Society of Sport Psychology."
– *Athanasios Papaioannou, University of Thessaly, Greece*

THE ROUTLEDGE INTERNATIONAL ENCYCLOPEDIA OF SPORT AND EXERCISE PSYCHOLOGY

The Routledge International Encyclopedia of Sport and Exercise Psychology integrates the topics of motor control, physical education, exercise, adventure, performance in sports, and the performing arts, in several important ways and contexts, drawing upon diverse cultural perspectives. More than 90 overarching topics have been systematically developed by internationally renowned experts in theory, research, and practice.

Each contribution delves into a thematic area with more nuanced vocabulary. The terminology drawn upon integrates traditional discourse and emerging topic matter into a state-of-the-art two-volume set. *Volume 1: Theoretical and Methodological Concepts* is comprised of theoretical topic matter, spanning theories and terminology from psychology contextualized to sport and physical activity, sport psychology-focused theories, and expansive discussions related to philosophy of science and methodology. *Volume 2: Applied and Practical Measures* draws upon practical concepts that bridge theory and research and practice. Broader issues that extend beyond sport and physical activity participants are embedded within the entries, intended to augment physical, mental, and social well-being.

This expansive encyclopedia is a must-have resource for all professionals, scholars, and students in the fields of sport psychology and sport science.

Dieter Hackfort is a retired professor of sport psychology. In his career he held professorships at the Center for Behavioral Medicine and Health Psychology at the University of South Florida, USA, the Institutes for Sport Science at the Universities in Heidelberg and Munich, Germany, and Qatar University in Doha, as well as an Honorary Professorship and a Guest Professorship at the Hubei University in Wuhan, China. Dr. Hackfort is former President of the German Association of Sport Psychology (ASP) and the International Society of Sport Psychology (ISSP). He also serves as a consultant for Olympic athletes, athletes in x-treme/adventurous sport activities, and professional athletes, including drivers in F1 and further motor sports.

Robert J. Schinke is President for the International Society of Sport Psychology (ISSP) and a Past President of the Association for Applied Sport Psychology (AASP). Robert is a Full Professor and the Canada Research Chair of Multicultural Sport and Physical Activity at Laurentian University, in Canada, and a Distinguished Honorary Professor at Tsing Hua University, in Taiwan. Robert has worked extensively with world champion professional boxers featured on major television networks, consults also with an assortment of professional sport athletes across disciplines, and has served as Mental Training Consultant with several Canadian male and female national teams each Olympic cycle since 1996.

INTERNATIONAL PERSPECTIVES ON KEY ISSUES IN SPORT AND EXERCISE PSYCHOLOGY

Series Editors: Robert J. Schinke, Thomas Schack, and Athanasios Papaioannou

International Perspectives on Key Issues in Sport and Exercise Psychology is a series of edited books published in partnership with the International Society of Sport Psychology. Each title reflects cutting edge research in the psychological study of high level sport, written by key researchers and leading figures in the field of sports psychology.

Books in this series:

Athletes' Careers across Cultures
Edited by Natalia B. Stambulova and Tatiana V. Ryba

Routledge Companion to Sport and Exercise Psychology: Global Perspectives and Fundamental Concepts
Edited by Athanasios Papaioannou and Dieter Hackfort

The Psychology of Sub-Culture in Sport and Physical Activity: Critical Perspectives
Edited by Robert J. Schinke and Kerry R. McGannon

Psychology in Professional Sports and the Performing Arts: Challenges and Strategies
Edited by Robert J. Schinke and Dieter Hackfort

Encyclopedia of Sport and Exercise Psychology: Volume 1: Theoretical and Methodological Concepts
Edited by Dieter Hackfort and Robert J. Schinke

Encyclopedia of Sport and Exercise Psychology: Volume 2: Applied and Practical Measures
Edited by Dieter Hackfort and Robert J. Schinke

THE ROUTLEDGE INTERNATIONAL ENCYCLOPEDIA OF SPORT AND EXERCISE PSYCHOLOGY

Volume 1: Theoretical and Methodological Concepts

Edited by Dieter Hackfort and Robert J. Schinke

International Society of Sport Psychology

Routledge
Taylor & Francis Group

LONDON AND NEW YORK

First published 2020
by Routledge
2 Park Square, Milton Park, Abingdon, Oxon OX14 4RN

and by Routledge
52 Vanderbilt Avenue, New York, NY 10017

Routledge is an imprint of the Taylor & Francis Group, an informa business

British Library Cataloguing-in-Publication Data
A catalogue record for this book is available from the British Library

Library of Congress Cataloging-in-Publication Data
A catalog record has been requested for this book

ISBN: 978-1-138-73441-8 (hbk)
ISBN: 978-1-315-18725-9 (ebk)

Typeset in Futura
by Swales & Willis, Exeter, Devon, UK

VOLUME 1 CONTENTS

VOLUME 2 CONTENTS

VOLUME 1: THEORETICAL AND METHODOLOGICAL CONCEPTS: BOARD OF EXPERTS

VOLUME 2: APPLIED AND PRACTICAL MEASURES: BOARD OF EXPERTS

Psychology of Sports – Intervention and Training
Gangyan Si, *Hong Kong Sports Institute, Hong Kong, China*
Joaquin Dosil, *Presidente Libredon, University of Vigo, Spain*

Exercise and Health Psychology
Yu'Kai Chang, *Department of Physical Education, National Taiwan Normal University, Taipei*
Young Ho Kim, *Department of Sport Sciences, Seoul National University of Science and Technology, Seoul, South Korea*

Talent, Career Development and Transitions
Natalia Stambulova, *School of Health and Welfare, Halmstad University, Sweden*
Kristoffer Henriksen, *Institute of Sport Science and Clinical Biomechanics, University of Southern Denmark, Odense, Denmark*

Education – Physical Education and Coaching
Cliff Mallett, *School of Human Movement and Nutrition Sciences, University of Queensland, Australia*

Mental Health and Clinical Issues in Sport Psychology
William Parham, *School of Education, Loyola Marymount University, Los Angeles, USA*

Neuro-cognitive Sport Psychology: Brain and Sport Performance
Ernest Tsung-Min Hung, *Department of Physical Education, National Taiwan Normal University*
Thomas Schack, *Faculty of Psychology and Sport Sciences, Bielefeld University, Germany*

Performance Issues
Ronnie Lidor, *The Academic College at Wingate, Wingate Institute, Wingate, Israel*

Professional Development, Practice, and Ethical Issues
Robert J. Schinke, *School of Human Kinetics, Laurentian University, Canada*
Dieter Hackfort, *Faculty of Human Sciences, University AF Munich, Germany*

FIGURES

TABLES

CONTRIBUTORS

Brandon L. Alderman
Department of Kinesiology and Health
The State University of New Jersey
Rutgers, NJ, USA

Danielle Alexander
Department of Kinesiology & Physical
   Education
McGill University
Montreal, Canada

Veronica Allan
School of Kinesiology and Health
   Studies
Queen's University
Canada

Duarte Araújo
Department of Sport and Health
University of Lisbon
Lisbon, Portugal

Christopher J. Armitage
Manchester Biomedical Research
   Centre
The University of Manchester
Manchester, UK

Atur V. Aturakhia
La Jolla Village
San Diego, CA, USA

Mitja D. Back
Department of Psychology
University of Münster
Münster, Germany

Joseph Baker
School of Kinesiology and Health Science
York University
Toronto, Canada

Lee Baldock
Faculty of Life Sciences
University of South Wales
Pontypridd, Wales, UK

Soledad Ballesteros Jimenez
Department of Basic Psychology II
Universidad Nacional de Educación
   a Distancia,
Madrid, Spain

Michael Bar-Eli
Department of Business Administration
Ben-Gurion University of the Negev
Beersheba, Israel

Jamie B. Barker
Centre for Sport, Health and Exercise
   Research
Loughborough University
Loughborough, UK

Vassilis Barkoukis
Department of Physical Education & Sport
    Sciences
Aristotle University of Thessaloniki
Thessaloniki, Greece

Patrick Belling
Mamba Sports Academy Venture Lab
Thousand Oaks, CA, USA

Alex J. Benson
School of Psychology
Western University
London, Canada

Marte Bentzen
Department of Physical Education
Norwegian School of Sport Sciences
Oslo, Norway

Nikita Bhavsar
School of Psychology
Curtin University
Perth, Australia

Amy T. Blodgett
School of Human Kinetics
Laurentian University
Sudbury, Canada

Gordon Bloom
Department of Kinesiology & Physical Education
McGill University
Montreal, Canada

Anthony J. Bocchine
Department of Kinesiology and Health
The State University of New Jersey
Rutgers, USA

Matt W. Boulter
Institute for the Psychology of Elite
    Performance
Bangor University
Bangor, Wales, UK

Christopher J. Brush
Department of Kinesiology and Health

The State University of New Jersey
Rutgers, NJ, USA

Robert Brustad
School of Sport and Exercise Science
University of Northern Colorado
Greeley, CO, USA

Timothy J. H. Budden
School of Human Sciences
The University of Western Australia
Perth, Australia

Suzanna Burton-Wylie
Department of Sport and Exercise Science
University of Portsmouth
Portsmouth, UK

Joanne Butt
Centre for Sport and Exercise Science
Sheffield Hallam University
Sheffield, UK

Massimiliano L. Cappuccio
School of Engineering and information
    Technology
University of New South Wales
Canberra, Australia

Sarah Castillo
Department of Psychology
National University
Carlsbad, CA, USA

Yu-Kai Chang
Department of Physical Education
National Taiwan Normal University
Taipei, Republic of China (Taiwan)

Nikos Chatzisarantis
School of Psychology
Curtin University
Perth, Australia

Feng-Tzu Chen
Department of Physical Education
National Taiwan Normal University
Taipei, Republic of China (Taiwan)

Ming-Yang Cheng
School of Psychology
University of Sport
Shanghai, China

Andrea Chirico
Faculty of Medicine and Psychology
Sapienza University of Rome
Rome, Italy

Stiliani "Ani" Chroni
Faculty of Social and Health Sciences
University of Applied Sciences
Elverum, Norway

Emma Conyers-Elliff
School for Science, Technology and
  Engineering
University of Suffolk
Ipswich, UK

Jean Côté
School of Kinesiology and Health Studies
Queen's University
Kingston, Canada

Stewart Cotterill
School of Psychology, Sport and Physical
  Activity
AECC University College
Bournemouth, UK

Tristan J. Coulter
School of Exercise and Nutrition Sciences
Queensland University of Technology
Brisbane, Australia

Ian Cowburn
Carnegie School of Sport
Leeds Beckett University
Leeds, UK

Anne E. Cox
Department of Educational Leadership, Sport
  Studies, and Educational/Counseling
  Psychology
Washington State University
Pullman, WA, USA

Brendan Cropley
Faculty of Life Sciences and Education
University of South Wales
Pontypridd, Wales, UK

Thomas Curran
Department of Psychological and Behavioural
  Sciences
London School of Economics and Political
  Science
London, UK

Koen De Brandt
Faculty of Physical Education and Physiotherapy
Vrije Universiteit Brussel
Brussels, Belgium

Paul De Knop
Faculty of Physical Education and
  Physiotherapy
Vrije Universiteit Brussel
Brussels, Belgium

James A. Dimmock
Department of Psychology
James Cook University
Townsville, Australia

Tracy C. Donachie
School of Sport
York St John University
York, UK

Mark G. Epp
College of Kinesiology
University of Saskatchewan
Saskatoon, Canada

Kai Essig
Faculty of Communication and Environment
Applied University Rhein-Waal
Kamp-Lintfort, Germany

M. Blair Evans
Department of Kinesiology
Pennsylvania State University
Stage College, PA, USA

Kirsten J. Fasey
Department of Sport Science
Nottingham Trent University
Nottingham, UK

Edson Filho
School of Psychology
University of Central Lancashire
Preston, UK

Cornelia Frank
Faculty of Psychology and Sports Science
Bielefeld University
Bielefeld, Germany

David W. Franklin
Department of Sport and Health Sciences
Technical University of Munich
Munich, Germany

Katrien Fransen
Department of Movement Sciences
University of Leuven
Leuven, Belgium

Katharina Geukes
Department of Psychology
University of Münster
Münster, Germany

Cole Giffin
Human Studies Program
Laurentian University
Sudbury, Canada

Diane L. Gill
Department of Kinesiology
University of North Carolina at
    Greensboro
Greensboro, USA

Daniel Gould
Institute for the Study of Youth Sports
Michigan State University
East Lansing, MI, USA

Scott A. Graupensperger
Department of Kinesiology

Pennsylvania State University
Stage College, PA, USA

Iain Greenlees
Institute of Sport
University of Chichester
Chichester, UK

Mathew Grey
Faculty of Health and Behavioural Sciences
The University of Queensland
Brisbane, Australia

Katie E. Gunnell
Carleton University
Ottawa, Canada

Dieter Hackfort
Faculty of Human Sciences
University AF Munich
Munich, Germany

John Elvis Hagan Jr.
Department of Health, Physical Education &
    Recreation
University of Cape Coast
Cape Coast, Ghana

Stephanie J. Hanrahan
School of Psychology
The University of Queensland
Brisbane, Australia

James Hardy
Institute for the Psychology of Elite Performance
School of Sport Health and Exercise Sciences
Bangor University
Bangor, Wales, UK

Michael A. Hemphill
Department of Kinesiology
University of North Carolina at Greensboro
Greensboro, NC, USA

Kristoffer Henriksen
Institute of Sport Science and Clinical
    Biomechanics
University of Southern Denmark
Odense, Denmark

Juan González Hernández
University of Granada
Granada, Spain

Andrew P. Hill
School of Sport
York St John University
York, UK

Nicola J. Hodges
School of Kinesiology
University of British Columbia
Vancouver, BC, Canada

Paul S. Holmes
Research Centre for Musculoskeletal Science
    and Sports Medicine
Manchester Metropolitan University
Manchester, UK

Nicholas L. Holt
Faculty of Kinesiology
Sport, and Recreation
University of Alberta
Edmonton, Canada

Ernst-Joachim Hossner
Institute of Sport Science
University of Bern
Bern, Switzerland

Tsung-Min Hung
Department of Physical Education
National Taiwan Normal
    University
Taipei, Taiwan

Jasmin Hutchinson
Department of Exercise Science and Athletic
    Training
Springfield College
Springfield, MA, USA

Jesús Ilundáin-Agurruza
Department of Philosophy
Linfield College
McMinnville, OR, USA

Ben Jackson
School of Human Sciences
The University of Western Australia
Perth, Australia

Helene Jørgensen
Faculty of Kinesiology, Sport, and Recreation
University of Alberta
Edmonton, Canada

Sophia Jowett
School of Sport, Exercise and Health Sciences
Loughborough University
Loughborough, UK

Anna Kavoura
Faculty of Sport and Health Sciences
University of Jyväskylä
Jyväskylä, Finland

Richard Keegan
Sport and Exercise Sciences
University of Canberra
Canberra, Australia

Göran Kenttä
Department of Sport and Health Sciences
Swedish School of Sport and Health Sciences
Stockholm, Sweden

Youngho Kim
Department of Sport Sciences
Seoul National University of Science and
    Technology
Seoul, South Korea

Nicola Kime
Bradford Institute for Health Research
Bradford Teaching Hospitals NHS Trust
Bradford, UK

Jens Kleinert
Institute of Psychology
German Sport University Cologne
Cologne, Germany

York-Peter Klöppel
Athlete Performance Center

Red Bull Salzburg
Thalgau, Austria

Camilla Knight
College of Engineering
Swansea University
Swansea, Wales, UK

Dirk Koester
Department of Sport Science
Bielefeld University
Bielefeld, Germany

Kent C. Kowalski
College of Kinesiology
University of Saskatchewan
Saskatoon, Canada

Ralf Kredel
Institute of Sport Science
University of Bern
Bern, Switzerland

Sylvain Laborde
Department of Performance Psychology
German Sport University Cologne
Cologne, Germany

Carsten Hvid Larsen
Department of Sports Science and Clinical
    Biomechanics
University of Southern Denmark
Odense, Denmark

Alexander T. Latinjak
School for Science, Technology and
    Engineering
University of Suffolk
Ipswich, UK

Benedikt Lauber
Department of Neurosciences and Movement
    Science
University of Fribourg
Fribourg, Switzerland

Lambros Lazuras
Department of Psychology, Sociology & Politics

Sheffield Hallam University
Sheffield, UK

Sae-Mi Lee
Department of Kinesiology
California State University
Chico, CA, USA

Ronnie Lidor
The Academic College at Wingate
Wingate Institute
Wingate, Israel

Christine Le Scanff
Sport and Human Movement Sciences
Université Paris-Sud
Paris, France

Lorenza Lozano-Sufrategui
School of Sport
Leeds Beckett University
Leeds, UK

Fabio Lucidi
Faculty of Medicine and Psychology
Sapienza University of Rome
Rome, Italy

Olivier Luminet
Psychological Sciences Research Institute
Université catholique de Louvain
Louvain, Belgium

John Lyle
Carnegie School of Sport
Leeds Beckett University
Leeds, UK

Clare MacMahon
School of Allied Health, Human Services, and
    Sport
La Trobe University
Melbourne, Australia

Daniel J. Madigan
School of Sport
York St John University
York, UK

Clifford J. Mallett
Faculty of Health and Behavioural Sciences
The University of Queensland
Brisbane, Australia

Sarah H. Mallinson-Howard
School of Sport
York St John University
York, UK

Harry Manley
Faculty of Psychology
Chulalongkorn University
Bangkok, Thailand

Warren Mansell
Faculty of Biology Medicine and Health
University of Manchester
Manchester, UK

Luc J. Martin
School of Kinesiology and Health Studies
Queen's University
Kingston, ON, Canada

Marina Mateos
Performance and Wellbeing
Melbourne, Australia

Dan P. McAdams
Department of Psychology
Northwestern University
Evanston, IL, USA

Kerry R. McGannon
School of Human Kinetics
Laurentian University
Sudbury, Canada

Stephen D. Mellalieu
School of Sport & Health Sciences
Cardiff Metropolitan University
Cardiff, Wales, UK

Antonio Hernández Mendo
Department of Social Psychology, Social
    Anthropology,
Social Work and Social Services

Universidad De Málaga
Malaga, Spain

Carine Meslot
Manchester Centre for Health Psychology
University of Manchester
Manchester, UK

Thierry R. F. Middleton
Human Studies Program
Laurentian University
Sudbury, Canada

Carolyn C. Morf
Institute of Psychology
University of Bern
Bern, Switzerland

Aidan Moran
School of Psychology
University College Dublin
Dublin, Ireland

Emma Mosley
School of Sport, Health and Social Sciences
Solent University
Southampton, UK

Mónica Muiños Durán
Faculty of Health Sciences
Universitat Jaume I
Castellón de la Plana, Spain

Bob Muir
Carnegie School of Sport
Leeds Beckett University
Leeds, UK

Aurelia Nattiv
Departments of Family Medicine and Ortho-
    paedic Surgery
University of California
Los Angeles, CA, USA

Rich Neil
School of Sport & Health Sciences
Cardiff Metropolitan University
Cardiff, Wales, UK

Christina G. L. Nerstad
Department of Public Administration and
   Leadership
Oslo Metropolitan University
Oslo, Norway

Steffen Nestler
Department of Psychology
University of Münster
Münster, Germany

Nikos Ntoumanis
School of Psychology
Curtin University,
Perth, Australia

Katherine A. O'Brien
Faculty of Health
Queensland University of Technology
Brisbane, Australia

Peter Olusoga
Centre for Sport and Exercise Science
Sheffield Hallam University
Sheffield, UK

Nicole T. Ong
School of Kinesiology
University of British Columbia
Vancouver, BC, Canada

Kurtis Pankow
Faculty of Kinesiology, Sport, and Recreation
University of Alberta
Edmonton, Canada

William D. Parham
School of Education
Loyola Marymount University
Los Angeles, CA, USA

Saengryeol Park
Department of Preventive Medicine
Kyung Hee University
Seoul, South Korea

Fabian Pels
Institute of Psychology

German Sport University Cologne
Cologne, Germany

Brennan Petersen
Human Studies Program
Laurentian University
Sudbury, Canada

Eva Pila
School of Kinesiology, Faculty of Health
   Sciences
Western University
Ontario, Canada

Nils Henrik Pixa
Department of Neuromotor Behavior and
   Exercise
University of Münster
Münster, Germany

Artur Poczwardowski
Sport and Performance Psychology in the
Graduate School of Professional Psychology
University of Denver
Denver, CO, USA

Leslie Podlog
Department of Health, Kinesiology, &
   Recreation
University of Utah
Salt Lake City, UT, U.S.A

Stefanie Podlog
School of Nursing
University of St. Augustine for Health
   Sciences
St. Augustine, FL, U.S.A

Zoë A. Poucher
Faculty of Kinesiology and Physical
   Education
University of Toronto
Toronto, Canada

Andy Pringle
College of Life and Natural Sciences
University of Derby
Derby, UK

Eleanor Quested
School of Psychology
Curtin University
Perth, Australia

Markus Raab
Institute of Psychology
German Sport University Cologne
Cologne, Germany

María Julia Raimundi
National Council of Scientific and Technical
    Research
University of Buenos Aires
Buenos Aires, Argentina

Susana Regüela
High Performance Center Sant Cugat
Barcelona, Spain

Rafael E. Reigal
Facultad de Psicología
University of Malaga
Malaga, Spain

Ryan E. Rhodes
School of Exercise Science
University of Victoria
Victoria, Canada

Claudio Robazza
Department of Medicine and Aging Sciences
"G. d'Annunzio" University of Chieti-Pescara
Chieti, Italy

Glyn C. Roberts
Department of Coaching and Psychology
Norwegian University of Sport Science
Oslo, Norway

Ross Roberts
Institute for the Psychology of Elite
    Performance
Bangor University
Bangor, Wales, UK

Noora Ronkainen
Department of Psychology

University of Jyväskylä
Jyväskylä, Finland

Julian Rudisch
Department of Neuromotor Behavior and
    Exercise
University of Münster
Münster, Germany

Montse C. Ruiz
Faculty of Sport and Health Sciences
University of Jyväskylä
Jyväskylä, Finland

Tatiana V. Ryba
Faculty of Sport and Health Sciences
University of Jyväskylä, Finland

Steven B. Rynne
Faculty of Health and Behavioural
    Sciences
The University of Queensland
Brisbane, Australia

Roy David Samuel
Baruch Ivcher School of Psychology
Interdisciplinary Center (IDC)
Herzliya, Israel

Mustafa Sarkar
Department of Sport Science
Nottingham Trent University
Nottingham, UK

Thomas Schack
Faculty of Psychology and Sport Science
Bielefeld University
Bielefeld, Germany

Robert J. Schinke
School of Human Kinetics
Laurentian University
Sudbury, Canada

Stefan Schneider
Institute of Movement and Neurosciences
German Sport University Cologne
Cologne, Germany

Jamie L. Shapiro
Sport and Performance Psychology in the
    Graduate School of Professional
    Psychology
University of Denver
Denver, CO, USA

Matthew J. Slater
Department of Sport and Exercise
Staffordshire University
Stoke-on-Trent, UK

Brett Smith
Department of Sport and Exercise
    Sciences
Durham University
Durham, UK

Martin M. Smith
School of Sport
York St John University
York, UK

Natalia B. Stambulova
School of Health and Welfare
Halmstad University
Halmstad, Sweden

Louise Kamuk Storm
Department of Sports Science and
    Clinical Biomechanics
University of Southern Denmark
Odense, Denmark

Ning Su
Hong Kong Sports Institute
Shatin, Hong Kong, China

Joel Suss
Faculty of Psychology
Wichita State University
Wichita, KS, USA

Katherine A. Tamminen
Faculty of Kinesiology and Physical
    Education
University of Toronto
Toronto, Canada

Wolfgang Taube
Department of Neurosciences and Movement
    Science
University of Fribourg
Fribourg, Switzerland

Gershon Tenenbaum
The Interdisciplinary Centre
B. Ivcher School of Psychology
Herzlia, Israel

Cecilie Thøgersen-Ntoumani
School of Psychology
Curtin University
Perth, Australia

Miquel Torregrossa
Facultat de Psicologia
Universitat Autònoma de Barcelona
Bellaterra, Spain

Atur V. Turakhia
Children, Youth & Prevention Behavioral
    Health Services
Orange County Health Care Agency
Orange County, CA, USA

Erlanger A. Turner
Faculty of Psychology
University of Houston-Downtown
Houston, TX, USA

Jennifer Turnnidge
School of Kinesiology and Health Studies
Queen's University
Kingston, Canada

Sarah Ullrich-French
Department of Educational Leadership, Sport
    Studies,
and Educational/Counseling Psychology
Washington State University
Pullman, WA, USA

Claudia Voelcker-Rehage
Department of Neuromotor Behavior and
    Exercise
University of Münster
Münster, Germany

Contributors

Kathryn E. Wilson
Department of Health Promotion
University of Nebraska Medical Center
Omaha, NE, USA

Svenja Wachsmuth
Institute of Sport Science
Eberhard Karls University
Heidelberg, Germany

Christopher R. D. Wagstaff
School of Sport, Health and Exercise
    Science
University of Portsmouth
Portsmouth, UK

Paul Ward
Department of Cognitive and Learning Sciences
Michigan Technological University
Michigan, MI, USA

Matthew Watson
Department of Performance Psychology
German Sport University Cologne
Cologne, Germany

Robert Weinberg
Department of Kinesiology and Health
Miami University
Miami, FL, USA

A. Mark Williams
Department of Health,
Kinesiology, and Recreation
University of Utah
Salt Lake City, UT, USA

Toni Louise Williams
Carnegie School of Sport
Leeds Beckett University
Leeds, UK

Kathryn E. Wilson
Department of Health Promotion
University of Nebraska Medical Center
Omaha, NE, USA

Stuart Wilson
School of Human Kinetics
University of Ottawa
Ottawa, Canada

Tim Woodman
Institute for the Psychology of Elite
    Performance
Bangor University
Bangor, Wales, UK

Svenja A. Wolf
Work and Organizational Psychology
    Program
University of Amsterdam
Amsterdam, The Netherlands

Emily Wright
Institute for the Study of Youth Sports
Michigan State University
East Lansing, MI, USA

David J. Wright
Research Centre for Musculoskeletal Science
    and Sports Medicine
Manchester Metropolitan University
    Manchester, UK

Paul Wylleman
Faculty of Physical Education and Physiotherapy
Vrije Universiteit Brussel
Brussel, Belgium

Jessica Zarndt
Departments of Family Medicine and Ortho-
    paedic Surgery
University of California
Los Angeles, CA, USA

Chunqing Zhang
Hong Kong Sports Institute
Shatin, Hong Kong, China

Stephan Zwolinsky
West Yorkshire & Harrogate Cancer
    Alliance
Wakefield, UK

KEYWORDS

(not covered by separate contributions; in addition to the subject index)

Keyword	Chapter (volume, chapter)
Accreditation	Quality management in sport and performance psychology programmes (2, 38)
Action	Career management – an action-theory approach (2, 8)
	Mental fitness (1, 19)
Action observation	Mental simulation and neurocognition: Advances for motor imagery and action observation training in sport (2, 28)
Action planning	Planning exploiting biopsychosocial cues (2, 34)
Action situation	Adventurous sport activities (1, 1)
	Career management – an action-theory approach (2, 8)
	Mental fitness (1, 19)
Adaptation	Mental fitness (1, 19)
	Performance of closed self-paced motor tasks (2, 33)
Adherence	Exercise behaviour models (2, 22)
Adjustment	Mental fitness (1, 19)
Adventure	Adventurous sport activities (1, 1)
Aerobic exercise	Depression: Prevention and treatment through exercise (2, 17)
Affect	Goals and emotions (1, 13)
Affiliation	Group cohesion (1, 14)
Affordances	Embodied cognition (1, 9)
	Talent development environments (2, 44)
Anorexia nervosa	Eating disorders and disordered eating in athletes (2, 18)
Arousal	Human performance pillars in elite sport (2, 25)
Audit	Evaluating interventions (2, 21)
Autonomy	Coaching athletes with a disability (2, 12)
Assessment	Narcissism (2, 27)
Athlete anxiety	Anxiety disorder and treatment (2, 3)
Athlete development	Expertise: Nature and nurture (1, 11)
	Talent development and expertise in sport (2, 43)
Athletic career	Career transitions (2, 9)
Athletic career model	Career development (2, 7)
Athletic retirement	Career transitions (2, 9)

(Continued)

Keyword	Chapter (volume, chapter)
Attention	Augmented feedback (2, 5)
Attitude	Planned exercise behaviour (1, 35)
Beliefs	Self-talk and emotions (2, 39)
Bias	Judgement and decision-making (1, 16)
Bias-perception conflict spiral	Conflict and communication in coach–athlete relationships (2, 14)
Bulimia nervosa	Eating disorders and disordered eating in athletes (2, 18)
Bullying	Positive youth development: A sport and exercise psychology perspective (1, 36)
Capability	Evaluating interventions (2, 21)
Capacity	Evaluating interventions (2, 21)
Career	Career management – an action-theory approach (2, 8)
Career competencies	Career development (2, 7)
Career counselling	Career management – an action-theory approach (2, 8)
Career decision-making	Career development (2, 7)
Career exploration	Career development (2, 7)
Career networking	Career management – an action-theory approach (2, 8)
Career transitions	Career assistance programmes (2, 6)
	Career management – an action-theory approach (2, 8)
Ceremonials	Organizational culture in sport (1, 28)
Certification	Accreditation (2, 1)
Change-event	Career transitions (2, 9)
Choice	Judgement and decision-making (1, 16)
Choking	Embodied cognition (1, 9)
Closed-Loop	Motor control (1, 25)
Closeness	Conflict and communication in coach–athlete relationships (2, 14)
Coaching	High-performance coaches (2, 24)
	Self-determination theory (1, 41)
Coefficient H	Validity and reliability (1, 47)
Cognition	Cognitive sport psychology (1, 5)
	Methods in cognitive sport psychology (1, 22)
Cognitive architecture	Neurocognitive psychology for sport (2, 30)
Cognitive defusion	Mindfulness training (2, 29)
Cognitive performance	Cognitive declines: Protection by physical activity (2, 13)
Commitment	Conflict and communication in coach–athlete relationships (2, 14)
	Evaluating interventions (2, 21)
Compassion fatigue	Trauma: The invisible tattoos (2, 46)
Competence	Ethical issues (2, 20)
Complementarity	Conflict and communication in coach–athlete relationships (2, 14)
Concussion	Injury (2, 26)
Confidence	Self-efficacy (1, 42)
Confidentiality	Ethical issues (2, 20)
Confirmatory factor analysis	Validity and reliability (1, 47)
Constructionism	Research philosophies (1, 39)
Constructivism	Research philosophies (1, 39)
Construct validity	Measurement quality (1, 18)
Context	Context-driven sport psychology: A cultural lens (1, 6)
Coordination	Motor control (1, 25)
Coping	Stress and well-being of those operating in groups (1, 45)

(Cont.)

Keyword	Chapter (volume, chapter)
Exploratory structural equation modelling	Validity and reliability (1, 47)
Extreme sports	Adventurous sport activities (1, 1)
	Embodied cognition (1, 9)
Eye–hand coordination	T'ai chi for improving brain function and cognition (2, 42)
Factor analysis	Validity and reliability (1, 47)
Fight-flight	Anxiety disorder and treatment (2, 3)
Flow	Adventurous sport activities (1, 1)
	Group flow (1, 15)
Formative evaluation	Evaluating interventions (2, 21)
Functional magnetic resonance imaging (fMRI)	Performance and brain in sport (2, 32)
Functional movement analysis	Practice (2, 36)
Generalizability	Meta-analysis and meta-synthesis (1, 21)
	Qualitative methods (1, 38)
Genes	Expertise: Nature and nurture (1, 11)
Goal aspirations	Self-determination theory (1, 41)
Goal planning	Goal-setting (2, 23)
Graduate training	Quality management in sport and performance psychology programmes (2, 38)
Group dynamics	Group cohesion (1, 14)
Harmony	Affect and music (2, 2)
Hazard perception	Anticipation and expertise (1, 3)
Health	Perfectionism (1, 29)
Hegemony	Power and privilege (1, 37)
Heuristic model	Cultural praxis (2, 16)
High-risk sport(s)	Adventurous sport activities (1, 1)
ICSpace	New technologies in sport psychology practice (2, 31)
Identity	Spirituality in sport (1, 44)
Ideology	Power and privilege (1, 37)
Idiographic	Personality assessment I: An integrative approach (1, 32)
Idiographic versus nomothetic	Personality assessment II: Within-person variability assessment (1, 33)
Impact evaluation	Evaluating interventions (2, 21)
Implicit person theories	Motivation: Achievement goal theory in sport and physical activity (1, 24)
Information processing	Cognitive sport psychology (1, 5)
Inner dialogue	Self-talk and emotions (2, 39)
Integrity	Ethical issues (2, 20)
Intention	Planned exercise behaviour (1, 35)
Internal consistency	Validity and reliability (1, 47)
Internalization	Exercise behaviour models (2, 22)
Knowledge	Judgement and decision-making (1, 16)
Knowledge of performance	Augmented feedback (2, 5)
Knowledge of result	Augmented feedback (2, 5)
Leadership	High-performance coaches (2, 24)
Licensing	Accreditation (2, 1)
Life skills	Positive youth development: A sport and exercise psychology perspective (1, 36)
	Positive youth development through sport (2, 35)

Keyword	Chapter (volume, chapter)
Martial arts	T'ai chi for improving brain function and cognition (2, 42)
Mastery climate	Motivation: Achievement goal theory in sport and physical activity (1, 24)
	Positive youth development: a sport and exercise psychology perspective (1, 36)
Measurement	Personality research: directions (1, 34)
Measurement theory	Methods in cognitive sport psychology (1, 22)
Melody	Affect and music (2, 2)
Member reflections	Qualitative methods (1, 38)
Mental imagery	Mental simulation and neurocognition: Advances for motor imagery and action observation training in sport (2, 28)
Mental practice	Mental simulation and neurocognition: Advances for motor imagery and action observation training in sport (2, 28)
Mental recovery	Mental fitness (1, 19)
Mental representation	New technologies in sport psychology practice (2, 31)
Mental robustness	Mental fitness (1, 19)
Mental toughness	Athletic talent development in relation to psychological factors (2, 4)
Mental health	Depression: Prevention and treatment through exercise (2, 17)
Meta-supervision	Professional development: Supervision, mentorship, and professional development in the career of an applied professional (2, 37)
Methodological nationalism	Transnational athletic career and cultural transition (2, 45)
Migration	Transnational athletic career and cultural transition (2, 45)
Mindful movement	Mindfulness and exercise (1, 23)
Mindset	Motivation: Achievement goal theory in sport and physical activity (1, 24)
Modelling	Mental imagery and neurocognition
Mood	Goals and emotions (1, 13)
Moral	Ethical issues (2, 20)
Motor control theory	Practice (2, 36)
Motor skills	Motor control (1, 25)
	Motor learning (1, 26)
Motivation	Human performance pillars in elite sport (2, 25)
Motivational climate	Motivation: Achievement goal theory in sport and physical activity (1, 24)
Movement representation	Neurocognitive psychology for sport (2, 30)
Multi-method personality assessment	Personality research: Directions (1, 34)
Narrative identity	Personality assessment I: An integrative approach (1, 32)
Naturalistic decision-making	Coaches' decision-making (2, 10)
Need support	Self-determination theory (1, 41)
Neurofeedback	Performance and brain in sport (2, 32)
Norms	Planned exercise behaviour (1, 35)
Omega and composite reliability	Validity and reliability (1, 47)
Open-loop	Motor control (1, 25)
Organizational resilience	Resilience in teams and organizations (1, 40)
Outcome goals	Goal-setting (2, 23)
Paradigm	Cognitive sport psychology (1, 5)
Peer debriefing	Measurement quality (1, 18)
Perceived behavioural control	Planned exercise behaviour (1, 35)
Perception action	Motor control (1, 25)

(Continued)

Keyword	Chapter (volume, chapter)
Sampling	Personality research: Directions (1, 34)
Self-confidence	Human performance pillars in elite sport (2, 25)
Self-determined motivation	Self-determination theory (1, 41)
Self-efficacy	Mental fitness (1, 19)
Self-reflexivity	Measurement quality (1, 18)
Self-reinforcing feedback loop	Conflict and communication in coach–athlete relationships (2, 14)
Self-regulation	Emotion regulation (2, 19)
	Goals and emotions (1, 13)
	Mental fitness (1, 19)
	Self-talk and emotions (2, 39)
Simple heuristic	Judgement and decision-making (1, 16)
Situation assessment	Anticipation and expertise (1, 3)
Situation awareness	Anticipation and expertise (1, 3)
Skill	Anticipation and expertise (1, 3)
Skill acquisition	Embodied cognition (1, 9)
	Motor learning (1, 26)
Social-cognitive theory	Self-efficacy (1, 42)
Social constructionism	Self-identity: Discursive and narrative conceptions and applications (1, 43)
Social involvement	Motivation: Achievement goal theory in sport and physical activity (1, 24)
Social relationships	Positive youth development: A sport and exercise psychology perspective (1, 36)
Social responsibility	Ethical issues (2, 20)
Sport coaching	Coaches' decision-making (2, 10)
State assessment	Personality assessment II: Within-person variability assessment (1, 33)
State fluctuations	Personality assessment II: Within-person variability assessment (1, 33)
Stigma	Mental health and wellness (1, 20)
Strength-building	Positive youth development: A sport and exercise psychology perspective (1, 36)
Stress	Injury (2, 26)
Stress mindset	Injury (2, 26)
Structure	Narcissism (2, 27)
Supervision	Quality management in sport and performance psychology programmes (2, 38)
Talent	Expertise: Nature and nurture (1, 11)
Talent development	Services for young talented athletes (2, 40)
Task involvement	Motivation: Achievement goal theory in sport and physical activity (1, 24)
Task space	Practice (2, 36)
Team building	Group cohesion (1, 14)
Team dynamics	Embodied cognition (1, 9)
Team personality	Personality and team effectiveness (1, 31)
Team resilience	Resilience in teams and organizations (1, 40)
Teams	Group cohesion (1, 14)
Test and testing	Qualitative methods (1, 38)
Thinking	Self-talk and emotions (2, 39)
Title usage	Ethical issues (2, 20)
Training	Expertise: Nature and nurture (1, 11)
Training environment	Talent development environments (2, 44)
Traits	Personality assessment I: An integrative approach (1, 32)

(Continued)

(Cont.)

Keyword	Chapter (volume, chapter)
Transfer	Motor learning (1, 26)
Transferability	Measurement quality (1, 18)
	Qualitative methods (1, 38)
Transnationalism	Transnational athletic career and cultural transition (2, 45)
Trial and error	Coaching athletes with a disability (2, 12)
Triangulation	Measurement quality (1, 18)
Trustworthiness	Measurement quality (1, 18)
Virtual reality	New technologies in sport psychology practice (2, 31)
Visual asymmetries	T'ai chi for improving brain function and cognition (2, 42)
Visuospatial abilities	T'ai chi for improving brain function and cognition (2, 42)
Volition	Planning exploiting biopsychosocial cues (2, 34)
Well-being	Ethical issues (2, 20)
X-treme sport(s)	Adventurous sport activities (1, 1)
Yoga	Mindfulness and exercise (1, 23)
Youth sport context	Services for young talented athletes (2, 40)

ORIENTATION FOR VOLUME 1

Volume 1 features the most relevant theoretical and methodological concepts in sport and exercise psychology. These contributions, derived from international scholars, are conceived in a manner whereby each reveals its own unique terminological network, from original foundations to context-specific relevance, with subordinate concepts and traditional and emerging discourse, written at a conceptual level. Meta-theoretical and methodological contributions are also found in this volume, often borrowed from a non-sport context and then contextualized for sport psychology researchers, to align with disciplinary requirements. The comprehensive landscape and in-depth theoretical and methodological exploration of each term are identified in the opening title. The orientation of Volume 1, then, is for both young and established sport psychology professionals to draw upon historical and up-to-date knowledge as a reference point to augment theoretical and scientific understanding, while encouraging academic progression and debate.

INTRODUCTION

Dieter Hackfort and Robert J. Schinke

The editors' mission through *The Routledge International Encyclopedia of Sport and Exercise Psychology* is threefold. First, this resource is intended to foster a better understanding of fundamental concepts, methodological approaches, and explanations of key terms embedded in the terminological network. Second, this project is positioned as a reference that can be used as a valuable information source and also as a tool to support teaching and research in classrooms, and among scholars of all stages. Finally, as an added value, this project was conceptualized to assist in the organization and management of applied strategies and practical measurements.

Background

The original idea of an encyclopedia, from its inception, was to have a collection of the entire (universal) knowledge available up to that point in time, an overview of cumulative knowledge across all subject areas. The concept 'encyclopedia' is founded in the work by Aristotle, and the term has its roots in the language of the ancient Greeks (see Fowers, 2012). However, the first encyclopedia was designed by the Romans. The *Naturalis Historia* (by Pliny the Elder, 77–79 A.D.) is regarded to be the oldest encyclopedia in good shape. The term 'encyclopedia' originated in the French word *encyclopédie* (1751–1780). Since then, the trend with encyclopedias has evolved, with some narrowing from universal to discipline-specific, such as in the case of the current project. The developmental path from which a given discipline is created and established, leading to sufficient content for an encyclopedia, accumulates over time. During this process, hallmarks of disciplinary evolution include the implementation of professorships, departments, institutes, and faculties in universities, the foundation of scientific organizations, and the formation of journals, all of which are essential in order to deepen disciplinary knowledge and credibility, while growing in practical knowledge and techniques. An encyclopedia, then, becomes a further, tangible indication that the discipline has achieved a certain level of formalized status and high standard, with sufficient depth and breadth in content to reveal an extensive, metaphorical geography of the domain.

Narrowing to the field of psychology and its formation, the statement by the German psychologist and pioneer in memory research Hermann Ebbinghaus, in 1907 (see Ebbinghaus,

1922), is that psychology has a long past but only a short history. Hence, the foundations are less specific and formal for psychology as compared with other scientific disciplines, such as the natural sciences. What we refer to as 'sport psychology' has its roots in various broad-based research areas, though it has been built on psychology theories and scholarship as its foundational literature. These diverse areas are known to include social psychology, occupational psychology, educational psychology, and clinical psychology. The interdisciplinary knowledge base that is referred to as sport psychology, which also includes exercise, has been, and is increasingly, informed from diverse countries and cultural backgrounds from across the global landscape. These disciplines and cultural perspectives weave together into a tapestry of knowledge that refers to the spheres of competitive sports and exercise; consequently, the discipline is labelled nowadays 'sport and exercise psychology'.

Development of the Discipline

Sport psychology as an academic discipline and area of research was developed in the 20th century. Briefly, after the foundation of the first laboratory for experimental psychology in Leipzig (Germany) by Wilhelm Wundt, in 1879, the first sport psychology laboratory was established in 1920 by Robert Werner Schulte at the German High School for Physical Education in Berlin. In the same year, in Russia, P. A. Rudik initiated a sport psychology laboratory at the Institute for Physical Culture. In Asia, Mitsuo Matsu organized sport psychology research in a laboratory at the National Institute of Physical Education located in Japan, in 1924. In the United States, Coleman Griffith opened a laboratory for sport psychology research in 1925 at the University of Illinois. However, the term 'sport psychology' was used, probably for the first time, by the French Baron Pierre de Coubertin (see de Coubertin, 1900), the founder of the modern Olympic Games and the organizer of the First International Congress on the Physiology and Psychology of Sport in 1913 (a second one was never organized).

From these initial well-known hallmark moments, sport and exercise psychology was launched and began to grow at a rapid pace. In the 1960s, the discipline was arranged in Europe (then comprised of Eastern and Western regions and ideologies) and in the United States by university professorships. With people from these regions, the International Society of Sport Psychology (ISSP) was founded in 1965, with additional engagement from South America (i.e., Brazil in 1965, followed by Argentina in 1973). Asia, though active in its continent, did not join the ISSP until 1973, followed by Africa in 1977 (i.e., Egypt). Since these points in time, scholarship founded in ISSP's flagship journal, first known as the *International Journal of Sport Psychology* and, more recently, the *International Journal of Sport and Exercise Psychology*, has become increasingly globalized. Broader leadership within continents and also in the ISSP has also integrated a closer balance of Eastern and Western perspectives, reflecting an ever-increasing, culturally diversified field (see www.issponline.org).

The discipline developed in the frame of sport science as a function of the increased interest in sport and exercise within modern society. Owing to the different terminology and concepts of sport/sports in various regions of the world, the differentiation between competitive/performance-oriented sport and health/fitness-oriented exercise resulted in what has become internationally the most used, comprehensive label of 'sport and exercise psychology' (see, e.g., the official journal of the ISSP – the *International Journal of Sport and Exercise Psychology*; the official journal of FEPSAC – *Psychology of Sport and Exercise*; and the official journal of NASPSA – the *Journal of Sport and Exercise Psychology*, as testament to the use of these terms side by side). More recently, the term 'performance', which referred from the very beginning to a fundamental phenomenon in sport psychology research and practice, has also begun to be used for a further differentiation and indication of the scope of sport psychology, as parameters continue to expand into parallel performance environments, such as combat and dance (see, e.g., the American Psychological Association's Division 47 journal, *Sport, Exercise, and Performance Psychology*).

However, the roots of sport and exercise psychology, including performance as well as adventure, can be traced back to pertinent ideas and practices found in various cultures for centuries, such as in Ancient Greece, India, and China. The meaning of physical activity, exercise, and sport for health and education purposes as well as sport performance was, and is, an essential issue across and within the evolution of cultures. On the one hand, the meaning of 'sport' is different in various cultures, with 'sport' and related terms being regarded as key elements of modern societies. Cultural developments are influencing significantly what is meant by 'sport' (see, e.g., Council of Europe, 2017), and, as a consequence, these understandings have influenced, and are influencing, the meaning of sport science and sport psychology.

At the beginning in this profession, institutionalized sport psychology focused on educational and performance issues. In interaction with the development of sport science, sport scientific disciplines, psychology, and requirements from sport and further related fields, the scope of interests and relevant issues to be covered in sport psychology was broadened, enlarged, and enriched. At present, the overall endeavour of sport and exercise psychology is to contribute to the quality of life of all human beings, and, for this mission, emphasis is given to the basic topics of health, well-being, fitness, performance, adventure, and sport. These topics are linked with a focus on educational (e.g., coaching, youth development, physical life skills), individual (e.g., motor learning, motor control, development of personality, self-concept), social (e.g., career management, team-building,

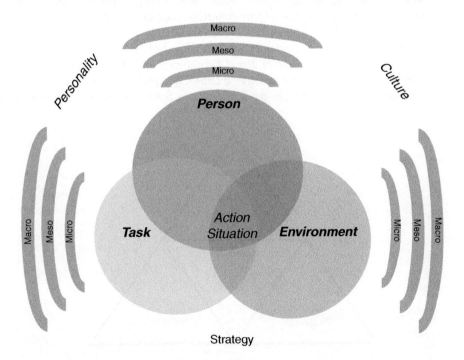

Figure 0.1 Relational systems, fundamental units of sport, and factors in sport psychology approaches

leadership), and exercise purposes, for which the fundamental psychic processes – affective, cognitive, motivational, and volitional – are analysed. The psychological analyses are realized across different levels and systems, such as the so-called micro-, meso-, and macro-systems, in regard to the interaction of individuals and their social or cultural environment, the interplay of emotional and cognitive processes (intra-psychic/system analyses), or cognitive and biological (neural) processes on a different level (inter-system analyses). Thus, the psychosocial perspective refers to the cultural system, and a more detailed psychophysiological perspective refers to the neural system – that is, from the macro- to the micro-level approaches to psychic processes (see Figure 0.1).

Sport activities as well as sport psychology research are embedded in an action situation, created by the actual person–task–environment constellation. This constellation can be regarded in terms of different systems and analysed by different methodological approaches and theoretical perspectives according to the interests and topics of the practitioner or researcher. This is taken into account in the compilation of the contributions to this encyclopedia.

Even though terms such as 'cultural sport psychology' or 'performance psychology' are used to indicate specific topic matter, as long as this is realized in regard to sport in a broad (classical) understanding, it is a subject and part of sport psychology as the overarching term and these issues, meaning the more specific aspects of sport, exercise, and performance found in this encyclopedia.

Despite sport psychology's relatively nascent history as a recognized field and discipline, there are numerous vibrant continental sport and exercise psychology organizations, suggestive of a flourishing domain. Each of these societies serves as an umbrella organization for its respective national societies. Several noteworthy societies, with origins in continental activities, such as conferences, include the Association for Applied Sport Psychology (AASP), founded in the United States, with strong support from Canada, and focused on practical application; the North American Society for the Psychology of Sport and Physical Activity (NASPSA), known for its academic and research focus, also in North America; the Asia South Pacific Association of Sport Psychology (ASPASP), representing the continent of Asia; the African Society of Sport Psychology (ASSP), representing Africa; the European Federation of Sport Psychology (FEPSAC), spanning Europe; and SOSUPE (Sociedad Sudamericana de Psicologia del Deporte), in South America. Though each of the

Figure 0.2 A multi-triangle framing of sport and exercise psychology

aforementioned societies has emerged from a continental focus, offerings from each society now attract engagement well beyond continental boarders. The ISSP was conceived as a global umbrella for established and emerging continental and national societies and continues to serve as a well-distributed global representative of sport psychology, with its activities rotating from one continent to the next in the aforementioned regions; additionally, the ISSP integrates several regions and their experts in regular global activities, such as publication projects, congresses, position stands, and think tanks. Sport and exercise psychology is a fundamental sport science discipline as well as a specialized branch in applied psychology. The establishment of this sport science discipline is a consequence of the development and differentiation of disciplines and subgroups of specialists in the scientific community. Sport and exercise psychology can be described through its synthesis in a large triangle (see Figure 0.2), with multiple embedded triangles.

Defining Sport and Exercise Psychology

Sport and exercise psychology is a scientific and professional stream of knowledge that focuses on various dimensions of sport and exercise behaviour. The general orientation of the discipline, similar to other domains (see, e.g., Nitsch & Hackfort, 2016), is to describe, explain, predict, and develop interventional methods to modify intentional organized and purposive behaviour (actions) in sports based on empirical research and ethical standards. More specifically, the intra- and interindividual, the psychophysiological, psychosocial, and psycho-ecological foundations, preconditions, configurations, processes, and consequences of actions in sports and exercise are investigated and clarified with the applied objective to optimize sport-related actions. Thereby, the psychological perspective in regard to sport and exercise is twofold: On the one hand, the analysis of how actions in sport and exercise are regulated by psychic processes (affective, cognitive, motivational, and volitional processes) is emphasized; on the other hand, the focus is on the analysis of how actions in sport and exercise regulate psychic phenomena (i.e., attitude, emotion, self-awareness, self-concept), with the intention to enhance a sound understanding (theoretical concepts) and to enlarge effective interventional tools (applied methods). Both of these perspectives are represented in this encyclopaedia.

Since sport and exercise psychology has developed into a respected and esteemed research domain, a scientific discipline taught in academic institutes and departments around the world, and a prominent field of expertise acquired by a broad range of people, including, but not limited to, athletes, coaches, physical education teachers and instructors, and those who are engaged in health promotion, the knowledge in, and the practice of, sport and exercise psychology have seen substantial growth. Based on the definition above, three general tasks of sport and exercise psychology can be distinguished:

(1) There is research, including the development of theoretical concepts on the general subject of sport- and exercise-related actions and acting in sports and exercise. There is the development of specific methodologies (and, embedded within these, methods), conceptualized and implemented as deemed necessary to ensure that they are reasonable for the subject and suitable for the action field, procedures for analyses and assessments, tests, and diagnostic instruments. And last but not least, there is the organization of qualitative and quantitative studies, structural and procedural analyses of the preconditions and circumstances, the regulation and control, and the effects and consequences of sport-related actions.

(2) There is education, teaching, and communication. Education and teaching refer to the students in sport and exercise psychology, the students in sport science and in psychology, practitioners such as coaches and teachers in physical education, and instructors in exercise. Communication and dissemination of knowledge, via publishing, lecturing, or presenting at congresses, and the exchange of experiences and skillsets through continuing education are essential tasks for the advancement and development of the discipline and the expertise of professionals.

(3) There is application, including counselling, mental coaching, performance enhancement, health promotion, and supporting recreation or adventure-oriented sport activities. This more practical aspect of the field bridges science and application, in what is an applied field. Sport and exercise psychology was conceptualized based on the needs of clients, and, as such, clients and participants serve as the basis of theory and empirical scholarship.

Each and all of the above serve as the background that led to the conceptualization of expert topics and the selection of section experts building the Board of Experts, as well as the subsequent selection of contributions to this encyclopaedia.

Key Topics

Applied sport and exercise psychologists are engaged in performance enhancement, counselling, injury rehabilitation, and promotion of physical activity for health maintenance, or in the design of adventure-oriented movement activities for special experiences. Research-oriented sport and exercise psychologists develop and test models and theories and undertake scientific investigations to understand sport- and exercise-related actions. Sport psychologists, whether researchers, practitioners, or professionals who balance both aspects to some degree, contribute to personal growth in conditions where exercise and sport are performed.

With regard to central values in modern societies, three key topics can be identified to build essential references for research in sport and exercise psychology and the application of corresponding knowledge. Health, performance, and experiences of the body and by the body, well-being, harmony (see, e.g., the topics of the ISSP World Congresses in Sydney, Australia, in 2005, or in Beijing, China, in 2013) of life and the self in extreme situations can be detected to be key topics across the popular and scientific literature in the field. The key issues associated with these values are health, well-being, fitness, fun, and adventure and they converge toward the core value of quality of life.

Formation of the Encyclopedia

This encyclopedia is supported by the ISSP. The ISSP continues to bring together and further initiate a global scientific community for the discipline, and this encyclopedia exemplifies the broader agenda of building capacity and exchanging ideas across a world of scholars and practitioners. The information within this two-volume set is characteristic of a discipline-specific encyclopedia, derived from fundamental thematic subject areas. It has been conceived to address the need for high-quality definitions and explanations of key terms. Hence, this encyclopedia can be used not only as a valuable information source, but also as a tool to support teaching, research, and practice. This project comprises the commission of more than 90 overarching contributions, each offering its own state-of-the-art description of a broad, key topic by providing context, reviewing key issues and findings, and tracing normative implications. The editors' mission for this work is for it to be grounded in the best scientific thought and understandings to present, and to meet the highest scientific standards of the field. The editors' vision, in turn, is, and will continue to be, for this project to be as inclusive as possible in regard to theoretical perspectives, methodologies, and practices.

Slightly more than 50 years after the foundation of the ISSP, its Publications Committee endorsed the development of the first ever ISSP *Encyclopedia of Sport and Exercise Psychology*. The individual authors of the more than 90 contributions are international experts in the fundamental topics found within the project from all continents around the globe. This first edition is anticipated and agreed with the publisher to be a "living, ongoing project", to be revisited, updated, and modernized at least twice each decade in hard copy, with live, timely updates of the e-version. Contributors were, and will continue to be, challenged with looking beyond their region at the topic they present and revisit with as international a perspective as is humanly possible.

The intention is to have a two-volume-set encyclopedia as close to one-stop shopping as there is for this field, covering the span of key thematic areas and key terms. What follows is an overview of the project's formation in the discipline of sport and exercise psychology as it can be characterized today, and how one might best draw upon the knowledge (i.e., uptake). The broad scope of topics and issues sport psychology is already covering were initially structured into sections defined by the editors in collaboration with outstanding experts, who built an expert panel, or the Board of Experts. The experts were then tasked with overseeing their proposed scope of key topics and charged with selecting appropriate contributions and the most suitable authors. Some of the topics chosen by the experts are classical, but nevertheless actual (i.e., coaching, goal-setting, motivation, motor control), whereas others are discussed at present in more detail or represent concepts that have been emphasized recently (i.e., career management, embodied cognition, mental fitness, cultural praxis). Methodological issues are also represented and discussed in various publications; as they are considered to be fundamental in the specific application and usage in sport and exercise psychology, the most relevant topics are included in this encyclopedia. Furthermore, some topics determined by the experts are not only relevant for sport psychologists, but also of special interest to a broader base of practitioners in sports, sport science experts, such as sport managers, and psychologists interested in adventure or performance, doctors and sport medicine people, teachers, and journalists. Hence, this encyclopedia, on the one hand, should comprise a broad scope of relevant topics, while, on the other hand, it must reflect the actual state of the field at the time of publication.

Key criteria for the selection of authors will always be their scientific standing and experience as scholars. Each of the contributors in the current project was asked to involve young, junior scientists and young researchers wherever appropriate, so as to bridge established and emerging scholars, while encouraging established and the most recent thinking within and across topics. This encyclopedia was derived with support from the experts, as an essential tool of quality assurance, prior to a final review by the editors. The panel of experienced scholars secured contributors from Europe, Africa, Asia, North America, and Australia, revealing current leading scholars who publish in English. However, it should be noted that an increasing number of scholars are being identified from emerging countries, such as in the continents of Africa and South America. These scholars are becoming emerging leaders, and they will be intentionally engaged in the subsequent editions of this project, in keeping with the ISSP's mandate of global capacity building. This deliberate ever-widening of international contributors will also ensure the broadest possible generation of knowledge, taking into account international diversity and a broad range of culturally infused perspectives.

The identification of key areas embedded in this project and the current list of experts are documented in the front matter of the encyclopedia.

Structure of This Encyclopedia

The ISSP encyclopedia is a two-volume set. Volume 1 is focused on "Theoretical and Methodological Concepts". Volume 2, denoted as "Applied and Practical Measures", contains topics that are delivered in a more practical manner. Both volumes, however, share a golden thread: They are built from extant literature and a sound knowledge base. Authors, be they scholars, practitioners, or scientist-practitioners (people who balance science and practice), have drawn on scholarship derived from their area(s) of interest. Approximately 200 contributing authors have referred to parent literature derived through sections focused on historical contexts, as well as existing research and practice, from their topic's inception to present day.

The content found in each volume has been alphabetized as opposed to having the content delivered by section, as that style of delivery would have matched with a handbook format, of which there are many available for our field. Rather, through alphabetized content, readers could easily find their sought-after topic area(s) within each volume and then delve more deeply into the expansive literature review associated with each contribution and its associated contributions (e.g., various aspects relating to coaching or careers).

The structure of each contribution ensures that, through an introduction and the contextualization of the subject providing a thematic classification, the topic is infused with keywords in its terminological network. The core topics are characterized by a key term in front of each contribution and mostly specified or differentiated by additional features or labelling elements in the title. Additional keywords, essential and explained in the various contexts and substantial for a comprehensive understanding of sport psychology, are listed in a separate index. Each contribution has its own keywords, which can be used to search out related entries with the help of the list of keywords in the preliminary pages. The intention is for the reader to conceptually link associated terms in relation to personal interest areas. This bridging process will be unique to each reader in terms of which ones bind together and how it is that they intersect.

The reader is also encouraged to draw upon contributions from both volumes concurrently to encourage a science-to-practice understanding, and vice versa, in relation to the topics. One's interests might be entirely scholarly or practical. However, the field itself naturally bridges research and practice. Hence, engaging with the two-volume set in relation to one's interests encourages a holistic understanding of an interest area. This bridging process might also encourage scholarship and practice that are theoretically informed, well founded, and yet practically understood.

References

de Coubertin, P. (1900). Psychologie du sport [Psychology of sport]. *Revue Des Deux Mondes, 160,* 167–179.

Council of Europe. (2017). Culture and sport. Retrieved from www.coe.int/en/web/compass/Culture-and-Sport June 08, 2019.

Ebbinghaus, H. (1922). *Abriss der Psychologie [Summary of psychology].* Berlin/Leipzig, Germany: Gruyter.

Fowers, B. J. (2012). An Aristotelian framework for the human good. *Journal of Theoretical and Philosophical Psychology, 32,* 10–23.

Nitsch, J. R., & Hackfort, D. (2016). Theoretical framework of performance psychology: An action theory perspective. In M. Raab, B. Lobinger, S. Hoffmann, A. Pizzera, & S. Laborde (Eds.), *Performance psychology. Perception, action, cognition, and emotion* (pp. 11–29). London: Elsevier.

1
ADVENTUROUS SPORT ACTIVITIES

Dieter Hackfort

Introduction

The interest in, or even devotion to, adventurous physical (including sport) activities (i.e., ultra-long-distance running such as the 100 km run, the 100-miles Barkley Marathon, or the Trans America Footrace; skydiving; skysurfing; deep-sea/ocean-diving; paragliding; wingsuit flying; big wave surfing), which are different to consumer experiences such as scat-diving (free fall into a safety net), hot rocket (vertical acceleration via a catapult), or the hereof almost traditional bungee jumping, is a trend (i.e., Schildmacher, 1998). According to a representative study by the B.A.T. Freizeit-Forschungsinstitut (leisure research institute in Hamburg, Germany) from 1994 (see Opaschowski, 1995), more than half a million German women would like to skydive, and almost a million men of the German population indicated skydiving, hang-gliding, or diving as their desired sport. The author (Opaschowski, 1995) argues that the reasons could be a hint of boredom with performing traditional sports and the need for challenges outside the workplace. From a psychological point of view, the described phenomenon for sure is interesting and may be, to some extent, also a complex problem.

The original event to experience adventure was probably Homer's Ulysses. Adventure education can also be traced back to the ancient Greeks, Plato and Aristotle (427–322 B.C.), who emphasized the learning of virtues by being impelled into adventurous situations. This idea was adopted in the 20th century, for example and most prominently, by the Outward Bound education programme (e.g., Hunt, 1990), which was also considered by the founder, Kurt Hahn (see Heckmair & Michl, 1993), to be a kind of therapy or preventive treatment.

Social and Socio-Psychological Considerations

Adventure sport as a kind of leisure or recreational sport allows one to exhaust emotional potentials through socially (morally and legally) accepted actions to an extent that is almost impossible to match or even beat. On the one hand, adventure and risk have vanished in everyday life through the industrial revolution, but, on the other hand, the risk-taking propensity has increased on the basis of the security (materialistic, social, existential) reached in the Western social systems. Some time ago, a German pedagogue, Von Cube (1990), made a statement, obviously influenced by his observations of members of Western societies, that a sense of security tempts the human to take risks, and he declared a misery maintenance law (orig. German: *Elendserhaltungsgesetz*). The idea behind this hypothetical law is based on the observation that the consequence of an increase in security is an increase in risk-taking, and this seems to be proportional – that is, the misery is always maintained and constant. From a behavioural biologist point of view, he recognized a functional meaning in it: Security is gained through the search for risks. Accordingly, he discusses the "dangerous security" and postulates a "security–risk law": The higher the sense of security, the more distinct the risk-taking propensity. The safer one feels with the brakes on a mountain bike or the ski binding, for example, the greater the tendency to ride even faster or to find an even more dangerous piste.

However, as early as the 18th century, Jean-Jacques Rousseau held the opinion that it is not those who have the most years/longest life, but those who feel life most strongly and have lived the most vivid live who life to its fullest. In line with this, some people are buried aged 100 years old, but already died at birth (original in French: "Lhomme qui a le plus vécu n'est pas celui qui a compté le plus d'années, mais celui qui a le plus senti la vie. Tel s'est fait enterrerà cent ans, qui mourut dès sa naissance", Rousseau, 1824, p. 24). Through Kurt Hahn and the Outward Bound courses (see Heckmair & Michl, 1993), which he understood as adventure education, or even therapy, and in which nature sports gained significant meaning, adventure pedagogy experienced an upsurge in the 1980s that developed into a boom in the 1990s (see Miles & Priest, 1990). This approach is not only used (if at all substantially) in the domain of leisure or in the framework of leisure pedagogy, but also within the scope of personnel and organizational development as a field of learning in nature–adventure pedagogy in management development (Rieper, 1995). Learning (as self-discovery or learning to work in a team) through discovery and experience in outdoor training is so popular that, in the *Süddeutsche Zeitung* (Southern German Newspaper; November 17, 1997, p. 13), the journalist Marco Althaus wrote the following title with a hint of sarcasm (translated by the author): "After the jump off the mast, group ritual practice – on high wires, on the climbing wall and in grass: personnel development in outdoor training". This article draws attention to the commercialization of pedagogically used adventurous sports activities.

Adventurous and high-risk sports activities have for quite some time been addressed in sport science from a pedagogical perspective (e.g., Hecker, 1989; Schleske, 1977) and in relation to self-reports (e.g., Aufmuth, 1983). In sport psychology, the orientation for taking up adventurous sport activities was originally to conceptualize a special programme to support the treatment of depression and, therefore, to broaden the spectrum of therapies (see Golz, Erkelenz, & Sack, 1990). From a psychological perspective, *high-risk sports*, such as motorcycling, are interesting in light of the analysis of the so-called *flow* state. Rheinberg (1991) reported interesting results that he interpreted as incentive triads: (1) enjoyment of unusual movement sensations, (2) experience of one's own competencies in emergency situations, and (3) a perception of danger that intensifies the event. Additionally, he described a "gladiator component" as the opportunity to present oneself as fearless. Klint (1990) argued, "if adventure experience can indeed enhance affective development, then planned adventure experiences could be considered attractive alternatives to therapeutic programming and human development" (p. 163). From this point of view, sports as a design of and for adventure also have a specific educational and therapeutic potential.

Terminological and Conceptual Framing

Adventure is relevant in various spheres and behavioural settings and for different purposes: such as, expeditions, scaling Mount Everest, exploring the deep ocean or outer space, and, in outward-bound pedagogy, survival trainings and similar adventure events to explore the self and team spirit in extreme situations. What is extreme or an adventure can be regarded to be a subjective definition and is determined by the individual potential (competences, skills), his or her experience, and the according appraisal processes performed by the person. Even though adventure is an individual experience, it is possible to happen and is often experienced in a group – for example, when an expedition is realized or river rafting is organized for a group to have an adventure experience in a group, with this group, and about the group. This kind of adventure can be described as "team adventure". In sport, *high-risk sports* or *x-treme sports* are regarded to be a separate and special field of sport associated with adventure experiences with a very high level of especially physical risk.

Looking for answers to the question "What is adventure", we can learn by a google search (e.g., www.dictionary.com/browse/adventure, https://dictionary.cambridge.org/dictionary/english/adventure) that adventure is, for example, characterized to be a risky undertaking with an unknown outcome, the willingness to commit to an uncertain outcome, an exciting and very unusual experience, an unusual, exciting, and possibly dangerous activity, a conscious exploration of unknown situations, an exploration and discovery resulting in an extension of the self, a physical and mental (or/and spiritual) experience. The term "adventure" is based on the Latin *advenire* – to happen to.

People in general, and athletes in particular, seek adventure to extend the limits and usage of their potential and competencies as well as to provoke and have the feeling of mastery and flow – *flow* with the meaning of "a kind of personal transcendence" (Mitchell, 1983, p. 153). In clarifying "the semantics of adventure education" (Priest, 1990, pp. 113–117), the author emphasized that adventurous activities are related to challenging tasks that involve problem-solving and require judgement and decision-making. "The challenge may take the form of testing one's competence against mental, social, or physical risks" (p. 114). Risk was defined by Priest (1990) to be "the potential to lose something of value" (p. 115), and "risk is created by the presence of dangers" (p. 115): for example, to break a leg (physical risk), to experience public disgrace (social risk), or to be faced with a situation of high value but uncertainty in regard to the actual competency of coping – that is, stress (mental risk). However, by phenomenological analyses of experts across various sports, it was detected (see Breivik, 2013) that athletes rely on conscious control in critical situations and in regard to highly skilled actions when the individual's security is at stake (Eysenck, 2004; see also Cappuccio & Ilundáin-Agurruza, Volume 1, Chapter 10, in this encyclopedia).

These notions contribute to clarifying, first, that result-oriented characteristics or external factors can be identified: Uncertain or unknown outcomes and also process-oriented characteristics or internal factors can be identified – excitement, dangerous activity, and so on. Thus, adventure is determined by specific actions in certain *action situations* (see Hackfort & Nitsch, 2019, pp. 2–3), which means that, for an adventure, an action is initiated to realize an intention and achieve an anticipated result (task) in a person–environment constellation. From this point of view, adventure is based on purposive, intentionally organized behaviour, and the special emphasis of the purpose is on exploration, extension, and/or expansion in the sense of gathering information and new experiences. A motivation of expansiveness in regard to both internal expansiveness – that is, self-exploration and self-discovery – and external expansiveness – that is, exploration and discovery of the world (nature, culture) – seems to be fundamental. Second, cognitive and affective processes of action regulation (see Nitsch & Hackfort, 2016) are emphasized: for example, calculation, judgement, and decision-making, as well as feelings of excitement and experiences of stress. Both processes are closely linked to the appraisal of competence and valence in regard to the *action situation* (see Nitsch & Hackfort, 1981). From an action-theory perspective, the relationship between self-efficacy and the situational demands, as well as the convergence between the limits of ability and anxiety, is of importance for the experience of challenge and risk. This concept (the action-theory approach) will be picked up again and elaborated in more detail later in this contribution.

For a characterization of aventurous sports activities, *high-risk* or *x-treme* sports, the following three features (as a kind of lowest common denominator) seem to be essential, even though these are not taken synonymously: For "adventure", the subjective interpretation (of novelty; exploration is the focus) is decisive; for "high risk", the objective constellation (difficulty of the task and and skills needed to cope with it) and individual calculation of competence and valence are decisive; and, for "x-treme", the absolute level (interindividual scale) and the individual judgement of the limit are decisive. Thus,

(1) maximal effort, a high degree of endeavour, and total commitment are required in regard to certain demands, challenges, and abilities,
(2) the situational structure (the task in this environment for this person) appears neither totally clear or particularly favourable nor completely inscrutable or unfavourable for a successful action, that is,
(3) the solvability of the task is appraised as minimal, but also not as impossible.

This implies a mental constellation of (a) a critical competence – that is, personal factors, environmental factors, and factors of the task need to be organized in an optimal fit – and (b) a challenge that is almost at the limit and of a very high valence, as the "body and soul" are in danger. The danger potential of the situation is created by a certain uncertainty, which originates from (a) a lack or surplus of information or (b) information ambiguity or discrepancy as it is typical for stress situations (see Nitsch, 1981; Nitsch & Hackfort, 1981). Therefore, to act in relative uncertainty (as nobody knows/can know by experience if all aspects have been considered sufficiently) in combination with a high potential for (physical) harm or loss (risk) is required – and desired. Facets of stress tolerance and tolerance for ambiguity and adversity are needed to organize appropriate actions and to be able to handle such situations successfully. Therefore, one should not discuss *high-risk, x-treme,* or adventure sport in the singular. It is more appropriate to use wording in the plural: adventurous sports or, even more precisely, "adventurous sport activities", as there are a variety of forms with different risk and experience potentials. This becomes apparent when comparing, for example, ultra-marathon runners (an example of *x-treme sports* in terms of effort), who withstand endurance demands with extreme physical strain (pain) by use of coping strategies, and speed-skiing (an example of *risk sports* in terms of courage) trying to beat speed records on skis, base-jumping (an example of adventurous sports in terms of exploration of new spheres and experiences), skydiving or wingsuit flying – for example, from rooftops – and big-wave surfing, which is highly demanding in terms of attention, concentration, fast decision-making, and reactions. Consequently, there can be no common, general explanation for such sports activities.

"Adventure sport" can – theoretically – cover a broad spectrum of experiential values (see Haubl, 1995). These can be used to differentiate and structure adventurous sport activities, similar to an approach by Schulze (1993), who assumed that social milieus can be differentiated in the adventure society as adventure milieus according to the orientation of different experiential values. In line with this assumption, credit would be given to Haubl (1995, p. 23), who adverted to not prematurely assuming a holistic level of motivation and who, in this context, also points out that, collectively, there is an appreciation of the hedonistic adventure orientation in postmodern sport culture. Therefore, experiential values from well-being via sociality through to *flow* and thrill could possibly be associated with sporting activity and be useful for the differentiation of adventure sports. Empirically, based on a comprehensive sample (n = ca. 1,400) and statistical calculations of the data, the study (see Haubl, 1995) pointed towards the fact that, on the one hand, adventure and risk are being associated with adventurous sport activities, but, on the other hand, risk and adventure cannot be clearly differentiated by empirical means or empirical proofs up to now. This issue is further considered hereafter.

Are we dealing with excesses of the "adventure society" (Schulze, 1993) or "risk society" (Beck, 1986) when looking at phenomena from hang-gliding, paragliding, and ice climbing, via rafting, air surfing, and canoeing, through to underground surfing (Beck, 1986), or are we confronted with (more and more?) pathological forms of the adventure society (Schulze, 1993)? In 1994, the German magazine *Der Spiegel* (no. 39) pursued the question, What drives athletes of *extreme sports*: death wish, vitality, or a risk addiction? The title of the issue was "Awesome feeling" (orig.: *Geiles Gefühl*). In the following years, the topic remained popular, and the magazine published a further article in 1996 (no. 37, p. 178) under the topic "Extreme sport/x-sport: eroticism of the rush" (orig.: *Erotik des Rausches*), in which journalists analysed and discussed what happened to the "population of poets and thinkers". To escape the boredom of their daily lives, German people are jumping off TV towers as bungee jumpers in their free time, they are climbing frozen waterfalls, or riding on rubber dinghies through wild water. Their conclusion: Someone who is devoted to experience anxiety is particularly crazy for happiness. Moreover, in an article on "Happy whilst canoeing – what drives extreme sport athletes and danger freaks close to death" (orig.: *Lustig beim Schluchting – Was Extremsportler und Dangerfreaks in Todesnähe treibt*) in the German newspaper *Süddeutsche Zeitung* (no. 122, May 29/30/31, 1993), the journalist Gerhard Pfeil drew the conclusion: "A case for the psychologist" (p. 34).

Approaches, Interpretations, and Explanations

There is certainly no lack of interpretive approaches. They range from an inherent curiosity behaviour, explorative behaviour (which is important for the survival and development of a species), or the anthropologically postulated "Odysseus-factor" via a constitutionally high production of neurotransmitters (e.g., adrenalin, dopamine, endorphins), personality traits (see, e.g., "sensation", Zuckerman, 1979a, 1991, or more general "stress-seeking", Klausner, 1986), through to spontaneous, socially induced tests of courage or character. In this context, it is also of interest that Rachman (1978) explained that courage does not mean the absence of anxiety, but that it is essential for courage not to avoid a danger although fear is growing. Of further interest are socio-cultural developments, as they are certainly influential and of psychological importance. In the following, approaches are introduced that have been most influential in regard to the description and explanation of adventurous and risky behaviour by focussing on a specific component of the action-orientation towards adventurous (here especially: sport) activities. In a final paragraph, a perspective on adventurous sport activities is introduced that provides an integrative framework for future empirical investigations and the further elaboration of a comprehensive and consistent conceptualization of adventurous sport activities as a model of adventurous activities in general. In this context, psychological aspects of adventurous sports and sports with high risk and the social preconditions and mental functionality are of utmost interest.

Social- and Personality-Psychology Perspectives

In this context, psychological aspects of adventurous sport activities and sports with high risk are of utmost interest. In the disciplinary discussion, one focus based on a social-psychology perspective is on the consequences of a perfectionistic control society (see prevention and contraception; airbag, birth control pill, social network, etc.), which could cause reactions or provocations of breaking routines and boredom, in which curiosity, creativity, and volition play a role. The huge influence of technology and urbanization could create a need for nature as a natural, primary experience. As a consequence of the increase in possibilities in digital communication (electronical networking), a decoupling in regard to face-to-face social interaction is taking place, as well as the thereby reduced experiences of sudden and direct interpersonal closeness and nonverbal contact and responses, which are important for self-awareness, self-development, self-improvement, and self-classification.

All of this could lead to a tendency towards compensatory experiences. The complexity of our life due to complex socio-economic, cultural, and ecological connections, as well as the rapid growth of complex technologies, is reflected in the experiences of uncertainty and insecurity. In this context, the search for risk and risk management could mediate the experience of overcoming uncertainty and insecurity. Furthermore, destructive behavioural impulses could be consequences of a supersaturated consumer society, and secondary world experiences (i.e., TV, video clips on the internet etc.) and artificial world experiences (e.g., reality TV, virtual reality) could spark a search for authentic self-experiences. Last, but not least, phenomena such as adventure tourism, extreme sports, and survival training could be related to the fact that, in everyday life, only weak stimuli and experiences are experienced, and, in partialized action interconnections, as they are typical in today's work life, merely a reduced self-awareness is possible, so that a search for holistic experiences (experience of psychophysical unity, biopsychosocial wholeness) is created through a synchronization of the channels of perception, through which an overcoming of disunity and orientation problems in everyday life is at least perceptible in the short term.

Experience orientation refers to self-occupation and self-experience, which indicates, if it occurs as a mass phenomenon, that it is not satisfied if it arises in work life or in traditional leisure-time activities. Facets of leisure sport such as recreational sports and adventurous sport activities therefore gain the functional meaning of either a compensation or a complementation as an alternative or additional action and experience sphere.

In social psychology, with a close link to sociology, a mass movement is detected and conceptualized in regard to the trend to individualize ("individualization"). Exclusivity and specificity (e.g., Himalayan trekking, helicopter skiing) become general offers through marketing, which creates a paradox. On the one hand, they lead to frustrating experiences and the (often disregarded) experience that offers of leisure-time events only lead to experiences through self-organized and internally attributed activities, whereby the experiences are not achieved through rational action strategies (alone). On the other hand, this supports the search for new niches and possibilities, which are included on the adventure market and also expand it. This creates a vicious (and frustrating) circle. Reflection and recollection of the adventure-constituting self-activity are needed here. The realization that offers of adventure simply suggest potentials for adventure could lead to a reorientation away from the quantitative focus (more often, more intensive) to a qualitative attitude (different, more specific) and an action-motivating attitude: Experiences in leisure sport are more dependent on the attitude than the offer, and they are directly and immediately connected to the actions of an individual.

The trend towards so-called adventure and high-risk sports is seized upon by commercial leisure activity providers. Paragliding, skydiving, and diving schools, expedition organizers, and providers of adventure weekends are experiencing a boom, which a look at the vast market of sports and leisure-time magazines illustrates.

Sport events simply become events and, ultimately, an arrangement of experiences for consumers, whose interest does not lie in the sport, but in everything else that has a value of entertainment ("desporting"). Complementary to achievement motivation and its differentiation, a kind of "experience motivation" and its components, "fear of missing out" or "hope for adventure", are possibly a driving force behind this.

The following characteristics of the commercial adventure offers warrant a critical observation from a psychological point of view: The experiences should be "delivered" (e.g., adventure weekends or expeditions), and other people control the action (e.g., tandem jump or bungee jumping).

These experiences, without any active option of control, without the conscientiousness to be responsible for one's own actions, and without any training of abilities and capabilities, do not appear to be suitable to satisfy a need for adventure in the long run. In particular, the aspect of an active control option seems to be important for a deep sense of adventure. According to Csikszentmihalyi and LeFevre (1975), this is a prerequisite for a state of *flow*. Csikszentmihalyi and Csikszentmihalyi (1990) reported that they have found in their studies:

> that people involved in adventurous pursuits such as rock climbing (Csikszentmihalyi, 1975; Mitchell, 1983), solo long-distance sailing (Macbeth, 1988), polar explorations (Logan, 1985) … and a variety of similar endeavours, report a state of optimal experience we have called flow. To understand why adventure is so attractive, it is important to understand what happens to people when they experience flow.
>
> *(pp. 149–150)*

In regard to prerequisites for a *flow* experience it seems to be essential that the activity is predominantly intrinsically rewarding, and extrinsic rewards are not important. The activity provides enjoyment and a feeling of competence.

> In a flow state there is characteristically a total involvement with the chosen activity, one that typically offers constant challenges that have to be met with appropriate skills, and the ability to match these provides immediate and gratifying feedback.
> *(Csikszentmihalyi & Csikszentmihalyi, 1990, p. 150)*

Moreover, it is assumed that activities that are able to produce *flow* in a person "are ways for people to test the limits of their being, to transcend their former conception of self by extending skills and undergoing new experience" (Csikszentmihalyi, 1975, p. 26).

These assumptions are supported, for example, by developments in bungee jumping, as people have started to perform tricks such as somersaults during the phase of bouncing up again. Apparently, the simple overcoming of fear or the confrontation with fear is not enough to uphold one's motivation for bungee jumping in the long run. In diving, two examples show an opposing development: On the one hand, in technical diving, the goal is to reach so-far unreachable places (deeper, caves, ice-diving). On the other hand, some divers attempt to have more intense diving experiences by changing the control options (physiological and psychological; e.g., free-diving). Similar developments can be observed when climbing (i.e., high-mountain tours without oxygen supply, free rock climbing in mountains, and ice climbing).

A further essential factor for the attraction of such activities is seen in the action competence experience (see Harter, 1978, 1981), especially for a long-term motivation for *high-risk sport*: Many divers, paraglider, skydivers, and so on, discover a deeper fascination of their actions only once they have reached a certain level of ability. It makes sense to assume that the ability and the experience of competence correlate up to a certain level.

Around 40 years ago, Zuckerman (see Zuckerman, 1979b, 1991) coined the concept of "sensation seeking", which differentiates people on the strength of their tendency to seek out situations with a risk factor. People with a strong tendency of sensation seeking expect less anxiety but strong positive feelings in risky situations, whereas people with a low value of sensation seeking are expected to be more likely to experience high levels of state anxiety and moderate-to-low levels of comfortable feelings. The distinct sensation seekers are more likely to be stressed with boredom and seek dangerous situations to escape their daily routines, sometimes even if this is associated with antisocial behaviours. They produce or provoke stress for themselves and others (Zuckerman, 1979c, 1991). Sensation seekers tend to display potentially dangerous behaviours, such as smoking or, of course, adventurous sport activities.

In 1986, Klausner published a book titled *Why Man Takes Chances*, in which he introduced the concept of "stress seeking". According to this concept, stress seekers approach dangerous situations (e.g., free-climbing) very rationally and they are self-centred. Furthermore, he (Klausner, 1986) described the stress-seeking personality as one where pain and pleasure are mixed. Stress seekers seek out situations that lead to an increase in physiological and psychological arousal. They perceive it as something positive when their arousal levels surpass normal levels.

Empirical studies regarding adventurous sport activities are scarce. Published works usually draw on personality psychology. A study by the Polish psychiatrist Ryn (1988), who described mountaineers as schizoid and asthenic-neurotic (only 4% of his sample proved to have normal personalities), serves as an example of this. He relied on data that had been collected using Cattell's 16 Personality Factor Questionnaire (16-PF) – a general, in terms of sport, unspecific, and unsuitable instrument (also, it was not reported whether the Polish translation was tested for its psychometric values). Csikszentmihalyi (1975) characterized mountaineers as motivated by an anti-structural tendency (among others), a tendency to regard conventional norms as provisional, and a tendency for self-actualization and personal fulfilment. Levenson (1990) also discovered that mountaineers are more contrarian (free-spirited) than others. In a classification study, he differentiated a variety of forms and types of risk-taking: drug consummation (antisocial risk seeking), heroic behaviour (e.g., firefighters who have been rewarded for their courage), and mountaineering (adventurous risk seeking).

A study by McMillan and Rachman (1988) illustrates the distinction between brave and fearless and overconfident individuals. They examined skydivers (n = 105), of which two-thirds belonged to the brave and less than 10% belonged to the category of those with overconfidence. In this regard, it is also important to point out that misjudgements about one's own abilities are often made, which could result from a comparison with others. Thus, the belief that one is in less danger than others in a risky situation ("optimistic misjudgement"; Weinstein, 1989; c.f. Allmer, 1995, p. 81), could lead to an overly brave behaviour and to a "rationalisation of future confrontations with risky situations" (Allmer, 1995, p. 81; "defensive optimism", according to Schwarzer, 1994). Schneider and Rheinberg (1995, p. 426) also describe this as a "risk-underestimation-tendency", which appears to be resistant to negative experiences.

A study by Freixanet (1991) examining the relationship between personality and participation in adventurous sport activities (n = 27 alpinists, n = 72 mountaineers, n = 221 other athletes, and n = 54 people who do not partake in any high-risk activities) showed that the personality profile of people participating in adventurous sport activities is identifiable: They appear to be extrovert, emotionally stable, compliant to social norms, and looking for thrills. In terms of extroversion and neuroticism, these results support the findings of Eysenck, Nias, and Cox (1982), who found that athletes are more extroverted and less neurotic compared with non-athletes. The results differ in regard to psychoticism (Eysenck et al. found higher values in athletes compared with non-athletes): No differences were found between athletes involved in adventurous sport activities and normal athletes. In an early empirical study in sport psychology using a standardized instrument (Cattell's 16-PF; see Cattell, 1946), Vanek and Hosek (1977) investigated athletes (n = 824 athletes from 27 different sports) and selected and analysed those who had been involved in risk sports. Self-security, hardiness/toughness, and unconventionality were found to be in close relation to the dangerousness of the sports activity (i.e., parachute jumping, wild-water canoeing), and high values in intelligence were measured in these athletes.

Such correlation studies provide empirical indications and, thereby, possibilities of descriptions, but they point to a theoretical integration to develop explanatory hypotheses.

Psychoanalytical Perspective

Psychoanalytically based explanations refer to the constructive aspect of overcoming fear (see Hackfort & Schwenkmezger, 1993) and to the fact that experiences of reality and of the core of the self are (only) possible in ultimate situations. On the basis that fear is an existential experience (in the wake of Kierkegaard), the overcoming of fear is a key moment of personal fulfilment and self-development.

To what extent a drive of fear should be assumed, which acts as the trigger of risk behaviour, which in turn means satisfaction of the drive of fear, is debatable and is empirically examined just as little as the assumption that risk behaviour is a way to learn strategies to overcome or at least to be able to handle the "fear of fear" (see also Semler, 1994). The classification of risk behaviour as a "contra phobic attitude" can be traced back to Fenichel (1939) and refers to the attempt to overcome fear, which stems from traumatic experiences in childhood. More generally, one puts oneself at risk in order to overcome it, instead of an inner fear.

The misleading term "anxiety pleasure" (orig. in German: *Angstlust*) was coined by Balint (1972) to explain the behaviour of *philobats*, who – in contrast to *ocnophiles* – constantly put themselves at risk, to prove to themselves that they can survive traumatic situations. He understands his psychoanalytic reflections on anxiety pleasure and regression (in German: *Angstlust* and *Regression*) as a contribution to psychological typology in which he differentiates between philobats and ocnophiles. He did not consider these two types to be independent alternatives, but as overlapping or also intermixing attitudes. The origin of his notions is the thrill, which is experienced at a funfair, for example, when people try to stimulate themselves through dangerous situations. Such a pleasure in anxiety or an enjoyment of fear is especially reachable through activities, many of which include speed, such as different forms of racing (motor sport or skiing), or circumstances that put the person in an exposed situation, such as diving, climbing, or gliding. Similar to the introvert (*sensu* Jung, 1972), based on his enjoyment of fear, the philobat manages to free himself and reaches a sense of harmony between himself and the world (the subject and the object). The ocnophile, on the other hand, similar to the extrovert (*sensu* Jung), needs to hold onto the objects to attempt to re-establish a lost harmony and is constantly being disappointed. The philobat has to leave the zone of safety and put himself at risk (Balint, 1972, p. 73), to assure himself that, after traumatic experiences (birth) and their consequences, he is now better at coping with new traumatic experiences.

In anxiety pleasure (*Angstlust*), in the interpretation of enjoyment in fear, or in thrill seeking, the psychoanalyst Kohut (1966) identified an expression of a neurotic disturbance: Such emotionally disturbed people can only reach self-assurance in extreme situations and experiences. More appropriate seems the interpretation of an enjoyment of the confrontation of fear, the overcoming of fear, and the anticipated satisfaction in case of success. The following part of an interview with Børge Ousland, who in 1997 was the first man to cross the Antarctic unsupported, provides evidence for this understanding:

> Fear is essential for me. It helps me to prepare my expedition. I need natural anxiety to make clever decisions, to act with care. ... fear is exciting, because it is exciting to overcome it. In bungee jumping, for example: you become stronger, when you beat your fear.
>
> *(orig. in German language, translated by the author; quote in the German magazine "Fit for Fun", 3/1997, p. 146)*

The experience of dealing with fear, to be competent while experiencing fear, and to be able to control anxiety as an emotional experience of competence are surely enough to strengthen self-awareness, especially in association with social recognition. Mediated by the increase in self-awareness, this experience also strengthens self-confidence as a confidence in one's own action competence, which always refers to a specific *action situation*. Accordingly, Schneider and Rheinberg (1995, p. 424) argued that, rather than the vital risk itself, the risk control through one's own competence is experienced as an appeal. This refers to the meaning of the action reference (reaction), which is discussed in more detail below.

Activation-Theoretical Perspective

The earlier (in the psychoanalytical context) mentioned "safety zone" also plays a role as a "protecting frame" in the attempted explanation of Apter (1992). The pleasure of the thrill unfolds as a search for stimulation in this frame, because – according to Apter's reversal theory, which is plausibly outlined, but is not verified and certainly not proven – the human needs an optimal situation and moves between the search for arousal and the avoidance of fear, as well as relaxation and the overcoming of boredom. If the balance (homeostasis) between these is interrupted, the result is either (in case of under-stimulation) a "thirst for adventure" or (in case of overstimulation) the search for relaxation.

An earmark of activation-theoretical conceptualizations is that they originate from optimal (usually medium) activation levels, which are perceived as pleasant.

> For an individual organism at a particular time there will be an optimal influx of arousal potential. Arousal potential that deviates in either an upward or downward direction from this optimum will be drive inducing or aversive.
>
> *(Berlyne, 1960, p. 194)*

Hence, exceedingly high levels of activation are perceived as unpleasant, and the reduction (relaxation) of these leads to positive experiences. The experience of reducing a short-term high activation level has a rewarding and reinforcing effect so that there is a tendency to repeatedly seek out such situations and also a tendency of an enhancement.

Also in Zuckermann's trait concept of sensation seeking (1974, 1979a, 1979b, 1979c, 1991; see above), this personality factor is closely linked to activation: The motivation for sensation and need for stimulation is individually manifested differently and corresponds with interindividual differences in optimal arousal. Thus, people who show high values in sensation seeking should also show a stronger tendency towards risky or dangerous situations or *adventurous sport activities*. This is not necessarily the case, as demonstrated by Schneider and Rheinberg (1995). These authors found that people with high values in sensation seeking are not only looking for *adventurous sport activities* but are engaged in different dangerous behaviours, such as drug use or risky behaviour in traffic. Moreover, Rossi and Cereatti (1993) argued that it would be needed to consider in detail the objective as well as subjective risks and the degree of predictability of the situation as it is combined with the sport activity to clarify the relation between sensation seeking and *adventurous sport activities*.

The concept of the optimal stimulation is also discussed by Spielberger, Peters, and Frain (1981; also see Spielberger & Starr, 1994). They reify it content-wise by assuming that, in distinctly stimulus-rich situations, a status of optimal experiences is reached, when feelings of joy or pleasure are interlinked or connected to feelings of anxiety. Examples of such situations are known by all from experiences on rollercoasters or ghost trains. These authors refer to previous studies on the relation between curiosity and anxiety.

Action-Theory Perspective

Adventurous sport activities are created by certain kinds of action in a specific class of situation (action situations). The *action situation* can be defined (see Hackfort & Nitsch, 2019; Nitsch & Hackfort, 1981) by the specific person–environment–task constellation, and what is perceived as adventurous, but nevertheless pleasant and attractive, depends on the individual intentional and instrumental reference systems (Nitsch & Hackfort, 1984). Depending on the initial situation, a gain in pleasure can be experienced in connection with an increase in tension (activation) or in consequence of a decrease in tension (relaxation), as described above. Furthermore, a certain activation level associated with a thrill is surely not only related to comfortable affective states, but more to blended emotions or an "emotional mixture" of pleasant and unpleasant emotions (Hackfort, 1991). Boesch (1975) mentioned feelings of triumph following an action and he characterized feelings of triumph as feelings induced by the perception of success in actions in which the subject was not sure about his or her action competence. Moreover, he explained that the insecurity of an action outcome is often experienced as a threat, and that the feeling of triumph is composed of the experience of relief that the threat did not come true (reality) and the pride based on the experience that the positive action outcome was a result of the subject's own skills (see Boesch, 1975, pp. 14–15).

The orientation of the action on the result, over the search for results through to the addiction to results, is labelled as the "internal" orientation (e.g., Schulze, 1993). However, in light of the action reference, a distinction between the internal and external orientation can be made. Accordingly, through the action referred external orientation and physically accentuated actions, *adventurous sport activities* appear to convey a gain in pleasure and satisfaction. Historically, this can be seen as a consequence of the more internal-oriented perspective favoured by the young generation in the 1960s and 1970s, when a physically accentuated activity was practised in the form of meditation to reach pleasure and satisfaction. Functionally, both orientations and activities would be seen as complementary to each other.

Whereas people used to find a way to their soul and to interact with it through meditation, nowadays an interaction with the environment and nature is practised as well – for some people, predominantly. The search for meaning (in life and for life), well-being, security, and adventure leads, on the one hand, to an inward way of action (contemplation) and, on the other hand, to an outward way of action (externalization like presentation). For one thing, this is related to a direct strategy of relaxation; for another thing, it is related to a resolving of tension – by progressive muscle relaxation, for example.

The search for adventure and curiosity are implemented in a "secure framework" (Apter, 1992) or a "security zone" (Balint, 1972), respectively, which can empirically be better distinguished from an *action-theory* perspective, with the "danger area" described by Fuchs (1976) between the ability and anxiety threshold. Through the overcoming of the anxiety threshold, the area of ability can be better exploited, which, among other things, can lead to the exploration and expansion of individual potentials, an increase in action competence (see also Schneider & Rheinberg, 1995) and self-control (see also Allmer, 1995), and the extension of the individual action scope (or leeway/"action leeway"), as well as lifting self-confidence and strengthening self-assurance. In this way, orientation problems related to socio-cultural developments (see above) or provoked by these developments can be individually addressed through missing sense and value systems (e.g., Le Breton, 1995). To what extent this would also have an effect on other areas or spheres of life – for example, the workplace – remains to be examined.

As a hypothesis, it can be assumed that transfers or generalizations are possible, so that the love for and practice of adventurous sport activities appear in a different light as to be crazy, incomprehensible, paradoxical, or mad, but the handling of stress in high-risk and adventurous sport activities can be considered to be a training situation for the handling of stress in other areas – for example, in the workplace, traffic, or further demanding situations in life. Tomlinson and Yorganci (1997, p. 7) argues that this is the appeal of *extreme sport* – more specifically, to be able to maintain perfect physical and mental control to achieve peak performances under difficult and even life-threatening conditions. In this sense, the above-mentioned statement by Semler (1994, p. 66), by which those who can deal with the most dangerous situations between sky and earth will not fail at mundane problems in their daily lives, should be taken up again and examined in empirical studies.

Unpublished studies by our research group indicate that, in individual cases, the assumption is certainly made that the practice of high-risk sports (e.g., skydiving, deep ocean diving) increases the competence of coping (related to the handling of stress and anxiety) and, in consequence, positively affects the private and professional life (i.e., "Maybe in some other situations I won't be so anxious anymore and I will have more self-confidence, if I have completed a tandem-skydive"; interview statement cited by Kuhlmann, 1998). Out of eight extreme sport athletes, five stated in the interviews, that they detected mental changes as an effect of extreme sport activities, which were an increase in self-confidence, the experience of higher subjective competence and self-efficacy, and a more self-secure presence overall. Four mentioned that the gained expansion of experiences through the experience of life-threatening situations and the connected affirmation of their own action control is a positive effect for their future life. Furthermore, three participants said they experienced more balance and calmness in their daily lives as a consequence of the confrontation with danger in sport. Moreover, three also stated that the required anxiety and stress control in extreme sport activities also leads to improved anxiety and stress control in daily situations. These statements can be interpreted in the sense of a generalization on one hand (see increase in self-confidence and action control) and in the sense of a transfer (see anxiety and stress control) on the other hand.

In a cross-sectional comparison of non-extreme sport athletes (n = 8; age: M = 25.25; SD = 1.67), novices in extreme sports (n = 8; age: M = 25.63; SD = 2.79) and experienced extreme sport athletes (n = 8; age: M = 26; SD = 2.20) regarding a variety of trait dimensions (among others, extroversion/introversion, friendliness/hostility, motivation/irresponsibility, neuroticism/emotional stability, intelligence/stupidity; perception of control, style of coping), no statistically significant differences could be found (Kuhlmann, 1998). All 24 male participants (students with the University AF, Munich) were very similar in regard to their personality traits. They scored highly in terms of readiness to take risks, performance orientation, and extraversion, are far more internally than externally oriented in their perception of control, and showed relatively high intolerance towards affective (physiological) arousal, which speaks for the fact that they strive to reduce an intensive affective state (Krohne, Schumacher, & Egloff, 1992); this is in line with the justification of the above-mentioned assumption, that the battle with stress in extreme sports as a training situation is used to improve the handling of stress in the workplace and in further life settings (which is initially observed and limited to this group).

On the basis of these observations, it remains to be clarified to what extent the practice of adventurous sport activities for the experience of an action competence in further fields of action is instrumentally and emotionally transferable to other action situations. This question refers to the existing or establishing transfer potential between two areas of actions and life experiences. The differently structured forms and types of sport on the one hand, and the different situations of work, traffic, leisure, and so on, and the various demands on the other hand, suggest that we need to assume different transfer potentials. How these are then used is a question of transfer management (Lemke, 1995), as the key message from Lemke (1995, p. 2) is that transfers can be managed. The indications of this development have not yet been examined for the psychology of *adventurous sport activities*.

Conclusion

The search for the experience of extraordinary affective states – for example, the experience of a combination of anxiety and enjoyment as is characteristic of adventurous activities – is regarded to be a consequence of the experience of boredom in everyday life situations for some people living in a society in which security is a typical feature of the system, but this is also associated with a certain degree of affective deprivation. Adventurous activities can be described as a search for extraordinary feelings and affective states induced by an activity-inherent attraction of the process of acting and, especially in sport, in regard to extraordinary experiences of the body (e.g., flying, diving) through these activities in extraordinary environments or circumstances (e.g., flying from skyscrapers, diving in the deep ocean or in caves). Such actions are motivated by and serve the expansion of self-experiences and self-realization, the extension of the scope of actions, and the extension of personal and human limits. These actions require and challenge self-control and coping competences. Thus, it is typical of athletes practising adventurous sport activities that they are totally committed and demonstrate very rational preparation and a systematic approach to adventurous sport projects.

Adventurous sport activities may be regarded to be a conceptual framework that also includes *risk sports* and *x-treme sports*, but these terms should not be used as synonyms. From an action-psychology perspective, adventurous actions and sports activities are primarily motivated by exploration and the extension of action spheres. Risk behaviour is associated with uncertainty based on a close balance of competences and demands and the appraisal of challenge and threat; actions characterizing high-risk sports are always in danger of inducing serious costs such as harm and loss in regard to mental, social, or/and physical well-being. X-treme sports are always in pursuit of the expansion of limits in terms of an absolute, interindividual level of these kinds of action. Thus, adventurous sports activities are not appropriately described as being irrational or even pathological and organized by pure daredevils, but are motivated by extraordinary motives, based on unusual self-concepts, associated with strong will-power, readiness for effort, and high stress tolerance.

Along with interpretative methods, single case studies are needed to search and uncover in detail combinations of mental characteristics (profiling) and, most important, functional (intra-mental, psychophysical, psychosocial, and psycho-ecological) interrelationships in the action-regulation system of athletes when practising adventurous sport activities. Such research could also be of interest for further behaviour settings, areas of action, and spheres of life such as military events or actions of people in the fire brigade.

Similar to a differentiation of performance psychology, adventure psychology also refers to a specific topic that is especially interesting and relevant in sport but not limited to sport. For sport psychology, a certain overlap is interesting to improve the understanding of adventurous sport activities and the people who turn towards this field of events, these kinds of action, and such experiences. For adventure psychology, the field of sport offers a broad scope of relevant opportunities to clarify the phenomena, functional interrelations, and decisive components for the organization and regulation of actions in regard to adventure experiences. For both sport and adventure psychology, an exchange of knowledge and cooperation should be promising for the development and support of applied measurements and interventional purposes such as therapy and education.

References

Allmer, H. (1995). "No risk – No fun" – Zur psychologischen Erklärung von Extrem-und Risikosport ["No risk – no fun" – For a psychological explanation of extreme- and risk- sport]. *Brennpunkte Der Sportwissenschaft, 9*(1/2), 60–90.

Apter, M. J. (1992). *The dangerous edge: The psychology of excitement*. New York: Free Press.

Aufmuth, U. (1983). Risikosport und Identitätsproblematik [Risk sport and the identity problem]. *Sportwissenschaft, 13*(3), 249–270.

Balint, M. (1972). *Angstlust und Regression. Beitrag zur psychologischen Typenlehre* [Anxiety pleasure and regression. Contribution to psychological tyoplogy]. Stuttgart: Klett-Cotta.

Beck, U. (1986). *Risikogesellschaft* [Risk society]. Frankfurt: Campus.

Berlyne, D. E. (1960). *Conflict, arousal, and curiosity*. New York: McGraw-Hill.

Boesch, E. E. (1975). *Zwischen Angst und Triumph* [Between anxiety and triumph]. Bern: Huber.

Breivik, G. (2013). Zombie-like or superconscious? A phenomenological and conceptual analysis of consciousness in elite sport. *Journal of the Philosophy of Sport, 40*, 85–106.

Cattell, R. B. (1946). *Description and measurement of personality*. Yonkers-on-Hudson, NY: World.

Csikszentmihalyi, M. (1975). *Beyond boredom and anxiety*. San Francisco, CA: Jersey-Boss.

Csikszentmihalyi, M., & Csikszentmihalyi, I. S. (1990). Adventure and the flow experience. In J. C. Miles & S. Priest (Eds.), *Adventure education* (pp. 149–155). State College, PA: Venture.

Csikszentmihalyi, M., & LeFevre, J. (1975). Optimal experience in work and leisure. *Journal of Personality and Social Psychology, 56*(5), 815–822.

Cube, F. V. (1990). *Gefährliche Sicherheit* [Dangerous security]. Munich: Piper.

Eysenck, H. J., Nias, D. K. B., & Cox, D. N. (1982). Sport and personality. *Advances in Behaviour Research and Therapy, 4*, 1–56.

Eysenck, M. W. (2004). *Psychology: An international perspective*. Hove: Psychology Press.

Fenichel, O. (1939). The counter-phobic attitude. *International Journal of Psycho-Analysis, 20*, 263–274.

Freixanet, M. G. (1991). Personality profile of subjects engaged in high physical risk sports. *Personality and Individual Differences, 12*, 1087–1093.

Fuchs, R. (1976). Furchtregulation und Furchthemmung des Zweckhandelns [Fear regulation and fear inhibition in purposive actions]. In A. Thomas Ed., *Psychologie der Handlung und Bewegung* [Psychology of action and movement] (pp. 97–159). Meisenheim am Glan: Hain.

Golz, N., Erkelenz, M., & Sack, H.-G. (1990). Ein erlebnisorientiertes Sportprogramm zur Behandlung von Depressionen. Theoretische Grundlagen und empirische Ergebnisse [A sport program for the treatment of depression oriented towards adventure. Theoretical foundations and empirical results]. *Report Psychologie, 4*, 12–19.

Hackfort, D. (Ed). (1991). *Research on emotions in sport*. Cologne: Sport und Buch Strauss.

Hackfort, D., & Nitsch, J. R. (2019). Action and action situation. In D. Hackfort, R. J. Schinke & B. Strauss (Eds.), *Dictionary of sport psychology* (pp. 2–3). London: Elsevier.

Hackfort, D., & Schwenkmezger, P. (1993). Anxiety. In R. N. Singer, M. Murphey, & L. K. Tennant (Eds.), *Handbook of research on sport psychology* (pp. 328–364). New York: MacMillan.

Harter, S. (1978). Effectance motivation reconsidered. Toward a developmental model. *Human Development, 21*, 34–64.

Harter, S. (1981). A model of mastery motivation in children: Individual differences and developmental change. In W. A. Collins (Ed.), *Aspects of the development of competence: The Minnesota symposia on child psychology* (Vol. 14, pp. 215–255). Hillsdale, NJ: Erlbaum.

Haubl, R. (1995). Des Kaisers neue Kleider? Struktur und Dynamik der Erlebnisgesellschaft [The emperor's new clothes? Structure and dynamic of the adventure society]. *Brennpunkte Der Sportwissenschaft, 9*(1/2), 5–27.

Hecker, G. (1989). Abenteuer und Wagnis im Sport – Sinn oder Unsinn [Adventure and risk in sport – Sense and nonsense]. *Deutsche Zeitschrift Für Sportmedizin, 40*(9), 328–331.

Heckmair, B., & Michl, W. (1993). *Erleben und Lernen* [Experience and learning]. Munich: Reinhardt.

Hunt, J. S., Jr. (1990). Philosophy of adventure education. In J. C. Miles & S. Priest (Eds.), *Adventure education* (pp. 119–128). State College, PA: Venture.

Jung, C. G. (1972). *Typologie* [Typology]. Olten: Walter.

Klausner, S. Z. (1986). Empirical analysis of stress-seekers. In S. Z. Klausner (Ed.), *Why man takes chances* (pp. 135–168). New York: Doubleday.

Klint, K. A. (1990). New directions for inquiry into self-concept and adventure experiences. In J. C. Miles & S. Priest (Eds.), *Adventure education* (pp. 163–172). State College, PA: Venture.

Kohut, H. (1966). Forms and transformations of narcissism. *Journal of the American Psychoanalytic Association, 1*, 243–272.

Krohne, H. W., Schumacher, A., & Egloff, B. (1992). Das Angstbewältigungs-Inventar (ABI) [The Mainz Coping Inventory, ABI]. *Mainzer Berichte Zur Persönlichkeitsforschung, 41*.

Kuhlmann, M. (1998). *Effekte der Ausübung von Extremsportarten auf andere Lebensbereiche* [Effects of practicing extreme sports in other spheres of life]. Munich: Unpublished diploma thesis, ISSW, University AF Munich.

Le Breton, D. (1995). *Lust am Risiko: Von Bungee-jumping, U-Bahn-surfen und anderen Arten, das Schicksal herauszufordern* [Pleasure of risk: About bungee-jumping, underground serving and further kinds to provoke fate]. Frankfurt: dipa.

Lemke, S. G. (1995). *Transfermanagement* [Management of transfer]. Göttingen: Verlag für Angewandte Psychologie.

Levenson, M. R. (1990). Risk taking and personality. *Journal of Personality and Social Psychology, 58*, 1073.

Logan, R. D. (1985). The flow experience in solitary ordeals. *Journal of Humanistic Psychology, 25*(4), 70–89.

Macbeth, J. (1988). Ocean cruising. In M. Csikszentmihalyi & I. S. Csikszentmihalyi (Eds.), *Optimal experience: Psychological studies of flow in conscious* (pp. 214–231). New York: Cambridge University Press.

McMillan, T. M., & Rachman, S. J. (1988). Fearlessness and courage in paratroopers undergoing training. *Personality and Individual Differences, 9*(2), 373–378.

Miles, J. C., & Priest, S. (Eds.). (1990). *Adventure education*. State College, PA: Venture.

Mitchell, R. G. (1983). *Mountain experience: The psychology and sociology of adventure*. Chicago, IL: University of Chicago Press.

Nitsch, J. R. (1981). Streßtheoretische Modellvorstellungen [Model types of stress theories]. In J. R. Nitsch (Ed.), *Stress* (pp. 52–141). Bern, Switzerland: Huber.

Nitsch, J. R., & Hackfort, D. (1981). Stress in Schule und Hochschule: Eine handlungspsychologische Funktionsanalyse [Stress in school and university: An action-psychology functional analysis]. In J. R. Nitsch (Ed.), *Stress* (pp. 263–311). Bern: Huber.

Nitsch, J. R., & Hackfort, D. (1984). Basisregulation interpersonalen Handelns im Sport [Tuning of interpersonal actions in sport]. In E. Hahn & H. Rieder Eds., *Sensumotorisches Lernen und Sportspielforschung* [Sensorimotor learning and research in sport games, pp. 148–166]. Cologne: bps.

Nitsch, J. R., & Hackfort, D. (2016). Theoretical framework of performance psychology: An action theory perspective. In M. Raab, B. Lobinger, S. Hoffmann, A. Pizzera & S. Laborde (Eds.), *Performance psychology. Perception, action, cognition, and emotion* (pp. 11–29). Amsterdam: Elsevier.

Opaschowski, H. W. (1995). *Freizeitökonomie: Marketing von Erlebniswelten* [Leisure economy: Marketing of worlds for adventure]. Opladen: Leske & Budrich.

Priest, S. (1990). The semantics of adventure education. In J. C. Miles & S. Priest (Eds.), *Adventure education* (pp. 113–117). State College, PA: Venture.

Rachman, S. J. (1978). *Fear and courage*. San Francisco, CA: Freeman.

Rheinberg, F. (1991). Flow-experience when motorcycling: A study of a special human condition. In R. Brendicke (Ed.), *Safety, environment, future* (pp. 349–362). Bochum: IfZ.

Rieper, G. (1995). Lernfeld Natur: Erlebnispädagogik in der Managemententwicklung [Learning field nature: Adventure pedagogy in management development]. *Personalführung, 27,* 924–930.

Rossi, B., & Cereatti, L. (1993). The sensation seeking in mountain athletes as assessed by Zuckerman's sensation seeking scale. *International Journal of Sport Psychology, 24,* 417–431.

Ryn, Z. (1988). Psychopathology in mountaineering – Mental disturbances under high-altitude stress. *International Journal of Sports Medicine, 9,* 163–169.

Schildmacher, A. (1998). Trends und Moden im Sport [Trends and fashions in sport]. *dvs-Informationen, 13* (2), 14–19.

Rousseau, J.-J. (1824). *Emile, ou de l'éducation.* Paris: Menard et Desenne.

Schleske, W. (1977). *Abenteuer, Wagnis, Risiko im Sport* [Adventure, venture, and risk in sport]. Schorndorf: Hofmann.

Schneider, K., & Rheinberg, F. (1995). Erlebnissuche und Risikomotivation [Seeking adventure and risk motivation]. In M. Amelang Ed., *Differentielle Psychologie* [Differential psychology] (pp. 407–439). Göttingen: Hogrefe.

Schulze, G. (1993). *Erlebnisgesellschaft* [Adventure society]. Frankfurt: Campus.

Schwarzer, R. (1994). Optimism, vulnerability and self-beliefs as self-related cognitions: A systematic overview. *Psychology and Health, 9,* 161–180.

Semler, G. (1994). *Die Lust an der Angst: Warum Menschen sich freiwillig extremen Risiken aussetzen* [The pleasure at anxiety: Why people expose themselves voluntarily to extreme risks]. Munich: Heyne.

Spielberger, C. D., Peters, R. A., & Frain, F. (1981). Neugier und Angst [Curiosity and anxiety]. In H. G. Voss & H. Keller (Eds.), *Neugierforschung. Grundlagen – Theorien – Anwendungen* [Curiosity research: Basics – theories – applications] (pp. 197–225). Weinheim: Beltz.

Spielberger, C. D., & Starr, L. M. (1994). Curiosity and exploratory behavior. In H. F. O'Neil, Jr. & M. Drillings (Eds.), *Motivation: Theory and research* (pp. 221–234). Hillsdale, NJ: Erlabaum.

Tomlinson, A., & Yorganci, I. (1997). Male coach/female athlete relations: Gender and power relations in competitive sport. *Journal of Sport and Social Issues, 21*(2), 134–155.

Vanek, M., & Hosek, V. (1977). *Zur Persönlichkeit des Sportlers* [To the personality of the athlete]. Schorndorf, Germany: Hofmann.

Weinstein, N. D. (1989). Effects of personal experience on self-protective behavior. *Psychological Bulletin, 105,* 31–50.

Zuckerman, M. (1974). The sensation seeking motive. In B. A. Maher (Ed.), *Progress in experimental personality research* (Vol. 7, pp. 80–148). New York: Academic Press.

Zuckerman, M. (1979a). *Sensation seeking: Beyond the optimal level of arousal.* Hillsdale, NJ: Erlbaum.

Zuckerman, M. (1979b). Attribution of success and failure revisited, or: The motivational bias is alive and well in attribution theory. *Journal of Personality, 47,* 245–287.

Zuckerman, M. (1979c). Sensation seeking and risk taking. In C. E. Izard (Ed.), *Emotion in personality and psychopathology* (pp. 163–187). New York: Plenum Press.

Zuckerman, M. (1991). *Psychobiology of personality* (Vol. 10). Cambridge: Cambridge University Press.

2

ALEXITHYMIA

Tim Woodman, Christine Le Scanff, and Olivier Luminet

Introduction

Alexithymia is a distinct personality trait (Luminet, Rokbani, Ogez, & Jadoulle, 2007; Mikolajczak & Luminet, 2006) that is also positively related to neuroticism and negatively related to extraversion and openness (Luminet, Bagby, Wagner, Taylor, & Parker, 1999). The word "alexithymia" derives from the Greek language and reflects a lack of ("a-") words ("lex") for feelings ("thymia").

Phenomenon and Concept

Initially developed from clinical observations of a deficit in emotion processing and regulation, alexithymia is characterized by difficulties in verbalizing emotions (Luminet & Zamariola, 2018; Parker, Bagby, Taylor, Endler, & Schmitz, 1993; Taylor & Bagby, 2013). It is widely considered that alexithymia comprises two principal components: a difficulty acknowledging emotions and feelings, and a difficulty verbalizing emotions and feelings to others (Sifneos, 1973; Taylor, Bagby, & Parker, 1997). Alexithymic individuals also tend to focus on external events rather than on internal feelings (Nemiah, Freyberger, & Sifneos, 1976; Taylor, 1984).

Although considered a subclinical trait, alexithymia is associated with many psychosomatic disorders such as fibromyalgia, chronic gastrointestinal distress, and medically unexplained symptoms (De Gucht, Fischler, & Heiser, 2004a, 2004b; Lumley, Stettner, & Wehmer, 1996). Alexithymia is also associated with indices of impoverished mental health and emotion regulation, such as anxiety and depression, and difficulties in interpersonal relationships (Corcos & Speranza, 2003; Taylor, 2000; Taylor et al., 1997), and is inversely related with emotional intelligence (Parker, Taylor, & Bagby, 2001). Alexithymia affects the processing of one's own emotions and the recognition of one's internal state (Murphy, Brewer, Hobson, Catmur, & Bird, 2018; van der Velde et al., 2013). Alexithymia also affects the ability to recognize emotions in words or in others' faces (e.g., Lane, Sechrest, Riedel, Shapiro, & Kaszniak, 2000; Lane et al., 1996; Parker, Prkachin, & Prkachin, 2005; Parker, Taylor, & Bagby, 1993; Pedrosa Gil et al., 2009; Starita, Borhani, Bertini, & Scarpazza, 2018).

Alexithymia in Sport

In sport and exercise settings, there is currently only a limited amount of research on alexithymia. For example, drawing upon the clinical literature (Pedrosa Gil, Scheidt, Hoeger, & Nickel, 2008), Andres, Castanier, and Le Scanff (2013) found that alexithymia mediated the relationship between attachment style (most notably maternal insecure attachment style) and alcohol use in a population of student athletes.

The vast majority of research on alexithymia in sport, however, is in the high-risk sport literature. Within this literature, researchers have typically viewed alexithymia as a possible underlying motive for engaging in the high-risk domain activity. According to Woodman, Hardy, Barlow, and Le Scanff's (2010) agentic emotion regulation theory, individuals high in alexithymia are attracted to the high-risk domain because of the emotions that they stand to experience therein, most notably fear and the regulation of fear (see also Castanier, Le Scanff, & Woodman, 2011; Cazenave, Le Scanff, & Woodman, 2007; Woodman, MacGregor, & Hardy, 2019). Specifically, the alexithymic difficulty in interpreting emotional signals, as well as the concomitant poor emotional communication, hampers interpersonal relationships (Taylor et al., 1997), which in turn reduces alexithymic individuals' feelings of agency in such relationships. This lack of felt agency in emotional relationships leads to an attraction to domains in which one can feel greater agency. Importantly for the alexithymic individual, this agency is related to the regulation of potentially intense emotion (e.g., the fear of dying). In essence, the high-risk domain provides the opportunity for alexithymic individuals to initiate emotions on their terms, rather than feel that others dictate their impoverished emotional experience (Woodman, Hardy, & Barlow, 2020).

Woodman et al. (2010) found support for this theoretical position when they conducted two in-depth, multi-method studies of trans-Atlantic rowing and expeditionary mountaineering, both of which are long-duration, arduous, high-risk activities. They found that both the rowers and the mountaineers had elevated alexithymia, which manifested specifically in the alexithymia factor difficulty verbalizing emotion. This difficulty was significantly greater than that of comparator norms, even when controlling for the (long) time spent away from home that is required to complete these high-risk activities. As such, it is not simply that alexithymic individuals choose to spend long periods away from the stressful home environment, but rather that they spend time away from home specifically to engage with high-risk activities. The specific emotional difficulty "at home" was in those relationships that involved a loving partner (more than in relationships with friends, work colleagues, etc.), which further lends credence to the position that it is specifically the emotionally laden relationships that alexithymic individuals find stressful (see also Barlow, Woodman, & Hardy, 2013; Taylor et al., 1997). As Lester (1983) noted in his in-depth study of Everest mountaineers, certain aspects of domestic life, particularly meaningful interpersonal romantic relationships, "were more stressful to the average team member than were the icy conditions in a fragile tent on a snowy ridge in a high wind with inadequate oxygen" (p. 34).

The idea that alexithymic individuals might be attracted to the high-risk domain was further supported by two studies conducted with skydivers (Woodman, Cazenave, & Le Scanff, 2008; Woodman, Huggins, Le Scanff, & Cazenave, 2009). In these studies, skydivers completed measures of anxiety three times before and after a skydive; the alexithymic groups consistently reported greater anxiety than their non-alexithymic counterparts did before their respective skydive. They also reported significant fluctuations in anxiety over the skydive timeline; this fluctuation did not occur for non-alexithymic participants. This finding supports the specific emotion regulation motive that appears to underpin the motive for participation for alexithymic individuals. That is, alexithymic individuals appear attracted to the high-risk domain specifically for the high-intensity emotions that they stand to glean therein.

Regarding whether alexithymic individuals genuinely feel emotional during these activities or simply report any experienced physical sensation as "emotion" is a question that remains unanswered. Specifically, in the skydiving studies, there were positive associations between alexithymia and trait anxiety and each of the state anxiety measurements (Woodman et al., 2008). At first sight, such an association might seem paradoxical given that alexithymia reflects a difficulty identifying and verbalizing emotions, and that anxiety inventories require participants specifically to identify and rate their experience of a specific emotion. As such, one might expect alexithymia to be negatively associated with anxiety. However, alexithymic individuals appear to experience anxiety as a nebulous psychological distress and thus feel a generalized negative affect, but they feel unable to identify and verbalize the specific emotion that they are feeling (Lundh & Simonsson-Sarnecki, 2001). Luminet et al. (1999) also found that alexithymia was positively associated with neuroticism. That is, alexithymic individuals appear to feel negative emotions such as anxiety in a stronger way than non-alexithymic individuals. Their specific difficulty appears to be in their understanding and differentiation of these emotions.

Building on the work of Castanier and colleagues (Castanier, Le Scanff, & Woodman, 2010), researchers have also found alexithymia to be a predictor of risk-taking within the high-risk sport domain. In a series of cross-sectional studies, Barlow et al. (2015) found that alexithymic high-risk sport participants consistently and purposefully took more risks and adopted fewer precautionary behaviours (see Woodman et al., 2013). They further revealed that these alexithymic participants suffered a greater number of accidents. This finding appears to corroborate further the previous motivational research, which revealed that alexithymic individuals participate in high-risk activities with the specific aim of gleaning a heightened emotional experience. It is noteworthy that these effects were consistent across all studies when controlling for sensation seeking. It is also noteworthy that Barlow et al. (2013) comprehensively demonstrated that the motives for high-risk activities are not uniform across high-risk activities. That is, whereas participants in high-intensity and low-duration high-risk activities (e.g., skydiving) appear more motivated by the satisfaction of a need for thrill and sensations, participants in longer-duration high-risk activities (e.g., mountaineering) appear more motivated by a need to regulate their emotions. As such, the alexithymic propensity to take greater risks and suffer from more accidents is likely driven more by a need to experience some form of emotion regulation than by reckless thrill seeking. This position requires further research.

There is a lack of alexithymia research in the competitive sport performance domain. However, competitive performance environments could be very motivationally appealing to alexithymic individuals. Indeed, the sport competition arena might provide a fruitful environment within which alexithymic sportspeople might regulate their otherwise impoverished emotional life (see Roberts & Woodman, 2015, 2016, 2017).

Indeed, as revealed in the high-risk sport literature above, high-risk environments provide alexithymic individuals with an emotion regulation opportunity because they allow for the experience and control of anxiety, an emotional clarity that is not experienced in everyday life. That is, the mastery of one's anxiety in these settings provides a relative sense of well-being after having engaged in the activity (Barlow et al., 2013). A transfer of emotion regulation benefits from the high-stress domain back into everyday life is a feature of the high-risk sport literature, such that individuals enjoy reductions in anxiety (Woodman et al., 2008, 2009) and a greater ability to deal with close relationships in everyday life (Woodman et al., 2010).

Potential of Alexithymia in Sport

Of course, traditional competitive sport environments are not the same as high-risk sport environments; in particular, they are not typically life-threatening. Nonetheless, competitive sport environments are "risky" environments because performers risk their ego in an inherently ego-threatening environment. That is, when competing against others, performers stand to be winners or losers. Performers often suffer pre-performance anxiety because of this threat (cf. Neil & Woodman, 2017; Woodman & Hardy, 2001). Such competitive environments might thus allow alexithymic athletes to experience, and then to master, their underlying anxiety – a fascinating research avenue.

Given the typically heightened emotional environment of competition, the alexithymic blunted emotional expression might in fact place them in an emotionally advantageous competitive position. That is, alexithymic individuals who suffer from an impoverished emotional experience may have somewhat of a competitive advantage over their comparatively emotionally attuned counterparts. Indeed, performance under pressure requires athletes to maintain control over their emotions. It is thus possible that the emotion regulation difficulties of the alexithymic person – which are a hindrance in most aspects of living (e.g., interpersonal relationships) – will confer a competitive advantage in high-pressure competition domains.

Furthermore, the relative emotional paucity in everyday life that is characteristic of alexithymia suggests that the motivation for competition might be rather more central to the alexithymic athlete's self-concept than it is for the comparatively emotionally attuned athlete (cf. Barlow et al., 2013). Indeed, it is likely that it is only in the competitive domain that the alexithymic athletes will "feel" anything. These suggestions are, of course, conjectural, although recent studies of interoception (the perception of one's internal states; e.g., via a heartbeat-counting task) support the view that alexithymic individuals do indeed "feel" less (Murphy et al., 2018).

Conclusion

Given that researchers have found that foundational life difficulties can lead to exceptional competitive performance in later life (Hardy et al., 2017), the idea that a typically limiting personality construct such as alexithymia might in fact be an advantage in sport is certainly worth exploring. There are likely many disadvantages also (e.g., impaired emotional regulation strategies, poor emotion signal reading, etc.). Regardless, this fascinating personality construct certainly deserves more research attention within sport and exercise settings.

References

Andres, F., Castanier, C., & Le Scanff, C. (2013). Attachment and alcohol use amongst athletes: The mediating role of conscientiousness and alexithymia. *Addictive Behaviours, 39,* 487–490.

Barlow, M., Woodman, T., Chapman, C., Milton, M., Dodds, T., & Allen, B. (2015). Who takes risks in high-risk sport? The role of alexithymia. *Journal of Sport & Exercise Psychology, 37,* 83–96.

Barlow, M., Woodman, T., & Hardy, L. (2013). Great expectations: Different high-risk activities satisfy different motives. *Journal of Personality & Social Psychology, 105,* 458–475.

Castanier, C., Le Scanff, C., & Woodman, T. (2010). Who takes risks in high-risk sports? A personality typological approach. *Research Quarterly for Exercise & Sport, 81,* 478–484.

Castanier, C., Le Scanff, C., & Woodman, T. (2011). Mountaineering as affect regulation: The moderating role of self-regulation strategies. *Anxiety, Stress, and Coping, 24,* 75–89.

Cazenave, N., Le Scanff, C., & Woodman, T. (2007). Psychological profiles and emotional regulation characteristics of women engaged in risk-taking sports. *Anxiety, Stress, & Coping, 20,* 421–435.

Corcos, M., & Speranza, M. (2003). *Psychopathologie de l'alexithymie.* [Psychopathology of alexithymia]. Paris: Dunod.

De Gucht, V., Fischler, B., & Heiser, W. (2004a). Neuroticism, alexithymia, negative affect, and positive affect as determinants of medically unexplained symptoms. *Personality and Individual Differences, 36,* 1655–1667.

De Gucht, V., Fischler, B., & Heiser, W. (2004b). Personality and affect as determinants of medically unexplained symptoms in primary care: A follow-up study. *Journal of Psychosomatic Research, 56,* 279–285.

Hardy, L., Barlow, M., Evans, L., Rees, T., Woodman, T., & Warr, C. (2017). Great British medallists: Psychosocial biographies of super-elite and elite athletes from Olympic sports. *Progress in Brain Research, 232,* 1–119.

Lane, R. D., Sechrest, L., Riedel, R., Shapiro, D. E., & Kaszniak, A. W. (2000). Pervasive emotion recognition deficit common to alexithymia and the repressive coping style. *Psychosomatic Medicine, 62,* 492–501.

Lane, R. D., Sechrest, L., Riedel, R., Weldon, V., Kaszniak, A., & Schwartz, G. E. (1996). Impaired verbal and nonverbal emotion recognition in alexithymia. *Psychosomatic Medicine, 58,* 203–210.

Lester, J. (1983). Wrestling with the self on Mount Everest. *Journal of Humanistic Psychology, 23,* 31–41.

Luminet, O., Bagby, R. M., Wagner, H., Taylor, G. T., & Parker, J. D. A. (1999). Relation between alexithymia and the five-factor model of personality: A facet-level analysis. *Journal of Personality Assessment, 73,* 345–358.

Luminet, O., Rokbani, L., Ogez, D., & Jadoulle, V. (2007). An evaluation of the absolute and relative stability of alexithymia in women with breast cancer. *Journal of Psychosomatic Research, 62,* 641–648.

Luminet, O., & Zamariola, G. (2018). Emotion knowledge and emotion regulation in alexithymia. In O. Luminet, G. J. Taylor & R. M. Bagby 2018, *Alexithymia: Advances in research, theory, and clinical practice* (pp. 49–77). Cambridge: Cambridge University Press.

Lumley, M. A., Stettner, L., & Wehmer, F. (1996). How are alexithymia and physical illness linked? A review and critique of pathways. *Journal of Psychosomatic Research, 41,* 505–518.

Lundh, L.-G., & Simonsson-Sarnecki, M. (2001). Alexithymia, emotion, and somatic complaints. *Journal of Personality, 69,* 483–510.

Mikolajczak, M., & Luminet, O. (2006). Is alexithymia affected by situational stress or is it a stable trait related to emotion regulation? *Personality & Individual Differences, 40,* 1399–1408.

Murphy, J., Brewer, R., Hobson, H., Catmur, C., & Bird, G. (2018). Is alexithymia characterised by impaired interoception? Further evidence, the importance of control variables, and the problems with the Heartbeat Counting Task. *Biological Psychology, 136,* 189–197.

Neil, R., & Woodman, T. (2017). Anxiety, arousal, and coping. In T. Horn & A. Smith (Eds.), *Advances in sport and exercise psychology* (4th ed., pp. 211–227). Champaign, IL: Human Kinetics.

Nemiah, J. C., Freyberger, H., & Sifneos, P. E. (1976). Alexithymia: A view of the psychosomatic process. In O. W. Hill (Ed.), *Modern trends in psychosomatic research* (Vol. 3, pp. 430–439). London: Buttersworth.

Parker, J. D., Taylor, G. J., & Bagby, R. M. (1993). Alexithymia and the recognition of facial expressions of emotion. *Psychotherapy and Psychosomatics, 59,* 197–202.

Parker, J. D. A., Bagby, R. M., Taylor, G. J., Endler, N. S., & Schmitz, P. (1993). Factorial validity of the 20-item Toronto Alexithymia Scale. *European Journal of Personality, 7,* 221–232.

Parker, J. D. A., Taylor, G. J., & Bagby, R. M. (2001). The relationship between emotional intelligence and alexithymia. *Personality and Individual Differences, 30,* 107–115.

Parker, P. D., Prkachin, K. M., & Prkachin, G. C. (2005). Processing of facial expressions of negative emotion in alexithymia: The influence of temporal constraint. *Journal of Personality, 73,* 1087–1107.

Pedrosa Gil, F., Ridout, N., Kessler, H., Neuffer, M., Schoechlin, C., Traue, H. C., & Nickel, M. (2009). Facial emotion recognition and alexithymia in adults with somatoform disorders. *Depression & Anxiety, 26,* E26–E33.

Pedrosa Gil, F., Scheidt, C. E., Hoeger, D., & Nickel, M. (2008). Relationship between attachment style, parental bonding and alexithymia in adults with somatoform disorders. *International Journal of Psychiatry in Medicine, 38,* 437–451.

Roberts, R., & Woodman, T. (2015). Contemporary personality perspectives in sport psychology. In S. Hanton & S. Mellalieu (Eds.), *Contemporary advances in sport psychology: A review* (pp. 1–27). London: Routledge.

Roberts, R., & Woodman, T. (2016). Personality and performance: Beyond the Big 5. In R. J. Schinke, K. R. McGannon & B. Smith (Eds.), *Routledge international handbook of sport psychology* (pp. 401–411). Oxford: Routledge.

Roberts, R., & Woodman, T. (2017). Personality and performance: Moving beyond the Big 5. *Current Opinion in Psychology, 16,* 104–108.

Sifneos, P. E. (1973). The prevalence of "alexithymic" characteristics in psychosomatic patients. *Psychotherapy and Psychosomatics, 22,* 255–262.

Starita, F., Borhani, K., Bertini, C., & Scarpazza, C. (2018). Alexithymia is related to the need for more emotional intensity to identify static fearful facial expressions. *Frontiers in Psychology, 9,* 929.

Taylor, G. J. (1984). Alexithymia: Concept, measurement, and implications for treatment. *American Journal of Psychiatry, 141,* 725–732.

Taylor, G. J. (2000). Recent developments in alexithymia theory and research. *Canadian Journal of Psychiatry, 45,* 134–142.

Taylor, G. J., & Bagby, M. R. (2013). Psychoanalysis and empirical research: The example of alexithymia. *Journal of the American Psychoanalytic Association, 61,* 99–133.

Taylor, G. J., Bagby, R. M., & Parker, J. D. A. (1997). *Disorders of affect regulation: Alexithymia in medical & psychiatric illness.* Cambridge: Cambridge University Press.

van der Velde, J., Servaas, M. N., Goerlich, K. S., Bruggeman, R., Horton, P., Costafreda, S. G., & Aleman, A. (2013). Neural correlates of alexithymia: A meta-analysis of emotion processing studies. *Neuroscience & Biobehavioral Reviews, 37,* 1774–1785.

Woodman, T., Barlow, M., Bandura, C., Hill, M., Kupciw, D., & MacGregor, A. (2013). Not all risks are equal: The risk-taking inventory for high-risk sports. *Journal of Sport & Exercise Psychology, 35,* 479–492.

Woodman, T., Cazenave, N., & Le Scanff, C. (2008). Skydiving as emotion regulation: The rise and fall of anxiety is moderated by alexithymia. *Journal of Sport & Exercise Psychology, 30,* 424–433.

Woodman, T., & Hardy, L. (2001). Stress and anxiety. In R. S. Singer, H. A. Hausenblas & C. M. Janelle (Eds.), *Handbook of sport psychology* (pp. 290–318). New York: Wiley.

Woodman, T., Hardy, L., & Barlow, M. (2020). High-risk sports. In G. Tenenbaum & R. Eklund (Eds.) *Handbook of sport and exercise psychology* (4th ed., pp. 177–189). Hoboken, NJ: John Wiley.

Woodman, T., Hardy, L., Barlow, M., & Le Scanff, C. (2010). Motives for participation in prolonged engagement high-risk sports: An agentic emotional regulation perspective. *Psychology of Sport & Exercise, 11,* 345–352.

Woodman, T., Huggins, M., Le Scanff, C., & Cazenave, N. (2009). Alexithymia determines the anxiety experienced in skydiving. *Journal of Affective Disorders, 116,* 134–138.

Woodman, T., MacGregor, A. L., & Hardy, L. (2019). Risk can be good for self-esteem: Beyond self-determination theory. *Journal of Risk Research.* Advance online publication. doi:10.1080/13669877.2019.1588913.

3

ANTICIPATION AND EXPERTISE

Paul Ward, Joel Suss, Patrick Belling, and A. Mark Williams

Introduction

Numerous researchers have described the expert's skill at recognizing familiar situations and selecting a corresponding course of action that is "good enough" (e.g., Klein, Calderwood, & Clinton-Cirocco, 1986). Moreover, scientists have detailed how experts leverage the environmental structure of recognized situations to generate real-time predictions about how situations will unfold. It is argued that successful performance in complex and dynamic environments, such as sport, depends heavily on this latter skill. It depends on the ability to accurately anticipate the future state of the current situation prior to acting on it, predict one's own future position relative to a target prior to pursuing an intended course of action, and predict how one's course of action will shape the future situational state (e.g., see Poulton, 1957). The current evidence supports the assertion that, relative to non-experts, experts are eminently more capable of making these types of decision even under temporal and/or informational constraint.

In this contribution, the focus is on perceptual anticipation and its central role in understanding expertise. First, the research on anticipation in sport is reviewed. Next, an overview is provided of research examining related constructs in other complex domains. Finally, the perceptual-cognitive mechanisms that have been proposed as responsible for superior performance are summarized.

Anticipation

De Groot (1947/1965) was among the first to study the perceptual-cognitive basis of anticipation, albeit quite indirectly. He studied expert chess players' ability to select their own next best move when presented with a given chess configuration (e.g., a mid-game chess position presented at a point when it was the participant's turn to move). This research is typically used to demonstrate experts' superiority in generating better moves through recognition of the current configuration and corresponding move options. Moreover, it is typically used as evidence for the absence of skill-based differences in heuristic search strategy, even though experts did consider higher-quality moves in more detail and deepened their search for better moves. Importantly, in de Groot's research, experts' search for better moves occurred in plies (e.g., potential moves for themself and predicted countermoves of their opponent). The implication from this research is that the expert chess players' higher-quality moves were generated, at least in part, based on predictions about their opponents' subsequent moves. In other words, their decision-making is based on their ability to anticipate possible future system states.

Poulton (1957) defined perceptual anticipation as the ability to predict the future state of a situation to coordinate and adapt an appropriate response relative to that future state. Poulton's original definition, which was based on basic experimental work in the laboratory, was concerned with adapting one's current action – in the moment – in response to changes in the immediate context (e.g., tracking a target to a predictable location). In a recent review, Suss and Ward (2015) extended this definition to include situations in which one's adaptations actively change the environment. In brief, these authors proposed that anticipation is a unifying concept that refers to the ability to generate real-time mental projections about how a situation may unfold in the immediate (e.g., seconds) or near (e.g., minutes, up to a few hours) future (see also Ward, Gore, Hutton, Conway, & Hoffman, 2018). Other researchers have reserved the term "mental projection" for the act of post hoc analysis of determining if a particular course of action would suffice given the current context (e.g., taking time out to check if a particular option works; Klein, 1989). It is argued that mental projection is used by experts in real time in a mode that has been previously termed "apperception" – the immediate comprehension of a pattern (based on one's existing knowledge) without requiring deliberative reasoning (see Wundt, 1896/1897). In other words, experts use anticipation as a means to immediately perceive, predict, and constrain the immediate future (see Kintsch, 1998; Poulton, 1957).

Anticipation, as a form of real-time mental projection, is consistent with the idea of integrating and updating one's situation model (e.g., Kintsch, 1998), and with the act of situation assessment in complex domains – an integral component of the Klein's recognition primed decision-making model (see below; e.g., see Klein et al., 2003). Numerous examples of skilled performers using anticipation in this dynamic manner have been reported. For instance, skilled athletes have been shown to "read the game" effectively (see Williams & Ward, 2007), expert pilots "fly ahead of the plane" (e.g., Doane, Sohn, & Jodlowski, 2004), advanced drivers anticipate hazards in the road ahead (e.g., McKenna & Horswill, 1999), and police officers predict perpetrators' intent (e.g., Ward, Suss, Eccles, Williams, & Harris, 2011). This research suggests that experts and skilled performers routinely anticipate the future by thinking – or apperceiving – ahead of the current situation.

Unlike chess or other self-paced domains where there is time to consider alternative future courses of action, when anticipation has been the focus of investigation, the domains are often more complex. Opportunities to anticipate the future are fleeting, often available for a split second before disappearing as other opportunities emerge dynamically. As a consequence, there is usually a limited amount of time available to make predictions of this type, and the consequences of missing such opportunities are typically reflected in a negative impact on performance. In the next two sections, the review focuses on the various ways in which anticipation and related concepts have been investigated as a key determinant of skilled performance across domains. First, a review of anticipation in sport is presented, and then the research on projection in dynamic domains and hazard perception in driving is examined as a means to better understand the universality of anticipation skill and the integral part it plays in expert sports performance.

Anticipation in Sport

There is a rich history of anticipation research in sport where athletes have limited time to respond (e.g., Abernethy, 1987; Haskins, 1965; for a recent review, see Williams, Fawver,

Broadbent, Murphy, & Ward, 2019). In some situations, such as one player versus one player in fast ball sports (e.g., tennis singles, soccer penalty kick, baseball pitch), to permit a timely response, athletes must anticipate their opponents' intentions based on advance cues available where their ecological validities (i.e., the information available on which a prediction can be based) are less than optimal. For instance, a tennis player must predict the outcome of a serve before the ball leaves the opponent's racket, a soccer goalkeeper has to predict before the penalty taker's kicking foot strikes the ball, and the baseball batter has to predict prior to the pitcher's ball release. Although ecological cue validities are typically much higher after such points in time (and other confirmatory cues, such as ball flight trajectory, are also available), initiating a later response, on average, leaves insufficient time to respond (see Williams, Davids, & Williams, 1999).

A number of researchers have used the temporal occlusion method to investigate skilled anticipation (e.g., Brenton, Müller, & Mansingh, 2016; see the contribution by Filho & Tenenbaum, Volume 1, Chapter 22, in this encyclopedia). In studies employing this method, participants view dynamic sequences of sports action (e.g., an opposing tennis player serving the ball), usually on video, from a first-person perspective. The videos are edited to occlude the stimuli (e.g., a tennis server is replaced with a blank screen) unexpectedly at various moments prior to the ecological validities being optimal (e.g., 120 milliseconds before racket–ball contact), at which point participants are asked to anticipate the situational outcome. Although the availability of information (e.g., postural cues) is limited prior to the point of occlusion (e.g., between 250 and 0 milliseconds prior to contact/release), experts are more successful than their novice counterparts at anticipating the future without additional information (see Williams, Ward, Knowles, & Smeeton, 2002).

In many sports, athletes use other situational information beyond the postural information available during the short window of time immediately prior to, for instance, ball–racket contact (e.g., Runswick, Roca, Williams, McRobert, & North, 2018). McRobert, Ward, Eccles, and Williams (2011) studied expert cricket batters and showed them either a limited amount of prior contextual information that was relevant (i.e., a single cricket bowl from one bowler, delivered after five other bowlers each bowling one ball) or more context that was more relevant (i.e., six balls bowled by the same cricket bowler). When participants faced the same bowler more frequently, they anticipated the outcome of the bowler's action more accurately relative to when exposed to the same bowler less frequently. These findings suggest that anticipation is based on the use of a host of contextual cues – for instance, opponent tendencies – beyond the immediately available postural information.

In many team sports, important cues are often distributed over space and time, such as in a pattern of play that involves multiple players interacting to produce a coordinated outcome (e.g., North, Hope, & Williams, 2016). Researchers have often used a spatial occlusion method to identify the important cues in such situations. In this method, participants typically view a similar pattern of play to that presented in the temporal occlusion method (without information being temporally occluded), but with some of the information cues (e.g., the actions and movements of other players on the field) obscured (i.e., using a dynamic mask) or removed via digital software (i.e., spatially occluded). Williams and Davids (1998) employed this method to examine skill-based differences in soccer skill at anticipating the outcome of an 11-player versus 11-player situation. The experts' ability to anticipate the outcome of the play was degraded when information other than the ball or player in possession of the ball was removed. Their data suggest that, in addition to the cues available from the player and ball, information available from the coordinated movements of multiple players over space and time is also used to anticipate the outcome of the play. These findings have been corroborated using reaction time methods (e.g., Williams et al., 2002) and eye-movement recordings (Williams & Davids, 1998; for a review, see Williams & Ward, 2007).

Other methods have also been used to examine sports anticipation. For instance, Ward and Williams (2003) adapted de Groot's (1965) move-selection task to measure the ability of skilled soccer players to identify the alternative options their opponent might pursue next. Participants viewed similar video stimuli to those used in the temporal occlusion method described earlier (albeit of an evolving offensive pattern of play by an opposing soccer team). Rather than being occluded at the critical moment, the last frame of action was frozen on screen. The participants' task was to predict the relevant ways (termed options) in which the current play might continue to evolve – for instance, by highlighting players on the opposing team in a good position to receive the ball and the movements they would make. Participants were then asked to prioritize those options in order of their future threat to the participant's defence. Elite soccer players identified more relevant options and fewer task-irrelevant options than sub-elite players and were better at prioritizing relevant options in the order of the threat posed. This *situation assessment* skill (i.e., skill at identifying and prioritizing relevant options) was correlated with skill at anticipating the actual outcome of the play (i.e., which option was actually pursued by the player with the ball), both of which combined to be the most predictive of skill level (see also Murphy, Jackson, & Williams, 2018; Williams, Reilly, & Franks, 1999).

Researchers have recently begun to test the application of commercial tools for training and assessing anticipation using some of these methods. In baseball, *pitch recognition* refers to the ability of the batter to anticipate the type of pitch (e.g., fastball, slider, curveball) being thrown by the pitcher. Using a touchscreen commercial application with a Division 1 NCAA team, Belling, Sada, and Ward (2015) demonstrated that the scores on a test of pitch recognition were predictive of the coaches' ratings of their hitting skill. Furthermore, Belling and Ward (2015) also demonstrated that a commercial training application was likely to have contributed to substantial improvement in a Division 1 NCAA team's hitting statistics, building on research with more experimental control (e.g., Fadde, 2006).

Collectively, the research in sport suggests that the ability to anticipate future events is key to attaining superior performance in this domain. Sports situations that involve dynamic interactions with an opponent or opponents are analogous to a wide range of other societally relevant situations in which highly developed anticipation is linked to expertise. In the next part, the review focuses on the role anticipation plays in these complementary, dynamic domains.

Anticipation in Other Complex Domains

In many other complex domains, anticipation has been studied under different guises, such as anticipatory thinking, foresight, hazard perception, prediction, and projection (a component of situation awareness). These concepts have emphasized, to varying degrees, the importance of anticipation as a reciprocal component of the decision-making process. In this section, the methods employed and the empirical data gathered are reviewed to examine some of these concepts as they relate to anticipation in a range of dynamic domains. This section begins with a look at the work on situation awareness, followed by research on hazard perception. The purpose of presenting these findings is to demonstrate the central role that anticipation plays in expert performance and to highlight the similarity in the mechanisms used to explain superior anticipation across diverse complex domains. The hope is that presentation of this research will motivate sports researchers to look beyond the realm of sport in an effort to identify more universal mechanisms capable of explaining superior performance.

Situation Awareness and Projection

When the concept of situation awareness (SA) was first popularized, it was used to describe some of the mental processes associated with a "dogfight" between aviation fighter pilots. In the dogfight, an aviator often tries to "get inside the head of the other pilot" – to predict what they might do next – as a means to gain a tactical advantage (R. Hoffman, personal communication). In essence, the first use of SA was in the context of skilled anticipation.

The ability of a human actor to anticipate a near-future state is an integral part of Endsley's (1995a) conceptualization of SA, defined as the "perception of the elements in the environment within a volume of time and space [Level 1 SA], the comprehension of their meaning [Level 2 SA], and the projection of their status in the near future [Level 3 SA]" (p. 36). It is the third level (projection to the immediate future) that captures the perceptual anticipation component, although all three levels likely contribute to successful anticipation. To identify task-critical situational information cues, what those cues mean, and how the situation will evolve, researchers have often conducted an a priori goal-directed task analysis where, for every decision made, the important cues, their meaning, and future state are documented, and relevant probe questions are devised to elicit information from participants about SA Level 1 (e.g., Which cues? Where is cue X), Level 2 (e.g., What does it mean?), and Level 3 (e.g., Where will X be in 5 seconds?; see Stanton, Salmon, Walker, Baber, & Jenkins, 2005).

Current measures of SA, including the situation awareness global assessment technique (SAGAT; Endsley, 1988, 1995b), are commonly designed to capture all three SA levels. The SAGAT is not too dissimilar to the temporal occlusion method used in sport – albeit, rather than occluding the scene, it is typically frozen on screen either at random (e.g., Hogan, Pace, Hapgood, & Boone, 2006) or critical points (e.g., Hogg, Follesø, Strand-Volden, & Torralba, 1995). When the scene is frozen, participants are presented with text-based probes about the aforementioned SA levels. The simulation then continues until the next freeze frame, when participants are probed again, and so on. Response accuracy is measured by comparing responses to the actual state of the simulator, and predictions to its future state, and/or by subject-matter expert evaluation. Variants of this method have been developed in which the probes are presented without pausing the simulator, which also permit response time to be recorded (e.g., situation present assessment method; Durso et al., 1998).

Although the emphasis on projection in each SA study has been variable, SA probes frequently include questions that address anticipation. Endsley, Sollenberger, Nakata, and Stein (1999) asked qualified air traffic controllers a number of questions: (a) Which pairs of aircraft will lose separation if they stay on their current (intended) course? (b) Which aircraft must be handed off to another sector/facility within the next 2 minutes? (c) Which aircraft will violate special airspace separation standards if they stay on their current (intended) paths? and (d) Which aircraft will weather be an impact on in the next 5 minutes along their current course?

Projection, or Level 3 SA, is thought to be the most advanced level (Endsley, 1995a). However, when data have been reported, rather than level-specific SA scores being presented individually, sometimes the data are presented as global scores (i.e., a total score that collapses data across all three SA levels; e.g., Hogan et al., 2006), or projection-related results are not reported (e.g., Endsley, 1995b, Studies 1 and 2; Strybel, Minakata, Nguyen, Pierce, & Vu, 2009), making it difficult to discern anticipation performance per se. Fortunately, a handful of researchers have leveraged these innovative methods to specifically describe skill-based differences in projection (cf. Endsley, 1995b; Endsley et al., 1999). For instance, Durso et al. (1998) examined whether different measures of SA and workload predicted performance (i.e., clearing the airspace) in an air traffic control task (ATC). Experienced air traffic controllers were presented with ATC scenarios and probed using the SAGAT method. Specifically, they were asked questions at Levels 1 and 2 (e.g., Which aircraft has the lower altitude, aircraft A or aircraft B?) and Level 3 (e.g., Will aircraft X and aircraft Y be traffic for each other?). Although workload and Levels 1 and 2 SAGAT queries combined to account for 74% of the variance in ATC performance, superior performance was positively associated with the speed and number of correct responses to Level 3 queries, but negatively related to the number of correct responses to Level 1 and 2 queries. These data suggest that focusing on the immediate future consequences of the current situation is an important component of superior performance in air traffic control. However, it also highlights that focusing on the future could be at the expense of missing current information (but, see Durso, Bleckley, & Dattel, 2006).

In a simulated study of air combat examining experienced fighter pilots' ability to predict what would happen next, Sulistyawati, Wickens, and Chui (2011) reported projection scores independently of the global SA score. Participants were presented with a simulation that was frozen either 10 seconds after enemy aircraft appeared on radar or when the pilot was within 25 nautical miles of the enemy aircraft. Participants responded to SAGAT probes including: (a) Will you be in a position to take shots at an enemy aircraft in the next 10 seconds? and (b) Will the enemy aircraft take shots at you within the next 30 seconds? The data revealed that more experienced pilots were able to predict their own ability, and that of their enemy, to get into a position to shoot with 67% accuracy. However, pilots with the least experience responded inappropriately to either Level 2 (i.e., comprehension) or Level 3 (i.e., projection) queries. The data from a regression analysis showed that the ability to project into the future positively predicted mission performance (i.e., the number of times the pilots were actually shot at by the enemy aircraft), whereas the level of overconfidence was a negative predictor.

Collectively, researchers who have measured Level 3 SA indicate that skill at anticipating a situation's future state is associated with higher levels of performance. The implications of this research for sport are vast. First, it suggests that similar anticipatory phenomena as those observed in sport are also observed in diverse domains such as aviation. Hence, these domains may provide additional avenues from which researchers could glean insights about superior anticipatory performance that could be directly applied to sport. Second, this perspective on anticipation suggests that the skill of anticipation – or projection in SA terms (Level 3 SA) – builds on attentional (Level 1 SA) and understanding-based (Level 2 SA) processes. Interestingly, the data also show that, on occasion, one's ability to direct attention to the future consequences of the current situational state can limit comprehension of the present situation, which could have serious implications for how athletes are trained to anticipate the immediate future. In other words, successful anticipation may be not just about having a sophisticated situational representation, but also about learning how to use that representation to predict the future without it impacting attention to the current evolving state.

Hazard Perception

Anticipation skill, under the guise of hazard perception, has also been examined in the everyday domain of car driving. Although each of these research programs has developed relatively independently, the research on hazard perception offers some complementary insights about skilled anticipation that could similarly inform how research on anticipation in sport is conducted.

Hazard perception, defined colloquially as the ability to "read the road ahead" or to identify potential traffic hazards, has been shown to be a reliable predictor of accident involvement (e.g., McKenna & Crick, 1994). Whereas skilled drivers are adept at identifying possible hazards in the road ahead, if less-skilled drivers spot hazards it often occurs much later in the process, when the hazard has moved from a potential danger to an imminent threat (Horswill & McKenna, 1999; McKenna & Horswill, 1999; see also Rumar, 1990).

As a means to test anticipation in driving, McKenna and Crick (1994) developed a hazard perception test. Participants were presented with a first-person-perspective, continuous video of road traffic and were required to respond to anything they thought might turn into a dangerous situation by pressing a button. Highly experienced police driving instructors detected more hazards than inexperienced drivers and responded much earlier in the video than both experienced civilian drivers and inexperienced drivers. These results have been replicated several times since the original study (see Jackson, Chapman, & Crundall, 2009; McKenna & Horswill, 1999; McKenna, Horswill, & Alexander, 2006; Vogel, Kircher, Alm, & Nilsson, 2003).

The hazard perception test has been adapted to examine the relationship between SA and anticipation by incorporating it in to a SAGAT procedure (see McGowan & Banbury, 2004). McGowan and Banbury (2004) presented the hazard perception test to relatively inexperienced drivers but, in approximately half of the hazardous events, the video was interrupted (i.e., paused). During each interruption, participants responded to a multiple-choice SA probe that included projection questions. Participants who were presented with interruptions and SA queries anticipated potential hazards 2 seconds faster than those in a control group. Consistent with research on anticipation in other domains, when relatively inexperienced drivers are primed to attend to aspects of the situation that may develop into hazards (via SA probes), they are better able to anticipate dangerous situations. Moreover, the number of correct responses to SA queries was positively and significantly correlated with the ability to anticipate the hazards. Unfortunately, results of the responses to Level 3 SA probes (projection) were not reported independent of the other SA data. Regardless, these data provide some preliminary evidence of convergent validity between SA and skilled anticipation and support the findings in sport – that anticipation and situation assessment skills, such as perceiving opponent threat, are interrelated (see Ward, Ericsson, & Williams, 2013; Ward & Williams, 2003).

Again, these findings have implications for sports researchers. First, they confirm the established findings in sport that experts are able to use advanced cues (such as placement of non-kicking foot in a penalty kick, or relative hip–shoulder rotation in a tennis groundstroke) that are not always obvious to detect (cf. potential hazards in the road ahead), whereas novices tend to wait for later occurring, more obvious information to appear (i.e., hazards that have become imminent threats), which experts use purely as confirmatory cues in sport. Second, like the SA research in aviation, the hazard perception and driving SA research offers a range of new methods (e.g., hazard perception test, SAGAT) that have yet to be exploited by sports researchers to further our understanding of expert anticipation. Third, like the SA research in aviation, the above research also has implications for training anticipation in sport. For instance, the findings suggest that cueing methods may be useful to improve the speed with which participants are able to anticipate future events. In the next section, the perceptual and cognitive mechanisms are described that have been used to explain anticipation, and the empirical evidence in favour of these and alternative mechanisms is discussed.

Mechanisms to Explain Skilled Anticipation

A handful of different mechanisms have been offered as potential explanations of skilled anticipation. For instance, the superior ability to perceive hazards has been explained as a consequence of having a predictive mental model of the driving environment (e.g., McKenna & Horswill, 1999). Similarly, superior SA has been explained as a product of superior comprehension mechanisms, such as those offered by Kintsch's (1988) construction-integration model (e.g., Durso, Rawson, & Girotto, 2007; Endsley, 1995a; Sohn & Doane, 2004). Others have pointed to the experts' superior indexing skill at encoding and their use of more sophisticated retrieval structures as a basis for expert anticipation (e.g., Ward, Suss, & Basevitch, 2009; Ward et al., 2011; Ward & Williams, 2003). Others, still, have pointed to adaptive sense-making mechanisms as a basis for superior situation assessment (e.g., Suss & Ward, 2018; Ward et al., 2018).

One common theory that has been used to explain superior anticipation is long-term working memory theory (LTWM; see Ericsson & Kintsch, 1995; Ericsson & Ward, 2007). This theory posits that, as a consequence of their extensive and deliberate involvement in a domain, experts build situation-specific memory representations. By integrating salient situational information cues with stored knowledge from long-term memory, the resulting "situation models" describe the semantic relations in the current situation. The current model remains updated by the incorporation of new situational information (and associated stored knowledge) that becomes available as the situation dynamically evolves. Having a constantly updating situation model permits performance to be effectively executed, future retrieval demands to be anticipated, and vital predictive inferences to be made (Kintsch, 1988; Zwaan & Radvansky, 1998). The situation model literature has its roots in text comprehension as a means to describe how skilled readers make predictive and other types of inferences from texts. More recently, the situation model-building process has been adapted to explain performance of expert aviation pilots and skilled computer programmers (Doane & Sohn, 2000; Doane, Sohn, McNamara, & Adams, 2000). In an extensive review of the literature, Ericsson and Kintsch (1995) argued that superior performance (rather than perceptual anticipation per se) in a range of domains could be explained via the use of a situation model-building process.

However, with the exception of medicine, many of the domains in this review that provided support for the use of these predictive situational models are relatively static in nature (e.g., chess, reading; see Kintsch, 1998). Surprisingly, there have been few empirical tests of specific hypotheses derived from LTWM that would provide support for the use of such mechanisms in more complex domains such as sport (but, see research by Ward and colleagues, below). Klein, Phillips, Rall, and Peluso (2007) proposed the data-frame (D/F) model (an alternative but conceptually similar model of "expert sense-making") as a means to further elaborate the mechanisms involved in the situation assessment phase of decision-making. Like LTWM's situation model-type retrieval structures, Klein et al.'s model relies on inference as a key mechanism in situation understanding, but, in addition, it supports the ability to detect and identify problems, make new discoveries, and generate insights in a way (e.g., via abduction) that might suggest an effective solution strategy (Klein et al., 2003; see also Ward et al., 2018).

Alternative mechanisms have been proposed to explain how experts predict the future courses of action to be taken by others (see Klein & Peio, 1989), such as the recognition-primed decision (RPD) model (Klein et al., 1986; for a review, see Klein, 1997). As the name suggests, this model was originally developed to explain the related ability of making superior decisions, but it applies equally to making decisions about (i.e., anticipating) an opponent's next move. It suggests that, with increasing experience in a domain, experts learn to recognize familiar situational patterns. In simple match situations (i.e., when a situation is recognized as familiar), based on one's goals, the available cues, and expectancies, these patterns elicit an associated response that is satisficing in nature. The response is satisficing because it is "good enough" (which is typically "very good" when generated by experts), rather than the absolute best possible response, and because time is not wasted comparing all possible options to find the best (on all possible dimensions). In essence, a satisficing response means going with the first, good-enough option generated, which alleviates the need to generate subsequent options. Although performers sometimes generate more than one option in a given situation (Johnson & Raab, 2003; Klein, Wolf, Militello, & Zsambok, 1995; cf. Klein et al., 1986; Phillips, Klein, & Sieck, 2004), the RPD model suggests that, as individuals become more skilled in a domain, they should generate fewer options until only one acceptable, if not the best possible, option is generated (see Yates, 2001).

To test the RPD model explicitly in situations where individuals had to predict what an opponent might do next, Klein and Peio (1989) presented a midgame chessboard configuration from an actual expert-level game. They asked chess players to predict the next moves that opposing expert players would take by first identifying their opponent's plausible next moves and then highlighting the move that their opponent would actually make next. Participants were given feedback about the move actually taken next by their opponent, and then they repeated the same task for the 20 subsequent moves. The findings were consistent with the RPD model. Compared with less-proficient players, skilled players generated fewer options per trial and predicted the experts' moves more often. Moreover, when they predicted their opponent's next move correctly, the skilled players generated that move first on significantly more occasions.

RPD has, of course, been used to explain one's own course-of-action decision-making. In a study on chess players, Klein et al. (1995) presented participants with a chessboard configuration from a real game and asked medium and highly skilled players to generate their next best course of action. Participants generated each of their next moves and then selected their final move, and the quality of each move was rated by a grandmaster chess player. Consistent with Klein and Peio's (1989) data and with the RPD model, chess players generated a relatively small number (i.e., three to five) of the possible legal moves, each of which were considered an acceptable level of quality, and then selected as their actual move (i.e., the move they considered most effective) one of the first moves generated. However, there were few differences in the option-generation strategies adopted at each level of skill, making it difficult to determine whether this strategy could adequately explain the superior move selection or prediction normally associated with expertise (see Klein & Peio, 1989).

Johnson and Raab (2003) proposed a mechanism that they named the take-the-first (TTF) heuristic and was conceptually consistent with the RPD model and its associated predictions, which they tested in a sports context. TTF is built on the premise that experts generate fewer rather than more options because of a hypothesized negative relationship between the number of options generated and the quality of a decision. Generating only a few options permits experts to choose from a set of higher-quality options (because each additional option generated would be of a lower quality), which results in a better decision (see also Goldstein & Gigerenzer, 2002). Hence, not adopting an RPD-type strategy (i.e., selecting the first option generated) would result in a greater likelihood of making a poorer decision. Johnson and Raab (2003) presented to moderately skilled handball players first-person-perspective video clips of high-level handball that (not unlike the SAGAT) were frozen on screen (for 45 seconds) at a point when an attacking player was in possession of the ball. Imagining themselves as the player with the ball, participants were asked to generate the option that first came to mind, then generate as many additional options as they could, and then select the best option from those they had generated. The moves generated were rated by expert coaches, who generally rated the first option generated as the highest-quality option, the second option as the next highest, and so on. The data demonstrated that experts were more likely to select a better option as their final choice when they generated fewer options. These findings were replicated in a subsequent study involving skilled and less-skilled handball players (Raab & Johnson, 2007).

To test Klein and Peio's (1989) claim that the RPD predictions could be extended to a dynamic and perceptual-motor context, and to contrast with the evidence presented by Raab and colleagues, Ward, Ericsson, and Williams (2013; see also Ward et al. 2011) adapted these approaches to measure skilled anticipation in soccer players. Participants were presented with short video clips of offensive patterns of soccer play taken from professional games, filmed from the defensive perspective. The videos ended unexpectedly (with the last frame either freezing or being replaced with a blank screen), when the opposing player with the ball was at a critical moment in the play (e.g., prior to passing the ball, making a run, shooting at goal). Skilled and less-skilled soccer players were then asked to generate plausible options, rank those options generated in order of threat posed to the defence, and then anticipate what the player with the ball actually did next.

Ward et al. (2013) first had a panel of expert coaches identify the task-relevant options (i.e., those that actually posed a threat to defence, of which the participants should be aware) and task-irrelevant options (i.e., those that did not pose a threat to defence and so could be ignored, relatively speaking). Participants generated similar numbers of total options as in the studies by Klein and Peio (1989) and Johnson and Raab (2003; Raab & Johnson, 2007) and generated better options first. However, skilled players generated more task-relevant options and fewer task-irrelevant options than the less-skilled players, were better at prioritizing those options in order of threat, and more successfully anticipated the next move. Ward et al. (2013) observed a positive relationship between the number of task-relevant options generated, which contrast with the predicted negative relationship between options generated and anticipation quality predicted by TTF. Rather than generating fewer options in total, skilled players generated fewer low-quality and more high-quality options than less-skilled players. These data were more consistent with explanations of expert sense-making (e.g., Klein et al., 2007) and with situation model-based explanations of expert performance (e.g., Ericsson & Kintsch, 1995; see Suss & Ward, 2018).

This approach has been extended to other domains, such as law enforcement (e.g., see Suss & Ward, 2018; Ward et al., 2011), and, importantly, to tests of both the situation assessment phase of decision-making, where anticipation is vital, and to intervention phases of decision-making, where participants are concerned about choosing their own course of action (e.g., see Belling, Suss, & Ward, 2015a, 2015b). In general, participants generate few options and typically select as best the first option they generated, irrespective of whether they are anticipating their opponent's intentions or deciding on a course of action for themselves. These data are consistent with use of relatively simple, more intuitive decision-making mechanisms (e.g., RPD simple match; TTF heuristic; see Johnson & Raab, 2003; Klein et al., 1986; Raab & Johnson, 2007).

However, sometimes the results were more consistent with the use of more complex mechanisms, such as the sense-making explanations of situational diagnosis (Klein et al., 2007) and situation model-based explanations of expert performance (e.g., Ericsson & Kintsch, 1995). For instance, Suss and Ward (2018) found that generating more (and not fewer) critical (i.e., task-relevant) situational assessment and intervention options was associated with making better decisions. Likewise, experts frequently generated more critical/task-relevant, and fewer non-critical/task-irrelevant options than novices (e.g., Suss & Ward, 2018; Belling et al., 2015a, 2015b; Ward et al., 2013). The fact that researchers have observed behaviour consistent with both intuitive and sense-making modes of decision-making can be understood in terms of the adaptive nature of expertise (see Ward et al., 2018). In familiar situations, experts quickly recognize the situation and identify an appropriate response. In less familiar or unfamiliar situations that are more complex and/or more uncertain, individuals may need to engage in rapid sense-making or situational diagnosis so that they can quickly comprehend the situation. The two theoretical approaches presented – that is, mechanisms to describe skilled decision-making (e.g., RPD, TTF) and mechanisms to describe expert sense-making (e.g., LTWM) – are likely to be much more complementary than competitive (see Kahneman & Klein, 2009).

Conclusion

In this contribution, the way in which anticipation and related constructs have been measured in sport and other dynamic domains was discussed, and the cognitive mechanisms that have been offered to explain superior anticipation were examined. Some of the earliest research that has informed our understanding of anticipation (e.g., de Groot, 1965; Poulton, 1957) suggests that successful performance is a product not just of effective action execution, but of the ability to anticipate how the system will unfold prior to the influence of one's actions, as well as the ability to anticipate the effect of one's actions on the future state of the system. The current research suggests that experts can successfully predict the immediate future, and that the mechanisms for doing so are consistent with those used to explain superior decision-making. The broader research suggests that anticipation and situation assessment are useful predictors of meaningful outcomes such as skill group membership and accident involvement, and that anticipation can be enhanced using task-specific interventions (see Ward et al., 2009).

In sports, this means superior decision-makers possess a well-developed mental representation of relevant situations that allows for better anticipation of teammates, opponents, and other environmental changes in situ. In fact, this ability is precisely what separates elite from non-elite athletes. This rather consistent empirical finding can be applied by sport organizations and coaches by using tests of anticipation and situation assessment (e.g., via simulation) to predict skilled athletes (as in baseball; Belling et al., 2015). Additionally, relevant scenarios can be used to train anticipation and situational assessment such that performance improvements are observed in real-world settings (as in baseball; Belling & Ward, 2015). More research is needed to quantify the effectiveness of applied tools for predicting and training skilled anticipation and situation assessment in additional sport settings. Researchers must also provide a more elaborate prescription for applied tools, detailing the types of situation that yield the highest utility for practitioners.

Disclaimer

Approved for Public Release; Distribution Unlimited. Public Release Case Number 19-1256.

Paul Ward's affiliation with the MITRE Corporation is provided for identification purposes only, and is not intended to convey or imply MITRE's concurrence with, or support for, the positions, opinions, or viewpoints expressed by the author.

References

Abernethy, B. (1987). Anticipation in sport: A review. *Physical Education Review, 10*, 5–16.

Belling, P., Suss, J., & Ward, P. (2015a). The effect of time constraint on anticipation, decision-making, and option-generation in complex and dynamic environments. *Cognition, Technology & Work, 17*, 355–366.

Belling, P., Suss, J., & Ward, P. (2015b). Advancing theory and application of cognitive research in sport: Using representative tasks to explain and predict skilled anticipation, decision-making and option-generation behavior. *Psychology of Sport and Exercise, 16*, 45–59.

Belling, P. K., Sada, J., & Ward, P. (2015). Assessing hitting skill in baseball using simulated and representative tasks. In *Proceedings of the International Conference on Naturalistic Decision Making*. McLean, VA: MITRE.

Belling, P. K., & Ward, P. (2015). Time to start training: A review of cognitive research in sport and bridging the gap from academia to the field. *Procedia Manufacturing, 3*, 1219–1224.

Brenton, J., Müller, S., & Mansingh, A. (2016). Discrimination of visual anticipation in skilled cricket batsmen. *Journal of Applied Sport Psychology, 28*, 483–488.

de Groot, A. D. (1965). *Thought and choice in chess* (1st ed.). The Hague: Mouton.

Doane, S. M., & Sohn, Y. W. (2000). ADAPT: A predictive cognitive model of user visual attention and action planning. *User Modeling and User-Adapted Interaction, 10*, 1–45.

Doane, S. M., Sohn, Y. W., & Jodlowski, M. T. (2004). Pilot ability to anticipate the consequences of flight actions as a function of expertise. *Human Factors, 46*, 92–103.

Doane, S. M., Sohn, Y. W., McNamara, D. S., & Adams, D. (2000). Comprehension- based skill acquisition. *Cognitive Science, 24*, 1–52.

Durso, F. T., Bleckley, M. K., & Dattel, A. R. (2006). Does situation awareness add to the validity of cognitive tests? *Human Factors, 48*, 721–733.

Durso, F. T., Hackworth, C. A., Truitt, T. R., Crutchfield, J., Nikolic, D., & Manning, C. A. (1998). Situation awareness as a predictor of performance for en route air traffic controllers. *Air Traffic Control Quarterly, 6*, 1–20.

Durso, F. T., Rawson, K., & Girotto, S. (2007). Comprehension and situation awareness. In F. T. Durso, R. Nickerson, S. Dumais, S. Lewandowsky & T. Perfect (Eds.), *Handbook of applied cognition* (2nd ed., pp. 163–193). Chichester: Wiley.

Endsley, M. R. (1988, May). Situation awareness global assessment technique (SAGAT). In *Proceedings of the National Aerospace and Electronics Conference* (pp. 789–795). New York: IEEE.

Endsley, M. R. (1995a). Toward a theory of situation awareness in dynamic systems. *Human Factors, 37*, 32–64.

Endsley, M. R. (1995b). Measurement of situation awareness in dynamic systems. *Human Factors, 37*, 65–84.

Endsley, M. R., Sollenberger, R., Nakata, A., & Stein, E. S. (1999). *Situation awareness in air traffic control: Enhanced displays for advanced operations (DOT/FAA/CT-TN00/01)*. Atlantic City, NJ: Federal Aviation Administration William J. Hughes Technical Center.

Ericsson, K. A., & Kintsch, W. (1995). Long-term working memory. *Psychological Review, 102*, 211–245.

Ericsson, K. A., & Ward, P. (2007). Capturing the naturally occurring superior performance of experts in the laboratory: Toward a science of expert and exceptional performance. *Current Directions in Psychological Science, 16*, 346–350.

Fadde, P. J. (2006). Interactive video training of perceptual decision-making in the sport of baseball. *Technology, Instruction, Cognition and Learning, 4*, 265–285.

Goldstein, D. G., & Gigerenzer, G. (2002). Models of ecological rationality: The recognition heuristic. *Psychological Review, 109*, 75–90.

Haskins, M. J. (1965). Development of a response-recognition training film in tennis. *Perceptual and Motor Skills, 21*, 207–211.

Hogan, M. P., Pace, D. E., Hapgood, J., & Boone, D. C. (2006). Use of human patient simulation and the Situation Awareness Global Assessment Technique in practical trauma skills assessment. *Journal of Trauma-Injury Infection and Critical Care, 61*, 1047–1052.

Hogg, D. N., Follesø, K., Strand-Volden, F., & Torralba, B. (1995). Development of a situation awareness measure to evaluate advanced alarm systems in nuclear power plant control rooms. *Ergonomics, 38*, 2394–2413.

Horswill, M. S., & McKenna, F. P. (1999). The development, validation, and application of a video-based technique for measuring an everyday risk- taking behavior: Drivers' speed choice. *Journal of Applied Psychology, 84*, 977–985.

Jackson, L., Chapman, P., & Crundall, D. (2009). What happens next? Predicting other road users' behaviour as a function of driving experience and processing time. *Ergonomics, 52*, 154–164.

Johnson, J. G., & Raab, M. (2003). Take the first: Option-generation and resulting choices. *Organizational Behavior and Human Decision Processes, 91*, 215–229.

Kahneman, D., & Klein, G. (2009). Conditions for intuitive expertise: A failure to disagree. *American Psychologist, 64*, 515–526.

Kintsch, W. (1988). The role of knowledge in discourse comprehension: A construction-integration model. *Psychological Review, 95*, 163–182.

Kintsch, W. (1998). *Comprehension: A paradigm for cognition.* Cambridge: Cambridge University Press.

Klein, G. (1989). Recognition-primed decisions. In W. B. Rouse (Ed.), *Advances in man-machine systems research, Vol. 5* (pp. 47–92). Greenwich, CT: JAI Press.

Klein, G. (1997). The recognition-primed decision (RPD) model: Looking back, looking forward. In C. E. Zsambok & G. Klein (Eds.), *Naturalistic decision making* (pp. 285–292). Hillsdale, NJ: Lawrence Erlbaum.

Klein, G., Calderwood, R., & Clinton-Cirocco, A. (1986). Rapid decision making on the fire ground. *Proceedings of the Annual Meeting of the Human Factors and Ergonomics Society, 30*, 576–580.

Klein, G., & Peio, K. J. (1989). Use of a prediction paradigm to evaluate proficient decision making. *The American Journal of Psychology, 102*, 321–331.

Klein, G., Ross, K. G., Moon, B. M., Klein, D. E., Hoffman, R. R., & Hollnagel, E. (2003). Macrocognition. *IEEE: Intelligent Systems, 18*, 81–85.

Klein, G., Wolf, S., Militello, L., & Zsambok, C. (1995). Characteristics of skilled option generation in chess. *Organizational Behavior and Human Decision Processes, 62*, 63–69.

Klein, G. A., Phillips, J. K., Rall, E. L., & Peluso, D. A. (2007). A data-frame theory of sensemaking. In R. R. Hoffman (Ed.), *Expertise out of context: Proceeding of the Sixth International Conference on Naturalistic Decision Making* (pp. 113–155). New York: Lawrence Erlbaum.

McGowan, A. M., & Banbury, S. (2004). Evaluating interruption-based techniques using embedded measures of driver anticipation. In S. Banbury & S. Tremblay (Eds.), *A cognitive approach to situation awareness: Theory and application* (pp. 176–192). Aldershot: Ashgate.

McKenna, F. P., & Crick, J. L. (1994). *Hazard perception in drivers: A methodology for testing and training* ([TRL Report 313]). Crowthorne: Transport Research Laboratory.

McKenna, F. P., & Horswill, M. S. (1999). Hazard perception and its relevance for driver licensing. *Journal of the International Association of Traffic and Safety Sciences, 23*, 26–41.

McKenna, F. P., Horswill, M. S., & Alexander, J. L. (2006). Does anticipation training affect drivers' risk taking? *Journal of Experimental Psychology: Applied, 12*, 1–10.

McRobert, A. P., Ward, P., Eccles, D. W., & Williams, A. M. (2011). The effect of manipulating context-specific information on perceptual–Cognitive processes during a simulated anticipation task. *British Journal of Psychology, 102*, 519–534.

Murphy, C. P., Jackson, R. C., & Williams, A. M. (2018). The role of contextual information during skilled anticipation. *The Quarterly Journal of Experimental Psychology, 71*, 2070–2087.

North, J. S., Hope, E., & Williams, A. M. (2016). The relative importance of different perceptual-cognitive skills during anticipation. *Human Movement Science, 49*, 170–177.

Phillips, J. K., Klein, G., & Sieck, W. R. (2004). Expertise in judgment and decision making: A case for training intuitive decision skills. In D. J. Koehler & N. Harvey (Eds.), *Blackwell handbook of judgment and decision making* (pp. 298–315). Malden, MA: Blackwell.

Poulton, E. (1957). On prediction in skilled movements. *Psychological Bulletin, 54*, 467–478.

Raab, M., & Johnson, J. G. (2007). Expertise-based differences in search and option-generation strategies. *Journal of Experimental Psychology: Applied, 13*, 158–170.

Rumar, K. (1990). The basic driver error: Late detection. *Ergonomics, 33*, 1281–1290.

Runswick, O. R., Roca, A., Williams, A. M., McRobert, A. P., & North, J. S. (2018). The temporal integration of information during anticipation. *Psychology of Sport and Exercise, 37*, 100–108.

Sohn, Y. W., & Doane, S. M. (2004). Memory processes of flight situation aware- ness: Interactive roles of working memory capacity, long-term working memory, and expertise. *Human Factors, 46*, 461–475.

Stanton, N. A., Salmon, P. M., Walker, G. H., Baber, C., & Jenkins, D. P. (2005). *Human factors methods: A practical guide for engineering and design.* Aldershot: Ashgate.

Strybel, T., Minakata, K., Nguyen, J., Pierce, R., & Vu, K.-P. L. (2009). Optimizing online situation awareness probes in air traffic management tasks. In G. Salvendy & M. Smith (Eds.), *Human interface and the management of information: Information and interaction* (Vol. 5618, pp. 845–854). Berlin: Springer.

Sulistyawati, K., Wickens, C. D., & Chui, Y. P. (2011). Prediction in situation awareness: Confidence bias and underlying cognitive abilities. *International Journal of Aviation Psychology, 21*, 153–174.

Suss, J., & Ward, P. (2018). Revealing perceptual-cognitive expertise in law enforcement: An iterative approach using verbal report, temporal-occlusion, and option-generation methods. *Cognition, Technology, & Work, 20*, 585–596.

Vogel, K., Kircher, A., Alm, H., & Nilsson, L. (2003). Traffic sense – Which factors influence the skill to predict the development of traffic scenes? *Accident Analysis and Prevention, 35*, 749–762.

Ward, P., Ericsson, K. A., & Williams, A. M. (2013). Complex perceptual–Cognitive expertise in a simulated task environment. *Journal of Cognitive Engineering and Decision Making, 7*, 231–254.

Ward, P., Gore, J., Hutton, R., Conway, G., & Hoffman, R. (2018). Adaptive skill as the *conditio sine qua non* of expertise. *Journal of Applied Research in Memory and Cognition, 7*, 35–50.

Ward, P., Suss, J., & Basevitch, I. (2009). Expertise and expert performance-based training (ExPerT) in complex domains. *Technology, Instruction, Cognition and Learning, 7*, 121–145.

Ward, P., Suss, J., Eccles, D. W., Williams, A. M., & Harris, K. R. (2011). Skill-based differences in option generation in a complex task: A verbal protocol analysis. *Cognitive Processing, 12*, 289–300.

Ward, P., & Williams, A. M. (2003). Perceptual and cognitive skill development in soccer: The multidimensional nature of expert performance. *Journal of Sport and Exercise Psychology, 25*, 93–111.

Williams, A. M., & Davids, K. (1998). Visual search strategy, selective attentive, and expertise in soccer. *Research Quarterly for Exercise and Sport, 69*, 111–128.

Williams, A. M., Davids, K., & Williams, J. G. (1999). *Visual perception and action in sport*. London: Routledge.

Williams, A. M., Fawver, B., Broadbent, D. P., Murphy, C. P., & Ward, P. (2019). Expert anticipation in sport: Past, present and future. In P. Ward, J. M. Schraagen, J. Gore & E. Roth (Eds.), *Oxford handbook of expertise: Research & applications*. Oxford: Oxford University Press. Retrieved from www.oxfordhand books.com/view/10.1093/oxfordhb/9780198795872.001.0001/oxfordhb-9780198795872-e-26

Williams, A. M., Reilly, T., & Franks, A. (1999). Identifying talented football players: A scientific perspective. *Insight: The FA Coaches Association Journal, 3*, 20–25.

Williams, A. M., & Ward, P. (2007). Anticipation and decision making: Exploring new horizons. In G. Tenenbaum & R. C. Eklund (Eds.), *Handbook of sport psychology* (3rd ed., pp. 203–223). Hoboken, NJ: John Wiley.

Williams, A. M., Ward, P., Knowles, J. M., & Smeeton, N. J. (2002). Anticipation skill in a real-world task: Measurement, training, and transfer in tennis. *Journal of Experimental Psychology: Applied, 8*, 259–270.

Wundt, W. (1897). *Grundriss der Psychologie*. Leipzig: Wilhelm Engelmann. (Original work published 1896).

Yates, J. F. (2001). "Outsider:" Impressions of naturalistic decision making. In E. Salas & G. Klein (Eds.), *Linking expertise and naturalistic decision making* (pp. 9–33). Mahwah, NJ: Lawrence Erlbaum.

Zwaan, R. A., & Radvansky, G. A. (1998). Situation models in language comprehension and memory. *Psychological Bulletin, 123*, 162–185.

4

CLIQUES AND SUBGROUPS

Luc J. Martin

Introduction

The effective functioning of a sport team, like many other performance groups, is contingent on how members work together as a collective (e.g., McDaniel & Salas, 2018; McEwan, Ruissen, Eys, Zumbo, & Beauchamp, 2017). Accordingly, and given that the overarching objective of sport is to outperform an opposing team, researchers have sought to understand the group dynamics that render one team more effective than another (e.g., Carron & Eys, 2012). Importantly, whereas the field of group dynamics in sport is burgeoning (Eys., Bruner, & Martin, 2019), much of the research has investigated constructs at the team level (e.g., cohesion, collective efficacy), overlooking the smaller groupings of members that exist within the total team—known as subgroups or cliques. Indeed, despite a rich research history in fields such as social and industrial/organizational (I/O) psychology, enquiry in sport is relatively recent and represents the main focus of the current chapter.

As a means of providing context for the concept of subgroups and cliques in sport, consider the following description of a hypothetical subset of team members. A group of 4–6 members from an ice hockey team (typically composed of 20–25 athletes) tends to gravitate towards each other for a variety of reasons. They are close to one another in age, have similar interests, and would likely be categorized as comparable in skill and motivation to excel in sport. The extent to which these members interact with one another, and the manner in which they do so, reinforces their distinctiveness from the total group, to the point where all team members are likely to identify them as a subgroup. In the subsequent sections, I hope to convey that this scenario is an inevitable occurrence within interdependent sport teams, but that its implications for member experiences and team functioning are nuanced and hinge predominantly on the subset of members' exhibited behaviours, rather than their mere existence or presence.

Description and Definition

Before discussing the implications that smaller subgroupings can have on individual athletes and a team as a whole, an important first step is to define them. At their most basic form, subgroups have been defined as individuals exhibiting tightly knit reciprocating relationships (Henrich, Kupermine, Sack, Blatt, & Leadbeater, 2000). Extending this description, Carton and Cummings (2012) reiterated the necessity for the presence of reciprocating relationships, while emphasizing the need for interactions that differ from those between other team members. Further, subgroup members must necessarily belong to the same total group, which should have overt task objectives and clear boundaries. In sport, similar descriptions have been advanced, situating them as an "inevitable, variable, and identifiable subgrouping of athletes within a team who exhibit particularly close task and/or social bonds" (Martin, Wilson, Evans, & Spink, 2015, p. 90). Accordingly, members of subgroups must belong to a total group, experience reciprocating relations, and be discernible from the remainder of the group.

Consider the previous definitions alongside the scenario provided above. Notably, all necessary characteristics are present. A subgroup of teammates spends more time together than with others from the same team, and their patterns of behaviour or grouping tendencies distinguish them as an observable entity. Yet, the mere fact that there *is* a noticeable smaller grouping of athletes tells us relatively little. Perhaps of greater importance to those interested in team dynamics is why or how these groupings develop, and to what extent they impact the team in adaptive or maladaptive ways. The omission of this information in the scenario was purposeful and meant to emphasize the perspective that subgroups develop for a wide variety of reasons, and that, in and of themselves, they are neither good nor bad. For example, those athletes could represent the informal leadership group, whereby they are the most skilled athletes, believe in and reinforce the team's values and norms, and engage with the remainder of their teammates to promote an inclusive and unified team culture. Conversely, they could be a group of athletes who have recently been receiving less playing time, have decreasing levels of motivation concerning the teams' objectives, and whose interests are veering towards social activities that are unrelated to—and often in direct conflict with—their sport performance.

Within the following section, I will: (a) briefly introduce perspectives from the broader psychology literature that inform our understanding of why subgroups develop and how they can impact those involved, (b) summarize the research conducted specifically in the sport setting, and (c) describe a preliminary organizing framework that can be used to differentiate groups considered to be either adaptive or non-value laden (i.e., subgroups) versus those that are more debilitative in nature (i.e., cliques).

Theory and Research

Why Subgroups Develop, and What They Mean for Those Involved

Humans are a social species, to the point where membership within groups is the norm (e.g., family, work teams, social circles) rather than the exception. Indeed, scholars (e.g., Baumeister & Leary, 1995; Forsyth, 2014) have suggested our tendency to coalesce with others and our innate need to belong to social groupings to be important human characteristics. This orientation is typically used to promote individual involvement in sport and to understand athlete experiences at the team level (e.g., Eys. et al., 2019); however, as you will see, subgroups are an inevitability in sport, and so understanding why they develop is important.

One perspective is that sport teams are typically composed of many members, so individuals will strive to conglomerate with a select few for affiliative and belongingness purposes. Evidence does suggest that a greater quantity of superficial relationships is less satisfying than a smaller number of high-quality relationships (e.g., Hawkley & Cacioppo,

2010). As such, bonds formed with a subset of teammates (as opposed to an entire team) may be better positioned to satiate the need for belonging. Forsyth (2014) supported this position, stating that:

> groups that create connections among their members, such as amateur athletic teams ... will reduce members' feelings of social loneliness, but only more intimate, involving types of groups—families, romantic couples, or very close friendship *cliques* —will meet members' social and emotional needs.
>
> (p. 67)

Brewer (2012) provided a similar perspective through the optimal distinctiveness theory (ODT), positioning individuals as seeking acceptance within a group that facilitates quality relations, while still maintaining autonomy and differentiation. The fundamental interpersonal relations orientation (FIRO; Schutz, 1958) also reinforces individual desire for inclusion, control, and affection—again, likely to be satiated in smaller groupings rather than a larger team. Aligned with these assumptions, sport teams offer athletes the opportunity for acceptance and belonging, yet their affiliation with a subgroup (or clique) enables differentiation and individual identity unique to that of the total team.

Another perspective relevant to sport includes purposeful motives beyond identity, belonging, and differentiation. Specifically, Carton and Cummings (2012) discuss the importance that individuals place on gaining relevant knowledge or acquiring resources to improve their standing within a group, in addition to establishing personal identity. As you would expect, knowledge-based subgroups develop when individuals interact with others to acquire or share information. Resource-based groupings revolve around the control or acquisition of resources, likely to influence power/status or hierarchies within a group. Lastly, identity-based subgroups involve individuals with similar values and social characteristics, and a shared sense of identity. Take the scenario depicted earlier in the chapter. The athletes might represent those with specialized roles (e.g., are members of the power play unit), who identify as the more skilled athletes on the team, obtain a greater amount of attention and playing time in this group, and specifically target more senior members to access information that might not otherwise be provided to first-year athletes. Each of Carton and Cummings' (2012) dimensions are represented in this scenario (i.e., knowledge, resources, identity), but it is worth noting that their presence is not necessary in all instances. The point of emphasis, rather, is that, through this perspective, grouping tendencies are a consequence of purposeful behaviour.

An alternative perspective as to why subgroups develop is that members are subject to grouping tendencies based on hypothetical "dividing lines" (e.g., faultlines) that are present in all groups. Lau and Murnighan's (1998) faultline theory suggests that the presence of inadvertent faultlines can increase proximity and promote interaction among certain members. The general notion is supported by the categorization-elaboration model (CEM; van Knippenberg, De Dreu, & Homan, 2004), whereby members desire similarity while also experiencing diversity. There are faultlines presented in the scenario provided earlier that reinforce this position. For instance, age is a common dividing feature that likely also informs stage of life and relative interests. Skill level in and of itself might not represent a faultline, yet where a skill set positions athletes in relation to ice time or status may. The important point here is that these are automatic, and do not necessarily determine the relative valence (i.e., the general positivity or negativity) that subsequent subgroups can have within a team, but that grouping tendencies can be unintentional. Clearly, there are many reasons why larger groups will experience subdivisions among their members, and many of these—as you will see in the subsequent sections—are relevant to sport.

In addition to understanding why subgroups exist, exploring how they impact those involved is equally necessary. This is particularly relevant for the current chapter, because, if subgroups or cliques had no behavioural influence or impact on the experiences of members, there would be little reason for their investigation. Across the field of psychology, research indicates the potential for group members to experience both adaptive and maladaptive outcomes. From an adaptive perspective, individuals can benefit from smaller, intimate groupings to learn accepted behaviours and important cultural knowledge (e.g., Adler & Adler, 1995; Pattiselanno, Dijkstra, Steglich, Vollebergh, & Veenstra, 2015), for improved self-perceptions (e.g., Tarrant, MacKenzie, & Hewitt, 2006), and levels of physical activity (e.g., Sawka et al., 2014). In addition, Cronin, Bezrukova, Weingart, and Tinsley (2011) noted that, when team members experience quality relations and understand the grouping tendencies of their total membership, potential benefits for team effectiveness can be associated with subgroup presence. Of course, evidence also points to myriad negative outcomes associated with smaller groupings. From an individual perspective, these can involve the likelihood of engaging in substance abuse and tobacco use (e.g., Fuqua et al., 2012; Gommans, Müller, Stevens, Cillessen, & Ter Bogt, 2017; Hussong & Chassin, 2002) or more general delinquent behaviours such as aggressive and bullying interpersonal interactions with others (e.g., Graham, Bellmore, & Maze, 2006; Lee et al., 2017; Pokhrel, Sussman, Black, & Sun, 2010; Schmitt-Rodermund & Silbereisen, 2008). From a team perspective, the presence of clear faultiness or smaller groups could negatively impact performance (Bezrukova, Spell, Caldwell, & Burger, 2016), lower perceptions of psychological safety (e.g., Edmondson, 1999), and cause identity-related issues (Hornsey & Hogg, 2000).

Taken as a whole, this brief introduction to the concept of subgroups and cliques from the broader psychology literature demonstrates their inherent complexities, not only in relation to why they develop, but also with respect to the relative impact that they have on individual members and teams more generally.

Subgroups and Cliques in Sport

Within this section, I aim to describe the research within the context of sport, but, as I do so, it is worthy of note that, although the direct investigation of subgroups and cliques has been limited, these topics have been explored as correlates to other relevant group variables. Further, the general discourse surrounding any distinguishable smaller entity within a sport team has traditionally been negative. I do not disagree that issues stemming from their presence are possible, but I emphasize that only a portion of the phenomenon, or one perspective, has been explored. Almost four decades ago, Carron and Chelladurai (1981) made several propositions to describe the cohesion–performance relationship in sport. Within those propositions, they described implications surrounding the division within a team pertaining to task-related interactions (i.e., coalitions) and socially oriented motives (i.e., cliques). The early research in sport appears to have focused predominantly on the socially oriented groups (i.e., cliques), while largely overlooking other potential smaller entities such as the coalitions advanced by Carron and Chelladurai (1981). In addition, and leaning on the broader psychology literature, there are many factors that dictate grouping tendencies and teammate interactions, and the manner in which they impact the team is likely more associated with how athletes experience them—both in terms of their immediate membership and the remainder of the team—rather than their presence or absence.

With the purview of adequately yet concisely depicting this body of work, I begin with studies that speak to the presence or implications of cliques, albeit from a more tangential perspective. As several examples, both Foley (1990) and Stratta (1995) made reference to their presence within their respective ethnographies. While exploring the potential for American football to serve as a ritual that socializes counterhegemonic cultural practices, Foley (1990) identified a particularly problematic group described as the "ex-player clique" that remained in town and negatively impacted the current adolescents' experiences. Similarly, by examining African American athletes' involvement within the National Collegiate Athletic Association (NCAA), Stratta (1995) noted issues surrounding racial cliques, reporting discourse pertaining to stereotypes and exhibiting little regard for multicultural awareness. Similar experiences in the NCAA have also been described in relation to clique development and the purposeful distancing from teammates based on sexual orientation (Blinde, Taub, & Han, 1994).

In addition to the references from collegiate and adolescent sport, other studies conducted during the late 1990s to the present day should be introduced. Fletcher and Hanton (2003) found elite athletes to report that cliques were a source of organizational strain owing to their tendency to divide teammates and deteriorate the team environment. Organizational-level cliques have also been reported, whereby specific rugby unions in New Zealand were described as "hunting in packs" to solidify commercial sustainability and access limited resources (Meiklejohn, Dickson, & Ferkins, 2016). Similarly, within Major League Baseball (MLB), Bezrukova and colleagues (2016) described the presence of clear faultlines at both the team and organizational levels to be negatively related to performance.

Cliques have also been featured during questionnaire development procedures for various group and developmental constructs. Notably, the presence of cliques has been used as an item indicative of negative experiences within the youth sport environment (MacDonald, Côté, Eys, & Deakin, 2012), youth athletes have identified the lack of cliques as an indication of a team's social cohesion (Eys, Loughead, Bray, & Carron, 2009), and young adults have described the presence of cliques resulting in intra-team conflict (Paradis, Carron, & Martin, 2014). With regard to the latter (i.e., conflict), Partridge and Knapp (2016) explored adolescent female experiences, noting that the presence of cliques formed based on athletic or social status contributed to discord within the team. Leggat, Smith, and Figgins (2019) emphasized the potential for cliques to serve as both an antecedent to, and a consequence of, conflict, also suggesting that their development could be instigated by the contributions of a single athlete. A good example of cliques being triggered by individuals can be found in Vealey's (2017) case study, whereby she began consulting with a team described as being "below zero" from a culture perspective, largely because the team was divided into two cliques, each led by one of two team captains.

Researchers interested in advancing the effectiveness of sport teams through team building (TB) have also discussed the implications of subgroups and cliques. For example, Yukelson (1997) noted that factions or cliques could divide loyalties and result in individuals becoming disconnected from the total team, and Brawley and Paskevich (1997) described one component of TB research to specifically involve the reduction or elimination of group properties (such as cliques) that hinder a group's development. These general notions have been supported with more specific examples, with Ryska, Yin, Cooley, and Ginn (1999) describing how coaches have stressed the need to promote social acceptance (vs. clique development and isolation) as a strategy for facilitating team cohesion. Similarly, Bloom, Loughead, and Newin (2008) cautioned against the use of simple team "get-togethers", advocating rather for targeted and purposeful activities that will not enable clique development and subsequent member isolation to be accentuated.

The previous examples of research in sport have predominantly situated "cliques" as problematic, with issues ranging from athlete marginalization, to associations with important group processes, to obstacles related to TB. Although this body of work has been instrumental in furthering our understanding, purposeful investigations pertaining to what constitutes a subgroup or clique, how they develop, and what they mean for those involved have gone largely unexplored in sport. This dearth of explicit research led colleagues and me to conduct a series of qualitative studies specifically exploring the nature of subgroups and cliques as the primary research question. The first study involved semi-structured interviews with intercollegiate athletes in Canada (Martin et al., 2015). These athletes believed the presence of subgroups or cliques to be inevitable, but also noted that their general structure (e.g., size, member composition) and associated behaviours (e.g., invitations to social activities) were quite variable. In addition, the athletes discussed a number of reasons for their development, ranging from clear faultlines, such as age or team tenure, to other factors, such as similarity in interests or physical proximity between teammates. Finally, the athletes also felt that, contingent on inclusive or exclusive behaviours, both adaptive (e.g., social acceptance, support) and maladaptive (e.g., desire to drop out, decreased performance) outcomes were possible.

The findings from the Martin et al. (2015) study with athletes reinforced the general complexity of groups within a group (e.g., Tichy, 1973) and supported the potential for benefits pertaining to group functioning (e.g., Cronin et al., 2011). In recognizing that coaches have a mandate to organize the structure and environment of a team, we subsequently sought to incorporate their perspectives within an elite sport context (Martin, Evans, & Spink, 2016). For instance, in addition to exploring their general perceptions and experiences with subgroups or cliques, an important extension was having coaches discuss strategies for their avoidance or management. Overall, coaches were in agreement with athlete perceptions in that the presence of smaller pockets of team members was seen as inevitable. Coincidentally, because of the perceived inevitability of subgroups, coaches acknowledged their efforts in becoming acutely aware of the social processes and grouping tendencies within their teams. The coaches in this study also emphasized expectations that subgroups would impact on their team's performance and elaborated on proactive measures used to decrease the potential deleterious effects.

Several important takeaways from this research extend previous TB literature. The coaches did not consider the presence of smaller entities within their teams to warrant an automatic "avoid at all costs" approach. They acknowledged that clique issues could certainly occur and reflected on the extensive amount of time that was spent considering the social structure of their teams. Similarly, they advanced a series of strategies used to mitigate their potential negative impact on their athletes. First, they discussed utilizing available resources to understand their groups (e.g., coaching or training staff, professors or instructors for intercollegiate athletes, billets for elite youth athletes). They also believed in proactive planning, whereby measures such as strict member selection criteria and purposeful early season TB efforts could reinforce the expected and desired culture within the team. Finally, direct athlete management strategies were advanced, ranging from frequent coach–athlete meetings to explicit discussions with athlete leaders to empower their ownership over team issues. It is important to reiterate that coaches described cliques as problematic but recognized that not all smaller groupings within a team are inherently an issue. Rather, the emphasis was on monitoring and being aware of athlete groupings to gain insight as to when they could be problematic and to proactively manipulate the environment to limit explicit faultlines and promote team member acceptance and inclusivity.

Although these two studies served to extend our understanding using various perspectives, several important questions remained. In addition, both studies involved one-time retrospective interviews, thus limiting our ability to adequately explore athletes' awareness of, responses to, and experiences in dealing with subgroups or cliques. Accordingly, a longitudinal repeated-interview case study design was conducted by Wagstaff, Martin, and Thelwell (2017) with an elite rugby union team across an entire season. Specific areas of interest involved the need to better understand the antecedents to either facilitative subgroups or debilitative cliques, their dynamic nature, the specific exhibited group behaviours, and to what extent (if any) they required management.

The athletes from the Wagstaff et al. (2017) study were able to identify the subgroupings within their teams and, more importantly, to differentiate them from the more problematic cliques (the latter representing those who demonstrated exclusive and conflict-oriented behaviours). In addition, they acknowledged thinking about the various groups often and discussed how they were an inevitable part of sport. The longitudinal nature of this study enabled us to see that, whereas certain clique members felt that they were acting in accordance with the teams' values and normative expectations (e.g., being inclusive, supportive, motivating teammates), other team members felt otherwise. This demonstrated a lack of self-awareness of clique members and also showed that the associated problems were perhaps not purposeful, but a misunderstanding of exhibited behaviours in relation to what was acceptable or helpful. Finally, membership variability within these smaller groups was evident, as follow-up interviews uncovered a number of athletes who had reported distancing themselves from previous groupings that no longer aligned with their or the teams' beliefs or objectives.

It is also worth noting that athletes described the deleterious impact of cliques in both favourable (e.g., winning streaks) and unfavourable (e.g., after a loss) situations. This is a particularly important result, as athletes discussed the potential for clique boundaries to become more accentuated and exclusive when successful, suggesting that winning does not necessarily overcome all issues. In building from this discussion, the athletes advocated that coaches should be aware of the grouping tendencies among team members, but that behaviours imposed by management should be used sparingly. Rather, including the athletes themselves throughout the process and undertaking authentic approaches to team management were preferred. They recommended avoiding typical strategies such as forced seating arrangements or rooming assignments and emphasized team values agreed upon by all members and speaking transparently about the various groupings within the team to explore how they can impact individual athletes and the team as a whole.

A final example of direct assessment in sport involves another season-long case study, but with an individual sport team and including more than one perspective (i.e., coaches and athletes; Saizew, 2018). Track and field was selected because it represented a sport composed of several smaller teams ranging in teammate interdependence and event types. Fifteen Canadian intercollegiate coaches and athletes engaged in semi-structured interviews at the beginning and end of their season. As a general summary, similar themes emerged in relation to the changing membership composition throughout the season, in addition to the misperception/misunderstanding of a group's impact on the team by members of particular cliques. Novel findings from this work demonstrated that numerous structural constraints inherent in the sport (e.g., sport and event type, facility/schedule limitations, team size) impacted teammate interactions and predisposed the team to subdivide. As a result, a large portion of the team's focus was directed toward the management of the social environment (e.g., athlete interactions, cooperation), which involved general TB and emphasized athlete leader ownership over the process to improve consistent and quality communication and buy-in. This research demonstrated the potential for sport-specific constraints to impact the grouping tendencies of teammates, suggesting that not all teams will experience subgroups in the same way, and that some sport types are more predisposed to divisions than others.

Taken together, it is clear that the sport literature has progressed from indirect assessment to more purposeful and direct investigation, and yet this line of enquiry remains in its infancy. Consequently, an important consideration for those interested in this topic would be to find novel ways of extending our understanding in sport. As several examples, the measurement of groups' physical presence within a team would be useful for predicting their impact on individual and group-level variables (e.g., Wölfer, Faber, & Hewstone, 2015) and could be combined with the advancement of self-report questionnaires (e.g., Kiesner, Cadinu, Poulin, & Bucci, 2002) or social-cognitive mapping (SCM; e.g., Cairns, Perrin, & Cairns, 1986) as ways of exploring athletes' perceptions of the various smaller groups present within their teams. In the meantime, however, the following organizing framework could be used as a helpful guide to reinforce the complexity of this phenomenon for future researchers in sport.

An Organizing Framework for Sport

Within the following section, a heuristic depiction is presented to consolidate what is currently known, with a slight adaptation from a previous version advanced for coaches and practitioners in sport (see Wagstaff & Martin, 2018). As can be seen in Figure 1, the presence of smaller entities is inevitable, and their member composition can be quite variable throughout the existence of a group (Basic Assumptions). There is also a myriad of reasons for their development, and these range from purposeful individual motives to more circumstantial and context-based causes (Antecedents/Precursors). The key feature within this depiction involves the nature of the smaller entities (Nature of Groupings), differentiated largely based on their general valence within the total group and their exhibited behaviours, resulting in the classification as either non-value laden or facilitative (i.e., subgroups) or more deleterious in

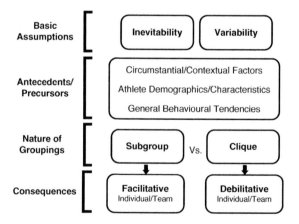

Figure 1 Organizing framework for subgroups and cliques in sport, adapted from Wagstaff and Martin (2018)

nature (i.e., cliques). Lastly, it is important to consider the relative impact that the specific entity has on the individual athletes or team involved (Consequences).

Basic Assumptions

Findings from specific research in sport, in combination with relevant literature from the broader field of psychology, suggest the inevitability of smaller entities. The desire for affiliation balanced with differentiation (e.g., Brewer, 2012; Forsyth, 2014) underscores the improbability that all members will interact in similar ways, in either quantity or quality. A second assumption relates to the complexity of these sub-entities (e.g., Kindermann, 2007), along with the transient nature of their member composition (e.g., Brown & Dietz, 2009). From the extant sport research (e.g., Martin et al., 2015; Wagstaff et al., 2017), athletes acknowledged their ever-changing landscape, attributing this to many of the precursors described below (e.g., injuries, changing personalities).

Antecedents/Precursors

When considering the reasons for the emergence of subgroups or cliques, it is clear that a range of factors must be considered. These range from purposeful motives (e.g., status, resource acquisition) to more faultline-based causes (e.g., cohort; Carton & Cummings, 2012; Lau & Murnighan, 1998). Based on the sport literature presented above, these can be considered in relation to circumstantial or contextual constraints (e.g., team size, proximity, performance issues), athlete demographics and characteristics (e.g., cohort, status, roles), and general behavioural tendencies (e.g., social habits, commitment level, objectives). Importantly, these themes are not exclusive, nor are they final.

Nature of Groupings

A novelty within the sport literature pertains to the differentiation of smaller entities based on general valence and exhibited behaviours. This departure has been informed by the sport-specific literature and reflects the manner in which relevant agents (i.e., athletes and coaches) have discussed the phenomenon. On one hand, subgroups are considered to be non-value laden to more facilitative. Both coaches and athletes have discussed non-value laden groupings as being largely circumstantial, whereby athletes may spend a significant amount of time together owing to factors such as carpooling needs or education programme enrolment, but these do not necessarily hold a positive or negative valence for those individuals or the team as a whole. Facilitative subgroups are seen as advancing the team's objectives or positively contributing to its culture, while also satisfying individual member needs. On the other hand, cliques are perceived as those inherently debilitative groups described as conflict-oriented, exclusive, and self-enhancing.

Consequences

One reason for the research attention in the broader literature is not only that subgroups feature saliently in the lives of most humans, but also that they can impact individuals and teams in a variety of ways, both adaptively and maladaptively. Extending from the nature of the groupings, subgroups are likely to influence individual athletes through perceptions of social support, belongingness, and identity, and teams more generally by creating an inclusive and safe environment and by demonstrating prototypically accepted and conducive normative behaviours. Conversely, cliques are likely to lead to debilitative outcomes, again, at both the individual (e.g., isolation, increased pressure) and team (e.g., conflict, poor performance) levels.

Circling back to the scenario presented earlier in the chapter, an organizing framework such as this could be used to explore the more salient features contributing to the various grouping tendencies within a team (why), the general valence attributed to or experienced by team members pertaining to the group (what), and the manner in which the respective group(s) is/are influencing the athletes involved (how). It is very likely that examples—such as those ice hockey players in the orienting example at the beginning of this chapter—exist across sport types, ages, and levels of competition, and, as demonstrated herein, recognizing the nuances associated with their presence will better position researchers to understand the phenomenon and practitioners to manage their team's social environment.

Conclusion

In 1993, Carron delivered the Coleman Roberts Griffith Address to the Association of Applied Sport Psychology, wherein he made the case for the complementarity of theory, research, and practice, advocating for applied work to be informed by theory, and for research to reflect a pragmatic stance using current issues to inform scientific enquiry. The coherence between research and practice is as critical today as it was then, and yet the paucity of systematic examination of subgroups and cliques in sport inhibits any potential comprehensive summary pertaining to practice and application. Whereas the body of literature reviewed previously is nascent, it is limited to a few studies, all qualitative in nature. Accordingly, the following represents a synthesis of the management strategies described by athletes and coaches within the literature, with attempts to incorporate relevant TB and intervention work where possible. The areas of focus for practice and application involve the importance of identification and awareness across team members and the benefits of authentic strategies grounded within a condition-setting approach.

Although there is support for the debilitative outcomes associated with cliques, findings do suggest that they are often a consequence of unintentional and misunderstood behaviours. Accordingly, a resounding practical implication is the need for coaches to have a "pulse" for the interaction tendencies of their athletes, and for athletes to be aware of how their behaviours are impacting others within the team. From a coach perspective, it is important to maintain dialogue with team members, ranging from athletes, training/support staff, and other coaches to important social agents, such as teachers or billet families (e.g., Martin et al., 2016). However, using the opening scenario as an example, understanding that those select few athletes gravitate towards each other will provide limited benefit if coaches are unable to differentiate between subgroup and clique characteristics. Recognizing beneficial features such as the provision of social support or the demonstration of productive norms versus the more debilitative antisocial or exclusionary behaviours is critical. For athletes, developing awareness of how their behaviours are impacting their teammates is necessary and can alleviate many of the potential issues attributed to cliques (e.g., Vealey, 2017; Wagstaff et al., 2017).

Direct interventions have not been conducted in this area, and yet examples pertaining to teammate interactions (Beauchamp, Maclachlan, & Lothian, 2005) and emotional intelligence (EI; e.g., Wagstaff, Fletcher, & Hanton, 2012a, 2012b) serve as useful templates. For instance, Beauchamp et al. (2005) proposed a framework for improved communication in team situations, emphasizing the need to understand the self and others and being able to adapt and to connect with others of varying interaction preferences. Using this general approach, Beauchamp, Lothian, and Timson (2008) implemented an intervention with an international-level co-acting sport team. By having athletes consider their and their teammates' personality and behaviour preferences and tendencies, they were able to decrease conflict and improve trust, team cohesion, and performance. This level of awareness also necessitates EI, whereby athletes should be able to understand the implications of, and manage, their and others' emotions (e.g., Wagstaff et al., 2012a, 2012b). Leaders, such as coaches, with higher levels of EI also have teams with stronger perceptions of cohesion and performance (e.g., Crombie, Lombard, & Noakes, 2009; Rapisarda, 2002). Further, research has shown that adaptive emotional regulation behaviours and EI can be taught (e.g., Wagstaff, Hanton, & Fletcher, 2013), which means that coaches and athletes could benefit from awareness-building activities to understand teammate grouping tendencies and to safeguard against unintended or misinterpreted problematic "clique" type behaviours.

A second general theme that is relevant for practice and application involves general strategies meant to manage the broader team environment. First, although a traditional perspective in the TB literature has been to remove or "break up" cliques, recent research suggests that carefully planned and authentic approaches to their management should be more effective (Martin et al., 2015; Wagstaff et al., 2017). Specifically, this approach aligns with the condition-setting perspective advanced by Hackman (2012), whereby providing fertile conditions for an organization will facilitate its effective functioning. The emphasis on planning and preparatory behaviours in relation to improving team functioning aligns with suggestions advanced within the TB literature (e.g., Brawley & Paskevich, 1997). Such activities can vary substantially; however, several relevant examples include bringing in the right people, establishing clear normative expectations for member conduct, and providing a supportive and safe environment (e.g., Hackman, 2011). Indeed, examples of clearly describing "ideal" team members and actively seeking such individuals during selection have been noted from a general team culture perspective (Hodge, Henry, & Smith, 2014) and more specifically in relation to avoiding clique issues (Martin et al., 2016). Coaches have also discussed the importance of utilizing leadership groups to regulate and improve the social dynamics in a team (e.g., Caron, Bloom, Loughead, & Hoffman, 2016), and athletes have emphasized their desire for ownership and autonomy to govern themselves in relation to establishing and reinforcing normative behaviours (Wagstaff et al., 2017). Finally, ensuring that athletes feel supported and that there are mechanisms put in place for them to voice their opinions or seek assistance have also been cited as critical (Martin et al., 2016; Ryska et al., 1999).

Finally, it is worth noting that management or intervention strategies should be authentic in nature, with an explicit emphasis on avoiding controlling and autocratic behaviours. For instance, athletes from Wagstaff et al. (2017) described being frustrated with coach-led, controlling-type strategies targeting athlete interactions. They described them as being "heavy-handed" and "forced and unnatural". Rather, they desired to be treated as adults and to have open conversations about the implications of cliques as a team. These perspectives were supported by Saizew's (2018) case study, whereby athletes discussed the added stress associated with too many forced TB activities. The preference was to have fewer, more meaningful and purposeful activities throughout the season, rather than frequent "get-togethers". This aligns with suggestions advanced in the sport literature, both in relation to the benefits of season-long TB efforts (Martin, Carron, & Burke, 2009) and in terms of cautioning against ill-prepared or simple team outings that can accentuate member isolation and grouping tendencies (Bloom et al., 2008).

References

Adler, P. A., & Adler, P. (1995). Dynamics of inclusion and exclusion in preadolescent cliques. *Social Psychology Quarterly, 58,* 145–162.

Baumeister, R. F., & Leary, M. R. (1995). The need to belong: Desire for interpersonal attachments as a fundamental human motivation. *Psychological Bulletin, 117*(3), 497–529.

Beauchamp, M. R., Lothian, J. M., & Timson, S. E. (2008). Understanding self and others: A personality preference-based intervention with an elite co-acting sport team. *Sport & Exercise Psychology Review, 4,* 4–20.

Beauchamp, M. R., Maclachlan, A., & Lothian, A. M. (2005). Communication within sport teams: Jungian preferences and group dynamics. *The Sport Psychologist, 19,* 203–220.

Bezrukova, K., Spell, C. S., Caldwell, D., & Burger, J. M. (2016). A multilevel perspective on faultlines: Differentiating the effects between group-and organizational-level faultlines. *Journal of Applied Psychology, 101*(1), 86–107.

Blinde, E. M., Taub, D. E., & Han, L. (1994). Sport as a site for women's group and societal empowerment: Perspectives from the college athlete. *Sociology of Sport Journal, 11*(1), 51–59.

Bloom, G. A., Loughead, T. M., & Newin, J. (2008). Team building for youth sport. *Journal of Physical Education, Recreation & Dance, 79,* 44–47.

Brawley, L. R., & Paskevich, D. M. (1997). Conducting team building research in the context of sport and exercise. *Journal of Applied Sport Psychology, 9*(1), 11–40.

Brewer, M. B. (2012). Optimal distinctiveness theory: Its history and development. In P. A. M. Van Lange, A. W. Kruglanski & E. T. Higgins (Eds.), *Handbook of theories of social psychology* (Vol. 2, pp. 81–98). Thousand Oaks, CA: Sage.

Brown, B. B., & Dietz, E. L. (2009). Informal peer groups in middle childhood and adolescence. In K. H. Rubin, W. M. Bukowski & B. Laursen (Eds.), *Handbook of peer interactions, relationships, and groups* (pp. 361–376). New York: Guildford Press.

Cairns, R. B., Perrin, J. E., & Cairns, B. D. (1986). Social structure and social cognition in early adolescence: Affiliative patterns. *The Journal of Early Adolescence, 5*(3), 339–355.

Caron, J. G., Bloom, G. A., Loughead, T. M., & Hoffmann, M. D. (2016). Paralympic athlete leaders' perceptions of leadership and cohesion. *Journal of Sport Behavior, 39*(3), 219–238.

Carron, A. V. (1993). The Coleman Roberts Griffith address: Toward the integration of theory, research, and practice in sport psychology. *Journal of Applied Sport Psychology, 5,* 207–221.

Carron, A. V., & Chelladurai, P. (1981). The dynamics of group cohesion in sport. *Journal of Sport Psychology, 3*(2), 123–139.

Carron, A. V., & Eys, M. A. (2012). *Group dynamics in sport* (4th ed.). Morgantown, WV: Fitness Information Technology.

Carton, A. M., & Cummings, J. N. (2012). A theory of subgroups in work teams. *Academy of Management Review, 37,* 441–470.

Crombie, D., Lombard, C., & Noakes, T. (2009). Emotional intelligence scores predict team sports performance in a national cricket competition. *International Journal of Sports Science and Coaching, 4,* 209–224.

Cronin, M. A., Bezrukova, K., Weingart, L. R., & Tinsley, C. H. (2011). Subgroups within a team: The role of cognitive and affective integration. *Journal of Organizational Behavior, 32*(6), 831–849.

Edmondson, A. (1999). Psychological safety and learning behavior in work teams. *Administrative Science Quarterly, 44,* 350.

Eys, M., Loughead, T., Bray, S. R., & Carron, A. V. (2009). Perceptions of cohesion by youth sport participants. *The Sport Psychologist, 23,* 330–345.

Eys, M. A., Bruner, M. W., & Martin, L. J. (2019). The dynamic group environment in sport and exercise. *Psychology of Sport and Exercise.* Online first publication. doi: 10.1016/j.psychsport.2018.11.001

Fletcher, D., & Hanton, S. (2003). Sources of organizational stress in elite sports performers. *The Sport Psychologist, 17*(2), 175–195.

Foley, D. E. (1990). The great American football ritual: Reproducing race, class, and gender inequality. *Sociology of Sport Journal, 7*(2), 111–135.

Forsyth, D. R. (2014). *Group dynamics* (6th ed.). Belmont, CA: Wadsworth Cengage Learning.

Fuqua, J. L., Gallaher, P. E., Unger, J. B., Trinidad, D. R., Sussman, S., Ortega, E., & Johnson, C. A. (2012). Multiple peer group self-identification and adolescent tobacco use. *Substance Use & Misuse, 47,* 757–766.

Gommans, R., Müller, C. M., Stevens, G. W., Cillessen, A. H., & Ter Bogt, T. F. (2017). Individual popularity, peer group popularity composition and adolescents' alcohol consumption. *Journal of Youth and Adolescence, 46*(8), 1716–1726.

Graham, S., Bellmore, A. D., & Maze, J. (2006). Peer victimization, aggression, and their co-occurrence in middle school: Pathways to adjustment problems. *Journal of Abnormal Child Psychology, 34*(3), 329–364.

Hackman, J. R. (2011). *Collaborative intelligence: Using teams to solve hard problems.* San Francisco, CA: Berrett-Koehler.

Hackman, J. R. (2012). From causes to conditions in group research. *Journal of Organizational Behavior, 33,* 428–444.

Hawkley, L. C., & Cacioppo, J. T. (2010). Loneliness matters: A theoretical and empirical review of consequences and mechanisms. *Annals of Behavioral Medicine, 40*(2), 218–227.

Henrich, C. C., Kupermine, G. P., Sack, A., Blatt, S. J., & Leadbeater, B. J. (2000). Characteristics and homogeneity of early adolescent friendship groups: A comparison of male and female clique and nonclique members. *Applied Developmental Science, 4,* 15–26.

Hodge, K., Henry, G., & Smith, W. (2014). A case study of excellence in elite sport: Motivational climate in a world champion team. *The Sport Psychologist, 28,* 60–74.

Hornsey, M. J., & Hogg, M. A. (2000). Assimilation and diversity: An integrative model of subgroup relations. *Personality and Social Psychology Review, 4,* 143–156.

Hussong, A. M., & Chassin, L. (2002). Parent alcoholism and the leaving home transition. *Development and Psychopathology, 14*(1), 139–157.

Kiesner, J., Cadinu, M., Poulin, F., & Bucci, M. (2002). Group identification in early adolescence: Its relation with peer adjustment and its moderator effect on peer influence. *Child Development, 73,* 196–208.

Kindermann, T. A. (2007). Effects of naturally existing peer groups on changes in academic engagement in a cohort of sixth graders. *Child Development, 78,* 1186–1203.

Lau, D. C., & Murnighan, J. K. (1998). Demographic diversity and faultlines: The compositional dynamics of organizational groups. *Academy of Management Review, 2,* 325–340.

Lee, S., Foote, J., Wittrock, Z., Xu, S., Niu, L., & French, D. C. (2017). Adolescents' perception of peer groups: Psychological, behavioral, and relational determinants. *Social Science Research, 65,* 181–194.

Leggat, F. J., Smith, M. J., & Figgins, S. G. (2019). Talented but disruptive: An exploration of problematic players in sports teams. *Journal of Applied Sport Psychology.* Online first publication. doi: 10.1080/10413200.2018.1549621

MacDonald, D. J., Côté, J., Eys, M., & Deakin, J. (2012). Psychometric properties of the youth experience survey with young athletes. *Psychology of Sport and Exercise, 13*(3), 332–340.

Martin, L. J., Carron, A. V., & Burke, S. M. (2009). Team building interventions in sport: A meta-analysis. *Sport and Exercise Psychology Review, 5,* 3–18.

Martin, L. J., Evans, M. B., & Spink, K. S. (2016). Coach perspectives of "groups within the group": An analysis of subgroups and cliques in sport. *Sport, Exercise, and Performance Psychology, 5*(1), 52–66.

Martin, L. J., Wilson, J., Evans, M. B., & Spink, K. S. (2015). Cliques in sport: Perceptions of intercollegiate athletes. *The Sport Psychologist, 29*(1), 82–95.

McDaniel, S. H., & Salas, E. (2018). The science of teamwork: Introduction to the special issue. *American Psychologist, 73*(4), 305–307.

McEwan, D., Ruissen, G. R., Eys, M. A., Zumbo, B. D., & Beauchamp, M. R. (2017). The effectiveness of teamwork training on teamwork behaviors and team performance: A systematic review and meta-analysis of controlled interventions. *PLoS One, 12,* e0169604.

Meiklejohn, T., Dickson, G., & Ferkins, L. (2016). The formation of interorganisational cliques in New Zealand rugby. *Sport Management Review, 19*(3), 266–278.

Paradis, K. F., Carron, A. V., & Martin, L. J. (2014). Athlete perceptions of intra-team conflict in sport. *Sport and Exercise Psychology Review, 10,* 4–18.

Partridge, J. A., & Knapp, B. A. (2016). Mean girls: Adolescent female athletes and peer conflict in sport. *Journal of Applied Sport Psychology, 28*(1), 113–127.

Pattiselanno, K., Dijkstra, J. K., Steglich, C., Vollebergh, W., & Veenstra, R. (2015). Structure matters: The role of clique hierarchy in the relationship between adolescent social status and aggression and prosociality. *Journal of Youth and Adolescence, 44*(12), 2257–2274.

Pokhrel, P., Sussman, S., Black, D., & Sun, P. (2010). Peer group self-identification as a predictor of relational and physical aggression among high school students. *Journal of School Health, 80*(5), 249–258.

Rapisarda, B. A. (2002). The impact of emotional intelligence on work team cohesiveness and performance. *The International Journal of Organizational Analysis, 10*, 363–379.

Ryska, T. A., Yin, Z., Cooley, D., & Ginn, R. (1999). Developing team cohesion: A comparison of cognitive-behavioral strategies of US and Australian sport coaches. *The Journal of Psychology, 133*(5), 523–539.

Saizew, K. (2018). *An examination of team structure and its implications for subgroups in an individual sport setting* (Doctoral dissertation). Online Repository: http://hdl.handle.net/1974/24973

Sawka, K. J., McCormack, G. R., Nettel-Aguirre, A., Blackstaffe, A., Perry, R., & Hawe, P. (2014). Associations between aspects of friendship networks, physical activity, and sedentary behaviour among adolescents. *Journal of Obesity, 2014*, 1–12.

Schmitt-Rodermund, E., & Silbereisen, R. (2008). The prediction of delinquency among immigrant and non-immigrant youth: Unwrapping the package of culture. *International Journal of Comparative Sociology, 49*(2–3), 87–109.

Schutz, W. C. (1958). *FIRO: A three-dimensional theory of inter-personal behavior.* New York: Holt, Rinehart & Winston.

Stratta, T. M. (1995). Cultural inclusiveness in sport—Recommendations from African American women college athletes. *Journal of Physical Education, Recreation & Dance, 66*(7), 52–56.

Tarrant, M., MacKenzie, L., & Hewitt, L. A. (2006). Friendship group identifcation, multidimensional self-concept, and experience of developmental tasks in adolescence. *Journal of Adolescence, 29*, 627–640.

Tichy, N. (1973). An analysis of clique formation and structure in organizations. *Administrative Science Quarterly, 18*, 194–208.

van Knippenberg, D., De Dreu, C. K. W., & Homan, A. C. (2004). Work group diversity and group performance: An integrative model and research agenda. *The Journal of Applied Psychology, 89*, 1008–1022.

Vealey, R. S. (2017). Conflict management and cultural reparation: Consulting "below zero" with a college basketball team. *Case Studies in Sport and Exercise Psychology, 1*(1), 83–93.

Wagstaff, C. R. D., Fletcher, D., & Hanton, S. (2012a). Positive organizational psychology in sport: An ethnography of organizational functioning in a national sport organization. *Journal of Applied Sport Psychology, 24*, 26–47.

Wagstaff, C. R. D., Fletcher, D., & Hanton, S. (2012b). Exploring emotion abilities and regulation strategies in sport organizations. *Sport, Exercise, and Performance Psychology, 1*, 268–282.

Wagstaff, C. R. D., Hanton, S., & Fletcher, D. (2013). Developing emotion abilities and regulation strategies in a sport organization: An action research intervention. *Psychology of Sport and Exercise, 14*, 476–487.

Wagstaff, C. R. D., & Martin, L. J. (2018). Managing groups and cliques. In R. Thelwell & M. Dicks (Eds.), *Professional advances in sports coaching: Research and practice* (pp. 295–317). Abingdon: Routledge.

Wagstaff, C. R. D., Martin, L. J., & Thelwell, R. C. (2017). Subgroups and cliques in sport: A longitudinal case study of a rugby union team. *Psychology of Sport and Exercise, 30*, 164–172.

Wölfer, R., Faber, N. S., & Hewstone, M. (2015). Social network analysis in the science of groups: Cross-sectional and longitudinal applications for studying intra-and intergroup behavior. *Group Dynamics: Theory, Research, and Practice, 19*, 45–61.

Yukelson, D. (1997). Principles of effective team building interventions in sport: A direct services approach at Penn State University. *Journal of Applied Sport Psychology, 9*(1), 73–96.

5

COGNITIVE SPORT PSYCHOLOGY

Aidan Moran

Introduction

Cognitive sport psychology is concerned with the scientific investigation of "cognitive" (derived from the Latin word *cognoscere* – "to know") processes in sport performers (Moran, 2009). These processes are mental or symbolic activities by which people acquire, store, and use knowledge. They are vital in everyday life because they help people in "constructing and in making sense not only of the world, but of themselves" (Bruner, 1990, p. 2). One of the most important cognitive activities is thinking, or the "internal processes involved in making sense of the environment, and deciding what action might be appropriate" (Eysenck & Keane, 2015, p. 1).

Over the past decade, the thinking processes of athletes have attracted considerable interest from researchers in cognitive sport psychology (e.g., see Brick, MacIntyre, & Campbell, 2015; Marlow & Uphill, 2017; Raab, Bar-Eli, Plessner, & Araújo, 2019; Samson, Simpson, Kamphoff, & Langlier, 2017). One way in which athletes' thoughts have been studied is through "think-aloud protocol" (TAP) analysis – a method pioneered by Ericsson and Simon (1980) in which data are collected from what people say as they verbalize everything that passes through their heads as they tackle a cognitive task in their specialist domain (see reviews of this method in Eccles & Arsal, 2017; Fox, Ericsson, & Best, 2011). Although the TAP has certain weaknesses (e.g., it is limited to consciously accessible thoughts), it is a popular and "nonreactive" method (i.e., it does not appear to alter cognitive processes and/or concurrent task performance during data collection; Fox et al., 2011) for recording ongoing cognitive activity. Crucially, participants in studies using the TAP are required only to verbalize their thoughts – not to explain or justify them. In sport psychology, Samson et al. (2017) used this method to capture the thoughts of long-distance athletes (defined as those who run a minimum of 20 miles per week) while they were engaged in a training run. Drawing on more than 18 hours of audio recordings, these researchers classified runners' thoughts into three distinct categories: "pace and distance", "pain and discomfort", and "environment". The first of these categories, which accounted for about 40 per cent of all the thoughts recorded in this study, comprised runners' reflections on monitoring pace and distance (e.g., "downhill, don't kill yourself, just cruise"); thoughts about strategies to maintain pace (e.g., using positive self-talk statements such as "you can do this ... don't walk, keep this pace") and thoughts about altering pace (e.g., "6:50 mile that's alright ... 2 miles to go ... 6:20, that's better").

The second category, which made up about 32 per cent of all thoughts, involved cognition about "pain and discomfort". Included here were thoughts about injuries and complaints (e.g., "my hips are a little tight. I'm stiff, my feet, my ankles, just killing me this morning"); thoughts about the causes of the runners' pain and discomfort (e.g., "my right foot is getting a little numb from going back up the hill"); and thoughts about how to cope with the pain and discomfort (e.g., "breathe, try to relax ..."). The final category, comprising some 28 per cent of all thoughts, concerned reflections on the running environment. Reported here were thoughts about geographical features (e.g., steep hills) and the weather (e.g., "I need it to start raining, it's hot, it's really hot, humid"); admiration for the environment, with the runners obviously having chosen scenic places to run (e.g., "oh my gosh, that's gorgeous ... it's so beautiful, the ocean, the mountains"); thoughts about wildlife (e.g., "hope I don't see any snakes"); and, finally, thoughts about traffic and other runners and cyclists (e.g. "ton of bikes out now ... I've been passed by 20 of them"). Overall, Samson et al.'s (2017) study showed that the majority (about 72 per cent) of runners' thoughts related to running and internal processes (e.g., maintaining pace, coping with pain and discomfort) rather than to external factors (e.g., the environment).

In a similar investigation of athletes' real-time cognitive activity, Whitehead et al. (2019) used the TAP to monitor the thoughts of cyclists over a 16.1 km time trial (TT). Results indicated that these athletes attended to different types of information depending on the phase of the race. Specifically, whereas thoughts relating to fatigue and pain were more likely to occur during the initial quartile of the event, thoughts relating to distance, speed, and heart rate increased throughout the event and were especially prominent during the final quartile.

Perhaps not surprisingly, contemporary research in cognitive sport psychology has been influenced significantly by theoretical developments in its parent discipline of cognitive psychology – a scientific field that explores how the mind works in acquiring, storing, and using knowledge. Of these developments, two "paradigms" or conceptual and methodological frameworks are especially important: the classical or information-processing approach (see history in Lachman, Lachman, & Butterfield, 1979) and a range of embodiment approaches (e.g., Glenberg, Witt, & Metcalfe, 2013; Willems & Francken, 2012). Broadly, the classical paradigm postulates that human knowledge is abstract and amodal (i.e., is stored in a format that is independent of any particular sensory modality), and that cognitive behaviour is best explained by brain-based mechanisms (e.g., the neural manipulation of internal symbols of knowledge). By contrast, embodiment theorists typically argue that cognitive processes are multimodal simulations or re-enactments of sensorimotor experience. Crucially, they also contend that cognitive activity involves more than mere symbol manipulation in the head: it entails constant interaction between the brain, the body, and the environment. Arising from this latter proposition, cognition has been portrayed as being embodied, enactive (i.e., tightly coupled with action), embedded (i.e., situated within specific environmental contexts that offer action possibilities: for example, a chair is directly perceived as encouraging sitting), and extended (i.e., cognition can be augmented and shaped by artefacts/technologies) – a set of ideas that is known collectively as the "4E" approach (see Newen, De Bruin, & Gallagher, 2018). Let us now explain these two preceding paradigms in more detail.

The Classical Paradigm in Cognitive Sport Psychology

The classical paradigm in cognitive psychology was shaped significantly by a symposium held on 11 September 1956 at Massachusetts Institute of Technology (MIT). At this symposium, an interdisciplinary group of cognitive researchers (i.e., Simon, Newell, Chomsky, and Miller) proposed that the mind could be studied as an information-processing system that functioned like a digital computer. According to this analogy, cognitive processes resemble the mind's "software", and the brain systems that implement them are likened to the mind's "hardware". At this point, the computational metaphor was born: the idea that the mind is an abstract, general-purpose, computational system or thinking machine that stores and manipulates symbolic representations of knowledge one step at a time (serial processing) in order to achieve its goals. Epitomizing this idea, Newell and Simon (1961, 1972) developed an information-processing theory of problem-solving. According to this theory, problem-solving involves a sequence of different knowledge states. In the first stage, the solver creates a "problem space" – a mental representation of the initial state of the problem, the goal state, details of any instructions and constraints, and all other relevant information retrieved from long-term memory (LTM). Subsequent stages of problem-solving involve strategy selection, strategy implementation, and, finally, evaluation of the distance between current and goal states. Using rational models such as that of Newell and Simon (1961), information-processing psychologists attempted to discover the nature of the mental processes that intervene between stimulus input and behavioural output. In this regard, Neisser (1967), who wrote the first modern textbook of cognitive psychology, likened the task of exploring cognitive processes to "trying to understand how a computer has been programmed" (p. 6).

Mind as a Representational System

The concept of the mind as a representational information-processing system revolutionized cognitive psychology for one major reason: it challenged the prevailing behaviourist view (e.g., as expressed by Watson, 1913, 1930) that, as mental processes were unobservable, they could not be studied scientifically. This latter claim was refuted by seminal cognitive researchers such as Bruner, Goodnow, and Austin (1956), who demonstrated that "thinking" not only involves the manipulation of internal (symbolic) representations of the external world but can also be investigated using objective empirical methods (e.g., card classification tasks). Taken together, the pioneering ideas of Bruner and the MIT symposium group showed that cognitive behaviour can be explained by invoking internal structures called "mental representations" that contain knowledge about the world and ourselves. But what exactly are these phenomena? Technically, mental representations are hypothetical cognitive structures in LTM that "stand in" mentally for the thing represented. Put simply, representations correspond to objects, ideas, or anything else that the brain is thinking about at any given moment (Ericsson & Pool, 2016). In other words, they are internal models of some aspect of our external reality. For example, as you read this paragraph, you are trying to decode the text on the page by forming mental representations of the meanings of the words and by relating them to what you already know. In this way, reading is a process of building and manipulating mental representations of written information.

Tenets of Classical Paradigm in Cognitive Sport Psychology

In cognitive sport psychology, the influence of the classical paradigm is evident in at least four propositions (Moran & Toner, 2017). First, the mind does not store knowledge directly, but instead "represents" it symbolically. This assumption dates back to the philosopher Kant (1929) who argued that people create internal representations of the world and use these cognitive templates to filter and interpret their everyday experience. As mental representations help people to make sense of the world, it is not surprising that they have been investigated by cognitive sport psychology researchers. In this regard, Schack and Mechsner (2006) began by postulating that athletes' representations of motor skills are memory structures that involve hierarchically organized clusters of "basic action concepts" (BACs). Note that the representations in this case are of the anticipated consequences of key movements (Mechsner, Kerzel, Knoblich, & Prinz, 2001). Typically, BACs correspond to functionally meaningful elements of a given skill. For example, in the case of the tennis serve, they include "ball throw", "bending the knee", and "racket follow-through". In studying BACs, Schack and Mechsner (2006) discovered that expert tennis players' mental representations of the serve were closely matched with the functional demands of this skill. By contrast, novice players' representations of the tennis serve were more variable and less well matched with such task demands.

The second tenet of the classical paradigm is the idea that "thinking" is a form of computation in which conscious knowledge is manipulated according to rules. These rules can be expressed formally as IF–THEN propositions. For example, a tennis player may be trained to respond to patterns of play such as, "if my opponent's return of serve is short, I'll attack it". In this case, when the player detects certain information on court (the IF part of the rule: namely, a short return of serve), an appropriate action is triggered (the THEN part of the rule: attacking the opponent's return). Similarly, consider the "take-the-first" (TTF) heuristic or rule of thumb in decision-making in sport (Raab & Gigerenzer, 2015). This strategy entails choosing the first option that comes to mind during a competitive event. Typically, it involves the operation of three types of rule: search rules that specify where to look for information, stopping rules that specify when to end the search, and decision rules that specify how to make a final choice. According to Raab and Gigerenzer (2015), the TTF uses a search rule that generates options from memory in the order of their validity. Option validity tends to be based on previous experience such that the option that facilitates the highest probability of success is generated first. In the earliest studies of TTF in sport (e.g., Johnson & Raab, 2003; Raab & Johnson, 2007), team handball players watched videos of offensive attack situations, cited potential moves that the player with the ball could perform, and then chose the best decision among those options. In general, results supported the predictions of the TTF approach. To explain, Johnson and Raab (2003) investigated the heuristic behaviour of handball players. After viewing videos from a handball match that were frozen after 10 seconds, participants were instructed to quickly identify the first option that came to mind. Then, they had to generate as many options as they could conceive of before finally choosing the option that they believed to be optimal for the specific situation. Results revealed a negative relationship between the total number of options generated and the quality of participants' final choice (as assessed based on the judgement of an expert panel). Interestingly, approximately 60 per cent of the time, participants chose the first option that they had generated – a fact that suggests that the handball players had a preference for "Type 1" (fast, intuitive, and unconscious) rather than "Type 2" (slow, deliberative, and conscious) thinking (see Kahneman, 2011).

The third tenet of the classical cognitive paradigm is that mental processes can be investigated objectively using methods such as laboratory simulations, eye-tracking technology, and brain-imaging techniques. To illustrate, consider the skill of anticipation in sport – the ability to predict accurately the outcome of upcoming events (e.g., an opponent's serve in tennis). This skill is crucial in enabling athletes to circumvent the spatiotemporal constraints typically encountered in sports such as tennis, baseball, and cricket (see review by Williams & Jackson, 2019). Put differently, the speed of play in fast ball sports precludes athletes from simply reacting to events. Instead, in order to be successful, they must use advance cues to anticipate likely future outcomes. Against this background, Causer, Smeeton, and Williams (2017) investigated the role of critical cues in the successful anticipation of penalty kicks by soccer goalkeepers who differed in their level of expertise. In particular, highly skilled and less-skilled soccer goalkeepers were required to anticipate the direction of a penalty kick under conditions of spatial and temporal occlusion or blockage. Briefly, the occlusion paradigm involves presenting participants with predictive tasks (e.g., estimating the likely direction of a kick/shot) based on obscured or incomplete information. By analysing how experts differ from novices in extrapolating from such obscured or incomplete information, researchers can evaluate the relative importance of different cues in predictive decisions-making situations. In spatial inclusion, viewers are required to make judgements about a visual scene from which certain parts have been either blocked from view or removed altogether. Temporal occlusion involves editing a video clip into specific time phases where progressively longer durations of a movement are presented. In the preceding study, Causer et al. (2017) tested the goalkeepers when viewing penalty kicks that had been occluded both spatially (full body, hip region) and temporally (±160 ms, ±80 ms before football contact). The skilled group performed better than the less-skilled group in all conditions. Furthermore, results showed that participants performed better in the full body condition than in the hip region condition. Performance in the hip only condition was significantly better than chance for the skilled group across all occlusion conditions. However, the less-skilled group's performance was no better than chance in the hip condition for the early occlusion points when predicting penalty direction and height. Later temporal occlusion conditions were associated with increased performance both in the correct response and correct direction analyses, but not for correct height. These data suggest that postural information solely from the hip region may be used by skilled goalkeepers to make accurate predictions of penalty kicks in football.

Another illustration of how mental processes can be measured scientifically comes from a study by Campbell and Moran (2014) of the little-investigated skill of "green reading" in golf – or trying to determine the slope of the putting surface prior to aiming the ball towards the hole. Briefly, these researchers used eye tracking technology to analyse the gaze behaviour of golfers of different skill levels (professional, elite amateur, and club-level players) as they attempted to "read" the slopes of virtual (computer-simulated) golf greens in a laboratory setting. The greens in question were virtual, three-dimensional, computer-generated surfaces. Based on a series of photographs of actual golf putts on real putting greens, Campbell and Moran (2014) used special effects software to create a simulated green and an immersive virtual tour of it. As in real life, this virtual tour enabled participants to view the golf putt from a number of different angles and positions around the green. Results showed that, when reading virtual greens, the professional golfers displayed a more economical gaze pattern than did their less-skilled counterparts.

A final tenet of the traditional information-processing paradigm is the controversial assumption that cognition is "sandwiched" between perception and action (Hurley, 2001). Based on this assumption, people's perceptual and motor systems were regarded as being subservient to thought – serving merely as "peripheral input and output devices" (Wilson, 2002, p. 625) for the mind. This classical sandwich model regards thinking as the primary focus (the "meat" in the sandwich) of cognitive research, with perception and action being seen as "slave" systems whose primary function is provide input to cognitive processors (in the case of perception) and to execute its commands (in the case of action). Clearly, the classical paradigm advocated a rather disembodied approach to the study of mental processes – one that soon attracted criticism.

Limitations of Classical Paradigm

Despite its strong influence on the study of cognitive processes in psychology, the classical paradigm has at least two obvious limitations. First, it provides little or no explanation of consciousness – the ability to be aware of one's own mental activities (Gazzaniga, Ivry, & Mangun, 2019). As Noë (2009) argued, "consciousness is not something the brain achieves on its own. Consciousness requires the joint operation of brain, body, and world" (p. 10). This idea that consciousness emerges dynamically from the interaction between the brain, body, and the external world is endorsed by embodiment approaches to cognition, which are described below. A second problem for the classical paradigm is its neglect of emotion. Briefly, for proponents of traditional information-processing psychology, the mind was a rational computational system that operated relatively independently of emotional experience. This view was caricatured by Claxton (1980), who claimed that the typical participant in a cognitive psychology experiment "does not feel hungry or tired or inquisitive; it does not think extraneous thoughts or try to understand what is going on. It is, in short, a computer" (p. 13). As research findings have accumulated (e.g., see Huntsinger & Schnall, 2013), however, it is now widely agreed that emotional factors play a crucial role in cognitive processing. In sport psychology, "emotions" are typically defined as appraisals of an event, either conscious or unconscious, that trigger a cascade of responses involving subjective experience, facial expression, cognitive processing, and physiological changes (Jones & Uphill, 2011). Since the pioneering studies of Hanin (2000), the role of emotion in athletic performance has been investigated extensively. For example, Woodman et al. (2009) discovered that, although the emotion of happiness did not affect performance, that of hope facilitated performance on reaction time tasks – and anger boosted performance of gross muscular activities. Emotions also influence cognitive processes. For example, in a recent study of anticipation in soccer, Broadbent, Gredin, Rye, Williams, and Bishop (2018) found that anxiety and prior contextual information affected participants' attentional resources independently of each other.

The Embodiment Paradigm in Cognitive Sport Psychology

Arising from the limitations of the information-processing paradigm, a range of embodiment approaches to the study of cognition emerged in psychology in the early 1990s (e.g., Varela, Thompson, & Rosch, 1991). These approaches proposed broadly that human cognition is shaped not only by bodily processes, but also by the interaction between the body and environmental factors. According to Goldinger, Papesh, Barnhart, Hansen, and Hout (2016), embodiment approaches range along a continuum, as follows: At one end lie "mild embodiment" researchers (e.g., Barsalou, 2008) who argue that all cognitive experiences are grounded in sensorimotor activity. For instance, when people describe something that they do not understand as being "over their heads", they are drawing metaphorically on their physical inability to see something that lies directly above them (McNerney, 2011). A good example of a mild embodiment theory is Barsalou's (2008) "grounded cognition" approach. This theory emphasizes the constant interaction between perception, action, the body, and the environment. Such interaction is governed by the principle of simulation or "the reenactment of perceptual, motor, and introspective states acquired during experience with the world, body, and mind" (Barsalou, 2008, p. 618). To illustrate this principle, consider action observation and movement planning. Briefly, research shows that, when people watch someone performing an action that is within their motor repertoire, their brains simulate performance of that action (Calvo-Merino, Glaser, Grèzes, Passingham, & Haggard, 2005). For mild embodiment researchers, cognitive processes are simulations or re-enactments of sensorimotor experience. Support for this concept of sensorimotor simulation comes from evidence that many of the brain circuits that are responsible for abstract thinking are inextricably linked to those that process sensory experience and motor action. Specifically, research shows that motor imagery (the covert rehearsal of an action without actually executing it) shares certain mental representations and neural structures with like-modality perception and with motor execution (see review by Moran, Guillot, MacIntyre, & Collet, 2012). For example, mentally simulated and executed actions activate many common brain areas such as the posterior parietal, premotor, and supplementary motor cortices, which are all involved in the planning of movements (Munzert, Lorey, & Zentgraf, 2009). At the other end of the embodiment continuum are "radical" theorists (e.g., Wilson & Golonka, 2013) who argue that mental representations are not necessary for the explanation of cognitive processes. In this regard, the term "radical" simply means "no representations" (see Stafford, 2015). Even among radical embodiment theorists, however, different theoretical perspectives exist. To explain, Baggs and Chamero (2018) distinguished between two radical embodiment approaches: that based on ecological psychology (Gibson, 1979; see below) and that arising from enactivism (Maturana & Varela, 1987). Although these approaches differ, they share a rejection of the assumption that cognition involves the computational manipulation of mental representations. Instead, radical embodiment theorists emphasize the importance of self-organization and nonlinear dynamical systems as the keys to understanding cognition. For further information on dynamical systems theory in sport, see Beek and Daffertshofer (2014) and Davids et al. (2014). An important difference between ecological and enactivist approaches, however, is that, whereas the former focuses on the nature of the environment that organisms perceive and act in, the latter emphasizes the agency of the organism. Encapsulating the main claim of radical embodiment, Wilson and Golonka (2013) argued that:

> the brain is not the sole cognitive resource that we have available to us to solve problems. Our bodies and their perceptually guided motions through the world do much of the work required to achieve our goals, *replacing* the need for complex internal mental representations.
>
> *(p. 1; original emphasis)*

Influence of Ecological Theory on Embodiment Approaches

As mentioned above, a key influence on radical embodiment approaches was Gibson's (1979) ecological theory of perception. Briefly, this theory suggested that, in order to understand how perception works, it is important to analyse the ecological functions that it serves for the organism. Intriguingly, according to Mather (2009), Gibson's (1979) theory was influenced by his research on aeroplane pilot training during the Second World War. Apparently, Gibson was enthralled by what pilots see from the cockpit when approaching the runway to land. For example, as the plane approaches the runway, its markings stream across the image projected on the eyes of the pilot, thereby creating an "optic flow field" or pattern of light caused by the relative movement between the observer and the environment. Accordingly, Gibson (1979) postulated that a perceiver's visual field can make sense of incoming stimuli *directly* – a possibility that renders mental representations unnecessary. More generally, Gibson (1979) argued that perception evolved in the service of action, and that people can extract information *directly* from the environment. Thus, he proposed that:

> perception of the environment ... is not mediated by retinal pictures, neural pictures, or mental pictures. Direct perception is the activity of getting information from the ambient array of light. I call this a process of information pickup, that involves ... looking around, getting around.
>
> *(p. 147)*

To illustrate direct perception in a sport situation, imagine that a golfer is looking for a ball that she drove up the fairway. As she walks towards the place where she thinks that the ball has landed, the image of this object on her retina changes, and the rate of expansion of that image offers important information about how close she is to the ball. In order to account for such direct information extraction from the environment, Gibson (1979) developed the concept of "affordance" or action possibility (i.e., a property of the environment that has functional significance for the individual) to account for the fact that people directly perceive the properties and functions of objects. For example, an object such as a cup invites or "affords" action possibilities such as grasping. So, an affordance is simply an opportunity for action – a latent feature of the environment that provides the possibility of behaviour. As a sporting example, whenever people look at a tennis racket, their perception of it is shaped by the presence of a handle that affords the actions of grasping and moving.

Evidence Supporting Embodiment Approaches

Evidence to support embodiment theories in psychology has emerged from numerous sources, especially in the field of perception. For example, some studies suggest that bodily information and action capabilities can influence people's perception in certain situations. Thus, Proffitt (2006) reported that the apparent slope of a hill tends to increase when people are tired or laden with a heavy backpack. He attributed this effect to "energetic considerations" or the idea that wearing a heavy backpack increases the energy required to walk up the hill. The logic here is that, if one feels very tired, one may need to rest. So, the act of perceiving a hill with a real slope of 5 degrees as a 15-degree slope may serve as a reminder to rest, which reduces the perceiver's energy expenditure significantly. It should be noted, however, that Proffitt's (2006) "backpack study" findings have been challenged on methodological grounds. For example, Durgin, Klein, Spiegel, Strawser, and Williams (2012) argued that they may be due to "demand characteristics" (i.e., pressure on participants that emanates from the experimental set-up and encourages them to respond in a certain manner; Orne, 1962). To explain, if participants are asked to judge the slope of a hill, then to wear a backpack, and, finally, to judge the slope of the hill again, they may intuitively guess the experimenter's hypothesis that the backpack will influence their judgement and respond accordingly. Turning to additional evidence in support of embodiment approaches, studies in sport psychology have shown that, in athletes, the perception of the size and speed of a moving ball is influenced by the ability to *act* on that object and is not determined solely by object characteristics (Gray, 2019). Similarly, bodily information and action abilities can influence people's perception in certain situations. For example, Witt et al. (2009) discovered that people who suffered from minor but chronic pain of the lower back tended to misperceive distances. In particular, their estimates of the distance between where they stood and cones placed at different points in a hallway were greater than those elicited from participants in a comparison group. Likewise, research shows that people who throw a heavy ball to a target tend to perceive that target to be farther away compared with people who throw a light ball (Witt, Proffitt, & Epstein, 2004). In reviewing the research literature on action-specific effects, Witt (2011) concluded that people's perception of the world "reflects the relationship between the environment and the perceiver's ability to act within it" (p. 205) – otherwise known as "action-specific theory". More recently, Gray (2014) evaluated available evidence supporting embodied perception in sport. In particular, he reviewed a variety of studies on three types of action-specific variable evident in sporting contexts: skill level (expert versus less-skilled counterparts), task difficulty, and task goals. For these variables, embodiment theory would make the following predictions.

First, if the level of expertise of a ball sports performer affects his or her perception, then balls should be perceived as appearing larger and moving slower as playing level increases, because the balls are more "hittable" at higher levels of ability. Evidence to support such size perception effects has emerged from studies on goal kicking in American football (Witt & Dorsch, 2009) and archery (Lee, Lee, Carello, & Turvey, 2012). Next, if a sporting task is made more difficult for athletes of a given level of ability, then embodiment theorists would predict that there should be changes in these athletes' perception of the target object. Again, there is evidence to support this hypothesis. Thus, Witt, Linkenauger, Bakdash, and Proffitt (2008) discovered that golfers perceived the hole as being larger when putting from close range (an easy task) as distinct from putting from a longer distance (a more difficult task). To explain, they conducted a series of studies on the relationship between golfing proficiency and perceived hole size. In one of them, they discovered that golfers who had played better than others after a specific round of golf subsequently estimated the hole to be bigger than did counterparts who had not played as well. But was this effect due to perceived hole size or remembered hole size? In order to arbitrate between these possibilities, Witt et al. (2008) conducted two follow-up laboratory studies. In these experiments, participants putted golf balls into a practice hole from a putting mat that was located either close to the hole (0.4 m from it) or farther away from it (2.15 m). Then, they had to judge the size of the hole either from memory (Study 2) or while actually viewing the hole (Study 3). Results showed that, in both experiments, estimates of the size of the hole that had been made after easy (i.e., close to the hole) putts were larger than those made after more difficult (i.e., farther away) putts. Note that the size estimates should have been similar if the only variables influencing participants' judgements were their visual abilities and the actual size of the hole. As these estimates were not similar, then it seems that size perception is influenced by the perceiver's current ability to act effectively. But what is not clear from these experiments is the direction of causality in this situation. This issue was raised by Witt et al. (2008) who wondered whether golfers putt better – and therefore see the hole as bigger – or see the hole as bigger first, and then putt better as a result. Clearly, research designed to address this question is required. In a related phenomenon, embodiment theorists argue that perceptual processes such as perceiving the size of a ball can be influenced by the current mental state of the athlete. Thus, Gray (2014) noted that peak performance states are often associated with qualitative perceptual changes in the performer in question. For example, John McEnroe, the seven-times grand-slam tennis champion, revealed that, when he played at his best, "things slow down, the ball seems a lot bigger and you feel like you have more time" (cited in McEnroe & Kaplan, 2002, p. 57). In a similar vein, anecdotal evidence suggests that, when athletes are performing exceptionally well, baseballs can appear as big as "grapefruits" (Will, 1990), and basketball hoops can seem as large as "oceans" (Nobles, 1995). Conversely, athletes who are playing poorly may experience a subjective perceptual shrinkage when looking at target objects. To illustrate, baseball players whose form has slumped may feel as though they are "swinging at aspirins" (Bradley, 2003).

Interestingly, embodiment theorists predict that objects that are deemed suitable for the attainment of a particular goal should be perceived as affording greater opportunity for successful action (e.g., being seen as larger and moving more slowly than usual) than do objects that are not deemed as suitable for goal attainment. Some evidence to support this prediction was reported by Gray (2013) using a baseball hitting task. In one of his experiments, expert baseball players were required to perform three different directional hitting tasks in a batting simulation and to make perceptual judgements about three ball parameters (speed, plate crossing location, and size). Results showed that perceived ball size was largest, and perceived speed was slowest, when the ball crossing location was optimal for the particular hitting task that the batter was performing. A possible explanation for this effect is that changes in perceived size and speed are examples of perceptual accentuation that occur when a performer focuses his or her attention on an object to be acted upon (Cañal-Bruland & van der Kamp, 2009). So, the ball may be perceived to be larger and moving more slowly when its trajectory is well suited for the hitter's goal simply because the batter is focusing attention on plate locations that are optimal for his or her goal.

Limitations of Embodiment Approaches

Despite the intuitive plausibility of its claims that cognitive processes are deeply rooted in bodily experiences and in bodily interaction with the world, embodiment theory has a number of limitations (see critique by Goldinger et al., 2016). For example, little consensus exists about the precise definition of the umbrella term "embodiment" (Wilson, 2002). Indeed, as mentioned earlier, mild and radical embodiment theorists use this term differently. In addition, Goldinger et al. (2016) raised doubts about the scientific validity and utility of the central tenet of embodiment approaches: the idea that cognition is influenced by the body. Specifically, they claimed that, "it appears extremely challenging" (p. 964) to incorporate this proposition into any meaningful type of formal, scientific model. Elaborating on this point, Goldinger et al. (2016) wondered, "how might we write an equation that expresses *embodiment*? How can the environment (such as the affordances of various objects) be parameterized?" (p. 964). Overall, these authors concluded that, although embodiment approaches can account elegantly and efficiently for certain motor cognitive phenomena (e.g., the ability of baseball outfielders to chase and catch fly balls), they are inadequate for the task of explaining many basic facts of mental life. For example, how can embodiment theory account for the fact that people can easily recognize a friend's face when scanning a crowded room – a feat that appears to derive from the existence of stored knowledge in the brain? In spite of their limitations, embodiment approaches offer a potentially fruitful theoretical perspective on the emerging topic of behavioural cognitive enhancement (see review by Zona, Raab, & Fischer, 2018). For example, Michalak, Troje, and Heidenreich (2010) demonstrated that mindfulness-based cognitive therapy for depressed patients can change their gait patterns, thereby highlighting the subtle interaction that occurs in everyday life between mind and body.

Conclusion

Research in cognitive sport psychology is influenced by two main theoretical paradigms – the classical or information-processing approach and a range of embodiment approaches. Whereas the classical paradigm postulates that the mind is a representational system, and that human knowledge is amodal and brain-based, embodiment theorists argue that cognitive processes are multimodal in nature and involve constant interaction between the brain, body, and environment. Although these rival paradigms have distinctive strengths, they each suffer from the limitations described above. So, how will the classical and embodiment paradigms influence new research horizons in cognitive sport psychology?

To begin with, the classical paradigm is likely to continue to influence studies of mental processes (e.g., thinking) that involve the transformation of knowledge states (mental representations) over time. However, a key methodological challenge persists in this area. Specifically, how can thinking, which is inherently subjective in nature, be studied objectively? Apart from TAP analysis, which was described earlier, other objective methods have been developed recently to investigate subtle features of people's thinking. For example, consider the task of measuring "mental effort" or the amount of processing resources required to pay attention to something. Research shows that pupillometry, or the objective measurement of task-evoked changes in the diameter of the pupil of the eye as a function of cognitive processing (see Laeng, Sirois, & Gredebäck, 2012), can provide a valid and reliable index of athletes' mental effort in a laboratory simulation of an equestrian setting (Moran et al., 2016). Typically, larger pupil diameters reflect the exertion of increased mental effort.

With regard to embodiment approaches in cognitive sport psychology, a recent handbook (Cappuccio, 2019) offers an overview of potentially fruitful new directions. For example, Reiner (2019) argued that virtual reality technology can be used to enhance affordances or action possibilities (Gibson, 1979) by evaluating and training athletes' adaptation to environmental cues in real time. In a similar vein, embodiment approaches offer new ways of exploring creativity in sport. Instead of focusing on the mental representations alleged to underlie creative behaviour (the classical account), embodiment researchers focus on how athletes manage to respond to the affordances of the environmental situation in which they perform (see Rucińska & Aggerholm, 2019). The emphasis here is on understanding creativity as an act that is always situated in a specific context.

References

Baggs, E., & Chamero, A. (2018). Radical embodiment in two directions. *Synthese*. doi:10.1007/s11229-018-02020-9

Barsalou, L. W. (2008). Grounded cognition. *Annual Review of Psychology, 59*, 617–645.

Beek, P. J., & Daffertshofer, A. (2014). Dynamical systems. In R. C. Eklund & G. Tenenbaum (Eds.), *Encyclopedia of sport and exercise psychology* (Vol. 1, pp. 223–227). London: Sage.

Bradley, J. (2003, 27 May). The flash. *ESPN The Magazine*. Retrieved May 3, 2019, from www.espn.com/magazine/vol5no11ichiro.html

Brick, N., MacIntyre, T., & Campbell, M. (2015). Metacognitive processes in the self-regulation of performance in elite endurance runners. *Psychology of Sport and Exercise, 19*, 1–9.

Broadbent, D., Gredin, N. V., Rye, J. L., Williams, A. M., & Bishop, D. T. (2018). The impact of contextual priors and anxiety on performance effectiveness and processing efficiency in anticipation. *Cognition and Emotion*. doi:10.1080/02699931.2018.1464434

Bruner, J. S. (1990). *Acts of meaning*. Cambridge, MA: Harvard University Press.

Bruner, J. S., Goodnow, J. J., & Austin, G. A. (1956). *A study of thinking*. New York: John Wiley.

Calvo-Merino, B., Glaser, D. E., Grèzes, J., Passingham, R. E., & Haggard, P. (2005). Action observation and acquired motor skills: An fMRI study with expert dancers. *Cerebral Cortex, 15*, 1243–1249.

Campbell, M. J., & Moran, A. P. (2014). There is more to green reading than meets the eye! Exploring the gaze behaviours of expert golfers on a virtual golf putting task. *Cognitive Processing, 15*(3), 363–372.

Cañal-Bruland, R., & van der Kamp, J. (2009). Action goals influence action-specific perception. *Psychonomic Bulletin & Review, 16*, 1100–1105.

Cappuccio, M. L. (Ed.). (2019). *Handbook of embodied cognition and sport psychology*. Cambridge, MA: MIT Press.

Causer, J., Smeeton, N. J., & Williams, A. M. (2017). Expertise differences in anticipatory judgements during a temporally and spatially occluded task. *PLoS ONE, 12*(2), e0171330.

Claxton, G. (1980). Cognitive psychology: A suitable case for what sort of treatment? In G. Claxton (Ed.), *Cognitive psychology: New directions* (pp. 1–25). London: Routledge.

Davids, K., Hristovski, R., Araújo, D., Balague Serre, N., Button, C., & Passos, P. (Eds). (2014). *Complex systems in sport*. London: Routledge.

Durgin, F. H., Klein, B., Spiegel, A., Strawser, C. J., & Williams, M. (2012). The social psychology of perception experiments: Hills, backpacks, glucose and the problem of generalizability. *Journal of Experimental Psychology: Human Perception and Performance, 38*, 1582–1595.

Eccles, D., & Arsal, G. (2017). The think aloud method: What is it and how do I use it? *Qualitative Research in Sport, Exercise and Health, 9*, 514–531.

Ericsson, K. A., & Pool, R. (2016). *Peak: How all of us can achieve extraordinary things.* London: Vintage.

Ericsson, K. A., & Simon, H. A. (1980). Verbal reports as data. *Psychological Review, 87,* 215–251.

Eysenck, M. W., & Keane, M. T. (2015). *Cognitive psychology: A student's handbook* (7th ed.). Hove: Psychology Press.

Fox, M. C., Ericsson, K. A., & Best, R. (2011). Do procedures for verbal reporting of thinking have to be reactive? A meta-analysis and recommendations for best reporting methods. *Psychological Bulletin, 137,* 316–344.

Gazzaniga, M., Ivry, R. B., & Mangun, G. R. (2019). *Cognitive neuroscience: Biology of the mind* (5th ed.; international student ed.). New York: W. W. Norton.

Gibson, J. J. (1979). *The ecological approach to visual perception.* Boston: Houghton Mifflin.

Glenberg, A. M., Witt, J. K., & Metcalfe, J. (2013). From the revolution to embodiment: 25 years of cognitive psychology. *Perspectives on Psychological Science, 8,* 573–585.

Goldinger, S. D., Papesh, M. H., Barnhart, A. S., Hansen, W. A., & Hout, M. C. (2016). The poverty of embodied cognition. *Psychonomic Bulletin & Review, 23,* 959–978.

Gray, R. (2013). Being selective at the plate: Processing dependence between perceptual variables relates to hitting goals and performance. *Journal of Experimental Psychology: Human Perception and Performance, 39,* 1124–1142.

Gray, R. (2014). Embodied perception in sport. *International Review of Sport and Exercise Psychology, 7,* 72–86.

Gray, R. (2019). Embodiment. In D. Hackfort, R. J. Schinke, & B. Strauss (Eds.), *Dictionary of sport psychology: Sport, exercise, and performing arts* (pp. 91–92). London: Academic Press/Elsevier.

Hanin, Y. L. (2000). Successful and poor performance and emotions. In Y. L. Hanin (Ed.), *Emotions in sport* (pp. 157–187). Champaign, IL: Human Kinetics.

Huntsinger, J. R., & Schnall, S. (2013). Emotion–cognition interactions. In D. Reisberg (Ed.), *Oxford handbook of cognitive psychology* (pp. 571–584). New York: Oxford University Press.

Hurley, S. (2001). Perception and action: Alternative views. *Synthese, 129,* 3–40.

Johnson, J. G., & Raab, M. (2003). Take the first: Option generation and resulting choices. *Organizational Behavior and Human Decision Processes, 91,* 215–229.

Jones, M., & Uphill, M. (2005). Emotion in sport: Antecedents and performance consequences. In J. Thatcher, M. Jones, & D. Lavallee (Eds.), *Coping and emotion in sport* (2nd ed., pp. 33–61). London: Routledge.

Jones, M., & Uphill, M. (2011). Emotion in sport: Antecedents and performance consequences. In J. Thatcher, M. Jones & D. Lavallee (Eds.), *Coping and emotion in sport* (2nd ed., pp. 33–61). London: Routledge.

Kahneman, D. (2011). *Thinking, fast and slow.* New York: Farrar, Straus & Giroux.

Kant, I. (1929). *Critique of pure reason.* N. K. Smith, Trans. London: Macmillan (Original work published in 1781).

Lachman, R., Lachman, J. C. L., & Butterfield, E. C. (1979). *Cognitive psychology and information processing.* Hillsdale, NJ: Lawrence Erlbaum.

Laeng, B., Sirois, S., & Gredebäck, G. (2012). Pupillometry: A window to the preconscious? *Perspectives on Psychological Science, 7,* 18–27.

Lee, Y., Lee, S., Carello, C., & Turvey, M. T. (2012). An archer's perceived form scales the "hitableness" of archery targets. *Journal of Experimental Psychology: Human Perception and Performance, 38,* 1125–1131.

Marlow, J. A. G., & Uphill, M. (2017). Exploring the nature of counterfactual thinking and their perceived consequences in an elite sporting context: An interpretative phenomenological analysis. *The Sport Psychologist, 31,* 369–381.

Mather, G. (2009). *Foundations of sensation and perception* (2nd ed.). Hove: Psychology Press.

Maturana, H. R., & Varela, F. J. (1987). *The tree of knowledge: The biological roots of human understanding.* New York: New Science Library/Shambhala.

McEnroe, J., & Kaplan, J. (2002). *You cannot be serious.* New York: G. P. Putnam's Sons.

McNerney, S. (2011, November 4). A brief guide to embodied cognition: Why you are not your brain. *Scientific American,* Retrieved March 5, 2019, from http://blogs.scientificamerican.com/guest-blog/a-brief-guide-to-embodied-cognition-why-you-are-not-your-brain/

Mechsner, F., Kerzel, D., Knoblich, G., & Prinz, W. (2001). Perceptual basis of bimanual coordination. *Nature, 414,* 69–73.

Michalak, J., Troje, N. F., & Heidenreich, T. (2010). Embodied effects of mindfulness-based cognitive therapy. *Journal of Psychosomatic Research, 68,* 312–313.

Moran, A. (2009). Cognitive psychology in sport: Progress and prospects. *Psychology of Sport and Exercise, 10,* 420–426.

Moran, A., Guillot, A., MacIntyre, T., & Collet, C. (2012). Re-imagining motor imagery: Building bridges between cognitive neuroscience and sport psychology. *British Journal of Psychology, 103,* 224–247.

Moran, A., Quinn, A., Campbell, M., Rooney, B., Brady, N., & Burke, C. (2016). Using pupillometry to evaluate attentional effort in Quiet Eye: A preliminary investigation. *Sport, Exercise, and Performance Psychology, 5,* 365–376.

Moran, A., & Toner, J. (ed.). (2017). *A critical introduction to sport psychology* (3rd ed.). Abingdon and Oxford: Routledge.

Munzert, J., Lorey, J., & Zentgraf, J. (2009). Cognitive motor processes: The role of motor imagery in the study of motor representations. *Brain Research Reviews, 60,* 306–326.

Neisser, U. (1967). *Cognitive psychology.* New York: Appleton-Century-Crofts.

Newell, A., & Simon, H. A. (1961). Computer simulation of human thinking. *Science, 134,* 2011–2017.

Newell, A., & Simon, H. A. (1972). *Human problem solving.* Englewood Cliffs: Prentice Hall.

Newen, A., De Bruin, L., & Gallagher, S. (Eds). (2018). *The Oxford handbook of 4E cognition.* Oxford: Oxford University Press.

Nobles, C. (1995, May 25). Scott fires first shots in magic arsenal. *The New York Times.* Retrieved from www.nytimes.com/1995/05/25/sports/basketball-scott-fires-first-shots-in-magic-arsenal.html

Noë, A. (2009). *Out of our heads: Why you are not your brain, and other lessons from the biology of consciousness.* New York: Hill & Wang.

Orne, M. T. (1962). On the social psychology of the psychological experiment: With particular reference to demand characteristics and their implications. *American Psychologist, 17,* 776–783.

Proffitt, D. R. (2006). Embodied perception and the economy of action. *Perspectives on Psychological Science, 1,* 110–122.

Raab, M., Bar-Eli, M., Plessner, H., & Araújo, D. (2019). The past, present and future of judgment and decision making in sport. *Psychology of Sport and Exercise, 42,* 25–32.

Raab, M., & Gigerenzer, G. (2015). The power of simplicity: A fast-and-frugal heuristics approach to performance. *Frontiers in Psychology, 6,* 1672.

Raab, M., & Johnson, J. G. (2007). Expertise-based differences in search and option-generation strategies. *Journal of Experimental Psychology: Applied, 13,* 158–170.

Reiner, M. (2019). Emerging technologies for sport performance enhancement: Embodied cognition and manipulation of brain rhythms. In M. L. Cappuccio (Ed.), *Handbook of embodied cognition and sport psychology* (pp. 333–355). Cambridge, MA: MIT Press.

Rucińska, Z., & Aggerholm, K. (2019). Embodied and enactive creativity in sports. In M. L. Cappuccio (Ed.), *Handbook of embodied cognition and sport psychology* (pp. 669–694). Cambridge, MA: MIT Press.

Samson, A., Simpson, D., Kamphoff, C., & Langelier, A. (2017). Think aloud: An examination of distance runners' thought processes. *International Journal of Sport and Exercise Psychology, 15,* 176–189.

Schack, T., & Mechsner, F. (2006). Representation of motor skills in human long-term memory. *Neuroscience Letters, 391,* 77–81. doi:10.1016/j.neulet.2005.10.009

Stafford, T. (2015, 5 March). Radical embodied cognition: An interview with Andrew Wilson. *Mind Hacks.* Retrieved December 26, 2019, from https://mindhacks.com/2015/03/05/radical-embodied-cognition-an-interview-with-andrew-wilson/

Varela, F. J., Thompson, E., & Rosch, E. (1991). *The embodied mind: Cognitive science and the human experience.* Cambridge, MA: MIT Press.

Watson, J. B. (1913). Psychology as the behaviorist views it. *Psychological Review, 20,* 158–177.

Watson, J. B. (1930). *Behaviorism* (revised ed.). Chicago, IL: University of Chicago Press.

Whitehead, A., Jones, H., Williams, E., Dowling, C., Morley, D., Taylor, J.A., & Polman, R. C. (2019). Changes in cognition over a 16.1 km cycling time trial using Think Aloud protocol: Preliminary evidence. *International Journal of Sport and Exercise Psychology, 17*(3), 266–274. doi:10.1080/1612197X.2017.1292302

Will, G. F. (1990). *Men at work: The craft of baseball.* New York: Macmillan.

Willems, R. M., & Francken, J. C. (2012). Embodied cognition: Taking the next step. *Frontiers in Psychology, 3,* 582.

Williams, A. M., & Jackson, R. C. (2019). Anticipation in sport: Fifty years on, what have we learned and what research still needs to be undertaken? *Psychology of Sport and Exercise, 42,* 16–24.

Wilson, A. D., & Golonka, S. (2013). Embodied cognition is not what you think it is. *Frontiers in Psychology, 4*(58), 1–13.

Wilson, M. (2002). Six views of embodied cognition. *Psychonomic Bulletin and Review, 9,* 625–636.

Witt, J. K. (2011). Action's effect on perception. *Current Directions in Psychological Science, 20,* 201–206.

Witt, J. K., & Dorsch, T. E. (2009). Kicking to bigger uprights: Field goal kicking performance influences perceived size. *Perception, 38,* 1328–1340.

Witt, J. K., Linkenauger, S. A., Bakdash, J. Z., Augustyn, J. S., Cook, A., & Proffitt, D. R. (2009). The long road of pain: Chronic pain increases perceived distance. *Experimental Brain Research, 192,* 145–148.

Witt, J. K., Linkenauger, S. A., Bakdash, J. Z., & Proffitt, D. R. (2008). Putting to a bigger hole: Golf performance relates to perceived size. *Psychonomic Bulletin & Review, 15,* 581–585.

Witt, J. K., Proffitt, D. R., & Epstein, W. (2004). Perceiving distance: A role of effort and intent. *Perception, 33,* 570–590.

Woodman, T., Davis, P., Hardy, L., Callow, N., Glasscock, I., & Yuill-Proctor, J. (2009). Emotions and sport performance: An exploration of happiness, hope, and anger. *Journal of Sport & Exercise Psychology, 3,* 169–188.

Zona, C. I., Raab, M., & Fischer, M. H. (2018). Embodied perspectives on behavioral cognitive enhancement. *Journal of Cognitive Enhancement.* doi:10.1007/s41465-018-0102-3

6

CONTEXT-DRIVEN SPORT PSYCHOLOGY

A Cultural Lens

Louise Kamuk Storm and Carsten Hvid Larsen

Introduction

Sport psychology is situated in a broader social and cultural context. Sports-specific cultures, socioeconomic factors, societal values, and policies all influence the work of a sport psychology practitioner. The relationship between the practitioner and client, the consultation, the specific events, processes, and situations are also contexts of sport psychology practice. In this chapter, we aim to address the term "context-driven sport and exercise psychology practice" that was recently introduced in sport psychology literature. This term builds from the special issue in the *Journal of Sport Psychology in Action* edited by Schinke and Stambulova (2017).

The purpose of this chapter is twofold. The first objective is to clarify the interrelated concepts and terms of context-driven sport and exercise psychology related to self-reflexivity (McGannon & Johnson, 2009), cultural competence (Ryba, Stambulova, Si, & Schinke, 2013), and cultural sensitivity (Schinke, McGannon, Parham, & Lane, 2012), each grounded in cultural sport psychology (Schinke & Hanrahan, 2009). The second objective is to describe three different context-driven case examples from, respectively, Canada, the UK, and Denmark. The authors wish to illustrate different examples of context-driven practice related to national culture and subculture across youth sport and elite senior sports. Finally, the authors discuss how the cases illustrate sociocultural aspects of context-driven sport psychology. The intention is to stimulate awareness and professional reflexivity and encourage practitioners and researchers towards an open exchange about subcultural contexts and how these contexts inform practice. Specifically, the goal is to illustrate how contexts inform and guide sport psychology delivery and that practitioners and researchers need to consider what (i.e., content), how (i.e., strategies, tools, assessment instruments), and why (i.e., theoretical frameworks, "local" research, professional philosophy) they work with their clients the ways they do (Schinke & Stambulova, 2016).

Situating Context-Driven Sport and Exercise Psychology Practice

Context-driven sport and exercise psychology practice (CDP) has been defined as practice that is "informed by reciprocal interactions between consultants, clients, and the cultural/sub-cultural contexts they are parts of" (Stambulova & Schinke, 2017, p. 131). CDP is a matter of widening practitioners' and researchers' lenses beyond the athletes, which means paying significant attention to the context and self (Schinke & Stambulova, 2017). A basic assumption for CDP is that people are influential on and influenced by their environments: "we cannot step outside culture, thus to ignore it would be to ignore a key matter that shapes all of us" (McGannon & Schinke, 2015, p. 5); it also acknowledges that, "every therapeutic encounter is cross-cultural in nature" (Comas-Díaz & Griffith, 1988, p. 869; see also Schinke & Moore, 2011).

Looking at *context* and *culture* as two concepts, there are differences and similarities that are relevant to consider. *Contexts* (i.e., events, processes within the organization) are dynamic, whereas *cultures* are more conservative and evolve more slowly (Stambulova & Schinke, 2017). *Contexts* relate to events and processes "that characterize a particular situation and have impact on an individual's behavior" (Reber, 1995, p. 159). The most important and influential elements from each context need to be understood in relation to the client, or organization, in advance of acting.

Culture is related to the motivations and meanings, the why and how, of practice. *Cultures* are both structured and structuring, and peoples' actions are neither totally determined by the confines of a *culture*, nor are they totally free (Hodkinson, Biesta, & James, 2008). Culture is "concerned with the production and exchange of meanings – the 'giving and taking of meaning' – between the members of a society or group" (Hall, 1997, p. 2). A description of *culture* could be related to overall national culture or sport culture, but culture is also about subcultures existing in youth sports being different from elite senior sports.

Understanding a given local cultural context, beyond its people, requires specific attention to both the places as *context*, the social relationships as *context*, and the institutions and the larger society as cultural contexts. The social structure and the power mechanisms – for example, the insider position – is central when speaking of context-driven sport psychology (e.g., Larsen, 2017; Mellalieu, 2017). It is important to identify the key gatekeepers, who are the people that support the researcher or practitioner to pull back the curtain and understand the sociocultural context. A lack of knowledge about the insider position will create a circumstance where the practitioner or researcher is an outsider. In CDP, the insider position is necessary to get access to and fully understand the given site and the cultural embedding mechanisms. Here, the knowledge or experience with the language of the subculture could be key (see Mellalieu, 2017, for an example). Hierarchy within the group or the organization is an important part of grasping the social order and thereby understanding the *context* and *culture*. The hierarchy is important in two ways: first, in relation to understanding a given site beyond its people – for example, the meaning of having teammates as "star makers" (Seanor, Schinke, Stambulova, Ross, & Kpazai, 2017); and second, in relation to obtaining an insider position as researcher or practitioner and displaying political acuity in the hierarchy of professional organizations (Larsen, 2017).

Clarifying Interrelated Terms in Context-Driven Practice

The term context-driven sport psychology practice is closely related to concepts such as cultural competence (Ryba et al., 2013), culturally informed sport psychology (Schinke & Moore, 2011), self-reflexive sport psychology practice (Schinke et al., 2012), cultural praxis (Ryba, Schinke, & Tennenbaum, 2010; Ryba & Wright, 2005), and cultural sensitivity and awareness (Schinke et al., 2012). These concepts acknowledge the practitioner and researcher as responsible in seeking an understanding of the cultural other, and becoming a reflexive practitioner can lead to culturally sensitive interventions. Recent discussions in cultural sport psychology have suggested that effective consulting requires moving beyond reflection (such as evaluating the effectiveness of an intervention) to include self-reflexivity (Ryba et al., 2013; Schinke et al., 2012; see also Hacker & Mann, 2017).

Self-reflexivity stresses the importance of the practitioner being aware of their own cultural background, biases, knowledge, and interests (McGannon & Johnson, 2009). Cultural sensitivity (Schinke et al., 2012) is the ability to act in a culturally sensitive manner and willingness to confront one's own background, biases, and interests in a self-reflexive manner (see also McGannon & Johnson, 2009; Schinke et al., 2012), whereas the notion of *cultural competence* (Ryba et al., 2013; Schinke & Moore, 2011) denotes a general approach intended to provide researchers and practitioners with a set of useful rules in advance of work with a group of people unfamiliar to them. Even though the notion of *cultural competence* is presented in relation to broader cultural contexts and traditionally regards skin colour, gender, sexual orientation, socio-economic and religious backgrounds, and how they influence practitioners' interventions (Schinke & Moore, 2011), it has also evolved into subcultures and microcultures (Schinke & McGannon, 2015). Cultural competence is, then, in line with what recently was termed contextual intelligence. The contextually intelligent practitioner has the ability to learn, reflect upon, understand, and take into account the contexts involved in working with clients (Stambulova & Schinke, 2017). However, in the understanding of the authors, the term contextually intelligent practitioner is more closely related to microsystems in which the clients are embedded. Microsystems are the immediate environment in which people live (Bronfenbrenner, 1979) and comprise, for example, the family, school, sports team, and peer group or community environment of the individual; the interactions within the microsystem involve relationships with peers, teammates, experts, and coaches. Contextually intelligent practitioners and CDP narrow the cultural understanding to the local level, considering the immediate context, peer affiliations, and community socialization.

All terms are outcomes of a general tendency in sport psychology to move focus away from looking at the athlete in isolation as a whole, singular, unified individual. Rather, the shift is towards an understanding of the athlete as a subject of multiple discourses and various identifications, a member of numerous social and cultural groups, and a part of sport as an institution immersed in a particular sociocultural and historical context (Ryba & Wright, 2005). After all, CDP regards not only the cultural standpoint of the client, but also that of the practitioner. Hence, it is not only a matter of understanding the other, but also oneself as a cultural being (McGannon & Johnson, 2009; Schinke & Moore, 2011).

Why Context Is Important in Service Delivery

Each context necessitates aspects of an idiosyncratic consulting approach that might include modes of communication, language terminology and jargon, dress, social norms, relational strategies, and how the practitioners position themselves and the field of sport psychology to clients. No two contexts are the same (e.g., Terry, 2009). Therefore, the reflection upon practice as locally influenced is crucial to better understand, assess, and intervene with clients (e.g., individuals, families, groups, organizations, and community) in order to promote more effective functioning (e.g., performance, relationships, climate, health, and well-being).

The Sport Psychologist journal published a special issue in 2012 on case studies in sport psychology (Giges & Van Raalte, 2012) that is a collection of detailed descriptions and discussions of different approaches and perspectives that illustrate sport psychology interventions as applied to specific individuals, teams, and situations (Giges & Van Raalte, 2012). The case studies presented in this special issue focus on particular practitioners, the working alliances, and the teams as having impact on an individual's behaviour. Together, the collected articles are an argument for the client–practitioner relationship to be a key contextual matter of sport psychology. In this special issue, Martindale and Collins (2012) provided an example of how the *consultation context* influenced service provision, the overall goal of support, the athletes' engagement in the support, and how the practitioner was integrated into the broader support network. Sport psychology is full of ethical dilemmas, which are also context. Sport psychology practitioners meet (unexpected) situations that create unexpected ethical dilemmas that need to be handled in situ. These dilemmas can also be rooted in the practitioner's experiences and self and, therefore, require self-reflexivity and awareness (for an example, see Dzikus, Fisher, & Hays, 2012).Special issues such as in *The Sport Psychologist* (2012) and *Journal of Sport Psychology in Action* (2017) are reasonable justification of why it is important to understand and use context as a part of one's practical approach. Together, they illustrate how contexts influence the practitioner's needs assessment, content, organization, and evaluation of their interventions. The effectiveness of service delivery is related to the athletes' contexts. Contextual awareness helps the practitioner to get a better sense of the client's needs, who is meeting those needs, or who potentially can.

However, the main purpose of paying attention to CDP is to increase contextual and cultural awareness and professional reflexivity among practitioners, because this benefits clients' performance, development, well-being, and mental health (Henriksen et al., 2019). Along these lines, Henriksen and colleagues (2019) recently argued that considering performers within their contexts is pivotal for mental health, as, without the ability to also broaden our practical lens, we will never understand any client's full story. We will then be able to best support excellence in and through sport.

The Contextually Intelligent Practitioner

The culturally competent or contextually intelligent practitioner acts skilfully in regard to several levels of the complex field of sport. In order to act in a culturally competent way, the practitioner becomes aware of and gains knowledge about the *culture* in which the practice is embedded, and, thereby, "space is made for individuals to be supported for exactly who they are as cultural beings" (Schinke & Moore, 2011, p. 285), and human development is also considered to be a mutual accommodation that takes place between an athlete and his or her contexts. The athlete–context interaction is considered irreducible as a unit of analysis.

Developing cultural competence is a fluid process that continuously transforms the practitioner's work (APA, 2019). Cultural competence takes diversity into sport psychology practice (Ryba et al., 2010), which means, in this particular use of the concept, that cultural competence is about diversity between social groups (e.g., young athletes, senior athletes, injured athletes, the newcomers, the migrants) and regards understanding of one's own *culture* and another's cultural background and the ability to act skilfully in accordance with these differences. Culturally competent practice means, first and foremost, that attention is directed towards an understanding of oneself as a cultural being, including an understanding of the other as being so. Taking into consideration that "one culture" is always most clearly identified in relation to "another culture", it becomes a very important resource for sport psychology practitioners to practise across diverse *contexts* and *cultures*.

The contextually intelligent practitioner develop an ability to learn, reflect upon, understand, and take into account the cultural contexts involved in working with athletes (Stambulova & Schinke, 2017). A part of acting in a contextually intelligent way is to immerse oneself in, and reflect upon, various contexts when planning and performing psychological interventions, which is a process of situating oneself and one's clients in their local contexts, and try to decipher the most important and influential elements from each cultural or subcultural layer (e.g., the culture of the club, the sport, group) in order to understand the context.

The contextually intelligent practitioner considers three intertwined levels: individual needs, group dynamics, and leadership and organizational culture in service delivery. First, individuals are cultural beings situated in a specific context. The practitioner brings values and preferences to a working alliance with an athlete and they will inevitably influence the effectiveness of that relationship, because they are a person first and a practitioner second (Terry, 2009). Herzog and Hays (2012) reflected upon the challenging continuum of providing sport psychology as psychotherapy versus the more didactic mental skills training. The nature of the referral, the client's preferences, the practitioner's perspective and skill sets, a continuous process of appraisal and adaptation, and the central importance of the athlete–practitioner relationship are considerations for a contextually intelligent practitioner. Context-driven sport psychology for smaller groups or teams is an issue of reflection upon and understanding of the shared practices and the processes of including and excluding members. The treatment of "newcomers" and "brokers" is a very important issue, whether these are migrants, injured players, or young talented athletes. The contextually intelligent practitioner could consider who belongs to the group on a regular basis and who are the "newcomers" and try to understand the processes of becoming a legitimate peripheral participant and how the group includes a newcomer. Lastly, at the organizational level, context-driven sport psychology can be an issue of understanding and sustaining the interconnected communities of practice through which an organization becomes effective and valuable as an organization. The importance of understanding how the organization operates, who are the gatekeepers, and what their formal and informal power structures are is important (Stambulova & Schinke, 2017). At the organizational level, the practitioner could reflect upon how the organization recruits new coaches, who it recruits, and why. How are the teams in the organization interconnected, and how is the organization connected to others outside? Thus, contextually intelligent practitioners have a possibility of cultivating the organizational cultures or microcultures operating in clubs, schools, or communities of practice by deciphering these organizational structures and cultures and working together with influential leaders. However, such reflections are simply also a part of the process of situating the individual athlete. Gaining insight into the unique world-view, the specific situation, and context of each individual athlete is a cornerstone of becoming a contextually intelligent practitioner (Terry, 2009).

How Context Guides Sport Psychology Delivery

CDP is: (a) based on a thorough analysis and understanding of the clients' contexts, with a particular focus on the local cultures; (b) related to positioning the clients and consultants within their local cultural contexts; (c) conducted mainly on the clients' sites; (d) carefully planned to fit clients and contexts; (e) spontaneous contact interventions to manage pressing issues in situ; (f) not always having an answer in advance of the problem (Hacker & Mann, 2017); (g) using language that is clear and accepted in the clients' contexts; (h) inclusive of the consultants' reflections before action, in action, and on action; (i) involving good cooperation with the staff and other experts (Stambulova & Schinke, 2017); and (j) aware of moving more closely to becoming cultural insiders (Mellalieu, 2017).

CDP can involve having an eye for organizations' cultural leaders, meaning those who are in the position to take responsibility for development, maintenance, and deliberate change of the organizational culture (Stambulova & Schinke, 2017). A group's underlying assumptions are "taught" to new team members as the correct way to perceive, think, feel, and act in relation to different challenges. CDP, as seen through a cultural lens, can include the role of a cultural leader when the target of the intervention is at group or organizational level. One powerful mechanism that cultural leaders have available is to communicate what they believe in or care about (Schein, 2010). The authors perceive cultural leadership to be the deliberate use of what Schein referred to as cultural embedding mechanisms (Henriksen, Storm, & Larsen, 2018). An example of an embedding mechanism could be how the practitioner reacts to critical incidents. Critical incidents and crises in a broad sense make people more susceptible to learning and change. Practitioners' actions in such situations are a powerful signal of personal priorities and goals. In this case, it is vital how practitioners communicate their values and expectations to the clients. Cultural leadership takes place all the time, but practitioners are not always aware of their potential roles as cultural leaders. Thus, when aiming to improve organizational culture, the role of a practitioner will often centre around being aware of their own behaviour, as well as teaching coaches and organizational leaders to be more aware of the ways in which their actions communicate values and expectations.

Cases from Different Cultural Contexts

In this section, we will describe three different examples from, respectively, Canada, the UK, and Denmark. The aim is to illustrate applied examples of context-driven sport psychology that pay particular attention to the cultural context and, subsequently, what practitioners need to consider when working in these specific cultural contexts.

The Need to Be Aware of How Results Affect Organizational Changes

Recently, Larsen (2017) described a sport psychology programme at a Danish professional soccer club. Studies in organizational psychology in sport and the experience of practitioners point to the fact that working within an environment means providing services where there are other distracting influences, such as organizational stress, change, pressure, external demands, media intrusion, contract negotiations, and the presence of agents (Nesti, 2010). Moreover, researchers highlight the existence of poor employment practices having direct and indirect implications for on-field performance following organizational changes (Wagstaff & Larner, 2015). The article highlights that the practitioner needs to be aware of how results affect organizational changes (e.g., changing coaches), and how organizational change affects their services in a professional sports organization. The article points to the fact that the practitioner needs to integrate the notions of self-reflexivity and cultural sensitivity into their professional philosophy when entering a professional sports organization and have an eye on several "logics" operating in the organization. The author described soccer culture as characterized by "short-termism" in regard to the need to win the next game, avoid relegation, and survive at all costs, thereby satisfying the sponsors' and fans' expectations. The practitioner was aiming at a long-term talent development focus for parts of his intervention. The short-termism was an important cultural context for the practical work with the talented young soccer players because it had a significant influence on priorities and focus areas among the managers of the club, which became clear during the period of "crisis" and adversity. The case illustrates how thorough cultural analytical work should be a continuous process for the practitioner, not just an initial act. However, this essential part of the job was in itself challenged by the dominant short-termism. One contextual learning point that the author highlighted is the need to have some political acuity, because the contexts are changing, and these circumstances imply that the practitioner needs to know that organizational changes will occur when results are poor. A similar organizational set-up can act differently according to shifting situations and processes within the club.

The Pivotal Position as Cultural Insider

In a British context, Mellalieu (2017) described his experiences of working within professional male rugby union in the South Wales region of the UK. This article describes the need for practitioners to be or become "embedded" in the culture of the sport. Mellalieu described his sustained engagement with professional rugby union as a player, coach, or practitioner for more than 20 years. To gain access and begin building working alliances within rugby, there is a need to be perceived as a mental skills/performance enhancement coach, as opposed to a sport psychology practitioner. The role of practitioner similarly needs to be considered as one of physical development or technical skills (passing, tackling, etc.). The professional male team sport environment is often a traditional, conservative, closed culture, resistant to change and suspicious of outsiders, and both staff and athletes can be sceptical about the value of new approaches or different regimes (Eubank, Nesti, & Cruickshank, 2014). Maybe this is an explanation of why Mellalieu experienced how important the insider position is. A valuable strategy to work towards integration with staff by seeking to understand the cultural environment of the team is to identify the key gatekeepers who provide access to the various subgroups within the team or organization. A key element of functioning in this macho environment was to gain trust and entry by focusing on "performance", but also supporting issues "away from the game" if required.

The Guided Walk as Key to Decipher Cultural Basic Assumptions

Within a Canadian context, Seanor and colleagues (2017) provided a cursory description of one high-performance artistic sport environment with a history of producing successful Olympians. The scope of the article was to take a preliminary step to inform practitioners about unique contextual factors present in an athlete talent development environment that supports athletes' development from grass roots to podium. Skyriders provides insight into how environmental factors can interact to create an organizational culture conducive to Olympic-level accomplishments. Practitioners open to learning from Skyriders will hopefully help future Olympians "catch the feeling of flying" in their own athletic ventures, building upon the ESF model (see Henriksen, Stambulova, & Roessler, 2010) derived from the holistic ecological approach to athlete talent development environments. The ESF model is designed to explain how contextual inputs in a sport environment, defined by preconditions and processes, interact to generate outputs from the environment in the form of the sport environment's organizational culture, individual and team achievements (including psychosocial competencies, such as autonomy and resilience, and athletic skills), and ultimately the overall success of the sport environment. Seanor and colleagues (2017) described how practitioners, in large and small sport environments alike, should consider if training sessions are structured to permit adequate opportunities for athletes to observe, support, and interact with each other. Training practices that facilitate interconnectedness among teammates will support the development of every athlete. Second, the athletes in this environment highlighted how teammates can inculcate each other with appropriate skills for elite-level success. Practitioners could further explore the influence of teammates as "star makers". Although "star makers" did not experience Olympic success, they were central to the development of each Olympian. Practitioners could help maximize athlete development by working with teams to evaluate the strengths and weaknesses of each athlete and arranging athletes in complementary pairings (i.e., partnering athletes together who have opposing strengths and weaknesses). Establishing complementary pairings could help athletes learn from each other and guide each other to a higher level. Third, practitioners embracing the scope would encourage a slow and steady approach that may help protect young athletes from the negative outcomes associated with early intense practice such as burn-out and manipulation by adults (Malina, 2010), while still nurturing their Olympic potential. Protecting young athletes early in their sport careers increases the likelihood that they will continue within a sport long enough to develop into elite competitors, potentially all the way to the podium.

Research Approaches

Context-driven sport and exercise psychology identifies research approaches that blend theory, lived culture, and social action with a self-reflexive sensibility to raise awareness as to how one's own values, biases, social position, and self-identity categories impact participants within research and/or consulting realms (McGannon & Johnson, 2009; Ryba & Wright, 2005). This cultural praxis model includes ethnography, narratives, and biographical approaches. For example, Seanor and colleagues (2017) raised an interesting point on research methodologies where CDP can be excavated. The authors embraced the stories and assumptions within a specific environment using a guided walk through the club together with the coaches. Mellalieu (2017) embraced group dynamics and power relationships within the "macho" culture of rugby. Relations of power shape the way the people interact when doing sports and affect the ways they learn (Hodkinson et al., 2008), and these processes can be hard to decipher. Thus, ethnography as a method involves direct and long-term immersion in the cultural life worlds of other people to grasp how they live, interact, and view life. The establishment of a personal role in the group is key to understanding the local culture (Atkinson, 2016). And, for example, the biographical approach was employed in the exploration of the prominent influences of becoming a coach (Lorimer & Holland-Smith, 2012).

Community-based participatory action research (Coghlan & Brannick, 2005) might also feature appropriate context-driven consultation processes and engaged group discussion. Participatory action research designs draw participants into a collaborative and democratic form of enquiry for and with people and thereby put power structures at the centre of the research by shifting the balance between researcher and participant (Schinke & Blodgett, 2016).

Case studies are suitable as research design and have been applied to a great extent by practitioners and researchers sharing knowledge. For example, a new journal (*Case Studies in Sport and Exercise Psychology*) was recently devoted to rigorous, in-depth examinations of particular cases to encourage sport and exercise psychologists to both share and receive feedback on their professional practice

Case studies are the examination of a complex functioning unit, a particular life event, organization, community, team, group, dyad, or individual (Hodge & Sharp, 2016). Adopting the case study as a methodological frame will enable a context-driven approach, because, as both emphasized and illustrated by Flyvbjerg (2006), "the case study produces the type of context-dependent knowledge that research on learning shows to be necessary to allow people to develop from rule-based beginners to virtuoso experts" (p. 221). From this viewpoint, case studies provide opportunities for sport psychology practitioners and researchers to learn from others experiences – as vicarious experiences. Thus, providing examples of localized approaches that bridge theory and situated practice as a reciprocal process have the potential to bring together sport psychology practitioners and create a community of practice that drives the field forward (Cotterill, Schinke, & Thelwell, 2016). For case studies to be context-driven, the process begins with paying special attention to the practitioners or the applied researchers themselves, their approach to practice, and their philosophy. Case studies provide transferability when the readers perceive an overlap with their own situation and then transfer the findings to their own contextual actions (Tracey, 2010). From this viewpoint, rich and transparent cases provide readers with a "virtual reality" (Flyvbjerg, 2006; Hodge & Sharp, 2016). The intention of case studies is not to provide objective measures of effect but, rather, to present a detailed description on the delivery of sport psychology services (see Henriksen, 2015, for an example).

Conclusion

Context-driven sport psychology includes three mutual influential processes: self-reflexivity, contextual awareness, and positioning. The three case examples together illustrate cultural awareness and sensitivity; the process of becoming a cultural insider and the dynamic interaction between practitioner and key people in the organization are essential aspects of context-driven sport psychology. Looking at the literature, the authors see that effective context-driven sport psychology practice is threefold: It regards self, context, and positioning in the client's context (if the practitioner works with or within the client's environment).

In CDP, the practitioner acknowledges their own background (e.g., education, ethnicity, gender, social status, experiences) and reflects on the ways in which their own views influence the practice. The self-reflexivity is important in the development of context-driven sport psychology. CDP is a process of building relationships, earning trust from the athletes and coaches in a club, and paying attention to presenting oneself as neutral, calm, and secure. According to social position (e.g., well-educated academic), CDP pays attention to how practitioners or researchers communicate and try to deliver simple and understandable messages for athletes, coaches, and staff. The practitioner could use a diary to reflect on their own practice and the reasons for how they are doing. An important "mirror" in this self-reflexive process is supervision sessions and sharing knowledge with other practitioners and researchers.

CDP acknowledges the existence and value of viewpoints outside one's own. To understand the context in which the client is embedded requires cultural competence and contextual intelligence, and a deliberate focus on what is unique about the present context. For example, being a practitioner in swimming and orienteering at the same time enables contextual awareness in the practitioner, because it is in the cultural comparison that the practitioner becomes aware of the uniqueness of, for example, the subculture of one sport. In the effort to become aware of the local culture, it is through comparison that one will see what is distinctive (Storm, 2015). Therefore, it is useful to work with different sports at the same time. When one is not solely working with one sport, one is able to draw experiences from other sports and "not become blind" to the one context in which one is working. The practitioner is able to reflect upon transferability regarding solutions, experiences, and differences from one context to another. Therefore, practitioners will benefit from openness and curiosity in regard to exploring their taken-for-granted assumptions in relation to others' cultures.

Practitioners and researchers need to be aware of their own positioning within the clients' contexts and determine how it influences the intervention. They should become "cultural insiders" by, for example, gathering knowledge about the sport and learning about the history and philosophy within the environment to competently communicate with the people. To stimulate reflexivity around positioning, it is important to consider what positions are presented. Is the practitioner close to the leaders or accepted by the captain of the team? What is the general perception of sport psychology, and how does it influence the legitimacy and position of the practitioner? Are they a legitimate participant in the group, and how did they pursue that position? What is their relationship to the people with formal and informal power (the management, the "star athlete")? The position within the group will influence the intervention and the ability to perform context-driven sport psychology. It is useful to focus on building relationships as a starting point of working with or within the athlete's environment. Additionally, it is useful to provide and receive feedback from colleagues and supervisors, because it enhances the cultural and contextual awareness. Supervision gives an opportunity for colleagues to challenge the choices of the practitioner. Sharing knowledge and experiences is a general way of moving towards contextual awareness, which could be included in education and professional sport psychology practice.

References

American Psychological Association (APA). (2019, April). Multicultural guidelines: An ecological approach to context, identity, and intersectionality. Retrieved from www.apa.org/about/policy/multicultural-guide lines.pdf

Atkinson, M. (2016). Ethnography. In B. Smith & A. Sparkes (Eds.), *Routledge handbook of qualitative research in sport and exercise* (pp. 49–62). New York: Routledge.

Bronfenbrenner, U. (1979). *The ecology of human development.* Cambridge, MA: Harvard University Press.

Coghlan, D., & Brannick, T. (2005). *Doing action research in your own organization* (2nd ed.). London: Sage.

Comas-Díaz, L., & Griffith, E. (Eds.). (1988). *Clinical guidelines in cross cultural mental health.* New York: John Wiley.

Cotterill, S. T., Schinke, R. J., & Thelwell, R. (2016). Writing manuscripts for case studies in sport and exercise psychology. *Case Studies in Sport and Exercise Psychology, 1,* 1–3.

Dzikus, L., Fischer, L., & Hays, K. (2012). Shared responsibility: A case of and for "real life" ethical decision-making in sport psychology. *The Sport Psychologist, 26,* 519–539.

Eubank, M., Nesti, M., & Cruickshank, A. (2014). Understanding high performance sport environments: Impact for the professional training and supervision of sport psychologists. *Sport and Exercise Psychology Review, 10,* 30–37.

Flyvbjerg, B. (2006). Five misunderstandings about case-study research. *Qualitative Inquiry, 12,* 219–245.

Giges, B., & Van Raalte, J. (2012). Special issue of the sport psychologist: Case studies in sport psychology. *The Sport Psychologist, 26,* 483–485.

Hacker, C. M., & Mann, M. E. (2017). Talking across the divide: Reflections and recommendations for context-driven, cultural sport psychology. *Journal of Sport Psychology in Action, 8,* 76–86.

Hall, S. (1997). *Representation: Cultural representations and signifying practices.* London: Sage.

Henriksen, K. (2015). Developing a high-performance culture: A sport psychology intervention from an ecological perspective in elite orienteering. *Journal of Sport Psychology in Action, 6,* 141–153.

Henriksen, K., Schinke, R. J., Moesch, K., McCann, S., Parham, W. D., Larsen, C. H., & Terry, P. (2019). Consensus statement on improving the mental health of high performance athletes. *International Journal of Sport and Exercise Psychology.* Advanced online publication. doi:10.1080/1612197X.2019.1570473

Henriksen, K., Stambulova, N. B., & Roessler, K. K. (2010). A holistic approach to athletic talent development environments: A successful sailing milieu. *Psychology of Sport and Exercise, 11,* 212–222.

Henriksen, K., Storm, L. K., & Larsen, C. H. (2018). Organisational culture and influence on developing athletes. In C. Knight, C. Harwood & D. Gould (Eds.), *Sport psychology for young athletes* (pp. 216–228). New York: Routledge.

Herzog, T., & Hays, K. (2012). Therapist or mental skills coach? How to decide. *The Sport Psychologist, 26,* 486–499.

Hodge, K., & Sharp, L.-A. (2016). Case studies. In B. Smith & A. Sparkes (Eds.), *Routledge handbook of qualitative research in sport and exercise* (pp. 62–75). New York: Routledge.

Hodkinson, P., Biesta, G., & James, D. (2008). Understanding learning culturally: Overcoming the dualism between social and individual views of learning. *Vocations and Learning, 1,* 27–47.

Larsen, C. H. (2017). Bringing a knife to a gunfight: A coherent consulting philosophy might not be enough to be effective in professional soccer. *Journal of Sport Psychology in Action, 8,* 121–130.

Lorimer, R., & Holland-Smith, D. (2012). Why coach? A case study of the prominent influences on a top-level UK outdoor adventure coach. *The Sport Psychologist, 26,* 571–583.

Malina, R. M. (2010). Early sport specialization: Roots, effectiveness, risks. *Current Sports Medicine Reports, 9,* 364–371.

Martindale, A., & Collins, D. (2012). A professional judgement and decision making case study. Reflection-in-action research. *The Sport Psychologist, 26,* 500–518.

McGannon, K. R., & Johnson, C. R. (2009). Strategies for reflective cultural sport psychology research. In R. J. Schinke & S. J. Hanrahan (Eds.), *Cultural sport psychology* (pp. 57–75). Champaign, IL: Human Kinetics.

McGannon, K. R., & Schinke, R. J. (2015). Situating the subculture of sport, physical activity and critical approaches. In R. J. Schinke & K. R. McGannon (Eds.), *The psychology of sub-culture in sport and physical activity. A critical perspective* (pp. 1–15). Hove, UK: Psychology Press.

Mellalieu, S. D. (2017). Sport psychology consulting in professional rugby union in the United Kingdom. *Journal of Sport Psychology in Action, 8,* 109–120.

Nesti, M. (2010). *Psychology in football.* New York: Routledge.

Reber, A. (1995). *Dictionary of psychology.* New York: Penguin.

Ryba, T. V., Schinke, R. J., & Tennenbaum, G. (2010). *The cultural turn in sport psychology.* Morgantown, WV: Fitness Information Technology.

Ryba, T. V., Stambulova, N. B., Si, G., & Schinke, R. J. (2013). ISSP position stand: Culturally competent research and practice in sport and exercise psychology. *International Journal of Sport and Exercise Psychology, 11,* 123–142.

Ryba, T. V., & Wright, H. K. (2005). From mental game to cultural praxis: A cultural studies model's implications for the future of sport psychology. *Quest, 57,* 192–212.

Schein, E. H. (2010). *Organizational culture and leadership* (4th ed.). San Francisco, CA: John Wiley.

Schinke, R. J., & Blodgett, A. (2016). Embarking on community-based participatory action research: A methodology that emerges from (and in) communities. In B. Smith & A. Sparkes (Eds.), *Routledge handbook of qualitative research in sport and exercise* (pp. 88–101). New York: Routledge.

Schinke, R. J., & Hanrahan, S. J. (2009). *Cultural sport psychology.* Champaign, IL: Human Kinetics.

Schinke, R. J., McGannon, K., Parham, W., & Lane, A. M. (2012). Toward cultural praxis and cultural sensitivity: Strategies for self-reflexive sport psychology practice. *Quest, 64,* 34–46.

Schinke, R. J., & McGannon, K. R. (Eds.). (2015). *The psychology of sub-culture in sport and physical activity. A critical perspective.* Hove, UK: Psychology Press.

Schinke, R. J., & Moore, Z. E. (2011). Culturally informed sport psychology: Introduction to the special issue. *Journal of Clinical Sport Psychology, 5,* 283–294.

Schinke, R. J., & Stambulova, N. B. (2016). Call for papers: Context-driven sport and exercise psychology. *Journal of Sport Psychology in Action, 7,* 56–57.

Schinke, R. J., & Stambulova, N. B. (2017). Context-driven sport and exercise psychology practice: Widening our lens beyond the athlete. *Journal of Sport Psychology in Action, 8,* 71–75.

Seanor, M., Schinke, R. J., Stambulova, N. B., Ross, R., & Kpazai, G. (2017). Cultivating Olympic champions: A trampoline development environment from grass roots to podium. *Journal of Sport Psychology in Action, 8,* 96–108.

Stambulova, N. B., & Schinke, R. J. (2017). Experts focus on the context. Postulates derived from the authors' shared experiences and wisdom. *Journal of Sport Psychology in Action, 8,* 131–134.

Storm, L. K. (2015). *"Colored by culture": Talent development in Scandinavian elite sport as seen from a cultural perspective.* (Doctoral dissertation). Department of Sport Science and Clinical Biomechanics, University of Southern Denmark.

Terry, P. (2009). Strategies for reflective cross-cultural sport psychology practice. In R. J. Schinke & S. J. Hanrahan (Eds.), *Cultural sport psychology* (pp. 79–89). Champaign, IL: Human Kinetics.

Tracey, S. J. (2010). Qualitative quality. Eight 'big tent' criteria for excellent qualitative research. *Qualitative Inquiry, 16,* 837–851.

Wagstaff, C., & Larner, R. J. (2015). Organisational psychology in sport: Recent developments and a research agenda. In S. Mellalieu & S. Hanton (Eds.), *Contemporary advances in sport psychology: A review* (pp. 91–110). Abingdon: Routledge.

7

CULTURE

Noora J. Ronkainen and Amy T. Blodgett

Introduction

It has been widely demonstrated that culture shapes and permeates human thoughts, feelings, and behaviours. Although there are hundreds of contested definitions of culture, in a simple form, culture has been defined as 'the shared way of life of a group of people' (Berry, Poortinga, Breugelmans, Chasiotis, & Sam, 2011, p. 4). In sport and exercise contexts, the need to develop cultural awareness (recognizing cultural influences on behaviour) and cultural competence (the application of culturally appropriate research methodology and interventions) has been highlighted by a growing number of scholars (e.g., Duda & Allison, 1990; Fisher, Butryn, & Roper, 2003; Lee, 2015; McGannon & Smith, 2015; Ryba & Wright, 2005). The increasing transnational flows of athletes, coaches, and even sport psychology researchers and practitioners imply that people involved in sport are likely to interact with people from different cultural backgrounds (Ryba, Schinke, Stambulova, & Elbe, 2018). From recreational contexts up to elite and professional levels, sport brings together individuals with diverse backgrounds in terms of race, ethnicity, nationality, class, gender, religion, sexual orientation, dis/ability, language, and so forth. It is important to consider these cultural aspects and their role in relation to who athletes are (identity), why they pursue sport, and how they are motivated, so that professionals in the field can effectively support each individual and address their unique needs (Schinke & Hanrahan, 2009). For instance, a number of sport psychology scholars have recently highlighted cultural challenges associated with athlete adaptation and acculturation (Brandão & Vieira, 2013; Ryba, Stambulova, & Ronkainen, 2016; Schinke, Blodgett, McGannon, & Ge, 2016) and the need to better understand cultural variability in motivation, communication, and meanings that athletes assign to sport (Ryba, 2009; Schinke & Hanrahan, 2009). Culture shapes research practices from the choice and formulation of theories and methods to the interpretation of findings (Ryba, Stambulova, Si, & Schinke, 2013), as well as applied sport psychology service delivery that needs cultural competence to be effective (Schinke & Hanrahan, 2009). Three distinct approaches to the study of culture – cross-cultural psychology, cultural psychology, and cultural praxis – have been introduced in sport psychology to respond to the need to better understand cultural issues (Ryba et al., 2013).

Cultural anthropologists' pioneering research on cultures, often using ethnographic fieldwork, provided a foundation for the psychological research on culture (Berry et al.,

2011). Early cultural anthropologists studied indigenous people and recorded their 'strange' rituals and beliefs, which were received with astonishment, but also with horror and condemnation (Shweder, 1991). One of the first anthropological definitions of culture was provided by Tylor (1871), who suggested that, 'culture, or civilization, taken in its broad, ethnographic sense, is that complex whole which includes knowledge, belief, art, morals, law, custom, and any other capabilities and habits acquired by man [*sic*] as a member of society' (p. 1). Initially, scholars in cultural anthropology focused more on 'external' markers of culture (e.g., material structures, national wealth or climate), and their work influenced how cross-cultural researchers operationalized culture for their research (Berry et al., 2011). A second view on culture, focused on 'internal' culture (of meanings, symbols, and social interactions), started to become influential in cultural anthropology from the 1970s (e.g., Geertz, 1973), inspiring cultural psychology scholars who challenged the theoretical foundations of cross-cultural psychology (e.g., Shweder, 1991). Since the 1950s, some anthropologists also started to emphasize the cognitive element of culture including symbols, systems of ideas, and meanings, giving rise to the strand of cognitive anthropology that had a close link to psychological research (D'Andrade, 1995). Cognitive anthropology sought to understand how people in different cultural locations think about and conceive their worlds, from material objects to abstract ideas, often focusing on the role of language in shaping human cognition. Today, many scholars have subscribed to a 'dual approach' to culture, emphasizing that culture has both 'external' (material culture, structures, institutions) and 'internal' (symbols and meanings) features, some of which are more durable, and others of which are subject to constant change and negotiation within social relationships (Berry, 2009; Berry et al., 2011; D'Andrade, 1995).

Cultural sport psychology (CSP) emerged in sport psychology as a call to engage with issues surrounding sociocultural difference, cultural diversity, and cultural competence in theorizing, research, and practice (McGannon & Smith, 2015; Ryba & Schinke, 2009; Ryba et al., 2013; Schinke & Hanrahan, 2009). The advocates of CSP have emphasized that it is impossible to take 'an objective stance' outside culture, and that dismissing it in psychological analysis and practice would be to ignore a key facet of peoples' lives (Ryba et al., 2013; Schinke & McGannon, 2015; Schinke, Stambulova, Lidor, Papaioannou, & Ryba, 2016). CSP has been proposed as an umbrella term for various ways of engaging with culture in sport psychology research to explore a wide range of topics and traditionally marginalized identities through methodologies that centralize culture. Ryba and Schinke (2009) conceptualized CSP as 'a discourse that encompasses a variety of ontological and epistemological underpinnings on a paradigmatic continuum that come *after* positivism' (Ryba & Schinke, 2009, p. 267), implying that the CSP genre mostly employs qualitative research methods grounded in a cultural psychology conceptualization of culture. As the interest in culture is still a relatively recent phenomenon in sport psychology, it is first important to outline the differences between two main approaches to defining and studying culture in psychology: the cross-cultural and the cultural approach.

Culture in Cross-Cultural Psychology

Cross-cultural psychology became an established research field within psychology in the mid 20th century and brought together the anthropologists' interest in culture with research methods established in psychology (Berry et al., 2011). In cross-cultural psychology, scholars assume a 'psychic unity' in people across cultures, while acknowledging that there is cultural variation in the manifestation of common psychological processes and functions. Within this so-called 'universalist' perspective, 'ultimately the assumption is that any theoretically meaningful psychological concept should make sense everywhere, despite large variations in behavior manifestations' (Berry et al., 2011, p. 12). Studying psychological phenomena in different cultures could help to test the generalizability of psychological theories and to make modifications to improve their universal applicability (Triandis, Malpass, & Davidson, 1971).

Cross-cultural scholars understand culture as an individual's membership in a particular group, most often based on nationality, language, or race/ethnicity. The cross-cultural perspective was introduced in sport psychology by Duda and Allison (1990) as a means to challenge researchers and practitioners to rethink theory and practice through a culturally aware lens. Since then, researchers have used the cross-cultural approach to compare athletes of different nationalities in terms of adaptation to career termination (Alfermann, Stambulova, & Zemaityte, 2004; Stambulova, Stephan, & Jäphag, 2007), coping styles (Anshell, Williams, & Hodge, 1997), and motivation for sport (Jowett et al., 2017). The cross-cultural perspective is most often grounded in the positivistic paradigm and typically (but not exclusively) employs quantitative research designs (Berry, 2009). In cross-cultural research projects, two groups of people from different cultures are typically compared in relation to a psychological variable (e.g., motivation, cognition, perceptions); participants' cultural contexts (e.g., ecological and sociocultural factors) are typically conceptualized as antecedent conditions, whereas psychological variables and behaviours are considered as consequents or outcomes (Berry et al., 2011).

The best-known cultural difference endorsed in cross-cultural psychology is the individualism/ collectivism divide (Hofstede, 1984), which has been associated with a variety of antecedents (e.g., affluence, family size), attributes (e.g., goal orientations, communication styles), and consequences (e.g., independence vs. interdependence; Triandis, McCusker, & Hui, 1990). Cross-cultural researchers have suggested that self-identity and sense of autonomy are particularly central concerns for people in individualistic cultures, whereas collectivistic cultures tend to centre on harmony, mutual obligations, and cooperation (Hofstede, 1984; Oyserman, Coon, & Kemmelmeier, 2002). As an example in sport, Asghar, Wang, Linde, and Alfermann (2013) compared the similarities and differences in anxiety, motivation, and self-concept in German (representatives of an individualistic country), Chinese, and Pakistani (representatives of collectivistic countries) youth athletes. They found mixed results in terms of somatic anxiety, but the athletes considered to represent individualistic cultural orientation were found to score higher on task orientation and lower on ego orientation and cognitive anxiety than the athletes representing collectivistic orientation. The authors concluded that, 'emphasizing group solidarity and norms in a [collectivistic] culture corresponds to an emphasis on cognitions that stress possible negative consequences in reputation and in evaluation from the own group' (Asghar et al., 2013, p. 240).

Culture in Cultural Psychology

Since the 1990s, a relativist view on culture known as cultural psychology has been introduced as an alternative approach to the cross-cultural perspective in mainstream psychology (Valsiner, 2014) and has primarily informed CSP (see Ryba & Schinke, 2009; Ryba et al., 2013). Shweder (2000) described cultural psychology as 'the study of ethnic and cultural sources of diversity in emotional and somatic functioning, self-organization, moral evaluation, social cognition, and human development' and 'psychological anthropology without the premise of psychic unity' (p. 210). Cultural psychology scholars have proposed that culture should be seen as having a constitutive, rather than a causal, role in human functioning. It is argued that psychological functioning is essentially different in different cultural locations, meaning that people inhabit different 'cultural modes of being' (Kitayama, Duffy, & Uchida, 2007, p. 161). For Shweder (1999), 'cultural psychology is premised on human existential uncertainty (the search for meaning) and on a (so-called) intentional conception of 'constituted' worlds' (p. 1). The idea of constituted worlds implies that sociocultural environments do not have distinct identities separate from meanings human beings assign to them, and, therefore, culture cannot be analytically considered as extrinsic to the psyche. In other words, there is no separation between the individual (psychology) and context (culture), because 'individuals and traditions, psyches and cultures, make each other up' (Shweder, 1991, p. 2). Therefore, the difference between people is not thought to occur only on the level of behavioural manifestations (as in cross-cultural psychology), but also in the underlying psychological processes. As Shweder (2000) put it, cultural psychology 'aims to reassess the uniformitarian principle of psychic unity and develop a credible theory of psychological pluralism' (p. 209).

Cultural (sport) psychology scholarship is interested in understanding the construction of meaning, rather than explaining cause or variation in behaviour (Kral, Burkhardt, & Kidd, 2002; Ryba et al., 2013; Valsiner, 2014). Scholars drawing on the cultural paradigm emphasize the need for reflexivity to avoid ethnocentrism and imposing Western cultural concepts on people, seeking instead to understand meanings from cultural members' own point of view (Geertz, 1973). For such purposes, cultural psychology researchers most often rely on qualitative methodologies (Kral et al., 2002). Valsiner (2014) suggested that, in addition to traditional forms of qualitative data (interviews, observations), fictional narratives (films, novels, myths) can be equally valuable forms of data because they can be analysed for cultural patterns of thinking and feeling. Cultural psychologists often adopt interdisciplinary perspectives and draw from anthropology, linguistics, and philosophy in analysing personal experiences in particular socio-historic contexts (Shweder, 1999). Cultural scholars also aim to avoid prior judgements or essentializing certain cultural markers such as class, ethnicity, and gender as the key categories that are assumed to produce the difference. The use of such categories is potentially problematic in that everyone in that particular category is assumed to be the same (e.g., all black women will have a similar experience of doing sport; see Ryba et al., 2013).

Culture in Cultural Sport Psychology

Following the growth of cultural psychology in mainstream psychology, sport psychology scholars have begun to engage with cultural issues in sport and exercise contexts. It is relatively recently – just over the past decade – that the 'cultural turn' has started to take place within the field (see Ryba, Schinke, & Tenenbaum, 2010; Ryba et al., 2013). Those working to advance the cultural turn have pointed out that sport psychology research has traditionally been embedded with a decidedly male and Western ethnocentric bias, which has misrepresented and disconnected many sport participants (such as women, people of colour, indigenous peoples, those with dis/abilities, and LGBTQ community members) from their ways of thinking, doing, and being (Duda & Allison, 1990; Fisher et al., 2003; Krane, 1994; Ryba & Wright, 2005, 2010). CSP researchers have thus been informed by a politically and ethically driven agenda to diversify sport psychology and address issues of representation, ethics of difference, and sociocultural justice through a centring of culture. There is a growing influx of research projects that have been conducted that centralize culture within meaning-making processes and modes of analysis in order to facilitate contextualized understandings of previously marginalized topics (Ryba et al., 2010; Schinke & McGannon, 2014; Stambulova & Ryba, 2013).

While recognizing the importance of cross-cultural studies as a foundational subset of CSP research, scholars have promoted cultural studies and cultural praxis (where culture is blended with theory, research, and practice, with an emphasis on transforming local contexts) as two trajectories for further advancing the CSP agenda (Ryba et al., 2013; Ryba & Wright, 2010). Particularly, it is emphasized how cultural studies and cultural praxis focalize local sport contexts as sites where people's lived bodies, and the experiences they have in those bodies, produce situated and fluid knowledge about what it means to be gendered, raced, aged, classed, sexually oriented, and dis/abled (Blodgett, Schinke, McGannon, & Fisher, 2015; Ryba et al., 2010; Ryba & Wright, 2005). Moreover, these contextually driven forms of research have the potential to help advance social missions within and through sport (see Schinke et al., 2016). Empirical research taken up as cultural studies is overviewed below, followed by emerging cultural praxis research. Studies on organizational culture in sport are also considered in the final section as a novel research trajectory that is expanding the CSP scholarship.

Cultural Studies

Cultural studies research is characterized by an openness to various theoretical and methodological approaches and content areas (Ryba & Schinke, 2009; Ryba & Wright, 2005, 2010). It can be taken up in a variety of ways grounded in a variety of epistemologies (e.g., social constructionism, post-positivism, critical realism, post-structuralism), although, to date, researchers within CSP have primarily drawn on social constructionism and critical approaches that bring forward issues of power and social inequality. The underlying goal is to bring forward the meanings of subgroups who are typically marginalized or excluded in the production of knowledge, as well as explore the subjectivities/positionings of researchers, in order to disrupt dominant discourses and power dynamics that disadvantage minority (in terms of power) sport participants (e.g., Blodgett, Schinke, Smith, Peltier, & Pheasant, 2011; Douglas, 2014; Schinke & McGannon, 2014, 2015).

In 2009, a foundational special issue of the *International Journal of Sport and Exercise Psychology* (Ryba & Schinke, 2009) highlighted CSP projects that engaged decolonizing methodologies to critically examine issues of power and sociocultural difference within research. As examples, decolonizing methodologies were used to facilitate reflexive awareness around issues of 'boundary crossing' (e.g., Smith, Collinson, Phoenix, Brown, & Sparkes, 2009) and whiteness (e.g., Butryn, 2009, 2010), emphasizing how we (researchers or practitioners) sometimes project our own perspectives on others and mispresent their views and needs. Decolonizing methodologies have also been used within participatory action research to centralize local indigenous ways of thinking and doing and facilitate more meaningful understandings of how to support Aboriginal athletes' identities and meanings of sport (e.g., Blodgett et al., 2014; Forsyth & Heine, 2010; Giles, 2013; McHugh, Coppola, & Sinclair, 2013). For a more comprehensive overview of issues of power and privilege, see Volume 1, Chapter 37, 'Power and Privilege'.

Narrative inquiry and discursive psychology have also been used to facilitate CSP research that foregrounds the constructed nature of identities and how they shape athletes' sport experiences and sense of well-being (McGannon & Smith, 2015; Ronkainen, Kavoura, & Ryba, 2016a, 2016b). Scholars have drawn on the concept of intersectionality to study how various cultural identities layer together and result in different configurations of power that, in turn, lead to some individuals feeling that they do not belong in particular sport contexts, that they are socially excluded or unsupported, and/or being discriminated against (e.g., Blodgett, Ge, Schinke, & McGannon, 2017; Kavoura, Ryba, & Chroni, 2015). Researchers have explored how an athletic identity intersects with other identities, including those surrounding gender, motherhood, disability, age, and race and ethnicity, each framed and interpreted within a particular sport context (e.g., Blodgett et al., 2014; Carless, Sparkes, Douglas, & Cooke, 2014; Krane, Ross, Sullivan Barak, Lucas-Carr, & Robinson, 2014; McGannon & Schinke, 2013; Ronkainen, Ryba, & Nesti, 2013; Smith, 2013; Smith, Bundon, & Best, 2016). Researchers have also argued that exclusive performance discourses/narratives that circulate high-performance sport cultures are potentially restrictive of athletes' identity development, and they have generated alternative narratives that are more empowering for recognizing athletes as holistic people (e.g., Carless & Douglas, 2012, 2013; Cosh, LeCouteur, Crabb, & Kettler, 2013; Douglas, 2014; Ronkainen & Ryba, 2017). These understandings of athletes have been further expanded through research on identity intersections, such as that presented in a special section of *Psychology of Sport and Exercise* (see Schinke & McGannon, 2015). For a more comprehensive review of identity research, see Volume 1, Chapter 43, 'Self-identity'.

More recently, researchers within CSP have focused on cultural transition and acculturation processes experienced by migrant athletes who move across national or cultural borders. Ryba (2017) reviewed this newly developing discourse and indicated how the concepts of transition and acculturation have been 're-articulated as culturally constituted processes that are complex, multifaceted, and dynamically produced within matrices of social power' (p. 123). Contextualized understandings of acculturation have been gleaned through research on acute cultural adaptation with Finnish swimmers (Ryba, Haapanen, Mosek, & Ng, 2012), transnational soccer players' career transitions (Agergaard & Ryba, 2014), and the acculturation pathways of immigrant athletes (Schinke et al., 2016; Schinke, McGannon, Battochio, & Wells, 2013) and relocated Aboriginal athletes (Blodgett & Schinke, 2015; Blodgett et al., 2014). These researchers have illustrated acculturation as an open-ended and ongoing process of cultural negotiations, which occur across all domains of daily life (see also the temporal model developed by Ryba et al., 2016). This scholarship has emphasized a critical need for researchers and practitioners to recognize transnational/migrant athletes' embeddedness within multiple cultural contexts, and to support practices that facilitate belonging in both the home and receiving cultures.

Cultural Praxis

Cultural praxis was first introduced to sport psychology by Ryba and Wright (2005, 2010) and has since been advocated as a critical form of CSP research that moves beyond academic knowledge production towards an agenda of social change (Blodgett et al., 2015; McGannon & Smith, 2015; Ryba & Schinke, 2009; Ryba et al., 2013). Cultural praxis operates as a 'heuristic' that blends together cultural studies theory, activism as practice, and empirical research as the mediator between theory and practice, 'with the various components held together with a progressive politics that focuses on social difference, equity, and justice' (Ryba & Wright, 2005, p. 201). Scholars advocating cultural praxis have called for researchers to transcend tradition and take up a reflexive sensibility towards local cultures and subjectivities, within both research and practice. Such research opens up space for culturally marginalized participants to share accounts of the sociocultural structures and social injustices that constrain their lives and contribute to knowledge production that is more critically connected to their interests and needs (Blodgett et al., 2015; Ryba & Wright, 2005; Schinke, McGannon, & Smith, 2013).

Stambulova and Ryba (2013, 2014) sought to move beyond theoretical discussions of cultural praxis and initiated a novel research trajectory termed *cultural praxis of athletes' careers*, wherein career theories, research, and assistance are interwoven and infused by culture. The authors articulated a set of conceptual and applied challenges for researchers to embrace sociocultural differences and generate knowledge that is meaningful in the lives of marginalized sport participants. Ryba (2017) noted that, in seven studies published in 2015–2016, researchers attempted to engage with some of these cultural praxis challenges. Researchers explicitly positioned within the cultural praxis of athletes' careers focused on the dual career transitions of adolescent Swedish athletes (Stambulova, Engstrom, Franck, Linner, & Lindahl, 2015), transnational athletes (Ryba, Stambulova, Ronkainen, Bundgaard, & Selänne, 2015), and Canadian Aboriginal athletes (Blodgett & Schinke, 2015). Notably, the researchers embraced a holistic developmental perspective of athletes to account for their simultaneous transitions within and outside sport; reflexively situated their projects within local sociocultural contexts to espouse culturally relevant meanings and experiences; and engaged idiosyncratic approaches that are sensitive to diversity in career patterns and experiences, and that further encourage idiosyncratic responses in career services. The researchers demonstrated how career decisions and the development of athletes 'on the move' unfold within shifting cultural dynamics, which create unique challenges and support needs.

Building on the career literature, Kavoura et al. (2015) used Foucauldian discourse analysis to examine the ways in which female Greek judokas constructed their sport careers and identities in relation to gender power dynamics that intersected with both the globalized judo culture and local Greek culture. Drawing on feminist cultural praxis, the researchers centralized the need for sport researchers and practitioners to support female martial artists in reconstructing martial arts as a field to which they possess the ability and right to belong. Multiple other scholars drawing on cultural praxis (Ronkainen & Ryba, 2017; Ronkainen, Watkins, & Ryba, 2016; Ryba, Ronkainen, & Selänne, 2015) have shared a focus on examining 'sporting narratives and gendered cultural practices that create a discursive field of athletic career from which athletes derive meanings underpinning their career construction' (Ryba, 2017, p. 125).

Outside athletes' careers, minimal research has been conducted with an explicit cultural praxis agenda. One notable example is decolonizing community research that was conducted with Aboriginal community members in Canada, aimed at centralizing local indigenous research perspectives through community members' narratives (Blodgett et al., 2011). Given that the cultural praxis research trajectory is still in its infancy, various CSP scholars have delineated possible directions and recommendations for future empirical research that centralizes cultural praxis tenets (Blodgett et al., 2015; McGannon & Smith, 2015; Ryba, 2017; Ryba et al., 2013; see also Volume 2, Chapter 16, 'Cultural Praxis').

Organizational Culture in Sport

Similar to the cultural praxis projects reviewed above, the study of organizational culture is an emerging trajectory in sport psychology (Bailey, Benson, & Bruner, 2017; Cruickshank & Collins, 2012; Cruickshank, Collins, & Minten, 2015; Eubank, Nesti, & Cruickshank, 2014; McCalla & Fitzpatrick, 2016; McDougall, Nesti, Richardson, & Littlewood, 2017). Although this research has not been explicitly framed as part of CSP, researchers exploring cultural issues in sport organizations have often adopted qualitative methodologies and highlighted the centrality of culture in understanding issues surrounding athlete development, well-being, and performance. After Fletcher and Wagstaff (2009) highlighted the lack of research on organizational culture in sport, a number of scholars started to explore cultural features of sport environments and their implications for individuals embedded in these organizations. Reviews of this literature (Maitland, Hills, & Rhind, 2015; Wagstaff & Burton-Wylie, 2018) have indicated that the scholarship has mainly focused on elite sport organizations and has been driven by an applied agenda aimed at creating more successful sport organizations.

Sport psychology scholarship has frequently drawn on Schein's (1990) conceptualization of organizational culture, which describes three levels of culture: artefacts, espoused values, and underlying assumptions (e.g., Bailey et al., 2017; Henriksen, 2015; Henriksen, Larsen, & Christensen, 2014; Larsen, Alfermann, Henriksen, & Christensen, 2013; McCalla & Fitzpatrick, 2016). For example, Henriksen, Larsen, and colleagues drew from this perspective and employed a holistic ecological approach to identify successful and less successful talent development environments in the Nordic context (Henriksen et al., 2014; Larsen et al., 2013). In addition to identifying values and practices that characterized successful environments (e.g., proximal role models, focus on long-term development, and support for the development of psychosocial skills), they suggested that the organizational culture in successful environments was coherent across Schein's (1990) three levels of culture. Furthermore, Henriksen (2015) documented a culture change intervention informed by Schein's model of culture and the holistic ecological approach.

Other researchers have further explored the processes of culture change and how it might be facilitated by key actors in sport organizations (Cruickshank & Collins, 2012; Cruickshank et al., 2015; Wagstaff, Fletcher, & Hanton, 2012). Eubank et al. (2014) discussed the potential role of a sport psychologist as a 'cultural architect' and the demands they will face in not only consulting individual athletes but also addressing organizational issues. However, several authors have raised concerns about the lack of training and expertise on organizational culture in sport psychology, suggesting that many novice practitioners are unprepared to address these issues in practical work (Fletcher & Arnold, 2011; Fletcher & Wagstaff, 2009). At the same time, the practice-focused approach has also been critiqued for not sufficiently addressing the theoretical foundations of the culture concept (Maitland et al., 2015; McDougall et al., 2017). Wagstaff and Burton-Wylie (2018) discussed the potential future trend of drawing on the spirit and approaches of CSP to develop a better balance between performance and well-being issues and to address power imbalances and fluid meanings in how organizational cultures in sport are constructed and negotiated.

Applied Practice

The CSP scholarship has several implications for sport and exercise psychology practitioners. Ryba et al. (2013) discussed cultural competence issues in applied sport psychology and highlighted three interrelated issues: (1) developing cultural awareness and reflexivity, (2) cultural competence in communication, and (c) designing interventions in a culturally competent manner. We will discuss each aspect briefly; for a more detailed discussion, see Ryba et al. (2013).

CSP researchers have highlighted the importance of recognizing different cultural identities of ourselves (as researchers/practitioners) and our clients/participants (Blodgett et al., 2017; McGannon & Smith, 2015; Sarkar, Hill, & Parker, 2015). For example, Sarkar et al. (2015) discussed specific issues when working with religious and spiritual athletes, encouraging practitioners not only to study basic knowledge about different religions, but also to reflect on their own beliefs and to experience different spiritual and religious practices to move beyond cognitive understandings of such issues. In relation to this, Blodgett et al. (2017) found that elite female boxers sometimes hid their religious and spiritual identities because they did not align with mainstream sport psychology practices and notions of being an athlete (where the focus is solely on developing mental and physical strength, not spiritual strength). A 'don't ask, don't tell' attitude was revealed around religion/spirituality, which at times left the athletes feeling unbalanced in their sport context.

For culturally competent communication, it is important for sport psychology practitioners to engage with athletes as holistic people and create safe spaces where clients can discuss various aspects of who they are (i.e., their cultural identities, including religious and spiritual beliefs, as well as various other facets). When individuals are given the opportunity to share self-stories and are met with understanding, support, and empathy, the experience lends to positive mental health, personal development, and empowerment (Blodgett et al., 2017; Douglas & Carless, 2009).

Finally, Ryba et al. (2013) raised awareness that the dominant models of sport psychology intervention draw upon Euro-American psychological theories and might not be appropriate for athletes with different cultural backgrounds, beliefs, and values. To return to the example of religion and spirituality, Balague (1999) suggested that interventions such as positive self-talk might not be appropriate for those Christian athletes for whom humility is a core religious virtue. As she noted, lack of understanding of the clients' world-view is likely to make the interventions ineffective, but also to lead the clients to lose trust in the practitioner who has been insensitive to their beliefs and values. Furthermore, scholars have explored cultural issues and their implications for applied sport psychology service delivery in non-Western national cultural contexts, including China (Si, Duan, Li, & Jiang, 2011) and Malaysia (Roy, Kuan, & Tenenbaum, 2016), highlighting the need to understand various dimensions of culture including ethnicity, race, religion and spirituality, and ideology when working with athletes.

A final question for consideration is the possibility for practitioners to work towards culture change. CSP scholars have highlighted the need for interventions to combat the potential detrimental effects of elite sport involvement on athletes' mental health and well-being (Carless & Douglas, 2013; Douglas, 2014), as well as issues in relation to marginalization and unequal opportunities for participation (Lee, Bernstein, Etzel, Gearity, & Kuklick, 2018; Schinke, Stambulova, et al., 2016). From the organizational psychology perspective, scholars have discussed the need for sport psychologists to contribute to the creation and modification of high-performance cultures to optimize elite sport environments' potential for success and to ensure the well-being of their members and employees (Cruickshank & Collins, 2012; Fletcher & Wagstaff, 2009; Henriksen et al., 2014). Although cultural praxis is action-oriented (i.e., it aims to promote social change and justice), it is recognized that attempting to change culture can be problematic, both because cultures are fragmented and fluid (rather than knowable and fixed entities) and because of the ethical issues involved in trying to change cultural insiders' beliefs and values. CSP scholars have specifically cautioned against trying to mould minority athletes' responses to fit the mainstream culture in the name of competitive success (Ryba et al., 2013), and that sport psychology practitioners might unintentionally contribute to a culture where athletes are exploited (Ryba, 2009). Therefore, sport psychology practitioners need to be aware of their potential role in perpetuating hegemonic cultural norms and critically examine whose interests are being served in their work towards culture change.

One potential way of working towards cultural change in a potentially problematic sport environment is to engage cultural insiders in dialogues that help them in becoming critically aware of the lived culture of their environment and thus potential agents for social change (Ryba, 2009). Sport psychology practitioners can challenge the dominant cultural ethos of the sport environment by identifying and actively promoting alternative cultural narratives that provide different ways of giving meaning to sport participation and, thus, challenge some of the taken-for-granted beliefs and values ingrained in the sport cultures (Carless & Douglas, 2013; Ronkainen & Ryba, 2017).

Conclusion

CSP researchers have provided a growing body of literature on cultural issues in sport to support the development of culturally competent practitioners. This will hopefully provide the future generation of consultants with readiness to encounter and work with culturally diverse athletes and to promote the creation of more culturally safe and inclusive spaces for sport participation and performance.

References

Agergaard, S., & Ryba, T. V. (2014). Migration and career transitions in professional sports: Transnational athletic careers in a psychological and sociological perspective. *Sociology of Sport Journal, 31,* 228–247.

Alfermann, D., Stambulova, N., & Zemaityte, A. (2004). Reactions to sport career termination: A cross-national comparison of German, Lithuanian, and Russian athletes. *Psychology of Sport and Exercise, 5,* 61–75.

Anshell, M. H., Williams, L. R. T., & Hodge, K. (1997). Cross-cultural and gender differences on coping style in sport. *International Journal of Sport Psychology, 28,* 141–156.

Asghar, E., Wang, X., Linde, K., & Alfermann, D. (2013). Comparisons between Asian and German male adolescent athletes on goal orientation, physical self-concept, and competitive anxiety. *International Journal of Sport and Exercise Psychology, 11,* 229–243.

Bailey, B., Benson, A. J., & Bruner, M. W. (2017). Investigating the organisational culture of crossFit. *International Journal of Sport and Exercise Psychology,* Advanced online publication. doi:1612197X.2017.1329223.

Balague, G. (1999). Understanding identity, value, and meaning when working with elite athletes. *The Sport Psychologist, 13,* 89–98.

Berry, J. W. (2009). A critique of critical acculturation. *International Journal of Intercultural Relations, 33,* 361–371.

Berry, J. W., Poortinga, Y. H., Breugelmans, S. M., Chasiotis, A., & Sam, D. L. (2011). *Cross-cultural psychology: Research and applications* (3rd ed.). Cambridge: Cambridge University Press.

Blodgett, A. T., Ge, Y., Schinke, R. J., & McGannon, K. R. (2017). Intersecting identities of elite female boxers: Stories of cultural difference and marginalization in sport. *Psychology of Sport and Exercise, 32,* 83–92.

Blodgett, A. T., & Schinke, R. J. (2015). 'When you're coming from the reserve you're not supposed to make it': Stories of aboriginal athletes pursuing sport and academic careers in 'mainstream' cultural contexts. *Psychology of Sport and Exercise, 21,* 115–124.

Blodgett, A. T., Schinke, R. J., McGannon, K. R., Coholic, D. A., Enosse, L., Peltier, D., & Pheasant, C. (2014). Navigating the insider-outsider hyphen: A qualitative exploration of the acculturation challenges of aboriginal athletes pursuing sport in Euro-Canadian contexts. *Psychology of Sport and Exercise, 15,* 345–355.

Blodgett, A. T., Schinke, R. J., McGannon, K. R., & Fisher, L. A. (2015). Cultural sport psychology research: Conceptions, evolutions, and forecasts. *International Review of Sport and Exercise Psychology, 8,* 24–43.

Blodgett, A. T., Schinke, R. J., Smith, B., Peltier, D., & Pheasant, C. (2011). In indigenous words: Exploring vignettes as a narrative strategy for presenting the research voices of aboriginal community members. *Qualitative Inquiry, 17,* 522–533.

Brandão, M. R. F., & Vieira, L. F. (2013). Athletes' careers in Brazil: Research and application in the land of ginga. In N. Stambulova & T. V. Ryba (Eds.), *Athletes' careers across cultures* (pp. 43–52). London: Routledge.

Butryn, T. M. (2009). (Re)examining whiteness in sport psychology through autonarrative excavation. *International Journal of Sport and Exercise Psychology, 7,* 323–341.

Butryn, T. M. (2010). Interrogating whiteness in sport psychology. In T. V. Ryba, R. J. Schinke & G. Tenenbaum (Eds.), *The cultural turn in sport psychology* (pp. 127–152). Morgantown, WV: Fitness Information Technology.

Carless, D., & Douglas, K. (2012). Stories of success: Cultural narratives and personal stories of elite and professional athletes. *Reflective Practice, 13,* 387–398.

Carless, D., & Douglas, K. (2013). Living, resisting, and playing the part of athlete: Narrative tensions in elite sport. *Psychology of Sport and Exercise, 14,* 701–708.

Carless, D., Sparkes, A. C., Douglas, K., & Cooke, C. (2014). Disability, inclusive adventurous training and adapted sport: Two soldiers' stories of involvement. *Psychology of Sport and Exercise, 15,* 124–131.

Cosh, S., LeCouteur, A., Crabb, S., & Kettler, L. (2013). Career transitions and identity: A discursive psychological approach to exploring athlete identity in retirement and the transition back into elite sport. *Qualitative Research in Sport, Exercise and Health, 5,* 21–42.

Cruickshank, A., & Collins, D. (2012). Culture change in elite sport performance teams: Examining and advancing effectiveness in the new era. *Journal of Applied Sport Psychology, 24,* 338–355.

Cruickshank, A., Collins, D., & Minten, S. (2015). Driving and sustaining culture change in professional sport performance teams: A grounded theory. *Psychology of Sport and Exercise, 20,* 40–50.

D'Andrade, R. G. (1995). *The development of cognitive anthropology.* Cambridge, MA: Cambridge University Press.

Douglas, K. (2014). Challenging interpretive privilege in elite and professional sport: One [athlete's] story, revised, reshaped and reclaimed. *Qualitative Research in Sport, Exercise and Health, 6,* 220–243.

Douglas, K., & Carless, D. (2009). Abandoning the performance narrative: Two women's stories of transition from professional sport. *Journal of Applied Sport Psychology, 21,* 213–230.

Duda, J. L., & Allison, M. T. (1990). Cross-cultural analysis in exercise and sport psychology: A void in the field. *Journal of Sport and Exercise Psychology, 12,* 114–131.

Eubank, M., Nesti, M., & Cruickshank, A. (2014). Understanding high performance sport environments: Impact for the professional training and supervision of sport psychologists. *Sport and Exercise Psychology Review, 10,* 30–36.

Fisher, L. A., Butryn, T. M., & Roper, E. A. (2003). Diversifying (and politicizing) sport psychology: A promising perspective. *The Sport Psychologist, 17,* 391–405.

Fletcher, D., & Arnold, R. (2011). A qualitative study of performance leadership and management in elite sport. *Journal of Applied Sport Psychology, 23,* 223–242.

Fletcher, D., & Wagstaff, C. R. (2009). Organizational psychology in elite sport: Its emergence, application and future. *Psychology of Sport and Exercise, 10,* 427–434.

Forsyth, J., & Heine, M. (2010). Indigenous research and decolonizing methodologies. In T. V. Ryba, R. J. Schinke & G. Tenenbaum (Eds.), *The cultural turn in sport psychology* (pp. 181–202). Morgantown, WV: Fitness Information Technology.

Geertz, C. (1973). *The interpretation of cultures.* New York: Basic Books.

Giles, A. R. (2013). It takes several northern communities to raise a reflexive and effective sport researcher. In R. J. Schinke & R. Lidor (Eds.), *Case studies in sport development: Contemporary stories promoting health, peace, and social justice* (pp. 119–131). Morgantown, WV: Fitness Information Technology.

Henriksen, K. (2015). Developing a high-performance culture: A sport psychology intervention from an ecological perspective in elite orienteering. *Journal of Sport Psychology in Action, 6,* 141–153.

Henriksen, K., Larsen, C. H., & Christensen, M. K. (2014). Looking at success from its opposite pole: The case of a talent development golf environment in Denmark. *International Journal of Sport and Exercise Psychology, 12,* 134–149.

Hofstede, G. (1984). *Culture's consequences: International differences in work-related values.* London: Sage.

Jowett, S., Adie, J. W., Bartholomew, K. J., Yang, S. X., Gustafsson, H., & Lopez-Jiménez, A. (2017). Motivational processes in the coach-athlete relationship: A multi-cultural self-determination approach. *Psychology of Sport and Exercise, 32,* 143–152.

Kavoura, A., Ryba, T. V., & Chroni, S. (2015). Negotiating female judoka identities in Greece: A Foucauldian discourse analysis. *Psychology of Sport and Exercise, 17,* 88–98.

Kitayama, S., Duffy, S., & Uchida, Y. (2007). Self as cultural mode of being. In S. Kitayama & D. Cohen (Eds.), *Handbook of cultural psychology* (pp. 136–173). New York: Guilford Press.

Kral, M. J., Burkhardt, K. J., & Kidd, S. (2002). The new research agenda for a cultural psychology. *Canadian Psychology/Psychologie Canadienne, 43,* 154–162.

Krane, V. (1994). A feminist perspective on contemporary sport psychology research. *The Sport Psychologist, 8,* 393–410.

Krane, V., Ross, S. R., Sullivan Barak, K., Lucas-Carr, C. B., & Robinson, C. L. (2014). Being a girl athlete. *Qualitative Research in Sport, Exercise and Health, 6,* 77–97.

Larsen, C. H., Alfermann, D., Henriksen, K., & Christensen, M. K. (2013). Successful talent development in soccer: The characteristics of the environment. *Sport, Exercise, and Performance Psychology, 2,* 190–206.

Lee, S. M. (2015). Cultural competence development in sport and exercise psychology graduate programs. *Athletic Insight, 7,* 269–289.

Lee, S. M., Bernstein, M. B., Etzel, E. F., Gearity, B. T., & Kuklick, C. R. (2018). Student-athletes' experiences with racial microaggressions in sport: A Foucauldian discourse analysis. *The Qualitative Report, 23,* 1016–1043.

Maitland, A., Hills, L., & Rhind, D. (2015). Organisational culture in sport – A systematic review. *Sport Management Review, 18,* 501–516.

McCalla, T., & Fitzpatrick, S. (2016). Integrating sport psychology within a high-performance team: Potential stakeholders, micropolitics, and culture. *Journal of Sport Psychology in Action, 7,* 33–42.

McDougall, M., Nesti, M., Richardson, D., & Littlewood, M. (2017). Emphasising the culture in culture change: Examining current perspectives of culture and offering some alternative ones. *Sport & Exercise Psychology Review, 13,* 47–59.

McGannon, K. R., & Schinke, R. J. (2013). 'My first choice is to work out at work; then I don't feel bad about my kids': A discursive psychological analysis of motherhood and physical activity participation. *Psychology of Sport and Exercise, 14,* 179–188.

McGannon, K. R., & Smith, B. (2015). Centralizing culture in cultural sport psychology research: The potential of narrative inquiry and discursive psychology. *Psychology of Sport and Exercise, 17,* 79–87.

McHugh, T.-L. F., Coppola, A. M., & Sinclair, S. (2013). An exploration of the meanings of sport to urban aboriginal youth: A photovoice approach. *Qualitative Research in Sport, Exercise and Health, 5,* 291–311.

Oyserman, D., Coon, H. M., & Kemmelmeier, M. (2002). Rethinking individualism and collectivism: Evaluation of theoretical assumptions and meta-analyses. *Psychological Bulletin, 128,* 3–72.

Ronkainen, N. J., Kavoura, A., & Ryba, T. V. (2016a). A meta-study of athletic identity research in sport psychology: Current status and future directions. *International Review of Sport and Exercise Psychology, 9,* 45–64.

Ronkainen, N. J., Kavoura, A., & Ryba, T. V. (2016b). Narrative and discursive perspectives on athlete identity: Past, present and, future. *Psychology of Sport and Exercise, 27,* 128–137.

Ronkainen, N. J., & Ryba, T. V. (2017). Rethinking age in athletic retirement: An existential-narrative perspective. *International Journal of Sport and Exercise Psychology, 15,* 146–159.

Ronkainen, N. J., Ryba, T. V., & Nesti, M. S. (2013). 'The engine just started coughing!' – Limits of physical performance, aging and career continuity in elite endurance sports. *Journal of Aging Studies, 27,* 387–397.

Ronkainen, N. J., Watkins, I., & Ryba, T. V. (2016). What can gender tell us about the pre-retirement experiences of elite distance runners in Finland? A thematic narrative analysis. *Psychology of Sport and Exercise, 22,* 37–45.

Roy, J., Kuan, G., & Tenenbaum, G. (2016). Sport psychology service delivery in Malaysia: An introduction to common cultural norms and experiences. *Journal of Physical Activity, Sport Psychology and Exercise, 1,* 22–29.

Ryba, T. V. (2009). Understanding your role in cultural sport psychology. In S. Hanrahan & R. J. Schinke (Eds.), *Cultural sport psychology* (pp. 33–44). Champaign, IL: Human Kinetics.

Ryba, T. V. (2017). Cultural sport psychology: A critical review of empirical advances. *Current Opinion in Psychology, 16,* 123–127.

Ryba, T. V., Haapanen, S., Mosek, S., & Ng, K. (2012). Towards a conceptual understanding of acute cultural adaptation: A preliminary examination of ACA in female swimming. *Qualitative Research in Sport, Exercise, and Health, 4,* 80–97.

Ryba, T. V., Ronkainen, N. J., & Selänne, H. (2015). Elite athletic career as a context for life design. *Journal of Vocational Behavior, 88,* 47–55.

Ryba, T. V., & Schinke, R. J. (2009). Methodology as a ritualized Eurocentrism: Introduction to the special issue. *International Journal of Sport and Exercise Psychology, 7,* 263–274.

Ryba, T. V., Schinke, R. J., Stambulova, N., & Elbe, A.-M. (2018). ISSP position stand: Transnationalism, mobility, and acculturation in and through sport. *International Journal of Sport & Exercise Psychology, 16,* 520–534.

Ryba, T. V., Schinke, R. J., & Tenenbaum, G. (Eds.). (2010). *The cultural turn in sport psychology.* Morgantown, WV: Fitness Information Technology.

Ryba, T. V., Stambulova, N., Si, G., & Schinke, R. J. (2013). ISSP position stand: Culturally competent research and practice in sport and exercise psychology. *International Journal of Sport and Exercise Psychology, 11,* 123–142.

Ryba, T. V., Stambulova, N. B., & Ronkainen, N. J. (2016). The work of cultural transition: An emerging model. *Frontiers in Psychology, 7,* 427.

Ryba, T. V., Stambulova, N. B., Ronkainen, N. J., Bundgaard, J., & Selänne, H. (2015). Dual career pathways of transnational athletes. *Psychology of Sport and Exercise, 21,* 125–134.

Ryba, T. V., & Wright, H. K. (2005). From mental game to cultural praxis: A cultural studies model's implications for the future of sport psychology. *Quest, 57,* 192–219.

Ryba, T. V., & Wright, H. K. (2010). Sport psychology and the cultural turn: Notes toward cultural praxis. In T. V. Ryba, R. J. Schinke, & G. Tenenbaum (Eds.), *The cultural turn in sport and exercise psychology* (pp. 3–27). Morgantown, WV: Fitness Information Technology.

Sarkar, M., Hill, D. M., & Parker, A. (2015). Reprint of: Working with religious and spiritual athletes: Ethical considerations for sport psychologists. *Psychology of Sport and Exercise, 17*, 48–55.

Schein, E. H. (1990). Organizational culture. *American Psychologist, 45*, 109–119.

Schinke, R., & Hanrahan, S. J. (2009). *Cultural sport psychology.* Champaign, IL: Human Kinetics.

Schinke, R. J., Blodgett, A. T., McGannon, K. R., & Ge, Y. (2016). Finding one's footing on foreign soil: A composite vignette of elite athlete acculturation. *Psychology of Sport and Exercise, 25*, 36–43.

Schinke, R. J., & McGannon, K. R. (Eds.). (2014). *The psychology of sub-culture in sport and physical activity: Critical perspectives.* New York: Routledge.

Schinke, R. J., & McGannon, K. R. (2015). Cultural sport psychology and intersecting identities: An introduction in the special section. *Psychology of Sport and Exercise, 17*, 45–47.

Schinke, R. J., McGannon, K. R., Battochio, R. C., & Wells, G. (2013). Acculturation in elite sport: A thematic analysis of immigrant athletes and coaches. *Journal of Sports Sciences, 31*, 1676–1686.

Schinke, R. J., McGannon, K. R., & Smith, B. (2013). Expanding the sport and physical activity research landscape through community scholarship: Introduction. *Qualitative Research in Sport, Exercise and Health, 5*, 287–290.

Schinke, R. J., Stambulova, N. B., Lidor, R., Papaioannou, A., & Ryba, T. V. (2016). ISSP position stand: Social missions through sport and exercise psychology. *International Journal of Sport and Exercise Psychology, 14*, 4–22.

Shweder, R. A. (1991). *Thinking through cultures: Expeditions in cultural psychology.* Cambridge, MA: Harvard University Press.

Shweder, R. A. (1999). Why cultural psychology? *Ethos, 27*, 62–73.

Shweder, R. A. (2000). The psychology of practice and the practice of the three psychologies. *Asian Journal of Social Psychology, 3*, 207–222.

Si, G., Duan, Y., Li, H. Y., & Jiang, X. (2011). An exploration into socio-cultural meridians of Chinese athletes' psychological training. *Journal of Clinical Sport Psychology, 5*, 325–338.

Smith, B. (2013). Sporting spinal cord injuries, social relations, and rehabilitation narratives: An ethnographic creative non-fiction of becoming disabled through sport. *Sociology of Sport Journal, 30*, 132–152.

Smith, B., Bundon, A., & Best, M. (2016). Disability sport and activist identities: A qualitative study of narratives of activism among elite athletes with impairment. *Psychology of Sport and Exercise, 26*, 139–148.

Smith, B., Collinson, J. A., Phoenix, C., Brown, D., & Sparkes, A. (2009). Dialogue, monologue, and boundary crossing within research encounters: A performative narrative analysis. *International Journal of Sport and Exercise Psychology, 7*, 342–358.

Stambulova, N., Stephan, Y., & Jäphag, U. (2007). Athletic retirement: A cross-national comparison of elite French and Swedish athletes. *Psychology of Sport and Exercise, 8*, 101–118.

Stambulova, N. B., Engstrom, C., Franck, A., Linner, L., & Lindahl, K. (2015). Searching for an optimal balance: Dual career experiences of Swedish adolescent athletes. *Psychology of Sport and Exercise, 21*, 4–14.

Stambulova, N. B., & Ryba, T. V. (Eds.). (2013). *Athletes' careers across cultures.* London: Routledge.

Stambulova, N. B., & Ryba, T. V. (2014). A critical review of career research and assistance through the cultural lens: Towards cultural praxis of athletes' careers. *International Review of Sport and Exercise Psychology, 7*, 1–17.

Triandis, H. C., Malpass, R. S., & Davidson, A. R. (1971). Cross-cultural psychology. *Biennial Review of Anthropology, 7*, 1–84.

Triandis, H. C., McCusker, C., & Hui, C. H. (1990). Multimethod probes of individualism and collectivism. *Journal of Personality and Social Psychology, 59*, 1006–1020.

Tylor, E. B. (1871). *Primitive culture: Researches into the development of mythology, philosophy, religion, language, art and custom.* London: J. Murray.

Valsiner, J. (2014). *An invitation to cultural psychology.* London: Sage.

Wagstaff, C., & Burton-Wylie, S. (2018). Organizational culture in sport: A conceptual, definitional, and methodological review. *Sport and Exercise Psychology Review, 14*, 32–52.

Wagstaff, C. R. D., Fletcher, D., & Hanton, S. (2012). Positive organizational psychology in sport. *International Review of Sport and Exercise Psychology, 5*, 87–103.

8

DEPRESSION AND ATHLETES

Erlanger A. Turner

Introduction

Major depressive disorder (MDD) is a serious public health concern across the developmental spectrum. According to the *Diagnostic and Statistical Manual of Mental Disorders*, Fifth Edition (American Psychiatric Association, 2013), the essential features of major depressive disorder consist of a period of depressed mood for at least 2 weeks during which the individual experiences either depressed mood or loss of interest or pleasure in almost all activities. Carrington (2006) also noted that symptoms of MDD may include: sadness, anhedonia (loss of pleasure), loss of motivation, reduced or no social activities or interactions, disturbances in sleeping patterns, eating patterns, or sexual functioning, difficulty concentrating or synthesizing, and memory losses.

Statistics show that depression is a frequent concern, and it is associated with economic, health, and social costs to society. Recent data indicate that one in five adults worldwide are diagnosed with depression and anxiety each year (Cuijpers, Kleiboer, Karyotaki, & Riper, 2017). It has been estimated that approximately 322 million people in the world are living with depression, with rates approximately 5.1% and 3.6% among females and males, respectively (World Health Organization, 2017). Furthermore, lifetime prevalence rates in the United States are approximately 17%, with rates of 20–25% for women and 9–12% for men, respectively (Craighead, Johnson, Carey, & Dunlop, 2015). Similarly, studies suggest similar findings among college students and college athletes, with prevalence rates of depression ranging from 15% to 21% (Wolanin, Gross, & Hong, 2015). The focus of this section will be to give an overview of the etiology of depression, highlight the connections between sports and mental health functioning, and conclude with a discussion of assessment and treatment.

Etiology of Depression

Several models have described how biological and environmental factors trigger depressive symptoms such as cognitive, interpersonal, and vulnerability stress models. According to the cognitive model of depression, depressive symptoms result from individuals' tendencies to negatively perceive themselves, the environment, and their future. Depressed individuals tend to view the environment as overwhelming, as presenting insurmountable obstacles that cannot be overcome, and as continually resulting in failure or loss (Young, Rygh, Weinberger, & Beck,

2007). In contrast, the interpersonal model of depression describes how individuals' interpersonal relationships play a role in the onset and maintenance of depressive symptoms (Craighead et al., 2015). Difficulties in interpersonal relationships may include four major problem areas: grief, interpersonal disputes, role transitions, and interpersonal deficits such as social isolation (Craighead, Hart, Craighead, & Ilardi, 2002). Furthermore, some individuals have a biological predisposition that may increase risk of developing depression. According to the vulnerability stress model, depression results from a predisposition for depression, and symptoms are then triggered by environmental stress such as loss of a relationship (Tompson, McNeil, Rea, & Asarnow, 2000). There is a significant amount of research that supports these multiple explanations. For example, research has shown that offspring of depressed parents are at a higher risk for the disorder owing to genetics (Brennan, Katz, Hammen, & LeBrocque, 2002).

Sports and Mental Health Outcomes

Among athletes in various sports, studies demonstrate the relationship between sports and mental health. According to Wolanin et al. (2015), approximately one out of five athletes experiences depression. Furthermore, some have noted that, because athletes deal with more stress than non-athletes, they may be at a higher risk of experiencing clinical mental health problems or developing subclinical mental ill health (Henriksen et al., 2019; Wolanin et al., 2015). Among college students, depression and anxiety are often comorbid with other problems such as sleep difficulties, which may exacerbate depressive and anxious symptoms, whether an athlete or non-athlete (Boehm, Lei, Lloyd, & Prichard, 2016). One study using college basketball players found that 15% met criteria for MDD, compared with 29.4% of non-athletes (Proctor & Boan-Lenzo, 2010). In a sample of 465 NCAA Division One athletes, another study found that 23.7% reported clinical levels of depression and 6.3% reported moderate to severe levels (Wolanin, Hong, Marks, Panchoo, & Gross, 2016). In one retrospective study, the authors (Wolanin et al., 2015) noted that athletes who experience injuries during the season tend to report higher depression symptoms compared with athletes without a history of injuries within the past year. Female athletes are also more likely to exhibit depression than their male counterparts. This may be owing to gender differences in depression (American Psychiatric Association, 2013). Wolanin and colleagues (2015) reported in their study that female athletes were 1.8 times more likely to meet diagnostic criteria for depression. Given these data, it is important to address depression in student athletes. Depressive symptoms may lead to decreased performance on the field or academic challenges in courses (Wolanin et al., 2015).

Another important consideration for athletes and mental health concerns such as depression is functioning after retirement. According to decades of research, poor mental health may be more likely depending on how an athlete's career is terminated (e.g., Werthner & Orlick, 1986; Wolanin et al., 2015). For example, published work indicates that voluntary termination (i.e., personal decision to retire) versus involuntary (i.e., injury, getting cut from team) career termination is associated with better adjustment, whereas involuntary career termination is more likely to result in depressive symptoms (Werthner & Orlick, 1986; Wolanin et al., 2015). Additionally, data from the National Football League (NFL) has indicated that retired players with a history of concussions were three times more likely to meet criteria for MDD than retired athletes with no history of concussions (Kerr, Marshall, Harding, & Guskiewicz, 2012). This is possibly one of the reasons why the NFL has sought to improve protection of players and address issues to prevention concussions.

Assessment of Major Depressive Disorder

Screening and assessment are important components of psychological treatment. Turner and Mills (2016) noted the following:

> Psychological assessment has several important purposes including: clarifying a diagnosis to facilitate communication among professionals which provides a clinical picture of the patient's difficulties, assisting the clinician in treatment planning and intervention selection consistent with evidence-based treatment, and monitoring treatment progress or outcomes to determine whether an individual continues to meet criteria for a diagnosis over the course of treatment.
>
> (p. 21)

Although it is important to engage in assessment, there is variability in what this process looks like across settings. For example, Jensen-Doss (2011) indicated that clinicians are not consistently following evidence-based assessment guidelines as recommended. According to current knowledge, practitioners primarily use unstructured clinical interviews to complete assessment and diagnosis (Jensen-Doss & Hawley, 2010). However, it is recommended that both unstructured and structured assessment methods be used to reduce bias and increase accuracy of diagnosis (e.g., Henriksen et al., 2019; Joiner, Walker, Pettit, Perez, & Cukrowicz, 2005).

With regard to assessment of depression, the evidence suggests that valid and reliable measures exist to screen for depression. Further, findings indicate no clear limitations with depression assessment measures regarding ethnicity and gender (Joiner et al., 2005). To identify depressive symptoms, screening measures or interviews may be used. Self-report measures are commonly used as an initial screening assessment to help capture symptoms. Evidence has supported the use of several self-report measures such as the Center for Epidemiological Studies Depression Scale (Radloff, 1977) and the Beck Depression Inventory (Beck, Steer, & Brown, 1996). Although they are useful for screening, some limitations may exist. For example, they capture the diagnostic criteria of depressive disorder but do not obtain information on the degree of functional impairment (Henriksen et al., 2019; Joiner et al., 2005). Consistent with evidence-based assessment, clinicians should consider incorporating structured interviews in their assessment process. However, Joiner and colleagues (2005) indicate that structured clinical interviews may not be practical for assessing symptom severity and change over multiple occasions. Therefore, it is imperative to rely on self-report measures to track clinical progress over the course of treatment.

Treatment Considerations for Depression

Although MDD is a significant public health concern, many individuals do not seek mental health treatment. Regardless of the diagnosis or mental health issue, some report that only approximately 35% of individuals who experience a mental health issue seek professional treatment (Turner et al., 2016). Additionally, studies document age, gender, and ethnic differences in treatment seeking. Numerous barriers may exist that influence these disparities in treatment seeking. For example, many individuals from ethnic and cultural groups may avoid treatment owing to lack of access, financial concerns, negative perceptions and attitudes, cultural beliefs, or preference for a same-race provider (Turner, Camarillo, Daniel, Otero, & Parker, 2017; Turner et al., 2016). Differences in recognizing and reporting depression have also been reported between athletes and non-athletes. Some studies indicate that athletes may be more likely to underreport symptoms of depression to portray themselves more favourably or to hide their difficulties from their coaches owing to fear of their coaches' reactions (Wolanin et al., 2015). One possible explanation for underreporting is that athletes may want to present as mentally prepared to take on the challenge of competing. As a result, there may be fear of not being allowed to compete by their coach.

According to decades of research, depression may result in personal and family suffering and societal burdens, such as role impairment and an increased use of mental and medical services (Craighead et al., 2015; Cuijpers et al., 2017). Given these issues, it is important to assist individuals with accessing treatment. Numerous studies have examined the efficacy of psychosocial treatments for depression. In the literature, effective psychosocial interventions for depression include cognitive behavioural therapy (CBT), interpersonal therapy (IPT), behaviour therapy (BT) such as behavioural activation, and problem-solving therapy (Aaronson, Katzman, & Moster, 2015; Craighead et al., 2015). Several clinical trials and meta-analytic studies have concluded that these interventions are effective either alone or in combination with pharmacological treatments (e.g., antidepressants). In a recent review (Cuijpers et al., 2017), the authors noted that these interventions are typically equally effective, but non-directive interventions appear less effective (e.g., psychodynamic therapies). Furthermore, when implementing psychological intervention with individuals from diverse backgrounds, it is also important to consider how multicultural competence influences the therapy relationship and intervention success (e.g., Hall, Ibaraki, Huang, Marti, & Stice, 2016; Turner, 2019). According to a recent meta-analysis, interventions targeting African Americans yield small-to-medium effect sizes compared with culturally adapted treatments (Jones, Huey, & Rubenson, 2018). Studies also report similar effect sizes with culturally sensitive therapies among other ethnic groups (Kalibatseva & Leong, 2014). The following sections will briefly describe some of the research on these interventions.

Research on Evidence-Based Interventions

CBT is based on the notion that thoughts, actions, and feeling are closely related. CBT is one of the most widely used evidence-based interventions for depression and other psychological disorders. According to Craighead and colleagues (2015), CBT is a short-term directive intervention that aims to reduce the individual's negative view of the self, world, and future. Therapy generally involves informing the client of the therapeutic process, implementing strategies to increase active behavioural performance, increasing monitoring of thoughts and behaviours, and changing negative or irrational beliefs that precipitate MDD (Craighead et al., 2015). Cognitive models propose that a number of processes (e.g., dysfunctional attitudes or beliefs, cognitive distortions, and negative attributional style) may play a role in the development and maintenance of MDD (Reinecke, Ryan, & DuBoise, 1998). In general, CBT appears to be effective in treating depression among adolescents and adult populations (Craighead et al., 2015; Cuijpers et al., 2017). Results tend to be positive whether treatment is delivered in individual or group formats. However, clinicians should be cautious with implementing CBT with ethnic and cultural groups. Some research suggests that culturally adapted interventions may result in greater reductions in depression symptoms (Carrington, 2006; Jones et al., 2018). For example, when working with international populations, it may be important to integrate aspects of faith into treatment.

In contrast to CBT, IPT is based on the notion that an individual's interpersonal relationships play a role in the onset and maintenance of depressive symptoms (Gillies, 2001). IPT is a time-limited therapy (12–16 weeks) that focuses on the identification and improvement of difficulties in interpersonal functioning associated with the current MDD episode (Craighead et al., 2015). Therapy focuses primarily on four problem areas: grief, interpersonal disputes, role transitions, and interpersonal deficits. Similar to CBT, decades of research on IPT exist on both youth and adult populations. For example, early adaptations of IPT for treating depression in adolescence sought to address adolescent developmental issues such as separation from parents, exploration of authority in relationship to parents, development of dyadic interpersonal relationships, experience with death of relatives or friends, and peer pressure (Mufson, Weissman, Moreau, & Garfinkel, 1999). Research on IPT with youth demonstrated significant decreases in depressive symptoms and improvement in functioning across numerous studies (Mufson & Fairbanks, 1996; Mufson et al., 1994). In adult populations, symptoms improvement has also been noted, with recovery ranging from 21% to 70% across studies (Craighead et al., 2015). Although IPT is useful for treating depression, Craighead et al. (2015) noted a caveat that the intervention may be more efficacious with acute depression.

Another common treatment for depression is based on principles of behaviourism. BT may involve monitoring and increasing positive daily activities, improving social and communication skills, increasing adaptive behaviours such as positive and negative assertion, increasing contingent positive reinforcement for adaptive behaviours, and decreasing negative life experiences (Craighead et al., 2015). One BT approach is behavioural activation (BA), which seeks to identify and promote engagement with activities and contexts that are reinforcing and consistent with an individual's goals (Dimidjian et al., 2006). Some studies have reported that behavioural activation may be as effective as cognitive therapy (CT). One study examined the effectiveness of BA compared with CT and medication, and the authors found that BA was comparable in efficacy to medication, and more efficacious than CT. Furthermore, the study reported that, among more severe cases of depression, BA and medication were comparable based on self-report clinical ratings. Several meta-analyses have also demonstrated that BA is effective across both youth and adult populations with medium-to-large effect sizes (for a complete review, see Mazzucchelli, Kane, & Rees, 2009; Tindall et al., 2017).

As the ethnic diversity of the United States continues to increase, treatment outcome studies generally do not include participants who adequately reflect the diversity of the population, which limits generalization. Some scholars and clinicians have been led to augment the literature to address this concern. For example, in a meta-analysis by Kalibatseva and Leong (2014), the authors reported on the examination of treatment as usual compared with cultural adaptations. In general, cultural adaptations were identified as more effective than no treatment ($d = 0.58$), treatment as usual ($d = 0.22$) and unadapted psychotherapy ($d = 0.32$; Kalibatseva & Leong, 2014). Furthermore, the authors noted that studies find that evidence-based treatments (EBTs) tested with ethnic and racial groups often show promising results. For example, Kalibatseva and Leong (2014) reported that CBT and IPT were effective treatments for African Americans and Latinos. Hall and colleagues (2016) also reported that CBT was effective with international populations. However, one of the challenges with interpreting the data on EBTs is that the studies or reviews combine traditional treatments and culturally sensitive elements, which reduces our understanding of the real treatment effects. Kalibatseva and Leong (2014) noted that adaptations often utilize a top–down approach by hiring bilingual and bicultural providers, offering all materials in the language of the group (e.g., Spanish, Mandarin), or adapting the materials and exercises to be culturally appropriate. In conclusion, culturally sensitive interventions appear effective, with effect sizes ranging from medium to large. (For a complete review, refer to Kalibatseva & Leong, 2014.)

Conclusion

Based on the literature, it appears that several EBTs are useful for addressing depression in athletes. Dismantling studies may continue to shed light on which specific treatment components may be most beneficial and for which populations. In the adult literature, there is no conclusive evidence suggesting that treatment modality selectively influences specific target behaviours. Imber and colleagues (1990) conducted a study comparing IPT, CBT, and imipramine. The results of the study did not show any significant mode-specific difference. However, common elements have been identified to be responsible for treatment improvements such as highly structured therapy, homework assignments, and training in skills (cognitive or behavioural) that the patient can use in handling their problems (Emmelkamp, 2004). Rossello and Bernal (1999) also suggested that integrating CBT and IPT may be promising for youth with depression. Given that both treatments are effective, a combination could be superior for patients who do not respond to one of these treatments individually. In the adult depression literature, results of combined treatment have been consistent with an additive model (e.g., Hollon & Beck, 2004).

With the increase in technology use and telepsychology, emerging areas for treating depression are being explored. For example, internet interventions are now being delivered through websites and the support by providers through secure messaging or mobile apps (e.g., Cuijpers et al., 2017). One large-scale clinical trial in the US examined the utility of Mobil apps to address mental health outcomes. Results of the study indicated that cognitive training and problem-solving apps demonstrated significant improvements in mood compared with the control app condition (Areán et al., 2016). In their review, Cuijpers and colleagues (2017) noted that internet and app interventions show promise for guided treatment and prevention. This emerging area may be particularly beneficial for athletes, given their practice and travel demands for games. Future work is needed to truly understand depression and treatment among athletes across all levels.

References

Aaronson, C. J., Katzman, G., & Moster, R. L. (2015). Combination pharmacotherapy and psychotherapy for the treatment of major depressive and anxiety disorders. In P. E. Nathan & J. M. Gorman (Eds.), *A guide to treatments that work* (4th ed., pp. 507–543). New York: Oxford University Press.

American Psychiatric Association. (2013). *Diagnostics and statistical manual of mental disorders* (5th ed.). Washington, DC: Author.

Areán, P. A., Hallgren, K. A., Jordan, J. T., Gazzaley, A., Atkins, D. C., Heagerty, P. J., & Anguera, J. A. (2016). The use and effectiveness of mobile apps for depression: Results from a fully remote clinical trial. *Journal of Medical Internet Research, 18*(12), e330.

Beck, A. T., Steer, R. A., & Brown, G. K. (1996). *Beck Depression Inventory-II (BDI-II)*. Toronto: The Psychological Corporation.

Boehm, M. A., Lei, Q. M., Lloyd, R. M., & Prichard, J. R. (2016). Depression, anxiety, and tobacco use: Overlapping impediments to sleep in a national sample of college students. *Journal of American College Health, 64*, 565–574.

Brennan, P., Katz, A., Hammen, C., & LeBrocque, R. (2002). Maternal depression, paternal psychopathology, and adolescent diagnostic outcomes. *Journal of Consulting and Clinical Psychology, 70*, 1075–1085.

Carrington, C. H. (2006). Clinical depression in African American women: Diagnoses, treatment, and research. *Journal of Clinical Psychology, 62*, 779–791.

Craighead, W. E., Hart, A. B., Craighead, L. W., & Ilardi, S. S. (2002). Psychosocial treatments for major depressive disorder. In P. E. Nathan & J. M. Gorman (Eds.), *A guide to treatments that work* (2nd ed., pp. 245–261). New York: Oxford University Press.

Craighead, W. E., Johnson, B. N., Carey, S., & Dunlop, B. W. (2015). Psychosocial treatments for major depressive disorder. In P. E. Nathan & J. M. Gorman (Eds.), *A guide to treatments that work* (4th ed., pp. 381–408). New York: Oxford University Press.

Cuijpers, P., Kleiboer, A., Karyotaki, E., & Riper, H. (2017). Internet and mobile interventions for depression: Opportunities and challenges. *Depression and Anxiety, 34,* 596–602.

Dimidjian, S., Hollon, S. D., Dobson, K. S., Schmaling, K. B., Kohlenberg, R. J., Addis, M. E., … Atkins, D. C. (2006). Randomized trial of behavioral activation, cognitive therapy, and antidepressant medication in the acute treatment of adults with major depression. *Journal of Consulting and Clinical Psychology, 74,* 658–670.

Emmelkamp, P. (2004). Behavior therapy with adults. In A. Bergin & S. Garfield (Eds.), *Handbook of psychotherapy and behavior change* (pp. 393–446). New York: Wiley.

Gillies, L. A. (2001). Interpersonal psychotherapy for depression and other disorders. In D. H. Barlow (Ed.), *Clinical handbook of psychological disorders* (pp. 309–331). New York: Guilford Press.

Hall, G. C. N., Ibaraki, A. Y., Huang, E. R., Marti, C. N., & Stice, E. (2016). A meta-analysis of cultural adaptations of psychological interventions. *Behavior Therapy, 47*(6), 993–1014.

Henriksen, K., Schinke, R., Moesch, K., McCann, S., Parham, W. D., Larsen, C. H., & Terry, P. (2019). Consensus statement on improving the mental health of high performance athletes. *International Journal of Sport and Exercise Psychology, 17,* 1–8.

Hollon, S., & Beck, A. (2004). Cognitive and cognitive behavioral therapies. In A. Bergin & S. Garfield (Eds.), *Handbook of psychotherapy and behavior change* (pp. 447–492). New York: Wiley.

Imber, S., Pilkonis, P., Sotsky, S., Elkin, I., Watkins, J., Collins, J., … Glass, D. (1990). Mode-specific effects among three treatments for depression. *Journal of Consulting and Clinical Psychology, 58,* 352–359.

Jensen-Doss, A. (2011). Practice involves more than treatment: How can evidence-based assessment catch up to evidence based treatment? *Clinical Psychology: Science and Practice, 18,* 173–177.

Jensen-Doss, A., & Hawley, K. M. (2010). Understanding barriers to evidence-based assessment: Clinician attitudes toward standardized assessment tools. *Journal of Clinical Child & Adolescent Psychology, 39,* 885–896.

Joiner, T. E., Jr, Walker, R. L., Pettit, J. W., Perez, M., & Cukrowicz, K. C. (2005). Evidence-based assessment of depression in adults. *Psychological Assessment, 17*(3), 267–277.

Jones, E., Huey, S. J., & Rubenson, M. (2018). Cultural competence in therapy with African Americans. In C. L. Frisby & W. T. O'Donohue (Eds.), *Cultural competence in applied psychology* (pp. 557–573). New York: Springer International.

Kalibatseva, Z., & Leong, F. T. L. (2014). A critical review of culturally sensitive treatments for depression: Recommendations for intervention and research. *Psychological Services, 11,* 433–450.

Kerr, Z. Y., Marshall, S. W., Harding, H. P., Jr, & Guskiewicz, K. M. (2012). Nine-year risk of depression diagnosis increases with increasing self-reported concussions in retired professional football players. *The American Journal of Sports Medicine, 40,* 2206–2212.

Mazzucchelli, T., Kane, R., & Rees, C. (2009). Behavioral activation treatments for depression in adults: A meta-analysis and review. *Clinical Psychology: Science and Practice, 16,* 383–411.

Mufson, L., & Fairbanks, J. (1996). Interpersonal psychotherapy for depressed adolescents: A one-year naturalistic follow-up study. *Journal of the American Academy of Child and Adolescent Psychiatry, 35,* 1145–1156.

Mufson, L., Moreau, D., Weissman, M., Wickramaratne, P., Martin, J., & Samoilov, A. (1994). Modification of interpersonal psychotherapy with depressed adolescents (IPT-A): Phase I and II studies. *Journal of the American Academy of Child and Adolescent Psychiatry, 33,* 695–705.

Mufson, L., Weissman, M., Moreau, D., & Garfinkel, R. (1999). Efficacy of interpersonal psychotherapy for depressed adolescents. *Archives of General Psychiatry, 26,* 573–579.

Proctor, S. L., & Boan-Lenzo, C. (2010). Prevalence of depressive symptoms in male intercollegiate student-athletes and nonathletes. *Journal of Clinical Sport Psychology, 4,* 204–220.

Radloff, L. S. (1977). The CES-D scale: A self-report depression scale for research in the general population. *Applied Psychological Measurement, 1*(3), 385–401.

Reinecke, M. A., Ryan, N. E., & DuBoise, D. L. (1998). Cognitive-behavioral therapy of depression and depressive symptoms during adolescence: A review and meta-analysis. *Journal of the American Academy of Child & Adolescent Psychiatry, 37*(1), 26–34.

Rossello, J., & Bernal, G. (1999). The efficacy of cognitive-behavioral and interpersonal treatments for depression in Puerto Rican adolescents. *Journal of Consulting and Clinical Psychology, 67,* 734–745.

Tindall, L., Mikocka, W. A., McMillan, D., Wright, B., Hewitt, C., & Gascoyne, S. (2017). Is behavioural activation effective in the treatment of depression in young people? A systematic review and meta-analysis. *Psychology and Psychotherapy: Theory, Research and Practice, 90,* 770–796.

Tompson, M., McNeil, F., Rea, M., & Asarnow, J. (2000). Identifying and treating adolescent depression. *Western Journal of Medicine, 172,* 172–176.

Turner, E. A. (2019). *Mental health among African Americans: Innovation in research and practice.* Lanham, MD: Rowman & Littlefield.

Turner, E. A., Camarillo, J., Daniel, S., Otero, J., & Parker, A. (2017). Correlates of psychotherapy use among ethnically diverse college student. *Journal of College Student Development, 58,* 300–307.

Turner, E. A., Cheng, H., Llamas, J., Tran, A. T., Hill, K., Fretts, J. M., & Mercado, A. (2016). Factors impacting the current trends in the use of outpatient psychiatric treatment among diverse ethnic groups. *Current Psychiatry Reviews, 12,* 199–220.

Turner, E. A., & Mills, C. (2016). Culturally relevant diagnosis and assessment of mental illness. In A. Breland-Noble, C. Al-Mateen, & N. Singh (Eds.), *Handbook of mental health in African American youth* (pp. 21–35). New York: Springer International.

Werthner, P., & Orlick, T. (1986). Retirement experiences of successful Olympic athletes. *International Journal of Sport Psychology, 17,* 337–363.

Wolanin, A., Gross, M., & Hong, E. (2015). Depression in athletes: Prevalence and risk factors. *Current Sports Medicine Reports, 14,* 56–60.

Wolanin, A., Hong, E., Marks, D., Panchoo, K., & Gross, M. (2016). Prevalence of clinically elevated depressive symptoms in college athletes and differences by gender and sport. *British Journal of Sports Medicine, 50,* 167–171.

World Health Organization. (2017). *Depression and other common mental disorders: Global health estimates.* Geneva: Author.

Young, J. E., Rygh, J. L., Weinberger, A. D., & Beck, A. T. (2007). Cognitive therapy for depression. In D. H. Barlow (Ed.), *Clinical handbook of psychological disorders: A step-by-step treatment manual* (4th ed., pp. 250–305). New York: Guilford Press.

9

EMBODIED COGNITION

Massimiliano L. Cappuccio and Jesús Ilundáin-Agurruza

Introduction

Embodied or 4E cognition (EC) approaches emphasize the defining and constitutive role that the body plays in mental activities. Sport psychologists are inclined to embrace EC because it appreciates how a full range of human experience that includes the affective, perceptual, and motoric, not just the intellectual, constitutes legitimate cognitive activity. EC stresses that sensorimotor skills and bodily affects (denoting moods, emotions, and feelings) enable and scaffold cognitive faculties such as perception, attention, control, communication, and memory, shaping and orienting the development of more intellectual capacities that involve language processing and rational judgement. Given the pervasive intertwining among psychophysical phenomena in sport performances (where does the "mental" game end and the physical one begin, when a bad case of the yips shakes a golfer's hands?), it is imperative to find philosophical accounts of the mind–body relation that are both non-dualistic and anti-reductionist. EC is strongly positioned to provide this. One reason is that it can meaningfully maintain a fundamental distinction between two forms of intelligence, representational and non-representational, while shedding light on how the former emerges from the latter. The representational forms of intelligence are intellectual, reflective, often linguistically mediated, and abstract – for example, a sportsperson or coach explicitly focuses on and analyses specific movements of the performance; the more basic, non-representational ones pertain to bodily engagements that are pre-reflective – that is, tacit, non-objectifying, and non-observational such that they perform unawares as it were. This chapter aims at illustrating how such understanding is needed to give a firm theoretical foundation to the efforts sport psychologists make to model sport performance and skilful expertise in athletes.

The Theory of Embodiment and the Embodied Approach to Cognition

Cognitive science is the interdisciplinary study of mental functions and intelligent systems at the level of their underlying processes and mechanisms. It aspires to answer fundamental questions about the functioning of human, animal, and artificial minds using a combination of empirical, synthetic, and phenomenological methods that involve both quantitative and qualitative analyses. Cognitive science can provide sport psychology with a theoretical and methodological foundation based on a concrete evidential and normative background. In order to achieve scientific validity, the protocols of practical intervention adopted by practitioner psychologists need to match the theoretical models, the empirical data, and the integrative methods introduced by cognitive science research.

EC is not the only theoretical approach available in this domain. It is necessary to distinguish between a cognitivist and an embodied approach to cognitive science. The traditional approach to cognitive science is often referred as "cognitivist" because it typically describes mental functions in computational and representational terms, as high-profile, logico-causal mechanisms designed to store and manipulate information encoded in a representational format. This approach tends to assume that the structure of cognitive processes is language-like in nature and endowed with semantic content. It presupposes that cognitive processes are essentially algorithmic and formal in nature, and that the details of their physical realization and contextual implementation cannot be a part of cognitive activity.

The premises of cognitivism are internalist, instructionist, symbolicist, and largely intellectualist, as they reduce even the most basic forms of practical know-how to temporally abstract, purely syntactic, amodal information processing. Cognitivism supposes that these systems operate by means of acontextual models of the world stored in the brain and decoupled from online interaction with real-life experiential contingencies. Burdened by such intellectualist assumptions, cognitivism lacks the conceptual resources required to appreciate that athletic skill (for example, wrestling) is a legitimate form of intelligence, because it involves cognitive faculties that are essentially different from linguistic and representational ones and that, despite this, are not less sophisticated or complex than – say – mathematical reasoning (Matthen, 2014).

EC stances represent the main alternative to the cognitivist approach. Embodied cognitive science studies how the mechanisms and processes underpinning cognition are not only causally integrated with, but also actively constituted by, bodily processes. Within EC, the approaches range from moderate versions that propose a minimal embodiment to more radical ones that reject cognitivist computational and representational views altogether. Far from being incidental contingencies, the details of bodily implementation deeply shape cognitive functions and define their reach. EC promotes a deeper understanding of the body that takes seriously the interdependency of body and mind. It maintains that the brain is not the only part of the body involved in cognitive activity, as mental activity is not reducible to the neurons that implement information-processing in the brain. In turn, the extra-neural body is not just a biological vessel necessary to keep the brain alive. The body is more than a system of sensors and actuators instrumental to cognition, or the location in space where mental processes materially occur.

Indeed, for EC, the body works as an open spatio-temporal horizon, a place of opportunities for action and discovery, a dynamical boundary that defines the self and world in processual, relational, and reciprocal terms – that is, as elements of a precarious stability that emerges from a context of continuous unfinished negotiation between organism and subpersonal environment. The body is the dimension in which the original link between personal and subpersonal components of the mind – that is, one person's consciousness and its underlying mechanisms and processes – can be clearly observed. EC studies this link using a "neurophenomenological" methodology that combines third-person empirical accounts and first-person phenomenological reports.

The phenomenological doctrines to which EC appeals conceive of the body as the place in which the self and world meet and constitute each other. They further see the body as the precondition under which their originating coupling is established. Thus, the body is a prerequisite to discover and make sense of the world as a meaningful experiential reality. The construction of the world through bodily perception and interaction is what allows embodied agents – athletes, for instance – to make sense of their environment as an open horizon of action possibilities. Revealing this horizon, the bodily experience actively scaffolds the capability to learn and articulate meaningful actions in the environment.

The EC programme – especially the radical trends that defend anti-computationalist, anti-representationalist, and dynamicist views (e.g., Chemero, 2009; Dreyfus, 2002; Hutto & Myin, 2017) – reflects this non-instrumental conception of the body as a precondition for experience and cognition. In this respect, EC opposes cognitivism and offers an alternative to its internalist and instructionist assumptions about the nature of cognition that relegate the body to a simple instrumental function.

The Key Tenets of EC

The fundamental principle of EC is that the reach and the very nature of mental functions constitutively depend on the material and temporal details of their implementation, including the history of interactions between the embodied agent and its world (Gallagher, 2005, 2011). A simple example is how an athlete's movements and experiences, say those of a mixed martial arts (MMA) fighter, are pervasively informed by the history of her engagements with specific opponents in particular locations and times. This principle has two important implications.

First, many "low-level" regulatory and adaptive processes (i.e., either physiological processes in the non-neural body or physical processes in the extra-bodily environment) actively participate in the most basic forms of cognition (sensorimotor, affective, adaptive), scaffolding their development and defining their scope. Not only are perception and action intrinsically intelligent, but also the hormonal and immune systems (Marin & Kipnis, 2013), autonomic and peripheral responses (Aranyosi, 2013), and highly selective saccadic reflexes (Mann, 2019) can play an intelligent role in certain tasks. For example, an expert MMA fighter's response to her opponent is modulated and highly grained: She readily and rapidly picks up the slight raise and twitch on her opponent's right shoulder as it signals a punch. In the context of how the fight is going, this may be read as potentially damaging (she may be reeling from a previous hit) and lead to a feeling of being intimidated so that a cascade of hormonal and emotional processes condition her (re)action – for example, protecting her ribs and face. Models in embodied robotics validate the hypothesis that the anatomical and postural specificity of the body, with its inherent material properties (hardness, elasticity, etc.), and the intrinsic biomechanical and morphological constraints of the actuators (degrees of freedom, weight distribution, etc.) can play a cognitive role. For example, in the design of passive artificial walkers (Pfeifer, Iida, & Lungarella, 2014), the pendulum-like configuration of one's body parts can contribute to reducing the computational complexity of a task of bipedal motion. To return to the MMA fighter, her training has shaped her body in specific ways that mean she can absorb and adapt to hits that would instantly disable a non-fighter: She readily positions her arms in specific configurations in response to her opponent's moves such that, much as a physical chess match, these may cancel possible lines of attack.

Second, competent embodied dispositions and habitual patterns of perception and action, emerging from dynamic forms of adaptive coupling between embodied agents and their environment, contribute significantly to scaffolding and shaping forms of cognition (inference, language, symbolic representation) that tend to appear "disembodied" – that is, less immediately dependent on the details of their bodily implementation. In truth, the body selectively modulates the development of "higher" cognitive faculties, such as abstract thought and rational decision, and filters or organizes their propositional contents. That is, although these faculties are not primarily aimed at sensorimotor engagement and physical interaction, they are nonetheless always informed by a primordial background of bodily familiarity and perceptual expertise. Strategic control and decision, perceptual discrimination, linguistic representation, memory, judgement, and creativity are not to be understood just as informational functions centrally controlled by the brain or abstract programmes detached from their material implementers: On the contrary, these cognitive functions can be correctly understood only when the fine-grained specificity of the physical and biological systems that instantiate them, and the real-life circumstances in which they have been developed and trained, are considered.

Bodily affects can dramatically curb perception and objective judgement for different reasons. In some cases, it may be that there are costs to our perceptual judgements, as when fatigue influences climbers' perception of how far they can reach (Pijpers, Oudejans, & Bakker, 2007). In other cases, we find how hunger or other possible extraneous conditions (mental fatigue, self-regulation resources) may influence a judge's rulings (Danziger, Levav, & Avnaim-Pesso, 2011). Accordingly, in his phenomenological account, Gallagher (2005) emphasizes that bodily dispositions and affordances in the environment can determine the outcome of evaluative and decisional processes more than any representation of the world internally stored by or manipulated within the central nervous system. Intelligent know-how, athletic skill, and embodied expertise emerge from the consolidation and diversification of an increasingly large repertoire of habitual interactions and affective patterns. By tapping into this repertoire, the agent finds the cognitive resources necessary to establish a structural coupling with real-world scenarios (Chiel & Beer, 1997).

Origins and Varieties of EC Approaches

The Embodied Mind (Varela, Thompson, Rosch, 1991), a seminal book that provided EC's original formulation, has exerted a remarkable influence over various disciplinary areas and is linked with a number of doctrines and theories. In philosophy of mind, EC proposes an emergentist variety of non-reductive physicalism; in epistemology, it defends radical constructivism and pragmatism; methodologically, it promotes pluralism through an integration of phenomenological (first-person) and empirical (third-person) investigations; in theoretical biology, it embraces the autopoietic model of the living; in psychology, it advances the developmental and ecological approaches based on the agent–environment coupling through the development of enactive dispositions and practical habits; and, in neuroscience, it endorses dynamical systems theory and the explanatory models based on free-energy principle and protean (anti-localizationist) brain hypothesis.

After generating a prominent debate in cognitive science and philosophy of mind, the EC approach to cognition is today fragmented into a constellation of varying – often conflicting – positions and views (reviewed by Gallagher, 2011; Menary, 2010) concerning the role played by the body in cognitive processes. The label of 4E cognition – embodied, embedded, enacted, extended – is frequently used but, in light of recent developments, it is now more a matter of terminological convenience. Indeed, EC has further splintered into a number of camps that include, at the extremes:

(a) Theories of minimal embodiment, which assert that the sensorimotor areas of the brain represent information in a "bodily format", scaffolding higher cognitive functions.

(b) Enactive (radical) theories of cognition, which claim that cognition builds on action–perception feedback loops emerging from the interaction between one's body and environment.

And, as intermediate positions:

(a) Embodied functionalism, claiming that some bodily systems, similar to other physical implementers, can at times play a non-trivial causal role in producing cognitive states and processes.
(b) Biological embodiment, which maintains that the details of biological embodiment define the unique cognitive possibilities of each organism.
(c) Semantic embodiment, which holds that the very nature of bodily experience shapes the possibilities of conceptualization and, in the case of humans, of linguistic categorization.

In particular, the interpretation of EC in cognitive philosophy is polarized around two leading approaches that contend the theoretical legacy of *The Embodied Mind*: the enactivist (or sensorimotor) and the extended (or distributed) approaches to cognition. Both accounts build on the premise that minds are causally co-determined and essentially co-constituted by the physical contingencies in which the body is contextually situated.

However, these two approaches hold different views about the major characteristics of embodiment: Enactivists, on the one hand, are generally oriented towards biological and dynamical accounts of the mind and stress that mental faculties are neither exactly localizable (because cognition is what the cognitive agent does, not an agent's component or property) nor language-like in nature (because basic forms of cognition are not syntactically organized and do not involve propositional contents detachable from their linguistic vessels). On the contrary, according to enaction theory, cognition holistically emerges in the continuous adaptive interplay between the organism and its ecological surroundings. The genetic/constitutive role played by the sensorimotor coupling between the agent and his/her world environment is particularly emphasized over offline forms of intelligence.

Extended mind theorists, on the other hand, are typically sympathetic to functionalist and mechanistic accounts of the mind, as they stress that intracranial (neuronal, usually organic) and extra-cranial (non-neuronal, possibly artificial) components and processes have in principle the same capability to realize cognitive processes and produce cognitive states. By virtue of their equal status, internal and external vehicles of cognition are in principle interchangeable or inherently complementary, depending on whether they replace or complete one another. The same cognitive function can be implemented either by the central nervous system, by extra-neuronal bodily systems, by extra-bodily systems, or by a combination of them, if the systems in question constitute suitable functional vehicles of cognitive processing and content representation. This implies that internal mental processes such as memory can and often are offloaded on to artificial devices or socio-culturally instantiated by multiple interactive agents, as in the case of language or other intersubjective practices.

Remarkably, if most psychologists and cognitive scientists who work on sport and performance tend to endorse one variant or the other, all of them seem naturally inclined to embrace at least the core general tenets of EC (see Beilock, 2008; Gray, 2014). Such proximity is not merely coincidental, as sport psychology and embodied cognitive science share theoretical and historical roots.

This communal root is shown first in the characterization of skill acquisition as progressive automatization of complex action patterns. Such characterization was offered by some of the pioneers of the EC programme, which can be traced back as early as William James (1890) and finds echo in the views of Dreyfus and Dreyfus (1980). These were in substantial accord with Fitts and Posner's (1967) model – a major contribution to establishing sport psychology as a scientific discipline – which posited that less cognitively demanding motor control is a distinctive mark of expertise. This is why experts can deliver their skilful performances in the form of unreflective action routines. More recently, the concept of reinvestment in motor skill acquisition research (Masters & Maxwell, 2008) congruently argues that, in expert action, subroutines are activated, and attention is reinvested into other attentional foci.

Precursor Theories – The Communal Roots of EC and Sport Psychology

EC resonates deeply with influential doctrines in developmental psychology and ecological psychology that paved the way for the foundation of sport psychology. These doctrines incarnate EC and sport psychology's common roots. Sport psychologists inherited important elements from both the Piagetian tradition (which stresses the pre-eminence attributed to "enactive learning" during early cognitive development) and the Gibsonian tradition (which has introduced the ecological concepts of "affordances" and "direct perception").

The legacy of ecological psychology is particularly remarkable for EC. The approach called "direct perception" or "direct realism" proposed by James J. Gibson (1966, 1979) stemmed, in many senses, from a reaction against the "computational" or "functionalist/ information processing" approach that had been growing in the 1960s, which was largely inspired by Putnam's theory of machine-state functionalism in philosophy of mind (Putnam, 1960). Putnam's theory presupposed both the computational theory of mind (the thesis that cognitive processes are fundamentally algorithmic in nature) and the principle of multiple-realizability (which states that a cognitive function, like any other algorithmic function, can be implemented by any material support capable of physically instantiating the relevant formal operations of symbolic manipulation; see Putnam, 1967). This computational and functionalist/information-processing approach is often associated with the internalist view (typically illustrated by means of Putnam's famous "brain-in-a-vat" thought experiment; Putnam, 1981) that human cognition is entirely realized and carried out by the central nervous system alone, and the extra-neural body and the extra-bodily environment do not play any properly constitutive role in mental activity because they allegedly do not participate in information-processing.

The ecological approach proposed by Gibson offers an alternative to this functionalist, computationalist, and internalist view. It affirms the principle that animal cognition evolved to serve movement and action in the environment. In the case of human cognition, it emerges from the integration of sensory and motoric capabilities. These coordinate to generate intelligent actions that need neither representational content nor abstract inferences in order to work. In its most radical version, the Gibsonian argument rejects internal representation, characterizing cognition as direct connection from perception to action through recurrent feedback loops (this idea is also one of the precursors of the enactive/sensorimotor account of the mental; see Noë, 2005; O'Regan & Noë, 2001).

According to many researchers inspired by Gibson, human performance is primarily determined by the physics and biology of human anatomy (the muscular and skeletal physiognomy, the geometry and degrees of freedom of the effectors), and only secondarily by planning and control algorithms mediated by internal representations of the external world. The anatomical and physiological properties of the body are in many cases sufficient to explain skilful action and expertise, minimizing the role of information-processing and de-emphasizing the importance of brain processes altogether (Carello & Turvey, 2016; Turvey, 1973; Kugler & Turvey, 1987).

The remarkable pre-eminence of Gibson's notion of affordance in the literature attests to the strong theoretical link between sport psychology and EC. The relationship between Gibsonian theory and EC is, however, multifaceted (see Chemero, 2009; Wilson & Golonka, 2013). The EC programme has tried to expand or revise the naïve realist epistemology embedded in direct perception theory, replacing it with the constructivist principle that cognition is a tentative process of unfinished negotiation and precarious adaptation to a world environment that is intelligible only to a living organism structurally coupled with it. EC has also updated some of the key ecological notions in light of recent empirical discoveries in the emerging neurosciences. For example, the notion of motor affordance was updated and expanded to accommodate the new data and models of action execution and motor control coming from neuropsychological research such as the discovery of canonical and mirror neurons in the premotor cortex.

In this updated ecological framework, EC does not emphasize just the action possibilities enabled by the physical structure of the body and the objects in the environment, but also the emotional, intentional, and motivational forces that fuel these actions, which are seen as fundamental components of skilful performance: built-in saliency detection and discrimination filters; powerful anticipatory mechanisms; adaptive systems for priority selection and allocation of interest, attention, and motivation; and flexible response habits.

The embodied nature of skill expertise does not only show the merely reactive and adaptive capability of the body. It also projects on to the capability to creatively improvise new actions: The notion of "enactive creativity" clarifies the experts' capability to strategically interpret their circumstances and adapt to unprecedented sensorimotor contingencies (Rucińska & Aggerholm, 2019; see also Hutto & Myin, 2017, for an enactivist account of imagination; Ilundáin-Agurruza, 2017, for a phenomenological and enactive analysis of imagination and improvisation). The embodied/enactive approach to cognition sees creativity as a capacity for active exploration of the limits of one's know-how. This capacity can be strengthened through training appropriately designed to diversify personal competences and adapted to unexpected opportunities.

In the last two decades, EC has proven advantageous for an expanding number of research areas pertaining to sport psychology. Below, to better connect theory with specific sport psychological applications, we discuss seven areas: skill acquisition and expertise; *risk sports*; attentional focus, flow, and choking in sports; tool use; social cognition; language processing in sports; and team dynamics.

Skill Acquisition and Expertise

The search for a global motor skill that would be the mark of skilled performers, posited as a "generalized motor ability" (GMA; McCloy, 1934; Schmidt, 1991) that underpins all other skills, never found sufficient supporting evidence. This led researchers to focus on specific skills with variations across groups and skill levels (Baker & Farrow, 2015). Today there are signs of a resurgence of interest in a GMA, endorsing an emergent and fluid model influenced by biology and environment over a lifespan (Hands, McIntyre, & Parker., 2018). EC can compellingly account for both GMA and specific abilities, as it relies on dynamic forms of adaptive coupling between embodied agents and their environment capable of describing the continuity between varying levels of generality in cognitive control. That is why EC can also explain the full range of expertise, from novice to advanced, while being particularly revealing with regard to experts' skills and their development. EC proves advantageous in both describing and explaining the complex dynamics at play in top performance, which draw upon automatized processes as well as fully immersive attunement with tasks.

Ericsson, Krampe, and Tesch-Römer's (1993) *deliberate practice* concept, which proposed that expertise develops from sustained and purposeful involvement and specific training, was pivotal to the development of sport psychology. A number of foundational and influential – but non-sport-specific – works (Bloom, 1985; Starkes & Allard, 1983) acted as trailblazers for sport-centred general research (Ericsson, 2003) and specific investigations thereof (Farrow, Baker, & MacMahon, 2013; Hodges & Williams, 2012; Vickers, 2016). An EC framework, given its emphasis on sportspersons' history of engagements within dynamic systems, may serve as a better theoretical foundation for such explanations.

Contemporary research in expert action in a variety of contexts is challenging long-held views in the field of sport psychology. Interestingly and controversially, opposing views in the current debate on skilful expertise correspond to different articulations of the EC approach. Fitts and Posner's principle, Dreyfus's contention, and reinvestment views posit that highly skilled performance is essentially unreflective, or that it operates solely subpersonally and by way of subroutines. Contrary to this view, more recent stances argue, from an ecological perspective, that expert athletes evince some measure of highly tuned self-awareness (Christensen, Sutton, & McIlwain, 2013, 2016; Sutton, McIlwain, Christensen, & Geeves, 2011). Experts rely not only on attuned motor control processes, but also on a tactical intelligence that dynamically adapts to contingent in-game conditions. To capture their connections, Sutton and colleagues propose a unitary model for the architecture of skilful action that integrates motor control with perception and cognition.

Risk Sports

Along these lines, *risk* or *extreme sports*, such as big wave surfing, free solo climbing (without using ropes or gear except for shoes and chalk), or wingsuit flying, push the practical and theoretical envelope. Ecological views (Immonen, Brymer, Davids, Liukkonen, & Jaakkola, 2018) highlight how traditional theory-laden psychological analyses of *extreme sports*, such as edgeworks, sensation-seeking, and psychoanalysis, have proven inadequate to capture the depth and nuances of experiences of risk sports participants – that is, such notions as adrenaline and thrill-seeking motivations prove too simple to capture the practitioners' deeply meaningful engagements. As an alternative, they advocate for studies that capture the phenomenology and ecological dynamics of these sports. Empirical evidence de-emphasizes the role of deliberate behaviour and top–down approaches that might counterbalance subpersonal routines by means of complex mental representations (Ericsson, 2006) when performers risk serious injury or even death, as Eriksen (2010) avows. That is, an EC approach is better positioned than alternative models to explain expert performances in high-stakes sports. Research on circus trapeze acrobats shows that, even if actions are highly automatized as subroutines, when much is on the line, performers rely on extensive conscious control (Eysenck, 2004). This reliance on explicit conscious control is corroborated by phenomenological analyses of experts across a range of sports (Breivik, 2013). Cognitivism is at odds with these findings: It posits subpersonal, amodal, syntactic processes that decouple online interaction from real-life experiential contingencies, whereas such studies show that the personal level and the body as attentional focus are constitutive elements of expert performance. Through neurophenomenology, EC precisely factors in both subpersonal and personal levels, advancing a holistic model of body–mind as the foundational locus for our dynamic worldly engagements – and not just a body or subcomponents thereof. That is why a highly discriminating attunement and fluid relation between online and offline processes are emblematic of EC.

Congruent with EC's framework, once a naturalistic perspective is adopted, even within cognitive systems engineering (CSE), the evidence corroborates that performers rely on a mix of formal, informal, and affective cognitive processes (Klein, 1998), and that experts depend less on formal aspects than novices (Beach & Lipshitz, 1993). Moreover, CSE forsakes informational models à la cognitivism in favour of modal description of cognitive workflows and supporting structures based on highly skilled performers' accounts (Lintern, Moon, Klein, & Hoffmann, 2018), something that neurophenomenological methodology is poised to elucidate. Moreover, the musculoskeletal, kinematic, neural, organic, and affective adaptations of expert athletes both constrain and enable the cognitive processes and reduce the cognitive load that underwrite superior performance.

The extent to which mental representations play a role in the type of intelligent and highly skilled action characteristic of experts is contested. EC approaches, by virtue of their dynamic, situated, online, and holistic (affective, intellectual, motoric) transactions with their environment, can accommodate hybrid online/offline situational requirements more parsimoniously than standard cognitivist and computational approaches. This is true even of more radical versions of enactivism that de-emphasize the role of representation in basic forms of cognition (Hutto & Myin, 2017). As previously mentioned, some EC variants – that is, enactive and biological ones – push against mental representation, opting for scaffolded cognitive models with both non-representational and representational features at different levels. Other versions – that is, minimal, functionalist, or semantic – accommodate representations all the way up and down the cognitive process. At stake is whether sport psychologists' and neuroscientists' notion of mental representation conforms to the canonical philosophical conception of representation, or whether representations are conceived as encoded neural and biological instantiations. The canonical conception understands representations in terms of veridicality, accuracy, or truth-functional conditions (do these accurately reflect states of affairs?), which is quite different from actual physiological embedment.

Enactive and biological variants support the latter view, and, indeed, the evidence seems to favour this. In the empirical literature, there are different notions of how sporting action and knowledge are represented, but none fit the canonical notion of mental representation. Even in cases where mental representations stand at the very centre of action control and organization, as in Schack and Land (2016), these correspond to dendrograms (diagrammatic taxonomic tree representations) derived from subjective labelling. Others, such as the abovementioned Lintern et al.'s (2018), explicitly discard information-processing and favour knowledge-elicitation to guide sportspersons' subjective reports, thereby operationalizing representations not as mental phenomena, but rather as a mapping tool for researchers. Accordingly, sport psychologists' notion of mental representations fit pictorial stand-ins for neurally encoded processes at best, instead of philosophical epistemic conditions.

Attention and Effort

Attentional focus, particularly in relation to effort and effortlessness, elicits less controversy, but the cognitive underpinning of effortless attention remains somewhat enigmatic. Judgement and decision-making are related to effort but distinct from it, as these involve testing of actual choices and judgements and rely on a different skillset and domain of applicability (Raab & MacMahon, Volume 1, Chapter 16, in this encyclopedia). Normally, the more effort an action requires, the harder it is to keep attention focused, with the effort eventually reaching a maximum point that it is not possible to surpass. Effort can be measured both objectively, in terms of metabolism (as in calories consumed, METs, or watt output), and subjectively, as how effortful a particular action is perceived to be. Puzzlingly, in some circumstances, the sportsperson, fully engaged in the activity, can reach a state in which action and attention seem effortless. The objective requirements do not change putatively, but the subjective exertion perplexingly remains the same and may even decrease. Current analyses fail to accommodate this, having neglected and often relegated this issue to the realm of esoteric explanations (Bruya, 2010). Csikzentmihalyi (1991) theorized this phenomenon as an autotelic experience – vernacularly known as "flow states" – which extends across many domains, including sport and performance (Jackson & Csikzentmihalyi, 1999). The phenomenon of *quiet eye* – a technique where gaze behaviour modification improves task outcome – has also been related to flow states and effortless attention (Vine, Lee, Moore, & Wilson, 2013). EC, broadly interdisciplinary and methodologically diverse, can integrate the objective accounts based on empirical findings with the subjective phenomenological accounts.

Novice and competent sportspeople generally experience flow states accidentally. Usually, these are seen as an epiphenomenon not under the control of the athlete. Hence, typically flow states are not expressly sought in Western sports. This contrasts with the deliberate cultivation of such states in its East Asian sport and martial practices (among others). Flow states are central to martial arts with a Buddhist undertone, such as Kyudo or Kendo, where they are referred to as *mushin* (lit. without mind) states (Ilundáin-Agurruza, 2016). In these practices, *mushin* is touted as a mark of highly skilled performers and their signature fluid action. Flow and *mushin* states are characterized by consistency, economy of movement, efficacy, accuracy, and improvisational effectiveness. Whereas these typify many sports, others that unfold in more chaotic circumstances (downhill skiing, big wave surfing) belie some of these elements. Exploring the similarities and differences between flow and *mushin* transactionally – that is, considering the physiological, phenomenological, and cultural levels – is beyond the cognitivist scope but well within EC's purview given its situated and extended view of mind–body–environment relations. Likewise, novice/expert and inter-sport variances in such states are best examined when understood as embodied dynamics that arise from adaptive agent–environment couplings.

Whether such effortless action and attention also lead to objectively improved performance is less clear, although there seems to be evidence to this effect (Swann, Keegan, Crust, & Piggott, 2016; Wulf, 2007; Wulf & Lewthwaite, 2010). This research, consistent with an EC model that endorses both subpersonal and reflective engagement in sports action, posits that it is external focus on movement, action targets, or stimuli, and not paying attention to internal sensations (whether these be proprioceptive, kinaesthetic, nociceptive, etc.), that leads to better results across the whole performance range. For example, when pedalling a bicycle, paying attention to cadence (revolutions per minute) results in better performance than focusing on muscular sensations in the quadriceps. In this case, explicit attention to external stimuli results in performance gains. Putatively, external foci allow for automatism of basic biomechanical actions and underlying mechanisms and processes. Such foci also centre attentional resources on objective target acquisition that correlates to performance objective maximization of performance goals: pedalling cadence correlates more readily with higher speeds, whereas muscular pain does not. Again, this is fruitfully analysed from an embodied perspective where physiological and mechanical conditions scaffold and structure performance as being intelligent and superior performance.

Sports Choking

Another challenging phenomenon that EC is poised to help clarify is choking under pressure in sport – the flip side to flow states, in a sense. At its simplest, when athletes choke, they fail to complete tasks that they have already mastered (Beilock, 2010). Normally, deliberative strategies lead to better performance, but real-world and do-or-die scenarios can increase the sense of effort and lead to worse results. This can become chronic or acute and develop into a pattern vernacularly referred to as "a slump". There are three main kinds of empirical account: (1) self-focus or self-monitoring theories (Baumeister, 1984), which attribute *choking* to paying too much attention to oneself and/or the task; (2) distraction theories, which posit that not enough attention is paid when, for instance, working memory is disrupted; and (3) overload views, in which cognitive demands overwhelm the sportsperson (these are usually conflated with and – for simplicity here – subsumed under distraction theories).

Integrating self-focus and distraction/overload accounts is not impossible, as they rely on two sets of explanations that do not entirely exclude each other (Beilock & Carr, 2001). Nonetheless, it is necessary to emphasize the different explanatory advantages of these two theories. Self-focus views best account for novice versus expert differences, particularly in terms of fast action conditions, and seem to better explain why distractors succeed in addressing choking problems (Beilock, Bertenthal, McCoy, & Carr, 2004; Beilock & Gray, 2012); distraction theories appear to more readily incorporate non-neural aspects (including environmental factors) as pressure conditions (Eysenck & Calvo, 1992). Both accounts share the underlying assumption that *choking* results from a misallocation of the attentional resources that make peak performance possible. What they contend is the nature of these attentional resources and the causes and specific modes of their misallocation.

One charge that applies to both theories is the ecological frugality that characterizes them. In other words, many of the experiments lack validity outside the laboratory and fail to reflect real-world conditions (Christensen et al., 2013; Montero, 2016). For instance, soccer players are told to dribble a ball while listening to aural cues (Beilock, Carr, MacMahon, & Starkes, 2002) or while paying attention to their feet (Ford, Hodges, & Williams, 2005), but these are not the sorts of task for which players train, nor do they mimic the competitive situations they face. Similarly, the role that pragmatic interests play in motivating athletes is sometimes underdetermined, and the modest monetary rewards offered to experiment participants as motivational stimulus hardly compare to being in contention for an Olympic medal.

EC, in virtue of the very plethora of theoretical stances and methodological resources, is well poised to supplement empirical findings, mediate in internecine theoretical disputes, and redress the ecological paucity that besets many studies. At the heart of sport psychology and embodied cognition – as the opening overture to this entry suggests – lies a recognition that cognitive activity is not merely intellectual, but also affective, perceptual, and motoric. Moreover, the high specificity inherent in sport means that, although there may be a general phenomenology to *choking* (Ilundáin-Agurruza, 2015), there are a variety of choking instances. A fully grained account of *choking* needs to account for the holistic continuities involved in skilled action and the disruptive discontinuities that characterize *choking*. To wit, physical qualities and skill, rather than isolated from each other, are so closely intertwined that skill and performance are affected by variables such as fatigue or pressure or affective state (Gabbet, 2015).

A number of studies can meet such demands from a variety of angles; for instance, Christensen et al. (2016) developed a theory they call Mesh, which "proposes that cognitive control plays an important ongoing role in advanced skill, with cognitive and automatic processes being closely integrated" such that performative responsibilities are assigned hierarchically (p. 280). This has the advantage of being able to explain in an ecologically thorough fashion how experts mesh or integrate cognitive and automatic processes or exploring how and when these decouple. Cappuccio (2017) and Cappuccio, Gray, Hill, Mesagno, and Carr (2019) assess *choking* in relation to consciousness and self-consciousness, respectively, from an EC perspective, maintaining that understanding how either factor is involved in choking episodes needs to discriminate and correlate with nine dimensions of consciousness and recognize that self-consciousness's effect on expert skills is articulated at multiple parallel levels and causal pathways (these include emotional, situational, and other factors). EC approaches combining radical enactivism and dynamic systems theory (Hutto & Sánchez-García, 2015) provide the requisite level of complexity for such a complex phenomenon. Some (Vine et al., 2013) have studied the relationship between *choking* and *quiet eye*. The studies have concluded that failure under pressure is due to disruptions in attentional control, demonstrating that "pressure has a greater impact on visual attention during the execution of the movement than it does during the preparation of the movement" (Vine et al., 2013). These findings further line up with EC, reflecting the constitutive role that it ascribes to sensorimotor processes and perception.

Tool Use

Tools add another level of complexity to theoretical and empirical sports research, as, in addition to the often theorized bodily and mental schemas, there is a need to integrate tool use as another layer of the performative workflow. Maravita and Iriki (2004) demonstrate how sportspersons incorporate tools and instruments into their body schema, much as Merleau-Ponty's (1962) blind man's cane becomes part of his body schematic processes. In athletics, this is often referred to as "transparent equipment": Athletes integrate a wide range of inputs, from varied tactile information (skin, temperature, pressure) to proprioceptive limb position or kinaesthetic dynamics (muscular, vestibular, nociceptive, etc.), and visual data. For example, Biggio, Bisio, Avanzino, Ruggeri, and Bove (2017) studied how, in measuring sportspeople's peripersonal space and its long-term modulation, expert tennis players accurately discriminated between their personal racquet and a common one such that "the tool daily used during sport activity is stably embodied in the peripersonal space of tennis players." (p. 54). Expert players had reached a much higher level of familiarity and integration. This can be extrapolated to many other sports where sportspeople rely on equipment – for example, cycling or surfing. The tight connection between our embodiment, our tools, and the sorts of sport we devise also leads to other interesting conundrums. Sporting equipment, for example, may afford different ways to modulate the transfer of skills such as gliding, which is usually operationalized in terms of the sense of balance. Research (Krenn, Werner, Lawrence, & Valero-Cuevas, 2015) shows that, in more static sports (rifle shooting, soccer, or golf), elite athletes show better balance, whereas, in the case of alpine skiing or surfing, it is not the case. Clearly, these issues fit the methodological and theoretical parameters and basic tenets that underlie the EC paradigm.

As remarked before, EC propounds that our cognition is extended: Out-of-skull extra-skin support systems such as notebooks or phones become constitutive of cognition and not merely causally relevant factors. Some favour a functionalist/mechanistic stance (Clark & Chalmers, 1998), whereas others endorse predictive and enactive positions (Kirchoff, 2015). Both argue that tools are fully integrated as de facto cognitive elements. The issue now is whether tool use is simply a causally relevant factor (Adams & Aizawa, 2008) or a constitutive element. Kirchoff (2015) argues that the pertinent sense of constitution is not synchronic; rather, body, brain, and environment (tool) dynamically couple diachronically. In this view, processes "distributed across different factors/levels (neural, behavioural, environmental) and across different timescales are constituted in a temporally integrated dynamic system" (Gallagher, 2016, p. 9). Thus, by EC's lights, sports equipment is not just an external object but becomes integrated as part of the performer's body schema. This theoretical framework, when combined with dynamic systems analyses, for instance, helps explore how embodiment constrains and enables our cognitive and skilled engagements.

Social Cognition – Embodied Approaches to Language and Action

The EC programme provides sport psychologists with updated theoretical tools to understand social interaction, informed by the recent advances in cognitive neuroscience. An example that sport psychologists (Beilock, 2015) particularly cite as evidence that neurocognitive functions and their bodily realizers must be studied together is that reading comprehension and memory improve if the subject, while reading the descriptions of certain physical activities (e.g., baseball actions), performs physical manipulations that are consistent with them (Glenberg, 2011). The "action-based" theory of reading comprehension, confirmed by neuroimaging studies, asserts that the sensory and motor systems are involved during the process of understanding, imagining, and remembering an action described in a written story, as if the reader were actually perceiving or executing that action (Glenberg & Gallese, 2012).

This investigation of the embodied scaffoldings of language confirms the results of Beilock, Lyons, Mattarella-Micke, Nusbaum, & Small (2008), who demonstrated in neuroimaging examinations of brain activation that fans of a sporting activity with scarce experience "on the field" and athletes who actually play the sport show different patterns of brain activation when watching videos of game play. Compared with fans, players' brains show much more activation in motor-planning and motor-control regions – the areas that would be active if the subjects were actually playing rather than merely watching a match.

This and similar results – for example, those concerning motor resonance during observation of basketball tasks (Abreu et al., 2012; Aglioti, Cesari, Romani, & Urgesi, 2008) – have been interpreted as evidence of a common embodied root of motor execution, imagination, and action understanding (Gallese, 2007; Beilock, 2015). According to this interpretation, TV sports fans reflectively evaluate those actions in a way detached from their motoric dimension, whereas expert players rely on their own motor repertoire to mentally re-enact the execution of the actions they are watching. As attested by brain imaging, performative familiarity with the execution of observed actions matters for the comprehension of those actions. According to Gallese (2007), what can be lived out in imagination and in remembering depends crucially on an internal "embodied" simulation of what has been previously experienced, which employs one's established reservoir of motor competences (for a similar conclusion suggested by a different body of evidence, see Witt, South, & Sugovic, 2014; for a review of the literature on embodied simulation informed by mirror neuron theory, see Ferrari & Rizzolatti, 2014; for a review more specifically related to sport and athletic skills, see Abreu, Esteves, & Aglioti, 2019; Ikegami, Nakamoto, & Ganesh, 2019).

Team Dynamics

Expanding the inquiry into team dynamics, the challenge is, much as with other aspects of sport, to properly analyse the many and varied kinds of team dynamics. Compared with other contexts, such as interview settings or workplace observation, Loehr, Kourtis, Vesper, Sebanz, and Knoblich (2013) confirm the unique and compounded challenges that team sports raise. EC addresses sport psychology's need for thick, flexible, and highly textured ecological accounts that can properly analyse the many and varied kinds of team dynamics. At one extreme we find synchronized, and at the other asynchronous, performances. In between, there is an array of possible team interactions – for example, military units, firefighters, surgery teams, and various types of team sports – with unique intersubjective manifestations, some of which are more collaborative than others and under more or less pressurized environments (Gallagher & Ilundáin-Agurruza, in press).

As far as synchronized performance, we find pre-reflective synchrony with teammates or partners. Musical performance is arguably the best and most studied example outside sport (Glowinski et al., 2013; Gnecco et al., 2013; Repp & Su, 2013). For instance, Soliman and Glenberg (2014) show that, when coordinating tasks such as cutting through candles with a wire that needs to be under tension, the participants modulate their actions in ways that are measurable both neuronally and behaviourally. In a sporting context, players would develop "joint body schemas" that integrate not only equipment, but also other players, inclusive of role as either adversary or ally (for joint action as a theory of event coding, see Hommel at al. 2001; for task sharing as in a doubles tennis table game, see Wenke et al., 2011). That is, rather than discrete individual body schemas, the EC stance would argue that such synchronous action is evidence for a larger system, based on joint-body schemas, that amounts to more than the sum of its parts (Gallagher & Ilundáin-Agurruza, in press). This fits best for cases where there is synchronization between or among agents, rather than situations with different constraints, as when antagonistic interactions are involved. At the other extreme, we find asynchronous interactions where there are adversaries who are actively working against one's own tactics and synchronized plays. If, in the former case, the level of attunement is high and consistent, in the latter, the adversarial factor means that such consistency is missing. Surprise is the norm. This results in phenomenological and performative differences between self- and other-awareness, as well as between effective attentional focus and letting go of such focus.

More specific to sports, as far as awareness of others is involved, whether of teammates or adversaries, we find on the one hand closed-skill team sports, where there are fixed sets of movements – for example, synchronized swimming. These are closer to the analysis where synchrony is central and finds parallels in non-improvised musical performance and dance. On the other hand, open-skill team sports such as rugby, which involve continuous and dynamic adjustment to competitors' moves, are quite different. Lacking any sort of pre-accorded movements or choreography, players must adapt to the opponents' attempts to thwart their tactics while trying to implement their own. That is, there is a need to synchronize with teammates while working with the asynchronous surprises that adversaries unfold. In this case, EC's methodological pluralism affords a more refined description of phenomena and more highly textured analysis at various levels of the complex dynamics involved, as there is a need to account for perceptual factors, affective states, physiological processes, biomechanical, kinetic, and kinaesthetic dynamics, and intersubjective relations, among others. Along these lines, Hoffmann et al. (2018) provide a multidisciplinary model that, taking into account the dimensions of movement dynamics, multivariate measures, and dynamic statistical parameters, aims at integrating action and cognition so as to be able to incorporate the dynamics of actions into theoretical advances.

Conclusion

EC theory can delineate a distinctive normative ideal to guide the disciplines that study sensorimotor abilities in sports activity, physical exercise, and athletic performance. Most of these disciplines focus exclusively on the medical and physiological aspects of sports performance – for example, the biomechanical and metabolic factors. The received story is that sport psychology differs from these disciplines because, unlike them, it is specifically concerned with the "mental" factors that affect sports activity. Said mental factors include the cognitive-behavioural, attitudinal, emotional, and motivational elements that underpin one's performance. It is true that sport psychology seeks to maximize performance by acting upon these elements, primarily to optimize training methods and skill development and, secondarily, to promote other distinctively "mental" dimensions of sport, such as talent identification, team consolidation, motivation building, and the pedagogy of sport ethics. But it is wrong to assume that a dichotomous view of the mind–body relation could accurately delineate the distinctive scope of sport psychology.

Insofar as it is expected to be compatible with the naturalistic paradigm of health and medicine research, sport psychology cannot afford to found its scientific status on such a dichotomous metaphysical understanding (whether based on a dualism of substances or functions). On the contrary, EC motivates sport psychology to interpret the mind–body as a reciprocal relationship of interconnected poles or, better yet, interrelated levels of the same complex systemic reality. EC and sport psychology naturally complement each other as they arise from the same endeavour to understand the human as a dynamic body–mind synthesis: On the one hand, embodied cognitive science plays a privileged role in defining the field of application of sport psychology by highlighting the reciprocal body–mind intertwinement in sporting activity; on the other hand, EC finds the most striking confirmations of its theoretical claims in the accounts of sport performance and athletic skill provided by scientific psychology. In conclusion, EC adequately responds to the foundational requirements of sport psychology and matches its practical expectations in various fields of applied research.

References

Abreu, A. M., Esteves, P. T., & Aglioti, S. M. (2019). Action understanding, motor resonance, and embodied simulation in sports: Bridging ecological and neuroscientific approaches. In M. Cappuccio (Ed.), *Handbook of embodied cognition and sport psychology.* (pp. 359–380). Cambridge, MA: MIT Press.

Abreu, A. M., Macaluso, E., Azevedo, P. T., Cesari, P., Urgesi, C., & Aglioti, S. M. (2012). Action anticipation beyond the action observation network: A functional magnetic resonance imaging study in expert basketball players. *European Journal of Neuroscience, 35*, 1646–1654.

Adams, F., & Aizawa, K. (2008). *The bounds of cognition.* Malden, MA: Blackwell.

Aglioti, S. M., Cesari, P., Romani, M., & Urgesi, C. (2008). Action anticipation and motor resonance in elite basketball players. *Nature Neuroscience, 11*, 1109–1116.

Aranyosi, I. (2013). *The peripheral mind.* Oxford: Oxford University Press.

Baker, J., & Farrow, D. (2015). A [very brief] review of the historical foundations of sport expertise. In J. Baker & D. Farrow (Eds.), *Routledge handbook of sport expertise* (pp. 1–7). London: Routledge.

Baumeister, R. F. (1984). Choking under pressure: Self-consciousness and paradoxical effects of incentives on skillful performance. *Journal of Personality and Social Psychology, 46*, 610–620.

Beach, L. R., & Lipshitz, R. (1993). Why classical decision theory is an inappropriate standard for evaluating and aiding most human decision making. In G. Klein, J. Orasanu, R. Calderwood & C. E. Zsambok (Eds.), *Decision making in action: Models and methods* (pp. 21–35). Norwood, NJ: Ablex.

Beilock, S. (2008). Beyond the playing field: Sport psychology meets embodied cognition. *International Review of Sport and Exercise Psychology, 1*(1), 19–30.

Beilock, S. (2010). *Choke: What the secrets of the brain reveal about getting it right when you have to.* New York: Simon & Schuster.

Beilock, S. (2015). *How the body knows its mind: The surprising power of the physical environment to influence how you think and feel.* New York: Atria Books.

Beilock, S. L., & Carr, T. H. (2001). On the fragility of skilled performance: What governs choking under pressure? *Journal of Experimental Psychology. General, 130*(4), 701–725.

Beilock, S., Carr, T. H., MacMahon, C., & Starkes, H. L. (2002). When paying attention becomes counterproductive: Impact of divided versus skill-focused attention on novice and experienced performance of sensorimotor skills. *Journal of Experimental Psychology Applied, 8*, 6–16.

Beilock, S. L., Bertenthal, B. I., McCoy, A. M., & Carr, T. H. (2004). Haste does not always make waste: Expertise, direction of attention, and speed versus accuracy in performing sensorimotor skills. *Psychonomic Bulletin & Review, 11*, 373–379.

Beilock, S. L., & Gray, R. (2012). From attentional control to attentional spillover: A skill-level investigation of attention, movement, and performance outcomes. *Human Movement Science, 31*, 1473–1499.

Beilock, S. L., Lyons, I. M., Mattarella-Micke, A., Nusbaum, H. C., & Small, S. L. (2008). Sports experience changes the neural processing of action language. *Proceedings of the National Academy of Sciences, 105*(36), 13269–13273.

Biggio, M., Bisio, A., Avanzino, L., Ruggeri, P., & Bove, M. (2017). This racket is not mine: The influence of the tool-use on peripersonal space. *Neuropsychologia, 103*, 54–58.

Bloom, B. S. (1985). *Developing talent in young people.* New York: Ballantine.

Breivik, G. (2013). Zombie-like or superconscious? A phenomenological and conceptual analysis of consciousness in elite sport. *Journal of the Philosophy of Sport, 40*, 85–106.

Bruya, B. (2010). *Effortless attention: A new perspective in the cognitive science of attention and action.* Cambridge, MA and London: MIT Press.

Cappuccio, M. L. (2017). Flow, choke, skill: The role of the non-conscious in sport performance. In Z. Radman (Ed.), *Before consciousness: In search of the fundamentals of mind* (pp. 323–371). Exeter: Imprint Academic.

Cappuccio, M. L., Gray, R., Hill, D. M., Mesagno, C., & Carr, T. H. (2019). The many threats of self-consciousness: Embodied approaches to choking under pressure in sensorimotor skills. In M. L. Cappuccio (Ed.), *Handbook of embodied cognition and sport psychology* (pp. 137–155). Cambridge, MA: MIT Press.

Carello, C, & Turvey M. (2016) Dynamic (effortful) touch. In T. Prescott, E. Ahissar, & E. Izhikevich (Eds.), *Scholarpedia of touch* (pp. 227–240). Paris: Atlantis Press.

Chemero, A. (2009). *Radical embodied cognitive science.* Cambridge, MA: MIT Press.

Chiel, H. J., & Beer, R. D. (1997). The brain has a body: Adaptive behavior emerges from interactions of nervous system, body and environment. *Trends in Neurosciences, 20*, 553–557.

Christensen, W., Sutton, J., & McIlwain, D. (2013). Cognitive control in skilled action. Online draft. https://waynechristensen.wordpress.com/2013/08/15/cognitive-control-in-skilled-action/

Christensen, W., Sutton, J., & McIlwain, D. J. (2016). Cognition in skilled action: Meshed control and the varieties of skill experience. *Mind & Language, 31*, 37–66.

Clark, A., & Chalmers, D. (1998). The extended mind. *Analysis, 58*, 7–19.

Csikzentmihalyi, M. (1991). *Flow: The psychology of optimal experience.* New York: Harper & Row.

Danziger, S., Levav, J., Avnaim-Pesso, L. (2011). Extraneous factors in judicial decisions. *Proceedings National Academy of Sciences USA, 108*, 6889–6892.

Dreyfus, H. L. (2002). Intelligence without representation: Merleau-Ponty's critique of mental representation. *Phenomenology and the Cognitive Sciences, 1*, 367–383.

Dreyfus, H. L. (2005). Overcoming the myth of the mental: How philosophers can profit from the phenomenology of everyday expertise. In *Proceedings and Addresses of the American Philosophical Association* (pp. 47–65). Newark, DE: American Philosophical Association.

Dreyfus, S. E., & Dreyfus, H. L. (1980). *A five-stage model of the mental activities involved in directed skill acquisition.* (No. ORC-80-2) Berkeley, CA: Berkeley Operations Research Center, California University.

Ericsson, A. (2003). How the expert performance approach differs from traditional approaches to expertise in sport: In search of a shared theoretical framework for studying expert performance. In J. L. Starkes & K. A. Ericsson (Eds.), *Expert performance in sports: Advances in research on sports expertise* (pp. 371–402). Champaign, IL: Human Kinetics.

Ericsson, K. A. (2006). The influence of experience and deliberate practice on development of superior expert performance. In K. A. Ericsson, N. Charness, P. J. Feltovich, & R. R. Hoffman (Eds.), *The Cambridge handbook of expertise and expert performance* (pp. 683–704). Cambridge: Cambridge University Press.

Ericsson, K. A., Krampe, R. T., & Tesch-Römer, C. (1993). The role of deliberate practice in the acquisition of expert performance. *Psychological Review, 100*, 363–406.

Eriksen, J. (2010). Mindless coping in competitive sport: Some implications and consequences. *Sport, Ethics and Philosophy, 4*, 66–86.

Eysenck, M. W. (2004). *Psychology: An international perspective.* Hove: Psychology Press.

Eysenck, M.W., & M.G. Calvo. (1992). Anxiety and performance: The processing efficiency theory. *Cognition & Emotion, 6*, 409–434.

Farrow, D., Baker, J., & MacMahon, C. (2013). *Developing sports expertise: Researchers and coaches put theory to practice.* Oxford: Routledge.

Ferrari, P. F., & Rizzolatti, G. (2014). Introduction: Mirror neuron research: the past and the future. *Philosophical Transactions of the Royal Society of London. Series B, Biological Sciences, 369*(1644), 1–4.

Fitts, P. M., & Posner, M. I. (1967). *Human performance.* Monterey, CA: Brooks/Cole.

Ford, P., Hodges, N. J., & Williams, A. M. (2005). Online attentional-focus manipulations in a soccer dribbling task: Implications for the proceduralization of motor skills. *Journal of Motor Behavior, 37,* 386–394.

Gabbet, T. (2015). Physical qualities of experts. In J. Baker & D. Farrow (Eds.), *The Routledge handbook of sport expertise* (pp. 121–129). London: Routledge.

Gallagher, S. (2005). *How the body shapes the mind.* Oxford: Oxford University Press.

Gallagher, S. (2011). Interpretations of embodied cognition. In W. Tschacher & C. Bergomi (Eds.), *The implications of embodiment: Cognition and communication* (pp. 59–70). Exeter: Imprint Academic.

Gallagher, S. (2016). The practice of thinking: Between Dreyfus and McDowell. In T. Breyer (Ed.), *The phenomenology of thinking* (pp. 134–146). London: Routledge.

Gallagher, S., & Ilundáin-Agurruza, J. (in press). Self- and other-awareness in joint expert performance. In E. Fridland & C. Pavese (Eds.), *Routledge handbook on skill and expertise.* London: Routledge.

Gallese, V. (2007). The shared manifold hypothesis: Embodied simulation and its role in empathy and social cognition. In T. F. D. Farrow & P. W. R. Woodruff (Eds.), *Empathy in mental illness and health* (pp. 448–472). Cambridge: Cambridge University Press.

Gibson, J. J. (1966). *The senses considered as perceptual systems.* Boston: Houghton Mifflin.

Gibson, J. J. (1979). *The ecological approach to visual perception.* Boston: Houghton Mifflin.

Glenberg, A. M. (2011). How reading comprehension is embodied and why that matters. *International Electronic Journal of Elementary Education, 4,* 5–18.

Glenberg, A. M., & Gallese, V. (2012). Action-based language: A theory of language acquisition, comprehension, and production. *Cortex: A Journal Devoted to the Study of the Nervous System and Behavior, 48,* 905–922.

Glowinski, D., Mancini, M., Cowie, R., Camurri, C., Chiorri, A., & Doherty, C. (2013). The movements made by performers in a skilled quartet: A distinctive pattern, and the function that it serves. *Frontiers in Psychology, 4,* 841.

Gnecco, G., Badino, L., Camurri, A., D'Ausilio, A., Fadiga, L., Glowinski, D., & Volpe, G. (2013). Towards automated analysis of joint music performance in the orchestra. In *International Conference on Arts and Technology* (pp. 120–127). Heidelberg: Springer.

Gray, R. (2014). Embodied perception in sport. *International Review of Sport and Exercise Psychology, 7,* 72–86.

Hands, B., McIntyre, F., & Parker., H. (2018). The general motor ability hypothesis: An old idea revisited. *Perceptual and Motor Skills, 125,* 213–233.

Hodges, N. J., & Williams, A. M. (2012). *Skill acquisition in sport.* London: Routledge.

Hoffmann, S., Borges, U., Bröker, L., Laborde, S., Liepelt, R., Lobinger, B. H., & Raab, J. M. (2018). The psychophysiology of action: A multidisciplinary endeavor for integrating action and cognition. *Frontiers of Psychology, 9,* 1423.

Hutto, D. D., & Myin, E. (2017). *Evolving enactivism: Basic minds meet content.* Cambridge, MA, and London, England: MIT Press.

Hutto, D. D., & Sánchez-García, R. (2015). Choking rectified: Embodied expertise beyond Dreyfus. *Phenomenology and the Cognitive Sciences, 14,* 309–331.

Ikegami, T., Nakamoto, H., & Ganesh, G. (2019). Action-driven and prediction-driven contagions in human actions. In M. L. Cappuccio (Ed.), *Handbook of embodied cognition and sport psychology* (pp. 381–411). Cambridge, MA: MIT Press.

Ilundáin-Agurruza, J. (2015). From clumsy failure to skillful fluency: A phenomenological analysis of and Eastern solution to sport's choking effect. *Phenomenology and the Cognitive Sciences, 14,* 397–421.

Ilundáin-Agurruza, J. (2016). *Holism and the cultivation of excellence in sports and performative endeavors: Skillful striving.* London: Routledge.

Ilundáin-Agurruza, J. (2017). Muscular imaginings—A phenomenological and enactive model for imagination. *Sport, Ethics and Philosophy, 11,* 92–108.

Immonen, T., Brymer, E., Davids, K., Liukkonen, J., & Jaakkola, T. (2018). An ecological conceptualization of extreme sports. *Frontiers in Psychology, 9*(1274), 1–9.

Jackson, S. A., & Csikzentmihalyi, M. (1999). *Flow in sports.* Champaign, IL: Human Kinetics.

James, W. (1890). *Principles of psychology*. New York: Dover.

Kirchoff, M. (2015). Extended cognition and the causal-constitutive fallacy: In search of a diachronic and dynamical conception of constitution. *Philosophy and Phenomenological Research, 90*, 320–360.

Klein, G. (1998). *Sources of power: How people make decisions*. Cambridge, MA: MIT Press.

Krenn, O., Werner, I., Lawrence, E., & Valero-Cuevas, F. J. (2015). The lower extremity dexterity text quantifies sensorimotor control for cross-country skiing. In E. Müller, J. Kröll, S. Lindiger, J. Pfusterschmied, & T. Stögl (Eds.), *Science and skiing V* (pp. 439–445). Aachen: Meyer & Meyer.

Kugler, P. N., & Turvey, M. T. (1987). *Information, natural law, and the self-assembly of rhythmic movement*. London: Routledge.

Lintern, G., Moon, B., Klein, G., & Hoffmann, R. R. (2018). Eliciting and representing the knowledge of experts. In A. K. Ericsson, R. R. Hoffman, A. Kozbelt, & M. Williams (Eds.), *The Cambridge handbook of expertise and expert performance* (2nd ed., pp. 165–191). Cambridge: Cambridge University Press.

Loehr, J. D., Kourtis, D., Vesper, C., Sebanz, N., & Knoblich, G. (2013). Monitoring individual and joint action outcomes in duet music performance. *Journal of Cognitive Neuroscience, 25*, 1049–1061.

Mann, D. (2019). Predictive processing in the control of interoceptive motor actions. In M. L. Cappuccio (Ed.), *Handbook of embodied cognition and sport psychology* (pp. 651–668). Cambridge MA: MIT Press.

Maravita, A., & Iriki, A. (2004). Tools for the body (schema). *Trends in Cognitive Sciences, 8*, 79–86.

Marin, I., & Kipnis, J. (2013). Learning and memory … and the immune system. *Learning and Memory, 20*, 601–606.

Masters, R., & Maxwell, J. (2008). The theory of reinvestment. *International Review of Sport and Exercise Psychology, 1*(2), 160–183.

Matthen, M. (2014). Debunking enactivism. *Canadian Journal of Philosophy, 44*, 118–128.

McCloy, C. H. (1934). The measurement of general motor capacity and general motor ability. *Research Quarterly, 5*(Supp. 1), 46–61.

Menary, R. A. (2010). Dimensions of mind. *Phenomenology and the Cognitive Sciences, 9*, 561–578.

Merleau-Ponty, M. (1962). *Phenomenology of perception* (trans. C. Smith). London: Kegan Paul.

Montero, B. G. (2016). *Thought in action: Expertise and the conscious mind*. Oxford: Oxford University Press.

Noë, A. (2005). *Action in perception*. Cambridge, MA: MIT Press.

O'Regan, J. K., & Noë, A. (2001). A sensorimotor account of vision and visual consciousness. *Behavioral and Brain Sciences, 24*, 939–973.

Pfeifer, R., Fumiya L., & Lungarella, M. (2014). Cognition from the bottom up: On biological inspiration, body morphology, and soft materials. *Trends in Cognitive Sciences, 18*, 404–413.

Pijpers, J. R., Oudejans, R. D., & Bakker, F. C. (2007). Changes in the perception of action possibilities while climbing to fatigue on a climbing wall. *Journal of Sports Science, 25*, 97–110.

Putnam, H. (1960). Minds and machines. In S. Hook. (Ed.), *Dimensions of mind* (pp. 138–164). London: Collier-Macmillan.

Putnam, H. (1967). Psychophysical predicates. In W. Capitan & D. Merrill. (Eds.), *Art, mind, and religion*. Pittsburgh, PA: University of Pittsburgh Press. Reprinted as "The nature of mental states," in H. Putnam (1975), *Mind, Language, and Reality* (pp. 429–440). Cambridge: Cambridge University Press.

Putnam, H. (1981). Brains in a vat. In H. Putnam (Ed.), *Reason, truth and history* (pp. 1–21). Cambridge: Cambridge University Press.

Repp, B. H., & Su, Y. H. (2013). Sensorimotor synchronization: A review of recent research (2006–2012). *Psychonomic Bulletin & Review, 20*, 403–452.

Rucińska, Z., & Aggerholm, K. (2019). Embodied and Enacted Creativity in Sports. In M. Cappuccio (Ed.), *Handbook on embodied cognition and sport psychology* (pp. 669–694). Cambridge, MA: MIT Press.

Schack, T., & Land, W. M. (2016). Mental representation and learning. In R. J. Schinke, K. R. McGannon & B. Smith (Eds.), *Routledge international handbook of sport psychology* (pp. 723–737). Abingdon, UK: Routledge.

Schmidt, R. A. (1991). *Motor learning and performance: From principles to practice*. Champaign, IL: Human Kinetics.

Soliman, T. M., & Glenberg, A. M. (2014). The embodiment of culture. In L. Shapiro (Ed.), *The Routledge handbook of embodied cognition* (pp. 207–220). London: Routledge.

Sutton, J., McIlwain, D., Christensen, W., & Geeves, A. (2011). Applying intelligence to the reflexes: Embodied skills and habits between Dreyfus and Descartes. *Journal of the British Society for Phenomenology, 42*, 78–103.

Swann, C., Keegan, R., Crust, L., & Piggott, D. (2016). Psychological states underlying excellent performance in professional golfers: "Letting it happen" vs. "making it happen". *Psychology of Sport and Exercise, 23,* 101–113.

Turvey, M. T. (1973). On peripheral and central processes in vision: Inferences from an information-processing analysis of masking with patterned stimuli. *Psychological Review, 80,* 1–52.

Varela, F. J., Thompson, E., & Rosch, E. (1991). *The embodied mind: Cognitive science and human experience.* Cambridge, MA: MIT Press.

Vickers, J. (2016). The quiet eye: Reply to sixteen commentaries. *Current Issues in Sport Science, 118,* 1–18.

Vine, S., Lee, D., Moore, L., & Wilson, M. (2013). Quiet eye and choking: Online control breaks down at the point of performance failure medicine and science. *Sports and Exercise, 45,* 1988–1994.

Wenke, D., Atmaca, S., Holländer, A., Liepelt, R., Baess, P., & Prinz, W. (2011). What is shared in joint action? Issues of co-representation, response conflict, and agent identification. *Review of Philosophy and Psychology, 2,* 147–172.

Wilson, A. D., & Golonka, S. (2013). Embodied cognition is not what you think it is. *Frontiers in Psychology, 4,* 58.

Witt, J. K., South, C. S., & Sugovic, M. (2014). A perceiver's own abilities influence perception, even when observing others. *Psychonomic Bulletin and Review, 2,* 384–389.

Wulf, G. (2007). *Attention and motor skill learning.* Champaign, IL: Human Kinetics.

Wulf, G., & Lewthwaite, L. (2010). Motor skill learning and performance: A review of influential factors. *Medical Education, 44,* 75–84.

10
EMOTIONAL INTELLIGENCE

Emma Mosley, Matthew Watson, and Sylvain Laborde

Introduction

The manifestations of emotions go hand in hand with sport and, as a result, have the ability to permeate sporting performance (Laborde, Dosseville, & Allen, 2015; Jones, 2012). Although emotions can be changeable in nature, more recent views on emotional dispositions suggest that emotional states may be more stable and specific to individuals (Lazarus, 2000). One particular theoretical standpoint linked to this is emotional intelligence (Goleman, 1995), which over the last two decades has demanded more interest within the sporting domain (Laborde, Allen, & Guillén, 2016). Therefore, the purpose of this entry is to define, contextualize, and showcase the application of emotional intelligence, specifically at the trait level, within sporting performance.

Emotional Intelligence: Definition and Theoretical Underpinning

Emotional intelligence (EI) is broadly defined as the individual responses to intrapersonal or interpersonal emotional information and incorporates the identification, expression, understanding, and regulation of one's own and others' emotions (Mayer & Salovey, 1997; Petrides & Furnham, 2003). Previous literature once argued that EI was split into separate opposing theoretical models, EI as an ability and EI as a trait (Stough, Saklofske, & Parker, 2009). The ability standpoint suggested EI can be trained and varies across different environments (Matthews, Zeidner, & Roberts, 2007), whereas the trait standpoint assumes EI is relatively stable (Petrides, 2009). However, since then, the tripartite model of EI has brought these opposing views together in a more holistic approach to understanding EI (Mikolajczak, 2009; Nelis, Quoidbach, Hansenne, & Mikolajczak, 2009).

The tripartite model suggests three levels of EI organization: knowledge, ability, and trait (Mikolajczak, 2009; Nelis et al., 2009). Knowledge is located within the first level of the model and it concerns the depth and breadth of the individual's emotion-related knowledge (Mikolajczak, 2009). In particular, Mikolajczak (2009) suggests that the knowledge is specifically related to what the person knows about emotions and how to cope with emotionally charged situations. In sport, an athlete may recognize that he/she is angry and link this to past experiences where the same emotion has occurred, such as when a footballer receives a red card. Ability is the second level of the model; it details the proficiency of an individual to draw on emotion-related abilities in emotional situations (Mikolajczak, 2009), such as an athlete's ability to draw on a breathing technique when he/she is experiencing anxiety. The third and final level of the model is trait EI, also known as dispositions, which is the typical behaviour an individual would exhibit in emotionally laden situations. For example, a captain high in trait EI would always remain calm under pressure to give clear instructions to his/her team. As trait EI is relatively stable and allows researchers and practitioners alike to examine behaviours in sporting situations, it is no wonder that EI has received large amounts of attention within sporting literature (Laborde, Dosseville, et al., 2015). Therefore, the purpose of this contribution is to focus on trait EI and its links to sporting performance.

Trait EI Conceptualization

Trait EI is considered a personality trait rather than a cognitive ability and involves self-perceptions that embrace the subjective nature of emotion (Petrides, Pita, & Kokkinaki, 2007). More specifically, it is defined as a constellation of emotional self-perceptions situated at the lower levels of personality hierarchies and it is made up of four main factors: well-being, self-control, emotionality, and sociability (Petrides et al., 2007). The well-being factor reflects a generalized sense of well-being that extends from past achievements to future expectations (Petrides, 2009). For example, if an athlete has previously done well in a competition, he/she will have a better sense of well-being approaching the next competition. Self-control is the ability to regulate emotions and impulses and manage external pressure and stress (Petrides & Furnham, 2003). For example, a rugby player with low self-control may not be able to control his or her impulses after a hard tackle and lash out. Emotionality allows individuals to better understand their own and others' emotions (Petrides, 2009). For example, a tennis player high in emotionality can better understand emotional cues from their opponent's body language. The factor of sociability directly links to the ability to use emotion management (influencing others), be assertive, and have good social awareness (Petrides, 2009). For example, a captain high in sociability will be better able to manage the emotions of his or her team and be assertive in emotionally charged situations.

Trait EI encompasses dispositions that are emotionally related, thus causing tendencies to behave in a predetermined manner in emotional situations (Nelis et al., 2009), and this makes it an interesting trait to examine within the sporting context. A systematic review of EI in sport and exercise emphasized the importance of EI in the sporting domain due to the need for athletes to motivate themselves to achieve long-term goals and manage the stressors of competition (Laborde, Dosseville et al., 2015). Within this context, athletes have to face emotionally charged situations, such as pressure. Individuals high in trait EI are said to effectively regulate, control, and modify emotions through implementing strategies (Gross & Thompson, 2007). These strategies differ in that emotion regulation is based on feedback processes and reduces the intensification of the activation caused by an emotion (Hackfort, 1999). Emotional control refers to the induction or reduction of a particular emotion through specific strategies – for example, slow breathing – and, finally, emotion modulation is where the athlete manages multiple and/or conflicting emotions (Hackfort, 1999). By successfully altering these emotional stimuli, trait EI promotes many beneficial effects that have a direct or indirect influence on sporting performance. For example, direct effects include higher levels of trait EI promoting better performance (Perlini & Halverson, 2006; Zizi, Deaner, & Hirschhorn, 2003), and indirect influences include facilitating coping under stress (Laborde, Brull, Weber, & Anders, 2011), enhanced physiological responses (Laborde et al., 2011;

Laborde, Lautenbach, & Allen, 2015; Laborde, Lautenbach, Herbert, Allen, & Achtzehn, 2014; Mosley, Laborde, & Kavanagh, 2018), and better emotional responses to competition (Lane et al., 2010; Lane & Wilson, 2011; Lu, Li, Hsu, & Williams, 2010). The next section describes how to measure trait EI.

Trait EI Measurement

Several questionnaires are used to measure trait EI in sports, such as the trait emotional intelligence questionnaire (Petrides, 2009), the Schutte emotional intelligence scale (Schutte et al., 1998), or the Bar-On Emotional Quotient Inventory (Bar-On, 2004). Even if the research on trait EI has sometimes come under the same umbrella (Petrides et al., 2016), the instrument used to measure trait EI should be carefully considered regarding the trait EI conceptualization on which it is based (Laborde & Allen, 2016). In sports, the questionnaire showing the most associations with a large range of outcomes is the trait emotional intelligence questionnaire (Petrides, 2009). This questionnaire exists in both a full- (153 items) and short- (30 items) form version, both providing a similar four-factor structure (Laborde, Allen, & Guillén, 2016); the short-form version has been shown to elicit higher results than the long-form one (Laborde, Guillén, & Watson, 2017). The other measures of trait EI, the Schutte emotional intelligence scale (Lane, Meyer, et al., 2009; Vaughan & Laborde, 2017) and the Bar-On Emotional Quotient Inventory (Stanimirovic & Hanrahan, 2012), showed some limitations with sport samples. Therefore, the recommended measure of trait EI within sporting samples would be the trait emotional intelligence questionnaire (Laborde, Dosseville, et al., 2015).

Questionnaires are currently the only way to measure trait EI; as a result, this poses some limitations when this method is used to determine the predictions of trait EI in sport. One limitation is that questionnaires are subject to bias, particularly if the construct in question is desirable within the sporting context, which the evidence suggests trait EI is. A suggestion to increase validity could be to use more objective measures of emotion and emotion regulation within performance settings. Examples such as cardiac vagal activity (Laborde, Lautenbach, et al., 2015) and cortisol (Laborde, Lautenbach, et al., 2014) have been associated with trait EI, and measuring these alongside self-report instruments may help to surmount some of the problems associated with a sole reliance on a single source of measurement.

The following paragraphs will detail how trait EI may directly and indirectly influence the sporting performance of athletes.

Direct Influences of Trait EI on Sports Performance

Across most research, it has been shown that higher levels of trait EI are related to better performance. A recent study by Rubaltelli, Agnoli, and Leo (2018) assessed the impact of trait EI on runners' finish time. They found that higher levels of trait EI predicted both actual finish time and athlete-predicted finish time, over and above training levels. Rubaltelli and colleagues suggested these effects were a result of EI enhancing the ability to control emotions related to fatigue, which in turn reduces fatigue and promotes performance (Rubaltelli et al., 2018). However, within this study, they did not use or acknowledge any other physiological measures related to performance – for example, anthropometric data or biomechanical variables, which have been shown to influence half-marathon finish times (Gomez-Molina et al., 2017; Knechtle et al., 2014). Examining the effects of trait EI on physiological effort, Tok & Morali (2009) found trait EI was associated with increased maximal isometric contractions. Although this study did not directly examine sporting performance, it does show that trait EI can influence physiological factors that are important for skill execution. In addition, from a longitudinal perspective, it has been found in baseball (Zizi et al., 2003) and ice hockey (Perlini & Halverson, 2006) that higher levels of trait EI are related to performance scores gathered over the course of a season. Specifically, trait EI moderately influenced pitching performance, but not hitting performance, in baseball (Zizi et al., 2003), and trait EI influenced the number of games played and national hockey league points in ice hockey (Perlini & Halverson, 2006).

Indirect Influences of Trait EI on Sports Performance

Trait EI has been shown to directly influence performance (Perlini & Halverson, 2006; Zizi et al., 2003); however, it can also facilitate processes that are useful within a performance domain such as subjective processes and physiological responses.

Trait EI and Subjective Processes in Sport

Trait EI has been shown to influence many subjective processes that are useful for performance. These include coping (Laborde, Dosseville, Guillén, & Chávez, 2014; Laborde, You, Dosseville, & Salinas, 2012), psychological skills usage (Lane, Thelwell, Lowther, & Devonport, 2009), and the experience of emotions in relation to sporting competition (Lane et al., 2010; Lane & Wilson, 2011; Lu et al., 2010). In relation to coping, Laborde, Dosseville, and colleagues (2014) found that higher trait EI is associated with better coping appraisals and lower competition stress; these, in turn, positively influenced performance satisfaction. More specifically, task-orientated coping, a coping method that specifically focuses on solving the problem at hand, is more likely to be used by athletes with higher levels of trait EI (Laborde et al., 2012). From Laborde et al. studies in 2012 and 2014 (Laborde et al., 2012; Laborde, Lautenbach, et al., 2014), trait EI was shown to positively influence coping, which is essential for sports performance (Nicholls & Polman, 2007). In addition to coping, other psychological skills have been highlighted with trait EI. Lane, Thelwell, et al. (2009) examined male athletes' psychological skill use alongside their trait EI. They found that those higher in trait EI had more frequent use of psychological skills within performance, and, specifically, self-talk, imagery, and activation were directly linked to athletes' ability to regulate their own emotions (Lane, Thelwell, et al., 2009). This finding shows that an athlete's higher awareness of his or her own emotional state may help to promote the use of specific psychological skills to help regulate that emotional state, which in turn may influence performance. In addition, the development of emotional intelligence enhances the emotional awareness of the individual, which in turn may influence the likelihood of adhering to interventions around emotional content (Devonport, 2007). It is important to consider that trait EI can also influence the emotions that actually manifest within the sporting environment. It has been found that, in relation to competitive performance, higher levels of trait EI can promote more pleasant emotional responses (Lane et al., 2010; Lane & Wilson, 2011) and reduced negative emotions (Lane & Wilson, 2011), such as anxiety (Lu et al., 2010). One key point to note around positive and negative emotions is that they relate to both a feeling (either a pleasant or unpleasant state) and the subsequent action regulation for that emotion (facilitating or debilitating to performance (Hackfort, 1999). For example, a swimmer high in trait EI may experience anxiety before a race, but has the ability to regulate this response and perceive this as excitement, which is then facilitative to performance.

Trait EI and Physiological Responses in Sport

Trait EI has been shown to directly influence physiological processes, with relationships being found at the neurophysiological level (Laborde et al., 2011; Laborde, Lautenbach, et al., 2015) and hormonal level (Laborde, Lautenbach, et al., 2014). At the neurophysiological level, individuals who have high trait EI exhibit more facilitative autonomic responses to stress (Laborde et al., 2011). Laborde et al. (2011) examined athletes under laboratory-induced stress, including negative imagery and crowd noise. They found that athletes lower in trait EI had a higher increase in sympatho-vagal ratio, which is considered an indicator of mental stress (Kristalboneh, Raifel, Froom, & Ribak, 1995), than their higher trait EI counterparts. This finding suggests that athletes higher in trait EI have better emotional regulation and, therefore, have a more functional physiological response to stress. The validity of the results could, however, be questioned, considering the lack of support for the sympatho-vagal ratio as a measure of mental stress within the current literature (Billman, 2013; Heathers, 2012; Laborde, Mosley, & Thayer, 2017). More recent work has focused on cardiac vagal activity, indexed through heart rate variability, which can be an indicator for emotion regulation (Laborde, Mosley, & Mertgen, 2018; Thayer, Hansen, Saus-Rose, & Johnsen, 2009).

Cardiac vagal activity has been explored in varying sporting scenarios, including laboratory (Laborde, Lautenbach, et al., 2015) and manipulated sporting competitions (Mosley et al., 2018). Laborde, Lautenbach, and colleagues (2015) tested visual search performance under pressure in line with a number of coping related variables that included trait EI. They found that trait EI well-being was the best predictor of resting cardiac vagal activity, which is in line with previous research examining resting cardiac vagal activity and well-being at rest (Geisler, Vennewald, Kubiak, & Weber, 2010). Well-being is associated with positive moods and a satisfaction with life (Geisler et al., 2010); a generalized sense of well-being can be assumed to be a result of effective self-regulation. Therefore, the link to higher levels of cardiac vagal activity makes theoretical sense (Thayer et al., 2009). During the pressurized visual search task, participants high in trait EI (emotionality) displayed higher cardiac vagal activity during the pressure task. This finding may indicate that those who were better able to understand their own emotions – and, thus, high in emotionality – had higher levels of cardiac vagal activity and, therefore, were better able to regulate their emotional response to the stressful task (Laborde, Lautenbach, et al., 2015). These findings support Laborde and colleagues' (2011) previous work and suggest that those higher in trait EI, the dimension of emotionality in particular, can better regulate emotions under pressure, which in turn can facilitate performance (Laborde, Lautenbach, et al., 2015). Mosley et al. (2018) also found a link between trait EI and cardiac vagal activity in a pressurized shooting task. Specifically, the factor of self-control increased cardiac vagal activity during the shooting task in both low- and high-pressure conditions (Mosley et al., 2018). As trait EI self-control is defined as the ability to regulate emotions and impulses and manage external pressure and stress (Petrides & Furnham, 2003), those higher in self-control may be better able to regulate themselves under stress, subsequently leading to higher cardiac vagal activity during stressful tasks.

At the hormonal level, trait EI has been found to predict cortisol secretion within a pressurized tennis serve task (Laborde, Lautenbach, et al., 2014). Specifically, Laborde, Lautenbach, and colleagues (2014) put 28 tennis players under pressure while they completed a series of serves; after this, they measured cortisol secretion, anxiety, and trait EI. Trait EI predicted cortisol secretion above and beyond anxiety levels; however, trait EI did not predict performance.

Training of Trait EI

To date, there have only been three studies that have examined the ability to train EI within sport (Campo, Laborde, & Mosley, 2016; Barlow & Banks, 2014; Crombie, Lombard, & Noakes, 2011); however, only two of the three studies have assessed trait EI as Crombie et al. (2011) examined ability EI. Barlow and Banks (2014) created a trait EI training intervention for 20 high-performance netball athletes, who were either assigned to a control group or an experimental group. Trait EI was measured in the experimental group only; both groups completed anxiety, self-efficacy, and team identification measures prior to the intervention. The experimental group took part in a half-hour individual coaching session that consisted of the coach explaining and feeding back on the athlete's EI scores. The control group had no intervention process. When compared with the control group, the experimental group had greater self-efficacy and reduced anxiety, thus suggesting that a short-term intervention that focuses on knowledge and understanding of trait EI is beneficial to other areas of athletes' psychological functioning (Barlow & Banks, 2014). However, this intervention was very brief, and they did not assess the long-term effects of the intervention on the athletes.

The second, and more recent, study by Campo and colleagues (2016) examined the influence of a 6-week training programme across a season using rugby union players. The intervention group delivery comprised of two sessions for pre- and post-testing of trait EI and four education sessions that covered (1) an introduction to EI and feedback on profiles; (2) education around emotions and the appraisal process; (3) introduction to arousal zones, emotional contagion, and regulation; and (4) application of knowledge through building performance routines. This was also supported by homework that involved the athletes improving the specific skills they had learned in the sessions. The control group sessions consisted of match analysis that focused on technical skills. The results showed partial support for the improvement of trait EI after the intervention. The intervention was effective with regard to enhancing specific aspects of trait EI (for example, social competence, emotion perception, and emotion management); however, global trait EI was not improved. Nevertheless, collectively, these studies show great support in both short- and longer-term interventions to enhance trait EI in athletes. As previously discussed, it is clear that trait EI is beneficial for sporting performance, and, as this can be enhanced through training, practitioners and researchers should address this further.

Trait EI in Other Sporting Populations

Not only is trait EI important for athletic performance, but it also bears much relevance to other populations who function within the sporting domain, such as coaches, officials, and spectators. The possession of a high degree of EI is a critical attribute in sports coaches, given the heightened emotional nature of this profession (Chan & Mallett, 2011; Latimer, Rench, & Brackett, 2007). For example, drawing on their ability EI, a coach may try to appear calm in the heat of a close game, in order to alleviate some of the pressure on his or her players, or become animated and vocal during a sluggish performance, in an attempt to energize the performance of his or her team. However, it is arguably the dispositional emotional behaviours (i.e., trait EI) routinely demonstrated by coaches in the long term (e.g., over the course of a season) that are of greater significance to the performance of their athletes or teams.

Coaches' EI is usually discussed in relation to coaches' interactions with their athletes or teams (Latimer et al., 2007). Related concepts also appear in research on coaching, but trait EI is popular given that it comprises both empathy (i.e., the understanding of someone else's perspective) and emotion perception (i.e., the decoding of intra- and interpersonal emotion). Numerous theoretical sources exist that highlight the role of coaches' EI in nurturing strong coach–athlete relationships, particularly through the interpersonal EI dimensions relating to the perception, understanding, and management of emotion in their athletes (Chan & Mallett, 2011). The perception and understanding of others' emotions (part of the trait EI factor of emotionality) allow coaches to establish deep, emotional connections with their athletes, which are necessary to inspire improved performance (O'Neil, 2011). Of course, accuracy in both of these dimensions is important, not just in terms of the correct identification of an emotion, but also in terms of its intensity and likely valence for the athlete. A coach that can accurately perceive and understand his or her athlete's emotion in this way will have a better idea of the athlete's psychological state and, in turn, the factors underlying his or her behaviour (Lorimer, 2013). Indeed, elite coaches speak of the necessity for high levels of EI in order to adapt their behaviour to the individual needs of their athletes (Lara-Bercial & Mallett, 2016).

Despite the support for the importance of coaches' EI and the depth of literature concerning athletes' EI, a recent systematic review of EI in sport identified only two studies that empirically examine coaches' EI (Laborde et al., 2016). Thelwell, Lane, Weston, and Greenlees (2008) found a number of associations between subscales of trait EI and coaching efficacy. Specifically, EI factors relating to both emotion regulation and social skills showed significant associations with coaches' perceived confidence to influence the psychological states and skills of their athletes. The appraisal of own emotions subscale was also significantly associated with the belief coaches had in their teaching and diagnostic skills (i.e., technique efficacy). These findings suggest that coaches' efficacy beliefs are partly influenced by their ability to detect and optimally regulate their emotions. Similarly, Hwang, Feltz, and Lee (2013) reported a relationship between EI and coaching efficacy, but further showed EI to be a significant predictor of coaches' training and instruction, positive feedback, social support, and situational consideration. One study has since examined coaches' trait EI and the motivational states of their athletes and found a relationship between coaches' self-control and the accuracy of their perception of athletes' competence satisfaction, although no direct effect of coaches' EI on athletes' motivation (Watson & Kleinert, 2018). It can be inferred from these findings that coaches with high trait EI are able to regulate their emotion so as to preserve or enter into their own optimal emotional state (i.e., he/she feels confident that he/she can overcome potentially unfavourable emotions) and also to enhance the effectiveness of their coaching behaviours (e.g., generating a positive mood to improve the provision of feedback).

The aforementioned results suggest an important role of the intrapersonal dimensions of trait EI for coaches, particularly those that, at least in part, pertain to the awareness of and ability to regulate their emotions, such as emotionality and self-control. As succinctly put by Cruickshank and Collins (2015) in their discussion of EI as a key attribute of coaches, "without the ability to recognize and regulate one's own responses … coaches will struggle to consistently select the best option or delivery style when interacting with their followers" (p. 163). Therefore, it may also be important to consider the type of emotion regulation coaches engage in. Gross and Thompson (2007) outline an array of emotion regulation processes, but cognitive reappraisal, an antecedent-focused form of emotion regulation, and expressive suppression, a response-focused form of emotion regulation, are commonly examined in research. Cognitive reappraisal involves actively changing the meaning and intensity of a stimulus to modify the emotional experience, and expressive suppression redirects attention to one's external expression of emotion. For example, a coach responding to a perceived bad call by a referee may accept it as part of the game and unlikely to determine the final result (reappraisal), or forcibly maintain a neutral expression despite an undercurrent of frustration (suppression). As cognitive reappraisal has shown favourable effects in terms of memory and affect in comparison with expressive suppression (Egloff, Schmukle, Schwerdtfeger, & Burns, 2006; Hayes et al., 2010), the type of emotion regulation a coach engages in could have a range of practical implications. If a coach engages in expressive suppression during critical phases of a game, his or her recollection of important details that occurred in these phases may be impaired, limiting the possibility of working on these situations in subsequent training sessions. If negative emotional reactions are suppressed, the lingering negative affect could impair subsequent interactions with his or her athletes (e.g., a critical outburst). Interestingly, coaches low in self-reported EI are more likely to experience emotional exhaustion as a result of suppressing emotion expression (or surface acting) than high-EI coaches (Lee & Chelladurai, 2015).

An emerging notion in the field of sport psychology, and one that could help to generate much-needed research attention in sports coaching, is that sports coaches are performers in their own right (Becker, 2009; Thelwell et al., 2008). This point seems particularly true from an emotional standpoint, as coaches must develop strong coach–athlete relationships, exercise emotional regulation, and be sensitive to emotional contagion. Indeed, elite athletes report favourably on the emotional consistency and stability of their coaches, as well as their abilities to use emotion to evoke a response in their athletes (Becker, 2009; Lara-Bercial & Mallett, 2016). One trait EI dimension that appears to be central to these aspects is self-control (comprising emotion regulation, stress management, and impulsiveness [low]). In comparison to individuals with low trait EI self-control, individuals high in trait EI self-control have been found to allocate more attention to negative emotional material while experiencing less mood deterioration in stressful conditions (Mikolajczak, Roy, Verstrynge, & Luminet, 2009). For sports coaches, therefore, self-control may be important to maintain an optimal emotional state and, as a result, observe relevant emotional cues emanating from their athletes, cues that may influence subsequent coaching decisions. However, very little research currently exists on self-control in coaches, although there is anecdotal evidence that hints at its importance. To quote revered ex-NBA coach Phil Jackson, "In a close game I check my pulse. I know if it gets over one hundred it's going to affect my thinking" (Mack & Casstevens, 2002, p. 28). Indeed, the interplay between trait EI self-control and physiological variables, such as cardiac vagal activity, may represent a fruitful avenue for further research in sports coaching, given recent findings relating to performance under pressure in athletes (Mosley et al., 2018).

Many of the aforementioned findings regarding EI in athletes and coaches are also of importance for other roles in sport, such as officials and spectators. Referees, for example, are passionate about their sport and susceptible to negative emotional experiences after committing an error, which may lead to subsequent biased decisions if they cannot control their emotion (Philippe, Vallerand, Andrianarisoa, & Brunel, 2009). Moreover, referees recognize the importance of building strong interpersonal relationships with players, noting the need to be highly sensitive to the emotional climate of a competition during their interactions (Morris & O'Connor, 2016). As such, the trait EI dimensions of self-control and sociability appear to be of particular importance to referees in order to regulate their emotions and appropriately assert themselves. In terms of spectators, individuals with higher EI have been found to more accurately predict their emotions regarding an upcoming basketball game than those with lower EI, an effect that was not moderated by team identification (Dunn, Brackett, Ashton-James, Schneiderman, & Salovey, 2007). For parents spectating at their children's football matches, EI has been negatively associated with maladaptive coping strategies such as venting negative emotion (Teques, Calmeiro, Martins, Duarte, & Holt, 2018). Beyond these findings, however, very little research has specifically examined the role of EI in officiating or spectator roles.

Conclusion

Across this contribution, we have shown how EI may have an influence on sports performance, trait EI in other sporting populations, and how we can train trait EI in sport. We recommend the continuation of this research in a number of ways. First, future theoretical development in the field has to consider the concept of emotional competences, which was suggested instead of emotional intelligence, based on the evidence that emotional intelligence can be trained (Brasseur, Grégoire, Bourdu, & Mikolajczak, 2013). Second, there is a need to conduct more longitudinal research within trait EI – for example, across an athletic career – to identify if this trait develops throughout the lifespan, alongside life events. Third, we encourage the development of the psychophysiological perspective of trait EI, given the holistic impact trait EI is suggested to have over the brain and body. Taking such an approach will allow researchers to objectify how self-reported trait EI may buffer stress and assist in emotion regulation within sporting settings. Fourth, it appears necessary to further assess training of trait EI across more sports, specifically individual athletes as it is not yet known how trait EI effects those competing on their own. Finally, research in individual differences in sport and exercise needs to clarify the unique contribution of trait emotional intelligence in contrast to other individual differences promoting adaptive functioning (Laborde, Guillén, Dosseville, & Allen, 2015; Laborde, Guillén, Watson, & Allen, 2017). The scope of this entry was to provide an overview of trait EI as a construct, how it is measured, and how it may influence the effects of sports performance, and it considered other trait EI in other sporting populations.

References

Barlow, A., & Banks, A. P. (2014). Using emotional intelligence in coaching high-performance athletes: A randomised controlled trial. *Coaching: An International Journal of Theory, Research and Practice, 7,* 132–139.

Bar-On, R. (2004). The Bar-On Emotional Quotient Inventory (EQ-i): Rationale, description and summary of psychometric properties. In G. Geher (Ed.), *Measuring emotional intelligence: Common ground and controversy* (pp. 115–145). Hauppage, NY: Nova Science.

Becker, A. (2009). It's not what they do, it's how they do it: Athlete experiences of great coaching. *International Journal of Sports Science and Coaching, 4,* 93–119.

Billman, G. E. (2013). The LF/HF ratio does not accurately measure cardiac sympatho-vagal balance. *Frontiers in Physiology, 4,* 1–5.

Brasseur, S., Grégoire, J., Bourdu, R., & Mikolajczak, M. (2013). The profile of emotional competence (PEC): Development and validation of a self-reported measure that fits dimensions of emotional competence theory. *PLoS ONE, 8,* 1–8. doi:10.1371/journal.pone.0062635

Campo, M., Laborde, S., & Mosley, E. (2016). Emotional intelligence training in team sports. *Journal of Individual Differences, 37*(3), 152–158.

Chan, J. T., & Mallett, C. J. (2011). The value of emotional intelligence for high performance coaching. *International Journal of Sports Science and Coaching, 6,* 333–336.

Crombie, D., Lombard, C., & Noakes, T. D. (2011). Increasing emotional intelligence in cricketers: An intervention study. *International Journal of Sports Science and Coaching, 6,* 69–86.

Cruickshank, A., & Collins, D. (2015). The sport coach. In I. O'Boyle, D. Murray, & P. Cummins (Eds.), *Leadership in sport* (pp. 155–172). Abingdon: Routledge.

Devonport, T. J. (2007). Emotional intelligence and the coping process amongst adolescent populations: A case study of student athletes. In A. M. Lane (Ed.), *Mood and human performance: Conceptual, measurement, and applied issues* (pp. 118–167). Hauppauge, NY: Nova Science.

Dunn, E. W., Brackett, M. A., Ashton-James, C., Schneiderman, E., & Salovey, P. (2007). On emotionally intelligent time travel: Individual differences in affective forecasting ability. *Personality and Social Psychology Bulletin, 33,* 85–93.

Egloff, B., Schmukle, S. C., Burns, L. R., & Schwerdtfeger, A. (2006). Spontaneous emotion regulation during evaluated speaking tasks: Associations with negative effect, anxiety expression, memory, and physiological responding. *Emotion, 6,* 356–366.

Geisler, F. C. M., Vennewald, N., Kubiak, T., & Weber, H. (2010). The impact of heart rate variability on subjective well-being is mediated by emotion regulation. *Personality and Individual Differences, 49,* 723–728.

Goleman, D. (1995). *Emotional intelligence.* New York: Bantam Books.

Gomez-Molina, J., Ogueta-Alday, A., Camara, J., Stickley, C., Rodriguez-Marroyo, J. A., & Garcia-Lopez, J. (2017). Predictive variables of half-marathon performance for male runners. *Journal of Sports Science and Medicine, 16,* 187–194.

Gross, J. J., & Thompson, R. A. (2007). Emotion regulation: Conceptual foundations. In J. J. Gross (Ed.), *Handbook of emotion regulation* (pp. 3–24). New York: Guilford Press.

Hackfort, D. (1999). The presentation and modulation of emotions. In R. Lidor & M. Bar-Eli (Eds.), *Sport psychology: Linking theory and practice* (pp. 231–244). Morgantown, WV: Fitness Information Technology.

Hayes, J. P., Morey, R. A., Petty, C. M., Seth, S., Smoski, M. J., McCarthy, G., & LaBar, K. S. (2010). Staying cool when things get hot: Emotion regulation modulates neural mechanisms of memory encoding. *Frontiers in Human Neuroscience, 4,* 230–240. doi:10.3389/fnhum.2010.00230

Heathers, J. A. J. (2012). Sympathovagal balance from heart rate variability: An obituary. *Experimental Physiology, 97*(4), 556.

Hwang, S., Feltz, D. L., & Lee, J. D. (2013). Emotional intelligence in coaching: Mediation effect of coaching efficacy on the relationship between emotional intelligence and leadership style. *International Journal of Sport and Exercise Psychology, 11,* 1–15.

Jones, M. V. (2012). Emotion regulation and sport performance. In S. M. Murphy (Ed.), *The Oxford handbook of sport and performance psychology* (pp. 154–172). New York: Oxford University Press.

Knechtle, B., Barandun, U., Knechtle, P., Zingg, M. A., Rosemann, T., & Rust, C. A. (2014). Prediction of half-marathon race time in recreational female and male runners. *Springerplus, 3,* 248. doi:10.1186/2193-1801-3-248

Kristalboneh, E., Raifel, M., Froom, P., & Ribak, J. (1995). Heart-rate-variability in health and disease. *Scandinavian Journal of Work Environment & Health, 21*(2), 85–95.

Laborde, S., & Allen, M. S. (2016). Comment: Measurement and the interpretation of trait EI research. *Emotion Review.* doi:10.1177/1754073916650498

Laborde, S., Allen, M. S., & Guillén, F. (2016). Construct and concurrent validity of the short- and long-form versions of the trait emotional intelligence questionnaire. *Personality and Individual Differences, 101,* 232–235.

Laborde, S., Brull, A., Weber, J., & Anders, L. S. (2011). Trait emotional intelligence in sports: A protective role against stress through heart rate variability?. *Personality and Individual Differences, 51*(1), 23–27.

Laborde, S., Dosseville, F., & Allen, M. (2015). Emotional intelligence in sport and exercise: A systematic review. *Scandinavian Journal of Medicine and Science in Sports, 26*(8), 862–874.

Laborde, S., Dosseville, F., Guillén, F., & Chávez, E. (2014). Validity of the trait emotional intelligence questionnaire in sports and its links with performance satisfaction. *Psychology of Sport and Exercise, 15*(5), 481–490.

Laborde, S., Guillén, F., Dosseville, F., & Allen, M. S. (2015). Chronotype, sport participation, and positive personality-trait-like individual differences. *Chronobiology International, 32,* 942–951.

Laborde, S., Guillén, F., & Watson, M. (2017). Trait emotional intelligence questionnaire full-form and short-form versions: Links with sport participation frequency and duration and type of sport practiced. *Personality and Individual Differences, 108,* 5–9.

Laborde, S., Guillén, F., Watson, M., & Allen, M. S. (2017). The light quartet: Positive personality traits and approaches to coping in sport coaches. *Psychology of Sport and Exercise, 32,* 67–73.

Laborde, S., Lautenbach, F., & Allen, M. S. (2015). The contribution of coping-related variables and heart rate variability to visual search performance under pressure. *Physiology & Behavior, 139,* 532–540.

Laborde, S., Lautenbach, F., Herbert, C., Allen, M. S., & Achtzehn, S. (2014). The role of trait emotional intelligence in emotion regulation and performance under pressure. *Personality and Individual Differences, 57,* 43–47.

Laborde, S., Mosley, E., & Mertgen, A. (2018). Vagal tank theory: The three Rs of cardiac vagal control functioning – resting, reactivity, and recovery. *Frontiers in Neuroscience, 12.* doi:10.3389/fnins.2018.00458

Laborde, S., Mosley, E., & Thayer, J. F. (2017). Heart rate variability and cardiac vagal tone in psycho-physiological research - Recommendations for experiment planning, data analysis, and data reporting. *Frontiers in Psychology, 8*, 1–18.

Laborde, S., You, M., Dosseville, F., & Salinas, A. (2012). Culture, individual differences, and situation: Influence on coping in French and Chinese table tennis players. *European Journal of Sport Sciences, 12*, 255–261.

Lane, A. M., Devonport, T. J., Soos, I., Karsai, I., Leibinger, E., & Hamar, P. (2010). Emotional intelligence and emotions associated with optimal and dysfunctional athletic performance. *Journal of Sports Science and Medicine, 9*(3), 388–392.

Lane, A. M., Meyer, B. B., Devonport, T. J., Davies, K. A., Thelwell, R., Gill, G. S., ... Weston, N. J. V. (2009). Validity of the emotional intelligence scale for use in sport. *Journal of Sports Science and Medicine, 8*(2), 289–295.

Lane, A. M., Thelwell, R. C., Lowther, J., & Devonport, T. (2009). Emotional Intelligence and psychological skill use among athletes. *Social Behaviour and Personality, 37*, 195–202.

Lane, A. M., & Wilson, M. R. (2011). Emotions and trait emotional intelligence among ultra-endurance runners. *Journal of Science and Medicine in Sport, 14*, 358–362.

Lara-Bercial, S., & Mallett, C. J. (2016). The practices and developmental pathways of professional and Olympic serial winning coaches. *Human Kinetics Journals, 3*, 221–239.

Latimer, A. E., Rench, T. A., & Brackett, M. A. (2007). Emotional intelligence: A frame- work for examining emotions in sport and exercise groups. In M. Beauchamp & M. Eys (Eds.), *Group dynamics advances in sport and exercise psychology: Contemporary themes* (pp. 3–22). New York: Routledge.

Lazarus, R. S. (2000). How emotions influence performance in competitive sports. *The Sport Psychologist, 14*, 229–252.

Lee, Y. H., & Chelladurai, P. (2015). Affectivity, emotional labor, emotional exhaustion, and emotional intelligence in coaching. *Journal of Applied Sport Psychology, 0*, 1–16. doi:10.1080/10413200.2015.1092481

Lorimer, R. (2013). The development of empathic accuracy in sports coaches. *Journal of Sport Psychology in Action, 4*, 26–33.

Lu, F. J., Li, G. S., Hsu, E. Y., & Williams, L. (2010). Relationship between athletes' emotional intelligence and precompetitive anxiety. *Perceptual and Motor Skills, 110*, 323–338.

Mack, G., & Casstevens, D. (2002). *Mind gym: An athlete's guide to inner excellence.* New York: McGraw-Hill.

Matthews, G., Zeidner, M., & Roberts, R. D. (2007). Measuring emotional intelligence: Promises, pitfalls, solutions?. In A. D. Van Ong & M. H. M. Van Dulmen (Eds.), *Oxford handbook of methods in positive psychology* (pp. 189–204). New York: Oxford University Press.

Mayer, J. D., & Salovey, P. (1997). What is emotional intelligence? In P. Salovey & D. Sluyter (Eds.), *Emotional development and emotional intelligence: Educational implications* (pp. 3–31). New York: Basic Books.

Mikolajczak, M. (2009). Going beyond the ability-trait debate: The three-level model of emotional intelligence. *E-Journal of Applied Psychology, 5*, 25–31.

Mikolajczak, M., Roy, E., Verstrynge, V., & Luminet, O. (2009). An exploration of the moderating effect of trait emotional intelligence on memory and attention in neutral and stressful conditions. *British Journal of Psychology, 100*, 699–715.

Morris, G., & O'Connor, D. (2016). Key attributes of expert NRL referees. *Journal of Sports Sciences.* doi:10.1080/02640414.2016.1194524

Mosley, E., Laborde, S., & Kavanagh, E. (2018). The contribution of coping-related variables and cardiac vagal activity on prone rifle shooting performance under pressure. *Journal of Psychophysiology,* 1–17. doi:10.1027/0269-8803/a000220

Nelis, D., Quoidbach, J., Hansenne, M., & Mikolajczak, M. (2009). Increasing emotional intelligence: (How) is it possible? *Personality and Individual Differences, 47*, 36–41.

Nicholls, A. R., & Polman, R. C. (2007). Coping in sport: A systematic review. *Journal of Sport Sciences, 25* (1), 11–31.

O'Neil, D. A. (2011). The value of emotional intelligence for high performance coaching: A commentary. *International Journal of Sports Science and Coaching, 6*, 329–332.

Perlini, A. H., & Halverson, T. R. (2006). Emotional intelligence in the national hockey league. *Canadian Journal of Behavioural Science, 38*, 109–119.

Petrides, K. V. (2009). *Technical manual for the Trait Emotional Intelligence Questionnaire (TEIQue)*. London: London Psychometric Laboratory.

Petrides, K. V., & Furnham, A. (2003). Trait emotional intelligence: Behavioural validation in two studies of emotion recognition and reactivity to mood induction. *European Journal of Personality, 17*, 39–57.

Petrides, K. V., Mikolajczak, M., Mavroveli, S., Sanchez-Ruiz, M. J., Furnham, A., & Perez-Gonzalez, J. C. (2016). Developments in trait emotional intelligence research. *Emotion Review, 8*, 335–341.

Petrides, K. V., Pita, R., & Kokkinaki, F. (2007). The location of trait emotional intelligence in personality factor space. *British Journal of Psychology, 98*, 273–289.

Philippe, F. L., Vallerand, R. J., Andrianarisoa, J., & Brunel, P. (2009). Passion in referees: Examining their affective and cognitive experiences in sport situations. *Journal of Sport and Exercise Psychology, 31*, 77–96.

Rubaltelli, E., Agnoli, S., & Leo, I. (2018). Emotional intelligence impact on half marathon finish times. *Personality and Individual Differences, 128*, 107–112.

Schutte, N. S., Malouff, J. M., Hall, L. E., Haggerty, D. J., Cooper, J. T., Golden, C. J., & Dornheim, L. (1998). Development and validation of a measure of emotional intelligence. *Personality and Individual Differences, 25*, 167–177.

Stanimirovic, R., & Hanrahan, S. (2012). Examining the dimensional structure and factorial validity of the Bar-On Emotional Quotient Inventory in a sample of male athletes. *Psychology of Sport and Exercise, 13*, 44–50.

Stough, C., Saklofske, D. H., & Parker, J. D. A. (2009). *Assessing emotional intelligence: Theory, research, and applications* (pp. 85–101). New York: Springer Science.

Teques, P., Calmeiro, L., Martins, H., Duarte, D., & Holt, N. L. (2018). Mediating effects of parents' coping strategies on the relationship between parents' emotional intelligence and sideline verbal behaviors in youth soccer. *Journal of Sport and Exercise Psychology, 40*, 153–162.

Thayer, J. F., Hansen, A. L., Saus-Rose, E., & Johnsen, B. H. (2009). Heart rate variability, prefrontal neural function, and cognitive performance: The neurovisceral integration perspective on self-regulation, adaptation, and health. *Annals of Behavioral Medicine, 37*, 141–153.

Thelwell, R. C., Lane, A. M., Weston, N. J. V., & Greenlees, L. A. (2008). Examining relationships between emotional intelligence and coaching efficacy. *International Journal of Sport and Exercise Psychology, 6*, 224–235.

Tok, S., & Morali, S. L. (2009). Trait emotional intelligence, the Big Five personality dimensions and academic success in physical education teacher candidates. *Social Behaviour and Personality, 37*, 921–932.

Vaughan, R., & Laborde, S. (2017). Psychometrics of the emotional intelligence scale in elite, amateur, and non-athletes. *Measurement in Physical Education and Exercise Science, 22*, 177–189.

Watson, M., & Kleinert, J. (2018). The relationship between coaches' emotional intelligence and basic need satisfaction in athletes. *Sports Coaching Review*. doi:10.1080/21640629.2018.1491669

Zizi, S. J., Deaner, H. R., & Hirschhorn, D. K. (2003). The relationship between emotional intelligence and performance among college baseball players. *Journal of Applied Sport Psychology, 15*, 262–269.

11
EXPERTISE
Nature and Nurture

Joseph Baker and Stuart Wilson

Introduction

Scientists and laypeople alike continue to argue over the roots of human achievement. To what extent is an individual's potential controlled by genes, and what proportion is due to learning and experience? The nature (i.e., genes) versus nurture (i.e., experience) dichotomy can be traced back to the work of Galton, a Victorian polymath active from the mid 1800s to early 1900s. His book *Hereditary Genius* (1869) represents the first scientific exploration of the factors related to human achievement and provided much of the stimulus for more systematic examinations of concepts such as talent, giftedness, and genius. His subsequent works, including *English Men of Science: Their Nature and Nurture* (1874), positioned individual differences in innate qualities as the primary mechanisms for explaining differences in exceptional achievement. Despite Galton's confidence in the primacy of nature over nurture, and over a century of additional work in this area, arguments among those in the scientific community persist. This is perhaps best epitomized by 'the two Watsons'. The first argument, from the behaviourist John B. Watson, reflects a strong position in the value of experience and opportunity.

> Give me a dozen healthy infants, well-formed, and my own specified world to bring them up in and I'll guarantee to take any one at random and train him to become any type of specialist I might select – doctor, lawyer, artist, merchant-chief and, yes, even beggar-man and thief, regardless of his talents, penchants, tendencies, abilities, vocations, and race of his ancestors. I am going beyond my facts and I admit it, but so have the advocates of the contrary and they have been doing it for many thousands of years.
>
> *(Watson, 1930, p. 82)*

The second is more recent and comes from Nobel Prize-winning biologist James Watson, famous for discovering the double helix structure of DNA and widely associated with the biological determinism approach: 'We used to think our fate was in the stars. Now we know, in large measure, our fate is in our genes' (Jaroff, 1989, p. 67). Without doubt, these two quotes represent extremes within the scientific community, with most scientists occupying the middle ground, but they also reflect the passion and emotion that are often brought to this discussion. In the sections below, we summarize the evidence for each side of this debate before moving on to a more inclusive approach to the development of expertise.

The Case for Nature

Researchers examining the role of hereditary characteristics typically examine these relationships using twins and/or members of a family. In this section, we summarize results from two of the largest and best-known genetic studies: the health, risk factors, exercise training, and genetics (HERITAGE) family study (Bouchard et al., 1995) and the Minnesota study of twins reared apart (MISTRA; Bouchard, Lykken, McGue, Segal, & Tellegen, 1990). Although other large-scale studies of genetic influences have been conducted (e.g., Fuentes, Perola, Nissinen, & Tuomilehto, 2002), these two particular studies are very extensive and present a common context from which to discuss the research findings. More importantly, they consider the role of genetics in distinctly different areas: health and exercise (HERITAGE) and psychological variables (MISTRA).

The HERITAGE Family Study

The objective of HERITAGE was 'to study the role of the genotype in cardiovascular, metabolic, and hormonal responses to aerobic exercise training and the contribution of regular exercise to changes in several cardiovascular disease and diabetes risk factors' (Bouchard et al., 1995, p. 722). The study has resulted in nearly 200 publications to date. Families in the study include both biological parents and at least three biological children. Further, all participants were essentially untrained (i.e., sedentary), but otherwise healthy, and had to meet medical requirements (e.g., related to body mass index and blood pressure). Participants completed a battery of tests including questionnaires related to health and physical activity, anthropometric measurements, and blood tests. In addition, they completed six maximal exercise tests: three prior to a 20-week standardized aerobic training programme and three at the conclusion of the training programme.

Results clearly implicate genes as constraints on several variables related to physical performance. Cardiorespiratory function, for example, reflected in measures such as maximal aerobic capacity (Bouchard et al., 1998), submaximal aerobic capacity (Pérusse et al., 2001), resting blood pressure (Gu et al., 1998), and resting heart rate (An et al., 1999), was strongly related to genetic factors. More interestingly for this discussion, an individual's response to training was influenced by genetic make-up (e.g., Bouchard et al., 1999; Rice et al., 2002). In activities where cardiorespiratory factors are related to performance (e.g., aerobic sports, particularly distance events such as marathon running), significant portions of interindividual variation in performance and in response to training can be explained by the presence or absence of specific genes.

The Minnesota Study of Twins Reared Apart

Despite the impressive amount of evidence generated by HERITAGE, some (Lykken, McGue, Tellegen, & Bouchard, 1992) have argued there are limits to what can be learned through family studies, suggesting some behaviours are the result of a complex interaction of genes that are only evident through examinations of individuals who share all of their genes. To this end, MISTRA examines genetic influences with twins and other 'multiples'. The study was unique in that it tried to account for a major obstacle for researchers examining genetic influences using twins – separating the effects of the shared environment from the effects of the shared DNA – by examining twins who were separated in infancy and reared apart. The number of twins who meet this criterion is obviously small, but MISTRA has had more than 100 sets of twins or triplets reared apart complete their weeklong battery of tests at the University of Minnesota, which includes approximately 50 hours of medical and psychological assessment.

MISTRA found genes account for significant interindividual variation in psychological measures such as general intelligence (Bouchard, 1997), work values (e.g., altruism and autonomy; Keller, Bouchard, Arvey, Segal, & Dawis, 1992), job satisfaction (Arvey, Bouchard, Segal, & Abraham, 1989), and several measures of personality (e.g., DiLalla, Carey, Gottesman, & Bouchard, 1996; Tellegen et al., 1988). As with the results of HERITAGE, this programme of research suggests genes will explain differences between performers in domains where these psychological characteristics are essential to the acquisition and demonstration of high levels of performance.

Although these results are compelling, there are a number of problems with applying findings from studies such as HERITAGE and MISTRA to those at the highest levels of performance, most notably the possibly limited relevance to elite athletes. HERITAGE, for example, examined only families that began sedentary and tracked performance changes after 20 weeks of training. In comparison, expert athletes have typically performed enormous amounts of structured training designed to perpetuate continual and often extreme physiological and cognitive adaptations in order to increase performance. The long-term effects of this type of training are not well understood, and studies of participants from the general population may have limited application to this group.

Moreover, the ultimate value of HERITAGE and MISTRA is in the consistency of their conclusions that genes account for significant variation between individuals. However, their results do not provide much specificity regarding which genes and why; as a result, it is difficult to determine whether they have any specific value for talent identification and/or development. Much has changed in genetic research since these studies were conducted in the 1990s. Most significantly, the human genome was mapped in 2001, a development that has revolutionized most fields of science (e.g., medical genetics, genomics, proteomics). Since this accomplishment, genetic research has noted several intriguing results in the search for the specific genes that might explain exceptional performance. For instance, genes for angiotensin-converting enzyme (Collins et al., 2004), COL5A1 (e.g., Collins, Mokone, September, van der Merwe, & Schwellnus, 2009; Mokone, Schwellnus, Noakes, & Collins, 2006), and alpha-actinin-3 (MacArthur & North, 2004) have differentiated athletes from non-athletes in several studies, although more work is needed to replicate and extend these results (e.g., with stronger models of gene × environment interaction).

The Case for Nurture

Although it is hard to refute that genetic factors affect an individual's likelihood of attaining greatness, there is compelling evidence that exceptional achievement is strongly related to the type of training and practice performed. For instance, the highly sophisticated anticipation and attention strategies noted by expert performances in time-constrained, decision-making sports (e.g., tennis, squash) are highly specific not only to the domain of expertise (i.e., skilled tennis players are generally no better than average individuals at anticipating when tested with stimuli outside their domain), but also to the context most often experienced (e.g., as the majority of the population is right-handed, skilled athletes become much better at anticipating the actions of right-handers compared with left-handers; Loffing, Schorer, Hagemann, & Baker, 2012). This suggests the frequency of exposure to conditions most similar to the domain they perform in is critical for the development of the cognitive, physiological, and psychological adaptations necessary for elite performance.

Understanding how to 'nurture' learning and skill development is a central concern in psychology. Beginning with Bryan and Harter's (1897, 1899) studies of the time course of learning Morse code, practical needs drove early research on how to improve skilled performance. Further investigations of typing (Book, 1925), mirror tracing (Snoddy, 1926), and cigar rolling (Crossman, 1959) established a strong relationship between practice and skill on simple motor tasks (Newell & Rosenbloom, 1981).

The benefits of practice for skilled performance occur through the learning of task-specific skills. Simon and Chase (1973; Chase & Simon, 1973) demonstrated that, in comparison with non-experts, expert chess players were excellent at recalling and recreating the positions of chess pieces in gameplay situations, but this advantage disappeared when the chess pieces had been randomly organized. The expert advantage among these players thus did not come from any superior memory ability, but from a learned cognitive skill specific to their domain.

This study was the stimulus for research focusing on the value of training in explaining elite/exceptional performance. The assumption underpinning this work was that exceptional performance is achieved when the correct domain-specific skills are applied through repetitive practice. Anders Ericsson and William Chase detailed the memory skill acquisition of an undergraduate student (SF) of average intelligence and memory ability. Over a 20-month period, SF progressed from displaying average (7-digit) recall abilities, to recalling 80 digits of randomly generated strings of numbers, bettering any known world bests at the time (Ericsson, Chase, & Faloon, 1980). This investigation was notable for recording SF's detailed, think-aloud descriptions of the self-generated cognitive strategies implemented to overcome what had been assumed to be biological barriers to memory. Strikingly, the authors later repeated the study with a subsequent student to even greater success (101-digit recall), specifically by having SF teach some of these cognitive strategies (Ericsson, 1985). Expert performance in these cases was achieved after only several hundred hours of practice, largely owing to the purposeful nature in which practices were designed.

Large volumes of practice are required to develop expert skills, but not all practice is equal in value. When Ericsson and colleagues examined the retrospective practice histories of students at the Music Academy of West Berlin, hours of music-related practice did not differentiate an elite group of expected international soloists from two lower-skill groups (i.e., 10 sub-elite students in the performance stream and 10 students in the lower teaching stream; Ericsson, Krampe, & Tesch-Römer, 1993). However, when counting only the hours of intensive practice performed alone, described by the musicians as most relevant to improving their performance, each successive skill group was found to have accumulated significantly more than the group below it. This study of musicians formed the initial evidence for the deliberate practice framework (DPF; Ericsson et al., 1993), which at its core predicts that individual differences in skill can be accounted for by accumulated time in deliberate practice, defined as (a) requiring high levels of effort, (b) being motivationally driven by performance improvement rather than enjoyment, and (c) purposefully designed to address areas of need to maximize improvement. According to the DPF, the accumulation of deliberate practice compounds steadily over time, but is constrained by the effort, motivation, and resources required for this intensive training.

The idea that the amount of intense, goal-directed practice determines future levels of expertise was immediately attractive to the domain of sport, with notable early studies of wrestlers (Hodges & Starkes, 1996), figure skaters (Starkes, Deakin, Allard, Hodges, & Hayes,

1996), martial artists (Hodge & Deakin, 1998), and soccer players (Helsen, Starkes, & Hodges, 1998) examining the tenets of deliberate practice in sport contexts. A review of deliberate practice in sport skill acquisition by Baker and Young (2014) found strong support for the basic tenet of the DPF: 16 of 17 included studies found significantly greater total accumulated deliberate practice for expert groups compared with non-expert groups. Moreover, experts were found to engage in greater amounts of the most relevant types of practice for skill improvement, such as advanced technical skills in figure skating (e.g., Deakin & Cobley, 2003) or one-on-one coach instruction, video training, and team practices in basketball, netball, and field hockey (Baker, Côté, & Abernethy, 2003).

It should be acknowledged that the DPF has been criticized by researchers in sport. Discrepancies with the DPF exist in that athletes often find the activities most relevant to their improvement to be the most enjoyable, and that team practice time is often more predictive of expertise than time in practice alone (for review, see Baker & Young, 2014). Additionally, the sufficiency of deliberate practice for explaining interindividual performance differences has been questioned, as a meta-analysis found that deliberate practice accounted for only 18% of the variation between performers in sport (Macnamara, Moreau, & Hambrick, 2016; c.f. Ericsson, 2016). The reviews and meta-analyses also highlighted that deliberate practice is often poorly defined in sport research and emphasized that several improvements in how this concept is operationalized and investigated must be made in order for this line of research to meaningfully progress.

Numerous factors affect the quality of interactions between athletes and their practice environments, ranging from broad, environmental variables to more proximal, immediate influences. For instance, the strategies used in youth sport to create balanced age groups (i.e., cut-off dates), promotes a phenomenon known as relative age effects (RAEs; Wattie, Schorer, & Baker, 2015). Although the purpose of age-grouping policies is to facilitate coaching and instruction of theoretically similar children, assumptions of homogeneity within age groups are in direct conflict with actual differences in chronological and developmental age between members of an age group. First identified through an over-representation of athletes born early in the year in both elite volleyball (Grondin, Deschaies, & Nault, 1984) and ice hockey (Barnsley, Thompson, & Barnsley, 1985; Grondin et al., 1984), RAEs have since been found in multiple sports (for a review, see Cobley, Baker, Wattie, & McKenna, 2009). RAEs generally develop when individual differences in physiological and psychological growth due to chronological age (e.g., height, perceptual-cognitive skill) are misinterpreted as potential talent and rewarded with better developmental training environments (Wattie et al., 2015). RAEs are extremely context-dependent, shifting to follow changes in cut-off dates (Cobley, Schorer, & Baker, 2008) and reversing for sports favouring delayed maturational development (e.g., gymnastics; Hancock, Starkes, & Ste-Marie, 2015).

Similarly, variables related to where an athlete is born seem to have a large effect on their likelihood of sporting success. Initial research by Côté, Macdonald, Baker, and Abernethy (2006) found that, in comparison with national census data, a greater proportion of North American high-performance athletes are born in cities of fewer than 500,000 people. This effect was suggested to occur because smaller cities provided a better developmental environment, with greater and safer access to resources and facilities (Baker & Logan, 2007; Côté et al., 2006). Spurred by some variation in results (Baker, Schorer, Cobley, Schimmer, & Wattie, 2009; Wattie, Schorer, & Baker, 2018), researchers have begun to explore the nuances of this effect, examining factors such as community size (Baker, Shuisky, & Schorer, 2014), population density (Hancock, Coutinho, Côté, & Mesquita, 2018), and proximity to sport clubs (Farah, Schorer, Baker, & Wattie, 2018). The variety of proxy measures that have produced significant results in this area suggest that, although currently undefined, powerful environmental influences exist in certain geographical contexts.

In addition to these broader social influences, more immediate factors are also critical. Familial variables, for example, appear to play a large role in an athlete's success. Based on interviews with talented performers and their families in a variety of fields (e.g., sport, music, art, science), Bloom (1985) described the home environment as crucial for establishing the work ethic and motivation required for high achievement. Côté (1999) furthered this line of inquiry by developing the domain-specific developmental model of sport participation. Similar to Bloom's model, parents were described as instrumental in providing different types of support throughout an athlete's development, shifting from a leadership role early on, to a facilitative role as athletes specialized in a sport, and finally to an advisory or supportive role when athletes committed to higher training levels. Athlete expertise has been associated with both parent (Wilson, Wilson, & Baker, 2018), and sibling sport involvement (Hopwood, Farrow, MacMahon, & Baker, 2015), further suggesting that the family home environment nurtures an athlete's progression in sport.

As the magnitude of parental influence diminishes throughout development, the role of coaching increases. If quality practice is of utmost importance for the development of expertise, coaches essentially moderate its influence through the management of training load, feedback, and instruction during skill acquisition, periodization of optimal performance, and the general construction of the training environment. Advancements in the domain of motor learning have highlighted the effect of implementing concepts such as the quiet eye (Vickers, 1996), decision training (Vickers, 2007), and focus of attention (Wulf, 2013) on optimal learning and skill development. Further, investigations have examined the feasibility of short-term interventions for the improvement of perceptual-cognitive training (Loffing, Hagemann, & Farrow, 2017), mental toughness (Gucciardi, Gordon, & Dimmock, 2009a, 2009b), and self-regulation (McCardle, Young, & Baker, 2017; Young, Medic, & Starkes, 2009).

Nature via Nurture? Interactive Approaches

With both the nature and nurture sides claiming victory in this debate, it is not surprising that practitioners are confused regarding how to use this research. Davids and Baker (2007) argued that an obstacle to forward movement in this field is the continual focus on dividing the influences on expertise development into 'nature' versus 'nurture', and that a more fruitful and evidence-based approach should focus on how these categories of influence interact. It is clear that neither category of factors provides enough explanatory power to account for all of the nuances of athlete development. Moreover, there is an argument to be made that focusing on the presence of individual genes ignores a considerable body of research noting that the influence of the environment comes through its interaction with genes. For example, the gene for COL5A1 (a collagen protein relevant to flexibility of ligaments and tendons) affects an individual's risk for Achilles tendon (Mokone et al., 2006) or anterior cruciate ligament injury (Posthumus et al., 2009), suggesting that athletes with the beneficial marker will be able to perform greater amounts of intense training than those with the disadvantageous marker (see also Heffernan et al., 2017). Importantly, this example focuses on a single gene as a marker for a specific type of injury to a specific type of tissue. This hypothetical example is too simple to reflect the function and behaviour of human systems, which are undoubtedly determined by complex networks of genes.

Recently, some researchers and practitioners (e.g., Davids & Baker, 2007; Phillips, Davids, Renshaw, & Portus, 2010) have argued for the use of a dynamical systems approach to the development of talent and expertise, where the myriad genetic and environmental variables dynamically interact over developmental time to produce exceptional achievement. Although logistically and philosophically complex, this approach likely better represents the subtleties and nuances of the extensive process(es) of athlete development. Moreover, it explains the sometimes-confusing reality of how two athletes with varying genotypes and developmental histories can end up at the same high level of attainment. This outcome, known as degeneracy in biological systems, occurs because elite performance is not defined in a single way (e.g., in basketball, players can be overly physical or good decision-makers or both) and, because of the complicated interactions of genes and environment over time, there is more than one pathway to greatness.

Conclusion

The past two decades have seen considerable attention to the factors affecting athlete development, both nature and nurture. This will undoubtedly continue as approaches to genetic analyses improve and attention to the practice and learning environment remains a hot topic for researchers in motor learning, expertise, and skill acquisition. That said, there is a need to improve the way research studies are conceptualized and positioned theoretically. For instance, there have been recent calls to better define key terms such as 'expert' (Baker, Wattie, & Schorer, 2015; Swann, Moran, & Piggott, 2014) and 'talent' (Baker, Wattie, & Schorer, 2019), which will increase clarity regarding what research results actually mean. This will be valuable as prior work in this area has often been vague and limiting. More thorough designs and better operational definitions will inform the development of better models for researchers and practitioners.

In addition to improving study design and conceptual models, several recent developments by researchers in this area highlight intriguing areas of future research. First, researchers exploring how training environments affect long-term athlete development have moved from examining total training exposure (e.g., number of hours of sport-specific training) to trying to understand how the quality of training (e.g., the microstructure of training) affects skill acquisition (see Baker, Young, Tedesqui, & McCardle, in press, for a more thorough discussion). Second, researchers have begun to explore novel statistical approaches to overcome some of the limitations of previous work. For instance, Güllich et al. (2019) used a machine-learning approach to pattern recognition to identify key factors that distinguished super-elite from elite athletes in the United Kingdom. Conceptually, this approach uses computational power to analyse possible patterns and interactions among a vastly superior number of variables than can be considered in traditional analyses. Although, ultimately, the user controls what variables are entered into the analysis and how they are measured, this approach may allow researchers to test more complex and dynamic models without the statistical power requirements of approaches such as analysis of variance or multiple regression. Third, the 'replication crisis' in psychology and other sciences (see Begley & Ioannidis, 2015; Pashler & Wagenmakers, 2012) serves as an important reminder to researchers in this area that science works when findings are continually challenged and replicated. Studies of athlete development are rarely replicated directly, which limits the quality of the evidence coaches and administrators can use when working with athletes. Moreover, replication often leads to more nuanced understanding of the relationships under examination (e.g., see original study of the 'birthplace effect' by Côté et al., 2006, and follow-up studies by Wattie et al., 2018; Farah et al., 2018). Researchers studying skilled athletes face unique constraints; for instance, the study designs typically have to use small samples that are difficult to track long term. Even when long-term studies are done, there is little follow-up with athletes who leave the sport, which makes 'loss to follow-up' analyses difficult. Given these issues, the need for replication in this field is arguably greater than other fields of sport science. As researchers in skill acquisition and sport expertise continue to explore these areas, design superior models, and create novel approach to analyses, our understanding of the role of biology and environment in determining skill and performance will continue to develop.

References

An, P., Rice, T., Gagnon, J., Borecki, I. B., Pérusse, L., Leon, A. S., … & Rao, D. C. (1999). Familial aggregation of resting blood pressure and heart rate in a sedentary population: The HERITAGE Family Study. *American Journal of Hypertension, 12*(3), 264–270.

Arvey, R. D., Bouchard, T. J., Jr., Segal, N. L., & Abraham, L. M. (1989). Job satisfaction: Environmental and genetic components. *Journal of Applied Psychology, 74*, 187–192.

Baker, J., Côté, J., & Abernethy, B. (2003). Learning from the experts: Practice activities of expert decision-makers in sport. *Research Quarterly for Exercise & Sport, 74*, 342–347.

Baker, J., & Logan, A. J. (2007). Developmental contexts and sporting success: Birthdate and birthplace effects in National Hockey League draftees 2000–2005. *British Journal of Sports Medicine, 41*, 515–517.

Baker, J., Schorer, J., Cobley, S., Schimmers, G., & Wattie, N. (2009). Circumstantial development and athletic excellence: The role of date and birthplace. *European Journal of Sport Science, 9*, 329–339.

Baker, J., Shuisky, K., & Schorer, J. (2014). Does size of one's community affect likelihood of being drafted into the NHL? Analysis of 25 years of data. *Journal of Sports Sciences, 32*, 1570–1575.

Baker, J., Wattie, N., & Schorer, J. (2015). Defining expertise: A taxonomy for researchers in skill acquisition and expertise. In J. Baker & D. Farrow (Eds.), *The Routledge handbook of sport expertise* (pp. 145–155). London: Routledge.

Baker, J., Wattie, N., & Schorer, J. (2019). A proposed conceptualization of talent in sport: The first step in a long and winding road. *Psychology of Sport and Exercise, 43*, 27–33.

Baker, J., & Young, B. (2014). 20 years later: Deliberate practice and the development of expertise in sport. *International Review of Sport and Exercise Psychology, 7*, 135–157.

Baker, J., Young, B. W., Tedesqui, R., & McCardle, L. (in press). New perspectives on deliberate practice and the development of sport expertise. In G. Tenenbaum & B. Eklund (Eds.), *Handbook of sport psychology* (4th ed.). Hoboken, NJ: John Wiley.

Barnsley, R. H., Thompson, A. H., & Barnsley, P. E. (1985). Hockey success and birthdate: The RAE. *Canadian Association of Health, Physical Education and Recreation, 51*, 23–28.

Begley, C. G., & Ioannidis, J. P. (2015). Reproducibility in science: Improving the standard for basic and preclinical research. *Circulation Research, 116*, 116–126.

Bloom, B. S. (1985). Generalizations about talent. In B. Bloom (Ed.), *Developing talent in young people* (pp. 507–549). New York: Ballantine Books.

Book, W. F. (1925). *The psychology of skill.* New York: Gregg.

Bouchard, C., An, P., Rice, T., Skinner, J. S., Wilmore, J. H., Gagnon, J., … & Rao, D.C. (1999). Familial aggregation of VO2max response to exercise training: Results from the HERITAGE family study. *Journal of Applied Physiology, 87*, 1003–1008.

Bouchard, C., Daw, W., Rice, T., Perusse, L., Gagnon, J., Province, M. A., … & Wilmore, J. H. (1998). Familial resemblance for VO2max in the sedentary state: The HERITAGE family study. *Medicine & Science in Sports and Exercise, 30*, 252–258.

Bouchard, C., Leon, A. S., Rao, D. C., Skinner, J. S., Wilmore, J. H., & Gagnon, J. (1995). Aims, design, and measurement protocol. *Medicine & Science in Sports and Exercise, 27*, 721–729.

Bouchard, T. J., Jr. (1997). IQ similarity in twins reared apart: Findings and response to critics. In R. J. Sternberg & E. Grigorenko (Eds.), *Intelligence, heredity, and environment* (pp. 126–160). Cambridge, MA: Cambridge University Press.

Bouchard, T. J., Jr., Lykken, D. T., McGue, M., Segal, N. L., & Tellegen, A. (1990). Sources of human psychological differences: The Minnesota study of twins reared apart. *Science, 250*, 223–228.

Bryan, W. L., & Harter, N. (1897). Studies in the physiology and psychology of the telegraphic language. *Psychological Review, 4*, 27–53.

Bryan, W. L., & Harter, N. (1899). Studies on the telegraphic language: The acquisition of a hierarchy of habits. *Psychological Review, 6*, 345–375.

Chase, W. G., & Simon, H. A. (1973). Perception in chess. *Cognitive Psychology, 4*, 55–81.

Cobley, S., Baker, J., Wattie, N., & McKenna, J. (2009). Annual age-grouping and athlete development: A meta-analytical review of relative age effects in sport. *Sports Medicine, 39*, 235–256.

Cobley, S., Schorer, J., & Baker, J. (2008). Relative age effects in professional German soccer: A historical analysis. *Journal of Sports Sciences, 26*, 1531–1538.

Collins, M., Mokone, G. G., September, A. V., van der Merwe, L., & Schwellnus, M. P. (2009). The COL5A1 genotype is associated with range of motion measurements. *Scandinavian Journal of Medicine and Science in Sports, 19*, 803–810.

Collins, M., Xenophontos, S. L., Cariolou, M. A., Mokone, G. G., Hudson, D. E., Anastasiades, L., & Noakes, T. D. (2004). The ACE gene and endurance performance during the South African ironman triathlons. *Medicine & Science in Sports & Exercise, 36*, 1314–1320.

Côté, J. (1999). The influence of the family on talent development in sport. *The Sport Psychologist, 13*, 395–417.

Côté, J., Macdonald, D. J., Baker, J., & Abernethy, B. (2006). When 'where' is more important than 'when': Birthplace and birthdate effects on the achievement of sporting expertise. *Journal of Sports Sciences, 24*, 1065–1073.

Crossman, E. R. F. W. (1959). A theory of the acquisition of speed-skill. *Ergonomics, 2*, 153–166.

Davids, K., & Baker, J. (2007). Genes, environment, and sport performance: Why the nature–nurture dualism is no longer relevant. *Sports Medicine, 37*, 961–980.

Deakin, J. M., & Cobley, S. (2003). An examination of the practice environments in figure skating and volleyball: A search for deliberate practice. In J. Starkes & K. A. Ericsson (Eds.), *Expert performance in sports: Advances in research on sport expertise* (pp. 90–113). Champaign, IL: Human Kinetics.

DiLalla, D. L., Carey, G., Gottesman, I. I., & Bouchard, T. J., Jr. (1996). Heritability of MMPI personality indicators of psychopathology in twins reared apart. *Journal of Abnormal Psychology, 105*, 491–499.

Ericsson, K. A. (1985). Memory skill. *Canadian Journal of Psychology/Revue Canadienne De Psychologie, 39*, 188–231.

Ericsson, K. A. (2016). Summing up hours of any type of practice versus identifying optimal practice activities: Commentary on Macnamara, Moreau, and Hambrick (2016). *Perspectives on Psychological Science, 11*, 351–354.

Ericsson, K. A., Chase, W. G., & Faloon, S. (1980). Acquisition of a memory skill. *Science, 208*(4448), 1181–1182.

Ericsson, K. A., Krampe, R. T., & Tesch-Römer, C. (1993). The role of deliberate practice in the acquisition of expert performance. *Psychological Review, 100*, 363–406.

Farah, L., Schorer, J., Baker, J., & Wattie, N. (2018). Population density and proximity to junior developmental teams affect the development of National Hockey League draftees. *Scandinavian Journal of Medicine and Science in Sports, 28*, 2427–2435.

Fuentes, R. M., Perola, M., Nissinen, A., & Tuomilehto, J. (2002). ACE gene and physical activity, blood pressure and hypertension: A population study in Finland. *Journal of Applied Physiology, 92*, 2508–2512.

Galton, F. (1869). *Hereditary genius: An inquiry into its laws and consequences*. London: Macmillan.

Galton, F. (1874). *English men of science: Their nature and nurture*. London: Macmillan.

Grondin, S., Deschaies, P., & Nault, L. P. (1984). Trimestre de naissance et participation au hockey et au volleyball. *La Revue québécoise de l'activité physique, 2*(3), 97–103.

Gu, C., Borecki, I. B., Gagnon, J., Bouchard, C., Leon, A. S., Skinner, J. S., … & Rao, D. C. (1998). Familial resemblance for resting blood pressure with particular reference to racial differences: Preliminary analyses from the HERITAGE family study. *Human Biology, 70*, 77–90.

Gucciardi, D. F., Gordon, S., & Dimmock, J. A. (2009a). Evaluation of a mental toughness training program for a youth-aged Australian footballers: I. A quantitative analysis. *Journal of Applied Sport Psychology, 21*, 307–323.

Gucciardi, D. F., Gordon, S., & Dimmock, J. A. (2009b). Evaluation of a mental toughness training program for a youth-aged Australian footballers: II. A qualitative analysis. *Journal of Applied Sport Psychology, 21*, 324–339.

Güllich, A., Hardy, L., Kuncheva, L., Laing, S., Barlow, M., Evans, L., … & Wraith, L. (2019). Developmental biographies of Olympic super-elite and elite athletes: A multidisciplinary pattern recognition analysis. *Journal of Expertise, 2*, 23–46.

Hancock, D. J., Coutinho, P., Côté, J., & Mesquita, I. (2018). Influences of population size and density on birthplace effects. *Journal of Sports Sciences, 36,* 33–38.

Hancock, D. J., Starkes, J. L., & Ste-Marie, D. M. (2015). The relative age effect in female gymnastics: A flip-flop phenomenon. *International Journal of Sport Psychology, 46, 714–725.*

Heffernan, S. M., Kilduff, L. P., Erskine, R. M., Day, S. J., Stebbings, G. K., Cook, C. J., ... & Pitsiladis, Y. P. (2017). COL5A1 gene variants previously associated with reduced soft tissue injury risk are associated with elite athlete status in rugby. *BMC Genomics, 18*(supplement 8), 820.

Helsen, W. F., Starkes, J. L., & Hodges, N. J. (1998). Team sports and the theory of deliberate practice. *Journal of Sport & Exercise Psychology, 20,* 12–34.

Hodge, T., & Deakin, J. M. (1998). Deliberate practice and expertise in the martial arts: The role of context in motor recall. *Journal of Sport & Exercise Psychology, 20,* 260–279.

Hodges, N. J., & Starkes, J. L. (1996). Wrestling with the nature of expertise: A sport specific test of Ericsson, Krampe, and Tesch-Römer's (1993) theory of deliberate practice. *International Journal of Sport Psychology, 27,* 400–424.

Hopwood, M., Farrow, D., MacMahon, C., & Baker, J. (2015). Sibling dynamics and sport expertise. *Scandinavian Journal of Medicine and Science in Sports, 25,* 724–733.

Jaroff, L. (1989, March). The gene hunt. *Time, 133,* 62–67.

Keller, L. M., Bouchard, T. J., Arvey, R. D., Segal, N. L., & Dawis, R. V. (1992). Work values: Genetic and environmental influences. *Journal of Applied Psychology, 77,* 79–88.

Loffing, F., Hagemann, N., & Farrow, D. (2017). Perceptual-cognitive training: The next step of the puzzle. In J. Baker, S. Cobley, J. Schorer & N. Wattie (Eds.), *The Routledge handbook of talent identification and development in sport* (pp. 207–220). London: Routledge.

Loffing, F., Schorer, J., Hagemann, N., & Baker, J. (2012). On the advantage of being left-handed in volleyball: Further evidence of the specificity of skilled visual perception. *Attention, Perception and Psychophysics, 74,* 446–453.

Lykken, D. T., McGue, M., Tellegen, A., & Bouchard, T. J. (1992). Emergenesis: Genetic traits that may not run in families. *American Psychologist, 47*(12), 1565.

MacArthur, D. G., & North, K. N. (2004). A gene for speed? The evolution and function of alpha-actinin-3. *Bioessays, 26,* 786–795.

Macnamara, B. N., Moreau, D., & Hambrick, D. Z. (2016). The relationship between deliberate practice and performance in sports: A meta-analysis. *Perspectives on Psychological Science, 11,* 333–350.

McCardle, L., Young, B., & Baker, J. (2017). Self-regulated learning and expertise development in sport: Current status, challenges, and future opportunities. *International Review of Sport and Exercise Psychology,* Advanced online publication. doi: 10.1080/1750984X.2017.1381141

Mokone, G. G., Schwellnus, M. P., Noakes, T. D., & Collins, M. (2006). The COL5A1 gene and Achilles tendon pathology. *Scandinavian Journal of Medicine and Science in Sports, 16,* 19–26.

Newell, A., & Rosenbloom, P. S. (1981). Mechanisms of skill acquisition and the law of practice. In J. R. Anderson (Ed.), *Cognitive skills and their acquisition* (pp. 1–55). Hillsdale, NJ: Erlbaum.

Pashler, H., & Wagenmakers, E.-J. (2012). Editors' introduction to the special section on replicability in psychological science: A crisis of confidence? *Perspectives on Psychological Science, 7,* 528–530.

Pérusse, L., Gagnon, J., Province, M. A., Rao, D. C., Wilmore, J. H., Leon, A. S., ... & Skinner, J. S. (2001). Familial aggregation of submaximal aerobic performance in the HERITAGE family study. *Medicine & Science in Sports and Exercise, 33,* 597–604.

Phillips, E., Davids, K., Renshaw, I., & Portus, M. (2010). Expert performance in sport and the dynamics of talent development. *Sports Medicine, 40,* 271–283.

Posthumus, M., September, A. V., Keegan, M., O'Cuinneagain, D., Van der Merwe, W., Schwellnus, M. P., & Collins, M. (2009). Genetic risk factors for anterior cruciate ligament ruptures: COL1A1 gene variant. *British Journal of Sports Medicine, 43,* 352–356.

Rice, T., Despres, J. P., Pérusse, L., Hong, Y., Province, M. A., Bergeron, J., ... & Bouchard, C. (2002). Familial aggregation of blood lipid response to exercise training in the health, risk factors, exercise training and genetics (HERITAGE) family study. *Circulation, 105,* 1904–1908.

Simon, H. A., & Chase, W. G. (1973). Skill in chess. *American Scientist, 61,* 394–403.

Snoddy, G. S. (1926). Learning and stability: A psychophysiological analysis of a case of motor learning with clinical applications. *Journal of Applied Psychology, 10,* 1–36.

Starkes, J. L., Deakin, J. M., Allard, F., Hodges, N. J., & Hayes, A. (1996). Deliberate practice in sports: What is it anyway? In K. A. Ericsson (Ed.), *The road to excellence: The acquisition of expert performance in the arts, sciences, sports and games* (pp. 81–106). Mahwah, NJ: Erlbaum.

Swann, C., Moran, A., & Piggott, D. (2014). Defining elite athletes: Issues in the study of expert perform-ance in sport psychology. *Psychology of Sport & Exercise, 16*, 3–14.

Tellegen, A., Lykken, D. T., Bouchard, T. J., Jr., Wilcox, K. J., Segal, N. L., & Rich, S. (1988). Personality similarities in twins reared apart and together. *Journal of Personality and Social Psychology, 54*, 1031–1039.

Vickers, J. N. (1996). Visual control when aiming at a far target. *Journal of Experimental Psychology: Human Perception and Performance, 22*, 342–354.

Vickers, J. N. (2007). *Perception, cognition and decision training: The quiet eye in action.* Champaign, IL: Human Kinetics.

Watson, J. B. (1930). *Behaviorism.* Chicago, IL: University of Chicago Press.

Wattie, N., Schorer, J., & Baker, J. (2015). The relative age effect in sport: A developmental systems model. *Sports Medicine, 45*, 83–94.

Wattie, N., Schorer, J., & Baker, J. (2018). Seeing the forest but not the trees: Heterogeneity in community size effects in Canadian ice hockey players. *Journal of Sports Sciences, 36*, 436–444.

Wilson, S. G., Wilson, M. J., & Baker, J. (2018). Parental sport achievement and the development of athlete expertise. *European Journal of Sport Science.* Advanced online publication. doi: 10.1080/17461391.2018.1551424

Wulf, G. (2013). Attentional focus and motor learning: A review of 15 years. *International Review of Sport and Exercise Psychology, 6*, 77–104.

Young, B. W., Medic, N., & Starkes, J. L. (2009). Effects of self-monitoring training logs on behaviors and beliefs of swimmers. *Journal of Applied Sport Psychology, 21*, 413–428.

12

FIVE-FACTOR MODEL (BIG 5) AND ITS RELATION TO SPORTING PERFORMANCE

Iain Greenlees

Introduction

Historically, a fundamental challenge for personality psychologists has been to summarize the numerous personality descriptors that exist (as evidenced through the thousands of words used to describe such characteristics) into a manageable number of constructs that adequately describe the organization of human traits (McCrae & Costa, 2008). Although the 1950s to the 1980s saw little agreement on the nature of such a structure, the 1990s saw the formation of a relatively stable consensus that endorses five broad and general dimensions. Indeed, since its emergence through the work of Paul Costa and Robert McCrae (McCrae & Costa, 1989, 1999, 2008; McCrae & John, 1992), the five-factor model (FFM or Big 5) has become, "unquestionably, the most ubiquitous and widely accepted trait framework in the history of personality psychology" (Judge & Zapata, 2015, p. 1150). Although there have been criticisms of the Big 5, and alternative structures have been suggested (e.g., Ashton & Lee., 2005), it does remain one of the most commonly used frameworks when conceptualizing and studying personality.

The fundamental postulate of the FFM (McCrae & Costa, 2008) is that personality traits can be classified under one of five superordinate dimensions. These genetically and environmentally determined dimensions, which develop throughout childhood but thereafter are relatively stable, are neuroticism, extraversion, openness to experience, agreeableness, and conscientiousness (see Table 1 for further information and an explanation of the key facets of each of the dimensions). By extension, McCrae and Costa assert that all individuals (across all cultures) can be characterized according to their standing on the five dimensions. Finally, in accord with the trait perspective, where an individual sits within each of these dimensions will predict typical patterns of thoughts, feelings and behaviours, and responses to different environments (McCrae & Costa, 2008).

Over the past 30 years, the FFM has served as an overarching structure for an extensive and fruitful examination of the impact of personality on human thought, emotions, action, and functioning in a variety of domains. Extensive meta-analyses have shown that the five personality dimensions are associated with various elements of human functioning such as coping strategies (Connor-Smith & Flachsbart, 2007), health-related behaviours (Bogg & Roberts, 2004), interpersonal conflict (Ford, Heinen, & Langkamer, 2007), and mental health issues (Kotov, Gamez, Schmidt, & Watson, 2010). Furthermore, within more general performance domains, the FFM has also been shown to be

Table 1 Big 5 dimensions and facets

Factor	Explanation	Example facets
Extraversion	Extraversion is concerned with tendencies towards sociability, dominance, liveliness, and activity	Warmth, gregariousness, assertiveness, activity, excitement-seeking Positive emotions, positive temperament, sociability, frankness
Neuroticism	Neuroticism is concerned with emotional stability and the ease and frequency with which someone experiences anxiety, low moods, and unpleasant emotions	Anxiety, angry hostility, depression, self-consciousness, impulsiveness, vulnerability, anger-proneness, depression Somatic complaints, envy
Openness to experience	Openness to experience is concerned with curiosity, creativity, and a preference for novelty and variety in life	Fantasy, aesthetics, feelings, actions, ideas, values, intellectance Novel experience-seeking, non-tradition alism
Agreeableness	Agreeableness is concerned with the tendency to be considerate and compassionate towards other people and with wanting to maintain positive relationships with other people	Trust, straightforwardness, altruism, compliance, modesty, Tender-mindedness, straightforwardness, empathy
Conscientiousness	Conscientiousness is concerned with an individual's level of self-control, determination, preference for order, and need for achievement	Competence, dutifulness, achievement striving, self-discipline, deliberation, order

associated with academic (Poropat, 2009) and job (Hurtz & Donovan, 2000) performance. Although the body of research examining, and supporting, the role of the FFM is impressive, a clear gap in the existing meta-analyses concerns the examination of sporting performance. This is perhaps surprising given the relative success that the FFM has achieved when applied to other performance domains, but perhaps unsurprising given the historical standing of personality research within sport (Aidman, 2007) and the impact of critical reviews in seminal sport psychology texts, by influential researchers, in the 1990s (e.g., Vealey, 2002).

FFM Research in Sport

Intuitively, it is relatively easy to make predictions concerning the nature of the relationships between the FFM and athletic success. For instance, Steca, Baretta, Greco, D'Addario, and Monzani (2018) argued that high-level athletes need to be high in conscientiousness (to put in the required effort to improve and to persist in the face of setbacks), emotionally stability (to cope with the various stressors involved with high-level sport), and agreeableness (to form the positive relationships with teammates and coaches that will promote development and performance, and to be willing and able to seek out and use social support as a coping mechanism). Despite this, research exploring such relationships has, hitherto, not been consistent, systematic, extensive, or always of the highest rigour (Allen, Greenlees, & Jones, 2013). However, although the handful of studies may not be sufficient to be worthy of systematic research synthesis, there is an emerging body of research that can be reviewed to provide some initial suggestions concerning the standing of the Big 5 in sport and to make suggestions for future research directions.

Relationships Between the FFM and Sporting Performance

A fundamental goal of early sport personality researchers appears to have been to examine whether the possession of certain personality characteristics enhances an individual's chances of sporting success. The first line of research that can be considered is research that has compared the personality characteristics of elite athletes and non-elite athletes. Unfortunately, this body of research has been consistently inconsistent, with some studies showing no differences between low- and high-level athletes (e.g., Elumaro, 2016; Lazarević, Petrović, & Damnjanović, 2012), some studies showing no differences between low- and high-level male athletes, but differences for female athletes (high-level athletes being more extraverted than low-level athletes; Frazier, 1987), and some studies showing differences (e.g., Egloff & Jan Gruhn, 1996; Gat & McWhirter, 1998; Williams & Parkin, 1980) between high- and low-level performers. However, across those supportive studies cited above, results are inconsistent. Egloff and Jan Gruhn showed that "outstanding" long-distance runners (classified by training intensities rather than level of achievement) were more extraverted than "average" runners; Gat and McWhirter showed that competitive cyclists were less agreeable (co-operation facet) than recreational cyclists, and Williams and Parkin showed that elite-level ice-hockey players displayed more agreeableness (trust, tendermindedness), extraversion, and neuroticism (confidence, emotional stability) than club/recreational performers. However, personality did not distinguish elite from province-level performers.

That such inconsistent results are observed in this literature is, perhaps, not surprising, given the overall level of quality of this research. In 1982, Eysenck, Nias, and Cox reviewed the state of sport personality research and argued that it was "of an unacceptably low standard" (p. 1). They went on to argue that low sample sizes, use of psychometrically questionable questionnaires, inconsistent use of questionnaires, and the use of heterogeneous samples with a consideration for the impact of type and level of sport all contributed to the confusion within the field. Given that the research mentioned above exhibits all of these weaknesses, it is clear that (a) inconsistent results were to be expected, and (b) the recommendations of Eysenck et al. have not always been heeded.

More recently, research that has utilized consistent, psychometrically reliable measures of the FFM, and much larger sample sizes have produced more consistent findings. Specifically, Allen, Greenlees, and Jones (2011), in a sample of more than 250 sports performers from 36 different sports, found that high-level athletes (international- and national-level competitors) were less neurotic and more conscientious and agreeable than lower levels of athletes, and Steca et al. (2018), in a sample of more than 750 male athletes from the sports of track and field, basketball, and soccer, also showed that performers who had attained high levels of performance (professional leagues or national-level competition) were more agreeable, conscientious, and emotionally stable than lower-level performers. Thus, it would appear as though there could be some more stable patterns emerging in this research. This notwithstanding, research that compares athletes of different levels of ability is very descriptive and tells us little about the nature of the relationship between personality and sporting performance.

A second, and potentially more fruitful, line of research has attempted to explore the associations between scores on the FFM dimensions and performance, either over the course of a season or in a single performance. The research examining the correlation of personality dimensions and a single (or short-term) performance have failed to provide support for the role of personality in sport, but this is perhaps not surprising, given the potential impact of external (luck, officiating decisions) and internal (injury status, preparation quality) factors on such performances (Allen et al., 2013) and given the idea that the impacts of personality will be more pervasive and long term (Aidman, 2007; Hogan, 1998). In line with this, research that has explored the association between personality and season-long performance has provided more promising evidence to support the role of the FFM in sport.

Piedmont, Hill, and Blanco (1999) explored the relationship between the Big 5 and season-long performance in a small (n = 79) sample of female soccer players. At the end of competitive season, the football players completed McCrae and Costa's (1987) bipolar adjective scale, and coaches provided information on playing statistics (goals scored, goal assists, shots on goal taken, and games played) and provided a rating of the players' coachability, athletic ability, game performance, team interaction (the degree to which the player got on with others), and work ethic. Piedmont et al. found that conscientiousness (positively) and neuroticism (negatively) predicted the coaches' ratings of the players, explaining 23% of the variance in coaches' ratings. For playing statistics, conscientiousness was found to explain 8% of the variance, with higher conscientiousness associated with better performance. These findings have been partially supported in two subsequent replication studies in soccer: Mirzaei, Nikbakhsh, and Sharififar (2013) and Teshome, Mengistu, and Beker (2015) both found that conscientiousness was associated with season-long football performance, albeit with very low associations being found by Mirzaei et al. (2013; 3% of variance in performance). However, the results of the Teshome et al. (2015) and the Piedmont et al. (1999) studies should be treated with some caution owing to the low sample size. For example, the regression analyses used by Piedmont et al. included only 58 participants for the game performance analysis. Thus, it would appear as though many of the criticisms of sport personality research first identified by Eysenck et al. (1982) are still prevalent in the literature.

Aidman (2007) has provided the only truly prospective, longitudinal study examining the ability of personality variables to predict long-term sporting success and achievement. A group of 32 elite junior Australian Rules football players completed personality assessments (using Cattell, Eber, & Tatsuoka's, 1970, 16 Personality Factors Inventory; 16PF) between the ages of 16 and 19 and were then tracked for the next 7 years. At this point, playing status (playing at an elite level versus not playing at an elite level) was determined and, additionally, an elite Australian Football League coach provided ratings of performance over each of the preceding seasons for all of the performers and also provided his ratings of the extent to which the player had coped with the transition from junior- to senior-level competition (from "struggling" to "cruising"). Aidman found that, when coach ratings of physical potential at 16–19 were controlled for, those players who had progressed to the professional ranks were less neurotic (scoring low on 16PF factor of tension), more extraverted (16PF factor of group orientation), less open to experience (16PF factor of radicalism), and more conscientious (16PF factor of conscientiousness). In addition, Aidman found that, when used in conjunction with coach ratings of physical potential, these four factors successfully predicted who would join the professional ranks and who would not. Finally, Aidman also showed that, although personality variables were not strong predictors of performance in the season after the assessments were completed, aspects of neuroticism (16PF factor of emotional stability) and extraversion explained nearly 61% of the variance in the coaches' ratings of their performances as professional players and 99.3% of the variance in coach ratings of the extent to which the performers had managed the transition from the junior to professional game. This study clearly hints at the potential for personality to be a strong determinant of long-term athletic development, but must be treated with some caution owing to the very low sample size and the reliance on single-item measures for many of the key dependent variables (e.g. transition to elite level).

The research of Piedmont et al. (1999) and Aidman (2007) clearly provides some evidence to support the utility of the FFM in predicting performance in sport. However, neither study is without key limitations (in the case of Piedmont et al., a small sample size; in the case of Aidman, the use of a personality measure that only indirectly assesses the Big 5, use of single-item ratings of performance, and a very low sample size), and so they must be treated with caution. What is needed is further research that employs larger sample sizes and more carefully considers how best to measure both performance and the Big 5. Ideally, the utilization of longitudinal research designs is needed.

Relationships Between the FFM and Factors That Contribute to Athletic Development

Although research examining the direct link between the Big 5 and sporting performance may be some way from maturity, a more fruitful line of inquiry has been the exploration of the relationships between the Big 5 and factors that contribute to long-term athletic development and achievement. More specifically, and in line with the contentions of Steca et al. (2018), such research has examined the relationships between the Big 5 and (a) the likelihood of experiencing adaptive pre-, during, and post-competitive cognitions and emotions; (b) the capacity to cope with sporting stressors; (c) motivation and the demonstration of motivated behaviours; and (d) the likelihood of developing positive social relationships with teammates and coaches.

The Experience of Adaptive Competitive Cognitions and Emotions

Kaiseler, Polman, and Nicholls (2012) explored the association between the Big 5 and the experience of stress. They found that, although the Big 5 was not associated with the types or numbers of stressors reported by a large sample (n = 482) of athletes, neuroticism was positively related to perceptions of stressor intensity and negatively related to perceived control over the stressor, agreeableness was negatively associated with stressor intensity, and conscientiousness predicted perceived control. Thus, it would appear that the Big 5 is associated with perceptions of stressors and, by extension, with emotional responses to competition. This has recently been supported, albeit with a very low sample size, by Balyan, Tok, Tatar, Binboga, and Balyan (2016), who examined the associations between the Big 5 and pre-competition arousal (as measured by electrodermal activity) and anxiety (measured using the Competitive Sports Anxiety Inventory-2; Martens, Burton, Vealey, Bump, & Smith, 1990) in male participants. They found that neuroticism predicted anxiety and arousal in competitive conditions. However, when exploring the association between the Big 5 and the meta-motivational states of challenge and threat (linked to the experience of positive and facilitative cognitions and emotions), Allen, Frings, and Hunter (2012) found no association, albeit in a small sample, between measures of the Big 5 and psychophysiological indices of challenge and threat states (cardiac output reactivity, total peripheral resistance reactivity, or the challenge and threat index).

In addition to influencing perceptions of stress and pre-competitive emotions, Allen, Greenlees, and Jones (2014) have also provided evidence to suggest that the Big 5 may also be associated with post-competitive emotional responses. They explored the associations between the Big 5 and emotional responses to poor performances and found that athletes low in agreeableness and openness to experience and high in extraversion and neuroticism tended to respond to poor performances with negative and persistent emotions. This highlights the role of the Big 5 in determining responses to competition. Given that such emotional responses may influence future levels of motivation and training behaviours, then it is clear how personality has the potential to influence long-term sporting involvement and experience.

Coping with Sporting Stressors

Research has also explored the extent to which the Big 5 may be related to the use of coping strategies and coping effectiveness. In the first of such studies, Allen et al. (2011) showed that neuroticism was positively associated with the tendency to use avoidance coping strategies (mentally or physically removing oneself from a stressor), whereas openness was negatively associated with such a tendency. They also showed positive associations between conscientiousness and the tendency to employ emotion-focused coping strategies (tackling the emotional consequences of being stressed) and extraversion and the use of problem-focused strategies (changing the nature of the stressor itself). Allen et al. (2014) partially supported these findings, and Kaiseler et al. (2012) supported the findings and also showed that neuroticism was associated with the selection of less adaptive strategies (avoidance and emotion-focused coping) and with lower perceptions of coping effectiveness. More recently, a similar study by Kaiseler, Levy, Nicholls, and Madigan (2017) has also shown an association between the Big 5 and coping. They revealed positive associations between task-oriented coping (conceptually similar to problem-focused coping but with elements of emotion-focused coping) and extraversion, agreeableness, and openness, positive associations between distraction-oriented coping (similar to avoidance coping, whereby attention is redirected away from the stressor) and neuroticism, and positive associations between disengagement-oriented coping (ceasing attempts to achieve goals) and neuroticism and extraversion. Negative associations emerged between agreeableness and conscientiousness and between disengagement-oriented coping and distraction-oriented coping. Finally, neuroticism was negatively associated with perceptions of coping effectiveness. Thus, taken as a whole, it would appear as though individuals who score highly on neuroticism are more likely to experience sport as more stressful, to experience more negative emotions prior to and after sporting competitions, and to cope less effectively with the demands of sport than more emotionally stable individuals.

Recent research has also indicated that the Big 5, specifically neuroticism, may influence the way in which individuals respond to stress. First, Barlow, Woodman, Gorgulu, and Voyzey (2016), in two experimental studies utilizing football and darts tasks, found neuroticism to be positively associated with stress-induced performance decrements and ironic performance errors (hitting a target area they were instructed to avoid). This suggests that neuroticism is associated with poorer responses to stressful situations. However, as this research did not control for the effects of state anxiety on performance, we cannot ascertain whether the decline in performance was because neuroticism is associated with higher levels of state anxiety or whether neuroticism influences the impact of anxiety on performance, or a combination of both.

Motivation and the Demonstration of Motivated Behaviours

Given the central role of commitment, persistence, and the expenditure of effort in the development of talent (Ericcson, Krampe, & Tesch-Römer, 1993), researchers have also explored how such behaviours may be associated with the Big 5. Although it is easy to predict that conscientiousness should be strongly associated with such behaviours, research indicates that this may not be entirely the case. One strand of research has explored how the Big 5 may be related to preparation quality. Woodman, Zourbanoz, Hardy, Beattie, and McQuillan (2010) demonstrated, in two separate studies utilizing gymnasts, positive associations between conscientiousness and self-reported quality of competition preparation, and between emotional stability and self-reported ability to cope with adversity in training. Favor (2011) examined the associations between facets of agreeableness (trust, morality, altruism, cooperation, modesty, and sympathy) and emotional stability (anxiety, anger, depression, immoderation – the lacking of restraint and tendency to indulge – self-consciousness, and vulnerability) and coach-rated coachability in female soccer players. The research indicated positive correlations between co-operation and coachability and negative correlations between facets of emotional stability (immoderation and anger) and coachability. In a further regression analysis, the combination of immoderation and anxiety predicted 8% of the variance in coachability. However, Favor's results should be treated with caution owing to the relatively low sample size used to deal with the number of predictor variables used and the use of bespoke measures of the Big 5 and coachability. In addition, Favor did not report associations at the domain level (i.e., agreeableness or neuroticism), but at the facet level. It is thus unclear whether the domain-level analysis yielded significant associations. However, taken together, the results from Favor and Woodman et al. do indicate that the Big 5 may influence an athlete's approach to training and their willingness to be guided by a coach.

Beyond these studies, attempts to explore the relationship between the Big 5 and motivation have been sporadic. Brinkman, Weinberg, and Ward (2016) showed that agreeableness and extraversion were positively associated with self-determined forms of motivation (implicated in determining levels of effort and persistence in sport), and neuroticism was associated with less self-determined forms of motivation and amotivation. Also of possible relevance here is a study by Malinauskas, Dumciene, Mamkus, and Venckunas (2014). They examined associations between the Big 5 and performance in a battery of physical and psychomotor tests (e.g., balance, hand–eye co-ordination, sprint speed, and power) conducted over 2 days in a sample of 376 young men. Although difficult to interpret owing to the sheer number of analyses reported, there were some correlations between emotional stability and fine motor skills (e.g., juggling) and between extraversion, agreeableness, openness, and conscientiousness and effort-based tasks during the second day of testing (sprint speed, pull-ups, and power output). The reasons for such associations remain unclear and tentative, but it could be that certain personality traits (e.g., conscientiousness and openness) may be associated with a willingness to exert the effort needed to attain higher levels of physical fitness (and so perform better in the tests conducted), or it could be that certain traits (e.g., agreeableness and conscientiousness) may be associated with a willingness to persist in strenuous tasks when requested to by a third party (in this case, the experimenters, but, in sport, the coaches). Taken as a whole, and accepting the limitations in each of the studies, the preceding research does implicate the influence of the Big 5 as possible determinants of training quality, a major determinant of eventual athletic success.

Development of Positive Sporting Relationships

Inspired by a large body of research that supports the role of the FFM in determining the quality of a range of interpersonal relationship types (e.g., Ford et al., 2007), Jackson, Dimmock, Gucciardi, and Grove (2010) found that, in sporting dyads, athletes' agreeableness, openness, and conscientiousness predicted their self-reported commitment to their sporting relationship and their perceptions of their partners' opinion of the relationship. Moreover, athletes' agreeableness and conscientiousness predicted how committed their partner reported being to the relationship. This suggests that not only does an individual's personality influence their approach to a relationship, but that the behaviours they engage in also create a more positive relationship for their partners. Further research in this area has also shown an impact of the Big 5 on the nature of the coach–athlete relationship. Jackson, Dimmock, Gucciardi, and Grove (2011) showed that, in coach–athlete dyads, athletes' conscientiousness, extraversion, and emotional stability predicted their self-reported commitment to the relationship, and conscientiousness also predicted coaches' commitment to the relationship. In addition, athletes' extraversion and agreeableness predicted their perceptions of closeness to the coach, and athletes' agreeableness and extraversion predicted coaches' perceptions of closeness. Subsequent studies have supported the association between athletes' Big 5 and athletes' and coaches' perceptions of relationship quality (positive associations with agreeableness and conscientiousness, negative associations with neuroticism; Yang, Jowett, & Chan, 2015) and athletes' perceptions of coach support and conflict within a relationship (Aşçi, Kelecek, & Altintaş, 2015).

Taken in their entirety, the preceding sections show that research does indicate that the Big 5 may be associated with how receptive to coaching an individual is, how effective their preparation is, and how able they are to cope with the barriers and setbacks they experience during training and competition. Given the central role of these elements in long-term athletic development and the maintenance of high levels of performance, it would appear as though personality may be an important component of sporting success.

Enhancing FFM Research in Sport

Although there is support for the utility of the Big 5 in sport psychology, it should be evident from the preceding review that there remain many more questions about its role than answers. The research conducted to date appears limited in quantity and consistency (predominantly owing to small sample size, but also owing to divergence in the measures employed and sample heterogeneity) and, perhaps worryingly, to not always appearing to have learned the lessons offered by Eysenck et al. (1982) nearly 40 years ago! What are clearly needed are longitudinal, as attempted by Aidman (2007), and sufficiently powered research programmes to provide more information concerning both the short- and long-term influence of the Big 5 on athletic achievement and development.

In addition to simply issuing a plea for larger and more ambitious research methods, the current review also issues a plea for a more nuanced consideration concerning the influence of the Big 5. The majority of research articles that have explored the Big 5 in sport appear to be conducted from a very strong trait perspective that predicts strong main effects of the Big 5. Although this approach is understandable, it is at odds with McCrae and Costa's (2008) five-factor theory (not to be confused with the five-factor model). Central to this theory (see McCrae and Costa, 2008, for further explanation) is the proposition that an individual's behaviours will be determined not simply by the Big 5, but also by prevailing characteristics of the situation and cultural contexts, self-concept, and biographical experiences. Thus, a greater emphasis on the interactive effects of the Big 5 is warranted. Where this has occurred, interesting results have been forthcoming. For instance, Balyan et al. (2016) found that neuroticism was associated with pre-competitive state anxiety, but only under high-pressure conditions. Similarly, as seen earlier, Woodman et al. (2010) provided evidence to suggest that conscientiousness is associated with training quality. However, they also showed that extraverts were only vulnerable to distractability in training when they were not encouraged to set goals, and individuals high in neuroticism only struggled to cope with adversity in training when they did not use emotional control strategies. Thus, this supports the view that aspects of the situation (e.g. competition importance, exposure to psychological skills training) will moderate the effect of personality on aspects associated with performance in sport and, additionally, highlights the importance of considering contextual variables when exploring the role of the Big 5 in sport.

A second way in which Big 5 research in sport could be more nuanced is for researchers to more carefully explore the interactive effects of the Big 5 dimensions, rather than solely exploring main effects. Although few would argue that an agreeable extravert would behave/achieve/cope in the same way as a disagreeable extravert, much of the research conducted with the Big 5 seems to assume this to be the case. The issue here is that much of the research involves simple main effects of the separate Big 5, rather than their interactive effects. The exploration of interaction effects has borne fruit when used in sports research. Allen et al. (2011) reported that problem-focused coping was predicted by the three-way interaction between extraversion, openness, and neuroticism (such that extraverts who were open and emotionally stable made more use of problem-focused coping strategies), and that emotion-focused coping was predicted by the three-way interaction between extraversion, openness, and agreeableness. Similarly, Kaiseler et al. (2017) reported a series of two-way interactions in their analysis of the role of the Big 5 in coping such that emotionally stable people open to experience and emotionally stable extraverts made more use of task-oriented coping, and agreeable, conscientious people made more use of distraction-focused coping. Thus, future research should also seek to explore the interactive, rather than simply main, effects of the Big 5 dimensions.

The final way in which a more sophisticated understanding of the role of the Big 5 could be achieved is by giving greater consideration to facet-level analysis (rather than simply focusing on the domains). It should be remembered that the Big 5 domains subsume a range of facets. Given that each of the five domains is made up of (at least) five facets (e.g. extraversion is made up of warmth, gregariousness, activity, excitement-seeking, and positive emotions), then it is clear to see that one highly extraverted person may be quantitatively distinct from another. This was explicitly acknowledged by McCrae, Costa, and Busch (1986) when they stated that assessment of the Big 5:

> gives a complete characterization of the person only at a global level. The factors represent groups of traits that covary, but are not necessarily interchangeable. A moderate score in Extraversion, for example, might be obtained by an individual who was energetic but aloof, or lethargic but friendly, or average on both energy level and sociability. For many purposes, these distinctions are essential.
>
> (p. 444)

Low sample sizes and questionnaire choice – the shorter (60-item) questionnaires, such as the NEO-FFI (Costa & McCrae, 1992) used by Allen et al. (2011, 2014) or the Big Five Inventory (John, Donahue, & Kentle, 1991) used by Kaiseler et al. (2012, 2017), do not provide facet-level scores – have limited the opportunities to perform such facet-level analysis, but personality research in general has benefitted from a finer-grained approach to studying the specific effects of the Big 5 (e.g., Rikoon et al., 2016), and Favor's (2011) work examining the relationship between Big 5 facets and coachability may also point to the utility of exploring facet-level effects.

To add further nuance to the facet-level analysis of the Big 5, it may also be important to look at the impact of combinations or clusters of facets. DeYoung, Quilty, and Peterson (2007) found that each of the Big 5 domains could be broken down into two (or three in the case of extraversion) clusters of facets. As an example, in De Young et al.'s analysis, neuroticism could be subdivided into volatility (associated with disinhibition and the outward expression of negative affect) and withdrawal (associated with inhibition and the internalization of negative affect). These two factors would be proposed to have very different consequences for behaviour and one's experience of sport. For example, volatility may be associated with acts of aggression in response to failure, whereas withdrawal may lead to excessive rumination. Such patterns of behaviour would be missed if researchers only ever considered personality at the Big 5 level. The utility of such an approach is also evident when one considers the relative success of research that has explored the influence of personality traits beyond the Big 5. Roberts and Woodman (2017) have argued that more specific traits, such as perfectionism and narcissism, may hold more promise for sport personality researchers and point to research that has supported such a view. Given that such traits may reflect combinations of facets (see Glover, Miller, Lynam, Grego, & Widiger, 2012), where possible, researchers should explore the influence of facets and facet clusters as well as the Big 5 domains.

Conclusion

The FFM holds much more promise for developing our understanding of the determinants of excellence in sport than was maybe proposed by authors such as Vealey (2002). However, what is also clear is that more concerted research efforts are needed in order to fully understand its role. Although initial attempts to explore the role of the Big 5 in sport could be considered to be inconsistent, largely opportunistic and unsystematic, sometimes naïve, and of variable quality, there seems to be an emerging body of evidence to suggest that the dimensions may have a meaningful role to play in long-term athletic development through many of the processes that underpin talent development (e.g., coachability, reactions to pressure and setbacks, goal-pursuit). If researchers can continue on the current trajectory, adopting more sophisticated approaches to research design (interactionist designs and analyses and/or the use of more longitudinal designs) and analysis (interaction effects of domains, facet-level analysis), then the future for this area of research looks good, and our broader understanding of the psychology of sport can be enhanced. Such research has enormous applied potential also as it may be able to further our understanding of the different environments that different personalities thrive in and the specific psychological skills training that may be able to offset some of the inherent maladaptive elements of specific traits (Woodman et al., 2010).

The proliferation of research into the Big 5 has seen a proliferation of measures designed to assess traits and facets associated with the model. However, as of yet, there is no single instrument that can lay claim to being the gold standard (John, Naumann, & Soto, 2008). Rather than advocate a single measure, the choice of measure will depend on practical issues (e.g., number of items likely to be tolerated by participants, commercial availability of the measure) and the aims of the specific research study (e.g., facet- versus trait-level analysis).

If the research is interested purely in examining trait-level predictions, there are a number of options that have been used in the literature. The NEO-FFI (Costa & McCrae, 1992) is a 60-item measure of the five facets that has, possibly, received the strongest support for its validity (John et al., 2008) but is commercially controlled. At 60 items, the NEO-FFI may also be unattractive for sports performers to complete. To counter this, there are shorter questionnaires available such as the recently validated short (30 items) and extra-short (15 items) Big Five Inventory (Soto & John, 2017a). If even shorter options are required (possibly in exploratory research, where many other questionnaires are being completed during the same testing session), the Ten Item Personality Inventory (Gosling, Rentfrow, & Swann, 2003) is available.

However, there may be substantial trade-offs with data quality in the use of such short measures (Gosling et al., 2003).

If a facet level of measurement is required, researchers have a number of options. The NEO-PI-R (Costa & McCrae, 1992) is commonly used. However, at 240-items long and with commercial copyright protection, this may be an unrealistic option for most. More commonly used (owing to its flexibility and its availability for use) is the International Personality Item Pool (Goldberg, 1999). Equally, the 60-item Big Five Inventory-2 (Soto & John, 2017b) offers a freely accessible and validated measure of the Big 5 and 15 facets. This is a pool of items that assess a range of facets that can be selected based on the specific aims of the research project.

References

Aidman, E. V. (2007). Attribute-based selection for success: The role of personality attributes in long-term predictions of achievement in sport. *The Journal of the American Board of Sport Psychology, 3*, 1–18.

Allen, M. S., Frings, D., & Hunter, S. (2012). Personality, coping and challenge and threat states in athletes. *International Journal of Sport and Exercise Psychology, 10*, 264–275.

Allen, M. S., Greenlees, I. A., & Jones, M. (2011). An investigation of the five-factor model of personality and coping behaviour in sport. *Journal of Sports Sciences, 29*, 841–850.

Allen, M. S., Greenlees, I. A., & Jones, M. (2013). Personality in sport: A comprehensive review. *International Review of Sport and Exercise Psychology, 6*, 184–208.

Allen, M. S., Greenlees, I. A., & Jones, M. (2014). Personality, counterfactual thinking and negative emotional reactivity. *Psychology of Sport and Exercise, 15*, 147–154.

Aşçi, F. H., Kelecek, S., & Altintaş, A. (2015). The role of personality-characteristics of athletes in coach–athlete relationships. *Perceptual and Motor Skills, 121*, 399–441.

Ashton, M. C., & Lee, L. (2005). Honesty-humility, the Big Five, and the five-factor model. *Journal of Personality, 73*, 1322–1354.

Balyan, K. Y., Tok, S., Tatar, A., Binboga, E., & Balyan, M. (2016). The relationship between personality, cognitive anxiety, somatic anxiety, physiological arousal and performance in male athletes. *Journal of Clinical Sport Psychology, 10*, 48–58.

Barlow, M., Woodman, T., Gorgulu, R., & Voyzey, R. (2016). Ironic effects of performance are worse for neurotics. *Personality of Sport and Exercise, 24*, 27–37.

Bogg, T., & Roberts, B. W. (2004). Conscientiousness and health-related behaviors: A meta-analysis of the leading behavioural contributors to mortality. *Psychological Bulletin, 130*, 887–919.

Brinkman, C. S., Weinberg, R. S., & Ward, R. M. (2016). The Big Five personality model and self-determined motivation in sport. *International Journal of Sport Psychology, 47*, 1–19.

Cattell, R. B., Eber, H. W., & Tatsuoka, M. M. (1970). *Handbook for the sixteen personality factor questionnaire (16PF)*. Champaign, IL: Institute for Personality and Ability Testing.

Connor-Smith, J. K., & Flachsbart, C. (2007). Relations between personality and coping: A meta-analysis. *Journal of Personality and Social Psychology, 93*, 1080–1107.

Costa, P. T., & McCrae, R. R. (1992). Trait psychology comes of age. In T. B. Sonderegger (Ed.), *Nebraska symposium on motivation: Psychology and aging* (pp. 169–204). Lincoln, NE: University of Nebraska Press.

DeYoung, C. G., Quilty, L. C., & Peterson, J. B. (2007). Between facets and domains: 10 aspects of the Big Five. *Journal of Personality and Social Psychology, 93*, 880–896.

Egloff, B., & Jan Gruhn, A. (1996). Personality and endurance sports. *Personality and Individual Differences, 21*, 223–229.

Elumaro, A. I. (2016). Personality, grit and sporting achievement. *IOSR-Journal of Sports and Physical Education, 3*, 14–17.

Ericcson, K. A., Krampe, R. T., & Tesch-Römer, C. (1993). The role of deliberate practice in the acquisition of expert performance. *Psychological Review, 100*, 363–406.

Eysenck, H. J., Nias, D. K., & Cox, D. N. (1982). Sport and personality. *Advances in Behaviour Research and Therapy, 4*(1), 1–56.

Favor, J. K. (2011). The relationship between personality traits and coachability in NCAA Divisions I and II female softball athletes. *International Journal of Sports Science and Coaching, 6*, 301–314.

Ford, M. T., Heinen, B. A., & Langkamer, K. L. (2007). Work and family satisfaction and conflict: A meta-analysis of cross-domain relations. *Journal of Applied Psychology, 92,* 57–80.

Frazier, S. E. (1987). Introversion-extraversion measure in elite and non-elite distance runners. *Perceptual and Motor Skills, 64,* 867–872.

Gat, I., & McWhirter, B. T. (1998). Personality characteristics of competitive and recreational cyclists. *Journal of Sport Behaviour, 21,* 408–420.

Glover, N., Miller, J. D., Lynam, D. R., Grego, C., & Widiger, T. A. (2012). The five-factor narcissism inventory: A five-factor measure of narcissistic personality traits. *Journal of Personality Assessment, 94,* 500–512.

Goldberg, L. R. (1999). A broad-bandwidth, public domain, personality inventory measuring the lower-level facets of several five-factor models. In I. Mervielde, I. Deary, F. De Fruyt, & F. Ostendorf (Eds.), *Personality psychology in Europe, Vol. 7* (pp. 7–28). Tilburg: Tilburg University Press.

Gosling, S. D., Rentfrow, P. J., & Swann, W. B., Jr. (2003). A very brief measure of the Big 5 personality domains. *Journal of Research in Personality, 37,* 504–528.

Hogan, R. (1998). Reinventing personality. *Journal of Social and Clinical Psychology, 17,* 1–10.

Hurtz, G. M., & Donovan, J. J. (2000). Personality and job performance: The Big Five revisited. *Journal of Applied Psychology, 85,* 869–879.

Jackson, B., Dimmock, J. A., Gucciardi, D. F., & Grove, J. G. (2010). Relationship commitment in athletic dyads: Actor and partner effects for Big Five self- and other-ratings. *Journal of Research in Personality, 44,* 641–648.

Jackson, B., Dimmock, J. A., Gucciardi, D. F., & Grove, J. G. (2011). Personality traits and relationship perceptions in coach–athlete dyads: Do opposites really attract? *Psychology of Sport and Exercise, 12,* 222–230.

John, O. P., Donahue, E. M., & Kentle, R. L. (1991). *The Big Five Inventory–Versions 4a and 54.* Berkeley, CA: University of California, Berkeley, Institute of Personality and Social Research.

John, O. P., Naumann, L. P., & Soto, C. J. (2008). Paradigm shift to the integrative Big-Five trait taxonomy: History, measurement, and conceptual issues. In O. P. John, R. W. Robins, & L. A. Pervin (Eds.), *Handbook of personality: Theory and research* (3rd ed. ed., pp. 114–158). New York: Guilford Press.

Judge, T. A., & Zapata, C. P. (2015). The person–situation debate revisited: Effect of situation strength and trait activation on the validity of the big five personality traits in predicting job performance. *Academy of Management Journal, 58,* 1149–1170.

Kaiseler, M., Levy, A., Nicholls, A. R., & Madigan, D. J. (2017). The independent and interactive effects of the Big-Five personality dimensions upon dispositional coping and coping effectiveness. *International Journal of Sport and Exercise Psychology,* doi:10.1080/1612197X.2017.1362459

Kaiseler, M., Polman, R. C. J., & Nicholls, A. R. (2012). Effects of the Big Five personality dimensions on appraisal coping, and coping effectiveness in sport. *European Journal of Sport Science, 12,* 62–72.

Kotov, R., Gamez, W., Schmidt, F., & Watson, D. (2010). Linking "big" personality traits to anxiety, depressive and substance abuse disorders: A meta-analysis. *Psychological Bulletin, 136,* 768–821.

Lazarević, L., Petrović, B., & Damnjanović, K. (2012). Personality traits of young gifted rhythmic gymnasts. *Physical Education and Sport, 10,* 115–126.

Malinauskas, R., Dumciene, A., Mamkus, G. S., & Venckunas, T. (2014). Personality traits and exercise capacity in male athletes and non-athletes. *Perceptual and Motor Skills, 118,* 145–161.

Martens, R., Burton, D., Vealey, R. S., Bump, L. A., & Smith, D. E. (1990). Development of the Competitive State Anxiety Inventory-2 (CSAI-2). In R. Martens, R. S. Vealey, & D. Burton (Eds.), *Competitive anxiety in sport* (pp. 117–190). Champaign, IL: Human Kinetics.

McCrae, R. R., & Costa, P. T. (1987). Validation of the five-factor model of personality across instruments and observers. *Journal of Personality, 57,* 17–40.

McCrae, R. R., & Costa, P. T. (1989). Reinterpreting the Myers–Briggs type indicator from the perspective of the five-factor model of personality. *Journal of Personality and Social Psychology, 52,* 81–90.

McCrae, R. R., & Costa, P. T., Jr. (1999). A five-factor theory of personality. In L. A. Pervin & O. P. John (Eds.), *Handbook of personality: Theory and research* (pp. 139–153). New York: Guilford Press.

McCrae, R. R., & Costa, P. T., Jr. (2008). The five-factor theory of personality. In O. P. John, R. W. Robins & L. A. Pervin (Eds.), *Handbook of personality: Theory and research* (pp. 159–181). New York: Guilford Press.

McCrae, R. R., Costa, P. T., Jr., & Busch, C. M. (1986). Evaluating comprehensiveness in personality systems: The California Q-Set and the five-factor model. *Journal of Personality, 54,* 430–446.

McCrae, R. R., & John, O. P. (1992). An introduction to the five-factor model and its applications. *Journal of Personality, 60,* 175–215.

Mirzaei, A., Nikbakhsh, R., & Sharififar, F. (2013). The relationship between personality traits and performance. *European Journal of Experimental Biology, 3,* 439–442.

Piedmont, R. L., Hill, D. C., & Blanco, S. (1999). Predicting athletic performance using the five-factor model of personality. *Personality and Individual Differences, 27, 769–777.*

Poropat, A. E. (2009). A meta-analysis of the five-factor model of personality and academic performance. *Psychological Bulletin, 135,* 322–338.

Rikoon, S. H., Brenneman, M., Kim, L. E., Khorramdel, L., MacCann, C., Burrus, J., & Roberts, R. D. (2016). Facets of conscientiousness and their differential relationships with cognitive ability factors. *Journal of Research in Personality, 61,* 22–34.

Roberts, R., & Woodman, T. (2017). Personality and performance: Moving beyond the Big 5. *Current Opinion in Psychology, 16,* 104–108.

Soto, C. J., & John, O. P. (2017a). Short and extra-short forms of the Big Five Inventory-2: The BFI-2-S and BFI-2-XS. *Journal of Research in Personality, 68,* 69–81.

Soto, C. J., & John, O. P. (2017b). The Next Big Five Inventory (BFI-2): Developing and assessing a hierarchical model with 15 facets to enhance bandwidth, fidelity, and predictive power. *Personality and Individual Differences, 113,* 117–143.

Steca, P., Baretta, D., Greco, A., D'Addario, M., & Monzani, D. (2018). Associations between personality, sports participation and athletic success: A comparison of Big 5 in sporting and non-sporting adults. *Personality and Individual Differences, 121,* 176–183.

Teshome, B., Mengistu, S., & Beker, G. (2015). The relationship between personality trait and sport performance: The case of national league football clubs in Jimma Town, Ethiopia. *Journal of Tourism, Hospitality and Sports, 11,* 25–32.

Vealey, R. (2002). Personality and sport behavior. In T. S. Horn (Ed.), *Advances in sport psychology* (pp. 43–74). Champaign, IL: Human Kinetics.

Williams, L. R., & Parkin, W. A. (1980). Personality factor profiles of three hockey groups. *International Journal of Sport Psychology, 11,* 113–120. http://psycnet.apa.org/psycinfo/1980-32564-001

Woodman, T., Zourbanoz, N., Hardy, L., Beattie, S., & McQuillan, A. (2010). Do performance strategies moderate the relationship between personality and training behaviours? An exploratory study. *Journal of Applied Sport Psychology, 22,* 183–197.

Yang, S. X., Jowett, S., & Chan, D. K. C. (2015). Effects of big-five personality traits on the quality of relationship and satisfaction in Chinese coach–athlete dyads. *Scandinavian Journal of Medicine and Science in Sports, 25,* 568–580.

13

GOALS AND EMOTIONS

Warren Mansell

Introduction

This chapter describes and explains emotions in terms of their relationship with goals using a control theory approach. A comprehensive and widely cited overview of goals in psychology defined a goal as 'internal representations of desired states, where states are broadly construed as outcomes, events or processes' (Austin & Vancouver, 1996, p. 338). Austin and Vancouver (1996) go on to give examples of these desired states, which include biological set points (e.g. body temperature) and abstractions of complex outcomes (e.g. career success, which could include achieving goals in sport), encompass wide-ranging durations from the present moment to the lifespan, and span the domains of the neurological, psychological, and social. Please note that goals in the psychological literature are much wider than the way that the term 'goal' is used in common parlance. A goal can include abstract, socially relevant set points such as being honest, worthwhile, or creative, as well as simple, concrete set points such as gripping a racquet tightly or keeping balance while in motion. Importantly, these authors found it necessary to use an organizing theoretical framework with specific operational definitions of its components for their review, and they used a form of control theory developed by Powers, often known as perceptual control theory (Powers, 1973, 2005).

This chapter will begin with a rationale for why emotions can be understood in relation to goals. The wider literature on goals and emotions will be reviewed in order to describe the current state of knowledge in this area, and then the control theory model will be used to elaborate and describe a mechanistic, functional account of the role of emotions. This account will be divided into the components of control theory, explaining their relevance to emotion, and it will conclude with the implications of a goal-oriented approach to emotion informed by control theory. The chapter begins with an open-minded approach to the role of emotion within what is often regarded as a relatively mechanistic and 'cold' account – 'goals' and 'control theory'. Yet the chapter converges on a conclusion that emotion exists in almost every feature of goal functioning, both unconscious and conscious, interpersonal and intrapersonal, and that emotions are a fundamental marker of the dynamic features of goals, such as conflict, higher-level perspective-taking, and change.

Why and How Emotions Are Particularly Relevant to Understanding Goals

Emotions are defined in ways that link the closely with goals; they are volitional, involved in action regulation, and they are seen to have *functional* roles including communication, orientation and activation in the context of purposeful activities such a meeting basic needs (food, water, safety), social engagements (meetings, parties, festivals) and competitive sports and past-times (Hackfort, 2019). Notably emotions are multi-modal constructs that span the domains of physiology, behaviour, cognitive and social interaction, as are goals (Austin & Vancouver, 1996). Second, emotional experience is closely tied to motivation – the essence of goals – and the evolutionary imperatives of survival and reproduction (Darwin, 1873). In particular, emotions appear to have a beneficial purpose, and theories of goals explain how humans achieve their purposes.

The majority of the literature on emotions and goals explores the nature of the goal(s) that are associated with specific emotional states. This literature is extremely broad and spans from work on basic emotions such as anger and fear through to more complex, most probably uniquely human, emotions such as pride, joy, and awe (Lench & Lench, 2018). In the section that follows, examples of these will be used to illustrate the control theory approach to understanding emotions. Yet this diverse literature will not be the topic of the chapter for a number of reasons. First, the aim of this chapter is to introduce a framework for understanding emotions in relation to goals, rather than to describe specific emotions and their relationship with specific goals. Second, this literature is too large to cover in a book chapter and is best analysed within systematic reviews (e.g. Ma, Tunney, & Ferguson, 2017; Stroebe, Schut, & Nauta, 2015). Third, and maybe most importantly, many of the findings appear to support contradictory accounts that fuel extended debate. For example, is anger a basic emotion that serves the goal of protecting the individual from physical threat, or does it serve the moral goal of restoring justice (Hutcherson & Gross, 2011)? As we shall see later, such debates regarding which goals are associated with which emotions do not make sense from a control theory perspective. Put simply, there are likely to be multiple, non-mutually exclusive goals related to the same emotion, and these are likely to vary across individuals, time, and context. Rather than debating these issues, the current chapter focuses on a single theoretical account that relates emotions to the principles of how goals are selected, managed, and prioritized, rather than attempting to pin specific emotions on specific goals.

Through understanding control theory, a range of complementary perspectives on the relationship between goals and emotions emerge. A starting point is to realize that nearly every goal can potentially have an emotional component. There is general agreement that a set of biologically derived, and evolutionarily prepared, goals are associated with emotions (Panksepp, 2004; Porges, 2011). Powers (2007, p. 1) echoes this account as follows:

> we must recognize that an experienced emotion is in fact a collection of inputs, perceptions that we call 'feelings', and at the same time, an output-caused change in physiological state: heart rate, respiration rate, vasoconstriction, metabolism, and motor preparedness – the 'general adaptation syndrome' in the case of avoidance or attack behavior.

Yet, in apparent contrast to the biological account, the interpersonal goals involved in the current situation appear to determine the nature of the emotion. Taking the constructionist stance to an extreme, it has been claimed that emotions are not biologically prepared, but that they emerge in the moment as the brain attempts to predict its perceptual experience (Hoemann, Gendron, & Barrett, 2017). Thus, there appears to be debate among theorists about the nature of emotion that has an impact on how we use goals to understand emotions. The theoretical stance towards emotion seems to depend in part on one's definition of the term 'emotion'. Is it always a conscious experience, or can it be unconscious? Is the physiological arousal component of an emotion sufficient to be called an emotion in itself? Is an emotion truly distinct from a mood?

The term 'emotion' appears to sit somewhere along a spectrum from an automatic physiological readiness for action (e.g. Frijda, Kuipers, & Terschure, 1989), through to an internal state than can be consciously recognized and used to inform decision-making (Damasio, 1996), to a 'mood' that persists despite no obvious trigger or goal. Indeed, the field of psychology as a whole often gets embroiled in debates about reified constructs such as 'working memory', 'intelligence', 'personality', 'psychiatric disorder', and 'emotion' because it endeavours to try to explain an entity for which there is no consensual definition. The converse approach is taken by proponents of control theory – first extract and define the core principles of psychological functioning, regardless of whether they relate to a well-known construct, and, second, imagine or simulate models of everyday activities that follow these principles and observe whether the models show properties or require features that resemble commonly observed constructs, such as 'emotion'. Earlier work has completed this exercise for constructs such as consciousness (Carey, 2018) and dissociation (Mansell & Carey, 2013), and two earlier publications have begun this work for emotion (Powers, 1973, 2007). Powers's earlier accounts will be integrated into the account presented here.

The Basics of a Control Theory Account of Goals and Emotion

Following Austin and Vancouver (1996), we now explain the control theory account of goals. According to Powers (1973), goals are reference specifications of perceived states of the self and the world that the individual seeks to achieve and maintain through their ongoing actions. Actions enable the reduction of *error*, which is the discrepancy between a current perception and the desired (goal, or reference) state for that perception. Error changes continuously as the perceptual input is compared with the reference value for that variable, and it is amplified (by a factor known as *gain*) error that drives the action against disturbances to goals within the environment. Thus, immediately, it is possible to identify three potential points at which 'emotion' might influence the functioning of a goal according to control theory: (1) at the perceptual component, where the features of the self and environment to be controlled are specified, identified, and monitored for changes; (2) at the reference values, where goals are stored as memories and compared with current experience; and (3) at the outputs, which prepare for, specify, and modulate the actions to be carried out in service of goals.

It is important to note that 'perceived states' in this account need not be consciously perceived; they simply need to represent afferent (inward) signals within the nervous system. In many ways, Powers (1973) pre-empted contemporary research on unconscious goals in this regard (e.g. Custers & Aarts, 2010) and, at the same time, echoed very early psychological accounts of emotion (James, 1894). Indeed, Powers (2007, p. 2) states:

> Consciousness and emotion are not directly related. Since an emotion arises when there is an error signal, and error signals can arise in control systems of which one is not currently aware, feelings can appear without any apparent cause or any apparent connection with the current objects of awareness.

In relation to this point, Powers (1973) explains how humans and other animals are biologically prepared with *intrinsic control systems* that keep a range of physiological variables as close as possible to *intrinsic reference values* to permit survival and reproduction. It is these intrinsic systems, operating outside conscious awareness, that guide the formation and refinement of the perceptual control system. For example, the intrinsic control of body temperature entails the perceptual experiences that provide warmth (e.g. closeness to caregiver, texture of warm cloths) when below the desired body temperature will be learned. Thus, within control theory, the main purpose of memories is their use as reference points for one's goals (Powers, 1973).

This control theory account comes very close to the premises of attachment theory, and this is no coincidence. Bowlby's (1969) attachment theory was not informed by behavioural, cognitive, or psychodynamic theory, but by the control systems approach to animal behaviour used within ethology. Indeed, some other authors have returned to control theory to understand and model attachment processes (Kobak, Cole, Ferenz-Gillies, Fleming, & Gamble, 1993; Mansell, 2005). In particular, Bowlby specified two control systems – one for safety seeking (with the caregiver in infancy) and one for exploration of the environment to enable learning and mastery. During the emergence of mobility in infancy, these two systems are in conflict, and, furthermore, child development involves learning to manage the balance between these two goals within various situations, throughout the lifespan. Rather than an 'internal working model' as specified by Bowlby, control theory specifies how perceptions of the self and world develop layer by layer to enable successful control, as intrinsic systems are kept in check. Memories are critical in this regard because they allow an individual to recognize the aspects of the self and world that restore and enhance control by matching these experiences with their desired states. I will return to attachment in the later section on collective control.

Memory is highly distributed, because perception itself is highly distributed within Powers's (1973) theory. As mentioned above, the infant develops the ability to control her perception of increasingly complex aspects of herself and the world in successive stages (van de Rijt-plooij & Plooij, 1992). Powers (1992) specified 11 levels of perception, though he anticipated that more would be identified. The 11 are: intensity, sensation, configuration, transitions, events, relationships, categories, sequences, programmes, principles, and system concepts. These perceptions are hierarchically related such that the highest-level control system achieves its own goal by setting the goals of the systems on the next level down, and so on. To take one emotionally relevant example, a woman may have a goal to be a compassionate person. Note that this goal does not need to be consciously experienced at every moment that this goal is being followed. Holding the goal of being a compassionate person entails that the woman upholds a number of principles, including being kind and honest, and she lives according to these principles through programmes (plans, routines) such as going over to her friend's house to support her after she loses her job. The programme can be broken down into sequences, one step of which involves maintaining the relationship of keeping physically close to her friend when she sees her. At one moment (an event), when her friend is particularly upset, the woman recognizes her friend's facial expression change (a configuration) and attempts to cheer her friend up by putting her hand on her shoulder (another relationship) and applying gentle pressure to keep a feeling of firmness in her touch (experienced as a sensation), which her friend finds comforting, close, kind, and indicative of compassion. This short vignette describes not a sequence of stages, but a hierarchy of controlled perceptions, all of which are active in the moment that the two women connect with one another. This is typical of the control theory account – it is not linear, but models the process of pursuing, achieving, and maintaining parallel, simultaneous, perceptual inputs while the person is acting within the environment to maintain these perceptual states.

A similar account could be provided in a sports context, for example. A cyclist may maintain her sense of being a worthwhile person through a number of goals, including success at sporting events. Imagine this to be a superordinate goal ('to feel worthwhile'), with a branching hierarchy of subgoals (e.g. 'to succeed at my sport', 'to be a good mother', 'to have good friends', etc.).

Her perception of sporting success would, in turn, be specified by a number of branching subgoals (e.g. 'to beat my best time', 'to win a competitive event'). Going further down the levels are the specifications of the 'programmes' (procedures/routines/plans) that help to achieve these goals. For example, one of these may involve trying to maintain a specific lap time within a race, which itself may be maintained by specifying a current speed, which would require variation in the current force exerted to the bicycle during a race. While these goals are being met at each level, the cyclist perceives an emotional state, possibly akin to the 'flow' experienced during smooth performance (Csikszentmihalyi, 1997). However, when error is experienced and not corrected for any length of time, the sense of urgency or even anxiety, may be felt.

There are two further features of goals in control theory that are critical to set the foundation for how emotions are involved. These are conflict and reorganization. Conflict occurs when two or more control systems, either within the same person or between individuals, have opposing goals for the same perception. For example, in a sporting context, conflict can occur when a boxer needs to experience anger in order to get aroused and activated for a boxing match, but he also is fearful of being angry because it might have an effect on his mood after the match. Indeed, many instances of conflict appear to involve emotion. The problem with conflict is that it cannot be solved by simply choosing one or other goal; both goals are often valid. A new solution, perspective, or insight is needed. This is where reorganization comes in.

Reorganization is a trial-and-error learning process that makes spontaneous changes in how we set, prioritize, balance, and implement goals, when our most important goals (at the highest level) and our intrinsic goals are not met. The challenge is making sure that reorganization occurs at the right place in the goal hierarchy. According to control theory, it is the goal superordinate to the two conflicting goals that needs to change. In the boxing example, the superordinate goal might be to gain and maintain respect from other people, because using anger to win a boxing fight and suppressing anger outside the match could both be motivated by the goal to gain respect. The actual goal will vary from person to person, but the principle is the same. The person in conflict needs to shift their awareness to the higher-order goal governing the conflicted goals and stay there to allow sufficient reorganization to make the right kind of difference – one that allows the person to achieve and maintain their most important goals. It is likely that this shift in the focus of reorganization can happen spontaneously, but that it is prevented in practice very often because the individual has other goals that get in the way. For example, if one had a goal to 'never think about what makes me angry', it would be very difficult to keep in awareness any goals that relate to feelings of anger (see the section where emotion regulation is introduced later on in the chapter). For this reason, a psychological therapy developed from control theory is directed entirely at helping people shift and sustain awareness to the source of goal conflict (Carey, 2006). Importantly, a key indicator of the therapeutic effect of the method of levels is regarded as emotional change (Carey, Mansell, & Tai, 2015).

Powers (2007) sums up the above account particularly succinctly:

> Normally, unidentified arousals draw our attention to them and we become aware of the perceptions in the control systems that are the source of the problem. But when the error arises because of conflict, there are two control systems involved, each part of its own context, while the conflict is expressed as a control process that is satisfying neither of the higher-order systems trying to use it. Such conflicts are ordinarily resolved by normal processes of reorganization as soon as they arise. But a person may find the conflict so painful that the whole subject is thrust aside – the person avoids getting into situations where either side of the conflict arises.
>
> *(Powers, 2007, p. 3)*

Following from the explanation above, my conclusion from the control theory account is that, across the lifespan, the intensity of the conscious experience of emotion may serve the purpose of enabling the necessary shifts and focus of awareness that are required to enable, restore, or enhance control. The primary direction of this mechanism is towards the external environment via the senses, allowing the gathering of information to meet basic goals or survival and reproduction (Porges, 2011), and the neurophysiological pathways of the sympathetic and parasympathetic nervous system are the substrates of this process. Also, through the external environment, the emotional state of the individual can have an array of functions that enable the enhancement of *collective control* – group actions such as marches or festivals, for example, and the upholding of shared principles such as kindness, honesty, and helping others. I will explain collective control in detail later.

The secondary direction of this same attentional mechanism is towards internally simulated perceptions from memory, through what Powers (1973) described as the *imagination mode*. This mode predominates when immediate action cannot fulfil a goal, most often owing to conflict with other goals. For example, a traumatized train passenger imagines trying to board a train, but she cannot bring herself to fully imagine her plan because she does not want to experience the intense fear that this involves. It is the emotions that 'pull' her awareness back to these goals day after day, leading her to try out a range of solutions: driving to work – but it takes too long; going with a friend to the station – but on some days her friend is not available; or looking at other jobs nearer to home – but no other jobs are available for her skill set. One could imagine that, eventually, by talking about a range of other fearful, but less traumatic, events she has experienced to a considerate friend, she realizes (through reorganization) that she can tolerate her emotion of fear when recalling the accident, and she is able to begin her plan of going to work on the train independently. Although not the topic of the current chapter, there is likely to be a specific neuroanatomic circuit involved in this process of conflict resolution: identification of conflict via the anterior cingulate, and two cortical structures – the ventromedial frontal cortex and orbital frontal cortex – that appear to be involved in evaluating the appropriate decision during goal conflicts (e.g. Cohen, Heller, & Ranganath, 2005).

Relating Emotion to Each Component of Goals According to Control Theory

The above account places emotion at the heart of a control theory account of goals, and the examples provided illustrate how emotional experiences appear relevant to each of the components and processes involved. In this section, each component of the control theory will be described in detail and the potential functions of emotions hypothesized within these accounts.

Intrinsic Control Systems

The notion of intrinsic control systems in Powers's (1973) theory, indicates that there are goals for a range of physiological variables, and that these are maintained through both internal, hormonally mediated pathways (e.g. breaking down glycogen for energy to keep body temperature at 37 degrees) and through actions in the outside world (e.g. putting on clothes to warm up). We return to the issue of definition. Would we call 'warmth' an emotion? On the face of it, physical warmth is not an emotion. Yet there is some evidence that physical and emotional warmth overlap to the degree that goals for each can be substituted, unconsciously, for one another in daily life (Bargh & Shalev, 2012).

Biological differences in temperament also have a potential role in the expression of emotion, via the relative 'strengths' of different intrinsic control systems that are associated with different 'emotional profiles' (Van Egeren, 2009). For example, the emotional dimension of fear versus comfort represents a biological preparedness to detect the source of threat and seek immediate safety, whereas an emotional dimension of excitement versus frustration may represent a biological preparedness to seek novelty through exploration. Therefore, it is likely that individual differences in these intrinsic control systems will bias the expression of certain emotions, even if the systems themselves are biological in nature and not directly open to conscious awareness.

An additional reason for implicating intrinsic systems in emotion is that intrinsic control systems are necessary for the learning of perceptual goals according to control theory (and in learning to resolve the conflict of exploration versus safety-seeking in attachment theory; Bowlby, 1969). In particular, during development, the human is able to perceive the detectable changes that co-occur or correlate with the activity of intrinsic systems – examples include heart rate increases, hairs standing up on the back of the neck, and muscle tension to prepare to seek safety. Thus, perceived physiological changes become markers for whether intrinsic systems are in error and help the individual – during early development – to become more aware of how to fulfil his or her own biological needs. This account, derived from control theory, overlaps with the somatic marker hypothesis (Damasio, 1996) and with accounts of interoceptive inference (e.g. Seth, 2013). Again, however, should we call a 'somatic marker' an emotion? The control theory explanation I am constructing here is moving from biological systems that do not require sensory perception to the domain of sensory perception that *may not* require consciousness (often known as 'intuition'; Dunn et al., 2010), and so this account has not fully arrived at the conscious experience of emotion.

Goal Hierarchies

The next way that goals provide a window to understanding emotion is to explore the hierarchy of goals within control theory. Working through Powers's (1992) hierarchy, the levels provide different breadths of lenses through which to consider emotion. Remember again, however, that there is no necessity within control theory for perceptions to be consciously experienced for them to be controlled. Nonetheless, according to Powers (1973), the mobile spotlight of awareness is located within the perceptual hierarchy, and so, through understanding the hierarchy in more detail, we are a step closer to understanding the conscious experience of emotion.

It may be no coincidence that the first level of the hierarchy – intensity – is the most common dimension that psychologists have used to ask people to rate their own emotions (Frijda, Ortony, Sonnemans, & Clore, 1992). Powers (1973) purposefully selected the perception of intensity to be at the bottom of his hierarchy because his experience with engineering control systems had taught him that a dimensional variable provided greater control. For example, contrast the control of lighting one gets from a light switch, which is binary, with that from a dimmer switch. By perceiving a continuum of intensity, an individual can make the tiny adjustments necessary – in light, sound, pressure, and so on, to achieve precise control. The second level in the hierarchy is sensation, which Powers (1973) characterized as a pattern of intensity change over time that can be perceived as a 'chunk' of perception in itself. However, a sensation does not have the shape, or form, that would qualify it for the third level of perception – configuration. One possibility, therefore, is that the felt sense of an emotion is the configuration of physical sensations across multiple systems – heart rate, muscle tension, thoughts, impulses, body temperature – that is distinctive, and differentiated between different emotions. The next level that Powers (1992) describes is the level of transition. This is the change in configuration over time, which potentially could be the level at which one experiences mixed emotions or shifts in emotional state. There are a number of further levels going upwards, but it is the level of principles, and system concepts, that again seems to have particular relevance to emotion. To perceive principles or system concepts, one needs to take account of oneself in a social context, often taking into account the goals of other people, including either their immediate intentions or their principles. Therefore, I will return to these levels in the next section on collective control.

Emotion and Collective Control

Collective control occurs when two or more individuals are both pursuing goals, either through being in the same physical environment as one another, or through various forms of communication (spoken language, text, social media, computer software, telephone, etc). These goals (reference values for the perceptual inputs) may overlap sufficiently to enable a group experience that no individual could achieve on their own. Alternatively, goals may be substantially discrepant from one another so that conflict between individuals or between groups of individuals occurs. The field of collective control is related to the fields of co-regulation (e.g. Sbarra & Hazan, 2008), interpersonal emotion regulation (Zaki & Williams, 2013), and attachment theory (Bowlby, 1969), and there are an array of social and psychological phenomena that emerge through collective control, such as joint attention, play, language development, sports performance, musical performance, theatre, dance, and, of course, the breadth of human social systems at various levels – families, communities, cities, nations, and so on. There is, without doubt, a role for emotion in these social systems, and emotions emerge in particular during instances of conflict (e.g. competitive sports, domestic violence, wars between nations) and, conversely, during instances of cooperation (e.g. live musical performances, weddings, festivals). Such diverse areas of research might seem a league away from the study of goals. However, there is a body of research using control theory to model collective control and show the emergence of phenomena that have been identified in real social systems (e.g. McClelland, 2004, 2014).

It is somewhat beyond the scope of this contribution to expand upon all of the different ways that individuals or groups of individuals can cooperate or conflict at various degrees of scale, through a wide variety of different media. Nonetheless, it is important to focus on the balance of control that can occur in different relationships owing to the different goals that each individual holds. The key starting point is the parent–child relationship. This is ideally a dynamic of mutually achieved goals that bring about feelings of love, comfort, and connectedness in both parties (Bowlby, 1969). As we know, intrinsic goals predominate in the infant, and so the parent needs to both help to meet these goals and forge physical experiences for the infant that help him to learn how to most reliably get his intrinsic goals met as he develops. There is emerging evidence for the necessity of this form of collective control. For example, parents who had greater sensitivity to their own somatic experiences during the first months of parenting had children with fewer somatic symptoms 6 months later (Abraham, Hendler, Zagoory-Sharon, & Feldman, 2019). Later in the chapter, I will elaborate on how the parent–child relationship needs to adapt throughout development to manage instances of conflict and learning through reorganization.

For the sake of contrast, it is important to describe how emotion relates to instances of collective control that involve conflict and in which one individual attempts to achieve his or her own goals despite the impact on others, such as during instances of manipulation, bullying, neglect, and torture. The dominating individual may experience the emotions of anger, contempt, and disgust towards the other person, and the dominated person may experience the emotions of fear, worthlessness, shame, and helplessness. However, the particular emotions experienced will clearly depend on the specific goals that are involved and their history of conflict. For example, intense fear would be experienced in the instance of an unknown attacker, whereas the emotions experienced during domestic abuse depend on the history of collective control between the couple involved. For example, often the victim experiences shame because he or she holds goals that he or she should have been a better spouse, or did not help his or her spouse to be a better person. As indicated earlier, the goals that are relevant in collective control are high-level ones – principles and system concepts (self-ideals, for example), and the complexity of their relationships is reflected by the wide range of emotions that are relevant to these relationships.

Emotions and Internal Conflict

The first point to clarify in relation to conflict, which informs the goal perspective on emotion, is that a degree of conflict is the norm. Indeed, psychological development could be regarded as a process of learning how not merely to control, but to resolve the conflicts between the many elements of the self and the environment that a person strives to control. Powers (1973) proposed that emotions are only transiently experienced unless there is conflict between goals. His rationale was that the physiological changes that occur as part of an emotion are preparing the individual to act on a goal – for example, to get away from a growling dog. To the extent that one can immediately act to achieve the goal of reaching a safe location, then the fear and its physiological effects will dissipate. On the other hand, if one is in a state of goal conflict – for example, the dog is your neighbour's, and she left you looking after the dog while she went out for the morning – then the emotion of fear remains because you actually want to be a reliable neighbour, and you do not achieve your goal of reaching safety. It is within this context that the persistent arousal of emotion can draw awareness back to persistent goal conflicts to facilitate conflict resolution (see the following section on reorganization). Lindner (2006) describes the close relationship between conflict and emotion and provides detailed case examples of how particular kinds of goal conflict relate to different specific emotions: fear, anger, guilt, humiliation, hope, confidence, and emotional warmth. A comprehensive review of goal conflict found that it is consistently associated with increased distress and poorer well-being, especially when assessed implicitly (Kelly, Mansell, & Wood, 2015).

When goal conflict persists unresolved for a lot longer than a single event – over weeks, months, and years – emotions become 'moods'; for example, the emotion of fear can be felt as anxiety. Indeed, it is the inability to tolerate that anxiety experienced during the uncertainty of goal conflict that may form the foundations for anxiety problems (Einstein & Mansell, 2016). Anxiety can take many forms, but one key source of anxiety involves performance, of which sports performance is a clear example. To a degree, the experience of anxiety leading up to any performance is a sign that the person cares about their performance. In control theory terms, this would be explained as the performance goal being hierarchically subordinate to a higher-level goal – to feel capable, to be respected, to be successful, for example. Feelings of anxiety themselves can be used as a reference point to strive for, because it indicates a readiness to perform. Indeed, when performance anxiety is minimal or non-existent, it may indicate that sports performance is no longer as important a higher-level life goal. Yet feelings of anxiety can also be experienced as too intense or enduring. Prolonged anxiety, as in the case of generalized anxiety disorder, becomes better described as 'free-floating', not tied to a specific situation or issue, when the inability and unwillingness to address the uncertainty of goal conflict becomes more pervasive.

Goal conflict has further impact on emotion in addition to detaching it from its associated goals. When goals are in conflict, they persist in trying to achieve their reference values by escalating their outputs in the short term, potentially drawing upon more energy and other resources, and reorganizing to enhance their gains (error sensitivities) in the medium term. Either one goal dominates and suppresses the expression of the others, or there is an oscillation in terms of which goal dominates, or some combination of the two. The dynamics, which can be modelled in computer simulations, are not dissimilar from a fight, battle, or war between two sides (Carey, 2008; McClelland, 2014). In terms of how these dynamics might appear as emotions, during oscillations between goals there may be obvious indicators of greater emotional intensity such as increasingly heightened physiological arousal, exaggerated behaviour, and a sense of loss of control over one's emotions. When one goal dominates, there is a profile of apparent up-regulation of some emotions at the expense of others, such as when a façade of happiness is used to suppress negative emotional states.

A third emergent property of goal conflict follows on from the above scenario. Emotional states, and their components, can become the targets of goals themselves. This becomes increasingly likely when emotions are experienced as out of control and, therefore, threatening in some way. The field of emotion regulation (Gross, 2007) is the domain of 'emotional states as goals'. The details of this area of research go well beyond the scope of this chapter. However, what is key to state here is that goal conflict, as described by control theory, may both generate the conditions that enhance motives for emotion regulation and, in fact, define when emotion regulation is problematic for the individual, rather than any specific regulation strategy (Dodd, Lockwood, Mansell, & Palmier-Claus, 2019; Koole, 2009). For example, it may be helpful for a surgeon to suppress feelings of anger while pursuing the goal of a successful heart transplant, and for a soldier to suppress feelings of sadness when the goal is to fight the enemy on the battlefield. However, these same feelings would be helpful when the same individuals have the opportunity to express them safely. For example, the surgeon may need to assert himself against the manager to get better facilities for the hospital, and the soldier may need to grieve for the loss of his companion. Thus, according to control theory, whether or not an emotion regulation goal, or indeed any goal, is problematic is entirely *relative* to the other goals held by that the person, and sometimes to the other people interacting with that person.

Emotion and the Function of Memory Within Goals

The study of memory and emotion is a further large domain of psychological science. Yet, as mentioned earlier, control theory implicates memory as having a crucial role – storing reference values for goals. Thus, potentially, memories of past experiences may involve the components of emotions, such as somatic experiences and facial expressions, at a relatively low, concrete level in a hierarchy, but also the stored 'felt sense' of higher-level perceptions, such as the feelings of guilt one experiences when one cannot uphold one's principle of helping others, or the feeling of incompetence one experiences when not able to master the goal of presenting one's work to a boardroom of colleagues. When stored as memories of this kind, emotions have the propensity to form the self-defining narratives of autobiographical memory. Indeed, one of the most influential psychological theories of autobiographical memory makes the case that hierarchies of autobiographical memories serve to maintain self-concept, and they are retained, forgotten, or distorted on the basis of whether they meet the self-ideal and whether they then form a coherent and consistent narrative with one another (Conway & Pleydell-Pearce, 2000).

Rather than reviewing the whole literature of memory and emotion, it is most pertinent to point out that a goal perspective appears to be vital to resolve the findings in this field (Kaplan, Van Damme, & Levine, 2012; Montagrin, Brosch, & Sander, 2013). Specifically, Levine and Safer (2002) conclude that memories of emotions provide condensed and accessible summaries of the relevance of past experiences to current goals. For example, studies show that emotional states are associated with the narrowing of the content of memory – for example, the barrel of a gun is remembered rather than the person carrying it. A review of this research concluded that it was the goal relevance of these memories, rather than simply the physiological arousal of the emotion, that is associated with this narrowing effect (Levine & Edelstein, 2009).

Emotion and Reorganization

As explained earlier, reorganization is the process through which learning occurs according to perceptual control theory. It is proposed that the systems governing our goals have parameters (e.g. error sensitivity or gain) and functions (e.g. the input functions that identify specific features of the self and the world) that change in a randomly specified direction whenever intrinsic control systems increase in error (e.g. after an injury). It is these parameters and functions that are reorganized during learning. This persists until the systems settle on a new, more adaptive organization that restores and enhances control.

There are a number of potential relationships between emotions and reorganization that build upon the components discussed earlier. First is the possible role of 'negative' and 'positive' emotions in setting the conditions for reorganizing goal conflict. Powers (1973) stated that it is the enhanced arousal, emerging from readiness to action that persists in the presence of goal conflict, that draws conscious awareness and sustained attention; we also introduced the role of the (calming) parasympathetic nervous system in sustained awareness and the role of prefrontal brain regions in the process of conflict resolution. There is evidence that this process of conflict resolution is facilitated by certain positive emotional states (e.g. hope, calmness), and, in particular, that these help broaden awareness of higher-level goals (Fredrickson, 2001). Notably, as mentioned earlier, it is this shift towards the higher-level goal driving the conflict, and sustaining attention there, that is thought to permit reorganization to continue long enough to stumble upon an adaptive organization of goals.

Resolving goal conflict can involve weighing up the relative priorities of two or more goals involving positive emotional states. These conflicts may be at a relatively low level in the hierarchy (e.g. the relative pleasure experienced in the choice of a chocolate ice cream versus coffee and a biscuit) or relatively high in the hierarchy (e.g. the sense of mastery achieved during a game of tennis after work versus the sense of responsibility experienced from staying longer at work to complete a project). Alternatively, the goal conflict may be marked by a negative emotion – which is simultaneously an awareness of an unmet goal (e.g. anger at oneself for taking a route to work that is scenic but slowed down by traffic) and an overarching positive emotion (e.g. hope, enthusiasm) that allows the individual to stay with the experience long enough to begin to resolve it (e.g. thinking of an alternative route). The parallels between this intrapsychic process of conflict resolution and the interpersonal co-regulation of a soothing parent with their distressed infant are not coincidental: They are mutually entrained systems. Indeed, van de Rijt-plooij and Plooij (1992) explain how this co-regulation is particularly important during periods when infants are themselves undergoing reorganization as they learn new input functions for the layers of the perceptual hierarchy that they develop regularly within the first 2 years of life. Furthermore, co-regulation through connectedness, affiliation, and often love, can continue throughout adulthood, as people in close relationships maintain environments for one another that allow their partners' goals to flourish and develop (Hazan & Shaver, 1987; Sternberg, 1986).

A second important relationship between emotions and reorganization emerges within the wider domains of collective control. Earlier, we discussed the role of emotional displays in forging cooperation within group and community activities, and in identifying group conflicts to be resolved through open expression and debate. Furthermore, there are collective activities in which the emotions appear to form components of learning and creativity through reorganization. Key examples are play and its verbal counterpart, humour. As in the example of a parent comforting a distressed child, play offers a positive emotional framing (e.g. excitement, pleasure, surprise) for a negative emotion experience (e.g. anger, fear, disgust). Play involves pushing the normal boundaries of one's goals within a safe environment so that learning and creativity are further enhanced – 'pushing the limits', 'thinking outside the box'. Consistent with this, the experience of play appears to enhance later problem-solving ability (Smith & Dutton, 1979).

The third relationship between emotion and reorganization is the spontaneous emergence of emotional responses when insights or novel solutions appear in awareness. Recent research has indicated a wide array of emotions described during moments of insight, even for apparently 'cold', cognitive tasks (Shen, Yuan, Liu, & Luo, 2016). Such findings underline the message from this chapter that emotion is part and parcel of human goal striving, whatever the domain of goals involved. Yet it also raises the question of why such moments of achievement, and attainment of certainty and control are marked by emotions.

Drawing from their own version of control theory, Carver and Scheier (1990) proposed that positive emotions are experienced when a person is reducing error (achieving control) faster than expected (i.e. accelerating), and that this *rate* of change of error is detected by a 'meta-monitoring' system. Thus, one would expect a sudden insight to be accompanied by an intense positive emotion. Carver and Scheier (1990) hypothesized that positive emotions in these instances permit a person to 'coast' – ease off effort – to invest their time and resources in other goals that would otherwise compete for time (Carver, 2003). Conversely, when the successful goal is prioritized at the expense of other goals, the detection of the rate, and even the acceleration, of its error reduction may also be a critical variable to enhance and optimize control without relying on error to actually decrease before learning through reorganization slows down. Thus, small trial-and-error 'tweaks' in the parameters of goals may be allowed to occur to further enhance skill and mastery, such as in sporting performance, motivated by the desire to maximize the positive feelings that this increasingly improved performance allows. Interestingly, in control theory models of goals that are optimized in this way, the parameter of gain (error sensitivity) can only increase to a threshold at which point the system becomes unstable because it begins to control for the effects of its own actions on the environment – leading to unstable oscillation and loss of control. Typically, such extremes are immediately reorganized such that the gain is reduced and kept at an optimal, but not exaggerated, level. It is feasible that this account may help to explain how the single-minded, highly specialized pursuit of perfection that is sometimes observed in highly ambitious individuals can become undermined without the opportunity for rest, disengagement from other goals, and reflection (conflict resolution, as described earlier).

Summary

By working through a control theory architecture of goals, it is evident that what people commonly describe as emotions appear to be intimately involved in nearly all aspects of goal functioning. Specifically, they help restore, maintain, and enhance control in multiple ways. As outputs from our nervous system, they prepare us to achieve and maintain our goals, both through preparing our body's physiology and through communicating with others to galvanize collective action to meet shared goals. As inputs to our nervous system, they form bodily markers we can use to help meet our biological needs, and the felt senses we use as guides to keep to our principles (higher-level goals) and judge their relative priority within conscious awareness. Emotions indicate the willingness for cooperation or conflict in others, and they draw attention to unresolved conflicts between our own goals. Yet emotions can themselves become exaggerated and counterproductive when they form the 'ammunition' of conflict that is left unresolved. The solution is to provide opportunities for conflict resolution, which requires a safe space for expression, time, a willingness to shift and sustain awareness to the higher-level goals driving conflict, and an openness to the spontaneous changes that may occur through reorganization.

The roots of connection between goals and emotion begin in parent–child co-regulation, and they persist within a wealth of collective pursuits such as play, sports, and family and community activities that can forge new alliances and potentially resolve long-standing group conflicts. It is the open expression of emotions and their goals through verbal communication, gesture, art, and the wider media that seems to be particularly potent for problem resolution in society as a whole. We experience positive emotions associated with learning, creativity, and insights as we continue to improve our goals, and that may permit us to widen our search for new opportunities to achieve and sustain some of our most foundational goals – our basic principles, self-ideals, and our system concepts of the families, communities, nations, and global networks to which we connect and belong.

References

Abraham, E., Hendler, T., Zagoory-Sharon, O., & Feldman, R. (2019). Interoception sensitivity in the parental brain during the first months of parenting modulates children's somatic symptoms six years later: The role of oxytocin. *International Journal of Psychophysiology, 136,* 39–48.

Austin, J. T., & Vancouver, J. B. (1996). Goal constructs in psychology: Structure, process, and content. *Psychological Bulletin, 120,* 338–375.

Bargh, J. A., & Shalev, I. (2012). The substitutability of physical and social warmth in daily life. *Emotion, 12* (1), 154–162.

Barrett, L. F. (2012). Emotions are real. *Emotion,* 12, 413–429.

Bowlby, J. (1969). *Attachment and loss: Vol. I. Attachment.* New York: Basic Books.

Carey, T. A. (2006). *The method of levels: How to do psychotherapy without getting in the way.* Hayward, CA: Living Control Systems.

Carey, T. A. (2008). Conflict, as the Achilles heel of perceptual control, offers a unifying approach to the formulation of psychological problems. *Counseling Psychology Review, 23,* 5–16.

Carey, T. A. (2018). Consciousness as control and controlled perception. *Annals of Behavioural Science, 4* (2), 3.

Carey, T. A., Mansell, W., & Tai, S. (2015). *Principles-based counselling and psychotherapy: A method of levels approach.* London: Routledge.

Carver, C. (2003). Pleasure as a sign you can attend to something else: Placing positive feelings within a general model of affect. *Cognition and Emotion, 17,* 241–261.

Carver, C. S., & Scheier, M. F. (1990). Origins and functions of positive and negative affect: A control-process view. *Psychological Review, 97,* 19–35.

Cohen, M. X., Heller, A. S., & Ranganath, C. (2005). Functional connectivity with anterior cingulate and orbitofrontal cortices during decision-making. *Cognitive Brain Research, 23,* 61–70.

Conway, M. A., & Pleydell-Pearce, C. W. (2000). The construction of autobiographical memories in the self-memory system. *Psychological Review, 107,* 261–288.

Csikszentmihalyi, M. (1997). *Finding flow: The psychology of engagement with everyday life.* New York: Basic Books.

Custers, R., & Aarts, H. (2010). The unconscious will: How the pursuit of goals operates outside of conscious awareness. *Science, 329*(5987), 47–50.

Damasio, A. R. (1996). The somatic marker hypothesis and the possible functions of the prefrontal cortex. *Philosophical Transactions of the Royal Society of London. Series B: Biological Sciences, 351*(1346), 1413–1420.

Darwin, C. (1873). *The expression of the emotions in man and animals.* London: Murray.

Dodd, A., Lockwood, E., Mansell, W., & Palmier-Claus, J. (2019). Emotion regulation strategies in bipolar disorder: A systematic and critical review. *Journal of Affective Disorders, 246,* 262–284.

Dunn, B. D., Galton, H. C., Morgan, R., Evans, D., Oliver, C., Meyer, M., … Dalgleish, T. (2010). Listening to your heart: How interoception shapes emotion experience and intuitive decision making. *Psychological Science, 21,* 1835–1844.

Einstein, D. A., & Mansell, W. (2016). The relevance of uncertainty and goal conflict to mental disorders, their prevention and management: A unifying approach. *The Cognitive Behaviour Therapist, 9,* e36.

Fredrickson, B. L. (2001). The role of positive emotions in positive psychology: The broaden-and-build theory of positive emotions. *American Psychologist, 56,* 218.

Frijda, N. H., Kuipers, P., & Terschure, E. (1989). Relations among emotion, appraisal, and emotional action readiness. *Journal of Personality and Social Psychology, 57,* 212–228.

Frijda, N. H., Ortony, A., Sonnemans, J., & Clore, G. (1992). The complexity of intensity: Issues concerning the structure of emotion intensity. *Review of Personality and Social Psychology, 13,* 60–89.

Gross, J. J. (Ed.). (2007). *Handbook of emotion regulation.* New York: Guilford Press.

Hackfort, D. (2019). Emotion. In D. Hackfort, R. J. Schinke & B. Strauss (Eds.), *Dictionary of sport psychology* (pp. 91–92). London: Elsevier.

Hazan, C., & Shaver, P. (1987). Romantic love conceptualized as an attachment process. *Journal of Personality and Social Psychology, 52,* 511–524.

Hoemann, K., Gendron, M., & Barrett, L. F. (2017). Mixed emotions in the predictive brain. *Current Opinion in Behavioral Sciences, 15,* 51–57.

Hutcherson, C. A., & Gross, J. J. (2011). The moral emotions: A social–functionalist account of anger, disgust, and contempt. *Journal of Personality and Social Psychology, 100,* 719–737.

James, W. (1894). Discussion: The physical basis of emotion. *Psychological Review, 1,* 516.

Kaplan, R. L., Van Damme, I., & Levine, L. J. (2012). Motivation matters: Differing effects of pre-goal and post-goal emotions on attention and memory. *Frontiers in Psychology, 3,* 404.

Kelly, R. E., Mansell, W., & Wood, A. M. (2015). Goal conflict and well-being: A review and hierarchical model of goal conflict, ambivalence, self-discrepancy and self-concordance. *Personality and Individual Differences, 85,* 212–229.

Kobak, R. R., Cole, H. E., Ferenz-Gillies, R., Fleming, W. S., & Gamble, W. (1993). Attachment and emotion regulation during mother–teen problem solving: A control theory analysis. *Child Development, 64,* 231–245.

Koole, S. L. (2009). The psychology of emotion regulation: An integrative review. *Cognition and Emotion, 23,* 4–41.

Lench, H. C., & Lench, H. (2018). *Function of emotions.* New York: Springer.

Levine, L. J., & Edelstein, R. S. (2009). Emotion and memory narrowing: A review and goal-relevance approach. *Cognition and Emotion, 23,* 833–875.

Levine, L. J., & Safer, M. A. (2002). Sources of bias in memory for emotions. *Current Directions in Psychological Science, 11,* 169–173.

Lindner, E. G. (2006). Emotion and conflict: Why it is important to understand how emotions affect conflict and how conflict affects emotions. In M. Deutch, P. T. Coleman, & E. C. Marcus (Eds.), *The handbook of conflict resolution* (2nd ed., pp. 268–293). San Francisco, CA: Jossey-Bass.

Ma, L. K., Tunney, R. J., & Ferguson, E. (2017). Does gratitude enhance prosociality? A meta-analytic review. *Psychological Bulletin, 143,* 601–635.

Mansell, W. (2005). Control theory and psychopathology: An integrative approach. *Psychology and Psychotherapy: Theory, Research and Practice, 78,* 141–178.

Mansell, W., & Carey, T. A. (2013). Perceptual control theory as an integrative framework for clinical interventions. In F. Kennedy, H. Kennerley, & D. Pearson (Eds.), *Cognitive behavioural approaches to the understanding and treatment of dissociation* (pp. 221–235). London: Routledge.

McClelland, K. (2004). The collective control of perceptions: Constructing order from conflict. *International Journal of Human-Computer Studies, 60*, 65–99.

McClelland, K. (2014). Cycles of conflict: A computational modeling alternative to Collins's theory of conflict escalation. *Sociological Theory, 32*, 100–127.

Montagrin, A., Brosch, T., & Sander, D. (2013). Goal conduciveness as a key determinant of memory facilitation. *Emotion, 13*, 622–628.

Panksepp, J. (2004). *Affective neuroscience: The foundations of human and animal emotions.* Oxford: Oxford University Press.

Porges, S. W. (2011). *The polyvagal theory: Neurophysiological foundations of emotions, attachment, communication, and self-regulation (Norton Series on Interpersonal Neurobiology).* New York: WW Norton.

Powers, W. T. (1973). In *Behavior: The control of perception.* New York: Hawthorne.

Powers, W. T. (1992). *Living control systems II: Selected papers of William T. Powers.* New Canaan CT: Benchmark.

Powers, W. T. (2005). *Behavior: The control of perception.* New Canaan, CT: Benchmark.

Powers, W. T. (2007). *On emotions and PCT: A brief overview.* www.livingcontrolsystems.com/intro_papers/on_emotions.pdf

Sbarra, D. A., & Hazan, C. (2008). Coregulation, dysregulation, self-regulation: An integrative analysis and empirical agenda for understanding adult attachment, separation, loss, and recovery. *Personality and Social Psychology Review, 12*, 141–167.

Seth, A. K. (2013). Interoceptive inference, emotion, and the embodied self. *Trends in Cognitive Sciences, 17*, 565–573.

Shen, W., Yuan, Y., Liu, C., & Luo, J. (2016). In search of the 'Aha!'experience: Elucidating the emotionality of insight problem-solving. *British Journal of Psychology, 107*, 281–298.

Smith, P. K., & Dutton, S. (1979). Play and training in direct and innovative problem solving. *Child Development, 50*, 830–836.

Sternberg, R. J. (1986). A triangular theory of love. *Psychological Review, 93*, 119–135.

Stroebe, M., Schut, H., & Nauta, M. (2015). Homesickness: A systematic review of the scientific literature. *Review of General Psychology, 19*, 157–171.

van de Rijt-plooij, H., & Plooij, F. X. (1992). Infantile regressions: Disorganization and the onset of transition periods. *Journal of Reproductive and Infant Psychology, 10*, 129–149.

Van Egeren, L. F. (2009). A cybernetic model of global personality traits. *Personality and Social Psychology Review, 13*, 92–108.

Zaki, J., & Williams, W. C. (2013). Interpersonal emotion regulation. *Emotion, 13*, 803–810.

14
GROUP COHESION

M. Blair Evans, Scott A. Graupensperger, and Svenja A. Wolf

Introduction

The social environment within sport often entails small groups, as athletes and others involved in sport are commonly structured into tight-knit, interactive, and interdependent groups such as teams and training groups. These small groups are fundamental to sport performances, and also influence whether or not youth and adults derive value from sport participation. Therefore, many researchers studying the social psychology of sport seek to identify and promote small group environments that optimize outcomes such as fostering adherence to sport, ensuring peak performance, and facilitating positive psychosocial experiences.

What are the characteristics of groups that optimize these outcomes? From the perspective of the public at large and within the media, unitedness appears as one intuitive hallmark. This is evidenced by the case of the 2017 Aiken high school cross-country running team (Cincinnati, USA). Fielding a roster of female and male runners for the first time, the programme was initiated to integrate youth from varying backgrounds, particularly immigrants and refugees, and capitalized on unitedness and involvement:

> "We have some members, they're able to survive war and immigration but what they can't survive is the acculturation process here and that's causing the most problems," [Coach] Parker said. The Aiken cross country team is a chance to change that. ... [A sophomore athlete] said the team changed her life positively, offering an opportunity to self-improve and make friends.
>
> *(Hatch, 2018)*

The value ascribed to team unity was similarly evident in media coverage of the 2018 Ryder Cup, a professional golf competition where one American team is pitted against a European team. In contrast with several preceding cup events where European team success was often linked to the bonds among members, reporting prior to the 2018 event praised the seemingly strong bonds among the American players. By the end of the competition, this script flipped after the Americans were yet again bested by their lower-ranking European counterparts, with Crouse (2018) from the *New York Times* claiming, "the harder the Americans try to manufacture a connection, a cohesion, the more spectacularly they fail."

Whereas several terms reflect the value of unity among team members – chemistry, closeness, morale, tight-knittedness – the construct of group cohesion has garnered the most substantial interest from sport researchers. In addition to the appeal of cohesive sport teams, researchers have empirically demonstrated the importance of group cohesion for key outcomes such as performance, sport adherence, and youth development (Carron & Eys, 2012). This contribution explores how the cohesiveness of sport groups has been studied. After describing how group cohesion has been defined, the contribution reviews key findings regarding the association between group cohesion and sport experiences, along with discussing central conceptual and methodological issues.

Defining and Measuring Sport Group Cohesion

The spectrum of terms used to describe teams comprising rich bonds and cooperation among members underpins the variability in ways to view cohesion and the importance of using a clear empirical definition. Formally, sport researchers describe group cohesion as "a dynamic process that is reflected in the tendency for a group to stick together and remain united in the pursuit of its instrumental objectives and/or for the satisfaction of member affective needs" (Carron, Brawley, & Widmeyer, 1998, p. 213). Numerous features of this definition delineate core aspects of group cohesion in sport. First, cohesion is a dynamic and emergent state that fluctuates over time. Second, group cohesion is fundamental to help members achieve group and individual tasks (i.e., instrumental) while being reflective of interpersonal bonds and feelings about their membership (i.e., affective). As a consequence of this, cohesion might be best accessed through the perceptions of members, that is, athletes' subjective evaluations. Third, and finally, the contrasting components of this definition highlight the multidimensional nature of the cohesion perceptions that members hold.

Although group dynamics theorists generally uphold this definition, group cohesion is admittedly an umbrella term that researchers from many domains have used to describe different types of positive evaluation of group membership (see Salas, Grossman, Hughes, & Coultas, 2015). Despite variability across domains, Carron, Widmeyer, Brawley, and colleagues cultivated a unique sport-specific perspective of cohesion when developing the Group Environment Questionnaire (GEQ). In this context, Carron, Widmeyer, and Brawley (1985) described the multidimensional nature of cohesion in the dimensions of group integration and individual attractions to the group. Group integration involves each member's assessment regarding the unitedness of the group as a whole. This is the "we" component. Meanwhile, individual attractions to the group focus on the "me" within the group, encompassing each member's assessment of personal group involvement and the costs or benefits of membership. For each of these dimensions, Carron and colleagues further distinguished cohesion perceptions based upon context. As such, cohesion evaluations assessed in relation to group tasks (i.e., performance-related) are unique from cohesiveness regarding social relationships and activities.

As represented within Table 2, these contrasts produce four dimensions of group cohesion: (a) individual attractions to group-task, (b) individual attractions to group-social, (c) group integration-task, and (d) group integration-social. Although investigators have occasionally collapsed the GEQ to fewer dimensions (e.g., Al-Yaaribi & Kavussanu, 2017), this conceptualization has produced meaningful findings that distinguish these as four unique evaluations (Eys & Brawley, 2018). Furthermore, investigations have supported the factor structure using unique analyses and in differing cultural contexts (Heuzé & Fontayne, 2002; Ohlert, 2012; Whitton & Fletcher, 2014). An exception to this factor structure is evident in group cohesion measures developed with children

Table 2 Key group cohesion measures in sport

Cohesion measure	Dimensional structure and example items	Notes pertaining to validity
Group Environment Questionnaire, ages 18 years and over (Carron et al., 1985)	**Group integration-task (5 items)**: *"Our team is united in trying to reach its goals for perform- ance."* **Group integration-social (4 items)**: *"Members of our team stick together outside of practices and games."* **Attraction to group-social (5 items)**: *"Some of my best friends are on this team."* **Attraction to group-task (4 items)**: *"I like the style of play on this team."*	• Original version included negatively worded items, although more recent research identifies the value of positive wording (Eys, Carron, Bray, & Brawley, 2007). • Additional investigations have supported validity (e.g., Whitton & Fletcher, 2014) • Further validation and translation into numerous languages (e.g., German: Ohlert, 2012; French: Heuzé & Fon- tayne, 2002)
Youth Sport Environment Questionnaire, ages 13–17 years (YSEQ; Eys et al., 2009) **Child Sport Cohesion Questionnaire**, ages 9–12 years (Martin et al., 2013)	**Social (8 items)**: *"We hang out with one another whenever possible"* **Task (8 items)**: *"I like the way we work together as a team"* **Social (7 items)** *"We stick together outside of sport"* **Task (7 items)** *"In games, we get along well"*	• Although based on the GEQ, were developed through unique item gen- eration processes

Notes. Whereas the GEQ and YSEQ are reported on a 1–9 scale, the Child Sport Cohesion Questionnaire is assessed on a 1–5 scale.

(Martin, Carron, Eys, & Loughead, 2013) and adolescents (Eys, Loughead, Bray, & Carron, 2009), wherein only overall task and social cohesion dimensions were distinguished (i.e., differentiations between individual attractions to the group and group integration did not emerge). Indeed, there is preliminary evidence that perceptions of group cohesion are more differentiated among older athletes (e.g., Eys et al., 2009), although there is limited knowledge regarding how evaluations of groups are acquired throughout development.

Emergence of Group Cohesion as a Topic of Research

The pivotal role of the conceptual growth during the process of developing the GEQ is evident when the historical timeline of cohesion research in sport is considered. The timeline presented in Figure 2 illustrates generalized periods that reflect key advances in sport group cohesion research. Throughout the 20th century, group dynamics emerged as a field of inquiry (e.g., Research Center for Group Dynamics; Lewin, 1945), and studies involving cohesion in organizational groups and other domains of social psychology became common (see Mathieu, Hollenbeck, van Knippenberg, & Ilgen, 2017). Subsequently, numerous sport-specific studies involving group cohesion emerged prior to the advent of the GEQ (Landers & Lüschen, 1974; Williams & Hacker, 1982), although these efforts were constrained by varying measures and definitions of cohesion. However, the conceptual and measurement advances of the GEQ produced a wave of research studying antecedents and consequences of group cohesion, along with applied interventions to promote cohesion. As a result, sport emerged as a unique context with an independent conceptualization and approach to measuring group cohesion. Sport group cohesion research nevertheless has continued to be closely bound to the topics and issues facing researchers studying group cohesion in other contexts (e.g., organizational psychology, management, social psychology).

Research efforts during the process of developing the GEQ also underpin the development of a domain of sport group dynamics research (i.e., efforts investigating the actions of groups and interactions within and between groups; Carron & Eys, 2012). Within this domain, three key developments are distinguished within Figure 2. One key development took place when researchers facing an increasing body of evidence sought to aggregate findings, especially pertaining to the link between cohesion and performance within sport teams and organizations (Carron, Colman, Wheeler, & Stevens, 2002). A subsequent development included efforts to extend measurement to broader cultural contexts and into younger age groups. More recently, researchers have directed attention toward advancing theory, methods, and methodological approaches in general groups research (Cronin, Weingart, & Todorova, 2011), along with sport-specific research (Eys, Bruner, & Martin, 2019). In the next section, findings produced across these empirical developments and focus on key correlates of group cohesion are highlighted.

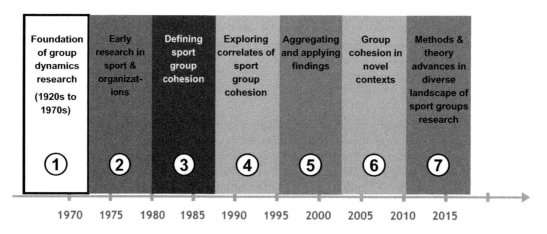

Figure 2 Timeline of the development of key issues and themes throughout the trajectory of sport group cohesion research

Note that periods are not mutually exclusive. For instance, although Period 4 (exploring correlates) was denoted during the early 1990s, studies continue to be conducted to examine correlates of cohesion; however, the focus on exploring associations was characterized as a key focus of sport group cohesion research at that time

Associations with Sport Experiences and Outcomes

When considering the associations between cohesion and sport experiences, it is first important to recognize that groups are complex. The complexity of groups is reflected in the conceptual framework employed by Carron and Eys (2012) to characterize the role of cohesion within broader group ecologies. This model identifies antecedents of cohesion (e.g., group structures and the group environment), which shape perceptions of group cohesion. These antecedents reflect the social context from which individuals derive cohesion perceptions. Ultimately, cohesion is also associated with the individual- and group-level outcomes of group membership. To help understand when and why cohesion predicts key outcomes, researchers often target associations with group processes (i.e., concrete and observable interactions among members) such as teamwork, team cognition, and member communication. Understanding small groups also entails recognizing that cohesion is one of several emergent states that are evaluations that members develop over the life of the team, stemming from experiences in the group (McEwan & Beauchamp, 2019). Below, key findings demonstrating the role of cohesion in relation to outcomes are introduced, before cohesion's associations with key group processes and emergent states are characterized. Given that there is enough evidence to dedicate entire chapters to associations between group cohesion and specific outcomes (e.g., group cohesion as a predictor of emotional states; see call-out box), we focus on only a subset of key associations below.

Call-Out Box: Team Cohesion and Emotions

What do we know? Among other benefits, athletes' perceptions of greater team cohesion link with more adaptive emotional responses – for example, to a pending competition. Specifically, athletes perceived greater cohesion to reduce their *precompetitive anxiety* (Wolf, Harenberg, Tamminen, & Schmitz, 2018), and perceptions of greater cohesion indeed predicted reduced precompetitive anxiety symptoms (in adults: Prapavessis & Carron, 1996; and in children: Martin et al., 2013), related to facilitative instead of debilitative interpretations of these symptoms (Eys, Hardy, Carron, & Beauchamp, 2003; Wolf, Eys, Sadler, & Kleinert, 2015), and, ultimately, decreased precompetitive anxiety while increasing *precompetitive excitement*. Group members who perceive higher group cohesion also likely experience:

- reduced *precompetitive tension, depression, irritation,* and *fatigue,* as well as enhanced *precompetitive vigour* (Terry et al., 2000),
- less intra-team *jealousy* (Kamphoff, Gill, & Huddleston, 2005), and
- enhanced *emotional agreement* with teammates, as captured by athletes' qualitative responses (Tamminen et al., 2016).

Why and how are these associations manifested? Whereas empirical findings revealing a link between cohesion and emotions are valuable, it is critical to understand the mechanisms behind this link. In line with cognitive-motivational-relational theory (Lazarus, 1999), team cohesion likely links to emotions via athletes' appraisal. Notably, reduced worries about letting teammates down and satisfying their expectations mediated the relationship between greater cohesion and reduced precompetitive anxiety symptoms (Prapavessis & Carron, 1996). Similarly, perceptions of greater cohesion predicted appraisals of enhanced prospects for coping with competitive demands (Wolf et al., 2015), which mediated the relationship between greater cohesion and decreased precompetitive anxiety and, respectively, increased precompetitive excitement (Wolf et al., 2018). These positive links between cohesion and coping prospects, in turn, likely are due to greater perceived social support (Tamminen, Sabiston, & Crocker, 2019; Wolf et al., 2018).

Summary: Owing to these adaptive effects and team cohesion's importance above and beyond a number of personal, environmental, and social variables, team cohesion likely holds unsourced potential as an avenue for effective and efficient emotion regulation.

Group Cohesion and Performance

Driven by the pursuit of optimal performance, early sport group cohesion research focused on the association between cohesion and performance in particular. It was presumed that group cohesion must be fundamental to peak group performances, to the extent that members experience task interdependence (i.e., cooperation during performance tasks; Carron & Chelladurai, 1981). Indeed, initial sport research employing varying operationalizations of group cohesion reported significant and positive associations with performance (Landers & Lüschen, 1974; Williams & Hacker, 1982). In the years that followed, this association has been explored through meta-analyses of a total of 63 sport-based studies (Carron et al., 2002; Filho, Dobersek, Gershgoren, Becker, & Tenenbaum, 2014), which revealed that cohesion and performance have a moderate bidirectional association across cohesion dimensions, genders, ages, competitive levels, and types of sport. Nonetheless, aggregated evidence suggested that task cohesion held a somewhat stronger association with performance than social cohesion, and that the link between cohesion and performance was stronger for female athletes (compared with males) and for sports involving lower levels of task interdependence (see Carron et al., 2002; Filho et al., 2014).

Recent advances in interpretation of the cohesion–performance relationship have employed methodological advances. As one example, researchers leveraging longitudinal multilevel models studied bidirectional associations across three time points within a season in elite youth sport (Benson, Šiška, Eys, Priklerova, & Slepička, 2016). In this study, mid-season performance was a significant predictor of end-of-season cohesion, whereas cohesion did not predict performance. Benson et al. (2016) described these findings by emphasizing the importance of recognizing the unique circumstances of a given context (in this case, elite youth sport) for understanding the cohesion–performance association.

Group Cohesion and Sport Participation

Another theme within the literature includes the tendency for researchers to consider how cohesion may increase commitment to the group and adherence to sport participation. Cross-sectional and longitudinal studies indeed support associations with athletes' intentions to return to sport (Spink, McLaren, & Ulvick, 2018) and actual return to teams (Spink, Wilson, & Odnokon, 2010). Despite this initial evidence for an association between group cohesion and sport adherence, there is limited evidence regarding the underlying mechanisms. Most previous studies have implied that cohesion satisfies belongingness needs (Baumeister & Leary, 1995). Whereas investigators have focused on the satisfaction of belongingness needs as a chief mechanism for the impact of group environments on sport adherence, this has not been empirically tested. There is also theoretical support for an expectation that groups likely have more comprehensive effects. For instance, group cohesion likely satisfies numerous fundamental needs (e.g., recognition of competence and establishing perceptions of autonomy; Ryan & Deci, 2000) that are, as yet, unstudied as mechanisms for their potential influence on sport participation (Greenaway et al., 2015).

Cohesion and Youth Development

Youth sport researchers commonly employ models of positive youth development (Holt et al., 2017) that could readily be applied to the study of groups. Interestingly, despite frequent claims that the experience of being required to cooperate with peers is a critical developmental asset gained through youth sport, empirical study of cohesion within the process of youth development is fairly novel. Nonetheless, findings seem promising. Specifically, Bruner, Eys, Wilson, and Côté (2014) examined associations between cohesion and youth-reported experiences in sport at the within-group (i.e., individual) and between-group (i.e., team) levels. Although between-group associations were more complex, within-group findings revealed that perceptions of task and social cohesion were significant and positive predictors of athlete-reported personal skill development, social skill development, initiative enhancement, and goal-setting. Other researchers have also demonstrated how variability in group cohesion throughout a season is positively associated with changes in self-regulation skills and the needs satisfied through sport (e.g., Erikstad, Martin, Haugen, & Høigaard, 2018). Group cohesion is, thus, likely to be a perception that is associated with personal development through sport.

Associations with Group Processes and Emergent States

Associations with the aforementioned key outcomes are commonly theorized to emerge via group processes (Carron & Eys, 2012). As such, iterative associations between group cohesion and group processes are useful for understanding associations with performance and development. As an example of a group process on the path from group cohesion to performance, perceptions of task and social cohesion are associated with perceptions of teamwork behaviours when preparing for performance and during execution (e.g., coordination, communication, cooperation; McEwan, Zumbo, Eys, & Beauchamp, 2018). As such, cohesion perceptions align closely with teammates' experiences of efficient team interactions. As an example relevant to youth development, cohesion is also associated with prosocial and antisocial behaviours among team members. When teammates engaged in higher levels of prosocial behaviour, such as encouraging one another, and less antisocial behaviour, members reported higher levels of cohesion (Al-Yaaribi & Kavussanu, 2017). Meanwhile, prospective research also demonstrates the opposing pathway, with cohesion predicting later prosocial and antisocial behaviour (Bruner, Boardley, & Côté, 2014). Experiences within cohesive groups may, thus, be a pathway to promote positive intragroup interactions and develop social skills.

Given its emergent instrumental and affective nature, group cohesion is also closely associated with other emergent states. For instance, cohesion can motivate members to invest effort, in the sense that higher perceptions of group cohesion are associated with lower perceptions of social loafing (De Backer, Boen, De Cuyper, Høigaard, & Vande Broek, 2015). Group cohesion is also associated with the strength with which members socially identify as members of a group. For instance, the in-group-ties dimension of social identity strength represents the strength of relationships with teammates and is closely associated with cohesion (e.g., Bruner et al., 2014). Although these are only several examples, they exemplify how cohesion is associated with group processes and emergent states in ways that are likely to influence key outcomes.

Building Cohesion

Considering the outcomes of cohesion, there is substantial interest in understanding its antecedents and in developing strategies to build cohesion. Regarding antecedents, a substantial evidence base supports claims that member attributes, team environments, and team structures shape cohesion perceptions (see Carron & Eys, 2012). As one example of the influence of group structure in the form of group size, Widmeyer, Brawley, and Carron (1990) conducted a quasi-experimental study with intramural teams of three, six, and nine members. Findings revealed that cohesion perceptions varied according to group size, whereby members perceived the highest cohesion and enjoyment in the smallest group size. As another example of structural and environmental influences on cohesion, Evans and Eys (2015) reported that cohesion perceptions within elite individual sport teams were highest among athletes who were task-interdependent (e.g., relay members). The authors also reported that cohesion perceptions were higher when athletes were proximal in time to an event with a team-level outcome, compared with when team-level competitions were several weeks away. In addition, group cohesion evaluations are also shaped by individuals' subjective perceptions of group structure. For instance, individuals with more clarity regarding their personal roles perceived increased cohesion (Eys & Carron, 2001).

Evidence regarding antecedents and outcomes has positioned group cohesion as a prime target for team-building. Generally, team-building refers to interventions or activities conducted with (or on) groups to promote the likelihood that (a) the group meets its task objectives, (b) belonging in the group satisfies members, and/or (c) the group provides a positive environment (Brawley & Paskevich, 1997). Specifically, team-building consists of a spectrum of strategies such as group goal setting, fostering interpersonal relationships and trust through formal and informal activities, or clarifying roles through communication and problem-solving tasks (e.g., Shuffler, DiazGranados, & Salas, 2011). Furthermore, team-building may differ with regard to when it is delivered (i.e., acute, or throughout a team's lifespan), and who delivers it (i.e., directly through a consultant, or indirectly through coaches or other leaders; Carron & Eys, 2012).

Across all of these possibilities, a meta-analysis of 17 sport-related team-building interventions reported overall positive outcomes (Martin, Carron, & Burke, 2009). Specifically, Martin et al. (2009) reported positive effects of team-building on group cohesion, team performance, and individual cognitions (e.g., confidence, trust, satisfaction). Furthermore, it emerged that team-building interventions that focused on goal setting were most commonly studied and were associated with the strongest effects (Martin et al., 2009). Although the existing knowledge base entails small and limited trials that increase the likelihood of biased results (i.e., no comparison or control groups; lack of randomization), existing research is useful for describing strategies that researchers, athletes, and coaches value and are willing to adopt.

The literature involving team-building in sport is represented through a few dominant approaches, particularly the approach outlined by Prapavessis, Carron, and Spink (1996). This conceptual framework describes an approach toward indirect team-building where the facilitator works as a partner with a group leader (e.g., coach). After introducing team-building concepts to coaches, the facilitator leads coaches when selecting potential strategies within their own groups and, in turn, delivering those strategies. This framework is distinguished by its approach to cluster strategies within varying domains of the group, including the team environment (e.g., distinctiveness-enhancing strategies), structure (e.g., fostering norms and ensuring conformity to them), and processes (e.g., activities that demand cooperation among members; Prapavessis et al., 1996). Beyond this approach, varying strategies have been linked to positive outcomes for athletes. For instance, personal disclosure and open discussion of group functioning at a critical juncture within a season was believed to strengthen interpersonal relationships among members and, in turn, perceptions of group cohesion (Pain & Harwood, 2009).

Although team-building is well established in sport, there are two areas of potential growth. One way for this literature to develop is to apply approaches for building teams in organizational psychology that focus on group processes rather than cohesion. For instance, organizational psychologists have contrasted traditional team-building with team-development strategies where practitioners enhance the instructions that members receive regarding interactions with teammates and conduct training to enhance members' capacity to work alongside one another (Shuffler et al., 2011). A similar approach was tested within recent sport research (McEwan & Beauchamp, 2019), including a teamwork training intervention that facilitated goal-setting (a common team-building strategy), combined with: (a) team-led simulation through anticipated competitive situations, and (b) briefing/debriefing through structured sessions before and after competition. Another way forward is to maintain a focus on building cohesion but, instead, consider a broader spectrum of outcomes. For example, team-building could be leveraged to optimize the types of peer influence exerted within groups, such as the aforementioned effects on behaviours related to peer behaviours and on substance use. Indeed, widespread prevention interventions such as the ATHENA substance use and weight-related intervention are conducted in team settings and impacted by group processes such as team norms (Ranby et al., 2009). Team-building strategies appear well suited to be integrated alongside prevention strategies, whereby increased cohesion around positive and prosocial norms may strengthen the messages conveyed in those interventions.

Theoretical and Conceptual Considerations

Throughout the development of an evidence base, the field of cohesion research has faced theoretical and practical considerations. Three considerations that continue to challenge researchers include (a) distinguishing cohesion from other group constructs, (b) operationalizing group cohesion in alternative ways, and (c) capturing the dynamic and multilevel nature of cohesion.

Challenge 1: Distinguishing Cohesion

The first consideration entails outlining what group cohesion is *not*. It is increasingly evident that cohesion is one of several emergent states that are important for group functioning. This raises challenges in distinguishing between group cohesion and other emergent states such as collective efficacy (Fransen, Mertens, Feltz, & Boen, 2017), groupness (Spink et al., 2018), and social identification (Bruner et al., 2014). Although the conceptual and theoretical foundation of cohesion distinguishes it from these contrasting emergent states, commonalities in theory or measurement complicate attempts to measure cohesion independently. As one example, the prevailing measure for social identification with sport teams entails some items that closely resemble those used to measure group cohesion (e.g., "I feel a sense of being 'connected' with other members in this team"; Bruner et al., 2014, p. 59). A related observation entails recognizing the distinction between cohesion as an emergent state and group processes. Given that processes represent what groups actually *do* (e.g., communicate, cooperate; McEwan & Beauchamp, 2019), a clear conceptual distinction exists with the personal nature of cohesion perceptions that are emergent. The measurement of group processes nevertheless often practically overlaps with cohesion, such as how items used to represent the cooperation component of teamwork (i.e., "Team members work together as one unit rather than a bunch of individuals"; McEwan et al., 2018, p. 66) share similarities with items for group integration.

A clear challenge for researchers moving forward is to demonstrate associations among group cohesion, emergent states, and group processes, while ensuring that conceptual distinctions are maintained. This is likely to entail clever integration of methodologies. Longitudinal approaches are one strategy to distinguish constructs that is employed in current research by testing prospective associations (e.g., Bruner et al., 2014). Another strategy is to diversify the way that constructs are measured, integrating alternative measurement approaches to reduce the potential for common-method bias. Finally, experimental methods could be critical, whereby researchers manipulate one group construct (e.g., perceptions of cohesion) to assess impacts on other emergent states or group processes.

Challenge 2: Alternative Theoretical Perspectives and Measures of Group Cohesion

A second challenge emerges in relation to how group cohesion is operationalized. Across the various research domains that study group cohesion (e.g., organizational psychology), there has been difficulty finding unanimity in its definition. Salas et al. (2015) conducted a review to collate operationalizations of group cohesion across domains and uncovered a mosaic of dimensions. Whereas they reported dimensions involving attraction based on interactions in task and social domains that are similar to sport measures (e.g., the GEQ), they also reported dimensions of belongingness (i.e., attraction among members), pride (i.e., members' liking for the status or importance of group membership), and morale (i.e., loyalty to other members). Further, Salas et al. (2015) reported how measures varied regarding whether respondents reported on their own attitudes or typical group behaviours. Contrasted with this variability, the consistent use of Carron et al.'s (1985) operationalization in sport seems like an advantage. Nonetheless, there may be substantial value in considering alternative operationalizations of cohesion in sport. This value may especially pertain to the expanding scope of cohesion research. For instance, researchers studying moral attitudes and intergroup behaviours may expect that dimensions related to member pride and morale may have particular salience for behaviours enacted with other group members.

Expanding our approach to studying cohesion may also entail introducing novel measurement strategies beyond self-report surveys. Although self-report instruments are psychometrically validated and align well with the conceptualization of cohesion as a subjective evaluation, novel approaches may overcome inherent limitations to scale-scored, Likert-style surveys (i.e., response biases), while also taking advantage of benefits that come with heterogeneity in measurement (i.e., minimizing common method variance). Eys and Brawley (2018) specifically identify potential assessments of interactions among members by tracking objective communication (e.g., social media), electronic tags that track physical locations and interactions, and other external observations of team functioning. In addition, sociometry is a promising approach. Although uncommon in sport research (for a notable example see Loughead et al., 2016), a sociometric evaluation of group cohesion would entail having members report their ties to one another and, in turn, producing group-level indices of tight-knittedness and structural cohesion along with individual-level analyses of people's position within the group. Such a measurement approach would recognize that cohesion is embedded in personal evaluations, while also enabling analytic approaches such as social network analysis that can reflect more complex group structures and relative member positions within the group. Warner, Bowers, and Dixon (2012) specifically note that social network analysis is ideally suited to complement the GEQ.

Thinking even more comprehensively, further consideration should be directed toward heterogeneity in how cohesion is perceived across populations. For example, early evidence of a stronger association between cohesion and performance in female teams (Carron et al., 2002) stimulated qualitative research into coaches' perceptions of cohesion salience and approaches to group management across male and female teams (Eys et al., 2015). Expanding on this notion, it is also important to investigate potential for broader influences to shape the nature and consequences of group cohesion. For example, although sport group cohesion has traditionally been conducted in mainstream sport, group cohesion entails unique salience and elements when reported on by parasport athletes (Caron, Bloom, Loughead, & Hoffmann, 2016).

Furthermore, our perspective of group cohesion has emerged predominately through research in North America and Western Europe. Meanwhile, orientations toward social relationships differ substantially across cultures, which is evident in research involving South Korean speed-skating Olympians (Nam, Kim, Marshall, Sung, & Mao, 2018). Although cohesion was not the focus of their study, Nam et al. (2018) described how South Korean national identity innately focused on the value of societal cohesion and loyalty, which placed pressures on athletes to compete for their country. This powerful national identity may shape how group cohesion is perceived and valued among members. As such, researchers should consider the ways that cohesion perceptions are likely to vary across individuals as a function of societal and cultural characteristics. The phenomenological methodology adopted by Nam et al. (2018) also reveals the value of adopting diverse philosophical and methodological approaches to studying group cohesion. Considering that sport group cohesion research emerged at a time when positivistic philosophies and quantitative methodologies prevailed, numerous qualitative methodologies are critical – especially when examining the cultural and social meaning of experiences within small groups.

Challenge 3: Advanced Quantitative Methods That Reflect the Multilevel Nature of Groups

A further point pertaining to the conceptualization and measurement of cohesion in quantitative research is its multilevel nature (Casey-Campbell & Martens, 2009). This issue was prevalent in early research, querying whether group cohesion perceptions are inherently individual or shared among members. This question was, to some extent, resolved empirically, revealing moderate agreement within teams (Carron, Brawley, Eys, Bray, Hall, & Terry, 2003). In other words, although members' perceptions of their own involvement with the group or the groups' greater integration are the level at which cohesion is measured, teammates' perceptions of cohesion tend to share variability because they refer to a common physical and psychological context. Group integration perceptions, in particular, reflect substantial group-level variability. Thus, contemporary researchers tend to hold interest in *both* the variability in cohesion that is shared among team members *and* variability that is unique for each member relative to his or her teammates.

When circumstances arise that demand a multilevel approach, how do researchers address the potential for member perceptions of cohesion to cluster within groups? Typically, researchers study the multilevel nature of team members' responses by calculating aggregated group-level cohesion perceptions shared by all group members, unique from members' own responses that are centred relative to their group mean. Doing so allows researchers to at least account for and factor out shared variance within teams (e.g., Wolf et al., 2015), but also provides opportunities to study the unique role of group-level cohesion. As an example, researchers could explore cross-level interactions, whereby the group cohesion perceptions shared in one's group may moderate associations at the individual level. Multilevel analyses are also well suited for considering another feature of cohesion: its dynamic nature. Indeed, the study of group dynamics has long been criticized for failing to use longitudinal analyses that are able to capture its dynamic nature (e.g., Cronin et al., 2011). Although group-level cohesion is anticipated to improve across the course of a season, individuals' perceptions of cohesion may be more volatile, even shifting from one practice to the next. Using perceptions of social identity (as opposed to cohesion), Benson and Bruner (2018) demonstrated the value in measuring group perceptions using intensive longitudinal designs (i.e., daily diary sampling) and multilevel analyses, finding, for example, that athletes reported a stronger social identity on days that they experienced a greater number of prosocial behaviours from teammates. Similar designs would expand our understanding of cohesion in sport (see Eys et al., 2019).

The Dark Side of Group Cohesion

Whereas the body of literature pertaining to cohesion in sport and exercise groups has primarily focused on positive effects of cohesion, researchers have also considered potential detrimental effects of cohesion. Hardy, Eys, and Carron (2005) were among the first to investigate whether teams featuring high levels of social or task cohesion may constrain member effort, produce exclusionary behaviours, or have other negative outcomes. Indeed, there are several potential dark sides of group cohesion.

For one, the strong interpersonal attraction and collectivity that make high cohesion so desirable may entail unwelcome side effects in the form of self-esteem threats or concerns about letting teammates down. First, although cohesive groups protect members against external self-esteem threats through increased social support, diffusion of evaluation, and shared responsibility for failure (e.g., Hill & Shaw, 2013), athletes who perceive greater cohesion may experience novel internal self-esteem threats in the form of increased self-presentational concerns. In other words, because cohesion represents a strong attraction to the group, members of cohesive groups likely place particular value on teammates' opinions and evaluations. As an empirical demonstration of this link to self-presentation, athletes who were prone to protect their self-esteem by self-handicapping were particularly likely employ such proactive excuse-making when they perceived high group cohesion (Carron, Prapavessis, & Grove, 1994). Second, although greater team cohesion seems to encourage members to invest greater personal effort through perceptions of increased social responsibility and indispensability (Gammage, Carron, & Estabrooks, 2001), these perceptions may induce concerns about affecting a collective task adversely. That is, because cohesion represents a strong integration of individual contributions, members of cohesive teams likely consider their personal performance as crucial to team performance. In line with this, perceptions of greater team cohesion linked with members appraising a pending team competition as more important (Wolf et al., 2015) and worries about letting teammates down (Hardy et al., 2005).

For another, research involving team cohesion may also be critical for understanding victimizing or exclusionary behaviour within a group. This is particularly the case when considering initiation rituals that athletes and coaches may believe can have beneficial effects on socialization (e.g., Johnson, Guerrero, Holman, Chin, & Signer-Kroeker, 2018). There is limited evidence for a direct link between hazing and group cohesion (Lafferty, Wakefield, & Brown, 2017). In fact, hazing may even be a way for members to ostracize or exclude others. For instance, martial artists required to pass through harmful or challenging rituals to progress in belt status only indicated stronger motives for pro-group action when they reported positive affective experiences in these rituals (Kavanagh, Jong, McKay, & Whitehouse, 2018). When members had poor experiences, hazing rituals did not influence their in-group views. Given the significance of group environments, further research involving links between cohesion and negative or harmful group behaviour is prudent.

Finally, cohesion also plays a role in athletes' health-risk behaviours. Although cohesion could hold associations with numerous health behaviours, alcohol use is one risky correlate of group cohesion. For instance, Zamboanga, Rodriguez, and Horton (2008) reported significant correlations between social cohesion and alcohol use in intercollegiate sport (although this association was non-significant when the time that members spent together in social settings was controlled for). Further research similarly reported a positive association between attraction to one's sport team and self-reported alcohol use (Grossbard, Hummer, LaBrie, Pederson, & Neighbors, 2009). Beyond direct associations, Grossbard et al. (2009) also reported a moderating effect, whereby the positive association between perceived norms for alcohol use and self-reported use was strongest when athletes reported high attraction to their team. These findings align with broader theoretical descriptions for how cohesion may also enhance the pressures felt by members to adhere to harmful group norms (e.g., Gammage et al., 2001). In sum, there is potential for cohesive teams to promote unique types of attitude, or for relatively higher levels of cohesion to produce pressures to conform to group standards and expectations.

Conclusion

Group cohesion represents the most commonly studied group attribute, and research involving this construct has been ongoing since early studies involving the dynamics of sport groups. Researchers have delineated numerous benefits that sport team members gain when they report high attractions to the group and demonstrate high group integration in task-related and social interactions. Correlational and experimental research has also revealed how group cohesion is shaped by group environments and group structures, and the dynamic relationships it has with group processes.

Researchers nevertheless face challenges when hoping to advance the study of groups generally and group cohesion specifically. Furthermore, researchers have introduced numerous important emergent states that increase our vocabulary to describe and understand groups but also obscure our existing understanding of the role of cohesion within sport groups. Promising strategies to advance understanding are evident in the increasing use of novel measures and analyses alongside dominant methodologies, as well as more comprehensive shifts in the lens through which researchers study groups. For instance, researchers are increasingly adopting multilevel analyses that distinguish correlates at individual and group levels. Network approaches are also an emerging approach, deriving estimates of group environments from the ties that bind each member within a group. Furthermore, the diverse spectrum of qualitative methodologies shows promise for extending the scope of cohesion research, particularly when examining the meanings that individuals ascribe to group cohesion in varying social and cultural contexts. By refining methodologies and conceptualizations of sport groups, it is likely that researchers will address existing challenges and continue to extend the trajectory of meaningful group cohesion research.

References

Al-Yaaribi, A., & Kavussanu, M. (2017). Teammate prosocial and antisocial behaviors predict task cohesion and burnout: The mediating role of affect. *Journal of Sport and Exercise Psychology, 39,* 199–208.

Baumeister, R. F., & Leary, M. R. (1995). The need to belong: Desire for interpersonal attachments as a fundamental human motivation. *Psychological Bulletin, 117,* 497–529.

Benson, A. J., & Bruner, M. W. (2018). How teammate behaviors relate to athlete affect, cognition, and behaviors: A daily diary approach within youth sport. *Psychology of Sport & Exercise, 34,* 119–127.

Benson, A. J., Šiška, P., Eys, M., Priklerova, S., & Slepička, P. (2016). A prospective multilevel examination of the relationship between cohesion and team performance in elite youth sport. *Psychology of Sport and Exercise, 27,* 39–46.

Brawley, L. R., & Paskevich, D. M. (1997). Conducting team building research in the context of sport and exercise. *Journal of Applied Sport Psychology, 9,* 11–40.

Bruner, M. W., Boardley, I. D., & Côté, J. (2014). Social identity and prosocial and antisocial behavior in youth sport. *Psychology of Sport and Exercise, 15,* 56–64.

Bruner, M. W., Eys, M. A., Wilson, K. S., & Côté, J. (2014). Group cohesion and positive youth development in team sport athletes. *Sport, Exercise, and Performance Psychology, 3,* 219.

Caron, J. G., Bloom, G. A., Loughead, T. M., & Hoffmann, M. D. (2016). Paralympic athlete leaders' perceptions of leadership and cohesion. *Journal of Sport Behavior, 39,* 17–29.

Carron, A. V., Brawley, L. R., Eys, M. A., Bray, S., Dorsch, K., Estabrooks, P., … Paskevich, D. (2003). Do individual perceptions of group cohesion reflect shared beliefs? An empirical analysis. *Small Group Research, 34,* 468–496.

Carron, A. V., Brawley, L. R., & Widmeyer, W. N. (1998). The measurement of cohesiveness in sport groups. In J. L. Duda (Ed.), *Advances in sport and exercise psychology measurement* (pp. 213–226). Morgantown, WV: Fitness Information Technology.

Carron, A. V., & Chelladurai, P. (1981). The dynamics of group cohesion in sport. *Journal of Sport Psychology, 3,* 123–139.

Carron, A. V., Colman, M. M., Wheeler, J., & Stevens, D. (2002). Cohesion and performance in sport: A meta-analysis. *Journal of Sport & Exercise Psychology, 24,* 168–188.

Carron, A. V., & Eys, M. A. (2012). *Group dynamics in sport* (4th ed.). Morgantown, WV: Fitness Information Technology.

Carron, A. V., Prapavessis, H., & Grove, J. R. (1994). Group effects and self-handicapping. *Journal of Sport and Exercise Psychology, 16,* 246–257.

Carron, A. V., Widmeyer, L. R., & Brawley, L. R. (1985). The development of an instrument to assess cohesion in sport teams: The Group Environment Questionnaire. *Journal of Sport Psychology, 7,* 244–266.

Casey-Campbell, M., & Martens, M. L. (2009). Sticking it all together: A critical assessment of the group cohesion–performance literature. *International Journal of Management Reviews, 11,* 223–246.

Cronin, M. A., Weingart, L. R., & Todorova, G. (2011). Dynamics in groups: Are we there yet? *The Academy of Management Annals, 5,* 571–612.

Crouse, K. (2018, Sept 30). In Ryder Cup, Europe leaves egos at door. Those of U.S. slam the door. *The New York Times.* Retrieved from: www.nytimes.com/2018/09/30/sports/golf/ryder-cup-europe-united-states-egos.html

De Backer, M., Boen, F., De Cuyper, B., Høigaard, R., & Vande Broek, G. (2015). A team fares well with a fair coach: Predictors of social loafing in interactive female sport teams. *Scandinavian Journal of Medicine & Science in Sports, 25,* 897–908.

Erikstad, M. K., Martin, L. J., Haugen, T., & Høigaard, R. (2018). Group cohesion, needs satisfaction, and self-regulated learning: A one-year prospective study of elite youth soccer players' perceptions of their club team. *Psychology of Sport and Exercise, 39,* 171–178.

Evans, M. B., & Eys, M. A. (2015). Collective goals and shared tasks: Interdependence structure and perceptions of individual sport team environments. *Scandinavian Journal of Medicine & Science in Sports, 25,* e139–e148.

Eys, M., Bruner, M. W., & Martin, L. J. (2019). The dynamic group environment in sport and exercise. *Psychology of Sport and Exercise, 42*, 40–47.

Eys, M. A., & Brawley, L. R. (2018). Reflections on cohesion research with sport and exercise groups. *Social and Personality Psychology Compass, 12*, e12379.

Eys, M. A., & Carron, A. V. (2001). Role ambiguity, task cohesion, and task self-efficacy. *Small Group Research, 32*, 356–373.

Eys, M. A., Carron, A. V., Bray, S. R., & Brawley, L. R. (2007). Item wording and internal consistency of a measure of cohesion: The Group Environment Questionnaire. *Journal of Sport & Exercise Psychology, 29*, 395–402.

Eys, M. A., Hardy, J., Carron, A. V., & Beauchamp, M. R. (2003). The relationship between task cohesion and competitive state anxiety. *Journal of Sport and Exercise Psychology, 25*, 66–76.

Eys, M. A., Loughead, T. M., Bray, S. R., & Carron, A. V. (2009). Development of a cohesion questionnaire for youth: The Youth Sport Environment Questionnaire. *Journal of Sport & Exercise Psychology, 31*, 390–408.

Eys, M. A., Ohlert, J., Evans, B., Wolf, S., Martin, L., Van Bussel, M., & Steins, C. (2015). Cohesion and performance for female and male sport teams. *The Sport Psychologist, 29*, 97–109.

Filho, E., Dobersek, U., Gershgoren, L., Becker, B., & Tenenbaum, G. (2014). The cohesion–performance relationship in sport: A 10-year retrospective meta-analysis. *Sport Sciences for Health, 10*, 165–177.

Fransen, K., Mertens, N., Feltz, D., & Boen, F. (2017). "Yes, we can!" review on team confidence in sports. *Current Opinion in Psychology, 16*, 98–103.

Gammage, K. L., Carron, A. V., & Estabrooks, P. A. (2001). Team cohesion and individual productivity: The influence of the norm for productivity and the identifiability of individual effort. *Small Group Research, 32*, 3–18.

Greenaway, K. H., Haslam, S. A., Cruwys, T., Branscombe, N. R., Ysseldyk, R., & Heldreth, C. (2015). From "we" to "me": Group identification enhances perceived personal control with consequences for health and well-being. *Journal of Personality and Social Psychology, 109*, 53–67.

Grossbard, J., Hummer, J., LaBrie, J., Pederson, E., & Neighbors, C. (2009). Is substance use a team sport? Attraction to team, perceived norms, and alcohol and marijuana use among male and female intercollegiate athletes. *Journal of Applied Sport Psychology, 21*, 247–261.

Hardy, J., Eys, M. A., & Carron, A. V. (2005). Exploring the potential disadvantages of high team cohesion. *Small Group Research, 36*, 166–187.

Hatch, C. (2018, Nov 19). The story behind Aiken's cross country program: Language, culture and unity. *Cincinnati Enquirer*. Retrieved from: www.cincinnati.com/story/sports/2018/11/19/story-behind-aikens-cross-country-program-language-culture-and-unity/2031229002/

Heuzé, J., & Fontayne, P. (2002). Questionnaire sur l'ambiance du groupe: A French-language instrument for measuring group cohesion. *Journal of Sport & Exercise Psychology, 24*, 42–67.

Hill, D. M., & Shaw, G. (2013). A qualitative examination of choking under pressure in team sport. *Psychology of Sport & Exercise, 14*, 103–110.

Holt, N. L., Neely, K. C., Slater, L. G., Camiré, M., Côté, J., Fraser-Thomas, J., … Tamminen, K. A. (2017). A grounded theory of positive youth development through sport based on results from a qualitative meta-study. *International Review of Sport and Exercise Psychology, 10*, 1–49.

Johnson, J., Guerrero, M. D., Holman, M., Chin, J. W., & Signer-Kroeker, M. (2018). An examination of hazing in Canadian intercollegiate sports. *Journal of Clinical Sport Psychology, 12*, 144–159.

Kamphoff, C. S., Gill, D. L., & Huddleston, S. (2005). Jealousy in sport: Exploring jealousy's relationship to cohesion. *Journal of Applied Sport Psychology, 17*, 290–305.

Kavanagh, C. M., Jong, J., McKay, R., & Whitehouse, H. (2018). Positive experiences of high arousal martial arts rituals are linked to identity fusion and costly pro-group actions. *European Journal of Social Psychology*. Advance online publication. doi: 10.1002/ejsp.2514.

Lafferty, M. E., Wakefield, C., & Brown, H. (2017). "We do it for the team" – Student-athletes' initiation practices and their impact on group cohesion. *International Journal of Sport and Exercise Psychology, 15*, 438–446.

Landers, D. M., & Lüschen, G. (1974). Team performance outcome and the cohesiveness of competitive coacting groups. *International Review of Sport Sociology, 9*, 57–71.

Lazarus, R. S. (1999). *Stress and emotion: A new synthesis*. New York: Springer.

Lewin, K. (1945). The research center for group dynamics at Massachusetts Institute of Technology. *Sociometry, 8*, 126–136.

Loughead, T. M., Fransen, K., Van Puyenbroeck, S., Hoffmann, M. D., De Cuyper, B., Vanbeselaere, N., & Boen, F. (2016). An examination of the relationship between athlete leadership and cohesion using social network analysis. *Journal of Sports Sciences, 34,* 2063–2073.

Martin, L. J., Carron, A. V., & Burke, S. M. (2009). Team building interventions in sport: A meta-analysis. *Sport and Exercise Psychology Review, 5,* 3–18.

Martin, L. J., Carron, A. V., Eys, M. A., & Loughead, T. (2013). Validation of the child sport cohesion questionnaire. *Measurement in Physical Education and Exercise Science, 17,* 105–119.

Mathieu, J. E., Hollenbeck, J. R., van Knippenberg, D., & Ilgen, D. R. (2017). A century of work teams in the *Journal of Applied Psychology. Journal of Applied Psychology, 102,* 451–452.

McEwan, D., & Beauchamp, M. R. (2019). Teamwork training in sport: A pilot intervention study. *Journal of Applied Sport Psychology.* Advance Online Publication. doi: 10.1080/10413200.2018.1518277.

McEwan, D., Zumbo, B. D., Eys, M. A., & Beauchamp, M. R. (2018). The development and psychometric properties of the multidimensional assessment of teamwork in sport. *Journal of Sport and Exercise Psychology, 40,* 60–72.

Nam, B. H., Kim, M. J., Marshall, R. C., Sung, S., & Mao, L. L. (2018). On the road to the Olympics: A phenomenological approach of national identity in South Korean national short-track speed skaters. *Sport in Society, 21,* 1917–1938.

Ohlert, J. (2012). Kohäsionsfragebogen für Individual- und Teamsport - Leistungssport (KIT-L): A German-language instrument for measuring group cohesion in individual and team sports. *International Journal of Sport & Exercise Psychology, 10,* 39–51.

Pain, M., & Harwood, C. (2009). Team building through mutual sharing and open discussion of team functioning. *The Sport Psychologist, 23,* 523–542.

Prapavessis, H., & Carron, A. V. (1996). The effect of group cohesion on competitive state anxiety. *Journal of Sport & Exercise Psychology, 18,* 64–74.

Prapavessis, H., Carron, A. V., & Spink, K. S. (1996). Team building in sport. *International Journal of Sport Psychology, 27,* 269–285.

Ranby, K. W., Aiken, L. S., MacKinnon, D. P., Elliot, D. L., Moe, E. L., McGinnis, W., & Goldberg, L. (2009). A mediation analysis of the ATHENA intervention for female athletes: Prevention of athletic-enhancing substance use and unhealthy weight loss behaviors. *Journal of Pediatric Psychology, 34,* 1069–1083.

Ryan, R. M., & Deci, E. L. (2000). Self-determination theory and the facilitation of intrinsic motivation, social development, and well-being. *American Psychologist, 55,* 68–82.

Salas, E., Grossman, R., Hughes, A. M., & Coultas, C. W. (2015). Measuring team cohesion: Observations from the science. *Human Factors, 57,* 365–374.

Shuffler, M., DiazGranados, D., & Salas, E. (2011). There's a science for that: Team development interventions in organizations. *Current Directions in Psychological Science, 20,* 365–372.

Spink, K. S., McLaren, C. D., & Ulvick, J. D. (2018). Groupness, cohesion, and intention to return to sport: A study of intact youth teams. *International Journal of Sports Science & Coaching, 13,* 545–551.

Spink, K. S., Wilson, K. S., & Odnokon, P. (2010). Examining the relationship between cohesion and return to team in elite athletes. *Psychology of Sport and Exercise, 11,* 6–11.

Tamminen, K. A., Palmateer, T. M., Denton, M., Sabiston, C., Crocker, P. R., Eys, M., & Smith, B. (2016). Exploring emotions as social phenomena among Canadian varsity athletes. *Psychology of Sport and Exercise, 27,* 28–38.

Tamminen, K. A., Sabiston, C. M., & Crocker, P. R. (2019). Perceived esteem support predicts competition appraisals and performance satisfaction among varsity athletes: A test of organizational stressors as moderators. *Journal of Applied Sport Psychology, 31,* 27–46.

Terry, P. C., Carron, A. V., Pink, M. J., Lane, A. M., Jones, G. J., & Hall, M. P. (2000). Perceptions of group cohesion and mood in sport teams. *Group Dynamics: Theory, Research, and Practice, 4,* 244–253.

Warner, S., Bowers, M. T., & Dixon, M. A. (2012). Team dynamics: A social network perspective. *Journal of Sport Management, 26,* 53–66.

Whitton, S. M., & Fletcher, R. B. (2014). The Group Environment Questionnaire: A multilevel confirmatory factor analysis. *Small Group Research, 45,* 68–88.

Widmeyer, W. N., Brawley, L. R., & Carron, A. V. (1990). The effects of group size in sport. *Journal of Sport & Exercise Psychology, 12,* 177–190.

Williams, J. M., & Hacker, C. M. (1982). Causal relationships among cohesion, satisfaction, and performance in women's intercollegiate field hockey teams. *Journal of Sport Psychology, 4,* 324–337.

Wolf, S. A., Eys, M. A., Sadler, P., & Kleinert, J. (2015). Appraisal in a team context: Perceptions of cohesion predict competition importance and prospects for coping. *Journal of Sport & Exercise Psychology, 37,* 489–499.

Wolf, S. A., Harenberg, S., Tamminen, K., & Schmitz, H. (2018). "'Cause you can't play this by yourself": Athletes' perceptions of team influence on their precompetitive psychological states. *Journal of Applied Sport Psychology, 30,* 185–203.

Zamboanga, B. L., Rodriguez, L., & Horton, N. J. (2008). Athletic involvement and its relevance to hazardous alcohol use and drinking game participation in female college athletes: A preliminary investigation. *Journal of American College Health, 56,* 651–656.

15

GROUP FLOW

Fabian Pels and Jens Kleinert

Introduction

Imagine a basketball team with perfect moves. Each individual player seems to know where to move and where to pass. The players' behaviours intertwine, resulting in perfectly coordinated behaviour between team members. The team appears to be a single unit, and it seems like there is a total understanding between the players without any strained communication. A basketball player once summarized such a state by saying that, "we played quietly and efficiently. We rarely spoke and played effortlessly and effectively. As teammates, we were 'in sync' with each other" (Jimerson, 1999, p. 13).

Such a state is a positive experience for the team members involved. They may describe or perceive it in unspecific terms (e.g., "I have had some of the most memorable and exhilarating gaming experiences of my life. As when we play well we play some amazing flowing football"; Kaye & Bryce, 2012, p. 28), but it may also be described or perceived as being specific in different regards. For instance, the experience may comprise a specific emotional aspect ("emotionally, you're just kind of floating"; Hart & Di Blasi, 2015, p. 284), specific thoughts ("It's just [...] freedom from your everyday thoughts"; Hart & Di Blasi, 2015, p. 281), a specific perception of group action ("everything seems to come naturally"; Sawyer, 2003, p. 44), or a specific perception of interpersonal relationship ("you definitely feel an affinity with the people you're playing with"; Hart & Di Blasi, 2015, p. 284). The entirety of all the aforementioned descriptions and the accompanying positive experiences illustrate the multifacetedness of the phenomenon called "group flow".

Taking into account the phenomenological characteristics, an integrative definition specifies group flow as:

> a shared state of balance within a group as represented by (a) fluent, positive inter-
> actions within the group, (b) a high collective competence of the group and (c)
> a collective state of mind of the group by means of positive relationships between
> group members, often resulting in optimal collective performance and creativity, and
> making group flow a positive collective experience.
>
> *(Pels, Kleinert, & Mennigen, 2018, p. 18)*

This definition addresses components (i.e., interaction, competence, state of mind), prerequisites (i.e. positive relationships), and consequences of group flow (i.e., positive experience, optimal performance, creativity). With regard to components, "fluent, positive interactions within the group" refers to well-coordinated task-related behaviour between group members (manifesting itself, for instance, in synchronization; Gloor, Oster, & Fischbach, 2013); "a high collective competence of the group" indicates that all group members optimally contribute their individual abilities in order to enable the group to perform the task (manifesting itself, for instance, in an integration of the skills of all group members; Kaye & Bryce, 2012); and "a collective state of mind" indicates that all group members share common emotions, cognitions, and motivational orientations (manifested, for instance, in collective expectancies regarding the capability to accomplish a task; Salanova, Rodriguez-Sanchez, Schaufeli, & Cifre, 2014).

The construct of group flow emanates from Csikszentmihalyi's (1975) concept of flow. In its original form, the concept of flow describes the experience of single individuals while they are absorbed in a task due to a flowing accomplishment of this task; hence, the name of flow or individual flow. Research has shown that the experience of individual flow is not restricted to solitary tasks (i.e., those performed in the absence of others) and it can also occur in social situations (for an overview, see Schiepe-Tiska & Engeser, 2012). In such social situations, an individual may experience the state of individual flow irrespective of whether others who are present are in a state of individual flow or not (Nakamura & Csikszentmihalyi, 2002). However, additional insights from both classical social psychology (e.g., Walker, 2010) and incidental anecdotal evidence (e.g., Sato, 1988) revealed another form of flow, namely group flow. These insights suggested that group flow was distinguishable from individual flow experiences in group settings (Nakamura & Csikszentmihalyi, 2002) and gave rise to specific conceptualizations and investigations of group flow based on Csikszentmihalyi's initial work (e.g., 1975, 1985, 2000) and the subsequent work of others (e.g., Jackson, 1995, 1996) on individual flow (for an overview of research on individual flow in sports, see Swann, Keegan, Piggott, & Crust, 2012).

As conceptualizations and investigations of group flow only began to emerge in the early 2000s, the scientific construct of group flow is still in the early stages of development. The aim of this chapter is to summarize currently existing theories of group flow, research on group flow, and topics of practice and application of group flow from a sport perspective.

Theory

In general, the starting point of all theoretical approaches to group flow is Csikszentmihalyi's (1975, 1985, 2000) concept of individual flow. Existing theoretical concepts of group flow extrapolate from the concept of individual flow in order to describe both the state of group flow and processes around group flow (i.e., how group flow occurs and the consequences of group flow). To date, there are four theoretical concepts of group flow:

The "group flow concept" of Sawyer (2003, 2006)) describes group flow as a collective state of synchrony of group members' interactions that results in group creativity. This interactional synchrony is an emergent property of the group, which is the reason why group flow is more than just an aggregation of individual flow states. Sawyer (2003, 2006)) assumes the need for parallel processing between group members for group flow to occur. This means that group members must simultaneously concentrate on and respond to each other's actions via different senses (e.g., hearing the velocity of another group member's steps in a basketball game) in order to keep the interactional synchrony flowing. Sawyer (2003, 2006) assumes that group flow is more likely to occur when there is a balance between the collective goals and pre-existing structures of the group members. The more extrinsic a goal is, the more pre-existing structures are required. Extrinsic goals are product-oriented (e.g., two points that need to be scored in the last second of a basketball game), whereas intrinsic goals are exploration-oriented (e.g., the improvisation skit of a group of jugglers in which the endpoint is unknown). Pre-existing structures are defined as "performance-related elements that are associated with a ritualized performance" (Sawyer, 2003, p. 168). More specifically, there are four types of pre-existing structure, which partly overlap (Armstrong, 2008; Sawyer, 2003): (1) having an overall outline of the performance that all group members know beforehand, (2) having a shared repertoire of ready-mades and knowing how they are usually sequenced, (3) having defined roles for each group member, and (4) having a common agreement on conventions.

Building upon Sawyer's (2003, 2006) group flow concept, the "networked flow model" (Gaggioli, Milani, Mazzoni, & Riva, 2011) describes group flow as a "a collective state of mind [...], a peak experience, a group performing at its top level of ability" (p. 41). This model assumes six phases in the development of group flow. More specifically, these stages are named (1) meeting (persistence), (2) reducing the distance, (3) liminality-parallel action, (4) networked flow, (5) networked flow – creation of an artefact, and (6) networked flow – application of the artefact in a social network. Phases (1)–(3) comprise the forming of a group with the development of shared intentions, similarities between group members and group identity, which are said to lead to the emergence of social presence, and collective intentions. Phases (4)–(6) describe the final state of group flow, distinguishing between (4), the onset of group flow with critical events such as a transformation of collective intentions into collective actions, (5), the creation of an artefact (i.e., some sort of product) as a further development of a pre-existing frame (e.g., the development of a new move in basketball), and (6), the application of this artefact to the social context of the group.

The 'multi-level model of flow in sociotechnical systems' (Duff, Giudice, Johnston, Flint, & Kudrick, 2014, p. 574) extrapolates Csikszentmihalyi's (1975, 1985, 2000) concept of individual flow across three levels. The model assumes that flow, in general, is an isomorphic construct. This means that flow occurs in a similar way on three different levels: (1) On the lowest level (i.e., the individual level), typical individual flow occurs. (2) On the mid-level (i.e., the group level), flow occurs in a group as a whole (i.e., group flow). Two kinds of flow can occur in a group as a whole. According to Duff et al. (2014), this can either be group flow while working on an individual task in the company of others (e.g., doing exercise on an ergometer next to others who are also exercising) or group flow while collaborating on a task with others (e.g., playing basketball). In flow, the social processes are harmonious and coordinated based on purposeful and clear communication. These processes result in innovative products. (3) On the highest level (i.e., the system level), flow occurs in a system (i.e., the entirety of all components, including individuals, teams, immediate environment, technology, etc.) as a whole.

The "channel model of group flow" (Kiili, Perttula, Arttu, & Tuomi, 2010) extrapolates Csikszentmihalyi's (1975, 1985, 2000) concept of individual flow by extending the traditional channel model. The traditional channel model (as the central component of an early version of the individual flow concept) assumes that individual flow occurs when there is a balance between challenges and skills for the present task (be it a balance of low challenges and low skills, a balance of medium challenges and medium skills, or a balance of high challenges and high skills). The corridor of balance is the so-called channel. By adding a group dimension to the traditional channel model, the channel model of group flow assumes a wider range of the challenge–skill balance to allow for group flow to occur. In other words, according to this model, the group's overall skills can be higher or lower than the challenges. This contrasts with the traditional channel model in which there is a very restricted range of challenge–skill balance for individual flow, with a necessity of a perfect fit between above-average challenges and skills.

To sum up, the theoretical concepts consistently describe balance within the group as a central characteristic of the state of group flow. Although using different words for balance (e.g., synchrony: Sawyer, 2003, 2006), the theoretical concepts only significantly differ with regard to the object of the balance that is assumed to be characteristic of the state of group flow (e.g., balance in behaviour: Sawyer, 2003, 2006; balance between a group's skills and challenges: Kiili et al., 2010). Moreover, the theoretical concepts consistently describe that group flow results in extraordinary products (e.g., innovative products: Duff et al., 2014; artefacts: Gaggioli et al., 2011). In terms of the processes around group flow, the theoretical concepts set different foci. Some concepts describe proximal processes (i.e., how a group enters or loses group flow or transitions between different forms of group flow; e.g., parallel processing: Sawyer, 2003, 2006), whereas others describe distal processes (i.e., preceding factors facilitating or impeding the occurrence of group flow; e.g. persistence across group members: Gaggioli et al., 2011).

Empirical Findings

Empirical research has rarely been conducted on group flow in the domain of sport and exercise. For sport and exercise, only two cross-sectional studies exist that have investigated correlates of group flow. In a study on soccer teams, Bakker, Oerlemans, Demerouti, Slot, and Ali (2011) found that performance feedback and support from the coach are positively associated with group flow. Moreover, the authors identified that group flow is higher when the outcome of a match is a draw or win for the respective team. A study on different kinds of group-based physical activity (e.g., aerobics, indoor cycling, football: Zumeta, Oriol, Telletxea, Amutio, and Basabe, 2015) found positive associations between group flow on the one hand and group identification and collective efficacy on the other hand, with group flow statistically mediating the relationship between group identification and collective efficacy.

Further studies on group flow have been conducted in the contexts of education (e.g., Admiraal, Huizenga, Akkerman, & Ten Dam, 2011), work (e.g., Primus & Sonnenburg, 2018), music (e.g., Gaggioli, Chirico, Mazzoni, Milani, & Riva, 2016), or digital gaming (e.g., Kaye & Bryce, 2012). In some of these studies, antecedents and consequences of group flow have been identified, inasmuch as the study design allowed for such a causal interpretation. Additionally, other studies have examined further correlates of group flow.

With regard to antecedents, studies identified aspects of (a) competence, (b) interaction, (c) action, and (d) relationship as influencing factors of group flow. For competence, having task-relevant skills across group members (Kaye & Bryce, 2012), knowing the other group members' skills (Kaye, 2016), and collective efficacy beliefs (Salanova et al., 2014) were found to be antecedents. In terms of interaction, collective collaboration (Kaye & Bryce, 2012), effective communication (Kaye, 2016), and decentralization within the group (i.e., decentralized control of the action; Armstrong, 2008) were identified. For action, effective group work (Kaye, 2016) and getting performance feedback (Gaggioli, Mazzoni, Milani, & Riva, 2015) were found to be influencing factors. Finally, for relationship, trust within the group (Armstrong, 2008) and social support among group members (Gaggioli et al., 2015) were identified as antecedents.

With regard to consequences, predominantly positive effects of group flow were detected. Positive effects of group flow were shown in terms of an increase in collective efficacy (Salanova et al., 2014), an improvement in the understanding of a task (Culbertson, Fullagar, Simmons, &

Zhu, 2015), an enhanced interest in a task (Culbertson et al., 2015), an increase in well-being (Zumeta, Basabe, Wlodarczyk, Bobowik, & Paez, 2016), a heightened fusion of identity with the group (Zumeta et al., 2016), and an increase in social integration (Zumeta et al., 2016). In contrast to these positive effects, successful performance was not found to be an inevitable consequence of group flow (Culbertson et al., 2015).

Furthermore, a number of studies identified correlates of group flow that partly contradicted the results relating to consequences of group flow. More specifically, two studies identified positive associations between group flow and performance (Admiraal et al., 2011; Gaggioli et al., 2015) that were not found in the aforementioned study that analysed performance as a consequence of group flow (cf. Culbertson et al., 2015). However, a positive association was found for group flow and empathy among group members (Hart & Di Blasi, 2015). No relationship was found for the association between group flow and learning (Admiraal et al., 2011).

To sum up, research on group flow is scarce, especially in the context of sport and exercise. The existing findings on antecedents, consequences, and correlates of group flow, thus, need to be confirmed (e.g., across contexts), clarified in the case of contradictory findings (e.g., by taking into account potential moderators), and extended (e.g., by systematically identifying antecedents in experiments) in a consecutive research programme.

Practice and Application in Research

Assessment

The existing instruments to assess group flow can be distinguished on two methodological dimensions. On the first dimension (source of data), instruments differ in whether they assess group flow from an internal perspective or from an external perspective. In more detail, instruments that assess group flow from an internal perspective focus on the individual perspective of the respective group member or group members, whereas instruments that assess group flow from an external perspective take into account the view of an external person (i.e., a person who is not part of the group action) regarding the entire group. On the second dimension (quality of data), instruments differ in whether they have a quantitative or a qualitative approach. More specifically, quantitative approaches are characterized by attempts to quantitatively measure group flow with the use of, for instance, highly structured protocols or highly structured questionnaires comprising a limited range of fixed-response options; in contrast, qualitative approaches emphasize processes and meanings of group flow with the use of, for instance, unstructured protocols or in-depth interviews (cf. Sale, Lohfeld, & Brazil, 2002).

Most of the existing tools to assess the internal perspective of group flow are quantitative self-report questionnaires. Of these, two different kinds of questionnaire can be distinguished. On the one hand, there are questionnaires that were originally designed to measure individual flow as conceptualized by Csikszentmihalyi (1975, 1985, 2000), but that were revised to assess group flow by relating the original items (e.g., stemming from the Flow State Scale-2; Jackson & Eklund, 2002) to the group. On the other hand, there are questionnaires that were newly developed to assess group flow. These were mostly derived from Sawyer's (2003, 2006) group flow concept.

In addition to these quantitative approaches, some qualitative tools exist to assess the internal perspective. To date, these qualitative assessments for the internal perspective are exclusively interviews. The interviews include questions regarding, for instance, the individual experience of group flow, which can subsequently be analysed by content analysis (e.g., Kaye & Bryce, 2012).

Existing assessments targeting the external perspective of group flow are scarce. To date, there is one quantitative approach that makes use of sociometric badges that assess the body movement energy levels of every single group member, by means of accelerometers, and the position of all group members relative to each other (Gloor et al., 2013). The result of an interindividual comparison of the intra-individual oscillations in the group members' body movements is taken as a measure of group flow, with synchronous oscillations indicating group flow. In addition, there are qualitative approaches using semi-structured group observations (e.g., Armstrong, 2008). Based on behaviour coding schemes, observers aim to identify whether group flow is present in a given group or not (e.g., by identifying whether group members perform the same gesture simultaneously; Armstrong, 2008).

Intervention

Treatments or interventions to enhance group flow have predominantly been designed for contexts outside sport and exercise. Only one such study exists in the context of sport and exercise, which examined different conditions systematically. Walker (2010) tested the extent of team members' interdependence during a tennis-like task as a predictor of group flow by manipulating two levels of interdependence (low interdependence: single players facing off and volleying cooperatively across the net; high interdependence: two-member teams passing the ball to each other at least once before volleying to the other team). Walker found more joy and challenge in the highly interdependent condition. Unfortunately, flow feelings were operationalized with feelings (i.e. cheerful, excited, focused, alive) only, which limits the conclusions for group flow as a multifaceted phenomenon.

Further studies on conditions that enhance group flow exist for digital gaming (Heyne, Pavlas, & Salas, 2011), music (Keeler et al., 2015), and design thinking (Primus & Sonnenburg, 2018). Of these, Heyne et al. (2011) found negative associations between group flow and the perceived complexity of the task. In a complex group task condition, group members had to simultaneously cooperate with other group members and react to hostile threats. Moreover, in this study, group flow related positively to sharing of information within the team, knowledge-building of the team, and the success of the team. In the study by Primus and Sonnenburg (2018), the authors tested the effect of a warm-up for group performance. The warm-up or preparation task showed positive effects on group flow. Finally, Keeler et al. (2015) present a rather weak research design making conclusions impossible owing to a very low sample size (i.e., four participants).

The aforementioned studies on the enhancement of group flow mainly focus on group task. Two aspects of the task have been distinguished, the task difficulty (i.e., level, complexity) and the task structure (including the form of the task result). In terms of task difficulty, the fit between the group's abilities and the given demands is of particular importance. Group abilities are both the entirety of the individuals' abilities and the group's overall knowledge and skills (e.g., the group members' ability to cooperate; Bachen & Raphael, 2011). The principle of a task–demand fit is already given in the concept of individual flow in which it is essential that the individual perceives their own capacities to act as corresponding to available opportunities or challenges (e.g., Wong & Csikszentmihalyi, 1991). However, in terms of group flow, a special harmonization seems necessary between the individual's opportunities and the group's opportunities and skills, the latter especially defined by collaborative skills (e.g., communication, sharing information, coordination of movements). It is currently unclear how communication and feedback should look to ensure group flow (e.g., emotional vs. rational, verbal vs. nonverbal).

In terms of task structure, the social task condition seems to be of particular importance to group flow. More specifically, a high interdependence, brought about by highly interactive or coactive skills (both leading to a collective result), might facilitate group flow more than sequential, rather independent group tasks (leading to additive group results). Therefore, task-induced coordination and cooperation, as well as the conjunctive and complementary nature of such cooperation, are recommended for group flow-enhancing tasks (Bachen & Raphael, 2011; Walker, 2010). This does not necessarily mean that all group members must share the same knowledge or competence. Instead, it seems to be more important that group members are able to fulfil their individual role (i.e., individual task) as a harmonic part of the group task as a whole. This harmonization manifests in smooth, fluent interactions, which are characterized by clear and presumably frequent implicit feedback loops between group members about their functional and emotional state during the task process. If group interactions are not smooth or fluent, the flow process will be impaired. Social interactions, therefore, might affect group flow in a positive or negative way. As such, flow experiences might be augmented or inhibited in team sport compared with individual sport. In examining this, Elbe, Strahler, Krustrup, Wikman, and Stelter (2010) examined male individual sport (running) and team sport (football) subjects and found no differences between these groups in flow experiences; however, in a second study with women, participants reported higher individual flow in running than in football.

Besides the social interaction during tasks, group flow can be also enhanced by treatments on an individual level. Aherne, Moran, and Lonsdale (2011) tested the effect of a mindfulness intervention on individual flow experiences during training sessions. The authors found some evidence for the assumed effect. Thus, it seems likely that a change in individual mindset may also change the likelihood of group flow experiences (e.g., owing to higher openness for and acceptance of team members).

Finally, external situational factors may play a role in flow experiences. In their experimental design with five athletes, Pain, Harwood, and Anderson (2011) found indices for the effect of music on flow experience (especially when combined with imagery). Therefore, a meaningful piece of music for a group (or a group song) might enhance feelings of flow, possibly mediated by a stronger social identity. Studies on flow feelings in music contexts may help to strengthen this research (Chirico, Serino, Cipresso, Gaggioli, & Riva, 2015). In conclusion, it is surprising that, even in individual flow, studies aiming to enhance flow, either experimentally or by means of an intervention, are rare (cf. Swann, Piggott, Schweickle, & Vella, 2018).

Conclusion

This chapter deals with the phenomenon of group flow, which emanates from Csikszentmihalyi's concept of individual flow (1975). Although the specific nature of group flow was anecdotally stressed as early as the 1980s (cf. Sato, 1988), conceptualizations and investigations of group flow only emerged in the early 2000s (cf. Sawyer, 2003). Accordingly, the scientific construct of group flow is still in an early stage of development. This chapter aimed to describe these developmental stages from theoretical, empirical, and practical standpoints.

From a theoretical standpoint, the existing literature mainly deals with the nature and the mechanisms of group flow. In terms of the nature, researchers consistently state that group flow is more than the sum of individual flow states. In addition to an individual-centred viewpoint, the relationships between group members are particularly stressed (especially in the form of balance between group members; Kiili et al., 2010; Sawyer, 2006). In terms of the mechanisms of group flow, the existing literature describes different distal or proximal processes that are likely to develop or enhance group flow (e.g., parallel processing: Sawyer, 2003; persistence across group members: Gaggioli et al., 2011).

One general conclusion of these theoretical approaches is that, in attempts to understand group processes or interpersonal processes of group flow, group flow concepts have largely neglected existing theories of social science. For instance, as far as balance and interpersonal relationships during group flow are concerned, social science offers established theories that enable the understanding of such interpersonal processes (e.g., social identity theory: Tajfel & Turner, 1979; optimal distinctiveness theory: Brewer, 1991; balance theory: Heider, 1958). It is very likely that the general social processes that can be explained by these theoretical approaches are important in group flow processes as well. Based on the integration of such theoretical input, it might be possible to systematically link aspects of states and processes in groups to understand group flow, which has yet to be done. An integration in this manner might lead to the creation of a comprehensive theoretical model that could be empirically tested.

From both a theoretical and an empirical standpoint, the group flow concept is still in its infancy. This is especially true for group flow research in sport and exercise, but also for research in other contexts (e.g., music, work) where research on group flow is scarce. As such, the existing findings on antecedents, consequences, and correlates of group flow need to be confirmed, clarified, and extended. Besides this need to increase the quantity of research, future empirical work should carefully handle theoretical and methodological issues. In terms of theory, research questions and research designs should consistently build upon given theoretical models. In terms of methods, research designs and assessments should be addressed that fit the given research questions (e.g., questions on causal mechanisms or processes require longitudinal or experimental designs).

The demand for adequate methods (e.g. assessments, interventions/treatments) in group flow research is currently hard to satisfy. Regarding assessments, this chapter has shown that current developments vary widely in their approaches (e.g., quantitative vs. qualitative; internal perspective vs. external perspective) and, more importantly, most of these methods are in a very early developmental stage.

In terms of interventions or treatments, research is not yet able to specify the circumstances (e.g. task structure, social structure) that enhance group flow. Accordingly, this chapter shows that given theories and current research, in particular, do not yet form a sufficient basis for practical applications based on the group flow concept. Although the findings discussed in this chapter provide some hints with regard to the potential beneficial effects of group flow, the conceptualization and evaluation of treatments or interventions are severely lacking. Therefore, the testing of interventions and treatments, formed on the basis of plausible theoretical models, should be a fundamental goal of future group flow research, as such studies will reveal the best approaches to help groups experience flow.

References

Admiraal, W., Huizenga, J., Akkerman, S., & Ten Dam, G. (2011). The concept of flow in collaborative game-based learning. *Computers in Human Behavior, 27,* 1185–1194.

Aherne, C., Moran, A. P., & Lonsdale, C. (2011). The effect of mindfulness training on athletes' flow: An initial investigation. *The Sport Psychologist, 25,* 177–189.

Armstrong, A. C. (2008). The fragility of group flow: The experiences of two small groups in a middle school mathematics classroom. *The Journal of Mathematical Behavior, 27,* 101–115.

Bachen, C. M., & Raphael, C. (2011). Social flow and learning in digital games: A conceptual model and research agenda. In M. Ma, A. Oikonomou, & L. C. Jain (Eds.), *Serious games and edutainment applications* (pp. 61–84). London: Springer.

Bakker, A. B., Oerlemans, W., Demerouti, E., Slot, B. B., & Ali, D. K. (2011). Flow and performance: A study among talented Dutch soccer players. *Psychology of Sport and Exercise, 12,* 442–450.

Brewer, M. B. (1991). The social self: On being the same and different at the same time. *Personality and Social Psychology Bulletin, 17,* 475–482.

Chirico, A., Serino, S., Cipresso, P., Gaggioli, A., & Riva, G. (2015). When music "flows". state and trait in musical performance, composition and listening: A systematic review. *Frontiers in Psychology, 6,* 906. doi:10.3389/fpsyg.2015.00906

Csikszentmihalyi, M. (1975). *Beyond boredom and anxiety.* San Francisco, CA: Jossey-Bass.

Csikszentmihalyi, M. (1985). Emergent motivation and the evolution of the self. *Advances in Motivation and Achievement, 4,* 93–119.

Csikszentmihalyi, M. (2000). The contribution of flow to positive psychology. In M. E. P. Seligman & J. Gillham (Eds.), *The science of optimism and hope* (pp. 387–395). Philadelphia, PA: Templeton Foundation Press.

Culbertson, S. S., Fullagar, C. J., Simmons, M. J., & Zhu, M. (2015). Contagious flow: Antecedents and consequences of optimal experience in the classroom. *Journal of Management Education, 39,* 319–349.

Duff, S. N., Giudice, K. D., Johnston, M., Flint, J., & Kudrick, B. (2014). A systems approach to diagnosing and measuring teamwork in complex sociotechnical organizations. *Proceedings of the Human Factors and Ergonomics Society Annual Meeting, 58,* 573–577.

Elbe, A.-M., Strahler, K., Krustrup, P., Wikman, J., & Stelter, R. (2010). Experiencing flow in different types of physical activity intervention programs: Three randomized studies. *Scandinavian Journal of Medicine & Science in Sports, 20,* 111–117.

Gaggioli, A., Chirico, A., Mazzoni, E., Milani, L., & Riva, G. (2016). Networked flow in musical bands. *Psychology of Music, 38,* 1–15.

Gaggioli, A., Mazzoni, E., Milani, L., & Riva, G. (2015). The creative link: Investigating the relationship between social network indices, creative performance and flow in blended teams. *Computers in Human Behavior, 42,* 157–166.

Gaggioli, A., Milani, L., Mazzoni, E., & Riva, G. (2011). Networked Flow: A framework for understanding the dynamics of creative collaboration in educational and training settings. *The Open Education Journal, 4,* 41–49.

Gloor, P. A., Oster, D., & Fischbach, K. (2013). JazzFlow - Analyzing "group flow" among jazz musicians through "honest signals". *KI – Künstliche Intelligenz, 27,* 37–43.

Hart, E., & Di Blasi, Z. (2015). Combined flow in musical jam sessions: A pilot qualitative study. *Psychology of Music, 43,* 275–290.

Heider, F. (1958). *The psychology of interpersonal relations.* Hillsdale, NJ: Erlbaum.

Heyne, K., Pavlas, D., & Salas, E. (2011). An investigation on the effects of flow state on team process and outcomes. *Proceedings of the Human Factors and Ergonomics Society Annual Meeting, 55,* 475–479.

Jackson, S. A. (1995). Factors influencing the occurrence of flow state in elite athletes. *Journal of Applied Sport Psychology, 7,* 138–166.

Jackson, S. A. (1996). Toward a conceptual understanding of the flow experience in elite athletes. *Research Quarterly for Exercise and Sport, 67,* 76–90.

Jackson, S. A., & Eklund, R. C. (2002). Assessing flow in physical activity: The flow state scale–2 and dispositional flow scale–2. *Journal of Sport and Exercise Psychology, 24,* 133–150.

Jimerson, J. B. (1999). Interpersonal flow in pickup basketball (dissertation). Indiana University, Bloomington, IN.

Kaye, L. K. (2016). Exploring flow experiences in cooperative digital gaming contexts. *Computers in Human Behavior, 55,* 286–291.

Kaye, L. K., & Bryce, J. (2012). Putting the "fun factor" into gaming: The influence of social contexts on experiences of playing videogames. *International Journal of Internet Science, 7,* 23–36.

Keeler, J. R., Roth, E. A., Neuser, B. L., Spitsbergen, J. M., Waters, D. J. M., & Vianney, J.-M. (2015). The neurochemistry and social flow of singing: Bonding and oxytocin. *Frontiers in Human Neuroscience, 9,* 518. doi:10.3389/fnhum.2015.00518

Kiili, K., Perttula, A., & Tuomi, P. (2010). Development of multiplayer exertion games for physical education. *IADIS International Journal on WWW/Internet, 8,* 52–69.

Nakamura, J., & Csikszentmihalyi, M. (2002). The concept of flow. In C. R. Snyder & S. J. Lopez (Eds.), *Handbook of positive psychology* (pp. 89–105). Oxford, New York: Oxford University Press.

Pain, M. A., Harwood, C., & Anderson, R. (2011). Pre-competition imagery and music: The impact on flow and performance in competitive soccer. *The Sport Psychologist, 25,* 212–232.

Pels, F., Kleinert, J., & Mennigen, F. (2018). Group flow: A scoping review of definitions, theoretical approaches, measures and findings. *PLoS ONE, 13*(12), e0210117. doi:10.1371/journal.pone.0210117

Primus, D. J., & Sonnenburg, S. (2018). Flow experience in design thinking and practical synergies with lego serious play. *Creativity Research Journal, 30,* 104–112.

Salanova, M., Rodriguez-Sanchez, A. M., Schaufeli, W. B., & Cifre, E. (2014). Flowing together: A longitudinal study of collective efficacy and collective flow among workgroups. *The Journal of Psychology, 148,* 435–455.

Sale, J. E. M., Lohfeld, L. H., & Brazil, K. (2002). Revisiting the quantitative-qualitative debate: Implications for mixed-methods research. *Quality & Quantity, 36,* 43–53.

Sato, I. (1988). Bosozoku: Flow in Japanese motorcycle gangs. In M. Csikszentmihalyi & I. S. Csikszentmihalyi (Eds.), *Optimal experience: Psychological studies of flow in consciousness* (pp. 92–117). Cambridge: Cambridge University Press.

Sawyer, R. K. (2003). *Group creativity: Music, theater, collaboration.* Mahwah, NJ: Lawrence Erlbaum.

Sawyer, R. K. (2006). Group creativity: Musical performance and collaboration. *Psychology of Music, 34,* 148–165.

Schiepe-Tiska, A., & Engeser, S. (2012). Flow in non-achievement situations. In S. Engeser (Ed.), *Advances in flow research* (pp. 87–107). New York: Springer.

Swann, C., Keegan, R. J., Piggott, D., & Crust, L. (2012). A systematic review of the experience, occurrence, and controllability of flow states in elite sport. *Psychology of Sport and Exercise, 13,* 807–819.

Swann, C., Piggott, D., Schweickle, M., & Vella, S. A. (2018). A review of scientific progress in flow in sport and exercise: Normal science, crisis, and a progressive shift. *Journal of Applied Sport Psychology,* 1–23. doi:10.1080/10413200.2018.1443525

Tajfel, H., & Turner, J. C. (1979). An integrative theory of intergroup conflict. In W. G. Austin & S. Worchel (Eds.), *The social psychology of intergroup relations* (2nd ed., Vol. 14, pp. 33–47). Monterey, CA: Brooks/Cole.

Walker, C. J. (2010). Experiencing flow: Is doing it together better than doing it alone? *The Journal of Positive Psychology, 5,* 3–11.

Wong, M. M., & Csikszentmihalyi, M. (1991). Affiliation motivation and daily experience: Some issues on gender differences. *Journal of Personality and Social Psychology, 60*(1), 154–164.

Zumeta, L., Basabe, N., Wlodarczyk, A., Bobowik, M., & Paez, D. (2016). Shared flow and positive collective gatherings. *Anales de Psicología, 32,* 717–727.

Zumeta, L. N., Oriol, X., Telletxea, S., Amutio, A., & Basabe, N. (2015). Collective efficacy in sports and physical activities: Perceived emotional synchrony and shared flow. *Frontiers in Psychology, 6,* 1960. doi:10.3389/fpsyg.2015.01960

16

JUDGEMENT AND DECISION-MAKING

Markus Raab and Clare MacMahon

Introduction

Judgement and decision-making (JDM) in sports are terms often used interchangeably: for instance, when referees judge a performance or decide on a penalty, a coach selects one player in the starting line-up over another, or a player chooses to pass the ball left. In science, judgements and decisions can be differentiated. For instance, in a widely accepted definition, judgements identify single objects in terms of certain qualitative or quantitative features, such as a score for an ice-skating performance (Eiser, 1990). Decisions, in contrast, can be unrelated to judgements and refer to choosing or deciding between two or more options, either presented in the external world or generated in the individual's internal mind (Johnson & Raab, 2003). For phenomena in sports, this differentiation may make sense in some cases. Typically, however, both constructs are used in describing behaviours and observable choices for sport stakeholders. Thus, for example, we refer to an athlete choosing to pass left as a JDM task.

An important differentiator between different JDM tasks in sport is the timeline, as choices, such as a playmaker's decision to pass to a teammate, can take mere milliseconds, up to much lengthier decisions that can take months or years, such as an athlete's choice to end her career. Moreover, the different levels and complexity of decision-making in sport are notable, and the relationship between decision-making, strategy, and tactics is often discussed. For instance, MacMahon and McPherson (2009) distinguished between decision-making as an action choice (e.g., pass left) that is influenced by strategy, which accounts for a performer's and their opponent's strengths and weaknesses (e.g., pass left because the defender on the right is too strong). Strategy is further seen to consider tactics, which are contemplated prior to a competition and based on the evolving action within a contest (Gréhaigne, Godbout, & Bouthier, 1999). A key distinction between decision-making, strategy, and tactics in sport is timeline, according to MacMahon and McPherson. Specifically, decision-making is the most local level of case-by-case action choices (e.g., to kick behind a player or run the ball forward) that are governed by a strategy, which can be adjusted as a competition evolves. For example, a strategy may change based on the responses of opposition or the field conditions (e.g., a rainy day may make ball-handling difficult and error prone). Tactics represents JDM at the broadest level and may be devised ahead of a game in general terms (e.g., to play an offensive, pressure-based game).

Another important distinction to consider in sports JDM is who is making the choice. For instance, in Bar-Eli, Plessner, and Raab (2011), literature on JDM has been organized by the stakeholder, such as athletes, managers and coaches, referees, and observers. It becomes evident that in the same basketball game the choices differ quite significantly between a playmaker's choice to shoot or pass, the coach's time-out decision, the referee's choice of penalty, and the fan's betting placement. These differences are also reflected in the knowledge base and specific cognitive skills of the different roles; although all of the roles have extensive experience with the sport and general knowledge and structure, they will excel at tasks related to their role such that an experienced referee will be superior at calling penalties, and a coach will be superior at identifying offensive structures (e.g., Allard, Deakin, Parker, & Rodgers, 1993; MacMahon et al., 2014; MacMahon, Starkes, & Deakin, 2009).

For the purposes of clarity, as well, JDM in sport is related to, but distinguished from, embodied cognition (see Cappuccio & Ilundáin-Agurruza, Volume 1, Chapter 9, in this encyclopedia) and anticipation and attention (see Ward, Suss, Belling, & Williams, Volume 1, Chapter 3, in this encyclopedia). Component skills, such as anticipating the next action of an opponent or the movement of the ball, and memory for patterns of play contribute to JDM in sport, but are different to testing actual action choices, judgements, or decisions. For example, a rugby referee anticipating the action of a player is distinct from his/hers evaluating an on-field action and choosing whether to award a penalty or not. That being said, the literature in these areas has established that anticipation, knowledge, and pattern recognition distinguish between experts and novices and are thus key component skills. JDM sports research has also frequently used similar research methods to those used in anticipation and pattern recall and recognition, namely the use of video clips and occlusion. For example, the standard laboratory-based approach uses game footage video of a key passage of play, with the video going blank just before a key action. The observer is then asked to choose the best next action (e.g., take a shot on goal), either verbally or by clicking on the screen. The full action is shown in the case of a refereeing decision, to provide the stimuli for choosing a call or no call. Variations of this method include animations or staged action that present the first-person point of view (Murphy, Jackson, & Williams, 2019), perception–action coupled methods with life-sized projection, and completion of the full skill (e.g., kicking towards the screen or wall; Helsen & Starkes, 1999). Additionally, think-aloud protocols involve measuring the knowledge base by discussing action choices during breaks in play. Occlusion anticipation studies have shown that those with greater expertise can do 'more with less' and anticipate actions with earlier occlusions or less information. Thus, anticipation contributes to decision-making, or action choice, but can be argued to be a component skill.

Theory and Research on Judgement and Decision-Making

Reviews of JDM research have shown that there are nearly 300 theories describing specific aspects of choices such as risk-taking, sequential choice, and other decision behaviours. From the huge list of potential theories that could have been applied to the sport context, only about a dozen have actually been tested in the sports domain (Bar-Eli et al., 2011). It should also be noted that JDM researchers from other decision domains (e.g., economics) agree that sport and sport JDM provide an excellent application area to test theories, given the complexity of problems and demands (e.g., Bar-Eli, 2018). Further, Raab, Bar-Eli, Plessner, and Araújo (2019), in a review of the research on JDM in sports, identified the four most influential perspectives and theoretical approaches as the (a) social cognitive, (b) economic, (c) cognitive, and (d) ecological dynamics views of JDM in sport. These views have been applied to predict and study decision behaviours, where sport is a rich context environment. From the social cognitive perspective, for example, decisions are made amid social influences, experience, and expectations. Owing to the fast pace and lack of information in sport and the associated decision tasks, accompanying cues such as prior exposure or context are often used to inform or at least influence judgements and decisions. Thus, a gymnastics judge's memory of a competitor's warm-up can influence expectations and the assessment of the competition performance, such that when the performance quality of a move differs between warm-up and competition, that move is judged less accurately, whether it is improved or impaired (Ste-Marie & Lee, 1991). Similarly, in gymnastics, Plessner (1999) found informal expectations that gymnasts will be organized to compete in rank order, from less to more skilled. This expectation influences judgements, and, indeed, the same athlete is rated higher if competing later in the line-up.

Given that JDM theory in economics is a well-developed area that examines behaviours and errors, the application of findings and theories to frame sport JDM is appealing. A classic case is the gambler's fallacy. Although gambling events such as a coin toss have independent outcomes, and, thus, probability is a useful tool for prediction of outcomes, sequential patterns are frequently used for this task. In this case, a coin flip, which has a 50% probability of a 'heads' outcome on each toss, is predicted at a much higher rate if three tails results have already taken place (Carlson & Shu, 2007). Reflection on the gambler's fallacy applied to sport in predicting basketball shot outcomes (miss or basket) and the 'hot hand' pattern brought the economic perspective of JDM research into sport. Specifically, the hot hand pattern predicts that a player can become 'hot', and, thus, successive successful basketball shots by one player, for example, lead to a prediction of continued success. There has been great debate around the existence of the hot hand pattern (are there streaks?), together with investigation of a number of factors that may need to be considered or that may have an influence on the pattern, such as game time (Yaari & Eisenmann, 2011) and player position (Csapo & Raab, 2014). Research on the hot hand in sport has thus moved from the question of whether streaks and the hot hand exist into an interest in understanding behaviours based on the *belief* in the pattern itself (e.g., Csapo, Avugos, Raab, & Bar-Eli, 2014). That is, whether or not a streak exists, the belief in a streak or a hot hand may influence whether teammates choose to pass to a perceived 'hot' player, or whether coaches choose to play and strategize around this player either in offence or defence (Csapo et al., 2014). This area of research and application of economic theory of JDM to sport highlighted to JDM researchers that sport provides an appealingly complex domain for theory development and, to cognitive sport researchers, that economic JDM research can provide paradigms and findings to help understand behaviour by multiple stakeholders in sport.

In addition to biases or decision tendencies that come to sport from the economic view of decision-making, there are also the study and use of heuristics, which are short cuts and rules of thumb and are considered to come from cognitive theories of JDM. For example, the rule of choosing the first option that becomes available is applicable to the time pressures inherent in many sports-based JDM scenarios, such as the player deciding on an action choice. Johnson and Raab (2003) showed that experts generated fewer, but higher-quality, decision options, when compared with novices, and that they often selected the first option they generated (Raab & Johnson, 2007). Raab and Laborde (2011) also showed that experts, compared with near-experts, generate faster, more appropriate options, rely more often on the first option they generate, and, thus, follow what is called a take-the-first heuristic (see Raab, 2012, for an overview in different domains and comparisons with other models). Given that there are a large number of possible decision heuristics that can be used to drive JDM (e.g., recognition, take-the-first, availability, simulation), Todd, Gigerenzer, and ABC Research Group (2012) further proposed that the appropriate or more successful heuristic is the one that is ecologically rational, meaning it should be selected based on its fit for the decision environment. A novice with few options or little expertise may not benefit from a take-the-first heuristic, for example. This acknowledgement of the demands and features of the decision environment are related to the ecological dynamics view of decision-making.

In the ecological dynamics view, JDM cannot be separated from the environment and the constraints imposed by the person, environment, and task. This theoretical approach to JDM in sport is also related to the area of perception and action (see Rudisch, Pixa, & Voelcker-Rehage, Volume 1, Chapter 25, in this encyclopedia). Thus, for example, an athlete who cannot kick more than 20 metres is constrained, and the action choice is influenced; a mountain climber who feels fatigued judges the possible next reaches differently to when in a non-fatigued state (Pijpers, Oudejans, Bakker, & Beek, 2006). Likewise, Russell, Renshaw, and Davids (2019) proposed decision-making in football officials as a process that operates within each game. This view emphasizes the need to understand decisions in context, with the authors drawing on Gibson's (1966) individual-environment-synergy ideas. Seeking to understand not simply what decisions soccer referees make, but why they make them, Russell et al. revealed four priorities that influence officiating decisions: safety, accuracy, fairness, and entertainment. Moreover, acknowledging the effects of game management in officiating decision-making (Mascarenhas, Collins, & Mortimer, 2002), wherein factors such as previous actions, game time, or a desire to maintain the flow of the contest are considered, Russell et al. also proposed a co-construction of the game decision-making standards and boundaries of behaviour: that these standards are controlled and enforced by referee decisions, but created between players and referees in each game.

Also related to the theoretical approach of ecological dynamics to sport is the naturalistic decision-making (NDM) model. The NDM – and, in particular, recognition-primed decision-making (RPDM) – is a specific type of naturalistic decision-making that takes place under time and information constraints. This approach comes from the human factors field of study to understand decision-making in domains such as aeronautics and emergency work (e.g., firefighting: e.g., Klein, 1989). From the NDM perspective, similar to that of ecological dynamics, the characteristics of the decision-making situation, such as time pressure, influence the decision process and outcome. For example, recent work with Australian rules football umpires used in-game communication to show that decisions and communication were influenced by the game context and the decision-making required at the time (Neville, Salmon, & Read, 2017). This analysis revealed that, like work using the RPD with players, the majority of decisions involve matching the situation to similar situations encountered previously to determine the best course of action. The next most frequent type of decision was those in which diagnosis of the situation is more critical in a search for similar previous situations. Neville et al. found that very few Australian Football League officiating decisions were of the type requiring mental simulation to test potential actions. These findings are similar to those advocated by the take-the-first heuristic (Raab & Johnson, 2007) and support that these theoretical approaches are all valuable for what they reveal about appropriate training and performance in different sports actors.

Research Findings: JDM in Sport

Sport JDM researchers using the main theoretical approaches we have reviewed have created a strong and growing knowledge base. There are clever and elegant studies, using various methods, and important findings. Some of the main key findings are grouped below.

Experts Are Better at JDM than Their Novice Counterparts

The study of action choice in sport was particularly accelerated with the use of and ability to easily edit video of gameplay. There are two main paradigms in this area: video-based decision-making and perception–action coupled decision-making (see also Filho & Tenenbaum, Volume 1, Chapter 22, in this encyclopedia).[1] In the former case, an athlete is typically seated at a computer and shown video of gameplay that is occluded at a key decision point. The athlete is then asked to indicate their choice of the best next action, which can be done verbally, through a mouse click, or through a touch screen indicating the area on the field, for example, where a kick might be directed. This method allows recording of both the speed of the response and the accuracy, typically compared with the choices made by expert coaches who have previously viewed the video clips. Researchers who are concerned with the execution of the action, and particularly those from the ecological dynamics school of thought who emphasize that action choices are inextricably linked to their performance, use the perception–action coupled approach, in which video is projected on a large scale in front of the athlete, who then must physically carry out the choice (e.g., kick the ball on to the place on the screen/projection wall representing where they would kick the ball in the actual game). Although there are some nuances to these methods, including the perspective of the video and the methods of scoring, the general findings are that expert athletes make better and faster decisions than their novice counterparts (Williams & Jackson, 2019) and have more available options, likely linked to their superior physical and skill capabilities (e.g., Bruce, Farrow, Raynor, & Mann, 2012). In addition, Sue McPherson's research provides an understanding of strategy and tactics, accessing the knowledge base of tennis players by asking them to report their thoughts between points (McPherson, 1994). Her research shows that experts have developed more tactical knowledge with sophisticated representations of the JDM problems within gameplay, using deep levels of analysis of the current situation as well as built-up knowledge of previous patterns with situation prototypes that guide the choice of action, as well as monitoring of the outcomes of these choices and their execution (McPherson, 1999). Taken together, McPherson's research suggests that experts are more tactical and have a sophisticated interpretation of game situations, with planning and monitoring of the events taking place within a competition. This work provides an indication of the mechanisms that drive more expert athletes' better action choices.

For one particular stakeholder – the sports official – knowledge base has long been acknowledged as a key component of superior JDM. Indeed, this role is often considered the key decision-maker in sports contests, with a number of decisions openly communicated. For example, Helsen and Bultynck (2004) calculated that soccer referees make an average of 137 observable decisions per game in the UEFA league, and they estimated an arguably conservative additional 63 unobservable decisions, to arrive at an estimated three to four decisions per minute. These decisions are based on knowledge of the rules of soccer, but also reflect what Mascarenhas, Collins, and Mortimer (2005) call the four cornerstones of successful officiating: (a) knowledge and application of the laws of the game, (b) contextual judgement, (c) fitness and positioning, and (d) personality and management skills. Although there are still limitations inherent in the use of video-based decision-making with officials, particularly with regards to capturing and replicating demands, this method of training and studying JDM has predominated, consistently showing that expert officials outperform novices across a number of sports (e.g., Gilis, Helsen, Catteeuw, & Wagemans, 2008; Larkin, Berry, Dawson, & Lay, 2011; Mascarenhas, Collins, Mortimer, & Morris, 2005). Though fewer in number, match-based assessments also show the same pattern of superior performance in decision-making by higher-level compared with lower-level officials (MacMahon et al., 2014).

Judgements and Decisions Are Influenced by Biases, Expectations, and Context

As mentioned, Mascarenhas, Collins, and Mortimer (2005) consider context for judgements so influential that contextual judgement is identified as a cornerstone of good officiating. Indeed, as alluded to, there is abundant evidence that context matters in sports JDM: Changing contextual factors can change a decision. The change may not necessarily be as dramatic as calling a foul where one factor is present and a no-foul when it is not, or kicking to the opposite side, but there are clear influences. One influence is the expectation of skill level based on reputation or the order in which an athlete is judged. Specifically, Findlay and Ste-Marie (2004) showed that figure-skating judges awarded higher technical marks to skaters who they knew, compared with skaters they were not familiar with, suggesting that there is a reputation bias. For athletes, reputation can also influence the perception of size of an opponent and, thus, specifics of the action choice. Mueller, Best, and Cañal-Bruland (2018) showed that not only were soccer goalkeepers with a good reputation perceived as taller than those with a 'lower' reputation, but shots to these keepers were farther from them, and consequently less successful. Similarly, simulating judges observing gymnasts warm up a routine created expectations for judges about how well particular skills would be performed, which was reflected in the marks and how accurately they were judged (Ste-Marie & Lee, 1991); as mentioned previously, skills performed in the same way as in warm-up (e.g., with or without error) were judged more accurately than those where a difference existed between warm-up and performance.

We have previously discussed how the hot hand belief leads to expectations for the success or failure of events such as basketball shots, based on beliefs around streaks. Even more indicative of the influence of context in sports JDM is work in soccer that shows that game time and sequencing of actions influence the likelihood of calling penalties. Plessner and Betsch (2001), for example, showed in an experimental study that participants are more likely to call penalties against one and then the other team, rather than two penalties in a row against the same team. Similarly, MacMahon and Starkes (2008) showed that ambiguous baseball pitches (borderline ball or strike) were more likely to be called as balls (missed the strike zone) after obvious strike pitches than after obvious ball pitches, or when there were three balls already in the pitch count, again showing a pattern of negative correlation. Subsequently, Unkelbach and Memmert (2008) introduced the idea that there are calibration effects to decision-making in soccer officiating, which can also apply to baseball umpiring, by showing that there are fewer yellow cards awarded at the beginning of soccer games compared with later in the game, with support for this effect found through experimental manipulations. They also supported the view that context has an influence by showing that fewer yellow cards were awarded when actions were judged in the context of a game sequence compared with when the same actions were shown in random order, a finding relevant to consider for the design and interpretation of performance in testing and training using video clips and game sequences.

Other seemingly less relevant factors have also been shown to influence judgements and decisions, such as the colour that competitors wear. In tae kwon do, protective equipment is either blue or red and is assigned randomly. Hagemann, Strauss, and Leißing (2008) used video editing to change the colour of this equipment and showed that, when competitors wore red, they were scored significantly higher and assigned more points than when in blue. Similarly, there has been investigation of colour effects in judo, wherein, although Julio et al. (2015) showed that competitors in blue uniforms (judogi) are more likely to win than those wearing white, Dijkstra, Preenen, and van Essen's (2018) more extensive analysis showed that the first competitor called, rather than the uniform colour, influenced winning probability.

Moreover, Dijkstra et al. argue that, although red may influence perceptions of dominance and aggression, which advantages red-wearing athletes in combat sports, blue has no clear associations and, when compared with white in judo, does not influence judgements. This has not been extensively tested; however, the point remains that sports JDM can be influenced, in tight contests, by expectations based on external factors, such as colour or order of being called to compete.

Athlete decisions are also influenced by indirect factors in the situation. For example, a number of researchers have investigated factors that influence decisions in penalty-taking in soccer and handball. Notably, van der Kamp and Masters (2008) showed that handball players behave in line with the Müller-Lyer illusion, in which arrows pointing out at the top of a line lead to the perception that it is longer than the same line with arrows pointing in. Specifically, shooters perceive goalkeepers standing with arms up, compared with out to the side, down, or parallel and tight to their body, as taller and, when they are faced with this posture, their throws are wider and lower. The suggestion is that standing with arms out, where the keeper seems smaller, will result in attackers choosing to throw closer to the keeper's body. Thus, this work shows that decision-makers can be subtly influenced by visual illusions. Finally, Levi and Jackson (2018) show that players themselves also acknowledge the influence of context on decision-making, with factors such as the game score, coach instructions, and the match importance being considerations in action choices.

Motor Experience Influences Judgements and Decision-Making

Ecological dynamicists and researchers from the field of embodied cognition regard judgements and decision-making as inextricably linked to physical capabilities, and there is evidence to support this. Pijpers et al. (2006) found that, when rock climbers are fatigued, their perception is that they cannot reach as high as they actually show they can. With officiating, Pizzera and Raab (2012) found that gymnastics judges who could perform or had previously performed the skills being judged made better judgements of gymnastics skills. In addition, when soccer referees were given more visual experience of watching simulations in which players fake a foul, they were better able to pick up that deception, and, interestingly, those trained to actually physically fake fouls themselves retained the advantage.

Experts Use Decision Shortcuts

JDM tasks in sport are difficult: They are time pressured and they lack information and/or include deceptive information. We know that, over time, experts operate with more efficiency and in a more automated manner (e.g., Beilock, Carr, MacMahon, & Starkes, 2002). Although the use of shortcuts may make our decisions and judgements more vulnerable to bias and error, it is also precisely what makes our JDM system more effective. In JDM, intuition may be a hallmark of this efficiency. Intuition is described as a faster, more surface-based analysis and choice-making that is difficult to explain or iterate, is based on experience, and is often influenced by affect. In a study by Raab and Laborde (2011), for example, expert handball players were more intuitive than near-expert and novice players. Moreover, the players who rated themselves with a higher preference for making intuitive decisions were also those who made faster and better choices. Similarly, Christensen (2009) found an emphasis on the use of intuition in talent identification on the part of soccer coaches at the national youth team level. The use of intuition in sports JDM can be contextually influenced, however. MacMahon, Bailey, Croser, and Weissensteiner (2019), for instance, showed evidence that Australian rules football talent recruiters' use of intuition was influenced by the nature of the coach–recruiter relationship: a high-engagement relationship seemed to facilitate intuition, and a low-engagement or conflict-based relationship was associated with deliberation. In this case, there may have been a need to use a more deliberative choice process if a recruiter felt that justification or rationalization was required in explaining decisions to the coach.

In JDM research, Gigerenzer looked at a number of different specific decision shortcuts or simple heuristics. A heuristic is a simplified mental strategy for decision-making that consists of three building blocks, a search, stop, and decision rule. For instance, if you have never heard of the construct simple heuristics and google it, you would search for important information from the top and stop searching after a fit to your search is found and you decide to click on the link. In sports, the execution of the movement itself has been argued to be another building block in heuristics, as both are important: what movement to choose, and how to process it in space and time to achieve a specific movement goal (Raab, Masters, & Maxwell, 2005). Recently, comparisons have been made between simple heuristics and other theories in sport psychology (e.g., Raab, 2012), as well as descriptions for many applications (Raab, 2020).

Mechanisms in Judgement and Decision-Making

Whereas much of the early work on cognition in sport was descriptive in nature, showing the major tasks on which experts and novices differ (e.g., Vickers, 2007) and testing visual function and the sport-specific or domain-general nature of this expertise (e.g., Baker & Hodges, 2015; Starkes, 1987), further work has examined the mechanisms that are responsible for these advantages. Specific to the area of JDM, we know that eye movements are linked to aspects of superior decision-making. Specifically, it is understood that there are eye movement differences between experts and novices, and that the patterns of eye movements and these differences also change, depending on the situation. For example, skilled soccer players use more fixations but of shorter duration in 11 versus 11 situations, but fewer fixations of longer duration when faced with a 3 versus 3 scenario. Further, in a one-on-one situation, the higher-skilled players use more specific fixation on the player's hip and ball compared with less skilled players, who primarily fixate only on the ball (see Roca, Ford, McRobert, & Williams, 2013 for a review).

Interestingly, although there is a dearth of research on eye movements related to decision-making in sports officials, some of this work shows a lack of expertise differences, regardless of differences in decision accuracy. Hancock and Ste-Marie (2013), for example, tested ice hockey referees' decisions and eye movements in response to video clips. In choosing between penalty/no-penalty decisions, the higher-level referees outperformed the lower-level referees; however, there were no accompanying differences in gaze patterns. Similarly, in a field study, Schnyder, Koedijker, Kredel, and Hossner (2017) found that, although expert assistant referees in soccer made more correct offside decisions compared with their near-expert counterparts, there were no differences in gaze patterns. It should be noted, however, that this study did also identify that, for both groups of referees, fixating the offside line, rather than any of the players, was associated with greater accuracy.

In a lifespan model of expert perceptual-motor performance, Starkes, Cullen, and MacMahon (2004) proposed that performers pass through an acquisition phase and a condensation and elaboration phase, to a third, routine expertise phase of performance. Notably, the model's fourth phase of perceptual-cognitive/perceptual-motor development is that of transcendent expertise, with innovation as a key hallmark. Whereas Starkes, Cullen, and MacMahon primarily identified the peak 'genius' performers who advance performance levels above those achieved before, or make significant advances in technique (e.g., Dick Fosbury, Mohammed Ali, Martina Navratilova, Wayne Gretzky, Serena Williams), within the skill of JDM, there is an acknowledgement that better performers are characterized by their creative decision-making and innovative problem-solving (Memmert & Roca, 2019). Moreover, creative decisions seem to be facilitated by specific eye movements. Specifically, Roca, Ford, and Memmert (2018) tested soccer players' physical action choices in response to life-sized projections of 11 versus 11 match video. The most creative players, whose decisions were innovative and who produced many different tactical options, used a broader focus of attention on the scene, fixating more, and more-informative locations, for shorter durations. These more creative players also picked up more of their teammates, earlier in the videos. These patterns presumably lead to more creative players acquiring more key information earlier, thus giving them more information and time on which to base their decisions.

A recent study focused on comparing creativity and intuitive decision-making, by Huettermann, Nerb, and Memmert (2018), compared soccer decision-making in near-elite Brazilian and German male players. Examining both the first intuitive option and the creative options generated, the results indicate that the constructs of intuition and creativity overlap in the option-generation of choices. Moreover, there was no difference, despite popular belief, between the Brazilian and German players in the measures of intuition and creativity or in performance on the video tests.

Similar to the approach of investigating superior JDM in sport using eye movements is work incorporating psychophysiological and neurophysiological measurement. A recent summary was provided in a book by Bilalic (2017) on the neuroscience of expertise. It exemplifies the need for a better understanding of the neurophysiological correlates of expertise in JDM and beyond (see Vartanian & Mandel, 2011, for an overview). Neurophysiological correlates of expertise seem to fit well with a less-is-more approach. That is, behavioural data show that experts use fewer fixations (Gegenfurtner, Lehtinen, & Säljö, 2011), generate fewer options (Raab & Johnson, 2007), and exhibit less brain activation for controlling and imagining actions (Bilalic, 2017). Additionally, in a more specific study comparing brain activation when imagining soccer movements of a top player (Neymar), experts showed less brain activation compared with less elite players. Even more interestingly, they also showed less activation than swimmers, a group that may have similar movement experiences with their feet but for very different movements (Naito & Hirose, 2014). This reveals the specific nature of movement experiences in brain activation patterns.

Brain-imaging in sports (Bachmann, Munzert, & Krueger, 2018), brain stimulation techniques (Colzato, 2017), and many more methods to understand sports performance and JDM have been recently summarized (Boecker, Hillman, Scheef, & Strüder, 2012). Further, psychophysiological explanations for some of the main JDM findings have been recently summarized (e.g., Hoffmann et al., 2018), with a focus on particular measures such as heart rate variability (HRV), studies in team sports (Laborde & Raab, 2013), EEG (Del Percio et al., 2010), and glucose (Haier et al., 1992).

Practice and Application

Knowing about the characteristics and responses of more skilled decision-makers, the factors that influence JDM in sport, and some of the mechanisms that may drive choices helps to inform practice and devise training methods. Moreover, adopting and testing training methods used in other domains is another approach that has been advocated by research into JDM in sports. Practice and applications do follow many different routes, and, thus, we present general training approaches, applications to a specific set of choices, as well as choices that are specific to different stakeholders in sports.

General Training Approaches for Decision-Making Skills

There has been a focus in sport on training visual skills such as anticipation and cue usage using the occlusion paradigm or measurement of eye movements, pattern recall and recognition, and use of implicit training techniques (see Filho & Tenenbaum, Volume 1, Chapter 22, and Ward et al., Volume 1, Chapter 3, in this encyclopedia). Although these are critical skills, they contribute to, but are not, decision-making as its own skill. Rather, choosing the next option that a player will carry out, or selecting an athlete to recruit from testing data are more central tasks. There is growing research in this area, which has tried to tackle the difficulty of a skill that involves both cognitive and physical abilities. Knowing that carrying out a chosen action is a key component of decision-making in sport, the perception–action coupling approach acknowledges the ecological dynamics approach and the importance this places on representative design (Brunswik, 1956). In this paradigm, one method involves large-scale projection of game stimuli, wherein an athlete is asked to physically carry out a chosen action in response. In addition, representative design (Simon, 1955) refers to the selection of stimuli, tasks, and their distribution in the real world. Simon and others (Ragni, Kola, & Johnson-Laird, 2018) have argued that, as we randomly assign participants to a condition, we should randomly draw from the stimuli, tasks, and their distribution in the real environment to be 'representative' in our designs. Recent overviews have shown how quality, quantity, and content of training have differential effects on performance (Ericsson & Lehmann, 1996) and its transfer (Buszard, Reid, Krause, Kovalchik, & Farrow, 2017). The discussion about effects for specific training regimes is certainly ongoing, and some demarcation lines have been discussed, such as whether perceptual training alone can improve decision-making (Abernethy, Schorer, Jackson, & Hagemann, 2012) or whether indicating a decision by pressing a response button in training represents the same transfer effects as more complex movements (Dicks, Button, & Davids, 2010).

Within the literature, different training approaches for athletes have been advocated that have been summarized as decision training (Vickers, 2007), ball school (Memmert & Roth, 2007), teaching games for understanding (Griffin, Mitchell, & Oslin, 1997), and Situation Model of Anticipated Response consequences in Tactical decisions – Extension and Revision (SMART-ER; Raab, 2015). Another approach that has recently received attention is the above-real-time training method that speeds up video training above the real video speed (e.g., in Australian rules football; Lorains, Ball, & MacMahon, 2013). Findings indicate improvements for the fast-speed group and superior short-term retention, but no advantage for longer-term retention. A further finding is that, following training, regardless of video speed, the eye movement fixation duration became longer compared with those who had no video training (Lorains, Panchuk, Ball, & MacMahon, 2014). This significant finding falls in line with previous research. Furthermore, analysis of eye movements showed that the above real-time training group spent a longer duration fixating on the best option after the retention test compared with other groups. These results provide a solid base for future research in sport to track changes in eye movements throughout training and learning (see Farahani, Javadi, O'Neill, & Walsh, 2017, for similar findings showing training effects not lasting beyond 2 weeks in soccer).

Like the above-real-time training effects in athletes, a study by Put, Wagemans, Pizzera, et al. (2016) suggests that referees make better decisions for normal and fast-speed videos than for slow speed. An explanation is that, if a referee sees a slow-motion video, they may be more inclined to believe that the player had more time to withdraw and avoid committing a foul and, thus, they indicate that the foul was intentional (Spitz, Put, Wagemans, Williams, & Helsen, 2017). Relying on referees' intuition and training with appropriate levels and amounts of feedback is another solution to training for improved JDM performance that has been validated (Schweizer, Plessner, Kahlert, & Brand, 2011). Finally, virtual reality as simulation training has become more and more important (Craig, 2013), and this has been applied in referee training in soccer (Put, Wagemans, Spitz, Williams, & Helsen, 2016) and in 3D training for athletes (Hohmann, Obelöer, Schlapkohl, & Raab, 2015).

Applications to a Set of Specific Choices

An important structure of applications of JDM research for training and performance is to consider the choice task. For instance, dimensions used to structure choice tasks are short-term and long-term (Raab, 2012), individual versus group decisions (Raab & Reimer, 2007), routine versus new choices (Betsch & Haberstroh, 2005), or discrete versus sequential choices (Raab, 2020), to name a few. This can be illustrated for the dimension of discrete versus sequential choices. A problem for applications of JDM research is often that, in laboratory studies, we provide athletes with a video test of multiple trials and, for a chosen manipulation, expert athletes show, on average, better performance than novices (Helsen & Starkes, 1999). However, averaging and keeping order of trials as discrete events is not what athletes do in real life. Rather, athletes believe in and regard choices in a game as having dependencies between events. Evidence of the effects of sequencing is present in a highly cited paper from Gilovich, Vallone, and Tversky (1985) and is well accepted. If athletes, coaches, or fans are asked whether a basketball player that just scored two or three baskets (hits) in a row has a higher chance of scoring again compared with the same player that just missed two or three attempts, the majority believe in the hot hand – that is, that positive streaks will continue. However, the analyses of actual shot sequences revealed that the shots are random in terms of hits and misses. Recently, the conclusion and analyses have been challenged by big data, alternative methods, or calculations (e.g., Csapo et al., 2014; Miller & Sanjurjo, 2018), and, thus, there may be evidence that the hot hand exists after all (Raab, Gula, & Gigerenzer, 2012). For application, whether the hot hand exists or not does not matter. Consider a basketball game with a score of 99:97; the trailing team is in possession of the ball for the last seconds of the game, and, in a timeout, the playmaker decides to either pass the ball to the player with the average highest base rate or to the player who just scored the last two or three baskets. Based on the literature reviewed above, players who believe in the hot hand would likely allocate the ball to the player who is hot (Raab et al., 2012). However, coaches instructing defensive strategies often double team the hot player, and, thus, for a specific moment in the game it is almost impossible to provide a sure decision strategy. On the other hand, over the course of a game, it seems likely that knowledge about player decision-making and instruction-specific strategies informed from research can have beneficial effects. For instance, new technology allows us to use big data to see individual and team performance from the perspective of sequential decision-making as introduced above (e.g., Csapo et al., 2014). The same logic could be applied for handball penalty throws or penalty shoot-outs (Bar-Eli, Azar, Ritov, Keidar-Levin, & Schein, 2007) and many more scenarios. The interactive nature of beliefs, behaviours, and strategies is thus illustrated, and the complexity this introduces for application.

Applications from the Choice Maker's Perspective

An important structure for applications is tuned to the person him- or herself. For instance, in the book *Judgment, Decision-Making and Success in Sport* (Bar-Eli et al., 2011), half of the chapters focus purely on the choices of an athlete, manager/coach, referee, or observer/fan. In each of these chapters, the choices the choice maker is confronted with and specific examples are given. A benefit of such a structure is the focus on a selection of the most important choices – for instance, for a coach who decides to develop game strategy or who selects the starting team for next weekend – which differ on dimensions of time, information needed, and decision strategy. Some of these differences, as highlighted at the start of this

Table 3 Applications and advice for athletes, coaches/managers, and referees

Athletes	Emotional and physical states might lead to underestimation of factual skills	Pijpers et al. (2006)
	The goalkeeper's posture influences the penalty-taker's actions	van der Kamp and Masters (2008)
	Experts and novices differ in JDM aspects such as analysing the situation or monitoring choice outcome	McPherson (1999)
Coaches/ managers	JDM in sports might be affected by expectations based on external factors (e.g., uniform colour)	Dijkstra et al. (2018)
	Intuitive decisions play an important role in JDM and might be used in talent identification	Christensen (2009)
	Above-real-time video training enhances learning/performance (but not long-term retention)	Lorains et al. (2013)
	The relationship between the coach and the recruiter influences the talent identification decision process	MacMahon et al., (2019)
	Creative decision-making and innovative problem-solving are associated with greater performance	Memmert and Roca (2019)
Referees	Reputation biases can influence referees' decisions	Findlay and Ste-Marie (2004)
	Successful JDM in officiating is summarized by four cornerstones: (1) knowledge and application of the laws of the game, (2) contextual judgement, (3) fitness and positioning, (4) personality and management skills	Mascarenhas, Collins, and Mortimer (2005)
	Immediate feedback on the correctness of decisions without further explanations increases decision accuracy	Schweizer et al. (2011)
	Assistant referees make better offside decisions when fixating the offside line rather than any of the players	Schnyder et al. (2017)

chapter, are substantial: from choices that must be made in a matter of milliseconds for an athlete, to a season-long evaluation of a player to consider renewal of a contract. Thus, specific theoretical starting points and applications can be produced. An even more extreme concept is to provide a book or review paper for each stakeholder. For instance, MacMahon et al. (2014) focused on referees, judges, and choices for officiating. Williams and Jackson (2019) focused mainly on athletes. Coaches and managers in sport and their judgements and decision-making have been summarized by Bar-Eli et al. (2011). Finally, a book on sport fans focused purely on observers (Strauß, 2012). Separating specific phenomena, theories, decision-making training, and mechanisms that explain choice behaviour systematically to different choice makers is not well established and could potentially prove to be a fruitful road for the future (see Table 3).

Conclusion

In conclusion, JDM in sport is a key critical skill. JDM research focuses on many dimensions, stakeholders, and applications. The introduction highlighted that JDM has benefitted from, and can continue to benefit from, knowledge produced in other domains and approaches. As usual, there are a variety of ways in which JDM in sport has been looked at, both theoretically and methodologically, and we indicated a number of current issues. An important development of interdisciplinary research is to integrate into JDM component skills that provide insights into complex and realistic behaviour in sports. We showed that, in the application and practical consequences of research, the variety of JDM tasks and actors may dictate the choice of approach and how good findings can be applied. In science, there is more work to do, and this has been helped by technology, big data methods, and different levels of description such as the increasing use of neurophysiological methods in sport. It is clear that there is much to gain from the continued development of JDM in sport.

Note

1 It should also be noted that a growing body of work looks at understanding decisions using methods such as open-ended interview (Russell et al., 2019), self-confrontation, or auto-confrontation interview (e.g., Boyer, Rix-Lièvre, & Récopé, 2015). These methods have the advantage of understanding judgements and decisions within their context and constraints. See comments in this section related to Sue McPherson's work.

References

Abernethy, B., Schorer, J., Jackson, R. C., & Hagemann, N. (2012). Perceptual training methods compared: The relative efficacy of different approaches to enhancing sport-specific anticipation. *Journal of Experimental Psychology: Applied, 18*, 143–153.

Allard, F., Deakin, J., Parker, S., & Rodgers, W. (1993). Declarative knowledge in a skilled motor performance: By product or constituent? In J. L. Starkes & F. Allard (Eds.), *Cognitive issues in motor expertise. Advances in psychology* (Vol. 102, pp. 95–107). Amsterdam: Elsevier.

Bachmann, J., Munzert, J., & Krueger, B. (2018). Neural underpinnings of the perception of emotional states derived from biological human motion: A review of neuroimaging research. *Frontiers in Psychology, 9*, 1763.

Baker, J., & Hodges, N. (2015). Sport expertise: A festschrift celebrating the contributions of Dr. Janet Starkes. *Special Issue of the International Journal of Sport Psychology, 46*.

Bar-Eli, M. (2018). *Boost! How the psychology of sports can enhance your performance in management and work*. Oxford: Oxford University Press.

Bar-Eli, M., Azar, O. H., Ritov, I., Keidar-Levin, Y., & Schein, G. (2007). Action bias among elite soccer goalkeepers: The case of penalty kicks. *Journal of Economic Psychology, 28*, 606–621.

Bar-Eli, M., Plessner, H., & Raab, M. (2011). *Judgment, decision-making and success in sport.* Chichester: Wiley-Blackwell.

Beilock, S. L., Carr, T. H., MacMahon, C., & Starkes, J. L. (2002). When paying attention becomes counter-productive: Impact of divided versus skill-focused attention on novice and experienced performance of sensorimotor skills. *Journal of Experimental Psychology: Applied, 8*, 6–16.

Betsch, T., & Haberstroh, S. (Eds.). (2005). *The routines of decision making.* Mahwah, NJ: Lawrence Erlbaum.

Bilalic, M. (2017). *The neuroscience of expertise.* Cambridge: Cambridge University Press.

Boecker, H., Hillman, C., Scheef, L., & Strüder, H. K. (2012). *Functional neuroimaging in exercise and sport sciences.* New York and Heidelberg: Springer Verlag.

Boyer, S., Rix-Lièvre, G., & Récopé, M. (2015). L'arbitrage de haut niveau, une affaire d'équipe [Elite refereeing, a team affair]. *Movement & Sport Sciences – Science & Motricité, 87*, 91–101.

Bruce, L., Farrow, D., Raynor, A., & Mann, D. (2012). But I can't pass that far! The influence of motor skill on decision making. *Psychology of Sport and Exercise, 13*, 152–161.

Brunswik, E. (1956). *Perception and the representative design of psychological experiments* (2nd ed.). Berkeley, CA: University of California Press.

Buszard, T., Reid, M., Krause, L., Kovalchik, S., & Farrow, D. (2017). Quantifying contextual interference and its effect on skill transfer in skilled youth tennis players. *Frontiers in Psychology, 8*, 1931.

Carlson, K. A., & Shu, S. B. (2007). The rule of three: How the third event signals the emergence of a streak. *Organizational Behavior and Human Decision Processes, 104*, 113–121.

Christensen, M. K. (2009). 'An eye for talent': Talent identification and the 'practical sense' of top level soccer coaches. *Journal of Sociology in Sport, 26*, 365–382.

Colzato, L. S. (2017). *Theory-driven approaches to cognitive enhancement.* New York: Springer.

Craig, C. (2013). Understanding perception and action in sport: How can virtual reality technology help? *Sports Technology, 6*, 161–169.

Csapo, P., Avugos, S., Raab, M., & Bar-Eli, M. (2014). How should 'hot' players in basketball be defended? The use of fast-and-frugal heuristics by basketball coaches and players in response to streakiness. *Journal of Sports Sciences, 33*, 1580–1588.

Csapo, P., & Raab, M. (2014). "Hand down, man down." Analysis of defensive adjustments in response to the hot hand in basketball using novel defense metrics. *PLoS One, 9*(12), e114184.

Del Percio, C., Infarinato, F., Iacoboni, M., Marzano, N., Soricelli, A., Aschieri, P., … Babiloni, C. (2010). Movement-related desynchronization of alpha rhythms is lower in athletes than non-athletes: A high-resolution EEG study. *Clinical Neurophysiology, 121*, 482–491.

Dicks, M., Button, C., & Davids, K. (2010). Examination of gaze behaviors under in situ and video simulation task constraints reveals differences in information pickup for perception and action. *Attention, Perception, & Psychophysics, 72*, 706–720.

Dijkstra, P. D., Preenen, P. T., & van Essen, H. (2018). Does blue uniform color enhance winning probability in judo contests? *Frontiers in Psychology, 9*, 45.

Eiser, J. R. (1990). *Social judgment.* Pacific Grove, CA: Brooks-Cole.

Ericsson, K. A., & Lehmann, A. C. (1996). Expert and exceptional performance: Evidence on maximal adaptations on task constraints. *Annual Review of Psychology, 47*, 273–305.

Farahani, J. J., Javadi, A. H., O'Neill, B. V., & Walsh, V. (2017). Effectiveness of above real-time training on decision-making in elite football: A dose–response investigation. *Progress in Brain Research, 234*, 101–116.

Findlay, L. C., & Ste-Marie, D. M. (2004). A reputation bias in figure skating judging. *Journal of Sport and Exercise Psychology, 26*, 154–166.

Gegenfurtner, A., Lehtinen, E., & Säljö, R. (2011). Expertise differences in the comprehension of visualizations: A meta-analysis of eye-tracking research in professional domains. *Educational Psychology Review, 23*, 523–552.

Gibson, J. J. (1966). *The senses considered as perceptual systems.* Boston, MA: Houghton Mifflin.

Gilis, B., Helsen, W., Catteeuw, P., & Wagemans, J. (2008). Offside decisions by expert assistant referees in association football: Perception and recall of spatial positions in complex dynamic events. *Journal of Experimental Psychology: Applied, 14*, 21–35.

Gilovich, T., Vallone, R., & Tversky, A. (1985). The hot hand in basketball: On the misperception of random sequences. *Cognitive Psychology, 17*, 295–314.

Gréhaigne, J. F., Godbout, P., & Bouthier, D. (1999). The foundations of tactics and strategy in team sports. *Journal of Teaching in Physical Education, 18*, 159–174.

Griffin, L. L., Mitchell, S. A., & Oslin, J. L. (1997). *Teaching sport concepts and skills. A tactical games approach*. Champaign, IL: Human Kinetics.

Hagemann, N., Strauss, B., & Leißing, J. (2008). When the referee sees red. *Psychological Science, 19*, 769–771.

Haier, R. J., Siegel, J. B., MacLachlan, V., Soderling, A., Lottenberg, E., & Buchsbaum, M. S. (1992). Regional glucose metabolic changes after learning a complex visuospatial/motor task: A positron emission tomographic study. *Brain Research, 570*(1–2), 134–143.

Hancock, D. J., & Ste-Marie, D. M. (2013). Gaze behaviors and decision making accuracy of higher-and lower-level ice hockey referees. *Psychology of Sport and Exercise, 14*, 66–71.

Helsen, W., & Bultynck, J. B. (2004). Physical and perceptual-cognitive demands of top-class refereeing in association football. *Journal of Sports Sciences, 22*, 179–189.

Helsen, W. F., & Starkes, J. L. (1999). A multidimensional approach to skilled perception and performance in sport. *Applied Cognitive Psychology, 13*, 1–27.

Hoffmann, S., Borges, U., Bröker, L., Laborde, S., Liepelt, R., Lobinger, B. H., ... Raab, M. (2018). The psychophysiology of action: A multidisciplinary endeavor for integrating action and cognition. *Frontiers in Psychology, 9*, 1423.

Hohmann, T., Obelöer, H., Schlapkohl, N., & Raab, M. (2015). Does training with 3D videos improve decision-making in team invasion sports? *Journal of Sports Sciences, 34*, 746–755.

Huettermann, S., Nerb, J., & Memmert, D. (2018). The role of regulatory focus and expectation on creative decision making. *Human Movement Science, 62*, 169–175.

Johnson, J. G., & Raab, M. (2003). Take the first: Option-generation and resulting choices. *Organizational Behavior and Human Decision Processes, 91*, 215–229.

Julio, U. F., Miarka, B., Rosa, J. P., Lima, G. H., Takito, M. Y., & Franchini, E. (2015). Blue judogi may bias competitive performance when seeding system is not used: Sex, age, and level of competition effects. *Perceptual and Motor Skills, 120*, 28–37.

Klein, G. (1989). Recognition-primed decisions. In W. B. Rouse (Ed.), *Advances in man–machine system research* (Vol. 5, pp. 47–92). Greenwich, CT: JAI.

Laborde, S., & Raab, M. (2013). The tale of hearts and reason: The influence of mood on decision making. *Journal of Sport and Exercise Psychology, 35*, 339–357.

Larkin, P. M., Berry, J., Dawson, B., & Lay, B. (2011). Perceptual and decision-making skills of Australian football umpires. *International Journal of Performance Analysis in Sport, 11*, 427–437.

Levi, H. R., & Jackson, R. C. (2018). Contextual factors influencing decision making: Perceptions of professional soccer players. *Psychology of Sport and Exercise, 37*, 19–25.

Lorains, M., Ball, K., & MacMahon, C. (2013). An above real time training intervention for sport decision making. *Psychology of Sport and Exercise, 14*, 670–674.

Lorains, M., Panchuk, D., Ball, K., & MacMahon, C. (2014). The effect of an above real time decision-making intervention on visual search behaviour. *International Journal of Sports Science & Coaching, 9*, 1383–1392.

MacMahon, C., Bailey, A., Croser, M., & Weissensteiner, J. (2019). Exploring the skill of recruiting in the Australian Football League. *International Journal of Sports Science & Coaching, 14*, 72–81.

MacMahon, C., Mascarenhas, D., Plessner, H., Pizzera, A., Oudejans, R. R. D., & Raab, M. (2014). *Sports officials and officiating: Science and practice*. London: Routledge.

MacMahon, C., & McPherson, S. L. (2009). Knowledge base as a mechanism for perceptual-cognitive tasks: Skill is in the details! *International Journal of Sport Psychology, 40*, 565–579.

MacMahon, C., & Starkes, J. L. (2008). Contextual influences on baseball ball-strike decisions in umpires, players, and controls. *Journal of Sports Sciences, 26*, 751–760.

MacMahon, C., Starkes, J. L., & Deakin, J. (2009). Differences in processing of game information in basketball players, coaches and referees. *International Journal of Sport Psychology, 40*, 403–423.

Mascarenhas, D. R., Collins, D., & Mortimer, P. (2002). The art of reason versus the exactness of science in elite refereeing: Comments on Plessner and Betsch (2001). *Journal of Sport and Exercise Psychology, 24*, 328–333.

Mascarenhas, D. R., Collins, D., & Mortimer, P. W. (2005). Elite refereeing performance: Developing a model for sport science support. *The Sport Psychologist, 19*, 364–379.

Mascarenhas, D. R., Collins, D., Mortimer, P. W., & Morris, B. (2005). Training accurate and coherent decision making in rugby union referees. *The Sport Psychologist, 19*, 131–147.

McPherson, S. L. (1994). The development of sport expertise: Mapping the tactical domain. *Quest, 46*, 223–240.

McPherson, S. L. (1999). Tactical differences in problem representations and solutions in collegiate varsity and beginner female tennis players. *Research Quarterly for Exercise and Sport, 70*, 369–384.

Memmert, D., & Roca, A. (2019). Tactical creativity and decision making in sport. In A. M. Williams & R. C. Jackson (Eds.), *Anticipation and decision making in sport: Theories and applications* (pp. 203–214). London: Routledge.

Memmert, D., & Roth, K. (2007). The effects of non-specific and specific concepts on tactical creativity in team ball sports. *Journal of Sports Sciences, 25*, 1423–1432.

Miller, J., & Sanjurjo, A. (2018). Surprised by the gambler's and hot hand fallacies? A truth in the law of small numbers. *Econometrica, 86*(6), 2019–2047.

Mueller, F., Best, J. F., & Cañal-Bruland, R. (2018). Goalkeepers' reputations bias shot placement in soccer penalties. *Journal of Sport and Exercise Psychology, 40*, 128–134.

Murphy, C. P., Jackson, R. C., & Williams, A. M. (2019). Informational constraints, option generation and, and anticipation. *Psychology of Sport and Exercise, 41*, 54–62.

Naito, E., & Hirose, S. (2014). Efficient foot motor control by Neymar's brain. *Frontiers in Human Neuroscience, 8*, 594.

Neville, T. J., Salmon, P. M., & Read, G. J. (2017). Analysis of in-game communication as an indicator of recognition primed decision making in elite Australian rules football umpires. *Journal of Cognitive Engineering and Decision Making, 11*, 81–96.

Pijpers, J. R., Oudejans, R. R. D., Bakker, F. C., & Beek, P. J. (2006). The role of anxiety in perceiving and realizing affordances. *Ecological Psychology, 18*, 131–161.

Pizzera, A., & Raab, M. (2012). Does motor or visual experience enhance the detection of deceptive movements in football? *International Journal of Sports Science & Coaching, 7*, 269–283.

Plessner, H. (1999). Expectation biases in gymnastics judging. *Journal of Sport and Exercise Psychology, 21*, 131–144.

Plessner, H., & Betsch, T. (2001). Sequential effects in important referee decisions: The case of penalties in soccer. *Journal of Sport and Exercise Psychology, 23*, 254–259.

Put, K., Wagemans, J., Pizzera, A., Williams, A. M., Spitz, J., Savelsbergh, G. J., & Helsen, W. F. (2016). Faster, slower or real time? Perceptual-cognitive skills training with variable video speeds. *Psychology of Sport and Exercise, 25*, 27–35.

Put, K., Wagemans, J., Spitz, J., Williams, A. M., & Helsen, W. F. (2016). Using web-based training to enhance perceptual-cognitive skills in complex dynamic offside events. *Journal of Sports Sciences, 34*, 181–189.

Raab, M. (2012). Simple heuristics in sports. *International Review of Sport and Exercise Psychology, 5*, 104–120.

Raab, M. (2015). SMART-ER: A situation model of anticipated response consequences in tactical decisions in skill acquisition – extended and revised. *Frontiers in Psychology*, (5), 1533. https://doi.org/10.3389/fpsyg.2014.01533.

Raab, M. (2020). Performance psychology. In G. Tenenbaum & R. Eklund (Eds.), *Handbook of sport psychology* (pp. 1113–1130). Hoboken, NJ: Wiley.

Raab, M., Bar-Eli, M., Plessner, H., & Araújo, D. (2019). The past, present and future of research on judgment and decision making in sport. *Psychology in Sport and Exercise, 42*, 25–32.

Raab, M., Gula, B., & Gigerenzer, G. (2012). The hot hand exists in volleyball and is used for allocation decisions. *Journal of Experimental Psychology: Applied, 18*(1), 81–94.

Raab, M., & Johnson, J. G. (2007). Expertise-based differences in search and option-generation strategies. *Journal of Experimental Psychology. Applied, 13*, 158–170.

Raab, M., & Laborde, S. (2011). When to blink and when to think: Preference for intuitive decisions results in faster and better tactical choices. *Research Quarterly for Exercise and Sport, 82*, 89–98.

Raab, M., Masters, R. S., & Maxwell, J. P. (2005). Improving the 'how' and 'what' decisions of elite table tennis players. *Human Movement Science, 24*, 326–344.

Raab, M., & Reimer, T. (2007). Expertise im Sport: Intuitive und deliberative Entscheidungen im Sport [Expertise in sports: Intuitive and deliberative decisions in sports]. In N. Hagemann, M. Tietjens, & B. Strauß (Eds.), *Psychologie der sportlichen Höchstleistung* [[Psychology of peak performance] (pp. 93–117). Göttingen: Hogrefe.

Ragni, M., Kola, I., & Johnson-Laird, P. N. (2018). On selecting evidence to test hypotheses: A theory of selection tasks. *Psychological Bulletin, 144*, 779–796.

Roca, A., Ford, P. R., McRobert, A. P., & Williams, A. M. (2013). Perceptual-cognitive skills and their interaction as a function of task constraints in soccer. *Journal of Sport and Exercise Psychology, 35,* 144–155.

Roca, A., Ford, P. R., & Memmert, D. (2018). Creative decision making and visual search behavior in skilled soccer players. *PLoS One, 13*(7), e0199381.

Russell, S., Renshaw, I., & Davids, K. (2019). How interacting constraints shape emergent decision-making of national-level football referees. *Qualitative Research in Sport, Exercise and Health, 11*(4), 573–588.

Schnyder, U., Koedijker, J. M., Kredel, R., & Hossner, E.-J. (2017). Gaze behaviour in offside decision-making in football: A field study. *German Journal of Exercise and Sport Research, 47,* 103–109.

Schweizer, G., Plessner, H., Kahlert, D., & Brand, R. (2011). A video-based training method for improving soccer referees' intuitive decision-making skills. *Journal of Applied Sport Psychology, 23,* 429–442.

Simon, H. A. (1955). A behavioral model of rational choice. *The Quarterly Journal of Economics, 69,* 99–118.

Spitz, J., Put, K., Wagemans, J., Williams, A. M., & Helsen, W. F. (2017). Does slow motion impact on the perception of foul play in football? *European Journal of Sport Science, 17,* 748–756.

Starkes, J. L. (1987). Skill in field hockey: The nature of the cognitive advantage. *Journal of Sport Psychology, 9*(2), 146–160.

Starkes, J. L., Cullen, J. D., & MacMahon, C. (2004). 12 A life-span model of the acquisition and retention of expert perceptual-motor performance. In A. M. Williams & N. J. Hodges (Eds.), *Skill acquisition in sport: Research, theory, and practice* (pp. 259–281). London: Routledge.

Ste-Marie, D. M., & Lee, T. D. (1991). Prior processing effects on gymnastic judging. *Journal of Experimental Psychology: Learning, Memory, and Cognition, 17,* 126–136.

Strauß, B. (Ed.). (2012). *Sportzuschauer* [Fans]. Göttingen: Hogrefe.

Todd, P. M., Gigerenzer, G., & ABC Research Group (2012). *Ecological rationality: Intelligence in the world.* New York: Oxford University Press.

Unkelbach, C., & Memmert, D. (2008). Game-management, context-effects and calibration: The case of yellow cards in soccer. *Journal of Sport and Exercise Psychology, 30,* 95–109.

van der Kamp, J., & Masters, R. S. W. (2008). The human Muller-Lyer illusion in goalkeeping. *Perception, 37,* 951–954.

Vartanian, O., & Mandel, D. R. (Eds.). (2011). *Neuroscience of decision making.* New York: Psychology Press.

Vickers, J. N. (2007). *Perception, cognition, and decision training: The quiet eye in action.* Champaign, IL: Human Kinetics.

Williams, A. M., & Jackson, R. (2019). *Perception and decision making in sports.* London: Routledge.

Yaari, G., & Eisenmann, S. (2011). The hot (invisible?) hand: Can time sequence patterns of success/failure in sports be modeled as repeated random independent trials? *PLoS One, 6*(10), e24532.

17
LEADERSHIP AND SOCIAL IDENTITY

Katrien Fransen, Jamie B. Barker, and Matthew J. Slater

Introduction

Teamwork is the fuel that allows ordinary sports teams to attain extraordinary results. In this vein, Gareth Southgate illustrated why the England soccer team in the 2018 FIFA World Cup outperformed many other teams, such as Portugal, Brazil, and Argentina, who each relied on one star player (i.e., Ronaldo, Neymar, Messi):

> We know where we are, we know we're not the finished article and I don't think we have loads of world-class players. There are other teams in the tournament who have a better collection of individuals but we've been a real team. We have some excellent players, no doubt about that, but the collective strength has been massive.
>
> *(Taylor, 2018, n.p.)*

As do many other coaches, Gareth Southgate here emphasized the strength of the collective, the strength of the 'we' and 'us' triumphing over the 'me' and 'I'. This contribution will outline the importance of this 'us' feeling, also termed social identity. Furthermore, the authors will elaborate on how leaders (i.e., both coaches and leaders within the team) can become more effective by capitalizing on their ability to cultivate and nurture this social identity in their team.

Social Identity

The social identity approach (Haslam, 2004; Tajfel & Turner, 1979) builds on the assumption that the psychology and behaviour of team members is shaped by their capacity to think, feel, and behave not only as individuals (in terms of their personal identity as 'I' and 'me'), but also, and often more importantly, as group members (in terms of their shared social identity as 'we' and 'us'). In other words, besides characteristics and qualities that distinguish us from others (i.e., personal identity), a significant part of people's self-concept is also derived from various group memberships (i.e., social identity).

Previous organizational researchers have shown that, when people internalize a sense of shared group membership, this collective identity is the basis for job satisfaction, motivation, commitment, in-role performance, and organizational citizenship behaviours (Ellemers, Spears,

& Doosje, 1997; Lee, Park, & Koo, 2015; Ng, 2015). Furthermore, when we perceive ourselves and others to share a group membership, this social identification also benefits our health and well-being (Cruwys, Haslam, Dingle, Haslam, & Jetten, 2014; Steffens, Haslam, Schuh, Jetten, & van Dick, 2017).

Although the benefits of a shared sense of 'we' and 'us' have been widely evidenced in organizational psychology, the social identity approach has largely been ignored in the history of sport and exercise psychology. In sports, researchers have mainly focused on the individual as centre of their analysis. Two key approaches that were often used in the past to explain sport phenomena were the self-determination theory (SDT; Deci & Ryan, 1985) and the theory of planned behaviour (TPB; Ajzen, 1991). Whereas SDT focuses on fundamental psychology needs that are essential for an individual's motivation, TPB is particularly concerned with predictors of an individual's behavioural intentions. To illustrate, the walking behaviour of an individual would be explained in terms of his/her motivation to walk or in terms of his/her intentions to walk. In other words, the individual is central, and no attention is paid to the social context (e.g., whether the environment is suited for walking, or whether the individual participates in a walking group with friends).

Only rarely have sports researchers taken into account the social context when explaining people's behaviours and actions. However, the social groups that people belong to (or, more precisely, perceive themselves to belong to) can have an important impact on their behaviour. For example, the enactment of someone's social identity as 'a member of a walking group' might stimulate their walking behaviour, whereas the perceived norms of another social identity (e.g., belonging to the group of older adults who are, on average, less physically active) might be a barrier to going walking. In the same vein, the social context in which physical activity takes place (e.g., walking alone or in a group) might be an essential element to explain behaviour, as this social context has the power to strengthen an individual's identification with the group and, therefore, might influence their motivation. To conclude, relying only on individual factors while not taking the social context into account does not provide us with full insight into why and how humans behave.

Since the last decade, a number of researchers have realized that the social context not only matters in organizations, but also has wider applicability. In this regard, several studies evidenced the applicability of the social identity approach in sports (for a review, see Rees, Haslam, Coffee, & Lavallee, 2015) and exercise contexts (for a review, see Stevens et al., 2017). Specifically within the sports context, it was shown that athletes who identified more strongly with their team experienced higher task cohesion and social cohesion in their team (Fransen, Decroos, Vande Broek, & Boen, 2016), engaged more in social labouring (i.e., going the extra mile for their team; De Cuyper, Boen, Van Beirendonck, Vanbeselaere, & Fransen, 2016), felt healthier and experienced fewer feelings of burnout (Fransen et al., 2020b), were more confident in their team's abilities, and ultimately also performed better (Fransen, Haslam, et al., 2015; Fransen, Steffens, et al., 2016; Slater, Haslam, & Steffens, 2018). In youth sport too, evidence has shown that high levels of team identification were associated with greater self-worth, commitment, and effort (Martin, Balderson, Hawkins, Wilson, & Bruner, 2017), and positive youth development (e.g., personal and social skills, goal setting; Bruner et al., 2017). Returning to the quote from Gareth Southgate, it seems that the ratio of 'we's to 'I's in the team indeed might have been a reliable indicator for the performances during the last world cup.

Several scholars in the field have recently shown that not only in organizations, but also in sports teams, being able to cultivate such a shared sense of 'us' (i.e., a joint social identity) is an important basis for effective leadership (e.g., Fransen, Haslam, et al., 2015; Slater & Barker, 2019). Before going into this aspect, the authors will first elaborate on the concept of leadership in sports teams.

Leadership in Sports

What turns some sports teams into perpetual champions and others into perennial runners-up? Researchers suggest that, besides having a shared social identity, leadership is another key factor that contributes to competitive advantage (Mallett & Lara-Bercial, 2016). In this contribution, the authors focus on two sources of leadership that are inherently associated with the sports team itself, namely the coach of the team and athletes within the team who take up important leadership roles (e.g., captains, vice-captains, informal leaders).

Coaches

Decades of research has produced a significant body of evidence indicating that coaches, being the formal leaders of their teams, are important drivers of the team's functioning and the team's success (Horn, 2008). More specifically, it has been reported that high-quality coaches had the capacities to strengthen players' identification with their team, as well as improving their perceptions of the team's cohesion (De Backer et al., 2011; Fransen, Decroos, et al., 2016). Furthermore, high-quality coaches succeeded in increasing their players' confidence in the team's abilities (Hampson & Jowett, 2014), engaging them in proactive behaviour (Van Puyenbroeck, Stouten, & Vande Broek, 2018), and nurturing their competence satisfaction, their intrinsic motivation, and ultimately also their performance (Fransen, Boen, Vansteenkiste, Mertens, & Vande Broek, 2018; Mertens, Boen, Vande Broek, Vansteenkiste, & Fransen, 2018). Research evidence also indicates that athletes who feel a strong psychological connection with their coach engage in more discretionary effort (Slater, Turner, Evans, & Jones, 2018) than those who to feel a poor connection with their coach.

Athlete Leaders

Although most research on leadership in sport has focused on the coach as formal leader of the team, in the last decade, a range of scholars have revealed that players within the team can also fulfil important leadership roles and as such become essential drivers of the team success (Cotterill & Fransen, 2016). Building upon a previous definition of leadership by Northouse (2010), Loughead, Hardy, and Eys (2006) defined athlete leadership as 'an athlete occupying a formal or informal role within a team who influences a group of team members (i.e., a minimum of two team members) to achieve a common goal' (p. 144). Important to note from this definition is that athlete leaders thus can be formally appointed as leader (e.g., as team captain), but can also gain their leadership status in an informal way through interactions with their teammates.

Besides this formal/informal distinction, we can also categorize athlete leaders depending on the leadership role they occupy. Further extending upon earlier leadership categorizations (Loughead et al., 2006; Rees & Segal, 1984), the most recent leadership classification distinguishes between four leadership roles athletes can occupy (Fransen, Vanbeselaere, De Cuyper, Vande Broek, & Boen, 2014). Two of these leadership roles are on-field roles, including the 'task leader', who masters the game plan and provides tactical advice, and the 'motivational leader', who motivates his or her teammates to perform at their best. Two leadership roles are off-field roles, including the 'social leader', who cultivates a positive team atmosphere, and the 'external leader', who represents the team in interactions with external parties (e.g., media).

A quickly growing research body has evidenced that effective athlete leaders can be a critical predictor of team success. To illustrate, teams having high-quality athlete leadership in the team also demonstrate greater resilience as a team when facing setbacks (Morgan, Fletcher, & Sarkar, 2013), greater task and social cohesion (Loughead, Fransen, Van Puyenbroeck, Hoffmann, & Boen, 2016; Price & Weiss, 2011), improved health and reduced feelings of burnout (Fransen et al., 2020b), and, ultimately, a better team performance (Crozier, Loughead, & Munroe-Chandler, 2013; Fransen et al., 2017).

Furthermore, experimental evidence reveals that athlete leaders who express high team confidence and provide positive feedback to their teammates can instigate a confidence contagion that quickly spreads throughout the team; the other team members will show higher confidence in their team, become more intrinsically motivated, exert more effort, and, ultimately, perform better (Fransen, Boen, et al., 2018; Fransen, Haslam, et al., 2015; Fransen, Steffens, et al., 2016; Fransen, Vansteenkiste, Vande Broek, & Boen, 2018). It should be noted, though, that leaders have the potential not only to make, but also to break, their teams. The above studies also reveal that a negative attitude shown by the leader, accompanied by competence-thwarting feedback (e.g., negative dressing-room banter), quickly infects the entire team, as a consequence of which teammates' confidence and motivation decline, and their performance deteriorates.

The fact that athlete leaders can not only make, but also break, a team emphasizes how essential it is to choose your athlete leaders wisely. Previous researchers have revealed that coaches do not always think this decision through. More specifically, with respect to the appointment of team captains, it was shown that, in contrast to the expectations of most athletes and coaches, the captains excelled in each of the four leadership roles in only 1% of the teams (Fransen, Vanbeselaere, et al., 2014). Even more noteworthy was that, in more than half of the teams, the team captain was not seen as best leader in any of these four roles, either on the field or off the field. It seems that coaches often rely on attributes not related to leadership, such as team tenure, age, or relations with sponsor or club management, to assign their captain (Fransen, Vanbeselaere, De Cuyper, Vande Broek, & Boen, 2018).

To overcome these barriers and appoint the best leaders in the team, it is essential to know what it is that makes leaders turn into great leaders. In this regard, a large cross-sectional study identifying the core traits and behaviours of high-quality athlete leaders (i.e., athletes who are perceived as very good leaders by their teammates) revealed that providing identity leadership is a key attribute that distinguishes the high-quality athlete leaders from their teammates (Fransen, Boen, Haslam, Steffens, & Vande Broek, 2020). This brings us back to the social identity approach and how this theory provides the perfect platform for effective leadership.

Leaders Cultivating the Social Identity

The social identity approach to leadership asserts that leaders are able to exert influence on team members (i.e., making them want to contribute to the achievement of shared goals) to the extent that they manage—that is create, embody, advance, and embed—a collective sense of 'us' (Platow, Haslam, Reicher, & Steffens, 2015; Steffens, Haslam, Reicher, et al., 2014). In sports terms, and in line with the previous quote from Gareth Southgate, this means that successful leaders cause athletes to think, feel, and behave as members of their sports team (i.e., as 'we' and 'us', in terms of their social identity), rather than as separate individuals (i.e., as 'I' and 'me', in terms of their personal identity).

Whereas earlier research on social identity leadership—shortened to identity leadership in this contribution—has focused primarily on identity prototypicality (i.e., the extent to which leaders are seen as being representative—or prototypical—of the groups they are leading;

Hogg, 2001; van Knippenberg, 2011), more recently, scholars have distinguished between four dimensions of effective identity leadership (Steffens, Haslam, Reicher, et al., 2014; van Dick et al., 2018). First, leaders need to be in-group prototypes (i.e., represent the unique qualities that define the group and what it means to be a group member). Second, leaders need to be in-group champions (i.e., advance and promote the core interests of the group). Third, leaders need to be entrepreneurs of identity (i.e., bring people together to create a shared sense of 'we' and 'us' within the group). Fourth and finally, leaders need to be embedders of identity (i.e., develop structures that facilitate and embed shared understanding, coordination, and success). In other words, leaders need not only to be 'one of us' (i.e., identity prototypicality), but also to 'do it for us' (i.e., identity advancement), to craft a sense of 'us' (i.e., identity entrepreneurship), and to make 'us' matter (i.e., identity impresarioship).

A large body of research in the organizational context testifies to the impact of leaders who succeed in creating, embodying, advancing, and embedding such a sense of 'we' and 'us', not only on team effectiveness (e.g., Haslam, Reicher, & Platow, 2011), but also on team members' health and well-being (Steffens, Haslam, Kerschreiter, Schuh, & Van Dick, 2014; Steffens et al., 2017; van Dick & Haslam, 2012). Despite this relatively long history in organizational research, only in the last decade has the social identity approach to leadership entered the sports arena. To illustrate, successful performance directors in the London 2012 Olympic Games were shown to mobilize their team members by consistently communicating a positive, distinctive, and enduring sense of social identity in their media communication (Slater, Barker, Coffee, & Jones, 2015). Not only performance directors, but also coaches and athlete leaders benefit from becoming cultural architects. By cultivating a sense of 'we' and 'us' in their team, coaches and athlete leaders can create an important leverage to enhance the team's functioning.

Coaches as Cultural Architects

Evidence has indicated that athletes' perceptions of their psychological connection (or the lack of such connection) with their coach has important motivational ramifications. To illustrate the influence of this relational identity aspect, Slater, Turner, et al. (2018) found that athletes were more mobilized towards a task to the extent that they felt a high (vs. low) level of connection with a hypothetical coach. In percentage terms, athletes were willing to practise on a task related to the coach's vision for 18.7% longer when feeling closely connected to the leader. Moreover, if that coach demonstrated identity leadership (e.g., had strong psychological connections with their team), athletes' intentions (i.e., what they were willing to do) and their effort increased even more. Additional evidence has demonstrated that, in addition, the creation of shared (vs. non-shared) values between leaders and followers further increased group members' behavioural motivation (Slater, Coffee, Barker, Haslam, & Steffens, 2019). Earlier research adds that, by creating this sense of 'we' and 'us', coaches not only strengthened athletes' motivation and effort, but also succeeded in building a stronger team confidence and team cohesion within their teams (Fransen, Decroos, et al., 2016). Recent research by Stevens, Rees, and Polman (2019) corroborated these findings not only in sports settings, but also in exercise settings. Their findings evidenced that leaders who represent, advance, create, and embed a shared sense of identity (i.e., a shared sense of 'us') among attendees promoted their participation in sport and exercise classes.

Athlete Leaders as Cultural Architects

Evidence reveals that not only coaches, but also leaders within the team (i.e., athlete leaders) benefit from cultivating a collective sense of 'us'. In this vein, Steffens, Haslam, Reicher, et al.

(2014) demonstrated that the four identity leadership dimensions of a team captain (i.e., identity prototypicality, advancement, entrepreneurship, and impresarioship) each had a unique contribution to different leadership outcomes. For example, while team captains' prototypicality predicted their influence (as perceived by teammates), their identity advancement skills predicted team members' team confidence; captains' identity entrepreneurship fostered the team identification in the team; and captains' impresarioship strengthened the team's task cohesion. Considering identity leadership in general, research further corroborated that athlete leaders' capacity to cultivate a shared sense of 'we' and 'us' within the team has been found to underpin their impact on the team's effectiveness (Fransen, Coffee, et al., 2014; Fransen, Decroos, et al., 2016; Fransen, Haslam, et al., 2015; Fransen, Steffens, et al., 2016; Slater et al., 2019), as well as their impact on the health and well-being of their team members (Fransen et al., 2020b).

Leadership Development Programmes Targeting Social Identity

The evidence outlined above clearly speaks to the importance of embracing an identity leadership approach, not only for coaches, but also for athlete leaders. Therefore, an important next step is to know how to teach leaders in sports teams to cultivate such sense of 'we' and 'us'. This question brings us to the final part of this contribution, namely the leadership development programmes specifically targeting these identity leadership skills. Despite the large body of evidence supporting the benefits of identity leadership, the application of this social identity theorizing to the practice of leadership training and development has been sparse. Two reasons might explain this lack in identity leadership programmes.

First, for a long time there were no validated instruments that could be used by practitioners to assess the identity leadership in the field (Haslam et al., 2017). Recently, however, the Identity Leadership Inventory (ILI; Steffens, Haslam, Reicher, et al., 2014) addressed this problem and provided a validated instrument to measure the extent to which leaders were able to create, advance, represent, and embed a shared social identity in their teams. This ILI has been validated across 20 different countries (van Dick et al., 2018).

A second and more fundamental reason for the lack of identity leadership programmes is that, for a long time, the sports context relied on more individual-oriented theories to explain athletes' behaviours and team outcomes (e.g., self-determination approach and achievement goal theory). Although these individual-oriented approaches have their merit, a lot of sports are practised in groups. A more recent theory such as the social identity approach, which captures the group as its centre of analysis, has, therefore, the potential to provide new insights to understand sports phenomena. Indeed, in the last decade, scholars have revealed that the widely evidenced benefits of the group-oriented social identity approach in organizational contexts also held in the sports arena (Rees et al., 2015). As a result, a few scholars have initiated the development of identity leadership programmes, thereby relying on the earlier developments in the organizational contexts, which we will discuss first.

Inspired by Organizational Research: The 5R Programme

To translate social identity theorizing into organizational practice, Haslam et al. (2017) further built on the earlier ASPIRe model (actualizing social and personal identity resources; Haslam, Eggins, & Reynolds, 2003; Peters, Haslam, Ryan, & Fonseca, 2013). More specifically, the authors argued that, to develop and manage identity effectively (i.e., to master the art of identity leadership), leaders have to take their teams through five phases: (1) readying session in which team members are educated about the importance of group and social identity processes for leadership and organizational behaviour; (2) reflecting on the nature of identities that are important for members of a given organization; (3) representing what those identities are about; and (4) realizing the identity-related ambitions of group members. A final reporting session that assesses progress towards relevant goals concludes the 5R programme. The first application of this programme with managers of Allied Health teams showed promising results. More specifically, the leaders participating in this programme experienced significant increases in their ability to engage in identity leadership and had an increased sense of procedural justice, team goal clarity, and team identification (Haslam et al., 2017).

Embracing a social identity leadership approach is advocated to lead to enhanced team effectiveness in both organizations and sports teams. This is not surprising given that previous research already emphasized that the principles of elite performance in sport are easily transferable to the business context, and also that sport has a considerable amount to learn from excellence in business (Fletcher, 2011; Wagstaff, 2017). Given the similar structure of organizations and sports teams (i.e., one hierarchical leader leading a team with clear performance-driven aims), the 5R programme has inspired the recent application of similar leadership programmes in the sports context.

Identity Leadership Development in the Sports Arena

Slater and Barker (2019) were the first to apply the three core phases of the 5R programme within an international disability sports team. To involve both coaches and athletes, the authors delivered the sessions to a senior leadership team, which included three members of the staff and four athletes (chosen by the staff). The senior leadership team was then asked to complete these activities with the wider team. Compared with baseline, data following the intervention indicated medium-to-large effect size increases in the strength of athletes' identification with their sports team (although only being statistically significant in the second year). The same increases were seen in athletes' perceptions of staff as identity leaders from pre- to post-programme. There were no increases in athletes' reported mobilization of effort, but there were marginal increases in the number of hours of practice athletes completed away from camps in the first and second years. The similar pattern of results seen in both years bolsters confidence in the application of the identity leadership programme in elite sporting environments, particularly in developing a team's sense of 'us'.

Where Slater and Barker (2019) focused on the senior leadership team (in which four athletes were selected by the coaching staff) for the delivery of the programme, the recent 5R^S Shared Leadership programme (5R^S) of Fransen et al. (2020a) aimed for a more in-depth integration of the implementation of a shared leadership structure and the identity leadership development of the appointed athlete leaders. First, to implement an effective structure of shared leadership, the authors chose to appoint the athletes who were perceived as best leaders by their team members. Having the staff appointing the leaders entails the risk that, when these leaders are not perceived as good leaders by their team members, team members will not be inclined to follow their guidance, and the team's leadership will not be effective. Therefore, the shared leadership mapping approach used in the 5R^S programme relied on social network analysis to take into account all team members' perceptions of the leadership qualities of all their teammates, not only on, but also off, the field. Based on all the resulting insights, athlete leaders were appointed to four different leadership roles: task, motivational, social, and external leadership (Fransen, Van Puyenbroeck, et al., 2015). To ensure continuity of leadership and to share the burden of leadership, shared leadership was applied not only across the different leadership roles, but also within each role (e.g., having multiple task leaders).

After implementing a shared leadership structure, the appointed athlete leaders then guide their team throughout the 5R phases, with a twofold aim: (1) by doing so, this process will strengthen leaders' identity leadership skills and, hence, will improve their perceived leadership quality; and (2) by crafting a shared sense of 'we' and 'us', they also create a lever to reach other important outcomes, such as increased team confidence, strengthened team cohesion, and improved performance. An important difference from the earlier described programme of Slater and Barker (2019) is that the workshops are delivered to the entire team, instead of only to the athlete leaders. In this way, all team members can provide input in the different phases, which maximizes the chances that all the resulting values, goals, and strategies will be truly shared by the entire team. The appointed leaders do get special responsibilities within the session and even more so in the follow-up, so that they can develop their leadership qualities.

The authors will shortly highlight the sport-specific content of the 5R phases. After informing participants why having a shared identity is important (i.e., readying phase), team members reflect on the core values of their team (i.e., reflecting phase). Also, they are asked to assemble these values in a trademark. Visualizing this trademark in the environment (e.g., in the dressing room, on T-shirts, in a yell) is a powerful reminder for the players about what is connecting them as a team. In the next, representing, phase, team members are asked to put this identity into practice by suggesting specific goals for the four aspects: task, motivational, social, and external goals. In the following, realizing, phase, team members concretize these goals even further by devising concrete strategies to reach each of the goals and by reflecting about possible hindrances or barriers that might get in the way (e.g., integrating new players by organizing social activities for the entire team or by appointing a senior player to each junior player to provide them with advice and guidance). The appointed leaders are given the responsibility to form an overview of the resulting goals and strategies for their specific role and are in charge of the follow-up afterwards. The final, reporting, phase, which follows after a few months, is designed to map the progress of the team on the different goals, to adjust the strategies if barriers have arisen, or, ideally, to design new goals if the previous ones have been achieved. As such, the feedback raised in this final phase provides the input to start the 5R process all over again, thereby transforming it into a cyclic process aimed at continuous improvement of the team functioning.

The initial implementation of this $5R^S$ programme within both an organizational and a sports team has revealed promising qualitative results (Fransen et al., 2020a). Further, Mertens et al. (2020) corroborated these findings by an intervention study in eight basketball teams, where four teams received the $5R^S$ programme (i.e., implementation of a shared leadership structure through the appointing of athlete leaders, followed by delivery of the 5R phases), and four teams served as control group. The teams who followed the $5R^S$ programme indeed reported that their athlete leaders demonstrated more identity leadership. Furthermore, the players in this condition identified more strongly with their team, were more intrinsically motivated, were more committed to the team goals, and even felt healthier than athletes in the control group.

Conclusion

Initial applications of the identity leadership programmes revealed promising results, in both qualitative and quantitative ways (Fransen et al., 2020a; Mertens et al., 2020; Slater & Barker, 2019). Nevertheless, it is important for future researchers to continue the validation and further optimization of these programmes in different types of sport, with male and female athletes, and at all levels of competition. Also, it would be interesting to conduct in-depth investigations to explore the precise elements of the identity leadership programmes that are perceived to be positively impactful. In this regard, deeper insight could be retrieved through intervention studies in which the different phases of the leadership programme are applied in different conditions (e.g., implementing a shared leadership structure vs. reflecting on a joint identity vs. putting this identity into practice by setting goals). Furthermore, as the effectiveness might vary from team to team, single-case research designs could help us to gain more insight into the idiosyncratic changes in social identity leadership interventions.

Furthermore, a fruitful avenue for future researchers would be to more broadly translate and apply the principles of social identity theorizing in leadership programmes in other settings. In this vein, research has established the importance of social identity in physical exercise contexts such as park runs (Stevens et al., 2017, 2019). Researchers could further capitalize on these results by designing intervention programmes that specifically strengthen people's identification with their exercise groups.

A final avenue for future researchers would be to provide more insight into the cross-cultural validity of the existing identity leadership programmes. Although previous research in sport psychology highlighted the important differences in sporting behaviours across cultures (Ryba, Stambulova, Si, & Schinke, 2013; Si & Lee, 2007), we have to note that both the 5R and the $5R^S$ programmes have been developed and tested only in Western cultures. When examining the applicability to other cultures, we have to consider the two key facets of the $5R^S$ programme—namely, the focus on strengthening the team's shared identity and the implementation of a shared leadership structure. With respect to shared identity, we could argue that the above programmes might even be more effective in collectivistic cultures (e.g., China), where the importance of the group and its needs and goals are much more essential than in individualistic cultures (e.g., US), where self-interests often have the upper hand.

With respect to the component of shared leadership, on the other hand, the effectiveness of shared leadership might be limited in collectivistic cultures, owing to the cultural element of power distance (Conger & Pearce, 2003). Power distance refers to the degree to which members of a culture accept and expect power in society to be distributed unequally (Hofstede, 2001). Whereas people in cultures low in power distance (e.g., Western societies) prefer less hierarchical leadership and more shared leadership, cultures high in power distance (e.g., Eastern cultures) will rather value and respect authority. Based on these findings, we might expect that teams in low power distance cultures will be more effective when leadership is shared, whereas teams in high power distance cultures might be more effective when hierarchically structured (Conger & Pearce, 2003). Given these assumed contrasting effects in different cultures, it is important that future research can provide more insight into the validity and effectiveness of the described identity leadership programmes across cultures.

We can conclude that the broadly evidenced advantages of providing identity leadership clearly speak to the benefits that (at least Western) coaches and athlete leaders could gain when following the described programmes. By learning how to create and cultivate a sense of 'we' and 'us' in their teams, coaches and athlete leaders not only become better leaders themselves, but also build their capacity to draw on this collective strength, thereby allowing ordinary sports teams to attain extraordinary results.

References

Ajzen, I. (1991). The theory of planned behavior. *Organizational Behavior and Human Decision Processes, 50*(2), 179–211. doi:10.1016/0749-5978(91)90020-T

Bruner, M. W., Balish, S. M., Forrest, C., Brown, S., Webber, K., Gray, E., ... Shields, C. A. (2017). Ties that bond: Youth sport as a vehicle for social identity and positive youth development. *Research Quarterly for Exercise and Sport, 88*(2), 209–214. doi:10.1080/02701367.2017.1296100

Conger, J. A., & Pearce, C. L. (2003). A landscape of opportunities: Future research on shared leadership. In J. A. Conger & C. L. Pearce (Eds.), *Shared leadership: Reframing the hows and whys of leadership* (pp. 285–304). Thousand Oaks, CA: Sage.

Cotterill, S. T., & Fransen, K. (2016). Athlete leadership in sport teams: Current understanding and future directions. *International Review of Sport and Exercise Psychology, 9*(1), 116–133. doi:10.1080/1750984X.2015.1124443

Crozier, A. J., Loughead, T. M., & Munroe-Chandler, K. J. (2013). Examining the benefits of athlete leaders in sport. *Journal of Sport Behavior, 36*(4), 346–364.

Cruwys, T., Haslam, S. A., Dingle, G. A., Haslam, C., & Jetten, J. (2014). Depression and social identity: An integrative review. *Personality and Social Psychology Review, 18*(3), 215–238. doi:10.1177/1088868314523839

De Backer, M., Boen, F., Ceux, T., De Cuyper, B., Hoigaard, R., Callens, F., … Vande Broek, G. (2011). Do perceived justice and need support of the coach predict team identification and cohesion? Testing their relative importance among top volleyball and handball players in Belgium and Norway. *Psychology of Sport and Exercise, 12*(2), 192–201. doi:10.1016/j.psychsport.2010.09.009

De Cuyper, B., Boen, F., Van Beirendonck, C., Vanbeselaere, N., & Fransen, K. (2016). When do elite cyclists go the extra mile? Team identification mediates the relationship between perceived leadership qualities of the captain and social laboring. *International Journal of Sport Psychology, 47*(4), 355–372. doi:10.7352/IJSP 2016.47

Deci, E. L., & Ryan, R. M. (1985). *Intrinsic motivation and self-determination in human behavior.* New York: Plenum.

Ellemers, N., Spears, R., & Doosje, B. (1997). Sticking together or falling apart: In-group identification as a psychological determinant of group commitment versus individual mobility. *Journal of Personality and Social Psychology, 72*(3), 617–626. doi:10.1037/0022-3514.72.3.617

Fletcher, D. (2011). Applying sport psychology in business: A narrative commentary and bibliography. *Journal of Sport Psychology in Action, 1*(3), 139–149. doi:10.1080/21520704.2010.546496

Fransen, K., Boen, F., Haslam, S. A., Steffens, N. K., & Vande Broek, G. (2020). Standing out from the crowd: Identifying the traits and behaviors that characterize high-quality athlete leaders on and off the field. *Scandinavian Journal of Medicine and Science in Sports*, In press. doi:10.1111/sms.13620.

Fransen, K., Boen, F., Vansteenkiste, M., Mertens, N., & Vande Broek, G. (2018). The power of competence support: The impact of coaches and athlete leaders on intrinsic motivation and performance. *Scandinavian Journal of Medicine and Science in Sports, 28,* 725–745. doi:10.1111/sms.12950

Fransen, K., Coffee, P., Vanbeselaere, N., Slater, M., De Cuyper, B., & Boen, F. (2014). The impact of athlete leaders on team members' team outcome confidence: A test of mediation by team identification and collective efficacy. *The Sport Psychologist, 28*(4), 347–360. doi:10.1123/tspp.2013-0141

Fransen, K., Decroos, S., Vande Broek, G., & Boen, F. (2016). Leading from the top or leading from within? A comparison between coaches' and athletes' leadership as predictors of team identification, team confidence, and team cohesion. *International Journal of Sports Science & Coaching, 11*(6), 757–771. doi:10.1177/1747954116676102

Fransen, K., Haslam, S. A., Mallett, C. J., Steffens, N. K., Peters, K., & Boen, F. (2017). Is perceived athlete leadership quality related to team effectiveness? A comparison of three professional sports teams. *Journal of Science and Medicine in Sport, 20,* 800–806. doi:10.1016/j.jsams.2016.11.024

Fransen, K., Haslam, S. A., Steffens, N., Mallett, C., Peters, K., & Boen, F. (2020a). *All for us and us for all: Introducing the 5R Shared Leadership Program.* Manuscript submitted for publication.

Fransen, K., Haslam, S. A., Steffens, N. K., Mallett, C., Peters, K., & Boen, F. (2020b). Making 'us' better: High-quality athlete leadership relates to health and burnout in professional Australian football teams. *European Journal of Sport Science*, In press. doi:10.1080/17461391.2019.1680736.

Fransen, K., Haslam, S. A., Steffens, N. K., Vanbeselaere, N., De Cuyper, B., & Boen, F. (2015). Believing in us: Exploring leaders' capacity to enhance team confidence and performance by building a sense of shared social identity. *Journal of Experimental Psychology: Applied, 21*(1), 89–100. doi:10.1037/xap0000033

Fransen, K., Steffens, N. K., Haslam, S. A., Vanbeselaere, N., Vande Broek, G., & Boen, F. (2016). We will be champions: Leaders' confidence in 'us' inspires team members' team confidence and performance. *Scandinavian Journal of Medicine and Science in Sports, 26*(12), 1455–1469. doi:10.1111/sms.12603

Fransen, K., Van Puyenbroeck, S., Loughead, T. M., Vanbeselaere, N., De Cuyper, B., Vande Broek, G., & Boen, F. (2015). Who takes the lead? Social network analysis as pioneering tool to investigate shared leadership within sports teams. *Social Networks, 43*, 28–38. doi:10.1016/j.socnet.2015.04.003

Fransen, K., Vanbeselaere, N., De Cuyper, B., Vande Broek, G., & Boen, F. (2014). The myth of the team captain as principal leader: Extending the athlete leadership classification within sport teams. *Journal of Sports Sciences, 32*(14), 1389–1397. doi:10.1080/02640414.2014.891291

Fransen, K., Vanbeselaere, N., De Cuyper, B., Vande Broek, G., & Boen, F. (2018). When is a leader considered as a good leader? Perceived impact on teammates' confidence and social acceptance as key ingredients. *International Journal of Psychology Research, 12*(1), 1–21.

Fransen, K., Vansteenkiste, M., Vande Broek, G., & Boen, F. (2018). The competence-supportive and competence-thwarting role of athlete leaders: An experimental test in a soccer context. *PLoS ONE, 13*(7), e0200480. doi:10.1371/journal.pone.0200480

Hampson, R., & Jowett, S. (2014). Effects of coach leadership and coach- athlete relationship on collective efficacy. *Scandinavian Journal of Medicine and Science in Sports, 24*(2), 454–460. doi:10.1111/j.1600-0838.2012.01527.x

Haslam, S. A. (2004). *Psychology in organizations: The social identity approach* (2nd ed.). London: Sage.

Haslam, S. A., Eggins, R. A., & Reynolds, K. J. (2003). The ASPIRe model: Actualizing social and personal identity resources to enhance organizational outcomes. *Journal of Occupational and Organizational Psychology, 76*, 83–113. doi:10.1348/096317903321208907

Haslam, S. A., Reicher, S. D., & Platow, M. J. (2011). *The new psychology of leadership: Identity, influence and power.* New York: Psychology Press.

Haslam, S. A., Steffens, N. K., Peters, K., Boyce, R. A., Mallett, C. J., & Fransen, K. (2017). A social identity approach to leadership development: The 5R program. *Journal of Personnel Psychology, 16*(3), 113–124. doi:10.1027/1866-5888/a000176

Hofstede, G. (2001). *Culture's consequences: Comparing values, behaviors, institutions, and organizations across nations* (2nd ed.). Thousand Oaks, CA: Sage.

Hogg, M. A. (2001). From prototypicality to power: A social identity analysis of leadership. In S. R. Thye & E. Lawler (Eds.), *Advances in group processes* (Vol. 18, pp. 1–30). Bingley, UK: Emerald.

Horn, T. S. (2008). Coaching effectiveness in the sport domain. In T. S. Horn (Ed.), *Advances in sport psychology* (pp. 239–267). Champaign, IL: Human Kinetics.

Lee, E. S., Park, T. Y., & Koo, B. (2015). Identifying organizational identification as a basis for attitudes and behaviors: A meta-analytic review. *Psychological Bulletin, 141*(5), 1049–1080. doi:10.1037/bul0000012

Loughead, T. M., Fransen, K., Van Puyenbroeck, S., Hoffmann, M. D., & Boen, F. (2016). An examination of the relationship between athlete leadership and cohesion using social network analysis. *Journal of Sports Sciences, 34*(21), 2063–2073. doi:10.1080/02640414.2016.1150601

Loughead, T. M., Hardy, J., & Eys, M. A. (2006). The nature of athlete leadership. *Journal of Sport Behavior, 29*, 142–158.

Mallett, C. J., & Lara-Bercial, S. (2016). Serial winning coaches: People, vision and environment. In M. Raab, P. Wylleman, R. Seiler, A.-M. Elbe, & A. Hatzigeorgiadis (Eds.), *Sport and exercise psychology research: Theory to practice* (pp. 289–322). Amsterdam: Elsevier.

Martin, L. J., Balderson, D., Hawkins, M., Wilson, K., & Bruner, M. W. (2017). Groupness and leadership perceptions in relation to social identity in youth sport. *Journal of Applied Sport Psychology, 29*(3), 367–374. doi:10.1080/10413200.2016.1238414

Mertens, N., Boen, F., Steffens, N. K., Cotterill, S. T., Haslam, S. A., & Fransen, K. (2020). Leading together towards a stronger 'us': An experimental test of the effectiveness of the 5R Shared Leadership Program in basketball teams. *Journal of Science and Medicine in Sport,* Manuscript accepted for publication.

Mertens, N., Boen, F., Vande Broek, G., Vansteenkiste, M., & Fransen, K. (2018). An experiment on the impact of coaches' and athlete leaders' competence support on athletes' motivation and performance. *Scandinavian Journal of Medicine and Science in Sports, 12*, 2734–2750. doi:10.1111/sms.13273

Morgan, P. B. C., Fletcher, D., & Sarkar, M. (2013). Defining and characterizing team resilience in elite sport. *Psychology of Sport and Exercise, 14*(4), 549–559. doi:10.1016/j.psychsport.2013.01.004

Ng, T. W. H. (2015). The incremental validity of organizational commitment, organizational trust, and organizational identification. *Journal of Vocational Behavior, 88*, 154–163. doi:10.1016/j.jvb.2015.03.003

Northouse, P. G. (2010). *Leadership: Theory and practice* (5th ed.). Thousand Oaks, CA: Sage.

Peters, K., Haslam, S. A., Ryan, M. K., & Fonseca, M. (2013). Working with subgroup identities to build organizational identification and support for organizational strategy: A test of the ASPIRe model. *Group & Organization Management*. doi:10.1177/1059601112472368

Platow, M. J., Haslam, S. A., Reicher, S. D., & Steffens, N. K. (2015). There is no leadership if no-one follows: Why leadership is necessarily a group process. *International Coaching Psychology Review, 10*(1), 20–37.

Price, M. S., & Weiss, M. R. (2011). Peer leadership in sport: Relationships among personal characteristics, leader behaviors, and team outcomes. *Journal of Applied Sport Psychology, 23*(1), 49–64. doi:10.1080/10413200.2010.520300

Rees, C. R., & Segal, M. W. (1984). Role differentiation in groups: The relationship between instrumental and expressive leadership. *Small Group Behavior, 15*(1), 109–123.

Rees, T., Haslam, S. A., Coffee, P., & Lavallee, D. (2015). A social identity approach to sport psychology: Principles, practice, and prospects. *Sports Medicine, 45*(8), 1083–1096. doi:10.1007/s40279-015-0345-4

Ryba, T. V., Stambulova, N. B., Si, G., & Schinke, R. J. (2013). ISSP position stand: Culturally competent research and practice in sport and exercise psychology. *International Journal of Sport and Exercise Psychology, 11*(2), 123–142. doi:10.1080/1612197X.2013.779812

Si, G., & Lee, H. (2007). *Cross-cultural issues in sport psychology research* (pp. 279–288). Champaign, IL: Human Kinetics.

Slater, M. J., & Barker, J. B. (2019). Doing social identity leadership: Exploring the efficacy of an identity leadership intervention on perceived leadership and mobilization in elite disability soccer. *Journal of Applied Sport Psychology, 31*(1), 65–86. doi:10.1080/10413200.2017.1410255

Slater, M. J., Barker, J. B., Coffee, P., & Jones, M. V. (2015). Leading for gold: Social identity leadership processes at the London 2012 Olympic Games. *Qualitative Research in Sport, Exercise and Health, 7*(2), 192–209. doi:10.1080/2159676X.2014.936030

Slater, M. J., Coffee, P., Barker, J. B., Haslam, S. A., & Steffens, N. K. (2019). Shared social identity content is the basis for leaders' mobilization of followers. *Psychology of Sport and Exercise, 43*, 271–278. doi:10.1016/j.psychsport.2019.03.012

Slater, M. J., Haslam, S. A., & Steffens, N. K. (2018). Singing it for "us": Team passion displayed during national anthems is associated with subsequent success. *European Journal of Sport Science, 18*(4), 541–549. doi:10.1080/17461391.2018.1431311

Slater, M. J., Turner, M. J., Evans, A. L., & Jones, M. V. (2018). Capturing hearts and minds: The influence of relational identification with the leader on followers' mobilization and cardiovascular reactivity. *The Leadership Quarterly, 29*(3), 379–388. doi:10.1016/j.leaqua.2017.08.003

Steffens, N. K., Haslam, S. A., Kerschreiter, R., Schuh, S. C., & Van Dick, R. (2014). Leaders enhance group members' work engagement and reduce their burnout by crafting social identity. *German Journal of Research in Human Resource Management, 28*(1–2), 173–194. doi:10.1688/ZfP-2014-01-Steffens

Steffens, N. K., Haslam, S. A., Reicher, S. D., Platow, M. J., Fransen, K., Yang, J., … Boen, F. (2014). Leadership as social identity management: Introducing the Identity Leadership Inventory (ILI) to assess and validate a four-dimensional model. *The Leadership Quarterly, 25*, 1001–1024. doi:10.1016/j.leaqua.2014.05.002

Steffens, N. K., Haslam, S. A., Schuh, S. C., Jetten, J., & van Dick, R. (2017). A meta-analytic review of social identification and health in organizational contexts. *Personality and Social Psychology Review, 21*(4), 303–335. doi:10.1177/1088868316656701

Stevens, M., Rees, T., Coffee, P., Steffens, N. K., Haslam, S. A., & Polman, R. (2017). A social identity approach to understanding and promoting physical activity. *Sports Medicine*. doi:10.1007/s40279-017-0720-4

Stevens, M., Rees, T., & Polman, R. (2019). Social identification, exercise participation, and positive exercise experiences: Evidence from parkrun. *Journal of Sports Sciences, 37*(2), 221–228. doi:10.1080/02640414.2018.1489360

Tajfel, H., & Turner, J. C. (1979). An integrative theory of intergroup conflict. In W. G. Austin & S. Worchel (Eds.), *The social psychology of intergroup relations* (pp. 33–47). Monterey, CA: Brooks-Cole.

Taylor, D. (2018). England delirium has Gareth Southgate and his tyros dreaming big. *The Guardian*. Retrieved from www.theguardian.com/football/2018/jul/08/england-gareth-southgate-semi-final

van Dick, R., & Haslam, S. A. (2012). Stress and well-being in the workplace: Support for key propositions from the social identity approach. In J. Jetten, C. Haslam, & S. A. Haslam (Eds.), *The social cure: Identity, health and well-being* (pp. 175–194). Hove and New York: Psychology Press.

van Dick, R., Lemoine, J. E., Steffens, N. K., Kerschreiter, R., Akfirat, S. A., Avanzi, L., ... Haslam, S. A. (2018). Identity leadership going global: Validation of the Identity Leadership Inventory (ILI) across 20 countries. *Journal of Occupational and Organizational Psychology, 91*, 697–728. doi:10.1111/joop.12223

van Knippenberg, D. (2011). Embodying who we are: Leader group prototypicality and leadership effectiveness. *Leadership Quarterly, 22*(6), 1078–1091. doi:10.1016/j.leaqua.2011.09.004

Van Puyenbroeck, S., Stouten, J., & Vande Broek, G. (2018). Coaching is teamwork! The role of need-supportive coaching and the motivational climate in stimulating proactivity in volleyball teams. *Scandinavian Journal of Medicine and Science in Sports, 28*(1), 319–328.

Wagstaff, C. R. D. (Ed.). (2017). *The organizational psychology of sport: Key issues and practical applications*. New York: Routledge.

18

MEASUREMENT QUALITY

Eva Pila, Mark G. Epp, and Kent C. Kowalski

Introduction

Evaluating measurement quality in sport psychology is intimately tied to the matter of research quality, as measurement does not occur in a vacuum independent from the researcher and the researched. This consideration of measurement quality is shaped from a realist ontological stance with a post-positive epistemology. As an example, Messick (1989a) intentionally used terms such as "scores" and "measurements", rather than "tests", as a way to recognize that it is only the responses to tests that have reliabilities and validities, but not the tests themselves. He stated that, "this is an important point because test responses are a function not only of the items, tasks, or stimulus conditions but of the persons responding and the context of measurement" (p. 14). The implication is that we cannot adequately discuss measurement quality without understanding the context within which the research takes place, as well as the quality of the research design.

Complicating matters further is that questions of measurement quality (and, more broadly, questions of research validity) vary greatly depending on whether the research uses a quantitative or qualitative approach. Quantitative and qualitative research approaches differ substantially in the underlying assumptions of the research, the types of question that are asked, the specific methods used by the researcher(s), and subsequently the types of measurement that might (or might not) be appropriate (Kowalski, McHugh, Sabiston, & Ferguson, 2018). Hence, to talk about measurement quality first requires a broader understanding of the concept of "quality" within the various research approaches used in sport psychology.

The concept of measurement quality most suitably aligns with a quantitative approach to research, whereby the goal is to obtain numerical (i.e., quantitative) data. Indeed, this quantitative approach is consistent with the underlying purpose of most forms of measurement in sport psychology research. For example, Brown, Arnold, Standage, and Fletcher (2017) were interested in knowing whether or not there are different responses to competitive encounters in sport from performers who thrive and those who do not thrive. To, in part, assess the construct of "thriving", participants competed a self-evaluation of their subjective performance on an 11-point scale ranging from 0 (i.e., totally dissatisfied with their sporting performance over the past month) to 10 (i.e., totally satisfied with their sporting performance over the past month). The resulting subjective performance score (with a group mean of 6.66) was found to be related to a wide range of other sport psychology variables, such as psychological skill use and the extent to which the coach created or thwarted a need-supportive environment. As another example, in their study of depression in elite Danish and Swedish football players, Jensen, Ivarsson, Fallby, Dankers, and Elbe (2018) assessed perfectionism using subscales from the Sport Multidimensional Perfectionism Scale (SMPS) and the Multidimensional Inventory of Perfectionism in Sport (MIPS). Both the SMPS and MIPS are multidimensional measures of perfectionism in sport that had reliability and/or validity evidence from previous research to justify their use (e.g., Dunn et al., 2006; Stoeber, Otto, Pescheck, Becker, & Stoll, 2007). Numerical data from the two perfectionism measures provided important evidence to support the researchers' conclusion that, "athletes on junior teams and athletes with high levels of perfectionistic concerns (and in connection with high anxiety) are vulnerable to depressive symptoms" (Jensen et al., 2018, p. 152). However, although it might seem relatively easy, the researchers' choice as to what specific measure to use in a study can often be challenging owing to the complexity of evaluating quantitative measurement quality.

The evaluation of quantitative measurement quality needs to be situated in the context of other forms of quality (i.e., validity). One important facet of validity concerns the choice of which measure to use in a research study. The choice of measure needs to follow logically from the researchers' research question(s) and their justification as to why the research study is important. For example, if a researcher were interested in the sport participation rates of different people from various geographical regions, using a measure of general physical activity levels would likely not be a suitable choice, no matter how useful that measure might be to other research studies. This type of validity can be referred to as logical validity and focuses on the logical flow within and across all aspects of a research study, including measurement (Kowalski et al., 2018). In addition to logical validity, researchers conducting quantitative research also need to consider both the internal and external validity of their study. Internal validity refers to a researcher's confidence to claim that any change in a study outcome is a result of the implemented intervention, as opposed to other extraneous factors, whereas external validity refers to how the research results can be reasonably expected to generalize to other populations beyond a researcher's study sample (Kowalski et al., 2018).

Measurement quality is important to both internal and external validity. For example, if a study outcome cannot be appropriately measured, researchers might draw incorrect conclusions as to whether any change (or absence of change) in the outcome is a "real" change or simply because of unreliability in the measure. Relatedly, without reliable and valid measurement tools, any results of a sport psychology study will be unlikely to generalize to other athletes, teams, or sporting environments. As such, logical, internal, and external validity are important to the consideration of measurement quality.

Another type of validity evidence—construct validity—lies at the centre of quantitative measurement. Construct validity focuses on whether a measure is adequately measuring what it intends to measure, and it integrates all forms of evidence that are needed to evaluate the interpretation or meaning of test scores (Messick, 1989a). Construct validity, above all other forms of validity, is most important to understanding quantitative measurement quality. Hence, the focus in the next section will be primarily on construct validity as it relates to quantitative research approaches. On the other hand, qualitative measurement quality is much harder to establish, as we discuss in an upcoming section on the measurement quality of qualitative research.

Measurement Quality in Quantitative Sport Psychology Research

Defining Psychological Constructs

Constructs such as motivation, emotion, and self-perception are highly relevant to the study of sport psychology. These and other constructs represent hypothetical abstractions that explain psychological phenomena, but they are not directly observable (MacCorquodale & Meehl, 1948; see also Filho & Tenenbaum, Volume 1, Chapter 22, in this volume). In order to study various sport psychology constructs within a quantitative research approach, precise methods of assessing or measuring these types of unobservable psychological phenomenon are required. Therefore, researchers *operationalize* psychological constructs through a process of assessing indicators, constituents, and representations that describe the phenomenon of interest (Thomas, Nelson, & Silverman, 2011). In other words, abstract constructs need to be translated into actual test scores as a part of the measurement process in order for researchers to have data to answer their research questions. By establishing an operational definition, an unobservable construct can be described and measured by the elements that constitute and characterize it.

An example of an operational definition can be seen in research on the emotional experience of competitive anxiety in sport. As an abstract construct, competitive anxiety is not directly observable or measurable, but components of anxiety can be measured by subjective assessments of self-report (e.g., Competitive State Anxiety Inventory 2 [CSAI-2]; Martens, Burton, Vealey, Bump, & Smith, 1990), rater observation, or objective assessments such as physiological markers (e.g., heart rate). The scores on each of these measures subsequently constitute the operational definition of anxiety in a study. There are various options for operationally defining and measuring anxiety in any given study, because state anxiety is an experience that has cognitive, physical, and social manifestations that can be both experienced by an individual and observed by others (e.g., teammates, competitors, coaches) in the sport context. Ideally, a researcher would assess all aspects of anxiety, but this might not be possible or desirable for a number of reasons, such as resource limitations, the scope of the research question, or the theoretical framework underlying the study.

State anxiety offers an excellent example to highlight the importance of operational definitions, because it is highly relevant to the social, evaluative, and competitive sporting environment. It has also been routinely studied with reference to performance outcomes (Craft, Magyar, Becker, & Feltz, 2003; Mellalieu, Hanton, & Fletcher, 2006). State anxiety is also often defined and assessed based on its distinct components (Ree, French, MacLeod, & Locke, 2008; Schwartz, Davidson, & Goleman, 1978). These include manifestations that are physical (e.g., trembling, elevated heart rate) and cognitive (e.g., excessive worrying, negative thoughts), thereby requiring different types of measurement and subsequently having different operational definitions in the literature.

The key point here is that psychological constructs, such as competitive state anxiety, can be distinctly defined from one study to another, and, therefore, identifying an operational definition helps the reader understand precisely what elements of a construct are being represented. In this way, it is important to recognize that, although the various components of state anxiety can be measured across various contexts and individuals, each represents an *indirect* index of anxiety, whereby the presence and degree of anxiety are inferred by way of its measurable or observable elements. As such, the quality of the measurement ultimately depends on the operationalization, method of assessment, and context in which it is assessed.

Construct Validity as an Index of Measurement Quality

A reminder that construct validity, which can more formally be defined as the degree to which a researcher's measurement of a construct is representative of the theoretical and observational phenomena on which the measure is based, is at the root of measurement quality in quantitative sport psychology research. Indeed, valid assessment of a construct is foundational to evaluating the merits and quality of any research study that is focused on understanding, labeling, and measuring psychological phenomena. Historically, construct validity was considered to be one among various types of measurement validity evidence (Cronbach & Meehl, 1955), typically alongside content validity (i.e., the degree to which a measure comprehensively represents the elements of a construct) and criterion validity (i.e., the degree to which a measure is related to an outcome). However, contemporary conceptualizations of construct validity define it as a unified and integrated conceptualization that subsumes other types of validity (Landy, 1986; Loevinger, 1957; Messick, 1995). In this view, measurement validity is considered a continuous and evolving process of evaluation of the constituents, interpretations, and values associated with the measured indicators of psychological constructs. Importantly, the consistently evolving nature of construct validation is key to the development and testing of psychological theories (Loevinger, 1957), and it is subsequently essential to understanding measurement quality in quantitative research.

As the construct validation process is iterative and continuous, each empirical investigation using a psychometric test is concurrently testing the validity of the scores in the measure, as well as the theoretical basis of the construct (Strauss & Smith, 2009). Let us consider this validation process by returning to our previous discussion of the construct of state anxiety relative to sport performance. Despite the popularity and extensive use of the CSAI-2, examination of construct validation evidence surrounding this measure has led to a series of concerns regarding the conceptualization and measurement of anxiety (e.g., Cerin, 2003; Craft et al., 2003; Woodman et al., 2009). For example, in a review of studies examining the relationship between competitive anxiety (assessed by the CSAI-2) and sport performance, Craft and colleagues (2003) reported a weak, non-significant relationship among each component of anxiety and sport performance. These findings have brought into question the quality of the CSAI-2 measure more generally. Owing to the inextricable links between psychometric tests and theory, these types of finding have led to further questions about the validity of the multidimensional theory of anxiety itself (Martens et al., 1990). The CSAI-2 is founded on the multidimensional theory of anxiety, which posits that somatic anxiety is linked to sport performance in an inverted-U relationship, whereas cognitive anxiety is associated with sport performance in a negative linear relationship. Weak support for this model challenges widely held beliefs that anxiety is typically detrimental to performance (Burton & Naylor, 1997). Further, this validation evidence adds support to the hypothesis that anxiety is a highly complex and varied emotional experience that often presents alongside other emotions, such as fear, sadness, guilt, and hostility and, therefore, might need to be reconceptualized in the competitive sport setting (Cerin, 2003). Taken together, the base of evidence described above illustrates the importance of construct validation being a continuous process to provide researchers with ongoing insight into the development and evaluation of what comprises a psychological construct, the quality psychometric measures used to assess it, and the theoretical frameworks that represent it.

Nomological Network

The process of developing a nomological network—a representation of constructs as they relate to one another (Cronbach & Meehl, 1955)—is an essential preliminary step as part of the construct validation process. A nomological network contains three key components, including (a) how the observable properties of a construct relate to one another, (b) how different constructs relate to each other, and (c) how theoretical constructs relate to the observable properties of a construct. Indeed, the development of a nomological network to establish construct validity is designed to link conceptual or theoretical constructs with how phenomena are observed in practice.

Sport psychologists have recently focused on the construct of mental toughness, which can be described as an attribute that promotes adaptive coping and engagement in adverse situations (Jones & Moorhouse, 2007; Weinberg, 2010). The construct of mental toughness has gained popularity in its application to sport psychology in large part because athletes often face high demands and pressures to perform and need effective psychological skills to deal with those demands and pressures. However, a significant challenge to the area is that there is a lack of consensus around what the construct of mental toughness does and does not represent (Gucciardi & Gordon, 2011). This lack of conceptual clarity presents a significant problem in the study of mental toughness as it relates to sport because researchers adopt varied definitions of what the construct actually *is*, thus hampering understanding of how the construct can be related to sport performance and athlete well-being. As such, researchers (e.g., Gucciardi, Hanton, Gordon, Mallett, & Temby, 2015) have urged for a unified conceptualization of mental toughness via the development of nomological networks. According to Cronbach and Meehl (1955), developing a construct is "a matter of elaborating the nomolgoical network in which it occurs, or of increasing the definiteness of the components" (p. 290). This means that empirical evidence is needed for the refinement of a construct, such as mental toughness, so that we know which constructs are analogous, which are related, and which are unique and independent of the construct of interest. Gucciardi and colleagues (2015) have contributed towards the development of a nomological network for mental toughness by showing how mental toughness—operationalized as a capacity to pursue achievement-oriented goals in the face of significant challenges, stressors, and adversities—is associated with conceptually related constructs such as perceived stress, adaptive coping, and performance across various achievement contexts, including sport. A nomological network sets the foundation for further empirical tests aimed at refining our understanding of the theoretical construct of mental toughness, its underlying dimensions, and its measurement properties.

Evaluation of Construct Validity

Whereas a nomological network can signify the relations among various constructs that researchers want to examine to evaluate construct validity, the specific evaluation of construct validity is also dependent on understanding the specific measurement tools that are used to assess psychological constructs of interest. Once researchers design a psychometric tool to assess a psychological construct and set up a nomological network, they need to then ensure that the measure is appropriately assessing and representing the construct of interest. Such an approach is needed to be able to draw meaning from the scores of a measure, as well as to interpret findings in light of how they inform psychological phenomena. Messick's (1989b, 1995) integrated, multifaceted framework of construct validity outlines a process for evaluating the quality of construct measurement. Influenced by Messick's initial conceptualization of validity, a modern framework of validity has subsequently been established. This most updated framework for validity is presented in *The Standards for Educational and Psychological Testing* (American Educational Research Association [AERA] et al., 2014).

Within the AERA et al. (2014) framework, construct validity can be evaluated based on five main sources of evidence: (a) test content (i.e., are test items appropriately measuring the construct?), (b) internal structure (i.e., do items on the measure align with the construct?), (c) response processes (i.e., do participants respond to the measure as intended?), (d) relations to other constructs (i.e., does the measure show convergence and discriminant evidence?), and (e) consequences of test (i.e., what are the potential consequences of using a measure?). According to the AERA et al. (2014) standards, "a sound validity argument integrates various strands of evidence into a coherent account of the degree to which existing evidence and theory support the intended interpretation of test scores for specific uses" (p. 21), thereby suggesting that instrument development ought to integrate various sources of validity (Zhu, 2012). Notably, several researchers (e.g., Gunnell et al., 2014; Hagger & Chatzisarantis, 2009; Zhu, 2012) have identified concerns with the current state of the field of sport psychology, which has not collectively adopted this contemporary view of validity. Gunnell and colleagues (2014) recommended that the utilization of a set of standards or framework, such as those recommended by AERA et al. (2014), is necessary for robust construct validation in sport psychology research. The set of standards are categorized within three clusters, aimed at defining (a) the use and interpretation of test scores, (b) samples and settings in the process of validation, and (c) specific forms of validity evidence.

Evaluation of Construct Validity Example

In sport psychology, one key instrument for which construct validity criteria have been applied is the Physical Self-Description Questionnaire (PSDQ; Marsh, Richards, Johnson, Roche, & Tremayne, 1994). The PSDQ is built upon the multidimensional, hierarchical physical self-concept model developed by Shavelson, Hubner, and Stanton (1976), which posits that the self-concept comprises various domains (e.g., social, academic, employment, moral, physical self) that are subsumed under global self-esteem. The physical-self domain specifically further comprises subdomains, each of which is measured by the PSDQ subscales. The full PSDQ is a 70-item measure that consists of nine physical self-perceptions, including perceptions of health, strength, body fat, physical activity, endurance, sports competence, coordination, appearance, flexibility, as well as the two higher-order constructs of global physical self-concept and self-esteem. Each item on the PSDQ represents a statement (e.g., "I have good sports skills") to which respondents indicate their agreement on a 6-point Likert scale ranging from 1 (false) to 6 (true). Eleven subscale scores can then be calculated by averaging of responses to items assessing each subscale, with higher scores representing more positive self-perceptions.

Knowing the construct validity evidence relevant to PSDQ scores is essential to justifying the use and interpretation of the measure, as well as to understanding and applying the physical self-concept in sport psychology research and practice more generally. Indeed, without strong construct validity evidence to support the PSDQ, the many conclusions researchers have drawn based on their use of the instrument would need to be accepted only with the most serious trepidation. Thus, it is no surprise the evaluation of the measurement quality of the PSDQ has received much attention in the sport psychology literature. And, despite the existing evidence to support the PSDQ specifically, Sabiston, Whitehead, and Eklund (2012) recognized the need for continued construct validation of physical self-concept measures more generally, based on the common confusion and blurred distinctions among researchers that continue to occur in the operationalization and measurement of constructs focused on the "self" in sport psychology. Because of this need, the application of the AERA et al. (2014) standards for construct validation with reference to the PSDQ is ideal to exemplify the validation process.

Evaluation of construct validity based on test content is typically conducted at the initial development stage of an instrument, during which items are refined based on wording, format, and links to theoretical constructs (AERA et al., 2014). Marsh and colleagues (1994) reported a preliminary content validation of items on the PSDQ based on comparing items with corresponding subscales of the Physical Self-Perception Profile (PSPP; Fox & Corbin, 1989) and the Richards Physical Self-Concept Scale (Richards, 1988), which represent other physical self-concept measures previously used in sport psychology research. The internal structure of the PSDQ has been evidenced to conform to hypothesized constructs via confirmatory factor analysis, demonstrating support for the distinct theoretical dimensions (and associated subscales) of the PSDQ, as well as gender invariance (Marsh, 1996b; Marsh et al., 1994). Meanwhile, evidence of response processes of the PSDQ has been more recently questioned (Freund, Tietjens, & Strauss, 2013) by critiques focused on the original six response categories of the PSDQ as not being suitable across populations, along with a recommendation that four response categories may be more appropriate. Evidence of relations to other constructs has been extensively integrated into the PSDQ validation process (Marsh, 1996a, 1997; Marsh et al., 1994). This fourth step has been identified as a critical part of the process of construct validation (Campbell & Fiske, 1959), such that construct validity can be established when a measure is linked in the expected direction to other theoretically supported psychological constructs (i.e., convergent validity) and by showing that the measure is *not* related to psychological constructs that are conceptually dissimilar (i.e., discriminant validity).

The evaluation of convergent validity and discriminant validity has been described as the multitrait-multimethod matrix methodology (Campbell & Fiske, 1959; see also Gunnell, Volume 1, Chapter 47, this encyclopedia). Evidence of convergent validity and divergent validity for the PSDQ scores has been found by examining correlations with other constructs assessing physical self-concepts (e.g., the PSPP), as well as with external measures of physical activity, body composition, strength, and flexibility (Marsh, 1996a). Convergent validity and discriminant validity have been further supported in cross-cultural studies by comparing subscales of the PSDQ with the PSPP across international samples (Marsh, Asci, & Tomas, 2002). Finally, the consequences of test interpretation and use may be particularly important for measures targeting constructs with an inherent focus on appraising the self. For example, if scores on the PSDQ were used to determine the need for adolescent athletes to partake in a self-esteem building programme, a biased instrument could lead to misclassification of at-risk athletes and them not receiving a beneficial intervention. Considering the potential implications of consequential validity evidence (Hubley & Zumbo, 2011), along with the paucity of consequential validity reporting in sport psychology literatures (Gunnell et al., 2014), continued validation of the consequences of the PSDQ are particularly warranted as part of the ongoing evaluation of construct validity process.

Measurement Quality in Qualitative Sport Psychology Research

Although measurement quality is typically associated with quantitative research, advocates of the qualitative approach employ parallel standards of rigour to evaluate the quality of qualitative research (Anfara, Brown, & Mangione, 2002). However, before beginning an examination of the measurement quality of qualitative research specifically, it is important to note that it would be inappropriate to judge the measurement quality of this approach by the same standards established for quantitative research. Qualitative research and quantitative research approaches have very different purposes, and, therefore, should each be judged on an ability to achieve their respective purpose, not the purpose of the other (Jasper, 1994).

Quantitative research has its origin in a belief that reality is both real and capable of capture, that findings are true and the result of objective assessment, and that the confirmation of hypotheses through quantitatively rigorous examination is the logical way to pursue knowledge (Guba & Lincoln, 1994). Alternatively, researchers taking a *qualitative* approach to research seek to understand the lived experiences of their research participants. Consequently, they embrace research principles associated with a social constructivist world-view in which multiple realities exist and meaning is varied and complex (Creswell, 2014). Denzin and Lincoln (2000) highlighted that the "constructivist paradigm assumes a relativist ontology (there are multiple realities), a subjectivist epistemology (knower and respondent co-create understandings), and a naturalistic (in the natural world) set of methodological procedures" (p. 21). The goal of qualitative research is to generate knowledge from the research participants' experiences of their own (and perhaps others') world(s) and, through inductive analysis based on the data generated, discern meaningful patterns from the information that has been shared (Creswell, 2014).

Most important to the discussion of measurement quality in qualitative research is that any examinations of quality must exist in harmony with the fundamental assumptions of constructivism that are core to qualitative research. Consequently, the term "trustworthiness" has been advocated as one of the key measuring sticks for qualitative measurement quality, in addition to other terms such as rigour and authenticity (Sparkes & Smith, 2009), as opposed to the quantitatively rooted terms of "reliability" and "validity" (Curtin & Fossey, 2007). As Curtin and Fossey described, trustworthiness represents the degree to which findings accurately reflect the experiences of those being studied. This conceptualization of trustworthiness accommodates the perspectives underlying the existence of qualitative research: a relativist ontology, a subjectivist epistemology, and a naturalistic methodology.

Trustworthiness

It is important to acknowledge that there is no template for trustworthiness that applies equally to all aspects of qualitative research within sport psychology, as plurality is an inherent dimension of qualitative research (Krefting, 1991). It is, however, possible to focus on key strategies that can enhance the trustworthiness of a qualitative research study (Kowalski et al., 2018). Because a deep, rich understanding of the experiences of the research participants is a key goal of the qualitative researcher (Creswell, 2014), the trustworthiness of researchers' work is tied to the accuracy with which those experiences are conveyed (Curtin & Fossey, 2007). As a result, trustworthiness in qualitative research is not attached to either a need to claim generalizability of the results or a need to establish causality among variables. Instead, although researchers taking a qualitative approach to research might hope to generate material from which generalizations might occur, it is equally appropriate for descriptive qualitative work to be sufficient in and of itself (Krefting, 1991). For example, a qualitative research study by Smith (2013) presented the health narratives of men who sustained a spinal injury through playing sport. In the results section, the narratives presented allow the reader entry into the worlds of the participants' experiences in a way that identifies a new narrative of health. The importance of narrative specifically is captured in the author's conclusion that, "throughout it was shown that narrative matters: narratives help conduct human life, shaping health behavior, doing things on, in, and for disabled men" (p. 118). This outcome of a narrative qualitative approach is unique and distinct from approaches that aim to generalize study results to other populations of athletes.

By disconnecting the concept of trustworthiness from the need for generalization and the need for causality, researchers can start to see how the measurement quality of qualitative work distances itself from the traditional quality control aims of "validity". McTaggart (1998), in justifying participatory action research (a research methodology in which researchers work collaboratively with participants to enact change), claimed that, "the dominant discourse of validity hinges upon the combination of two key quests: the quest for generalization, and the quest for causality. Implicit in both quests is an aspiration for replicability, prediction and control which transcends time" (p. 212). Although the dominant viewpoint in quantitative approaches, this conceptualization of validity is not applicable to qualitative work, and, if it is applied to assess the measurement quality of qualitative research, it effectively undermines the inherent value of that research (Sandelowski, 1993). To further emphasize this point, Sandelowski stated:

> It is as if, in our quasi-materialistic zeal to neutralize bias and to defend our projects against threats to validity, we were more preoccupied with building fortifications against attack than with creating the evocative, true-to-life, and meaningful portraits, stories, and landscapes of human experience that constitute the best test of rigor in qualitative work.
>
> (p. 1)

For example, in an effort to exemplify the assessment of quality in sport-specific community-based research, Schinke, Smith, and McGannon (2013) used a relativist approach to posit that qualitative community research ought to be evaluated based on characteristics that represent capacity-building between communities and researchers, with a commitment to community betterment.

Establishing the Trustworthiness of Qualitative Research

Curtin and Fossey (2007) highlighted six criteria by which the trustworthiness of qualitative research can be measured: (a) reflexivity, (b) transferability, (c) researcher–participant collaboration, (d) member-checking, (e) triangulation, and (f) descriptions that are thick in nature. Creswell (2014) emphasized additional trustworthiness criteria in the context of qualitative validity, such as the importance of researchers spending prolonged time in the field and the importance of having a trusted and knowledgeable colleague to support a peer debriefing process. Each of these criteria will be presented as components critical to an understanding of trustworthiness, and consequently qualitative measurement quality. Further, the criteria have been summarized in Table 4.

Self-Reflexivity

Researchers conducting qualitative research need to acknowledge that their interpretations of qualitative data are shaped, in part, by their own values. These value-laden interpretations are not viewed as a weakness, but rather a recognition of the reality of any human interpretive experience. Denzin and Lincoln (2000) went so far as to say, "all research is interpretive; it is guided by a set of beliefs and feelings about the world and how it should be understood and studied" (p. 19). Importantly, the value-laden interpretations of qualitative research do not

Table 4 Summary of criteria for establishing trustworthiness in qualitative research

Criteria	What is it?	Example
Reflexivity	Researcher reflects on how personal perspective may inform research study	Researcher reflects on her role as an athlete when interviewing members of sports teams
Transferability	Extent to which findings may apply to other contexts or individuals	Indigenous athletes' experiences accessing mental health services may inform experiences of other marginalized groups
Researcher–participant collaboration	Researcher and participants partner throughout all stages of research process	Athletes and coaches are involved with defining research question and making meaning of data on athlete–coach relationships
Member-checking	Enlist study participants to review and engage in generated data	Researchers engage in discussions with participants about focus group findings to appropriately convey experiences of childhood sport specialization
Triangulation	Collating several sources of data	Utilizing interviews, focus groups, and researcher observations in a study examining team-based sport dynamics
Thick descriptions	Rich and comprehensive summary of findings to appropriately represent complexity of generated data	Presenting detailed descriptions and contextual information of the nuances of women's unique experiences with body image in sport across the lifespan
Sustained engagement	Spending extended time interacting or observing participants or phenomena of study	Multiple and repeated one-on-one interviews with athletes throughout a competitive season
Peer debriefing	Critically reflect on study findings with other researcher(s)	Engage with trusted colleagues and mentors about the meanings and interpretations generated from focus group data discussing competitive anxiety in elite sport

compromise its trustworthiness, but simply acknowledge that the research-generated data are, at a minimum, the product of (at least) two people's experiences (the researcher and the research participant). Self-reflexivity, or introspection, is a process by which researchers contextualize their personal identities within the research process, thus allowing for the awareness of how one's status, power, and social position can be expressed, while maintaining the integrity of the culture of the researched (Schinke, McGannon, Parham, &

Lane, 2012). For example, in a case study approach to explore interpersonal emotion regulation within a team of varsity volleyball athletes, Palmateer and Tamminen (2018) discussed the role of self-reflexivity as an important parameter for methodological rigour. In their study, the interviewer's personal history as a varsity athlete was carefully considered in the design, collection, and interpretation of the data, and this was aided by the use of a reflective journal throughout the research process. In this way, qualitative researchers can be reflexive by acknowledging the presence of their own lens in the shaping of the research findings (Pillow, 2003). Though Pillow (2003) recognized that researchers might need to pursue elevated levels of sophistication in their self-reflexivity, researcher acknowledgement of personal connectedness to the research process nonetheless has the potential to enhance the trustworthiness of the findings.

Transferability

Though it is imprecise to state that the findings of qualitative research are generalizable per se, it is more accurate to state that the findings have the potential to be transferable. This means the findings may have applicability to other people in similar contexts. Transferability is one measure of assessing the trustworthiness of qualitative research, and one way of increasing that likelihood is to provide significantly detailed descriptions throughout the study (Curtin & Fossey, 2007). These descriptions enable readers to compare the experiences of the groups and individuals in the study with themselves, other people, or other research. A detailed description of qualitative work allows the findings to serve as an example to others in terms of possible implications for their own similar circumstances. As Flyvbjerg (2006) stated, "formal generalization is overvalued as a source of scientific development, whereas 'the force of example' is underestimated" (p. 228). To facilitate transferability in sport psychology research, Smith (2018) suggested utilizing creative methods of representing qualitative interpretations, such as storytelling, ethnodramas, or documentaries.

Researcher–Participant Collaboration and Partnership

To accurately represent the lived experiences of participants, researchers (Curtin & Fossey, 2007) urge heightened "collaboration and partnership between the participants and the researchers to be developed" (p. 88). The qualitative approach to research encourages researchers and affords them the freedom to collaborate with their participants throughout the entire research process, beginning with the identification of research questions through to a final representation of findings. In addition to enhancing trustworthiness, the presence of significant researcher–participant collaboration potentially provides a significant boost to the quality of learning that qualitative research can generate. For example, McHugh, Holt, and Anderson (2015) utilized a community-based participatory research approach to explore indigenous people's experiences of sport and community, whereby the participants and researchers were equal partners in constructing meaning across all phases of the research process. Acknowledging that collaboration can take many forms that are tied to the nature of the project, the topic matter, and the subjects who are engaged, the authors advocate for the inclusion of collaborative practices in sports psychology. Similarly, Flyvbjerg (2006) claimed, if research is to be a process of learning, the most effective learning occurs the closer researchers get to the phenomenon they are learning about. The best way to come closer to a phenomenon that is known to the participants in a study is to work collaboratively with them throughout.

Member Checking

Member checking involves researchers inviting participants to review the data generated by the research and to make any changes they feel are necessary to more accurately reflect their experiences (Creswell, 2014). Through the process of member checking, researchers ensure participants have had an opportunity to read and provide feedback on their raw and transcribed (i.e., typed word for word) interview data. However, it is important to note that member checking is not universally accepted as a thorough means of enhancing the trustworthiness of qualitative research. Smith and McGannon (2017) claimed that member checking does not adequately support trustworthiness, because neither the researcher nor participant can eliminate subjectivity from the member checking process. Instead, the authors recommended "member reflections", whereby sport psychology researchers and participants enhance and expand the data by collectively discussing the similarities and differences in their interpretations, with full recognition that there is no universal right answer.

Methodological Triangulation

Trustworthiness of qualitative findings is also enhanced through the use of methodological triangulation (Curtin & Fossey, 2007). Methodological triangulation refers to the incorporation of at least two methods for doing research or at least two techniques for collecting data (Farmer, Robinson, Elliot, & Eyles, 2006). It is a way for researchers to cross-check their interpretations and findings using multiple methodologies. Kowalski et al. (2018) highlighted the combination of participant observation and one-on-one interviews as one example of methodological triangulation. As an example, if a sport psychology researcher were interested in understanding the experiences of varsity athletes accessing mental health services in the university setting, a method of triangulation might be to conduct one-on-one interviews with athletes, focus groups with mental health service providers, and observational accounts of mental health conversations in the team context. According to Krefting (1991), this process of methodological triangulation can contribute to or confirm certain aspects of the study, or alternatively provide a more complete picture of the phenomenon of interest.

Thick Descriptions

"Thick descriptions" refer to rich, detailed descriptions of the context and circumstances pertaining to the phenomenon under study, which are important so the researcher can ensure that the meaning of behaviours is fully understood (Curtin & Fossey, 2007). Thick descriptions also have the potential power to transport the reader to the experience being described (Creswell, 2014) and, notably, can serve to improve the transferability of qualitative research (Curtin & Fossey, 2007). For example, in a study aimed at exploring emotion and body image among older women, Bennett and colleagues (2017) showcased the rich, deep stories provided by women detailing their physical activity experiences as they relate to the ageing body. Thick descriptions enhance the research results in terms of richness and realism (Creswell, 2014), and it is this enhancement that potentially contributes to elevating the trustworthiness of the results.

Sustained Engagement

Sustained engagement in the research field can enhance research quality in several ways. For example, sustained engagement can enable the researcher to generate a comprehensive and detailed awareness of the phenomenon being studied (Creswell, 2014). As Creswell argued, the more time researchers spend with research participants, the more accurate their findings become. Specifically, sustained engagement results in broader and more frequent participant observation, thereby allowing the researcher to understand differences between stable and consistent versus fluctuating and malleable occurrences. Additionally, sustained engagement can help participants become accustomed to the presence of the researcher and, therefore, is advantageous in mitigating against the tendency for some research participants to bias their words and actions in a socially desirable direction (Krefting, 1991). One excellent example of sustained engagement is a study by Debois and colleagues (2012), where the researchers aimed to understand an elite female fencer's sports career using a lifespan narrative approach over a 14-year span. The prolonged engagement and exposure between the researcher and the researched promote a comprehensive and inclusive representation of the participant's perspective and allow for the richness and depth of the research collaboration to contribute towards the trustworthiness of the findings.

Peer Debriefing

The "peer debrief" trustworthiness criterion enables the researcher to be held accountable by a peer who will review and ask questions about the research and plays an important role in improving the preciseness of the research (Creswell, 2014). The peer debriefing function applies to both data generation and data analysis (Spillett, 2003), and the person conducting the peer debrief must be considered impartial (Krefting, 1991). The peer debrief process should be thorough and extensive, which then contributes to the worthiness, honesty, and believability of the research (Spall, 1998). Essentially, the trustworthiness of the research is enhanced by peer debriefing because the research is now subject to "interpretation beyond the researcher" (Creswell, p. 202). In sport psychology research, Smith and McGannon (2017) advocated for the utilization of critical friends— peers who can act in the process of sharing research interpretations and critically consider the meaning construction of qualitative data. The role of this peer debrief and/or engagement of a critical friend is an important step in promoting rigour in qualitative sport psychology research.

The Measurement Quality of the Qualitative Researcher

Although trustworthiness is important, ensuring measurement quality in qualitative research requires more than careful monitoring of methodology. It also requires ethical conduct on the part of the administrator of the methodology (i.e., the researcher). In qualitative research, the researcher is often considered to be the instrument of data collection, as opposed to that instrument being other external tests or measures (Krefting, 1991). Therefore, rather than focusing on tests and measures, it is really researchers' commitment to a high level of ethical conduct that is of paramount importance to the measurement quality of qualitative research. For example, imagine a scenario in which a researcher has the opportunity to present her qualitative findings, which, if shared as an accurate reflection of a young athlete's experience, have the potential to place the young athlete in harm's way. Allen (2009) suggested that some argue the first responsibility of a researcher is the pursuit of scientific knowledge; however, he also stated that others "assert that the protection of children is of the utmost importance for society and that professionals who come in contact with children, including researchers are directly responsible for providing that protection" (p. 16). Therefore, a likely conclusion is that the potentially harmful material needs to be withheld from the public record because of the unethical actions that would be required to present the findings. In this case, the measurement quality (i.e., the quality of the measurement instrument, which is the researcher herself) would be the highest when the researcher acts in a way that is consistent with the most ethical action. This perspective on measurement quality is fundamentally different from thinking of an evaluation of measurement residing in an external quantitative measure, even one that considers the persons responding and the context of measurement, as Messick (1989a) had envisioned in the context of construct validity.

Clearly enunciated ethical principles are required for ethical decisions, and non-maleficence (the responsibility to do no harm) is arguably the foundational ethical principle any individual in a service profession, including research, needs to adhere to (Welfel, 2006). Therefore, in the example above, the researcher, while being committed to presenting accurate findings, should only do so to the point at which the reporting of those findings is not placing the participant in harm's way. However, complicating matters, researchers also need to demonstrate a high level of respect for the ethical principle of autonomy, or acting in a manner that preserves the "inherent freedom and dignity of each person" (Welfel, 2006, p. 32). Thereby, researchers can be placed in an ethical dilemma in which the participants' autonomous decision might place them in harm's way (i.e., the only way to prevent harm would be to undermine a participant's autonomous choice). These are difficult situations that researchers might need to navigate through because there is no clear, most ethical path, and having an effective ethical decision-making model as part of the research process is essential (Kowalski et al., 2018). Ultimately, because of the challenges that ethical dilemmas can pose researchers, one measure of measurement quality is the quality of a researcher's ethical decision-making process, which goes far beyond any data that are generated in the research process.

Conclusion

In conclusion, the identification of measurement quality is an integral part of the research process in sport psychology and varies considerably depending on the approach to research. To establish measurement quality in quantitative research, we need to consider the concept of construct validity, and the role of the nomological network helps establish what evidence we need to look at to evaluate construct validity. It is only when we have a complete representation of construct validity that we can claim the highest standard of measurement quality for a quantitative measure. When there is sufficient support for construct validity, it is only then that we should have confidence in the measurement quality of a particular instrument or tool in our research. Alternatively, because of the social constructivist roots of qualitative research, measurement quality in qualitative research is tied to the trustworthiness of the research. Though the plurality of qualitative research makes it impossible to establish a template of trustworthiness that applies equally to all qualitative methodologies (Krefting, 1991), it is possible to highlight key strategies that have the potential to enhance the trustworthiness of qualitative work. Some of these strategies include self-reflexivity, transferability, member checking, methodological triangulation, thick descriptions, sustained engagement, and peer debriefing. In qualitative research, researchers are often considered to be the instruments of data generation and, consequently, they must abide by clear ethical guidelines to help ensure the trustworthiness, and hence measurement quality, of their research. In sum, regardless of the research approaches utilized, thoughtful considerations and evaluations of measurement quality are integral to the development and advancement of the field of sport psychology.

References

Allen, B. (2009). Are researchers ethically obligated to report suspected child maltreatment? A critical analysis of opposing perspectives. *Ethics and Behavior, 19*, 15–24.

American Educational Research Association (AERA), American Psychological Association, & National Council on Measurement in Education, Joint Committee on Standards for Educational, & Psychological Testing (US). (2014). *Standards for educational and psychological testing*. Washington, DC: American Educational Research Association.

Anfara, V. A., Brown, K. M., & Mangione, T. L. (2002). Qualitative analysis on stage: Making the research process more public. *Educational Researcher, 31*, 28–38.

Bennett, E. V., Clarke, L. H., Kowalski, K. C., & Crocker, P. R. (2017). From pleasure and pride to the fear of decline: Exploring the emotions in older women's physical activity narratives. *Psychology of Sport and Exercise, 33*, 113–122.

Brown, D. J., Arnold, R., Standage, M., & Fletcher, D. (2017). Thriving on pressure: A factor mixture analysis of sport performers' responses to competitive encounters. *Journal of Sport and Exercise Psychology, 39*, 423–437.

Burton, D., & Naylor, S. (1997). Is anxiety really facilitative? Reaction to the myth that cognitive anxiety always impairs sport performance. *Journal of Applied Sport Psychology, 9*, 295–302.

Campbell, D. T., & Fiske, D. W. (1959). Convergent and discriminant validation by the multitrait-multimethod matrix. *Psychological Bulletin, 56*, 81–105.

Cerin, E. (2003). Anxiety versus fundamental emotions as predictors of perceived functionality of pre-competitive emotional states, threat, and challenge in individual sports. *Journal of Applied Sport Psychology, 15*, 223–238.

Craft, L. L., Magyar, T. M., Becker, B. J., & Feltz, D. L. (2003). The relationship between the competitive state anxiety inventory-2 and sport performance: A meta-analysis. *Journal of Sport and Exercise Psychology, 25*, 44–65.

Creswell, J. W. (2014). *Research design: Qualitative, quantitative, and mixed methods approaches* (4th ed.). Los Angeles, CA: Sage.

Cronbach, L. J., & Meehl, P. E. (1955). Construct validity in psychological tests. *Psychological Bulletin, 52*, 281–302.

Curtin, M., & Fossey, E. (2007). Appraising the trustworthiness of qualitative studies: Guidelines for occupational therapists. *Australian Occupational Therapy Journal, 54*, 88–94.

Debois, N., Ledon, A., Argiolas, C., & Rosnet, E. (2012). A lifespan perspective on transitions during a top sports career: A case of an elite female fencer. *Psychology of Sport and Exercise, 13*, 660–668.

Denzin, N. K., & Lincoln, Y. S. (2000). Introduction: The discipline and practice of qualitative research. In N. Denzin & Y. Lincoln (Eds.), *Handbook of qualitative research* (2nd ed.,, pp. 1–28). Thousand Oaks, CA: Sage.

Dunn, J. G. H., Causgrove Dunn, J., Gotwals, J. K., Vallance, J. K. H., Craft, J. M., & Syrotuik, D. G. (2006). Establishing construct validity evidence for the sport multidimensional perfectionism scale. *Psychology of Sport and Exercise, 7*, 57–59.

Farmer, T., Robinson, K., Elliott, S., & Eyles, J. (2006). Developing and implementing a triangulation protocol for qualitative health research. *Qualitative Health Research, 16*, 377–394.

Flyvbjerg, B. (2006). Five misunderstandings about case-study research. *Qualitative Inquiry, 12*, 219–245.

Fox, K. R., & Corbin, C. B. (1989). The physical self-perception profile: Development and preliminary validation. *Journal of Sport and Exercise Psychology, 11*, 408–430.

Freund, P. A., Tietjens, M., & Strauss, B. (2013). Using rating scales for the assessment of physical self-concept: Why the number of response categories matters. *Measurement in Physical Education and Exercise Science, 17*, 249–263.

Guba, E. G., & Lincoln, Y. S. (1994). Competing paradigms in qualitative research. In N. K. Denzin & Y. S. Lincoln (Eds.), *Handbook of qualitative research* (pp. 105–117). Thousand Oaks, CA: Sage.

Gucciardi, D., & Gordon, S. (2011). *Mental toughness in sport: Developments in theory and research*. Abingdon: Routledge.

Gucciardi, D. F., Hanton, S., Gordon, S., Mallett, C. J., & Temby, P. (2015). The concept of mental toughness: Tests of dimensionality, nomological network, and traitness. *Journal of Personality, 83*, 26–44.

Gunnell, K. E., Schellenberg, B. J. I., Wilson, P. M., Crocker, P. R. E., Mack, D. E., & Zumbo, B. D. (2014). A review of validity evidence presented in the *Journal of Sport and Exercise Psychology* (2002–2012):

Misconceptions and recommendations for validation research. In B. D. Zumbo & K. H. Chan (Eds.), *Validity and validation in social, behavioral, and health sciences* (pp. 137–156). New York: Springer.

Hagger, M. S., & Chatzisarantis, N. L. D. (2009). Assumptions in research in sport and exercise psychology. *Psychology of Sport and Exercise, 10,* 511–519.

Hubley, A. M., & Zumbo, B. D. (2011). Validity and the consequences of test interpretation and use. *Social Indicators Research, 103,* 219–230.

Jasper, M. A. (1994). Issues in phenomenology for researchers of nursing. *Journal of Advanced Nursing, 19,* 309–314.

Jensen, S. N., Ivarsson, A., Fallby, J., Dankers, S., & Elbe, A.-M. (2018). Depression in Danish and Swedish elite football players and its relation to perfectionism and anxiety. *Psychology of Sport and Exercise, 36,* 147–155.

Jones, G., & Moorhouse, A. (2007). *Developing mental toughness: Gold medal strategies for transforming your business performance.* Oxford: Spring Hill.

Kowalski, K. C., McHugh, T.-L., Sabiston, C. M., & Ferguson, L. J. (2018). *Research methods in kinesiology.* Don Mills, ON: Oxford University Press.

Krefting, L. (1991). Rigor in qualitative research: The assessment of trustworthiness. *American Journal of Occupational Therapy, 45,* 214–222.

Landy, F. J. (1986). Stamp collecting versus science: Validation as hypothesis testing. *American Psychologist, 41,* 1183–1192.

Loevinger, J. (1957). Objective tests as instruments of psychological theory. *Psychological Reports, 3,* 635–694.

MacCorquodale, K., & Meehl, P. E. (1948). On a distinction between hypothetical constructs and intervening variables. *Psychological Review, 55,* 95–107.

Marsh, H. W. (1996a). Physical self-description questionnaire: Stability and discriminant validity. *Research Quarterly for Exercise and Sport, 67,* 249–264.

Marsh, H. W. (1996b). Construct validity of physical self-description questionnaire responses: Relations to external criteria. *Journal of Sport and Exercise Psychology, 18,* 111–131.

Marsh, H. W. (1997). The measurement of physical self-concept: A construct validation approach. In K. Fox (Ed.), *The physical self: From motivation to well-being* (pp. 27–58). Champaign, IL: Human Kinetics.

Marsh, H. W., Asci, F. H., & Tomas, I. M. (2002). Multitrait-multimethod analyses of two physical self-concept instruments: A cross-cultural perspective. *Journal of Sport and Exercise Psychology, 24,* 99–119.

Marsh, H. W., Richards, G. E., Johnson, S., Roche, L., & Tremayne, P. (1994). Physical self-description questionnaire: Psychometric properties and a multitrait-multimethod analysis of relations to existing instruments. *Journal of Sport and Exercise Psychology, 16,* 270–305.

Martens, R., Burton, D., Vealey, R. S., Bump, L. A., & Smith, D. E. (1990). Development and validation of the Competitive State Anxiety Inventory-2 (CSAI-2). In R. Martens, R. S. Vealey, & D. Burton (Eds.), *Competitive anxiety in sport* (pp. 193–208). Champaign, IL: Human Kinetics.

McHugh, T.-L. F., Holt, N. L., & Andersen, C. (2015). Community-based sport research with Indigenous youth. *Retos: Nuevas Tendencias en Educación Física, Deporte y Recreación, 28,* 219–224.

McTaggart, R. (1998). Is validity really an issue for participatory action research? *Studies in Cultures, Organizations, and Societies, 4,* 211–236.

Mellalieu, S. D., Hanton, S., & Fletcher, D. (2006). A competitive anxiety review: Recent directions in sport psychology research. In S. Hanton & S. D. Mellalieu (Eds.), *Literature reviews in sport psychology* (pp. 1–45). Hauppauge, NY: Nova Science.

Messick, S. (1989a). Validity. In R. L. Linn (Ed.), *Educational measurement* (3rd ed., pp. 13–103). New York: Macmillan.

Messick, S. (1989b). Meaning and values in test validation: The science and ethics of assessment. *Educational Researcher, 18,* 5–11.

Messick, S. (1995). Validity of psychological assessment: Validation of inferences from persons' responses and performances as scientific inquiry into score meaning. *American Psychologist, 50,* 741–749.

Palmateer, T., & Tamminen, K. (2018). A case study of interpersonal emotion regulation within a varsity volleyball team. *Journal of Applied Sport Psychology, 30,* 321–340.

Pillow, W. S. (2003). Confession, catharsis, or cure? Rethinking the use of reflexivity as methodological power in qualitative research. *International Journal of Qualitative Education, 16,* 175–196.

Ree, M. J., French, D., MacLeod, C., & Locke, V. (2008). Distinguishing cognitive and somatic dimensions of state and trait anxiety: Development and validation of the State-Trait Inventory for Cognitive and Somatic Anxiety (STICSA). *Behavioural and Cognitive Psychotherapy, 36,* 313–332.

Richards, G. E. (1988). *Physical self-concept scale.* Sydney: Australian Outward Bound Foundation.

Sabiston, C., Whitehead, J. R., & Eklund, R. (2012). Exercise and self-perception constructs. In G. Tenenbaum, R. Eklund, & A. Kamata (Eds.), *Measurement in sport and exercise psychology* (pp. 227–237). Champaign, IL: Human Kinetics.

Sandelowski, M. (1993). Rigor or rigor mortis: The problem of rigor in qualitative research revisited. *Advances in Nursing Science, 16,* 1–8.

Schinke, R. J., McGannon, K. R., Parham, W. D., & Lane, A. M. (2012). Toward cultural praxis and cultural sensitivity: Strategies for self-reflexive sport psychology practice. *Quest, 64,* 34–46.

Schinke, R. J., Smith, B., & McGannon, K. R. (2013). Pathways for community research in sport and physical activity: Criteria for consideration. *Qualitative Research in Sport, Exercise and Health, 5,* 460–468.

Schwartz, G. E., Davidson, R. J., & Goleman, D. J. (1978). Patterning of cognitive and somatic processes in the self-regulation of anxiety: Effects of meditation versus exercise. *Psychosomatic Medicine, 40,* 321–328.

Shavelson, R. J., Hubner, J. J., & Stanton, G. C. (1976). Self-concept: Validation of construct interpretations. *Review of Educational Research, 46,* 407–441.

Smith, B. (2013). Disability, sport and men's narratives of health: A qualitative study. *Health Psychology, 32,* 110–119.

Smith, B. (2018). Generalizability in qualitative research: Misunderstandings, opportunities and recommendations for the sport and exercise sciences. *Qualitative Research in Sport, Exercise and Health, 10,* 137–149.

Smith, B., & McGannon, K. R. (2017). Developing rigor in qualitative research: Problems and opportunities within sport and exercise psychology. *International Review of Sport and Exercise Psychology.* Advanced online publication. doi: 10.1080/1750984X.2017.1317357.

Spall, S. (1998). Peer debriefing in qualitative research: Emerging operational models. *Qualitative Inquiry, 4,* 280–292.

Sparkes, A. C., & Smith, B. (2009). Judging the quality of qualitative inquiry: Criteriology and relativism in action. *Psychology of Sport and Exercise, 10,* 491–497.

Spillett, M. A. (2003). Peer debriefing: Who, what, when, why, how. *Academic Exchange Quarterly, 7,* 36–40.

Stoeber, J., Otto, K., Pescheck, E., Becker, C., & Stoll, O. (2007). Perfectionism and competitive anxiety in athletes: Differentiating striving for perfection and negative reactions to imperfection. *Personality and Individual Differences, 42,* 959–969.

Strauss, M. E., & Smith, G. T. (2009). Construct validity: Advances in theory and methodology. *Annual Review of Clinical Psychology, 5,* 1–25.

Thomas, J. R., Nelson, J. K., & Silverman, S. J. (2011). *Research methods in physical activity* (6th ed.). Champaign, IL: Human Kinetics.

Weinberg, R. (2010). *Mental toughness for sport, business, and life.* Bloomington, IN: Author House.

Welfel, E. R. (2006). *Ethics in counseling and psychotherapy: Standards, research, and emerging issues* (3rd ed.). Belmont, CA: Thomson Brooks/Cole.

Woodman, T., Davis, P. A., Hardy, L., Callow, N., Glasscock, I., & Yuill-Proctor, J. (2009). Emotions and sport performance: An exploration of happiness, hope, and anger. *Journal of Sport and Exercise Psychology, 31,* 169–188.

Zhu, W. (2012). Measurement practice in sport and exercise psychology: A historical comparative, and psychometric view. In G. Tenenbaum, R. C. Eklund,, & A. Kamata (Eds.), *Measurement in sport and exercise psychology* (pp. 293–302). Champaign, IL: Human Kinetics.

19

MENTAL FITNESS

Dieter Hackfort and York-Peter Klöppel

Introduction

The term "fitness" is colloquially used for a variety of concepts. Most commonly, people refer to a person's physical fitness or appearance when using the word "fit" or "fitness". Furthermore, the term is used internationally in a number of different language contexts. For example, in the German language, the word *Fitnessstudio* is used for a specific kind of gym. According to the Oxford Dictionary (2018b; see catchword), in the English language, "fitness" is defined as "the condition of being physically fit and healthy", but also as "the quality of being suitable to fulfil a particular role or task". In this chapter, (1) the concept of fitness is elaborated from an action-theory perspective and characterized as a multidimensional concept including physical, mental, and social fitness. Next, (2) the concept of mental fitness is elaborated in accordance with this framework, and components and facets of mental fitness are described. Finally, (3) the operationalization and a self-evaluation method for the assessment of a key factor of mental fitness, namely mental robustness, is presented.

Theoretical Framework and Definition

The conceptualization of fitness presented here is ascribed to a relational fitness construct. Fitness refers to adaptations of the human being as a biopsychosocial system to his fields of living and acting. Long before the term was colloquially used to describe a person's physical fitness, especially in terms of sport, Spencer (1864) coined the term in reference to his renowned "survival of the fittest" hypothesis, which was later taken up by Darwin in his evolution theory. Darwin already understood fitness as a relationship phenomenon and, therefore, as an *adaptation*. The person–environment–task constellation (*action situation*; see Hackfort & Nitsch, 2019; Nitsch & Hackfort, 2016) sets the framework for *adaptation* in reference to human action. Indeed, *adaptation* is generally defined as "the process of change by which an organism or species becomes better suited to its environment" (Oxford Dictionary, 2018a; see catchword). Moreover, Piaget (1981) conceptualized *adaptation* as a continuous process between organisms and their environment. Fitness, therefore, refers to the relationship between the conditions (environment and task component of the action situation) and the person (as a component of the action situation) and, thus, represents an adaptation potential for or in specific action situations (Hackfort, Klämpfl, & Klöppel, 2019). In the context of sport, however, fitness can be described more specifically as an *adjustment*. Athletes striving for excellence have to adjust to small changes in their environment during competitions or training. Hackfort and Schinke (2019a) define *adjustment* as a:

> process of managing discrepancies in affective, cognitive, motivational, or/and volitional experiences in a given action situation, as one attempts to move toward a state of equilibrium or a fit in regard to a certain standard, such as an increased level of performance or health.
>
> *(pp. 6–7)*

The ability to effectively apply these processes in a given situation is described by the term fitness. Thus, fitness is not equal to a person's level of performance, as it is assumed frequently. Furthermore, *adjustment* (in conjunction with *adaptation*; Hackfort & Schinke, 2019b) appears to be the better-suited term, in a social science context, to describe fitness, as *adaptation* was developed and predominantly used in a bioscience context.

To further establish and bring specific meaning to this definition of fitness, one must first clarify the terminological relationship of fitness to related terms such as health and performance. Although fitness and health are related, and one often influences the other, they are not prerequisites for each other. In other words, a healthy person can have a low level of (physical, mental, or social) fitness, and a "fit" person can lack health. Paralympic athletes are classed as having a disability from a medical perspective and are restricted in their health status by definition, but they are "fitter" than numerous people in various ways. To give another example, long-term illness will most likely lead to a decrease in fitness, and vice versa. The fact that performance and fitness are not the same construct or prerequisites for one another becomes obvious when we look at the variety of body shapes in elite athletes across different sports. Comparing an elite rugby forward, an elite triathlete, and an elite snooker player, we see three athletes who are entirely different in their physical appearance and their physical fitness. However, they are all capable of producing the highest level of performance in their respective sport. Moreover, despite the snooker player possibly being regarded as being physically less fit than the other two, he will most probably always beat them at a game of snooker.

In reference to the biopsychosocial model for health (Engel, 1977), fitness is multidimensionally differentiated. More specifically, fitness can be grouped into (1) biological aspects with a focus on physical fitness; (2) psychological aspects with a focus on mental fitness; and (3) social aspects with a focus on social fitness, which has largely been neglected to date. Therefore, this comprehensive model of fitness contains three dimensions, which are not directly related, although they can influence each other. This multidimensional view of fitness allows not only for a more differentiated understanding, but also for a more specific assessment and intervention or fitness training than concepts in everyday language would suggest.

This framework, which has been developed from an action-theory perspective (see, e.g. Nitsch & Hackfort, 2016) for a general conceptualization of fitness, presumes the concept of the action situation as a person–environment–task constellation to be the fundamental relational unit or system of analysis. Furthermore, actions are considered to be intentional behaviours in regard to this system. If we refer to situations in sport and, therefore, sport-related fitness (or fitness in sport) or actions in sport, we consequently emphasize the psychophysiological adjustment potential of athletes in relation to mastering tasks and challenges in sport. The *adjustment* of the individual's resources (physical, mental, and social) to the situation-specific demands is central to this idea. Beyond the domain of sport, a holistic view on fitness is also of vital interest in the workplace. The demands of the workplace require individuals to use their individual resources to continuously produce adequate performance and be resilient to, and recover efficiently from, stressors. By implementing a concept that considers the potentials for performance, *resilience*, and *recovery* as components of fitness, it is possible to systematically analyse a person's strengths and weaknesses and to organize individualized training if necessary. This may help, for example, to maintain performance in challenging situations and reduce the risk of choking under pressure. Finally, the concept is a prerequisite for methods to counteract the constant rise in stress-induced psychological illnesses such as burnout and depression in the workplace and in sport. In the following section, a holistic concept of fitness based on an action-theory perspective is presented in more detail.

An Action-Theory-Based Concept of Fitness

Each of the aforementioned dimensions of fitness (physical, mental, and social) can potentially interact with each other. In fact, it is difficult to solely train one fitness dimension, as training to improve one's physical fitness in a gym, for example, will also affect, to some extent, one's mental and social fitness. Mental facets, such as concentration and *mental toughness*, will most likely also be improved as an epiphenomenon of the physical training. Figure 3 illustrates the holistic fitness concept consisting of three dimensions. Each dimension is further differentiated into three components, namely the potentials for performance, resilience, and recovery. These

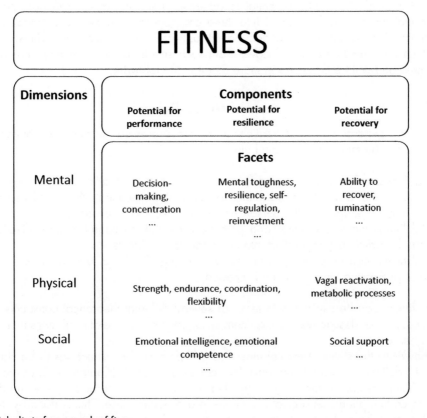

Figure 3 A holistic framework of fitness

components are further subdivided by facets. The list in Figure 3 is not a complete list of facets for each component in each dimension, but simply serves to give the reader some examples. Further related constructs can be embedded in the concept as facets of the relevant component within the applicable dimension.

More specifically, the physical fitness dimension refers to the physical potential to accomplish an action situation and can be further differentiated into health-related and skill-related physical fitness (Pate, 1983). Physical fitness consists of several facets, such as cardiorespiratory endurance, muscular endurance, muscular strength, body composition, coordination, flexibility, and metabolic processes.

Social fitness entails facets such as social competence and emotional intelligence and refers to the potential of an individual to manage social tasks or social demands in interindividual actions. Emotional intelligence has recently been defined as the ability to deal with intra- or interpersonal aspects of emotions (Laborde & Mosley, 2019; see the contribution in this encyclopedia). Amid an ongoing discussion on whether emotional intelligence should be considered as a trait or an ability, the term *emotional competence* emerged to describe an individual's trainable and improvable ability to cope with intra- and interpersonal emotional aspects. Brasseur, Grégoire, Bourdu, and Mikolajczak (2013) detected identification, expression, understanding, regulation, and use of one's own or others' emotions as further facets of emotional competence. Social support as a facet of social fitness is especially crucial for the component of the potential for recovery.

The final dimension, namely mental fitness, is the focus of this contribution. Mental fitness refers to an individual's mental potential to adjust to a specific action situation. As Figure 3 shows, mental fitness is differentiated into three components, exactly like physical fitness and social fitness. The potentials to render mental performance, to mentally withstand stressful action situations, and to mentally recover from such situations form the three components of mental fitness and will be discussed in more detail in the following.

Status of Mental Fitness

Based on the general conceptualization of fitness presented in this contribution, several propositions can be made about mental fitness:

(a) Mental fitness refers to a fit (being fit in a specific action situation, thus, situational) or an adaptation (the process of adapting to an action situation, thus, processual) within a system that is shaped by the person–environment–task constellation.
(b) Mental fitness includes abilities and potentials, as well as cognitive and affective factors that can be structurally separated into components and facets.
(c) Mental fitness can be a state, in the sense of being "fit" for a task, or a potential, in the sense of possessing fitness when it is needed.

Mental fitness can be explained in terms of several different theoretical constructs. Whether mental fitness is a descriptive or explicative, a personal or relational construct is briefly discussed below.

First, however, the status of mental fitness as a hypothetical construct has to be clarified. "A construct is defined as something built by mental synthesis" (Kaplan & Saccuzzo, 2005, p. 148). Such mental syntheses (or hypothetical theories or constructs) are used to give meaning to certain phenomena or observations in a broader sense. This is done by integrating empirical issues (observations) into theoretical frameworks. These observations thereby become indicators of a certain concept. Consequently, additional indicators can be identified in the research process so that more and more explicit statements can be made about the construct. The research and development of a construct and its corresponding theory are, therefore, continuously ongoing. Furthermore, Nitsch (2000) argues that theories help us make reality more comprehensible and feasible, as well as structure and systematize our knowledge, research processes, and research findings.

Differences in the theoretical status of mental fitness become evident in reference to the aforementioned propositions. The different uses of the term (processual or situational; as a state or as a potential) point to different functions of mental fitness, as signified by the discrimination between an explicative and a descriptive construct (e.g. Herrmann, 1969).

A descriptive construct describes a particular constellation of empirical issues (in this case, fitness) as a state. This constellation of issues as a descriptive construct always contains multiple elements. The key questions in clarifying the construct concern which elements correlate, and how they are related to each other. Mental, emotional, and behavioural elements are measured and diagnosed to further explain and specify the construct. In light of this, mental fitness as a descriptive construct is best defined with the adjective "fit" to describe the state of being fit.

The purpose of explicative constructs is, as the name suggests, the clarification (explanation) of functional relationships in relation to empirical issues. In terms of fitness, individual differences in the causality of fitness or the change of empirically observable attributes in the fitness state of a person or the effect of fitness are explained. Therefore, explicative constructs explain the relationships between the empirical issues that are described by the descriptive construct. Consequently, the term fitness should be used to describe the potential to actively reach the state of being fit. Such a potential always refers to a framework, which is why another theoretical construct is being presented here.

In contrast to a personal construct, which describes personality traits such as emotionality or intelligence, a relational construct emphasizes the aspect, which is implemented by interaction or transaction theories. As a specific action, which aims to reach a state of fitness, indicates a situation that an acting subject has to deal with, and that presents the challenges that provoke an action, fitness should always be seen in relation to its respective person–task–environment constellation (action situation; Hackfort, 1986; Hackfort & Nitsch, 2019). Therefore, fitness should also be identified as a relational construct.

Structure of Mental Fitness

Mental fitness in this conceptualization as an adjustment potential is differentiated into three components: the potential to (1) render mental performance (potential for performance); (2) mentally withstand stressful action situations (potential for resilience); and (3) mentally recover from such situations (potential for recovery). A similar structural approach in the conceptualization of psychological fitness in regard to the US military was used by Bates (2010). The potentials for performance and resilience have also been mentioned from a sport psychology perspective by Schinke, Battochio, Dube, Tenenbaum, and Lane (2012). They comment on the potentials of elite athletes to react to stressors competently; however, they focus on emotional and psychological balance, which is achieved by techniques such as self-regulation. The conceptualization presented here is based on the differentiation of cognitive and affective regulation processes and the interrelation of these basic mental processes. Consequently, in consideration of the international terminology, the term mental fitness appears better suited for a holistic conceptualization of the mental adjustments to stressful situations. The aforementioned three components are outlined below.

(1) The performance component describes a person's potential to render mental performance. The requirements for mental performance are an individual's mental abilities. These abilities, such as directing one's attention to concentrate, to make decisions, or to regulate one's memory, are the facets of the potential for mental performance. In the context of sport, such facets include, for example, mental training (imagery) or tactical thinking.

(2) The resilience component describes the potential to withstand stressful situations with as little performance loss as possible. Many constructs are related to the component, such as resilience, perceived self-efficacy, *mental toughness*, self-regulation, emotional stability, and reinvestment.

(3) The recovery component describes the potential to regenerate from stressful situations as quickly as possible and to be ready to perform in upcoming tasks. Identically to the potential for mental performance and the potential for mental resilience, this concept also consists of facets. Two key facets characterize the potential for mental recovery, namely rumination and the ability to recover.

As shown in Figure 3, each component is further explained by facets. The number of facets for each component is theoretically limitless, as the components are highly complex constructs owing to humans being extremely complex beings. Each additional facet will help to further explain the component and, therefore, fitness as a whole. The facets presented here are considered to be the key facets for each component, but this is not an exhaustive list.

The selection and specific definition of facets related to the potential for mental performance are guided by the task-specific demands in the way in which they are relevant for the action organization and regulation. As an example, two key facets (decision-making and attention/concentration) are described below.

Decision-making refers to "the process of making a choice from a set of options, with the consequences of that choice being crucial" (Bar-Eli, Plessner, & Raab, 2011, p. 6). The process for making an adequate decision depends on the task complexity, from which the mental demands of a task result, and the integration of perceived information from previous experiences. Decision-making processes are often closely related to other facets of the potential for mental performance – for example attention, perception, anticipation, memory, and learning (Raab, 2019). Owing to the vast amount of research on decision-making in psychology (more than 250 identified theories; Raab, 2019), "decision-making competencies" is used as an umbrella term by some, encompassing all the abilities and skills that expert decision-makers develop over time. This is an example of how some facets within a dimension of mental fitness can be even further differentiated. One example of a theory for decision-making is the multi-attribute decision theory (Keeney & Raiffa, 1976), which is relatively extensive and explains how preferences over multiple objectives can be quantified. Furthermore, the theory elaborates on the processes of calculation, which are vital in conjunction with the planning processes in the anticipation phase of actions (see Nitsch & Hackfort, 2016). However, quick decisions are usually taken intuitively. Gigerenzer (2007) characterizes intuition as a quick judgement that is not based on contemplation or conscious reasoning, but is still strong enough to act upon. Intuitive decisions happen automatically and rest upon unconscious associations between the perceived situation and the execution of an action. Affective processes ("good feelings") influence intuitive decisions more than cognitive processes (Chaudhry, Parkinson, Hinton, Owen, & Roberts, 2009). Intuitive decision-making occurs according to a strategy called a "heuristic". A heuristic "ignores part of the information, with the goal of making decisions more quickly, frugally, and/or accurately than more complex methods" (Gigerenzer & Gaissmaier, 2011, p. 454). In sport, heuristics have been studied in a number of aspects including discrete choice tasks and the "hot hand fallacy". Furthermore, the theory of "take the first heuristic", which describes the phenomenon of choosing the first option that comes to mind, has been shown to explain up to 90% of athletes' decisions (Hepler & Feltz, 2012).

Concentration has most recently been defined as "the ability to exert mental effort on the task at hand, or on what is most important in any situation, while ignoring distractions" (Moran, 2019, pp. 57–58). Attention, on the other hand, describes the conscious perception or observance of an object (e.g. process, object, idea; Häcker & Stapf, 2004). In sport psychology, concentration is described as the ability not only to direct one's attention to a task, but also to maintain the attentional focus without being distracted by external (e.g. noise) or internal (e.g. negative thoughts) stimuli (Wilson, Peper, & Schmid, 2006). The reason why concentration and attention are listed collectively here is because of the synonymous usage of the terms in sports psychology and everyday language. Again, similar to decision-making, attention can be further differentiated. One possible conceptualization by Etzel (1979; cf. Moran, 2016) describes attention as a multidimensional construct encompassing four factors: (1) capacity – amount of mental energy for processing task-relevant information in a given situation; (2) duration – ability to maintain concentration over time (also called vigilance); (3) flexibility – ability to change area and focus of attention with ease; (4) selectivity – selection of activities to analytically process information. In fact, the fourth factor mentioned (selectivity) is what is best described as concentration (Moran, 2019).

From a theoretical perspective, the potential for mental resilience as a component of mental fitness contains a large number of facets. Self-efficacy, *mental toughness*, self-regulation, resilience, emotional stability, and reinvestment are presented here as examples of the many more theoretical constructs developed in the past.

Different definitions exist for the term *resilience*. It is a polysemic term that has been applied across various different disciplines, including mechanical engineering, ecological systems, child psychology, security and emergency management, and organizational science (Mukherjee & Kumar, 2017; cf. Fletcher, 2019). To find a common ground and in the context of the theoretical framework for mental fitness, *resilience* is characterized here as an explicative construct that refers to a personal (or group) potential. Moreover, Fletcher (2019) defines resilience in sport psychology as "an individual's, group's, or organization's ability to withstand or adapt to demanding environments" (p. 248). As this definition and the terminology suggest, *resilience* is the overarching term for this component, but also a facet in itself. Resilient individuals are optimistic and emotionally stable and have a high enjoyment of life and vital (life) energy.

Perceived *self-efficacy* is a construct originally developed within the framework of social cognitive theory and was first defined by Bandura (1977). He defined efficacy expectations as "the conviction that one can successfully execute the behavior required to produce the outcomes" (Bandura, 1977, p. 193). More specifically, in the context of sport, *self-efficacy* usually refers to the cognitive process by which people make judgements about their abilities to accomplish a certain goal. In other words, it describes what people think they can do rather than their actual physical ability and is, therefore, closely related to motivation. People with high *self-efficacy* are more likely to endure a stressful situation, as their strong belief in their own abilities will have motivational effects. Feltz (2019) also proposed that self-efficacy beliefs can influence "thought patterns, such as worries, goal intentions, and causal attributions, as well as such emotional reactions as pride, shame, happiness, and sadness" (p. 261).

Another polysemic term that has gained a lot of interest among academic and sporting communities in the past two decades is called *mental toughness*. A recent definition of *mental toughness* highlights the idea that mental fitness (and its components and facets) is a potential (i.e. a resource). Gucciardi (2017) defines the concept as "a state-like psychological resource that is purposeful, flexible, and efficient in nature for the enactment and maintenance of goal-directed pursuits" (p. 18). Furthermore, theories on *mental toughness* commonly use the term as a collective for several related constructs (e.g. self-efficacy or self-regulation). Most relevant to this conceptualization of mental fitness, however, seems to be the 4Cs model (Clough, Earle, & Sewell, 2002). This model and its conceptualization of *mental toughness* have integrated the construct of hardiness and updated this framework with the concept of confidence. Clough et al. (2002) conceptualize *mental toughness* as a personality trait containing four dimensions: (1) control – believing that you control your own destiny and emotions; (2) commitment – the ability to stick to tasks (dedication); (3) challenge – perceiving challenging situations as an opportunity; and (4) confidence – being confident in your own abilities to cope with and overcome negative life events.

Self-regulation has been described as both adjustable, depending on the situation, and as a stable personality trait. As a situation-depending concept, self-regulation "refers to the processes by which individuals modify or modulate their thoughts, feelings, and behaviors to attain goals" (Robazza & Ruiz, 2019). In this sense, self-regulation implies a cognitive, affective, behavioural, and attentional modulation through deliberate or automatic application of specific mechanisms or skills. As a stable personality trait, on the other hand, self-regulation entails emotional and attentional regulation, as well as self-efficacy beliefs, which are also conceptualized as stable constructs for their part (Luszczynska, Diehl, Gutiérrez-Dona, Kuusinen, & Schwarzer, 2004). The strength model of self-regulation (Baumeister & Vohs, 2016) suggests that the self-regulation of thoughts, emotions, and behaviours requires energy, which can be depleted over time by repeated exertion. This highlights the notion that self-regulation is also a potential that an individual can utilize in stressful situations.

A further facet of mental resilience is *emotional stability*, which, together with its opposite concept, emotional lability, makes up one of the traits of the five-factor model (Digman, 1990), namely neuroticism. Emotional stability describes the ability to control one's own emotions, to overcome stressful situations, and to recover from such situations quickly. People at the opposite end of the neuroticism spectrum (emotional lability) tend to be anxious, self-conscious, vulnerable, angry, and/or depressed.

In a sporting context, the concept of *reinvestment* describes the application of an internal direction of attention to one's own conscious control of body movements by using explicit knowledge about the movement. Reinvestment theory proposes that athletes' performances decrease under pressure when they direct conscious attention to the execution of the skill, rather than allowing the skill to be executed automatically (Masters & Maxwell, 2008). This is especially relevant for skills that have already been learned and are usually executed automatically. In a situation of mental pressure (e.g. a competition), people tend to regulate their movements consciously in order to feel more in control (Masters & Maxwell, 2008). Therefore, reinvestment is a potential underlying mechanism of "choking under pressure".

The description of resilience, self-efficacy, mental toughness, self-regulation, emotional stability, and reinvestment has shown that these facets depict personality factors of the potential for mental resilience. Furthermore, contentual similarities between these personality factors become apparent. In fact, demarcation problems between resilience, perceived self-efficacy, and hardiness have been reported (Schumacher, Leppert, Gunzelmann, Strauß, & Brähler,

2005). Empirical correlations have been found between self-efficacy and resilience (r = 0.68–0.70; Schumacher et al., 2005), mental toughness (r = 0.22–0.50; Madrigal, Hamill, & Gill, 2013; Nicholls et al., 2015), self-regulation ($r > 0.65$; Luszczynska, Gutiérrez-Doña, & Schwarzer, 2005), and emotional lability (r = –0.42; Schwarzer, 2014). Moreover, correlations between mental toughness and resilience (r = 0.63; Nicholls et al., 2015) and emotional lability (r = –0.64; Horsburgh, Schermer, Veselka, & Vernon, 2009) have also been found.

The third component of mental fitness, the potential for *mental recovery*, also contains a number of different facets. There are several terms to describe the concept of recovery (e.g. regeneration, rest, or recuperation); however, recovery is considered the umbrella term (Heidari & Kellmann, 2019) and has, therefore, been used in this conceptualization. The two facets described in detail here are antagonistic. From a theoretical perspective, they describe the two opposite ends of the spectrum of mental recovery.

On the one hand, *rumination* describes a process of pondering (ruminating) about the current emotional state or past events, which are usually related to unsuccessful performances. Individuals with a tendency to ruminate experience more negative agitations, worry more, and perform worse on cognitive tasks (Scott & McIntosh, 1999). Therefore, rumination is a negative stress-processing strategy that does not lead to problem-solving. Instead, this process "traps" people in their own thoughts, requiring (mental) energy rather than helping the recovery process. Furthermore, it can lead to under-recovery, overtraining, and burn-out.

On the other hand, the ability to recover describes an individual's competence to recover from a stressful situation efficiently. Recovery has been described from different perspectives (e.g. physiological, behavioural, social, etc.). In sport psychology, recovery has been described as "a restorative, psychophysiological process that aims at the reestablishment of depleted resources" (Heidari & Kellmann, 2019, p. 242). Furthermore, it helps an organism to regain homeostatic and biorhythmic balance after it has been exposed to stressful events and situations (Kellmann, 2002). Krajewski, Mühlenbrock, Schnieder, and Seiler (2011) characterize the ability to recover as the appropriate selection of compensatory methods to balance out the current stress level. This ability is further described by the readiness to recover and the capability to recover.

In summary, mental fitness is characterized as a relational construct that refers to an action situation. This construct brings a combination of three personality components (potential for performance, resilience, and recovery) into relation with task- and environment-specific demands. Cognitive and affective processes are required to overcome these demands.

Operationalization of Mental Fitness

For the operationalization and assessment of the three presented components, a multimethod approach is needed. The resulting profile created by the analysis of data collected through measurements characterizes the individual kind or state of mental fitness. An overview of the methodological approach is given in Figure 4.

One possible tool to diagnose and train the potential for mental performance is a computer-based test, the movement detection test (MDT; Hackfort, Herle, & Debelak, 2010) available in the mental test and training system (MTTS; Hackfort, Kilgallen, & Hao, 2009). As the MTTS has already been outlined in detail (see Hackfort et al., 2009), and its manual (Hackfort et al., 2010) provides comprehensive information on the MDT, the focus here is on a new measurement developed specifically in the context of the operationalization of mental fitness.

For the assessment of two components of mental fitness, namely the potentials of resistance and recovery, a multifactorial summative self-evaluation method has been developed. In the

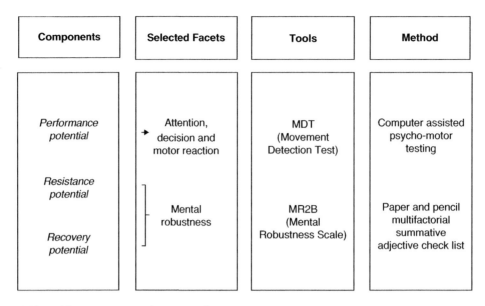

Figure 4 Mental fitness operationalization and assessment

design of this assessment, the potentials for mental *resilience* and *mental recovery* have been combined to form the construct of *mental robustness*. Moreover, mental robustness comprises two components derived from the two fundamental processes, namely the cognitive and affective potential for resilience and recovery of an individual with respect to all kinds of stress exposure. In other words, this construct of mental robustness represents the potential of an individual to resist different kinds of strain and moderate the perception and experience of, and reaction to, stress with as minimal performance losses as possible, as well as recovering from these types of experience as quickly as possible to be ready for upcoming performance tasks. This construct is closely related, on the one hand, to the construct of resilience or resistance and, on the other hand, to the construct of regeneration (see Figure 5), as they are essential components in the concept of fitness and especially mental fitness, as outlined above.

Mentally robust people can access the potential for mental performance even in stressful situations and subsequently recover quickly from these situations. On the other hand, people with less mental robustness will have difficulty reaching their full mental performance potential.

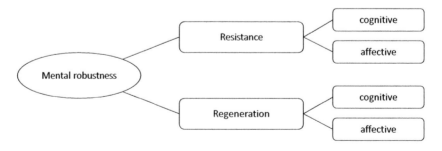

Figure 5 Conceptual structure of mental robustness

Development of the Mental Robustness Scale

Based on the concept of mental robustness, an economical scale was developed (MR2B; Hackfort et al., 2019). This scale enables the operationalization and multifactorial diagnostic of this construct. This scale was originally developed in German for German clients.

In order to develop an economical scale, a summative procedure needs to be employed. Rather than a cumulation of items adding up to a factor, the scale only consists of marker items for the factors to capture an individual's self-assessment (Hackfort, 2014; Hackfort & Schlattmann, 1995). Such a procedure has two major advantages. First, the application is flexible. In other words, the resulting scale can be used as a state (the current condition) or trait (in general, across different situations and times) measure. Second, the resulting scale can be used to measure direct differences (before vs. after) over a short period of time. To develop such an economical scale, the following steps must be performed:

(1) Selection of instruments
(2) Identification of marker items
(3) Transformation to a consistent response category – for example, adjectives
(4) Verification of factor structure
(5) Validation
(6) Compilation of norm values

All six steps were carried out to systematically develop the MR2B. There follows a detailed description of the steps in order. Based on the presented facets for the potential of resilience and recovery above, suitable measurements were examined and selected for their methodological and conceptual suitability. The following instruments were considered for each facet:

Resilience: The superordinate construct of resilience was used from the revised short version of the resilience scale by Leppert and colleagues (RS-13; 2008). Other measures include the long version of the resilience scale (RS-25; Wagnild & Young, 1993) and the short version in German (RS-11; Schumacher et al., 2005). However, these were not considered for the development of the MR2B for economical (RS-25) or statistical (RS-11) reasons. Furthermore, the Connor–Davidson resilience scale (Connor & Davidson, 2003) and the resilience scale for adults (Friborg, Hjemdal, Rosenvinge, & Martinussen, 2003) were not used, as at the time of development no German versions existed of these scales.

Self-efficacy: Despite the construct of self-efficacy being based on situation-specific assumptions, the *Skala der Allgemeinen Selbstwirksamkeitserwartung* (general self-efficacy scale, SWE, by Schwarzer & Jerusalem, 1999) measures a more stable fundamental belief about one's abilities. Two other measures, both developed by Riggs, Warka, Babasa, Betancourt, and Hooker (1994), namely the personal efficacy scale and the collective efficacy scale, were not used for the development of the MR2B owing to their lack of relevance in this context.

Mental toughness: For this concept, the mental toughness questionnaire (MTQ-48; Clough et al., 2002; German version: Gerber et al., 2012) was selected. Other measures are based on unidimensional concepts and were, therefore, not used in this project (mental toughness index: Gucciardi, Hanton, Gordon, Mallett, & Temby, 2015; mental toughness scale: Madrigal et al., 2013).

Self-regulation: Only one scale was deemed suitable to measure the concept of self-regulation. The self-regulation scale (SRS; Schwarzer, Diehl, & Schmitz, 1999) measures the ability to maintain complex tasks in spite of negative impacts on the motivation and attention of an individual.

Emotional stability (ES): The subscale "neuroticism" of the NEO five-factor inventory (Costa & McCrae, 1992; German version: Borkenau & Ostendorf, 1993) is used to measure an individual's emotional stability (lability). An alternative measure is represented by the subscale of the Bochumer Inventar zur berufsbezogenen Persönlichkeitsbeschreibung (Bochum inventory of occupational personality characterization) developed by Hossiep and Paschen (2003).

Reinvestment: Reinvestment is also relevant in the field of decision-making, and the tendency towards it can be measured with the decision-specific reinvestment scale (DSRS; Kinrade, Jackson, & Ashford, 2010; German version: Laborde et al., 2015). It is believed that mentally robust individuals are less prone to reinvesting.

Rumination: The tendency to reflect over bad decisions made in the past can be measured with the subscale "rumination" of the DSRS (Kinrade et al., 2010; German version: Laborde et al., 2015). Alternatively, the subscale Gedankliche Weiterbeschäftigung (continued mental engagement) of the Stressverarbeitungsfragebogen (stress processing questionnaire; SVF 78, SVF 120; Erdmann & Janke, 2008) or the Scott–McIntosh rumination inventory (Scott & McIntosh, 1999) could be considered.

Potential to recover: This potential is measured through the short version of the Erholungskompetenzskala (recovery competency scale; Krajewski et al., 2011). In the field of sport science, the situation-specific comprehensive recovery stress questionnaire for athletes (Kellmann & Kallus, 2001) is often used.

In order to form representative and summative factor items, first the marker items for each factor of the selected instruments had to be determined. An item was identified as a marker item when it showed the highest loadings or the best power scores within a factor when tested for validity. In this way, up to three marker items were identified for each factor. In some cases, the power scores from the English version of an instrument were used, when no detailed information on the validity was published for the German version of an instrument.

Following the identification of the marker items, representative adjectives were derived from the marker items. First, a group of two experts collected possible adjectives, before, with the help of a third expert, they selected the best representative adjective for each identified marker item. For example, the marker item "Ich behalte an vielen Dingen Interesse [I stay interested in many things]" from the resilience scale was derived to the adjective "interested".

Finally, the design of a "cloud" was formed and filled with the three derived adjectives that initially represent the original factor of the instrument. In this way, 13 "cloud items" were initially developed that contained both positively and negatively polarized items. The chosen four-point response scale ranged from 1 (does not apply) to 4 (fully applies). In order to determine the factor structure, construct validity, and reliability of the designed scale, an online and paper-and-pencil survey was conducted. A total of 503 participants (online: n = 383; paper-and-pencil: n = 117; age: M = 34.1 years, SD = 14.3, range = 11–77; female = 30.6%) completed the survey.

Based on the conceptual framework, a binary structure analysis (BISTRAN; Nitsch, 1974) was conducted to test the factor structure of the constructed scale of mental robustness. The binary structure analysis is based on a conceptual dual perspective and the binary itemization principle by which opposite factors are extracted through factorial analysis methods in a hierarchical stepwise approach.

The first calculations revealed that the cloud item "self-analysing, self-reflective, self-observant" (originally representing reinvestment) could not be unambiguously allocated to a factor and was, therefore, excluded from any further calculations.

Next, all items were split into two factors via an oblique rotation (binary factors, Stage 1). The oblique rotation implies that the dimensions are correlated – that is, scoring high on one factor of the questionnaire correlates with high scores on the other factor. Subsequently, each item was allocated to one of the two factors according to their factor loadings. In the next step, all items within each factor were divided into two more factors using an oblique rotation again (binary factors, Stage 2). At this stage, the procedure was ended, as a further distribution into more factors would be ineffective. The factor analysis, therefore, resulted in a two-tier binary structure with a total of six binary factors.

The content description of the factors refers to the corresponding items and the correlations with other constructs. Mental robustness (MR; ES: $r = .61$; SWE: $r = .58$; RS: $r = .56$; MTQ: $r = .56$) is the superordinate factor. The next stage of binary factors revealed robustness booster (RBO; RS: $r = .55$; SWE: $r = .55$; ES: $r = .46$) and robustness barriers (RBA; ES: $r = -.62$; MTQ: $r = -.50$; SRS: $r = -.42$). Robustness boosters are further differentiated on the next factor level into self-assurance (SeAs; Items 3–6 and 11; SWE: $r = .50$; RS: $r = .49$; MTQ: $r = .42$) and self-esteem (SeEs; Items 9 and 10; RS: $r = .45$; SWE: $r = .45$; MTQ: $r = .41$). Robustness barriers are further differentiated on the next factor level into emotional lability (EmLa; Items 2, 7, and 8; ES: $r = -.57$; MTQ: $r = -.48$; SRS: $r = -.46$) and recovery insufficiency (ReIn; Items 1 and 12; ES: $r = -.39$; RUM: $r = .34$; EKS: $r = -.32$).

The scoring of the MR2B works by substituting the raw item scores (self-reported scores of the participant) with the transformed z'-scores (McCall procedure; McCall, 1939). Next, the z'-scores are added up for each factor. Finally, the summarized z'-scores are assigned to the corresponding norm values.

Psychometric Properties of the MR2B

In this section, a report is given on the psychometric properties of the MR2B scale. The data obtained through the aforementioned survey (n = 503) were used to calculate the psychometric values such as validity.

The reliability is an indication for the accuracy of measurements and how reliable specific results of an instrument are. Reliability measures include item difficulty, item discrimination power, internal consistency, and test-retest reliability.

Item difficulty indicates the general response tendency of an item. In this way, items that generate a similar response across all participants can be excluded from an instrument for being too easy or too difficult to answer. A score between .20 and .80 is considered acceptable (Fisseni, 1997). All items of the MR2B show acceptable scores, apart from Items 7 and 11, which are slightly too easy.

Item discrimination power refers to and provides a score of how well an item can differentiate between individuals with high and low construct characteristics. Scores between .30 and .50 are regarded as optimal (Fisseni, 1997), with all of the items of the MR2B showing optimal scores, apart from Items 1 and 12, which appear to have low discrimination.

Internal consistency describes the extent to which the items of an instrument correlate with one another. Cognitive tests are expected to show scores higher than .80 and performance tests higher than .70. For psychometric tests, a consistency lower than .70 can also be acceptable (Field, 2009). Three sub-scores of the MR2B show an internal consistency lower than .70, with recovery insufficiency most notably low ($\alpha = .218$).

Test-retest reliability ensures that measurements obtained at one point in time are representative and stable over time. A sufficient stability is reached with scores above .70 (Bühner, 2011). The first test-retest sample consisted of 91 participants of the original survey (age: M = 36.0 years, SD = 14.1; female = 31.9%). The time between the two measurements was 3–8 months. Owing to this, the scores varied between .28 and .60. The second test-retest sample consisted of 29 university students (M = 21.9 years, SD = 4.4; female = 17.2%). The time between the two measurements was 2 weeks for all participants. However, similar scores to those in the first sample were found.

Consistent with convergent validity, the factors of the MR2B should correlate with related constructs of other psychometric instruments. As mentioned before, the survey consisted of an array of psychometric instruments. Significant and positive correlations are especially noteworthy between MR and self-efficacy, self-regulation, resilience, and mental toughness. Furthermore, significant and negative correlations exist between MR and rumination and emotional lability. RBOs correlate similarly to the superordinate factor, MR. RBAs, on the other hand, correlate reciprocally with the other constructs. In summary, a satisfactorily convergent validity of the MR2B is assumed.

Another form of validity is the correlation between parameters of the instrument with different criteria that are to be expected owing to the theoretical background of the construction of the instrument. Therefore, mentally robust individuals should perform better in cognitive stress tests than individuals who score less highly on the scale of MR. Using the MR2B to identify mentally robust (n = 5; MR > 6; age: M = 23 years, SD = 1.4) and less mentally robust (n = 7; MR < 4; age: M = 23 years, SD = 3.2) individuals in a study containing 40 participants, two cognitive tests on the Vienna test system (Schuhfried, 2014) were used to confirm criterion validity. The determination test (Schuhfried, 2010) is a complex, multi-stimuli reaction test involving the presentation of both coloured stimuli and acoustic signals, thereby assessing reactive stress tolerance, attention, and reaction speed in the respondent. The Stroop test (Schuhfried, 2009) is a sensorimotor speed test that measures speed in reading words and naming colours. To measure the arousal levels of the participants in relation to a resting state, the heart rate was recorded. At the end of each session, the participants rated how mentally stressful they felt the tests were on a scale of 0 (not at all) to 9 (completely stressful).

The determination test revealed that the mentally robust group was more resilient than the less mentally robust group in terms of reaction speed (right answers): $t(6.789) = -3.49$, $p = .011$. However, no significant differences were found between the two groups in relation to the ability to concentrate on easy cognitive tasks over a longer period of time (wrong answers: $t(10) = 0.51$, $p = .619$; missed answers: $t(10) = -.78$, $p = .454$). Although the Stroop test did not reveal any significant differences between the two groups, there is a clear trend that shows that the mentally robust group answered more tasks correctly. A larger sample size would probably confirm this trend. The same is the case for differences in the heart rate and subjective ratings of the tests, which showed no significant differences; however, a trend was noticeable.

In summary, there is a tendency to show criterion validity. With larger group sizes, it is expected that the observable trends would become statistically significant. Furthermore, differences between people with mental illnesses and mentally healthy people would also show criterion validity, as it is expected that athletes, for example, are more mentally robust than people with mental illnesses.

Scale Interpretation

The scale consists of one superordinate factor and six hierarchically ordered binary factors. The superordinate factor, MR, characterizes an individual's potential to resist strain or withstand stressful situations with as little performance loss as possible (potential for mental resilience) and the potential to recover from stressful situations as quickly as possible and be ready to perform in upcoming tasks (potential for mental regeneration). Mentally robust individuals (scoring above average in MR) are more able to perform at their maximum mental performance level in stressful situations and recover more efficiently than individuals with lower (scoring below average in MR) MR.

The first factor level distinguishes between RBOs and RBAs. As the terms suggest, RBOs have a facilitative effect on MR, whereas mental barriers have a debilitative effect. RBOs can be associated with self-confidence. Self-confidence can be defined as "the belief in one's abilities to accomplish a certain goal" (Feltz & Moss, 2019, p. 257), as well as the belief in one's self-worth. Indeed, RBOs are further broken down into self-assurance and self-esteem on the next factor level, two concepts closely related to self-confidence. Individuals scoring high on RBOs are more self-confident than individuals with lower scores, which in turn means that they are more self-assured about their abilities and possess stronger self-esteem about themselves. RBAs, on the other hand, inhibit MR, hence negatively effecting the mental performance potential of a person in a stressful situation. Individuals scoring high on RBAs will have difficulties regulating their own emotions, enduring or withstanding stressful situations, relaxing or unwinding, and efficiently recovering from stressful situations. They tend to be emotionally labile and unable to mentally regenerate. The second factor level also identifies RBAs differentiated into emotional lability and regeneration insufficiency.

Conclusion

Mental fitness as a dimension of a holistic fitness concept, which stands in reference to the human as a biopsychosocial system, refers as a relational construct to an adjustment in the action situation as a person–environment–task constellation. The mental dimension of fitness entails cognitive and affective factors and can be internally differentiated into three components, namely the potential for performance, resilience, and recovery. These components can be further broken down into facets. The facets of the potential for mental performance include (not exclusively) decision-making and attention/concentration. The key facets of the potential for mental *resilience* are *self-efficacy*, *mental toughness*, *self-regulation*, *emotional stability*, and *reinvestment*. Finally, the potential for *mental recovery* includes *rumination* and the potential to recover as facets. These facets reflect (facilitative) RBOs on the one hand and (inhibiting) RBAs on the other. This structure offers an approach to the diagnostics of mental fitness, as well as possible ideas for a training system to improve an individual's mental fitness.

Different methods are used for the operationalization of this concept. Regarding the potential for mental performance, the utilization of an attention decision test – for example, the MDT – is recommended. To diagnose the potential for *mental resilience* and *recovery*, a recently developed scale, namely the MR2B, was introduced. Both of these tools are easy to use owing to their economic values and are open to the possibility of intervention techniques.

Future research should analyse the emergence of the facets and determine the antecedents of mental fitness. Distal antecedents of mental fitness should be considered in light of socialization and lifestyle, whereas proximal antecedents should be determined by investigating the individual effect of the facets (e.g. potential to recover, self-assurance, self-confidence). Furthermore, it is important to reiterate that mental fitness is a relational construct ("mentally fit" for what?) and should, therefore, in practice, always be considered specific to a given action situation; This means that the ascertainment or accentuation of the facets has to be adjusted to a specific situation (according to the fitness concept). Thus, the importance or relevance of the facets of mental fitness varies across different types of sport and competition. Therefore, a most relevant task for future research in regard to the professional practice and improvement of the application of sport psychology knowledge is to seek for and determine those facets that are the most relevant and important for each sport.

References

Bandura, A. (1977). Self-efficacy: Toward a unifying theory of behavioral change. *Psychological Review, 84*, 191–215.

Bar-Eli, M., Plessner, H., & Raab, M. (2011). *Judgment, decision-making and success in sport*. West Sussex: Wiley-Blackwell.

Bates, M. J., Bowles, S., Hammermeister, J., Stokes, C., Pinder, E., Moore, M., & Myatt, C. (2010). Psychological fitness. *Military Medicine, 175*(suppl_8), 21–38.

Baumeister, R. F., & Vohs, K. D. (2016). Strength model of self-regulation as limited resource: Assessment, controversies, update. In J. M. Olson & M. P. Zanna (Eds.), *Advancec in experimental social psychology* (Vol. 54, pp. 67–127). London: Elsevier.

Borkenau, P., & Ostendorf, F. (1993). *NEO-Fünf-Faktoren Inventar (NEO-FFI). Handanweisung [NEO Five-Factor Inventory (NEO-FFI). Manual]*. Göttingen, Germany: Hogrefe.

Brasseur, S., Grégoire, J., Bourdu, R., & Mikolajczak, M. (2013). The profile of emotional competence (PEC): Development and validation of a self-reported measure that fits dimensions of emotional competence theory. *PLoS ONE, 8*(5), 1–8.

Bühner, M. (2011). *Einführung in die Test-und Fragebogenkonstruktion* [Introduction to test and questionnaire construction]. Hallbergmoos, Germany: Pearson Deutschland.

Chaudhry, A. M., Parkinson, J. A., Hinton, E. C., Owen, A. M., & Roberts, A. C. (2009). Preference judgements involve a network of structures within frontal, cingulate and insula cortices. *European Journal of Neuroscience, 29*(5), 1047–1055.

Clough, P., Earle, K., & Sewell, D. (2002). Mental toughness: The concept and its measurement. In I. M. Cockerill (Ed.), *Solutions in sport psychology* (pp. 32–46). London: Thomson Learning.

Connor, K., & Davidson, J. (2003). Development of a new resilience scale: The Connor–Davidson resilience scale (CD-RISC). *Depression and Anxiety, 18*, 76–82.

Costa, P. T., & McCrae, R. R. (1992). *Revised NEO personality inventory (NEO-PI-R) and NEO five factor inventory. Professional manual*. Odessa: Psychological Assessment Resources.

Digman, J. M. (1990). Personality structure: Emergence of the five-factor model. *Annual Review of Psychology, 41*, 417–440.

Engel, G. L. (1977). The need for a new medical model: A challenge for biomedicine. *Science, 196*(4286), 129–136.

Erdmann, G., & Janke, W. (2008). *Stressverarbeitungsfragebogen: SVF; Stress, Stressverarbeitung und ihre Erfassung durch ein mehrdimensionales Testsystem* [Stress processing questionnaire: SVF; Stress, stress processing and its measurement via a multidimensional test system.]. Göttingen, Germany: Hogrefe.

Etzel, Jr, E. F. (1979). Validation of a conceptual model characterizing attention among international rifle shooters. *Journal of Sport Psychology, 1*, 281–290.

Feltz, D. (2019). Self-efficacy. In D. Hackfort, R. J. Schinke,, & B. Strauss (Eds.), *Dictionary of sport psychology* (p. 260). London: Elsevier.

Feltz, D. L., & Moss, T. (2019). Self-confidence. In D. Hackfort, R. Schinke, & B. Strauss (Eds.), *Dictionary of sport psychology* (pp. 257–258). London: Elsevier.

Field, A. (2009). *Discovering statistics using SPSS*. London: Sage.

Fisseni, H. J. (1997). *Lehrbuch zur psychologischen Diagnostik: Mit Hinweisen zur Intervention* [Textbook on psychological diagnostics: With references to intervention] (2nd ed.). Göttingen, Germany: Hogrefe.

Fletcher, D. (2019). Resilience. In D. Hackfort, R. J. Schinke,, & B. Strauss (Eds.), *Dictionary of sport psychology* (p. 248). London: Elsevier.

Friborg, O., Hjemdal, O., Rosenvinge, J., & Martinussen, M. (2003). A new rating scale for adult resilience: What are the central protective resources behind healthy adjustment? *International Journal of Methods in Psychiatric Research, 12*, 65–76.

Gerber, M., Kalak, N., Lemola, S., Clough, P. J., Pühse, U., Elliot, C., & Brand, S. (2012). Adolescents' exercise and physical activity are associated with mental toughness. *Mental Health and Physical Activity, 5*, 35–42.

Gigerenzer, G. (2007). *Gut feelings: The intelligence of the unconscious.* Melbourne, Australia: Penguin.

Gigerenzer, G., & Gaissmaier, W. (2011). Heuristic decision making. *Annual Review of Psychology, 62,* 451–482.

Gucciardi, D. F. (2017). Mental toughness: Progress and prospects. *Current Opinion in Psychology, 16,* 17–23.

Gucciardi, D. F., Hanton, S., Gordon, S., Mallett, C. J., & Temby, P. (2015). The concept of mental toughness: Tests of dimensionality, nomological network, and traitness. *Journal of Personality, 83,* 26–44.

Häcker, H. O., & Stapf, K.-H. (Eds.). (2004). *Dorsch Psychologisches Wörterbuch* [Dorsch psychological handbook] (14th ed.). Bern, Switzerland: Huber.

Hackfort, D. (1986). *Theorie und Analyse sportbezogener Ängstlichkeit* [Theory and analysis of sport-related anxiety]. Schorndorf, Germany: Hofmann.

Hackfort, D., Herle, M., & Debelak, R. (2010). *MDT – Bewegungs-Detektions-Test* [MDT – Movement detection test]. Mödling, Austria: Schuhfried.

Hackfort, D., Kilgallen, C., & Hao, L. (2009). The action theory-based mental test and training system (MTTS). In E. Tsung-Min Hung, R. Lidor,, & D. Hackfort (Eds.), *Psychology of sport excellence* (pp. 9–14). Morgantown, WV: Fitness Information Technology.

Hackfort, D., Klämpfl, M., & Klöppel, Y.-P. (2019). Mentale Fitness [Mental fitness]. In A. Güllich & M. Krüger (Eds.), *Sport in Kultur und Gesellschaft* [Sport in culture and society] (pp. 1–19). Heidelberg, Germany: Springer. doi:10.1007/978-3-662-53385-7_51-1

Hackfort, D., & Nitsch, J. R. (2019). Action and action situation. In D. Hackfort, R. J. Schinke, & B. Strauss (Eds.), *Dictionary of sport psychology* (pp. 2–3). London: Elsevier.

Hackfort, D., & Schinke, R. J. (2019a). Adjustment. In D. Hackfort, R. J. Schinke, & B. Strauss (Eds.), *Dictionary of sport psychology* (pp. 6–7). London: Elsevier.

Hackfort, D., & Schinke, R. J. (2019b). Adaptation. In D. Hackfort, R. J. Schinke, & B. Strauss (Eds.), *Dictionary of sport psychology* (pp. 5–6). London: Elsevier.

Hackfort, D., & Schlattmann, A. (1995). Die Stimmungs- und Befindensskalen (SBS) [The mood and condition scales]. *Arbeitsinformation Sportwissenschaft (AIS), 7,* 1–35.

Hackfort, G. (2014). Möglichkeiten eines Assessments psycho-physischer Belastbarkeit im Kontext der Personalauswahl [Possibilities for an assessment of psychophysical resilience in the context of personnel selection]. (Dissertation, University FAF Munich). Retrieved from https://athene-forschung.unibw.de/doc/92071/92071.pdf

Heidari, J., & Kellmann, M. (2019). Recovery. In D. Hackfort, R. J. Schinke,, & B. Strauss (Eds.), *Dictionary of sport psychology* (pp. 242–243). London: Elsevier.

Hepler, T. J., & Feltz, D. L. (2012). Take the first heuristic, self-efficacy, and decision-making in sport. *Journal of Experimental Psychology: Applied, 18*(2), 154.

Herrmann, T. (1969). *Lehrbuch der empirischen Persönlichkeitsforschung* [Textbook of empirical personality research]. Göttingen, Germany: Hogrefe.

Horsburgh, V. A., Schermer, J. A., Veselka, L., & Vernon, P. A. (2009). A behavioural genetic study of mental toughness and personality. *Personality and Individual Differences, 46*(2), 100–105.

Hossiep, R., & Paschen, M. (2003). *Bochumer Inventar zur berufsbezogenen Persönlichkeitsbeschreibung (BIP)* [Bochum inventory of occupational personality characterization] (2nd ed.). Göttingen, Germany: Hogrefe.

Kaplan, R. M., & Saccuzzo, D. P. (2005). *Psychological testing: Principles, applications and issues.* Belmont, CA: Thomson Wadsworth.

Keeney, R., & Raiffa, H. (1976). *Decisions with multiple objectives: preferences and value trade-offs.* New York: Wiley.

Kellmann, M. (2002). Underrecovery and overtraining: Different concepts – similar impact? In M. Kellmann (Ed.), *Enhancing recovery: Preventing underperformance in athletes* (pp. 3–24). Champaign, IL: Human Kinetics.

Kellmann, M., & Kallus, K. W. (2001). *The recovery-stress questionnaire for athletes: User manual.* Champaign, IL: Human Kinetics.

Kinrade, N. P., Jackson, R. C., & Ashford, K. J. (2010). Dispositional reinvestment and skill failure in cognitive and motor tasks. *Psychology of Sport and Exercise, 11,* 312–319.

Krajewski, J., Mühlenbrock, I., Schnieder, S., & Seiler, K. (2011). Wege aus der müden (Arbeits-) Gesellschaft: Erklärungsmodelle, Messansätze und Gegenmaßnahmen [Escaping drowsiness: Models, measures and countermeasures]. *Zeitschrift Für Arbeitswissenschaft, 65*(2), 97–115.

Laborde, S., & Mosley, E. (2019). Emotional intelligence. In D. Hackfort, R. J. Schinke, & B. Strauss (Eds.), *Dictionary of sport psychology* (p. 92). London: Elsevier.

Laborde, S., Musculus, L., Kalicinski, M., Klämpfl, M. K., Kinrade, N. P., & Lobinger, B. H. (2015). Reinvestment: Examining convergent, discriminant, and criterion validity using psychometric and behavioral measures. *Personality and Individual Differences, 78,* 77–87.

Leppert, K., Koch, B., Brähler, E., & Strauß, B. (2008). Die Resilienzskala (RS) – Überprüfung der Langform RS-25 und einer Kurzform RS-13 [The resilience scale (RS) – Review of the long version RS-25 and the short version RS-13]. *Klinische Diagnostik Und Evaluation, 1,* 226–243.

Luszczynska, A., Diehl, M., Gutiérrez-Dona, B., Kuusinen, P., & Schwarzer, R. (2004). Measuring one component of dispositional self-regulation: Attention control in goal pursuit. *Personality and Individual Differences, 37,* 555–566.

Luszczynska, A., Gutiérrez-Doña, B., & Schwarzer, R. (2005). General self-efficacy in various domains of human functioning: Evidence from five countries. *International Journal of Psychology, 40*(2), 80–89.

Madrigal, L., Hamill, S., & Gill, D. L. (2013). Mind over matter: The development of the mental toughness scale (MTS). *The Sport Psychologist, 27,* 62–77.

Masters, R., & Maxwell, J. (2008). The theory of reinvestment. *International Review of Sport and Exercise Psychology, 1,* 160–183.

McCall, W. A. (1939). *Measurement.* New York: Macmillan.

Moran, A. (2019). Concentration (skills). In D. Hackfort, R. J. Schinke, & B. Strauss (Eds.), *Dictionary of sport psychology* (pp. 57–58). London: Elsevier.

Moran, A. P. (2016). *The psychology of concentration in sport performers: A cognitive analysis.* Hove: Psychology Press.

Mukherjee, S., & Kumar, U. (2017). Psychological resilience: A conceptual review of theory and research. In U. Kumar (Ed.), *The Routledge international handbook of psychological resilience* (pp. 3–32). New York: Routledge.

Nicholls, A. R., Perry, J. L., Jones, L., Sanctuary, C., Carson, F., & Clough, P. J. (2015). The mediating role of mental toughness in sport. *The Journal of Sports Medicine and Physical Fitness, 55*(7–8), 824–834.

Nitsch, J. R. (1974). Die hierarchische Struktur des Eigenzustandes - ein Approximationsversuch mit Hilfe der Binärstrukturanalyse (BISTRAN) [The hierarchical structure of the self: An application of binary structural analysis (BISTRAN)]. *Diagnostika, 20,* 142–164.

Nitsch, J. R. (2000). Handlungstheoretische Grundlagen der Sportpsychologie [Action-theoretical foundations of sport psychology]. In H. Gabler, J. Nitsch, & R. Singer (Eds.), *Einführung in die Sportpsychologie* [Introduction to sport psychology] (pp. 43–164). Schorndorf, Germany: Hofmann.

Nitsch, J. R., & Hackfort, D. (2016). Theoretical framework of performance psychology: An action theory perspective. In M. Raab, B. Lobinger, S. Hoffmann, A. Pizzera, & S. Laborde (Eds.), *Performance psychology. Perception, action, cognition, and emotion* (pp. 11–29). London: Elsevier.

Oxford Dictionary. (2018a). Adaptation. Retrieved from https://en.oxforddictionaries.com/definition/adaptation

Oxford Dictionary. (2018b). Fitness. Retrieved from https://en.oxforddictionaries.com/definition/fitness

Pate, R. R. (1983). A new definition of youth fitness. *The Physician and Sportsmedicine, 11*(4), 77–83.

Piaget, J. (1981). *Die Entwicklung des Kindes* [The development of the child]. Frankfurt/Main: Fischer.

Raab, M. (2019). Decision making. In D. Hackfort, R. J. Schinke, & B. Strauss (Eds.), *Dictionary of sport psychology* (pp. 69–70). London: Elsevier.

Riggs, M. L., Warka, J., Babasa, B., Betancourt, R., & Hooker, S. (1994). Development and validation of self-efficacy and outcome expectancy scales for job related applications. *Educational and Psychological Measurement, 54,* 793–802.

Robazza, C., & Ruiz, M. C. (2019). Self-regulation. In D. Hackfort, R. J. Schinke, & B. Strauss (Eds.), *Dictionary of sport psychology* (pp. 264–265). London: Elsevier.

Schinke, R. J., Battochio, R. C., Dube, T. V., Lidor, R., Tenenbaum, G., & Lane, A. M. (2012). Adaptation processes affecting performance in elite sport. *Journal of Clinical Sport Psychology, 6*(2), 180–195.

Schuhfried, G. (2009). *Manual. Stroop. Stroop interference test. Version 23.00.* Mödling, Austria: Schuhfried.

Schuhfried, G. (2010). *Manual. DT. Determination test. Version 33.00.* Mödling, Austria: Schuhfried.

Schuhfried, G. (2014). *Vienna test system. Psychological tests. For personal-, clinical neuro-, traffic-, and sport psychology.* Mödling, Austria: Schuhfried.

Schumacher, J., Leppert, K., Gunzelmann, T., Strauß, B., & Brähler, E. (2005). Die Resilienzskala–Ein Fragebogen zur Erfassung der psychischen Widerstandsfähigkeit als Personmerkmal [The resilience scale –

A questionnaire to assess the psychic resilience capabilities as a personality trait]. *Zeitschrift für Klinische Psychologie, Psychiatrie und Psychotherapie, 53,* 16–39.

Schwarzer, R. (2014). Everything you wanted to know about the general self-efficacy scale but were afraid to ask. Accessed at: Retrieved from http://userpage.fu-berlin.de/%7Ehealth/faq_gse.pdf

Schwarzer, R., Diehl, M., & Schmitz, G. S. (1999). Self-regulation scale. Accessed at:. Retrieved from www.userpage.fu-berlin.de/~health/selfreg_g.htm

Schwarzer, R., & Jerusalem, M. (Ed.). (1999). *Skalen zur Erfassung von Lehrer- und Schülermerkmalen. Dokumentation der psychometrischen Verfahren im Rahmen der wissenschaftlichen Begleitung des Modellversuchs Selbstwirksame Schulen* [Scales to measure teacher and pupil characteristics. Documentation of psychometric methods in terms of scientific support of the model trial self-efficient schools]. Berlin, Germany: Free University of Berlin.

Scott, V. B., & McIntosh, W. D. (1999). The development of a trait measure of ruminative thought. *Personality and Individual Differences, 26,* 1045–1056.

Spencer, H. (1864). *Principles of biology.* London: Williams & Norgate.

Wagnild, G. M., & Young, H. M. (1993). Development and psychometric evaluation of the resilience scale. *Journal of Nursing Measurement, 1,* 165–178.

Wilson, V. E., Peper, E., & Schmid, A. (2006). Training strategies for concentration. In J. M. Williams (Ed.), *Applied sport psychology: Personal growth to peak performance* (5th ed., pp. 404–422). Boston, MA: McGraw Hill.

20
MENTAL HEALTH AND WELLNESS

William D. Parham

Introduction

Despite the apparent spike in interest over the last 2 years relative to the mental health and well-being of athletes, the topic of mental health and wellness within athletic communities is not a new area of investigative inquiry. As far back as the 1960s, the importance of acknowledging athletes as human beings and not simply as performers began to surface among US scholars (Ogilvy & Tutko, 1966), and this interest in athlete emotional well-being continued through the 1980s (Chartrand & Lent, 1987), 1990s (Danish, Petipas, & Hale, 1993; Pargman, 1993), and 2000s (Friesen & Orlick, 2010; Ranglin, 2001; Rice et al., 2016; Uphill, Sly, & Swain, 2016). The mental health and well-being of elite athletes (Rice et al., 2016), as well as collegiate athletes (Etzel, 2009; Etzel, Ferrante, & Pinkney, 1991; Parham, 1993; Pinkerton, Hinz, & Barrow, 1987), continues to represent an important research focus.

International scholars (Gouttebarge, Kerkhoff, & Lambert, 2016; Gulliver, Griffiths, Mackinnon, Batterham, & Stanimirovic, 2015; Hughes & Leavey, 2012; Uphill, Sly, & Swain, 2016) are addressing mental health and well-being in athletic communities across the globe, and several consensus statements, including those of the International Olympic Committee (Reardon et al., 2019), International Society of Sport Psychology (Henriksen et al., 2019), European Federation of Sport Psychology (FEPSAC; Moesch et al., 2018), International Society of Sport Psychology (Schinke, Stambulova, Si, & Moore, 2018), and Neal et al. (2013), assert the importance of understanding and appreciating mental health and well-being as essential components of acknowledging the whole-person performer. Lastly, sport psychiatry (Begel & Burton, 2000; Hughes & Leavey, 2012; McDuff, 2012; Reardon & Factor, 2010; Strohle, 2018) has joined conversation relative to the mental health and wellness of athletes.

The World Health Organization (WHO) articulated a perspective of mental health and well-being globally (WHO, 2017) that acknowledged that life can be stressful but recognized the potential in every human being to respond adaptively to life's inevitable ups and downs while moving forward productively and with purpose. Asserted in its document is that mental health is a universal concern requiring across-country collaborations relative to "promoting mental health and preventing mental disorders; reducing stigmatization, discrimination and human rights violations; and which is responsive to specific vulnerable groups across the lifespan, and integrated within the national mental health and health promotion strategies" (p. 49). The Centers for Disease Control and Prevention (CDC, 2011, p. 2) added that, "mental illness refers collectively to all diagnosable mental disorders and is characterized by sustained, abnormal observations in thinking, mood, or behavior associated with distress and impaired functioning".

Fast forward to the fall of 2018, when a small group of sport psychology professionals with varied backgrounds and from different parts of the globe came together to explore current application and research approaches to athlete mental health and well-being. A resultant document, "Consensus Statement on Improving the Mental Health of High Performance Athletes" (Henriksen et al., 2019), offered for consideration six observation-based recommendations aimed at broadening the definitions of mental health and well-being and suggesting implications for applied, research, and consultation sport psychology practices. The contextual frame within which the observation-based recommendations are placed illuminates a cardinal thesis that mental health and well-being represent dynamic life experiences that are inextricably a part of the human condition. The six propositions included the following: (1) mental health is a core component of a culture of excellence; (2) mental health in a sport context should be better defined; (3) research on mental health in sport should broaden the scope of assessment; (4) athlete mental health is a major resource for the whole career of an athlete and life post-athletic career; (5) the environment can nourish or malnourish athlete mental health; and (6) mental health is everybody's business but should be overseen by one or a few specified members. Emphasized therein is that mental health and wellness experiences are not unique to professional sports, nor are they recent phenomena within professional sports. Mental health and wellness challenges within athletic communities, both domestic and global, are long-standing, and inferences that their recent emergence in conversations evidences a rise in mental health and wellness concerns within athlete populations merit further examination (Henriksen et al., 2019; Moesch et al., 2018; Reardon et al., 2019; Schinke et al., 2018).

Contextual Parameters

Mental health and wellness experiences represent complex human challenges that manifest across generations, the developmental spectrum (e.g., childhood, adulthood, old age), dimensions of personal identity (e.g., culture, race, ethnicity, age, gender, religion, disability, LGBTQ, political affiliation, country of origin, etc.), community profiles (e.g., rural, urban, cosmopolitan), academic settings (e.g., elementary, secondary, high school, college/ university), occupational pathways (e.g., blue collar, white collar), and the variety of life circumstances within contextual trappings of social class (e.g. poverty, middle class, upper class; Black & Stone, 2005; Frost, Lehavot, & Meyer, 2015; Green 2005; Rosenfield, 2012; Seng, Lopez, Sperlich, Hamana, & Reed, 2012; Thoits, 2010).

Mental health disorders are among the most common health conditions in the United States (World Health Organization, 2017). According to the CDC, more than 50% of the population will be diagnosed with a mental illness or disorder at some point in their lifetime. Further, 20% of Americans will experience a mental illness in a given year, and 4% of Americans live with a serious mental illness, such as schizophrenia, bipolar disorder, or major depression. Estimates suggest that 6.8 million adults in the United States are affected by generalized anxiety. Social anxiety impacts 13% of the US population. Panic disorder, obsessive compulsive disorder (OCD), and post-traumatic stress disorder (PTSD) have equally attention-worthy statistics (CDC, 2011).

Despite these and other data profiles, mental health and wellness challenges cannot be understood fully using statistical data alone, nor can they be appreciated when viewed dichotomously (e.g., either you have or do not have mental health and wellness). Rather, mental health and wellness experiences are more fully understood and appreciated when viewed along a continuum, with "significantly unhealthy" anchoring one end and "completely healthy" anchoring the other end, and with an admixture of variations of the two end points in-between (FEPSAC, 2018; ISSP, 2017, 2019). Schinke et al. (2018) describe the mental health continuum as including five points along a continuum designed to better understand athlete psychological well-being, distress levels, and levels of functioning. The five points include: (a) active mental illness, (b) subsyndromal illness, (c) normal, (d) good mental health, and (e) flow or zone states.

In the Beginning

It is important to note that clues to unravelling the complexities of the "significantly unhealthy" lived experiences of athletes may be found in the Kaiser Permanente/Center for Disease Control Adverse Childhood Experiences-ACE study (Felitti et al., 1998). Suggested therein is that adverse childhood experiences are common, they often occur in clusters, and there is a strong relationship between adverse childhood experiences and the development of problems including, but not limited to, physical health, social, relational, and high-risk behaviours occurring throughout the lifespan and sometimes resulting in premature death. Approximately 65% of adults have experienced at least one adverse childhood experience, and approximately 20% have experienced up to four. Adverse childhood experiences include abuse (e.g., physical, sexual, emotional), neglect (e.g., emotional, physical), and family/household challenges (e.g., mother treated violently, household substance abuse, parental separation and divorce, mental illness in the household, criminal household member).

Spotting Symptoms

Very much related, outward and ongoing expressions of anger, chronic anxiety, depression, isolation, "slumps" in performance, fighting, off-court personal and familial troubles, and more, often represent symptoms of a much deeper problem. Symptoms can be problematic in that persistence of problematic behaviours can lead to significant inauspicious consequences. However, symptoms are never the problem. Symptoms can be analogous to a home "smoke detector". When smoke detectors sound an alarm, it is not an indication that it is broken. Rather, it is an indication that it is working and sounding the alert to possible danger. In like manner, outward and ongoing behavioural, cognitive, and emotional expressions of distress by athletes represent cries for help and often signal that deeper-seated issues warrant attention.

In short, not all athletes struggle with mental health and well-being challenges to the same degree. Some athletes lead lives of balance, optimism, and feeling in control of their life's trajectory, prepared to respond in healthy ways to expected and unexpected challenges along the way. Other athletes lead lives experiencing significant cognitive, behavioural, and affective disequilibrium, pessimism, and feeling not in control of their life's trajectory and respond with fear and trepidation to expected and unexpected life challenges. Apropos to this latter observation is the scholarship on athlete burn-out (Crosswell & Eklund, 2004; Fender, 1989; Gustafsson, Kentta, & Hassmen, 2011; Lonsdale, Hodge & Ross, 2009) that illuminates the importance of identifying early warning signs and designing viable intervention strategies.

Hiding in Plain Sight

As suggested earlier in this narrative, mental health and well-being experiences represent dynamic human circumstances that vary considerably by persons and are influenced by myriad contextual parameters (e.g., environmental, developmental, social, gender, culture, race, ethnicity, intrapersonal), the understanding and appreciation of which position applied practitioners, researchers, and consultants to fully grasp the person before the performer. For example, when viewed through the contextual lenses of gender and socially sanctioned ways of communicating, a female athlete meeting the *Diagnostic and Statistical Manual of Mental Disorders*, 5th edition (DSM-5; American Psychiatric Association, 2013), diagnostic criteria for depression might, more accurately, be experiencing anger, and possibly rage at the extreme. However, expressing their distress verbally, behaviourally, and with animated affect, and running the risk of misinterpretation, influences choices to express their true concerns in socially sanctioned ways that do not draw attention to their central experiences. Male athletes, on the other hand, meeting the diagnostic criteria for anger, necessitating consideration of anger management as an intervention, might, more accurately, be experiencing depression. Expressing emotional truth, however, and running the risk of misinterpretation influence choices to camouflage their distress and express it in socially acceptable ways.

It should also be noted that whole person approaches to responding to athlete mental health and well-being challenges must factor in an understanding and appreciation of the lived experiences of domestic as well as international athletes. There are similarities between domestic and international athletes relative to, for example, their skills, talents, and abilities to execute sport-specific behaviours. At the same time, however, there are many substantial differences that need to be acknowledged, understood, and appreciated. For instance, international athletes may struggle with: (a) leaving their countries of origin where familiarity, customs, and traditions exist and in which they felt comfort; (b) feeling pressures to represent community and country in the midst of very unfamiliar environments; and (3) adjusting to new environments complete with new demands, not least of which may include developing conversance with language, learning about political systemic structures, and developing daily, weekly, and monthly routines reflecting balances between pre- and post-adjustment realities (Schinke & McGannon, 2014; Schinke, Yukelson, Bartolacci, & Bartolacci, 2011; Terry & Si, 2015).

Stigma

Stigma, disgrace, shame, and public disapproval represent significant roadblocks to addressing mental health and well-being challenges, irrespective of an athlete's domestic or international origin. Stigma, relative to mental health, represents emotional experiences that are influenced by the complex interplay of both intra-personal factors (e.g., self-esteem, confidence, motivation, ignominy, public embarrassment), interpersonal factors (e.g., relational capital), and external factors (e.g., systemic structures within and across medical models of pathology, and financial profit models that are hallmarks of insurance and pharmaceutical companies). Mental health and wellness literacy (Jorm, 2000; Jorm, Barney, Christensen, Highet, & Kelly, 2006; Kelly, Jorm, & Wright, 2007) campaigns represent important educational strategies to consider when designing programmes aimed at deconstructing stigma and setting the stage for emotional healing. In parallel, addressing the mental health and wellness of professional athletes requires developing, maintaining, and periodically re-examining interdependent relationships between (a) owners, (b) team executive leadership, (c) coaches, (d) trainers, and (e) players. Further, top-tier mental health and wellness programmes for professional athletes require fiscal, capital, and human resources and a designated mental health professional at the helm tasked accountably with developing, maintaining, and evaluating the mental health and wellness programmes (Henriksen et al., 2019). Lastly, reconciling important questions represents additional cornerstone prerequisites for establishing viable mental health and wellness programmes. One example of a critical question invites the following consideration: "Has professional sport failed at meaningfully and viably addressing athlete mental health and wellness, or has professional sport succeeded at not meaningfully and viably addressing athlete mental health and wellness?" Organizational and systemic motivation, drives, and incentives for establishing as well as maintaining mental health and wellness programmes for athletes deserve ongoing and honest contemplative self-reflection.

Final Thoughts

The DSM-5 lists in excess of 150 diagnostic categories, the exhumation and examination of which are beyond the scope of this project. The limitations of the DSM-5 (Thomason, 2014; Wakefield, 2016), though also beyond the scope of this project, nonetheless deserve attention relative to the framing of the forthcoming entries. In short, the disorders listed in the DSM-5 can be misleading and often confusing. "Symptom", for example, is used interchangeably with "disorders", and pharmaceutical interventions are given primacy consideration over evidence-based research relative to psychotherapy treatment effectiveness. Vulnerability to overdiagnosis represents another alleged shortcoming.

The substance and quality of the phenomena under investigation, however, are more important than the number of listed disorders or the labels used to differentiate one condition from another. With the forgoing as a prelude, contained herein are narratives that reflect some of the more common mental health and wellness challenges found in athletic communities – elite, professional, and collegiate, as well as across sports. The following chapters strike a balance between using strict DSM-5 labelling nomenclature with behavioural and cognitive approaches to conceptualizations and treatments that are rooted in evidence-based practices. Explicated in this section are entries that spotlight the invisible tattoos of trauma, anxiety, depression, disordered eating, substance abuse, and the psychological impact of concussions. Each entry utilizes a four-part template as a way of organizing and presenting the material. The four component parts of the template include: (a) framing and defining each topic as lived experiences, (b) unveiling best practices relative to assessment, (c) identifying treatment considerations, and (d) deciding on ways to evaluate outcomes. The "person before the performer" surfaces as the guiding and overarching principle relative to responding to the mental health and well-being of domestic and international athletes.

References

American Psychiatric Association. (2013). *Diagnostic and statistical manual of mental disorders* (5th ed.). Washington, DC: Author.

Begel, D., & Burton, R. W. (2000). *Sport psychiatry.* New York: W. W. Norton.

Black, L. L., & Stone, D. (2005). Expanding the definition of privilege: The concept of social privilege. *Journal of Multicultural Counseling and Development, 33*(4), 243–255.

Centers for Disease Control and Prevention (CDC). (2011). *Mental illness surveillance among adults in the United States* (pp. 1–32). Atlanta, GA: Author.

Chartrand, J. M., & Lent, R. W. (1987). Sports counseling: Enhancing the development of the athlete. *Journal of Counseling and Development, 66*, 164–167.

Crosswell, S. L., & Eklund, R. C. (2004). The athlete burnout syndrome: Possible early signs. *Journal of Science and Medicine in Sport, 7*(4), 481–487.

Danish, S. J., Petipas, A. J., & Hale, B. D. (1993). Life development interventions for athletes: Life skills through sports. *The Counseling Psychologist, 21*, 352–385.

Etzel, E. (Ed.). (2009). *Counseling and psychological services for college student-athletes*. Morgantown, WV: Fitness Information Technologies.

Etzel, E., Ferrante, A. P., & Pinkney, J. (Eds.). (1991). *Counseling college student-athletes: Issues and interventions*. Morgantown, WV: Fitness Information Technologies.

Felitti, V. J., Anda, R. F., Nordenberg, D., Williamson, D. F., Spitz, A. M., Edwards, V., … Marks, J. S. (1998). Relationship of childhood abuse and household dysfunction to many of the leading causes of death in adults. *American Journal of Preventive Medicine, 14*, 245–258.

Fender, L. K. (1989). Athlete burnout: Potential for research and intervention strategies. *The Sport Psychologist, 3*(1), 63–71.

Friesen, A., & Orlick, T. (2010). A qualitative analysis of holistic sport psychology consultants' professional philosophies. *The Sport Psychologist, 24*, 227–244.

Frost, M., Lehavot, K., & Meyer, I. H. (2015). Minority stress and physical health among sexual minority individuals. *Journal of Behavioral Medicine, 38*(1), 1–8.

Gouttebarge, V., Kerkhoff, G., & Lambert, M. (2016). Prevalence and determinants of symptoms of common mental disorders in retired professional rugby union players. *European Journal of Sport Science, 16*, 595–602.

Green, B. (2005). Psychology, diversity, and social justice: Beyond hetereosexism and across the social divide. *Counseling Psychology Quarterly, 18*(4), 295–306.

Gulliver, A., Griffith, K. M., Mackinnon, A., Batterham, P. J., & Stanimirovic, R. (2015). The mental health of Australian elite athletes. *Journal of Science and Medicine in Sport, 18*, 255–261.

Gustafsson, H., Kentta, G., & Hassmen, P. (2011). Athlete burnout: An integrated model and future research directions. *International Review of Sport and Exercise Psychology, 4*(1), 3–24.

Henriksen, K., Schinke, R. J., Moesch, K., McCann, S., Parham, W. D., Larsen, C. H., & Terry, P. (2019). Consensus statement on improving the mental health of high-performance athletes. *International Journal of Sport and Exercise Psychology*. Advanced online publication. doi: 10.1080/1612197X.2019.1570473.

Hughes, L., & Leavey, G. (2012). Setting the bar: Athletes and vulnerability to mental illness. *British Journal of Psychiatry, 200*(2), 95–96.

Jorm, A. F. (2000). Mental health literacy: Public knowledge and beliefs about mental disorders. *The British Journal of Psychiatry, 177*(5), 396–401.

Jorm, A. F., Barney, L. J., Christensen, N., Highet, N. J., & Kelly, C. M. (2006). Research on mental health literacy: What we know and what we still need to know. *Australian and New Zealand Journal of Psychiatry, 40*(1), 3–5.

Kelly, C., Jorm, A. F., & Wright, A. (2007). Improving mental health literacy as a strategy to facilitate early intervention for mental disorders. *Medical Journal of Australia, 187*(S7), S26–S30.

Lonsdale, C., Hodge, K., & Ross, E. (2009). Athlete burnout in elite sport: A self-determination perspective. *Journal of Sport Sciences, 27*(8), 785–795.

McDuff, D. R. (2012). *Sport psychiatry: Strategies for life balance and peak performance*. Washington, DC: American Psychiatric Association.

Moesch, K., Kentta, G., Kleinert, J., Quignon-Fleuret, C., Cecil, S., & Bertollo, M. (2018). FEPSAC position statement: Mental health disorders in elite athletes and models of service provision. *Psychology of Sport and Exercise, 38*, 61–71.

Neal, T. L., Diamond, A. B., Goldman, S., Klossner, D., Morse, E. D., Pajak, D. E., … Welzant, V. (2013). Inter-association recommendation for developing a plan to recognize and refer student-athletes with psychological concerns at the collegiate level: An executive summary of a consensus statement. *Journal of Athletic Training, 48*(5), 716–720.

Ogilvy, B., & Tutko, T. (1966). *Problem athletes and how to handle them*. New York: Pelham Books.

Pargman, D. (Ed.). (1993). *Psychological basis of sport injuries*. Morgantown, WV: Fitness Information Technologies.

Parham, W. D. (1993). The intercollegiate athlete: A 1990s profile. *The Counseling Psychologist, 21*, 411–429.

Pinkerton, R., Hinz, L., & Barrow, J. (1987). The college student-athlete: Psychological considerations and interventions. *Journal of American College Health, 37*, 218–226.

Ranglin, J. S. (2001). Psychological factors in sport performance: The mental health model revisited. *Sports Medicine, 31*(12), 875–890.

Reardon, C. L., & Factor, R. M. (2010). Sport psychiatry: A systematic review of diagnosis and medical treatment of mental illness in athletes. *Sports Medicine, 40*(11), 961–980.

Reardon, C. L., Hainline, B., Aron, C. M., Baron, D., Baum, A., Bindra, A., … Derevensky, J. L. (2019). Mental health and elite athletes: International Olympic Committee consensus statement. *British Journal of Sport Medicine, 53*(11), 667–699.

Rice, S. M., Purcell, R., DeSilva, S., Mawren, D., McGorry, P. D., & Parker, A. G. (2016). The mental health of elite athletes: A narrative systematic review. *Sport Medicine, 46*(9), 1333–1353.

Rosenfield, S. (2012). Triple jeopardy? Mental health at the intersection of gender, race and class. *Social Science and Medicine, 74*(11), 1791–1801.

Schinke, R. J., & McGannon, K. R. (2014). The acculturative experience of (and with) immigrant athletes. *International Journal of Sport and Exercise Psychology, 12*(1), 64–75.

Schinke, R. J., Stambulova, N. B., Si, G., & Moore, Z. (2018). International society of sport psychology position stand: Athletes' mental health, performance, and development. *International Journal of Sport and Exercise Psychology, 16*(6), 622–639.

Schinke, R. J., Yukelson, G., Bartolacci, R. C., & Bartolacci, K. (2011). The challenges encountered by immigrated elite athletes. *Journal of Sport Psychology in Action, 2*(1), 10–20.

Seng, J. S., Lopez, W. D., Sperlich, M., Hamana, L., & Reed, C. D. (2012). Marginalized identities, discrimination burden, and mental health: Empirical exploration of an interpersonal-level approach to modeling intersectionality. *Social Science of Medicine, 75*(12), 2437–2445.

Strohle, A. (2018). Sport psychiatry: Mental health and mental disorders in athletes and exercise treatment of mental disorders. *European Archives of Psychiatry and Clinical Neuroscience.* doi:10.1007/s00406-018-0891-5

Terry, P. C., & Si, G. (2015). Introduction to special issue on providing sport psychology support for Olympic athletes: International perspectives. *International Journal of Sport and Exercise Psychology, 13*(1), 1–3.

Thoits, P. A. (2010). Stress and health: Major findings and policy implications. *Journal of Health and Science Behavior, 51*(1), 41–53.

Thomason, T. C. (2014). Criticisms, limitations and benefits of the DSM-5. *Arizona Counseling Journal.* Retrieved from http://works.bepress.com/timothy_thomason/11

Uphill, M., Sly, D., & Swain, J. (2016). From mental health to mental wealth: Looking back and moving forward. *Frontiers in Psychology.* doi:10.3389/fpsyg.2016.00935

Wakefield, J. C. (2016). Diagnostic issues and controversies in DSM-5: Return of the false positive problem. *Annual Review of Clinical Psychology, 12*, 105–132.

World Health Organization. (2017). *Mental health atlas.* Geneva: Author.

21
META-ANALYSIS AND META-SYNTHESIS

Thomas Curran and Toni Louise Williams

Introduction

Just like other scientific disciplines, progress in sport and exercise psychology is made with the painstaking accrual of empirical evidence. Researchers typically refer to this evidence as a body of literature. Within each body of literature, it is seldom that a single study would be deemed sufficient to settle a hypothesis on a particular phenomenon. Instead, researchers compare and contrast findings from a body of incremental advancements in order to reach conclusions. Hence, comparisons of study findings – in the form of reviews of research – are integral to knowledge generation.

In sport and exercise psychology, the most common form of review is narrative – that is, a review that draws an informal inference about a specific phenomenon. Book chapters, for instance, typically contain narrative reviews, as do introductions to journal articles. Yet narrative reviews have several limitations, which include convenience sampling of studies, a lack of systematic review methodology, and a reliance on statistical significance rather than effect size (Johnson & Eagly, 2014). Accordingly, reliable and valid review strategies have emerged to obviate these limitations. Meta-analysis is a quantitative review strategy used to statistically aggregate tests of a particular phenomenon (Glass, 1976). More recently, meta-synthesis has emerged to systematically search, critically appraise, and synthesize the results of qualitative studies (Jensen & Allen, 1996). In this contribution, we overview meta-analysis and meta-synthesis and give a practical guide to their application in sport and exercise psychology.

Meta-Analysis

Meta-analysis is a quantitative form of systematic review in which results from studies are pooled and aggregated mathematically. The methodology guiding meta-analysis has several key steps. Each step directly informs the next, and groundwork in the early stages pays dividends when it comes to reporting and writing in the latter stages. These steps include: (a) generating the research question, (b) inclusion and exclusion criteria, (c) literature searching, (d) coding and data extraction, (e) calculating and interpreting the weighted average effect size, and (f) testing for moderation and publication bias. In what follows, the procedures and considerations across each of these steps are outlined.

Step 1: Generating the Research Question

A meta-analysis is only as good as the research question it is testing. A mistake many researchers make is to assume that aggregating many papers on a particular phenomenon is sufficient to warrant a meta-analysis. Unfortunately, the aggregation of a lot of individual studies yields just a summary statement. A worthwhile meta-analysis, instead, is undertaken to both aggregate and resolve some controversial issue that is under debate in the literature. When undertaking a meta-analysis, it is, therefore, important to ask: What is new, what will I learn, and how will the findings move the literature significantly forward?

The most common way to address these questions is to test how effects pattern across studies. Specifically, a certain theory or perspective may suggest that a third variable would influence the association of our focal independent and dependent variables. In statistical parlance, this third variable is known as the moderator (Hayes & Rockwood, 2017). It determines when and under what conditions the sign or magnitude of an effect varies. With this approach, Hill and Curran (2016) showed that the positive relationship between perfectionism and burn-out was significantly larger in work contexts than in school or sport – an important finding with implications for both perfectionism theory and organizational practice. In this example, the context of workplace or sport was the moderator. The acronym PICO (population, intervention, comparator, outcomes) is useful for researchers when clarifying their research questions (see Table 5; Schardt, Adams, Owens, Keitz, & Fontelo, 2007).

Table 5 Description of PICO elements with example

PICO element	Description	Study example (Lindheimer, O'Connor, & Dishman, 2015)
Population	What is the age range, gender, ethnic background, or clinical make-up of the population of interest? For example, one might be interested in the effects of high-intensity exercise training in cancer survivors, or only those who have had a particular cancer diagnosis	Healthy adults, with no clinical background
Intervention	What is the treatment, intervention, drug, food supplement, training schedule, or clinical practice of interest? For example, one might be interested in the effects of a high-intensity exercise intervention	A randomized trial with participants allocated to any exercise treatment
Comparator	Is the comparison a placebo, normal care, active control, passive control, or waiting list? For example, one might be interested in the effects of a high-intensity exercise intervention versus an aerobic exercise control	Study must include a control arm and an arm that delivered an exercise placebo
Outcomes	What are the focal outcome variables of interest? For example, one might be interested in the effects of high-intensity exercise training on affect	Anxiety, cognitive performance, depression, energy, or fatigue

Step 2: Inclusion and Exclusion Criteria

Once the research question is set, researchers need to make decisions regarding which studies should (and should not) be reviewed. In other words, they must resolve to include all studies in their review that satisfy inclusion criteria and omit those that meet exclusion criteria. For the most part, the inclusion criteria are guided by the population, intervention, comparator, and outcome(s) of interest (PICO). For example, Lindheimer, O'Connor, and Dishman's (2015) meta-analysis of placebo effects in exercise for mental health included only randomized trials with: (a) adults (population), (b) a treatment arm, control arm, placebo arm (comparator), (b) a treatment group engaging in at least 4 weeks of exercise training (intervention), and (c) outcome data for anxiety, cognitive performance, depression, energy, or fatigue (outcomes). If a researcher is in interested in meta-analysing correlational research, which is increasingly common in sport and exercise psychology, then inclusion criteria are only necessary on the population, intervention (viz. predictor variables), and outcome (viz. criterion variables).

Exclusion criteria, on the other hand, are a little more contentious. Oftentimes, researchers will exclude studies based on methodological rigour, with obviously flawed studies removed from the analysis in what is known as the best evidence synthesis (Greenwald & Russell, 1991). However, there are few absolute standards for methodological quality, and thus researchers must outline the methodological flaws that are to be the basis of exclusion criteria (Johnson & Eagly, 2014). Another issue that sometimes arises is the retrieval of studies with extremely atypical populations (e.g., clinical populations). In this case, the selection criteria should be modified to exclude them. Lastly, a contentious topic in the setting of exclusion criteria is whether to omit non-published research. It is well understood that the withholding and non-publication of non-significant findings is a widespread problem in psychology – an issue termed the 'file drawer problem' (Rosenthal, 1979). As well, beyond the 'file drawer problem', there is a large amount of unpublished data contained within theses and dissertations. For these reasons, it is recommended that researchers do not exclude research because of publication status.

Step 3: Literature Searching

Once selection criteria are defined, researchers can move to retrieving the relevant literature. For obvious reasons, the importance of meta-analysis increases commensurately with the number of studies it synthesizes. Hence, researchers should seek to retrieve as many studies as is possible in their literature search. There are several ways in which researchers can find relevant studies, and it is generally advisable that they use them all. First, computer searches of databases will yield most (but not all) of the literature. In the psychological sciences, PsychINFO, Medline, Web of Science, and Google Scholar are extremely useful and should be first in line for literature searches. Other databases, such as ProQuest and EOTS (Index to Theses and Electronic Online Theses Service), cover dissertations and should also be inspected. Finally, researchers are advised to contact authors or groups of authors to request in press or unpublished data.

To permit the replication of search procedures, researchers should describe in detail their search methods. These include: (a) the date of the search, (b) the names of the databases searched, (c) the period covered by the search, and (d) the keywords used. It is becoming generally advisable to also document the search comprehensively in PRISMA format, which describes the flow of the search process, listing the number of included and excluded studies at each discrete stage (see Figure 6; Moher, Liberati, Tetzlaff, & Altman, 2009). An exhaustive

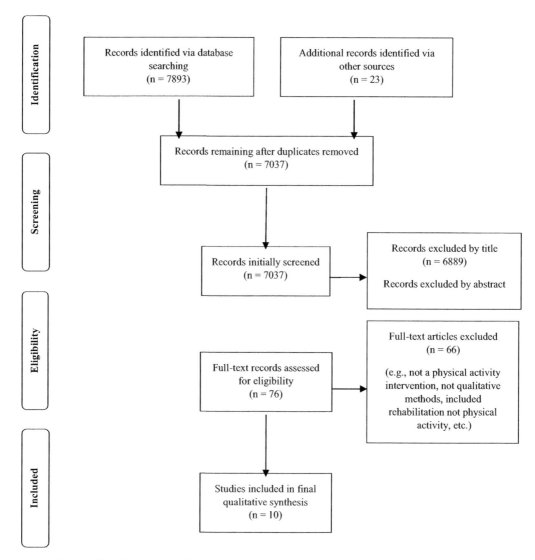

Figure 6 PRISMA flowchart (adapted from Williams et al., 2017)

search will retrieve many studies, of which only a fraction will be included. For instance, Curran and Hill (2019) screened 1,763 abstracts of studies on perfectionism in college students, but only 146 fit their inclusion criteria.

Step 4: Coding and Data Extraction

In systematically generating a research question and inclusion criteria, the researcher should have developed ideas regarding what study characteristics need to be coded from the retrieved literature. In most cases, the salient study characteristics are the moderators (or mediators). For example, in their meta-analysis of relationships between passion and intrapersonal outcomes, Curran, Hill, Appleton, Vallerand, and Standage (2015) coded two categorical (domain and culture of each study) moderators and one continuous (mean age of study participants) moderator. Sample size and the observed standard deviation(s) of treatment means (for studies that deal with mean differences) are also important characteristics to code because they are central to weighing calculations for the statistical procedures (see below). Beyond these essential characteristics, it is generally advisable to code for as much information as is available (e.g., date of publication, mean age of participants, gender), because a broad overview of study characteristics helps to provide context for the nature of the studies included in the review.

Alongside the coding of study characteristics, researchers must extract effect sizes or the necessary data to calculate effects sizes from their retrieved literature. Effect sizes provide a common, comparable index for the aggregation and synthesis of discrete studies. There are many metrics that can be meta-analysed, and a good review is provided by Shelby and Vaske (2008). In sport and exercise psychology, correlation coefficients and standardized mean differences are most frequently reported. Focus on these indexes is emphasized herein.

When the objective of a meta-analysis is to investigate the magnitude and moderators of associations between variables, the correlation coefficient is the effect size of interest (i.e., Pearson's product-moment r). For example, Hill, Mallinson-Howard, and Jowett (2018) meta-analysed studies reporting correlation coefficients between multidimensional perfectionism and a range of motivation, emotion/well-being, and performance outcomes in sport. The correlation coefficient is a metric quantifying the degree of covariation between two standardized variables. It runs from -1 to +1, with the sign indicating the direction of covariation (i.e., negative vs positive), and the level indicating the magnitude of covariation (small $r = .10$, medium $r = .30$, large $r = .50$; Cohen, 1992).

If, by contrast, the objective of the meta-analysis is to investigate the magnitude of differences between treatments, the standardized mean difference is the effect size of interest (i.e., Cohen's d or Hedge's d).[1] For example, Lawlor and Hopker (2001) meta-analysed studies reporting standard mean differences from randomized controlled trials that used exercise as an intervention in the management of depression. This metric reflects the ratio of the difference between the treatment and control group to the standard deviation of the control group. Unlike the correlation coefficient, the standardized mean difference can exceed ±1 because it is a z-score and quantifies the advantage (or disadvantage) of the experimental group in units of standard deviation. Like correlation coefficients, the sign and level of the standardized mean difference indicates the direction and magnitude of the effects (small $d = .20$, medium $d = .50$, large $d = .80$; Cohen, 1992).

When extracting data, it is not uncommon to find that some authors fail to report effect sizes or, worse, contain insufficient information to calculate them. If the effect size is not reported, but there is sufficient information to calculate it (i.e., means and SDs), researchers should use available formulae (see Lipsey & Wilson, 2001). Where there is insufficient information reported to calculate the effect size, researchers are advised to contact authors and request either: (a) the effect size(s), or (b) the raw data. In our experience, polite requests for such information yield reasonable success (just under half of contacted authors typically respond).

Accurate coding and data extraction are, of course, essential for valid meta-analysis. Hence, it is recommended that at least two researchers code study characteristics and extract all data independently. Commonly, the percentage of agreement between coders is used as a metric of reliability, with disagreements resolved by discussion. When multiple coding of the entire literature is not feasible, random sampling may be used, in which an independent coder codes and extracts data from a random subset of studies (typically 25%; Card, 2012). The best procedure, however, is to double-code all studies (Johnson & Eagly, 2014).

Step 5: Calculating and Interpreting the Weighted Average Effect Size

Once the research question has been set, the selection criteria have been implemented, the literature has been retrieved, and the data extracted, researchers can move to analysing for the pooled effect of interest. Statistical pooling within meta-analysis is, however, not as simple as an arithmetic mean of effect sizes. Across any given literature, there will be much between-study variance in sample size and, therefore, the precision of effects. Hence, meta-analysis not only averages effect sizes but also weights them for these differences. As studies with larger sample sizes have greater precision than those with smaller samples sizes (i.e., smaller error), a meta-analysed weighted average effect size gives larger sample sizes more influence.

An initial step in meta-analysis is to combine study outcomes by averaging effects from k studies, with each effect size (T) for each study (j) weighted by sample size (correlation coefficients) or reciprocal variance (standardized mean differences; ω).[2] The product, or weighted average effect size (T_+), is a weighted average of all effect sizes extracted from the literature search.

$$T_+ = \frac{\sum_{j=1}^{k} \omega_j T_j}{\sum_{jw1}^{k} \omega_j}$$

Weights (ω) can be simply defined as a function of within-study sampling error. In this case, researchers follow a fixed-effects assumption that between-study heterogeneity in effect sizes is attributable to differences in the precision of effect size estimation (i.e., the sample size or reciprocal variance). Alternatively, researchers can calculate weights to include an additive estimate of between-study variance in the population (τ^2; see Hedges & Vevea, 1998, for methods of estimation). Here, researchers follow a random-effects assumption that between-study heterogeneity in effect size is attributable to both sampling error and variance arising from differences between studies in terms of their procedures and settings. Unless under very restrictive conditions (e.g., $k < 5$), random-effects meta-analysis is considered superior to fixed-effect meta-analysis because it permits generalization beyond the pool of studies included in the review (Schmidt, Oh, & Hayes, 2009).

Alongside the weighted average effect, it is informative for researchers to report two estimates of effect size heteronomy, namely Cochran's Q and I^2. The primary reason for this is that significant heteronomy in effect sizes provides justification for moderator analyses that seek to explain between-study differences. Cochran's (1954) Q is a chi-square statistic that tests the null hypothesis that individual effects sizes T_j do not differ from the weighted average effect size T_+. A significant Q, then, is evidence of effect size heterogeneity. Values of Q, however, are influenced by the number of effect sizes that make up the statistic (Johnson & Eagly, 2014). It can, therefore, be a problematic statistic when the number of effect sizes in an analysis is large. Moreover, it is a difficult statistic to compare across meta-analyses. Higgins and Thompson (2002) addressed these issues by developing another heterogeneity statistic, I^2, which uses Q but controls for its degrees of freedom (i.e., number of studies in the analysis). I^2 reflects the percentage of variability among effect sizes, with high values indicating more variability, and zero indicating perfect homogeneity. Values of 25%, 50%, and 75% indicate small, moderate, and large amounts of heterogeneity, respectively (Johnson & Eagly, 2014).

Finally, statistical inference about the weighted average effect size is typically gleaned from a 95% confidence interval. Such an interval is calculated using the standard deviation (*SD*) of the weighted average effect size, $T_+ \pm 1.96 \sqrt{SD}$, where 1.96 is the critical value of significance at the p < .05 level. A confidence interval that does not contain zero permits the conclusion that there is a significant association or difference between the variables of interest. By contrast, if the confidence interval does include zero, then the conclusion is that there is no association or difference in the population. Under conditions of substantial effect size heterogeneity, weighted average effect sizes are more likely to reach significance under fixed-effects assumptions (owing to a lack of account for between-study variance). Hence, making fixed-effects assumptions about the weighted average effect size is a hazardous strategy of statistical inference and another reason why random-effects models should be preferred (Johnson & Eagly, 2014).

Step 6: Testing for Moderation and Publication Bias

As discussed, the weighted average effect size provides a summary statement. Yet it is often the case that researchers are more interested in how the effect sizes that make up this weighted average pattern across studies. Here, it is necessary to assess whether study characteristics (and other potential moderators) explain between-study variance in the effect size. To do so, researchers typically employ subgroup (for categorical moderators) or meta-regression (for continuous moderators) analyses. Although these tests can have different procedures, they are analogous – underpinned by weighted ordinary least squares regression with categorical variables dummy coded as necessary. For example, in their meta-analytic test of whether perfectionism was rising over time, Curran and Hill (2019) found that perfectionism (the effect size of interest) was positively correlated with year of data collection (continuous moderator) and was higher among American college students than among British and Canadian college students (dummy-coded categorical moderator).

As Curran and Hill (2019) show in their example, continuous and categorical moderators can be tested simultaneously. Yet many researchers in sport and exercise choose to examine them separately. For categorical moderators, the total heterogeneity of effect sizes (i.e., Cochran's Q) can be partitioned into heterogeneity explained by the categorization (Q_b) and the residual error heterogeneity (Q_e). Statistically significant heterogeneity explained by the categorization (Q_b) indicates that there are differences between categories in terms of their effects sizes and provides a strong basis for inferring moderation. For continuous moderators, the weighted effect size can be regressed on moderating variables of influence. The unstandardized beta coefficient provides a test of significance of the moderator's relationship with the magnitude of effect sizes. Meta-analytic software provides options for the incorporation of random-effects assumptions in subgroup and meta-regression analyses (we recommend the metaphor R package; Viechtbauer, 2010). Such analyses are typically termed mixed-effects models because differences between groups of effect sizes (i.e., the slopes) are fixed, whereas the intercepts are permitted to vary randomly (Johnson & Eagly, 2014).

Beyond hypothesized moderators, another potential source of between-study heterogeneity is publication bias. It is, therefore, an essential step in meta-analysis to test the possibility that published results differ from those that are not published (Sutton, 2009). To do so, several approaches can be adopted. First, researchers might employ subgroup analyses on published and unpublished studies to ascertain whether there is a difference. Second, researchers can plot inverse variance (study weighting) against effect size and observe the result. If the plot resembles a funnel, with smaller studies at the bottom showing more scatter than larger studies at the top, there is good evidence that no publication bias is evident. Finally, there are a number of statistical indexes of publication bias available to researchers, which include Rosenthal's (1979) 'fail-safe N' (the number of additional studies needed to bring the weighted average effect size to non-significance), Egger's test (a test for asymmetry in the funnel plot; Egger, Smith, Schneider, & Minder, 1997), and the trim and fill technique (a test of whether asymmetry in the funnel plot would change the significance of the weighted average effect size; Duval & Tweedie, 2000).

Meta-Analysis Conclusion

This overview of meta-analysis is timely for the burgeoning field of sport and exercise psychology. As literatures continue to accrue studies, the appetite for comprehensive reviews grows. We hope we have stressed the importance of high standards and rigour in the conducting of these reviews. To summarize, several key components of meta-analysis emerge from this section:

(1) Outline a research question that is specific and testable and adds something new to the existing literature beyond a summary statement. Then, define any hypotheses regarding the direction of effects and moderating influences.
(2) Adopt explicit selection criteria for the inclusion and exclusion of studies and adopt these a priori.
(3) Retrieve as much literature as possible through exhaustive literature searches that include both published and unpublished studies.
(4) Code study characteristics and extract data diligently, with the use of multiple coders where possible.
(5) Analyse the data using meta-analytic procedures that maintain fidelity to the appropriate fixed- versus random-effects assumptions.

A limitation of meta-analysis is that it is a statistical tool that synthesizes quantitative data. Yet researchers are increasingly exploring phenomena in sport and exercise psychology using qualitative methods to obviate the interpretative limitations of numerical output (Culver, Gilbert, & Sparkes, 2012; Meredith, Dicks, Noel, & Wagstaff, 2018). Rather than metrics, qualitative research focuses on people's lived experience, documenting in rich detail 'the way people interpret and make sense of their experiences and the world in which they live' (Sparkes & Smith, 2014, p. 14). Like quantitative research, the accumulation of qualitative research in sport and exercise psychology necessitates methods of synthesis. One such technique is meta-synthesis.

Meta-Synthesis

A meta-synthesis of qualitative research is comparable to a meta-analysis of quantitative research. Both methods involve the systematic review of literature followed by a secondary analysis of empirical data. The aim of a meta-synthesis is to rigorously search, critically appraise, and synthesize qualitative research to produce themes, concepts, or theories that go beyond the findings of the individual studies under review to reveal new knowledge concerning a specific research topic (Williams & Shaw, 2016). As such, a meta-synthesis can be undertaken to identify gaps of knowledge in a research area, inform future research directions, complement or contrast results of meta-analyses, reveal new understandings in relation to generalizability, and provide evidence to support policy and practice (Finfgeld-Connett, 2014; Paterson, 2012; Shaw, Larkin, & Flowers, 2014; Smith, 2018). Systematic review and synthesis of qualitative research evidence are well-established actions within health and social sciences. However, there are far fewer examples within the field of sport and exercise science, as researchers are only just beginning to embrace the possibility of meta-synthesis to conceptually advance the field (Williams & Shaw, 2016).

There are many methods available to synthesize qualitative research. These methods of meta-synthesis are largely integrative or interpretative (see Barnett-Page & Thomas, 2009; Gough, Thomas, & Oliver, 2012; Grant & Booth, 2009; Shaw, 2011). Integrative approaches seek to identify and describe the current evidence base to produce practical recommendations to policymakers (Gough et al., 2012). On the other hand, interpretative approaches are more exploratory and involve developing a theoretical understanding of the current knowledge base (Shaw, 2011). In practice, it is useful to view these approaches on a continuum, as most methods include elements of integration and interpretation. However, the choice of meta-synthesis undertaken will depend upon the research question and purpose of the review. Here, we will focus upon the approach of thematic synthesis owing to the flexibility of this method allowing it to address a range of different research questions. Accordingly, thematic synthesis is an adaptable integrative and interpretative method that aims to address research questions relating to intervention need, appropriateness, acceptability, and effectiveness (Thomas & Harden, 2008).

In terms of conducting a meta-synthesis, there are two main phases. The first phase relates to the purpose of the review, a systematic search and screen of papers, and the appraisal of qualitative research studies. These are steps that, with a few notable exceptions, echo those of meta-analysis. The final phase involves the secondary analysis of data and synthesis of the selected studies. This is where the method varies depending on what type of meta-synthesis is being undertaken. Here, the steps involved in a thematic synthesis are illustrated, and working examples and critical reflections with this method are provided, derived from Williams, Ma, and Martin Ginis (2017).

Step 1: Developing a Research Question

Like meta-analysis, the first step of a meta-synthesis involves developing a clear, focused, and answerable research question (Shaw, 2011). This step is important as the research question will guide the search strategy and inclusion/exclusion criteria used to identify relevant literature in the following steps. If the review question is not clear, or is unfocused, this will result in uncertainty in the next steps and may waste both time and effort. As Soilemezi and Linceviciute (2018) note, adequate consideration must be taken when designing a research question. On the one hand, too broad a research question will lead to an ineffective search strategy and a lack of clarity regarding the inclusion/exclusion criteria. On the other hand, too narrow a research question means that the review might not fully cover a phenomenon, and too few studies might be identified to allow for a meaningful analysis. It is also important in this first step to develop a review protocol that is a detailed and transparent plan of action. In some instances, the review protocol can be published to promote transparency, minimize potential bias, enable public access, and avoid duplication (Moher et al., 2015).

In the example of Williams et al. (2017), the rationale to conduct the review was justified by the need to better understand disabled peoples' experiences and perceptions of physical activity enhancing interventions. This information could then be used by researchers, interventionists, healthcare professionals, and policymakers to inform the design of more effective physical activity interventions. As a result, the purpose of the meta-synthesis was to:

(1) systematically search and appraise the qualitative research evidence on physical activity behaviour change interventions for disabled people
(2) synthesize knowledge regarding the perceived impact of the interventions on physical activity behaviour change
(3) based on the results, propose improvements to inform future interventions, policies, and practices designed to increase long-term physical activity in these populations.

Given these objectives, the following research question was formulated: 'What does the published qualitative research evidence contribute to our empirical knowledge of the experiences and perceptions of people with physical impairments and mobility limitations who have participated in physical activity behaviour change interventions?'

Step 2: Identifying Relevant Papers

The next step of a meta-synthesis is to identify published papers and determine their relevance to the purpose of the review. Like meta-analysis, most methods of meta-synthesis involve a comprehensive and systematic search strategy to locate relevant peer-reviewed published papers and any related grey literature (Thomas & Harden, 2008; Williams & Shaw, 2016). This is achieved through searching electronic databases and hand-searching relevant journals, papers, policy documents, professional guidelines, and so on, identified through reference lists, bibliographies, citation searching, and contact with experts. To ensure maximum coverage of the literature, and to provide transparency in the search process, it is important that specific key terms are used to retrieve primary studies. It is useful to make a list of all the relevant keywords, terms, and synonyms related to the review question to help guide the search strategy.

To help identify these keywords, it is also recommended to draw upon one of the design tools to break a review question down into its key components. Beyond the PICO tool introduced earlier, helpful strategies for meta-synthesis include CHIP (context of the study; how it was conducted; issues investigated; and population involved) and SPIDER (sample, phenomenon of interest, design, evaluation, research type; Booth et al., 2016; Shaw, 2011). Table 6 illustrates how the CHIP tool applies to the example used by Williams et al. (2017) to guide the search strategy.

At this point, it is worthwhile consulting with one's university librarian to draw upon their breadth of knowledge concerning literature searches and database coverage. Their support

Table 6 CHIP tool to inform search strategy

Context	Disabled people subject to a physical activity behaviour change intervention
How	*Intervention*: 'intervention stud*' or 'programme' or 'curriculum' or 'physical education' or 'promotion' or 'initiative' or 'behaviour change' or 'strateg*'
Issues	*Physical activity*: 'physical activity' or 'exercise' or 'physical fitness' or 'sports' or 'exercise therapy'
Population	*Physical impairment*: 'disabled person*' or 'stroke' or 'cerebral palsy' or 'amputee' or 'spinal cord injur*' or 'multiple sclerosis' or 'arthritis' or 'Parkinson'

Note: The use of truncation terms (*) broadens the utility of the search term (e.g., 'spinal cord injur*' would retrieve injury, injuries, etc.) but may be different across databases can be invaluable when one is navigating the different subject headings and thesaurus terms used within databases to develop an efficient search strategy (Soilemezi & Linceviciute, 2018). In our example, to conduct a thorough and systematic search, we entered these search terms into databases with interdisciplinary coverage (such as Medline) and more specific databases (e.g., PsycINFO) without a limit on the date of publication. The next part of this stage is to screen the papers retrieved for relevance to the research question.

Papers should first be screened based on the relevance of the title to the research question. Once the irrelevant papers have been removed, the abstracts of the remaining papers should be screened based upon (a) relevance to the research question, (b) qualitative methodology, and (c) inclusion/exclusion criteria. At this point, it is important to be over-inclusive when screening papers (Shaw, 2011). For example, where the title and/or abstract suggests potential relevance to the research question or does not include enough information to apply inclusion/exclusion criteria, the full text of the article should be read. As in meta-analysis, it is recommended that more than one reviewer screens papers to minimize bias in meta-synthesis (Booth et al., 2016; Soilemezi & Linceviciute, 2018). Furthermore, akin to meta-analysis, it is important to keep a detailed report of the screening process using a PRISMA flowchart (see Figure 6).

Step 3: Appraising Studies for Research Quality

The third step of a meta-synthesis involves appraising the quality of the final selection of papers under review. Appraising the quality of these papers has been proposed as a vital stage in the process to avoid drawing unreliable or misleading conclusions from studies with perceived theoretical, methodological, or analytical deficiencies (Hannes & Macaitis, 2012; Paterson, 2012; Thomas & Harden, 2008). That said, judging the quality of qualitative research is not a straightforward task and is a topic of great debate and critique. Some scholars suggest that the quality appraisal should not be done owing to inflexible checklists and lack of reviewer agreement, and others argue that low-quality studies should be removed as they contribute minimally to the final synthesis (see Carroll & Booth, 2015; Soilemezi & Linceviciute, 2018). In practice, studies perceived to be of low quality are not necessarily excluded. Rather, their contribution to the synthetic output can be checked in the latter stages to ensure the final themes or concepts are not guided by research deemed 'inferior'.

Conversely, there is no one agreed method by which to appraise the final studies, and multiple structured quality assessment checklists and tools are available (see Majid & Vanstone, 2018). There has been little guidance as to how to choose a checklist or tool, or which one might be most suitable (Soilemezi & Linceviciute, 2018). However, to address this issue, Majid and Vanstone (2018) have sought to provide a description of some common existing appraisal tools and evaluated the limitations of each when synthesizing qualitative literature. In our experience, we have used Garside's (2014) recommendation that qualitative papers should be appraised for quality and rigour based on a flexible list of questions concerning trustworthiness, theoretical considerations, and practical considerations. Examples of questions include:

(1) Trustworthiness: Are the design and execution appropriate to the research question? How well supported by the data are any conclusions?
(2) Theoretical considerations: Does the study connect to a wider body of knowledge or existing theoretical framework? Does the article develop explanatory concepts for the findings?
(3) Practical considerations: Does the study usefully contribute to the review? Does this study provide evidence relevant to the policy setting?

In the meta-synthesis by Williams et al. (2017), all authors appraised the final studies under review based on these three elements. First, in the assessment of trustworthiness, each article was designed and executed appropriately to answer the research questions, and all conclusions were supported with data. Second, theoretical considerations were easier to appraise when authors made explicit reference to their conceptual/theoretical framework in their design and analysis, demonstrated reflexivity, or identified appropriate criteria for judging their method of inquiry. Although this level of methodological detail was not evident across all studies, this was not considered to influence the usability of the results for the synthesis. Third, in relation to practical considerations, it was deemed by all authors that each article usefully contributed to the review. Using these guidelines, no papers were excluded in the appraisal process.

Step 4: Developing Descriptive Themes

Steps 1–3 broadly follow the meta-analytic review protocol (with a few notable differences, e.g., quality screening). The next two steps are unique to the method of thematic synthesis. The fourth step involves extracting data, coding the text, and developing descriptive themes. In line with thematic synthesis methodology, any text labelled 'results' or 'findings', including within the abstract or discussion, can be extracted as 'raw data' for coding (Thomas & Harden, 2008). These raw data extracted for synthesis can include participant quotations and author interpretations of these data. In the example by Williams et al. (2017), additional quotes included as part of figures within the text, or in the appendices to support themes, were also extracted for coding. However, in line with the purpose of the review, only quotations from disabled people partaking in the intervention were utilized for synthesis. The views and perceptions of disabled people within the control group – and, therefore, not taking part in the physical activity intervention – and other participants (e.g., physiotherapists, intervention staff, peers) were excluded. Further descriptive information from each study, such as the aim, sample, characteristics of intervention, and methodology employed, should also be extracted and included in a tabulated summary of review articles.

The next part of this stage is to code the text line by line according to both its meaning and context. As Thomas and Harden (2008) propose, coding the data allows for translation, which, in this context, refers to the 'process of taking concepts from one study and recognizing the same concepts in another study, though they may not be expressed using identical words' (p. 3). For Williams et al. (2017), participants' experiences and perceptions of physical activity interventions were coded inductively, without restriction to a prior framework, to encourage new concepts to be identified in the data. More than one author can code the text to identify aspects of the data that relate to the purpose of the review. However, coding in this manner is not undertaken to seek inter-rater reliability and ensure 'reliable' coding, as can be seen in a meta-analysis. This is because inter-rater reliability is an ineffective measure to ensure reliable qualitative research (Smith & McGannon, 2018). Instead, multiple researchers can act as critical friends to scrutinize the audit trail in terms of data collection and analysis and encourage reflection and exploration of alternative interpretations and explanations (Sparkes & Smith, 2014).

Once data have been coded, it is important researchers look for similarities and differences in the codes to group them into descriptive themes across studies (Thomas & Harden, 2008). This phase of coding data and generating descriptive themes is representative of the method of thematic analysis as described by Braun and colleagues (2016). In the paper by Williams et al. (2017), codes were initially identified as (a) expectations of the intervention or reasons for participating, (b) factors perceived to be good about the intervention, (c) facilitators of continued exercise (during intervention or in the community), (d) barriers to exercise (completion of intervention or continuing exercise), and (e) participant suggestions for improvements to the intervention. The codes were then colour-coded (e.g., expectations were coloured black, good factors of the intervention were coloured green, etc.) to ensure that the context of the code was not lost when descriptive themes were created.

Step 5: Interpretation and Conceptual Synthesis

The final step of a thematic synthesis is to construct analytical themes, or overarching concepts, through interpretation and conceptual synthesis. At this point in the synthesis, the descriptive themes are very close to the findings of the original studies. However, a key feature of thematic synthesis is a clear distinction between generating 'data-driven' descriptive themes in Step 4 and constructing 'theory-driven' analytical themes in Step 5 (Thomas & Harden, 2008). This is where the defining characteristic of going beyond the findings of the original studies to reveal new or enhanced knowledge concerning the research topic is achieved. The process of constructing analytical themes involves interrogating the descriptive themes considering the current literature, theoretical frameworks, and purpose of the review. This stage also involves the continuous comparison of codes and descriptive themes to ensure that analytical themes are grounded in the data from the original studies. That said, this final step of synthesis is hard to describe. As Hannes and Macaitis (2012) note, there can be a 'black box between what people claim to use as a synthesis approach and what is actually done in practice' (p. 434). Therefore, it is imperative that authors are transparent throughout and keep a reflexive journal and audit trail of the decision-making process at each stage of the synthesis (Williams & Shaw, 2016). For example, the reflexive journal should be used to record decisions regarding the inclusion/exclusion of papers and how analytical themes were created from descriptive themes. Furthermore, the audit trail should illustrate where the codes from each paper have

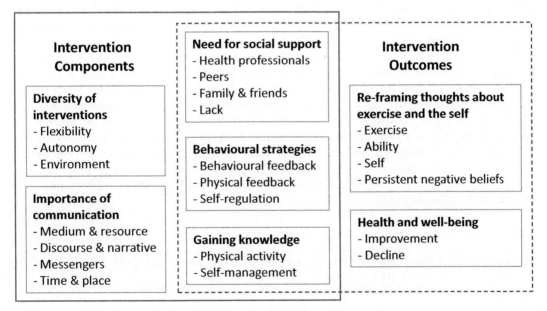

Figure 7 Final interpretation and conceptual synthesis (adapted from Williams et al., 2017)

contributed to each analytical theme and may be submitted as a supplementary file at the request of dissertation supervisors or journal editors.

One challenge of this final step is to write up the findings and draw conclusions and recommendations based on the synthesized results to inform research and practice (Soilemezi & Linceviciute, 2018). For Williams et al. (2017), the interpretation and conceptual synthesis resulted in the creation of seven interrelated concepts. When they returned to the purpose of the review, it became apparent that these concepts represented both components of an intervention and desired outcomes of an intervention (see Figure 7). Thus, the results of this thematic synthesis indicated that a combination of informational, social, and behavioural interventions components is necessary to promote physical activity initiation and maintenance. Furthermore, these results provided insight as to why each type of intervention is important and revealed several implications for the design of future interventions, policies, and practices to facilitate physical activity among disabled people.

Conclusion

We have presented a brief overview of the stages involved in the systematic review and thematic synthesis of qualitative research evidence. By now, the reader will be aware that the recommendations provided for the research question and literature search for meta-synthesis are not dissimilar to those for meta-analysis. However, there are crucial differences in terms of coding and analysis. Here, we highlight the unique aspects of the qualitative research review process that specifically relate to meta-synthesis. These include (a) ensuring that the purpose of the review is the driving factor when deciding which type of meta-synthesis should be undertaken, (b) how to appraise eligible studies and deal with perceived low-quality studies, and (c) how to describe and evidence the final extraction and synthesis of data. There are also aspects worthy of further consideration such as how to make a transparent and explicit assessment that the synthesized results provide a 'reasonable representation' of the phenomenon under review (see Lewin et al., 2018). That said, we hope that this overview of meta-synthesis stimulates further use and critical interest in the methodology to conceptually advance the field of sport and exercise psychology.

As research continues to accumulate in sport and exercise psychology, comparisons of study findings – in the form of reviews of research – become highly salient. The aim of this chapter was to provide an overview of literature review techniques used by researchers to synthesize quantitative and qualitative research. We first introduced the reader to meta-analysis, a review technique that aggregates data from quantitative studies. We then provided an overview of meta-synthesis, a review technique that collates data from qualitative studies. It is our hope that this section has highlighted the salience of study integration and has given the reader confidence in both conducting and interpreting a literature review. We urge researchers to harness the opportunities offered by meta-analysis and meta-synthesis to address new and existing research problems.

Notes

1 Cohen's *d* is sometimes referred to as the 'uncorrected effect size' to distinguish it from Hedge's *d*, which is corrected for sample size (see Johnson & Eagly, 2014).
2 Calculation for the reciprocal variance of a two-group comparison can be found in Johnson and Eagly (2014).

References

Barnett-Page, E., & Thomas, J. (2009). Methods for the synthesis of qualitative research: A critical review. *BMC Medical Research Methodology, 9,* 59.

Booth, A., Noyes, J., Flemming, K., Gerhardus, A., Wahister, P., van der Wilt, G. J., & Rehfuess, E. (2016). Guidance on choosing qualitative evidence synthesis methods for use in health technology assessments of complex interventions [online]. Retrieved from www.integrate-hta.eu/downloads/

Braun, V., Clarke, V., & Weate, P. (2016). Using thematic analysis in sport and exercise research. In B. Smith & A. C. Sparkes (Eds.), *International handbook of qualitative methods in sport and exercise* (pp. 274–288). London: Routledge.

Card, N. A. (2012). *Applied meta-analysis for social science research.* New York: Guildford Press.

Carroll, C., & Booth, A. (2015). Quality assessment of qualitative evidence for systematic review and synthesis: Is it meaningful, and if so, how should it be performed? *Research Synthesis Methods, 6,* 274–288.

Cochran, W. G. (1954). The combination of estimates from different experiments. *Biometrics, 10,* 149–154.

Cohen, J. (1992). A power primer. *Psychological Bulletin, 112,* 101–129.

Culver, D., Gilbert, W., & Sparkes, A. C. (2012). Qualitative research in sport psychology journals: The next decade 2000–2009 and beyond. *The Sport Psychologist, 26,* 155–159.

Curran, T., & Hill, A. P. (2019). Perfectionism is increasing over time: A meta-analysis of birth cohort differences from 1989 to 2016. *Psychological Bulletin, 145,* 261–281.

Curran, T., Hill, A. P., Appleton, P. R., Vallerand, R. J., & Standage, M. (2015). The psychology of passion: A meta-analytical review of a decade of research on intrapersonal outcomes. *Motivation and Emotion, 39,* 410–429.

Duval, S., & Tweedie, R. (2000). Trim and fill: A simple funnel-plot–based method of testing and adjusting for publication bias in meta-analysis. *Biometrics, 56,* 631–655.

Egger, M., Smith, G. D., Schneider, M., & Minder, C. (1997). Bias in meta-analysis detected by a simple, graphical test. *BMJ, 315,* 455–463.

Finfgeld-Connett, D. (2014). Metasynthesis findings: Potential versus reality. *Qualitative Health Research, 24,* 629–634.

Garside, R. (2014). Should we appraise the quality of qualitative research reports for systematic reviews, and if so, how? *Innovation: The European Journal of Social Science Research, 27,* 1581–1591.

Glass, G. V. (1976). Primary, secondary, and meta-analysis of research. *Educational Researcher, 5,* 67–79.

Gough, D., Thomas, J., & Oliver, S. (2012). Clarifying differences between review designs and methods. *Systematic Reviews, 1,* 28.

Grant, M. J., & Booth, A. (2009). A typology of reviews: An analysis of 14 review types and associated methodologies. *Health Information and Libraries Journal, 26,* 91–108.

Greenwald, S., & Russell, R. L. (1991). Assessing rationales for inclusiveness in meta-analytic samples. *Psychotherapy Research, 1,* 91–108.

Hannes, K., & Macaitis, K. (2012). A move to more systematic and transparent approaches in qualitative evidence synthesis: Update on a review of published papers. *Qualitative Research, 12,* 17–24.

Hayes, A. F., & Rockwood, N. J. (2017). Regression-based statistical mediation and moderation analysis in clinical research: Observations, recommendations, and implementation. *Behaviour Research and Therapy, 98,* 402–442.

Hedges, L. V., & Vevea, J. L. (1998). Fixed- and random-effects models in meta-analysis. *Psychological Methods, 3*(4), 39–57.

Higgins, J. P., & Thompson, S. G. (2002). Quantifying heterogeneity in a meta-analysis. *Statistics in Medicine, 21,* 1539–1558.

Hill, A. P., & Curran, T. (2016). Multidimensional perfectionism and burnout: A meta-analysis. *Personality and Social Psychology Review, 20,* 269–288.

Hill, A. P., Mallinson-Howard, S. H., & Jowett, G. E. (2018). Multidimensional perfectionism in sport: A meta-analytical review. *Sport, Exercise, and Performance Psychology, 7,* 235–270.

Jensen, L. A., & Allen, M. N. (1996). Meta-synthesis of qualitative findings. *Qualitative Health Research, 6,* 553–560.

Johnson, B. T., & Eagly, A. H. (2014). Meta-analysis of social-personality psychological research. In H. T. Reis & C. M. Judd (Eds.), *Handbook of research methods in social and personality psychology* (2nd ed., pp. 675–707). London: Cambridge University Press.

Lawlor, D. A., & Hopker, S. W. (2001). The effectiveness of exercise as an intervention in the management of depression: Systematic review and meta-regression analysis of randomised controlled trials. *BMJ, 322,* 763.

Lewin, S., Booth, A., Glenton, C., Munthe-Kaas, H., Rashidian, A., Wainwright, M., & Noyes, J. (2018). Applying GRADE-CERQual to qualitative evidence synthesis findings: Introduction to the series. *Implementation Science, 13*(Suppl 1), 2.

Lindheimer, J. B., O'Connor, P. J., & Dishman, R. K. (2015). Quantifying the placebo effect in psychological outcomes of exercise training: A meta-analysis of randomized trials. *Sports Medicine, 45*, 693–711.

Lipsey, M. W., & Wilson, D. B. (2001). *Practical meta-analysis.* Thousand Oaks, CA: Sage.

Majid, U., & Vanstone, M. (2018). Appraising qualitative research for evidence syntheses: A compendium of quality appraisal tools. *Qualitative Health Research, 28*, 2115–2131.

Meredith, S. J., Dicks, M., Noel, B., & Wagstaff, C. R. D. (2018). A review of behavioural measures and research methodology in sport and exercise psychology. *International Review of Sport and Exercise Psychology, 11*, 25–46.

Moher, D., Liberati, A., Tetzlaff, J., Altman, D. G., & Group, P. (2009). Reprint—Preferred reporting items for systematic reviews and meta-analyses: The PRISMA statement. *Physical Therapy, 89*, 873–880.

Moher, D., Shamseer, L., Clarke, M., Ghersi, D., Liberati, A., Petticrew, M., & Stewart, L. A. (2015). Preferred reporting items for systematic review and meta-analysis protocols (PRISMA-P) 2015 statement. *Systematic Reviews, 4*, 1.

Paterson, B. L. (2012). 'It looks great but how do I know if it fits?': An introduction to meta-synthesis research. In K. Hannes & C. Lockwood (Eds.), *Synthesising qualitative research: Choosing the right approach* (pp. 1–21). Chichester: John Wiley.

Rosenthal, R. (1979). The file drawer problem and tolerance for null results. *Psychological Bulletin, 86*, 638–641.

Schardt, C., Adams, M. B., Owens, T., Keitz, S., & Fontelo, P. (2007). Utilization of the PICO framework to improve searching PubMed for clinical questions. *BMC Medical Informatics and Decision Making, 7*, 16.

Schmidt, F. L., Oh, I. S., & Hayes, T. L. (2009). Fixed-versus random-effects models in meta-analysis: Model properties and an empirical comparison of differences in results. *British Journal of Mathematical and Statistical Psychology, 62*, 97–128.

Shaw, R. L. (2011). Identifying and synthesising qualitative literature. In D. Harper & A. Thompson (Eds.), *Qualitative research methods in mental health and psychotherapy: An introduction for students and practitioners* (pp. 9–22). Chichester: Wiley Blackwell.

Shaw, R. L., Larkin, M., & Flowers, P. (2014). Expanding the evidence within evidence-based healthcare: Thinking about the context, acceptability and feasibility of interventions. *BMJ Evidence Based Medicine, 19*, 9–22.

Shelby, L. B., & Vaske, J. J. (2008). Understanding meta-analysis: A review of the methodological literature. *Leisure Sciences, 30*, 201–203.

Smith, B. (2018). Generalizability in qualitative research: Misunderstandings, opportunities and recommendations for the sport and exercise sciences. *Qualitative Research in Sport, Exercise and Health, 10*, 96–110.

Smith, B., & McGannon, K. R. (2018). Developing rigor in qualitative research: Problems and opportunities within sport and exercise psychology. *International Review of Sport and Exercise Psychology, 11*, 137–149.

Soilemezi, D., & Linceviciute, S. (2018). Synthesizing qualitative research: Reflections and lessons learnt by two new reviewers. *International Journal of Qualitative Methods, 17*, 1–14.

Sparkes, A. C., & Smith, B. (2014). *Qualitative research methods in sport, exercise & health: From process to product.* London: Routledge.

Sutton, A. J. (2009). Publication bias. In H. Cooper, L. V. Hedges,, & J. C. Valentine (Eds.), *The handbook of research synthesis and meta-analysis* (pp. 435–452). New York: Russell Sage Foundation.

Thomas, J., & Harden, A. (2008). Methods for the thematic synthesis of qualitative research in systematic reviews. *BMC Medical Research Methodology, 8*, 45.

Viechtbauer, W. (2010). Conducting meta-analyses in R with the Metafor package. *Journal of Statistical Software, 36*, 1–48.

Williams, T. L., Ma, J. K., & Martin Ginis, K. A. (2017). Participant experiences and perceptions of physical activity-enhancing interventions for people with physical impairments and mobility limitations: A meta-synthesis of qualitative research evidence. *Health Psychology Review, 11*, 179–196.

Williams, T. L., & Shaw, R. L. (2016). Synthesizing qualitative research. In B. Smith & A. C. Sparkes (Eds.), *International handbook of qualitative methods in sport and exercise* (pp. 274–287). London: Routledge.

22

METHODS IN COGNITIVE SPORT PSYCHOLOGY

Edson Filho and Gershon Tenenbaum

Introduction

There is great interest in capturing and measuring the inner processes of the brain. The measurement of "thoughts" enables us to comprehend human emotional states and behavioural tendencies. In this chapter, we discuss current methodological approaches to measuring cognitive states and patterns in sport psychology. We start by defining cognition and discussing reliability and validity in light of measurement theory. We then comment on the complex, multidimensional, and relative nature of cognitive states and patterns. We proceed by outlining the importance of measuring biopsychosocial markers of latent abstract constructs and subscribing to theory-based methodology in the design of experimental research in sport psychology. We also review transdisciplinary and key domain-specific research paradigms. We comment on core principles of qualitative, quantitative, and psychophysiological measurement and discuss future trends in cognitive sport psychology.

Cognition

Cognitive psychology pertains to the study of the mind (Braisby & Gellatly, 2012), and cognition refers to "mental operations involving information processing and thus includes processes such as perception, problem solving, memory recall, and decision making" (Tenenbaum & Filho, 2014, p. 141). Importantly, cognition manifests in states and patterns. States are moment-to-moment sense-making and reasoning, whereas patterns are trait-like tendencies that predispose someone to think in a certain way (Tenenbaum & Filho, 2017). Simply put, cognition pertains to thinking, and we know from our own lived experiences and previous empirical research that thinking is a fundamental part of human life. Descartes' philosophy "I think, therefore I am" captures how important thinking is for all of us. Without thinking, we cannot play sports or send a spacecraft to the moon. However, measuring the so-called "matter of thought" is not easy, because thoughts are arguably an abstract phenomenon (Tenenbaum & Filho, 2015). Notwithstanding this inherent difficulty of measuring thought, researchers concur that different methodological approaches are needed to study cognitive states and patterns (Cacioppo, Tassinary, & Berntson, 2007).

Sport psychologists should keep in mind that cognitive states and patterns are entangled with affective and behavioural states and patterns, something that has been called the "cognitive-affective-behavioural linkage" (Tenenbaum, Basevitch, Gershgoren, & Filho, 2013). At times, we must change how we think (i.e., cognitive therapy) to change how we feel and behave. Other times, changing how we behave (i.e., behavioural interventions) can change how we think and feel (see Orlick, 2015). Notably, the relationship among cognition, affect, and behaviour is not explained by a one-to-one rule. In other words, it is not always the case that cognition influences (directly or indirectly) and is influenced by affective and behavioural states and patterns. For instance, people might understand a situation but not feel good about it or know how to behave in it (e.g., fight in a football stadium). Alternatively, individuals might experience cognitive overload in a given situation, but still enjoy it greatly (e.g., rollercoaster ride). Accordingly, sport psychologists should keep in mind that the reliability and validity of cognitive states and patterns co-vary (to a greater or lesser extent) with affective and behavioural variables.

Reliability and Validity of Cognitive Measures

An in-depth discussion of reliability and validity of cognitive measures is available elsewhere (see Tenenbaum, Eklund, & Kamata, 2012, and contribution by Gunnel, Volume 1, Chapter 47, in this encyclopedia). To inform our discussion on methodological approaches in cognitive sport psychology, we reiterate that cognitive measures should be: (a) reliable, in the sense that they should be accurate and error-free as much as possible; and (b) valid, in the sense that they should provide us with the information we wish to obtain when measuring a given variable (Tenenbaum & Filho, 2015). Sport psychologists have used different types of validity method to assess the content, convergent, discriminant, and predictive validity of cognitive variables in the form of introspection (Tenenbaum & Filho, 2018). For the remainder of this section, we use anxiety, one of the most studied topics in sport psychology (Filho & Tenenbaum, 2015), to exemplify the ideas of reliable and valid measurement of cognitive states and patterns.

To measure any cognitive state or pattern researchers must first propose an operational definition for the variable of interest. For instance, anxiety has been broadly defined as "worry-ness" that is expressed through cognitive and somatic channels (Smith, Smoll, & Schutz, 1990). Based on this operational definition, researchers have created written questionnaire items to reflect the abstract notion of trait and state anxiety. The extent to which these items reflect (see "reflective indicators" in Hoyle, 2011) the concept of anxiety is what we call "content validity". Notably, any measure designed to capture the theorem of anxiety, or any other cognitive state or pattern, must also possess "temporal stability" (see test-retest reliability in Tenenbaum et al., 2012). Without temporal stability, a measure cannot be reliable or, by extension, a valid measure of a cognitive state or trait. Importantly, the greater the temporal stability for a given measure, the more likely this measure is tapping into a cognitive trait rather than a cognitive state.

Another key idea in measurement pertains to the notions of "convergent validity" and "discriminant validity", which are, in a sense, opposite sides of the same coin. Convergent validity refers to the extent that two different measures are related, whereas discriminant validity refers to the extent that two different measures are independent of one another. To establish convergent and discriminant validity, researchers often correlate individuals' scores on different measures. For instance, psychologists have correlated measures of anxiety with questionnaires on confidence and depression to evaluate differences among these theorems. By triangulating different measures, researchers are able to test theoretical differences among cognitive constructs so that, in practice, anxiety can be differentiated from confidence and depression, for example.

Researchers and practitioners are also interested in "discriminant validity" and "predictive validity". If scores on a given anxiety questionnaire are sensitive enough to differentiate expert from novice athletes, then the test has high discriminant validity. If scores on an anxiety test are predictive of performance in a reaction time task, then the test has high predictive validity. These concepts are important because sport psychologists are often trying to discriminate between optimal and suboptimal performance and well-being levels, as well as trying to predict output variables (e.g., performance and well-being) from myriad biopsychosocial input variables.

In essence, to measure cognitive states and traits, researchers and practitioners must be attuned to the notion of reliability and validity. The ideas of temporal stability, and content, convergent, discriminant, and predictive validity are particularly important to the measurement of cognitive states and traits in sport, a highly complex, multidimensional, and relative domain of human performance.

The Complex, Multidimensional, and Relative Nature of Measuring Cognition

The measurement and interpretation of cognition are complex matters that extend beyond the understanding of reliability and validity. This complexity is partially due to the fact that cognitive variables do not always behave linearly over time or share a linear relationship with other variables. For instance, the relationship between cognitive arousal and performance has been modelled through linear, curvilinear, and exponential functions (see Weinberg & Gould, 2018). Similarly, working memory over the lifespan has been shown to change abruptly over time, and the learning of a new cognitive task is often described by a sinusoidal-like (s-shape) function (Wang & Chen, 2014). Generally speaking, most biopsychosocial variables (cognitive or otherwise) tend to reach an asymptote over time. For instance, one's height and salary tend to stagnate at some point, rather than continue to increase linearly. It follows that: (a) the length of time that a cognitive variable is measured matters; and (b) we recommend the use of non-linear statistical functions to model the relationship between cognitive and biopsychosocial variables.

Cognitive variables are also multidimensional and, thus, are usually described by reflective indicators or are constituted of formative indicators. For instance, flow-feeling is described using nine different dimensions (e.g., challenge and skill balance, intense concentration; see Csikszentmihalyi & Csikszentmihalyi, 1975), and dementia is a syndrome constituted by manifold symptoms (e.g., memory loss, poor judgement; see Barkhof & van Buchem, 2016). Importantly, the various dimensions of a given cognitive construct might be more or less interrelated. Accordingly, when measuring cognitive variables, researchers must conceptualize and account for the different reflective or formative indicators, as well as the relationship (oblique or orthogonal) among these indicators.

The measurement of cognitive states and patterns is influenced by personal, task, and contextual effects (Filho, Bertollo, Robazza, & Comani, 2015; see also "action theory" in Schack & Hackfort, 2007). For instance, the normative value for a given cognitive variable usually depends on the person (e.g., adults vs. elderly), the task (e.g., simple reaction time vs. multi-reaction time), and the context (e.g., Western vs. Eastern societies) being measured. Put differently, many advancements in applied psychology have been made through design and experimental manipulations targeting different person, task, or contextual variables. The use of advanced multivariate statistics, such as multilevel structural equation modelling, is also a fruitful way to measure and interpret how individuals' cognitive states and patterns influence and are influenced by person–task–context factors.

Variables of Interest

Consistent with the importance of examining human behaviour and health from a dynamic biopsychosocial standpoint (Lehman, David, & Gruber, 2017), we recommend that scholars and practitioners manipulate and measure biological, psychological, and sociological factors when studying and proposing interventions in the field. In other words, one can manipulate biopsychosocial factors to operationalize an independent variable, or measure biopsychosocial states to operationalize a dependent variable.

The number of biological factors that can be measured by applied psychologists is endless. In essence, however, we understand that scholars and practitioners are interested in measuring central and peripheral physiological responses associated with cognitive activity. By central responses, we refer to brain-related activity (Tenenbaum & Filho, 2015). Peripheral physiological responses are those unconsciously regulated by the parasympathetic and sympathetic systems, such as hormonal changes and temperature (McArdle, Katch, & Katch, 2010). There is also focused interest in measuring perceptual-sensory responses as related to our five senses of sight, hearing, taste, smell, and touch (Braisby & Gellatly, 2012). To date, most research in sport psychology has been focused on the visual system, and thus we encourage novel research on the other four senses. There is also a plethora of research targeting the motor system, particularly studies targeting central markers of control of movement and action in the motor cortex (Wang & Chen, 2014).

The list of psychological variables related to cognitive phenomena is also extensive. It is clear from the literature that perception, attention, decision-making, anticipation, and memory are some of the most studied cognitive phenomena in sport psychology (Braisby & Gellatly, 2012; Tenenbaum & Filho, 2014). These cognitive processes are all intertwined, and, thus, the challenge for scholars is to design reliable and valid methods to measure them. The time it takes to react to a stimulus and the number of items recalled in a memory test are well-known examples of dependent variables used to study cognitive processes.

Manipulating social factors can bring about a number of independent variables. For instance, priming and audience effects have been shown to influence cognitive functioning (Kuzyakov, Friedel, & Stahra, 2000). Also, changing socio-contextual factors, such as practice structure (e.g., blocked vs. random practice; see Wang & Chen, 2014), can influence learning and performance. Social factors can also serve as covariates, as cultural background and team tenure in sport teams might influence cognitive functioning. More recently, applied psychologists have examined inter-brain coupling to study socio-cognitive theoretical frameworks, including the notion of team mental models and theory of mind (Filho & Tenenbaum, 2019). In fact, theory-driven methodologies are paramount to advance the field, as we elaborate on next.

Theory-Based Methodology

Reliable measurement of cognitive variables is required to advance theoretical models, which, in turn, must inform practice. This rationale is akin to the well-established notion of evidence-based practice (Moore, 2007). On the other hand, theory should also inform methodology, especially given the multitude of complex, multidimensional, and relative cognitive phenomena that can be measured through biopsychosocial means. Accordingly, in the remainder of this section, we comment on different types of theory that can be advanced by sport psychologists.

First, we differentiate between "descriptive" and "explanatory" theoretical models. Descriptive models list the features proper to a given phenomenon, whereas explanatory models discuss input–throughout–output relations among a set of variables. For instance, as noted elsewhere: "some scholars in chemistry and physics have focused on describing what the elements in the periodic table are, while others have tried to explain how and why the linkages among certain elements take place in the natural world" (Filho, in press, p. 2). In our field, sport psychologists have described different socio-cognitive constructs such as cohesion and shared mental models and related them systemically in a nomological (input–throughput–output) network (Filho, Tenenbaum, & Yang, 2015). The literature on emotion also illustrates how some psychologists tried to describe the several different emotions that individuals experience, whereas others have tried to explain how the by-product of two affective states (e.g., activation and pleasantness) might account for the spectrum of emotional experiences (see Russell, 1980).

Second, we differentiate between "systemic" and "holistic" theories. Systemic theories discuss the relationship among a subset of variables, whereas holistic theories try to describe "the whole". For instance, physicists are working towards "a theory of everything", and we know that psychologists and physiologists try to identify thresholds (e.g., working memory capacity, maximum heart rate) that apply to everybody. Thus, holistic theories are about establishing a single overarching rule. Systemic theories are, again, about explaining the relations among a set of constructs, such as in the case of long-term working memory. Specifically, Ericsson and Kintsch (1995) explain how experts' perceptual and memory structures are related in a manner that allows them to exceed their working memory computational capacities (7 ± 2 bits of information) in their respective domains of expertise.

Third, we differentiate between "nomothetic" and "idiographic" models. Nomothetic models are probabilistically based models aimed at describing the mean (and variability around the mean) for a given variable of interest. In other words, nomothetic models represent "a regression to the mean" of a given variable and, thus, focus on describing and predicting trends within the general population. Conversely, idiographic models emphasize individual differences in the population. By shedding light on outliers, idiographic models teach us about the nuances of a given cognitive phenomenon. Importantly, we need both nomothetic and idiographic models of thinking to help sport actors to perform optimally. For instance, a classic example pertains to the inverted-U hypothesis which describes that, on average, athletes perform better when experiencing moderate levels of psychophysiological activation. However, according to the individual zones of optimal functioning theory, different athletes show unique levels of activation associated with peak performance experiences. Knowing the population mean effect provides us with a norm that allows for the prediction of population trends; however, practitioners should also keep in mind that they often work with unique individuals operating in singular contexts and with singular performance pressures.

Overall, it is important that sport psychologists continue to refine their theoretical models by contrasting descriptive, explanatory, systemic, and holistic frameworks, as well as by considering both nomothetic and idiographic ways of thinking. Foremost, as Popper (2005) has taught us, theoretical models should be falsifiable, and, thus, sport psychologists should try to disprove their models rather than search for evidence to prove them right. It is the contrast of thesis and antithesis that leads to novel synthesis that in turn catalyses better research paradigms across domains of human interest.

Research Paradigms

A paradigm denotes the ways of thinking shared by scholars to address problems within a field (Kuhn, 1962). More specifically, according to Chilisa and Kawulich (2012), a research paradigm is a set of assumptions and propositions about the nature of reality (i.e., ontology), the different ways of knowing (i.e., epistemology), and ethics and values systems (i.e., axiology). Of note, scholars across a number of areas of interest have relied primarily on four broad research paradigms, namely "positivist/post-positivist", "constructivist/interpretative", "transformative/emancipatory", and "postcolonial/indigenous" (Chilisa, 2011).

In the positivist/post-positivist paradigm, scholars assume there is one reality that must be studied through quantifiable methods and described under the law of probability. For instance, experimental methods in cognitive sport psychology have been used to study the brain dynamics underpinning skilled and automatic performance in self-paced tasks (Bertollo et al., 2016). In the constructivist/interpretative paradigm, scholars defend the notion that multiple realities exist, as "reality" depends on the person and context under study. For instance, we have used a constructivist paradigm to study team cognition in sports and observed that teammates possess both a shared (communal) understanding of reality and complementary (idiosyncratic) mental representations (Filho, Gershgoren, Basevitch, Schinke, & Tenenbaum, 2014; Filho & Rettig, 2019). In the transformative/emancipatory paradigm, scholars challenge status quo interpretations of reality in order to empower people and transform society – for instance, the research on the cognitive and affective experiences of black men and women coaches trying to make it to the professional level in soccer, a sport that is usually dominated by male Caucasian coaches (Rankin-Wright, Hylton, & Norman, 2017). Finally, in the postcolonial/indigenous paradigm, scholars challenge the world-views shaped by the colonizers over the colonized. For instance, the cognitive-affective self-adaptation strategies of indigenous aboriginal elite athletes in North America has been studied in sport psychology (Schinke et al., 2006).

Key Research Paradigms in Cognitive Sport Psychology

Beyond these broader transdisciplinary paradigms, there are domain-specific paradigms, as Kuhn (1962) has noted in his classic book *The Structure of Scientific Revolutions*. Within cognitive sport psychology, researchers have used several paradigms to study cognitive phenomena. It is beyond the remit of this chapter to review all possible paradigms. Nevertheless, we discuss recurrent research paradigms used in the field, namely (a) the expert–novice paradigm, (b) the expert performance approach, (c) perturbation paradigms, and (d) the learning paradigm.

The Expert–Novice Paradigm

The expert–novice paradigm is straightforward: Researchers compare higher-level athletes with lower-level athletes (i.e., between-subject design), and/or more and less proficient performances within athletes (within-subject design). By doing so, scholars can describe and explain differences between experts and novices, as well as the underlying mechanisms of optimal and suboptimal performances (Filho & Tenenbaum, 2015). For instance, previous research based on the expert–novice paradigm has shown that experts use fewer fixations of long durations (i.e., context control strategy) than novices, who show the precisely opposite gaze behaviour (see Tenenbaum, 2003). Put differently, experts look at the right environmental cues for a longer time, whereas novices look everywhere because they are not certain where crucial information is in the environment.

The Expert Performance Approach

The purpose of the expert performance approach is to identify representative tasks (domain-specific tasks predictive of superior performance in a given domain) that can be objectively measured and studied in laboratory conditions. Once a task has been identified and shown to capture reproducibly superior performance in laboratory conditions, scholars can study the cognitive processes mediating expertise by using manifold biopsychosocial methods, including protocol analysis, eye-tracking, and electroencephalogram (Ericsson, 2015; Ericsson, Whyte, & Ward, 2007).

Perturbation Paradigms

Perturbation paradigms consist of disturbing the rate (quantitative features) and/or nature (qualitative features) of a given stimulus to explore the underpinning cognitive mechanisms (e.g., perception, attention, decision-making, anticipation, and memory) associated with performance or learning. For instance, in the classic "odd-ball paradigm", the effects of a deviant stimulus on cognitive mechanisms are explored (García-Larrea, Lukaszewicz, & Mauguiére, 1992). In the "occlusion paradigm", an ongoing video-clip is frozen (or the screen "goes black"), and then individuals are asked to perform a task designed to assess their perceptive, anticipatory, or decision-making skills (Mann, Williams, Ward, & Janelle, 2007). In the "juggling paradigm", team cognition (i.e., shared and complementary mental models) is studied through the continuous monitoring of the psychophysiological states of individuals engaged in an interactive juggling task of increased difficulty (Filho et al., 2015). Maximal effort tests (e.g., 1RM, VO_2 max; see McArdle et al., 2010), wherein individuals are asked to perform a physical task until they reach a maximum threshold, are also examples of perturbation-based paradigms that have been used to study cognitive constructs, such as mental fatigue and executive cognitive functioning. Notably, in perturbation-based paradigms, scholars use either an event or block design to study changes in biopsychosocial variables. In "event designs", changes in biopsychosocial variables are examined around (before or after) the presentation of a timed (t_0) stimulus. In "block designs", a block of trials or time is used as the unit of analysis, and scores on a given biopsychosocial variable are averaged for the block (see Blascovich, Vanman, Mendes, & Dickerson, 2011).

The Learning Paradigm

In addition to studying performance through the above-mentioned paradigms, sport psychologists are also interested in studying how people learn (for a review, see Wang & Chen, 2014). In essence, the learning paradigm consists of the following steps: (a) identifying a novel task; (b) measuring baseline performance at this task (pre-test); (c) allowing individuals to practice or not (in the case of a control group), and under different conditions (e.g., feedback and no-feedback); and (d) observing which practice condition yields better learning outcomes at a post-test (measured after a pre-established time interval) and at a transfer condition consisting of a different task or situation (e.g., pressure vs. no-pressure manipulation). The learning paradigm has been around for decades, but it still has great promise for the field, as the emergence of new technology allows for broader and deeper insights into the biopsychosocial changes resulting from learning (Tenenbaum & Filho, 2015). Specifically, the effect of neural stimulation techniques on the learning of cognitive and motor tasks is an emerging trend in the field (see Carlstedt & Balconi, 2019).

Analytical Approaches

Depending on the question under study, sport psychologists use "qualitative", "quantitative", and "psychophysiological" methods to generate and analyse data. Numerous books on each of these analytical approaches exist in the field, and, thus, we do not review the different types of quantitative, qualitative, and neuroscientific method that exist. In fact, the American Psychological Association has recently published guidelines that should inform the reporting of quantitative and qualitative research in psychology (see Appelbaum et al., 2018; Levitt et al., 2018), and current guidelines for psychophysiological analyses are also available in the literature (Carlstedt & Balconi, 2019). As such, in the remainder of this section, we highlight some key ideas linked to each one of these analytical approaches.

Qualitative approaches are mainly about purposeful samples. Scholars are interested in studying unique cases, such as how Olympic gold medallists' problem-solve under pressure (e.g., Gould, Dieffenbach, & Moffett, 2002; Orlick, 2015). Accordingly, it is important to employ a sampling strategy that targets information-rich cases who are able to provide quality insights on the topic under study. Furthermore, the triangulation of participants, methods (e.g., interviews, document analysis, observations), researchers (e.g., critical friend reviews), and theoretical outlooks is important to enhance the trustworthiness of qualitative findings (Patton, 2015). Analysing negative or divergent cases, considering both emic and etic approaches in cross-cultural studies, and inviting external researchers (i.e., external audits review) to scrutinize the raw data and researchers' subjective assessments are also ways to increase the credibility of qualitative research (Patton, 2015).

In quantitative research, scholars must clearly specify the design they are using (e.g., within, between, mixed), as well as provide a clear operational definition for each variable (dependent, independent, and covariate) under study. It is important to provide detailed information on the research design and variables to address the replicability crisis in psychology (Appelbaum et al., 2018). Also, we know that wrong premises often lead to wrong conclusions (Popper, 2005). Therefore, the assumptions of any given statistical analysis should not be disregarded. Statistical power should be reported so it is clear whether a study has appropriate power, or whether its results are under- or overpowered. Bayesian statistical models are also increasingly being used to relate input and output variables in psychology. Finally, statistical models addressing input–output relationships among a set of variables should test for alternative equivalent (same statistical fit indexes) and non-equivalent models and aim for parsimony rather than over-parametrization (Tenenbaum & Filho, 2015).

The analysis of psychophysiological data also has to be considered in light of some core ideas. First, scholars must capture that psychophysiological relations can be assessed in terms of "generality" (context-dependent vs. context-independent relations), "specificity" (from "one-to-one" to "many-to-many" relations) and "sensitivity" (low to high), as detailed elsewhere (for a review, see Cacioppo et al., 2007). Second, scholars must consider the importance of baseline intakes, which are used to ensure that the data being collected are reliable and within normal ranges and to serve as an experimental manipulation check (Tenenbaum & Filho, 2018). Third, different physiological signals must be sampled at different sampling rates, usually at a rate four to eight times greater than the naturally occurring frequency of the signal (e.g., heart rate) under study (Stern, Ray, & Quigley, 2001). Fourth, psychophysiological signals are subject to the law of initial values (Stern et al., 2001). That is, there is less room for variability if an individual's baseline heart rate is at a higher (150 bpm) as opposed to lower (75 bpm) level. Finally, it is important to rely on multimodal assessments, as different individuals might manifest their cognitive-affective-behavioural states and patterns through different channels (e.g., galvanic skin response, heart rate), and a given stimulus might lead to myriad changes in various psychophysiological systems akin to the notion of "directional fractionation" (see Stern et al., 2001). Notably, we expect psychophysiological approaches to become increasingly prevalent in the field.

Trends in Cognitive Measurement

Robotics and information technology, genetics, and brain mapping and stimulation are trends likely to continue to grow in the field (Raab, 2017; Tenenbaum & Filho, 2016). In fact, the miniaturization and popularization of high-tech hardware and software have enabled more sport actors to monitor biopsychosocial variables linked to cognitive states and patterns (Filho & Tenenbaum, 2018). New hardware and software are launched every year, with sport-specific gear allowing athletes to monitor myriad variables (e.g., cardiovascular responses, sleeping patterns, and kinematic behaviour).

Sport-related genetics testing and genetic-tailored training and medicine (gene therapy) also promise to change our research praxis and intervention protocols in cognitive sport psychology (Wagner & Royal, 2012). Importantly, we must remain critical regarding the reliability and validity of genetic testing and engineering in sports and beyond, and advance ethical considerations to cope with the moral challenges that follow (see Lucidi, Chirico, & Hackfort, Volume 2, Chapter 20, in this encyclopedia). Gene doping, which can be operationalized through molecular biology technology, is also an emerging area of research in sport (Friedmann, 2010; Friedmann, Rabin, & Frankel, 2010).

Brain imaging and stimulation techniques are also a ripe and ever-growing area of research and practice in the field (Carlstedt & Balconi, 2019). Two challenges in our field regarding brain imaging and stimulation are to (a) advance applied and ecologically valid research concerning movement and interactive approaches, as most research about the brain remains tied to static lab settings and observational approaches; and (b) develop safe and ethically sound neuro-feedback interventions. Hyper-brain studies (i.e., monitoring of two or more brains at the same time) are another promising avenue of research that might advance our knowledge of the neural markers of team processes, such as cooperation, leadership, and team mental models (Astolfi et al., 2012; Dumas, Martinerie, Soussignan, & Nadel, 2012; Filho et al., 2016; Sänger, Müller, & Lindenberger, 2013).

Also, it is noteworthy that the ageing population around the world will likely influence the willingness of funding agencies to support research and professional training in the field (Raab, 2017). The phenomenon of esports, video-gaming, and exergaming might catalyse new research and intervention protocols (Filho, Di Fronso, Robazza, & Bertollo, 2018). Finally, as the world continues to shrink, with international travelling becoming faster and cheaper, research and practitioners will need to develop "cultural intelligence" to compete and thrive in a global market.

Conclusion

Methodological approaches to cognitive sport psychology must be reliable and valid. Researchers and practitioners must keep in mind that cognitive states and patterns might be nonlinear, possess multidimensional indicators, and vary greatly according to person–task–context circumstances. Accordingly, we recommend a multimodal approach to the measurement of cognitive processes, considering biopsychosocial variables. Importantly, the measurement of cognitive states and patterns should be in tandem with theory; that is, theoretical models should inform the development of measurement tools, which in turn catalyse novel theories and research paradigms in the field. It is important to keep an open mind to research and practice in cognitive sport psychology, as different research paradigms and evidence-based approaches might be more or less suited to the research question under study or practical issue of interest. Finally, we must remain tuned to the fast-paced advancements in technology, genetics, and brain techniques that will continue to revolutionize the measurement of cognitive processes in sports and beyond.

References

Appelbaum, M., Cooper, H., Kline, R. B., Mayo-Wilson, E., Nezu, A. M., & Rao, S. M. (2018). Journal article reporting standards for quantitative research in psychology: The APA Publications and Communications Board task force report. *American Psychologist, 73*(1), 3.

Astolfi, L., Toppi, J., Borghini, G., Vecchiato, G., He, E. J., Roy, A., … Babiloni, F. (2012). *Cortical activity and functional hyperconnectivity by simultaneous EEG recordings from interacting couples of professional pilots.* Paper presented at the IEEE Engineering in Medicine and Biology Society Annual Conference (pp. 4752–4755). doi:10.1109/EMBC.2012.6347029

Barkhof, F., & van Buchem, M. A. (2016). Neuroimaging in dementia. In J. Hodler, R. A. Kublik-Huch, & G. K. von Schulthess (Eds.), *Diseases of the brain, head and neck, spine 2016–2019* (pp. 79–85). Cham: Springer.

Bertollo, M., Di Fronso, S., Filho, E., Conforto, S., Schmid, M., Bortoli, L., … Robazza, C. (2016). Proficient brain for optimal performance: The MAP model perspective. *PeerJ,* 1–26.

Blascovich, J., Vanman, E., Mendes, W. B., & Dickerson, S. (2011). *Social psychophysiology for social and personality psychology.* Thousand Oaks, CA: Sage.

Braisby, N., & Gellatly, A. (Eds.). (2012). *Cognitive psychology.* Oxford, UK: Oxford University Press.

Cacioppo, J. T., Tassinary, L. G., & Berntson, G. G. (2007). Psychophysiological science: Interdisciplinary approaches to classic questions about the mind. In J. T. Cacioppo, L. G. Tassinary, & G. G. Berntson (Eds.), *Handbook of psychophysiology* (pp. 1–16). New York: Cambridge University Press.

Carlstedt, R., & Balconi, M. (Eds.). (2019). *Handbook of sport neuroscience and psychophysiology.* New York: Routledge.

Chilisa, B. (2011). *Indigenous research methodologies.* Thousand Oaks, CA: Sage.

Chilisa, B., & Kawulich, B. B. (2012). Selecting a research approach: Paradigm, methodology and methods. In C. Wagner, B. Kawulich, & M. Garner (Eds.), *Doing social research: A global context* (pp. 51–61). London: McGraw Hill.

Csikszentmihalyi, M., & Csikszentmihalyi, I. (1975). *Beyond boredom and anxiety* (Vol. 721). San Francisco, CA: Jossey-Bass.

Dumas, G., Martinerie, J., Soussignan, R., & Nadel, J. (2012). Does the brain know who is at the origin of what in an imitative interaction? *Frontiers in Human Neuroscience, 6,* 1–11. doi:10.3389/fnhum.2012.00128

Ericsson, K. A. (2015). Acquisition and maintenance of medical expertise: A perspective from the expert-performance approach with deliberate practice. *Academic Medicine, 90*(11), 1471–1486.

Ericsson, K. A., & Kintsch, W. (1995). Long-term working memory. *Psychological Review, 102*(2), 211.

Ericsson, K. A., Whyte IV, J., & Ward, P. (2007). Expert performance in nursing: Reviewing research on expertise in nursing within the framework of the expert-performance approach. *Advances in Nursing Science, 30*(1), E58–E71.

Filho, E. (in press). Team dynamics theory: Nomological network among cohesion, team mental models, coordination, and collective efficacy. *Sport Sciences for Health.*

Filho, E., Bertollo, M., Robazza, C., & Comani, S. (2015). The juggling paradigm: A novel social neuroscience approach to identify neuropsychophysiological markers of team mental models. *Frontiers in Psychology,* 1–6.

Filho, E., Bertollo, M., Tamburro, G., Schinaia, L., Chatel-Goldman, J., Di Fronso, S., Robazza, C., & Comani, S. (2016). Hyperbrain features of team mental models within a juggling paradigm: A proof of concept. *PeerJ,* 1–38.

Filho, E., Di Fronso, S., Robazza, C., & Bertollo, M. (2018). Exergaming. In S. Razon & M. Sachs (Eds.), *Applied exercise psychology: The challenging journey from motivation to adherence* (pp. 122–134). New York: Routledge.

Filho, E., Gershgoren, L., Basevitch, I., Schinke, R., & Tenenbaum, G. (2014). Peer leadership and shared mental models in a college volleyball team: A season long case study. *Journal of Clinical Sport Psychology, 8,* 184–203.

Filho, E., & Rettig, J. (2019). Team coordination in high-risk circus acrobatics. *Interaction Studies, 19,* 501–520.

Filho, E., & Tenenbaum, G. (2015). Sports psychology. *Oxford Bibliographies.* Oxford, UK: Oxford University Press.

Filho, E., & Tenenbaum, G. (2018). Advanced technological trends in exercise psychology. In S. Razon & M. Sachs (Eds.), *Applied exercise psychology: The challenging journey from motivation to adherence* (pp. 111–121). New York: Routledge.

Filho, E., & Tenenbaum, G. (2019). We think, therefore we are: A social neuroscience perspective on team dynamics, hyperbrains, and collective minds. In R. A. Carlstedt & M. Balconi (Eds.), *Handbook of sport neuroscience and psychophysiology* (pp. 320–332). New York: Routledge.

Filho, E., Tenenbaum, G., & Yang, Y. (2015). Cohesion, team mental models, and collective efficacy: Towards an integrated framework of team dynamics in sport. *Journal of Sports Sciences, 33*, 641–653.

Friedmann, T. (2010). How close are we to gene doping? *Hastings Center Report, 40*, 20–22.

Friedmann, T., Rabin, O., & Frankel, M. S. (2010). Gene doping and sport. *Science, 327*, 647–648.

García-Larrea, L., Lukaszewicz, A. C., & Mauguiére, F. (1992). Revisiting the oddball paradigm. Non-target vs neutral stimuli and the evaluation of ERP attentional effects. *Neuropsychologia, 30*(8), 723–741.

Gould, D., Dieffenbach, K., & Moffett, A. (2002). Psychological characteristics and their development in Olympic champions. *Journal of Applied Sport Psychology, 14*(3), 172–204.

Hoyle, R. H. (2011). *Structural equation modeling for social and personality psychology*. Thousand Oaks, CA: Sage.

Kuhn, T. (1962). *The structure of scientific revolutions*. Chicago, IL: University of Chicago Press.

Kuzyakov, Y., Friedel, J. K., & Stahra, K. (2000). Review of mechanisms and quantification of priming effects. *Soil Biology and Biochemistry, 32*, 1485–1498.

Lehman, B. J., David, D. M., & Gruber, J. A. (2017). Rethinking the biopsychosocial model of health: Understanding health as a dynamic system. *Social and Personality Psychology Compass, 11*(8), e12328.

Levitt, H. M., Bamberg, M., Creswell, J. W., Frost, D. M., Josselson, R., & Suárez-Orozco, C. (2018). Journal article reporting standards for qualitative primary, qualitative meta-analytic, and mixed methods research in psychology: The APA Publications and Communications Board task force report. *American Psychologist, 73*(1), 26.

Mann, D. T., Williams, A. M., Ward, P., & Janelle, C. M. (2007). Perceptual-cognitive expertise in sport: A meta-analysis. *Journal of Sport and Exercise Psychology, 29*(4), 457–478.

McArdle, W. D., Katch, F. I., & Katch, V. L. (2010). *Exercise physiology: Nutrition, energy, and human performance*. Philadelphia, PA: Lippincott Williams & Wilkins.

Moore, Z. E. (2007). Critical thinking and the evidence-based practice of sport psychology. *Journal of Clinical Sport Psychology, 1*(1), 9–22.

Orlick, T. (2015). *In pursuit of excellence*. Champaign, IL: Human Kinetics.

Patton, M. Q. (2015). *Qualitative research & evaluation methods: Integrating theory and practice*. Washington, DC: Sage.

Popper, K. (2005). *The logic of scientific discovery*. New York: Routledge.

Raab, M. (2017). Sport and exercise psychology in 2050. *German Journal of Exercise and Sport Research, 47*(1), 62–71.

Rankin-Wright, A. J., Hylton, K., & Norman, L. J. (2017). Negotiating the coaching landscape: Experiences of Black men and women coaches in the United Kingdom. *International Review for the Sociology of Sport, 54*(5), 603–621.

Russell, J. A. (1980). A circumplex model of affect. *Journal of Personality and Social Psychology, 39*(6), 1161–1178.

Sänger, J., Müller, V., & Lindenberger, U. (2013). Directionality in hyperbrain networks discriminates between leaders and followers in guitar duets. *Frontiers in Human Neuroscience, 7*, 1–14. doi:10.3389/fnhum.2013.00234

Schack, T., & Hackfort, D. (2007). An action theory approach to applied sport psychology. In G. Tenenbaum & R. C. Eklund (Eds.), *Handbook of sport psychology* (3rd ed., pp. 332–351). New York: John Wiley.

Schinke, R. J., Michel, G., Gauthier, A. P., Pickard, P., Danielson, R., Peltier, D., ... Peltier, M. (2006). The adaptation to the mainstream in elite sport: A Canadian Aboriginal perspective. *The Sport Psychologist, 20*(4), 435–448.

Smith, R. E., Smoll, F. L., & Schutz, R. W. (1990). Measurement and correlates of sport-specific cognitive and somatic trait anxiety: The sport anxiety scale. *Anxiety Research, 2*(4), 263–280.

Stern, R. M., Ray, W. J., & Quigley, K. S. (2001). *Psychophysiological recording*. New York: Oxford University Press.

Tenenbaum, G. (2003). Expert athletes: An integrated approach to decision-making. In J. Starkes & A. Ericsson (Eds.), *Expert performance in sports: Advances in research on sport expertise* (pp. 192–218). Champaign, IL: Human Kinetics.

Tenenbaum, G., Basevitch, I., Gershgoren, L., & Filho, E. (2013). Emotions-decision-making in sport: Theoretical conceptualization and experimental evidence. *International Journal of Sport and Exercise Psychology, 11*, 151–168.

Tenenbaum, G., Eklund, R. C., & Kamata, A. (2012). *Measurement in sport and exercise psychology.* Champaign, IL: Human Kinetics.

Tenenbaum, G., & Filho, E. (2014). Cognitive styles. In R. C. Eklund & G. Tenenbaum (Eds.), *Encyclopedia of sport and exercise psychology* (Vol. 3, pp. 141–143). Thousand Oaks, CA: Sage.

Tenenbaum, G., & Filho, E. (2015). Measurement considerations in performance psychology. In M. Raab, B. Lobinger, S. Hoffmann, A. Pizzera, & S. Laborde (Eds.), *Performance psychology: Perception, action, cognition, and emotion* (pp. 31–44). Philadelphia, PA: Elsevier.

Tenenbaum, G., & Filho, E. (2016). Overt-covert behaviors' linkage: Forecasting the future of the sport psychology science. In R. J. Schinke, K. R. McGannon, & B. Smith (Eds.), *Routledge international handbook of sport psychology* (pp. 559–571). New York: Routledge.

Tenenbaum, G., & Filho, E. (2017). Decision-making in sports: A cognitive and neural basis perspective. In *Reference module in neuroscience and biobehavioral psychology.* Philadelphia, PA: Elsevier.

Tenenbaum, G., & Filho, E. (2018). Psychosocial measurement issues in sport and exercise settings. In *Oxford research encyclopedia of psychology.* Oxford, UK: Oxford University Press.

Wagner, J. K., & Royal, C. D. (2012). Field of genes: An investigation of sports-related genetic testing. *Journal of Personalized Medicine, 2*(3), 119–137.

Wang, J., & Chen, S. (2014). *Applied motor learning in physical education and sports.* Morgantown, WV: Fitness Information Technology.

Weinberg, R. S., & Gould, D. S. (2018). *Foundations of sport and exercise psychology.* Champaign, IL: Human Kinetics.

23
MINDFULNESS AND EXERCISE

Sarah Ullrich-French and Anne E. Cox

Introduction

Mindfulness is a popular construct that has been targeted both as an intervention or a mechanism for exercise-related outcomes and as an outcome itself of exercise. There is a substantial empirical evidence base that supports the health benefits of mindful movement more broadly and the quality of exercise experiences and regulation of exercise behaviour specifically. There is also evidence that movement or exercise experiences can be used as an effective vehicle for cultivating the development of mindfulness. Therefore, mindfulness shows great promise for promoting adaptive physical activity and exercise experiences and behaviour. Perhaps the greatest impediment to the study of mindfulness in exercise psychology has been the lack of consistent definitions, measurement, effective methodology, and comprehensive theoretical frameworks that tie mindfulness to core concepts that are explored in the field of exercise psychology. In this chapter, mindfulness will be conceptualized as both a trait and a state to capture dispositional tendencies as well as the in-the-moment experience of being mindful while engaging in physical activity. We will address how mindfulness fits within this contemporary emphasis on the quality of the exercise experience and conditions under which exercise takes place, as well as how mindfulness aligns with the popular motivational framework of self-determination theory (SDT) and may serve as a strategy to foster intrinsic or autonomous physical activity motivation. Current trends in exercise psychology research highlight the dual processes of both explicit and implicit variables involved in understanding exercise behaviour. This chapter explores the role of mindfulness in affecting explicit processes, implicit processes, and the relationship between the two. Strategies for incorporating mindfulness into exercise highlight traditional mind-body exercise, such as yoga, but also address how mindfulness can be introduced to possibly enhance affective experiences during other forms of exercise such as walking. We conclude by identifying gaps in the literature and offer some key future research directions. Ideally, the information in this chapter can be used to pave the way for a more systematic, theory-driven examination of mindfulness in the context of exercise moving forward.

Mindfulness Defined

How mindfulness is defined has important implications for theory, measurement, and practice. The definitions of mindfulness in the broader literature reflect some variability; however, there is considerable agreement that there are two key components to mindfulness. The first is attention to and awareness of the present moment (Bishop, et al., 2004; Brown & Ryan, 2003; Kabat-Zinn, 2003; Tanay & Bernstein, 2013). One can be mindfully aware as both internal and external stimuli pass in and out of consciousness. Imagine how, as you are walking down a beautiful wooded path, you can be aware of the feeling of your breath, your thoughts, your emotions, and your feet making contact with the path (internal), as well as the trees, grass, and sunlight (external) as they naturally move in and out of your field of awareness. One can also pay mindful attention to a particular stimulus, which reflects focus or concentration. For example, you could focus your attention only on the sensations in the soles of your feet while walking and repeatedly bring attention back to this target every time you become distracted. Both mindful awareness and attention take on specific characteristics that distinguish them from other states of consciousness – this is the second key component of mindfulness. The quality of mindful attention and awareness includes an attitude of openness, receptivity, curiosity, non-judgement, and acceptance. The state of consciousness that results from this type of attention and awareness is one of vividness and clarity (Brown & Ryan, 2003). Thus, mindfulness has been considered an optimal state of functioning that confers many psychological benefits.

An important distinction is between mindfulness as a disposition or trait and mindfulness as a state (i.e., situational). Individuals' tendency or disposition to be in a mindful state across a range of activities throughout their day reflects trait mindfulness. State mindfulness, on the other hand, reflects one's degree of mindful attention and awareness in the current moment or situation. Differences exist between people in the degree to which they are typically mindful throughout the day (i.e., interindividual differences), and mindfulness fluctuates throughout the day within individuals (i.e., intra-individual differences; Brown & Ryan, 2003). Research evidence supports the independent effects of trait and state mindfulness predicting various indices of well-being (Brown & Ryan, 2003). In addition, state and trait mindfulness are positively correlated, supporting the notion that a higher tendency to be mindful predicts higher state mindfulness in a given situation. Brown and Ryan state that mindfulness is inherently a state, and, presumably, the impact of various mindfulness interventions is based on increasing mindful states. Despite this, in most of the research, mindfulness is by and large assessed as a trait.

State mindfulness within the context of exercise may be particularly relevant for the prediction of physical activity-related cognitions, affect, and behaviour. The development of the State Mindfulness Survey for Physical Activity (SMS-PA; Cox, Ullrich-French, & French, 2016) provides a tool to begin pursuing new research questions utilizing novel research designs. Cox et al. created the SMS-PA based on the State Mindfulness Survey (SMS) developed by Tanay and Bernstein (2013). The original measure included a subscale for mental targets of mindfulness (e.g., thoughts, emotions) and physical targets of mindfulness (e.g., physical sensations). However, the physical targets of mindfulness needed to be contextualized to a physical activity setting to increase the relevance of the scale items for movement-based settings. Owing to the salience of physical sensations related to exertion during physical activity, items that better captured awareness of bodily movement were included, and two subscales emerged that reflect the mental and physical targets of attention and awareness during physical activity participation. In this chapter, we will explore the roles of both state and trait mindfulness relative to exercise and physical activity.

Mindfulness Related to Exercise Motivation and Behaviour

Initial evidence suggests mindfulness is an important factor related to physical activity. Early research on mindfulness and physical activity largely demonstrated a positive association between dispositional mindfulness and self-reported physical activity behaviour (Gilbert & Waltz, 2010; Kangasniemi, Lappalainen, Kankaanpää, & Tammelin, 2014) and motivation (Kang, O'Donnell, Strecher, & Falk, 2017). In addition to dispositional or trait mindfulness, engaging in mindfulness practices associates with physical activity behaviour. For example, those who self-report engaging in mindfulness meditation are less likely to be inactive and more likely to meet physical activity recommendations (Strowger, Niken, & Ramcharran, 2018). Exercise mode has emerged as an important factor to consider. Greater trait mindfulness is associated with more time spent participating in yoga, whereas time spent doing cardio-based exercise is associated with lower trait mindfulness (Martin, Prichard, Hutchinson, & Wilson, 2013). This introduces a chicken and egg question. Are those who are more mindful attracted to mind-body exercises such as yoga, or does participation in yoga cultivate greater trait mindfulness? There is no clear answer to this question, as this evidence has largely been atheoretical and cross-sectional in nature.

Mindfulness consistently predicts self-reported exercise or physical activity; however, there are inconsistent or non-significant relationships with objectively measured physical activity behaviour (Kang et al., 2017; Kangasniemi, Lappalainen, Kankaanpää, Tolvanen, & Tammelin, 2015). Stronger, consistent associations are found for dispositional mindfulness and exercise-related cognitions and emotions (e.g., self-determined motivation) compared with behavioural outcomes (e.g., Kang et al., 2017; Kangasniemi et al., 2015). Furthermore, when mindfulness is assessed contextualized to the physical activity experience (i.e., how mindful one typically is during physical activity) or as a state, trait mindfulness appears to either be unrelated or indirectly related to physical activity through physical activity contextualized mindfulness (Tsafou, Lacroix, Van Ee, Vinkers, & De Ridder, 2017; Ulmer, Stetson, & Salmon, 2010). These findings point to the potential value in examining the experience of being mindful during physical activity specifically or state mindfulness within physical activity contexts owing to greater proximity or relevance to the outcome behaviour (Brown & Ryan, 2003). Tsafou, De Ridder, van Ee, and Lacroix (2016) similarly found that contextualized mindfulness during physical activity positively related to self-report physical activity, whereas trait mindfulness did not relate. Furthermore, this study also found that satisfaction with physical activity mediated the association between mindfulness during physical activity and physical activity behaviour. Despite evidence for the association between mindfulness and exercise behaviour, there has been little theory-based explanation for how this relationship manifests. Investigations of mindfulness and exercise behaviour have suffered from insufficient theoretical foundations for understanding the mechanisms explaining how mindfulness relates to exercise behaviour.

Key Theoretical Frameworks

Both theory and empirical evidence point to the significant role that mindfulness can play in the facilitation of physical activity behaviour. The major theoretical perspectives that will be discussed in this chapter position mindfulness as (a) a critical piece in the autonomous regulation of behaviour, (b) a key facilitator of positive affective experiences, and (c) a key psychological factor that may increase concordance between implicit and explicit motivational processes. The following sections will present the integration of mindfulness within SDT and dual process models, as current and popular exercise psychology theoretical perspectives, followed by relevant empirical support.

Self-Determination Theory

SDT (Deci & Ryan, 2002; Ryan & Deci, 2007) provides one of the most comprehensive frameworks for understanding exercise motivation and behaviour and provides a logical home for the examination of mindfulness within this context. The organismic integration mini-theory of SDT (Deci & Ryan, 2002) describes how motivation ranges from being completely autonomous or volitional to controlled. The most autonomous form is intrinsic motivation, in which the source of motivation emanates from internal sources of satisfaction and pleasure from the very act of engaging in the activity. The next two autonomous forms of motivation are integrated regulation, which reflects motivation that stems from one's very sense of self (e.g., deeply held beliefs), and identified regulation, in which the person is motivated based on how much they value or the importance they place on the activity. Finally, the two more controlling forms of motivation include introjected and external regulations. Introjected regulation represents an internalized pressure due to a desire to experience positive emotions (e.g., pride) and avoid unpleasant ones (e.g., shame). External regulation is the most controlled form in which individuals are motivated to meet external contingencies such as avoiding punishment or earning rewards. Finally, amotivation represents a state in which the source of behavioural regulation is unclear, and motivation is lacking. Individuals high in amotivation lack intention and fail to see a connection between their effort and desired outcomes.

More autonomous forms of motivation, and intrinsic motivation in particular, are most effective for sustaining long-term physical activity behaviour (Teixeira, Carraça, Markland, Silva, & Ryan, 2012). In order to support the development of more autonomous forms of motivation, SDT asserts that the basic psychological needs for competence (i.e., perceived ability or effectiveness), autonomy (i.e., a sense of choice and control), and relatedness (i.e., feeling of connection) need to be met. Thus, the vast majority of research on how to support autonomous motivation for physical activity has focused on how various social-contextual variables (e.g., instructor behaviours) either support, fail to support, or thwart these three key psychological needs. However, the role of intrapersonal psychological processes such as mindfulness, which may facilitate autonomous motivation, has received far less attention.

Deci and Ryan (1980) specifically highlighted the role of mindfulness in the facilitation of more volitional or autonomous behaviours almost 40 years ago. They described how the quality of attention that is characteristic of mindfulness may allow individuals to interrupt compulsive, automatic, or reactive patterns that are maladaptive in nature and make decisions that are more in line with their values, needs, and interests. Acting in line with one's values and clearly responding to one's needs represent a form of motivation that is more integrated and autonomous. Brown and Ryan (2003) echo this assertion by stating the importance of open and attentive awareness to the internal landscape of thoughts, feelings, and sensations in order to support autonomous decision-making. Greater awareness and attention to one's true underlying needs may facilitate behaviours that lead to the fulfilment of the needs for competence, autonomy, and relatedness, thus supporting autonomous motivation. Despite these clear articulations of the role of mindfulness in the facilitation of autonomous motivation, in addition to more recent writing on the topic through the SDT lens (Brown, Ryan, & Creswell, 2007; Deci, Ryan, Schultz, & Niemiec, 2015; Niemiec, Ryan, & Brown, 2008), empirical tests in the context of physical activity are quite limited.

Although not in a physical activity context, Brown and Ryan (2003) provided some of the strongest evidence of the roles of state and trait mindfulness in the autonomous regulation of behaviour. Utilizing a daily diary approach, participants were prompted three times each day to record their current affect (i.e., feelings of pleasantness and unpleasantness), state mindfulness, and degree of autonomous regulation of the activity they were currently engaged in. Trait mindfulness was assessed at baseline. Their findings demonstrated that individuals who reported greater trait mindfulness also reported higher state mindfulness on a day-to-day basis. Further, higher state and trait mindfulness was associated with greater autonomous regulation of their behaviour, higher positive affect (state mindfulness only), and lower negative affect. Importantly, the effects of state and trait mindfulness were independent, with the effects of state mindfulness being stronger. This means that individuals can derive benefits from state mindfulness even if they lack a general disposition towards mindfulness. Also notable was that only state mindfulness related to positive affect. Brown and Ryan (2003) also demonstrated positive associations between trait mindfulness and global measures of perceived competence, autonomy, and relatedness in their research. Thus, the stage was set for examining how these intrapersonal processes impact physical activity behaviour. Collectively, these findings open the door to dozens of specific research questions that could be addressed with respect to exercise motivation. What are the roles of state and trait mindfulness in the autonomous regulation of exercise behaviour? What is the role of state mindfulness in predicting affective responses during exercise? Does need satisfaction mediate the relationship between state and trait mindfulness and autonomous exercise motivation? Some answers to these questions are slowly emerging.

Empirical evidence suggests that trait mindfulness is associated with autonomous physical activity motivation and behaviour. Those who are higher in trait mindfulness also report higher levels of autonomous physical activity motivation and lower levels of controlling forms of motivation (Kang et al., 2017; Ruffault, Bernier, Juge, & Fournier, 2016). With the exception of amotivation, these relationships between trait mindfulness and motivation regulations are small. Trait mindfulness has also been explored as a strategy for strengthening the relationship between motivation and behaviour. Some evidence suggests that trait mindfulness moderates the relationship between intrinsic motivation and physical activity behaviour (Ruffault et al., 2016). That is, individuals with higher dispositional mindfulness have stronger concordance between their self-reported intrinsic motivation and physical activity behaviour. Therefore, trait mindfulness appears to have a weak association with motivation regulations, but may serve to increase congruency between intrinsic motivation and behavioural outcomes.

In addition to trait mindfulness, state mindfulness of the body, in particular, may hold significant relevance to the regulation of behaviour in the context of physical activity. In line with SDT, open, non-judgemental awareness of what individuals are experiencing in the body may afford them the opportunity to make decisions during physical activity that support both feelings of competence and autonomy. Mindfulness has been described as a state of consciousness that creates a mental space within which individuals can experience more volition and choice behind their actions, rather than acting in a compulsive or reactive manner. For example, a non-conscious reaction to pain experienced during exercise might be to immediately quit or alternatively to grit it out and push through, depending on past behavioural patterns. However, the key here is not the behavioural choice itself, but that a compulsive behavioural reaction is not made with intention or conscious thought about what might best serve the individual's innate needs in that moment. On the other hand, using mindfulness to view the pain from a more detached, accepting, and clear perspective might allow the individual to make a choice that better serves them. Options might include slowing down, stretching, shifting their form, or even stopping the exercise if that is the best option. Making choices in this manner will feel more volitional, supporting autonomy, and better serve the body, which may support feelings of competence. In line with SDT, individuals are motivated to make decisions that support these innate psychological needs because this leads to better integration within the self, which may be facilitated by mindful practice.

A series of studies over the past few years are in support of the theoretical role that state mindfulness of the body may play in supporting the autonomous regulation of physical activity behaviour. State mindfulness of the body during various forms of physical activity (e.g., strength training, aerobic, yoga) has demonstrated positive associations with all three autonomous forms of physical activity motivation in samples of older adolescents and adults (Cox, Ullrich-French, & French, 2016; Ullrich-French, González Hernández, & Hildago Montesinos, 2017). In a longitudinal study, how mindful participants were of their physical experience during the practice of yoga predicted how much they increased on internal reasons for exercise over a period of 8 weeks (Cox, Ullrich-French, Cole, & D'Hondt-Taylor, 2016). There is yet to be research on how state mindfulness might relate to need satisfaction, but, given the natural conceptual links as well as empirical evidence from other settings (Brown & Ryan, 2003), these relationships need to be tested within the context of physical activity. Other possibilities include examining the role of state mindfulness of the mind (e.g., thoughts, emotions) in physical activity motivation, as well as the interplay between trait mindfulness and state mindfulness during physical activity, for predicting physical activity motivation. The development of the SMS-PA allows researchers to explore these kinds of research question within an SDT framework, and initial findings within the context of physical activity are consistent with theoretical predictions that date back to 1980. This line of research provides a good example of theoretically grounded investigations of mindfulness within the context of physical activity motivation and behaviour, which shows promise for advancing our understanding of the regulatory properties of mindfulness.

Dual Process Models

A rapidly expanding area of research in exercise psychology involves the interplay between implicit and explicit processes in predicting future exercise behaviours, referred to as dual process models (e.g., Brand & Ekkekakis, 2018). The primary reason for the recent elevation in interest in these models is that the dominant theoretical perspectives in exercise psychology that rely on explicit knowledge and processes to understand exercise behaviour have simply fallen short of robustly explaining exercise behaviour (Rhodes, McEwan, & Rebar, 2018), producing small effects at best (e.g., Chatzisarantis & Hagger, 2005; Johnson, Scott-Sheldon, & Carey, 2010). Common examples of explicit focused theories include self-efficacy theory (Bandura, 1989) and the theory of planned behaviour (Ajzen, 1985). Despite the intuitive appeal of humans as rational decision-makers, recent evidence suggests that, in fact, many behaviours, including exercise, are driven by impulsive, irrational, implicit processes such as the degree of pleasure experienced during the activity.

Dual process models such as the elaboration likelihood model suggest there are two pathways of processing information, a low-elaboration pathway (implicit, heuristic approach) and a high-elaboration pathway (explicit cognitive effort; Petty & Cacioppo, 1986). When one uses explicit processes, cognitive resources are needed; however, this pathway often leads to stronger, longer-lasting beliefs. Explicit knowledge is required to understand the content of an exercise programme or to anticipate health benefits derived from exercise behaviour. Implicit knowledge is obtained through the direct experience of exercise – for example, through interoceptive cues. Both explicit and implicit knowledge is involved in the enactment of exercise behaviour. Individuals can cognitively (explicitly) understand what they should do to exercise and the benefits they may accrue, may even desire or intend to exercise, but struggle to enact the exercise behaviour, particularly when exercise is not enjoyable. This suggests that explicit processes are not sufficient. Mindfulness may play a couple of key roles within a dual process model framework. First, it may serve to enhance the pleasure that one experiences during exercise. Second, it may increase the concordance or consistency between explicit and implicit processes. In both of these cases, mindfulness may act as a means of increasing exercise behaviour. Given the typically weak correlation between explicit processes such as exercise intentions and exercise behaviour, there is a current trend towards examining the role of implicit processes, largely through the exploration of how affective experiences impact exercise behaviour (Deutsch, Gawronski, & Hofmann, 2017; Hagger, 2016).

Affective experiences during exercise have recently received considerable attention in exercise psychology owing to their role in predicting future exercise intentions and behaviour (Rhodes & Kates, 2015; Williams et al., 2008, 2016). Core affect refers to the most basic, irreducible affective response that can range from very pleasant to very unpleasant and is not derived from reflective processes (Russell, 1980). Related, but distinct from affect experienced during exercise, negative remembered affect associated with exercise may undermine the execution of exercise behaviour (Zenko, Ekkekakis, & Ariely, 2016). Negative affect can trigger a defensive response that often is counterproductive to goals and can lead to avoidant behaviour. When explicit intentions to exercise are at odds with the implicit negative associations with exercise, an individual must rely upon explicit self-regulation or self-control, which is effortful and can be easily depleted, in order to counteract defensive and avoidant responses. Understandably, then, interventions or strategies that can be applied to make exercise more pleasurable are an important trend in the literature. Ironically, the highly effortful explicit process of directing mindful attention and awareness to the physical sensations of exercise could play a key role in supporting positive affective responses. Dispositional mindfulness may support behaviour through reduced negative affect, tempering affective beliefs that can interfere with behavioural enactment. It may be that dispositional mindfulness may modulate implicit processes by reducing affective reactivity in the brain (Creswell, Way, Eisenberger, & Lieberman, 2007; Desbordes et al., 2012). One of the most robust findings in the mindfulness literature is the positive association between mindfulness (particularly state mindfulness) and affective responses across a range of daily activities (e.g., Brown & Ryan, 2003; Snippe, Nyklíček, Schroevers, & Bos, 2015).

Interestingly, dissociation, a popular strategy for enhancing positive affect during exercise, takes quite the opposite approach from mindfulness (Lind, Welch, & Ekkekakis, 2009). This strategy is based on the premise that many avoid exercise owing to unpleasant implicit affective responses to the act of exercising, particularly at higher levels of exercise intensity. There is clear evidence supporting the affective advantages of dissociating from the sometimes unpleasant physiological and psychological experiences during exercise through strategies such as listening to music (e.g., Hutchinson et al., 2018). Although often leading to more pleasurable experiences, this approach does not tap into implicit knowledge about the bodily experience of exercise. A further limitation to dissociative strategies is that the ability to dissociate from interoceptive cues diminishes at higher intensities. For example, whereas music may serve as a distraction at lower intensities, at higher intensities one no longer can ignore the stronger interoceptive experience of physical exertion. An alternative to dissociation is using an associative attentional strategy during exercise, but with the qualities of openness, acceptance, and curiosity. Although greater associative focus of attention has been assumed to result in more negative affective responses (see Hutchinson & Karageorghis, 2013), mindfulness may represent a special case. When one focuses attention on physical, cognitive, and affective experiences during exercise in a manner that is free of judgement and evaluation, then a space is created to experience the stimuli anew with openness and a fresh perspective that may override automatic associations. Open, non-judgemental, curious attention to the physical and mental sensations of exercise may allow one to experience the inherently pleasurable aspects of moderate-intensity exercise (see Ekkekakis, Parfitt, & Petruzzello, 2011), thus building or strengthening implicit positive associations with exercise. Such positive associations with interoceptive cues could carry over to higher intensities or at least elicit less negative affective responses to the physiological responses of high-intensity exercise. Therefore, tuning into the experience of exercise with the qualities of mindfulness could be a critical strategy that can be used to counteract the negative automatic associations with the execution of exercise behaviour.

Despite the intuitive appeal of applying mindfulness to enhance affect during exercise, rigorous tests of its role in the exercise experience are lacking. In one example that supports this approach, Ivanova and colleagues (Ivanova, Jensen, Cassoff, Gu, & Knäuper, 2015) taught half of the women in a randomized controlled trial how to be open to and accept (rather than push away or reject) unpleasant emotions and physical sensations while exercising to exhaustion on a cycle ergometer. These strategies were grounded in acceptance and commitment therapy (ACT; Hayes, Luoma, Bond, Masuda, & Lillis, 2006) in which mindfulness serves as a core mechanism for change. The women in the experimental ACT group were able to exercise longer, had lower perceived effort, and reported higher enjoyment following exercise compared with the control group, although in-task affect did not differ between the groups. This, coupled with recent interest in the role of remembered affect, suggests that higher reports of how enjoyable they found the exercise after the fact is important. More experimental research is needed to replicate these findings and test the acute effects of being more mindful on a variety of exercise experiences. Future study designs could employ experimental conditions that direct participants' attention mindfully to their physical sensations, thoughts, and emotions during the very act of engaging in the exercise (e.g., Cox, Roberts, Cates, & McMahon, 2018) and consider additional outcome variables such as remembered and anticipated affect.

Dual process models are typically based on the premise that implicit, automatic processes will dominate except under conditions in which they have the appropriate motivation or self-control to do otherwise. Thus, there is often a disconnect between implicit and explicit processes, and this disconnection has been shown to be greater in certain populations such as inactive adults. In one study, inactive adults reported lower expected enjoyment prior to exercising compared with active adults, but similar levels of actual enjoyment experienced during a 30-minute exercise session (Loehr & Baldwin, 2014). One might also tune into the experiences of exercise in order to build confidence, to observe the functionality afforded by moving one's body, or to notice the positive sensations of movement. Thus, mindfulness can serve to strengthen both implicit and explicit processes that can be harnessed to increase and sustain exercise behaviour. The other key role that mindfulness may play within a dual process model framework is the impact it has on the relationship between implicit and explicit processes. In fact, mindfulness may serve to foster the intention–behaviour relationship in physical activity, where those who are more mindful show a stronger link between intentions and behaviour (Chatzisarantis & Hagger, 2007) or autonomous motivation and behaviour (Ruffault et al., 2016). The field is wide open to begin exploring the integration of implicit and explicit processes through mindfulness within the context of physical activity. Although many variables have been examined as potentially useful in aligning the concordance between implicit and explicit processes involved in predicting physical activity behaviour (e.g., behavioural regulations, explicit attitudes; Berry, Rodgers, Markland, & Hall, 2016), we are only beginning to consider the role of mindfulness in the context of physical activity.

In the general psychology literature, we know that there is greater concordance between implicit and explicit measures of affect for those with higher dispositional mindfulness (e.g., Brown & Ryan, 2003). Mindfulness may play distinct roles in relationship to healthy (e.g., physical activity) compared with unhealthy behaviours (e.g., smoking, impulsive eating). Whereas mindfulness may disrupt habitual impulse behaviours that may be counterproductive to one's goals, mindfulness has not been found to disrupt habitual physical activity behaviour

(Tsafou et al., 2016). Thus, mindfulness may not necessarily disrupt behaviour that is aligned with a productive and healthy goal. In this way mindfulness may serve as a tool to align one's behaviour patterns in a productive, intentional, and non-impulsive way (Baer, Fischer, & Huss, 2005). However, research is needed that directly tests or manipulates the concordance between implicit and explicit factors related to physical activity.

There is preliminary evidence supporting further exploration of dual process perspectives through not just implicit processes, but the combination of both implicit and explicit processes (Rebar et al., 2016). Affective experience during exercise contributes to a memory association with exercise and can strengthen the relationship between exercise intentions and behaviour (Kwan & Bryan, 2010). Mindfulness may serve as a conduit for supporting positive affective experiences during exercise as well as aligning implicit and explicit processes in order to facilitate exercise behaviour. Affective experiences are an important target because affective beliefs have been more robust predictors of behavioural choices than more instrumental beliefs (e.g., goals, intentions; Morris, Lawton, McEachan, Hurling, & Conner, 2016). What has become clear is that the experience of exercise itself is a critical factor in understanding future exercise behaviours. And, mindfulness has potential to enhance the quality of exercise experiences in adaptive ways. Thus, the integration or interaction of both explicit and implicit processes through mindfulness shows promise for furthering our understanding of exercise behaviour and strategies that can be used to increase exercise behaviour.

Where Mindfulness and Exercise Merge: Mindful Movement

Mindful movement reflects an explicit and deliberate presence to fully experience physical activity through "whole practice" where one can objectively self-observe core elements of physical movement, breath, feelings, and thoughts (Asztalos et al., 2012). As explained by Brown et al. (2007), the detached element of mindfulness may afford unbiased information processing or an adaptive psychological space that allows an explicit process to complement an implicit process. For example, a feature of implicit processes is the automaticity that does not rely upon evaluative or meaning attachment that is reflected in mindfulness. What mindfulness can do is to allow a greater awareness of the implicit experience of moving. When this awareness takes place from a detached perspective, mindful movement is an opportunity for physical, mental, and spiritual wellness. Therefore, the degree of engagement in mindful movement may be a critical mechanism explaining variance in the broad mental health benefits associated with physical activity (Asztalos et al., 2012).

Yoga is a quintessential example of mindful movement and one that has significantly increased in popularity over the last 5 years (Clarke, Barnes, Black, Stussman, & Nahin, 2018). Hatha yoga, a popular form, naturally infuses physical activity with mindfulness by focusing on being present in one's body and responding to bodily cues with awareness and acceptance of the physical and psychological experience. A key feature of the yoga experience is the use of intentional cues directing attention to the physical experience, such as breath and body alignment, as well as the psychological experience, such as thoughts and emotions. The positive physical and psychological outcomes associated with yoga participation are strong (Chu, Gotnik, Yeh, Goldie, & Hunink, 2016; Klatte, Pabst, Beelmann, & Rosendahl, 2016). An important explanation for such widespread positive outcomes is that the practice of mindfulness within yoga may facilitate emotion regulation and distress tolerance, which in turn may be useful in combating negative associations with, or uncomfortable sensations of, exercise. This may translate to increased exercise adherence, and there is some evidence supporting that introducing an inactive sample to yoga can increase exercise adherence

(Bryan, Zipp, & Parasher, 2012). Yoga may provide an especially impactful experience in terms of both physical and psychological outcomes, over and above non-movement mindful practice (Hunt, Al-Braiki, Dailey, Russell, & Simon, 2018). Through studies following participants longitudinally across sustained yoga participation, we have found increases in state mindfulness, body appreciation, internal reasons for exercise and intrinsic motivation for physical activity, as well as reductions in body surveillance or concerns about the appearance of one's body (Cox, Ullrich-French, Cole, et al., 2016; Cox, Ullrich-French, Howe, & Cole, 2017).

In addition to yoga, there are a variety of examples of mindful movement used as both forms of exercise and to target physical therapy and movement rehabilitation (e.g., t'ai chi, Pilates, qigong, Feldenkrais). Pilates is another type of mind–body-focused exercise that includes key principles of concentration, body awareness, and breath. In addition to producing physiological benefits, Pilates has been found to increase trait mindfulness, at least partially explaining other physical and psychological benefits (Caldwell, Adams, Quin, Harrison, & Greeson, 2013; Caldwell, Harrison, Adams, Quin, & Greeson, 2010), as well as leading to increased positive affect and decreased negative affect (Tolnai, Szabó, Köteles, & Szabo, 2016). There is increased popularity of various forms of mindful movement, as the benefits of both moving and mindfulness appear to produce a particularly powerful context for promoting well-being.

Mindfulness-based movement has served as an intervention to address a variety of indices of well-being ranging from targeting reduction of physical or psychological symptoms in clinical populations to enhancing well-being in young, healthy populations (e.g., Robert-McComb et al., 2015; Tsang, Chan, & Cheung, 2008). Tailored mindful moving interventions (e.g., Robert-McComb et al., 2015), participation in mind–body exercise (Tsang et al., 2008), and simply assessing situational mindfulness while moving (e.g., Yang & Conroy, 2018a) all support the benefits of moving mindfully. Next, we focus on how mindfulness serves as a mechanism for facilitating physical activity and exercise as well as how physical activity, and mindful movement in particular, may serve as a means to foster mindfulness.

Mindfulness Interventions to Increase Exercise and Physical Activity

Mindfulness has also been included as part of interventions aimed to increase physical activity (e.g., Kangasniemi et al., 2015). Intervention research using randomized control trial (RCT) methodology, with the ability to provide strong empirical evidence for intervention effectiveness overall, supports the use of mindfulness within interventions to produce physical activity behaviour changes. Most of this work has framed interventions within mindfulness and acceptance perspectives (e.g., mindfulness-based stress reduction (MBSR), ACT, and self-compassion), which are about how one experiences thoughts and emotions. These perspectives are grounded in healthy psychological functioning, but are not developed to explain exercise behaviour. Thus, the experience or state of mindfulness is taught and practised through these interventions.

Lazarus and Folkman's (1984) transactional model of stress (TMS) largely provides the basis for MBSR interventions. TMS places the primary appraisal process as critical in determining the extent to which an event is perceived as stressful, and, thus, leads to different strategies to cope with and respond to the perceived level of stress. Within this model, mindfulness fosters a balanced response appraisal of potentially stressful events rather than habitual or impulsive cognitive and physiological reactions. In the exercise context, when one encounters unpleasant sensations, it is not uncommon for a stress response to result in avoidant behaviours (e.g., quitting or avoiding exercise). However, if one could appraise the process in a detached or decentred manner and accept the experience without judgement, then more accurate appraisals are likely, leading to more potential coping responses (e.g., modify the exercise) compared with avoidance. Mindfulness would provide a psychological space from which to appraise the event and respond in a less reactive or habitual pattern and, thus, a longer-term adaptive coping response. ACT shares similar perspectives on psychological processes, placing mindfulness as a critical element of adaptive psychological functioning, or psychological flexibility as opposed to avoidance. These perspectives are widely supported through extensive empirical support for greater cognitive and behavioural flexibility in those with greater mindfulness and acceptance (see Gotink et al., 2015). However, theoretical tests of the TMS or ACT perspectives themselves have not received much empirical attention in mindfulness-focused exercise research.

Experimental research using RCT methodology largely supports the effectiveness of mindfulness interventions in positively impacting exercise behaviour. A number of ACT-based RCT interventions resulted in significantly greater increases in physical activity behaviour from baseline to 6-month follow-up compared with a control condition (e.g., Butryn, Forman, Hoffman, Shaw, & Juarascio, 2011; Tapper et al., 2009). Similar results have been found with MBSR interventions in objectively measured physical activity compared with aerobic exercise training (Meyer et al., 2018). Interventions incorporating mindfulness, ACT, and self-compassion have also shown increases in physical exercise (Palmeira, Pinto-Gouveia, & Cunha, 2017). Robust evidence is, thus, emerging to support these types of physical activity behaviour intervention.

A movement towards incorporating mindfulness in school-based interventions also shows promise in fostering the psychological well-being (Yook, Kang, & Park, 2017) and physical activity of youth (Salmoirago-Blotcher et al., 2018). School-based health education including mindfulness training produced higher physical activity compared with the health education control condition, suggesting that mindfulness training could be an effective strategy to increase physical activity, especially for male and more active adolescents (Salmoirago-Blotcher et al., 2018). An interesting feature of this study was that the effects of mindfulness training were stronger for those who started as more active, suggesting that, if individuals have a base of experience with physical activity, then they may be more aware of their bodies and, thus, may be more receptive to attending to their physical experience (e.g., proprioception). Although less research applying mindfulness to youth physical activity exists, this is a growing area of research.

Mindfulness as an Outcome of Physical Activity

Research on mindfulness clearly demonstrates the role that both trait mindfulness and state mindfulness can play in the facilitation of physical activity motivation and behaviour. However, another useful angle is to consider how engagement in physical activity can be used as a means to promote the development of trait mindfulness. From this perspective, movement is a strategy to foster mindfulness. The physical sensations associated with movement can be used as a focal point of attention that can enhance mindfulness skills (Segal, Williams, & Teasdale, 2002). Some empirical evidence using experience sampling methodology (ESM) suggests that mindful movement can be an effective strategy to maintain mindfulness skills following a mindfulness intervention (Gotink et al., 2016). Using ESM, state mindfulness was found to predict state affect, and more mindful walking bouts resulted in improved mindfulness and mood. There are a number of physical activity programmes and interventions that have been developed for the purpose of cultivating trait mindfulness as well as other general indices of well-being (e.g., perceived stress, sleep quality). In these studies, mindfulness is either intentionally incorporated into the movement programme or specific forms of movement are selected based on foundations in mindfulness (e.g., yoga, Pilates). Evidence shows these programmes to be effective at increasing levels of trait mindfulness.

In fact, practising mindfulness through movement has been shown to be more effective than other mindfulness practices (e.g., body scans and seated meditation) for predicting some facets of mindfulness and general well-being (Carmody & Baer, 2008). Movement-based mindfulness practices may provide a more accessible entryway towards mindfulness relative to more static practices. Unlike traditional practices in mindfulness-based stress reduction programmes that require sitting quietly and just focusing on the breath, or slowly moving attention through the body in a body scan, movement provides a dynamic and potentially more engaging focus of attention. In practices such as yoga, participants are frequently directed to attend to their breath as well as various physical sensations and kinaesthetic feedback as they move through the various poses or asanas. In addition, the movement may serve to settle the sympathetic nervous system response, making it easier to mindfully attend to relevant stimuli in the here and now. Dispositional mindfulness may even be enhanced through non-mindful movement exercise. Aerobic exercise has been found to increase dispositional mindfulness more than relaxation or wait-list control conditions in men (Mothes, Klaperski, Seelig, Schmidt, & Fuchs, 2014). Moving, thus, provides a good foundation for practising mindfulness.

Conclusion

There is evidence to suggest that being mindful during formal exercise or other forms of movement plays a positive role in positive affective experiences, the regulation of exercise behaviour, and the development of the tendency to be more mindful in daily life (i.e., trait mindfulness). Given the relevance of mindfulness to several exercise motivation frameworks, and initial empirical findings, the possibilities are vast for future investigations of mindfulness in exercise. Some future avenues to consider include consistency between the conceptualization and measurement of mindfulness, the examination of mindfulness as both a process and an outcome in theory-based models, testing the role of both trait and state mindfulness on affective experiences and both objectively measured and long-term behaviour, and using rigorous research designs to study mindfulness in the context of exercise and movement.

First and foremost, future research needs to carefully consider and provide a strong rationale for the selection of instruments used to assess mindfulness. The selection of a measurement tool should be consistent with the conceptualization of mindfulness that is being used in a particular study. Measures of trait mindfulness vary widely and tap into different aspects of mindfulness that are situated in very different conceptualizations of this construct. For example, one of the most popular assessments of trait mindfulness, the mindful attention and awareness scale (Brown & Ryan, 2003), captures the degree to which individuals are mindless (e.g., "I find it difficult to stay focused on what's happening in the present"). Although Brown and Ryan do provide evidence that mindfulness and mindlessness are closely related, their conceptualization of mindfulness places primary importance on the focus of attention, consistent with their measure that positions mindfulness as the opposite of inattention. Another popular measure of trait mindfulness is the five-facet mindfulness questionnaire, which measures five different dimensions of mindfulness (i.e., observing, describing, acting with awareness, non-judging of inner experience, and non-reactivity to inner experience). This measure clearly goes beyond simply paying attention to the present, and there is considerable debate around which characteristics are really at the heart of mindfulness. At a minimum, researchers need to be intentional with their selection of mindfulness instruments and discuss the implications of research findings in light of the measure being used. Similarly, the recently developed state mindfulness scale for physical activity (Cox, Ullrich-French, & French, 2016) includes items that assess attention paid to one's physical sensations, thoughts, and emotions but does not assess the quality of that attention (e.g., non-judgement, acceptance) directly. The development of mindfulness instruments that capture the qualities of present-oriented attention while engaging in physical activity would allow researchers to investigate the relative importance of these different aspects of mindfulness for predicting different outcomes. Alignment of measurement to test theoretical processes is imperative for grounding future research on the mechanisms by which mindfulness exerts effects on exercise.

Another area to pay attention to in future research is the theoretical relevance of state versus trait mindfulness. For example, most of the existing research has tested the role of trait mindfulness in increasing concordance between implicit and explicit processes and predicting physical activity motivation and behaviour. However, non-judgemental awareness and attention to one's physical sensations during the act of exercise (state mindfulness) may be even more relevant for supporting adaptive exercise-related variables and require investigation. Similarly, it would be interesting to explore the relationship between mindfulness during physical activity and affective responses in the context of exercise. For example, Yang and Conroy (2018a) found, through the use of momentary assessment, that negative affect was lower when participants were more mindful while walking compared with being less mindful while walking. It is possible that this non-judgemental, accepting focus of attention on the physical experience of moving could enhance an awareness of the naturally pleasant experience of moderate intensity exercise (i.e., below the ventilatory threshold) and potentially rewrite old, unconscious negative associations that have been inhibiting physical activity behaviour. A direction for future research is to investigate the role of state mindfulness during physical activity in predicting affective, motivation, and behavioural outcomes within dual process and/or SDT perspectives. Working with these theoretical perspectives is valuable because what is lacking is evidence consistently linking mindfulness to objective, long-term exercise behaviour. Future research exploring theoretical mechanisms for how mindfulness translates to behavioural outcomes is needed.

Given the relevance of mindfulness for supporting positive affect in daily activities, investigating the nuances of the relationship between state mindfulness and affect during physical activity lends itself to expanded areas of inquiry that tap into regulatory processes. It makes sense that the bodily awareness and acceptance of both pleasant and unpleasant physical and mental experiences would lead to a tolerance of uncomfortable physical sensations (Dutton, 2008) that would increase the likelihood of sustained exercise behaviour over time. Further insight into the connection between mindfulness and interoception (perception of the state of the body – internal functioning) and proprioception (perception of the position/movement of the body) will be important to determine the mechanisms by which mindfulness increases awareness of the sensory system and, in turn, how we regulate emotions that are closely tied to the sensory system. When there are sensory system problems, one may be overly sensitive (heightened sensory awareness triggers negative or extreme affective responses) or may lack sensitivity (lack of sensory awareness interferes with the ability to self-regulate needs). If mindfulness can provide a psychological distance or space to observe bodily cues during exercise, then there is an increased likelihood that one may regulate a dysfunctional emotional responses (e.g., a threat response) to unpleasant bodily cues. Mindfulness, thus, can elucidate positive or pleasant experiences while also providing an

315

adaptive way to cope with negative or unpleasant experiences during physical activity. Research that can tap into these regulatory processes, especially relative to why and how to harness affective responses, will be important to understanding how mindfulness is best incorporated within physical activity.

Finally, when investigating the impact of mindful exercise or movement interventions such as walking or yoga, better methods are needed to capture the role of mindfulness in the intervention and select appropriate control groups (see Hunt et al., 2018). In studies that lack a suitable control group or any measure of mindfulness while engaging in the physical activity, it is difficult to determine the role that mindfulness plays in predicting the outcome variables above and beyond the role of exercise. In other words, what benefits does mindful movement provide above and beyond what would simply be expected from physical activity? Assessing mindfulness in the intervention either by documenting the degree to which mindfulness was taught or implemented (e.g., curriculum or detailed description of the programme) or via the mindful experiences of the participants in the intervention (e.g., self-reported state mindfulness) would better enable us to determine the role of mindfulness. In addition, utilizing various control or comparison groups in which participants are also engaging in some form of movement will allow researchers to draw more specific conclusions about the role that mindfulness plays during movement. For example, one could design a mindful walking experiment with three separate walking groups: (a) walking with no instruction, (b) walking with instruction to pay attention to physical sensations, and (c) walking with instruction to pay attention to physical sensations with openness and non-judgement. This type of study design might provide information about the role of various aspects of mindfulness when applied during easily practised activities, such as walking.

The research on mindfulness and exercise is relatively new, and, despite conceptual and empirical promise for the near universal positive effects of mindfulness, there is much to learn about mindfulness. Some pause is needed as there is much to be learned about the mechanisms underlying mindful exercise experiences. For example, at higher intensities of exercise, such as exercise above the ventilatory threshold, it is not clear how increased mindful attention – even with non-judgement – to the largely unpleasurable interoceptive cues (e.g., muscle pain, perspiration, increased heart rate) may benefit the affective experience or long-term behavioural choices. Another cause for caution is outlined through the constrained action hypothesis, which suggests that internal focus of attention interferes with automatic processes of motor control (McNevin, Shea, & Wulf, 2003). As such, it is unknown what types of motor behaviour effect occur with an internal focus that is fostered by mindful practice during physical activity. It may be that, for certain types of exercise or at certain stages of learning, mindfulness may not facilitate safe or appropriate motor skill execution. Walking, as a well-practised motor behaviour, may provide an ideal mind–body movement pair. However, when learning new and complex motor coordination patterns (e.g., safely executing a dead lift), it is imperative to focus attention on the appropriate cues needed to safely execute certain exercises, and how qualities of openness and curiosity play a role is unknown. Identifying specific modes of exercise or the timing of introducing mindfulness will be important rather than recommending generic, one-size-fits-all interventions.

Given the advantages of moving mindfully for core affect, self-regulatory processes, and the development of trait mindfulness, realistic, practical recommendations are needed. There are many forms of movement or exercise that formally incorporate various mindfulness practices such as being present with the breath, at one with one's body, or even emphasizing non-judgement and being with one's own experience (e.g., yoga, t'ai chi, Pilates). Engaging in these types of activity provides a nice introduction to practising mindfulness while moving, with the benefit of being guided by an instructor. Important points to consider when selecting a class are the expertise and background of the instructor and the description of the class. Physical activities such as yoga can vary widely in the way they are taught and may incorporate more or less mindfulness into the practice. Another simple and accessible way to incorporate mindfulness into daily movement is during walking (e.g., Yang & Conroy, 2018b). This could include during formal exercise sessions of walking or simply while walking to and from the car or down the hall during the workday. Every time we engage in walking, we can choose to attend to the sensations of our feet making contact with the ground and other physical sensations as our feet are alternately lifted and placed in front of us (e.g., Gotink et al., 2016). Slowing down our normal walking pace just a bit will increase our ability to bring mindful attention and awareness to the act of walking. Finally, we can extend the experiences we have during mind–body exercises or mindful walking to many other physical activities that may or may not typically be thought of as formally mindful. For example, while running or cycling, we can purposefully bring open, accepting attention to the sensations of our breath and in our muscles throughout our body as we work. This practice of intentional mindfulness of physical sensations during exercise may serve to enhance affect and promote the development of trait mindfulness, as well as overall well-being. As the literature base extends our knowledge, we can further refine strategies for enhancing both mindfulness and physical activity.

References

Ajzen, I. (1985). From intentions to actions: A theory of planned behavior. In J. Kuhl and J. Beckmann (Eds.), *Action control* (pp. 11–39). Berlin: Springer.

Asztalos, M., Wijndaele, K., De Bourdeaudhuij, I., Philippaerts, R., Matton, L., Duvigneaud, N., & Cardon, G. (2012). Sport participation and stress among women and men. *Psychology of Sport and Exercise, 13*, 466–483.

Baer, R. A., Fischer, S., & Huss, D. B. (2005). Mindfulness and acceptance in the treatment of disordered eating. *Journal of Rational-emotive and Cognitive-behavior Therapy, 23*, 281–300.

Bandura, A. (1989). Human agency in social cognitive theory. *The American Psychologist, 44*, 1175–1184.

Berry, T. R., Rodgers, W. M., Markland, D., & Hall, C. R. (2016). Moderators of implicit–Explicit exercise cognition concordance. *Journal of Sport and Exercise Psychology, 38*, 579–589.

Bishop, S. R., Lau, M., Shapiro, S., Carlson, L., Anderson, N. D., Carmody, J., & Devins, G. (2004). Mindfulness: A proposed operational definition. *Clinical Psychology: Science and Practice, 11*, 230–241.

Brand, R., & Ekkekakis, P. (2018). Affective–reflective theory of physical inactivity and exercise. *German Journal of Exercise and Sport Research, 48*, 48–58.

Brown, K. W., & Ryan, R. M. (2003). The benefits of being present: Mindfulness and its role in psychological well-being. *Journal of Personality and Social Psychology, 84*, 822–848.

Brown, K. W., Ryan, R. M., & Creswell, J. D. (2007). Mindfulness: Theoretical foundations and evidence for its salutary effects. *Psychological Inquiry, 18*, 211–237.

Bryan, S., Zipp, G. P., & Parasher, R. (2012). The effects of yoga on psychosocial variables and exercise adherence: A randomized, controlled pilot study. *Alternative Therapies in Health & Medicine, 18*(5), 50–59.

Butryn, M. L., Forman, E., Hoffman, K., Shaw, J., & Juarascio, A. (2011). A pilot study of acceptance and commitment therapy for promotion of physical activity. *Journal of Physical Activity and Health, 8*, 516–522.

Caldwell, K., Adams, M., Quin, R., Harrison, M., & Greeson, J. (2013). Pilates, mindfulness and somatic education. *Journal of Dance & Somatic Practices, 5*, 141–153.

Caldwell, K., Harrison, M., Adams, M., Quin, R. H., & Greeson, J. (2010). Developing mindfulness in college students through movement-based courses: Effects on self-regulatory self-efficacy, mood, stress, and sleep quality. *Journal of American College Health, 58*, 433–442.

Carmody, J., & Baer, R. A. (2008). Relationships between mindfulness practice and levels of mindfulness, medical and psychological symptoms and wellbeing in a mindfulness-based stress reduction program. *Journal of Behavioral Medicine, 31*, 23–33.

Chatzisarantis, N. L., & Hagger, M. S. (2007). Mindfulness and the intention–behavior relationship within the theory of planned behavior. *Personality and Social Psychology Bulletin, 33*, 663–676.

Chatzisarantis, N. L. D., & Hagger, M. S. (2005). Effects of a brief intervention based on the theory of planned behavior on leisure time physical activity participation. *Journal of Sport and Exercise Psychology, 27*, 470–487.

Chu, P., Gotink, R. A., Yeh, G. Y., Goldie, S. J., & Hunink, M. M. (2016). The effectiveness of yoga in modifying risk factors for cardiovascular disease and metabolic syndrome: A systematic review and meta-analysis of randomized controlled trials. *European Journal of Preventive Cardiology, 23*, 291–307.

Clarke, T. C., Barnes, P. M., Black, L. I., Stussman, B. J., & Nahin, R. L. (2018). *Use of yoga, meditation, and chiropractors among U.S. adults aged 18 and over. NCHS Data Brief*, no 325. Hyattsville, MD: National Center for Health Statistics.

Cox, A., Ullrich-French, S., Cole, A., & D'Hondt-Taylor, M. (2016). The role of mindfulness during yoga in predicting self-objectification and reasons for exercise. *Psychology of Sport and Exercise, 22*, 321–327.

Cox, A., Ullrich-French, S., & French, B. (2016). Validity evidence for state mindfulness scale scores in a physical activity context. *Measurement in Physical Education and Exercise Science, 20*, 38–49.

Cox, A., Ullrich-French, S., Howe, H., & Cole, A. (2017). A pilot yoga physical education curriculum to promote positive body image. *Body Image, 23*, 1–8.

Cox, A. E., Roberts, M. A., Cates, H. L., & McMahon, A. K. (2018). Mindfulness and affective responses to treadmill walking in individuals with low intrinsic motivation to exercise. *International Journal of Exercise Science, 11*, 609.

Creswell, J. D., Way, B. M., Eisenberger, N. I., & Lieberman, M. D. (2007). Neural correlates of dispositional mindfulness during affect labeling. *Psychosomatic Medicine, 69*, 560–565.

Deci, E. L., & Ryan, R. M. (1980). The empirical exploration of intrinsic motivational processes. In L. Berkowitz (Ed.), *Advances in experimental social psychology* (Vol. 13, pp. 39–80). New York: Academic Press.

Deci, E. L., & Ryan, R. M. (2002). *Handbook of self-determination research*. Rochester, NY: University of Rochester Press.

Deci, E. L., Ryan, R. M., Schultz, P. P., & Niemiec, C. P. (2015). Being aware and functioning fully: Mindfulness and interest-taking within self-determination theory. In K. W. Brown, J. D. Creswell, & R. M. Ryan, *Handbook of mindfulness: Theory, research, and practice* (pp. 112–129). New York: Guilford Press.

Desbordes, G., Negi, L. T., Pace, T. W., Wallace, B. A., Raison, C. L., & Schwartz, E. L. (2012). Effects of mindful-attention and compassion meditation training on amygdala response to emotional stimuli in an ordinary, non-meditative state. *Frontiers in Human Neuroscience, 6*, 292.

Deutsch, R., Gawronski, B., & Hofmann, W. (Eds.). (2017). *Reflective and impulsive determinants of human behavior*. New York: Psychology Press.

Dutton, G. R. (2008). The role of mindfulness is health behavior change. *ACSM's Health & Fitness Journal, 12*(4), 7–12.

Ekkekakis, P., Parfitt, G., & Petruzzello, S. J. (2011). The pleasure and displeasure people feel when they exercise at different intensities. *Sports Medicine, 41*, 641–671.

Gilbert, D., & Waltz, J. (2010). Mindfulness and health behaviors. *Mindfulness, 1*, 227–234.

Gotink, R. A., Chu, P., Busschbach, J. J. V., Benson, H., Fricchione, G. L., & Huniink, M. G. M. (2015). Standardised mindfulness-based interventions in healthcare: An overview of systematic reviews and meta-analyses of RCTs. *PLoS One, 10*(4), 2015 Apr 16, e0124344.

Gotink, R. A., Hermans, K. S., Geschwind, N., De Nooij, R., De Groot, W. T., & Speckens, A. E. (2016). Mindfulness and mood stimulate each other in an upward spiral: A mindful walking intervention using experience sampling. *Mindfulness, 7*, 1114–1122.

Hagger, M. S. (2016). Non-conscious processes and dual-process theories in health psychology. *Health Psychology Review, 10*, 375–380.

Hayes, S. C., Luoma, J. B., Bond, F. W., Masuda, A., & Lillis, J. (2006). Acceptance and commitment therapy: Model, processes and outcomes. *Behavioral Research and Therapy, 44*, 1–25.

Hunt, M., Al-Braiki, F., Dailey, S., Russell, R., & Simon, K. (2018). Mindfulness training, yoga, or both? Dismantling the active components of a mindfulness-based stress reduction intervention. *Mindfulness, 9*, 512–520.

Hutchinson, J. C., Jones, L., Vitti, S. N., Moore, A. N., Dalton, P. C., & O'Neil, B. J. (2018). The influence of self-selected music on affect-regulated exercise intensity and remembered pleasure during treadmill running. *Sport, Exercise, and Performance Psychology, 7*, 80–92.

Hutchinson, J. C., & Karageorghis, C. I. (2013). Moderating influence of dominant attentional style and exercise intensity on responses to asynchronous music. *Journal of Sport & Exercise, & Psychology, 35*, 625–643.

Ivanova, E., Jensen, D., Cassoff, J., Gu, F., & Knäuper, B. (2015). Acceptance and commitment therapy improves exercise tolerance in sedentary women. *Medicine & Science in Sports & Exercise, 47*, 1251–1258.

Johnson, B. T., Scott-Sheldon, L. A., & Carey, M. P. (2010). Meta-synthesis of health behavior change meta-analyses. *American Journal of Public Health, 100*, 2193–2198.

Kabat-Zinn, J. (2003). Mindfulness-based interventions in context: Past, present, and future. *Clinical Psychology: Science and Practice, 10*, 144–156.

Kang, Y., O'Donnell, M. B., Strecher, V. J., & Falk, E. B. (2017). Dispositional mindfulness predicts adaptive affective responses to health messages and increased exercise motivation. *Mindfulness, 8*, 387–397.

Kangasniemi, A. M., Lappalainen, R., Kankaanpää, A., & Tammelin, T. (2014). Mindfulness skills, psychological flexibility, and psychological symptoms among physically less active and active adults. *Mental Health and Physical Activity, 7*, 121–127.

Kangasniemi, A. M., Lappalainen, R., Kankaanpää, A., Tolvanen, A., & Tammelin, T. (2015). Towards a physically more active lifestyle based on one's own values: The results of a randomized controlled trial among physically inactive adults. *BMC Public Health, 15*, 260.

Klatte, R., Pabst, S., Beelmann, A., & Rosendahl, J. (2016). The efficacy of body-oriented yoga in mental disorders: A systematic review and meta-analysis. *Deutsches Ärzteblatt International, 113*(12), 195.

Kwan, B. M., & Bryan, A. (2010). In-task and post-task affective response to exercise: Translating exercise intentions into behaviour. *British Journal of Health Psychology, 15*, 115–131.

Lazarus, R. S., & Folkman, S. (1984). *Stress, appraisal, and coping.* New York: Springer.

Lind, E., Welch, A. S., & Ekkekakis, P. (2009). Do 'mind over muscle' strategies work? *Sports Medicine, 39* (9), 743–764.

Loehr, V. G., & Baldwin, A. S. (2014). Affective forecasting error in exercise: Differences between physically active and inactive individuals. *Sport, Exercise, and Performance Psychology, 3*, 177–183.

Martin, R., Prichard, I., Hutchinson, A. D., & Wilson, C. (2013). The role of body awareness and mindfulness in the relationship between exercise and eating behavior. *Journal of Sport & Exercise Psychology, 35*, 655–660.

McNevin, N., Shea, C., & Wulf, G. (2003). Increasing the distance of an external focus of attention enhances learning. *Psychological Research, 67*, 22–29.

Meyer, J. D., Torres, E. R., Grabow, M. L., Zgierska, A. E., Teng, H. Y., Coe, C. L., & Barrett, B. P. (2018). Benefits of 8-wk mindfulness-based stress reduction or aerobic training on seasonal declines in physical activity. *Medicine and Science in Sports and Exercise, 50*, 1850.

Morris, B., Lawton, R., McEachan, R., Hurling, R., & Conner, M. (2016). Changing self-reported physical activity using different types of affectively and cognitively framed health messages, in a student population. *Psychology, Health & Medicine, 21*, 198–207.

Mothes, H., Klaperski, S., Seelig, H., Schmidt, S., & Fuchs, R. (2014). Regular aerobic exercise increases dispositional mindfulness in men: A randomized controlled trial. *Mental Health and Physical Activity, 7*, 111–119.

Niemiec, C. P., Ryan, R. M., & Brown, K. W. (2008). The role of awareness and autonomy in quieting the ego: A self-determination theory perspective. In H. A. Wayment & J. J. Bauer (Eds.), *Transcending self-interest: Psychological explorations of the quiet ego* (pp. 107–115). Washington, DC: APA Books.

Palmeira, L., Pinto-Gouveia, J., & Cunha, M. (2017). Exploring the efficacy of an acceptance, mindfulness & compassionate-based group intervention for women struggling with their weight (Kg-Free): A randomized controlled trial. *Appetite, 112*, 107–116.

Petty, R. E., & Cacioppo, J. T. (1986). The elaboration likelihood model of persuasion. In L. Berkowitz (Ed.), *Advances in experimental social psychology* (Vol. 19, pp. 123–205). New York: Academic Press.

Rebar, A. L., Dimmock, J. A., Jackson, B., Rhodes, R. E., Kates, A., Starling, J., & Vandelanotte, C. (2016). A systematic review of the effects of non-conscious regulatory processes in physical activity. *Health Psychology Review, 10*, 395–407.

Rhodes, R. E., & Kates, A. (2015). Can the affective response to exercise predict future motives and physical activity behavior? A systematic review of published evidence. *Annals of Behavioral Medicine, 49*, 715–731.

Rhodes, R. E., McEwan, D., & Rebar, A. L. (2018). Theories of physical activity behaviour change: A history and synthesis of approaches. *Psychology of Sport and Exercise.* Advanced online publication. doi:10.1016/j.psychsport.2018.11.010

Robert-McComb, J. J., Cisneros, A., Tacón, A., Panike, R., Norman, R., Qian, X.-P., & McGlone, J. (2015). The effects of mindfulness-based movement on parameters of stress. *International Journal of Yoga Therapy, 25*, 79–88.

Ruffault, A., Bernier, M., Juge, N., & Fournier, J. F. (2016). Mindfulness may moderate the relationship between intrinsic motivation and physical activity: A cross-sectional study. *Mindfulness, 7*, 445–452.

Russell, J. A. (1980). A circumplex model of affect. *Journal of Personality and Social Psychology, 39*, 1161–1178.

Ryan, R. M., & Deci, E. L. (2007). Active human nature: Self-determination theory and the promotion and maintenance of sport, exercise, and health. In M. S. Hagger & N. L. D. Chatzisarantis (Eds.), *Intrinsic motivation and self-determination in exercise and sport* (pp. 1–19). Champaign, IL: Human Kinetics.

Salmoirago-Blotcher, E., Druker, S., Frisard, C., Dunsiger, S. I., Crawford, S., Meleo-Meyer, F., & Pbert, L. (2018). Integrating mindfulness training in school health education to promote healthy behaviors in adolescents: Feasibility and preliminary effects on exercise and dietary habits. *Preventive Medicine Reports, 9*, 92–95.

Segal, Z. V., Williams, J. M. G., & Teasdale, J. D. (2002). *Mindfulness-based cognitive therapy for depression: A new approach to preventing relapse.* New York: Guilford Press.

Snippe, E., Nyklíček, I., Schroevers, M. J., & Bos, E. H. (2015). The temporal order of change in daily mindfulness and affect during mindfulness-based stress reduction. *Journal of Counseling Psychology, 62*, 106–114.

Strowger, M., Niken, L. G., & Ramcharran, K. (2018). Mindfulness meditation and physical activity: Evidence from 2012 National Health Interview Survey. *Health Psychology, 37*, 924–928.

Tanay, G., & Bernstein, A. (2013). State mindfulness scale (SMS): Development and initial validation. *Psychological Assessment, 25*, 1286–1299.

Tapper, K., Shaw, C., Ilsley, J., Hill, A. J., Bond, F. W., & Moore, L. (2009). Exploratory randomised controlled trial of a mindfulness-based weight loss intervention for women. *Appetite, 52*, 396–404.

Teixeira, P. J., Carraça, E. V., Markland, D., Silva, M. N., & Ryan, R. M. (2012). Exercise, physical activity, and self-determination theory: A systematic review. *International Journal of Behavioral Nutrition and Physical Activity, 9*, 78.

Tolnai, N., Szabó, Z., Köteles, F., & Szabo, A. (2016). Physical and psychological benefits of once-a-week Pilates exercises in young sedentary women: A 10-week longitudinal study. *Physiology & Behavior, 163*, 211–218.

Tsafou, K. E., De Ridder, D. T., van Ee, R., & Lacroix, J. P. (2016). Mindfulness and satisfaction in physical activity: A cross-sectional study in the Dutch population. *Journal of Health Psychology, 21*, 1817–1827.

Tsafou, K. E., Lacroix, J. P., Van Ee, R., Vinkers, C. D., & De Ridder, D. T. (2017). The relation of trait and state mindfulness with satisfaction and physical activity: A cross-sectional study in 305 Dutch participants. *Journal of Health Psychology, 22*, 1221–1232.

Tsang, H. W. H., Chan, E. P., & Cheung, W. M. (2008). Effects of mindful and non-mindful exercises on people with depression: A systematic review. *British Journal of Clinical Psychology, 47*, 303–322.

Ullrich-French, S., González Hernández, J., & Hildago Montesinos, M. D. (2017). Validity evidence for the adaptation of the state mindfulness scale for physical activity (SMS-PA) in Spanish youth. *Psicothema, 29*, 119–125.

Ulmer, C. S., Stetson, B. A., & Salmon, P. G. (2010). Mindfulness and acceptance are associated with exercise maintenance in YMCA exercisers. *Behaviour Research and Therapy, 48*, 805–809.

Williams, D. M., Dunsiger, S., Ciccolo, J. T., Lewis, B. A., Albrecht, A. E., & Marcus, B. H. (2008). Acute affective response to a moderate-intensity exercise stimulus predicts physical activity participation 6 and 12 months later. *Psychology of Sport and Exercise, 9*, 231–245.

Williams, D. M., Dunsiger, S., Emerson, J. A., Gwaltney, C. J., Monti, P. M., & Miranda, J. R. (2016). Self-paced exercise, affective response, and exercise adherence: A preliminary investigation using ecological momentary assessment. *Journal of Sport and Exercise Psychology, 38,* 282–291.

Yang, C. H., & Conroy, D. E. (2018a). Momentary negative affect is lower during mindful movement than while sitting: An experience sampling study. *Psychology of Sport and Exercise, 37,* 109–116.

Yang, C. H., & Conroy, D. E. (2018b). Feasibility of an outdoor mindful walking program for reducing negative affect in older adults. *Journal of Aging and Physical Activity,* 1–33. doi:10.1123/japa.2017-0390

Yook, Y. S., Kang, S. J., & Park, I. (2017). Effects of physical activity intervention combining a new sport and mindfulness yoga on psychological characteristics in adolescents. *International Journal of Sport and Exercise Psychology, 15,* 109–117.

Zenko, Z., Ekkekakis, P., & Ariely, D. (2016). Can you have your vigorous exercise and enjoy it too? Ramping intensity down increases postexercise, remembered, and forecasted pleasure. *Journal of Sport and Exercise Psychology, 38,* 149–159.

24
MOTIVATION

Achievement Goal Theory in Sport and Physical Activity

Glyn C. Roberts and Christina G. L. Nerstad

Introduction

The term motivation is a very overused and vague term. Whether it is business leaders trying to motivate people in the workplace, the health industry trying to halt the rise in obesity and sedentary lifestyles, parents and teachers bemoaning the study habits of children and adolescents, or coaches and administrators within the sport and performance communities wondering how to get better "results": all address motivation in one form or another. Our cues from everyday life suggest it may be associated with arousal, such as the "motivational" tirades of coaches in the locker room. Some believe it is a measure of confidence, a winning attitude that motivates one to better performance. Some believe it is a simple matter of positive thinking: Believe and you will achieve! Some believe it is a personal entity, or is genetically endowed — you either "have it, or not"! However, these beliefs do not begin to capture the complexity and richness of contemporary motivational theory and research.

It is no different within psychology: Motivation is defined so broadly by some as to incorporate the whole field of psychology, or so narrowly by others as to be almost useless as an organizing construct. There are at least 32 theories of motivation that have their own definitions and explanations of the construct (Ford, 1992). However, Ford only reviewed the psychological literature, whereas Davis, Campbell, Hildon, Hobbs, and Michie (2015) reviewed health interventions across four scientific disciplines—psychology, sociology, anthropology, and economics—and found evidence for 82 theories. The solution for many has been to abandon the term and use descriptions of cognitive processes such as self-regulation or self-systems (e.g. Bandura & Wood, 1989), or discuss processes such as personal goals and goal setting (e.g. Locke & Latham, 1985; Nicholls, 1989), or emotional processes (e.g. Weiner, 1985), or universal needs (e.g. Deci & Ryan, 2000; Dweck, 2017).

In sport contexts, two theories tend to dominate. One is self-determination theory (SDT), which assumes that three basic needs drive the motivational engine: the needs of competence, relatedness, and autonomy (Deci & Ryan, 1985, 2000). SDT stipulates that individuals in achievement settings will adopt a more or less self-determined motivational style because of the perceived level of satisfaction and fulfilment of these three basic needs. When all three basic psychological needs are satisfied within an activity, individuals will feel a high degree of autonomous and self-determined motivation. The second is termed achievement goal theory (AGT). AGT is a social-cognitive theory that assumes that the individual is an intentional, rational, goal-directed organism, and that achievement goals govern achievement beliefs and guide subsequent decision-making and behaviour in achievement contexts. It is these goals that reflect the purposes of achievement striving. Once adopted, the achievement goal determines the integrated pattern of beliefs that energize approach and avoid strategies, the differing engagement levels, and the differing responses to achievement outcomes. Goals are what give an activity purpose or meaning (Kaplan & Maehr, 2007; Maehr & Nicholls, 1980).

Which theory should we use? Well, that clearly depends on one's understanding of how the psyche works. If one believes that satisfying basic needs drive the human organism, then SDT is the theory of choice. If one believes that the human organism is rational and intentional and is driven by how one perceives the social context, or believes in trying to demonstrate either task- or ego-involved competence, then AGT is the theory of choice. SDT is a more global theory of personality; AGT is limited to achievement tasks that are valued by the person. It is a choice, but the predictions of both theories are remarkably similar. It would seem that trying to integrate the theories is not viable at this time (Marsh, Craven, Hinkley, & Debus, 2003). However, in this chapter, it is our remit to discuss AGT.

Achievement Goal Theory and Research

The 50-year history and development of AGT in sport has been reviewed in several recent and older publications (e.g., Duda, 2005; Harwood, Spray, & Keegan, 2008; Lochbaum, Kazak Cetinkalp, Graham, Wright, & Zazo, 2016; Roberts, 2012; Roberts, Nerstad, & Lemyre, 2018; Roberts, Treasure, & Conroy, 2007). We will not exhaustively review the literature in the present encyclopedia entry; rather, we will focus on identifying key constructs, tenets, and constraints to the theory. We review the original basic conceptual infrastructure (see Figure 8) and empirical support within the sport and physical activity context, and later present proposals for expanding and/or restructuring the approach (e.g., Elliot & Thrash, 2001), with some rebuttals and counterpoints.

As stated above, AGT is a social-cognitive theory that assumes that goals are what give an activity purpose or meaning (Kaplan & Maehr, 2007; Maehr & Nicholls, 1980). Recognizing the importance of the meaning of behaviour makes it clear that there may be multiple goals of action, not one (Maehr & Braskamp, 1986). Thus, an individual's investment of personal resources such as effort, talent, and time in an activity is dependent on the achievement goal of the individual. The overall energizing construct in AGT is the individual's desire to develop and demonstrate competence and to avoid demonstrating incompetence (Nicholls, 1984). Figure 8 illustrates the overall dynamic process of motivation in AGT. Individuals learn through their socialization experiences that demonstrated competencies are valued attributes in the home, in school, and on the playing field. Individuals learn over time which achievement goals are most valued by parents, teachers, coaches, and peers. The goal becomes demonstrating or developing a valued competence. However, competence has more than one meaning. Based on previous research on learned helplessness (Dweck, 1975) and his own work on children's understanding of the concepts of effort and ability (Nicholls, 1976), Nicholls argued that more than one conception of ability exists, and that achievement goals and behaviour differ depending on the conception of ability held by the person. Two conceptions of ability (at least; Maehr & Nicholls, 1980, also included social involvement in 1980, but the concept was never fully developed at the time) manifest themselves in achievement contexts. The first is a *task-involved* conception, where ability and effort are not differentiated by the individual. The more effort one exerts, the more likely competence is developed or demonstrated. The second is an

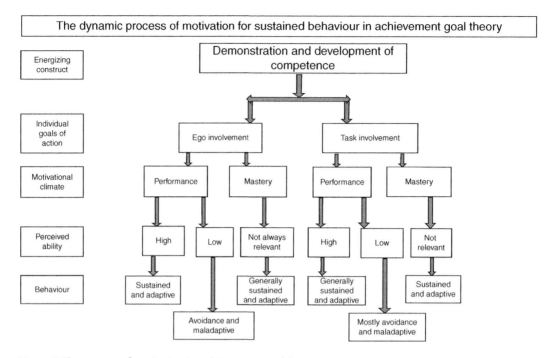

Figure 8 The process of motivation in achievement goal theory

ego-involved conception, where ability and effort are differentiated (Nicholls, 1984, 1989). Demonstrating competence with little effort is evidence of even higher competence. Following a series of experiments, Nicholls (Nicholls, 1978; Nicholls & Miller, 1984) argued that children tend to be task-involved and associate ability with learning through effort, so that the more effort one puts forth, the more learning (and ability) one achieves. However, by age 12, children begin to adopt a more adult perception and see ability as capacity, and that the demonstration of competence may involve outperforming others. In terms of effort, high ability is inferred when outperforming others and expending equal or less effort or performing equal to others while expending less effort.

An individual will approach a task or activity with certain goals of action reflecting their personal perceptions and beliefs about the form of ability they wish to demonstrate (Nicholls, 1984, 1989). They interpret their performance in terms of these perceptions and beliefs and form a personal theory of achievement in the activity (Nicholls, 1989) that reflects their perception of how things work in achievement situations. This perception is experiential and learned over time, in the home and school and on the playing field. The adopted personal theory of achievement (Dweck, 2006, terms this as an implicit person theory) affects one's beliefs about how to achieve success and avoid failure at the activity. Therefore, based on their personal theory of achievement, people will differ in which of the conceptions of ability and criteria of success and failure they use.

State of Involvement

The two conceptions of ability thereby become the source of the criteria by which individuals assess success and failure. When task-involved, the goal of action is to develop mastery of a valued competence and show improvement or learning, and the demonstration of ability is self-referenced, internal, and autonomous (see Figure 8). Success is realized when mastery or improvement is attained, and the individual sustains achievement striving. Perceived normative ability becomes less relevant as the individual is trying to demonstrate or develop mastery at the task rather than demonstrate normative ability. The achievement behaviours are adaptive in that the individual is more likely to persist in the face of failure, to exert effort, select challenging tasks, and be intrinsically interested in the task (e.g., Nicholls, 1989; Roberts, 2012; Roberts et al., 2018).

When ego-involved, the goal of action is to demonstrate competence relative to others or to outperform others, making ability other-referenced and external. Success is realized when the performance of others is exceeded, especially when one is expending less effort (Nicholls, 1984, 1989). Perceived normative competence is relevant as the individual is trying to demonstrate normative ability, or avoid demonstrating inability, to determine how his/her ability fares in comparison with others. The ego-involved person is inclined to use the least amount of effort to realize the goal of action (Nicholls, 1989). If the perception of ability is low, then the individual recognizes that competence is unlikely to be demonstrated, and he/she manifests maladaptive achievement behaviours such as avoiding the task, avoiding challenge, reducing persistence in the face of difficulty, exerting little effort, and, in sport, even dropping out if the desired goal appears unachievable (Nicholls, 1989). Whereas the participant may view these avoidance behaviours as adaptive, because a lack of competence is disguised, they are considered maladaptive in terms of achievement behaviour (see Figure 8).

An important tenet of AGT is that the states of involvement are mutually exclusive (e.g., Nicholls, 1989; Roberts et al., 2018; Treasure, 2001; Treasure et al., 2001). One is either ego- or task-involved, and motivational involvement ranges on a continuum from task to ego. The goal state is very dynamic and can change from moment to moment as information is processed (Gernigon, d'Arripe-Loungeville, Delignères, & Ninot, 2004). An athlete may begin a task with strong task-involved motivation, but contextual events may make the athlete wish to demonstrate superiority to others (e.g., when a coach publicly highlights a mistake), and the athlete becomes ego-involved in the task. Similarly, an athlete may begin a competitive event with a strong ego-involved state of involvement, but, as the event unfolds, the athlete may realize he/she will win easily (or lose emphatically) and, therefore, begin to work on mastery criteria instead and become task-involved. Thus, goal states are dynamic and ebb and flow depending on the perception of the athlete (as illustrated in Figure 8).

In this entry, when we refer to the motivated state of involvement of the individual, we use the terms ego- and task-involvement to be consistent with Nicholls's use of the terms. However, other theorists use different terms such as mastery and performance (e.g., Ames, 1992c; Dweck, 1986). In addition, when we refer to individual dispositions, we use the terms *task* and *ego orientation* to be consistent with Nicholls. Again, other motivation theorists (e.g., Dweck, 1986, 2006; Elliot, 1999; Maehr & Braskamp, 1986) have used different terms (e.g., self-schemas, personal theories of achievement, implicit person theories, personal investment) to describe the same phenomena.

Goal Orientations, an Individual Difference Variable

When individuals are predisposed (through their personal theory of achievement) to act in an ego- or task-involved manner, these predispositions are called *achievement goal orientations* (Nicholls, 1989). Individual differences in the disposition to be ego- or task-involved are probably the result of socialization through task- or ego-involving contexts in the home or other significant achievement contexts (classrooms, sport). In other words, individuals learn that the criterion of success that is important in the present context is to demonstrate mastery (task-involved) or to demonstrate normative competence (ego-involved). The way Elliott and Dweck (1988) explain it is that each of the achievement goals runs off a different programme with different commands, decision rules, and inference rules, and hence, with different cognitive, affective, and behavioural consequences. Each goal, in a sense, creates and organizes its own world—each evoking different thoughts and emotions and calling forth different behaviours (p. 11).

Goal orientations are not "traits" or based on needs. They are cognitive schemas that are dynamic and subject to change as information pertaining to one's performance on the task is processed. The orientations have some stability over time and are relatively enduring in sport (Duda & Whitehead, 1998; Roberts, Treasure, & Balague, 1998). Thus, being task- or ego-oriented refers to the predisposition of the individual to be task- or ego-involved in an achievement task. When task-oriented, the individual is likely to focus on mastering the task, developing skills, and becoming better over time. When ego-oriented, the individual is likely to wish to demonstrate relative competence to others, to enter into competition deliberately with peers in order to show superiority.

The Research Evidence

In previous, comprehensive reviews, the hypotheses pertinent to the goal orientations are supported (Duda, 2001; Lochbaum et al., 2016). Task orientation is associated with adaptive achievement strategies, positive affect, well-being, less cheating, better performance, and intrinsic forms of motivation. Ego orientation is associated with maladaptive achievement strategies, negative affect, cheating, ill-being, and extrinsic forms of motivation. An important attribute of achievement goal orientations is that they are orthogonal: One can be high or low in each or both orientations at the same time. It is possible for an individual to be high or low in both task and ego goal orientation, or high in one and low in the other (Nicholls, 1989). In the sport and exercise literature, this orthogonality has been supported many times (e.g. Lemyre, Ommundsen, & Roberts, 2000; Lochbaum et al., 2016; Pensgaard & Roberts, 2000; Roberts & Ommundsen, 1996; Roberts, Treasure, & Kavussanu, 1996; Walling & Duda, 1995). For qualitative reviews, see Duda and Whitehead (1998) and Roberts (2012) and colleagues (2018). The implications of the orthogonality of goal orientations are important. The research evidence in sport suggests that individuals with high task *and* high ego or high task and low ego orientations have the most adaptive motivational profiles and are more likely to sustain achievement behaviour (e.g., Fox, Goudas, Biddle, Duda, & Armstrong, 1994; Hodge & Petlichkoff, 2000; Pensgaard & Roberts, 2002; Roberts et al., 1996; Smith, Balaguer, & Duda, 2006). As one would expect, when an individual has been high in ego and low in task, or high in task and low in ego, then the findings are consistent with the findings reported above for task and ego orientation (task orientation is adaptive; ego orientation, especially when coupled with low perception of competence, is generally maladaptive). However, researchers have found that high ego orientation, when coupled with high (or moderate) task orientation, is not maladaptive (e.g., Cumming, Hall, Harwood, & Gammage, 2002; Harwood, Cumming, & Fletcher, 2004; Lochbaum et al., 2016; Pensgaard & Roberts, 2002; Smith et al., 2006; Wang & Biddle, 2001). Therefore, rather than focusing on whether an individual is task- or ego-oriented, it is important to consider the simultaneous combination of task and ego orientation.

Researchers in sport have used cluster analysis (Hair, Anderson, Tatham, & Black, 1998) to investigate goal orientations and, in general, have supported the use of cluster analysis to produce goal orientation profiles (e.g., Cumming et al., 2002; Harwood et al., 2004; Hodge & Petlichkoff, 2000; Smith et al., 2006; Wang & Biddle, 2001). The clusters have varied across these studies, but, importantly, participants with high ego/high task and high task/ moderate or low ego goal orientations have consistently reported more desirable responses on the variables under study (e.g., greater imagery use, more physical activity, higher self-determination, better social relationships). Thus, the motivational implications of the orthogonality of goals are a very important attribute of AGT because it is the joint influence of the goals that determines whether an individual is motivated to sustain achievement striving.

Elite athletes are likely to be high task and high ego (e.g., Pensgaard & Roberts, 2000) or high ego and low or moderate in task orientation. In sport, the individuals most at risk are the high ego- and low task-oriented. These are the people most likely to exhibit maladaptive motivation and drop out, and most likely to burn out when they believe they cannot demonstrate competence (Lemyre, Roberts, & Stray-Gundersen, 2007). The low ego and low task people are the least motivated and may not even commit to achievement tasks. The important conclusion in the present discussion is that the orthogonality of the goal orientations has been demonstrated quite conclusively (see Lochbaum et al., 2016, for details), and the orthogonality of the goals is an important factor determining sustained motivated behaviour in sport.

Mindsets and Goal Orientation

Dweck (e.g., 2012) draws on Nicholls's (1989) initial ideas concerning conceptions of intelligence in that she proposes that there exist specific individual difference variables that stimulate the pursuit of different goals. These variables are *mindsets* or *implicit person theories* (IPTs). Mindsets are beliefs athletes have about themselves and their assumptions about the plasticity of personal characteristics such as abilities (e.g., athletic), personality, and intelligence that guide human behaviour (Dweck, 1986). Typically, IPTs are referred to as implicit because they are not explicitly articulated in the mind of the individual holding them (Burnette, O'Boyle, VanEpps, Pollack, & Finkel, 2013). Dweck (1986, 2012) distinguishes between two types of IPT: a "growth mindset" and a "fixed mindset". Individuals with a growth mindset assume that it is possible to change personal attributes, and that, with effective strategies, effort, and guidance, all individuals can develop their abilities over time (Dweck, 1999, 2006). In contrast, individuals with a fixed mindset believe that personal attributes cannot be changed or developed much over time because they are entities that exist within individuals (Dweck, 2000, 2012).

Mindsets are considered to be relatively stable dispositions (Dweck, 1999; Dweck, Chiu, & Hong, 1995; Dweck & Leggett, 1988), although they may also be modified through interventions (Sisk, Burgoyne, Sun, Butler, & Macnamara, 2018). Changes in mindsets and behaviour have been found to withstand for periods of 6–9 weeks (e.g., Aronson, Fried, & Good, 2002; Heslin, Latham, & Vandewalle, 2005).

Measurement of Mindset

When it comes to the measurement of mindset, there exist at least two views. One view is that mindsets form a continuum and are measured accordingly (Dweck, 2006; Ehrlinger, 2008). This means that individuals typically lie somewhere along a continuum between the growth and fixed mindset prototypes, where the ends of the continuum represent beliefs that individuals' abilities are either fixed or capable of growth (Heslin & Vandewalle, 2008). Thus, one of the IPTs is likely to be dominant (Heslin & Vandewalle, 2008; Spray, Wang, Biddle,

Chatzisarantis, & Warburton, 2006). Measurement of mindsets based on this view typically involves asking individuals to respond to an eight-item scale which is measured on a Likert scale (e.g., 1 = fixed; 7 = growth mindset). A mindset score is computed for each individual as the average across the eight questions. This follows the necessary adjustments with respect to reverse-coded items.

The other view is that it may be beneficial and possible for individuals to hold a combination of both growth and fixed mindsets (Dweck & Leggett, 1988; C. G. Harwood et al., 2008). This may be, for example, when individuals recognize differences in relative ability, although they value growth in ability at the same time. Accordingly, mindset may even be an orthogonal construct, meaning that it could be possible for athletes to score high or low in each or both mindsets at the same time. In sport and physical education, measures have been developed to facilitate the independent assessment of the mindsets (e.g., Wang, Liu, Biddle, & Spray, 2005). Empirical research (Biddle, Wang, Chatzisarantis, & Spray, 2003; Spray et al., 2006; Wang et al., 2005) has indicated a negative, but weak, correlation between the two dimensions, which facilitates support for such combined mindsets (cf. Dweck & Leggett, 1988).

According to Dweck (1986, 1999), individuals have different goal orientations in achievement settings, and these goals have their basis in the individuals' IPTs. In such a person-oriented approach to goal orientation, personality plays a major role in goal adoption (Dweck, 2017; Maehr & Zusho, 2009). The performance or mastery goals that individuals endorse help generate helpless- or mastery-oriented responses (Dweck, 1999). Athletes with a fixed mindset are more likely to adopt performance goals (normative ability judgements), which creates susceptibility to a helpless behavioural pattern, particularly when their perceived competence is low (Dweck & Leggett, 1988; Maehr & Zusho, 2009). When helpless, athletes attribute their failures to deficient abilities and personal inadequacies and experience negative affect (cf. Dweck, 1999; Dweck & Leggett, 1988). Athletes with a growth mindset rather view their ability as improvable over time and they are, therefore, more likely to endorse mastery goals (Dweck, 1999; Dweck & Leggett, 1988; Payne, Youngcourt, & Beaubien, 2007).

The Research Evidence

In the following paragraph, we briefly review the main findings from several achievement domains, concentrating on sport and physical education. Meta-analytic (e.g., Burnette et al., 2013) evidence suggest that individuals can embrace different IPTs in different achievement domains such as in sport, and growth and fixed mindsets are endorsed approximately equally. In sport and physical education research, a growth mindset predicts mastery goals, whereas a fixed mindset has been found to predict performance goals (e.g., Biddle, Soos, & Chatzisarantis, 1999; Biddle et al., 2003; Cury, Da Fonseca, Rufo, & Sarrazin, 2002; Ommundsen, 2001a, 2001b; Spray et al., 2006). Meta-analytic evidence facilitates support for Dweck's (1986, 1999) predictions that a fixed mindset is negatively correlated with a mastery orientation and positively correlated with performance orientation (Payne et al., 2007). However, the effect sizes were very small, suggesting limited evidence for Dweck's (1986) propositions of mindsets being the primary underlying predictors of goal orientations.

To some extent contradicting these findings, a more recent meta-analysis (Burnette et al., 2013) found that mindsets predict distinct self-regulatory processes including performance and mastery orientation, helpless and mastery strategies, negative emotions and expectations (e.g., likelihood of meeting one's desired progress rate). These self-regulatory processes further predicted goal achievement. Specifically, growth mindset was a significant negative predictor of performance orientation and helpless strategies, but a positive predictor of mastery orientation and mastery-oriented strategies. The effects on goal orientation and helpless/ mastery strategies were stronger in the absence, rather than presence, of ego threats such as failure feedback. These findings somewhat contradict the findings of Payne et al. (2007) by providing additional support for Dweck's initial propositions that mindsets are imperative antecedents of individual goal orientation. It, therefore, seems important that future research clarifies the role of IPTs as predictors of goal orientations (Vandewalle, Nerstad, & Dysvik, 2019).

In the sport domain, goal orientations have been found to play a relevant mediating role in the relationship between mindsets and various outcomes. For example, a growth mindset has been found to positively predict satisfaction, enjoyment, and reduced acceptance of cheating behaviour through a mastery goal orientation (e.g., Biddle et al., 2003; Corrion et al., 2010; Ommundsen, 2001c). In contrast, a fixed mindset of ability has been linked to increased self-reported levels of anxiety, reduced levels of satisfaction, decrease in motivation, and more acceptance of cheating behaviour, partially through a performance goal orientation.

More recently, (Dweck, 2017) has proposed a more comprehensive theory that purports to integrate motivation, personality, and development into one framework. Departing from a purely social-cognitive approach, Dweck combines both classic AGT and mindset research with more recent needs-based approaches to motivation. She argues that motivation derives from basic human needs, including psychological needs, that give rise to achievement goals designed to meet the needs. The theory proposes that, as individuals experience the needs, they pursue goals designed to fulfil the needs and develop representations of their experiences fundamental to ongoing motivation. Departing from classic self-determination theory (e.g., Deci & Ryan, 2000), Dweck argues that, although there are three basic needs, the needs she argues for are competence, acceptance, and predictability, which give rise to three emergent needs of trust, control, and self-esteem. A final emergent need is self-coherence, which is the hub of all the needs. The needs serve as the energizing constructs within the theory, and the goals become the impetus to satisfy the needs. Goals direct the energy into action to satisfy the goals. Dweck claims that her proposal can be the beginning of a unifying theory to integrate motivation, development, and personality. However, Dweck is careful to point out that the theory is new and highly tentative and meant to be a stimulus to ongoing research and theory development.

Extensions and Criticisms of AGT

A provocative theory claiming to revise and extend AGT has emerged from work on the hierarchical model of achievement motivation (e.g., Elliot & Conroy, 2005; Elliot & Thrash, 2001). The theory is based on the premise that approach and avoidance motivation are also important when considering achievement striving. Several researchers have suggested that an approach and an avoid motivation exist (e.g., Elliot, 1997; Middleton & Midgley, 1997; Skaalvik, 1997), and that individuals strive to be competent (an appetitive or approach valence) or strive to avoid appearing incompetent (an aversive or avoid valence). Thus, it is possible to differentiate goals based on their valence or the degree to which the focal outcome is pleasant or unpleasant.

In reviewing the achievement goal literature, Elliot (e.g., Elliot & Harackiewicz, 1996; Elliot & Thrash, 2001) observed that performance goals that focus on the pleasant possibility of demonstrating competence (approach goals) lead to different outcomes than performance goals focused on the unpleasant possibility of demonstrating incompetence (avoidance goals). Performance avoidance goals reduce both free-choice behaviour and self-reported interest in a task, whereas performance approach goals did not have any consistent effect on intrinsic motivation indices (Rawsthorne & Elliot, 1999). This finding led to the introduction of a tripartite model of achievement goals comprising mastery, performance-approach, and performance-avoidance goals (Elliot & Harackiewicz, 1996). Following a series of studies (e.g., Cury, Da Fonséca, Rufo, Peres, & Sarrazin, 2003; Cury, Elliot, Sarrazin, Da Fonseca, & Rufo, 2002) within sport, the model expanded to include a fourth possible achievement goal: mastery-avoidance goal (e.g., Elliot & Conroy, 2005). Thus, the argument was proffered that achievement goals should consider both the definition of competence and the valence of the striving. The model then became a two-by-two model, with two definitions of competence (mastery vs. performance) and two valences of striving (approaching competence vs. avoiding incompetence). The four goals became mastery approach, mastery avoidance, performance approach, and performance avoidance (see Papaioannou, Zourbanos, Kromidas, & Ampatzoglou, 2012; Roberts et al., 2007).

Elliot and colleagues (e.g., Murayama, Elliot, & Yamagata, 2011) introduced a third component arguing that competence may be defined as doing well or poorly based on three evaluative standards—task, self, and other. Task-based goals use the absolute demands of the task as the evaluative reference; self-based goals use self-referenced criteria of doing well or poorly relative to one's past or future potential achievement; other-based goals use the performance of others to evaluate competence. Thus, self-based goals are introduced, forming a three-by-two model of goals. The goals then became task, self, and other approach goals, and task, self, and other avoidance goals. Elliot and colleagues (e.g., Murayama et al., 2011) view the three-by-two model as a logical extension of the two-by-two model that has its own distinct framework applicable to any achievement setting. They argue that the model produces conceptual, empirical, and applied advances that keep achievement goals at the forefront of achievement motivation literature.

Although we would agree with the conclusions of Elliot and colleagues, the introduction of the hierarchical model has challenged many of the tenets and underlying assumptions of traditional AGT. In particular, it expanded the mastery and performance dichotomy to introduce valence and expanded the theory from two goals to four goals (e.g., Elliot & Conroy, 2005) and then, in 2011, expanded the theory to six goals. A body of evidence has accumulated to support these assertions, and some argue that the new model is a "better" theory to explain motivated behaviour (e.g., Elliot & Conroy, 2005; Murayama et al., 2011). However, the extension is criticized in that it violates some of the basic tenets of AGT (e.g., it negates the orthogonality of orientations), adds little conceptual understanding to the motivational equation (e.g., Maehr & Zusho, 2009; Midgley, Kaplan, & Middleton, 2001; Papaioannou et al., 2012), and undermines the parsimony and elegance of AGT (Roberts, 2012). Midgley and colleagues (2001) state that there is some evidence that performance-approach goals are more facilitative for boys than for girls, and for older students than for younger students, in competitive learning environments, but only when mastery goals are also espoused, supporting the orthogonality of achievement goals. The authors argue that the cost of performance-approach goals in terms of the use of avoidance strategies, cheating, and reluctance to cooperate with peers is problematical, and they conclude that the suggested reconceptualization of AGT by Elliot and colleagues is simply not warranted. This is echoed by Roberts (2012) and colleagues (2007), who argued that the hierarchical model may be a valid theory in itself, but it is not an extension of AGT as claimed by Elliot and colleagues (e.g., Elliot & Conroy, 2005; Murayama et al., 2011). For a more detailed criticism of the hierarchical model, see Roberts (2012, pp. 34–36).

A second criticism of the traditional model of AGT comes from Harwood and colleagues (Harwood & Hardy, 2001; Harwood, Hardy, & Swain, 2000; Harwood et al., 2008), who raise conceptual and methodological concerns. Harwood and colleagues argued that AGT was not as useful in sport as in education and they argued that task involvement, as a state, did not exist in sport because of the ego-involving nature of the sport experience: The goal pertinent to sport was termed "self-referenced ego involvement" (Harwood et al., 2000, p. 244). However, in a later treatise (Harwood et al., 2008), the three states of involvement were termed task involvement process, task involvement product, and norm-referenced ego involvement. As task involvement per se did not exist, it was a focus on the process of performing within the competitive sport experience. Task involvement product was the new term for self-referenced ego involvement, where the athlete would focus on competing against others, but only to determine relative competence and improvement. Norm-referenced ego involvement was whether the athlete could outperform other athletes. Others have also argued for similar multiple goals, such as process, performance, and outcome goals (e.g., Burton & Weiss, 2008; Gould, 2006). The core of the argument is that there needs to be a new goal to reflect the nature of the sport experience. For example, Harwood and colleagues (2008) argue that researchers need to adjust their use of the core concepts of AGT to drive "at the heart of sport subcultures and specific concepts" (p. 167). The arguments revolve around the concept of task involvement and how it may be "corrected" and made to characterize what really happens in sport, and that task involvement is not present in competitive sport because, by definition, competitive sport is ego-involving.

However, these arguments were rebutted by Treasure and colleagues (2001) and Roberts (2012), where the conceptual logic behind the multiple states of involvement was seriously questioned (for more detail, see Roberts, 2012, pp. 36–40). Harwood and colleagues may be focusing on goals from a content perspective and on what individuals are trying to achieve in a specific situation. The same is true for the introduction of other goals such as social goals (e.g., Dowson & McInerney, 2001), where individuals may want to achieve in order to win friends. Maehr and Zusho (2009) argue that we may need to reconsider the distinction between goal (reason) and goal objective (target) as a first step in reconciling the various operationalizations of the achievement goal construct. In this way, we may facilitate a better understanding of achievement goal theory by renewing a focus on issues of goal hierarchy and multiple goal endorsement. More recently, Sommet and Elliot (2017) proposed a systematic approach to disentangling the shared and unique variance explained by achievement goals, reasons for goal pursuit, and specific goal–reason combinations. In a series of studies, Sommet and Elliot demonstrated that striving for task mastery, striving for autonomous reasons, and a combination of task mastery goal and autonomous reason for striving all made separate positive combinations to beneficial achievement-related outcomes. The same was true for performance goals and a specific performance goal–autonomous reason combination. Sommet and Elliot conclude that achievement goals and reasons for striving are distinct and overlapping constructs, and that neither eliminates the influence of the other. Both type of goal and type of reason are important for a full understanding of achievement motivation and offer "the most promising avenue for a full account of competence motivation" (p. 1141). Only the ebb and flow of subsequent data on the shoals of theory will determine the efficacy of the approach.

Another critique of AGT is that it tends to mainly focus on conscious (e.g., controlled, intentional, reflective, planned) processes, while ignoring the role of non-conscious processes (e.g., spontaneous, implicit, automatic evaluations) when explaining behaviour and affect.[1] This may to some extent limit AGT, particularly given that an exclusive focus on conscious processes may not provide a complete or realistic understanding of behaviour in settings such as sport and physical education (cf. Hagger, 2016). More recently, emphasis has been given to dual-process theories because they argue that behaviours are determined by a combination of conscious and non-conscious processes (e.g., Bargh, 1989, 1990; Levesque, Copeland, & Sutcliffe, 2008). For example, when repeatedly associated with an external situation where athletes feel that they have to demonstrate their ability and engage in rivalry with team members, they may come to automatically associate various situations with feelings of having to demonstrate their abilities. Thus, an ego involvement goal can be activated or triggered without their conscious will, intention, or intervention (Levesque et al., 2008). Nicholls (e.g., 1984) argues that ego and task orientations are the function of socialization processes in the home, school, and activity contexts, and, therefore, it could well be argued that the orientations do become automatic and non-conscious. Friedman and colleagues (Friedman, Deci, Elliot, Moller, & Aarts, 2010) investigated whether simply observing the motivational orientation of others (behaviour implying intrinsic versus extrinsic orientation) can prime the motivational behaviour of an observer. Exposure to an intrinsically motivated target led observers to engage in greater levels of free-choice behaviour and performance. Future research is needed to explore the relevance of non-conscious processes and whether goal involvement could be automatically activated and under which conditions. For example, would exposing athletes to ego- and task-involved words activate the goals to pursue their performance and their way of relating to other peers?

The above documents the various approaches to arguing for the emergence of goal orientations and goal processes within the study of motivation. Both Elliot and colleagues (e.g., (Sommet & Elliot, 2017) and Dweck (2017) have proposed more comprehensive approaches to understanding motivation. Only the future will determine the more robust approach when data inform theory.

The Motivational Climate: Mastery and Performance Criteria

One of the most powerful aspects of AGT is that it incorporates not only the individual difference variables of task and ego orientations, or growth and entity orientations, but also the situational determinants of task and ego involvement. The situation plays a central role in the motivation process. Consistent with other motivation research that has emphasized the situational determinants of behaviour (e.g., deCharms, 1976; Deci & Ryan, 2000; Ntoumanis, 2012), research within AGT has examined how the structure of the environment can make it more or less likely that an individual will become task- or ego-involved (Ames, 1992a, 1992b, 1992c; Nicholls, 1984, 1989). The premise of this line of research is that the individual perceives the degree to which task and ego criteria are salient within the context. The individual then decides on the behaviours necessary to achieve success and/or avoid failure (Ames, 1992c; Roberts et al., 2018). The achievement behaviours, cognition, and affective responses of individuals are determined by the perceived cues in the context. When describing the achievement cues within the context, the schemas emerging from achievement situations, we will be consistent with Ames (1992c) and refer to the task-involving aspect of the context as *mastery* criteria and the ego-involving aspect of the context as *performance* criteria (see Figure 8).

A performance climate is created when the criteria of success and failure are other-referenced and ego-involving (Ames, 1992c), and the individual perceives that the demonstration of normative ability is valued. A mastery climate is created when the criteria of success and failure are self-referenced and task-involving (Ames, 1992c), and the individual perceives that the demonstration of mastery and learning is valued. The individual will adopt adaptive achievement strategies (namely, to work hard, seek challenging tasks, persist in the face of difficulty) in the climate in which he or she feels comfortable. For most people, and especially children, this is in the climate that emphasizes mastery (e.g., Biddle, 2001; Roberts et al., 2018, 2007; Roberts, Treasure, & Kavussanu, 1997; Treasure, 1997; Treasure & Roberts, 2001). In mastery-oriented situations, an individual is assumed to adopt adaptive achievement strategies such as working hard, seeking challenging tasks, and persisting in the face of difficulty (Harwood, Keegan, Smith, & Raine, 2015; Roberts, 2012). Certainly, the extant research supports that assumption (e.g., Treasure, 2001). However, some people function well in a performance climate. These are people who are high in perceived competence at the activity and who wish to demonstrate their competence and enjoy demonstrating superiority to others (see Figure 8). As long as the perception of high ability lasts, these people seek challenging tasks and revel in demonstrating their ability. But, as soon as the perception of ability wavers, because of age, injury, or an individual enters into a more elite context, then these people are likely to adopt maladaptive achievement strategies (namely, seek easy tasks, reduce effort or give up in the face of difficulty, cheat in order to win, etc).

The Research Evidence

The creation of a mastery motivational climate is important in optimizing positive attributes (i.e., well-being, sportspersonship, persistence, task perseverance, adaptive achievement strategies) and attenuating negative attributes (i.e., overtraining, self-handicapping, stress responses, burn-out, cheating; e.g., Fry & Gano-Overway, 2010; Hogue, Fry, & Fry, 2017; Iwasaki & Fry, 2016; Kuczka & Treasure, 2005; Ommundsen & Roberts, 1999; Sarrazin, Roberts, Cury, Biddle, & Famose, 2002; Standage, Duda, & Ntoumanis, 2003; Standage, Treasure, Hooper, & Kuczka, 2007; Treasure & Roberts, 2001). This pattern of findings has been confirmed in a comprehensive qualitative and quantitative review using 104 studies (n = 34,156) that found that perceptions of a mastery climate were associated with adaptive motivational outcomes including perceived competence, self-esteem, objective performance improvement, intrinsic motivation, positive affective states, experienced flow, and less cheating (Harwood et al., 2015). On the other hand, perceptions of a performance climate were associated with extrinsic motivation, negative affective states, maladaptive performance strategies, perfectionism, and greater likelihood of cheating. The extant evidence, therefore, supports the position that perceptions of a mastery motivational climate are associated with more adaptive motivational and affective response patterns than perceptions of a performance climate in the context of sport.

For the purposes of the present discussion, it is as well to realize that dispositional goal orientations and perceptions of the climate are two independent dimensions of motivation within AGT that interact to affect behaviour (Nicholls, 1989). However, the powerful and parsimonious aspect of AGT is that both the individual dispositions and the perception of the motivational climate are encompassed by the theory. It is true that research to date primarily deals with dispositional goal orientations and perceptions of the motivational climate as separate constructs isolated from each other (Harwood et al., 2015; Lochbaum et al., 2016). It has been suggested that an interactionist approach that looks to combine both variables promises to provide a more complete understanding of achievement behaviours in the sport and physical education experience (e.g., Duda, Chi, Newton, & Catley, 1995; Papaioannou et al., 2012; Roberts, 2012; Roberts & Treasure, 1992; Roberts et al., 2007; Treasure, 2001; Treasure & Roberts, 2001).

In a qualitative review, Roberts (2012) argued that, instead of looking at achievement goals and the motivational climate separately, as is the custom, AGT should focus on an integrated perspective, because dispositional goal orientations and the perceived motivational climate are part of the same theoretical platform, and the energizing force for motivated behaviour is the resultant state of involvement. It supports meaningful relationships between personal goals of achievement and/or the perceived criteria of success and failure in the motivational climate, with cognitive and affective beliefs about involvement in physical activity, as well as achievement striving. However, there are few studies that have investigated the interactive effect of both the goal orientations and the motivational climate within the same study. An exception is a study conducted by Cury and colleagues (1996). In this study, the researchers utilized structural equation modelling (SEM) to examine the interest of adolescent girls in physical education. The researchers conclude by suggesting that their findings support the positive effects of a mastery-oriented motivational climate in physical education and offer evidence of a possible shaping effect of the climate on an individual's goal orientation. This finding is replicated in more recent studies (e.g., Iwasaki & Fry, 2016).

Multilevel structural equation modelling (MSEM) may be an appropriate technique to examine potential relationships among achievement goals and perceptions of the motivational climate, including the testing of interactive effects (Morin, Marsh, Nagengast, & Scalas, 2014; Preacher, Zyphur, & Zhang, 2016). Particularly, the MSEM approach may provide some interesting insights into how goal orientations and the motivational climate may interact by simultaneously accounting for the individual and group level of analysis (cf. Lam, Ruzek, Schenke, Conley, & Karabenick, 2015).

Research has found interesting relationships between orientations and the climate (e.g., Harwood & Swain, 1998; Swain & Harwood, 1996; Treasure & Roberts, 1998). Swain and Harwood found that separate main effects as well as significant interactions occurred between the dispositional and situational predictors of the different goal states. Specifically, social perceptions and competitive race-specific criteria were the major predictors of ego involvement, whereas the level of task orientation combined with the above situational factors seemed to exert greater influence in determining the intensity of task involvement in age-group swimmers. In a later study, Harwood and Swain (1998) found that perceptions of significant others, the achievement value of the match, and perceptions of ability were the major predictors of task involvement. The pre-match intensity of ego involvement was predicted by ego orientation combined with perceptions of significant others and match value. They concluded by stating that the findings reinforce the need for researchers to consider the importance of both dispositional and situational variables when predicting goal involvement in competitive contexts. More recently, Granero-Gallegos and colleagues (2017) concurred and found that a perceived mastery-oriented motivational climate was positively related to a task-centred goal orientation, enjoyment, and a belief that success may be achieved through effort. In contrast, a perceived performance-oriented training climate was linked to an ego-centred goal orientation, boredom or lack of enthusiasm, and a belief that the path to success in handball involves the use of deception techniques.

Although moderated hierarchical analysis does enable researchers to examine the separate, as well as the interactive, effects of goal orientations and the motivational climate, this type of analysis is not powerful. The fact that significant main effects emerged for both climate and orientations appears to confirm the validity of investigating the effects of goal orientations and perceptions of the motivational climate separately, as the majority of achievement goal research has done to date. However, as documented above, evidence is accumulating to demonstrate that both goal orientations and the motivational climate need to be considered within the AGT model to fully understand the manifestation of achievement striving in sport and physical activity (e.g., Buch, Nerstad, Aandstad, & Säfvenbom, 2016). This research has also been pursued in other settings, such as work (Nerstad, Richardsen, & Roberts, 2018). However, we have to agree with Harwood et al. (2008) and Roberts and colleagues (2018) that research in sport has not yet fully examined the interaction of dispositions and the situational criteria of the motivational climate in the manifestation of goal involvement.

Conclusion

There are two important conclusions we may draw from the evidence of the research effort on AGT over the past 40 years (Roberts et al., 2018). The first one is that ego-involving goals are more likely to lead to maladaptive achievement behaviour, especially when participants perceive their competence to be low, have an entity IPT, are concerned with failure, or are invested in protecting self-worth. In such circumstances, the evidence is quite clear: Motivation ebbs, task investment is low, persistence is low, performance suffers, satisfaction and enjoyment are lower, peer relationships suffer, cheating is more likely, burn-out is more likely, and participants feel more negatively about themselves and the achievement context. But, as we have been at pains to note, this does not mean that ego-involving goals are always negative; in some situations, for some people, they are positive. When one is ego-oriented with a high perception of competence, then that goal is facilitative of achievement and functions as a motivating construct (e.g., Pensgaard & Roberts, 2002). This is precisely why being ego-involved in sport can be very motivating and lead to sustained achievement behaviour. But even then, ego-involving goals are more "fragile" and can lead to maladaptive achievement striving as context information is processed (Dweck & Leggett, 1988), such as when age begins to become a factor in elite sport performance, or when injury strikes.

Second, the research is unequivocal that task-involving (mastery) and growth goals are adaptive. When task-involved, whether through personal dispositions or because participants perceive mastery criteria in the context, or both, then motivation is optimized, participants are invested in the task and persist longer, performance is higher, satisfaction and enjoyment are higher, peer relationships are fostered, burn-out and cheating are less likely, and participants feel more positively about themselves and the task. Being task-involved has been consistently associated with desirable cognitive, affective, and achievement-striving responses. The research is clear that if we wish to optimize motivation in sport and physical activity we ought to promote task involvement. It does not matter whether we do it through enhancing socialization experiences (encouraging parents to be more task-involving in the home, or teacher/coaches in school and sport contexts), so that the individual has a task goal orientation and is naturally, and perhaps unconsciously, task-involved (Nicholls, 1989), or we structure the physical activity context to be more task-involving (Ames, 1992b; Treasure & Roberts, 2001). The crucial issue is that the participant has task-involving goals of achievement. The evidence has led many sport psychologists to conclude that being task-involved better enables participants to manage motivation in the sport experience (e.g., Brunel, 2000; Hall & Kerr, 1997; Hogue, Fry, & Iwasaki, 2018; Iwasaki & Fry, 2016; Pensgaard & Roberts, 2002; Roberts, 2012; Roberts et al., 2018; Theeboom, DeKnop, & Weiss, 1995; Treasure & Roberts, 1995).

We can never have equality of achievement, but we can have equality of motivation: That was the mission of John Nicholls (1979). His goal was "equality of optimal motivation" (p. 1071), so that everyone should achieve the best that is possible for them to fulfil their potential. This enshrines the conceptual basis of enhancing motivation from an AGT perspective.
Note

Note

1 We would like to thank Dr. Nikos Ntoumanis for his valuable comments on this section.

References

Ames, C. (1992a). Achievement goals and the classroom motivational climate. In D. Schunk & J. Meece (Eds.), *Student perceptions in the classroom* (pp. 327–348). Hillsdale, NJ: Erlbaum.

Ames, C. (1992b). Achievement goals, motivational climate, and motivational processes. In G. C. Roberts (Ed.), *Motivation in sport and exercise* (pp. 161–176). Champaign, IL: Human Kinetics.

Ames, C. (1992c). Classrooms: Goals, structures, and student motivation. *Journal of Educational Psychology, 84,* 261–271.

Aronson, J., Fried, C. B., & Good, C. (2002). Reducing the effects of sterotype threat on African American college students by shaping theories of intelligence. *Journal of Experimental Social Psychology, 38,* 113–125.

Bandura, A., & Wood, R. E. (1989). Effect of perceived controllability and performance standards on self-regulation of complex decision making. *Journal of Personality and Social Psychology, 56,* 805–814.

Bargh, J. A. (1989). Conditional automaticity: Varieties of automatic influence in social perception and cognition. In J. S. Uleman & J. A. Bargh (Eds.), *Unintended thought* (pp. 3–51). New York: Guilford Press.

Bargh, J. A. (1990). Auto-motives: Preconscious determinants of social interaction. In E. T. Higgins & R. M. Sorrentino (Eds.), *Handbook of motivation and cognition* (Vol. 2, pp. 93–132). New York: Guilford Press.

Biddle, S. (2001). Enhancing motivation in physical education. In G. C. Roberts (Ed.), *Advances in motivation in sport and excercise* (pp. 101–127). Champaign, IL: Human Kinetics.

Biddle, S. J. H., Soos, I., & Chatzisarantis, N. (1999). Predicting physical activity intentions using a goal perspectives approach: A study of Hungarian youth. *Scandinavian Journal of Medicine and Science in Sports, 9,* 353–357.

Biddle, S. J. H., Wang, C. K. J., Chatzisarantis, N. L. D., & Spray, C. M. (2003). Motivation for physical activity in young people: Entity and incremental beliefs concerning athletic ability. *Journal of Sports Sciences, 21,* 973–989.

Brunel, P. C. (2000). Achievement motivation: Toward interactive effects of dispositional and situational variables on motivation and social cognition. Habilitation à diriger les recherches. Limoges: University of Limoges Press.

Buch, R., Nerstad, C. G. L., Aandstad, A., & Säfvenbom, R. (2016). Exploring the interplay between the motivational climate and goal orientation in predicting maximal oxygen uptake. *Journal of Sport Sciences, 34,* 267–277.

Burnette, J. L., O'Boyle, E. H., VanEpps, E. M., Pollack, J. M., & Finkel, E. J. (2013). Mind-sets matter: A meta-analytic review of implicit theories and self-regulation. *Psychological Bulletin, 139,* 655–701.

Burton, D., & Weiss, C. L. (2008). The fundamental goal concept: The path to process and performance success. In T. Horn (Ed.), *Advances in sport psychology* (3rd ed., pp. 339–375). Champaign, IL: Human Kinetics.

Corrion, K., D'Arripe-Longueville, F., Chalabaev, A., Schiano-Lomoriello, S., Roussel, P., & Cury, F. (2010). Effect of implicit theories on judgement of cheating acceptability in physical education: The mediating role of achievement goals. *Journal of Sport Sciences, 28,* 909–919.

Cumming, J., Hall, C., Harwood, C. G., & Gammage, K. (2002). Motivational orientations and imagery use: A goal profiling analysis. *Journal of Sports Sciences, 20,* 127–136.

Cury, F., Biddle, S., Famouse, J.-P., Goudas, M., Sarrazin, P., & Durand, M. (1996). Personal and situational factors influencing intrinsic interest in adolecent girls in school physical education: A structural equation modelling analysis. *Educational Psychology, 16,* 305–315.

Cury, F., Da Fonséca, D., Rufo, M., Peres, C., & Sarrazin, P. (2003). The trichotomous model and investment in learning to prepare for a sport test: A mediational analysis. *British Journal of Educational Psychology, 73,* 529–543.

Cury, F., Da Fonseca, D., Rufo, M., & Sarrazin, P. (2002). Perceptions of competence, implicit theory of ability, perception of motivational climate, and achievement goals: A test of the trichotomous conceptualization of endorsement of achievement motivation in the physical education setting. *Perceptual and Motor Skills, 95,* 233–244.

Cury, F., Elliot, A., Sarrazin, P., Da Fonseca, D., & Rufo, M. (2002). The trichotomous achievement goal model and intrinsic motivation: A sequential mediational analysis. *Journal of Experimental Social Psychology, 38,* 473–481.

Davis, R., Campbell, R., Hildon, Z., Hobbs, L., & Michie, S. (2015). Theories of behaviour change across the social and behavioural sciences: A scoping review. *Health Psychology Review, 9,* 323–344.

deCharms, R. (1976). *Enchancing motivation: Change in classroom.* New York: Irvington.

Deci, E. L., & Ryan, M. R. (1985). The general causality orientation scale: Self-determination in personality. *Journal of Research in Personality, 19,* 109–134.

Deci, E. L., & Ryan, R. M. (2000). The "what" and "why" of goal pursuits: Human needs and the self-determination of behaviour. *Psychological Inquiry, 11,* 227–268.

Dowson, M., & McInerney, D. M. (2001). Psychological parameters of students' social and work avoidance goals: A qualitative analysis. *Journal of Educational Psychology, 93,* 35–42.

Duda, J. L. (2001). Achievement goal research in sport: Pushing the boundaries and clarifying some issues. In G. C. Roberts (Ed.), *Advances in motivation in sport and exercise* (pp. 129–183). Champaign, IL: Human Kinetics.

Duda, J. L. (2005). Motivation in sport. In A. J. Elliot & C. S. Dweck (Eds.), *Handbook of competence and motivation* (pp. 318–335). New York: Guilford Press.

Duda, J. L., Chi, L., Newton, M. D., & Catley, D. (1995). Task and ego orientation and intrinsic motivation in sport. *International Journal of Sport Psychology, 26,* 40–63.

Duda, J. L., & Whitehead, J. (1998). Measurement of goal perspectives in the physical domain. In J. L. Duda (Ed.), *Advances in sport and exercise psychology measurement* (pp. 21–48). Morgantown, WV: Fitness Information Technology.

Dweck, C. S. (1975). The role of expectations and attributions in the alleviation of learned helplessness. *Journal of Personality and Social Psychology, 31,* 674–685.

Dweck, C. S. (1986). Motivational processes affecting learning. *American Psychologist, 41,* 1040–1048.

Dweck, C. S. (1999). *Self-theories: Their role in motivation, personality, and development.* Philadelphia, PA: Psychology Press.

Dweck, C. S. (2000). *Self-theories: Their role in motivation, personality, and development.* New York: Routledge.

Dweck, C. S. (2006). *Mindset: The new psychology of success.* New York: Random House.

Dweck, C. S. (2012). Mindsets and human nature: Promoting change in the Middle East, the schoolyard, the racial divide, and willpower. *American Psychologist, 67,* 614–622.

Dweck, C. S. (2017). From needs to goals and representations: Foundations for a unified theory of motivation, personality, and development. *Psychological Review, 124*(6), 689–719.

Dweck, C. S., Chiu, C., & Hong, Y. Y. (1995). Implicit theories and their role in judgements and reactions: A word from two perspectives. *Psychological Inquiry, 6,* 267–285.

Dweck, C. S., & Leggett, E. L. (1988). A social-cognitive approach to motivation and personality. *Psychological Review, 95,* 265–273.

Ehrlinger, J. (2008). Skill level, self-views and self-theories as sources of error in self-assessment. *Social and Personality Psychology Compass, 2,* 382–398.

Elliot, A. J. (1997). Integrating the "classic" and "contemporary" approaches to achivment motivation: A hierarchical model of approach and avoidance achievement motivation. In M. L. Maehr & P. R. Pintrich (Eds.), *Advances in motivation and achievement goals* (Vol. 10, pp. 143–179). Greenwich, CT: JAI Press.

Elliot, A. J. (1999). Approach and avoidance motivation and achievement goals. *Educational Psychologist, 34,* 169–189.

Elliot, A. J., & Conroy, D. E. (2005). Beyond the dichotomous model of achivment goals in sport and exercise psychology. *Sport and Exercise Psychology Review, 1,* 17–25.

Elliot, A. J., & Harackiewicz, J. M. (1996). Approach and avoidance achievement goals and intrinsic motivation: A mediational analysis. *Journal of Personality and Social Psychology, 70,* 461–475.

Elliot, A. J., & Thrash, T. M. (2001). Achievement goals and the hierarchical model of achievment motivation. *Educational Psychological Review, 13,* 139–156.

Elliott, E. S., & Dweck, C. S. (1988). Goals: An approach to motivation and achievement. *Journal of Personality and Social Psychology, 54,* 5–12.

Ford, M. E. (1992). *Motivating humans: Goals, emotions, and personal agency beliefs.* Newbury Park, CA: Sage.

Fox, K., Goudas, M., Biddle, S., Duda, J. L., & Armstrong, N. (1994). Children's task and ego goal profiles in sport. *British Journal of Educational Psychology, 64*, 253–261.

Friedman, R., Deci, E. L., Elliot, A. J., Moller, A. C., & Aarts, H. (2010). Motivational synchronicity: Priming motivational orientations with observations of others' behaviors. *Motivation and Emotion, 34*, 34–38.

Fry, M. D., & Gano-Overway, L. A. (2010). Exploring the contribution of the caring climate to the youth sport experience. *Journal of Applied Sport Psychology, 22*, 294–304.

Gernigon, C., d'Arripe-Loungeville, F., Delignères, D., & Ninot, G. (2004). A dynamical systems perspective on goal involvement states in sport. *Journal of Sport & Exercise Psychology, 26*, 572–596.

Gould, D. (2006). Goal setting for peak performance. In J. M. Williams (Ed.), *Applied sport psychology: Personal growth to peak performance* (pp. 240–259). New York: McGraw-Hill.

Granero-Gallegos, A., Gómez-López, M., Rodríguez-Suárez, N., Abraldes, J. A., Alesi, M., & Bianco, A. (2017). Importance of the motivational climate in goal, enjoyment, and the causes of success in handball players. *Frontiers in Psychology, 8*, 2081.

Hagger, M. S. (2016). Non-conscious processes and dual-process theories in health psychology. *Health Psychology Research, 10*, 375–380.

Hair, J. F., Jr., Anderson, R. E., Tatham, R. L., & Black, W. C. (1998). *Multivariate data analysis* (5th ed.). Upper Saddle River, NJ: Prentice-Hall.

Hall, H. K., & Kerr, A. W. (1997). Motivational antecedents of precompetitive anxiety in youth sport. *Sport Psychologist, 11*, 24–42.

Harwood, C. G., Cumming, J., & Fletcher, D. (2004). Motivational profiles and psychological skills use within elite youth sport. *Journal of Applied Sport Psychology, 16*, 318–332.

Harwood, C. G., & Hardy, L. (2001). Persistence and effort in moving achievement goal research forward: A response to Treasure and colleagues. *Journal of Sport and Exercise Psychology, 23*, 330–345.

Harwood, C. G., Hardy, L., & Swain, A. B. J. (2000). Achievement goals in sport: A critique of conceptual and measurement issues. *Journal of Sport and Exercise Psychology, 22*, 235–255.

Harwood, C. G., Keegan, R. J., Smith, J. M. J., & Raine, A. S. (2015). A systematic review of the intrapersonal correlates of motivational climate perceptions in sport and physical activity. *Psychology of Sport and Excercise, 18*, 9–25.

Harwood, C. G., Spray, C. M., & Keegan, R. (2008). Achievement goal theories in sport. In T. S. Horn (Ed.), *Advances in sport psychology* (pp. 157–186). Champaign, IL: Human Kinetics.

Harwood, C. G., & Swain, A. B. J. (1998). Antecedents of pre-competition achievement goals in elite junior tennis players. *Journal of Sport Sciences, 16*, 357–371.

Heslin, P. A., Latham, G. P., & Vandewalle, D. (2005). The effect of implicit person theory on performance appraisals. *Journal of Applied Psychology, 90*, 842–856.

Heslin, P. A., & Vandewalle, D. (2008). Manager's implicit assumptions about personnel. *Current Directions in Psychological Science, 17*, 219–223.

Hodge, K., & Petlichkoff, L. (2000). Goal profiles in sport motivation: A cluster analysis. *Journal of Sport & Exercise Psychology, 22*, 256–272.

Hogue, C. M., Fry, M. D., & Fry, A. C. (2017). The differential impact of motivational climate on adolescents' psychological and physiological stress responses. *Psychology of Sport and Exercise, 30*, 118–127.

Hogue, C. M., Fry, M. D., & Iwasaki, S. (2018). The impact of the perceived motivational climate in physical education classes on adolescent greater life stress, coping appraisals, and experience of shame. *Sport, Exercise, and Performance Psychology.* doi:10.1037/spy0000153

Iwasaki, S., & Fry, M. D. (2016). Female adolescent soccer players' perceived motivational climate, goal orientations, and mindful engagement. *Psychology of Sport and Exercise, 27*, 222–231.

Kaplan, A., & Maehr, M. L. (2007). The contributions and prospects of goal orientation theory. *Educational Psychological Review, 19*, 141–184.

Kuczka, K. K., & Treasure, D. C. (2005). Self-handicapping in competitive sport: Influence of the motivational climate, self-efficacy, and perceived importance. *Psychology of Sport and Exercise, 6*, 539–550.

Lam, A. C., Ruzek, E. A., Schenke, K., Conley, A. M., & Karabenick, S. A. (2015). Student perceptions of classroom achievement goal structure: Is it appropriate to aggregate? *Journal of Educational Psychology.* doi:10.1037/edu0000028

Lemyre, P. N., Ommundsen, Y., & Roberts, G. C. (2000). Moral functioning in sport: The role of dispositional goals and perceived ability. *International Journal of Psychology, 35*, 23.

Lemyre, P. N., Roberts, G. C., & Stray-Gundersen, J. (2007). Motivation, overtraining, and burnout: Can self-determined motivation predict overtraining and burnout in elite athletes? *European Journal of Sport Science, 7*, 115–126.

Levesque, C., Copeland, K. J., & Sutcliffe, R. A. (2008). Conscious and nonconscious processes: Implications for self-determination theory. *Canadian Psychology, 49*, 218–224.

Lochbaum, M. R., Kazak Cetinkalp, Z., Graham, K.-A., Wright, T., & Zazo, R. (2016). Task and ego goal orientations in competitive sport: A quantitative review of the literature from 1989 to 2016. *Kinesiology, 48*, 3–29.

Locke, E. A., & Latham, G. P. (1985). The application of goal setting to sports. *Journal of Sport Psychology, 7*, 205–222.

Maehr, M. L., & Braskamp, L. A. (1986). *The motivation factor: A theory of personal investment*. Lexington, MA: Lexington Books/Heath.

Maehr, M. L., & Nicholls, J. G. (1980). Culture and achievement motivation: A second look. In N. Warren (Ed.), *Studies in cross-cultural psychology* (Vol. 2, pp. 221–267). New York: Academic Press.

Maehr, M. L., & Zusho, A. (2009). Achievement goal theory: The past, present, and future. In K. R. Wentzel & A. Wigfield (Eds.), *Handbook of motivation at school* (pp. 77–104). New York: Routledge.

Marsh, H. W., Craven, R. G., Hinkley, J. W., & Debus, R. L. (2003). Evaluation of the big-two-factor theory of academic motivation orientations: An evaluation of jingle-jangle fallacies. *Multivariate Behavioral Research, 38*, 189–224.

Middleton, M. J., & Midgley, C. (1997). Avoiding the demonstration of lack of ability: An underexplored aspect of goal theory. *Journal of Educational Psychology, 89*, 710–718.

Midgley, C., Kaplan, A., & Middleton, M. (2001). Performance-approach goals: Good for what, for whom, under what circumstances, and at what cost? *Journal of Educational Psychology, 93*, 77–86.

Morin, A. J. S., Marsh, H. W., Nagengast, B., & Scalas, L. F. (2014). Doubly latent multilevel analyses and classroom climate: An illustration. *The Journal of Experimental Education, 82*, 143–167.

Murayama, K., Elliot, A. J., & Yamagata, S. (2011). Separation of performance-approach and performance-avoidance achievement goals: A broader analysis. *Journal of Educational Psychology, 103*, 238–256.

Nerstad, C. G. L., Richardsen, A. M., & Roberts, G. C. (2018). Who are the high achievers at work? Perceived motivational climate, goal orientation profiles, and work performance. *Scandinavian Journal of Psychology, 59*, 661–677.

Nicholls, J. G. (1976). Effort is virtuous, but it's better to have ability: Evaluative responses to perceptions of effort and ability. *Journal of Research in Personality, 10*, 306–315.

Nicholls, J. G. (1978). The development of the concepts of effort and ability, perception of academic attainment, and the understanding that difficult tasks require more ability. *Child Development, 49*, 800–814.

Nicholls, J. G. (1979). Quality and equality in intellectual development: The role of motivation in education. *American Psychologist, 34*, 1071–1084.

Nicholls, J. G. (1984). Conceptions of ability and achievement motivation. In C. Ames & R. Ames (Eds.), *Research on motivation in education: Goals and cognitions* (Vol. 3, pp. 39–73). San Diego, CA: Academic Press.

Nicholls, J. G. (1989). *The competitive ethos and democratic education*. Cambridge, MA: Harvard University Press.

Nicholls, J. G., & Miller, A. T. (1984). Development and its discontents: The differentiation of the concept of ability. In J. G. Nicholls (Ed.), *Advances in motivation and achievement: The development of achievement motivation* (Vol. 3, pp. 185–218). Greenwich, CT: JAI Press.

Ntoumanis, N. (2012). A self-determination theory perspective on motivation in sport and physical education: Current trends and possible future research directions. In G. C. Roberts & D. C. Treasure (Eds.), *Advances in Motivation in sport and exercise* (Vol. 3, pp. 91–128). Champaign, IL: Human Kinetics.

Ommundsen, Y. (2001a). Pupils' affective responses in physical education classes: The association of implicit theories of the nature of ability and achievement goals. *European Physical Education Review, 7*, 219–242.

Ommundsen, Y. (2001b). Self-handicapping strategies in physical education classes: The influence of implicit theories of the nature of ability and achievement goal orientations. *Psychology of Sport and Exercise, 2*, 139–156.

Ommundsen, Y. (2001c). Students' implicit theories of ability in physical education classes: The influence of motivational aspects of the learning environment. *Learning Environments Research, 4*, 139–158.

Ommundsen, Y., & Roberts, G. C. (1999). Effect of motivational climate profiles on motivational indices in team sport. *Scandinavian Journal of Medicine and Science in Sports, 9,* 389–397.

Papaioannou, A., Zourbanos, N., Kromidas, H., & Ampatzoglou, G. (2012). The place of achievement goal in the social context of sport: A comparison of Nicholls' and Elliot's models. In G. C. Roberts & D. Treasure (Eds.), *Advances in motivation in sport and exercise* (Vol. 3, pp. 59–91). Champaign, IL: Human Kinetics.

Payne, S. C., Youngcourt, S. S., & Beaubien, M. J. (2007). A meta-analytic examination of goal orientation nomological net. *Journal of Applied Psychology, 92,* 128–150.

Pensgaard, A.-M., & Roberts, G. C. (2000). The relationship between motivational climate, perceived ability and sources of distress among elite athletes. *Journal of Sport Sciences, 18,* 191–200.

Pensgaard, A.-M., & Roberts, G. C. (2002). Elite athletes' experiences of the motivational climate: The coach matters. *Scandinavian Journal of Medicine and Science in Sports, 12,* 54–60.

Preacher, K. J., Zyphur, M. J., & Zhang, Z. (2016). Multilevel structural equation models for assessing moderation within and accross levels of analysis. *Psychological Methods, 21,* 189–205.

Rawsthorne, L. J., & Elliot, A. J. (1999). Achievement goals and intrinsic motivation: A meta-analytic review. *Personality and Social Psychology Review, 3,* 326–344.

Roberts, G. C. (2012). Motivation in sport and exercise from an achievement goal theory perspective: After 30 years, where are we? In G. C. Roberts & D. Treasure (Eds.), *Advances in motivation in sport and exercise* (Vol. 3, pp. 5–58). Champaign, IL: Human Kinetics.

Roberts, G. C., Nerstad, C. G. L., & Lemyre, P. N. (2018). Motivation in sport and performance. In O. Brodikk (Ed.), *Oxford research encyclopedia of psychology* (pp. 1–38). Oxford, UK: Oxford University Press doi:10.1093/acrefore/9780190236557.013.150.

Roberts, G. C., & Ommundsen, Y. (1996). Effect of goal orientation on achievement beliefs, cognition and strategies in team sport. *Scandinavian Journal of Medicine & Science in Sports, 6*(1), 46–56.

Roberts, G. C., & Treasure, D. C. (1992). Children in sport. *Sport Science Review, 1,* 46–64.

Roberts, G. C., Treasure, D. C., & Balague, G. (1998). Achievement goals in sport: The development and validation of the perception of success questionnaire. *Journal of Sport Science Review, 16,* 337–347.

Roberts, G. C., Treasure, D. C., & Conroy, D. E. (2007). Understanding the dynamics of motivation in sport and physical activity. In G. Tenenbaum & R. C. Eklund (Eds.), *Handbook of sport psychology* (3rd ed., pp. 3–30). Hoboken, NJ: John Wiley.

Roberts, G. C., Treasure, D. C., & Kavussanu, M. (1996). Orthogonality of achivement goals an its relationship to beliefs about success and satisfaction in sport. *The Sport Psychologist, 10,* 398–408.

Roberts, G. C., Treasure, D. C., & Kavussanu, M. (1997). Motivation in physical activity contexts: An achievement goal perspective. In P. Pintrich & M. Maehr (Eds.), *Advances in motivation and achievement* (Vol. 10, pp. 413–447). Stamford, CT: JAI Press.

Sarrazin, P., Roberts, G. C., Cury, F., Biddle, S., & Famose, J.-P. (2002). Exerted effort and performance in climbing among boys: The influence of achievement goals, perceived ability, and task difficulty. *Research Quarterly for Exercise and Sport, 73,* 425–436.

Sisk, V. F., Burgoyne, A. P., Sun, J., Butler, J. L., & Macnamara, B. N. (2018). To what extent and under which circumstances are growth mind-sets important to academic achievement? Two meta-analyses. *Psychological Science, 29,* 549–571.

Skaalvik, E. M. (1997). Self-enhancing and self-defeating ego orientation: Relations with task and avoidance orientation, achievement, self-perceptions, and anxiety. *Journal of Educational Psychology, 89,* 71–81.

Smith, A. L., Balaguer, I., & Duda, J. L. (2006). Goal orientation profile differences on perceived motivational climate, perceived peer relatioships, and motivation-related responses of youth athletes. *Journal of Sport Sciences, 24,* 1315–1327.

Sommet, N., & Elliot, A. J. (2017). Achievement goals, reasons for goal pursuit, and achievement goal complexes as predictors of beneficial outcomes: Is the influence of goals reducible to reasons? *Journal of Educational Psychology, 109,* 1141–1162.

Spray, C. M., Wang, C. K. J., Biddle, S. J. H., Chatzisarantis, N. L. D., & Warburton, V. E. (2006). An experimental test of self-theories of ability in youth sport. *Psychology of Sport and Excercise, 7,* 255–267.

Standage, M., Duda, J. L., & Ntoumanis, N. (2003). A model of contextual motivation in physical education: Using constructs from self-determination and achievement goal theories to predict physical activity intentions. *Journal of Educational Psychology, 95,* 97–110.

Standage, M., Treasure, D. C., Hooper, K., & Kuczka, K. (2007). Self-handicapping in school physical education: The influence of the motivational climate. *British Journal of Educational Psychology, 77,* 81–99.

Swain, A. B. J., & Harwood, C. G. (1996). Antecedents of state goals in age-group swimmers: An interactionist perspective. *Journal of Sport Sciences, 14,* 111–124.

Theeboom, M., DeKnop, P., & Weiss, M. R. (1995). Motivational climate, psychological responses, and motor skill development in children's sport: A field based intervention study. *Journal of Sport & Exercise Psychology, 17,* 294–311.

Treasure, D. (1997). Perceptions of the motivational climate and elementary school children's cognitive and affective response. *Journal of Sport and Exercise Psychology, 19,* 278–290.

Treasure, D., & Roberts, G. C. (1998). Relationship between female adolescents' achievement goal orientations, perceptions of the motivational climate, belief about success and sources of satisfaction in basketball. *International Journal of Sport Psychology, 29,* 211–230.

Treasure, D. C. (2001). Enhancing young people's motivation in youth sport: An achievement goal approach. In G. C. Roberts (Ed.), *Advances in motivation in sport and exercise* (pp. 79–100). Champaign, IL: Human Kinetics.

Treasure, D. C., Duda, J. L., Hall, H. K., Roberts, G. C., Ames, C., & Maehr, M. L. (2001). Clarifying misconceptions in achievement goal research in sport: A response to Harwood, Hardy, and Swain. *Journal of Sport & Exercise Psychology, 23,* 317–329.

Treasure, D. C., & Roberts, G. C. (1995). Applications of achievement goal theory to physical education: Implications for enhancing motivation. *Quest, 47,* 475–489.

Treasure, D. C., & Roberts, G. C. (2001). Students' perceptions of the motivational climate, achievement beliefs and satisfaction in physical education. *Research Quarterly for Exercise and Sport, 72,* 165–175.

Vandewalle, D., Nerstad, C. G. L., & Dysvik, A. (2019). Goal orientation: A review of the miles traveled and the miles to go. *Annual Review of Organizational Psychology and Organizational Behavior, 6,* 115–144.

Walling, M. D., & Duda, J. L. (1995). Goals and their associations with beliefs about success in and perceptions of the purpose of physical education. *Journal of Teaching in Physical Education, 14,* 140–156.

Wang, C. K. J., & Biddle, S. J. H. (2001). Young people's motivational profiles in physical activity: A cluster analysis. *Journal of Sport & Exercise Psychology, 23,* 1–22.

Wang, C. K. J., Liu, W. C., Biddle, S. J. H., & Spray, C. M. (2005). Cross-cultural validation of the conceptions of the nature of athletic ability questionnaire version 2. *Personality and Individual Differences, 38,* 1245–1256.

Weiner, B. (1985). An attributional theory of achievement motivation and emotion. *Psychological Review, 92,* 548–573.

25
MOTOR CONTROL

Julian Rudisch, Nils Henrik Pixa, and Claudia Voelcker-Rehage

Introduction

Coordinated control of body movements is the most central function of the nervous system for humans and other animals and the basis for interacting with our environment. Without the coordinated control of our muscles, we could not perform any basic activities such as eating, talking, or walking. Beyond activities of daily life, humans also possess the capacity to control highly complex skilled actions, such as, for example, those of which elite gymnasts are capable. It is obvious, from these examples, that motor actions comprise a vast range of skill sets, some of which are fundamental to our daily life and others of which are very specific to certain groups of people, such as athletes. Starting from very basic up to highly complex movements, motor control can be defined as "the interactions between the central nervous system, the body, and the environment during the production of voluntary and involuntary movements" (Latash & Zatsiorsky, 2016, p. xii). Hence, motor control is directly influenced by the individual, the task, and the environment.

On a structural level, motor skills can be further classified on different continua (see Figure 9), such as by their amount and type of involved muscles (i.e., fine and gross motor skills), their duration (i.e., discrete and continuous), and their regularity (i.e., open and closed skills). Furthermore, the level of complexity, difficulty, and familiarity can differ strongly between different skills. Taxonomies, as shown in Figure 9, can be used to classify motor skills for the study of motor control (and learning).

This chapter aims to review the central neurobiological structures and functions that are necessary for motor control and the central theories, frameworks, and associated concepts that have been developed over the last century. The central questions these concepts try to answer are: (a) What are the parameters that are being controlled? (b) What are the related mechanisms? And (c) how are they stored in the central nervous system (CNS)? Finding an answer to these questions is not trivial, especially when considering the complexity of the sensorimotor system and the abundance (or rather redundancy) of degrees of freedom (DOFs) that need to be coordinated for any action (Bernstein, 1967). Generally speaking, DOFs are all parts of a system that can be varied independently and that determine the system's state. The motor system has many DOFs on different levels of analysis, such as joints, muscles, or neurons. As a result of this abundance, the motor system is inherently redundant; that is, the

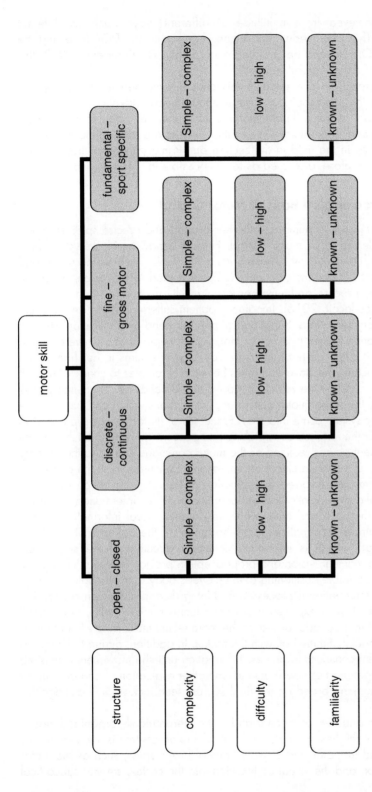

Figure 9 Taxonomy for motor skills. Classification of skills is often undertaken on a structural level (e.g., fine vs. gross motor skills. Furthermore, skills are often classified by virtue of complexity, difficulty, and familiarity (reprinted with permission from Voelcker-Rehage, 2008)

same action goal can be achieved in a multitude of different ways (such as different combinations of joint angles). That also means that, when changes in one DOF (affecting the system state) occur, all other DOFs have to be changed accordingly. For Bernstein (1967), this was the fundamental problem of motor control research.

The different theoretical perspectives presented in this chapter emerged mostly during the last century, and they reflect the philosophical and methodological advances of different decades. Experiments in support of the different motor control theories often focus on very specific classes of movements, and generalizations to other classes are often difficult to proof experimentally. The main theories in the field in the section on "Primary theories, frameworks, and associated concepts" are, therefore, discussed as far as possible in chronological order.

Neurobiological Basis of Motor Control

One of the most striking characteristics of humans is the fine-graded and precise spatiotemporal control of movements that is referred to as motor control. Human behaviour in everyday life is made up of movements that are controlled by several parts of the CNS, such as the motor and sensory systems. Important to note is that motor control is not restricted to movement execution only, but relies on sensorimotor process and emerges as a result of perception, action, and cognition (Shumway-Cook & Woollacott, 2016). Imagine a patient suffering from a neurological disorder that affects somatosensory sensations. If that patient puts her hand on a stove top, she will not receive the information about whether it is hot or not, which might lead to severe injury. However, she has learned that it might be hot and might cause severe burns to her hand. That knowledge prevents her from touching the stove and gives her other strategies to check whether it is hot or not. In another situation, consider the voluntary, goal-directed behaviour of a tennis player training to serve. For that action, the sensorimotor system and interactions within and between the several levels of the sensorimotor system come into play. Processes of motor planning proceed to create the best movement plan for the required serve, taking into account the need to hit the service court. Following this, the movement plan is realized as the motor command passes to the primary motor cortex (M1) to execute the serve (hierarchical organization). Concurrent with the movement execution, several sensory systems are involved in evaluation of the ongoing action based on proprioception and vision (parallel organization). Proprioception provides information about the player's body and body parts in space and time, while, in parallel, visual information is also processed and delivers, for example, information about the height of the ball after it has been thrown above the player's head, which is important for timely direction of the subsequent movements to hit the ball. At that moment, vision and proprioception provide essential information for the brain to compute the most suitable positioning of the player's body to hit the ball optimally. Ultimately, all available sensory information is processed and integrated in a multisensory fashion and is further combined with the player's experience of earlier tennis serves. Finally, many small adjustments of the initial motor plan are made, based on the more recent multisensory information, in order for the player to appropriately hit the ball with the racket. In addition, during the ongoing execution, the sensorimotor system continues to process information until the movement is finished and the ball has either hit the target area or not. That leads to further evaluation of and adjustment to the finally executed motor command based on the final sensory feedback as well as cognitive appraisal.

The CNS comprises the brain and the spinal cord and is the hierarchically organized master command in motor control. The highest processing level of motor control is located in the cerebral cortex and is processed in motor and sensory cortical brain areas, such as the motor cortex, the somatosensory cortex, and the visual cortex. Beneath the cortex, several subcortical structures are involved in motor control such as the basal ganglia, the cerebellum, and the brainstem. The lowest level of motor control is the spinal cord. Together, these structures plan, execute, control, and evaluate our movements and enable us to keep our posture and balance, move our body and limbs in space and time, move our eyes, and express ourselves in speech, gesture, and mimics. Besides voluntary and goal-directed movements, very fast movements caused by specific stimuli, namely reflexes, can be processed at the spinal cord level without the involvement of higher-order centres of motor control (Carlson, 2010). In the following, the structures of the CNS most directly involved in motor control will be briefly outlined with regard to their specific function.

At the cortical level, motor and sensory areas are widely distributed over the cerebral cortex. Whereas motor regions are allocated to the frontal cerebral lobe, sensory regions spread over the parietal and occipital lobe. Motor cortical areas are the M1, the premotor cortex (PMC), the supplementary motor area, the frontal eye field, and the parietal cortex (Pinel, 2015). These motor cortical areas are primarily involved in planning and executing voluntary and goal-directed movements and can, therefore, be associated with (motor) action. Sensory information – for example, somatosensory, visual, and auditory stimuli – is processed in specific sensory brain regions, such as the somatosensory, visual, and auditory cortices. Somatosensory and motor cortical areas are sometimes referred to as the sensorimotor cortex, because of their neuroanatomical proximity. The complex flow of sensory and motor information is organized and integrated within the association cortices, such as the somatosensory association cortex, the visual association cortex, and the auditory association cortex. Within these association cortices, the transition from perception to action is processed, including higher-level abstract cognitive processing.

At the subcortical level, the basal ganglia (basal nuclei) play an essential part in movement planning, initiation, and evaluation. The basal ganglia are formed by a functional network of different nuclei and receive input via the striatum (caudate nucleus and putamen) and send output via the globus pallidus internus and the substantia nigra reticularis. Further structures of the basal ganglia are the globus pallidus externus, nucleus subthalamicus, and the substantia nigra compacta. The cerebellum is located behind the cerebral cortex, attached to the brainstem. Key motor functions are the execution of smooth movements, postural control, especially balance, and the coordination of posture and goal-directed movements. A further important function is the optimization of motor control due to the adjustment and correction of planned and executed movements, especially when movements are visually guided. The cerebellum receives sensory input via the cortex, the brainstem, and the spinal cord, and its output is sent to the motor cortex; it is further involved in movements of the eyes. The brainstem can be further divided into the pons, the medulla oblongata, and the formatio reticularis. As the brainstem receives much sensory information, it is involved in postural control via reflex loops and also in the execution of goal-directed movements. Moreover, various internal physiological processes such as cardiorespiratory mechanisms are controlled by the brainstem (Kandel, Jessell, Schwartz, Siegelbaum, & Hudspeth, 2013). Finally, the spinal cord, as the lowest processing level of motor control, is strongly involved in basal reflexes, such as the patellar reflex. Moreover, the spinal cord is not restricted to reflexes, as it is also involved in more complex movements and enables voluntary motion patterns, such as building the basis of locomotion.

Taken together, voluntary movements are mediated via the different hierarchical as well as parallel organized levels of the CNS, elucidating a direct connection between the cerebral cortex and the spinal cord. Within that sensorimotor system, a complex flow of information is processed to integrate and organize sensory and motor aspects of the control of movement.

Numerous neurobiological studies have allowed researchers to map structural and functional neural networks of sensorimotor information processing with very high precision (for an in-depth description of neurobiological structures and processes please refer to, e.g., Carlson, 2010). However, neurophysiological studies of motor control using electrical and magnetic brain imaging techniques, such as electroencephalography (EEG) and functional magnetic resonance imaging (fMRI), as well as methods of brain stimulation, such as transcranial magnetic stimulation and transcranial current stimulation, are mostly restricted to simple movements performed in mainly stationary experimental settings. Despite the great technical advances of these methods, there are still strong limitations owing to the immobility of the devices and sensitivity of motion artefacts (e.g., bad signal quality) that hinder or challenge neurophysiological investigations of more complex, naturalistic movements. It is noteworthy that there is a vast body of knowledge from neuroscience, and yet, still, little is known to answer the central questions mentioned: What aspects in a movement are controlled? What are the related functional mechanisms? And, how are movements stored in the CNS?

Primary Theories, Frameworks, and Associated Concepts

Scientist from different disciplines such as sport and exercise science, neuroscience, psychology, and engineering have developed different theoretical approaches to answer these questions, the most important of which are discussed in the following sections: (a) servo- and equilibrium-point models of motor control, (b) motor programmes, (c) concepts of information processing, (d) systems dynamics, and v) accounting for noise and variability in motor control.

Servo- and Equilibrium-Point Models of Motor Control

From the late 19th century onwards, motor control research focused strongly on the function of the spinal cord in the generation of movement (Eccles & Sherrington, 1930; Sherrington, 1906) as well as the dependence of muscle forces on length and tension (Bernstein, 1935, 1967). In the subsequent decades, different models were developed that incorporate these length–tension characteristics and spinal reflexes as the principal parameters and mechanisms that are being controlled by the CNS. The underlying assumption of such so-called servo- or equilibrium-point models is that the end-point of a movement (e.g., a specific muscle length) is set, and spinal reflexes or spring-like muscle tendon characteristics are exploited for the muscle to adjust towards it.

The theoretical basis for these models was provided by the mathematician Wiener (1948). The field of cybernetics, which he founded, focuses on feedback loops as the principle mechanisms of control. In such a closed-loop control system, the current system state (the actual value) is compared with a desired final state (the target value). If the two values do not match, the system adjusts to achieve the target value. The servo-hypothesis, which was subsequently conceptualized by Merton (1953), represents the first cybernetic closed-loop control theory with a concrete reference to motor control. Merton assumed that the target value of the muscle length is coded via the γ motoneurons, and the system state — that is, the actual muscle length — is detected via the muscle spindle, so that the two values can be gradually adjusted via the path of spinal reflexes. However, the servo-hypothesis did not withstand later experimental testing (Latash, 2008; Vallbo, 1970). One of the weak points is that the model does not explain the simultaneous activation of α and γ motoneurons during motor action (Vallbo, 1970). In addition, the muscle tension actually achieved in experimental studies is less than the tension that would theoretically be necessary to assume that the spinal stretch reflex is the sole basis of closed-loop motion control (Latash, 2008). Based on Merton's original hypothesis, however, further models were developed with the aim of eliminating the original shortcomings — so-called equilibrium point (EP) models. These include models by Feldman (1966, 1986), as well as Bizzi and colleagues (1991). In his λ model based on physiological measurement data in humans, Feldman formulated the assumption that an EP serves to control the length change of a muscle. The EP is a result of the length (λ) of the muscle, from which a stretch reflex is triggered, and the external force acting on the muscle. In contrast, Bizzi explains the mechanism to achieve the EP in the α model with mechanical mass-spring properties (an excellent summary of the different EP concepts can be found McIntyre & Bizzi, 1993). It is likely that neuromuscular closed-loop mechanisms are used to control certain parameters of a movement, such as joint stiffness. However, several streams of evidence from deafferentation studies (cf. below) as well as philosophical problems have been presented that show the limitations of these EP concepts.

Motor Programmes

Complex or sequentially executed actions require highly coordinated control of many redundant DOFs. It has, therefore, been proposed by many researchers that a specific representation of the action—that is, a motor programme—is stored in the CNS to manage the number of DOFs for a given action.

The idea of a motor programme implies that an internal image or model of an action and the steps necessary to complete that action are programmed prior to its execution. Therefore, sensory information may be processed and used during the programming process, but does not necessarily play a role during execution owing to the "open-loop" nature of the control processes. This is in contrast to the closed-loop nature of regulatory control mechanisms (cf. servo- and equilibrium-point models). With the response-chaining hypothesis, James (1890) offered an early explanatory approach to the execution of sequential movements underlying specific actions based on open-loop control mechanisms. James assumed that muscular contractions were caused by certain external and internal information. Sensory information resulting from the initial muscle contraction in turn serves as information for the subsequent movement. Complex movements would, thus, result from a series of successive response chains. Lashley (1917), on the other hand, provided evidence to disprove the response chaining hypothesis by examining a patient with a loss of sensory pathways in the knee as a result of a gunshot wound. Lashley showed that his patient was able to perform complex movement sequences despite a lack of sensory information. From this he concluded that the sequence of motion must already be centrally represented (Lashley, 1951). Influenced by, among other things, Lashely's work, Keele (1968, p. 387) formulated a first comprehensive definition of motor programmes as a set of instructions for muscle activation that is already present before the initiation of movement and can run independently of sensory information processing. Schmidt (1975), however, showed that, as attractive as Keele's definition may sound, it has two fundamental weaknesses, namely that (1) the number of movement sequences that one needs to control are so numerous that the storage capacity of the nervous system would not be sufficient to store all individual movements (with all muscle contractions involved), and (2) the learning of new movement sequences cannot be explained by this. As a direct response, Schmidt (1975) formulated the theory of generalized motor programmes (GMPs). He assumed that movements are not stored as specific unchangeable programmes, but rather as abstract schemata or classes from which concrete specifications for a movement can be extracted as required. One of the biggest disadvantages of motor programme theories is that they are often based on theoretical considerations and behavioural data, and that the neurophysiological basis is not clear. Bernstein (1935, 1967) argued for the existence of motor programmes (or engrams) storing topological features of the movement. For Henry and Rogers (1960), on the other hand, such programmes rather consisted of the exact neuromotor details (i.e., muscle activation patterns) of a specific action.

Perhaps the most appropriate physiological equivalents to motor programmes are so-called central pattern generators (CPGs). Brown (1911) has documented (roughly) coordinated gait actions in a deafferented cat (i.e., section afferent fibres from the cat's hind limbs) after additional decerebration (i.e., section of the brain stem and disruption of connections to higher centres). The sequenced activation of flexor and extensor muscles of the two limbs has subsequently been shown to be caused by a circular neural network, a CPG, that codes the timing of muscle activity. Further studies confirmed the existence of CPGs in other animals (see Marder & Bucher, 2001, for a review) and also for different coordination modes (Forssberg, Grillner, Halbertsma, & Rossignol, 1980).

By means of electrically stimulating different areas of the primary sensory and motor cortices, Penfield and Boldrey (1937) were able to demonstrate that specific regions of the body are encoded by localized areas in the primary motor and sensory cortices. This later led to the well-known abstraction of the somatotopic organization of body parts in the cerebral cortex related to motor functions and sensory sensation, as the motor and sensory homunculus (Penfield, 1958). However, the motor responses in Penfield's studies were not goal-directed and had little to do with specific actions—for example, as performed in everyday life. It was not until the early 2000s that Graziano, Taylor, Moore, and Cooke (2002) were able to show that a prolonged (500 ms) stimulation of the PMC in monkeys actually triggers goal-directed movement sequences, such as a feeding movement, in which the hand is led to the mouth and the mouth is opened simultaneously. Interestingly, the movement was performed by stimulating the same area with the same aim, even if the initial position of the hand was changed. It was concluded that the somatotopic maps of the motor cortex do not refer to specific muscle groups, but to velocities and positions in space—that is, to potential targets of movements in the proximal gripping area.

Given the results derived from neurophysiological studies of CPGs, it is evident that certain aspects of an action are stored in functional neural networks. The term "motor programme", on the other hand, may be misleading as it suggests stereotypical activation sequences for any given action. Preprogramming, for example, of joint torques, muscle activation, end-point displacement, and so on, would not be appropriate to control an action as these are clearly dependent on external and internal conditions that are different every time we execute an action. Therefore, theories on motor control clearly need to incorporate the dynamic interaction between the individual and the many DOFs with the environment. This dynamic interaction has been considered within theories on perception and action (cf. below).

Concepts of Information Processing

In addition to the basic concepts of the organization of motor control described above, a large body of research has been concerned with the speed of sensorimotor information processing and the underlying cognitive mechanisms. Donders (1868, cf. Donders, 1969) asked participants to perform a series of tasks that are similar but, however, require different steps of information processing (e.g., stimulus identification or response selection). He used a systematic subtractive method to infer the processing time these different steps require (assuming serial processing). As has been shown since, these processing steps are not as simple as Donders imagined and may not just run serially, but also, to an extent, in an overlapping fashion. In addition, the number of stimuli (or bits of information that have to be processed) in choice reaction time tasks have a strong impact on the speed of execution. Hick (1952) and Hyman

(1953) discovered this relation between the number of bits to be processed in a choice reaction time task and the corresponding response time and that this relation can be modelled extremely well using a logarithmic function of the form $T = b * \log_2(n - 1)$, where T is the reaction time, b is a constant (to be determined empirically), and n denotes the number of bits to be processed. Briefly, after the discovery of this so-called Hick–Hyman law, a similar discovery was made for the relationship between movement time and requirements for precision and movement amplitude (or distance) in precision tasks. Fitts (1954) showed the difficulty index (*ID*) of a given task is defined by a logarithmic relationship of the precision (*W*) amplitude (*D*) quotient: $ID = \log_2\left(\frac{2D}{W}\right)$, and that movement time and *ID* are linearly related.

Such studies on the relationship between the perception of information and the time required to produce an appropriate movement contribute to understanding of the cognitive mechanisms that are involved in sensorimotor information processing. They are, however, limited with respect to the insight they provide about the mechanisms underlying the execution of actions coordinated with the environment based on sensorimotor control mechanisms. This coordinated interaction between perception and action is discussed in the next section.

Perception and Action

So far, the theoretical approaches that were being discussed focused on the neuromuscular control mechanisms (cf. section on servo- and equilibrium-point models), neurocognitive aspects of motor control (cf. section on motor programmes and information processing), and information processing (cf. section on concepts of information processing). Goal-directed actions in any situation, however, not only require the execution of stereotypical movement sequences, but also afford coordination of our actions with the environment. Imagine riding a bike through city traffic during rush hour or downhill on a narrow, single trail. In both cases, our actions need to be coordinated with the environment, with little time to process the excessive amount of visual information around us. In that respect, the 1970s signify a paradigm shift in that perception was considered less of a passive aspect of information processing but rather an active part, emphasizing the dynamic interaction between perception and action in the control of movements.

In a study on the visual control of stance, Lee and Lishman (1975) highlighted the direct impact of visual flow fields (i.e., visually perceived motion) on posture. He showed that, by changing the projection size of an object on the retina, it is very easy to calculate the time of contact (time to contact) with this object. From this, Lee (1976, 1998) deduced that the integration of visual information into the motor process is likely to occur via the variable tau (τ). Lee subsequently created a time-to-contact or τ-theory using information on the time to close (visual) gaps as a control parameter for actions (Lee, 1976, 1998).

A generalized theory on the dynamic interaction between visual perception and motor action was described shortly after Lee's introduction of τ-theory by Gibson (1979) in his work *The Ecological Approach to Visual Perception*. According to Gibson, perceiving our environment is an entirely active process. The way humans (or animals) perceive the world strongly depends on their actions and skills. When we observe a specific tool or piece of sports equipment, for example, we perceive the different possibilities of interacting with it. We perceive objects (or situations) differently if we know how we can (inter)act with them. These so-called "affordances" of an object or situation thus strongly depend on our motor skills, and, further, the perception directly influences the motor action. "Locomotion and manipulation [...] are controlled not by the brain, but by information, that is, by seeing oneself in the world" (Gibson, 1979, p. 225).

Several lines of evidence from neurocognitive and physiological studies further highlighted the close relationship between perception and action. In this vein, Prinz (1997) proposed a common coding—that is, some overlap between the neural coding of sensory perceived stimuli and motor actions, based on different classes of neurocognitive paradigms, namely: induction paradigms in which perception of certain stimuli enhances actions by virtue of similarity, and interference paradigms by which perception of certain stimuli interferes with actions by virtue of (dis)similarity. With the discovery of mirror neurons in the macaque brain, on the other hand, di Pellegrino, Fadiga, Fogassi, Gallese, and Rizzolatti (1992) provided direct physiological evidence of such a common coding. The group showed that specific neurons in the area F5 (corresponding to the human premotor area) displayed the same activation pattern when the monkey performed a specific grasp action and when it observed the experimenter performing the same action. To date, a direct proof of mirror neurons in the human brain has not been found, mainly owing to the difficulty of measuring the activity of single neurons in humans. Measures of larger network activity—for example, using EEG or fMRI—are indicative of the existence of human mirror neuron systems, however.

Systems Dynamics

Like many systems in nature such as climate, planet, or social systems, the human body is far from being static or linearly organized, but is rather a complex dynamical system that has states being determined by different system components. Such states often show a macroscopic order—for example, atmospheric circulation, planetary orbits, or swarm behaviour—and they are able to maintain different steady system states. Furthermore, a complex interaction of many elemental variables determines the state of the system (for an in-depth introduction into system dynamics, please refer to Kelso, 1995). Following the development of chaos theory in the second half of the 20th century (Lorenz, 1963), researchers in physics began to study the behaviour of complex dynamical systems extensively. The field of mathematics is particularly concerned with predicting the behaviour of "seemingly" chaotic systems by use of nonlinear differential equations. The theory of "synergetics" (Haken, 1977), initially being developed as an explanation of the laser effect, soon became a generalized theory—also in humanities and social sciences—explaining the formation of coordinated patterns in complex dynamical systems, following principles of self-organization. Central to this theory is the concept of low-dimensional order parameters—that is, variables that describe the macroscopic state of a system. Further, the principle of enslaving is used to explain the emergence of order with respect to the many DOFs in a complex system. That is, lower-dimensional (long-lasting) quantities enslave the higher-dimensional (short-lasting) quantities and, thus, determine their behaviour. For example, when thinking of walking, the relative phase between the legs can be seen as a lower-dimensional order parameter (i.e., when one leg is in its stance phase, the other is in the swing phase). Each joint is now enslaved to be flexed or extended according to the task dynamics of the relative phase.

Soon thereafter, the systems dynamics view became central to the explanation of human physiological and behavioural functioning in general and of coordinated movement patterns in particular. Kugler, Kelso, and Turvey (1980) presented an important milestone in the development of the dynamic systems theory of motor control. Their concept of "coordinative structures" denotes the motor control equivalent of a dissipative structure. Dissipative structures are reproducible states of order that can emerge in a dissipative system—for example, atmospheric convection. In that respect, coordinative structures are functional units that are created on different levels, such as groups of body segments, muscles (i.e., synergies), or neurons. This concept is in drastic contrast to the programme-oriented and cybernetic concepts of motor control that prevailed before, in which fixed circuits or preprogrammed sets of instructions are assumed to be the central control structures (Kugler et al., 1980).

Empirical testing of the theoretical assumptions and predictions that arise from the dynamical systems perspective on motor control has focused on a rhythmic (oscillating) bimanual movement task. Kelso (1984) observed that in-phase bimanual coordination modes (i.e., simultaneous activation of homologous muscles during continuous ab- and adduction movements of the index fingers) are more stable, showing fewer fluctuations compared with antiphase modes (i.e., alternating muscle activation). Particularly at higher frequencies, sudden phase transitions are observable when less stable antiphase coordination modes are shifted to in-phase. Central concepts and predictions of the theory were developed and tested using Kelso's experimental paradigm, later being termed the Haken–Kelso–Bunz model (Haken, Kelso, & Bunz, 1985): (a) The relative phase of the fingers in the movement cycle are the lower-order collective variables (order parameters) that describe the current state (or coordination mode) of a system. (b) Different coordination modes (i.e., in-phase and antiphase) exist that are stable under certain conditions. (c) The stability of the antiphase coordination mode is lost with increasing movement frequency, and the system is subsequently governed by the in-phase mode. The movement frequency is, thus, a control parameter that guides the system through its different states. The phase transitions occur suddenly and in a nonlinear fashion. (d) A hysteresis effect is found—that is, the attractiveness of currently existing system states and dwelling of the system in that particular state. A great example of the hysteresis of the motor system has been provided by Diedrich and Warren (1995) for locomotor phase transitions—that is, the change from walking to running that occurs spontaneously at a certain velocity. This velocity has been shown to be higher in individuals when changing from walking to running than vice versa.

Accounting for Noise and Variability in Motor Control

Noise in information processing and variability of action execution are fundamental characteristics of human movement. Noise can occur at all levels of sensorimotor information processing (Faisal, Selen, & Wolpert, 2008). It arises from random spontaneous activity within the cortex and the body systems. Moreover, spontaneous activity could show a highly coherent spatiotemporal structure, and therewith it is assumed that the pattern of this spontaneous activity may shape neural responses (Fiser, Chiu, & Weliky, 2004).

Variability of action execution, on the other hand, can be found at different levels. Imagine trying to throw a dart at the same spot on the board again and again. Even highly professional darts players will not be able to hit the exact same spot, let alone novices. On the other hand, one may have to produce alike actions under different environmental conditions— for example, hitting the dartboard in almost the spot from different positions. Professional darts players would not have any difficulties doing so. Variable action execution may, thus, either be seen as a source of error affecting the performance, or as a way to flexibly adjust to changing environmental conditions or stochastic perturbations (e.g. noise). Although the theoretical motor programme framework often rather takes the former perspective on movement variability (i.e., a source of error), the complex dynamical systems perspective rather takes the latter perspective and, furthermore, provides a reasonable account to explain how the motor system deals with the "immanent noise".

When measuring elements of an action, such as movement kinematics, force production, or electrophysiological signals, the stochastic noise may become apparent on an effector level.

These fluctuations, on the other hand, may not necessarily have a large effect on the task performance. When younger adults produce a constant grip force, for example, high-frequency random fluctuations in force production have been shown. These fluctuations disappear in older and highly aged adults, resulting in greater regularity in the produced force. On the other hand, task performance (i.e., maintaining the same force level) is reduced in older adults (Vaillancourt & Newell, 2003). These random fluctuations are assumed to be a signature of redundant (neuromuscular) DOFs that stabilize the task in a self-organized manner (i.e., the task goal is stabilized without each DOF being controlled separately). On the other hand, when the task is constrained by a different dynamic, such as producing a regular pattern in the form of a sine-wave, the DOFs are enslaved by the new task dynamics, and the random fluctuations are reduced, a function that is likewise affected in individuals with reduced systems complexity—for example, following healthy ageing or disease (Lipsitz & Goldberger, 1992).

The complexity of the motor system and the redundancy or rather abundance of DOFs for any given action, which Bernstein (1967) once referred to as the central problem of control, can also be seen as a possible solution by which action goals can be kept stable despite constantly changing external and internal conditions. The abundance of DOFs provides the system with not just one, but a manifold of solutions for any given task. The uncontrolled manifold hypothesis (Scholz & Schöner, 1999) is an operationalized concept relating the presence of noise or variability on the level of the elemental variables to that of the task variables. In a high-dimensional set of combinations of all elemental DOFs that determine the system state, the uncontrolled manifold is the subspace of combinations that yield the correct task goal. Imagine a redundant bimanual force control task, for example, where the index finger of each hand (i.e., two DOFs) have to produce a specific total force (i.e., one DOF) by combining the force produced by each index finger. The uncontrolled manifold would be a one-dimensional space including all possible combinations of left and right finger force that meet the task demand. Variability in direction of the uncontrolled manifold does not affect the task performance. Variability in the orthogonal direction, on the other hand, does affect the task. Several studies have shown that good motor control is characterized by an increased variance in direction and a decreased variance orthogonal to the uncontrolled manifold (Latash, Scholz, & Schoner, 2007; Scholz & Schöner, 1999). However, motor control research is often conducted in highly controlled experimental settings where the DOFs are reduced to a minimum. Hence, only fine, simple sensorimotor tasks (often including only one DOF) are used for investigations, rather than more complex, sport-related (e.g., gross motor) tasks.

Evidently, the capacity to achieve the same action goal in multiple ways is not a disadvantage for motor control, and healthy motor systems seem to exploit this variability to a certain extent. These observations lead (back) to the questions of which aspects of a movement are controlled, and what the guiding principles of an action are. It is probable that the sensorimotor system does not seek a single solution, but rather a kind of "solution space" for a given action. Within that solution space, the most stable task performance is striven for, which is least affected by the presence of stochastic noise (Sternad, Abe, Hu, & Müller, 2011).

Conclusion

Motor control is the ability to direct movements in a given environment (e.g., on the tennis court) and for a given task (e.g., to perform a tennis serve). In summary, this chapter briefly describes fundamental structures of the CNS involved in the control of movements, which are the *cerebral cortex*, the *basal ganglia*, the *cerebellum*, and the *spinal cord*. Further, central theories, frameworks, and concepts of motor control are presented, including the *servo-* and equilibrium-point models of motor control, the *theory of motor programmes*, the *concept of action and perception*, the *systems dynamics theory*, and *theoretical approaches accounting for noise and variability in motor control*. This broad overview of theoretical considerations also provides a brief historical evolution of the field of motor control and shows the abundance of scientific disciplines involved in motor control research. Altogether, these theories create a framework for interpreting how humans control their manifold movements in everyday life and also in special environments, such as sports. Although some theoretical frameworks and approaches were conceptualized more than 100 years ago, the field of motor control is still expanding, and the problem of DOFs is still not solved. It is noteworthy that, owing to the broad theoretical perspectives of motor control and growing knowledge about neurobiological structures and processes, our understanding of motor control has increased enormously So far, however, a mechanistic incorporation of theoretical concepts of motor control into neurobiological substrates is widely missing.

To conclude, the complex phenomenon of motor control cannot completely be handled by one theory, but needs to be approached from different perspectives. This holistic perspective on motor control might contribute to the development and validation of theoretical aspects, hypotheses, and studies of motor control, as well as to practical applications, such as optimization of clinical practice or sports training.

References

Bernstein, N. A. (1935). The problem of interrelation between coordination and localization. *Archives of Biological Sciences, 38*, 1–34.

Bernstein, N. A. (1967). *The co-ordination and regulation of movements.* Oxford, UK: Pergamon Press.

Bizzi, E., Mussa-Ivaldi, F., & Giszter, S. (1991). Computations underlying the execution of movement: A biological perspective. *Science, 253*, 287–291.

Brown, T. G. (1911). The intrinsic factors in the act of progression in the mammal. *Proceedings of the Royal Society of London. Series B, Containing Papers of a Biological Character, 84*, 308–319.

Carlson, N. R. (2010). *Physiology of behavior* (10th ed.). Boston, MA: Pearson/Allyn & Bacon.

Di Pellegrino, G., Fadiga, L., Fogassi, L., Gallese, V., & Rizzolatti, G. (1992). Understanding motor events: A neurophysiological study. *Experimental Brain Research, 91*, 176–180.

Diedrich, F. J., & Warren, W. H., Jr. (1995). Why change gaits? Dynamics of the walk–run transition. *Journal of Experimental Psycholology: Human Perception and Performance, 21*, 183–202.

Donders, F. C. (1868). Over de snelheid van psychische processen. *Onderzoekingen gedaan in het Physiologisch Laboratorium der Utrechtsche Hoogeschool, 1868–1869*(II), 92–120.

Donders, F. C. (1969). On the speed of mental processes. *Acta Psychologica, 30*, 412–431.

Eccles, J. C., & Sherrington, C. S. (1930). Numbers and contraction-values of individual motor-units examined in some muscles of the limb. *Proceedings of the Royal Society of London. Series B, Containing Papers of a Biological Character, 106*, 326–357.

Faisal, A. A., Selen, L. P., & Wolpert, D. M. (2008). Noise in the nervous system. *Nature Reviews Neuroscience, 9*, 292–303.

Feldman, A. G. (1966). On the functional tuning of the nervous system in movement control or preservation of stationary pose. II. Adjustable parameters in muscles. *Biofizika, 11*, 498–508.

Feldman, A. G. (1986). Once more on the equilibrium-point hypothesis (λ model) for motor control. *Journal of Motor Behavior, 18*, 17–54.

Fiser, J., Chiu, C., & Weliky, M. (2004). Small modulation of ongoing cortical dynamics by sensory input during natural vision. *Nature, 431*, 573–578.

Fitts, P. M. (1954). The information capacity of the human motor system in controlling the amplitude of movement. *Journal of Experimental Psychology, 47*, 381–391.

Forssberg, H., Grillner, S., Halbertsma, J., & Rossignol, S. (1980). The locomotion of the low spinal cat. II. Interlimb coordination. *Acta Physiologica Scandinavica, 108*(3), 283–295.

Gibson, J. J. (1979). *The ecological approach to visual perception.* Boston, MA: Houghton, Mifflin.

Graziano, M. S., Taylor, C. S., Moore, T., & Cooke, D. F. (2002). The cortical control of movement revisited. *Neuron, 36*, 349–362.

Haken, H. (1977). *Synergetics—an introduction: Nonequilibrium phase transitions and self-organization in physics, chemistry, and biology.* Berlin: Springer.

Haken, H., Kelso, J. A. S., & Bunz, H. (1985). A theoretical model of phase transitions in human hand movements. *Biological Cybernetics, 51*, 347–356.

Henry, F. M., & Rogers, D. E. (1960). Increased response latency for complicated movements and a "memory drum" theory of neuromotor reaction. *Research Quarterly of the American Association for Health, Physical Education, & Recreation, 31*, 448–458.

Hick, W. E. (1952). On the rate of gain of information. *The Quarterly Journal of Experimental Psychology, 4*, 11–26.

Hyman, R. (1953). Stimulus information as a determinant of reaction time. *Journal of Experimental Psychology, 45*, 188–196.

James, W. (1890). *The principles of psychology* (Vol. I). New York: Henry Holt.

Kandel, E. R., Jessell, T. M., Schwartz, J. H., Siegelbaum, S. A., & Hudspeth, A. J. (2013). *Principles of neural science* (5th ed.). New York: McGraw-Hill Education.

Keele, S. W. (1968). Movement control in skilled motor performance. *Psychological Bulletin, 70*, 387–403.

Kelso, J. A. S. (1984). Phase transitions and critical behavior in human bimanual coordination. *American Journal of Physiology, 246*, R1000–1004. doi:10.1152/ajpregu.1984.246.6.R1000

Kelso, J. A. S. (1995). *Dynamic patterns: The self-organization of brain and behavior.* Cambridge, MA: MIT Press.

Kugler, P., Kelso, J. A. S., & Turvey, M. T. (1980). On the concept of coordinative structures as dissipative structures: I theoretical lines of convergence. In G. E. Stelmach & J. Requin (Eds.), *Advances in psychology* (Vol. 1, pp. 3–47). Amsterdam: North-Holland.

Lashley, K. S. (1917). The accuracy of movement in the absence of excitation from the moving organ. *American Journal of Physiology, 43*, 169–194.

Lashley, K. S. (1951). The problem of serial order in behavior. In *Cerebral mechanisms in behavior; the Hixon Symposium.* (pp. 112–146). Oxford, UK: Wiley.

Latash, M. L. (2008). Evolution of motor control: From reflexes and motor programs to the equilibrium-point hypothesis. *Journal of Human Kinetics, 19*(19), 3–24.

Latash, M. L., Scholz, J. P., & Schoner, G. (2007). Toward a new theory of motor synergies. *Motor Control, 11*, 276–308.

Latash, M. L., & Zatsiorsky, V. M. (2016). *Biomechanics and motor control: Defining central concepts.* London: Elsevier.

Lee, D. N. (1976). A theory of visual control of braking based on information about time-to-collision. *Perception, 5*, 437–459.

Lee, D. N. (1998). Guiding movement by coupling taus. *Ecological Psychology, 10*, 221–250.

Lee, D. N., & Lishman, J. R. (1975). Visual proprioceptive control of stance. *Journal of Human Movement Studies, 1*, 87–95.

Lipsitz, L. A., & Goldberger, A. L. (1992). Loss of "complexity" and aging. Potential applications of fractals and chaos theory to senescence. *Jama, 267*, 1806–1809. doi:10.1001/jama.1992.03480130122036

Lorenz, E. N. (1963). Deterministic nonperiodic flow. *Journal of the Atmospheric Sciences, 20*, 130–141.

Marder, E., & Bucher, D. (2001). Central pattern generators and the control of rhythmic movements. *Current Biology, 11*, R986–996. doi:10.1016/S0960-9822(01)00581-4

McIntyre, J., & Bizzi, E. (1993). Servo hypotheses for the biological control of movement. *Journal of Motor Behavior, 25*, 193–202.

Merton, P. A. (1953). Speculations on the servo-control of movement. In J. Malcolm & J. A. B. Gray (Eds.), *Ciba foundation symposium—the spinal cord* (p. 247). Boston, MA: Little, Brown and Co.

Penfield, W. (1958). *The excitable cortex in conscious man.* Springfield, IL: C. C. Thomas.

Penfield, W., & Boldrey, E. (1937). Somatic motor and sensory representation in the cerebral cortex of man as studied by electrical stimulation. *Brain, 60*, 389–443.

Pinel, J. P. J. (2015). *Biopsychology* (8th ed.). Boston, MA: Allyn & Bacon.

Prinz, W. (1997). Perception and action planning. *European Journal of Cognitive Psychology, 9*, 129–154.

Schmidt, R. A. (1975). A schema theory of discrete motor skill learning. *Psychological Review, 82*, 225–260.

Scholz, J. P., & Schöner, G. (1999). The uncontrolled manifold concept: Identifying control variables for a functional task. *Experimental Brain Research, 126,* 289–306.

Sherrington, C. S. (1906). *The integrative action of the nervous system.* New Haven, CT: Yale University Press.

Shumway-Cook, A., & Woollacott, M. H. (2016). *Motor control: Translating research into clinical practice.* Alphen: Wolters Kluwer.

Sternad, D., Abe, M. O., Hu, X., & Müller, H. (2011). Neuromotor noise, error tolerance and velocity-dependent costs in skilled performance. *PLoS Computational Biology, 7*(9), e1002159–e1002159. doi:10.1371/journal.pcbi.1002159

Vaillancourt, D. E., & Newell, K. M. (2003). Aging and the time and frequency structure of force output variability. *Journal of Applied Physiology, 94,* 903–912.

Vallbo, Å. B. (1970). Discharge patterns in human muscle spindle afferents during isometric voluntary contractions. *Acta Physiologica Scandinavica, 80,* 552–566.

Voelcker-Rehage, C. (2008). Motor-skill learning in older adults—A review of studies on age-related differences. *European Review of Aging and Physical Activity, 5,* 5–16.

Wiener, N. (1948). *Cybernetics; or control and communication in the animal and the machine.* Oxford, UK: John Wiley.

26
MOTOR LEARNING

Nicole T. Ong and Nicola J. Hodges

Introduction

Motor learning involves processes that develop with experience, which changes an individual's behaviours and internal state. These processes are evidenced by "relatively permanent improvements in the potential or capability for skilled behaviour" (Schmidt & Lee, 2011, p. 327). Examples of processes or internal states that change with learning are: attention, memory, perception, and neuromuscular patterns of activation. Although developmental influences, such as a learner's physical and cognitive maturation, will affect an individual's capability for skilled behaviour, motor learning is specifically defined with respect to changes that occur as a consequence of experience or dedication to practice. Other terms that also refer to the phenomenon of motor learning are: motor skill acquisition, perceptual-motor learning, psychomotor learning, and sensorimotor learning.

Effective practice for motor learning tends to be goal-oriented and may involve as few or as many trials as demanded by the complexity of the task and the corresponding skill of the learner. Improvement in an individual's capability for skilled movement may consist of a change in quality of movement production (such as increased motor efficiency leading to decreased energy expenditure, faster reaction time, or greater force production) and/or a greater likelihood of success in achieving desired outcome goals, such as improvement in response consistency or a reduction in error. Researchers are often concerned with determining how these variables relating to learning efficiency and effectiveness can be improved through manipulations to information and conditions of practice, such as instructions, feedback, and task scheduling.

Though learning is best indexed by changes in behavioural outcomes, the processes and internal states influencing an individual's current performance are not necessarily related to learning. For instance, fatigue after a long practice session may result in markedly diminished performance, or the presence of a monetary incentive could spur an individual to an elevated, but atypical, level of performance. Thus, immediate conclusions made on the efficacy of a practice intervention could be masked by these temporary performance factors. Hence, researchers control for the impact of such performance factors on assessments of learning by measuring performance on a retention or transfer test, typically administered after a period of delay known as the retention interval (see the sections below on "Retention" and "Transfer" for further discussion). The "gold standard" for the retention interval that motor learning researchers apply is ~24 hours, but others have measured performance for longer periods in order to draw conclusions about stable changes in performance and the degree of forgetting.

Learning is also possible without any overt changes in performance. Sometimes this is referred to as "overlearning" (Schmidt & Lee, 2011), which manifests as a period of performance plateau or saturation during practice. Although there are no indicators of behavioural change, changes are occurring in the processes underpinning motor control. As an illustration, attentional processes tend to shift from more "controlled" to more "automatic" (i.e., from attention-demanding to not demanding) with increased skill (Fitts & Posner, 1967). There may not be an overt change in performance, as skill execution becomes more autonomous, but an individual is better able to simultaneously perform a secondary, attention-demanding task without interference (see the section below on "Progressions in learning based on a reduction or change in higher-level cognitive processes"). A lack of change in performance may also signal a failure to measure appropriate aspects of performance or use a sensitive enough measure (such as moving from looking at outcomes to movement form or from number of target hits to millimetre differences in target accuracy).

Primary Theories, Frameworks, and Associated Concepts

We discuss four general theoretical approaches that are most frequently cited in motor learning research. These comprise: (1) cognitive/information processing, (2) ecological dynamics, (3) neurophysiological models and mechanisms, and (4) psychosocial perspectives. These approaches reflect differential emphasis on internal "representational" processes (information processing) versus non-representational, behavioural dynamics' approaches (ecological dynamics), as well as different levels of analysis (neurophysiological) versus behavioural. They also result from differences in methods and experimental tasks, which we expand upon below (e.g., discrete actions versus continuous actions).

Cognitive/Information Processing

Cognitive information-processing accounts share similarities in that these approaches to motor learning are heavily influenced by determination of the cognitive processes that mediate performance and learning. Error processing and feedback are important facets of these theories and frameworks detailed below.

Adam's Closed-Loop Theory

Adam's closed-loop theory emphasizes the importance of processing information related to movement outcomes (or knowledge of results) and sensory feedback for motor learning (Adams, 1971). Two traces or states of memory are thought to guide movement. The memory trace provides the motor commands to drive the initial portion of a movement, and the perceptual trace provides a "reference of correctness". This latter memory state is important for the detection of discrepancies between sensory feedback and an intended movement, affording what is termed "closed-loop" (feedback-based) control until movement completion. Experience strengthens these memory traces.

In initial learning, when an individual does not have correct experiences of a motor skill, the perceptual trace of the correct movement would be weak as there are relatively few correct movement traces compared with incorrect traces. The learner is heavily dependent on outcome-related feedback, typically provided by external sources, to help guide any repetitions if the task goal was not achieved. As the performer improves with practice, the perceptual trace for the correct movement increases in strength, as a relatively large number of correct perceptual traces are accumulated compared with incorrect ones. Dependence on external feedback diminishes as the correct perceptual trace is strengthened and proficiency increases.

One of the long-lasting legacies of this theory is the importance placed on various types of feedback for minimizing error and guiding performers towards increasing accuracy. With practice, there is an increased reliance on response-produced sensory/intrinsic feedback rather than externally provided/augmented feedback. This theory prompted much research into the role of feedback for motor learning and the importance of the development of error-detection mechanisms for effective motor performance. Although the theory is still widely cited in many textbooks, it is rarely cited in current motor learning research.

Schema Theory

Schema theory was developed by Richard Schmidt, a student of Adams (Schmidt, 1975). The main difference between this theory and that of Adam's is that, in schema theory, the movement can be controlled by the motor trace (or motor programme) and executed without influence from sensory feedback (termed "open-loop" control). As such, the motor programme contains motor commands that are specified in advance of the movement. This idea of a motor programme was not, however, unique to schema theory (e.g., Keele, 1968). As with Adam's theory, there are two memory states: (1) the recall memory/schema, which controls movement execution; and (2) the recognition memory/schema, which provides a reference of correctness for comparing sensory feedback, allowing for error evaluation at the end of the movement or after the motor programme has run. Similar to closed-loop theory, feedback is essential for motor learning in schema theory, as knowledge of movement outcomes is necessary for developing the recall and recognition schemas.

A key aspect of schema theory for motor learning is the idea that individuals acquire "generalized" motor programmes (GMPs). Rather than specific programmes for every action, the idea was that individuals develop and store abstract representations for a class of motor skills that contains "invariant" features (e.g., the proportion of time between onset and offset of muscles) which stay relatively consistent despite changes to the effectors used or the overall duration of an action. With practice, relations are developed between specific parameters (i.e., overall timing, overall force, the limb or muscles used) and contextual factors and various outcomes or sensory consequences. These relations are referred to as schemas. For instance, to pitch a baseball to a catcher, a pitcher would have stored a template of a pitch that would contain relatively invariant features. Taking into account the desired outcome (e.g., a 60-ft pitch) and contextual conditions, they would specify the effector (e.g., dominant right arm) and the absolute force (e.g., 15 N) that would be needed to cover the desired distance. Even if the pitcher had not pitched that distance before, if they had pitched to similar distances, they would be able to use the stored schema to select parameters that would likely produce the novel action. Hence, schema theory provides an explanation for how individuals are able to execute novel variations of a motor task with unexpected proficiency.

In contrast to closed-loop theory, errors during practice are not detrimental to learning as they provide information that informs the schema. Considerable empirical evidence exists supporting this idea through what is known as variability of practice research (Van Rossum, 1990). More variable practice around a criterion task tends to lead to poorer immediate performance than constant practice of the same task but, importantly, results in more robust long-term learning and transfer to new, unpractised conditions (e.g., Shea & Kohl, 1991). Variation in task parameters strengthens the recall and recognition schemas for a motor skill such that, with increased movement experiences, not only is execution accuracy increased via the recall schema (i.e., correct selection of parameters), but the recognition schema gives a more accurate prediction of anticipated sensory effects, improving fast, feedforward-based error detection. As stated below, these ideas concerning feedforward- and feedback-based error correction strategies are central to computational theories of motor control and the idea of internal models, which have tended to dominate laboratory-based research into motor learning processes over the past decade.

Internal Models

Motor learning entails the mastery of sensorimotor transformations or mappings relating motor commands to sensory feedback. Computational neuroscientists and engineers have made significant progress in studying and modelling how these transformations are learned through the concept of internal models (e.g., Wolpert, Ghahramani, & Jordan, 1995; Wolpert, Miall, & Kawato, 1998). Major overlaps exist between the functions of internal models and memory representations based on schema theory. Two types of internal model have been conceptualized. Analogous to the concept of recognition memory in schema theory, the forward model captures the causal relationship between inputs (motor commands) and outputs (sensory consequences) of the motor system in a given context. The function of the inverse model is similar to recall memory in that it inverts the causal relationship between sensory consequences and motor commands to provide an estimation of the motor commands for generating a desired outcome.

To acquire and maintain reliable internal models for motor control, an individual learns to associate repeated pairings of motor commands with the corresponding sensory consequences. For learning or behavioural adaptations to take place, and for these internal models to be updated, the learner must experience a discrepancy between the expected and actual sensory consequences as a result of movement execution. Hypothetically, a copy of the motor command is generated, termed an "efference copy", that interacts with the forward model to give a prediction of the sensory consequences of an action (i.e., feedforward processing). When discrepancies are experienced, both the forward and inverse internal models are updated, so that motor commands are essentially modified to suit the new sensorimotor mapping. It has been suggested that the forward model is updated before the inverse model and plays a role in the training of the inverse model.

Empirical work on internal models is typically based on what are termed visuomotor or dynamical (force-field) adaptation tasks. In adaptation studies, perturbations are introduced so that a sensory discrepancy is experienced, requiring modifications to motor commands. With sufficient practice, learners adapt to the perturbation, and error is reduced (e.g., aiming at targets that are inverted or rotated). Upon removal of these perturbations, "after-effects" are noted, which are compensatory actions opposite to the direction of the perturbation. These after-effects arise even when performers are informed that the environment is normal, and, hence, are unintentional (or implicit). They are taken as evidence that a performer's internal models or sensorimotor mappings for the task have been updated, and, hence, some learning has occurred. Recent debates in this area are often centred around the neurophysiological mechanisms underpinning the various models and the independence of error signals that drive implicit updating and explicit/strategic changes to motor plans (e.g., Huang & Shadmehr, 2007; Taylor & Ivry, 2014).

Cognitive Effort and Challenge

Motor learning is not merely influenced by the amount of practice, but also by the quality of the practice. Two well-studied practice conditions are often cited in support of practice quality effects on motor learning: the contextual interference effect (Shea & Morgan, 1979), related to practice organization of multiple skills; and the guidance hypothesis (Winstein & Schmidt, 1990), related to the impact of augmented feedback on motor learning.

An interference that occurs when a motor skill is practised in the context of other skills is termed the contextual interference (CI) effect. This interference is actually good for longer-term learning, but not for short-term performance. When practice is organized in a more random manner, by the interleaving of the practice trials of all skills so that each skill is typically not repeated more than once, overall performance is degraded in comparison with that achieved with blocked practice. In blocked practice, trials of one skill are performed repetitively before a switch to practising the next skill, such that CI is low. However, on retention or transfer tests, an "acquisition-retention reversal" is typically observed, where the presence of greater interference in the practice context (random practice) results in longer-lasting learning benefits compared with low-interference, blocked practice. These CI effects are thought to be due to differences in cognitive-processing activities. Random practice promotes deeper processing and understanding of each skill ("elaborative processing hypothesis"; Shea & Zimny, 1983) or/and increased cognitive effort in organizing plans of actions during practice ("forgetting and reconstruction hypothesis"; Lee & Magill, 1983) compared with blocked practice. In general, conditions that make practice more challenging or effortful are more beneficial to motor learning.

Research on the guidance hypothesis underscores the importance of practice quality, related to cognitive processing, on motor learning. The guidance hypothesis arose out of research related to the frequency and timing of augmented (also termed extrinsic) feedback, particularly information related to the outcome of the movement, termed knowledge of results (KR). Augmented feedback, which can be provided by a coach or teacher, or perhaps by some technical device such as a phone video app, serves to guide the learner through the immediate highlighting of errors in performance. However, when provided too soon or too frequently, augmented feedback can be detrimental to learning, eliciting an acquisition-retention reversal, as discussed for the CI effect. So, for example, more frequent KR (e.g., KR provided on 100% of trials) is detrimental to learning relative to less frequent KR (e.g., Sullivan, Kantak, & Burtner, 2008).

According to the guidance hypothesis, the prescriptive aspect of KR prevents individuals from processing their own intrinsic feedback, thus impairing error detection and correction processes. The result is that learners become dependent on the extrinsic KR feedback and are unable to apply appropriate adjustments or corrective strategies when this source of feedback is unavailable. Withholding or delaying KR or providing summary feedback only after several trials serves to reduce the guidance effects of KR on motor learning (Schmidt & Lee, 2011). When participants have been asked to estimate their error on each trial before receiving KR on 100% of the trials, this strategy has also been effective in reducing the negative retention effects of practising with a high frequency of KR (e.g., Guadagnoli & Kohl, 2001). Here, engaging in effortful activities related to detection of error benefited learning.

The principle common to both contextual interference and the guidance hypothesis of augmented feedback is that effortful or challenging practice benefits learning while potentially suppressing practice performance. Yet, there are documented cases where too much challenge was found to be a hindrance to learning. For instance, when random and blocked practices were separately administered to two groups of novices that were learning a nominally (or inherently) difficult task, longer-term learning in the random practice group was diminished compared with the blocked practice group (Guadagnoli, Holcomb, & Weber, 1999). It was argued that task and individual factors moderated the gains that could be attained from incorporating challenge into practice. Guadagnoli and Lee (2004) proposed the challenge point framework to help explain how challenge and learning interact. A moderate degree of practice challenge, or what they term "functional task difficulty", is optimal for learning. Functional task difficulty is a measure of difficulty that accounts for the interaction of nominal task difficulty and a performer's skill level. According to the challenge point framework, practising at a functional task difficulty level too low or too high for an individual is suboptimal for learning. The challenge point framework nicely illustrates the relation between short-term performance in practice and longer-term learning. Performing at a more challenging level in practice, which would result in poorer short-term performance, should lead to more gains in terms of learning and improvement than those associated with low challenge and low error practice.

Ecological Dynamics

A departure from the cognitive perspectives discussed thus far, and borrowing key ideas from ecological psychology and complex dynamical systems to theorize about human motor learning, an ecological dynamics approach to understanding learning processes was developed (also referred to as a constraints-led approach; e.g., Davids, Button, & Bennett, 2008; Kelso, 1994; Kugler & Turvey, 1988; Newell, 1986). The ecological dynamics approach was established on the notion of self-organization in biological systems, where adaptive movement behaviours emerge from continuous interactions between individuals, their task, and the environment in which they perform. An example of self-organization can be seen in gait transition as speed of locomotion is increased in a walking individual. As speed (the control parameter) increases, the relative timing and step characteristics (order parameters) are spontaneously reorganized to transition from walking gait to jogging gait. Self-organization is also seen in coordination dynamics research involving bimanual inter-limb movements. Decoupling the limbs to perform relative phase patterns other than in-phase (symmetrical flexion/extension of both limbs, 0° phasing) or anti-phase (alternating flexion/extension, 180° phasing), which are termed intrinsic attractors, is difficult and produces instability. With increasing movement velocity, that is, a change in some control parameter, the dynamical system will transition back to a more stable attractor state (Haken, Kelso, & Bunz, 1985). Hence, learning is conceptualized as a change in the attractor landscape and one of self-organization and stability–instability transitions. Where previous, more cognitive-based theories have been good at describing and explaining discrete actions or sequences of action (with clearly defined beginning and end points), continuous actions have been well described through an ecological dynamics approach.

Behavioural outcomes in such self-organizing systems are considered to be mostly independent of high-level executive input and are governed by structural (body-related) and informational (visually related) constraints. Movement "patterns" that emerge are a result of perception–action coupling, wherein perceptual information guides or regulates action directly, independent of any type of pre-planned motor programme. A fundamental feature of the ecological dynamics approach to motor learning is that there is inherent neurobiological "degeneracy" in the perceptual and action systems (Edelman & Gally, 2001). This means that multiple functionally equivalent ways of attaining the same outcome goals can be generated through various biomechanical configurations of the physical body. Degeneracy is illustrated in the different types of pass a Frisbee player could make (e.g., forehand, backhand, hammer throw) and biomechanical variations in how these passes may be executed that would achieve the same performance outcome of hitting a target. A Russian scientist, named Nikolai Bernstein, was one of the first researchers to consider the influence of context and fluctuations in the internal and external factors impacting skill performance (Bernstein, 1996). He posited that the same motor commands would not achieve identical outcomes from one trial to another, as the internal states vary in an individual from trial to trial owing to inherent noise in the motor system. The same could be said for the variability in the performance context. Accordingly, it is the process of solving variations of motor problems that prepare a learner to adapt to ever-changing interactions in constraints. Bernstein advocated for variability in practice that encourages exploration of motor solutions that achieve the same task objective, rather than mere repetitive practice of a single motor solution. This guideline for structuring practice is especially applicable to acquisition of "open skills" (see the first paragraph of the section on "Psychosocial models", below).

A constraint-led framework is often adopted to promote motor learning under the ecological dynamics approach. Imposing various task (e.g., equipment or rule adaptation) and/or environmental (e.g., weather, playing surface) constraints, given the individual constraints (e.g., age, skill level), can direct learners to "specifying information" (i.e., relevant information for regulating a movement) and "affordances" (i.e., movement possibilities). A constraints-led coaching or instructional design is founded on ecological dynamics principles and the idea that behaviours emerge as a consequence of manipulation to constraints rather than as a result of a specific aim to produce one type of motor pattern or solution (Davids et al., 2008). Although there is considerable evidence that constraints can change behaviours in the absence of specific intentions to change, there is less evidence that this way of instructing, where movements are brought about through a discovery- and constraints-heavy environment, is better for performance and learning than a more prescriptive approach where learners are directed to a particular motor solution. Importantly, both an information-processing and a constraints-led approach to behaviour change would encourage active effort on the part of the learner, with practice environments that are designed to maximize the match between conditions encountered in test or competition.

Neurophysiological Models and Mechanisms

With advancements in technology and increased accessibility to brain imaging and neurophysiological tools, researchers have begun to detail the neural processes and circuitry involved in motor learning (e.g., Seidler, 2010). These neural processes have been detailed in relation to memory consolidation (e.g., Shadmehr & Holcomb, 1997), that is, the offline processes that take place outside of practice and serve to make short-term memories longer term. As well, these processes have been detailed with respect to different forms of learning such as use-dependent, error-based, and reinforcement learning (e.g., Huang, Haith, Mazonni, & Krakauer, 2011).

Neurophysiological work on use-dependent (also known as Hebbian) learning has shown that movement repetition induces short-term neural plasticity (e.g., Classen, Liepert, Wise, Hallett, & Cohen, 1998). In Hebbian learning, when a neuron fires and elicits activity in another, or when a stimulus elicits a certain pattern of neural activity, the synaptic connections between these neurons strengthen (a cellular process known as long-term potentiation; LTP). This strengthening means that the stimulus will tend to elicit the same neural activity on subsequent occasions. The reverse – that is, a lack of/no association between neural activity and synaptic connections – results in long-term depression (LTD), a weakening of the strength of synaptic transmissions. Repeated elicitations of such synaptic connections are strengthened irrespective of feedback regarding error or outcome efficacy in Hebbian learning. Hebbian learning is underpinned by neural plasticity within and between areas of the cerebral cortex, including the primary motor and somatosensory cortices (Buonomano & Merzenich, 1998; Classen et al., 1998). In supervised or error-based learning, feedback is pertinent for error correction and adaptation to a changing environment (Seidler, Kwak, Fling, & Bernard, 2013). Augmented or intrinsic sensory feedback, containing information on magnitude and direction of error, is used to update subsequent motor commands and predictions of sensory consequences. Error-based learning is thought to be driven by neural plasticity (particularly LTD) in the cerebellum, which is based on sensory prediction errors (e.g., Diedrichsen, Hashambhoy, Rane, & Shadmehr, 2005; Ito, Yamaguchi, Nagao, & Yamazaki, 2014).

A reinforcement learning mechanism is also thought to be involved in learning from errors, involving the midbrain dopamine system, anterior cingulate cortex (ACC), basal ganglia, and other higher brain-level cortical areas. When consequences of a response are worse than predicted, a negative dopaminergic signal (i.e., decrease in dopaminergic neuronal firing) is elicited and projected to various cortical structures. This dopamine signal reaches the ACC and results in neural disinhibition, which can be seen by electroencephalography measures of error-related negativity in frontal/central regions of the brain (Holroyd & Coles, 2002). When consequences are better than predicted, the dopamine signal is reversed. Dopaminergic neurons in other cortical regions also show phasic activations corresponding to rewards and reward-predicting stimuli that appear to be crucial for reinforcement learning (as well as memory consolidation – see next paragraph; McGaugh, 2000; Wadden, Borich, & Boyd, 2012). At the cellular level, dopamine influences synaptic plasticity via LTP and LTD. Notably, when dopaminergic projections to the primary motor cortex were blocked (through surgical lesions) in rodents, new skill learning was reduced, whereas existing skills were not impacted (Hosp, Pekanovic, Rioult-Pedotti, & Luft, 2011).

Memory consolidation processes are also linked to neurobiological evidence alluding to the importance of dopamine for learning. These consolidation processes are subsumed within the definition of motor learning. Consolidation refers to offline neurobiological processes that serve to stabilize or enhance memory, whereas motor learning is the relatively permanent improvement in capacity for skilled movement that is due to both online (during practice) and offline processes that happen at all levels of the sensory-motor system. During memory consolidation, neurophysiological processes influence a memory trace in two distinct time frames (Karni et al., 1998). The fast (synaptic) consolidation involves synaptic protein synthesis and strengthening of synaptic transmissions that are active during skill performance. The slow (systems) consolidation, which can last for weeks, involves reorganization of neural networks. Memories, which were encoded and dependent on the hippocampus for retrieval, are relieved of this dependency and moved to the neocortical system for long-term storage through this slow system. Both types of consolidation are necessary to induce permanent changes to memory and motor skills.

Events that happen during practice and post-practice can impact memory consolidation, serving to augment and facilitate or negatively impact and interfere. For example, immediate practice of a counter-rotation after first adapting to an opposite visuomotor rotation (a virtual environment whereby visual feedback representing hand movement is rotated in relation to actual hand movement) usually induces (retroactive) interference resulting in significant reduction in retention of the first rotation (see discussion on visuomotor adaptation in the final paragraph of the section on "Internal models" discussed above and "Transfer" in the final sections below). In a task involving fast rhythmic finger movements, a non-invasive electromagnetic procedure that interferes with local brain function, known as repetitive transcranial magnetic stimulation, disrupted memory consolidation when applied to the primary motor cortex immediately after practice (Muellbacher et al., 2002). A lack of sufficient sleep or rest after skill practice has also been shown to interfere with consolidation processes. For example, when learners were sleep-deprived on the first night after a practice session, they showed less pronounced offline improvement in a motor sequence task at a 48-hour delayed retention test compared with learners who had two regular nights of sleep after practice (Fischer, Hallschmid, Elsner, & Born, 2002).

Psychosocial Models

The psychological construct of motivation, defined as the direction, intensity, and persistence of effort in certain behaviours (Vallerand & Thill, 1993, cited in Crocker, 2007, p. 75), has received renewed attention as a potential motor learning mechanism. Motivation is thought to influence motor learning based on processes related to competence, social-relatedness, and autonomy (Deci & Ryan, 2000). Although motivation has always been regarded as important in exerting temporary energizing effects on performance and the quality or amount of practice, researchers have accumulated evidence supporting the idea that motivation-related processes have a direct impact on motor learning. This has led Wulf and Lewthwaite (2016) to propose the OPTIMAL (optimizing performance through intrinsic motivation and attention for learning) model. The OPTIMAL model groups together learning-related effects that are thought to be driven by the satisfaction of basic psychological needs of competence and autonomy coupled with an externally related attentional focus. Practice interventions that enhance expectancies in performers (e.g., self-efficacy, perceived competency, or success expectations) and perceived autonomy (a sense of agency and control) have benefited motor learning.

The authors of the OPTIMAL model propose that meeting the basic psychological needs of competence and autonomy increases energy expenditure, cognitive effort, and positive affect, which exerts a positive impact on motor performance and learning. Elevated competency perceptions and autonomy also tend to be associated with other cognitive and attentional states that have enhanced performance and learning, such as improved goal-setting, concentration, adoption of an external focus of attention, or lowered debilitating concerns about one's lack of ability. Neurobiochemical processes related to consolidation and dopamine release have also been used to explain how motivation might directly impact motor learning. Although the OPTIMAL model is based on empirical evidence and combines a variety of potential effects and mechanisms into an integrated model, it is relatively new and awaits verification. Because it is a rather all-encompassing framework, it is difficult to refute the model, but there has been evidence that serves to question the moderating role of motivation in learning effects (e.g., Carter, Smith, & Ste-Marie, 2016; Ong, Lohse, & Hodges, 2015). On the positive side, this model has led to a greater appreciation of psychosocial influences on mechanisms of motor control and learning, which until now had mostly been, at best, controlled or, at worst, discounted or ignored.

Learning Phases and Stages

Researchers and practitioners have noted certain patterns and characteristics of performance as motor skills are acquired, which has led to various conceptualizations about phases or stages that describe learning and the progression through skill levels (from novice/beginner to expert). Although these stages are sometimes described as discrete and separated in such a way as to appear independent, most researchers acknowledge that skill progressions are likely blended and continuous in nature. Moreover, there is consensus that there is considerable variation between individuals with respect to how they learn. In this way, phases represent general observations about processes likely to be operating at a specific point in time, rather than being predictive of how people will learn when looking across different time scales. Below we consider two primary ways skill progressions have been considered, which we have broadly divided into progressions based on higher-level cognitive processes and progressions based on lower-level motor system reorganization. However, we also acknowledge that these phases have also been considered at a computational level (e.g., in terms of fast and slow processes), at a brain systems level (e.g., in relation to progressions from cortical to cerebellar brain structures), as well as at a cellular level (related to potentiation of neurons and synaptic connections), which we do not discuss here.

Progressions in Learning Based on a Reduction or Change in Higher-Level Cognitive Processes

Several theorists have proposed that acquisition of motor skills begins in a cognitively demanding ("cognitive") stage (e.g., Fitts & Posner, 1967). In this stage, performance is initially characterized by large errors and inconsistency. Working memory and attentional resources are heavily tapped during this early stage of learning, referred to as "controlled processing" (Schneider & Shiffrin, 1977). Novice performers are thought to consciously control skill execution, attending to how the skill is performed and the mechanics of the action. Declarative knowledge (i.e., facts, rules, and strategies) on "what to do" (or what not to do) is accumulated in the cognitive stage (e.g., Anderson, 1982). If learners are overloaded with a second task to perform, a decrement in performance (or interference) is likely to be observed on either or both tasks. In this stage, performance tends to improve quickly (i.e., exponentially – or what has been referred to as the power law of practice; Crossman, 1959; Newell & Rosenbloom, 1981), and consistency in outcome attainment and movement production typically improves in concert with overall accuracy. People have referred to graphs illustrating acquisition rate over time with respect to some measure of performance as performance or learning curves (Schmidt & Lee, 2011). These can be at an individual or group (mean) level. The rate of acquisition is aided by such methods as instructions, error feedback, appropriate task constraints, and observational learning, which enable the performer to generate an adequate movement solution and get the movement "in the ballpark".

Subsequent to the cognitive stage, performance continues to improve with practice, although the gains are usually gradual past the initial stage of learning. This intermediate, "fixation" stage (Fitts & Posner, 1967) may consist of periods of trial and error or discovery of motor solutions, in which skill execution is likely to be defined mostly by controlled processing. As performances become more consistent and biomechanically efficient, movement production becomes more autonomous. Hence, the final stage of learning is aptly named the "autonomous" stage (Fitts & Posner, 1967). Here, performance error is low, and outcome consistency is high. Instead of relying on declarative knowledge, learners have proceduralized their knowledge on "how to" perform the task, such that it is less accessible to conscious awareness and, hence, less verbalizable. Skill execution occurs with automaticity or "automatic processing", meaning little cognitive effort or attention is required for the skill to be performed well. With automatic processing, a performer is able to perform a second task with little to no interference. There are many sport-related empirical studies showing that expert performers (e.g., in golf) are able to perform just as well in a single-task condition (e.g., putting only) as in second-task conditions (additionally performing a listening word search task; e.g., Beilock & Carr, 2001). Given that such findings define skilled but not novice performers, this suggests that, with advancing skill, a level of automaticity in the primary task allows resources to be allocated to other tasks (such as monitoring other players or reading the lie of the ground in putting).

At the autonomous stage, performance can be negatively impacted by an inward shift towards the self, known as "self-focused attention", or skill-focused attention, which is a shift towards use of declarative knowledge and step-by-step conscious processing of skills (e.g., Gray, 2004; Wulf, 2013). Other concepts similar to skill-focused attention are the "explicit monitoring hypothesis" (e.g., Beilock & Carr, 2001), "constrained action hypothesis" (e.g., Wulf, McNevin, & Shea, 2001), and the "reinvestment hypothesis" (e.g., Masters & Maxwell, 2004). The principle central to these accounts is a hypothesized regression towards an early cognitive control stage and monitoring of skill that interferes with the automaticity and effectiveness of skill execution. In high-stake contests, this regression leads to performance akin to "choking", the term that describes uncharacteristic performance decrements for an individual performing under pressure conditions. In accordance with the reinvestment hypothesis, experienced performers would be more likely to "choke" under stressful or attention-demanding situations if they accumulated a wealth of declarative knowledge early in learning (i.e., in the cognitive stage). This propensity for reinvestment is not only dependent on how skills were acquired and the amount of declarative knowledge, but also on characteristics of the individual and their propensity to reinvest (Masters, Polman, & Hammond, 1993).

Although there is significant evidence that motor learning of novel skills is typically defined by explicit, declarative processes related to how to perform, this way of learning is not necessarily ubiquitous for all skills, nor is it necessarily the best way of learning. We can learn to kick or throw a ball or jump without explicit knowledge as to how we are performing these skills. To learn implicitly refers to acquisition of a skill without conscious awareness of the products of learning or regularities that govern performance success. In other words, implicit motor learning bypasses the accumulation of declarative knowledge while procedural knowledge is acquired (e.g., Masters & Maxwell, 2004). In contrast, explicit motor learning normally follows guided or prescriptive learning environments whereby learners become consciously aware of knowledge (e.g., task structure, strategies) relevant to the skill they have acquired. Patients with amnesia who acquire new motor skills provide evidence for this implicit mode of learning, as, although these patients have clearly acquired procedural knowledge to perform the tasks, they can neither recollect the learning experience nor verbally report explicit knowledge relevant to the skill (Nissen, Willingham & Hartman, 1989). There is some empirical evidence that practice methods that are more implicit in nature, such as progressing through practice environments where errors are minimized (e.g., easy to difficult) or providing instructions that promote an external focus of attention, are effective for preventing performance decrements when participants later are tested under high-stress or high-demand tasks that exceed attentional capacity (e.g., Maxwell, Masters, Kerr & Weedon, 2001; Ong, Bowcock, & Hodges, 2010; Wulf, 2013). By learning implicitly, learners avoid accumulating declarative or explicit knowledge of a skill and, hence, do not reinvest or revert to a conscious mode of control under pressure that could hamper performance.

Learning Progressions Based on Lower-Level, Motor System Adaptations

The idea of spontaneous neural reorganization (i.e., self-organization) as a result of experience is central to ideas about motor behaviour being an emergent property of various internal and external constraints. Consistent with what is now termed the ecological-dynamics perspective (Davids et al., 2008; Kelso, 1994; Kugler & Turvey, 1988; Newell, 1986), the Russian physiologist Bernstein proposed that motor behaviour generally, and motor learning more specifically, could be conceptualized as a problem of solving degrees of freedom (Bernstein, 1996). He argued that a central command system in the brain, like that defined in early ideas of a motor programme, would be overwhelmed with the copious degrees of freedom (i.e., independent units or dimensions) that would need to be controlled for successful motor skill execution. For example, in an underarm softball pitch to a batter, at least 20 muscles would require independent specification, at any point of time in the movement.

To overcome the degrees of freedom problem, Bernstein postulated that the first stage of learning essentially involves a constraining or freezing of some degrees of freedom. By fixating certain muscles/joints, or coupling the movement of one muscle or joint to another, such as seen in the inefficient co-contraction of agonist and antagonist muscles around a joint, computational load at any given point in time is reduced. In the softball-pitching example, a novice pitcher can limit the movements in the elbow and wrist joints, relying only on the rotation around the shoulder to generate momentum for ball release. As learning progresses, there would be a "freeing" of these degrees of freedom and an associated increase in independence between joints or muscles. Correspondingly, relative motion of joints involved in a motor task becomes less coupled and manifests as decreased correlation in relative motion between joints (see Newell & McDonald, 1994; Vereijken, Emmerik, Whiting, & Newell, 1992). In the softball-pitching example, we might see a decrease in correlation between the relative motions of the elbow and wrist joints as the pitcher starts to flex the elbow and wrist joints at different moments in the pitch. In the final stage of motor learning, it is proposed that the motor system becomes more mechanically and energy efficient through exploitation of the mechanical-inertial properties of the limbs (e.g., extension of the more proximal shoulder joint would result in passive torques at the more distal elbow and wrist joints). Higher-skilled softball pitchers are more likely to exploit the dynamic interactions between joint motions, activating different muscle groups at different times during the pitching motion, so as to maximize the angular momentum transferred to the ball at release.

Depending on the nature of the task, tighter couplings between joints could also be seen at a more advanced stage of learning. The emergence of coordinative structures – that is, relations between components of the motor system that serve a functional purpose – with increasing expertise might reflect better control of task-relevant versus non-task-relevant variability. Couplings that emerge later in practice will be those that matter most for task success (usually the timing and position of distal joints in throwing-type actions).

Learning Goals

It should be apparent to practitioners that the type of task and goal of learning are important considerations for structuring practice and assessing learning. Motor skills have often been categorized along a continuum of closed to open skills (e.g., Gentile, 1972; Poulton, 1957). Closed skills are motor tasks that are performed in a predictable or stable environment, devoid of variability that would arise from the influence of external factors, whereas open skills are executed in unpredictable environments subject to external influence.

Retention

If the goal of practice is to learn a closed skill or produce only one variant of a motor skill accurately and consistently, we would be most interested in the performers' long-term retention of the skill. A retention test typically assesses performance of the same task that was executed in practice (Schmidt & Lee, 2011). To enhance learning and best prepare performers to execute the practised task under real-world "test" conditions, the practice context should match the test conditions as closely as possible. This guideline for structuring practice is known as the "specificity of learning" or "practice specificity" principle (e.g., Barnett, Ross, Schmidt, & Todd, 1973; Proteau, Marteniuk, & Lévesque, 1992). As mentioned in the section on "Primary theories, frameworks, and associated concepts" above, retention tests are usually administered after a period of delay, allowing time for temporary performance influences to dissipate before learning is assessed. Absolute measures of performance at retention, especially when compared with pre-practice levels or control group levels, provide an indication of the extent of (relatively) permanent behavioural changes that have transpired with practice. Relative measures, such as difference scores between the end of practice and retention or percentage change in pre-practice to retention, offer alternative ways of quantifying learning (or forgetting).

Some empirical evidence from research on memory consolidation suggests that skill retention is impacted by the achievement of performance stability (e.g., Hauptmann, Reinhart, Brandt, & Karni, 2005). Within a practice session, stability is achieved when the performance curve begins to level out, termed asymptotic performance. In addition to practice amount, we also know that there are many ways of manipulating practice quality to impact retention. Conditions that make practice conditions harder and more effortful are often shown to be the conditions that result in the strongest retention effects (Lee, Swinnen, & Serrien, 1994). There is some minor disagreement about whether delayed tests of learning conducted in the absence of a variable present in practice should be called "retention" or "transfer" tests. Regardless of their label, we do know that such tests (e.g., the no-KR retention test) provide valuable information about what has been retained independently from its potential guiding role in practice. As discussed earlier with respect to memory consolidation, events following motor practice can also exert positive or negative effects on retention (e.g., rewards, sleep, or subsequent practice of new tasks; e.g., Fischer et al., 2002; Larssen, Ong, & Hodges, 2012; Stickgold, 2005).

Transfer

For motor tasks that are categorized as open skills, a learner's goal would be to enhance the capacity for response adaptability, which increases the odds that optimal movement solutions would be selected in varying contexts or under varying constraints. Practice protocols that promote problem-solving and experience of a variety of movement solutions would allow generalizability across a range of performance contexts. In motor learning studies, the capacity for generalization is assessed through transfer tests (Schmidt & Lee, 2011). Transfer is a critical measure of learning as rarely are the conditions of practice the same as the conditions of test (such as in sports competition or in functional tasks of everyday life following rehabilitation). According to the practice specificity principle, transfer would be elicited with increased similarity between the practice and criterion tasks. These similarities may be in the perceptual-motor elements of the tasks and its performance context, or in the cognitive processes underlying performance of both tasks (also referred to as transfer-appropriate processing: Graf & Ryan, 1990; Lee, 1988; encoding specificity: Tulving & Thomson, 1973; and representative task design: Pinder, Davids, Renshaw, & Araújo, 2011).

For increased training fidelity, performers would practise in performance contexts that are identical or closely matched to test conditions that they would later be tested on (often with added pressure). This type of transfer is referred to as "near" or specific transfer (Schmidt & Lee, 2014). Conversely, transfer effects observed with large disparities between the training environment and a later test phase would be considered "far" or general transfer. In reality, high-fidelity training may be cost-prohibitive, risky, or difficult to achieve. For instance, the cost and risks of training fighter pilots to operate a real aircraft are remarkably greater than if training them in a flight simulator. It is challenging in itself for practitioners to recreate conditions that would be experienced by performers under test or match contexts. Besides an interest in structuring practice for high-fidelity training, researchers and practitioners are also concerned with questions on how "far-reaching" the transfer effects of their practice might be. How much dissimilarity can exist between practice and criterion skills, or how closely matched must these conditions be, for transfer effects to be significant and meaningful? Transfer designs allow a probe of what has been acquired and how abstract that learning might be (e.g., if something transfers to the non-practised hand then we know learning was not specific to the muscles involved in the training phase). In this way, transfer tasks help to inform learning theory and can tell us what is acquired and the level of specification of learning.

Transfer can also be considered with respect to how learning episodes of different skills potentially facilitate or impede performance and learning of another skill. Proactive transfer is the term used to describe how previous practice in one activity impacts on performance of a second activity, such as that observed moving from practice playing tennis to practice playing squash (Schmidt & Lee, 2011). Another form of transfer is retroactive transfer. This was previously mentioned in relation to memory consolidation and it describes how the immediate and subsequent practice of a closely related skill could interfere with the performance of a previously practised skill (e.g., how tennis is affected by interspersed practice of squash; e.g., Krakauer, 2009). Researchers have shown that retroactive interference from practice of a second skill is possible up to 4–5 hours after practice of an initial skill (e.g., Brashers-Krug, Shadmehr, & Bizzi, 1996; Press, Casement, Pascual-Leone, & Robertson, 2005). The directional influence of transfer can be positive or negative. Positive transfer refers to a facilitative effect, and negative transfer indicates interference. Transfer effects, whether positive or negative, may be expected between motor performances in net-type games, such as in tennis and badminton. Positive transfer may result from improved anticipation of an opponent's actions, hence leading to more optimal response selection, as comparable tactical decision-making and strategies exist in tennis and badminton. However, there is likely to be negative transfer in stroke execution between the two activities. The badminton forehand consists of a wrist snap, whereas the tennis forehand typically involves a fixed wrist (except for elite players). Transfer would not be expected from unrelated skills that feature vastly disparate perceptual-motor elements or do not share similar cognitive-related processes.

Skill Refinement, Relearning, and Technique Change

Much of our discussion of motor learning has been focused on acquisition of new skills, reflecting the general course of research in the field. Yet, performers often find themselves making refinements to their motor responses, whether they are attempting to adjust their movements so that performance may be more accurate, powerful, or consistent (e.g., greater use of legs and shorter pole push while double poling in cross-country skiing), or adopting a new technique altogether (e.g., Fosbury flop in high jump) while aiming to achieve the same task goal. The ease with which performers are able to effect change or refine a skill appears to be associated with the level of expertise acquired on an existing motor skill.

As discussed earlier, one of the distinguishing characteristics of skilled performance is the extent to which a motor skill is autonomously controlled without demands on attentional resources. Based on this cognitive perspective of motor learning, any modification to movement coordination is arguably easier to accomplish before automaticity is attained. To modify a well-learned skill in a significant manner (also known as shifting, relearning, or habit change), it is thought that a performer must first "de-automatize" its control and decouple existing perceptual-motor associations to avoid spontaneous and undesired production of the old movement pattern in future performance scenarios (Carson & Collins, 2018). Suggested methods to aid movement de-automatization have often included some form of explicit comparing, contrasting, and cueing between a "new way" and the "old way" (akin to cognitive processing described in the elaboration hypothesis of the contextual interference effect), followed by extensive practice of the new way until automaticity or stability is achieved (e.g., Lyndon, 1989). Depending on the performance context, a new technique may be acquired either to replace an old one or as an additional skill to apply in new situations (related to the idea of "bifurcations" in ecological dynamics; Davids et al., 2008). How well a new skill is learned is influenced by the degree of perceptual-motor and processing similarities between the new and existing skills (see discussion in the section on "Transfer"). The greater the similarity between the new and existing skills, the greater the interference or competition between these skills.

Owing to the scarcity of research on technique change, questions as to whether an existing movement pattern can actually be replaced by another, or whether closely related techniques can co-exist without competition, remain relatively unanswered. From an ecological dynamics perspective, there is evidence that the learning of a new pattern, coupled with increased stability of this pattern over time, would change the stability and appearance of behaviours that are "close by" in terms of coordination demands (e.g., Zanone & Kelso, 1992). This has been referred to as a change in the attractor landscape. One interesting observation in dynamics research based on motor learning of new coordination patterns is that these attractors might only show up under certain conditions (such as high speeds, high attention demands; Haken et al., 1985). As such, undesirable movement patterns can be "replaced", but they may not truly be annihilated.

Technique change can be brought about by direct and indirect means – that is, through more prescriptive instructional means or through a change to the task constraints forcing adaptation on behalf of the learner. For example, both an abrupt and a gradual introduction of a novel split-belt treadmill pattern (independent belts for each limb that move at different speeds) led to similarly adapted walking patterns in healthy adults (Roemmich & Bastian, 2015). However, the additive effects of an abrupt introduction and extended practice on the novel task enhanced retention of the new walking pattern the most. This suggests that an explicit awareness of task regularities and characteristics distinguishing a new skill might aid the stability and co-existence of both new and old skills.

Conclusion

In summary, we have defined motor learning and discussed the various ways it has been studied and conceptualized. In addition to thinking about learning at various levels of the motor system, including cognitive, neurophysiological, and biomechanical levels, motor learning has also been considered with respect to principles based on self-organization under constraints as well as in relation to acquisition of memory structures. In motor learning research, considerable evidence has accumulated showing that methods that promote active engagement on the part of the learner during practice, related to variable practice conditions and active problem-solving, are best for longer-term learning. Moreover, when these conditions of practice are most closely matched to conditions where test or transfer is required, the efficacy of the practice will be heightened.

With respect to the history and future of the field, there has been a growing trend for research and associated theories that are rooted in neurophysiology, likely owing to the comparative ease with which brain-related functioning can be measured today compared with in the past and because of a growing appreciation of skill acquisition principles for rehabilitation. Schema theory (Schmidt, 1975) has all but been replaced by internal model-based frameworks and terminology (e.g., Wolpert et al., 1995), mostly owing to a surge in the computational engineering fields, where models of control have been formulated to help explain and potentially engineer adaptive movements in the fields of robotics. In sport, the constraints-based, ecological dynamics framework has had a significant impact in practical coaching settings, although empirical, evidence-based interventions for practice methods and instructions are still mostly based on cognitive frameworks. With improvements in technology and potential for enhanced measurement of actions through wearables, phone apps, and so on, there is a strong likelihood that principles concerning what to do with information, how to design simulations, and how best to promote efficient and effective learning and relearning will continue to be developed and researched. The future of motor learning from an interdisciplinary perspective looks to be rich and vibrant.

References

Adams, J. A. (1971). A closed-loop theory of motor learning. *Journal of Motor Behavior, 3*, 111–150.

Anderson, J. R. (1982). Acquisition of cognitive skill. *Psychological Review, 89*, 369–406.

Barnett, M. L., Ross, D., Schmidt, R. A., & Todd, B. (1973). Motor skills learning and the specificity of training principle. *Research Quarterly, 44*, 440–447.

Beilock, S. L., & Carr, T. H. (2001). On the fragility of skilled performance: What governs choking under pressure? *Journal of Experimental Psychology: General, 130*, 701–725.

Bernstein, N. A. (1996). On motor control. In M. L. Latash & M. T. Turvey (Eds.), *Dexterity and its development* (pp. 25–44). Mahwah, NJ: Lawrence Erlbaum.

Brashers-Krug, T., Shadmehr, R., & Bizzi, E. (1996). Consolidation in human motor memory. *Nature, 382* (6588), 252–255.

Buonomano, D. V., & Merzenich, M. M. (1998). Cortical plasticity: From synapses to maps. *Annual Review of Neuroscience, 21*, 149–186.

Carson, H. J., & Collins, D. (2018). Refining motor skills in golf: A biopsychosocial perspective. In M. Toms (Ed.), *Routledge international handbook of golf science* (pp. 196–206). New York: Routledge.

Carter, M. J., Smith, V., & Ste-Marie, D. M. (2016). Judgments of learning are significantly higher following feedback on relatively good versus relatively poor trials despite no actual learning differences. *Human Movement Science, 45*, 63–70.

Classen, J., Liepert, J., Wise, S. P., Hallett, M., & Cohen, L. G. (1998). Rapid plasticity of human cortical movement representation induced by practice. *Journal of Neurophysiology, 79*, 1117–1123.

Crocker, P. R. E. (2007). *Sport and exercise psychology: A Canadian perspective*. Toronto: Pearson Canada.

Crossman, E. R. F. W. (1959). A theory of the acquisition of speed skill. *Ergonomics, 2*, 153–166.

Davids, K. W., Button, C., & Bennett, S. J. (2008). *Dynamics of skill acquisition: A constraints-led approach*. Champaign, IL: Human Kinetics.

Deci, E. L., & Ryan, R. M. (2000). The "what" and "why" of goal pursuits: Human needs and the self-determination of behavior. *Psychological Inquiry, 11*, 227–268.

Diedrichsen, J., Hashambhoy, Y., Rane, T., & Shadmehr, R. (2005). Neural correlates of reach errors. *Journal of Neuroscience, 25*, 9919–9931.

Edelman, G. M., & Gally, J. (2001). Degeneracy and complexity in biological systems. *Proceedings of the National Academy of Sciences, 98*, 13763–13768.

Fischer, S., Hallschmid, M., Elsner, A. L., & Born, J. (2002). Sleep forms memory for finger skills. *Proceedings of the National Academy of Sciences, 99*, 11987–11991.

Fitts, P. M., & Posner, M. I. (1967). *Human performance*. Belmont, CA: Brooks/Cole.

Gentile, A. M. (1972). A working model of skill acquisition with application to teaching. *Quest, 17,* 3–23.

Graf, P., & Ryan, L. (1990). Transfer-appropriate processing for implicit and explicit memory. *Journal of Experimental Psychology: Learning, Memory, & Cognition, 16,* 978–992.

Gray, R. (2004). Attending to the execution of a complex sensorimotor skill: Expertise differences, choking, and slumps. *Journal of Experimental Psychology: Applied, 10,* 42–54.

Guadagnoli, M. A., Holcomb, W. R., & Weber, T. (1999). The relationship between contextual interference effects and performer expertise on the learning of a putting task. *Journal of Human Movement Studies, 37,* 19–36.

Guadagnoli, M. A., & Kohl, R. M. (2001). Knowledge of results for motor learning: Relationship between error estimation and knowledge of results frequency. *Journal of Motor Behavior, 33,* 217–224.

Guadagnoli, M. A., & Lee, T. D. (2004). Challenge point: A framework for conceptualizing the effects of various practice conditions in motor learning. *Journal of Motor Behavior, 36,* 212–224.

Haken, H., Kelso, J. S., & Bunz, H. (1985). A theoretical model of phase transitions in human hand movements. *Biological Cybernetics, 51,* 347–356.

Hauptmann, B., Reinhart, E., Brandt, S. A., & Karni, A. (2005). The predictive value of the leveling off of within session performance for procedural memory consolidation. *Cognitive Brain Research, 24,* 181–189.

Holroyd, C. B., & Coles, M. G. (2002). The neural basis of human error processing: Reinforcement learning, dopamine, and the error-related negativity. *Psychological Review, 109,* 679–709.

Hosp, J. A., Pekanovic, A., Rioult-Pedotti, M. S., & Luft, A. R. (2011). Dopaminergic projections from midbrain to primary motor cortex mediate motor skill learning. *The Journal of Neuroscience, 31,* 2481–2487.

Huang, V. S., Haith, A., Mazzoni, P., & Krakauer, J. W. (2011). Rethinking motor learning and savings in adaptation paradigms: Model-free memory for successful actions combines with internal models. *Neuron, 70,* 787–801.

Huang, V. S., & Shadmehr, R. (2007). Evolution of motor memory during the seconds after observation of motor error. *Journal of Neurophysiology, 97,* 3976–3985.

Ito, M., Yamaguchi, K., Nagao, S., & Yamazaki, T. (2014). Long-term depression as a model of cerebellar plasticity. *Progress in Brain Research, 210,* 1–30.

Karni, A., Meyer, G., Rey-Hipolito, C., Jezzard, P., Adams, M. M., Turner, R., & Ungerleider, L. G. (1998). The acquisition of skilled motor performance: Fast and slow experience-driven changes in primary motor cortex. *Proceedings of the National Academy of Sciences, 95,* 861–868.

Keele, S. W. (1968). Movement control in skilled motor performance. *Psychological Bulletin, 70,* 387–403.

Kelso, J. A. S. (1994). The informational character of self-organized coordination dynamics. *Human Movement Science, 13*(3–4), 393–413.

Krakauer, J. W. (2009). Motor learning and consolidation: The case of visuomotor rotation. In D. Sternad (Ed.), *Progress in motor control* (pp. 405–421). New York: Springer.

Kugler, P. N., & Turvey, M. T. (1988). Self-organization, flow fields, and information. *Human Movement Science, 7*(2–4), 97–129.

Larssen, B. C., Ong, N. T., & Hodges, N. J. (2012). Watch and learn: Seeing is better than doing when acquiring consecutive motor tasks. *PLoS One, 7*(6), e38938.

Lee, T. D. (1988). Transfer-appropriate processing: A framework for conceptualizing practice effects in motor learning. *Advances in Psychology, 50,* 201–215.

Lee, T. D., & Magill, R. A. (1983). The locus of contextual interference in motor-skill acquisition. *Journal of Experimental Psychology: Learning, Memory, and Cognition, 9,* 730–746.

Lee, T. D., Swinnen, S. P., & Serrien, D. J. (1994). Cognitive effort and motor learning. *Quest, 46,* 328–344.

Lyndon, H. (1989). Research into practice. *Australasian Journal of Special Education, 13,* 32–37.

Masters, R. S., & Maxwell, J. P. (2004). Implicit motor learning, reinvestment and movement disruption: What you don't know won't hurt you. In A. M. Williams & N. J. Hodges (Eds.), *Skill acquisition in sport: Research, theory and practice* (pp. 207–228). New York: Routledge.

Masters, R. S. W., Polman, R. C. J., & Hammond, N. V. (1993). "Reinvestment": A dimension of personality implicated in skill breakdown under pressure. *Personality and Individual Differences, 14,* 655–666.

Maxwell, J. P., Masters, R. S. W., Kerr, E., & Weedon, E. (2001). The implicit benefit of learning without errors. *The Quarterly Journal of Experimental Psychology Section A, 54,* 1049–1068.

McGaugh, J. L. (2000). Memory – A century of consolidation. *Science, 287*(5451), 248–251.

Muellbacher, W., Ziemann, U., Wissel, J., Dang, N., Kofler, M., Facchini, S., & ... Hallett, M. (2002). Early consolidation in human primary motor cortex. *Nature, 415*(6872), 640–644.

Newell, A., & Rosenbloom, P. S. (1981). Mechanisms of skill acquisition and the law of practice. In J. R. Anderson (Ed.), *Cognitive skills and their acquisition* (pp. 1–56). Hillsdale, NJ: Lawrence Erlbaum.

Newell, K. M. (1986). Constraints on the development of coordination. In M. G. Wade & H. T. A. Whiting (Eds.), *Motor development in children. Aspects of coordination and control* (pp. 341–360). Dordrecht: Martinus Nijhoff.

Newell, K. M., & McDonald, P. V. (1994). Learning to coordinate redundant biomechanical degrees of freedom. In S. P. Swinnen, H. Heuer, J. Massion, & P. Casaer (Eds.), *Interlimb coordination: Neural, dynamical, and cognitive constraints* (pp. 515–536). San Diego, CA: Academic Press.

Nissen, M. J., Willingham, D., & Hartman, M. (1989). Explicit and implicit remembering: When is learning preserved in amnesia? *Neuropsychologia, 27,* 341–352.

Ong, N. T., Bowcock, A., & Hodges, N. J. (2010). Manipulations to the timing and type of instructions to examine motor skill performance under pressure. *Frontiers in Psychology, 1.* https://doi.org/10.3389/fpsyg.2010.00196

Ong, N. T., Lohse, K. R., & Hodges, N. J. (2015). Manipulating target size influences perceptions of success when learning a dart-throwing skill but does not impact retention. *Frontiers in Psychology, 6,* 1378.

Pinder, R. A., Davids, K., Renshaw, I., & Araújo, D. (2011). Representative learning design and functionality of research and practice in sport. *Journal of Sport and Exercise Psychology, 33,* 146–155.

Poulton, E. C. (1957). On prediction in skilled movements. *Psychological Bulletin, 54,* 467–478.

Press, D. Z., Casement, M. D., Pascual-Leone, A., & Robertson, E. M. (2005). The time course of off-line motor sequence learning. *Cognitive Brain Research, 25,* 375–378.

Proteau, L., Marteniuk, R. G., & Lévesque, L. (1992). A sensorimotor basis for motor learning: Evidence indicating specificity of practice. *The Quarterly Journal of Experimental Psychology, 44,* 557–575.

Roemmich, R. T., & Bastian, A. J. (2015). Two ways to save a newly learned motor pattern. *Journal of Neurophysiology, 113,* 3519–3530.

Schmidt, R. A. (1975). A schema theory of discrete motor skill learning. *Psychological Review, 82,* 225–260.

Schmidt, R. A., & Lee, T. D. (2011). *Motor control and learning: A behavioral emphasis* (5th ed.). Champaign, IL: Human Kinetics.

Schmidt, R. A., & Lee, T. D. (2014). *Motor learning & performance: From principles to application* (5th ed.). Champaign, IL: Human Kinetics.

Schneider, W., & Shiffrin, R. M. (1977). Controlled and automatic human information processing: I. Detection, search, and attention. *Psychological Review, 84,* 1–66.

Seidler, R. D. (2010). Neural correlates of motor learning, transfer of learning, and learning to learn. *Exercise and Sport Sciences Reviews, 38,* 3–9.

Seidler, R. D., Kwak, Y., Fling, B. W., & Bernard, J. A. (2013). Neurocognitive mechanisms of error-based motor learning. *Advances in Experimental Medicine and Biology, 782,* 39–60.

Shadmehr, R., & Holcomb, H. H. (1997). Neural correlates of motor memory consolidation. *Science, 277*(5327), 821–825.

Shea, C. H., & Kohl, R. M. (1991). Composition of practice: Influence on the retention of motor skills. *Research Quarterly for Exercise and Sport, 62,* 187–195.

Shea, J. B., & Morgan, R. L. (1979). Contextual interference effects on the acquisition, retention, and transfer of a motor skill. *Journal of Experimental Psychology: Human Learning and Memory, 5,* 179–187.

Shea, J. B., & Zimny, S. T. (1983). Context effects in memory and learning movement information. In R. A. Magill (Ed.), *Memory and control of action* (pp. 345–366). Amsterdam: Elsevier.

Stickgold, R. (2005). Sleep-dependent memory consolidation. *Nature, 437*(7063), 1272–1278.

Sullivan, K. J., Kantak, S. S., & Burtner, P. A. (2008). Motor learning in children: Feedback effects on skill acquisition. *Physical Therapy, 88,* 720–732.

Taylor, J. A., & Ivry, R. B. (2014). Cerebellar and prefrontal cortex contributions to adaptation, strategies, and reinforcement learning. *Progress in Brain Research, 210,* 217–253.

Tulving, E., & Thomson, D. M. (1973). Encoding specificity and retrieval processes in episodic memory. *Psychological Review, 80,* 359–380.

Van Rossum, J. H. A. (1990). Schmidt's schema theory: The empirical base of the variability of practice hypothesis. *Human Movement Science, 9,* 387–435.

Vereijken, B., Emmerik, R. E. V., Whiting, H. T. A., & Newell, K. M. (1992). Free(z)ing degrees of freedom in skill acquisition. *Journal of Motor Behavior, 24,* 133–142.

Wadden, K. P., Borich, M. R., & Boyd, L. A. (2012). Motor skill learning and its neurophysiology. In N. J. Hodges & A. M. Williams (Eds.), *Skill acquisition in sport: Research, theory and practice* (pp. 247–265). New York: Routledge.

Winstein, C. J., & Schmidt, R. A. (1990). Reduced frequency of knowledge of results enhances motor skill learning. *Journal of Experimental Psychology: Learning, Memory, and Cognition, 16*, 677–691.

Wolpert, D., Ghahramani, Z., & Jordan, M. (1995). An internal model for sensorimotor integration. *Science, 269*, 1880–1882.

Wolpert, D. M., Miall, R. C., & Kawato, M. (1998). Internal models in the cerebellum. *Trends in Cognitive Sciences, 2*, 338–347.

Wulf, G. (2013). Attentional focus and motor learning: A review of 15 years. *International Review of Sport and Exercise Psychology, 6*, 77–104.

Wulf, G., & Lewthwaite, R. (2016). Optimizing performance through intrinsic motivation and attention for learning: The OPTIMAL theory of motor learning. *Psychonomic Bulletin & Review, 23*, 1382–1414.

Wulf, G., McNevin, N., & Shea, C. H. (2001). The automaticity of complex motor skill learning as a function of attentional focus. *The Quarterly Journal of Experimental Psychology: Section A, 54*, 1143–1154.

Zanone, P. G., & Kelso, J. A. (1992). Evolution of behavioral attractors with learning: Nonequilibrium phase transitions. *Journal of Experimental Psychology: Human Perception and Performance, 18*, 403–421.

27

NARCISSISM

Katharina Geukes, Carolyn C. Morf, and Mitja D. Back

Introduction

At its heart, competitive sport is about winning—winning competitions, winning against oneself and against opponents, setting records and winning medals, winning glory and admiration. The outcomes of sports competitions—similarly at any competitive level—determine who wins or loses, who experiences success or failure, who breaks records and achieves gold medals, and who writes sports history. As such, and combined with spectators', fans', opponents', officials', and especially the media's attention, the competitive sports context provides an ideal environment for narcissistic individuals: It offers rich opportunities for admiration and glory and, thus, greatly serves their foremost goal to maintain their grandiose selves. Therefore, narcissism is assumed to be a crucial factor predicting selecting into and experiencing, behaving, and succeeding in the sports context. Likewise, presumably, it provides an ideal environment for researchers to study the fascinating concept of narcissism.

Despite a comprehensive history of narcissism research within mainstream psychology, research on narcissism within sport and exercise psychology is relatively young. Therefore, this contribution provides a summary of fundamental insights into the narcissism concept gained within relevant psychological disciplines and, subsequently, those gained within sport psychology, focusing on two groups of protagonists—athletes and coaches. On a final note, a brief outlook is given on potential future directions in narcissism research within sport psychology.

The History of Narcissism and Narcissism Research

The history of *narcissism* can be traced back to Greek mythology, specifically to the third book of Ovid's *Metamorphoses* that, among others, involves the popular tragedy of Narcissus (and Echo). The beautiful young man, Narcissus, disdained those who loved him (including the nymph Echo) and was proud to do so. At a pool of water one day, he fell in love with his own reflection, not recognizing that his object of desire was only his mirror image. Ultimately, he lost his will to live and died in despair.

The history of narcissism research can be traced back to scholars such as Henry Havelock Ellis who, inspired by Narcissus's tragedy, was among the first to describe "narcissus-like" attributes (e.g., self-absorption linked to mental disorders). Subsequently popularizing the concept, Sigmund Freud (Freud, 1914/1990), as well as Heinz Kohut (1977) and Otto Kernberg (1975), provided more detailed theories on the origins and development of narcissism. Based on this clinical, psychoanalytic foundation, narcissism was first added to the *Diagnostic and Statistical Manual of Mental Disorders* (DSM-III; American Psychiatric Association, 1980) in the early 1980s. This inclusion promoted the subsequent development of tools for the assessment of narcissism as a subclinical personality trait.

Nowadays, narcissism is a well-studied concept across scientific disciplines (e.g., psychology, economics, sociology) and particularly across psychological disciplines (e.g., clinical, organizational, social, developmental, personality psychology). Much of the popularity and fascination of the narcissism concept originates from its contradictory and sometimes even paradoxical associations with antecedents and consequences (e.g., grandiose vs. fragile self-views, charming vs. aggressive behaviours, prestigious vs. unpopular reputations, or occupational success vs. failure). Furthermore, narcissism represents a prime example of a trait that is interpersonal at its core, which, therefore, allows researchers to explore long-standing psychological questions on individual complexities in a social world as well as in a social sport world.

The Concept of Narcissism

Narcissism is defined as a multifaceted personality trait describing relatively stable individual differences in the degree of feelings of grandiosity, entitlement, and vulnerability, and in strivings for admiration, superiority, and approval. Behaviours exhibited include charmingness, aggressiveness, and impulsiveness. The degree to which individuals are narcissistic is reflected in scores on a continuous dimension that ranges from low (= non-narcissistic) to high (= very narcissistic). Narcissism as a subclinical personality trait needs to be distinguished from pathological manifestations that are marked by intrapersonal and interpersonal maladjustment, as they appear in *narcissistic personality disorder*. Vulnerable, approval-seeking, and impulsive aspects of narcissism, however, bridge subclinical and clinical manifestations (Pincus & Lukowitsky, 2010).

In recent history, researchers have differentiated between grandiose narcissism, capturing agentic and antagonistic aspects, and vulnerable narcissism (Cain, Pincus, & Ansell, 2008; Wink, 1991), capturing antagonistic and particularly neurotic aspects (see Miller et al., 2011). In the last few years, however, a three-dimensional structure of narcissism has been proposed that captures all three aspects—aspects of agency (extraversion), antagonism (disagreeableness), and vulnerability (neuroticism; see Back & Morf, in press; Krizan & Herlache, 2017; Miller et al., 2016; Wright & Edershile, 2018)—that jointly describe subclinical expressions of narcissism. Grandiose narcissism involves agentic/extraverted (such as dominance, self-esteem, and a need for power) and antagonistic/disagreeable attributes (such as entitlement, hostility, and a low need for intimacy), so that individuals high on grandiose narcissism have been described as "disagreeable extraverts" (Paulhus, 2001). Vulnerable narcissism involves antagonistic/disagreeable as well as vulnerable/neurotic attributes (such as insecurity, emotional instability, and anxiety). Analogously, vulnerable narcissists could be described as "disagreeable neurotics". Grandiose and vulnerable narcissism, thus, share the antagonistic/disagreeable aspects, which are assumed to conceptually lie in-between agentic and neurotic aspects of narcissism (Back, Küfner, & Leckelt, 2018; Back & Morf, in press; Miller et al., 2016), but distinctly cover agentic/extraverted and vulnerable/neurotic aspects, respectively.

The Measurement of Narcissism

Researchers have traditionally used the Narcissistic Personality Inventory (NPI; Raskin & Terry, 1988), which is a 40-item forced-choice self-report questionnaire. For each item, respondents have to choose between a narcissistic and a non-narcissistic statement (e.g., "I am more capable than other people." vs. "There is a lot that I can learn from other people."). The number of selected narcissistic statements represents the individual narcissism score. Examination of the item content reveals that the NPI primarily covers agentic aspects of narcissism. Antagonistic aspects of narcissism are only represented in a few items (Grosz et al., 2017), and neurotic aspects are not assessed. Thus, total NPI scores reflect individual differences in grandiose (agentic and—less so and rather unreliably—antagonistic), but not in vulnerable (neurotic), narcissism.

With the aim to capture the multidimensionality of the narcissism concept and to overcome psychometric inconsistencies of the NPI (Ackerman et al., 2011; Brown, Budzek, & Tamborski, 2009; Grosz et al., 2017; Rosenthal, Montoya, Ridings, Rieck, & Hooley, 2011), a number of further broad (targeting at least two aspects), as well as specific (targeting one aspect), narcissism measures have been developed. Among the broad measures are the Five Factor Narcissism Inventory (Glover, Miller, Lynam, Crego, & Widiger, 2012), which covers all three aspects of narcissism, the Pathological Narcissism Inventory (Pincus et al., 2009), which primarily covers antagonistic and vulnerable aspects, as well as the Narcissistic Admiration and Rivalry Questionnaire (Back et al., 2013), which covers agentic and antagonistic aspects. Among the specific narcissism measures are, for example, the unpublished Grandiose Narcissism Scale (Rosenthal, Hooley, & Steshenko, 2007), assessing agentic aspects, the Psychological Entitlement Scale (Campbell, Bonacci, Shelton, Exline, & Bushman, 2004), assessing antagonistic aspects, as well as the Hypersensitivity Narcissism Scale (Hendin & Cheek, 1997), assessing neurotic aspects of narcissism.

The Determinants of Narcissism

Determinants of narcissism—as for any other trait—are found in individuals' nature (i.e., genes) and nurture (i.e., environment). Neurotic aspects of narcissism, for example, have a substantial genetic component (e.g., Livesley, Jang, & Vernon, 1998). When differentiating between agentic and antagonistic aspects of grandiose narcissism, modest heritability coefficients were found for both aspects (Luo, Cai, & Song, 2014), with largely distinct genetic and environmental sources of variation.

Focusing on environmental sources that promote the development of narcissism, early conceptual approaches emphasized the importance of inadequate parental care—that is, either parental devaluation (Kernberg, 1975; Kohut, 1977) or parental overvaluation (Millon, 1981). These theoretical propositions were supported by cross-sectional empirical evidence (Thomaes, Brummelmann, Reijntjes, & Bushman, 2013). Evidence of studies using longitudinal designs suggests that parental overvaluation may primarily predict grandiose and particularly agentic aspects of narcissism (Brummelman, Nelemans, Thomaes, & Orobio de Castro, 2017; Brummelman et al., 2015), whereas parental devaluation predicts neurotic aspects of narcissism (Horton, 2011). Additionally, parental hostility and lack of monitoring were found to be linked to antagonistic aspects (Wetzel & Robins, 2016).

The Development of Narcissism

Differences in narcissism between individuals tend to be stable from young adulthood onwards (Orth & Luciano, 2015)—a stability that is comparable to other broad personality traits

(Brummelman et al., 2015; Wetzel & Robins, 2016). There are, however, differences across genders and cultures. Men, compared with women, usually report higher scores on grandiose but not on vulnerable narcissism (Grijalva et al., 2015). Persons from individualistic cultures, compared with collectivistic cultures, report greater grandiose narcissism on average (Foster, Campbell, & Twenge, 2003; Miller et al., 2015). Such cultural differences may also be reflected in the sport context and might, for example, point at mean-level differences across national teams (e.g., Team USA presumably holding a higher average narcissism score than Team China, for example). Importantly, such cultural differences might influence and, therefore, help explain whether and how narcissism develops, both inside and outside the sport context (for overviews see, for example, Kontos & Breland-Noble, 2002; Schinke & Hanrahan, 2009). However, apart from descriptive, quantitative mean-level differences in grandiose narcissism across cultures, grandiose narcissism might simply (i.e., qualitatively, conceptionally) be different in collectivistic, compared with individualistic, cultures: The assumption is that narcissism in collectivistic cultures involves inflated self-views on communal, rather than agentic, traits at its core (see Sedikides, Gaertner, & Toguchi, 2003).

Within individuals, narcissism typically shows a decline over the lifespan, with a peak in young adulthood followed by a decrease of scores over middle and old adulthood (Cramer, 2011). Comparing the average narcissism expression of generational cohorts, it is heavily disputed whether current younger generations are more narcissistic than previous ones, with some evidence suggesting that they are (Twenge & Foster, 2010) and other that they are not (Wetzel et al., 2017). Research aiming at explaining individual narcissism development has proposed potential sources within peers, colleagues, romantic partners, stressful life events, and active and elite sport participation but have as yet only rarely been examined (see, for example, Orth & Luciano, 2015).

The Prevalence of Narcissism in the Sport Domain

Although it is easy to recall anecdotal evidence of narcissistic athletes, it is an open empirical question whether athletes, on average, are indeed more narcissistic than the general population or whether the anecdotal evidence just mirrors an existing but invalid stereotype. Initial evidence (Elman & McKelvie, 2003) supports this stereotype, with athletes (here: soccer players) being perceived as more narcissistic than non-athletes. The stereotypical perceptions, however, were found to be only partly valid because they exaggerated reality. In fact, the investigated soccer players were found to score only slightly higher on narcissism than non-athletes did (Elman & McKelvie, 2003). Such small group differences were also found in a study by Carroll (1989). She comparatively studied the narcissism of bodybuilders, other athletes, and non-athletes and found bodybuilders to report higher scores on the self-absorption subscale of the NPI, but equally high scores on all other subscales. These studies only provide initial evidence, and more research is needed that systematically targets the prevalence of narcissism and aspects of narcissism within the sport context. Here, future research efforts will, for example, address group differences between athletic and non-athletic groups, within the athletic group (e.g., elite vs. recreational athletes), between types of sport (e.g., individual vs. team sport), and within types of sport (e.g., striker vs. defender).

Assuming that athletes may hold slightly increased narcissism scores, it is still unclear whether athletes' narcissism scores are (a) due to narcissistic individuals selecting themselves more frequently into active sport participation (i.e., selection effects) or/and (b) due to active sport participation feeding back into and presumably reinforcing individuals' narcissism levels over time (i.e., socialization effects). To empirically distinguish these two effects, longitudinal research is needed that repeatedly monitors narcissism levels in (to-be) athletes through their sport careers. Such efforts will clarify the role of active and elite sport participation in the intra-individual development of narcissism and be able to test whether selection or socialization effects or both jointly explain potentially amplified narcissism in athletes.

The Consequences of Narcissism

Narcissism is consequential for many important life outcomes both, outside as well as inside the sport domain. In this section, a summary of narcissism effects found in mainstream psychology is provided, relating them, whenever possible, to potential implications for the role of narcissism in the sport domain. Because, at its heart, sport is about winning, particular attention is paid to narcissism effects on performance and career success.

Narcissism revolves around maintaining a grandiose self. As such, agentic aspects of narcissism relate to positive self-views and to favourable consequences, such as measures of self-esteem, optimism, positive affect, life satisfaction, and subjective health (e.g., Sedikides, Rudich, Gregg, Kumashiro, & Rusbult, 2004). Hence, individuals high in agentic narcissism typically report being well adjusted. Antagonistic and particularly neurotic aspects of narcissism, however, are often found to be related to fragile self-views and unfavourable intrapersonal outcomes (Back et al., 2013; Back & Morf, in press; Geukes et al., 2017; Gregg & Sedikides, 2010; Miller et al., 2011; Miller, Lynam, Hyatt, & Campbell, 2017; Morf & Rhodewalt, 1993; Morf et al., 2017; Zeigler-Hill & Besser, 2013). Because narcissistic individuals with more vulnerable features often show self-, emotional, and behavioural dysregulation in response to ego threats or self-enhancement failures, it is especially the neurotic aspect of narcissism that represents a close link to maladjustment and psychopathology (e.g., Pincus, Cain, & Wright, 2014). These intra-individual consequences should also translate into the sport domain, with agentic aspects of narcissism promoting, and antagonistic and neurotic aspects of narcissism hindering, adjustment.

Social consequences of narcissism depend not only on the aspect of narcissism considered but, additionally, on the relationship type, its duration, and the social and situational context (Back et al., 2018; Campbell & Campbell, 2009; Leckelt, Küfner, Nestler, & Back, 2015). Individuals scoring high on grandiose narcissism are often more popular among peers at first sight (Back, Schmukle, & Egloff, 2010), but this popularity declines over time. Specifically, whereas the agentic aspects of narcissism lead to early popularity, its antagonistic aspects lead to unpopularity in later relationship stages (Küfner, Nestler, & Back, 2013; Leckelt et al., 2015; Paulhus, 1998). These findings derive from peer relationships or friendships, but also translate into the romantic relationship context where narcissism is related to success in the short-term dating phase but to problems in long-term committed relationships (Campbell, Brunell, & Finkel, 2006; Wurst et al., 2017). Within the sport domain, individuals are part of both short-term and long-term social contexts. A superficial interaction with an opponent or the opponent's coach, a brief statement to a journalist after the competition, and some small talk with fans in front of the arena represent short-term social contexts in which individuals high on agentic narcissism, especially, should garner applause and popularity. A long training history with a coach and team mates, a rehabilitation phase with a physiotherapist after a severe injury, and regular counselling sessions with a sport psychologist represent long-term social contexts in which antagonistic and potentially neurotic aspects of narcissism might lead to social conflicts and interpersonal problems in the long run. Initial supporting evidence, for example, has shown that narcissistic individuals engage in social loafing behaviours, which negatively influence group outcomes, such as cohesion or satisfaction (Woodman, Roberts,

Hardy, Callow, & Rogers, 2011). Negative social outcomes such as these might even be more pronounced and, therefore, more consequential within team sports, compared with individual sports, where the focus is on each team member's contribution to collective rather than individual success.

Regarding performance outcomes, narcissistic individuals exhibit optimistic expectations, engage in positive and superior evaluations of their own performances, and pursue a self-serving attributional style (Farwell & Wohlwend-Lloyd, 1998; Gabriel, Critelli, & Ee, 1994). Contrasting this positive subjective view on performances, however, their objective performances—across domains and tasks—are generally found to be no better than those of non-narcissistic individuals (Gabriel et al., 1994)—for example, in group interactions (John & Robins, 1994), supervisor ratings of work performance (Judge, LePine, & Rich, 2006), oral presentations (Robins & John, 1997), socio-cognitive tasks (Mota et al., 2019), and intelligence tests (Gabriel et al., 1994). Thus, even though performances of narcissistic individuals are not found to be substantially better than those of non-narcissistic individuals per se, their positive performance expectations, evaluations, and attributions, as well as their desire to win and be better than others, might at least predispose them to select themselves, engage in, and ultimately also succeed in competitive activities such as sport.

Regarding career success, narcissistic individuals appear to be fairly successful at building an occupational career: Narcissism is associated with high-ranking jobs (Ahmetoglu et al., 2016; Board & Fritzon, 2005), leadership emergence and positions (Braun, 2017; Brunell et al., 2008; Campbell, Hoffman, Campbell, & Marchisio, 2011; Grijalva, Harms, Newman, Gaddis, & Fraley, 2015), high compensations (O'Reilly, Doerr, Caldwell, & Chatman, 2014), and wealth (Leckelt et al., 2018). At the same time, however, narcissism is related to risky institutional behaviours (Foster, Reidy, Misra, & Goff, 2011) and corporate failure in the long run (e.g., Maccoby, 2014). Recent meta-analyses suggest that agentic aspects of narcissism drive the career-promoting effects, whereas counter-productive work behaviours are associated with antagonistic aspects of narcissism (Grijalva et al., 2015; Grijalva & Newman, 2015). Longitudinal research, however, will need to clarify whether these outcomes are the results of selection or socialization influences. In parallel, narcissism is likely to have divergent effects on sports careers, depending on the aspect of narcissism considered. Agentic narcissism should be more likely to foster successful career paths, for example, via positive self-views and extraversion. Antagonistic and neurotic aspects, in contrast, might be more detrimental via more negative self-views and disagreeable and emotionally unstable tendencies, because they are typically found, albeit only weakly, to be negatively associated with success (e.g., Barrick & Mount, 1991).

The Dynamics of Narcissism

All of these consequences do not, of course, happen by chance, but are grounded in narcissistic dynamics, with their core being the aim of maintaining a grandiose self (e.g., Back et al., 2013; Morf, Torchetti, & Schürch, 2011). To achieve this aim, narcissistic individuals engage in characteristic ways of wanting, feeling, thinking, and behaving, which can be related to the threefold structure of narcissism and which were specified by several conceptual models: for example (in alphabetical order), the contextual reinforcement model (Campbell & Campbell, 2009), the dynamic self-regulatory processing model (Morf & Rhodewalt, 2001; Morf et al., 2011), the extended agency model (Campbell & Foster, 2007), the narcissistic admiration and rivalry concept (Back et al., 2013), and the narcissism spectrum model (Krizan & Herlache, 2017). In essence, the intra- and interpersonal dynamics relate to how individuals select and construe situations, how they perceive and behave in situations, and how they evaluate and react to situations (e.g., Geukes, van Zalk, & Back, 2018; Heckhausen, 1991).

Agentic aspects of narcissism are characterized by approach motivation (Foster & Trimm, 2008) and aiming at "getting ahead" rather than at "getting along" (Campbell & Foster, 2007; Morf & Rhodewalt, 2001). In social situations, agentic aspects are linked to exploiting self-presentational opportunities and to perceiving others as a source of admiration (e.g., Back et al., 2010; Holtzman & Strube, 2010; Vazire, Naumann, Rentfrow, & Gosling, 2008). Typical reactions of agentic aspects of narcissism are (over-)attributing successes to innate abilities (e.g., Rhodewalt & Morf, 1998) and accompanying emotions of pride (Tracy, Cheng, Martens, & Robins, 2011). By contrast, antagonistic and neurotic aspects of narcissism are both characterized by avoidance motivation (Foster & Trimm, 2008). In social situations, antagonistic aspects are linked to disagreeable strivings for self-protection (Back et al., 2013) and to inconsiderate and bold reactions when feeling criticized (Krizan & Johar, 2015; Leckelt et al., 2015). Typical reactions of antagonistic aspects of narcissism involve external attributions of failures by blaming or devaluing others (Kernis & Sun, 1994) and experiencing malicious envy (Lange, Crusius, Hagemeyer, 2016). Neurotic aspects of narcissism are linked to heightened affective dysregulation and negative interpersonal schemas (Foster & Trimm, 2008). Typical reactions of neurotic aspects of narcissism reflect a hostile attribution bias such as believing others' intentions to be malevolent and accompanying emotions of shame (Tracy et al., 2011).

The Role of Narcissism in the Sports Domain

Sport psychological research on narcissism is relatively young and spans about the last two decades. Mirroring the clinical origins of narcissism research, much of the early sport psychological research focused on athletes and revolved around psychopathological issues such as anxiety (e.g., Akehurst & Thatcher, 2010; Spano, 2001), exercise dependence and addiction (e.g., Bruno et al., 2014; Hausenblas & Downs, 2002; Lichtenstein, Christiansen, Elklit, Bilenberg, & Støving, 2014; Miller & Mesagno, 2014), body image and esteem (e.g., Davis, Claridge, & Brewer, 1996; Davis, Claridge, & Cerullo, 1997), and disturbed eating behaviours and eating disorders (e.g., Davis & Strachan, 2001; Goldfield, Harper, & Blouin, 1998). More recent sport psychological research efforts have targeted subclinical questions regarding the consequences of athlete narcissism (e.g., Arthur, Woodman, Ong, Hardy, & Ntoumanis, 2011; Geukes, Mesagno, Hanrahan, & Kellmann, 2012, 2013; Jones, Woodman, Barlow, & Roberts, 2017; Roberts, Woodman, Lofthouse, & Williams, 2015; Woodman et al., 2011), as well as the consequences of coach narcissism in the sport domain (Matosic et al., 2017; Matosic, Ntoumanis, Boardley, Stenling, & Sedikides, 2016). Therefore, the focus is on summarizing findings on these two groups of protagonists in the sport domain: athletes and coaches.

Narcissism in Athletes

As the competitive sport context might greatly serve the narcissistic individuals' goal to maintain a grandiose self, researchers assume that they might benefit from their positive self-views, expectations, evaluations, and attributions (cf. Farwell & Wohlwend-Lloyd, 1998). Specifically, narcissistic individuals are thought to succeed in high-stakes situations, which might be threatening and involve pressure (Roberts, Woodman, & Sedikides, 2018). Thus, this assumption implies that the link between narcissism and relevant outcomes in performance situations is moderated by situational features describing a person–situation interaction. Empirically, it has indeed been found that the influence of narcissism on outcomes in performance situations largely depends on situational characteristics. In situations that provide opportunity for glory, admiration, as well as prestige and status attainment, narcissistic individuals are more strongly motivated and perform better than non-narcissistic individuals (Geukes et al., 2012; Wallace & Baumeister, 2002). In situations, however, that do not offer these opportunities, narcissism and motivation, as well as narcissism and performance, are either unrelated or even negatively related (e.g., Geukes et al., 2013; Roberts et al., 2019; Roberts, Woodman, Hardy, Davis, & Wallace, 2013; Wallace & Baumeister, 2002; Woodman et al., 2011).

Considering different high-pressure situations, findings indicate that narcissism positively predicts performance in public pressure situations, when performing in front of a large audience, but not in more private situations, even if pressure is still involved through motivational incentives (Geukes et al., 2012, 2013). In an attempt to explain why narcissistic individuals perform better in situations in which they detect an opportunity for glory and competition, researchers have emphasized the crucial role of effort (Arthur et al., 2011; Wallace & Baumeister, 2002), as well as enjoyment and intrinsic motivation (Morf, Weir, & Davidov, 2000). Narcissistic individuals have been found to increase effort in such situations, and initial evidence points at them "trying harder" (i.e., investing more effort) rather than "trying smarter" (i.e., investing effort more effectively; Roberts et al., 2018; Woodman et al., 2011).

Given their natural ability to thrive when the stakes are high, researchers (e.g., Roberts, Callow, Hardy, Woodman, & Thomas, 2010; Roberts et al., 2013) have also addressed the question of whether narcissistic individuals further profit from the use of psychological skills (e.g., imagery, self-talk, relaxation, emotional control). They found narcissism to moderate the association between psychological skill use and performance, with narcissistic individuals benefitting from external visual imagery, relaxation, and self-talk, but not from internal visual imagery and emotional control (e.g., Roberts et al., 2010, 2013). Based on these important initial insights, future sport psychology research needs to further determine how (i.e., strength and directionality of effects), when (i.e., situational dependencies of effects), and why (i.e., underlying processes of effects) athletes' narcissism and its different aspects affect performance. Successful performance, however, is a result of both an optimal mental state that enables peak performance when it counts and a thorough preparation through hard and regular work aimed at constantly increasing the respective motor ability (Ericsson, 2006, 2014). Thus, sport psychological research has provided important insights regarding the former, highlighting that narcissistic individuals are predisposed to excel under pressure. Regarding the latter, however— whether narcissistic individuals are capable of rigorously keeping up with a sustained training regimen that is needed to be successful—current empirical knowledge is sparse. Because training settings, compared with competitions, usually are rather lacking in external motivational features and any directly contingent opportunity for glory, this ability might be a matter of individuals' achievement motivation (e.g., Emmons, 1989). If their achievement motivation primarily relates to competitiveness (i.e., to the desire to be better than others), individuals might indeed be challenged by the demands of overly strict training schedules lacking performance comparisons. If, however, their achievement motivation also, or even primarily, relates to mastery (i.e., to the desire to attain competence), they might be well able to devote themselves to the hard work necessary for the desired success (e.g., Elliot & Thrash, 2001). In case these considerations find empirical support, they might also provide starting points of how to optimally design training schedules (i.e., to involve competitions and rewards) to keep narcissistic individuals consistently motivated throughout preparation phases.

Narcissism in Coaches

The behaviour of coaches is thought to have a substantial impact on athletes' motivation, behaviour, performance, and well-being (e.g., Ntoumanis & Mallet, 2014). Evidence from organizational psychology underlines that narcissistic leaders are likely to be seen as charismatic figures who convincingly communicate bold and daring visions, and who act in a forward-driven manner (Braun, 2017). These narcissistic attributes (e.g., charisma, dominance, charmingness, self-assuredness, and need for power) might also apply to the sport context and contribute to effective coaching behaviours. The resulting assumption is that narcissistic individuals might be "born leaders or coaches". However, the organizational literature also points at negative outcomes of narcissistic leadership, even when considering its grandiose aspects. Narcissistic leaders lack concern for others, and their self-view as transformational leaders often remains unshared by followers (Greaves, Zacher, McKenna, & Rooney, 2014; Judge et al., 2006). Moreover, narcissistic leadership was found to be associated with negative consequences for followers' emotions (e.g., malicious envy; Braun, Aydin, Frey, & Peus, 2016) and behaviours (e.g., counterproductivity; Martin, Côté, & Woodruff, 2016) and with rather unsustainable, risky, and short-sighted activities (e.g., Petrenko, Aime, Ridge, & Hill, 2016). In sports, the role of narcissism in leadership has only received little empirical attention, and initial findings so far seem to support the negative rather than at the positive side. Narcissism in coaches was found to be linked to controlling behaviours, with this relationship being mediated via a lack of empathetic concern (Matosic et al., 2017). Importantly, controlling coaching behaviours were further linked to relevant unfavourable outcomes in athletes such as frustrated needs and positive doping attitudes (Matosic et al., 2016). Although these findings might be counter-intuitive at first sight, they are well in line with insights on narcissistic leadership emergence and maintenance and peer popularity gained within organizational, social, and personality psychology (e.g., Campbell & Campbell, 2009; Grijalva et al., 2015; Rosenthal & Pittinsky, 2006). Here, it was found that narcissistic individuals are indeed seen as "born leaders" and as popular initially, but these positive perceptions decrease over time (e.g., Back et al., 2013, 2010; Carlson & DesJardins, 2015; Czarna, Leifeld, Śmieja, Dufner, & Salovey, 2016; Ong, Roberts, Arthur, Woodman, Akehurst, 2016; Paulhus, 1998). Importantly, focusing on the processes behind the decline of narcissistic individuals' peer popularity, researchers identified distinct behavioural and perceptual pathways (Back et al., 2018; Küfner et al., 2013). Agentic aspects of narcissism were found to relate to dominant and assertive behaviours, which are perceived as positive, especially in early, more superficial stages of interaction. Antagonistic aspects of narcissism, however, were found to relate to arrogant and aggressive behaviours, which are perceived as negative and typically only come to light once relationships become more intimate and involve more potential for conflict (Leckelt et al., 2015). Thus, insights gained in personality psychology more broadly illustrate potential processes behind narcissistic leadership emergence and maintenance that might also be applicable to evolving as well as existing coach–athlete relationships.

Future Prospects for Sport Psychological Narcissism Research

Research on narcissism within sport psychology is young, and the sports context promises to be an ideal environment to systematically study narcissism, its prevalence, development, consequences, and dynamics. To advance research on the prevalence and development of narcissism in the sport domain, comprehensive studies are needed to determine differences in narcissism across populations, cultures, and groups (e.g., to what degree athletes and other sport populations are more narcissistic than non-athletes and general populations) and to longitudinally disentangle selection (to what degree narcissistic individuals select themselves into the sport domain) and socialization effects (to what degree individuals become more narcissistic during sports participation over time). To further advance research on the consequences of narcissism (e.g., in what ways narcissism is positively related to performance) and their underlying dynamics (e.g., how and why is narcissism positively related to performance and a rigorous training regime), it will be necessary to obtain a longitudinal, rather than cross-sectional, and process-oriented perspective. Moreover, representative designs are needed that incorporate multiple methods and data sources (e.g., self-reports, behavioural observations, other-reports), as well as multiple social perspectives (self, others, observers; for an example, see Leckelt et al., 2015) to fully account for the complexities in narcissistic dynamics. In doing so, it will be necessary to consider the threefold conceptualization of narcissism involving agentic, antagonistic, and neurotic aspects. To date, unidimensional conceptualizations of mainly grandiose narcissism are still frequently used in the sport domain (for an exception, see, for example, Davis et al., 1997), but the three-dimensional distinction will help to disentangle differentiated effects that are typical for different aspects of narcissism and the processes by which they unfold. Finally, as the competitive sport domain as a whole provides a range of systematically different (selection and socialization) contexts regarding, for example, competitive tasks and modes, types of sport, present norms and values, as well as cultural backgrounds, it is especially promising to make use of this natural variation to target boundary conditions of effects on and of narcissism and to target the mechanisms underlying these associations.

Conclusion

Narcissism is a subclinical, relatively stable, multifaceted personality trait that captures agentic (extraverted), antagonistic (disagreeable), and vulnerable (neurotic) aspects and can be assessed using self-report questionnaires. Narcissism has genetic as well as environmental origins, peaks in early adulthood, and declines thereafter over the lifespan. Initially, researchers were left puzzled by its enigmatic ambiguity in correlates and consequences, because associations were found to be contradictory and sometimes even paradoxical. More recently, however, both, the threefold distinction of subclinical narcissism and an intensified focus on underlying processes have helped to unravel previously mixed findings. Whereas agentic aspects of narcissism were found to be largely linked to favourable correlates and adaptive consequences via functional processes, antagonistic and especially neurotic aspects of narcissism were found to be largely linked to unfavourable antecedents and maladaptive consequences via more dysfunctional processes, bridging subclinical and pathological research. Sport psychological research on the role of narcissism is relatively young and particularly focused on consequences of narcissism for athletes (e.g., psychopathology, performance) as well as coaches (e.g., leadership). Future research on narcissism in sports will aim at gaining a better understanding of its determinants, development, consequences, and processes within and across different protagonists, within and across different competitive tasks and modes, within and across different types of sport, as well as within and across different cultures. These efforts might benefit from incorporating the three-dimensional structure of narcissism and from adopting a longitudinal, multi-methodological, process-based perspective to provide answers on the question of which role narcissism plays in the sport domain. Because, at its heart, competitive sport is about winning, which presumably serves a grandiose self, the sport arena reflects an ideal tumbling ground for further systematic narcissism research in its protagonists.

References

Ackerman, R. A., Witt, E. A., Donnellan, M. B., Trzesniewski, K. H., Robins, R. W., & Kashy, D. A. (2011). What does the narcissistic personality inventory really measure? *Assessment, 18*, 67–87.

Ahmetoglu, G., Dobbs, S., Furnham, A., Crump, J., Chamorro-Premuzic, T., & Bakhshalian, E. (2016). Dark side of personality, intelligence, creativity, and managerial level. *Journal of Managerial Psychology, 31*, 391–404.

Akehurst, S., & Thatcher, J. (2010). Narcissism, social anxiety and self-presentation in exercise. *Personality and Individual Differences, 49*, 130–135.

American Psychiatric Association [APA]. (1980). *Diagnostic and statistical manual of mental disorders* (3rd ed.). Washington, DC: Author.

Arthur, C. A., Woodman, T., Ong, C. W., Hardy, L., & Ntoumanis, N. (2011). The role of athlete narcissism in moderating the relationship between coaches' transformational leader behaviors and athlete motivation. *Journal of Sport and Exercise Psychology, 33*, 3–19.

Back, M. D., Küfner, A. C. P., Dufner, M., Gerlach, T. M., Rauthmann, J. F., & Denissen, J. J. A. (2013). Narcissistic admiration and rivalry: Disentangling the bright and dark sides of narcissism. *Journal of Personality and Social Psychology, 105*, 1013–1037.

Back, M. D., Küfner, A. C. P., & Leckelt, M. (2018). Early impressions of grandiose narcissists: A dual-pathway perspective. In A. D. Hermann, A. Brunell & J. Foster (Eds.), *The Handbook of trait narcissism: Key advances, research methods, and controversies* (pp. 309–316). New York: Springer.

Back, M. D., & Morf, C. C. (in press). Narcissism. In V. Zeigler-Hill & T. K. Shackelford (Eds.), *Encyclopedia of personality and individual differences*. New York: Springer.

Back, M. D., Schmukle, S. C., & Egloff, B. (2010). Why are narcissists so charming at first sight? Decoding the narcissism–popularity link at zero acquaintance. *Journal of Personality and Social Psychology, 98*, 132–145.

Barrick, M. R., & Mount, M. K. (1991). The big five personality dimensions and job performance: A meta-analysis. *Personnel Psychology, 44*, 1–26.

Board, B. J., & Fritzon, K. (2005). Disordered personalities at work. *Psychology, Crime & Law, 11*, 17–32.

Braun, S. (2017). Leader narcissism and outcomes in organizations: A review at multiple levels of analysis and implications for future research. *Frontiers in Psychology, 8*, 773.

Braun, S., Aydin, N., Frey, D., & Peus, C. (2016). Leader narcissism predicts malicious envy and supervisor-targeted counterproductive work behavior: Evidence from field and experimental research. *Journal of Business Ethics, 151*, 725–741.

Brown, R. P., Budzek, K., & Tamborski, M. (2009). On the meaning and measure of narcissism. *Personality and Social Psychology Bulletin, 35*, 951–964.

Brummelman, E., Nelemans, S. A., Thomaes, S., & Orobio de Castro, B. (2017). When parents' praise inflates, children's self-esteem deflates. *Child Development, 88*, 1799–1809.

Brummelman, E., Thomaes, S., Nelemans, S. A., Orobio de Castro, B., Overbeek, G., & Bushman, B. J. (2015). Origins of narcissism in children. *Proceedings of the National Academy of Sciences of the United States of America, 112*, 3659–3662.

Brunell, A. B., Gentry, W. A., Campbell, W. K., Hoffman, B. J., Kuhnert, K. W., & DeMarree, K. G. (2008). Leader emergence: The case of the narcissistic leader. *Personality and Social Psychology Bulletin, 34*, 1663–1676.

Bruno, A., Quattrone, D., Scimeca, G., Cicciarelli, C., Romeo, V. M., Pandolfo, G., ... Muscatello, M. R. A. (2014). Unraveling exercise addiction: The role of narcissism and self-esteem. *Journal of Addiction.*. http://dx.doi.org/10.1155/2014/987841.

Cain, N. M., Pincus, A. L., & Ansell, E. B. (2008). Narcissism at the crossroads: Phenotypic description of pathological narcissism across clinical theory, social/personality psychology, and psychiatric diagnosis. *Clinical Psychology Review, 28*, 638–656.

Campbell, W. K., Bonacci, A. M., Shelton, J., Exline, J. J., & Bushman, B. J. (2004). Psychological entitlement: Interpersonal consequences and validation of a self-report measure. *Journal of Personality Assessment, 83*, 29–45.

Campbell, W. K., Brunell, A. B., & Finkel, E. J. (2006). Narcissism, interpersonal self-regulation, and romantic relationships: An agency model approach. In K. D. Vohs & E. J. Finkel (Eds.), *Self and relationships: Connecting intrapersonal and interpersonal processes* (pp. 57–83). New York: Guilford Press.

Campbell, W. K., & Campbell, S. M. (2009). On the self-regulatory dynamics created by the peculiar benefits and costs of narcissism: A contextual reinforcement model and examination of leadership. *Self and Identity, 8,* 214–232.

Campbell, W. K., & Foster, J. D. (2007). The narcissistic self: Background, an extended agency model, and ongoing controversies. In C. Sedikides & S. Spencer (Eds.), *Frontiers in social psychology: The self* (pp. 115–138). Philadelphia, PA: Psychology Press.

Campbell, W. K., Hoffman, B. J., Campbell, S. M., & Marchisio, G. (2011). Narcissism in organizational contexts. *Human Resource Management Review, 21,* 268–284.

Carlson, E. N., & DesJardins, N. M. L. (2015). Do mean guys always finish first or just say that they do? Narcissists' awareness of their social status and popularity over time. *Personality and Social Psychology Bulletin, 41,* 901–917.

Carroll, L. (1989). A comparative study of narcissism, gender, and sex-role orientation among bodybuilders, athletes, and psychology students. *Psychological Reports, 64,* 999–1006.

Cramer, P. (2011). Narcissism through the ages: What happens when narcissists grow older? *Journal of Research in Personality, 45,* 479–492.

Czarna, A. Z., Leifeld, P., Śmieja, M., Dufner, M., & Salovey, P. (2016). Do narcissism and emotional intelligence win us friends? Modeling dynamics of peer popularity using inferential network analysis. *Personality and Social Psychology Bulletin, 42,* 1588–1599.

Davis, C., Claridge, G., & Brewer, H. (1996). The two faces of narcissism: Personality dynamics of body esteem. *Journal of Social and Clinical Psychology, 15,* 153–166.

Davis, C., Claridge, G., & Cerullo, D. (1997). Reflections on narcissism: Conflicts about body-image perceptions in women. *Personality and Individual Differences, 22,* 309–316.

Davis, C., & Strachan, S. (2001). Elite female athletes with eating disorders: A study of psychopathological characteristics. *Journal of Sport & Exercise Psychology, 23,* 245–253.

Elliot, A. J., & Thrash, T. M. (2001). Narcissism and motivation. *Psychological Inquiry, 12,* 216–219.

Elman, W., & McKelvie, S. (2003). Narcissism in football players: Stereotype or reality. *Athletic Insight, 5,* 38–46.

Emmons, R. A. (1989). Exploring the relations between motives and traits: The case of narcissism. In D. M. Buss & N. Cantor (Eds.), *Personality psychology: Recent trends and emerging directions* (pp. 32–44). New York: Springer.

Ericsson, K. A. (2006). The influence of experience and deliberate practice on the development of superior expert performance. In K. A. Ericsson, N. Charness, R. R. Hoffman & P. J. Feltovich (Eds.), *The Cambridge handbook of expertise and expert performance* (pp. 39–68). New York: Cambridge University Press.

Ericsson, K. A. (2014). *The road to excellence: The acquisition of expert performance in the arts and sciences, sports, and games.* New York: Psychology Press.

Farwell, L., & Wohlwend-Lloyd, R. (1998). Narcissistic processes: Optimistic expectations, favorable self-evaluations, and self-enhancing attributions. *Journal of Personality, 66,* 65–83.

Foster, J. D., Campbell, W. K., & Twenge, J. M. (2003). Individual differences in narcissism: Inflated self-views across the lifespan and around the world. *Journal of Research in Personality, 37,* 469–486.

Foster, J. D., Reidy, D. E., Misra, T. A., & Goff, J. S. (2011). Narcissism and stock market investing: Correlates and consequences of cocksure investing. *Personality and Individual Differences, 50,* 816–821.

Foster, J. D., & Trimm, R. F. (2008). On being eager and uninhibited: Narcissism and approach-avoidance motivation. *Personality and Social Psychology Bulletin, 34,* 1004–1017.

Freud, S. (1990). Zur Einführung des Narzißmus [On narcissism: An introduction]. In A. Freud, E. Bibring, & W. Hoffer (Eds.), *Gesammelte Werke* (8th ed. vol. X, pp. 137–171). Frankfurt, Germany: S. Fischer. (Original published 1914).

Gabriel, M. T., Critelli, J. W., & Ee, J. S. (1994). Narcissistic illusions in self-evaluations of intelligence and attractiveness. *Journal of Personality, 62,* 143–155.

Geukes, K., Mesagno, C., Hanrahan, S. J., & Kellmann, M. (2012). Testing an interactionist perspective on the relationship between personality traits and performance under public pressure. *Psychology of Sport and Exercise, 13,* 243–250.

Geukes, K., Mesagno, C., Hanrahan, S. J., & Kellmann, M. (2013). Activation of self-focus and self-presentation traits under private, mixed, and public pressure. *Journal of Sport and Exercise Psychology, 35,* 50–59.

Geukes, K., Nestler, S., Hutteman, R., Dufner, M., Küfner, A. C. P., Egloff, B., ... Back, M. D. (2017). Puffed up but shaky selves: State self-esteem level and variability in narcissists. *Journal of Personality and Social Psychology, 112,* 769–786.

Geukes, K., van Zalk, M., & Back, M. D. (2018). Understanding personality development: An integrative state process model. *International Journal of Behavioral Development, 42,* 43–51.

Glover, N., Miller, J. D., Lynam, D. R., Crego, C., & Widiger, T. A. (2012). The five-factor narcissism inventory: A five-factor measure of narcissistic personality traits. *Journal of Personality Assessment, 94,* 500–512.

Goldfield, G. S., Harper, D. W., & Blouin, A. G. (1998). Are bodybuilders at risk for an eating disorder? *Eating Disorders, 6,* 133–151.

Greaves, E. C., Zacher, H., McKenna, B., & Rooney, D. (2014). Wisdom and narcissism as predictors of transformational leadership. *Leadership & Organization Development Journal, 35,* 335–358.

Gregg, A. P., & Sedikides, C. (2010). Narcissistic fragility: Rethinking its links to explicit and implicit self-esteem. *Self and Identity, 9,* 142–161.

Grijalva, E., Harms, P. D., Newman, D. A., Gaddis, B. H., & Fraley, R. C. (2015). Narcissism and leadership: A meta-analytic review of linear and nonlinear relationships. *Personnel Psychology, 68,* 1–47.

Grijalva, E., & Newman, D. A. (2015). Narcissism and counterproductive work behavior (CWB): Meta-analysis and consideration of collectivist culture, big five personality, and narcissism's facet structure. *Applied Psychology, 64,* 93–126.

Grijalva, E., Newman, D. A., Tay, L., Donnellan, M. B., Harms, P. D., Robins, R. W., & Yan, T. (2015). Gender differences in narcissism: A meta-analytic review. *Psychological Bulletin, 141,* 261–310.

Grosz, M. P., Emons, W. H., Wetzel, E., Leckelt, M., Chopik, W. J., Rose, N., & Back, M. D. (2017). A comparison of unidimensionality and measurement precision of the narcissistic personality inventory and the narcissistic admiration and rivalry questionnaire. *Assessment, 26,* 281–293.

Hausenblas, H. A., & Downs, D. S. (2002). Exercise dependence: A systematic review. *Psychology of Sport and Exercise, 3,* 89–123.

Heckhausen, H. (1991). Historical trends in motivation research. In J. Heckhausen & H. Heckhausen (Eds.), *Motivation and action* (pp. 15–65). New York: Springer.

Hendin, H. M., & Cheek, J. M. (1997). Assessing hypersensitive narcissism: A reexamination of Murray's Narcism Scale. *Journal of Research in Personality, 31,* 588–599.

Holtzman, N. S., & Strube, M. J. (2010). Narcissism and attractiveness. *Journal of Research in Personality, 44,* 133–136.

Horton, R. S. (2011). Parenting as a cause of narcissism: Empirical support for psychodynamic and social learning theories. In W. K. Campbell & J. D. Miller (Eds.), *The handbook of narcissism and narcissistic personality disorder: Theoretical approaches, empirical findings, and treatments* (pp. 181–190). Hoboken, NJ: John Wiley.

John, O. P., & Robins, R. W. (1994). Accuracy and bias in self-perception: Individual differences in self-enhancement and the role of narcissism. *Journal of Personality and Social Psychology, 66,* 206–219.

Jones, B. D., Woodman, T., Barlow, M., & Roberts, R. (2017). The darker side of personality: Narcissism predicts moral disengagement and antisocial behavior in sport. *The Sport Psychologist, 31,* 109–116.

Judge, T. A., LePine, J. A., & Rich, B. L. (2006). Loving yourself abundantly: Relationship of the narcissistic personality to self-and other perceptions of workplace deviance, leadership, and task and contextual performance. *Journal of Applied Psychology, 91,* 762–776.

Kernberg, O. (1975). *Borderline conditions and pathological narcissism.* New York: Aronson.

Kernis, M. H., & Sun, C.-R. (1994). Narcissism and reactions to interpersonal feedback. *Journal of Research in Personality, 28,* 4–13.

Kohut, H. (1977). *The restoration of the self.* New York: International Universities Press.

Kontos, A. P., & Breland-Noble, A. M. (2002). Racial/ethnic diversity in applied sport psychology: A multicultural introduction to working with athletes of color. *The Sport Psychologist, 16,* 296–315.

Krizan, Z., & Herlache, A. D. (2017). The narcissism spectrum model: A synthetic view of narcissistic personality. *Personality and Social Psychology Review, 22,* 3–31.

Krizan, Z., & Johar, O. (2015). Narcissistic rage revisited. *Journal of Personality and Social Psychology, 108,* 784–801.

Küfner, A. C. P., Nestler, S., & Back, M. D. (2013). The two pathways to being an (un-)popular narcissist. *Journal of Personality, 81,* 184–195.

Lange, J., Crusius, J., & Hagemeyer, B. (2016). The evil queen's dilemma: Linking narcissistic admiration and rivalry to benign and malicious envy. *European Journal of Personality, 30,* 168–188.

Leckelt, M., Küfner, A. C. P., Nestler, S., & Back, M. D. (2015). Behavioral processes underlying the decline of narcissists' popularity over time. *Journal of Personality and Social Psychology, 109,* 856–871.

Leckelt, M., Richter, D., Schröder, C., Küfner, A. C. P., Grabka, M. M., & Back, M. D. (2018). The rich are different: Unraveling the perceived and self-reported personality profiles of high net-worth individuals. *British Journal of Psychology..* Advance online https://onlinelibrary.wiley.com/doi/abs/10.1111/bjop.12360

Lichtenstein, M. B., Christiansen, E., Elklit, A., Bilenberg, N., & Støving, R. K. (2014). Exercise addiction: A study of eating disorder symptoms, quality of life, personality traits and attachment styles. *Psychiatry Research, 215,* 410–416.

Livesley, W. J., Jang, K. L., & Vernon, P. A. (1998). Phenotypic and genetic structure of traits delineating personality disorder. *Archives of General Psychiatry, 55,* 941–948.

Luo, Y. L. L., Cai, H., & Song, H. (2014). A behavioral genetic study of intrapersonal and interpersonal dimensions of narcissism. *PLoSOne, 9,* e93403.

Maccoby, M. (2014). Narcissistic leaders: The incredible pros, the inevitable cons. *Harvard Business Review, 78,* 68–77.

Martin, S. R., Côté, S., & Woodruff, T. (2016). Echoes of our upbringing: How growing up wealthy or poor relates to narcissism, leader behavior, and leader effectiveness. *Academy of Management Journal, 59,* 2157–2177.

Matosic, D., Ntoumanis, N., Boardley, I. D., Sedikides, C., Stewart, B. D., & Chatzisarantis, N. (2017). Narcissism and coach interpersonal style: A self-determination theory perspective. *Scandinavian Journal of Medicine & Science in Sports, 27,* 254–261.

Matosic, D., Ntoumanis, N., Boardley, I. D., Stenling, A., & Sedikides, C. (2016). Linking narcissism, motivation, and doping attitudes in sport: A multilevel investigation involving coaches and athletes. *Journal of Sport and Exercise Psychology, 38,* 556–566.

Miller, J. D., Hoffman, B. J., Gaughan, E. T., Gentile, B., Maples, J., & Campbell, W. K. (2011). Grandiose and vulnerable narcissism: A nomological network analysis. *Journal of Personality, 79,* 1013–1042.

Miller, J. D., Lynam, D. R., Hyatt, C. S., & Campbell, W. K. (2017). Controversies in narcissism. *Annual Review in Clinical Psychology, 13,* 291–315.

Miller, J. D., Lynam, D. R., McCain, J. L., Few, L. R., Crego, C., Widiger, T. A., & Campbell, W. K. (2016). Thinking structurally about narcissism: An examination of the five-factor narcissism inventory and its components. *Journal of Personality Disorders, 30,* 1–18.

Miller, J. D., Maples, J. L., Buffardi, L., Cai, H., Gentile, B., Kisbu-Sakarya, Y., … Siedor, L. (2015). Narcissism and United States' culture: The view from home and around the world. *Journal of Personality and Social Psychology, 109,* 1068–1089.

Miller, K. J., & Mesagno, C. (2014). Personality traits and exercise dependence: Exploring the role of narcissism and perfectionism. *International Journal of Sport and Exercise Psychology, 12,* 368–381.

Millon, T. (1981). *Disorders of personality.* New York: Wiley.

Morf, C. C., & Rhodewalt, F. (1993). Narcissism and self-evaluation maintenance: Explorations in object relations. *Personality and Social Psychology Bulletin, 19,* 668–676.

Morf, C. C., & Rhodewalt, F. (2001). Unraveling the paradoxes of narcissism: A dynamic self-regulatory processing model. *Psychological Inquiry, 12,* 177–196.

Morf, C. C., Schürch, E., Küfner, A., Siegrist, P., Vater, A., Back, M. D., … Schröder-Abé, M. (2017). Expanding the nomological net of the Pathological Narcissism Inventory: German validation and extension in a clinical inpatient sample. *Assessment, 24,* 419–443.

Morf, C. C., Torchetti, L., & Schürch, E. (2011). Narcissism from the perspective of the dynamic self-regulatory processing model. In W. K. Campbell & J. D. Miller (Eds.), *The handbook of narcissism and narcissistic personality disorder: Theoretical approaches, empirical findings, and treatments* (pp. 56–70). Hoboken, NJ: Wiley.

Morf, C. C., Weir, C. R., & Davidov, M. (2000). Narcissism and intrinsic motivation: The role of goal congruence. *Journal of Experimental Social Psychology, 36,* 424–438.

Mota, S., Leckelt, M., Geukes, K., Nestler, S., Humberg, S., Schröder-Abé, M., … Back, M. D. (2019). A comprehensive examination of narcissists' self-perceived and actual socioemotional cognition ability. *Collabra: Psychology, 5,* 6.

Ntoumanis, N., & Mallet, C. (2014). Motivation in sport: A self-determination theory perspective. In A. Papaioannou & D. Hackfort (Eds.), *Routledge companion to sport and exercise psychology: Global perspectives and fundamental concepts* (pp. 67–82). Hove: Routledge.

O'Reilly, C. A., Doerr, B., Caldwell, D. F., & Chatman, J. A. (2014). Narcissistic CEOs and executive compensation. *The Leadership Quarterly, 25*, 218–231.

Ong, C. W., Roberts, R., Arthur, C. A., Woodman, T., & Akehurst, S. (2016). The leader ship is sinking: A temporal investigation of narcissistic leadership. *Journal of Personality, 84*, 237–247.

Orth, U., & Luciano, E. C. (2015). Self-esteem, narcissism, and stressful life events: Testing for selection and socialization. *Journal of Personality and Social Psychology, 109*, 707–721.

Paulhus, D. L. (1998). Interpersonal and intrapsychic adaptiveness of trait self-enhancement: A mixed blessing. *Journal of Personality and Social Psychology, 74*, 1197–1208.

Paulhus, D. L. (2001). Normal narcissism: Two minimalist accounts. *Psychological Inquiry, 12*, 228–230.

Petrenko, O. V., Aime, F., Ridge, J., & Hill, A. (2016). Corporate social responsibility or CEO narcissism? CSR motivations and organizational performance. *Strategic Management Journal, 37*, 262–279.

Pincus, A. L., Ansell, E. B., Pimentel, C. A., Cain, N. M., Wright, A. G., & Levy, K. N. (2009). Initial construction and validation of the Pathological Narcissism Inventory. *Psychological Assessment, 21*, 365–379.

Pincus, A. L., Cain, N. M., & Wright, A. G. (2014). Narcissistic grandiosity and narcissistic vulnerability in psychotherapy. *Personality Disorders: Theory, Research, and Treatment, 5*, 439–443.

Pincus, A. L., & Lukowitsky, M. R. (2010). Pathological narcissism and narcissistic personality disorder. *Annual Review of Clinical Psychology, 6*, 421–446.

Raskin, R., & Terry, H. (1988). A principal-components analysis of the Narcissistic personality inventory and further evidence of its construct validity. *Journal of Personality and Social Psychology, 54*, 890–902.

Rhodewalt, F., & Morf, C. C. (1998). On self-aggrandizement and anger: A temporal analysis of narcissism and affective reactions to success and failure. *Journal of Personality and Social Psychology, 74*, 672–685.

Roberts, R., Callow, N., Hardy, L., Woodman, T., & Thomas, L. (2010). Interactive effects of different visual imagery perspectives and narcissism on motor performance. *Journal of Sport & Exercise Psychology, 32*, 499–517.

Roberts, R., Cooke, A., Woodman, T., Hupfeld, H., Barwood, C., & Manley, H. (2019). When the going gets tough, who gets going? An examination of the relationship between narcissism, effort and performance. *Sport, Exercise, and Performance Psychology, 8*, 93–105.

Roberts, R., Woodman, T., Hardy, L., Davis, L., & Wallace, H. M. (2013). Psychological skills do not always help performance: The moderating role of narcissism. *Journal of Applied Sport Psychology, 25*, 316–325.

Roberts, R., Woodman, T., Lofthouse, S., & Williams, L. (2015). Not all players are equally motivated: The role of narcissism. *European Journal of Sport Science, 15*, 536–542.

Roberts, R., Woodman, T., & Sedikides, C. (2018). Pass me the ball: Narcissism in performance settings. *International Review of Sport and Exercise Psychology, 11*, 190–213.

Robins, R. W., & John, O. P. (1997). Effects of visual perspective and narcissism on self-perception: Is seeing believing? *Psychological Science, 8*, 37–42.

Rosenthal, S. A., Hooley, J. M., & Steshenko, Y. (2007). *Distinguishing grandiosity from self-esteem: Development of the Narcissistic grandiosity scale.* Manuscript in preparation.

Rosenthal, S. A., Montoya, R. M., Ridings, L. E., Rieck, S. M., & Hooley, J. M. (2011). Further evidence of the Narcissistic Personality Inventory's validity problems: A meta-analytic investigation—Response to Miller, Maples, and Campbell (this issue). *Journal of Research in Personality, 45*, 408–416.

Rosenthal, S. A., & Pittinsky, T. L. (2006). Narcissistic leadership. *The Leadership Quarterly, 17*, 617–633.

Schinke, R., & Hanrahan, S. J. (2009). *Cultural sport psychology.* Champaign, IL: Human Kinetics.

Sedikides, C., Gaertner, L., & Toguchi, Y. (2003). Pancultural self-enhancement. *Journal of Personality and Social Psychology, 84*, 60–79.

Sedikides, C., Rudich, E. A., Gregg, A. P., Kumashiro, M., & Rusbult, C. (2004). Are normal narcissists psychologically healthy? Self-esteem matters. *Journal of Personality and Social Psychology, 87*, 400–416.

Spano, L. (2001). The relationship between exercise and anxiety, obsessive-compulsiveness, and narcissism. *Personality and Individual Differences, 30*, 87–93.

Thomaes, S., Brummelman, E., Reijntjes, A., & Bushman, B. J. (2013). When Narcissus was a boy: Origins, nature, and consequences of childhood narcissism. *Child Development Perspectives, 7*, 22–26.

Tracy, J. L., Cheng, J. T., Martens, J. P., & Robins, R. W. (2011). The emotional dynamics of narcissism: Inflated by pride, deflated by shame. In W. K. Campbell & J. D. Miller (Eds.), *The handbook of narcissism and narcissistic disorder: Theoretical approaches, empirical findings, and treatments* (pp. 330–343). Hoboken, NJ: Wiley.

Twenge, J. M., & Foster, J. D. (2010). Birth cohort increases in narcissistic personality traits among American college students, 1982–2009. *Social Psychological and Personality Science, 1*, 99–106.

Vazire, S., Naumann, L. P., Rentfrow, P. J., & Gosling, S. D. (2008). Portrait of a narcissist: Manifestations of narcissism in physical appearance. *Journal of Research in Personality, 42*, 1439–1447.

Wallace, H. M., & Baumeister, R. F. (2002). The performance of narcissists rises and falls with perceived opportunity for glory. *Journal of Personality and Social Psychology, 82*, 819–834.

Wetzel, E., Brown, A., Hill, P., Chung, J. M., Robins, R. W., & Roberts, B. W. (2017). The narcissism epidemic is dead; long live the narcissism epidemic. *Psychological Science, 28*, 1833–1847.

Wetzel, E., & Robins, R. W. (2016). Are parenting practices associated with the development of narcissism? Findings from a longitudinal study of Mexican-origin youth. *Journal of Research in Personality, 63*, 84–94.

Wink, P. (1991). Two faces of narcissism. *Journal of Personality and Social Psychology, 61*, 590–597.

Woodman, T., Roberts, R., Hardy, L., Callow, N., & Rogers, C. H. (2011). There is an "I" in TEAM: Narcissism and social loafing. *Research Quarterly for Exercise and Sport, 82*, 285–290.

Wright, A. G., & Edershile, E. A. (2018). Issues resolved and unresolved in pathological narcissism. *Current Opinion in Psychology, 21*, 74–79.

Wurst, S. N., Gerlach, T. M., Dufner, M., Rauthmann, J. F., Grosz, M. P., Küfner, A. C. P., & Back, M. D. (2017). Narcissism and romantic relationships: The differential impact of narcissistic admiration and rivalry. *Journal of Personality and Social Psychology, 112*, 280–306.

Zeigler-Hill, V., & Besser, A. (2013). A glimpse behind the mask: Facets of narcissism and feelings of self-worth. *Journal of Personality Assessment, 95*, 249–260.

28

ORGANIZATIONAL CULTURE IN SPORT

Christopher R. D. Wagstaff and Suzanna Burton-Wylie

Introduction

Sport environments are increasingly isomorphically organized as global influences, and knowledge sharing has led to developments in sport science, medicine, technology, and the growing use of centralized operational and funding systems (cf. Wagstaff, 2017). Yet, despite this move towards isomorphic environments, sport organizations are also culturally complex and often influenced by volatile influences and performance challenges. Indeed, the concept of organizational culture, identified in its broadest sense as 'an umbrella concept describing cultural and symbolic phenomena or aspects in organizations' (Wagstaff & Burton-Wylie, 2018, p. 43), has recently received growing research attention as scholars attempt to understand and support sport organizations. In this chapter, we provide a review of organizational culture in sport and a treatment of definitional, conceptualization, and measurement considerations.

To provide a historical and conceptual foundation for this review, we will begin by offering a brief overview of the emergence of research on organizational culture. Organizational culture received substantial research attention within industrial and organizational psychology in the early 1980s and was a prominent focus of change initiatives within large corporations during this period. Although a full review of the thousands of early publications on organizational culture is beyond this review, several excellent reviews exist that provide the reader with an insight into these beginnings (e.g., Pettigrew, 1979; Roberts, 1970; Schein, 1985; Smircich, 1983). In a cross-cultural literature review related to organizational behaviour, Roberts (1970) found researchers adopted various vantage points when investigating organizations, with some concerned with individual behaviours, others hierarchical and functional subunits, and yet others examined the interactions of organizations with one another. In concluding, Roberts noted that studies of attitudes and values, management, perception, and personality variables were the most dominant areas under examination, with a predominance of individual behaviours. Further, researchers lacked consensus and adopted poorly considered methods often devoid of theoretical underpinning. Roberts (1970) called for 'more effort to be invested in understanding behaviour in a single culture, developing middle-level theories to guide explorations, and seeking the relevant questions to ask across cultures' (p. 347). In her review of organizational analysis, Smircich (1983) examined the significance of the conceptualizations of organizational culture, classifying the foregoing perspectives in five categories, two of which referred to organizational culture as either an independent or dependent, external or internal, organization variable, whereby culture is considered a background factor influencing the development and reinforcement of beliefs. The remaining three themes were distinguished from those that view culture as a variable, preferring to refer to organizational culture as a root metaphor, whereby organizations were considered as a particular form of human expression. Researchers perceiving culture as a variable identified culture through the themes of: comparative management (e.g., culture is imported through membership, influencing development and reinforcing beliefs) and *corporate culture* (e.g., distinctive culture through artefacts such as rituals and ceremonies). Researchers who perceived culture as a root metaphor identified culture through: organizational cognition (e.g., culture is a shared system of knowledge and beliefs influencing behaviours and emotions); organizational symbolism (e.g., culture is shared through symbols and meanings, focusing on how individuals interpret and relate to action); and unconscious processes and organization (e.g., culture is shared through forms and practices and understood through unconscious processes). This early work by Smircich demonstrated the varying basic assumptions and conceptions of organizational culture that researchers held, and demonstrated a lack of general consensus on its meaning and use of methods that has characterized much of the subsequent work on this concept.

Schein (1985) used a leadership approach to study organizational culture, adopting the view that researchers could not understand organizational culture without understanding the leaders within a given organization. In this early work, Schein argued that any organization with a history has a culture, and it is this that determines the criteria of leadership and subsequently drives behaviour. Moreover, Schein noted that leaders should be aware of three fundamental levels of culture within an organization (i.e., artefacts, espoused values, basic assumptions) and two dimensions (i.e., external environment and internal integration) of organizational culture. Moreover, leaders were advised to acknowledge the multidimensional aspect of organizational culture by displaying sensitivity when integrating subcultures.

The importance of organizational culture in sport has been intimated by a sporadic and siloed body of literature within the field of sport psychology. For example, researchers have identified organizational culture as having a significant influence on talent development (e.g., Henriksen, 2015) and performance outcomes at the Olympic Games (e.g., Gould, Greenleaf, Guinan, & Chung, 2002; Greenleaf, Gould, & Dieffenbach, 2001). Moreover, leaders in sport have increasingly acknowledged the salience of organizational culture for improving the welfare and duty of care for those engaged in elite sport (see Grey-Thompson, 2017). Indeed, UK Sport, the funders of elite sport in Great Britain and Northern Ireland, recently launched a cultural health check across all Olympic and Paralympic sports to understand what it takes to be the best in the world at culture, governance, and integrity in sport for both organic optimization and funding purposes. Indeed, the UK is not alone in seeking to monitor and influence organizational culture in sport, with similar examples in the Australian cricket team (ball tampering), South African Sports Confederation and Olympic Committee (irregularities and financial mismanagement), the Danish orienteering team (secrete filming of bathroom and sleeping arrangements), and US gymnastics (the fallout of the Larry Nassar abuse case) demonstrating the potential impact of undesirable organizational cultures. Nevertheless, despite this growing scholarly and practice attention, recent reviews of organizational culture in sport (see Maitland, Hills, & Rhind, 2015; Wagstaff & Burton-Wylie, 2018) have noted definitional, conceptual, and methodological concerns. In the next section, we provide an overview of common definitions and conceptualizations of organizational culture in sport. We then provide a detailed review of the methods typically employed to examine the levels and forms of organizational culture in sport, before concluding with typically examined recommendations for future research and practice.

Definitions of Organizational Culture in Sport

Commonalties in the characteristics and functions of organizational culture are shared among researchers (e.g., Alvesson, 2002; Martin, 2002; Schein, 1991), who regard it to: be grounded in history and tradition, shared, stable, and transmitted to new members; provide order to and rules for organizational existence; and be a source of collective identity. Despite these commonalities, culture is generally characterized as a family of concepts and a frame of reference (Pettigrew, 1990), and, therefore, it is perhaps not surprising that definitions of organizational culture are many and varied.

Alvesson (2000) described culture as somewhere between the heads of a group of people, observed through language and communication that are adopted by members of an organization and expressed through everyday social interactions (e.g., meetings, travel) and performance. Taking this view, culture can be conceived as a set of norms defined by shared rules designed to direct cognition and affect within members of an organization (Kunda, 1992). In recent reviews of organizational culture in sport (see Maitland et al., 2015; Wagstaff & Burton-Wylie, 2018), it has been noted that the majority of definitions used by those researching organizational culture in sport derive from general organizational culture literature (e.g., Girginov, 2006), with only a small number of researchers adopting a sport-based definition (e.g., Doherty & Chelladurai, 1999). Further, recent reviews have identified that the most commonly adopted definition of organizational culture in sport (see Cresswell & Eklund, 2007; Mills & Hoeber, 2013) is the one originally outlined by Schein (1985, 2010)), who defined organizational culture as:

> A pattern of shared basic assumptions learned by a group as it solved its problems of external adaptation and internal integration, which has worked well enough to be considered valid and, therefore, to be taught to new members as the correct way to perceive, think, and feel in relation to those problems.
>
> *(p. 18)*

Despite ambivalence in the way researchers define organizational culture, as a term it is often used within sporting organizations to describe shared qualities, consensus, homogeneity, and integration. As a result, most definitions within sport-based research have been aligned with an integration perspective, as outlined in Meyerson and Martin's (1987) three-perspective framework. It is towards this framework and other cultural conceptualizations that we now turn our attention.

Conceptualization of Organizational Culture

A common way that researchers in sport psychology have characterized the concept of organizational culture is by approaching it as something organizations 'have' or by something organizations 'are'. Researchers adopting the approach that culture is something organizations 'have' view culture as a variable that can be manipulated to better understand the relationship between culture and a desired outcome (e.g., performance, effectiveness). This approach, which Alvesson (1993) referred to as an objectivist-functionalist approach to organizational culture, is frequently adopted in the field of sport management (see Choi & Scott, 2008;

Weese, 1996) where culture is a leader-led initiative, supporting the leader's vision of change, and guides the sport psychologist in effective service delivery (McDougall & Ronkainen, 2018). It should be noted, however, that Alvesson (1993) warned scholars to ensure they attempt to develop an understanding of the organization (e.g., subcultures) before attempting to manipulate its environment. In contrast to 'the organizations have a culture' approach, there are those researchers who adopt the view that organizational culture is something that organizations 'are'. These researchers and practitioners strive to understand the culture of an organization by taking an insider's view to cognize how underlying assumptions are interpreted and drive the behaviour of people that operate in it. Alvesson (1993) referred to this perspective as a subjectivist-interpretivist approach to organizational culture, whereby researchers characterize culture as hermeneutic (i.e., understanding how culture is created in organizations through verbal and nonverbal communication) or emancipatory (i.e., review the extent organizational leaders control personal autonomy; see Alvesson & Willmott, 1992). In contrast to those who perceive culture as a variable, researchers adopting this approach place focus on symbolism and meaning, observing culture through narratives, myths, and rituals within an organization (see Cresswell & Eklund, 2007; Henriksen, Stambulova, & Roessler, 2010a, 2010b, 2011). Whereas the objectivist-functionalist approach is linked directly to behaviour and measured through quantitative research, the subjectivist-interpretivist approach is more complex, complicated, and impractical, requiring interpretive qualitative research designs (Alvesson, 2000).

Martin and Meyerson's Three-Perspective Framework

An alternative to the objectivist-functionalist and subjectivist-interpretivist approaches to conceptualizing organizational culture is to use Martin's three-perspective framework (Martin, 1992, 2002). According to this framework, scholars describe organizational culture through one of three perspectives (viz. integration, differentiation, and fragmentation). McDougall and Ronkainen (2018) articulated the value of this approach, noting that it offers researchers 'a theoretically credible and empirically supported means of challenging prevailing ideas about organizational culture that exist in sport psychology literature' (p. 15). Researchers adopting the integration perspective imply culture is organizationally led, placing explicit focus on consensus and consistency on what is shared, and overlooking conflict within the organization. Martin (2002) observed that studies distinguished by this perspective typically focus on senior management level and prioritize general consensus (e.g., assumptions) over internal conflict (e.g., Frontiera, 2010; Schroeder, 2010b). Those adopting the differentiation perspective imply organizations lack general consensus, instead distinguishing organizational culture as inconsistent interpretations between subcultures, with studies typically focusing on functional levels within the organization (e.g., Colyer, 2000; Parent & MacIntosh, 2013). Researchers adopting this perspective place general consensus within subcultures (e.g., subcultural integration), instead focusing on the conflict between subcultures (Martin, 1992). Lastly, those adopting the fragmentation perspective place ambiguity at the centre of their focus, distinguishing organizational culture as a loosely connected web of individuals whose involvement and identity can fluctuate depending on their view of a situation at a given time (Martin, 1992).

Despite having numerous advantages, Martin's framework is not without critics. Indeed, one major advantage emanates from Martin's call to researchers and practitioners to challenge the homogeneity of culture and avoid cultural 'blind spots' by considering the individual differences of members in the way they interpret, evaluate, and enact culture. Yet Ehrhart,

Schneider, and Macey (2014) questioned whether the three perspectives represent the different lenses to view an organization's culture or they are, in fact, typologies of culture. Ehrhart et al. also noted that confusion may arise owing to Martin's (2002) examples of fragmentation studies, which demonstrate a consensus among employees regarding the presence of ambiguity in the organization, thereby seemingly combining the integration and fragmentation perspectives. Further, scholars (e.g., Alvesson, 1993, 2002; Schein, 1991; Trice, 1991) have questioned whether an organization can have a culture at all without a consensus. Nevertheless, these same researchers have also noted a general acceptance of the three-perspective framework and concur with the presence of ambiguity in organizational culture (e.g., Alvesson, 2002). Trice (1991) agreed that the contradictions and ambiguities central to the fragmentation perspective appear in organizations, yet went on to state that organizations would fail to function effectively without the shared perspectives and assumptions of individuals and subgroups within an organization. McDougall and Ronkainen (2018) recently supported the use of the three-perspective framework in sport and challenged researchers to move away from the dominant discourse of typically neat and idealistic descriptions of organizational culture hitherto common in the sport psychology and management literatures. Indeed, researchers within the sport psychology domain have almost uniformly conceptualized culture by what is shared, placing greater emphasis on a search for homogeneity and harmony (i.e., integration) while neglecting conflict (i.e., differentiation) and ambiguity (i.e., fragmentation). Although the merits of adopting an integration perspective are clear for those in leadership positions (and perhaps psychologists tasked with supporting aligned change) who aim to achieve success and excellence through the manipulation of culture, McDougall and Ronkainen (2018) state that researchers and practitioners who ground their work in the idea of a shared ideology are at risk of restricting culture by seeking out meaning and interpretations consistent with their views and developing 'blind spots' (e.g., downplaying, dismissing) towards sources of culture and marginalizing those who do not conform to this view. Moreover, using the three perspectives simultaneously to adopt a broad and inclusive view of culture is how Martin and Meyerson intended their work to be used, as this enables researchers and practitioners to interpret what has, and has not, been learned from culture work. Such an interpretive approach allows scholars to accommodate the complexities of everyday organizational life, focusing their cultural lens on all members and acknowledging the individual differences that influence the experience and applied cultural meaning. Indeed, several sport management researchers have used a multilevel approach employing a lens of integration and differentiation (Girginov, Papadimitriou, & Lopez De D'Amico, 2006) and integration, differentiation, and fragmentation (Girginov, 2011) for studying organizational culture, leading to interesting advancements in the field. In the next section of this chapter, we offer further considerations for researchers and practitioners relating to the potential value of creating and maintaining organizational culture through the use of metaphor.

Culture as a Metaphor

Conceptualizing culture as a metaphor provides greater room for ambiguity, promotes organizations as expressive forms, provides critical examination for how our thinking is shaped, and offers both researchers and practitioners accessible terms for the communication of organizational culture (Alvesson, 2002; Smircich, 1983). In his work on organizational culture, Alvesson (2002) created eight metaphors to communicate how culture has been conceptualized. These are outlined in Table 7.

Table 7 Metaphors for conceptualizing organizational culture (adapted from Alvesson, 2002)

Culture as *exchange-regulator*	Culture acts to indirectly control individuals' behaviours through shared social knowledge of the relational exchange between individuals and their organizations
Culture as *compass*	Culture provides individuals and teams with a shared set of values that guide their goal-directed behaviour in the pursuit of effectiveness
Culture as *social glue*	Culture as shared beliefs and norms that bring individuals and teams towards a harmonious and consensual existence
Culture as *sacred cow*	Culture as core values that individuals emotionally identify with, are committed to, and ultimately view as sacred
Culture as *affect regulator*	Culture as a means to communicate rules for appropriate emotional expressions and as a mechanism to manage the emotional expression of individuals
Culture as *disorder*	Culture as a jungle of ambiguity, characterized by uncertainty, contradiction, irony, and confusion
Culture as *blinders*	Culture as an unconscious and largely inaccessible concept, with limited individual access or understanding of its effects
Culture as a *world-closure*	Culture as a leader-created social reality that restricts individuals' or teams' autonomy and runs counter to their interests

Although researchers may state their perspective on organizational culture, Martin (1992) argued that it is the manifestations of culture that scholars typically use to influence and study organizational culture in practice. Frequently studied cultural manifestations include: forms (e.g., rituals), practices (e.g., tasks), and content themes (e.g., deeply held group assumptions), as discussed in the next section of this chapter.

Levels of Organizational Culture

A central debate within organizational culture research has been the depth or level of analysis. This consideration should not be confused with rigour and reflects the extent to which cultural content is objectively viewed or unobservable. In short, questions of level relate to how much 'digging' is required to unearth the cultural information that is taken for granted and ingrained within organizational life. The principle distinction for approaches adopted by researchers is between what can objectively be observed or espoused versus what is 'really' going on at a deeper level (Ehrhart et al., 2014). A widely used categorization of organizational culture level is that outlined by Schein (1985; for a recent review, see Schein, 2010), which includes three levels of organizational culture: artefacts, espoused values and beliefs, and underlying assumptions. Artefacts and symbols are at the surface of the organization, visible elements not only accessible to employees but observable to those outside the organization, although their meaning may not be explicit without further insight. They include corporate clothing, architecture, structure, processes, brand, logos, stories, rituals, and language. Importantly, although these artefacts may appear to be similar across organizations, the meaning they have for individuals and teams will vary. It is common for studies of organizational culture to begin with an investigation of the artefacts and follow this with an examination of their symbolic meaning to individuals. The espoused values of an organization relate to the standards, values, and rules of conduct articulated by leaders (e.g., performance directors), which may or may not reflect the values or beliefs of followers (e.g., athletes, coaches, support staff). Problems may arise when the espoused values of the leaders are not in line with those of their followers. In addition to these idealistic values, of equal importance are those that are communicated and shared through strategies, objectives, and social interaction, and the behaviours of individuals have been labelled the values in use. The challenge of ascertaining what is 'really going on' in a given sport organization is arguably why qualitative researchers have had a long-held interest in organizational culture research. Indeed, penetrating the espoused values facade is immeasurably important, but difficult to achieve via questionnaire methods alone. Basic underlying assumptions are deeply embedded in the core of organizational culture, they influence the daily behaviours of individuals, and are often unconscious and taken for granted experiences that individuals within the organization are unable to recognize or articulate. Indeed, these basics assumptions form around deeper dimensions of human existence about how the world works, originating from experience and perception. Rousseau (1990) proposed two additional levels to Schein's framework: patterns of behaviour (e.g., how members interact to solve problems) and behavioural norms (i.e. beliefs about acceptable and unacceptable behaviour).

In practice, the levels of organizational culture outlined by Schein (1985) can be represented as an onion model (see Figure 10). Composed of different layers, the deeper the layer the more difficult and resistant to change. The outer layer represents artefacts and symbols and can be changed with relative ease. The middle layer represents espoused values, while at the core and most difficult to change is the basic underlying assumptions.

Forms of Organizational Culture

In addition to considering the level at which they conduct their work, researchers might seek forms of organizational culture in their endeavours to understand and influence what they will focus on. Cultural forms include dress, rules, behavioural norms, traditions, stories, myths, jargon, jokes, slogans, rituals, rewards, ceremonies, and celebrations. Martin and Frost (1996) distinguished between the study of organizational culture forms according to those that might be labelled generalist (i.e., holistic descriptions of culture with a variety of manifestations) and that of those that might be termed specialist (i.e., a singular focus on one cultural manifestation). Alternatively, Trice and Beyer (1984) noted that, 'culture has two basic components: (1) its substance, or the networks of meanings contained in its ideologies, norms and values; and (2) its forms, or the practices whereby these meanings are expressed, affirmed, and communicated to

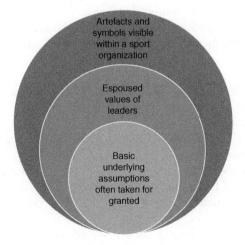

Figure 10 Onion model of organizational culture

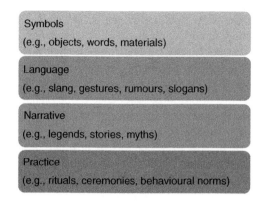

Figure 11 Categorization of forms of organizational culture (methods for researching organizational culture)

members (p. 654). Trice and Beyer (1991) organized these manifestation forms into four categories: symbols, language, narrative, and practices (see Figure 11). Now that we have discussed the level and forms that researchers need to consider when studying organizational culture, we will direct our focus towards the methods that can be used to study this topic.

As alluded to in earlier sections of this chapter, there remains much debate regarding the definition and conceptualization of organizational culture, and, therefore, unsurprisingly, the methodology adopted by researchers when studying this topic also lacks consistency. Moreover, researchers have often failed to define or state their perspective on organizational culture in their work (for reviews, see Maitland et al., 2015; Wagstaff & Burton-Wylie, 2018), leaving the reader unclear on the intentions of the research and appropriateness of the methods. Culture is a multifaceted concept, and, therefore, asking researchers to conform their work to a 'one-size-fits-all' design would be unfair and impossible. Instead, when attempting to influence organizational culture, we recommend that researchers align their method with their underlying assumptions on culture – that is, to aim for conceptual congruence. This conceptual precision will ensure a consistent thread across the conceptual, definitional, methodological, and interpretive elements of their work, while supporting researchers to take their organizational analysis in varied, promising directions.

Researchers have offered guidance to their peers in the past, with Pettigrew (1990) highlighting seven methodological 'issues' commonly faced by researchers when studying organizational culture:

(1) The levels issue: It is difficult to study deeply held beliefs and assumptions.
(2) The pervasiveness issue: Organizational culture encompasses a broad number of interlocking organizational elements.
(3) The implicitness issue: Organizational culture is taken for granted and rarely explicitly acknowledged and discussed.
(4) The imprinting issue: Culture has deep ties to the history of the organization.
(5) The political issue: Cultural issues are tied to differences in power or status in the organization.
(6) The plurality issue: Organizations rarely have a single culture, but instead have multiple subcultures.
(7) The interdependency issue: Culture is interconnected with a broad number of other issues, both internal and external to the organization.

Elsewhere, Davey and Symon (2001) recommended that researchers divide organizational culture into two methodologically related categories: (1) psychological perspectives that are positivist (i.e., reliant on experiments) and functionalist (i.e., common values held essential for the integration and development of a culture) in their approach; and (2) anthropological and sociological (i.e., the study of human society) perspectives that are more subjective and interpretive in their approach. Next, we provide further recommendations on what methodological approach researchers might adopt, depending on their epistemological perspective of culture.

Quantitative Methods

Researchers who perceive culture as something organizations 'have' are compatible with the objective-functionalist paradigm (Alvesson, 1993) in that they share similar basic assumptions about the nature and social world of organizations. These researchers and practitioners attempt to understand the relationships between variables to explain organizational culture. Researchers aligned with this paradigm are likely to adopt quantitative methods (and, to a lesser degree, qualitative or mixed methods) to explore outside perspectives and describe differences across cultures. This is similar to etic accounts of organizational culture, whereby scholars adopt a deductive approach to compare across different cultures. Researchers utilize quantitative measures to isolate components of culture and examine whether they influence or predict change. By way of an example recommendation, researchers examining organizational culture through leader-led approaches, including effectiveness of transformational leadership for performance (Scott, 1997; Weese, 1995, 1996), application of shared values for managing cultural diversity (Doherty & Chelladurai, 1999), and leadership and organizational culture transformation (Frontiera, 2010), could adopt a questionnaire methodology to understand how leaders influence the culture of an organization.

Qualitative Methods

Researchers who perceive culture as something organizations 'are' adopt an subjective-interpretivist paradigm (Alvesson, 1993) to describe and document human expression within organizational culture. In employing qualitative methods, these researchers attempt to gain an inside perspective, describing culture from a native's point of view. This approach is similar to emic accounts of organizational culture, whereby scholars adopt an inductive approach to observe a single cultural group. Researchers aligned with this approach also typically adopt qualitative methods to gain an insider's view to understand organizations as cultures. As an example recommendation, researchers might explore organizational culture through the environment's symbolism and practice (Zevenbergen, Edwards, & Skinner, 2002), artefacts (Mills & Hoeber, 2013), individual perspectives on gender differences (Pfister & Radtke, 2009), and individual differences (e.g., family, religion, gender, ethnicity), or could adopt an interview and observation approach to understand how the environment influences an organization's culture.

Recent reviews (see Maitland et al., 2015; Wagstaff & Burton-Wylie, 2018) have noted that adopting a mixed-methods approach to studying organizational culture would likely benefit the field if epistemological fidelity can be assured (see also McDougall & Ronkainen, 2018; Wagstaff & Burton-Wylie, 2019). Taking a mixed methods approach has potential merits because of opportunities afforded to researchers to acknowledge the environment and accommodate subcultural differences through qualitative methods while examining how leaders can influence positive culture change through quantitative methods.

General Recommendations for Researchers

Researchers are advised to avoid applying a 'quick-fix' leader-led approach to organizational culture change. Organizations consist of complex subgroups with inherent conflict, power flux, and inequality, and oversimplifying the meaning of culture would merely skirt the true complexities and challenges inherent in culture work. Instead, researchers and practitioners are advised to embrace the organizational complexities by considering the multiple perspectives when designing their research or practice. Adopting multiple perspectives affords sport psychologists, as culture change agents, the potential to influence an organization's 'strong', 'unified', 'old-school', or 'healthy' culture to maximize performance (i.e., integration), while appreciating the possibility of intergroup conflicts and different identities, opinions, personal investments, and interests (i.e., differentiation). Similarly, researchers should look beyond a primary focus on espoused values or self-reported behavioural norms as the route to understanding and influencing organizational culture, given individuals are likely to present behaviours that conform to managerial ideals in order to serve impression management, yet reject these behaviours when operating more autonomously and authentically. Instead, researchers should gain an in-depth understanding of naturalistic behaviour within an environment through participant observations and context-specific insights. Further, for organizations to embed deep-rooted positive culture, the 'story' needs to resonate with as many members of the organization as possible, while change agents 'work at the seams' of conflict, fluctuating alignment, and disharmony, rather than seeking – in vain – total alignment or imposition of the values and thoughts of senior management. Acknowledging the different understandings of an organization may be an important step to help facilitate positive culture change.

The Value of Language

One area of potential interest to researchers and practitioners alike is the use of language in sport organizations. Ravasi (2016) addressed the confusion surrounding similar concepts and the language used by researchers when exploring 'organizational identity' (internal members' perceptions), 'organizational culture' (self-referent claims and understandings that constitute what is commonly referred to as organization identity), and 'organizational image' (external stakeholder perceptions or 'reputation'). In this review of literature, Ravasi (2016) referred to 'identity' as a narrower set of meaning structures focused on how members 'fit in' and perceive their organization as different, and 'organizational culture' as a broader term shaping behaviour within an organization. Understanding these concepts when exploring organizational culture in sport is important not only to ensure researchers are consistent in what they are studying, but to acknowledge the cultural complexities that exist within organizations, including contended views on identity or image and how individuals' new identities and beliefs may influence organizational culture.

Making Sense of Culture

A second area of importance to our field and closely linked to language is sense-making in organizations. In their systematic review, Brown, Colville, and Pye (2015) referred to sense-making as, 'the process by which people seek plausibility to understand ambiguous, equivocal or confusing issues or events' (p. 266). Brown et al.'s review provided some insight into some of the ways sense is made in organizations: 'discourse' (i.e., stories and narratives) to gain insight into individuals' emotional responses and intellectual positions in organizations; 'politics and power' to enact, guide, and control processes for self-interest; from 'micro to macro', through identified mechanisms of priming, editing, and triggering; 'identities' – by making sense of their world, individuals make sense of themselves, which assists in 'steering action' and reducing feelings of isolation; and 'individual and collective decision-making for organizational change' through deliberate and dynamic social interactions of agreement, disagreement, and reflexive processes. Acknowledgement by researchers and practitioners of these routes to sense-making are important to understanding behaviours, processes, decision-making, and culture change in the turbulent landscape of sport environments.

The Practice of Rites and Ceremonies

A third area of potential interest to researchers and practitioners is the practice of rites and ceremonies. Trice and Beyer (1984) focused on the social consequences of *rites* (i.e., number of discrete cultural forms, integrated for public performance) and *ceremonials* (i.e., the event or occasion that connects these rites together) to uncover networks of interacting meanings that characterized organizational cultures and affected organizational life. Rites and ceremonies are usually performed for the benefit of an audience, requiring deliberate planning and time spent rehearsing. In performing these rites and ceremonies, other cultural forms such as language and gestures are used to express the shared meaning of the occasion and are conveyed to the audience through narrative such as myths and stories. For further detail on the different types of rite, their manifestations and expressions (through ceremonies), and the social consequences of these events, see Trice and Beyer (1984). We would recommend that researchers and practitioners consider the practice of rites and ceremonies when studying or attempting to influence an organization's culture. The social expression of these events locates rites and ceremonies as a convenient and accessible method for researchers and practitioners to observe, enabling them to learn a great deal about the meaning that exists at the core of organizational culture.

Conclusion

Organizational culture is anecdotally and empirically a salient construct in sport, yet this broadly used term lacks global consensus on definitional and conceptual perspectives and the most appropriate methodological approaches for associated research. In this chapter, we have attempted to provide an overview of these issues and the challenges facing researchers and practitioners. Not least of these is that there exists no consensus or sport-specific definition of organizational culture: Scholars and practitioners have conceptualized organizational culture in a multitude of ways, using conceptual, level, form, metaphoric, and methodological distinctions for its characterization. It is possible that conceptualizing organizational culture as a metaphor provides greater room for ambiguity and offers both researchers and practitioners accessible terms for the communication of organizational culture (Alvesson, 2002; Smircich, 1983). Nevertheless, it remains the case that the level of cultural information that researchers aim to understand requires substantial amounts of 'digging' commonly reflected by Schein's (1985, 2010) three levels of organizational culture (viz. artefacts, espoused values and beliefs, and underlying assumptions). Moreover, culture change attempts often fail when the top–down espoused values of leaders are not in line with those of their followers, and where these values are rejected by subcultures within the organization. Hence, researchers might also consider what forms of culture they will focus on in their work, such as symbols, language, narrative, and practice (cf. Trice & Beyer, 1991). Methods for studying or monitoring organizational culture should be in line with a researcher's epistemological perspective on culture, with quantitative methods recommended for those who view culture as something an organization 'has', and qualitative methods for those who view culture as something an organization 'is'. Alternatively, adopting a mixed-methods design may enable researchers to better acknowledge environment factors beyond leader-led values and accommodate subcultural differences, while examining how leaders can influence positive culture change.

References

Alvesson, M. (1993). Organizations as rhetoric: Knowledge-intensive firms and the struggle with ambiguity. *Journal of Management Studies, 30,* 997–1015.

Alvesson, M. (2000). Social identity and the problem of loyalty in knowledge-intensive companies. *Journal of Management Studies, 37,* 1101–1124.

Alvesson, M. (2002). *Understanding organizational culture.* London: Sage.

Alvesson, M., & Willmott, H. (1992). On the idea of emancipation in management and organization studies. *The Academy of Management Review, 17,* 432–464.

Brown, A. D., Colville, I., & Pye, A. (2015). Making sense of sensemaking in organization studies. *Organization Studies, 36,* 265–277.

Choi, Y. S., & Scott, D. K. (2008). Assessing organisational culture using the competing values framework within American Triple-A baseball. *International Journal of Sport Management, 4,* 33–48.

Colyer, S. (2000). Organizational culture in selected Western Australian sport organizations. *Journal of Sport Management, 14,* 321–341.

Cresswell, S. L., & Eklund, R. C. (2007). Athlete burnout and organizational culture: An English rugby replication. *International Journal of Sport Psychology, 38,* 365–387.

Davey, K. M., & Symon, G. (2001). Recent approaches to the qualitative analysis of organizational culture. In C. Cooper, S. Cartwright, & P. Earley (Eds.), *The international handbook of organisational culture and climate* (pp. 123–142). New York: John Wiley.

Doherty, A. J., & Chelladurai, P. (1999). Managing cultural diversity in sport organizations: A theoretical perspective. *Journal of Sport Management, 13,* 280–297.

Ehrhart, M., Schneider, B., & Macey, W. (2014). *Organizational climate and culture.* New York: Routledge.

Frontiera, J. (2010). Leadership and organizational culture transformation in professional sport. *Journal of Leadership & Organizational Studies, 17,* 71–86.

Girginov, V. (2006). Creating a corporate anti- doping culture: The role of Bulgarian sports governing bodies. *Sport in Society, 9,* 252–268.

Girginov, V. (Ed.). (2011). *Sport management cultures.* London: Routledge.

Girginov, V., Papadimitriou, D., & Lopez De D'Amico, R. (2006). Cultural orientations of sport managers. *European Sport Management Quarterly, 6,* 35–66.

Gould, D., Greenleaf, C., Guinan, D., & Chung, Y. (2002). A survey of US Olympic coaches: Variables perceived to have influenced athlete performances and coach effectiveness. *The Sport Psychologist, 16,* 229–250.

Greenleaf, C., Gould, D., & Dieffenbach, K. (2001). Factors influencing Olympic performance: Interviews with Atlanta and Nagano US Olympians. *Journal of Applied Sport Psychology, 13,* 154–184.

Grey-Thompson, T. (2017). *Duty of care in sport review.* Independent report to government. Available at www.gov.uk/government/publications/duty-of-care-in-sport-review

Henriksen, K. (2015). Developing a high-performance culture: A sport psychology intervention from and ecological perspective in elite orienteering. *Journal of Sport Psychology in Action, 6,* 141–153.

Henriksen, K., Stambulova, N., & Roessler, K. K. (2010a). Holistic approach to athletic talent development environments: A successful sailing milieu. *Psychology of Sport & Exercise, 11,* 212–222.

Henriksen, K., Stambulova, N., & Roessler, K. K. (2010b). Successful talent development in track and field: Considering the role of environment. *Scandinavian Journal of Medicine & Science in Sports, 20,* 122–132.

Henriksen, K., Stambulova, N., & Roessler, K. K. (2011). Riding the wave of an expert: A successful talent development environment in kayaking. *Sport Psychologist, 25,* 341–362.

Kunda, Z. (1992). Can dissonance theory do it all? *Psychological Inquiry, 3,* 337–339.

Maitland, A., Hills, L. A., & Rhind, D. J. (2015). Organisational culture in sport: A systematic review. *Sport Management Review, 18,* 501–516.

Martin, J. (1992). *Cultures in organizations: Three perspectives.* Oxford, UK: Oxford University Press.

Martin, J. (2002). *Organizational culture: Mapping the terrain.* London: Sage.

Martin, J., & Frost, P. (1996). The organizational culture war games: A struggle for intellectual dominance. In S. R. Clegg, C. Hardy, & W. Nord (Eds.), *Handbook of organization studies* (pp. 599–621). London: Sage.

Martin, J., & Meyerson, D. (1987). Organizational culture and the denial, channelling and acknowledgement of ambiguity. In L. R. Pondy, R. Boland, & H. Thomas (Eds.), *Managing ambiguity and change* (pp. 93–125). New York: Wiley.

McDougall, M., & Ronkainen, N. J. (2018). Organisational culture is not dead ... yet: Response to Wagstaff and Burton-Wylie. *Sport and Exercise Psychology Review, 15,* 13–19.

Meyerson, D., & Martin, J. (1987). Cultural change: An integration of three different views. *Journal of Management Studies, 24,* 623–647.

Mills, C., & Hoeber, L. (2013). Exploring organizational culture through artefacts in a community figure skating club. *Journal of Sport Management, 27,* 482–496.

Parent, M. M., & MacIntosh, E. W. (2013). Organizational culture evolution in temporary organizations: The case of the 2010 Olympic Winter Games. *Canadian Journal of Administrative Sciences, 30,* 223–237.

Pettigrew, A. (1990). Organizational climate and culture: Two constructs in search of a role. In B. Schneider (Ed.), *Organizational climate and culture* (pp. 413–433). San Francisco, CA: Jossey-Bass.

Pettigrew, A. M. (1979). On studying organizational cultures. *Administrative Science Quarterly, 24,* 570–581.

Pfister, G., & Radtke, S. (2009). Sport, women and leadership: Results of a project on executives in German sport organizations. *European Journal of Sport Science, 9,* 229–243.

Ravasi, D. (2016). Organisational identity, culture and image. In M. Schultz, B. E. Ashforth, & D. Ravasi (Eds.), *The Oxford handbook of organizational identity* (pp. 65–78). Oxford, UK: Oxford University Press.

Roberts, K. H. (1970). On looking at an elephant: An evaluation of cross-cultural research related to organizations. *Psychological Bulletin, 74,* 327–350.

Rousseau, D. M. (1990). New hire perceptions of their own and their employer's obligations: A study of psychological contracts. *Journal of Organizational Behavior, 11,* 389–400.

Schein, E. H. (1985). *Organizational culture and leadership.* San Francisco, CA: Jossey-Bass.

Schein, E. H. (1991). *What is culture?* Newbury Park, CA: Sage.

Schein, E. H. (2010). *Organizational culture and leadership.* San Francisco, CA: Jossey-Bass.

Schroeder, P. J. (2010b). Changing team culture: The perspectives of ten successful head coaches. *Journal of Sport Behavior, 33,* 63–88.

Scott, D. K. (1997). Managing organizational culture in intercollegiate athletic organizations. *Quest, 49,* 403–415.

Smircich, L. (1983). Concepts of culture and organizational analysis. *Administrative Science Quarterly, 28* (3), 33–358.

Trice, H. M. (1991). Comments and discussion. In P. J. Frost, L. F. Moore, M. R. Louis, C. C. Lundberg, & J. Martin (Eds.), *Reframing organizational culture* (pp. 298–308). Newbury Park, CA: Sage.

Trice, H. M., & Beyer, J. M. (1984). Studying organizational cultures through rites and ceremonials. *Academy of Management Review, 9,* 653–669.

Trice, H. M., & Beyer, J. M. (1991). Cultural leadership in organizations. *Organization Science, 2,* 149–169.

Wagstaff, C. R. D. (2017). Organizational psychology in sport: An introduction. In C. R. D. Wagstaff (Ed.), *The organizational psychology of sport: Key issues and practical applications* (pp. 1–8). Abingdon: Routledge.

Wagstaff, C. R. D., & Burton-Wylie, S. (2018). Organisational culture in sport: A conceptual, methodological and definitional review. *Sport & Exercise Psychology Review, 14*, 32–52.

Wagstaff, C. R. D., & Burton-Wylie, S. (2019). 'Alive and kicking': Securing the health of organisational culture in sport – A response to McDougall and Ronkainen. *Sport and Exercise Psychology Review, 15*, 20–25.

Weese, W. J. (1995). Leadership and organizational culture: An investigation of the Big Ten and American Conference campus recreation administrations. *Journal of Sport Management, 9*, 119–134.

Weese, W. J. (1996). Do leadership and organizational culture really matter? *Journal of Sport Management, 10*, 197–206.

Zevenbergen, R., Edwards, A., & Skinner, J. (2002). Junior golf club culture: A Bourdieuian analysis. *Sociology of Sport Online, 5*, 1–15.

29

PERFECTIONISM

Andrew P. Hill, Daniel J. Madigan, Martin M. Smith,
Sarah H. Mallinson-Howard, and Tracy C. Donachie

Introduction

Great Britain's Tom Daley won the gold medal in the men's 10 metre platform dive at the 2017 World Aquatics Championships in Budapest. In winning the medal, Daley was awarded 12 perfect scores across six dives. Chen Aisen, the double gold winner at the 2016 Summer Olympics, was awarded three perfect scores of his own and won the silver medal. In this case, three instances of perfection simply were not enough to win the competition. It is scenarios such as this that underscore why the study of perfectionism is so important in sport. In most other areas of life, perfection is ambiguous, elusive, and irrational. In sport, though, perfection can be more tangible, objective, and, for athletes at the very highest levels, attainable. These factors may explain why so many athletes identify themselves as perfectionists, and why some researchers and practitioners have come to view perfectionism as a hallmark characteristic of elite performers (e.g., Gould, Dieffenbach, & Moffett, 2002).

It is important to bear in mind, however, that, from a personality perspective, perfectionism is more than the standards people have for themselves. Rather, perfectionism is an engrained way of thinking, feeling, and behaving that, paradoxically, can quite easily undermine athlete motivation, performance, and well-being (Flett & Hewitt, 2014). As it is common to find perfectionistic people in sport, and because perfectionism is so easily misunderstood, perfectionism is a valuable addition to an encyclopaedia of sport psychology. The entry is structured around four topics. The topics covered are: (1) the multidimensional structure of perfectionism, (2) its trans-contextual nature, (3) whether 'healthy' perfectionists exist, and (4) the likely consequences of perfectionism in sport. These are key topics in this area of research and will provide a valuable reference for students, researchers, and practitioners interested in perfectionism.

Perfectionism Is Multidimensional

Perhaps the biggest advancement in perfectionism research in the last 40 years has been the reconceptualization of perfectionism as multidimensional. Prior to this development, perfectionism was conceptualized as unidimensional (i.e., a total perfectionism score) and considered largely in terms of self-related irrational beliefs (e.g., 'I should be perfect all of the time'). Multidimensional models (e.g., Hewitt & Flett, 1991) bought to the fore a wide array of dimensions indicative of perfectionism and shifted emphasis to studying the different dimensions. Some of the dimensions include, for example, an emphasis on interpersonal aspects of perfectionism, such as beliefs about how others should behave (e.g., 'Other people should perform perfectly') and beliefs about what other people think (e.g., 'Other people expect me to be perfect'). The result of the development of a multidimensional conceptualization of perfectionism has been a fuller account of its various manifestations and its consequences, as well as the ability to intervene in a more effective manner.

There are now at least six multidimensional models of perfectionism. With so many different models (and accompanying measures) of perfectionism, research can be difficult to navigate. However, in actuality, these models show considerable overlap. Notably, all models include dimensions that capture high, exceptionally high, or excessively high personal standards. Thereafter, models differ in the dimensions they include. However, typically, the additional dimensions pertain to less desirable aspects of perfectionism. These dimensions capture the thoughts and feelings that accompany achievement-oriented behaviour such as an intense aversion to mistakes, chronic doubts about performance, and negative reactions to imperfection. These dimensions are key to differentiating perfectionism from other achievement-related traits (Frost, Marten, Lahart, & Rosenblate, 1990). They are also important for understanding how the consequences of perfectionism differ between people.

Additional support for the notion that perfectionism should be studied as multidimensional has been provided by the higher-order model of perfectionism. Adopting a broad definition of perfectionism ('high standards of performance *which are accompanied by tendencies for overly critical evaluations of one's own behaviour*'; Frost et al., 1990, p. 450; italics in original), the higher-order model distinguishes between two factors: perfectionistic strivings (PS) and perfectionistic concerns (PC). PS are 'aspects of perfectionism associated with self-oriented striving for perfection and the setting of very high personal performance standards' (Gotwals, Stoeber, Dunn, & Stoll, 2012, p. 264), whereas PC are 'aspects associated with concerns over making mistakes, fear of negative social evaluation, feelings of discrepancy between one's expectations and performance, and negative reactions to imperfection' (Gotwals et al., 2012, p. 264). This model is not a theory of perfectionism. However, it is a useful heuristic based on factor analytical studies of different measures of perfectionism (e.g., Bieling, Israeli, & Antony, 2004) and the notion of functional homogeneity whereby the constitutes of the two higher-order factors tend to have similar effects (Gaudreau & Verner-Filion, 2012). Therefore, regardless of the specific model of perfectionism adopted, evidence supports a multidimensional conceptualization of perfectionism with at least two distinct dimensions (PS and PC).

Perfectionism Is Trans-Contextual

A further important issue is whether perfectionism is a trait or disposition. The confusion is understandable. Both terms are used interchangeably (and sometimes in combination) in sport and personality research. Drawing on the work of McAdams and Pals (2006), here, traits are considered to be 'broad dimensions of individual differences between people, accounting for inter-individual consistency and continuity in behaviour, thought, and feelings across situations and over time' (p. 207). By contrast, dispositions are considered to be an adaptation to one's character that is bound or 'contextualized in time, place, and/or social role' (p. 208). Examples of character adaptations include personal motives, goals, plans, values, and virtues. As such, a disposition is something that is less consistent than a trait and shows lower stability over time and across situations and contexts. With regard to perfectionism, there are currently two opposing positions on this issue. On the one hand, researchers have argued that perfectionism is best considered a trait (or is at least 'trait-like'; e.g., Hill, 2016). On the other hand, other researchers have argued that perfectionism is best considered a disposition and domain-specific (e.g., Stoeber, 2018). The two positions are revisited below.

Hill (2016) offered three main arguments to support the notion that perfectionism is best considered a trait or trait-like. First, research examining domain-specific perfectionism has found the tendency to exhibit perfectionism in one domain is highly correlated with a tendency to exhibit perfectionism in other domains (e.g., Dunn, Craft, Dunn, & Gotwals, 2011). Second, related to the first point, most people who report being 'perfectionistic' identify multiple domains in which they are perfectionistic, rather than only one (see Stoeber & Stoeber, 2009). Third, and finally, in twin studies examining perfectionism, a substantial proportion of variability in perfectionism can be attributed to common genetic factors (up to 42%; e.g., Iranzo-Tatay et al., 2015). The amount of variance for some dimensions of perfectionism is similar to other personality characteristics normally considered traits (e.g., Big Five; Bouchard & McGue, 2003).

Stoeber (2018), by contrast, has argued that perfectionism is best considered a disposition, not a trait. He also offers three main arguments for why this is the case. First, evidence of heritability aside, theoretical models of the development of perfectionism suggest that perfectionism is most likely something learned from early experiences, particularly in response to parental behaviours (see Flett, Hewitt, Oliver, & MacDonald, 2002). Second, individuals who report that they are perfectionistic in all domains are rare. Most people have a very limited number of domains in their lives in which they are perfectionistic. Finally, longitudinal studies often show changes in perfectionism over relatively short periods that reflect more immediate changes in experiences and expectations. Stoeber argues that changes of this kind would be unlikely to occur if perfectionism was a trait.

This debate has yet to be resolved. In revisiting it here, a recent study by Franche and Gaudreau (2016) may help move it forward somewhat. Franche and Gaudreau advocated that perfectionism be best studied as a multilevel characteristic that varies between individuals and within individuals, and illustrated how the cross-domain manifestation of perfectionism can be taken into account when studying its effects. The approach is based on the work of Fleeson (2001; Fleeson & Noftle, 2008), who argued that both typical behaviour *and* variability in that behaviour can reflect stable individual differences and meaningful aspects of personality. In other words, consistent inconsistency can denote personality in the same way that consistency does. In this regard, the presence of perfectionism in some domains (domains that carry especial personal meaning or value), and its predictable absence in others (domains with no personal meaning or value), can be considered to be itself part of an overall pattern of expression that signals perfectionism is unlikely to be a contextually bound disposition. Rather, perfectionism has a structure that stretches beyond contexts; it is a trans-contextual trait (McCrae & Costa, 1984).

Perfectionists Who Are 'Healthy' Do Not Exist

The third topic pertains to an ongoing controversy regarding the existence of so-called 'healthy' perfectionists (also referred to as 'adaptive' or 'functional' perfectionists). Some sport psychologists believe perfectionism may be desirable for athletes when exhibited as a healthy type (e.g., Sarkar & Fletcher, 2014). However, reasoned examination of perfectionism highlights that the notion of 'healthy' perfectionists is a misnomer, and that there is little empirical basis for the existence for such a type of perfectionist. The case against the use of the term 'healthy perfectionist' centres on three issues: (1) whether types of perfectionist exist, (2) whether it is advisable to label a trait in a manner that presumes its effects, and (3) whether dimensions of perfectionism are being confused with types of perfectionism. These issues are discussed below.

The first issue is whether 'perfectionists' actually exist. People are often surprised to learn that, in all likelihood, there is no such thing as a perfectionist. We use the term perfectionist as shorthand when describing people who exhibit dimensions of perfectionism to some varying, typically high, degree. The evidence to support the existence of different types of perfectionism (a taxonomy), such as healthy and unhealthy perfectionists, is questionable (see Hill & Madigan, 2017). Rather, the evidence that does exist supports the notion that perfectionism has a continuum-based structure (Broman-Fulks, Hill, & Green, 2008). That is, like most personality traits, all people exhibit perfectionism to some degree. As such, it would be advisable to use the term 'perfectionistic' to signal the trait, rather than perfectionist. This is something that others have recently advocated when describing other traits (e.g., narcissistic versus narcissist; Aslinger, Manuck, Pilkonis, Simms, & Wright, 2018). In short, if there are no perfectionists, there can be no healthy (or even unhealthy) perfectionists.

The second issue is whether, if there is benefit to studying typology regardless, 'healthy' is a suitable moniker. A number of researchers have argued against the use of the term 'healthy' and similar terms on various grounds (e.g., Gaudreau, 2013). Principally, it is a label that emphasizes what the trait is related to, not what it is, thus making the construct and its effects practically inseparable. This is evident in the tautological arguments that follow (e.g., healthy perfectionism is characterized by, well, good health). As a label, it also presupposes the effects of a trait that are likely to be exceedingly complex. Is healthy perfectionism healthy for everyone, under all circumstances, all of the time? Few people would argue that this is the case. By adopting such a black-and-white approach we also divert attention away from the role of personal and situational factors that will be important in determining its effects and the more meaningful question of when and for whom perfectionism is likely to contribute to good or bad health. There is already preliminary evidence, for example, that the effects of dimensions of perfectionism in sport may be moderated by gender, age, sport type, and the instrument used to measure perfectionism (see Hill, Mallinson-Howard, & Jowett, 2018).

The third, and final, issue is whether proponents of healthy perfectionism are confusing dimensions of perfectionism with types of perfectionism. Typically, it is perfectionistic strivings that are seized upon when advocating the notion of healthy perfectionists. Obviously, this is not a type of perfectionism; it is a dimension of perfectionism. It is also only one part of a two-factor higher-order model. The two factors can, of course, be examined separately and statistically analysed in a manner that allows examination of their unique effects, and each can be examined in context of high or low levels of the other. However, PC cannot be ignored when the intention is to understand the consequences of perfectionism. One cannot separate the 'good' from the 'bad' without subsequently examining something that is not actually perfectionism (see also Stoeber, 2011).

Research Examining Perfectionism Reveals It to Be Complex

The final topic discussed is the likely consequences of perfectionism for athletes. Research examining perfectionism in athletes extends across 25 years. This research has not revealed perfectionism to be either uniformly good or bad. Rather, perfectionism has been revealed to be complex. We are, however, beginning to gain a better understanding of the typical effects one can expect when athletes report higher and lower levels of PS and PC. We briefly summarize the results of two recent large reviews in sport below to illustrate how this is the case.

The first review is a meta-analysis of research examining perfectionism in sport (Hill et al., 2018). The meta-analysis included 52 studies and 697 effect sizes for 29 criterion variables that spanned motivation, performance, and emotion/well-being. Based on research in the review, there was little evidence of any discernible benefits of PC for athletes. Rather, motivationally, PC were characterized by a pattern of achievement goals (e.g., ego orientation, mastery avoidance, and performance avoidance) and motivation regulation (combination of introjected, external, and amotivation) that is unlikely to provide the basis for long-term participation and expertise development. Rather, PC appeared likely to place a heavy toll on the well-being of athletes in the form of greater anxiety, self-criticism, and depressive symptoms. In regard to performance, research has yet to find any evidence of an impact of PC on athletic performance. However, given how PC influence well-being, it is difficult to comprehend how they would not indirectly undermine an athlete's ability to regularly perform to their potential.

PS were revealed to be much more ambiguous. In regard to motivation, it included a mix of achievement goals (task and ego orientation) and almost all motivation regulations (with the exception of amotivation). PS are, therefore, likely to be highly energizing but are also likely to give rise to a complex pattern of achievement behaviour that reflects the presence of both high-quality/optimal motivation and low-quality/suboptimal motivation (Deci & Ryan, 2008). The result of this combination appears to be evident regarding performance and emotion/well-being. Unlike PC, PS were positively related to athletic performance. However, their impact on emotion/well-being was mixed. On the one hand, PS were positively related to self-esteem, self-confidence, and enjoyment, but, on the other hand, they were also positively related to anxiety, worry, and self-criticism. In regard to unpicking this complexity, additional analyses revealed that some of the ambiguity of PS is attributable to their relationship with PC. Specifically, accompanying levels of PC are one major source of problems for athletes higher in PS.

The second review was a reanalysis of research in sport, dance, and exercise with a focus on outcomes associated with different combinations of dimensions of perfectionism (Hill, Mallinson-Howard, Madigan, & Jowett, in press). In the review, the 2 × 2 model proposed by Gaudreau and Thompson (2010) was adopted wherein within-person combinations of perfectionism are examined: non-perfectionism (low PS/low PC), pure perfectionistic strivings (pure PS; high PS/low PC), pure perfectionistic concerns (pure PC; low PS/high PC), and mixed perfectionism (high PS/high PC).[1] The model includes a number of formalized hypotheses regarding differences between each combination. Hypothesis 1 states that pure PS will either be associated with better (H1a), poorer (H1b), or no different (H1c) outcomes than non-perfectionism. Hypothesis 2 states that non-perfectionism will be associated with better outcomes than pure PC (H2). Hypothesis 3 states that mixed perfectionism will be associated with better outcomes than pure PC (H3). Finally, Hypothesis 4 states that pure PS will be associated with better outcomes than mixed perfectionism (H4).

With these hypotheses in mind, the reanalysis included 63 studies and 1,772 effect sizes. Hypothesis 1a was supported on 312 of 443 occasions (70% of the time). Hypothesis 2 was supported on 416 of 443 occasions (94% of the time). Hypothesis 3 was supported on 309 of 443 occasions (70% of the time). Hypothesis 4 was supported on 416 of 443 occasions (94% of the time). In other words, as expected, typically, pure PS were associated with better outcomes than non-perfectionism and mixed perfectionism, and non-perfectionism and mixed perfectionism were associated with better outcomes than pure PC. However, based on instances in which hypotheses were in the opposite direction to expectations (H1b supported on 131 occasions, or 30% of the time, and H3 contradicted on 134 occasions, or 30% of the time), it is likely that pure PS and mixed perfectionism carry the potential to be associated with both better *and* worse outcomes than non-perfectionism and pure PC. On this basis, it was concluded that it was likely that all combinations of perfectionism carry at least some potential for motivation, well-being, and (therefore) performance difficulties.

Future Directions

Although understanding of perfectionism in sport has increased a great deal, there is still much to be learned. There are three immediate priorities. Researchers need to identify factors that moderate the effects of perfectionism in sport. This research is required to provide answers to key questions regarding when and for whom perfectionism is likely to contribute to good or bad health and better or worse performance outcomes. Some of the most important studies in this regard will be those that examine how different combinations of dimensions of perfectionism interact to determine how athletes respond to routine success and failure. This work has begun and is suggestive of the notion that higher levels of both perfectionistic strivings and concerns may provide the basis for greater emotional difficulties following failure (e.g., Curran & Hill, 2018). However, this work is in its infancy and has yet to examine these relationships in more meaningful, 'real-world' achievement scenarios.

Another priority for future research is to examine different aspects of perfectionism in sport other than trait perfectionism. Research outside sport has included an additional focus on cognitive elements of perfectionism – frequent cognitions about the attainment of ideal standards – and social aspects of perfectionism – perfectionistic self-presentational styles. A very small number of studies have examined perfectionistic cognitions in athletes (e.g., Donachie, Hill, & Hall, 2018) and perfectionistic self-presentational styles have been examined in exercisers but, as yet, not athletes (Hill, Robson, & Stamp, 2015). This initial research suggests that these aspects of perfectionism may have important implications in sport and warrant examination alongside trait perfectionism. Just as moderating factors are important to revealing the consequences of perfectionism, these aspects of perfectionism, too, will provide a fuller picture of its likely effects.

A final priority for research is to give the relationship between perfectionism and mental health outcomes in sport its due attention. Again, some research exists in this regard (e.g., Shanmugam, Jowett, & Meyer, 2011). However, when one considers the mounting meta-analytical evidence that has implicated perfectionism in a range of mental health difficulties outside sport (e.g., Limburg, Watson, Hagger, & Egan, 2017), it is apparent sport psychology is severely lagging. In addition to the call for more research of this kind here, hopefully, impetus for this research might also be provided by inclusion of perfectionism as a risk factor for poorer mental health in elite athletes in a recent IOC consensus statement (Reardon et al., 2019). This research is most important in regard to contextualizing suggestions that perfectionism may exist in a healthy form or that athletes may, in some ways, benefit from higher levels of perfectionism.

Conclusion

Perfectionism is common but often misunderstood in sport. In considering key topics in this area of research, we argue perfectionism is a multidimensional trait that manifests in areas of people's lives that are important. In addition, there is little evidence to support the existence of types of perfectionist, healthy or otherwise. Instead, perfectionism most likely exists in everyone to some degree, with its consequences dependent on the level of perfectionism, the particular dimensions exhibited, and other personal and situational moderating factors. Research to date suggests that the effects of PS are ambiguous: perhaps beneficial for athletic performance some of the time, but most likely bad for the athlete most of the time. By contrast, PC are likely to be problematic for most athletes, most of the time. This pattern of findings is also evident in research examining combinations of the different dimensions of perfectionism.

Note

1 These dimensions are actually referred to as non-perfectionism (low PS/low PC), pure personal standards perfectionism (pure PSP; high PS/low PC), pure evaluative concerns perfectionism (pure ECP; low PS/high PC), and mixed perfectionism (high PS/high PC). We have retained the language of the higher-order model to avoid confusion and for ease of the reader.

References

Aslinger, E. N., Manuck, S. B., Pilkonis, P. A., Simms, L., & Wright, A. G. (2018). Narcissist or narcissistic? Evaluation of the latent structure of narcissistic personality disorder. *Journal of Abnormal Psychology, 127*, 496–502.

Bieling, P. J., Israeli, A. L., & Antony, M. M. (2004). Is perfectionism good, bad, or both? Examining models of the perfectionism construct. *Personality and Individual Differences, 36*, 1373–1385.

Bouchard, T. J., Jr, & McGue, M. (2003). Genetic and environmental influences on human psychological differences. *Journal of Neurobiology, 54*, 4–45.

Broman-Fulks, J. J., Hill, R. W., & Green, B. A. (2008). Is perfectionism categorical or dimensional? A taxometric analysis. *Journal of Personality Assessment, 90*, 481–490.

Curran, T., & Hill, A. P. (2018). A test of perfectionistic vulnerability following competitive failure among college athletes. *Journal of Sport and Exercise Psychology, 40*, 269–279.

Deci, E. L., & Ryan, R. M. (2008). Facilitating optimal motivation and psychological well-being across life's domains. *Canadian Psychology, 49*, 14–23.

Donachie, T. C., Hill, A. P., & Hall, H. K. (2018). The relationship between multidimensional perfectionism and pre-competition emotions of youth footballers. *Psychology of Sport and Exercise, 37*, 33–42.

Dunn, J. G., Craft, J. M., Dunn, J. C., & Gotwals, J. K. (2011). Comparing a domain-specific and global measure of perfectionism in competitive female figure skaters. *Journal of Sport Behavior, 34*, 25–46.

Fleeson, W. (2001). Toward a structure- and process-integrated view of personality: Traits as density distributions of states. *Journal of Personality and Social Psychology, 80*, 1011–1027.

Fleeson, W., & Noftle, E. (2008). The end of the person–situation debate: An emerging synthesis in the answer to the consistency question. *Social and Personality Psychology Compass, 2*, 1667–1684.

Flett, G. L., & Hewitt, P. L. (2014). The perils of 'perfectionism in sports' revisited: Toward a broader understanding of the pressure to be perfect and its impact on athletes and dancers. *International Journal of Sport Psychology, 45*, 395–407.

Flett, G. L., Hewitt, P. L., Oliver, J. M., & MacDonald, S. (2002). Perfectionism in children and their parents: A developmental analysis. In G. L. Flett & P. L. Hewitt (Eds.), *Perfectionism: Theory, research, and treatment* (pp. 89–132). Washington, DC: American Psychological Association.

Franche, V., & Gaudreau, P. (2016). Integrating dispositional perfectionism and within-person variations of perfectionism across life domains into a multilevel extension of the 2 × 2 model of perfectionism. *Personality and Individual Differences, 89*, 55–59.

Frost, R. O., Marten, P., Lahart, C., & Rosenblate, R. (1990). The dimensions of perfectionism. *Cognitive Therapy and Research, 14*, 449–468.

Gaudreau, P. (2013). The 2 × 2 model of perfectionism: Commenting the critical comments and suggestions of Stoeber (2012). *Personality and Individual Differences, 55*, 351–355.

Gaudreau, P., & Thompson, A. (2010). Testing a 2 × 2 model of dispositional perfectionism. *Personality and Individual Differences, 48*, 532–537.

Gaudreau, P., & Verner-Filion, J. (2012). Dispositional perfectionism and well-being: A test of the 2 × 2 model of perfectionism in the sport domain. *Sport, Exercise, and Performance Psychology, 1*, 29–43.

Gotwals, J. K., Stoeber, J., Dunn, J. G., & Stoll, O. (2012). Are perfectionistic strivings in sport adaptive? A systematic review of confirmatory, contradictory, and mixed evidence. *Canadian Psychology/Psychologie Canadienne, 53*, 263–279.

Gould, D. R., Dieffenbach, K., & Moffett, A. (2002). Psychological characteristics and their development in Olympic champions. *Journal of Applied Sport Psychology, 14*, 172–204.

Hewitt, P. L., & Flett, G. L. (1991). Perfectionism in the self and social contexts: Conceptualization, assessment, and association with psychopathology. *Journal of Personality and Social Psychology, 60*, 456–470.

Hill, A. P. (2016). Conceptualizing perfectionism: An overview and unresolved issues. In A. P. Hill (Ed.), *The psychology of perfectionism in sport, dance and exercise* (pp. 3–30). London: Routledge.

Hill, A. P., & Madigan, D. J. (2017). A short review of perfectionism in sport, dance, and exercise: Out with the old, in with the 2 x 2. *Current Opinion in Psychology, 108*, 220–224.

Hill, A. P., Mallinson-Howard, S. H., & Jowett, G. E. (2018). Multidimensional perfectionism in sport: A meta-analytical review. *Sport, Exercise, and Performance Psychology, 7*, 235–270.

Hill, A. P., Mallinson-Howard, S. H., Madigan, D. J., & Jowett, G. E. (in press). Perfectionism in sport, dance, and exercise: An extended review and reanalysis. In G. Tenenbaum & R. C. Eklund (Eds.), *Handbook of sport psychology* (4th ed., pp. 00-00). Hoboken, NJ: John Wiley.

Hill, A. P., Robson, S. J., & Stamp, G. M. (2015). The predictive ability of perfectionistic traits and self-presentational styles in relation to exercise dependence. *Personality and Individual Differences, 86*, 176–183.

Iranzo-Tatay, C., Gimeno-Clemente, N., Barberá-Fons, M., Rodriguez-Campayo, M. Á., Rojo-Bofill, L., Livianos-Aldana, L., & Rojo-Moreno, L. (2015). Genetic and environmental contributions to perfectionism and its common factors. *Psychiatry Research, 230*, 932–939.

Limburg, K., Watson, H. J., Hagger, M. S., & Egan, S. J. (2017). The relationship between perfectionism and psychopathology: A meta-analysis. *Journal of Clinical Psychology, 73*, 1301–1326.

McAdams, D. P., & Pals, J. L. (2006). A new Big Five: Fundamental principles for an integrative science of personality. *American psychologist, 61*(3), 204–217.

McCrae, R. R., & Costa, P. T., Jr. (1984). Personality is transcontextual: A reply to Veroff. *Personality and Social Psychology Bulletin, 10*, 175–179.

Reardon, C. L., Hainline, B., Aron, C. M., Baron, D., Baum, A. L., Bindra, A., & Derevensky, J. L. (2019). Mental health in elite athletes: International Olympic Committee consensus statement (2019). *British Journal of Sports Medicine, 53*, 667–699.

Sarkar, M., & Fletcher, D. (2014). Psychological resilience in sport performers: A review of stressors and protective factors. *Journal of Sports Sciences, 32*, 1419–1434.

Shanmugam, V., Jowett, S., & Meyer, C. (2011). Application of the transdiagnostic cognitive behavioral model of eating disorders to the athletic population. *Journal of Clinical Sport Psychology, 5*, 166–191.

Stoeber, J. (2011). The dual nature of perfectionism in sports: Relationships with emotion, motivation, and performance. *International Review of Sport and Exercise Psychology, 4*, 128–145.

Stoeber, J. (2018). The psychology of perfectionism: Critical issues, open questions, and future directions. In J. Stoeber (Ed.), *The psychology of perfectionism: Theory, research, applications* (pp. 333–352). London: Routledge.

Stoeber, J., & Stoeber, F. S. (2009). Domains of perfectionism: Prevalence and relationships with perfectionism, gender, age, and satisfaction with life. *Personality and Individual Differences, 46*, 530–535.

30
PERSONALITY AND PHYSICAL ACTIVITY

Ryan E. Rhodes and Kathryn E. Wilson

Introduction

Regular physical activity, performed for approximately 150 minutes per week in the moderate-to-vigorous intensity range, has been established as critical in reducing the risk of most major chronic diseases such as heart disease, type 2 diabetes, several cancers, and musculoskeletal disorders (Lee et al., 2012; Rhodes, Bredin, Janssen, Warburton, & Bauman, 2017; Warburton, Charlesworth, Ivey, Nettlefold, & Bredin, 2010). Furthermore, regular physical activity has also been linked to the prevention and rehabilitation of psychological disorders such as depression and anxiety (Rebar et al., 2015). Despite these considerable health benefits, very few people in developed nations engage in this recommended level of physical activity (Hallal et al., 2012). Thus, an understanding of the antecedents of regular physical activity are needed to inform effective population health promotion initiatives.

Physical activity is a complex behaviour with antecedents ranging from biological and genetic factors to environmental and policy aspects (Bauman et al., 2012). Thus, an understanding of physical activity spans from individuals to society and the built (e.g., neighbourhood infrastructure) and social (e.g., programmes and services) environment. One aspect at the individual end of this spectrum that has seen considerable research aiming at understanding of physical activity is the role of personality traits.

Overview of Personality

According to the American Psychological Association, personality is defined as systematic variation in the way people think, feel, and behave (American Psychological Association, 2018). Overall, personality traits are conceptualized as enduring and consistent individual-level differences across the lifespan (McCrae et al., 2000; Roberts, Walton, & Viechtbauer, 2006).

Although the expression of personality traits is generally considered a culturally conditioned manifestation of several factors (Eysenck, 1970; Funder, 2001; McCrae et al., 2000), the basis of personality is considered biological (Gray, 1991; Zuckerman, 2005). Common themes that emerge across biological theories include individual differences in reactivity (stimulus/response threshold), arousal (tonic neural activity), and self-regulation (recovery from evoked responses; Depue & Collins, 1999; Gray & McNaughton, 2000; Zuckerman, 2005). Personality is also moderately to highly heritable (Bouchard & Loehlin, 2001; De Moor et al., 2012), suggesting an evolutionary basis.

Contemporary personality trait research and theory have followed a common higher-order trait taxonomy that acts as a determinant of lower-order sub-traits with greater specificity and detail. Thus, primary personality traits represent the peak of a conceptual hierarchy, linking individual biological differences to individual-level behaviour. This approach has helped bridge the gap between specific sub-traits and more general factors that created a disparate field of study in early personality trait psychology (Digman, 1990; Goldberg, 1993). Early factor analysis work by Cattell (1947), followed by the pioneering biological models of extraversion and neuroticism by Eysenck (Eysenck, 1970), provided a platform for the big five model of personality used most often in contemporary personality research (McCrae & Costa, 2008; Revelle, Wilt, & Condon, 2011).

The five-factor model of personality suggests that neuroticism (e.g., tendency to be emotionally unstable, anxious, self-conscious, and vulnerable), extraversion (e.g., tendency to be sociable, assertive, energetic, seek excitement, and experience positive affect), openness to experience/intellect (e.g., tendency to be perceptive, creative, reflective and appreciate fantasy, and aesthetics), agreeableness (e.g., tendency to be kind, cooperative, altruistic, trustworthy, and generous), and conscientiousness (e.g., tendency to be ordered, dutiful, self-disciplined, and achievement-oriented) are the basic factors of personality structure. These common-factor taxonomies are thought to represent the basic building blocks of personality and subsequently interact with one's environmental exposures to cause the expression of more specific sub-traits, (Goldberg et al., 2006; McCrae & Costa, 1995). For example, individuals high in extraversion may express this higher-order trait through excitement-seeking, sociability, a positive outlook, or energetic activity, depending on an outlet that is feasible and socially conditioned in their environment. The organization of sub-traits relative to their relationships with primary factors is inconsistent between theories. However, most theorists propose that personality interacts with external factors to produce narrower, more contextualized social cognitive and motivational characteristics that subsequently determine behavioural action (Ajzen, 1991; Bogg, Voss, Wood, & Roberts, 2008; McCrae & Costa, 1999; Mischel & Shoda, 1999; Rhodes, 2006). In the context of this meta-theoretical perspective, the way an individual responds to any external or internal stimulus is moderated by their underlying personality at the highest level (which is reflective of individual differences in neurobiological arousal and reactivity in relevant neural networks). Personality is expected to moderate the impact of environment on cognitions, affect, and behaviour. An understanding of how personality and physical activity are related may be of great practical value in explaining systematic variability in physical activity level, as well as reach and effectiveness of behavioural interventions. Such a perspective can also shed light on systematic variability in the affective response to physical activity and exercise, and psychological and physiological responses to acute or chronic exercise. Using an integrative framework of the personality system may allow researchers to tease out cognitive and biological mechanisms responsible for systematic variation in the way people respond to exposures relevant to physical activity and exercise promotion (Coulter, Mallett, Singer, & Gucciardi, 2016; Ferguson, 2013; Wilson, in press).

The following sections provide an abbreviated overview of the evidence linking physical activity to personality traits. Contemporary perspectives can also be read elsewhere (Allen & Laborde, 2014; Coulter et al., 2016; De Moor & De Geus, 2018; Laborde & Allen, 2016; Rhodes & Boudreau, 2017; Wilson, in press).

Personality and Physical Activity

Research on personality and physical activity has spanned almost 50 years, with intermittent attention. Personality researchers typically apply a hierarchical structure to understanding personality that includes primary traits as broad dimensions of thoughts, feelings, and action, followed by finer-grained lower-order traits that are reflective of individuals' cumulative relevant experiences and underlying personality (Costa & McCrae, 1992). We address the research on physical activity and these primary and lower-order traits in the sections below.

Primary Traits

Although some personality research has been focused more on sport performance (Allen, Greenlees, & Jones, 2013; Eysenck, Nias, & Cox, 1982), three meta-analyses (Rhodes & Smith, 2006; Sutin et al., 2016; Wilson & Dishman, 2015) have been conducted to appraise the relationship between the primary traits of the five-factor model and physical activity. In the first meta-analysis on this research topic, Rhodes and Smith (2006) found small positive associations between extraversion ($r = .23$) and conscientiousness ($r = .20$) and physical activity and a small negative relationship between physical activity and neuroticism ($r = -.11$) among 35 samples. They further used a narrative analysis to evaluate potential moderators of these findings, concluding that sex, age, and study design did not appear to affect the findings. In contrast, they found that European studies had a lower association of extraversion and physical activity compared with North American studies, suggesting there may be some cultural differences with how extraversion is expressed in physical activity.

More recently, Wilson and Dishman (2015) conducted a meta-analysis of 64 studies on the application of the five-factor model and physical activity. Sutin and colleagues (2016) also completed a more recent, selected meta-analysis of 16 population samples. Similar to that of Rhodes and Smith, both meta-analyses found positive associations between extraversion (both $r = .11$) and conscientiousness (both $r = .10$) and physical activity in the small effect-size range. All other associations were within the trivial effect size classification (Cohen, 1992; Gignac & Szodorai, 2016). Design characteristics of the studies were formally examined as moderators of the effects. There were some significant differences noted in Wilson and Dishman (2015), but almost all of the deviations were small, even in the context of guidelines for individual differences research (Cohen, 1992; Gignac & Szodorai, 2016). The exception was the association between conscientiousness and physical activity, where conscientiousness was linked more to the frequency of activity ($r = .21$) than other types of assessment such as general quantity ($r = .06$) or volume ($r = .07$). Taken together, physical activity has a reliable, yet small, positive association with extraversion and conscientiousness. Neuroticism may have a negative relationship with physical activity, but the practicality of this association remains unclear (Rhodes & Boudreau, 2017). Overall, the evidence suggests these relationships are invariant with demographic characteristics and study design.

Lower-Order Traits

A systematic review by Rhodes and Pfaeffli (2012) was performed to examine current evidence for lower-order personality traits and their association with physical activity. The lower-order personality trait review included 42 samples with conclusions that could be drawn for Type A, optimism, industriousness, sociability, and activity.

Specifically, the review showed that Type A (i.e., blend of competitiveness and hostility with agitated behaviour) was associated with physical activity in the small-to-medium effect size range, whereas sociability (i.e., preference for the company of others and social situations) and optimism (i.e., generalized expectations of positive outcomes) were not (Rhodes & Pfaeffli, 2012). The most robust correlates of physical activity, however, were conscientiousness's industriousness–ambition trait and extraversion's activity trait. Industriousness–ambition (also labelled self-discipline in some cases) is a sub-facet of conscientiousness. Industriousness–ambition comprises aspects of achievement-striving and self-discipline, and a natural extension of this type of disposition could be regular physical activity, given its challenge, and self-regulatory demands. It may also represent the central mediator for associations between conscientiousness and physical activity. Rhodes and Pfaeffli (2012) pointed out, however, that the association between industriousness–ambition and physical activity does not seem to hold constant once extraversion's activity trait is controlled for in multivariate analyses. Thus, many of the aspects of conscientiousness and industriousness–ambition that relate to physical activity are likely accounted for within the activity trait.

The activity trait represents a disposition toward being high-energy and fast-talking, having a fast lifestyle, and keeping busy, as opposed to a more laissez-faire disposition. Although the facet is organized under extraversion, it also has been suggested as a sub-trait of conscientiousness owing to the organizational properties and goal achievement necessary for this trait to manifest (Costa & McCrae, 1995). Rhodes and Pfaeffli (2012) found that all studies measuring this trait showed correlations with physical activity in the medium-to-large effect size range. Further, direct tests that compared the predictive capacity of the activity trait with general extraversion showed the activity trait mediated the relationship (Adams & Mowen, 2005; Rhodes & Courneya, 2003; Rhodes, Courneya, & Jones, 2002). Thus, activity appears to be the underlying driver of the relationship between extraversion and physical activity. The reasons for this finding have not been explored, but physical activity may be a natural behaviour of choice, given its energy and organizational/self-regulatory demands (Rhodes & Pfaeffli, 2012).

Rhodes and Boudreau (2017) recently updated the prior review of lower-order traits to include an analysis of both Type D personality and grit. People with Type D (distressed) personalities have tendencies to experience higher levels of social inhibition and negative affect (Denollet, 1998). Participants scoring high on Type D personality were found to participate in significantly less physical activity than non-Type D personalities (Borkoles, Polman, & Levy, 2010). The facet trait of grit is the tendency to persevere and be passionate about long-term goals (Duckworth, Peterson, Matthews, & Kelly, 2007). Those high on grit were associated with better adherence to a moderate- or high-intensity exercise programme compared with their low-grit counterparts (Reed, Pritschet, & Cutton, 2012). Similar to grit, Gerber et al. (2012) found that higher levels of mental toughness were more closely associated with meeting physical activity guidelines for adolescents compared with lower levels of mental toughness.

Personality and Specific Physical Activity Attributes

Physical activity is a collection of behaviours that involve movement with different skill requirements and energy expenditure demands (Ainsworth et al., 2011; Pate et al., 1995). Thus, individual differences in preferences for physical activity (e.g., types, frequency, intensity, duration, and progression) may be influenced by personality factors (Eysenck et al., 1982). Several studies have supported this conjecture. For example, Courneya and Hellsten (1998) found that extraversion was related to preferences for exercising with people (i.e., in a group or with a supervisor), and openness was related to a preference for outdoor (rather than home or gym), recreational (rather than competitive), unsupervised, and spontaneous (rather than scheduled) exercise, and a preference for walking rather than modes such as skating or weight-training. Furthermore, conscientiousness was related to a preference for scheduled exercise and high-intensity, rather than moderate-intensity, exercise. Additionally, those who preferred high intensity to moderate intensity scored low for neuroticism, and those who preferred aerobics to weight-training scored higher on agreeableness.

Explorations of different physical activity behaviours and personality showed some similar findings to the study on preferences (Courneya & Hellsten, 1998). The Rhodes and Smith (2006) review, for example, outlined five studies that explored personality with a particular mode or modes of physical activity. They found that neuroticism was negatively associated with aerobic activity, whereas extraversion was positively associated with this form of activity. Howard, Cunningham, and Rechnitzer (1987), in a more focused assessment of physical activity modes, found that extraverts were more likely to engage in swimming, aerobic conditioning, dancing, and tennis than introverts. By contrast, introverts were more inclined to engage in gardening and home improvement. The results of this study, however, showed no associations between extraversion and walking, jogging, golf, and cycling. Rhodes, Courneya, Blanchard, and Plotnikoff (2007) replicated and extended these results by showing no relationship between neuroticism, extraversion, or conscientiousness and leisure-time walking. The most robust evidence for these differences, however, was identified through moderator analyses performed in the Wilson and Dishman meta-analysis (2015). Specifically, the relationship between extraversion and physical activity was weaker in studies that reported physical activity as the amount of mild-to-moderate-intensity physical activity than it was in other studies, suggesting that the relationship between extraversion and physical activity might be intensity-dependent, in agreement with theory (Eysenck et al., 1982). Specifically, extraverts are expected to experience positive hedonic tone at greater stimulus intensities than those who are lower in extraversion. Taken together, the results support more robust relationships between personality traits and specific attributes of physical activities, such as aesthetics and social qualities (e.g., social, outdoor/indoor), structure (exercise vs. spontaneous activity), extreme energy requirements (intensity), competitiveness, and skill.

Mechanisms of the Personality and Physical Activity Relationship

Most research on personality and physical activity has been focused on answering the question of whether there is a basic relationship between these two variables. In the sections below, we discuss the evidence for the direction of this relationship over time, the potential mediators of this relationship, the genetic basis for personality and physical activity, and evidence for whether personality can be used in physical activity intervention.

Direction of Influence (Longitudinal Evidence)

Although past meta-analyses and reviews have summarized the relationship between personality traits and behaviour, the findings have been largely based on bivariate correlations in cross-sectional or very short-prospective designs (Allen & Laborde, 2014). Snapshots of how traits relate to behaviour across a sample are interesting, but the interconnected relationship between personality and physical activity across time and through periods of change is a relatively unexplored research topic. Research with these more sophisticated designs, however, has yielded interesting findings. For example, a 40-year longitudinal trial showed that extraversion and neuroticism were predictive of physical activity changes across time whereas openness and agreeableness were not (Kern, Reynolds, & Friedman, 2010). Multiple assessments over time also allow for within-person and between-person effects of personality and physical activity. For example, Mõttus, Epskamp, and Francis (2017) showed that, whereas extraversion and conscientiousness predict between-person physical activity, differences in neuroticism within people over time were also predictive of physical activity, with higher levels of neuroticism predicting lower activity.

Longitudinal designs also allow for an examination of whether physical activity practices shape personality. For example, regular physical activity has been shown to reduce sub-traits of neuroticism, presumably owing to its anxiolytic and anti-depressive effect (DiLorenzo et al., 1999). A recent 20-year study also showed that lower physical activity was associated with declines in conscientiousness, openness, extraversion, and agreeableness, although the effect sizes were very small (Stephan, Sutin, Luchetti, Bosselut, & Terracciano, 2018). Similarly, two longitudinal studies of personality change in adulthood found that physically active adults declined significantly less on many five-factor traits (conscientiousness, extraversion, openness, and agreeableness) compared with those who were less active (Stephan, Boiché, Canada, & Terracciano, 2014; Stephan, Sutin, & Terracciano, 2014). How these effects may occur requires study, but it may be a mix of psychobiology (lessened cognitive decline) and a more engaged lifestyle. Such observations suggest that the relationship between personality and physical activity is bidirectional, though this hypothesis has mixed support (Allen, Magee, Vella, & Laborde, 2017). Indeed, relationships between personality and physical activity appear stable across the lifespan for the most part. A population-based study using the Netherlands Twin Registry collected survey data from adolescent and adult twins and their families every 2 years from 1991 to 2002 and showed that exercisers were significantly more extraverted and generally more emotionally stable (low neuroticism) than non-exercisers across age categories ranging from 10–15 years to > 60 years (De Moor, Beem, Stubbe, Boomsma, & De Geus, 2006). Overall, this supports the stability of personality and physical activity associations across adulthood.

Mediation via Social Cognitive Constructs

As noted previously, personality is not hypothesized to affect behaviour directly, but rather through social cognitions (e.g., perceptions, attitudes, norms, self-efficacy), habits, or social and environmental access to a behaviour, which in turn influence the health behaviour (Ajzen, 1991; Bogg et al., 2008; McCrae & Costa, 1995; Rhodes, 2006). The review by Rhodes and Pfaeffli (2012) noted 17 studies where social cognitive constructs were examined as mediators of personality and physical activity relationships, congruent with this theorizing. Most of these studies employed Ajzen's (1991) theory of planned behaviour (with constructs of intention, attitude, subjective norm, and perceived behavioural control) as the intermediary. Rhodes and Pfaeffli (2012) found that almost all studies were able to establish a significant relationship between personality and physical activity, that personality was related to theory of planned behaviour constructs, and that these constructs were related to physical activity. The final mediation test, however, was only supported in two samples (Bryan & Rocheleau, 2002; Hagan, Rhodes, Hausenblas, & Giacobbi, 2009). In these cases, extraversion's activity trait was mediated through attitude and perceived behavioural control (Hagan et al., 2009), and extraversion was mediated through perceived behavioural control (Bryan & Rocheleau, 2002). All other studies showed that personality had significant direct effects on physical activity. The finding is interesting because it shows that personality may have another route to behaviour beyond reflective social cognitions (e.g., intention, attitude, perceived control). Dual processes theories (Deutsch & Strack, 2006), where behaviour is a composition of planned "cold" conscious deliberation and "hot" impulsive drives may help explain these findings with personality. It may be that extraversion, for example, primes or determines impulsive behaviour to approach/avoid physical activity independent of initial intentions (Rhodes & Boudreau, 2017). More research is needed to explore this possibility.

Given that intention is considered the proximal determinant of behaviour in most social cognition models (Conner & Norman, 2015), personality has also been examined as a moderator of the intention–physical activity relationship. In a systematic review of intention–behaviour moderators, Rhodes and Dickau (2013) found convincing evidence that those higher in conscientiousness were more likely to follow through with original intentions than those low on conscientiousness. The result was further supported in a meta-analysis (Wilson & Dishman, 2015). Conner and Abraham (2001) were among the first researchers to test this association and theorized that the disposition toward organization and achievement keeps high-conscientiousness individuals from slipping in their original physical activity goals. Rhodes and Dickau (2013) also noted that there was some evidence that extraversion moderated the intention–behaviour relationship, with extraverts more likely to follow through on intentions than introverts. Most recently, Smith, Williams, O'Donnell, and McKechnie (2017) demonstrated that conscientiousness interacted with competency to set exercise goals (conceptually similar to intention) to predict objectively measured physical activity. Those who scored low for conscientiousness and reported poor goal-setting skills appeared to be at risk for inactivity compared with others.

Rhodes, Courneya, and Hayduk (2002) have suggested that individuals high on extraversion may facilitate their intentions through gravitating toward active environments more than introverted individuals. Further, neuroticism has been evaluated as a moderator of the intention–behaviour relationship in three studies (Hoyt, Rhodes, Hausenblas, & Giacobbi, 2009; Rhodes, Courneya, & Hayduk, 2002; Rhodes, Courneya, & Jones, 2005) and in a retrospective assessment of exercise intention and behaviour following breast cancer (Rhodes, Courneya, & Bobick, 2001). Of those, two provided evidence for moderation (Hoyt et al., 2009; Rhodes et al., 2001), where participants higher in neuroticism had a smaller intention–behaviour relationship than participants scoring lower in neuroticism. These mixed findings, along with a limited literature, suggest that more research is required before any definitive conclusions about neuroticism's moderation capacity can be drawn.

Genetic Determinants of Personality and Physical Activity

As noted previously, personality is considered to have a partially genetic basis. For example, heritability estimates for the big five traits range from 41% to 61% (Jang, Livesley, & Vernon, 1996; Riemann, Angleitner, & Strelau, 1997; Vukasovic & Bratko, 2015). Physical activity is heritable in the range of 48% to 71% (De Moor & De Geus, 2012; Stubbe et al., 2006); thus, an interesting contemporary area of study is the application of the shared heritability of personality and physical activity. Early assessments support rather strong heritability. For example, a Croatian sample of 399 twin pairs, ranging in age from 15 to 22 years, reported that 100% of the correlation between physical activity and extraversion and 86–100% of the correlation between physical activity and neuroticism were due to genetic overlap, after controlling for age and sex (Butkovic, Vukasovic Hlupic, & Bratko, 2017). Most recently, a longitudinal structural equation model of 10,105 twins, surveyed from 1991 to 2009, supported that genetic pleiotropy between personality and physical activity, rather than causal effects, explained the small phenotypic correlations between physical activity and neuroticism (De Moor & De Geus, 2018). By contrast, a combination of genetic pleiotropy between physical activity and personality and a causal effect of extraversion on physical activity explained the small phenotypic correlations between physical activity and extraversion. This research begins to tease apart causal effects and shared variance in the physical activity and personality relationship. Additional research is needed to test the reproducibility and generalizability of these observations in more diverse samples.

Physical Activity Interventions Using Personality Traits

Given the importance of shifting the population's physical activity behaviour, a move from descriptive research on personality to its role in physical activity promotion is welcomed. Unlike social cognitive or social-environmental variables, an association between personality and physical activity represents a potentially challenging obstacle and not a target for change. Indeed, it resembles other intractable correlates of physical activity such as age, disability, or gender. Thus, health promoters need to consider responsive interventions for personality types. Personality assessments may help clinicians and public health professionals recommend activities with features that have been reported to appeal to people according to their traits. For example, research has shown that extraverts prefer being active with others, and open individuals prefer unsupervised, outdoor activities (Courneya & Hellsten, 1998). Thus, it seems reasonable to assume that practitioners may be able to assist an extraverted, open individual with adhering to exercise by recommending an unsupervised, socially supported (i.e., recruit a walking buddy), outdoor walking programme. By contrast, practitioners may enable better exercise adherence in more introverted individuals through recommendations that include individual activities. Personality may also interact with recruitment materials and/or strategies and might moderate intervention strategies to impact adherence and subsequent intervention effectiveness. Finally, personality might predict which people are likely to maintain behaviour change following programme cessation and which may be at risk for dropout or poor behavioural maintenance, which is essential information for practitioners.

As noted above, the proposal for personality-matched interventions has appeal but very limited research on this approach at present. Rhodes and Matheson (2008) examined whether a planning intervention among low-conscientiousness individuals could help improve physical activity over a control group. The effects were null, but it may have been from an ineffective intervention as most of the participants reported that they did not even complete the planning worksheet. By contrast, Why and colleagues (Why, Huang, & Sandhu, 2010) examined the effects of a walking intervention and found that messages were more effective in increasing walking behaviour among conscientious individuals than among their less conscientious counterparts. The results underscore that personality traits may need targeting to help less conscientious individuals (Smith et al., 2017). Most recently, Lepri and colleagues (Lepri, Staiano, Shmueli, Pianesi, & Pentland, 2016) showed some evidence for how extraversion and neuroticism may affect the utility of physical activity interventions on mobile phones. Extraverts and those higher on neuroticism were found to increase physical activity under a social comparison strategy but not when peer pressure was used. A continuation of this research is needed, however, to ascertain the utility of personality-matched intervention.

Conclusion

Personality and physical activity have been studied for nearly half a century, but much of this work has been conducted with healthy young adult samples and relatively static designs. Overall, much of the recent research has been with the five-factor model (neuroticism, extraversion, openness, agreeableness, and conscientiousness). Meta-analytic reviews suggest that conscientiousness and extraversion have small positive associations with physical activity, with some mixed evidence for a small negative relationship with neuroticism (Rhodes & Smith, 2006; Wilson & Dishman, 2015). The effect appears to be most pronounced with vigorous physical activities and less so with lower-intensity activities, but relatively invariant to age and gender. Because most of the reviewed literature involved adult samples, it is unclear how useful personality may be for understanding physical activity among children and adolescents.

Research conducted on specific lower-order traits shows that the activity facet of extraversion and the industriousness–ambition facet of conscientiousness have larger associations with particular types of physical activity than the more basic traits (Rhodes & Pfaeffli, 2012). The process by which personality affects physical activity is not entirely understood, but some of this covariance may be through engendering more positive attitudes and a sense of control/self-efficacy or by facilitating/inhibiting the intention–behaviour relationship (Rhodes & Dickau, 2013; Rhodes & Pfaeffli, 2012). Much of the evidence linking personality to physical activity level through social cognitive variables has been limited to the framework of the theory of planned behaviour, and other approaches such as dual process models are warranted.

More recent research has also investigated the role that physical activity practices may have on personality. There are some mixed results, but it appears that personality stability over several years is influenced by physical activity level (Stephan et al., 2014). The full understanding of these complex relationships, however, remains incomplete. A burgeoning area of research is focusing on the genetic covariance of personality traits and physical activity, with promising initial results but too few studies to reach conclusions at present. Similarly, personality-informed physical activity interventions may be a promising area of promotion. Traits may interact with socio-demographic characteristics, personal history relevant to physical activity and exercise, or even other traits within individuals to influence relationships between personality and intentions to be active. This has seen too little research at present for any conclusion about its efficacy. In order to use personality differences to ultimately help people adhere to a physically active lifestyle, there is a need for more integrative research that applies dynamic theories of personality and health in the personalized physical activity context.

References

Adams, T. B., & Mowen, J. C. (2005). Identifying the personality characteristics of healthy eaters and exercisers: A hierarchical model approach. *Health Marketing Quarterly, 23*, 22–41.

Ainsworth, B. E., Haskell, W. L., Herrmann, S. D., Meckes, N., Bassett, D. R., Tudor-Locke, C., … Leon, A. S. (2011). 2011 Compendium of physical activities. *Medicine & Science in Sports & Exercise, 43*, 1575–1581.

Ajzen, I. (1991). The theory of planned behavior. *Organizational Behavior and Human Decision Processes, 50*, 179–211. doi:10.1016/0749-5978(91)90020-T

Allen, M. S., Greenlees, I., & Jones, M. V. (2013). Personality in sport: A comprehensive review. *International Review of Sport and Exercise Psychology, 6*, 184–208.

Allen, M. S., & Laborde, S. (2014). The role of personality in sport and physical activity. *Current Directions in Psychological Science, 23*, 460–465.

Allen, M. S., Magee, C. A., Vella, S. A., & Laborde, S. (2017). Bidirectional associations between personality and physical activity in adulthood. *Health Psychology, 36,* 332. doi:10.1037/hea0000371

American Psychological Association. (2018). Personality. www.apa.org/topics/personality/

Bauman, A., Reis, R. S., Sallis, J. F., Wells, J. C., Loos, R. J. F., Martin, B. W., & Lancet Physical Activity Series Working Group. (2012). Correlates of physical activity: Why are some people physically active and others not? *Lancet, 380,* 258–271.

Bogg, T., Voss, M. W., Wood, D., & Roberts, B. W. (2008). A hierarchical investigation of personality and behavior: Examining neo-socioanalytic models of health related outcomes. *Journal of Research in Personality, 42,* 183–207.

Borkoles, E., Polman, R., & Levy, A. (2010). Type-D personality and body image in men: The role of exercise status. *Body Image, 7,* 39–45.

Bouchard, T. J., & Loehlin, J. C. (2001). Genes, evolution, and personality. *Behavior Genetics, 31,* 243–273.

Bryan, A. D., & Rocheleau, C. A. (2002). Predicting aerobic versus resistance exercise using the theory of planned behavior. *American Journal of Health Behavior, 26,* 83–94.

Butkovic, A., Vukasovic Hlupic, T., & Bratko, D. (2017). Physical activity and personality: A behaviour genetic analysis. *Psychology of Sport & Exercise, 30,* 128–134.

Cattell, R. B. (1947). Confirmation and clarification of primary personality factors. *Psychometrica, 12,* 197–220.

Cohen, J. (1992). A power primer. *Psychological Bulletin, 112,* 155–159. doi:10.1037/0033-2909.112.1.155

Conner, M., & Abraham, C. (2001). Conscientiousness and the theory of planned behavior: Toward a more complete model of the antecedents of intentions and behavior. *Personality and Social Psychology Bulletin, 27,* 1547–1561.

Conner, M., & Norman, P. (2015). *Predicting health behaviour: Research and practice with social cognition models.* Maidenhead, UK: Open University Press.

Costa, P. T., & McCrae, R. R. (1992). *Revised NEO Personality Inventory (NEO-PI-R) and NEO Five Factor Inventory (NEO-FFI) professional manual.* Odessa, FL: Psychological Assessment Resources.

Costa, P. T., & McCrae, R. R. (1995). Domains and facets: Hierarchical personality assessment using the revised NEO Personality Inventory. *Journal of Personality Assessment, 64,* 21–50.

Coulter, T. J., Mallett, C. J., Singer, J. A., & Gucciardi, D. F. (2016). Personality in sport and exercise psychology: Integrating a whole person perspective. *International Journal of Sport and Exercise Psychology, 14,* 23–41.

Courneya, K. S., & Hellsten, L. A. (1998). Personality correlates of exercise behavior, motives, barriers and preferences: An application of the five-factor model. *Personality and Individual Differences, 24,* 625–633.

De Moor, M., Beem, A. L., Stubbe, J. H., Boomsma, D. I., & De Geus, E. J. C. (2006). Regular exercise, anxiety, depression and personality: A population-based study. *Preventive Medicine, 42,* 273–279.

De Moor, M., Costa, P. T., Terracciano, A., Krueger, R. F., De Geus, E. J. C., Toshiko, T., & Boomsma, D. I. (2012). Meta-analysis of genome-wide association studies for personality. *Molecular Psychiatry, 17,* 337–349.

De Moor, M., & De Geus, E. J. (2018). Causality in the associations between exercise, personality, and mental health. In H. Budde & M. Wegner (Eds.), *The exercise effect on mental health* (pp. 67–99). New York: Routledge.

De Moor, M., & De Geus, E. J. C. (2012). Genetic influences on exercise behavior. In J. M. Rippe (Ed.), *Lifestyle medicine* (pp. 1367–1378). Boca Raton, FL: Taylor & Francis.

Denollet, J. (1998). Personality and risk of cancer in men with coronary heart disease. *Psychological Medicine, 28,* 991–995.

Depue, R. A., & Collins, P. F. (1999). Neurobiology of the structure of personality: Dopamine, facilitation of incentive motivation, and extraversion. *Behavioral and Brain Sciences, 22,* 491–517.

Deutsch, R., & Strack, F. (2006). Duality models in social psychology: From dual processes to interacting systems. *Psychological Inquiry, 17,* 166–172.

Digman, J. M. (1990). Personality structure: Emergence of the five-factor model. *Annual Review of Psychology, 41,* 417–440.

DiLorenzo, T. M., Bargman, E. P., Stucky-Ropp, R., Brassington, G. S., Frensch, P. A., & LaFontaine, T. (1999). Long-term effects of aerobic exercise on psychological outcomes. *Preventive Medicine, 28,* 75–85.

Duckworth, A. L., Peterson, C., Matthews, M. D., & Kelly, D. R. (2007). Grit: Perseverance and passion for long-term goals. *Journal of Personality and Social Psychology, 92,* 1087–1101.

Eysenck, H. J. (1970). *The structure of human personality* (3rd ed.). London: Methuen.

Eysenck, H. J., Nias, D. K. B., & Cox, D. N. (1982). Sport and personality. *Advances in Behaviour Research and Therapy, 4,* 1–56.

Ferguson, E. (2013). Personality is of central concern to understand health: Towards a theoretical model for health psychology. *Health Psychology Review, 7*(1), S32–S70.

Funder, D. C. (2001). Personality. *Annual Review of Psychology, 52,* 197–221.

Gerber, M., Kalak, N., Lemola, S., Clough, P. J., Puhse, U., Elliot, C., & Brand, S. (2012). Adolescents' exercise and physical activity are associated with mental toughness. *Mental Health and Physical Activity, 5,* 35–42.

Gignac, G. E., & Szodorai, E. T. (2016). Effect size guidelines for individual differences researchers. *Personality and Individual Differences, 102,* 74–78.

Goldberg, L. R. (1993). The structure of phenotypic personality traits. *American Psychologist, 48,* 26–34.

Goldberg, L. R., Johnson, J. A., Eber, H. W., Hogan, R., Ashton, M. C., Cloninger, C. R., & Gough, H. C. (2006). The international personality item pool and the future of public-domain personality measures. *Journal of Research in Personality, 40,* 84–96.

Gray, J. A. (1991). The neuropsychology of temperament. In J. Strelau & A. Angleitner (Eds.), *Explorations in temperament* (pp. 105–128). New York: Plenum Press.

Gray, J. A., & McNaughton, N. (2000). *The neuropsychology of anxiety: An enquiry into the functions of the septo-hippocampal system* (2nd ed.). Oxford, UK: Oxford University Press.

Hagan, A. L., Rhodes, R. E., Hausenblas, H., & Giacobbi, P. R. (2009). Integrating five-factor model facet level traits with the theory of planned behavior and exercise. *Psychology of Sport & Exercise, 10,* 565–572.

Hallal, P. C., Andersen, L. B., Bull, F. C., Guthold, R., Haskell, W., Ekelund, U., & Wells, J. C. (2012). Global physical activity levels: Surveillance progress, pitfalls, and prospects. *The Lancet, 380,* 247–257.

Howard, J. H., Cunningham, D. A., & Rechnitzer, P. A. (1987). Personality and fitness decline in middle-aged men. *International Journal of Sport Psychology, 18,* 100–111.

Hoyt, A. L., Rhodes, R. E., Hausenblas, H., & Giacobbi, P. R. (2009). Integrating five-factor model facet level traits with the theory of planned behavior and exercise. *Psychology of Sport & Exercise, 10,* 565–572.

Jang, K. L., Livesley, W. J., & Vernon, P. A. (1996). Heritability of the big five personality dimensions and their facets: A twin study. *Journal of Personality, 64,* 577–591.

Kern, M. L., Reynolds, C. A., & Friedman, H. S. (2010). Predictors of physical activity patterns across adulthood: A growth curve analysis. *Personality and Social Psychology Bulletin, 36,* 1058–1072.

Laborde, S., & Allen, M. S. (2016). Personality-trait-like individual differences: Much more than noise in the background for sport and exercise psychology. In M. Raab, P. Wylleman, R. Seiler, A. M. Elbe, & A. Hatzigeorgiadis (Eds.), *Sport and exercise psychology research from theory to practice* (pp. 201–210). Amsterdam: Elsevier.

Lee, I. M., Shiroma, E. J., Lobelo, F., Puska, P., Blair, S. N., & Katzmarzyk, P. T. (2012). Effect of physical inactivity on major non-communicable diseases worldwide: An analysis of burden of disease and life expectancy. *Lancet, 380,* 219–229.

Lepri, B., Staiano, J., Shmueli, E., Pianesi, F., & Pentland, A. (2016). The role of personality in shaping social networks and mediating behavioral change. *User-Model User Adaptation Interface, 26,* 143–175.

McCrae, R. R., & Costa, P. T. (1995). Trait explanations in personality psychology. *European Journal of Personality, 9,* 231–252.

McCrae, R. R., & Costa, P. T. (1999). A five-factor theory of personality. In L. A. Pervin & O. P. John (Eds.), *Handbook of personality: Theory and research* (2nd ed., pp. 139–153). New York: Guilford Press.

McCrae, R. R., & Costa, P. T. (2008). The five-factor theory of personality. In O. P. John, R. W. Robins & L. A. Pervin (Eds.), *Handbook of personality: Theory and research* (3rd ed., pp. 159–181). New York: Guilford Press.

McCrae, R. R., Costa, P. T., Ostendorf, F., Angleitner, A., Hrebickova, M., Avia, M. D., … Smith, P. B. (2000). Nature over nurture: Temperament, personality, and life-span development. *Journal of Personality & Social Psychology, 78,* 173–186.

Mischel, W., & Shoda, Y. (1999). Integrating dispositions and processing dynamics within a unified theory of personality: The cognitive-affective personality system. In L. A. Pervin & O. P. John (Eds.), *Handbook of Personality: Theory and Research* (2nd ed., 139–153). New York: Guilford Press.

Mõttus, R., Epskamp, S., & Francis, A. (2017). Within- and between individual variability of personality characteristics and physical exercise. *Journal of Research in Personality, 69*, 139–148.

Pate, R. R., Pratt, M., Blair, S., Haskell, W. L., Macera, C. A., & Bouchard, C. (1995). Physical activity and public health: A recommendation from the Centers of Disease Control and Prevention and the American College of Sports Medicine. *Journal of the American Medical Association, 273*, 402–407.

Rebar, A., Stanton, R., Geard, D., Short, C. E., Duncan, M., & Vandelanotte, C. (2015). A meta-meta-analysis of the effect of physical activity on depression and anxiety in non-clinical adult populations. *Health Psychology Review, 9*, 366–378.

Reed, J., Pritschet, B. L., & Cutton, D. M. (2012). Grit, conscientiousness, and the transtheoretical model of change for exercise behaviour. *Journal of Health Psychology, 18*, 612–619.

Revelle, W., Wilt, J., & Condon, D. (2011). Individual differences and differential psychology: A brief history and prospect. In T. Chamorro-Premuzic, S. von Stumm, & A. Furnham (Eds.), *The Wiley Blackwell handbook of individual differences* (pp. 3–38). Malden, MA: John Wiley.

Rhodes, R. E. (2006). The built-in environment: The role of personality with physical activity. *Exercise and Sport Sciences Reviews, 34*, 83–88.

Rhodes, R. E., & Boudreau, P. (2017). *Physical activity and personality traits.* Oxford, UK: Oxford Press.

Rhodes, R. E., Bredin, S. S. D., Janssen, I., Warburton, D. E. R., & Bauman, A. (2017). Physical activity: Health impact, prevalence, correlates and interventions. *Psychology and Health, 32*, 942–975.

Rhodes, R. E., & Courneya, K. S. (2003). Relationships between personality, an extended theory of planned behaviour model, and exercise behaviour. *British Journal of Health Psychology, 8*, 19–36.

Rhodes, R. E., Courneya, K. S., Blanchard, C. M., & Plotnikoff, R. C. (2007). Prediction of leisure-time walking: An integration of social cognitive, perceived environmental, and personality factors. *International Journal of Behavioral Nutrition and Physical Activity, 4*, 51.

Rhodes, R. E., Courneya, K. S., & Bobick, T. M. (2001). Personality and exercise participation across the breast cancer experience. *Psycho-Oncology, 10*, 380–388.

Rhodes, R. E., Courneya, K. S., & Hayduk, L. A. (2002). Does personality moderate the theory of planned behavior in the exercise domain? *Journal of Sport and Exercise Psychology, 24*, 120–132.

Rhodes, R. E., Courneya, K. S., & Jones, L. W. (2002). Personality, the theory of planned behavior, and exercise: The unique role of extroversion's activity facet. *Journal of Applied Social Psychology, 32*, 1721–1736.

Rhodes, R. E., Courneya, K. S., & Jones, L. W. (2005). The theory of planned behavior and lower-order personality traits: Interaction effects in the exercise domain. *Personality and Individual Differences, 38*, 251–265.

Rhodes, R. E., & Dickau, L. (2013). Moderators of the intention–behavior relationship in physical activity: A systematic review. *British Journal of Sports Medicine, 47*(4), 215–225. doi:10.1136 bjsports-2011-090411

Rhodes, R. E., & Matheson, D. H. (2008). Does personality moderate the effect of implementation intentions on physical activity? *Annals of Behavioral Medicine, 35*, S209.

Rhodes, R. E., & Pfaeffli, L. A. (2012). Personality and physical activity. In E. O. Acevedo (Ed.), *The Oxford handbook of exercise psychology* (pp. 195–223). New York: Oxford University Press.

Rhodes, R. E., & Smith, N. E. I. (2006). Personality correlates of physical activity: A review and meta-analysis. *British Journal of Sports Medicine, 40*, 958–965.

Riemann, R., Angleitner, A., & Strelau, J. (1997). Genetic and environmental influences on personality: A study of twins reared together using the self- and peer report NEO-FFI scales. *Journal of Personality, 65*, 449–475.

Roberts, B. W., Walton, K. E., & Viechtbauer, W. (2006). Patterns of mean-level change in personality traits across the life course: A meta-analysis of longitudinal studies. *Psychological Bulletin, 132*, 1–25.

Smith, G., Williams, L., O'Donnell, C., & McKechnie, J. (2017). The influence of social-cognitive constructs and personality traits on physical activity in healthy adults. *International Journal of Sport and Exercise Psychology, 15*, 540–555.

Stephan, Y., Boiché, J., Canada, B., & Terracciano, A. (2014). Association of personality with physical, social, and mental activities across the lifespan: Findings from US and French samples. *British Journal of Psychology, 105*, 564–580.

Stephan, Y., Sutin, A. R., Luchetti, M., Bosselut, G., & Terracciano, A. (2018). Physical activity and person-ality development over twenty years: Evidence from three longitudinal samples. *Journal of Research in Personality, 73,* 173–179.

Stephan, Y., Sutin, A. R., & Terracciano, A. (2014). Physical activity and personality development across adulthood and old age: Evidence from two longitudinal studies. *Journal of Research in Personality, 49,* 1–7.

Stubbe, J. H., Boomsma, D. I., Vink, J. M., Cornes, B. K., Martin, N. G., Skytthe, A., & De Geus, E. J. (2006). Genetic influences on exercise participation in 37,051 twin pairs from seven countries. *PLoS One, 1,* e22.

Sutin, A. R., Stephan, Y., Luchetti, M., Artese, A., Oshio, A., & Terracciano, A. (2016). The five-factor model of personality and physical inactivity: A meta-analysis of 16 samples. *Journal of Research in Per-sonality, 63,* 22–28.

Vukasovic, T., & Bratko, D. (2015). Heritability of personality: A meta-analysis of behavior genetic studies. *Psychological Bulletin, 141,* 769–785.

Warburton, D. E. R., Charlesworth, S., Ivey, A., Nettlefold, L., & Bredin, S. S. D. (2010). A systematic review of the evidence for Canada's physical activity guidelines for adults. *International Journal of Behav-ioral Nutrition and Physical Activity, 7,* 39.

Why, Y. P., Huang, R. Z., & Sandhu, P. K. (2010). Affective messages increase leisure walking only among conscientious individuals. *Personality and Individual Differences, 48,* 752–756.

Wilson, K. E. (in press). Personal characteristics and exercise. In M. H. Anshel & S. J. Petruzzello (Eds.), *APA's handbook of sport and exercise psychology* (Vol. 2). American Psychological Association.

Wilson, K. E., & Dishman, R. K. (2015). Personality and physical activity: A systematic review and meta-analysis. *Personality and Individual Differences, 72,* 230–242.

Zuckerman, M. (2005). *Psychobiology of personality* (2nd ed.). Cambridge: Cambridge University Press.

31

PERSONALITY AND TEAM EFFECTIVENESS

James Hardy, Alex J. Benson, and Matt W. Boulter

Introduction

Much like many industrial organizations where employees are structured using teams, the experiences of athletes (and exercisers) are heavily shaped by their involvement with teams and group-related factors (e.g., leadership, team goals). This includes athletes who are members of task-interdependent sports team (e.g., rugby, soccer), as well as those competing in an individual sport but practising as part of a training squad (e.g., gymnastics, track and field; Evans, Eys, & Bruner, 2012). The importance of considering athlete personalities in team settings is highlighted by the inevitable fact that every team is comprised of individuals each of whom brings their own unique set of characteristics and propensities. As team members' characteristic thoughts, feelings, and behaviours impact both the task-focused actions of team members and how those individuals react and relate to one another, it is evident that the personality composition of teams may be crucial to team functioning and performance (e.g., LePine, Buckman, Crawford, & Methot, 2011; LePine, Colquitt, & Erez, 2000). Nevertheless, despite the intertwined coexistence of personality and teams, the stated importance of personality for team effectiveness (McEwan & Beauchamp, 2014), and, hence, calls for research on this topic (Allen, Greenlees, & Jones, 2013; Beauchamp, Jackson, & Lavallee, 2007), there remains a distinct lack of empirical investigation by sports researchers.

A traditional perspective on understanding team effectiveness in the organizational psychology literature adopts an input–process–output basis (e.g., Mathieu, Maynard, Rapp, & Gilson, 2008). Recently, a similar approach has been utilized by McEwan and Beauchamp (2014) in the sports literature. Common to this school of thought is that team members' personalities are conceptualized as an input inherent within the team. Although this explicitly acknowledges the potential relevance of personality, very little concrete steer is provided concerning personality's specific role or how best to conceptualize *team personality* and the investigation of personality within the context of a team setting. Given the limited examination of team personality within sport, in this present contribution, the authors draw largely from relevant organizational psychology research and nascent lines of inquiry in sport and expand on salient points using sports-based examples. Directions for future research are highlighted throughout.

Conceptualizing Team Personality

Researchers have conceptualized team personality in a number of ways that reflect both team-level effects (i.e., how the confluence of personalities within a team relates to group processes and outcomes) and the influence of individuals within teams. However, these perspectives have not been investigated to equal extents. An interesting perspective on team personality that places clear emphasis on team-level effects has been termed collective personality. Stewart (2003) suggested that personality terms used to describe individual personality can also be applied to depict the behavioural regulation of teams as a whole. For example, Manchester United Football Club teams, under Sir Alex Ferguson, frequently scored winning goals late in matches, building a reputation as being gritty teams who never give up. However, when David Moyes took over as manager of virtually the same set of players, the aura of being a winning team evaporated. This speaks to Hofmann and Jones's (2005) assertions that, although individual and collective personalities are functionally isomorphic (i.e., they can describe behaviour at both levels using similar terminology), the development of their relevant underpinning processes can differ. As an interpersonal construct, collective personalities develop over time, reflecting shared experiences, and are shaped by more than just team members' individual personalities (e.g., in the aforementioned example, the coaches' roles in shaping the teams' collective personality are highlighted). An example of a collective personality that has attracted more systematic investigation by researchers is collective narcissism predicting intergroup aggressiveness (see de Zavala, Cichocka, Eidelson, & Jayawickreme, 2009, for more details). Despite the potential relevance of collective personality, the overall scarcity of research examining team personality in this collective manner makes this perspective an avenue of future research sport psychologists ought to consider.

To date, the most common approach to examining personality within team contexts has been to operationalize personality through a Big Five lens and utilize individual data to represent the team personality composition (TPC). For instance, researchers have aggregated individual reports to create a mean team score, a variance team score, as well as maximum and minimum scores of members on a team (e.g., Bell, 2007). Collectively, these methods reflect both the degree of a personality characteristic and the variability of these individual differences within teams, enabling insight regarding the importance of the extent of a personality trait on a team or the diversity of it within the team.

A final approach to researching personality within teams is investigating the constituent components of teams by examining the roles of individual team members within their teams (Cameron, Cameron, Dithurbide, & Lalonde, 2012). Rather than examining the effect of personality in a way that assumes a trait acts in a diffused manner across all team members in the same way, this alternative perspective focuses on how the personality characteristics of specific team members (e.g., a team captain) influence team performance and the underpinning team processes that facilitate superior team effectiveness (Kim, Gardant, Bosselut, & Eys, 2018).

Given the popularity of input–process–output models for understanding antecedents of team performance and coupled with the aforementioned conceptualizations of team personality, as well as the nature of personality–team performance research conducted so far, we use the schematic shown in Figure 12 to shape our review.

Accordingly, we acknowledge the complex ways in which personality may impact team performance through both individual- and team-level effects, as well as via direct and indirect pathways (cf. LePine et al., 2011). Owing to the focus of the review, writing is prioritized to

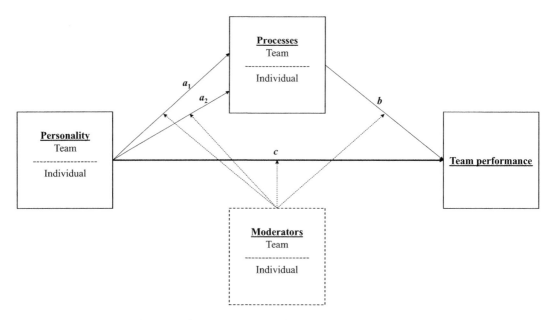

Figure 12 Personality and team performance overview framework

cover the a_1, a_2, and c paths depicted in Figure 12, as well as to advance reasoning why sport psychologists should also consider the moderating function of team personality.

Personality and Team Performance (c Path)

As mentioned above, the majority of research conducted follows a TPC perspective, operationalizing team personality as a mean team score, a variance team score, as well as maximum and minimum scores. Although this research has yielded findings that are relatively challenging to interpret, meta-analytical summaries of this work enable some clarity. For instance, Bell (2007) reported overall (i.e., no differentiation between team mean, team variance, etc.) associations between the Big Five conceptualization of TPC and team performance whereby agreeableness (corrected population correlation, ρ = .12), conscientiousness (ρ = .11), and extroversion (ρ = .09) were mildly and positively correlated with performance, but emotional stability and openness to experience were not significantly correlated. Further, moderator analyses revealed some practically helpful information for sport psychologists interested in team personality. Of particular relevance to the discipline, consistently stronger associations between personality and team performance emerged from field rather than lab-based settings: agreeableness: field ρ = .31 versus lab ρ = .03; conscientiousness: ρ = .30 versus .04; emotional stability: ρ = .06 versus .03; extraversion: ρ = .15 versus .06; and openness to experience: ρ = .20 versus .00. Consequently, sport appears to provide a fruitful setting in which to examine team personality. Corroborating this point, Prewett, Walvoord, Stilson, Rossi, and Brannick (2009) also reported larger effects for field-based and physical teams compared with lab and conceptual teams (e.g., teams working on creative tasks). Additional moderator analyses revealed that how researchers conceptualize TPC also influences its association with team performance (Bell, 2007). More specifically, mean scores across the Big Five dimensions nearly always revealed the largest effect sizes. The exception was agreeableness, where both the mean and minimum team score operationalizations exhibited similarly positive relations with team performance (team mean: ρ = .17; minimum score: ρ = .19). It is perhaps for this reason why the majority of research has traditionally operationalized team personality from the mean score perspective. One relatively recent example of a sports-oriented examination of the relation between team personality and team performance utilized rowing crews as the unit of analysis and focused on perfectionism (Hill, Stoeber, Brown, & Appleton, 2014). Mean crew perfectionism was significantly and positively related to performance over a 4-day regatta. Not all aspects of perfectionism were salient, but crews expecting perfection from their teammates outperformed crews not holding such high performance expectations of their colleagues.

When surveying the existing TPC literature, it is apparent that team personality influences team performance, although only to a relatively modest extent. As a result, researchers and practitioners alike should continue to consider alternative TPC concepts beyond the traditional mean score approach to fully understand the implications of personality for team dynamics. Drawing from task-oriented theories of team personality might provide a useful steer regarding which aggregation methods are likely most relevant for the sports teams being investigated. LePine, Hollenbeck, Ilgen, and Hedlund (1997) used Steiner's (1972) classic classification of group tasks to propose how trait scores derived from individual team members should be transformed into appropriate team scores. For additive tasks (e.g., gymnastics, wrestling teams), where team performance is theorized to increase proportionate to each member's contributions to task execution, the mean method is preferred. For disjunctive tasks (e.g., four-ball golf pairings/teams), when team performance is dependent on the team member who contributes the most, the maximum score approach is commended for consideration. Last, for conjunctive tasks (e.g., mountaineering team), where all team members must successfully complete the task and team performance is most sensitive to the team's "weakest link", the minimum method is salient. Moving forward, it would be interesting to see how these alternative aggregation methods, and particularly the team perfectionism minimum score perspective, predict rowing crew performance. When considering the relevance of different TPC perspectives, researchers are reminded to keep the nature of the trait at the forefront of their theorizing. For instance, for some traits (e.g., narcissism), the maximum TPC approach might be particularly problematic, but the minimum score would be beneficial for team effectiveness.

One of the proposed reasons why the predictive power of traditional TPC measures is relatively small with regard to team performance is that its influence is averaged across different situations a team encounters (Bradley, Klotz, Postlethwaite, & Brown, 2013; Schmidt, Ogunfowora, & Bourdage, 2012). Alternatively, modelling TPC as a moderator allows researchers to "zoom in" on which personality conditions are conducive or destructive to team performance. For instance, Bradley and colleagues (2013) considered the relationship between task conflict and team performance to be contingent on the personality of the team (mean TPC). More specifically, for teams characterized by high emotional stability and openness to experience, task conflict enabled divergent viewpoints to be heard without hostility, contributing to a constructive environment to resolve task-related issues and work toward optimal solutions. Findings supported this theorizing. Task conflict and team performance were positively correlated with each other when both team mean openness to experience and emotional stability were high. Conversely, a negative relationship emerged when the mean TPCs were low, providing empirical support for an alternative conceptualization for role of TPC.

Viewing team personality as a moderator, however, is not the only approach available to address the lack of predictive power associated with orthodox TPC findings. A classic person–situation approach provides a powerful lens through to which examine the individual nature and role of personality in team outcomes, represented by the multilevel investigation of individual (Level 1) personality variables within the context of team level (Level 2) moderators (Bell, 2007; Bradley et al., 2013). Trait activation theory (Tett & Burnett, 2003) forms the basis for the notion that individuals' behaviours are a product of their personality and their environment. Within this context, high mean team (Level 2) conscientiousness reflects a hard-working, motivated, and well-organized environment that will "activate" and encourage an individual (Level 1) to further increase his/her work effort, facilitating superior performance. On the other hand, a negative effect might be expected for a highly conscientious individual within a low team conscientiousness environment (Schmidt et al., 2012). This theorizing compares well with the rise of French footballer, N'Golo Kante. Described as a very hard-working individual, his performances were not consistently observed and recognized until he moved from lower-league French football to Leicester City in the English Premier League. Transferred to a motivating, hard-working environment, Kante's performances helped Leicester City win the Premier League 2015–16 title and was named the PFA Player of the Year.

Schmidt and colleagues (2012) applied this cross-level approach to evaluate whether team conscientiousness moderated the relation between individual conscientiousness and the performance of Canadian football players. They documented support for the moderating effect of team conscientiousness in relation to both objective and subjective performance. Specifically, there was a significant positive relationship with individual player conscientiousness at higher levels of team conscientiousness; however, this relationship was non-significant at lower levels of team conscientiousness. Conscientious individuals want to contribute to group goals and elevated performance when placed with others who hold similar values, whereas they are unmotivated when in an environment where the group is less motivating and hard working. Although Schmidt et al. focused on individual performance, the authors believe that there are relevant principles worth examining in the context of team performance. That said, it remains unclear if such person–environment interactions are activated when other personality traits are considered, as well as what underpinning team process might be at work. Moreover, it is reasonable to assume that not all team members view their team environment the same way, giving support to the adoption of a person-centred approach within such investigations.

Personality and Team-Level Processes (a_1 Path)

Consistent with the model in Figure 12, team personality may also influence team performance through team processes (e.g., communication, intra-group conflict, organizational citizenship behaviours, team cohesion, etc). Team processes refer to cognitive or behavioural activities that contribute to a team's pursuit of its collective goals (Marks, Mathieu, & Zaccaro, 2001). Although there is literature investigating personality and team processes, unfortunately very little research has explicitly tested the mediating role of team processes on the personality–performance relation. Instead, researchers have tended to infer an indirect effect based on their interpretation of the literature (LePine et al., 2011). For instance, numerous studies have examined the relationship between task/social cohesion and performance. Carron, Colman, Wheeler, and Stevens's (2002) meta-analysis provided robust support for a positive relationship between cohesion and performance in sports teams (i.e., the *b* path of the indirect effect). When considering team personality, Barrick, Neubert, Mount, and Stewart (1998) argued social cohesion to be a marker of effective performance as it reflects positive communication and conflict resolution, as well as effective workload sharing. They examined mean, variance, maximum, and minimum TPC and reported effects for agreeableness, extraversion, and emotional stability on social cohesion. Mean and minimum TPC perspectives had a positive relationship for agreeableness ($r = .32$ and $.38$, respectively), as did emotional stability ($r = .53$ and $.34$). Variance and maximum TPC approaches were both negatively correlated with agreeableness ($r = -.23$ and $-.39$), but not emotional stability. Meanwhile, extraversion was positively related to all operationalizations of TPC: mean ($r = .36$), variance ($r = .35$), minimum ($r = .24$), and maximum ($r = .33$), thus, offering some support for the presence of a relationship on the a_1 path of the team personality–team performance indirect effect. Van Vianen and De Dreu (2001) extended these findings by focusing on task cohesion. Both mean conscientiousness and agreeableness were positively related to task cohesion, and variance in team conscientiousness and extraversion was negatively associated with task cohesion.

Another example of a team process investigated in the context of personality is organizational citizenship behaviours (Organ, 1988), described as "discretionary behaviors that are not a formal requirement of an employee's role, that nevertheless promote effective functioning of the organization" (p. 4). In sport, citizenship behaviours reflect the tendency for athletes to go above and beyond their role for the team. Although studied at the individual rather than team level, Chiaburu, Oh, Berry, Li, and Gardner's (2011) meta-analysis revealed small-to-moderate correlations for conscientiousness ($\rho = .20$), agreeableness ($\rho = .19$), emotional stability ($\rho = .12$), and openness ($\rho = .20$); a null-to-small effect was reported for extraversion ($\rho = .02$). Research examining TPC in relation to organizational citizenship behaviours would complement these findings, as would applying the person–situation (Level 1– Level 2) approach advanced in the previous team performance section. In fact, the general lack of personality research investigating emergent team processes and their expected mediating role leads to the conclusion that future research attention is warranted in order to develop an empirical understanding of how and why team personality influences team performance.

Personality and Individual Level Processes (a_2 Path)

Another approach to studying personality characteristics in relation to sports team effectiveness is through a role-based lens at the individual level of analysis. Several scholars have drawn attention to how attending to personality differences among team members can be leveraged to gain insight into why certain roles emerge in teams, and why individuals may adopt specific roles (Humphrey & Aime, 2014; LePine et al., 2011). Some athletes are known for their larger-than-life personalities and strive for the spotlight, such as Randy Moss, who is considered one of the all-time-great wide receivers in the National Football League. Others, however, focus on leading quietly by their actions, such as the captain of the Chicago Blackhawks, Jonathan Toews. A role refers to the contextually situated behavioural expectations for a team member. Role expectations may develop through explicit communication by an authority figure within the team (i.e., a formally assigned role) or more naturally through repeated interactions with group members over time (i.e., informal roles; Mabry & Barnes, 1980). In both cases, personality factors have been recognized as a factor in shaping whether athletes choose to accept and embrace a specific role and the type of role that is expected of a given athlete (Benson, Surya, & Eys, 2014). Nonetheless, personality characteristics are likely to be more relevant to the emergence and adoption of informal roles than formal roles, because the strength of the relation between personality and behaviours tends to be attenuated under conditions of high situational strength (i.e., when there is clarity, consistency, constraints, and consequences tied to specific behaviour), and formal roles are characterized by higher situational strength (Meyer, Dalal, & Hermida, 2010).

As a key structural feature of sports teams, roles function to organize and coordinate team processes by delineating who is responsible for whom (i.e., hierarchical boundaries) and the tasks for which each member is responsible (i.e., functional boundaries; Eys, Schinke, Surya, & Benson, 2014). Indeed, mounting evidence shows that the roles athletes occupy, as well as the perceptions they harbour in relation to such roles, are linked to several team dynamics variables, including role acceptance (Benson, Eys, Surya, Dawson, & Schneider, 2013), satisfaction (Eys, Carron, Bray, & Beauchamp, 2003), and team member performance (e.g., Beauchamp, Bray, Eys, & Carron, 2002). Consider, for example, the 2004 United States Olympic men's basketball "Dream Team"—a team uniformly agreed to have the most talented roster, and yet they were unable to capture gold. Although several factors contributed to this (under) performance, team members seemingly struggled to establish roles that complemented and maximized their effectiveness as a unit.

Despite being a new area of inquiry in sport, there is growing interest in how personality characteristics contribute to the adoption of roles in sports teams. Role adoption may, in part, be driven by individual differences in preferences for specific roles. Akin to the concept of job crafting (e.g., Wrzesniewski & Dutton, 2001), athletes may attempt to revise or redefine a formally assigned role based on their personality characteristics and preferences (Benson et al., 2014). There is some evidence, for example, that more narcissistic athletes may be resistant to followership roles. In a study with sports teams, athletes higher in narcissism were less satisfied with their role, perceived their role to be a less accurate reflection of their ability, and engaged in fewer citizenship behaviours, but only when they occupied a lower-status role within the group (Benson, Jordan, & Christie, 2016). These findings from sports teams align with three experimental studies where participants were assigned either a leader (i.e., project manager) or follower (i.e., employee) role (Studies 1–3; Benson, Jordan, et al., 2016). Similarly, other findings from the sport domain suggest that more narcissistic followers are less likely to be motivated to exert additional effort by displays of a coach's transformational leadership (Arthur, Woodman, Ong, Hardy, & Ntoumanis, 2011). Considering these findings together, athletes higher in narcissism may actively avoid occupying roles that do not align with their grandiose self-views and, instead, pursue roles that afford the power and status they covet.

Several lines of inquiry provide insight into the relation between personality characteristics and the emergence of informal roles within sports teams. For example, an ethnographic study of an outdoor expedition group emphasized that role emergence is driven by an array of factors, including the personality characteristics of team members (Carreau, Bosselut, Ritchie, Heuzé, & Arppe, 2016). However, this study did not provide details regarding which personality characteristics were relevant to specific roles. In a separate study exploring negative informal roles in sports teams, several coaches reported that athletes who occupied a "team cancer" role also tended to possess Machiavellian (e.g., manipulative) and narcissistic characteristics (Cope, Eys, Schinke, & Bosselut, 2010). Although these findings suggest that individuals believe that personality differences may predispose athletes to behave in a certain way, neither study examined whether personality differences explained variance in the emergence and adoption of specific team roles.

Recent work has addressed this gap in the literature by evaluating whether informal role occupants—measured via self-identification and teammate identification—differed in trait levels on the Big Five personality characteristics (Kim et al., 2018). Athletes responded to a list of 12 informal roles, derived from previous work (Cope et al., 2010). Kim et al. found that the team comedian role and the distractor role corresponded to higher levels of extraversion, but only the distractor corresponded to lower levels of conscientiousness. In addition, athletes who were identified by their teammates as occupying a mentor role scored lower on neuroticism, whereas athletes identified as the star player by their teammates scored lower on agreeableness. Less clear, however, were the results related to leadership roles. Self-identification as the nonverbal leader corresponded to higher levels of extraversion in Study 1 but not in Study 2. In contrast, self-identification as the verbal leader corresponded to higher levels of extraversion in Study 2 but not in Study 1 (Kim et al., 2018). Despite these mixed findings, research outside the sport domain provides insight into the relations between personality characteristics and leadership role emergence.

Individuals high in narcissism, in particular, are confident in their ability to lead and enjoy opportunities to do so (Benson, Jordan, et al., 2016; Brunell et al., 2008). Interestingly, one study found narcissism to be a predictor of leadership emergence among unacquainted individuals, even though leader narcissism contributed to worse intra-team communication and, ultimately, poorer group performance (Nevicka, Ten Velden, De Hoogh, & Van Vianen, 2011). The ability of individuals scoring high in narcissism to elevate their social status during group interactions is partly driven by their social assertiveness (Leckelt, Küfner, Nestler, & Back, 2015). Despite emerging as leaders during short-term interactions, the charm of highly narcissistic individuals tends to wane over time or with frequent interactions (Nevicka, Van Vianen, De Hoogh, & Voorn, 2018; Ong, Roberts, Arthur, Woodman, & Akehurst, 2016). Together, these findings suggest that athletes who are higher in narcissism may emerge as leaders owing to their social boldness, but their potency as leaders wanes with time, becoming ineffective or disruptive in such roles owing to their sense of entitlement and exploitativeness. Overall, studying how athlete personality characteristics are associated with the adoption of roles appears to be a promising area of inquiry for advancing our understanding of how personality contributes to team effectiveness through its effect on individual-level variables.

Promising Perspectives on Personality and Teams

Here, approaches to studying personality in relation to team effectiveness that are theoretically promising, but have yet to receive empirical attention in the sport domain, are advanced. Until now, the authors have described studies wherein the focus is on the effect of specific personality traits (e.g., conscientiousness) in relation to key outcomes (e.g., team performance), with minimal attention to how multiple traits combine within individuals to produce distinct personality profiles. Latent profile analysis enables researchers to detect potentially complex configurations among multiple personality traits and examine how these distinct profiles relate to variables of interest (Daljeet, Bremner, Giammarco, Meyer, & Paunonen, 2017). This approach to studying personality assumes that there are subgroups in a population that share similar scores on multiple traits. For example, Daljeet et al. (2017) used latent profile analysis with the HEXACO model of personality (an expanded version of the Big Five that encompasses the honesty–humility dimension) and documented support for distinct personality profiles across two independent samples. They labelled these profiles as socially considerate, self-confident, goal-oriented, withdrawn, and maladjusted. Relating back to the role-based perspective, sport researchers could apply latent profile analysis to identify distinct athlete personality profiles at the individual level of analysis and examine how these profiles contribute to role behaviours within teams. In the context of the TPC models described earlier, sport researchers could examine whether there are distinct *team personality profiles* at the group level of analysis (e.g., O'Neill, McLarnon, Hoffart, Woodley, & Allen, 2018). Overall, given that personality traits do not operate in isolation from one another, sport researchers may benefit from embracing an analytical approach that enables insight into the ways that personality traits jointly operate (i.e., athlete personality profiles and/or team personality profiles) and the potential consequences of such profiles on team outcomes.

Driskell, Goodwin, Salas, and O'Shea (2006) present an alternative take on team personality that to date remains unexamined. Driskell et al.'s theorizing places an emphasis on (a) individual player personality, (b) specific and discrete facets of team personality, and (c) the larger situation of personality in the context of teamwork, a concept that has largely escaped systematic research in the sports literature. Accordingly, Driskell and co-workers argued that the prevailing approach of aggregating to the team level neglects the effect of the individual. They also argued that the global Big Five trait approach is too simplistic, as lower or first-order facets can have differing or even contradictory effects. For example, although affiliation and dominance are both facets of the global trait of extraversion, they are expressed very differently. On the one hand, affiliation reflects how easy-going and friendly an individual is, whereas, on the other hand, dominance reflects domineering autocratic behaviours. A problematic upshot of this masking is that researchers are unable to discern which facets are of greatest relevance, limiting the practical value of the research. Drawing from the above principles, Driskell et al. (2006) put forward that:

> Good team players are not controlling or domineering. They are sociable, perceptive and empathic, and interpersonally expressive. They are emotionally stable and confident They are adaptive, trust other team members, and are cooperative. Finally, good team players are reliable, have a strong sense of loyalty or duty to the team, and they work hard for the team goals.
>
> (p. 257)

This view is consistent with sports-oriented data documenting high-level coaches' descriptions of ideal followership (Benson, Hardy, & Eys, 2016). Of note, as Driskell and colleagues couched their theorizing within the context of teamwork, coupled with research establishing that teamwork includes a set of dimensions or roles and responsibilities to effectively coordinate the team towards its common goal (Ilgen, 1999), Driskell et al. considered there to be specific personality facets associated with teamwork dimensions. This approach is consistent with person–team fit theory (Hollenbeck et al., 2002), whereby personality and outcomes are contingent on the task. Based on research conducted with naval teams and aircrews (e.g., Cannon-Bowers, Tannenbaum, Salas, & Volpe, 1995; Morgan, Glickman, Woodard, Blaiwes, & Salas, 1986), Driskell et al. presented precise hypotheses linking first-order facets of personality to eight teamwork dimensions: adaptability, shared situational awareness, performance monitoring and feedback, team management, interpersonal relationships, coordination, communication, and decision-making. Figure 13 highlights the relevant facets of personality characterizing team players. However, for more in-depth coverage of the expected influence of personality on the specific dimensions of teamwork, the interested reader is referred to Driskell et al. (2006).

Although Driskell and colleagues advanced an interesting and well-grounded perspective on personality in team settings that appears to be highly relevant to sports team dynamics, their predictions nonetheless await empirical examination. Similar to the previously raised promising research perspective, Driskell et al.'s hypotheses can be thought of as involving profiles of personality, and so are also well aligned to the use of latent profile type analyses.

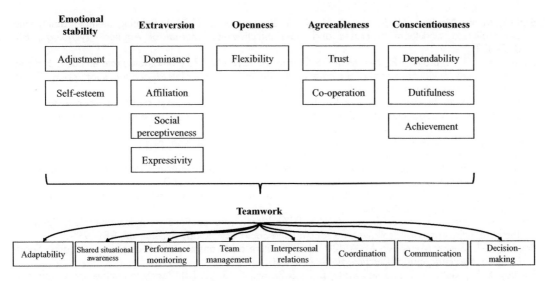

Figure 13 Adaptation of Driskell and colleagues' (2006) personality facet–teamwork mapping

Conclusion

In this review of personality considered in the context of sports teams, the authors initially presented a number of different conceptualizations of team personality as evident in the (almost exclusively organizational) literature. Then, the summarized findings of empirical research focusing on team performance, as well as both team and more individually oriented underpinning processes, were covered. Existing data support the idea that team personality is a relevant construct for sports teams and their performance. Furthermore, meta-analytic reviews flag sport as a setting of particular suitability for the continued investigation of team personality in its various guises. The structure of this contribution, in line with other contemporary theoretical frameworks of team personality (e.g., LePine et al., 2011), emphasizes the latter's influence at both team and individual levels. To energize continued work in this area, a number of approaches were presented. Future sport researchers would do well to consider these aspects when investigating team personality. A major thrust of the avenues for future research revolve around the notion of bearing in mind the individual nature of personality—"putting the I in team"—when considering the effectiveness of sports teams. Where appropriate, the authors also highlight particular literature (e.g., narcissism research) in an attempt to shift thinking beyond a traditional "main effects" Big Five viewpoint towards more theoretically grounded perspectives of team personality.

References

Allen, M. S., Greenlees, I., & Jones, M. V. (2013). Personality in sport: A comprehensive review. *International Review of Sport and Exercise Psychology, 6*, 184–208.

Arthur, C. A., Woodman, T., Ong, C. W., Hardy, L., & Ntoumanis, N. (2011). The role of athlete narcissism in moderating the relationship between coaches' transformational leader behaviors and athlete motivation. *Journal of Sport & Exercise Psychology, 33*, 3–19.

Barrick, M. R., Neubert, M. J., Mount, M. K., & Stewart, G. L. (1998). Relating member ability and personality to work-team processes and team effectiveness. *Journal of Applied Psychology, 83,* 377–391.

Beauchamp, M. R., Bray, S. R., Eys, M. A., & Carron, A. V. (2002). Role ambiguity, role efficacy, and role performance: Multidimensional and mediational relationships within interdependent sport teams. *Group Dynamics: Theory, Research, and Practice, 6,* 229–242.

Beauchamp, M. R., Jackson, B., & Lavallee, D. (2007). Personality processes and intra-group dynamics in sport teams. In M. Beauchamp & M. Eys (Eds.), *Group dynamics in exercise and sport psychology: Contemporary themes* (pp. 25–42). Oxford, UK: Routledge.

Bell, S. T. (2007). Deep-level composition variables as predictors of team performance: A meta-analysis. *Journal of Applied Psychology, 92,* 595–615.

Benson, A. J., Eys, M., Surya, M., Dawson, K., & Schneider, M. (2013). Athletes' perceptions of role acceptance in interdependent sport teams. *The Sport Psychologist, 27,* 269–280.

Benson, A. J., Hardy, J., & Eys, M. (2016). Contextualizing leaders' interpretations of proactive followership. *Journal of Organizational Behavior, 37,* 949–966.

Benson, A. J., Jordan, C. H., & Christie, A. M. (2016). Narcissistic reactions to subordinate role assignment: The case of the narcissistic follower. *Personality and Social Psychology Bulletin, 42,* 985–999.

Benson, A. J., Surya, M., & Eys, M. A. (2014). The nature and transmission of roles in sport teams. *Sport, Exercise, and Performance Psychology, 3,* 228–240.

Bradley, B. H., Klotz, A. C., Postlethwaite, B. E., & Brown, K. G. (2013). Ready to rumble: How team personality composition and task conflict interact to improve performance. *Journal of Applied Psychology, 98,* 385–392.

Brunell, A. B., Gentry, W. A., Campbell, W. K., Hoffman, B. J., Kuhnert, K. W., & DeMarree, K. G. (2008). Leader emergence: The case of the narcissistic leader. *Personality and Social Psychology Bulletin, 34,* 1663–1676.

Cameron, J. E., Cameron, J. M., Dithurbide, L., & Lalonde, R. N. (2012). Personality traits and stereotypes associated with ice hockey positions. *Journal of Sport Behavior, 35,* 109–124.

Cannon-Bowers, J. A., Tannenbaum, S. I., Salas, E., & Volpe, C. E. (1995). Defining competencies and establishing team training requirements. In R. Guzzo & E. Salas (Eds.), *Team effectiveness and decision making in organizations* (pp. 333–380). San Francisco, CA: Jossey-Bass.

Carreau, J. M., Bosselut, G., Ritchie, S. D., Heuzé, J.-P., & Arppe, S. (2016). Emergence and evolution of informal roles during a canoe expedition. *Journal of Adventure Education and Outdoor Learning, 16,* 191–205.

Carron, A. V., Colman, M. M., Wheeler, J., & Stevens, D. (2002). Cohesion and performance in sport: A meta-analysis. *Journal of Sport and Exercise Psychology, 24,* 168–188.

Chiaburu, D. S., Oh, I.-S., Berry, C. M., Li, N., & Gardner, R. G. (2011). The five-factor model of personality traits and organizational citizenship behaviors: A meta-analysis. *Journal of Applied Psychology, 96,* 1140–1166.

Cope, C. J., Eys, M. A., Schinke, R. J., & Bosselut, G. (2010). Coaches' perspectives of a negative informal role: The "cancer" within sport teams. *Journal of Applied Sport Psychology, 22,* 420–436.

Daljeet, K. N., Bremner, N. L., Giammarco, E. A., Meyer, J. P., & Paunonen, S. V. (2017). Taking a person-centered approach to personality: A latent-profile analysis of the HEXACO model of personality. *Journal of Research in Personality, 70,* 241–251.

de Zavala, A. G., Cichocka, A., Eidelson, R., & Jayawickreme, N. (2009). Collective narcissism and its social consequences. *Journal of Personality and Social Psychology, 97,* 1074–1096.

Driskell, J. E., Goodwin, G. F., Salas, E., & O'Shea, P. G. (2006). What makes a good team player? Personality and team effectiveness. *Group Dynamics, 10,* 249–271.

Evans, M. B., Eys, M. A., & Bruner, M. W. (2012). Seeing the "we" in "me" sports: The need to consider individual sport team environments. *Canadian Psychology, 53,* 301–308.

Eys, M., Carron, A., Bray, S., & Beauchamp, M. (2003). Role ambiguity and athlete satisfaction. *Journal of Sports Sciences, 21,* 391–401.

Eys, M. A., Schinke, R. J., Surya, M., & Benson, A. J. (2014). Role perceptions in sport groups. In M. Beauchamp & M. Eys (Eds.), *Group dynamics in sport and exercise psychology: Contemporary themes* (2nd ed., pp. 131–146). Oxford, UK: Routledge.

Hill, A. P., Stoeber, J., Brown, A., & Appleton, P. R. (2014). Team perfectionism and team performance: A prospective study. *Journal of Sport & Exercise Psychology, 36,* 303–315.

Hofmann, D. A., & Jones, L. M. (2005). Leadership, collective personality, and performance. *Journal of Applied Psychology, 90,* 509–522.

Hollenbeck, J. R., Moon, H., Ellis, A. P. J., West, B. J., Ilgen, D. R., Sheppard, L., & Wagner, J. A. (2002). Structural contingency theory and individual differences: Examination of external and internal person-team fit. *Journal of Applied Psychology, 87,* 599–606.

Humphrey, S. E., & Aime, F. (2014). Team microdynamics: Toward an organizing approach to teamwork. *The Academy of Management Annals, 8,* 443–503.

Ilgen, D. R. (1999). Teams embedded in organizations: Some implications. *American Psychologist, 54,* 129–139.

Kim, J., Gardant, D., Bosselut, G., & Eys, M. (2018). Athlete personality characteristics and informal role occupancy in interdependent sport teams. *Psychology of Sport and Exercise.* Advance online publication. doi: 10.1016/j.psychsport.2018.07.011

Leckelt, M., Küfner, A. C., Nestler, S., & Back, M. D. (2015). Behavioral processes underlying the decline of narcissists' popularity over time. *Journal of Personality and Social Psychology, 109,* 856–871.

LePine, J. A., Buckman, B. R., Crawford, E. R., & Methot, J. R. (2011). A review of research on personality in teams: Accounting for pathways spanning levels of theory and analysis. *Human Resource Management Review, 21,* 311–330.

LePine, J. A., Colquitt, J. A., & Erez, A. (2000). Adaptability to changing task contexts: Effects of general cognitive ability, conscientiousness, and openness to experience. *Personnel Psychology, 53,* 563–593.

LePine, J. A., Hollenbeck, J. R., Ilgen, D. R., & Hedlund, J. (1997). Effects of individual differences on the performance of hierarchical decision-making teams: Much more than g. *Journal of Applied Psychology, 82,* 803–811.

Mabry, E. A., & Barnes, R. E. (1980). *The dynamics of small group communication.* Englewood Cliffs, NJ: Prentice Hall.

Marks, M. A., Mathieu, J. E., & Zaccaro, S. J. (2001). A temporally based framework and taxonomy of team processes. *Academy of Management Review, 26,* 356–376.

Mathieu, J., Maynard, M. T., Rapp, T., & Gilson, L. (2008). Team effectiveness 1997-2007: A review of recent advancements and a glimpse into the future. *Journal of Management, 34,* 410–476.

McEwan, D., & Beauchamp, M. R. (2014). Teamwork in sport: A theoretical and integrative review. *International Review of Sport and Exercise Psychology, 7,* 229–250.

Meyer, R. D., Dalal, R. S., & Hermida, R. (2010). A review and synthesis of situational strength in the organizational sciences. *Journal of Management, 36,* 121–140.

Morgan, B. B., Glickman, A. S., Woodard, E. A., Blaiwes, A. S., & Salas, E. (1986). *Measurement of team behaviors in a Navy environment.* Report No. NTSC TR-86-014. Orlando, FL: Naval Training Systems Center.

Nevicka, B., Ten Velden, F. S., De Hoogh, A. H., & Van Vianen, A. E. (2011). Reality at odds with perceptions narcissistic leaders and group performance. *Psychological Science, 22,* 1259–1264.

Nevicka, B., Van Vianen, A. E., De Hoogh, A. H., & Voorn, B. (2018). Narcissistic leaders: An asset or a liability? Leader visibility, follower responses, and group-level absenteeism. *Journal of Applied Psychology, 103,* 703–723.

O'Neill, T. A., McLarnon, M. J., Hoffart, G. C., Woodley, H. J., & Allen, N. J. (2018). The structure and function of team conflict state profiles. *Journal of Management, 44,* 811–836.

Ong, C. W., Roberts, R., Arthur, C. A., Woodman, T., & Akehurst, S. (2016). The leader ship is sinking: A temporal investigation of narcissistic leadership. *Journal of Personality, 84,* 237–247.

Organ, D. W. (1988). *Organisational citizenship behaviour: The good soldier syndrome.* Lexington, MA: Lexington.

Prewett, M. S., Walvoord, A. A. G., Stilson, F. R. B., Rossi, M. E., & Brannick, M. T. (2009). The team personality–team performance relationship revisited: The impact of criterion choice, pattern of workflow, and method of aggregation. *Human Performance, 22,* 273–296.

Schmidt, J. A., Ogunfowora, B., & Bourdage, J. S. (2012). No person is an island: The effects of group characteristics on individual trait expression. *Journal of Organizational Behavior, 33,* 925–945.

Steiner, I. D. (1972). *Group processes and productivity.* New York: Academic Press.

Stewart, G. L. (2003). Toward an understanding of the multilevel role of personality in teams. In M. R. Barrick & M. R. Ryan (Eds.), *Personality and work: Reconsidering the role of personality in organizations* (pp. 183–204) San Francisco, CA: Jossey-Bass.

Tett, R. P., & Burnett, D. D. (2003). A personality trait-based interactionist model of job performance. *Journal of Applied Psychology, 88,* 500–517.

Van Vianen, A. E., & De Dreu, C. K. (2001). Personality in teams: Its relationship to social cohesion, task cohesion, and team performance. *European Journal of Work and Organizational Psychology, 10,* 97–120.

Wrzesniewski, A., & Dutton, J. E. (2001). Crafting a job: Revisioning employees as active crafters of their work. *Academy of Management Review, 26,* 179–201.

32

PERSONALITY ASSESSMENT I

An Integrative Approach

Tristan J. Coulter, Clifford J. Mallett, and Dan P. McAdams

Introduction

The starting point for applied sport psychologists should be a comprehensive framework for understanding the person (Taylor, 2018). Understanding people well, in this domain, has many reported benefits, including opportunities to (a) develop meaningful relationships (e.g., a strong coach–athlete relationship), (b) better understand how different athletes think, feel, and behave (e.g., in different groups, when under competitive stress), and (c) provide clients with information that leads them to achieving greater self-awareness and self-concept clarity (Tabano & Portenga, 2018). To attain these benefits, a common approach in the field is to profile people's personalities and, specifically, where they stand (e.g., high, low, average) in comparison with others on a series of attributes. These attributes often involve an assessment of people's general well-being (e.g., their self-esteem). They also tend to focus on generalized personality (e.g., via the five-factor model; McCrae & Costa, 1999) and/or more circumscribed constructs considered relevant to sport performance (e.g., perfectionism, mental toughness, narcissism, optimism; Laborde, Guillén, Watson, & Allen, 2017; Roberts & Woodman, 2017).

A notable theme linking these descriptive attributes together – and, equally, much of the focus in this encyclopaedia – is the inclination sport and exercise psychologists have for personality traits as the basic, and often sole, constructs through which to know the person. This observation is not problematic per se. As discussed later, there is a lot to be learned about a person through the assessment of his or her trait profile. Rather, the issue lies more in the fact that many people in the sport psychology community seem to accept a trait discourse as the main way to think and talk about personality. For instance, in most sport and exercise psychology textbooks and journal articles, personality is often defined as (something similar to) this: "psychological qualities that contribute to an individual's enduring and distinctive patterns of feeling, thinking, and behaving" (Pervin & Cervone, 2010, p. 8). For many, these qualities equate to *dispositional traits* and denote the main measurable features of human variation that distinguish one athlete or exercise participant from another.

In this contribution, it is argued that an approach based solely on dispositional traits results in a limited understanding of the person in that it fails to reflect the person's full experience in the world. Moreover, an exclusive reliance on traits falls well short of the integrative mandate for personality psychology spelled out in many classic (e.g., Allport, 1937; Murray, 1938) and contemporary (e.g., Dunlop, 2015; Mayer & Allen, 2013) sources in the field (McAdams & Pals, 2006). As Taylor (2018) suggested, to understand the athlete as a person encompasses every aspect of who he or she is. It includes, he suggested, gathering information about his or her innate dispositions and tendencies (e.g., degree of extroversion), values and priorities (i.e., goals), and beliefs about his or herself (e.g., self-identity). Psychologists – both researchers and practitioners – ought to collect and integrate different types of personality construct for the purpose of generating a comprehensive description of a person's psychological individuality.

To make the case for a holistic assessment of personality in sport and exercise, McAdams's (1995, 2015) integrative framework is utilized to examine the whole person. For more than two decades, now, this framework has received wide acclaim in the field of personality psychology (e.g., Campbell, 2008; Dunlop, 2015), but only recently has it received attention in sport and exercise psychology (see Coulter, Mallett, & Singer, 2018; Coulter, Mallett, Singer, & Gucciardi, 2016). The framework's basic feature is its psychological depiction of the person in terms of three broad metaphors: the self as actor, agent, and author (McAdams & Cox, 2010). These metaphors represent three different and increasingly complex perspectives from which the human self can be seen to operate.

In what follows, these three metaphors are unpacked and used to explain how they are useful to understanding the whole person in the sport and exercise domain. The issue of data integration is also considered. McAdams's framework requires psychologists to integrate different types of data in personality assessment, and how different data sets are combined to form a coherent interpretation of personality will be a focus in the chapter. Lastly, a case study of an actual performer – specifically, a world-class coach (cf. Swann, Moran, & Piggott, 2015) – will be used to illustrate the approach. This individual – henceforth "Mel" (an alias) – is in her 50s and has won multiple national and international titles in her sport, as both a coach and an athlete. Using real case data will help to clarify the conceptual features of McAdams's actor, agent, and author, and the value these three metaphors have for generating an integrated, multilayered assessment of personality in sport and exercise psychology.

Actors, Agents, and Authors

The Social Actor: Dispositional Traits

At a very basic level, personality captures broad individual differences in social behaviour (socio-emotional functioning) that are expressed in relatively consistent ways across time and context. What does this mean for knowing the person? Simply put, it means personality attributions such as these: Mike and Sue are obsessive and vain. Jon is optimistic and trusting, but Jenny is shy and downright mentally tough! These descriptors, and others like them, capture those widely observed differences people show with respect to their social performances (Goffman, 1959; Hogan, 1982). They are differences displayed early on in life, as a mark of human temperament. Over time and with significant environmental input, these differences gradually evolve into readily apparent and measurable dispositional personality traits (McAdams & Olson, 2010). Hence, traits represent the self as a social actor. They are the recurring and recognizable styles people display on the human stage of life, observed and commented upon by other social actors who, in a sense, serve as each other's audiences. When people are profiled against their basic traits – how high or low they score for neuroticism, agreeableness, conscientiousness, and the like – one gets an indication of their broad abilities to function appropriately and successfully in society (e.g., their tendencies to regulate emotion effectively, get along with each other in groups, and to compete successfully to get ahead).

On the sporting stage, people who consistently perform their roles in conscientious, extroverted, and emotionally stable ways tend to be the ones who make it to the top (Allen & Laborde, 2014). Those performers who are confident, perfectionistic, narcissistic, ruthless, emotionally "flat", and resilient do pretty well too, it seems, especially under high-pressure conditions (Rees et al., 2016, 2016; Roberts & Woodman, 2017). The traits subsumed within the Big Five taxonomy, as well as other broad dispositions observed and inferred (by self and others), capture broad individual differences in the social performances of actors who participate in sport and physical activity.

Turning attention to the personality of the world-class coach, Table 8 shows Mel's Big Five profile after completing the self-report form of the NEO-PI-3 (McCrae & Costa, 2010).

A quick review of Table 8 displays several highlights about Mel as a social actor. Compared with the majority of adult women, she is very well adjusted and rarely experiences psychological distress. She is hardworking, self-disciplined, and strives for excellence. Mel is like most other women, as far as extraversion goes, but stands out for being forceful and socially dominant – preferring to lead than follow. She is fairly open to experience, but considers daydreaming a waste of time and is not particularly interested in intellectual pursuits. As for agreeableness, she is sincere and trusting of others, but tends to put her own needs first. The uniform and distinctive nature of Mel's neuroticism (very low) and conscientiousness (high) scores suggest her style of impulse control is a cardinal feature of her personality. These two traits denote that she is very focused on achieving her goals and can tolerate many setbacks and frustrations on this path.

The Big Five have dealt us a broad sketch of Mel's personality as a social actor – the type of person she is, compared with most. There are, of course, various other traits one could have collected about Mel, such as those thought to be more specific or relevant to sport (e.g., how emotionally intelligent, narcissistic, or perfectionistic she is). But, no matter how many more traits are collected and how narrow or confined they are to sport and exercise settings, the assessment is still limited to her style of social-emotional performance as an actor. For the most part, traits do not take the reader into the mind of Mel. They do not tell us anything about what she wants in her life (sport or otherwise), what she values, or how she makes sense of who she is. Trait assessment provides a good initial sketch of action tendencies and functioning styles that people display as social actors. But traits are not equipped to explain it all. When it comes to understanding the whole person, dispositional traits are the best starting point, but there is more to personality than traits (McAdams, 2015).

Table 8 Mel's NEO-PI-3 summary report

Scale	Range*
Factors	
Neuroticism	Very low
Extraversion	Average
Openness	Average
Agreeableness	Average
Conscientiousness	High
Neuroticism facets	
Anxiety	Low
Angry hostility	Very low
Depression	Very low

(*Continued*)

Table 8 (Cont.)

Scale	Range*
Self-consciousness	Low
Impulsiveness	Very low
Vulnerability	Low
Extraversion facets	
Warmth	Average
Gregariousness	Average
Assertiveness	High
Activity	Average
Excitement-seeking	Average
Positive emotions	Average
Openness facets	
Fantasy	Low
Aesthetics	Average
Feelings	Average
Actions	Average
Ideas	Low
Values	Average
Agreeableness facets	
Trust	High
Straightforwardness	High
Altruism	Low
Compliance	Average
Modesty	Average
Tender-mindedness	Average
Conscientiousness facets	
Competence	High
Order	High
Dutifulness	High
Achievement striving	High
Self-discipline	High
Deliberation	Average

* Note: *Very low*: at least two standard deviations below a mean score of 50; *low*: between one and two standard deviations below mean; *average*: within one standard deviation of mean; *high*: between one and two standard deviations above mean; *very high*: at least two standard deviations above mean

The Motivated Agent: Goals, Motives, Plans, and Values

If dispositional traits account for the consistent differences in the actor's characteristic style of performance, internalized goals and values reflect a second line in personality – the motivated agent. The motivated agent is the metaphor in McAdams's framework that represents what people want in their lives and what they strive to obtain in particular domains and contexts. It is the aspect of personality that acknowledges people's internalized desires, plans, and strategies to achieve valued ends (i.e., goals) in the social world (McAdams, 2015).

Research in developmental psychology conclusively shows that, between the ages of 5 and 7 years, children make impressive strides in becoming planful and goal-oriented agents (McAdams & Olson, 2010). Even before they move into adolescence, they come to establish motivational agendas that speaks to what they want in life and how they plan to get it. By this point, personality is no longer just about traits – such as how introverted, agreeable, or optimistic a person is. It now comprises a second aspect of psychological individuality, layered over traits, that identifies the way in which a person is a motivated agent who pursues specific goals and values, situated in time and context.

Returning to Mel, her personality traits indicate the style or manner in which she tends to behave in pursuit of her goals. For example, as a social actor scoring very low in neuroticism, Mel tends to track her goals in a distinctly calm and relaxed manner. However, her low scores on neuroticism, as well as her scores on other dispositional traits, do not tell us very much about what she wants and values, and how those wants and values apply to some domains and not others, or how they change in response to social (e.g., family, peers, institutional, the media, culture) and developmental demands (McAdams & Olson, 2010).

What, then, does the 50-something-year-old Mel want? To answer this question, the reader needs to examine her goals and the complex psychological infrastructure that surrounds them – the types of goal she pursues, their importance, purpose, and difficulty, their value and nature, and the sets of beliefs and other mental constructions she has developed to help her pursue her goals with success. For McAdams, and other personality psychologists interested in human motivation, accessing people's goals – the particular goals they have set for themselves, the plans and strategies they use to meet those ends, and the progress they perceive they are making toward the fulfilment of those goals – is a key step to understanding their personality and social behaviour. Goals are a window into the self as a motivated agent.

Goals are a familiar and well-established topic in sport and exercise psychology (for a review, see Moran & Toner, 2017). Sport practitioners and health professionals help athletes and exercisers set "good" (e.g., SMART) goals all the time. Similarly, popular goal-related theories (e.g., achievement goal theory: Nicholls, 1984; self-determination theory: Deci & Ryan, 1985) and measures (e.g., Task and Ego Orientation in Sport Questionnaire; Duda, 1989) have been widely applied in the field for many decades. In personality psychology, goals can be understood in a hierarchy of motivational constructs (see Figure 14). These constructs range from people's fundamental motives (Level 1) to the contextually specific action sequences they engage in to achieve their desired projects and tasks (Level 4).

At Level 2 in the motivational hierarchy, personal strivings represent what people are typically trying to achieve through their daily behaviour (Emmons, 1989). They can be thought of as unifying constructs that condense a cluster of secondary goals (projects, actions) around a common quality or theme. Examining personal strivings is useful because it gives access to people's long-standing motivational concerns that are tied to particular situations, roles, and time periods. From a goal hierarchy perspective (see Figure 14), personal strivings are not so specific and immediate that they lose sight of the larger picture of personality, neither are they so broad and decontextualized as to be classed as motives similar in structure and purpose to personality traits. In this sense, personal strivings offer an ideal "middle-level" construct (Emmons, 1989) to measure people's goal orientations. They provide an effective insight into the recurring and enduring aspects of what people want and value that is reasonably comprehensive, stable, and context-specific.

So that Mel's personal strivings could be assessed, she was asked to complete Emmons's (2003) personal striving assessment task. This task required her to record the things she is

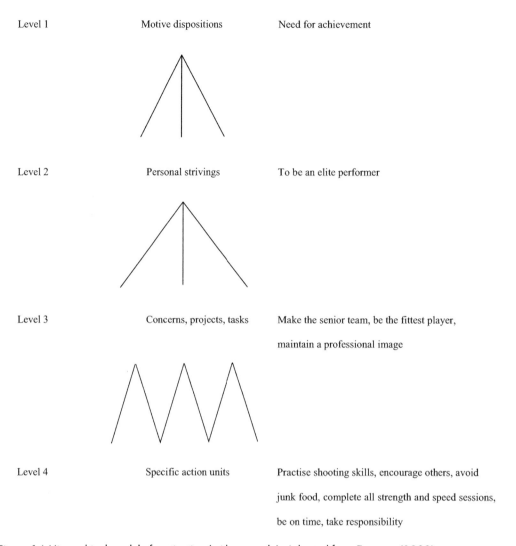

Level 1   Motive dispositions   Need for achievement

Level 2   Personal strivings   To be an elite performer

Level 3   Concerns, projects, tasks   Make the senior team, be the fittest player, maintain a professional image

Level 4   Specific action units   Practise shooting skills, encourage others, avoid junk food, complete all strength and speed sessions, be on time, take responsibility

Figure 14 Hierarchical model of motivation (with example). Adapted from Emmons (1989)

"typically trying to achieve on a daily basis" and, afterwards, rate each striving across a series of dimensions (e.g., commitment, past success). Table 9 provides a list of Mel's personal strivings (rank ordered for goal commitment), which reflect two main interconnecting themes.

The first theme is communion and the realization that Mel is driven to both connect with and promote the interests of others (e.g., her players, staff, child). The second is power and her desire to positively influence others around her (e.g., be a positive role model, nurture young talent). Although there are other interesting aspects in Table 9 (e.g., how approach-focused and adaptive Mel's strivings are), together, these two themes clarify her personality as a motivated agent – she is driven to use her position/ability to "do good" for other people. The content of her strivings also suggests an underlying moral purpose to her personality. Ranked first, in terms of goal commitment, is to be a "good person". We can also see themes

Table 9 Mel's personal strivings

(1)	I typically try to ... be a good person
(2)	I typically try to ... be well organized everyday
(3)	I typically try to ... be a positive role model
(4)	I typically try to ... connect genuinely in my relationships with people
(5)	I typically try to ... speak to staff to ensure they are feeling supported, encouraged, and engaged
(6)	I typically try to ... have "me" time to recharge mind and energy to give full attention to the players
(7)	I typically try to ... look after my [child]
(8)	I typically try to ... take a personal interest in others to help them achieve their goals
(9)	I typically try to ... nurture young talent
(10)	I typically try to ... have fun

of generativity in her strivings that emphasize her desire to develop and grow the next generation.

With the exception of the seventh item ("look after my [child]"), Mel stated that all her remaining strivings meaningfully connect with her life as a coach. This knowledge subsequently provides a richer picture of her personality and refines the prominence of her traits in this role. For example, having collected Mel's strivings, the reader now sees that her high conscientiousness (e.g., persistence, self-discipline, organization) links to her coaching efforts to develop and nurture others; her high assertiveness (facet of extraversion) to be a leader reflects her desires for power in sport and her agenda to be a positive role model in this position; Mel's low level of altruism – initially painting a rather self-centred individual – can now be understood from the perspective of her concern for self-care as a prerequisite to better serve her players, and the highly adaptive nature of her strivings – in particular, the total lack of avoidance themes found in them – is consistent with her very low neuroticism, which reinforces a perception that she is a hardy and emotionally stable coach.

Acknowledging the goals Mel values is an insight into her life as a motivated agent. However, this particular pattern of characteristic adaptations in her personality raises other questions, especially concerning themes of importance and timing: How long have these strivings been important to Mel? Are they goals she has developed in recent years, as both a coach and mother, or have they always been a part of her underlying motivational agenda? We dig deeper into answering some of these questions, in due course, when we get to McAdams's third layer of personality. But, for now, it is worth mentioning that, compared with traits, what people want and value and the goals they are driven to achieve are influenced, to a greater degree, by social forces that impact the content, timing, and importance of different characteristic adaptations (McAdams & Pals, 2006). In essence, why Mel chooses to invest her energy in these particular goals at this particular time of her life is more likely to be shaped by her cultural surroundings (e.g., family, community, religion, sport) than any predisposed genetic disposition. These surroundings set limits on expected and valued forms of behaviour and contour how she understands herself as a motivated agent. From this perspective, the reader can speculate that Mel has lived and developed in communities where people of influence and responsibility give back to others and strive to act as positive role models for the next generation.

As a social actor, Mel's traits capture her current performance on the social stage: She is someone who is resilient, assertive, and hard-working. As a motivated agent, her goals and values project her into the future, presenting the image of a coach who strives to connect with and nurture the people she feels responsible for. Beyond the actor and agent, however, there is still more to know about Mel in order to understand her as a whole person. According to McAdams (1995, 2015), knowing the whole person also involves exploring the ways in which the self functions as an autobiographical author.

The Autobiographical Author: Life Stories

By the time people reach late adolescence and the emerging-adulthood years, they are faced with the normative developmental task of forming an identity (Erikson, 1963). According to McAdams (2015), a key feature of this identity task is to develop and internalize an evolving, self-defining life story that explains how the person came to be (the past) and where he or she may be going (the future). People's life stories are not a recollected biography of facts and events, but instead the way they integrate those facts and events into a meaningful narrative account. Personality psychologists call this account "narrative identity", which is the story people tell themselves (and others) about who they are and how they became the person they are becoming. Layered on top of the actor's traits and agent's goals, then, is an internalized and evolving life story, what McAdams describes as a third layer of personality to join the psychological repertoire. This layer depicts the self as an autobiographical author, whose job it is to reconstruct the past and imagine the future in such a way as to give one's life some semblance of unity, purpose, and temporal coherence (McAdams, 2015).

A good way to access people's *narrative identities* is to conduct a life-story interview. In this interview (see McAdams, 2008), people are asked to think about the key events and chapters in their lives that stand out as being particularly significant to them (e.g., the main high points, low points, or turning points they have experienced). The interviewer asks the person to reflect on poignant memories, such as life's hard challenges and regrets, and to describe what they believe to be their core values and ideologies. He or she also asks them to consider what is coming next in their lives and where they see their lives heading in the near and distant future. Beyond the content or detail of any life story, an important goal for the psychologist is to prompt the person to think about what it all means. That is, when they look back on the various chapters, events, and challenges in their lives, what does it mean to them, today, and how do they weave their story together in such a way that gives an insight into the person they believe themselves to have been in the past, who they are in the present, and who they may become in the future? To this end, the goal of these activities is to understand the individual's uniquely crafted *personal myth*, which represents the imaginative act that integrates the different parts of people's lives into a purposeful and convincing whole (McAdams, 1993). To illustrate how people create their personal myths, reflect on the following extract taken from an interview with a top British athlete in Hardy et al.'s (2017) recent psychosocial development study of super-elite performers:

> [At] 4–5 years old, I remember going for runs with my Dad, in the snow, before he went to work at 6 am. To have that one-to-one time with someone who is a very motiv-ated person … I ended up picking up a lot of those traits from him … If there was anything that [my Dad] was not good at he would find a book and make himself better at it. So I had that as a role model … he instilled that in me … The one kernel of everything was "if you can't do something, find a way of doing it" and "if there's someone who's giving you a problem, you get over it".
>
> *(pp. 13–14)*

The quote demonstrates how people acquire a capacity to create meaning and develop prominent attitudes about themselves (and the world) from their standout memories and experiences, where imaginary connections are made between instances of fact (e.g., at 4–5 years old I went running with my dad in the snow) and fiction (because of dad, and those runs, I developed the necessary traits to get through life's challenges). This ability to autobiographically reason and form meaning about one's life is the crux to understanding the person at Layer 3 – the self as an autobiographical author.

In analysing and interpreting people's life-story interviews, it is important to consider not only *what* was said, but *how* it was said (for useful resources on coding narrative interviews, see Adler et al., 2017; Smith, 2016). There are various key components and structural themes one can look for in people's narratives that contribute to understanding their author-selves (Douglas & Carless, 2006; Marcia, 1966; McAdams, 1988; Singer & Salovey, 1993). Some of these components and themes are shown in Table 10.

Table 10 Commonly assessed life-story components

Narrative category/ elements	Description/variables
Motivational currents	*Agency* – the degree of self-mastery and control, status striving, achievement and power in the story *Communion* – the emphasis placed on togetherness, harmony, help, connection, and care for others in the story *Growth goals* – the degree of self-development and direction in the story, oriented toward personal growth
Affective themes	*Contamination* – good things turn to bad outcomes *Redemption* – bad things turn to good outcomes *Positive resolution* – making peace with a challenging event
Structural elements	*Coherence* – degree of unity in the story *Complexity* – simple versus complex/multilayered *The plot* (e.g., decline then progress, rise and fall) *Tone* – optimistic versus pessimistic *Self-defining memories* – nuclear episodes (e.g., high points, turning points) that determine people's life choices and goals *Ideological setting* – background values or belief systems people use to evaluate how the world around them functions (e.g., how just, trustworthy, or competitive is the world?) *Generative script* – How the story will end. How will the author be remembered? *Main characters* – Key archetypes that reflect core values, goals, strategy, and fears
Integrative meaning	Degree of *meaning-making* in the story (from positive or negative events)
Identity status	*Diffusion, moratorium, foreclosure,* and *achievement*
Dominant sport narrative	*Performance* – win at all costs *Relational* – relationships are most important *Discovery* – sport is a conduit to living a fuller life

What kind of story does Mel construct about her life that tells us about her narrative identity? After a near 5-hour interview, conducted over two sessions, the main points can be summarized as follows (note, the detail is purposely absent to protect Mel's identity):

On the surface, Mel's life story tracks the events of a highly successful athlete, who quickly reaches the heights of the game and sustains success for many years at world level. Post playing career, she subsequently makes the effective transition to high-performance coaching and is responsible for leading the necessary culture shift that radically transforms the fortunes of an organization so that it achieves multiple national championships.

Below this initial plot in the story, however, is a deeper theme that defines the person she was and, now, is. Specifically, the main plot in Mel's life story is that of a woman who experiences great fulfilment and liberation following the decision to finally accept and address her lingering anxiety and the insecurities that have caused her to "run away" from various career-related challenges and life opportunities. It is a plot that puts caring, supportive relationships at the centre of its storyline, as the necessary platform upon which people fully develop themselves and, later, thrive. It is a narrative about taking ownership of her problems – in particular, addressing her very high levels of self-doubt throughout her entire sporting life – and the development of a leader who is understanding and sensitive to the personal needs of those individuals she is accountable for.

This sensitivity to the personal needs of others connects profoundly with the two main characters in her story. The first character is her father – and "hero" – through whom Mel portrays an endearing image and mix of vivid childhood memories of successes, strength, competitiveness, and loving connection. His mental health problems, however, are a dominant theme in the story that follows – the painful decline of a man who eventually succumbs to suicide at a time when Mel was at the very peak of her athletic career. This event is the most dramatic scene in Mel's life story, and it reveals to her the devastating impact mental illness can have on people. The scene also functions as a key motivating influence underpinning her desire for self-care and efforts to look after the person behind the performer. The second character is Mel's long-time coach, who, coincidentally, lived only metres away from her when she was a child. This individual was the prominent figure in both Mel's junior and senior athletic days and, because of her important status in the sporting world, continues to be involved in her coaching life today. In discussing this character, the tone significantly sours, as a reflection of the great strain and bitterness in the relationship – namely, a perceived lack of warmth, understanding, and mentorship from this individual. The bond described represents a dysfunctional mother–daughter relationship that, even now (after approximately 40 years), remains unresolved. In short, this second main character personifies the antithesis of what Mel values in a high-performance coach. This life-narrative character is distant, critical, and authoritarian, which contrasts with the strong emphasis Mel places on valuing and making connections with the people she leads.

Mel's story splits into two halves. The first half portrays a very vulnerable character, who struggles to deal with her anxieties, despite the great accolades and championships she achieves in her sport. The second half, though, displays a redemptive tale about Mel getting through her problems, where her coaching successes are testament to an ability to believe in herself and take risks from the safety and structure that she craves. Today, she is much more self-assured, where her story strongly mirrors the emotional stability and grit reported in her NEO profile. But, to know Mel is to know the journey she has been through to take ownership of her life, face her demons, and recognize the critical role supportive others have played to liberate her to become the person she now is – someone who no longer "runs away" from the challenges ahead.

This secure sense of self and unity in her identity underlies her self-described legacy to nurture the next generation of young players:

> That's my job, to make sure that the environment that I am providing for these [people] is the best – that it is going to help facilitate their growth, their learning, and it is going to nurture them to get the best out of themselves.

To know Mel is to know this part of her story and how much she sees herself as a key person who can support and scaffold the positive development of others:

> It is more important for me to be giving to somebody else, and getting satisfaction out of that, than me just as a single entity. I have more value, and I get better emotionally, when I am able to help people or be involved in their life in a positive way.

Mel's concern for generativity (i.e., preparing and safeguarding future generations) connects profoundly with her memories of growing up in a safe, competitive, and free environment. It links with some of the key archetypes and characters who she admires and made her feel good, as a quiet, anxious, and introverted child. It is associated with her own best playing days, where connection and care in the coach–athlete relationship were present. Lastly, it resonates with the very personal challenges she has experienced in dealing with her own and others' (namely, her father's) mental health issues. In summary, Mel draws heavily on themes of connection, support, and relationship in telling her story, backgrounding other possible narrative themes and forms. For instance, even when she discusses stories of success and winning (more often associated with a performance narrative), the reason for these achievements tend to relate to a relationship theme, as the basic dimension upon which such success is founded.

To finish, Mel's key message about her life story is this:

> Life is a roller coaster and when you get knocked down you have to pick yourself back up, dust yourself off, and get on with it … You can put barriers up to protect yourself, but there comes a time when that road block – you need to find a way around it … I have got around those road blocks. I have gone through it and I am really relaxed with who I am. I am content. I am happy with where I am, today.

Despite knowing Mel as a social actor (the type of person she is on the social stage) and motivated agent (what she wants and values in her life), we do not know her well enough unless we also know her story. Here, the epistemological lens moves away from talk about Mel's traits and goals in the direction of more existential and phenomenological aspects of her personality, namely, the internalized narrative she lives by that explains "why the actor does what it does, why the agent wants what it wants, and who the self was, is, and will be as a developing person in time" (McAdams, 2013, p. 273). Specifically, Mel's story is about the fulfilment that comes with having the guts to make the necessary changes in life to experience a better existence. It is about the critical role, she believes, significant others played in enabling this possibility to occur for her and how, today, as a result of this and other events in her story, she sees herself as someone who can custom an environment that encourages others to do the same. Most importantly, though, she is now content with who she is and has unity in her identity. Once the victim of debilitating insecurities, as both an athlete and a coach, Mel's narrative identity is the adopted tale of a self-assured and liberated leader whose pledge is to support and nurture people – especially young athletes – to "be the best they can be".

Who Mel is, then, stems from the way in which she authors her life, up to this point in time, which underscores her motivational agenda to look out for others and get the best from them. It is this story she creates – and the meaning she attaches to the various events and chapters of her life – that enables us to understand why she is so invested in her strivings (see Table 10) and why she now acts in such a confident, assertive, and self-assured way (see Table 10).

Building a Psychological Portrait

To understand a person in a comprehensive way, sport and exercise psychologists are encouraged to collect and bring together diverse data regarding the self as a social actor, a motivated agent, and an autobiographical author (Coulter et al., 2016). Currently, too many experts in the field dismiss people's life stories as peripheral to the main stuff of personality, which they often suggest is traits. Similarly, the goals and values people strive for tend to be backgrounded and given much less attention than their dispositional counterparts. However, a full accounting of personality requires analysis from all three of these distinct psychological standpoints (McAdams, 1995, 2015).

The current contribution – and the multilayered assessment of Mel's personality – has provided some guidance and clarification for the way in which different personality constructs can be integrated to create a richer understanding of people's complexity. Human beings are complex creatures by nature and design. Hence, on this foundation alone, a single-dimensional (trait) approach to understanding the person in sport and exercise is restricted in how fully it reflects an individual's real-world experience.

To integrate and organize personality assessment data across the three perspectives of actor, agent, and author, it is proposed that sport and exercise psychologists follow an approach similar to the one taken here, which charts the logic of person perception. Starting with traits, psychologists get a "first cut" of personality from a trait score that reflects the individual's overall socio-emotional functioning. Subsequent assessments of people's goals, and then life stories, provide much deeper levels of understanding – and require greater work and intimacy (rapport) on behalf of the psychologist – to gain a more complete and satisfying psychological portrait. This logic emulates the views of Levak, Hogan, Beutler, and Song (2011), who set out guidelines for organizing multiple data sets when conducting an integrated assessment. Although these guidelines are described in the context of creating a clinical personality report, they are, nonetheless, valuable to sport and exercise psychologists looking for guidance in making decisions about the cardinal and coherent features of any given individual's personality. In summary, these guidelines emphasize:

(1) The generation of preliminary anchor hypotheses (e.g., derived from trait data/generalized personality constructs, such as the Big Five or sport-specific traits).
(2) Expanding the anchor hypotheses by incorporating outputs from Layers 2 (goals and values) and 3 (narrative identity), similar to that described above (Mel).
(3) Address conflicting data across the three layers (where there is a lack of coherence). Avoid dismissing contradictory findings and seek to blend the data together using clinical experience and judgement.

(4) Prepare feedback for the individual client that emphasizes personality highlights.

(5) Check and discuss with the client the perceived accuracy of the report and collaborate with him or her to establish a comprehensive assessment of personality that fairly reflects the actor, agent, and author self.

Challenges and Opportunities

It is worth highlighting some of the practical challenges and opportunities when taking a holistic approach to personality assessment in sport and exercise. As others have noted (Prophet, Singer, Martin, & Coulter, 2017), the most obvious challenge to taking a three-layer approach to assessing personality is the time it takes to collect and analyse the various forms of data. Compared with a single trait-based approach, the assessment of personality across multiple layers is a time-intensive (and labour-intensive) strategy. However, it is important to weigh up the value proposition of any particular approach before judging its efficacy. As viewed in this contribution, the time spent early to understand the person as an actor, agent, and author is a worthwhile investment for several reasons. The biggest payoff is, arguably, the level of rapport built between the practitioner and client. Following a three-layer approach to assessing personality tends to build strong bonds that subsequently lay down a platform for delivering successful interventions. A deep, accelerated focus on the person – that goes beyond surface traits – also increases the prospect of developing a quality relationship sooner. Examining people over three layers of personality saves substantial time understanding them in the future and is particularly evident after the completion (and analysis) of the life-story interview. Some readers might have been surprised to learn that Mel's life-story interview took nearly 5 hours to complete (note, the average time is approximately 2 hours). However, the potential benefits for a practitioner learning about and spending time with this person – who might very well be the most important individual in the whole organization – cannot be undervalued. In this case, knowing what Mel is driven to achieve and why she is so passionate about it is privileged information that can only truly come to the surface through a whole-person approach.

It is noteworthy that integrating the three data sets is challenging, particularly for the novice psychologist. This challenge is exacerbated when the data from each layer are incongruent. Nonetheless, over time, experience improves the efficiencies in making sense of the data and one's ability to detect potential patterns across the different layers. Participants have also reported how much they enjoyed the process and the insights gained. For example, they often say that the procedure helps them to establish self-concept clarity. People who have clarity in their self-concepts know who they are and where they are going in life. They understand the nature of their personalities and where they stand on important attitudes and values. This ability to organize knowledge about themselves is afforded by the inherent design of McAdams's framework. The three metaphors of actor, agent, and author provide a simple, yet comprehensive, understanding of a human life that ties together what is, essentially, a great amount of psychological complexity.

The current contribution has mainly focused on the applied aspect of using McAdams's framework in personality assessment in sport and exercise psychology. However, before finishing, it is worth noting some of the potential research benefits to be had when adopting the framework in the field. First, the most significant of these benefits is the redefinition of personality and the acknowledgement that people vary according to their traits, goals, and narrative identities. In short, McAdams's framework acts "as an overarching conception organizing the many constructs potentially relevant to studying people participating in sport and exercise" (Coulter et al., 2016, p. 34). Second, the framework lends itself to the development of sophisticated research questions that encourage an integrated and interdisciplinary approach. For example, what interrelationships exist between athlete and exerciser traits, goals, and narratives? How do sport and exercise contexts differently shape people's actor, agent, and author? Developmentally, how does personality evolve across the three layers, and what longitudinal opportunities exist to track athletes and exercisers across the lifespan, when considering the whole person? The opportunities are many to both ask and answer such questions and incorporate major areas of psychology (e.g., developmental, social, cognitive) that will only benefit the reestablishment of personality research in sport and exercise psychology in the years to come. Lastly, any endorsement of the use of McAdams's framework to conduct research in the sport and exercise domain adds to the emerging body of literature seeking to explore the predictive power of the three layers as incrementally valid features of personality. In this way, sport and exercise researchers have the opportunity to contribute to knowledge development in mainstream personality psychology by way of examining the necessity of the actor, agent, and author in the personalities of people participating in sport and exercise.

Conclusion

By focusing most of their attention on the actor's trait profile, sport and exercise psychologists continue to underplay the historical mission of personality psychology, which is to study the full gamut of human personality in all of its richness and complexity. To address this issue, and with the help of an actual case study, the purpose of this chapter was to introduce readers to a holistic approach to personality assessment that draws on McAdams's integrative framework and the tripartite view of the self as a social actor, a motivated agent, and an autobiographical author. This approach to psychological assessment is a new way to think about personality in sport and exercise psychology and a practical approach to understanding the whole person in this field.

References

Adler, J. M., Dunlop, W. L., Fivush, R., Lilgendahl, J. P., Lodi-Smith, J., McAdams, D. P., & Syed, M. (2017). Research methods for studying narrative identity: A primer. *Social Psychological and Personality Science, 8*, 519–527.

Allen, M. S., & Laborde, S. (2014). The role of personality in sport and physical activity. *Current Directions in Psychological Science, 23*, 460–465.

Allport, G. W. (1937). *Personality: A psychological interpretation*. New York: Holt, Rinehart & Winston.

Campbell, J. B. (2008). Modern personality theories: What have we gained? What have we lost? In G. Boyle, G. Matthews, & D. Saklofske (Eds.), *The Sage handbook of personality theory and assessment. Vol. 1. Personality theories and models* (pp. 190–212). Los Angeles, CA: Sage.

Coulter, T. J., Mallett, C. J., & Singer, J. A. (2018). A three-domain personality analysis of a mentally tough athlete. *European Journal of Personality, 32*, 6–29.

Coulter, T. J., Mallett, C. J., Singer, J. A., & Gucciardi, D. F. (2016). Personality in sport and exercise psychology: Integrating a whole person perspective. *International Journal of Sport and Exercise Psychology, 14*, 23–41.

Deci, E. L., & Ryan, R. M. (1985). *Intrinsic motivation and self-determination in human behavior*. New York: Plenum.

Douglas, K., & Carless, D. (2006). Performance, discovery, and relational narratives among women professional tournament golfers. *Women in Sport and Physical Activity Journal, 15*, 14–27.

Duda, J. L. (1989). The relationship between task and ego orientation and the perceived purpose of sport among male and female high school athletes. *Journal of Sport and Exercise Psychology, 11*, 318–335.

Dunlop, W. L. (2015). Contextualized personality, beyond traits. *European Journal of Personality, 29*, 310–325.

Emmons, R. A. (1989). The personal striving approach to personality. In L. A. Pervin (Ed.), *Goal concepts in personality and social psychology* (pp. 87–126). Hillsdale, NJ: Lawrence Erlbaum.

Emmons, R. A. (2003). *The psychology of ultimate concerns: Motivation and spirituality in personality.* New York: Guildford Press.

Erikson, E. H. (1963). *Childhood and society* (2nd ed.). New York: Norton.

Goffman, E. (1959). *The presentation of self in everyday life.* Garden City, NY: Doubleday.

Hardy, L., Barlow, M., Evans, L., Rees, T., Woodman, T., & Warr, C. (2017). Great British medalists: Psychosocial biographies of super-elite and elite athletes from Olympic sports. In V. Walsh, M. Wilson, & B. Perkin (Eds.), *Progress in brain research* (Vol. 232, pp. 1–119). London: Elsevier.

Hogan, R. (1982). A socioanalytic theory of personality. In M. M. Page (Ed.), *Nebraska symposium on motivation: Vol. 29. Personality: Current theory and research* (pp. 55–89). Lincoln, NE: University of Nebraska Press.

Laborde, S., Guillén, F., Watson, M., & Allen, M. S. (2017). The light quartet: Positive personality traits and approaches to coping in sport coaches. *Psychology of Sport and Exercise, 32*, 67–73.

Levak, R. W., Hogan, R. S., Beutler, L. E., & Song, X. (2011). Applying assessment information: Decision making, patient feedback and consultation. In T. M. Harwood, L. E. Beutler, & G. Groth-Marnat (Eds.), *Integrative assessment of adult personality* (3rd ed., pp. 373–412). New York: Guildford Press.

Marcia, J. E. (1966). Development and validation of ego-identity status. *Journal of Personality and Social Psychology, 3*, 551–558.

Mayer, J. D., & Allen, J. L. (2013). A personality framework for the unification of psychology. *Review of General Psychology, 17*, 196–202.

McAdams, D. P. (1988). *Power, intimacy and the life story: Personological inquiries into identity.* New York: Guildford Press.

McAdams, D. P. (1993). *The stories we live by: Personal myths and the making of the self.* New York: Guilford Press.

McAdams, D. P. (1995). What do we know when we know a person? *Journal of Personality, 63*, 365–396.

McAdams, D. P. (2008). The life story interview. Retrieved from www.sesp.northwestern.edu/foley/instruments/interview/

McAdams, D. P. (2013). The psychological self as actor, agent, and author. *Perspectives on Psychological Science, 8*, 272–295.

McAdams, D. P. (2015). *The art and science of personality development.* New York: Guildford Press.

McAdams, D. P., & Cox, K. S. (2010). Self and identity across the life span. In R. Lerner, A. Freund & M. Lamb (Eds.), *Handbook of life span development* (Vol. 2, pp. 158–207). New York: Wiley.

McAdams, D. P., & Olson, B. D. (2010). Personality development: Continuity and change over the life course. *Annual Review of Psychology, 61*, 517–542.

McAdams, D. P., & Pals, J. L. (2006). A new big five: Fundamental principles for an integrative science of personality. *American Psychologist, 61*, 204–217.

McCrae, R. R., & Costa, P. T., Jr. (1999). A Five-Factor theory of personality. In L. A. Pervin & O. P. John (Eds.), *Handbook of personality: Theory and research* (pp. 139–153). New York: Guilford Press.

McCrae, R. R., Costa, P. T., & Jr,. (2010). *NEO inventories for the NEO Personality Inventory-3 (NEO-PI-3), NEO Five-Factor Inventory-3 (NEO-FFI-3), NEO Personality Inventory-Revised (NEO PI-R): Professional manual.* Odessa, FL: Psychological Assessment Resources.

Moran, A., & Toner, J. (2017). *A critical introduction to sport psychology.* Abingdon: Routledge.

Murray, H. A. (1938). *Explorations in personality.* New York: Oxford University Press.

Nicholls, J. G. (1984). Achievement motivation: Conceptions of ability, subjective experience, task choice, and performance. *Psychological Review, 91*, 328–346.

Pervin, L. A., & Cervone, D. (2010). *Personality: Theory and research* (11th ed.). New York: Wiley.

Prophet, T., Singer, J., Martin, I., & Coulter, T. J. (2017). Getting to know your athletes: Strengthening the coach–athlete dyad using an integrative personality framework. *International Sport Coaching Journal, 4*, 291–304.

Rees, T., Hardy, L., Güllich, A., Abernathy, B., Côte, J., Woodman, T., & Warr, C. (2016). The Great British medallist project: A review of current knowledge on the development of the world's best sporting talent. *Sports Medicine, 46*, 1041–1058.

Roberts, R., & Woodman, T. (2017). Personality and performance: Moving beyond the Big 5. *Current Opinion in Psychology, 16*, 104–108.

Singer, J. A., & Salovey, P. (1993). *The remembered self.* New York: Free Press.

Smith, B. (2016). Narrative analysis. In E. Lyons & A. Coyle (Eds.), *Analysing qualitative data in psychology* (2nd ed., pp. 202–221). London: Sage.

Swann, C., Moran, A., & Piggott, D. (2015). Defining elite athletes: Issues in the study of expert performance in sport psychology. *Psychology of Sport and Exercise, 16,* 3–14.

Tabano, J., & Portenga, S. (2018). Personality tests: Understanding the athlete as person. In J. Taylor (Ed.), *Assessment in applied sport psychology* (pp. 73–82). Champaign, IL: Human Kinetics.

Taylor, J. (2018). Importance of assessment in sport psychology consulting. In J. Taylor (Ed.), *Assessment in applied sport psychology* (pp. 73–82). Champaign, IL: Human Kinetics.

33

PERSONALITY ASSESSMENT II
Within-Person Variability Assessment

Katharina Geukes and Steffen Nestler

Introduction

In competitive sports, often only milliseconds, millimetres, or one-hundredth of a point make the difference between victory and defeat, joy and disappointment, pride and shame. And, as we (un)fortunately all know, in recreational sports, often only minor details make the difference between ambition and indifference, hard work and laziness, putting on the running shoes and watching Netflix. Thus, within the sporting domain, athletes experience and show a variety of states – that is, a variety of feelings, thoughts, behaviours, and performances. Importantly, across time and situations, athletes differ in average states (e.g., the mean of repeated self-esteem states) but also in how strongly they fluctuate in states (e.g., the variability of repeated self-esteem states), also called within-person variability.

To target within-person variability, the vivid and diverse sporting domain can be regarded as an ideal research environment. Owing to the different types of sport, different competition modes and rules, different skill requirements and tasks, different performance quantifications and evaluations, different goal and success definitions, different behavioural norms and interpersonal affordances, the sporting domain provides a unique combination of systematic situational variation and field-based ecological validity. This rare combination enables a thorough investigation of within-person variability (e.g., psychometric properties), its determinants (e.g., Who fluctuates in states? Does neuroticism predict individual differences in state fluctuations?), and its consequences (e.g., Are state fluctuations adaptive or not? What are the boundary conditions determining their (mal)adaptiveness?).

Despite the assumed relevance of within-person variability in the sporting domain and despite its unique suitability as a respective research environment, sport psychology researchers have only recently started to consider interindividual differences in how people fluctuate across time and situations and their consequences (e.g., Amorose, 2001; Baranowski, Smith, Thompson, Baranowski, & Hebert, 1999; for a review on personality in sport, see Allen, Greenlees, & Jones, 2013). Within personality psychology, however, state fluctuations in affect and self-esteem have been targeted for quite some time (e.g., Savin-Williams & Demo, 1983; Wessman & Ricks, 1966). More comprehensive work, also targeting behaviour, has been done over the last two decades and was considerably facilitated by important advances in theory (e.g., Back et al., 2011; Baumert et al., 2017; Fleeson & Jayawickreme, 2015; Wrzus

& Roberts, 2017), assessment (e.g., Scollon, Prieto, & Diener, 2009; Wrzus & Mehl, 2015), and data analysis (e.g., Baird, Le, & Lucas, 2006; Jahng, Wood, & Trull, 2008; Wang, Hamaker, & Bergeman, 2012). Given the current lack of state variability research in sport, the aim of this contribution is to demonstrate sport psychology's opportunity to contribute relevant knowledge on within-person variability and the conceptional value of incorporating within-person variability into the understanding of personality. Thus, it is the authors' hope that this contribution may stimulate more variability research both inside and outside the sporting domain.

Theory: From a Nomothetic to a More Idiographic Perspective

Traditionally, personality researchers have adopted a nomothetic perspective and understood personality as relatively stable interindividual differences in how people generally feel, think, and behave (e.g., Allport, 1961; Carver & Scheier, 2004). In fact, the trait perspective is one of the great success stories of psychology: Personality traits have been found to be determined by nature and nurture (e.g., Briley & Tucker-Drob, 2014; Kandler et al., 2010; Riemann, Angleitner, & Strelau, 1997), to systematically develop across the lifespan (e.g., Lodi-Smith & Roberts, 2007; Roberts, Walton, & Viechtbauer, 2006), and to be consequential for individuals' health, relationships, and occupational outcomes (Ozer & Benet-Martinez, 2006; Roberts, Kuncel, Shiner, Caspi, & Goldberg, 2007). Despite the success of the trait perspective on personality, however, it has been severely challenged within the person–situation debate (Epstein & O'Brien, 1985). Initiated by a seminal publication of Walter Mischel (1968), in which he claimed the concept of traits to be untenable, the controversy regarded whether the person (behaviour is consistent) or the situation (behaviour is inconsistent) is more influential in determining an individual's behaviour (or state). What followed for decades was a lively exchange of arguments about, among others, the consideration of relative or absolute trans-situational (in)consistency of behaviour (or states), the evaluation of sizes of correlations, and the meaning of aggregation (see Funder, 2006; Kenrick & Funder, 1988). In the 1990s, the person–situation debate finally found its end in an integrative consensus, labelled the interactionist perspective (e.g., Ekehammar, 1974; Endler, 1981, 1993; Krahé, 1992). This perspective summarizes that (1) main effects of personality, (2) main effects of situations, and (3) the interactions between the two jointly predict behaviour (or states). As a matter of fact, this perspective was not entirely novel to personality research. In contrast, the interactionist perspective on personality has its early origins in the works of Lewin (1935, 1936), who had already formalized the reciprocal interaction of the individual and the environment (cf. Lewin's equations; Lewin, 1936), and of Murray (1938), who postulated a need-press theory of personality, with the essential characteristic being the interaction between the person and situational factors (see Endler & Edwards, 1986). Nowadays, within personality and social psychology and, fortunately, increasingly so within sport psychology, most researchers base their work on an interactionist understanding of behavioural (and state) expressions.

This long-desired and promising consensus (Fleeson & Noftle, 2009) has led to important theoretical advancements regarding a state-based personality conception (e.g., Fleeson, 2001, 2004), as well as interactive and process-based approaches to psychological phenomena (e.g., Back et al., 2011; Baumert et al., 2017; Wrzus & Roberts, 2017). With the whole trait theory (Fleeson, 2007, 2012; Fleeson & Jayawickreme, 2015), Fleeson (2001) has integrated the putatively opposing perspectives of the person–situation debate into a state-based conception of personality. He proposed that personality dimensions are best operationalized as density distributions of individuals' states across many situations. Interindividual differences, accordingly, manifest in multiple characteristics that describe state distributions, such as their location, size, and shape. Therefore, a single characteristic or value (e.g., a trait score or the distribution's mean) only represents a parsimonious reduction of the rich information available. Moreover, novel approaches to psychological phenomena targeted person–situation interactions (Tett & Guterman, 2000), as well as underlying processes (e.g., personality development, personality effects), aiming at explaining why and how exactly these effects occur (Back et al., 2011: PERSOC: personality and social relationships framework; Baumert et al., 2017; Geukes, van Zalk, & Back, 2018; Wrzus & Roberts, 2017: TESSERA: triggering situations, expectancy, states/state expressions, and reactions). All of these theoretical advancements have put personality psychologists in a comparatively convenient position: Having successfully defended and established the concept of stable personality traits and having extended the trait perspective to be more *idiographic*, personality research now also incorporates intra-individual, dynamic, and also contextualized aspects, such as interindividual differences in within-person variability (Vazire & Sherman, 2017).

Assessment: From Trait Assessment to Experience Sampling

To delve beyond traditional self-report trait measurements (e.g., McCrae & Costa, 1987) and to acknowledge the more idiographic perspective on personality, researchers have increasingly targeted states. These states involve individuals' momentary feelings, thoughts, and behaviour, as well as the quality of behavioural outcomes, such as performances, across time and situations of their daily lives. To repeatedly assess states, researchers typically use intensive longitudinal methodologies summarized under the term experience sampling (Larson & Csikszentmihalyi, 1983; also, for example, daily diary method, ecological momentary assessment, ambulatory assessment). The advantages of experience sampling lie in the opportunities to (1) increase psychology's ecological validity by accessing people's real lives; (2) overcome some of the shortcomings associated with traditional trait self-reports, such as memory biases and the use of global heuristics; and (3) adopt an idiographic, within-person perspective on psychological phenomena (Scollon et al., 2009). Therefore, owing to technological advances related to the availability of stationary (personal computers, laptops) and especially mobile devices (smartphones, tablets), involving stable internet connection, experience-sampling methods are still on the rise (Wrzus & Mehl, 2015).

Even (long) before the person–situation debate had started, the early origins date back to a first experience-sampling study published in 1925 (Fluegel, 1925). In this study, Fluegel used a self-report, paper-and-pencil approach to monitor "feeling and emotion in everyday life" across 30 days (p. 318). Later, from the 1960s and 1970s onwards, researchers (e.g., Csikszentmihalyi, Larson, & Prescott, 1977; Larson, Csikszentmihalyi, & Graef, 1980; Prescott, Csikszentmihalyi, & Graef, 1981; Savin-Williams & Demo, 1983; Wessman & Ricks, 1966) further developed the experience-sampling approach to study state affect and self-evaluations in naturalistic contexts. In the study by Savin-Williams and Demo (1983), for example, participants carried a paging device (beeper) for the 1-week duration of the study. During waking hours, each participant was signaled on a random schedule, six to eight times daily, but not during school hours, in which four fixed time points were defined. At each beep or defined time point, participants were asked to complete a "beep sheet" – a paper-and-pencil questionnaire involving questions, among others, regarding the location and their momentary self-feelings. In retrospect, this historic study design appears far ahead of its time because it involves all typical attributes of modern experience sampling and only differs in one minor aspect: the manual data entry.

Nowadays, using stationary or mobile devices, manual data entry is no longer required (for overviews, see Mehl & Conner, 2012; Wrzus & Mehl, 2015). The sampling of state assessments can be scheduled at regular time intervals (i.e., time-based) or contingent on specified events (i.e., event-based; Bolger & Laurenceau, 2013; Gosling & Johnson, 2010). To set up an experience-sampling study, both standard survey technologies (e.g., Qualtrics, 2005) and more powerful software solutions that allow for highly flexible programming are available (e.g., formr: Arslan & Tata, 2015; ExperienceSampler: Thai & Page-Gould, 2018; Survey Signal: Hofmann & Patel, 2015). Moreover, the rise of smartphone usage provides powerful and unobtrusive access to mobile sensor data (e.g., Wi-Fi and GPS scans, accelerometer, light, microphone, proximity sensors, calls, sms logs) that can be used to infer rich information about individuals' behaviours and the environment they select (for overviews, see Chittaranjan, Blom, & Gatica-Perez, 2013; Harari et al., 2016; Schmid Mast, Gatica-Perez, Frauendorfer, Nguyen, & Choudhury, 2015).

In sport psychology research, the experience-sampling approach was and is used to answer performance-oriented research questions in competitive sports as well as health-related research questions within recreational sports and exercise. Regarding performance-oriented research, in most experience-sampling studies, researchers primarily focused on current states (e.g., emotions, mood, affect, anxiety, thoughts, flow) leading up to and partly even during competitions (e.g., Cerin, Szabo, & Williams, 2001; Dickens, Van Raalte, & Hurlburt, 2018; Hanton, Thomas, & Maynard, 2004; Kimiecik & Stein, 1992; Schüler & Brunner, 2009; Stein, Kimiecik, Daniels, & Jackson, 1995; Totterdell, 2000). Although the experience-sampling approach allows access to athletes' real lives, it still faces crucial limitations at least for some types of sport, competition modes, and tasks regarding a close-to and in-competition or in-game state assessment. Here, researchers will presumably need to complement the experience-sampling approach with behavioural observations on the spot or based on video footage to comprehensively portray athletes' competitive lives (and psychological states).

Regarding health-oriented research, researchers used the experience-sampling approach to target questions that, above all, regard affective and emotional consequences of physical activity, as well as exercise withdrawal and attrition (Gauvin, Rejeski, & Norris, 1996; Gauvin & Szabo, 1992; Kirshnit, Ham, & Richards, 1989; Lutz et al., 2008). Related to the experience-sampling approach, a novel research focus also concerns the potential effects of pedometers, apps, and self-tracking wearables to improve users' health – that is, their diet, physical activity, and sedentary behaviour (e.g., Clemes, Matchett, & Wane, 2008; Clemes & Parker, 2009; Schoeppe et al., 2016).

Independent from a specific research question at hand, all of these efforts result in intensive, longitudinal intra-individual state data. These data follow a nested data structure because the repeated assessments (time points) are nested within persons, and this needs to be considered when selecting an appropriate analytic strategy.

Data Analyses: From Variability Indices to One-Step Analyses

With the aim of quantifying a person's within-person variability based on repeated assessments of states, researchers can select from a plethora of suggested statistical indices. Traditionally, researchers have used the standard deviation (or the variance) of the repeated assessments (e.g., Eid & Diener, 1999; Larson et al., 1980; Zeigler-Hill & Abraham, 2006). Although straight-forward, this statistical index is problematic, because it contains information not only on variability, but also on the average state (see Baird et al., 2006) and developmental trends potentially occurring during the study (Jahng et al., 2008). To circumvent these problems, researchers have suggested using mean- or trend-corrected versions of this index. A mean correction can, for example, be realized by using the residuals obtained from regressing the means and the squared means on to the individuals' standard deviations in follow-up analyses (see Baird et al., 2006). Similarly, a trend-corrected index can, for example, be obtained by computing the standard deviation across the residuals from an individual regression model in which a time variable has been used to predict a person's state variable (i.e., detrending).

Although this (mean- or trend-corrected) statistical index is able to quantify the overall instability of repeatedly assessed states, it simultaneously ignores important additional information: the temporal (in)dependency (cf. Larsen, 1987). In fact, based on such an index of variation, two people with the consecutive values of 2, 2, 2, 6, 6, 6 (Person A) and 2, 6, 2, 6, 2, 6 (Person B) would receive identical variability values, although presumably contradicting our intuition that assumes Person B to fluctuate more than Person A. A measure that does refer to the temporal (in)dependency of state values is autocorrelation, with lower values indicating greater variability (i.e., lower dependency). Thus, based on the autocorrelation, Person A would have received a lower variability score than Person B, which is different from the rank order based on the instability index but in line with our intuition. The autocorrelation, however, comes with a different problem: Imagine Person B, described above, and Person C with consecutive values of 1, 7, 1, 7, 1, 7. These persons would receive identical values for the autocorrelation, although we would intuitively assume, based on the size of successive changes, that Person C fluctuates more than Person B. Accordingly, the autocorrelation does not capture the size of changes from one time point to the next, as it fails to reflect the overall instability (Ebner-Priemer, Eid, Kleindienst, Stabenow, & Trull, 2009).

To provide a statistical quantification of variability that accounts for both overall instability and temporal dependency of state values over time, a further index has been suggested, namely the mean square successive difference (introduced by Von Neumann, Kent, Bellinson, & Hart, 1941; for more details, see Jahng et al., 2008), reflecting, as the name suggests, the average of the squared difference between successive observations at occasions $i + 1$ and i. Thus, on the basis of repeated assessments of states, interindividual differences in intra-individual variability can be described via indices of variation, which should at best capture both overall instability and temporal dependency, and are particularly accurate once mean level and trend information is removed.

When studying within-person variability, researchers not only aim to describe interindividual differences, but also, for example, to study its associations with determinants, antecedents, and consequences. When analysing such associations, many researchers follow a two-step procedure in which they calculate a statistical index of intra-individual variation in the first step and then use this variable as an independent or dependent variable in the second step. This two-step procedure, however, is problematic (see Wang et al., 2012, for a critical discussion) because it assumes that the index being computed in the first step is an error-free estimate of a person's variability, which is typically not the case. Rather, the index is a composite of the true parameter and measurement error. Because this error is not considered in the second step of the analysis, the results may not be trustworthy, and the standard errors might be biased.

An accessible option to overcome the problems of the two-step procedure is to use a one-step approach, such as the mixed-effects location scale model (Hedeker, Mermelstein, & Demirtas, 2008; Lin, Raz, & Harlow, 1997; Nestler, Geukes, & Back, 2018; see Geukes et al., 2016, for an example). This model is an extension of multilevel growth models, often used to model repeated measurements of an individual (see Nestler, Grimm, & Schönbrodt, 2015, for an introduction, or Verbeke & Molenberghs, 2009, for an extensive treatment of this model). As in standard multilevel growth models, repeated observations of persons are modelled as a function of time, allowing the inclusion of person-level variables (e.g., a trait) to predict interindividual differences in the intercept and slope (reflecting the mean level and change of the state, respectively). In contrast to the standard growth model, this model allows between-person heterogeneity in the residual variance (i.e., intra-individual variability), which can again be predicted by person-level covariates (e.g., Hedeker, Demirtas, & Mermelstein, 2009; Hedeker et al., 2008). Thus, the mixed-effects location scale model is well suited to empirically test associations of overall instability in one single analytical step.

To run such a model as typical for multilevel modelling, the state data need to be stored in the long format instead of the wide format. Whereas, in the wide format, one row corresponds to one person, in the long format, each row corresponds to one time point per person, making identification variables for persons and time points necessary. The state information per person and time point would then be stored in one or more state variables, depending on how many states were assessed. Finally, if assessed and of interest, a second data set in the wide format entails information on the person-level covariates.

To calculate mixed-effects location scale models, one can, for example, use R, a free software environment for statistical computing and graphics. An example code for R using WinBUGS software (Spiegelhalter, Thomas, Best, & Lunn, 2003), via the R-package RtoWinBUGS (Sturtz, Ligges, & Gelman, 2005), can be found at www.osf.io/2yvfk/ (Geukes et al., 2016). In this example, we investigated the effects of narcissism (i.e., admiration and rivalry) and the Big Five personality dimensions on state self-esteem level and variability across three studies (Geukes, Nestler, Hutteman, Küfner, & Back, 2017). For each study, there is a folder labelled "1 Effects of personality on variability", in which one can find (1) state data on self-esteem (Daten#studyname_AV_Final); (2) trait data on the personality predictors (Daten#studyname_PR_Final); and (3) the R-Code (#studyname_Variability_Models). The R-Code involves some data preparation steps (e.g., definition of consecutive and ascending ID numbers, centring of the time variable, z-standardization of all variables within the sample, handling of missing values) and commands to run the mixed-effects location scale models (i.e., null-model without predictors, models including predictors).

Relevant parameters are the expected a posteriori or Bayes mean estimate (EAP), the median a posteriori or Bayes median estimate (MAP), and the Bayesian confidence interval (BCI; sometimes also called credibility intervals). Within the null model, one would be interested in the average state level (intercept) and the variance of state level, as well as the average state variability (residual variance) and the variance of state variability. Plus, one receives information on the correlation of state level with state variability. Within the model including predictors, one would be interested in the effects of the predictors (here, narcissistic admiration and rivalry) on state level and state variability, also indicated via EAP, MAP, and BCI. If respective confidence intervals do not include zero, they can be considered significant and can be interpreted in terms of size and directionality.

In its basic form, the mixed-effects location scale model considers interindividual differences in instability only, not in temporal dependency. To model both types of variability simultaneously, however, extensions of the approach within the Bayesian framework have been suggested in recent years (e.g., Wang et al., 2012).

Empirical Findings: From Recent Insights to Future Prospects

Empirical efforts on within-person variability have been particularly devoted to investigating this individual difference variable and to establishing it as meaningful. Indeed, if within-person variability is meaningful and "trait-like", researchers should be able to (1) reliably measure it, (2) predict these measures by determinants, and (3) use these measures to predict consequences.

First, empirical research has shown that statistical indices of intra-individual state variation capture systematic information on interindividual differences because positive associations have been found among indicators of variability (e.g., Oosterwegel, Field, Hart, & Anderson, 2001; Santangelo et al., 2017), as well as with conceptually related concepts (e.g., cross-role variability or self-pluralism; e.g., Baird et al., 2006). Regarding the stability of within-person variability, findings regarding the stability of affective, self-esteem, and behavioural variability indicate that variability is sufficiently stable to be considered a trait (see Baird et al., 2006; Eaton & Funder, 2001; Eid & Diener, 1999; Fleeson, 2001; Kernis, 1993, 2003; Kernis, Cornell, Sun, Berry, & Harlow, 1993).

Second, regarding the determinants of state fluctuations, most research has addressed the associations between within-person variability measures and the Big Five personality traits. Unsurprisingly, perhaps, neuroticism (or emotional instability) and also openness have been found to be positively associated with state fluctuations (see Fleeson & Gallagher, 2009; Kuppens, Oravecz, & Tuerlinkx, 2010; Miller, Vachon, & Lynam, 2009; Zeigler-Hill et al., 2015). Accordingly, persons who score highly on neuroticism and openness report greater fluctuations in their states across time points. Findings regarding the role of extraversion, as well as agreeableness and conscientiousness, respectively, indicate that these traits are either negatively related or unrelated to variability measures (cf. Fleeson & Gallagher, 2009; Geukes et al., 2017). Thus, extravert, agreeable, and conscientious persons either fluctuate less in their states across time points or just as much as their low-scoring counterparts.

Third, regarding the consequences of within-person variability, comprehensive theorizing has led to two opposing assumptions: Within-person variability should either be adaptive because it reflects a functional flexibility (Paulhus & Martin, 1988), with individuals being able to appropriately adapt to changing situational circumstances, or it should be maladaptive because it reflects a weak sense of self (Donahue, Robins, Roberts, & John, 1993), as, for example, also evident in psychopathology, such as borderline or narcissistic personality disorders (see Bosson et al., 2008; Zeigler-Hill, & Abraham, 2006). Empirical findings suggest that within-person variability is, indeed, rather a sign of psychological maladjustment (e.g., Kernis, 2005; Kuppens, Van Mechelen, Nezlek, Dossche, & Timmermans, 2007; Larson et al., 1980; Zeigler-Hill & Besser, 2013; Zeigler-Hill & Wallace, 2012). When correcting variability indices for the mean, however, most of the positive associations between variability and psychological maladjustment vanished to become insignificant, indicating that the variability effects were largely driven by the mean levels of the construct (Baird et al., 2006).

As a matter of fact, empirical research on within-person variability is still in its infancy. Therefore, a comprehensive research programme is necessary that is devoted (1) to fundamental questions regarding the psychometric properties of within-person variability, targeting its conceptualization, reliability, and validity (e.g., Baird et al., 2006; Eid & Diener, 1999; Jahng et al., 2008; Moskowitz & Zuroff, 2004; Wang & Grimm, 2012) in comparative analyses across state domains (feelings, cognitions, behaviours); and (2) to answering exciting new research questions, regarding variability's origins and development (e.g., Eaton & Funder, 2001; Eid & Diener, 1999; Röcke, Li, & Smith, 2009), determinants, and consequences across different samples, domains, and contexts (e.g., Xanthopoulou, Bakker, & Ilies, 2012; Zeigler-Hill et al., 2013). Finally, as within-person variability is a truly contextualized measure, further incorporating situational information (e.g., similarity of situations, obtained social roles, present interaction partners, training vs. competition) promises to be key to further understanding what drives state variability (see Frederiksen, 1972; Furr & Funder, 2004; Geukes et al., 2017; Magnusson & Ekehammar, 1978).

Conclusion

Facilitated by advances in theory, assessment, and data analysis, researchers have become increasingly interested in the study of within-person variability – that is, in how individuals fluctuate in momentary feelings, thoughts, behaviour, and performance across time and situations. Respective mean- and/or trend-corrected quantifications should capture both overall instability and temporal dependency of repeated states, and analyses should rather follow a one-step than a two-step approach. Empirical evidence indicates that within-person variability exhibits trait-like characteristics as it is found to be reliably measurable, predictable by determinants, and potentially consequential for people's lives. Future research on within-person variability will need to further target its psychometric properties, its origins and development, and its determinants and consequences. In fact, the sporting domain appears to be an ideal environment to study within-person variability, because athletes regularly experience a diversity of states, and it provides a unique combination of systematic situational variation and field-based ecological validity (Allen et al., 2013). A novel focus on this trait-like characteristic promises to provide important insights into interindividual differences in athletes' intra-individual functioning, ultimately leading to more comprehensive explanations of athletes' sporting success (e.g., victory vs. defeat) and their health and well-being (e.g., putting on the running shoes vs. watching Netflix).

References

Allen, M. S., Greenlees, I., & Jones, M. V. (2013). Personality in sport: A comprehensive review. *International Review of Sport and Exercise Psychology, 6*, 184–208.

Allport, G. W. (1961). *Pattern and growth in personality.* New York: Holt, Rinehart & Winston.

Amorose, A. J. (2001). Intraindividual variability of self-evaluations in the physical domain: Prevalence, consequences, and antecedents. *Journal of Sport and Exercise Psychology, 23*, 222–244.

Arslan, R. C., & Tata, C. S. (2015). formr.org survey software (Version v0.8.2).

Back, M. D., Baumert, A., Denissen, J. J., Hartung, F. M., Penke, L., Schmukle, S. C., ... Wrzus, C. (2011). PERSOC: A unified framework for understanding the dynamic interplay of personality and social relationships. *European Journal of Personality, 25*, 90–107.

Baird, B. M., Le, K., & Lucas, R. E. (2006). On the nature of intraindividual personality variability: Reliability, validity, and associations with well-being. *Journal of Personality and Social Psychology, 90*, 512–527.

Baranowski, T., Smith, M., Thompson, W. O., Baranowski, J., & Hebert, D. (1999). Intraindividual variability and reliability in a 7-day exercise record. *Medicine and Science in Sports and Exercise, 31*, 1619–1622.

Baumert, A., Schmitt, M., Perugini, M., Johnson, W., Blum, G., Borkenau, P., ... Jayawickreme, E. (2017). Integrating personality structure, personality process, and personality development. *European Journal of Personality, 31*, 503–528.

Bolger, N., & Laurenceau, J. P. (2013). *Intensive longitudinal methods.* New York: Guilford Press.

Bosson, J. K., Lakey, C. E., Campbell, W. K., Zeigler-Hill, V., Jordan, C. H., & Kernis, M. H. (2008). Untangling the links between narcissism and self-esteem: A theoretical and empirical review. *Social and Personality Psychology Compass, 2*, 1415–1439.

Briley, D. A., & Tucker-Drob, E. M. (2014). Genetic and environmental continuity in personality development: A meta-analysis. *Psychological Bulletin, 140*, 1303–1331.

Carver, C. S., & Scheier, M. F. (2004). *Perspectives on personality.* Boston, MA: Allyn & Bacon.

Cerin, E., Szabo, A., & Williams, C. (2001). Is the experience sampling method (ESM) appropriate for studying pre-competitive emotions? *Psychology of Sport and Exercise, 2*, 27–45.

Chittaranjan, G., Blom, J., & Gatica-Perez, D. (2013). Mining large-scale smartphone data for personality studies. *Personal and Ubiquitous Computing, 17*, 433–450.

Clemes, S. A., Matchett, N., & Wane, S. L. (2008). Reactivity: An issue for short-term pedometer studies? *British Journal of Sports Medicine, 42*, 68–70.

Clemes, S. A., & Parker, R. A. (2009). Increasing our understanding of reactivity to pedometers in adults. *Medicine and Science in Sports and Exercise, 41*, 674–680.

Csikszentmihalyi, M., Larson, R., & Prescott, S. (1977). The ecology of adolescent activity and experience. *Journal of Youth and Adolescence, 6,* 281–294.

Dickens, Y. L., Van Raalte, J., & Hurlburt, R. T. (2018). On investigating self-talk: A descriptive experience sampling study of inner experience during golf performance. *The Sport Psychologist, 32,* 66–73.

Donahue, E. M., Robins, R. W., Roberts, B. W., & John, O. P. (1993). The divided self: Concurrent and longitudinal effects of psychological adjustment and social roles on self-concept differentiation. *Journal of Personality and Social Psychology, 64,* 834–846.

Eaton, L. G., & Funder, D. C. (2001). Emotional experience in daily life: Valence, variability, and rate of change. *Emotion, 1,* 413–421.

Ebner-Priemer, U. W., Eid, M., Kleindienst, N., Stabenow, S., & Trull, T. J. (2009). Analytic strategies for understanding affective (in) stability and other dynamic processes in psychopathology. *Journal of Abnormal Psychology, 118,* 195–202.

Eid, M., & Diener, E. (1999). Intraindividual variability in affect: Reliability, validity, and personality characteristics. *Journal of Personality and Social Psychology, 76,* 662–676.

Ekehammar, B. (1974). Interactionism in personality from a historical perspective. *Psychological Bulletin, 81,* 1026–1048.

Endler, N. S. (1981). Persons, situations, and their interaction. In A. I. Rabin, J. Aronoff, A. M. Barclay, & R. A. Zucker (Eds.), *Further explorations in personality* (pp. 114–151). New York: Wiley.

Endler, N. S. (1993). Personality: An interactional perspective. In P. J. Hetterma & I. J. Deary (Eds.), *Foundations of personality* (pp. 251–268). Dordrecht: Kluwer.

Endler, N. S., & Edwards, J. M. (1986). Interactionism in personality in the twentieth century. *Personality and Individual Differences, 7,* 379–384.

Epstein, S., & O'Brien, E. J. (1985). The person-situation debate in historical and current perspective. *Psychological Bulletin, 98,* 513–537.

Fleeson, W. (2001). Toward a structure- and process-integrated view of personality: Traits as density distributions of states. *Journal of Personality and Social Psychology, 80,* 1011–1027.

Fleeson, W. (2004). Moving personality beyond the person-situation debate: The challenge and the opportunity of within-person variability. *Current Directions in Psychological Science, 13,* 83–87.

Fleeson, W. (2007). Situation-based contingencies underlying trait-content manifestation in behavior. *Journal of Personality, 75,* 825–861.

Fleeson, W. (2012). Perspectives on the person: Rapid growth and opportunities for integration. In K. Deaux & M. Snyder (Eds.), *The Oxford handbook of personality and social psychology* (pp. 33–63). New York: Oxford University Press.

Fleeson, W., & Gallagher, P. (2009). The implications of Big Five standing for the distribution of trait manifestation of behavior: Fifteen experience-sampling studies and a meta-analysis. *Journal of Personality and Social Psychology, 97,* 1097–1114.

Fleeson, W., & Jayawickreme, E. (2015). Whole trait theory. *Journal of Research in Personality, 56,* 82–92.

Fleeson, W., & Noftle, E. E. (2009). In favor of the synthetic resolution to the person-situation debate. *Journal of Research in Personality, 43,* 150–154.

Fluegel, J. C. (1925). A quantitative study of feeling and emotion in everyday life. *British Journal of Psychology. General Section, 15,* 318–355.

Frederiksen, N. (1972). Toward a taxonomy of situations. *American Psychologist, 27,* 114–123.

Funder, D. C. (2006). Towards a resolution of the personality: Persons, situations and behavior. *Journal of Research in Personality, 40,* 21–34.

Furr, R. M., & Funder, D. C. (2004). Situational similarity and behavioral consistency: Subjective, objective, variable-centered and person-centered approaches. *Journal of Research in Personality, 38,* 421–447.

Gauvin, L., Rejeski, W. J., & Norris, J. L. (1996). A naturalistic study of the impact of acute physical activity on feeling states and affect in women. *Health Psychology, 15,* 391–397.

Gauvin, L., & Szabo, A. (1992). Application of the experience sampling method to the study of the effects of exercise withdrawal on well-being. *Journal of Sport and Exercise Psychology, 14,* 361–374.

Geukes, K., Nestler, S., Hutteman, R., Dufner, M., Küfner, A. C. P., Egloff, B., ... Back, M. D. (2016). Puffed up but shaky selves: State self-esteem level and variability in narcissists. *Journal of Personality and Social Psychology, 112,* 769–786.

Geukes, K., Nestler, S., Hutteman, R., Küfner, A. C., & Back, M. D. (2017). Trait personality and state variability: Predicting individual differences in within-and cross-context fluctuations in affect, self-evaluations, and behavior in everyday life. *Journal of Research in Personality, 69,* 124–138.

Geukes, K., van Zalk, M., & Back, M. D. (2018). Understanding personality development: An integrative state process model. *International Journal of Behavioral Development, 42*, 43–51.

Gosling, S. D., & Johnson, J. A. (2010). *Advanced methods for conducting online behavioral research.* Washington, DC: American Psychological Association.

Hanton, S., Thomas, O., & Maynard, I. (2004). Competitive anxiety responses in the week leading up to competition: The role of intensity, direction and frequency dimensions. *Psychology of Sport and Exercise, 5*, 169–181.

Harari, G. M., Lane, N. D., Wang, R., Crosier, B. S., Campbell, A. T., & Gosling, S. D. (2016). Using smartphones to collect behavioral data in psychological science: Opportunities, practical considerations, and challenges. *Perspectives on Psychological Science, 11*, 838–854.

Hedeker, D., Demirtas, H., & Mermelstein, R. J. (2009). A mixed ordinal location scale model for analysis of ecological momentary assessment (EMA) data. *Statistics and Its Interface, 2*, 391–402.

Hedeker, D., Mermelstein, R. J., & Demirtas, H. (2008). An application of a mixed-effects location scale model for analysis of ecological momentary assessment (EMA) data. *Biometrics, 64*, 627–634.

Hofmann, W., & Patel, P. V. (2015). SurveySignal: A convenient solution for experience sampling research using participants' own smartphones. *Social Science Computer Review, 33*, 235–253.

Jahng, S., Wood, P. K., & Trull, T. J. (2008). Analysis of affective instability in ecological momentary assessment: Indices using successive difference and group comparison via multilevel modeling. *Psychological Methods, 13*, 354–375.

Kandler, C., Bleidorn, W., Riemann, R., Spinath, F. M., Thiel, W., & Angleitner, A. (2010). Sources of cumulative continuity in personality: A longitudinal multiple-rater twin study. *Journal of Personality and Social Psychology, 98*, 995–1008.

Kenrick, D. T., & Funder, D. C. (1988). Profiting from controversy: Lessons from the person–situation debate. *American Psychologist, 43*, 23–24.

Kernis, M. H. (1993). The roles of stability and level of self-esteem in psychological functioning. In R. F. Baumeister (Ed.), *Self-esteem: The puzzle of low self-regard* (pp. 167–182). New York: Springer.

Kernis, M. H. (2003). Toward a conceptualization of optimal self-esteem. *Psychological Inquiry, 14*, 1–26.

Kernis, M. H. (2005). Measuring self-esteem in context: The importance of stability of self-esteem in psychological functioning. *Journal of Personality, 73*, 1569–1605.

Kernis, M. H., Cornell, D. P., Sun, C., Berry, A., & Harlow, T. (1993). There's more to self-esteem than whether it is high or low: The importance of stability of self-esteem. *Journal of Personality and Social Psychology, 65*, 1190–1204.

Kimiecik, J. C., & Stein, G. L. (1992). Examining flow experiences in sport contexts: Conceptual issues and methodological concerns. *Journal of Applied Sport Psychology, 4*, 144–160.

Kirshnit, C. E., Ham, M., & Richards, M. H. (1989). The sporting life: Athletic activities during early adolescence. *Journal of Youth and Adolescence, 18*, 601–615.

Krahé, B. (1992). *Personality and social psychology: Towards a synthesis.* Thousand Oaks, CA: Sage.

Kuppens, P., Oravecz, Z., & Tuerlinkx, F. (2010). Feelings change: Accounting for individual differences in the temporal dynamics of affect. *Journal of Personality and Social Psychology, 99*, 1042–1060.

Kuppens, P., Van Mechelen, I., Nezlek, J. B., Dossche, D., & Timmermans, T. (2007). Individual differences in core affect variability and their relationship to psychological adjustment. *Emotion, 7*, 262–274.

Larsen, R. J. (1987). The stability of mood variability: A spectral analytic approach to daily mood assessments. *Journal of Personality and Social Psychology, 52*, 1195–1204.

Larson, R., & Csikszentmihalyi, M. (1983). The experience sampling method. *New Directions for Methodology of Social and Behavioral Science, 15*, 41–56.

Larson, R., Csikszentmihalyi, M., & Graef, R. (1980). Mood variability and the psychosocial adjustment of adolescents. *Journal of Youth and Adolescence, 9*, 469–490.

Lewin, K. (1935). *A dynamic theory of personality. Selected papers.* New York: McGraw-Hill.

Lewin, K. (1936). *Principles of topological psychology.* New York: McGraw-Hill.

Lin, X., Raz, J., & Harlow, S. D. (1997). Linear mixed models with heterogeneous within- cluster variances. *Biometrics, 53*, 910–923.

Lodi-Smith, J., & Roberts, B. W. (2007). Social investment and personality: A meta-analysis of the relationship of personality traits to investment in work, family, religion, and volunteerism. *Personality and Social Psychology Review, 11*, 68–86.

Lutz, R., Lochbaum, M. R., Carson, T., Jackson, S., Greenwood, M., & Byars, A. (2008). Are we underestimating the affective benefits of exercise? An experience sampling study of university aerobics participants. *Journal of Sport Behavior, 31*, 166–186.

Magnusson, D., & Ekehammar, B. (1978). Similar situations – similar behaviors? A study of the intraindividual congruence between situation perception and situation reactions. *Journal of Research in Personality*, *12*(1), 41–48.

McCrae, R. R., & Costa, P. T. (1987). Validation of the five-factor model of personality across instruments and observers. *Journal of Personality and Social Psychology*, *52*, 81–90.

Mehl, M. R., & Conner, T. S. (2012). *Handbook of research methods for studying daily life*. New York: Guilford Press.

Miller, D. J., Vachon, D. D., & Lynam, D. R. (2009). Neuroticism, negative affect, and negative affect instability: Establishing convergent and discriminant validity using ecological momentary assessment. *Personality and Individual Differences*, *47*, 873–877.

Mischel, W. (1968). *Personality and assessment*. New York: Wiley.

Moskowitz, D. S., & Zuroff, D. C. (2004). Flux, pulse, and spin: Dynamic additions to the personality lexicon. *Journal of Personality and Social Psychology*, *86*, 880–893.

Murray, H. A. (1938). *Explorations in personality*. Oxford, UK: Oxford University Press.

Nestler, S., Geukes, K., & Back, M. D. (2018). Modeling intraindividual variability in three-level models. *Methodology*, *14*, 95–108.

Nestler, S., Grimm, K. J., & Schönbrodt, F. D. (2015). The social consequences and mechanisms of personality: How to analyse longitudinal data from individual, dyadic, round-robin, and network designs. *European Journal of Personality*, *29*, 272–295.

Oosterwegel, A., Field, N., Hart, D., & Anderson, K. (2001). The relation of self-esteem variability to emotion variability, mood, personality traits, and depressive tendencies. *Journal of Personality*, *69*, 689–708.

Ozer, D. J., & Benet-Martinez, V. (2006). Personality and the prediction of consequential outcomes. *Annual Review of Psychology*, *57*, 401–421.

Paulhus, D. L., & Martin, C. L. (1988). Functional flexibility: A new conception of interpersonal flexibility. *Journal of Personality and Social Psychology*, *55*, 88–101.

Prescott, S., Csikszentmihalyi, M., & Graef, R. (1981). Environmental effects on cognitive and affective states: The experiential time sampling approach. *Social Behavior and Personality: an International Journal*, *9*, 23–32.

Qualtrics. (2005). *Qualtrics*. Provo, UT. 2015 www.qualtrics.com

Riemann, R., Angleitner, A., & Strelau, J. (1997). Genetic and environmental influences on personality: A study of twins reared together using the self-and peer report NEO-FFI scales. *Journal of Personality*, *65*, 449–475.

Roberts, B. W., Kuncel, N. R., Shiner, R., Caspi, A., & Goldberg, L. R. (2007). The power of personality: The comparative validity of personality traits, socioeconomic status, and cognitive ability for predicting important life outcomes. *Perspectives on Psychological Science*, *2*, 313–345.

Roberts, B. W., Walton, K. E., & Viechtbauer, W. (2006). Patterns of mean-level change in personality traits across the life course: A meta-analysis of longitudinal studies. *Psychological Bulletin*, *132*, 1–25.

Röcke, C., Li, S. C., & Smith, J. (2009). Intraindividual variability in positive and negative affect over 45 days: Do older adults fluctuate less than young adults? *Psychology and Aging*, *24*, 863–878.

Santangelo, P. S., Reinhard, I., Koudela-Hamila, S., Bohus, M., Holtmann, J., Eid, M., & Ebner-Priemer, U. W. (2017). The temporal interplay of self-esteem instability and affective instability in borderline personality disorder patients' everyday lives. *Journal of Abnormal Psychology*, *126*, 1057–1065.

Savin-Williams, R. C., & Demo, D. H. (1983). Situational and transituational determinants of adolescent self-feelings. *Journal of Personality and Social Psychology*, *44*, 824–833.

Schmid Mast, M., Gatica-Perez, D., Frauendorfer, D., Nguyen, L., & Choudhury, T. (2015). Social sensing for psychology: Automated interpersonal behavior assessment. *Current Directions in Psychological Science*, *24*, 154–160.

Schoeppe, S., Alley, S., Van Lippevelde, W., Bray, N. A., Williams, S. L., Duncan, M. J., & Vandelanotte, C. (2016). Efficacy of interventions that use apps to improve diet, physical activity and sedentary behaviour: A systematic review. *International Journal of Behavioral Nutrition and Physical Activity*, *13*, 127.

Schüler, J., & Brunner, S. (2009). The rewarding effect of flow experience on performance in a marathon race. *Psychology of Sport and Exercise*, *10*, 168–174.

Scollon, C. N., Prieto, C. K., & Diener, E. (2009). Experience sampling: Promises and pitfalls, strength and weaknesses. In E. Diener (Ed.), *Assessing well-being* (pp. 157–180). Dordrecht: Springer.

Spiegelhalter, D. J., Thomas, A., Best, N. G., & Lunn, D. (2003). *Win-BUGS version 1.4 users' manual*. MRC Biostatistics Unit, Cambridge. Retrieved from www.mrc-bsu.cam.ac.uk/bugs/

Stein, G. L., Kimiecik, J. C., Daniels, J., & Jackson, S. A. (1995). Psychological antecedents of flow in recreational sport. *Personality and Social Psychology Bulletin, 21*, 125–135.

Sturtz, S., Ligges, U., & Gelman, A. (2005). R2WinBUGS: A package for running WinBUGS from R. *Journal of Statistical Software, 12*, 1–16.

Tett, R. P., & Guterman, H. A. (2000). Situation trait relevance, trait expression, and crosssituational consistency: Testing a principle of trait activation. *Journal of Research in Personality, 34*, 397–423.

Thai, S., & Page-Gould, E. (2018). ExperienceSampler: An open-source scaffold for building smartphone apps for experience sampling. *Psychological Methods, 23*, 729–739.

Totterdell, P. (2000). Catching moods and hitting runs: Mood linkage and subjective performance in professional sport teams. *Journal of Applied Psychology, 85*, 848–859.

Vazire, S., & Sherman, R. A. (2017). Introduction to the special issue on within-person variability in personality. *Journal of Research in Personality, 69*, 1–3.

Verbeke, G., & Molenberghs, M. (2009). *Linear mixed models for longitudinal data*. New York: Springer.

Von Neumann, J., Kent, R. H., Bellinson, H. R., & Hart, B. T. (1941). The mean square successive difference. *The Annals of Mathematical Statistics, 12*, 153–162.

Wang, L. & Grimm, K. J. (2012). Investigating reliabilities of intraindividual variability indicators. *Multivariate Behavior Research, 47*, 1–31.

Wang, L., Hamaker, E., & Bergeman, C. (2012). Investigating inter-individual differences in short-term intra-individual variability. *Psychological Methods, 17*, 567–581.

Wessman, A. E., & Ricks, D. F. (1966). *Mood and personality*. Oxford, UK: Holt, Rinehart & Winston.

Wrzus, C., & Mehl, M. (2015). Lab and/or field? Measuring personality processes and their social consequences. *European Journal of Personality, 29*, 250–271.

Wrzus, C., & Roberts, B. W. (2017). Processes of personality development in adulthood: The TESSERA framework. *Personality and Social Psychology Review, 21*, 253–277.

Xanthopoulou, D., Bakker, A. B., & Ilies, R. (2012). Everyday working life: Explaining within-person fluctuations in employee well-being. *Human Relations, 65*(9), 1051–1069.

Zeigler-Hill, V., & Abraham, J. (2006). Borderline personality features: Instability of self-esteem and affect. *Journal of Social and Clinical Psychology, 25*, 668–687.

Zeigler-Hill, V., & Besser, A. (2013). A glimpse behind the mask: Facets of narcissism and feelings of self-worth. *Journal of Personality Assessment, 95*, 249–260.

Zeigler-Hill, V., Holden, C. J., Enjaian, B., Southard, A. C., Besser, A., Li, H., & Zhang, Q. (2015). Self-esteem instability and personality: The connections between feelings of self-worth and the Big Five dimensions of personality. *Personality and Social Psychology Bulletin, 41*, 183–198.

Zeigler-Hill, V., Li, H., Masri, J., Smith, A., Vonk, J., Madson, M. B., & Zhang, Q. (2013). Self-esteem instability and academic outcomes in American and Chinese college students. *Journal of Research in Personality, 47*, 455–463.

Zeigler-Hill, V., & Wallace, M. T. (2012). Self-esteem instability and psychological adjustment. *Self and Identity, 11*, 317–342.

34
PERSONALITY RESEARCH
Directions

Harry Manley and Ross Roberts

Introduction

It is evident that this area of research (i.e., personality) is having something of a resurgence, and the current wave of personality research is really helping to further what we know about the influence of individual differences in this domain. Focus herein is placed on a number of issues to consider for future personality researchers within sport and exercise in the domain to ensure that the quality and impact of any further work is maximized.

Broad and Narrow Traits

When discussing the five-factor model of personality in the entries within this encyclopedia, the focus has largely been on the broad, higher-order traits of extraversion, conscientiousness, neuroticism, openness, and agreeableness. However, each of these traits can also be considered hierarchically, with two facet levels (DeYoung, Quilty, & Peterson, 2007) that can then be further broken down in to six lower-order sub-facets, as specified by the NEO-PI-R (Costa & McCrae, 1992).

Consequently, because of the broad/narrow distinction available within the Big Five, researchers working in this area can choose to examine broad traits and/or finer-grained aspects of personality at facet and sub-facet level. The overwhelming majority of research examining personality in sport has adopted a broad approach. However, studying relevant lower-order traits may be important for predicting specific performance-related outcomes (for an illustration of the relevance of facets and job performance, see Judge, Rodell, Klinger, Simon, & Crawford, 2013). In the sporting domain, neuroticism is an example of a broad-level trait that it may be highly relevant to examine at the lower-order level. At the broad level, neuroticism is associated with generalized anxiety, but, at the facet level, it can be divided into volatility and withdrawal. Neuroticism–withdrawal is associated with a heightened tendency to internalize negative affect, engage in rumination and experience worry, and adopt a pessimistic outlook and interpretation of events (DeYoung et al., 2007). In contrast, neuroticism–volatility is associated with greater sensitivity to threat and the tendency to easily anger, react with hostility, and openly display negative affect. These two facets may have different implications when considering how individuals respond in demanding performance domains and, at an applied level, what psychological strategies are most effective for helping athletes. For example, van Doorn and Lang (2010) examined the effect of neuroticism facets on the regulation of mental resources and performance in a visual search task. When the task was highly demanding, withdrawal and volatility were associated with contrasting effects of effort on performance, such that increased effort benefited performance for individuals high in withdrawal but impaired the performance of those high in volatility.

Therefore, future personality research in sport is encouraged to give more consideration to the broad/narrow trait distinction and examine the influence of both broad overarching traits and facet-level aspects of personality. Given the heterogeneity in the effect of broad traits on performance, examining these effects at the facet level is likely to have greater predictive validity and will lead to the development of a fuller understanding of how these different aspects influence behaviour.

Statistical and Analytic Concerns

As emphasized in the entries on personality, a better understanding of the effects of personality on performance will most likely be gained through greater focus on how personality interacts with other factors to predict important outcomes, rather than simply considering the main effects of personality traits (see also Roberts & Woodman, 2017). Consequently, researchers are strongly encouraged to consider interactions when designing research studies on the effect of personality traits. However, an important caveat to the examination of interactions is that the typical effect sizes of interactions are considerably smaller than what are observed for main effects. For example, in a review of the effect sizes reported for interactions across more than 600 applied psychology and management studies, the median observed effect (f^2) was as low as .002 (Aguinis, Beaty, Boik, & Pierce, 2005). Thus, researchers should ensure studies are adequately powered to detect smaller interaction effects. One obvious solution is to increase sample size. However, where this is not possible for practical reasons (e.g., accessing limited research populations of elite athletes), it is recommended that researchers would benefit from careful attention to maximizing measurement reliability (Aguinis & Gottfredson, 2010). Consider the example of a researcher studying the interaction between two constructs that can be measured via self-report (x and y) to predict task performance. If the reliability of x is .70, and y also has reliability of .70, the reliability of the interaction term is .49 (assuming imagery and y are uncorrelated). Thus, more than half of the variance in the interaction score is attributable to random error. Contrast this with the situation when a researcher uses two scales with .90 reliability, which would produce a product term with a reliability of .81, where only 19% of the variance is attributable to random error. For more details and specific recommendations to improve measurement reliability (e.g., through aggregating scores from multiple raters), see Aguinis and Gottfredson (2010).

A Call for Large and Diverse Sampling

Researchers would also benefit from using not only larger, but also more diverse, samples than is typically the case in psychological research (Henrich, Heine, & Norenzayan, 2010). Although personality–performance outcome effects appear highly replicable (Soto, 2019), there is relatively limited consideration of how the effects of personality traits on performance outcomes may generalize and differ across cultures. It seems reasonable to assume that traits such as conscientiousness would be associated with beneficial effects (e.g., greater diligence in training), irrespective of the culture. However, the effect of other traits may be more strongly influenced by characteristics of the culture in which the athlete is embedded. For example, the self-centred, agentic, and highly extraverted characteristics of a narcissistic athlete may be well tolerated in cultures that value independence (e.g., the US), but would be less socially accepted in cultures that value communal qualities (e.g., Thailand), and this may influence how these athletes are treated by fans, teammates, and coaches within their respective cultures. At a practical level, researchers interested in addressing such issues are encouraged to explore resources such as StudySwap (Chartier, Riegelman, & McCarthy, 2018) to identify and connect with potential global collaborators.

Multi-Method Personality Assessment

The dominant approach to personality assessment in sport psychology (and personality/social psychology) is through self-report measures. However, this is despite a consensus that multi-method assessments benefit the reliability and validity of personality measurement (Vazire, 2006). Informant reports of personality are typically provided by well-known acquaintances (e.g., friends or family members) and can be aggregated across observers to increase their reliability. The use of informant reports may be especially relevant when assessing traits for which individuals either lack accurate self-knowledge or when individuals are unwilling to honestly report their attitudes and cognitions. Informant reports can also be used to obtain reliable outcome measures, such as assessing mental toughness behaviour. For example, if a researcher is interested in understanding the mental toughness of narcissistic athletes, self-report measures of the construct may be susceptible to socially desirable responding (e.g., Kowalski, Rogoza, Vernon, & Schermer, 2018), with athletes overestimating their mental toughness to make themselves appear in a more positive light. Instead, researchers can ask coaches to rate how their athletes behave/perform across a range of situations (e.g., Hardy, Bell, & Beattie, 2014). Although informant ratings can be considered to provide a more objective measure of personality, they are also susceptible to similar biases. A coach who manages a disagreeable athlete who they often argue with may be far from objective in their broader ratings of the characteristics of this athlete. Thus, a multi-method approach integrating both self- and informant ratings would be useful for a fuller understanding of the effects of personality on outcome measures.

Another potential application of informant responses is to obtain personality ratings for individuals who cannot be assessed using self-report or knowledgeable informants (e.g., coaches). A researcher interested in studying the effect of personality traits on the performance of elite soccer players is unlikely to have the necessary access to these players to administer a detailed self-report personality questionnaire. Alternatively, it would be possible to ask multiple informants (e.g., fans of each player's club) who have observed the players across a range of situations (i.e., during competition, in press conferences, on social media, etc.) to provide personality ratings for players and then use the aggregate of their responses. Although there is no direct evidence to validate such an approach, there is evidence (Borkenau, Mauer, Riemann, Spinath, & Angleitner, 2004) that people are capable of making accurate personality inferences from 'thin slices of behaviour' (i.e., brief interactions with and observations of others), and supportive anecdotal evidence of this nature does exist (e.g., McGannon, Gonsalves, Schinke, & Busanich, 2015). Thus, fans should be well placed to make personality inferences about players. This information could be combined with text mining of players' autobiographies and the use of machine-learning techniques to predict personality traits on social media (Golbeck, Robles, Edmondson, & Turner, 2011). On a cautionary note, although people's social media profiles have been shown to accurately reflect their personalities (Back et al., 2010), it is unclear whether this is also true for athletes who are aware that their posts and information are subject to public scrutiny and may be more guarded in the information they present to the public. Informant reports also only allow one to get at the more overt and/or behavioural expressions of personality, and so no one measurement approach on is likely to capture everything about an individual's personality. Nonetheless, researchers are encouraged to go beyond thinking solely about self-report in studies of personality.

Biological Basis of Personality

A clearer picture of how individual difference factors can affect sport and exercise performance is also likely to be gained through greater understanding of the biological basis of personality traits. Recent efforts in personality neuroscience have focused on identifying the neural regions involved in each of the Big Five traits (e.g., DeYoung, 2010), and yet the immediate utility of identifying neural correlates of Big Five traits is not fully apparent, given that these traits were originally derived using a factor analytic approach (Costa & McCrae, 1992) and, consequently, may not easily map on to biological substrates.

However, one biologically based theory of personality that may be particularly relevant (and especially for understanding performance in the sporting domain) is reinforcement sensitivity theory (RST; Gray, 1970; Gray & McNaughton, 2000). RST is noteworthy in its conceptual development, inferring motivational systems from the study of animal behaviour and pharmacological effects to describe a conceptual nervous system that ties together motivational processes and neurobiological structures (Gray & McNaughton, 2000). According to RST, distinct motivational systems mediate physiological, emotional, and behavioural responses to facilitate approach to reward, avoidance of punishment, and the resolution of conflict between competing motivations.

The behavioural approach system mediates goal-directed behaviours to move an individual towards rewarding stimuli. Two parallel defensive systems regulate responses to threats and can be distinguished according to defensive direction (McNaughton & Corr, 2004; Perkins & Corr, 2006). The fight-flight-freeze system (FFFS) mediates avoidance of highly aversive threats, whereas the behavioural inhibition system (BIS) regulates defensive approaches, prompting cautious behaviours and inhibiting ongoing responses (e.g., pausing to ruminate over an upcoming situation). These defensive systems are each hierarchically organized along a gradient of defensive distance whereby the specific physiological and behavioural response is determined by the perceived proximity of the threat (Blanchard, Hynd, Minke, Minemoto, & Blanchard, 2001; McNaughton & Corr, 2004; Perkins & Corr, 2006).

This hierarchical organization of defensive responses is adaptive because different neural regions can mediate either complex preparatory processes or reactive responses, depending on what is most appropriate, given the proximity of threat (Mobbs, Hagan, Dalgleish, Silston, & Prevost, 2015). Distal threats (either spatial or temporal) that pose no imminent danger activate the dorsal prefrontal cortex and posterior cingulate (Mobbs et al., 2007), mediating ruminative processes that include potential threat assessment (Fiddick, 2011) and the simulation and prediction of future environments and behaviours (Suddendorf & Corballis, 2007). In contrast, more proximal threats activate lower-level neural regions such as the septo-hippocampal system, which mediates conflict resolution, the medial hypothalamus mediating risk assessment (Canteras, 2002), and, at the very lowest neural level, the periaqueductal gray that inhibits prepotent responses leading to defensive inactivity (McNaughton & Corr, 2004).

Thus, RST provides a theoretical framework for understanding how perceived proximity to threat may give rise to different emotional and cognitive responses (e.g., panic or rumination), and how individual differences in the sensitivity of these systems may lead to distinct outcomes. Given the potential for RST to explain individual differences in behavioural responses to threat and reward, it is perhaps surprising that there have been limited attempts to apply RST to understand how people perform in stressful performance environments. Indeed, the sporting domain is characterized by the combined presence of threatening (e.g., physical pain, embarrassment) and rewarding (e.g., money, admiration) stimuli, and, thus, it would appear that RST offers considerable utility in this regard. However, recent efforts have attempted to understand how individual differences in the sensitivity of the systems described by RST might influence performance. For example, there is evidence that heightened threat sensitivity (BIS and FFFS) can be adaptive for athletes because it drives earlier detection of potential threats (Hardy et al., 2014) and earlier implementation of effective coping strategies (Manley, Beattie, Roberts, Lawrence, & Hardy, 2018). However, as would be predicted by RST, the benefits of punishment sensitivity are only present when athletes are insensitive to reward. When athletes are highly sensitive to reward, heightened threat sensitivity is negatively related to mental toughness (potentially) owing to greater conflict between approach and avoidance systems that leads to inhibited decision-making and behavioural responses that harm performance when rapid responses are required (Hardy et al., 2014; Manley et al., 2018). Consequently, future researchers are encouraged to pay greater attention to the theoretical implications of RST when considering individual differences in the sporting domain.

Outside the RST framework, attention has been directed to understanding how biological factors that reflect stable individual differences relate to performance. One area in particular that has received recent attention is the effect of individual differences in dopaminergic synthesis capacity on performance in high-incentive domains (Aarts et al., 2014). Dopamine (DA) is implicated in the effective regulation of cognitive control (Cools & D'Esposito, 2010) and exhibits an inverted U-shape function such that optimal cognitive control is associated with moderate levels of DA, whereas excessively high or low levels of DA lead to impaired cognitive control (Aarts et al., 2014; Yerkes & Dodson, 1908). To study the effect of DA on cognitive control, one approach is to examine performance on a cognitive control task after promising high and low monetary rewards for success that either increase or are unrelated to DA levels, respectively (Aarts et al., 2014). Because of the inverted U-shape of DA and cognitive control, the influence of high incentives on cognitive control may be highly dependent on baseline levels of DA. For example, an individual with low baseline DA may be able to exert good cognitive control in high-incentive domains, because high incentives have a facilitative effect on dopaminergic levels and, therefore, cognitive control. In contrast, the same high incentives may be detrimental to cognitive control for individuals with high baseline DA.

In a notable recent study that supports the theorizing above, Aarts et al. (2014) used a modified Stroop task with low and high trial incentives. Individual differences in baseline DA synthesis predicted cognitive control during high-incentive tasks. Higher baseline dopamine synthesis predicted better performance on congruent trials (i.e., brought about by greater motivation) but detrimental effects on incongruent trials (i.e., indicating less cognitive flexibility). These effects are interpreted as indicating that, for individuals with a high baseline capacity for dopamine synthesis, a promised bonus overdoses the dopaminergic system, thereby impairing rather than improving cognitive control.

In another recent study, Lee and Grafton (2015) used a bimanual motor task resembling the game Snake that required a cursor to be moved into a target by both the velocity and direction of the cursor being controlled. They measured performance in response to varying levels of potential reward incentives and found a quadratic relationship between reward and performance; performance was better for $10 incentives but worse for $5 and $40 trials. Their main finding was that the level of connectivity between the prefrontal cortex (a brain region associated with top–down control) and motor cortex prior to movement initiation predicted whether participants would choke. However, of considerable relevance here was evidence that individual differences in self-reported impulsivity predicted greater performance impairments on the high-incentive trials. Impulsive individuals were less likely to be able to increase connectivity between prefrontal regions and the motor cortex during the pressure trials, which suggests they 'just go for it' and, therefore, perform worse. In explaining these results, Lee and Grafton proposed that impulsive individuals could have either been more sensitive to the potential rewards, or that their engagement of top–down control was simply less effective than that of people with low trait impulsivity.

Altogether, these and related studies (Aarts et al., 2014; Chib, De Martino, Shimojo, & O'Doherty, 2012; Chib, Shimojo, & O'Doherty, 2014; Lee & Grafton, 2015; Mobbs et al., 2009) point to the growing relevance of studying individual difference factors in combination with an understanding of the relevant neurobiological processes and the potential connectivity with top–down regulatory processes to understand behaviour.

Applied Issues with the Measurement of Latent Variables

Given the above consideration of the neurobiological basis of personality, the measurement of latent personality traits using self-report measures can also present complex issues for the sport psychology researcher. One way to illustrate this is through a consideration of the potential problems associated with trying to infer an individual's level of effortful control (i.e., their ability to inhibit responses and self-regulate emotional and behavioural reactivity), distinct from their sensitivity to threat. In this example, imagine an individual's average behaviour manifests such that the responses to questionnaire items designed to assess these constructs indicate they have moderate levels of effortful control and moderate sensitivity to threat. The problem is that the latent traits that give rise to an individual's behaviour could reflect a variety of different combinations of the lower-order traits. For example, moderate levels of effortful control may indicate an insensitivity to threat but an inability to inhibit fear/anxiety (because of low effortful control) or, similarly, it could manifest from the individual being highly sensitive to threat but having high levels of effortful control to suppress the behavioural effects of threat sensitivity. Recent neuroimaging evidence emphasizes this complexity; in an elegant approach, Hahn et al. (2013) compared the relationship between amygdala–hippocampus connectivity and scores on questionnaire measures of threat sensitivity. For some individuals, self-reported sensitivity to threat was driven by stronger amygdala activation, whereas, for others, threat sensitivity was associated with weak inhibitory connections from the hippocampus. This finding suggests that, despite the same behavioural manifestation (i.e., reporting the same level of sensitivity to threat), threat sensitivity can either be driven by greater reactivity to threats or an inability to exert control to downregulate the threat response. The distinctions regarding the cause of threat sensitivity are not trivial and may have important practical implications when athletes are taught techniques to regulate their anxiety. For instance, Hahn et al. (2013) speculate that relaxation techniques (e.g., mindfulness and breathing techniques) may be most effective in reducing anxiety driven by amygdala reactivity, whereas cognitive reappraisals may be more effective for individuals with poor hippocampal–amygdala connectivity. Although it is unlikely that practitioners will readily have access to the sophisticated measures required to discern the different anxiety profiles of athletes, it is worth being aware that the efficacy of emotion regulation strategies may vary across athletes, and what works best for one athlete may not work for another.

Conclusion

At the beginning of this contribution, it was noted that personality research in sport appears to be stepping out from its less than illustrious past and is now firmly back on the research agenda. The contributions on personality in this encyclopedia provide an outstanding overview of where the research literature now is, and much more is now known about the influence of individual differences in personality in relation to sport and exercise behaviour. However, with increases in knowledge come more questions and other issues to consider. It is anticipated that personality research really is on the cusp of something special. The next generation of personality research has the potential to hugely advance our understanding in this area, providing the work takes heed of some of the issues we have identified above, so that any future endeavours do not fall foul of the same problems as the early efforts in our domain.

References

Aarts, E., Wallace, D. L., Dang, L. C., Jagust, W. J., Cools, R., & D'Esposito, M. (2014). Dopamine and the cognitive downside of a promised bonus. *Psychological Science, 25,* 1003–1009.

Aguinis, H., Beaty, J. C., Boik, R. J., & Pierce, C. A. (2005). Effect size and power in assessing moderating effects of categorical variables using multiple regression: A 30-year review. *The Journal of Applied Psychology, 90,* 94–107.

Aguinis, H., & Gottfredson, R. K. (2010). Best-practice recommendations for estimating interaction effects using moderated multiple regression. *Journal of Organizational Behavior, 31,* 776–786.

Back, M. D., Stopfer, J. M., Vazire, S., Gaddis, S., Schmukle, S. C., Egloff, B., & Gosling, S. D. (2010). Facebook profiles reflect actual personality, not self-idealization. *Psychological Science, 21,* 372–374.

Blanchard, D. C., Hynd, L., Minke, K., Minemoto, T., & Blanchard, R. J. (2001). Human defensive behaviors to threat scenarios show parallels to fear- and anxiety-related defense patterns of non-human mammals. *Neuroscience and Biobehavioral Reviews, 25,* 761–770.

Borkenau, P., Mauer, N., Riemann, R., Spinath, F. M., & Angleitner, A. (2004). Thin slices of behavior as cues of personality and intelligence. *Journal of Personality and Social Psychology, 86,* 599–614.

Canteras, N. S. (2002). The medial hypothalamic defensive system: Hodological organization and functional implications. *Pharmacology, Biochemistry, and Behavior, 71,* 481–491.

Chartier, C. R., Riegelman, A., & McCarthy, R. J. (2018). StudySwap: A platform for interlab replication, collaboration, and resource exchange. *Advances in Methods and Practices in Psychological Science, 4,* 574–579.

Chib, V. S., De Martino, B., Shimojo, S., & O'Doherty, J. P. (2012). Neural mechanisms underlying paradoxical performance for monetary incentives are driven by loss aversion. *Neuron, 74,* 582–594.

Chib, V. S., Shimojo, S., & O'Doherty, J. P. (2014). The effects of incentive framing on performance decrements for large monetary outcomes: Behavioral and neural mechanisms. *Journal of Neuroscience, 34,* 14833–14844.

Cools, R., & D'Esposito, M. (2010). Dopaminergic modulation of flexible cognitive control in humans. In A. Björklund, S. Dunnett, & L. Iversen (Eds.), *Dopamine handbook* (pp. 249–260). Oxford, UK: Oxford University Press.

Costa, P. T., & McCrae, R. R. (1992). The five-factor model of personality and its relevance to personality disorders. *Journal of Personality Disorders, 6,* 343–359.

DeYoung, C. G. (2010). Personality neuroscience and the biology of traits. *Social and Personality Psychology Compass, 4,* 1165–1180.

DeYoung, C. G., Quilty, L. C., & Peterson, J. B. (2007). Between facets and domains: 10 aspects of the Big Five. *Journal of Personality and Social Psychology, 93,* 880–896.

Fiddick, L. (2011). There is more than the amygdala: Potential threat assessment in the cingulate cortex. *Neuroscience and Biobehavioral Reviews, 35,* 1007–1018.

Golbeck, J., Robles, C., Edmondson, M., & Turner, K. (2011). Predicting personality from twitter. *Proceedings of the 3rd International Conference on Social Computing*, 149–156.

Gray, J. A. (1970). The psychophysiological basis of introversion-extraversion. *Behaviour Research and Therapy, 8,* 249–266.

Gray, J. A., & McNaughton, N. (2000). *The neuropsychology of anxiety: An enquiry into the functions of the septo-hippocampal system* (2nd ed.). Oxford, UK: Oxford University Press.

Hahn, T., Heinzel, S., Notebaert, K., Dresler, T., Reif, A., Lesch, K. P., ... Fallgatter, A. J. (2013). The tricks of the trait: Neural implementation of personality varies with genotype-dependent serotonin levels. *NeuroImage, 81,* 393–399.

Hardy, L., Bell, J. J., & Beattie, S. (2014). A neuropsychological model of mentally tough behavior. *Journal of Personality, 82,* 69–81.

Henrich, J., Heine, S. J., & Norenzayan, A. (2010). The weirdest people in the world? *Behavioral and Brain Sciences, 33*(2–3), 61–83.

Judge, T. A., Rodell, J. B., Klinger, R. L., Simon, L. S., & Crawford, E. R. (2013). Hierarchical representations of the five-factor model of personality in predicting job performance: Integrating three organizing frameworks with two theoretical perspectives. *Journal of Applied Psychology, 98,* 875–925.

Kowalski, C. M., Rogoza, R., Vernon, P. A., & Schermer, J. A. (2018). The dark triad and the self-presentation variables of socially desirable responding and self-monitoring. *Personality and Individual Differences, 120,* 234–237.

Lee, T. G., & Grafton, S. T. (2015). Out of control: Diminished prefrontal activity coincides with impaired motor performance due to choking under pressure. *NeuroImage, 105,* 145–155.

Manley, H., Beattie, S., Roberts, R., Lawrence, G. P., & Hardy, L. (2018). The benefit of punishment sensitivity on motor performance under pressure. *Journal of Personality, 86,* 339–352.

McGannon, K. R., Gonsalves, C. A., Schinke, R. J., & Busanich, R. (2015). Negotiating motherhood and athletic identity: A qualitative analysis of Olympic athlete mother representations in media narratives. *Psychology of Sport & Exercise, 20,* 51–59.

McNaughton, N., & Corr, P. J. (2004). A two-dimensional neuropsychology of defense: Fear/anxiety and defensive distance. *Neuroscience and Biobehavioral Reviews, 28,* 285–305.

Mobbs, D., Hagan, C. C., Dalgleish, T., Silston, B., & Prevost, C. (2015). The ecology of human fear: Survival optimization and the nervous system. *Frontiers in Neuroscience, 9,* 1–22.

Mobbs, D., Hassabis, D., Seymour, B., Marchant, J. L., Weiskopf, N., Dolan, R. J., & Frith, C. D. (2009). Choking on the money. *Psychological Science, 20,* 955–962.

Mobbs, D., Petrovic, P., Marchant, J. L., Hassabis, D., Weiskopf, N., Seymour, B., ... Frith, C. D. (2007). When fear is near: Threat imminence elicits prefrontal-periaqueductal gray shifts in humans. *Science, 317,* 1079–1083.

Perkins, A. M., & Corr, P. J. (2006). Reactions to threat and personality: Psychometric differentiation of intensity and direction dimensions of human defensive behaviour. *Behavioural Brain Research, 169,* 21–28.

Roberts, R., & Woodman, T. (2017). Personality and performance: Moving beyond the big 5. *Current Opinion in Psychology., 16,* 104–108.

Soto, C. J. (2019). How replicable are links between personality traits and consequential life outcomes? The life outcomes of personality replication project. *Psychological Science, 30,* 711–727.

Suddendorf, T., & Corballis, M. C. (2007). The evolution of foresight: What is mental time travel, and is it unique to humans? *The Behavioral and Brain Sciences, 30,* 299–313.

van Doorn, R. R. A., & Lang, J. W. B. (2010). Performance differences explained by the neuroticism facets withdrawal and volatility, variations in task demand, and effort allocation. *Journal of Research in Personality, 44,* 446–452.

Vazire, S. (2006). Informant reports: A cheap, fast, and easy method for personality assessment. *Journal of Research in Personality, 40,* 472–481.

Yerkes, R., & Dodson, J. D. (1908). The relation of strength of stimulus to rapidity of habit-formation. *Journal of Comparative Neurology and Psychology, 18,* 459–482.

35
PLANNED EXERCISE BEHAVIOUR

Vassilis Barkoukis and Lambros Lazuras

Introduction

Physical inactivity and lack of exercise represent the fourth leading cause of death worldwide, and efforts are needed to improve physical activity and exercise at a population level (Kohl et al., 2012). The benefits of physical exercise are well documented in the international literature (Warburton, Nicol, & Bredin, 2006), and a large body of research has shown that frequent exercise is associated with (a) improved cardiovascular functioning (Wilson, Ellison, & Cable, 2016); (b) increased life expectancy and quality of life in later years (Halaweh, Willen, Grimby-Ekman, & Svantesson, 2015; Wen et al., 2011); (c) improved executive functions in older individuals, with and without cognitive impairment (Hsu et al., 2018); (d) improved bone density and reduced risk for osteoporosis in older individuals (Bolam, Van Uffelen, & Taaffe, 2013). Accordingly, exercise reduces the risk for mental disorders, chronic disorders, and unhealthy behaviours, such as depression (McKercher et al., 2014; Mura, Moro, Patten, & Carta, 2014), osteoporosis (Beck, Daly, Singh, & Taaffe, 2017), Type 2 diabetes (Colberg et al., 2016), anxiety (Greenwood, Loughridge, Sadaoui, Christianson, & Fleshner, 2012), smoking, and other substance use (Haasova et al., 2014; Lynch, Peterson, Sanchez, Abel, & Smith, 2013).

Additionally, Ruegsegger and Booth (2018) and Wasser, Vasilopoulos, Zdziarski, and Vincent (2017) indicated that physical exercise delays the onset of approximately 40 chronic diseases. Furthermore, exercise can be beneficial to people suffering from multiple sclerosis (Motl & Pilutti, 2012; Motl & Sandroff, 2015), breast cancer (Murphy et al., 2011; Mutrie et al., 2012), traumatic brain injury (Wise, Hoffman, Powell, Bombardier, & Bell, 2012), Alzheimer's and Parkinson's diseases (Hernandez et al., 2015; Paillard, Rolland, & de Souto Barreto, 2015), and coronary heart disease (Lavie et al., 2015). Despite the well-known benefits of exercise for public health, epidemiological studies demonstrate that between 30% and 50% of adults and children are inactive or do not exercise regularly enough to experience the health-promoting effects of exercise (Fried, 2016; Wasser et al., 2017).

Theory of Planned Behaviour

Several approaches have been utilized in past research to explain the decisions involved in exercise uptake patterns. Among this research tradition, social-cognitive variables – that is, people's beliefs about exercise and their intentions to voluntarily engage in and adhere to exercise – have been extensively studied. Therefore, this contribution focuses specifically on the role of social-cognitive variables in exercise behaviour. To this end, the theory of planned behaviour (TPB) has been extensively used and found effective for comprehending the decision-making process towards fostering exercise behaviour. Furthermore, TPB has been proliferated as an appropriate approach and, among the best-accepted perspectives, is conceptualized exercise-related social cognition. In this contribution, the applicability of the TPB (Ajzen, 1991) and related models is discussed in detail, and recent evidence about the need to employ alternative approaches that will help the reader better understand, predict, and change exercise behaviour is presented.

The TPB is a social-cognitive theory designed to explain voluntary and overt behaviour – that is, actions that can be directly observed and measured and that result from people's volition and free will (Ajzen, 1991). The origins of the TPB can be traced in early work on subjective expected utility models and related decision-making. In these seminal works, Ajzen and Fishbein (1969, 1970) proposed that behaviour and decision-making are a function of one's behavioural intentions (BIs). BIs represent the motivational drivers of behaviour and are reflected in one's determination and planning to perform the behaviour in question (e.g., I intend to act; I am determined to act; I plan to act). According to Ajzen and Fishbein (1970), BIs are necessary and sufficient for the prediction of overt behaviours.

In turn, behavioural intentions are predicted by attitudes and by normative beliefs. Attitudes reflect outcome expectations (e.g., exercise will improve my health), as well as people's evaluations of the importance of those outcomes (e.g., improving my health through exercise is important to me), and are relevant to specific behaviours in well-defined situations. In this respect, attitudes to acting are specific to the behaviour in question and are not to be confused with more abstract and context-free evaluations of the behaviour or related objects/people. The evaluation of the outcome can be either instrumental, describing the usefulness of the behaviour, or relating to the quality of the experiences corresponding to perceptions and feelings while engaging in the behaviour (Fishbein & Ajzen, 2011; Knabe, 2012). Normative beliefs, on the other hand, were initially believed to represent personal beliefs about what other people expect of the actor to do in a given situation, and the motivation to comply to such expectations. According to Ajzen and Fishbein (1970), voluntary and overt behaviours could be predicted by the following algebraic formula,[1] which also expresses the core theoretical tenets of the theory of reasoned action (TRA; Ajzen & Fishbein, 1980; Fishbein, 1979):

$$B \sim BI = [A-act]w_0 + [NBs]w_1$$

A few years after the introduction of the TRA, Ajzen (1985) argued that voluntary and overt behaviours are also determined by people's subjective expectancies of their capability to successfully perform the behaviour in question – in other words, their perceived behavioural control (PBC). Interestingly, PBC was initially seen as an alternative name for Bandura's (1977, 1997) concept of self-efficacy (i.e., the belief that one is capable of successfully performing the action in question). Ajzen (1985) distinguished between the TRA and TPB by suggesting that:

> the two theories are identical when the subjective probability of success and the degree of control of internal and external factors reach their maximum values [...] When subjective probabilities of success and actual control are less than perfect, how-ever, we enter the domain of Planned Behavior.
>
> *(p. 36)*

To the extent that PBC reflects actual behavioural control (e.g., access to resources, knowledge about performing the behaviour successfully, availability of opportunities to perform the behaviour), PBC can directly predict behaviour. In summary, Ajzen's (1991) TPB presents a useful conceptual and theoretical framework to understand how ability (PBC) and motivation (intentions) predict human behaviour.

The implications of the TPB are simple but profound. First of all, as Ajzen (1991) argued, human behaviour is rather complex and influenced by a wide range of factors. To this end, the TPB provides a parsimonious model that enables researchers and students of human behaviour to understand the key driving forces behind voluntary actions. The parsimony of the TPB is one of the main reasons that made this theory widely appealing and applied inside and outside psychological research (Ajzen, 2011). Second, the three main predictors of intentions in the TPB (attitudes, subjective norms, and PBC) are related to each other, but, at the same time, they represent distinct psychological processes, each of which plays an important role in motivating people to act in a specific way. In this respect, personal evaluations of exercise (e.g., attitudes = exercise is good for my health) can be associated with expected modes of behavioural conduct (e.g., subjective norms = most people who are important to me think that I should exercise frequently) and with personal self-efficacy beliefs (e.g., PBC = If I want to exercise, I know how and where to do this successfully). Third, the TPB purports that more positive attitudes towards the behaviour, stronger subjective norms, and greater perceived control over the behaviour in question are associated with stronger intentions to act, which, in turn, predict actual behaviour. Fourth, Ajzen (1991) emphasized the principle of specificity: Attitudes, subjective norms, and PBC that are specific to a given behaviour are more predictive of concomitant intentions and actual behaviour than more general attitudinal, normative, and self-efficacy beliefs. To illustrate, attitudes, subjective norms, and PBC beliefs towards cycling are more predictive of cycling intentions and actual cycling compared with general beliefs about the health benefits of exercise. Finally, Ajzen (1991) further suggested that attitudes, norms, and PBC represent the most immediate predictors of intentions, and that the effects of other influences (e.g., personality, demographic characteristics) on intentions and behaviour should be mediated by attitudes, subjective norms, and PBC beliefs. This "mediation hypothesis" has been explicated further in the integrative model of behavioural prediction (e.g., Fishbein, 2009), which is described in more detail later in the contribution.

The TPB was published in 1991 and, ever since, has been cited more than 60,000 times, has spawned or inspired other models of intentions behaviour (e.g., technology acceptance model; for a review, see Holden & Karsh, 2010), and has been successfully applied in a wide variety of behavioural domains, from health-promoting and health-risk behaviour (Ajzen, 2011; Fishbein & Ajzen, 2011; Montano & Kasprzyk, 2015) to pro-environmental action (De Groot & Steg, 2007; Han, Hsu, & Sheu, 2010), gambling (Martin et al., 2010), and even choice of travelling (Bamberg, Ajzen, & Schmidt, 2003) and hunting (Hrubes, Ajzen, & Daigle, 2001). According to Nosek et al. (2010), the TPB has had a significant impact in social psychology research in the USA and Canada.

Applications of the Theory of Planned Behaviour in Exercise Settings

Conner and Armitage (1998) and Armitage and Conner (2001) summarized the evidence about the predictive validity of the TPB and found that the model predicted 39% of the variance in intentions and 27% of the variance in behaviour. In light of their findings, Armitage and Conner (2001) argued that a large proportion of the variance in both intentions and behaviour was still left unexplained and further emphasized the small-to-medium effect sizes observed in the correlation between intentions and behaviour. Their findings were further corroborated by a meta-analysis of experimental studies that showed that medium-to-large changes in intentions yielded to small-to-medium changes in actual behaviour (Webb & Sheeran, 2006). Nevertheless, three different meta-analyses of TPB studies in the exercise and physical activity context have provided different findings.

Hausenblas, Carron, and Mack (1997) meta-analysed the findings from 31 studies that used the TRA and TPB to predict exercise intentions and behaviour and found, across studies and based on a total sample of more than 10,000 participants, that the effect of exercise intentions on behaviour was large, suggesting that intentions to exercise predicted, to a large extent, actual exercise participation. Additionally, PBC exerted a large effect on both intentions and actual behaviour. Finally, attitudes to exercise had a large effect on both intentions and exercise behaviour, whereas subjective social norms had a moderate effect on intention and a zero-order effect on behaviour. It was concluded that the TPB presents a "superior" and more complete model, compared with the TRA, for understanding and predicting exercise behaviour, and that attitudes and PBC are the strongest predictors of exercise intentions and behaviour.

Hagger, Chatzisarantis, and Biddle (2002) published a meta-analytic review of 79 studies that used the TRA and TPB to predict exercise intentions and behaviour, and also accounted for the effects of demographic variables (i.e., age), past behaviour, and self-efficacy as an alternative measure to PBC. Their results corroborated the findings reported by Hausenblas et al. (1997) regarding the superiority of the TPB over the TRA in predicting exercise intentions and actual behaviour, and with respect to the large effect sizes in the relationships between attitudes and intentions and attitudes and behaviour. Measures of self-efficacy were distinct from PBC and added significant variance in predicting exercise intentions, suggesting that both dimensions of internal control/agency over the behaviour are important in explaining how exercise intentions are formed. Finally, past behaviour moderated the effects of attitudes on intentions, and the effects of PBC and intentions on behaviour. Hagger et al. (2002) concluded that the TPB provided a useful framework for understanding and predicting exercise behaviour, and the predictive validity of the TPB, as well as our understanding of the associations between TPB variables, exercise intentions, and actual behaviour, can be improved by the consideration of alternative measures of behavioural control (e.g., self-efficacy) and past exercise behaviour. Downs and Hausenblas' (2005) meta-analysis provided similar findings. After examining 111 studies that used the TRA or the TPB to predict exercise intentions and behaviour, they found that intentions and PBC had the strongest relationship with actual behaviour. Also, attitudes and PBC had the strongest effect on exercise intentions. Finally, a recent meta-analysis (Plotnikoff, Costigan, Karunamuni, & Lubans, 2013) of the application of different social-cognitive theories in adolescent physical activity participation showed that the studies that used TPB predicted between 28% (in African American girls; Trost et al., 2002) and 73% (among Greek pupils; Hagger et al., 2007) of the variance in intentions, and between 5% (in African American girls; Trost et al., 2002) and 59.1% (among Singaporean pupils; Hagger et al., 2007) of the variance in actual physical activity participation. Further evidence in support of the applicability of the TPB in exercise contexts across cultures and in different age and gender groups was provided by Nigg, Lippke, and Maddock (2009). They demonstrated that the relationships between the TPB variables, exercise intentions, and actual behaviour were invariantly significant in both males and females, younger and older individuals, and across ethnic groups.

Although physical activity and exercise uptake are important, exercise adherence (i.e., maintaining exercise habits in the long term) is perhaps most important, because it signifies long-term behaviour change and increases the prospects for sustainable healthy lifestyles. Armitage (2005) used the TPB to predict exercise participation and adherence in a sample of adult gym users over 4 months. He found that exercise habits were developed in the first 5 weeks, the successful enactment of exercise behaviour improved PBC beliefs, and that PBC predicted both exercise intentions and actual behaviour. Jekauc et al. (2015) compared the effect of TPB, social-cognitive theory, and physical activity maintenance theory in predicting exercise adherence. Attitudes and perceived behavioural control, as measured in the TPB, emerged as significant predictors of exercise behaviour. Furthermore, variables that are common between social-cognitive theory and the TPB (e.g., self-efficacy) were significantly associated with exercise adherence.

Taken together, the aforementioned findings that have derived from a range of meta-analytic, cross-sectional, longitudinal, and cross-cultural studies suggest that the TPB provides a useful theoretical framework for understanding and predicting exercise participation and adherence in diverse populations, independent of demographic factors, such as age, gender, and ethnic background. Furthermore, although habit formation and past behaviour are important in determining future behaviour, the studies reviewed above clearly show that, when past behaviour and habit are controlled for, the TPB variables (and especially attitudes and PBC) are still significantly associated with both exercise intentions and actual behaviour.

Theory of Planned Behaviour and Exercise in Clinical Populations

The TPB has been used to predict exercise adherence in diverse clinical populations. For instance, Blanchard et al. (2003) found that the TPB predicted 30% of the variance in exercise intentions and 12% of the variance in exercise adherence among cardiac patients during Phase II cardiac rehabilitation (i.e., cardiac rehabilitation through self-regulated and self-monitored exercise following hospital discharge).

Courneya and Friedenreich (1997, 1999) used the TPB to predict exercise among patients in cancer treatment. They demonstrated that attitudes and subjective norms predicted exercise intentions. In turn, intentions and PBC predicted actual exercise behaviour. Intentions significantly predicted exercise participation and adherence in cancer patients attending a 10-week programme (Courneya, Friedenreich, Sela, Quinney, & Rhodes, 2002). These findings were further replicated by Blanchard, Courneya, Rodgers, and Murnaghan (2002) in a sample of females diagnosed with breast cancer. It was found that the TPB variables were significantly associated with exercise intentions, which, in turn, predicted 30% of the variance in exercise behaviour. Similar findings were reported in studies with adolescent cancer survivors (Keats, Culos-Reed, Courneya, & McBride, 2007) and patients with kidney (Trinh, Plotnikoff, Rhodes, North, & Courneya, 2012) and prostate (Blanchard et al., 2002) cancer. Husebø, Dyrstad, Søreide, and Bru (2012) reviewed the evidence about the applicability of the TPB in exercise behaviour among cancer patients and found that PBC and intentions were the stronger predictors of exercise behaviour and adherence.

The TPB has been further applied to predict exercise behaviour among patients diagnosed with diabetes. Plotnikoff, Courneya, Trinh, Karunamuni, and Sigal (2008) demonstrated that, across 3 months, the TPB explained 8% and 10%, respectively, of the variance in aerobic physical activity and resistance training among patients with Type II diabetes. The TPB also accounted for 39% (aerobic physical activity) and 45% (resistance training) of the variance in intentions. Plotnikoff, Lippke, Trinh Courneya, Birkett, and Sigal (2010) further showed that attitudes, subjective norms, and PBC were significantly associated with intentions, which in turn predicted physical activity participation in patients with Type I and Type II diabetes. Lastly,

White et al. (2012) showed that a TPB-based intervention significantly predicted exercise participation among older patients with Type II diabetes and cardiovascular disease.

Extended TPB Models and Exercise Behaviour

Despite its parsimony and focus on social-cognitive determinants of intentions and behaviour, the TPB has received a lot of criticism that has, sometimes, inspired the development of augmented or refined TPB models (Conner, 2015) and, in other cases, led to calls for discarding the model overall (e.g., Ogden, 2003; Sniehotta, Presseau, & Araújo-Soares, 2014). According to different meta-analyses and review articles (e.g., Armitage & Conner, 2001; Conner & Armitage, 1998; McEachan, Conner, Taylor, & Lawton, 2011; Rivis & Sheeran, 2003b), some of the most notable limitations of the TPB include (a) lack of consideration of affective variables, such as anticipated emotions, in the decision-making and action-planning process; (b) narrow focus of social normative influences on subjective norms; and (c) limited insight into the psychological variables that may explain the intention–behaviour gap.

In order to overcome these limitations and to improve the predictive validity of the TPB, researchers have been considering the addition of theory-relevant psychological constructs to the original TPB corpus (a practice also known as theoretical "augmentation" of the TPB; Conner, 2015; Rivis, Sheeran, & Armitage, 2006). Justification for the theoretical augmentation of the TPB comes from Ajzen's (1991) recognition that:

> The theory of planned behavior is, in principle, open to the inclusion of additional predictors if it can be shown that they capture a significant proportion of the variance in intention or behavior after the theory's current variables have been taken into account. The theory of planned behavior in fact expanded the original theory of reasoned action by adding the concept of perceived behavioral control
>
> (p. 199)

With respect to the addition of beliefs that capture affective processes in decision-making, it has been recommended that anticipated regret represents a suitable candidate (Conner & Armitage, 1998). In support of this argument, researchers (e.g., Zeelenberg, 1999; Zeelenberg & Pieters, 2007) have shown that most human decisions are based not solely on the expected utility of their outcomes (e.g., if I exercise I will improve my fitness levels), but also on their anticipated affective impact, especially for regrettable outcomes (e.g., anticipating regret from failing to exercise). Although one may argue that TPB measures of attitudes incorporate an affective element (e.g., affective evaluation of exercise as good or bad, positive or negative, harmful or beneficial), anticipated regret represents a distinct psychological construct that can predict intentions and motivate behaviour over and above attitudes and other TPB components (Conner, McEachan, Taylor, O'Hara, & Lawton, 2015; Sandberg & Conner, 2008). A recent meta-analysis showed that anticipated regret predicted both intentions and actual behaviour across a variety of health-related behaviours (Brewer, DeFrank, & Gilkey, 2016). In a series of studies on exercise behaviour, anticipated regret was incorporated in the TPB. In particular, Abraham and Sheeran (2003, Study 1) showed that baseline measures of anticipated regret did not predict exercise behaviour after 2 weeks, but it significantly moderated the association between intentions and behaviour, so that participants who intended to exercise were more likely to do so if they anticipated more regret from failing to exercise. Similarly, exercise intentions at baseline measures were more strongly associated with actual behaviour 2 weeks later among participants who were asked to focus on anticipated regret prior to declaring their exercise intentions (Abraham & Sheeran, 2003, Study 2). In subsequent studies, Abraham and Sheeran (2004) showed that anticipated regret significantly predicted exercise intentions on top of past behaviour and other TPB variables (Study 1), and that participants induced to think about anticipated regret reported stronger exercise intentions, as compared with control participants (Study 2). In line with regret management theory (e.g., Zeelenberg & Pieters, 2007), these findings suggest that people are motivated to act on their intentions in ways that will reduce the likelihood of experiencing regret in the future. Nevertheless, it should be noted that the findings reported by Abraham and Sheeran (2003, 2004)) can be attributed to methodological artefact. More specifically, as Ajzen (2011) argued, the effect of anticipated regret on intentions and behaviour is only significant when regret is measured with respect to inaction (e.g., failing to exercise) and all the other TPB variables are measured with respect to action (e.g., intending to exercise, believing that exercise is good). When regret and TPB variables are measured in the same direction (e.g., action–action), then the effect of regret on intentions and behaviour becomes non-significant (see Ajzen & Sheikh, 2013). However, other studies have shown that, even when regret and TPB variables are measured in the same direction, anticipated regret has a significant effect on intentions over and above other TPB variables (e.g., Lazuras, Barkoukis, Mallia, Lucidi, & Brand, 2017; Lazuras, Barkoukis, & Tsorbatzoudis, 2015). The "action-inaction" effect has not been extensively examined in the exercise context, and, therefore, future research is needed to establish if anticipated regret effects on exercise intentions and behaviour reflect affective processes in decision-making or should be attributed to methodological artefacts.

With regard to the effects of social norms on behaviour, the TPB has mostly focused on the perceived social approval or disapproval of a given behaviour on intentions (Ajzen, 1991). In exercise settings, this concept of social norms has been weakly associated with exercise intentions and behaviour (Hagger et al., 2002; Hausenblas et al., 1997). An alternative measure of social norms reflects the perceived prevalence of a given behaviour in referent groups (e.g., how many people of my age and gender engage in exercise) and has been commonly described as *descriptive* social norms in other theories of normative influence and intention formation (see Cialdini, 2007; Cialdini, Kallgren, & Reno, 1991; Nolan, Schultz, Cialdini, Goldstein, & Griskevicius, 2008; Rimal, 2008; Rimal & Real, 2005). In the context of the TPB, research has shown that descriptive norms added significant variance in the prediction of intentions and behaviour, on top of subjective norms and other TPB measures (Rivis & Sheeran, 2003a). However, research on the effects of descriptive norms on exercise intentions and behaviour has provided mixed findings. In particular, Rivis and Sheeran (2003b) showed that descriptive norms were significantly associated with exercise intentions, and that the interaction between descriptive norms and prototype similarity (i.e., perceived similarity to the type of person who engages in exercise) predicted actual exercise behaviour on top of other TPB variables among adolescents. Similarly, Smith-McLallen and Fishbein (2008) showed that descriptive norms were associated with exercise intentions over and above other TPB variables among adults aged between 40 and 70 years, but the observed effect size was medium ($\beta = 0.088$, $p < .001$). Other studies (Rhodes & Courneya, 2003; Rivis et al., 2006) did not find a significant association between descriptive norms and exercise intentions when other TPB variables were controlled for. A possible explanation of these findings is that descriptive norms may be associated with more unplanned, spontaneous, and cue-driven action initiation that cannot be captured by TPB measures (e.g., Rivis & Sheeran, 2003a). Nevertheless, further research is needed to better understand how normative influences (and their decomposed measures) are associated with planned and unplanned exercise behaviour.

Another area of research addressed the intention–behaviour gap in exercise settings. Conner, Sandberg, and Norman (2010) found that baseline measures of exercise intentions PBC explained 50% of the variance in exercise behaviour after 2 weeks, and that action planning (i.e., plans that specified when, where, how, and for how long participants would exercise) mediated the effects of exercise intentions on actual behaviour. The mediation effect of action planning was stronger among individuals with higher scores in exercise intentions.

Accordingly, de Bruijn, Rhodes, and van Osch (2012a) showed that attitudes and PBC predicted exercise intentions and behaviour, but the relationship between exercise intentions and actual behaviour was mediated by action planning (i.e., specific plans about where, when and how often to exercise, with whom to exercise, and what type of exercise activity to do). These findings were further corroborated by de Bruin et al. (2012b), who showed that self-regulatory processes, such as monitoring goal progress and responding to discrepancies between goals and actions, explained the association between exercise intentions and actual behaviour.

Beyond the Theory of Planned Behaviour: A Meta-theory Perspective

Meta-theories are theoretical frameworks that try to predict and explain human behaviour by synthesizing aspects and processes derived from different individual theories. The integrative model of behavioural prediction, or, for short, the integrative model (Fishbein, 2000, 2009; Fishbein & Yzer, 2003), is a meta-theory that is directly relevant to the TPB because it incorporates constructs from the TRA, TPB, social-cognitive theory, and the health belief model. Similar to the TPB, the integrative model maintains that attitudes, social norms (descriptive and subjective norms), and behavioural control beliefs (e.g., PBC and self-efficacy) predict intentions, and intentions are recognized as both dependent variables as well as predictors of actual behaviour (Bleakley, Hennessy, Fishbein, & Jordan, 2011; Fishbein, 2000). However, unlike the TPB, the integrative model further distinguishes between two types of predictor variable: Proximal predictors refer to the most immediate antecedents of intentions (i.e., attitudes, social norms, and behavioural control beliefs), and distal (or background) variables represent individual differences in risk perception, personality traits, demographic characteristics, past behaviour, and social influence factors, such as media exposure. In line with the TPB's mediation hypothesis (see Armitage & Conner, 2001; Conner & Armitage, 1998), the integrative model further purports that the effects of distal/background variables on behavioural intentions are fully mediated by the proximal predictors (Fishbein, 2000; Fishbein & Ajzen, 2011). Finally, the relationship between intentions and actual behaviour in the integrative model is determined by environmental constraints on behaviour and by the actor's skills and abilities to successfully perform the behaviour in question.

Although the integrative model has been proposed as an effective psychosocial model in the context of health promotion (Fishbein, 2009; Fishbein & Cappella, 2006), it has been mostly applied in the domain of sexual health and safe sex practices (e.g., Bleakley et al., 2011; Rhodes et al., 2007). In the field of sport and physical activity, the integrative model has informed research on the use of performance-enhancing drugs in sports (e.g., Barkoukis, Lazuras, Tsorbatzoudis, & Rodafinos, 2013; Lazuras et al., 2015), but has not been extensively applied in the study of physical activity and exercise participation and adherence as yet. The available evidence has shown that the integrative model can be usefully applied to predict physical activity participation and screen-time use in children, and that intentions and PBC were associated with physical activity, and attitudes, perceived social norms, and PBC were associated with intentions (Branscum & Crowson, 2017). Nevertheless, one could argue that the application of the integrative model does not offer greater insights into our capacity to understand and predict physical activity participation compared with the TPB (e.g., see McEachan et al., 2011). However, future studies are needed to determine if the theoretical integration of background/distal predictors of the integrative model (e.g., mood, personality traits, demographic variables, etc.) and their assumed mediated effect on intentions generate added value and novel research findings compared with the findings obtained from studies using the original or augmented versions of the TPB in the context of physical activity and exercise participation.

Using the TPB to Inform Physical Activity and Exercise Participation Interventions

The TPB has been used in behaviour change interventions as a guiding theoretical framework to either inform the development of the interventions or to guide the assessment of key outcome variables, such as intentions (Hardeman et al., 2002). Darker, French, Eves, and Sniehotta (2010) used the TPB in an intervention designed to increase walking in the general population that included strategies to improve PBC and walking intentions. It was found that the intervention was effective in increasing PBC, attitudes and intentions towards walking, and actual walking behaviour. Importantly, walking behaviour was maintained 6 weeks following the implementation of the intervention. These findings were further replicated by French, Darker, Eves, and Sniehotta (2013), who used an extended version of the TPB to inform a brief intervention that targeted walking behaviour. They incorporated motivational and volitional strategies in the TPB in an attempt to improve PBC and walking efficacy and found that participants in the intervention group reported significantly stronger self-efficacy and intentions immediately after the intervention, followed by significant increases (mean increase of 87 minutes per week) in objectively assessed walking behaviour 6 weeks post-intervention.

In addition, Chatzisarantis and Hagger (2005) examined the effect of two persuasive communications (i.e., salient belief vs. non-salient belief) based on TPB in promoting physical activity-related cognition and behaviour. This study showed that a salient belief message based on TPB produced more positive attitudes and stronger intentions towards physical activity. Another example of an intervention utilizing the TPB is the one implemented by Haerens et al. (2006) in a school setting. The intervention involved modification of a number of personal (e.g., physical fitness) and environmental (e.g., school activities promoting physical activity) activities related to physical activity and healthy nutrition. Students received tailored feedback about their intentions, attitudes, self-efficacy, social support, knowledge, benefits, and barriers related to physical activity and health nutrition based on the premises of TPB. The results showed that the intervention increased physical activity participation and reduced fat intake. Overall, the findings presented in this section suggest that the TPB can be used to inform interventions aimed to improve physical activity participation in different populations. However, as Michie and Abraham (2004) noted, the reported interventions seldom specify the behaviour change techniques used, and the correspondence between theoretical inspiration and adoption of particular behaviour change techniques tends also to be unclear.

Conclusion

The TPB originated in early work on subjective expected utility theories and is a direct "descendant" of the theory of reasoned action (Ajzen, 1985). The TPB is used to explain volitional behaviours and suggests that intentions to act represent the motivational impetus and the most proximal predictor of actual behaviour. In turn, intentions are shaped on the basis of people's evaluations of the behaviour and its outcomes (attitudes), perceived social approval of the behaviour in question (subjective social norms), and their ability to control the behaviour (PBC); to the extent that PBC reflects actual behavioural control, it is possible that PBC can directly predict behaviour without necessarily requiring the mediation of intentions (Ajzen, 1991). The theoretical parsimony of the TPB has made it a popular and, at the same time, successful theory in numerous studies examining intentional behaviours, including physical activity and exercise participation. Several meta-analyses and review papers have systematically shown that the TPB adequately predicted and explained physical activity and exercise behaviour in different populations and across cultures (Hagger et al., 2002; Hausenblas et al., 1997; Plotnikoff et al., 2013), compared with other social-cognitive theories. Importantly, the TPB has been successfully used to predict exercise intentions and behaviour in both healthy and clinical populations (e.g., Plotnikoff et al., 2008, 2010). However, criticisms of the theory's capacity to leave a large proportion of the variance in intentions and behaviour unexplained, as well as the intention–behaviour gap, have spawned extended versions of the TPB – models that have added theoretically relevant variables to the traditional TPB corpus in order to increase the prediction of intentions and behaviour and/or to improve the predictability of behaviour from intention measures (Conner et al., 2015; Montano & Kasprzyk, 2015). This approach is compatible with Ajzen's recommendation to consider an extended version of the TPB, given that the additions to the model are theoretically relevant, meaningful, and justifiable, and that the prediction of intentions and behaviour is improved by those additions. Importantly, the TPB and its extended variants have informed behaviour-change interventions that successfully improved exercise and physical activity-related behaviour, such as walking behaviour (e.g., French et al., 2013). Nonetheless, the intention–behaviour gap still remains, and some scholars (e.g., Sniehotta et al., 2014) have even argued that it is time to abandon the TPB and consider alternative approaches to predict and explain volitional as well as automatically activated behaviours. So far, however, the TPB has fared well in predicting exercise and physical activity.

Note

1 B = overt behaviour; BI = behavioural intentions; A-act = attitudes to act; NBs = normative beliefs; w = empirically determined weights (e.g., regression coefficients) for each variable in predicting intentions.

References

Abraham, C., & Sheeran, P. (2003). Implications of goal theories for the theories of reasoned action and planned behaviour. *Current Psychology: Developmental, Learning, Personality, Social, 22,* 264–280.

Abraham, C., & Sheeran, P. (2004). Deciding to exercise: The role of anticipated regret. *British Journal of Health Psychology, 9,* 269–278.

Ajzen, I. (1985). From intentions to action: A theory of planned behavior. In J. Kuhl & J. Beckman (Eds.), *Action-control: From cognition to behaviour* (pp. 11–39). Heidelberg: Springer.

Ajzen, I. (1991). The theory of planned behavior. *Organizational Behavior and Human Decision Processes, 50,* 179–211.

Ajzen, I. (2011). The theory of planned behaviour: Reactions and reflections. *Psychology & Health, 26,* 1113–1127.

Ajzen, I., & Fishbein, M. (1969). The prediction of behavioral intentions in a choice situation. *Journal of Experimental and Social Psychology, 5,* 400–416.

Ajzen, I., & Fishbein, M. (1970). The prediction of behavior from attitudinal and normative variables. *Journal of Experimental Social Psychology, 6,* 466–487.

Ajzen, I., & Fishbein, M. (1980). *Understanding attitudes and predicting social behavior.* Englewood Cliffs, NJ: Prentice-Hall.

Ajzen, I., & Sheikh, S. (2013). Action versus inaction: Anticipated affect in the theory of planned behavior. *Journal of Applied Social Psychology, 43*, 155–162.

Armitage, C. J. (2005). Can the theory of planned behavior predict the maintenance of physical activity? *Journal of Health Psychology, 24*, 235–245.

Armitage, C. J., & Conner, M. (2001). Efficacy of the theory of planned behaviour: A meta-analytic review. *British Journal of Social Psychology, 40*, 471–499.

Bamberg, S., Ajzen, I., & Schmidt, P. (2003). Choice of travel mode in the theory of planned behavior: The roles of past behavior, habit, and reasoned action. *Basic and Applied Social Psychology, 25*, 175–188.

Bandura, A. (1977). Self-efficacy: Toward a unifying theory of behavioural change. *Psychological Review, 84*, 191–215.

Bandura, A. (1997). *Self-efficacy: The exercise of control.* New York: W. H. Freeman/Times Books/Henry Holt.

Barkoukis, V., Lazuras, L., Tsorbatzoudis, H., & Rodafinos, A. (2013). Motivational and social cognitive predictors of doping intentions in elite sports: An integrated approach. *Scandinavian Journal of Medicine & Science in Sports, 23*, 330–340.

Beck, B., Daly, R., Singh, M. F., & Taaffe, D. (2017). Exercise and Sports Science Australia (ESSA) position statement on exercise prescription for the prevention and management of osteoporosis. *Journal of Science and Medicine in Sport, 20*, 438–445.

Blanchard, C. M., Courneya, K. S., Rodgers, W. M., Fraser, S. N., Murray, T. C., Daub, B., & Black, B. (2003). Is the theory of planned behavior a useful framework for understanding exercise adherence during Phase II cardiac rehabilitation? *Journal of Cardiopulmonary Rehabilitation, 23*, 29–39.

Blanchard, C. M., Courneya, K. S., Rodgers, W. M., & Murnaghan, D. M. (2002). Determinants of exercise intention and behavior in survivors of breast and prostate cancer: An application of the theory of planned behavior. *Cancer Nursing, 25*, 88–95.

Bleakley, A., Hennessy, M., Fishbein, M., & Jordan, A. (2011). Using the integrative model to explain how exposure to sexual media content influences adolescent sexual behavior. *Health Education & Behavior, 38*, 530–540.

Bolam, K. A., Van Uffelen, J. G., & Taaffe, D. R. (2013). The effect of physical exercise on bone density in middle-aged and older men: A systematic review. *Osteoporosis International, 24*, 2749–2762.

Branscum, P., & Crowson, H. M. (2017). The association between environmental and psychosocial factors towards physical activity and screen time of children: An application of the integrative behavioural model. *Journal of Sports Sciences, 35*, 982–988.

Brewer, N. T., DeFrank, J. T., & Gilkey, M. B. (2016). Anticipated regret and health behavior: A meta-analysis. *Health Psychology, 35*, 1264–1275.

Chatzisarantis, N. L., & Hagger, M. S. (2005). Effects of a brief intervention based on the theory of planned behavior on leisure-time physical activity participation. *Journal of Sport and Exercise Psychology, 27*, 470–487.

Cialdini, R. B. (2007). Descriptive social norms as underappreciated sources of social control. *Psychometrika, 72*, 263–268.

Cialdini, R. B., Kallgren, C. A., & Reno, R. R. (1991). A focus theory of normative conduct: A theoretical refinement and reevaluation of the role of norms in human behavior. In M. P. Zanna (Ed.), *Advances in experimental social psychology* (pp. 201–234). New York: Academic Press.

Colberg, S. R., Sigal, R. J., Yardley, J. E., Riddell, M. C., Dunstan, D. W., Dempsey, P. C., & Tate, D. F. (2016). Physical activity/exercise and diabetes: A position statement of the American Diabetes Association. *Diabetes Care, 39*, 2065–2079.

Conner, M. (2015). Extending not retiring the theory of planned behaviour: A commentary on Sniehotta, Presseau and Araújo-Soares. *Health Psychology Review, 9*, 141–145.

Conner, M., & Armitage, C. J. (1998). Extending the theory of planned behavior: A review and avenues for further research. *Journal of Applied Social Psychology, 28*, 1429–1464.

Conner, M., McEachan, R., Taylor, N., O'Hara, J., & Lawton, R. (2015). Role of affective attitudes and anticipated affective reactions in predicting health behaviors. *Health Psychology, 34*, 642–652.

Conner, M., Sandberg, T., & Norman, P. (2010). Using action planning to promote exercise behavior. *Annals of Behavioral Medicine, 40*, 65–76.

Courneya, K. S., & Friedenreich, C. M. (1997). Relationship between exercise pattern across the cancer experience and current quality of life in colorectal cancer survivors. *Journal of Alternative and Complementary Medicine, 3*, 215–226.

Courneya, K. S., & Friedenreich, C. M. (1999). Physical exercise and quality of life following cancer diagnosis: A literature review. *Annals of Behavioral Medicine, 21,* 171–179.

Courneya, K. S., Friedenreich, C. M., Sela, R. A., Quinney, H. A., & Rhodes, R. E. (2002). Correlates of adherence and contamination in a randomized controlled trial of exercise in cancer survivors: An application of the theory of planned behavior and the five factor model of personality. *Annals of Behavioral Medicine, 24,* 257–268.

Darker, C. D., French, D. P., Eves, F. F., & Sniehotta, F. F. (2010). An intervention to promote walking amongst the general population based on an "extended" theory of planned behaviour: A waiting list randomised controlled trial. *Psychology and Health, 25,* 71–88.

de Bruijn, G. J., Rhodes, R. E., & van Osch, L. (2012a). Does action planning moderate the intention–habit interaction in the exercise domain? A three-way interaction analysis investigation. *Journal of Behavioral Medicine, 35,* 509–519.

de Bruin, M., Sheeran, P., Kok, G., Hiemstra, A., Prins, J. M., Hospers, H. J., & van Breukelen, G. J. (2012b). Self-regulatory processes mediate the intention-behavior relation for adherence and exercise behaviors. *Health Psychology, 31,* 695–704.

De Groot, J. I. M., & Steg, L. (2007). Value orientations and environmental beliefs in five countries: Validity of an instrument to measure egoistic, altruistic and biospheric value orientations. *Journal of Cross-Cultural Psychology, 38,* 318–332.

Downs, D. S., & Hausenblas, H. A. (2005). The theories of reasoned action and planned behavior applied to exercise: A meta-analytic update. *Journal of Physical Activity and Health, 2,* 76–97.

Fishbein, M. (1979). A theory of reasoned action: Some applications and implications. In H. Howe & M. Page (Eds.), *Nebraska symposium on motivation* (pp. 65–116). Lincoln, NE: University of Nebraska Press.

Fishbein, M. (2000). The role of theory in HIV prevention. *AIDS Care, 12,* 273–278.

Fishbein, M. (2009). An integrative model for behavioral prediction and its application to health promotion. In R. J. DiClemente, R. A. Crosby, & M. C. Kegler (Eds.), *Emerging theories in health promotion practice and research* (pp. 215–234). San Francisco, CA: Jossey-Bass.

Fishbein, M., & Ajzen, I. (2011). *Predicting and changing behavior: The reasoned action approach.* New York: Psychology Press.

Fishbein, M., & Cappella, J. N. (2006). The role of theory in developing effective health communications. *Journal of Communication, 56,* 1–17.

Fishbein, M., & Yzer, M. C. (2003). Using theory to design effective health behaviour interventions. *Communication Theory, 13,* 164–183.

French, D. P., Darker, C. D., Eves, F. F., & Sniehotta, F. F. (2013). The systematic development of a brief intervention to increase walking in the general public using an "extended" theory of planned behavior. *Journal of Physical Activity and Health, 10,* 940–948.

Fried, L. P. (2016). Interventions for human frailty: Physical activity as a model. *Cold Spring Harbor Perspectives in Biology, 6*(6), a025916.

Greenwood, B. N., Loughridge, A. B., Sadaoui, N., Christianson, J. P., & Fleshner, M. (2012). The protective effects of voluntary exercise against the behavioral consequences of uncontrollable stress persist despite an increase in anxiety following forced cessation of exercise. *Behavioural Brain Research, 233,* 314–321.

Haasova, M., Warren, F. C., Ussher, M., Van Rensburg, K. J., Faulkner, G., Cropley, M., & Taylor, A. H. (2014). The acute effects of physical activity on cigarette cravings: Exploration of potential moderators, mediators and physical activity attributes using individual participant data (IPD) meta-analyses. *Psychopharmacology, 231,* 1267–1275.

Haerens, L., Deforche, B., Maes, L., Cardon, G., Stevens, V., & De Bourdeaudhuij, I. (2006). Evaluation of a 2-year physical activity and healthy eating intervention in middle school children. *Health Education Research, 21,* 911–921.

Hagger, M. S., Chatzisarantis, N. L. D., Barkoukis, V., Wang, C. K. J., Hein, V., & Pihu, M. (2007). Cross-cultural generalizability of the theory of planned behavior among young people in a physical activity context. *Journal of Sport & Exercise Psychology, 29,* 2–20.

Hagger, M. S., Chatzisarantis, N. L. D., & Biddle, S. J. H. (2002). A meta-analytic review of the theories of reasoned action and planned behavior in physical activity: Predictive validity and the contribution of additional variables. *Journal of Sport & Exercise Psychology, 24,* 3–32.

Halaweh, H., Willen, C., Grimby-Ekman, A., & Svantesson, U. (2015). Physical activity and health-related quality of life among community dwelling elderly. *Journal of Clinical Medicine Research, 7,* 845–852.

Han, H., Hsu, L. T., & Sheu, C. (2010). Application of the theory of planned behavior to green hotel choice: Testing the effect of environmental friendly activities. *Tourism Management, 31,* 325–334.

Hardeman, W., Johnston, M., Johnston, D., Bonetti, D., Wareham, N., & Kinmonth, A. L. (2002). Application of the theory of planned behaviour in behaviour change interventions: A systematic review. *Psychology and Health, 17,* 123–158.

Hausenblas, H. A., Carron, A. V., & Mack, D. E. (1997). Application of the theories of reasoned action and planned behavior to exercise behavior: A meta-analysis. *Journal of Sport & Exercise Psychology, 19,* 36–51.

Hernandez, S. S., Sandreschi, P. F., da Silva, F. C., Arancibia, B. A., da Silva, R., Gutierres, P. J., & Andrade, A. (2015). What are the benefits of exercise for Alzheimer's disease? A systematic review of the past 10 years. *Journal of Aging and Physical Activity, 23,* 659–668.

Holden, R. J., & Karsh, B. T. (2010). The technology acceptance model: Its past and its future in health care. *Journal of Biomedical Informatics, 43,* 159–172.

Hrubes, D., Ajzen, I., & Daigle, J. (2001). Predicting hunting intentions and behavior: An application of the theory of planned behavior. *Leisure Sciences, 23,* 165–178.

Hsu, C. L., Best, J. R., Davis, J. C., Nagamatsu, L. S., Wang, S., Boyd, L. A., & Liu-Ambrose, T. (2018). Aerobic exercise promotes executive functions and impacts functional neural activity among older adults with vascular cognitive impairment. *British Journal of Sports Medicine, 52,* 184–191.

Husebø, A. M. L., Dyrstad, S. M., Søreide, J. A., & Bru, E. (2012). Predicting exercise adherence in cancer patients and survivors: A systematic review and meta-analysis of motivational and behavioural factors. *Journal of Clinical Nursing, 22*(1-2), 4–21.

Jekauc, D., Völkle, M., Wagner, M. O., Mess, F., Reiner, M., & Renner, B. (2015). Prediction of attendance at fitness center: A comparison between the theory of planned behavior, the social cognitive theory, and the physical activity maintenance theory. *Frontiers in Psychology, 6,* 1–8.

Keats, M. R., Culos-Reed, S. N., Courneya, K. S., & McBride, M. (2007). Understanding physical activity in adolescent cancer survivors: An application of the theory of planned behavior. *Psychooncology, 16,* 448–457.

Knabe, A. (2012). *Applying Ajzen's theory of planned behavior to a study of online course adoption in public relations education* (Doctorate dissertation). Marquette University, Milwaukee. Retrieved from http://epublications.marquette.edu/dissertations_mu/186 (Paper 186).

Kohl, H. W., Craig, C. L., Lambert, E. V., Inoue, S., Alkandari, J. R., Leetongin, G., &, & Lancet Physical Activity Series Working Group. (2012). The pandemic of physical inactivity: Global action for public health. *The Lancet, 380,* 294–305.

Lavie, C. J., Arena, R., Swift, D. L., Johannsen, N. M., Sui, X., Lee, D. C., & Blair, S. N. (2015). Exercise and the cardiovascular system: Clinical science and cardiovascular outcomes. *Circulation Research, 117*(2), 207–219.

Lazuras, L., Barkoukis, V., Mallia, L., Lucidi, F., & Brand, R. (2017). More than a feeling: The role of anticipated regret in predicting doping intentions in adolescent athletes. *Psychology of Sport and Exercise, 30,* 196–204.

Lazuras, L., Barkoukis, V., & Tsorbatzoudis, H. (2015). Toward an integrative model of doping use: An empirical study with adolescent athletes. *Journal of Sport & Exercise Psychology, 37,* 37–50.

Lynch, W. J., Peterson, A. B., Sanchez, V., Abel, J., & Smith, M. A. (2013). Exercise as a novel treatment for drug addiction: A neurobiological and stage-dependent hypothesis. *Neuroscience & Biobehavioral Reviews, 37,* 1622–1644.

Martin, R. J., Usdan, S., Nelson, S., Umstattd, M. R., LaPlante, D., Perko, M., & Shaffer, H. (2010). Using the theory of planned behavior to predict gambling behavior. *Psychology of Addictive Behaviors, 24,* 89–97.

McEachan, R. R. C., Conner, M., Taylor, N. J., & Lawton, R. J. (2011). Prospective prediction of health-related behaviours with the theory of planned behaviour: A meta-analysis. *Health Psychology Review, 5,* 97–144.

McKercher, C., Sanderson, K., Schmidt, M. D., Otahal, P., Patton, G. C., Dwyer, T., & Venn, A. J. (2014). Physical activity patterns and risk of depression in young adulthood: A 20-year cohort study since childhood. *Social Psychiatry and Psychiatric Epidemiology, 49,* 1823–1834.

Michie, S., & Abraham, C. (2004). Interventions to change health behaviours: Evidence-based or evidence-inspired? *Psychology & Health, 19,* 29–49.

Montano, D., & Kasprzyk, D. (2015). Theory of reasoned action, theory of planned behavior, and the integrated behavioral model. In K. Glanz, B. K. Rimer, & K. Viswanath (Eds.), *Health behavior: Theory, research, and practice* (pp. 95–124). San Francisco, CA: Jossey-Bass.

Motl, R. W., & Pilutti, L. A. (2012). The benefits of exercise training in multiple sclerosis. *Nature Reviews Neurology, 8,* 487–497.

Motl, R. W., & Sandroff, B. M. (2015). Benefits of exercise training in multiple sclerosis. *Current Neurology and Neuroscience Reports, 15,* 62.

Mura, G., Moro, M. F., Patten, S. B., & Carta, M. G. (2014). Exercise as an add-on strategy for the treatment of major depressive disorder: A systematic review. *CNS Spectrums, 19,* 496–508.

Murphy, E. A., Davis, J. M., Barrilleaux, T. L., McClellan, J. L., Steiner, J. L., Carmichael, M. D., & Green, J. E. (2011). Benefits of exercise training on breast cancer progression and inflammation in C3(1) SV40Tag mice. *Cytokine, 55*(2), 274–279.

Mutrie, N., Campbell, A., Barry, S., Hefferon, K., McConnachie, A., Ritchie, D., & Tovey, S. (2012). Five-year follow-up of participants in a randomised controlled trial showing benefits from exercise for breast cancer survivors during adjuvant treatment. Are there lasting effects? *Journal of Cancer Survivorship, 6,* 420–430.

Nigg, C. R., Lippke, S., & Maddock, J. E. (2009). Factorial invariance of the theory of planned behavior applied to physical activity across gender, age, and ethnic groups. *Psychology of Sport and Exercise, 10,* 219–225.

Nolan, J. P., Schultz, P. W., Cialdini, R. B., Goldstein, N. J., & Griskevicius, V. (2008). Normative social influence is underdetected. *Personality and Social Psychology Bulletin, 34,* 913–923.

Nosek, B. A., Graham, J., Lindner, N. M., Kesebir, S., Hawkins, C. B., Hahn, C., & Tenney, E. R. (2010). Cumulative and career-stage citation impact of social-personality psychology programs and their members. *Personality and Social Psychology Bulletin, 36,* 1283–1300.

Ogden, J. (2003). Some problems with social cognition models: A pragmatic and conceptual analysis. *Health Psychology, 22,* 424–428.

Paillard, T., Rolland, Y., & de Souto Barreto, P. (2015). Protective effects of physical exercise in Alzheimer's disease and Parkinson's disease: A narrative review. *Journal of Clinical Neurology, 11,* 212–219.

Plotnikoff, R. C., Costigan, S. A., Karunamuni, N., & Lubans, D. R. (2013). Social cognitive theories used to explain physical activity behavior in adolescents: A systematic review and meta-analysis. *Preventive Medicine, 56,* 245–253.

Plotnikoff, R. C., Courneya, K. S., Trinh, L., Karunamuni, N., & Sigal, R. J. (2008). Aerobic physical activity and resistance training: An application of the theory of planned behavior among adults with Type 2 diabetes in a random, national sample of Canadians. *International Journal of Behavioral Nutrition and Physical Activity, 5*(61), 1–14.

Plotnikoff, R. C., Lippke, S., Trinh, L., Courneya, K. S., Birkett, N., & Sigal, R. J. (2010). Protection motivation theory and the prediction of physical activity among adults with Type 1 or Type 2 diabetes in a large population sample. *British Journal of Health Psychology, 15,* 643–661.

Rhodes, R. E., & Courneya, K. S. (2003). Investigating multiple components of attitude, subjective norm, and perceived control: An examination of the theory of planned behaviour in the exercise domain. *British Journal of Social Psychology, 42,* 129–146.

Rhodes, S. D., Eng, E., Hergenrather, K. C., Remnitz, I. M., Arceo, R., Montaño, J., & Alegria-Ortega, J. (2007). Exploring Latino men's HIV risk using community-based participatory research. *American Journal of Health Behavior, 31,* 146–158.

Rimal, R. V. (2008). Modeling the relationship between descriptive norms and behaviors: A test and extension of the theory of normative social behavior (TNSB). *Health Communication, 23,* 103–116.

Rimal, R. V., & Real, K. (2005). How behaviors are influenced by perceived norms: A test of the theory of normative social behaviour? *Communication Research, 32,* 389–414.

Rivis, A., & Sheeran, P. (2003a). Social influences and the theory of planned behaviour: Evidence for a direct relationship between prototypes and young people's exercise behaviour. *Psychology and Neuroscience, 18,* 567–583.

Rivis, A., & Sheeran, P. (2003b). Descriptive norms as an additional predictor in the theory of planned behaviour: A meta-analysis. *Current Psychology, 22,* 218–233.

Rivis, A., Sheeran, P., & Armitage, C. J. (2006). Augmenting the theory of planned behaviour by the prototype/willingness model: Predictive validity of actor versus abstainer prototypes for adolescents' health protective and health risk intentions. *British Journal of Health Psychology, 11,* 483–500.

Ruegsegger, G. N., & Booth, F. W. (2018). Health benefits of exercise. *Cold Spring Harbor Perspectives in Medicine, 8,* 1–16.

Sandberg, T., & Conner, M. (2008). Anticipated regret as an additional predictor in the theory of planned behaviour: A meta-analysis. *British Journal of Social Psychology, 47,* 589–606.

Smith-McLallen, A., & Fishbein, M. (2008). Predictors of intentions to perform six cancer-related behaviours: Roles for injunctive and descriptive norms. *Psychology, Health & Medicine, 13*, 389–401.

Sniehotta, F. F., Presseau, J., & Araújo-Soares, V. (2014). Time to retire the theory of planned behaviour. *Health Psychology Review, 8*, 1–7.

Trinh, L., Plotnikoff, R. C., Rhodes, R. E., North, S., & Courneya, K. S. (2012). Physical activity preferences in population-based sample of kidney cancer survivors. *Supportive Care in Cancer, 20*, 1709–1717.

Trost, S. G., Pate, R. R., Dowda, M., Ward, D. S., Felton, G., & Saunders, R. (2002). Psychosocial correlates of physical activity in white and African-American girls. *Journal of Adolescent Health, 31*, 226–233.

Warburton, D. E., Nicol, C. W., & Bredin, S. S. (2006). Health benefits of physical activity: The evidence. *Canadian Medical Association Journal, 174*, 801–809.

Wasser, J. G., Vasilopoulos, T., Zdziarski, L. A., & Vincent, H. K. (2017). Exercise benefits for chronic low back pain in overweight and obese individuals. *PM&R, 9*, 181–192.

Webb, T. L., & Sheeran, P. (2006). Does changing behavioral intentions engender behavior change? A meta-analysis of the experimental evidence. *Psychological Bulletin, 132*, 249–268.

Wen, C. P., Wai, J. P. M., Tsai, M. K., Yang, Y. C., Cheng, T. Y., Lee, M. C., & Wu, X. (2011). Minimum amount of physical activity for reduced mortality and extended life expectancy: A prospective cohort study. *The Lancet, 378*, 1244–1253.

White, K. M., Terry, D. J., Troup, C., Rempel, L. A., Norman, P., Mummery, K., & Kenardy, J. (2012). An extended theory of planned behavior intervention for older adults with Type 2 diabetes and cardiovascular disease. *Journal of Aging and Physical Activity, 20*, 281–299.

Wilson, M. G., Ellison, G. M., & Cable, N. T. (2016). Basic science behind the cardiovascular benefits of exercise. *British Journal of Sports Medicine, 50*, 93–99.

Wise, E. K., Hoffman, J. M., Powell, J. M., Bombardier, C. H., & Bell, K. R. (2012). Benefits of exercise maintenance after traumatic brain injury. *Archives of Physical Medicine and Rehabilitation, 93*, 1319–1323.

Zeelenberg, M. (1999). Anticipated regret, expected feedback, and behavioral decision making. *Journal of Behavioral Decision Making, 12*, 93–106.

Zeelenberg, M., & Pieters, R. (2007). A theory of regret regulation 1.0. *Journal of Consumer Psychology, 17*, 3–18.

36

POSITIVE YOUTH DEVELOPMENT

A Sport and Exercise Psychology Perspective

Diane L. Gill and Michael A. Hemphill

Introduction

Positive youth development (PYD) has become a popular topic in sport and exercise psychology in recent years. As Weiss (2016) pointed out in her chapter titled "Old wine in a new bottle", the topic is not really new, but repackaged. And, with the newer wave, we have some sport-specific models/frameworks, programmes, and research findings.

So, what is PYD? First, it is about youth development and, more specifically, it is about holistic development, including psychosocial, emotional, and cognitive, as well as physical, development. Second, it is positive, and, in line with positive psychology, PYD focuses on strength-building and assets. Holt et al. (2017) draw from the major developmental psychology work to define PYD as: "a strength-based conception of development in which children and adolescents are viewed as having 'resources to be developed' rather than problem's to be solved" (p. 1). Holt is one of the active sport and exercise scholars of PYD today, but we can find work that we would now identify as PYD much earlier.

Historical Perspective on PYD

Early Roots

The roots of PYD in sport and physical activity extend back to early physical education works, before sport and exercise psychology (SEP) was an identifiable field. Williams, a key leader in early physical education, was known for his call for "education through the physical", widely distributed in the first edition of his *The Principles of Physical Education* (1927) and multiple editions after that. Williams essentially was calling for emphasis on holistic development, through physical education. McCloy (1930), another early leader, published his article "Character Building through Physical Education" in the first year of the *Research Quarterly*. In that article, McCloy wrote, "Physical educators have for years claimed to be builders of character ... the evidence is not impressive" (p. 41). McCloy is often set up on one side of the "of the physical" versus "through the physical," debate, but, in his 1940 book, he specifically called on the field to move beyond the "old mind–body dualism". McCloy (1940, p. 116) stated: "Education of the physical? Education through the physical? We need to forget this division, which smacks too much of the old mind–body dualism. We cannot separate them." Indeed, like Williams, McCloy took a holistic view of development. His 1930 article presented a challenge to scholars to develop the evidence base for what we now know as PYD.

As with many topics in SEP, we can find earlier roots in early psychology works. Developmental psychology is the obvious source, but here we take a sidetrack to highlight the work of Lewin (the first author's social psychology hero). Lewin's work is familiar and widely cited in SEP, particularly his deceptively simple model of behaviour, $B = f(P, E)$ (Lewin, 1935), which denotes the complex, dynamic interaction of person and environment characteristics in determining behaviour, and his often-quoted statement, "there is nothing so practical as a good theory". That classic line is from a call to scholars to look to the real world:

> This can be accomplished … if the theorist does not look toward applied problems with highbrow aversion or with a fear of social problems, and if the applied psychologist realizes that there is nothing so practical as a good theory.
>
> *(Lewin, 1951, p. 169)*

Both Lewin's recognition of the complexity of behaviour and his call for scholars to address real-world problems are particularly relevant to PYD. Youth development is a complex, dynamic process influenced by multiple factors. And PYD, at its best, applies psychology to address real-world problems. Furthermore, Lewin lived up to his calls. He is widely recognized as the originator of "action research" and devoted much of his efforts to social development and social justice.

PYD in Sport and Exercise Psychology

As SEP was developing as an identifiable field in the 1970s and 1980s, several scholars focused on youth development in sport, most notably Weiss and Gould, who have continued that work and mentored many students and colleagues along the way. The later sections of this chapter highlight much of that research. At the same time that SEP had scholars focusing on youth development, other scholars branched out from traditional physical education pedagogy to focus on more holistic development within physical education, often extending into community-based programmes. Hellison's (e.g., 1983) early innovative community work with underserved youth, focusing on teaching personal and social responsibility, is particularly notable. Several scholars coming from pedagogy backgrounds have followed Hellison's model or developed lines of community-based youth development programmes, and much of that work is reviewed in later sections. Although the SEP and pedagogy scholars come from differing backgrounds and sub-areas, the research lines on PYD overlap in many ways, including the focus on holistic development and in their guiding models and frameworks.

PYD Models and Frameworks

Most of the current SEP work on PYD draws from developmental psychology models, and some scholars have drawn from those models to develop models more specific to sport and physical activity programmes. In the concluding chapter of Holt's 2016 book, Holt, Deal, and Smyth (2016) offered the following guiding definition: PYD through sport is intended to facilitate youth development via experiences and processes that enable participants in adult-supervised programmes to gain transferable personal and social *life skills* along with physical competencies. These skill and competency outcomes will enable participants in youth sport programmes to thrive and to contribute to their communities, both now and in the future (p. 231). That guiding definition highlights elements particularly relevant to PYD research and programmes in sport and physical activity. First, sport is clearly defined as encompassing all forms of sport and physical activity, such as recreational sport and after-school activity programmes. In our PYD programmes, adult leaders have a key role in designing and providing experiences and processes. The target outcomes are life skills that are generalizable and transferable outside the specific programme, and those outcomes include physical competencies. Finally, the programmes serve communities as well as individual participants; indeed, many sport-based PYD programmes are community-based.

PYD Frameworks

The leading SEP researchers and current PYD work (e.g., Gould & Carson, 2008; Petitpas, Cornelius, Van Raalte, & Jones, 2005; Weiss, 2011) draw from Benson's developmental assets, Lerner's 5Cs and Larson's developmental or growth experiences. Benson's (2006) developmental assets include 20 internal or personal assets (e.g., integrity, self-esteem, competence) and 20 external or social assets (e.g., family support, positive peer influence). The 5Cs approach (Lerner, Almerigi, Theokas, & Lerner, 2005) includes character, caring, competence, confidence, and connection, with a sixth C – contribution – added as a result of demonstrating all five Cs. In Larson's (2000) developmental model, youth develop personal skills (e.g., initiative, problem-solving) and interpersonal skills (group process skills, peer relationships) through growth experiences. In all these approaches, PYD, in line with positive psychology, focuses on developing strengths.

PYD programmes have often been developed for underserved or marginalized youth. In recognition of the profound influence of social class, ethnicity, race, and other cultural factors on development, scholars have extended the models and research. Coll and colleagues (1996) developed an integrative model for developmental research with minority children, based on social stratification theory, that explicitly emphasizes the role of racism, prejudice, discrimination, oppression, and segregation in creating promoting/inhibiting environments and the development of minority children and families. More recently, a special issue of *American Psychologist* focused on the contributions of the Coll et al. (1996) model and reconsideration of guiding models for work with youth experiencing marginalization. In the lead article introducing that special issue, Causadias and Umaña-Taylor (2018) defined marginalization as a multidimensional, dynamic, context-dependent, and diverse web of processes, rooted in power imbalance and systematically directed toward specific groups and individuals, with probabilistic implications for development (p. 707). Many aspects of that definition align with PYD frameworks, while highlighting the multiple, powerful ways the sociocultural context influences development. In an article in that special issue, Gaylord-Harden, Barbarin, Tolan, and McBride Murry (2018) specifically adopt a PYD framework, focusing on strengths and using development assets, along with adaptive calibration to contextual challenges, to account for prosocial development of African American boys and young men.

Much of the SEP PYD research adopts those developmental frameworks in focusing on the development of personal and interpersonal skills or assets and creating a supportive, learning-oriented climate. Also, as nearly everyone who has developed programmes or conducted research related to PYD has noted, youth sport programmes do not automatically result in positive outcomes; character is not caught in youth sport, but must be taught by trained, informed leaders; interventions can promote PYD, but only when they are intentionally designed to do so.

Models for Sport and Physical Activity

Several SEP scholars have drawn from the psychology frameworks to develop models specific to sport and physical activity. Based on the youth sport literature at the time, Petitpas et al. (2005) proposed that positive psychological growth is most likely to occur when young athletes: (a) are engaged in a desired activity within an appropriate environment (context), (b) are surrounded by caring adult mentors and a positive group or community (external assets), (c) learn or acquire skills (internal assets) that are important for managing life situations, and (4) benefit from the findings of a comprehensive system of evaluation and research.

Gould and Carson (2008) presented a model of life skills development through sport that begins with internal and external assets from the developmental assets profile. The next part focuses on the sport experience, with emphasis on coach competencies and both direct and indirect teaching of life skills. The middle component offers possible explanations for the development of life skills, first in terms of social environment influences and second with the utility of the life skill strategies themselves. The final component of the model focuses on the transferability of life skills to nonsporting aspects of life.

Hodge Model

Hodge and colleagues (Hodge, Danish, Forneris, & Miles, 2016; Hodge, Danish, & Martin, 2012) developed a model that integrates the three basic needs (autonomy, competence, relatedness) and need-supportive motivational climate from self-determination theory into the life development intervention framework, which focuses on self-directed, goal-directed change into their life skills development model. More specifically, the model suggests that, when the life skills programme creates a need-supportive motivational climate, and the basic needs are then satisfied, then the desired outcome – enhanced personal and interpersonal competence – can be achieved.

Holt Model

Most recently, Holt and colleagues (2017) used a grounded theory approach with results from a qualitative meta-study to create a model of PYD through sport. That model begins by highlighting the social-ecological systems that frame the context and also considers individual characteristics. Those distal systems and individual characteristics affect behaviours and the PYD climate. Within the PYD programme, the social climate (relationships with adults and peers) affects outcomes. The meta-study also highlighted the key role of a life skill programme focus, involving life skill building activities and transfer activities. Holt et al. (2017) explicitly proposed that the combined effects of a PYD climate and life skills focus will produce more PYD outcomes than a PYD climate alone. Finally, gaining PYD outcomes (social, personal, physical) will facilitate transfer and enable youth to thrive and contribute to their communities.

Both the Hodge and Holt models stem from continuing SEP research on PYD in sport and draw from the development models (e.g., Lerner et al., 2005) discussed earlier. Two other models prominent in youth development take different approaches. Hellison's model stems from his community-based programme and focuses on personal-social development with little attention to physical skill development. In contrast, Côté and colleagues' model emphasizes talent development in sport. Although those two models seem at opposite extremes, Harwood and Johnston (2016) suggested that it is possible, and desirable, to combine PYD with talent development.

Developmental Model of Sport Participation

Côté and colleagues (Côté, Baker, & Abernethy, 2007; Côté, Hancock, & Abernethy, 2014) proposed the developmental model of sport participation (DMSP) with the following three stages:

1 Sampling years (age 6–13). Emphasis is on play and a wide range of activities.
2 Specializing years (age 13–15). Youth invest significantly more time and effort in a few sports, with a balance between deliberate play and practice.
3 Investment years (ages 15–20). The focus switches to achieving elite levels in one sport with considerable time and effort dedicated to deliberate practice.

Côté and colleagues' developmental model works for most elite athletes; whereas a few successfully specialize very early, many more reach elite levels through the DMSP. More importantly, the DMSP is clearly the better path for the 99.9% of youth participants who will never reach elite levels. In early stages, the emphasis is on fun and sampling a range of sport and physical activities. By emphasizing play (vs. practice and training) and with encouragement and support in the early years, parents and leaders provide opportunities for children to develop fundamental motor skills as well as enhancing motivation and positive attitudes. Côté et al. argue that, even in later stages, emphasis on developing physical skills and literacy within holistic PYD models better serves the wide range of youth participants.

Teaching Personal and Social Responsibility

The teaching personal and social responsibility (TPSR) framework includes core values and assumptions, the levels of responsibility, and moves into programme leader responsibilities, programme format, strategies, problem-solving, and assessment. Hellison (2011) describes the core value underlying the programme as putting kids first or being youth-centred. Holistic self-development is a complementary value, noting that physical development takes place along with emotional, social, and cognitive development in TPSR. As a final value, Hellison describes TPSR as not a way of teaching, but a way of being.

Levels of responsibility are the most visible and widely cited part of TPSR. The five levels and the components of each (Hellison, 2011) are listed below.

1 Level I: Respecting the rights and feelings of others. Components of respect are self-control, right to peaceful conflict resolution, and right to be included and to have cooperative peers.
2 Level II: Effort and cooperation. The components are self-motivation, exploration of effort and new tasks, and getting along with others.
3 Level III: Self-direction. The components are on-task independence, goal-setting progression, and courage to resist peer pressure.
4 Level IV: Helping others and leadership. The components are caring and compassion, sensitivity and responsiveness, and inner strength.
5 Level V: Transfer outside the gym. The components are trying these ideas in other areas of life and being a positive role model for others, especially for younger kids.

Each higher level encompasses all lower levels. People can, and often do, function at multiple levels. For example, a student may engage in self-directed play and cooperate with others one minute and shout at and blame another player the next minute. Although the levels are highlighted, TPSR is broader and more nuanced, relying on adult leaders who guide and gradually shift responsibility so that students have opportunities to feel empowered, purposeful, and connected to others, as well as to experience responsible behaviour, persevere, and acknowledge activities that impinge upon others.

Typical TPSR sessions start with brief relational time before the actual lesson begins with awareness talks in which students learn about the importance of the levels. During the lesson, in which physical activity takes the most time, students experience the levels in action. For example, students may play an inclusion game to stress that everyone has a right to participate. Opportunities for individual decision-making, such as choosing activities, are built into instruction. The lessons always close with reflection time in which students discuss the degree to which they have been respectful of others, involved in the programme, self-directed, and helpful to others.

These models and frameworks have guided the expanding research on PYD and also helped to refine the models and provide direction for PYD programmes. The following sections review that research.

PYD Research

Several of the works on models cited in the previous section have also reviewed the related research. This section first highlights some of the major findings and conclusions based on the research reviews, focusing on several research programmes that extend over multiple studies, and then highlights current research on the primary PYD psychosocial outcomes, as well as recent work on the "old" topic of character development and moral behaviour.

Several of the reviews and earlier works have highlighted the need for research, as well as the challenges particular to PYD research. In 1982, Gould reviewed youth sport research and called for future research focusing on developing theory, using multiple methods, and conducting interrelated rather than isolated studies. Several scholars have followed that approach, but, as Weiss (2016) noted, evaluation research, which is common in broader PYD, is rare in sport-related PYD. Research on PYD programmes faces many challenges. Programmes typically have multiple components and variations, making it difficult to draw any conclusion about why or how the programme might promote PYD. It must also be recognized that youth development is a complex ongoing process that occurs in multiple contexts; development in one PYD programme necessarily presents a limited view. Assessment is also a persistent issue, not only for measuring outcomes, but also for assessing programme components. Finally, for some PYD leaders, academic scholarship is low priority, as their focus is on serving the youth and communities. Despite those challenges, several reviews of the growing scholarship provide some consistent findings, and several researchers have developed programmatic studies that lead to continuing advances in our understanding of PYD in sport and physical activity.

Bean and colleagues (Bean, Harlow, Mosher, Fraser-Thomas, & Forneris, 2018) have taken a step toward advancing programme evaluation with the programme quality assessment in youth sport observation measure. They used that measure with 24 sport programmes and formed two clusters – high- and low-quality programmes. Survey results of athletes in those programmes of needs support, needs satisfaction, and developmental experiences revealed that athletes in high-quality programmes perceived greater opportunities for autonomy, relatedness, and choice, and lower negative experiences compared with athletes in low-quality programmes.

PYD Research Reviews

Weiss, Kipp, and Bolter (2012) framed their extensive review of PYD through sport research in Lerner et al.'s 5Cs model and grouped research into social, psychological, and physical assets. Social assets include peer group acceptance, friendship quality, and morale development, as well as relationships with peers, coaches, and parents. Psychological assets included self-conceptions, emotions, and motivational orientations. Physical assets included fundamental motor skills, sport-specific skills, fitness, physical activity, and physical health – all critical in promoting a physically active lifestyle. Weiss (2016) is a persistent advocate for including the physical domain in PYD and notably puts the emphasis on physical activity rather than sport.

In their review, Eime, Young, Harvey, Charity, and Payne (2013) concluded that there is substantive evidence for many psychological and social benefits, but cautioned that the evidence was limited and largely cross-sectional, with no randomized control studies.

Gould, Cowburn, and Shields (2014) summarized the evidence on psychological and social outcomes of youth sport participation, noting that there is good evidence for benefits, such as enhanced confidence, prosocial values, positive affect, formation of positive relationships, and teamwork skills. Several studies have used the Youth Experiences Scale (Hansen & Larson, 2007), which assesses a wide range of developmental outcomes, with youth sport (Gould & Carson, 2011; Gould, Flett, & Lauer, 2012; Larson, Hansen, & Moneta, 2006). Those results show that young athletes learn personal skills (e.g., setting goals, exerting effort, problem-solving, time management), as well as social skills (e.g., compromising, giving/receiving feedback, leadership). Gould et al. (2014) highlighted the importance of climate, specifically a mastery motivational climate and a caring climate, in achieving positive developmental outcomes.

Holt et al. (2017), in their more recent qualitative meta-study and review, found similar major PYD outcomes grouped into three main domains – personal, social, and physical. Personal outcomes were primarily self-perceptions, including confidence and self-esteem, academic benefits, perseverance, respect, independence and taking personal responsibility, problem-solving skills, and stress management. Social outcomes reported in the research included friendships, teamwork, leadership, and communication skills. Physical outcomes included fundamental movement skills and skills for healthy active living. Notably, there were far fewer reports of physical outcomes: Only 7 studies reported outcomes in the physical domain, whereas outcomes in the personal and social domains were reported in 30 and 32 studies, respectively.

PYD Programme Research

Several PYD programmes have extended over time, with ongoing evaluative assessments. For example, Project Effort and its expanded Youth Leader Corps, a TPSR-based, after-school programme led by Tom Martinek, has been operating successfully over 25 years (e.g., Hemphill & Martinek, 2017; Martinek & Hellison, 2016). TPSR-based programmes have been implemented successfully in school physical education (Hemphill, Templin, & Wright, 2015), as well as after-school programmes (Gordon, Jacobs, & Wright, 2016).

Other sport-based PYD programmes have been implemented in community settings. Although squash might seem an unlikely candidate for a sport-based PYD programme with youth from disadvantaged communities, Chucktown Squash Scholars, a partnership with the College of Charleston and 11 Title I schools, provides a model (Hemphill & Richards, 2016). That programme was affiliated with the National Urban Squash and Education Association, which developed a model emphasizing academic and life skills development. The Charleston programme included equal time with activity (squash) and academic learning skills and mentoring.

In one of the few comprehensive evaluations of PYD programmes, Weiss and colleagues (Weiss, 2008; Weiss, Bolter, & Kipp, 2014, 2016; Weiss, Stuntz, Bhalla, Bolter, & Price, 2013) conducted a longitudinal evaluation of the First Tee programme. The First Tee is a sport-based PYD programme teaching life skills and promoting positive psychosocial and behavioural outcomes through the sport of golf. In the first phase (Weiss et al., 2013), they conducted focus groups and interviews with youth, coaches, and parents on the curriculum, coaching, and generalization of life skills learned in the programme. They reported converging evidence for programme effectiveness on developing interpersonal and emotion management skills. In the second phase (Weiss et al., 2014), they used Phase 1 results to develop and validate quantitative measures of life skill transfer. In the third phase, they included youth in other organized activities for comparison on life skill transfer and development outcomes. The First Tee youth compared favourably with youth in other activities on most dimensions of life skills transfer and developmental outcomes. The findings provide evidence that the First Tee has a positive effect on promoting life skills and core values among youth participants within a golf context, and also in the transfer to other domains. They further suggested that the programme is effective because of the synergy among the context (golf), external assets (delivery by trained coaches), internal assets (life skills guided by intentional curriculum), and development outcomes.

All sport-based PYD programmes focus on life skills that generalize and transfer outside the programmes. However, transfer is one of the major challenges in the programmes, and in research. As noted earlier, transfer is the highest and most challenging level in the TPSR model. Walsh, Ozaeta, and Wright (2010) found youth were able to transfer some TPSR goals from the gym to school when instructors used deliberate strategies to promote transfer. Others found transfer more challenging, prompting Martinek and Lee (2012) to propose a framework for transfer with three interconnected elements: (1) participants' awareness of values, (2) school's awareness and support of programme goals, and (3) a set of transfer strategies. Jacobs and Wright (2016) offered practical suggestions, including imagery, for youth leaders to promote transfer. More recently, they offered a model for transfer of life skills focusing on a cognitive bridging process, with youth coming to understand life skills and how they can apply beyond sports (Jacobs & Wright, 2018). Turnnidge, Côté, and Hancock (2014) outlined issues and challenges with transfer in PYD programmes and specifically noted the importance of fostering continued participation and providing opportunities for excitement, skills development, and connections with peers.

Overall, PYD programmes are in line with developmental theories and research, and the research within SEP provides evidence that well-designed programmes that intentionally target psychological and social development in a mastery-oriented, caring climate do indeed foster positive developmental skills. However, we seem to have lost sight of physical development. PYD includes physical development, although it receives little attention in developmental psychology, but physical development is a primary and unique target for many sport and physical activity programmes. Dzewaltowski and Rosenkranz (2014) argue that PYD should more explicitly focus on physical activity as the primary outcome to promote lifelong participation. As Weiss and Wiese-Bjornstal (2009) emphasized, physical competencies contribute to psychosocial development and commitment to physical activity. Fundamental motor skills are prerequisite to mastering sport-specific skills, and, more importantly, physical skills and physical literacy are keys to maintaining lifelong physical activity with all its related health benefits. Weiss (2011) contends that PYD should include both motor skills development and physical activity and health goals.

PYD and Social Missions

The role of sport and physical activity in social development has extended beyond individual social skills. As discussed in a 2016 ISSP position stand (Schinke, Stambulova, Lidor, Papaioannou, & Ryba, 2016), SEP is expanding to social missions that aim to promote social change leading to betterment for individuals, groups, communities, countries, and world regions. Social missions using sport include PYD and often extend to broader social issues such as sport for peace or sport for cultural exchange and social justice.

As Schinke et al. note, a long-standing belief in the social virtues of sport (character development) has prompted use of sport for social missions. They also note that sport can foster violence, exploitation, discrimination, and nationalism. Critical sport studies scholars have rightly criticized sport for development programmes, particularly those that go into underdeveloped countries or target underserved populations with little understanding of the particular cultural context. As with all PYD programmes, programmes with social missions must be intentionally designed to foster positive outcomes, with attention to the needs and cultural context of participants. Some PYD researchers have developed extended programmes following those guidelines.

Maro, Roberts, and Sørensen (2009) developed a community-based soccer programme in Tanzania aimed at reducing the high rate of HIV infection in youth aged 15–25. In the programme, peer coaches were trained to teach not only soccer skills, but also HIV/AIDS prevention strategies. The project also involved a soccer group with a mastery motivational climate and two control groups, one receiving regular school education on the topic and another with no education. HIV/AIDS education was more effective with the two soccer groups.

Whitley, Forneris, and Barker, who have each been involved in community-based youth development programmes using TPSR or PYD life skills approaches, have outlined the issues and challenges involved in implementing, sustaining, and evaluating programmes in a series of articles (Forneris, Whitley, & Barker, 2013; Whitley, Forneris, & Barker, 2014, 2015). Although each of the programmes involved faced some unique challenges, common challenges that are faced by many programmes with social missions also arose. Similarly, many of their recommendations, or lessons learned, reflect those in the ISSP position statement, as well as PYD models and guidelines. For example, Forneris et al. (2013) recommended involving community members in the planning and implementation and maintaining consistent contact with leaders and organizations during and after the programme. Training for all staff, recruiting bilingual leaders, and having resources for leaders are also in line with ISSP recommendations. Sustaining the programme is always an issue, and an especially important one for social development and PYD programmes. Challenges, such as building strong relationships with community partners, knowledge translations, and funding, may be addressed with strategies of planning, capacity building, recruitment, and evaluation. In reviewing PYD programmes with marginalized populations, Forneris, Bean, and Halsall (2016) identified key strategies as providing a safe and fun environment, intentional activities to develop life skills, and intentional opportunities to provide leadership roles that can lead to greater capacity building. They also called for more rigorous evaluation research, including long-term research, research on life skills transfer, and research extending beyond the individual to community impact. Finally, they cited the critical importance of knowledge translation into the community.

Blom and colleagues (2015) described their experiences with US and international sport for development and peace programmes. They highlighted the importance of establishing partnerships, developing curriculum, training programme staff, monitoring and evaluation, and sustaining programmes. All these recommendations and the ISSP position stand call for advance planning, continuing involvement of community partners, culturally relevant approaches, and continued reflection and evaluation. Perhaps one of the strongest recommendations for anyone considering such a programme is to go in with the long view – start by planning for a programme that will continue and be self-sustaining, even if you are no longer there. Those sentiments are echoed by the major researchers and programme leaders in PYD.

Current PYD Research

As well as the major findings evident in the reviews, some recent studies shed some insight on PYD processes within sport and physical activity. Ullrich-French and Cole (2018) looked at changes in psychosocial outcomes in the Girls on the Run (GOTR) programme. GOTR is a national programme based on PYD principles. In their first study they looked at changes in self-perceptions and tested a measure of physical self-worth, perceived competence, and emotional self-efficacy, as well as autonomy support. As well as getting support for their measure, they found increases in perceived competence and self-worth, and moreover, those changes were predicted by autonomy support. Those specific findings highlight the important role of a supportive, empowering climate in PYD. In their second study, they looked at individual characteristics and found that girls who started low (less positive self-perceptions) made the greatest gains.

Bruner and colleagues (Bruner et al., 2017) focused on social identity and social relationships in PYD. With a large sample of youth in recreational sports, they found that social identity, including perceptions of belonging, bonding, and importance of being a team member, were positively associated with personal and social skills. Those findings reflect Weiss and Kipp's (2018) key point in their chapter in the Tucker Center Report on developing physically active girls. As their title stated, "Social relationships rock!" More to the point, they reviewed considerable evidence and concluded that the key differences between positive and negative outcomes for girls in organized sport and physical activity concern quality of interactions and relationships with parents, coaches, and teammates.

Moral Development and Prosocial Behaviour

Before PYD was a major topic in SEP, some scholars, particularly Bredemeier, Shields, and colleagues, focused on moral development. Bredemeier and Shields (1986, 1995, 2014; Shields & Bredemeier, 2014) took a developmental approach to moral behaviour in sport and applied Haan's (1991) interactional model, which emphasizes moral reasoning and balancing interests of self and others. As people mature, moral reasoning becomes more comprehensive and complex, moving from self-concern, to other-concern, to principled social welfare. However, as they suggested with their work on game reasoning and bracketed morality, the context of sport may promote a morality different from that of everyday life. Importantly, Shields and Bredemeier (2014) applied the theories and research to promote moral reasoning and reduce antisocial behaviour in sport. Specifically, they call for dialogue as a key strategy. That is, coaches, youth leaders, or parents should engage participants in discussion about moral issues to promote higher levels of reasoning and reduce antisocial behaviour. Those calls are in line with key components of PYD programmes and models.

Shields and Bredemeier (2014) have extended their research to character development, which includes intellectual character (e.g., curiosity, critical thinking), civic character (e.g., social organization, rights and responsibilities), and performance character (e.g., resilience, emotional control), as well as moral character. Similarly, the Fair Play for Kids programme, developed more than 20 years ago, draws on the moral behaviour and development literature. Fair Play for Kids incorporates fair play principles (e.g., respect for rules and others, and self-control) into all classroom settings. Gibbons, Ebbeck, and Weiss (1995) investigated the effects of Fair Play for Kids on the moral judgement, reasoning, intention, and behaviour of fourth- and sixth-graders. After 7 months, groups incorporating Fair Play for Kids scored higher than the control groups on moral judgement, reasoning, intention, and behaviour. In a follow-up study, Gibbons and Ebbeck (1997) found higher moral judgement, intention, and behaviour in only 4 months and concluded that the systematic implementation of effective teaching strategies led to student growth in moral reasoning. As with more recent PYD research, the findings suggest intentional design- and life skill-focused activities are key.

Maria Kavussanu and colleagues have conducted much of the research on aggression and moral behaviour in SEP (e.g., Kavussanu, 2014), and some of that research focuses on youth programmes. That research has identified both individual and situational factors as antecedents of aggressive behaviour. The main individual factors are goal orientations and moral disengagement. Goal orientation refers to the extent to which an individual is task-oriented (self-referenced, focusing on mastery and improvement) or ego-oriented (focused on comparison with others and competitive outcomes). Generally, research indicates that those who are high in task orientation are more likely to engage in prosocial behaviours, whereas those high in ego orientation are more likely to engage in antisocial behaviours. Moral disengagement refers to cognitive mechanisms people use to justify antisocial behaviour without experiencing negative emotions (e.g., guilt). For example, athletes might displace responsibility to the coach, blame the victim, or downplay the negative consequences.

The social environment also has a strong influence on moral behaviour. As Bredemeier and Shields (1986, 2014) suggest, the sport context has unique moral features. For example, sport competition has opposing teams, so that pursuit of self-interest is expected, and moral responsibility is concentrated in the roles of officials.

Motivational climate is the environmental factor that has received the most research attention – both in SEP research on moral behaviour and PYD. Motivational climate parallels goal orientation, but climate is environmental and typically is created by coaches, teachers, or parents. Competitive outcomes are emphasized in a performance climate, whereas mastery and improvement are emphasized in a mastery climate. Research shows that a mastery climate is associated with prosocial behaviour, as well as overall PYD. Although most SEP research on moral behaviour involves aggression in sport, research has been extended to other physical activity settings and a wider range of moral behaviours, more relevant to PYD, including *bullying*.

Bullying

Bullying is clearly antisocial behaviour and relevant to SEP; much bullying takes place in schools, often in sport and physical activity settings. Hymel and Swearer (2015), in an introduction to a special issue of the *American Psychologist* on school bullying, defined bullying as "a subcategory of interpersonal aggression characterized by intentionality, repetition, and an imbalance of power, with abuse of power being a primary distinction between bullying and other forms of aggression" (p. 293).

Gano-Overway and her colleagues (Fry & Gano-Overway, 2010; Gano-Overway, 2013; Gano-Overway et al., 2009) have conducted several studies on prosocial and antisocial behaviour, focusing on the climate, and specifically on a caring climate, in which each participant is treated in a caring, supportive manner. More explicitly, Fry and Gano-Overway (2010) described the caring climate as an overarching context characterized by engrossment (listening, accepting, and attending), motivational displacement (honouring interests, supporting and helping the achievement of goals, empowering), and respect (trust, sensitivity). Research in non-sport settings suggests a caring climate reduces bullying, and one key mechanism is the development of empathy.

Gano-Overway et al. (2009) looked at the role of caring climate on prosocial and antisocial behaviours with a large sample of participants in the National Youth Sport Program and also looked at self-regulatory efficacy and empathic self-efficacy as mediators. As expected, a perceived caring climate positively related to prosocial behaviour and negatively predicted antisocial behaviour. Furthermore, mediation effects suggested that the caring climate develops youths' ability to self-regulate positive affect, which in turn enhances their belief in their ability to empathize. As they concluded, where a caring climate is intentionally structured in youth sport, youth reap important social, emotional, and psychological benefits – that is, PYD.

Helping youth develop emotional and cognitive control skills is a key strategy for reducing antisocial behaviour and promoting prosocial behaviour. Similarly, the development of social competence (empathy, perspective-taking, conflict management) can enhance social development. These skills are fostered in a positive, caring climate.

Conflict Resolution and PYD

One current programme (Hemphill, Janke, Gordon, & Farrar, 2018) takes a PYD approach to resolve conflicts in youth sport. More specifically, Hemphill and colleagues follow the TPSR model and, in an innovative move, combined TPSR with restorative practices in their applied model of conflict resolution in sport-based youth development programmes. As discussed in an earlier section, TPSR (Hellison, 2011) is a PYD model that seeks to empower youth to be responsible in their conduct (personal responsibility) and in how they treat others (social responsibility). TPSR provides a model and strategies to encourage transfer of personal and social skills to other areas of life outside sport. Research suggests TPSR has a positive effect on personal and social development (Martinek & Hellison, 2016), can be implemented by teachers and coaches (Hemphill et al., 2015), and can connect with other youth development initiatives in schools (Escarti, Llopis-Goig, & Wright, 2018). Research with TPSR suggests the model can promote social and emotional learning when implemented with a high level of fidelity (Gordon et al., 2016).

Restorative practices, which are an extension of the restorative justice movement, are a more innovative approach to PYD. Restorative justice argues that those who suffer from wrong-doing should have their needs addressed, and also that those who commit the wrong-doing should take responsibility for the actions (Zehr, 2002). Restorative practices include strategies for addressing harm, as well as proactive relationship development strategies more commonly used in educational settings (Macready, 2009). Hemphill et al. developed their applied model within the context of New Zealand schools, which have established expectations for restorative practices in the schools. The research team took a community-engaged approach emphasizing reciprocal, asset-based, mutually beneficial university–community partnerships. They interviewed a wide range of professionals involved in related roles, including professors and teachers, community programme leaders, youth development professionals, and restorative justice practitioners. Overall, they found great potential for restorative practices to be integrated into youth sport programmes, but also missed opportunities in that restorative practices had made few inroads into sports.

Given those findings, they developed a new restorative youth sports model incorporating the TPSR framework, grounded in an asset-based community development approach. More specifically, their applied model includes three major components similar to those used with restorative practices in education – restorative youth sports essentials, awareness circles, and team meetings. The restorative essentials include a relational approach, effective communication, and the TPSR goals (respect, effort, self-direction, leadership, and transfer). Awareness circles provide space for restorative conversations and should be routine (e.g., at the beginning/end of practice). The circles provide space for considering ways to repair harm when conflicts occur. Team meetings provide space for coaches and teachers to address conflict, as well as apply problem-solving. The process should help participants identify harm and restore the team. To implement the model, Hemphill et al. offer the following principles: (a) youth should be gradually empowered, (b) restorative practices should be integrated into the sport experience, (c) efforts should be made to transfer learning outside sports, (d) individuals are interconnected as members of a team and community, and (e) participants have accountability for individual actions and impact on others. Overall, as with other PYD programmes, the applied model recognizes the centrality of relationships to the well-being of youth and provides intentional strategies to promote positive relationships through sports.

Practical Applications

Many of the PYD programmes and related research provide guidance for implementation and application in PYD programmes. For example, the restorative practice model offers specific guidelines. Similarly, at the end of their Tucker Center chapter, Weiss and Kipp (2018) offer specific recommendations of evidence-based best practices for parents, coaches, and programme leaders. Guides for parents include enabling opportunities, encouraging and supporting interests, reinforcing mastery attempts, being positive role models, planning family activities, and being involved. Coaches are advised to give frequent instructional feedback, create a mastery motivational climate, and inspire through transformational leadership. Advice for programme leaders includes training coaches on developmentally appropriate feedback, encouraging social support, and regularly evaluating coaching behaviours.

Hook and Newland (2018), in the applied *Journal of Sport Psychology in Action (JSPA)*, offer specific tips on how coaches can foster a mastery climate and provide autonomy support, both of which promote PYD. Coaching behaviours to foster autonomy support include providing choice within limits, providing change-oriented feedback, and allowing athletes to own their team. Specific coaching behaviours to foster a mastery climate include focusing on improvement, evaluating players individually, and celebrating failing forward (making mistakes while striving for improvement). Coaching behaviours to foster a caring climate include developing caring relationships, modelling caring behaviours, creating opportunities for caring, and *ubantu*, an African philosophy meaning "my humanity is caught up, is inextricably bound up, in yours".

In another article in *JSPA*, Mac Intosh and Martin (2018) provide information on the Ross Initiative in Sports for Equality (RISE) high school leadership programme intended to improve race relations and drive social progress. They connect classic social psychology with PYD principles, specifically focusing on assets to build development within a safe, structured environment. RISE uses activities that challenge and empower youth, as well as the mentoring role of the coach. They reported positive changes, although there was no comparison group. They recognize the challenges in the programme but see potential in the ability of coaches to be effective mentors and positioning sport as a context in which difficult conversations can take place.

Conclusion

Youth sport and physical activity programmes have great potential to foster PYD, but, as virtually everyone who has written about PYD through sport has argued, positive outcomes are not automatic. Programmes much be intentionally designed and conducted in line with PYD models and guidelines. A caring, supportive climate that emphasizes mastery and learning is key. That climate is created and maintained by adult leaders who guide and empower youth participants. Programmes focus on developing life skills, including physical literacy, as well as social and personal skills that are generalizable and transferable outside the programme. Transfer is a particular challenge, both in programming and evaluation, but successful programmes take up the challenge by building transfer strategies into the programmes.

References

Bean, C., Harlow, M., Mosher, A., Fraser-Thomas, J., & Forneris, T. (2018). Assessing differences in athlete-reported outcomes between high and low-quality youth sport programs. *Journal of Applied Sport Psychology, 30, 456–472*.

Benson, P. L. (2006). *All kids are our kids: What communities must do to raise caring and responsible children and adolescents* (2nd ed.). San Francisco, CA: Jossey-Bass.

Blom, L. C., Judge, L., Whitley, M. A., Gerstein, L., Huffman, A., & Hillyer, S. (2015). Sport for development and peace: Experiences conducting U.S. and international programs. *Journal of Sport Psychology in Action, 6, 1–16*.

Bredemeier, B. J., & Shields, D. L. (1986). Game reasoning and interactional morality. *Journal of Genetic Psychology, 147, 257–275*.

Bredemeier, B. J. L., & Shields, D. L. L. (1995). *Character development and physical activity*. Champaign, IL: Human Kinetics.

Bredemeier, B. L., & Shields, D. L. (2014). Moral reasoning. In R. C. Eklund & G. Tenenbaum (Eds.), *Encyclopedia of sport and exercise psychology* (pp. 465–469). Thousand Oaks, CA: Sage.

Bruner, M. W., Balish, S. M., Forrest, C., Brown, S., Webber, K., Gray, E., ... Shields, C. A. (2017). Ties that bond: Youth sport as a vehicle for social identity and positive youth development. *Research Quarterly for Exercise and Sport, 88, 209–214*.

Causadias, J. M., & Umaña-Taylor, A. J. (2018). Reframing marginalization and youth development: Introduction to the special issue. *American Psychologist, 73, 707–712*.

Côté, J., Baker, J., & Abernethy, B. (2007). Practice and play in the development of sport expertise. In G. Tenenbaum & R. Eklund (Eds.), *Handbook of sport psychology* (3rd ed., pp. 184–202). Hoboken, NJ: Wiley.

Côté, J., Hancock, D. J., & Abernethy, B. (2014). Nurturing talent in youth sport. In A. G. Papaionnou & D. Hackfort (Eds.), *Routledge companion to sport and exercise psychology: Global perspectives and fundamental concepts* (pp. 22–33). London: Routledge.

Dzewaltowski, D. A., & Rosenkranz, R. R. (2014). Youth development: An approach for physical activity behavioral science. *Kinesiology Review, 3, 92–100*.

Eime, R. M., Young, J. A., Harvey, J. T., Charity, M. J., & Payne, W. R. (2013). A systematic review of the psychological and social benefits of participation in sport for children and adolescents: Informing development of a conceptual model of health through sport. *The International Journal of Behavioral Nutrition and Physical Activity, 10, 98*.

Escarti, A., Llopis-Goig, R., & Wright, P. M. (2018). Assessing the implementation fidelity of a school-based teaching personal and social responsibility program in physical education and other subject areas. *Journal of Teaching in Physical Education, 37, 12–23*.

Forneris, T., Bean, C., & Halsall, R. (2016). Positive youth development programming with marginalized populations. In N. L. Holt (Ed.), *Positive youth development through sport* (2nd ed., pp. 168–177). London: Routledge.

Forneris, T., Whitley, M. A., & Barker, B. (2013). The reality of implementing community-based sport and physical activity programs to enhance the development of underserved youth: Challenges and potential strategies. *Quest, 65*, 313–331.

Fry, M. D., & Gano-Overway, L. A. (2010). Exploring the contribution of the caring climate to the youth sport experience. *Journal of Applied Sport Psychology, 22*, 294–304.

Gano-Overway, L. A. (2013). Exploring the connections between caring and social behaviors in physical education. *Research Quarterly for Exercise and Sport, 84*, 104–114.

Gano-Overway, L. A., Newton, M., Magyar, T. M., Fry, M. D., Kim, M., & Guivernau, M. (2009). Influence of caring youth sport contexts on efficacy-related beliefs and social behaviors. *Developmental Psychology, 45*, 329–340.

Coll, C. G., Lamberty, G., Jenkins, R., McAdoo, H. P., Crnic, K., Wasik, B. H., & Vázquez García, H. (1996). An integrative model for the study of developmental competencies in minority children. *Child Development, 67*, 1891–1914.

Gaylord-Harden, N. K., Barbarin, O., Tolan, P. H., & McBride Murry, V. (2018). Understanding development of African American boys and young men: Moving from risks to positive youth development. *American Psychologist, 73*, 753–767.

Gibbons, S. L., & Ebbeck, V. (1997). The effect of different teaching strategies on moral development of physical education students. *Journal of Teaching Physical Education, 17*, 85–98.

Gibbons, S. L., Ebbeck, V., & Weiss, M. R. (1995). Fair play for kids: Effects on the moral development of children in physical education. *Research Quarterly for Exercise and Sport, 66*, 247–255.

Gordon, B., Jacobs, J. M., & Wright, P. M. (2016). Social and emotional learning through a teaching personal and social responsibility based after-school program for disengaged middle school boys. *Journal of Teaching in Physical Education, 35*, 358–369.

Gould, D. (1982). Sport psychology in the 1980s: Status, direction and challenge in youth sports research. *Journal of Sport Psychology, 4*, 203–218.

Gould, D., & Carson, S. (2008). Life skills development through sport: Current status and future directions. *International Review of Sport and Exercise Psychology, 1*, 58–78.

Gould, D., & Carson, S. (2011). Young athletes' perceptions of the relationship between coaching behaviors and developmental experiences. *International Journal of Coaching Science, 5*(2), 3–29.

Gould, D., Cowburn, I., & Shields, A. (2014). "Sports for All" – Summary of the evidence of psychological and social outcomes of participation. *Elevate Health: Research Digest of the President's Council on Fitness, Sports & Nutrition, Series, 15*(3). Special Issue 2014 www.fitness.gov/resource-center/research-and-reports/

Gould, D., Flett, M. R., & Lauer, L. (2012). The relationship between psychosocial developmental and the sports climate experienced by underserved youth. *Psychology of Sport and Exercise, 13*, 80–87.

Haan, N. (1991). Moral development and action from a social constructivist perspective. In W. M. Kurtines & J. L. Gerwitz (Eds.), *Handbook of moral behavior and development: Vol. 1. theory* (pp. 251–273). Hillsdale, NJ: Erlbaum.

Hansen, D. M., & Larson, R. (2007). Amplifiers of developmental and negative experiences in organized activities: Dosage, motivation, lead roles, and adult-youth ratios. *Journal of Applied Developmental Psychology, 28*, 360–374.

Harwood, C., & Johnston, J. (2016). Positive youth development and talent development. In N. L. Holt (Ed.), *Positive youth development through sport* (pp. 113–125). London: Routledge.

Hellison, D. (1983). Teaching self-responsibility (and more). *Journal of Physical Education, Recreation and Dance, 54*(23), 28.

Hellison, D. (2011). *Teaching personal and social responsibility through physical activity* (3rd ed.). Champaign, IL: Human Kinetics.

Hemphill, M. A., Janke, E. M., Gordon, B., & Farrar, H. (2018). Restorative youth sports: An applied model for resolving conflicts and building positive relationships. *Journal of Youth Development, 13*, 76–96.

Hemphill, M. A., & Martinek, T. J. (2017). Community engagement through sport: University partnerships to promote youth development. *Kinesiology Review, 6*(4), 311–316.

Hemphill, M. A., & Richards, K. A. R. (2016). "Without the academic part, it wouldn't be squash": Youth development in an urban squash program. *Journal of Teaching in Physical Education, 35*, 263–276.

Hemphill, M. A., Templin, T. J., & Wright, P. M. (2015). Implementation and outcomes of a responsibility-based continuing professional development protocol in physical education. *Sport, Education, and Society, 20*, 398–419.

Hodge, K., Danish, S., Forneris, T., & Miles, A. (2016). Life skills and basic needs: A conceptual framework for life skills interventions. In N. L. Holt (Ed.), *Positive youth development through sport* (2nd ed., pp. 45–55). London: Routledge.

Hodge, K., Danish, S., & Martin, J. (2012). Developing a conceptual framework for life skills interventions. *The Counseling Psychologist, 41*, 1125–1152.

Holt, N. L., Deal, C. J., & Smyth, C. (2016). Future directions for positive youth development through sport. In N. L. Holt (Ed.), *Positive youth development through sport* (2nd ed., pp. 229–240). London: Routledge.

Holt, N. L., Neely, K. C., Slater, L. G., Camire, M., Côté, J., Fraser-Thomas, J., ... Tamminen, K. A. (2017). A grounded theory of positive youth development through sport based on results from a qualitative meta-study. *International Review of Sport and Exercise Psychology, 10*, 1–49.

Hook, R., & Newland, A. (2018). A basic needs coaching paradigm for coaches of intercollegiate and high school athletes. *Journal of Sport Psychology in Action, 9*, 182–195.

Hymel, S., & Swearer, S. M. (2015). Four decades of research on school bullying: An introduction. *American Psychologist, 70*, 293–299.

Jacobs, J. J., & Wright, P. M. (2016). An alternative application of imagery in youth sport: Promoting the transfer of life skills to other contexts. *Journal of Sport Psychology in Action, 7*, 1–10.

Jacobs, J. M., & Wright, P. M. (2018). Transfer of life skills in sport-based youth development programs: A conceptual framework bridging learning to application. *Quest, 70*, 81–99.

Kavussanu, M. (2014). Moral behavior. In R. C. Eklund & G. Tenenbaum (Eds.), *Encyclopedia of sport and exercise psychology* (pp. 454–456). Thousand Oaks, CA: Sage.

Larson, R. (2000). Toward a psychology of positive youth development. *American Psychologist, 55*, 170–183.

Larson, R. W., Hansen, D. M., & Moneta, G. (2006). Differing profiles of developmental experiences across types of organized youth activities. *Developmental Psychology, 42*, 849–863.

Lerner, R. M., Almerigi, J. B., Theokas, C., & Lerner, J. V. (2005). Positive youth development: A view of the issues. *Journal of Early Adolescence, 25*, 10–16.

Lewin, K. (1935). *A dynamic theory of personality.* New York: McGraw Hill.

Lewin, K. (1951). *Field theory in social science.* New York: Harper.

Mac Intosh, A., & Martin, E. M. (2018). Creating athlete activists: Using sport as a vehicle to combat racism. *Journal of Sport Psychology in Action, 9*(3), 159–171.

Macready, T. (2009). Learning social responsibility in schools: A restorative practice. *Educational Psychology in Practice, 25*(3), 211–220.

Maro, C., Roberts, G. C., & Sørensen, M. (2009). Using sport to promote HIV/AIDS education for at-risk youths: An intervention using peer coaches in football. *Scandinavian Journal of Medicine & Science in Sports, 19*, 129–141.

Martinek, T., & Hellison, D. (2016). Learning responsibility through physical activity. In N. L. Holt (Ed.), *Positive youth development through sport* (2nd ed., pp. 180–190). New York: Routledge.

Martinek, T., & Lee, O. (2012). From community gyms to classrooms: A framework for values transfer in schools. *Journal of Physical Education, Recreation, and Dance, 83*, 33–51.

McCloy, C. H. (1930). Character building through physical education. *Research Quarterly, 1*(3), 41–60.

McCloy, C. H. (1940). *Philosophical bases for physical education.* New York: F. S. Crofts.

Petitpas, A. J., Cornelius, A. E., Van Raalte, J. L., & Jones, T. (2005). A framework for planning youth sport programs that foster psychosocial development. *The Sport Psychologist, 19*, 63–80.

Schinke, R. J., Stambulova, N. R., Lidor, R., Papaioannou, A., & Ryba, T. V. (2016). ISSP position stand: Social missions through sport and exercise psychology. *International Journal of Sport and Exercise Psychology, 14*, 4–22.

Shields, D. L., & Bredemeier, B. L. (2014). Promoting morality and character development. In A. G. Papaionnou & D. Hackfort (Eds.), *Routledge companion to sport and exercise psychology: Global perspectives and fundamental concepts* (pp. 636–649). London: Routledge.

Turnnidge, J., Côté, J., & Hancock, D. J. (2014). Positive youth development from sport to life: Explicit or implicit transfer? *Quest, 66*, 203–217.

Ullrich-French, S., & Cole, A. M. (2018). Exploring participant characteristics in an assessment of changes in psychosocial outcomes in a physical activity-based positive youth development programme for girls. *International Journal of Sport and Exercise Psychology, 16*, 535–554.

Walsh, D. S., Ozaeta, J., & Wright, P. M. (2010). Transference of responsibility model goals to the school environment: Exploring the impact of a coaching club program. *Physical Education and Sport Pedagogy, 15*, 15–28.

Weiss, M. R. (2008). "Field of dreams": Sport as a context for youth development. *Research Quarterly for Exercise and Sport, 79*, 434–449.

Weiss, M. R. (2011). Teach the children well: A holistic approach to developing psychosocial and behavioral competencies through physical education. *Quest, 63*, 55–65.

Weiss, M. R. (2016). Old wine in a new bottle: Historical reflections on sport as a context for youth development. In N. L. Holt (Ed.), *Positive youth development through sport* (2nd ed., pp. 7–20). London: Routledge.

Weiss, M. R., Bolter, N. D., & Kipp, L. E. (2014). Assessing impact of physical activity-based youth development programs: Validation of the Life Skills Transfer Survey (LSTS). *Research Quarterly for Exercise and Sport, 85*, 263–278.

Weiss, M. R., Bolter, N. D., & Kipp, L. E. (2016). Evaluation of the First Tee in promoting positive youth development: Group comparisons and longitudinal trends. *Research Quarterly for Exercise and Sport, 87*, 271–283.

Weiss, M. R., & Kipp, L. E. (2018). Social relationships rock! How parents, coaches, and peers can optimize girls' psychological development through sport and physical activity. In Tucker Center for Research on Girls & Women in Sport (Ed.), *The 2018 Tucker Center research report: Developing physically active girls: An evidence-based multidisciplinary approach* (36–54). Minneapolis, MN: University of Minnesota, Author.

Weiss, M. R., Kipp, L. E., & Bolter, N. D. (2012). Training for life: Optimizing positive youth development through sport and physical activity. In S. M. Murphy (Ed.), *The Oxford handbook of sport and performance psychology* (pp. 448–475). New York and Oxford, UK: Oxford University Press.

Weiss, M. R., Stuntz, C. P., Bhalla, J. A., Bolter, N. D., & Price, M. S. (2013). "More than a game": Impact of the first tee life skills programme on positive youth development: Project introduction and year 1 findings. *Qualitative Research in Sport, Exercise, and Health, 5*, 214–244.

Weiss, M. R., & Wiese-Bjornstal, D. M. (2009). Promoting positive youth development through physical activity. *President's Council on Physical Fitness and Sports Research Digest, 10*(3), 1–8.

Whitley, M. A., Forneris, T., & Barker, B. (2014). The reality of evaluating community-based sport and physical activity programs to enhance the development of underserved youth: Challenges and potential strategies. *Quest, 66*, 218–232.

Whitley, M. A., Forneris, T., & Barker, B. (2015). The reality of sustaining community-based sport and physical activity programs to enhance the development of underserved youth: Challenges and potential strategies. *Quest, 67*, 409–423.

Williams, J. F. (1927). *The principles of physical education*. Philadelphia, PA: W. B. Saunders.

Zehr, H. (2002). *The little book of restorative justice*. Intercourse, PA: Good Books.

37
POWER AND PRIVILEGE

Sae-Mi Lee and Stephanie J. Hanrahan

Introduction

In recent years, there have been numerous sporting events that have brought forth issues related to social justice. For example, Colin Kaepernick, who was previously the quarterback for the San Francisco 49ers, a professional American football team in the National Football League (NFL), gathered national attention during the 2016–2017 season when he sat, and subsequently kneeled, during the national anthem to protest the racial injustices that Black people face, especially in North America (Jones, 2017). Since then, the protest has grown, and numerous athletes across various sports have joined in (Félix, 2017); even US politicians have shared their views regarding using sport as a vehicle for social change (Hoffman, 2017; Watkins, 2017). In the aftermath of the protest, Colin Kaepernick became a free agent but remains jobless, which some consider an act of retaliation by the NFL owners for his activism (Moore, 2018). His and other social justice protests have been considered controversial, with some arguing that sport should not be a political platform, that speaking about social issues is a distraction (Jones, 2017), and that athletes such as professional basketball player Lebron James should "shut up and dribble" (Chavez, 2018, n.p.). Others argued that sport has always been political, and that athletes have the right to engage in activism (Campanelli, 2017).

Sport, exercise, and performance psychology (SEPP) has remained relatively mute on issues related to social justice. The same arguments about the proper place for social justice discussions and protests are present when speaking up about social inequities in SEPP. Some have argued that SEPP should be an apolitical space that focuses on performance enhancement (i.e., Johnson, 2018; Myers, 2017). Others, however, have acknowledged that sport, and SEPP, is a microcosm of society where society's inequitable power structures are reflected (e.g., Fisher, Butryn, & Roper, 2003; Ryba, Schinke, & Tenenbaum, 2010). Traditionally, issues of power have been addressed by sport sociologists rather than SEPP professionals. Recently, however, the study of culture, identities, power, and privilege has increased in SEPP, primarily through a new research genre called cultural sport psychology (CSP). CSP is a framework that infuses multiple genres of work that are focused on the "cultural" in sport and exercise psychology. CSP researchers have adopted and applied the work of prominent critical theorists such as Gramsci and Marx to critique the exclusion of traditionally marginalized, non-Eurocentric viewpoints in SEPP and examined the various consequences of such inequalities (e.g., Krane, 2001a; Roper, Fisher, & Wrisberg, 2005).

Moreover, CSP professionals have argued for the promotion of "athletes-as-citizens" (Fisher et al., 2003, p. 398), where athletes can be seen as holistic beings who are affected by, and take part in, various social injustices that occur on and off the field.

In recent years, the International Society of Sport Psychology (ISSP) has released position stands on cultural competence outlining tasks that SEPP professionals should undertake to improve their cultural competence in an ever-evolving, culturally diverse world (Ryba, Stambulova, Si, & Schinke, 2013). They proposed that SEPP professionals analyse the ethnocentric assumptions underlying all aspects of the field (including research, theories, and practice) and shift towards a more culturally reflexive lens (Ryba et al., 2013). This task involves individual practitioners and the profession as a whole recognizing the importance of power, because power and politics determine what is considered ethical and good (Ryba et al., 2013). Moreover, the ISSP position stand on "Social Missions through Sport and Exercise Psychology" advocated that sport is not only in an ideal situation to promote positive social change, but also the professionals working in that space have the responsibility to do so (Schinke, Stambulova, Lidor, Papaioannou, & Ryba, 2016). These position stands clearly indicate that SEPP professionals have the responsibility to understand the relevance of power and privilege in their work and competently address social justice-related concerns.

As one can see from current events, the (re)emergence of athlete activism, and the ongoing disagreements about social injustices, sport and SEPP are not exempt from discussions of social justice and identity politics. Given their job to help professionals, many SEPP professionals' relative muteness on the cases listed above are troubling. It seems timely that SEPP professionals should facilitate "social consciousness, political awareness, and democratic engagement" (Fisher et al., 2003, p. 399). The authors' goal for this contribution is to help SEPP professionals make explicit connections between how understanding power can help SEPP professionals understand the academic concept of privilege (McIntosh, 1988) and social injustices. Ideally SEPP professionals can understand and address historical and ongoing systemic and interpersonal injustices such as racism, sexism, homophobia, and transphobia that, inevitably, continue to affect their work. Below, the authors introduce theoretical perspectives on power and provide suggestions for how SEPP professionals can integrate understandings of power and privilege to promote social change and help *all* communities.

Theory and Research: Power

Although it is common to think of power as having control over somebody (e.g., parents make their children eat their vegetables), there are various theories on what power is and how power works in society. Below, power is approached from a relativist ontological stance, an epistemological stance of social constructionism, and a critical theoretical perspective. Specifically, in this section, the historical and chronological development of how power has been understood and interrogated by three prominent critical scholars – Karl Marx, Antonio Gramsci, and Michel Foucault – will be outlined. The basic principles of the three scholars' theoretical perspectives on power – ideological power, hegemonic power, and discursive power – will be explained. Each theoretical explanation will be followed by a brief review of critical SEPP research. For alternative ontological and theoretical discussions of power, see Guzzini (2013).

Ideological Power

Karl Marx is regarded as one of the most influential thinkers who theorized about power inequities and the struggle between economic classes (Allen, 2011; Molnar & Kelly, 2013).

Marx theorized that capitalist society left power in the hands of the ruling class, the bourgeoisie, with the means of production and left the subordinate working class, the proletariat, participating in an exploitative system (Marx & Engels, 1848). "Since the parties to this trading in labour are not equal … the propertyless must submit to the bad conditions laid down by the bourgeois" (Marx & Engels, 1848, p. 38). Marx viewed class and the capitalist production model as the root of social inequalities.

Marx further explained that the fundamental class divide in capitalist society was justified through the use of ideologies (Molnar & Kelly, 2013). According to Marx, ideologies are systems of values and ideas that reflect and support the established order and manifest themselves in everyday actions, decisions, and practices, usually without people being aware of their presence (Brookfield, 2005). Marx asserted that societal values and norms are products of *ideology*, and that ideologies represent the interests of the ruling class rather than the subordinate class (Marx & Engels, 1848). "Over time, ideologies become taken for granted and accepted as universally valid by most members of a society … [and] ideologies help to validate worldviews that help dictate our attitudes and behaviors" (Allen, 2011, p. 32). An example of dominant ideology is the ideology of meritocracy, where society believes that rich people are rich because they worked hard and poor people are poor because they are lazy (Allen, 2011). Such an ideology works to justify the current social order and hierarchy.

Marx heavily critiqued capitalism and the ideologies developed within the capitalist system to justify its dominance. Marxist theorists stated that power is held by those in the ruling class because they created the material realities and the subsequent ideologies that exploited the general public and justified their rule (Marx & Engels, 1848). Thus, to achieve social change, liberation, and equality, Marxist theorists advocated for education to raise the consciousness and collaborative activism of the working class. They also advocated altering material reality by finding alternative solutions to capitalist production. Marx ultimately believed the proletariat would revolt to overthrow the capitalist system in favour of a more equitable communist society. Nevertheless, the socialist revolution that Marx predicted never arrived (Molnar & Kelly, 2013). Subsequently, scholars tried to make sense of why the subordinate class went along with oppressive systems, which led to the articulation of a concept called *hegemony* (described below).

Ideological Power in SEPP Research

Research on the different theoretical perspectives of power have been scant in SEPP. Despite the overlap between capitalism and sport, as can be seen in the rising ticket costs of professional sport or coaching salaries (Molnar & Kelly, 2013), to the authors' knowledge, research drawing on a traditional Marxist perspective is absent in the field of SEPP. The few dominant ideologies examined in SEPP research have been about race or gender, rather than class and economics. For example, recent research on racial microaggressions, the casual and often subtle degradation of any marginalized group (Sue, 2010), helped researchers illustrate the dominance of colour-blind ideology in sport contexts, which lead to racial discriminations being overlooked and dismissed (Burdsey, 2011; Carter & Davila, 2017). Burdsey (2011) found that the colour-blind ideology in UK cricket was so pervasive that even athletes of colour, specifically British-Asian cricket players, adhered to this ideology. Ideological power led the athletes to minimize their experiences with racial microaggressions in sport, despite microaggressions being perpetrated by coaches, teammates, referees, and fans. Future research on dominant ideologies in sport could allow SEPP professionals to examine how dominant ideas work to justify the current social order and hierarchies and overlook social injustices.

Hegemonic Power

Antonio Gramsci, a Marxist philosopher, broadened Marx's concept of ideology by describing how social power is exercised through consent and ideology, rather than through violence and force (Gramsci, 1999). Gramsci expanded on the concept of hegemony to understand why the socialist revolution that Marx predicted never occurred and the bourgeoisie continued to maintain societal control. Gramsci (1999) observed that, when ideologies become learned, lived, and engrained in everyday decisions, social structures, and practices, these ideas become pervasive and represent what is perceived as common sense. Although ideologies represent the interest of the ruling class, they become so pervasive that the subordinate class adopts the interests of the bourgeoisie and identifies them as its own (Gramsci, 1999). Hegemony is created through complex processes of consent and coercion by the socialization process of these ideologies through various social institutions, such as schools, families, and mass media. As a result, rather than revolting, members of the subordinate class help maintain the status quo by adopting dominant ideologies and believing their place in society is *"right and natural"* (Ross & Shinew, 2008, p. 42; emphasis in original).

Although both Marx and Gramsci critiqued the capitalist production model, Gramsci departed from Marx's economic determinism to emphasize culture as the superstructure that divides the dominators and dominated. An example of the relevance of Gramsci's departure from economics as the core of power differentials is society's perceptions of those with old money versus those with new money. In some cultures, there is the perception that people with old money are more elite than those with new money, and that upper class means "for the most part, people who are ethnically WASP [White, Anglo-Saxon, Protestant] and possess ... 'old money'" (Ortner, 1998, p. 8). As seen from this example, wealth itself is not the single determining factor for who and what are considered at the top of the social hierarchy. Rather than being a stable unilateral force, hegemonic power is created and reproduced through "ongoing social action" (Stoddart, 2007, p. 201). Finally, Gramsci disagreed that power is possessed solely by the powerful (Pringle, 2005). He also rejected that power is always repressive; rather, Gramsci theorized power as productive, because it socializes, rather than forces, society into the status quo (Pringle, 2005). Therefore, Gramsci asserted that consciousness-raising about socialization is required to promote social justice (Stoddart, 2007). He explained that social change occurs as people become aware that what they take for granted as truth is the result of socialization (Stoddart, 2007).

Gramsci's theorization of hegemonic power has important implications for understanding how all individuals promote and resist power relations. If the powerful create and maintain their power through ideas that are embedded and transmitted through the socialization process, power is pervasive and subtle. These ideas are taught in schools, religion, science, and even in sport, eventually becoming common-sense, taken-for-granted assumptions. When these ideas become so pervasive, one considers these sets of beliefs as legitimate even when they do not serve the interests of those being dominated.

For example, cultural SEPP researchers have critiqued the Eurocentric assumptions of the field of SEPP as remaining unacknowledged and unchallenged (Ryba & Schinke, 2009; Ryba et al., 2013). When the Eurocentrism of SEPP goes unacknowledged, and minimal representation of traditionally marginalized perspectives exists (Kamphoff, Gill, Araki, & Hammond, 2010), the Eurocentric ways of knowing can seem like the only true way of knowing. The ideology of Eurocentrism becomes hegemonic as one adopts and adheres to beliefs and values one has been socialized to adopt. This process can lead to ethnocentric monoculturalism, which is the belief that one's own cultural beliefs and values are more valid than others (Sue, 2004), or not even considering there may be alternative beliefs and values. Ethnocentric monoculturalism serves as a form of cultural oppression and contributes to one's inability to see one's self as a cultural being (Sue, 2004).

Hegemonic Power in SEPP Research

Although hegemonic power has been explored by many sport sociologists (e.g., Bridges & Pascoe, 2014; Carney & Chawansky, 2016; Comeaux & Martin, 2018; Messner, 1990), only a few SEPP researchers have examined hegemonic power structures in sport, primarily as they relate to gender. In interviews with 10 male basketball players who served as practice opposition for a successful intercollegiate women's team, Fink, LaVoi, and Newhall (2016) found that, even though the male athletes acknowledged that the athletic abilities of males and females were fluid and overlapping, and often the women were better players, they continued to uphold traditional gender stereotypes, including beliefs that men are inherently and naturally superior to women. This inconsistency was accomplished by the male players thinking these particular women played like men, and this women's team was a special case (Fink et al., 2016). Throughout the interviews, the male athletes called male players men and female players girls, marginalizing women by infantilization. In another study, Krane (2001b) examined how hegemonic femininity manifested in sport. Krane found that athletes who did not appear straight or overtly feminine were discriminated against, which led to female athletes adopting and presenting hyperfeminine behaviours and attitudes. On the other hand, feminine athletes in this study were also scrutinized and sexualized, while their athletic achievements were overlooked. These studies served as an example of how our ideas of gender become hegemonic and are adopted and contested within sporting contexts.

Discursive Power

Although influenced by other critical theorists such as Marx and Gramsci, Michel Foucault significantly departed from Marx and Gramsci in his theorization of power. There are some similarities in Gramsci's and Foucault's views on power. First, both theorists viewed power as being omnipresent (Pringle, 2005). Rather than viewing power as something that could be possessed by dominant groups, they viewed power as fluid and relational (Pringle, 2005). The theorists also viewed power as being productive rather than repressive, because it produces meaning within society (Pringle, 2005). Finally, they both acknowledged that power relations are inequitable as they currently lie, but that they can be changed, shifted, and resisted. Where Gramsci and Foucault disagreed was on how the powerful become powerful and how unequal power relations are formed.

Many commonly understand power to be top–down within a binary hierarchical relationship, which Foucault (1995) called repressive power. For example, coaches have power over athletes and can make them come to morning practice or they can cut players from the team. Teachers have power over students because they are designing the class and grading the students. However, Foucault (1995) observed that the form of power shifted over time; he called this new form of power discursive power. Discursive power is the understanding that power is not centralized and held by a powerful other but exercised through discourse. Discourse is how we dialogue and make sense of the world. Rather than emphasizing an economic or cultural superstructure that divides the powerful from the powerless, Foucault and other poststructuralist theorists focused on the role of language and its role in knowledge production.

Although there are multiple discourses, not all are legitimized equally. Some discourses are more widely circulated and considered more valid than others. For example, there are multiple discourses about gender, such as the gender binary (i.e., everyone is either female or male) or gender as a spectrum. However, the gender binary discourse is socially dominant, and this discourse is further legitimized through social practices such as legally regulating which gendered bathrooms one can use. Because society rarely refers to a cis-gender male (i.e., a male who identifies with the gender assigned at birth) as a cis-gender male (they are simply referred to as male), while specifically calling transgender males transgender males, society upholds the norm of the gender binary while "othering" transgender individuals as different, exotic, or abnormal. As a result, transgender people or gender non-conforming individuals have to fight for the right to be recognized and validated (Lucas-Carr & Krane, 2011).

Similar to hegemony, the widely circulated discourses can eventually become so dominant they become taken-for-granted notions of truth. We consider these truths as common sense, and they appear difficult to challenge or change (Weedon, 1997). These socially legitimized discourses "determine what is considered 'normal' in a setting, who belongs, who is allowed to participate and who is not" (Dortants & Knoppers, 2013, p. 537). To go back to the example of gender discourses, the discourse of gender binary is more socially legitimate, not because it is truer, but because it is more widely circulated through our everyday reference to gender. For example, asking one another about the pronouns they use is uncommon, because the assumption is that pronouns will either be he or she; the discourse of gender binary is embedded within, and legitimized through, our everyday practices. Thus, discourse does not reflect reality; discourse constitutes reality (Weedon, 1997).

Although Foucault recognized there was a power divide between the rulers and ruled, he viewed the dual/binary divide as a consequence and outcome of the power process rather than a given assumption (Foucault, 1995). More specifically, he asserted that the powerful achieved power through the strategic use of discourse, which society takes for granted and considers *normal* (Foucault, 1995). For example, it is not solely the government or a powerful group of people who purposefully alienate and the transgendered community. All societal members contribute to the marginalization of transgender people by normalizing the gender binary discourse through everyday language, assumptions, and social practices. Bathrooms and locker rooms are built for people who fit the gender binary, and official pronouns are limited to either he or she.

When people understand power in this way, they can see how power is more insidious and pervasive than they may have thought. Individuals can understand why the ways in which they engage in dialogue and how they frame things (i.e., discourse) are important because discourse constitutes knowledge and contributes to what society considers real, true, good, and normal (Weedon, 1997; Willig, 2013). Thus, to negotiate power dynamics, SEPP professionals are tasked to continuously question their taken-for-granted ways of thinking and being.

Discursive Power in SEPP Research

McGannon and Mauws (2000, 2002) were among the first to take a discursive approach within SEPP. They addressed the limitations of social cognitive theory, which was the main theoretical approach to understanding exercise behaviour, and suggested discursive psychology as an alternative approach to understanding exercise adherence. The authors discussed the productive, rather than reflective, nature of language and advocated for the need to trace people's discursive understandings of exercise, because language shapes and limits how individuals think, feel, and behave when engaging in exercise behaviour (McGannon & Mauws, 2000). For example, if a mother discursively constructs being a "good mother" as someone who prioritizes meeting her children's needs first, she may feel guilty for exercising because she feels as though she is putting her own needs first (McGannon & Mauws, 2002). This way of thinking can subsequently lead her to live a sedentary lifestyle to fit the discursive construction of a "good mother". To increase her physical activity and exercise adherence, SEPP professionals would need to help her examine how she is constructing the identity of a good mother (McGannon & Mauws, 2002). Alternative constructions of being a good mother might include assuring one lives long enough to see their children through to adulthood or pursuing empowerment and happiness in themselves as a way to set positive examples for their children (McGannon, McMahon, & Gonsalves, 2017; McGannon & Schinke, 2013).

Since these pioneering articles, discursive approaches in SEPP research have expanded to include more Foucauldian approaches, which have a more explicit focus on uncovering the influences of power. Through a Foucauldian genealogical approach, Ryba (2005) traced the historical origins of sport psychology and "the discursive formations of that historical conjecture that shaped the way sport psychology was conceptualized, theorized, practiced and institutionalized" (p. 40). Through a poststructuralist approach, Ryba troubled the seemingly singular and coherent historical origins of SEPP by identifying narratives overlooked. Ryba and Wright (2005, 2010) further outlined the potential and promise of theorizing the field of SEPP through a cultural studies lens, which broadens our ways of understanding identities and behaviours within sociocultural and historical contexts and power relations.

In recent years, more researchers have incorporated a Foucauldian poststructuralist perspective into their SEPP work (e.g., Kavoura, Kokkonen, Chroni, & Ryba, 2017; Kavoura, Ryba, & Chroni, 2015; Lee, Bernstein, Etzel, Gearity, & Kuklick, 2018). These studies outlined the multiple and, at times, contradictory discourses athletes draw upon to make sense of their gendered and racialized experiences and identities. For example, Kavoura et al. (2015) and Lee et al. (2018) both found the dominant discourse in sport contexts was often that individual identities do not matter in sport. However, the sub-discourses participants drew from indicated that this idea of sport as a meritocratic space does not exist. Drawing from other sub-discourses such as those of racism or feminism allowed athletes to consider the gendered or racialized nature of their experiences and identities. The dominant discourse conflicted with the experiences of many participants.

These studies illustrate how athletes continuously negotiate multiple competing discourses to make sense of their experiences in sport with regards to race and gender. Which experiences need to be ignored, and what parts of one's identity need to be silenced for them to uphold dominant discourses about what sport is and what it means to be an athlete? Although it is common and ideal to consider sport as a unifying practice that transcends identities, it is important to realize this discourse can lead to the silencing and invalidation of the gendered and racialized realities of athletes. It was by seeking multiple competing and even contrasting discourses rather than seeking a single master narrative that researchers illustrated how discursive power is circulated through everyday talk and social practices and considered its subsequent consequences.

Theory and Research: Privilege

Privilege is a concept introduced by Peggy McIntosh in 1988. McIntosh (1988) defined privilege as "an invisible package of unearned assets which I can count on cashing in each day, but about which I was 'meant' to remain oblivious" (p. 1). Although McIntosh first examined privilege in the context of whiteness, the concept has extended to recognize other types of interconnected and intersecting privilege such as class privilege and heterosexual privilege. Although the concept is widely used nowadays, privilege still remains misunderstood, which can evoke defensiveness in those who have privilege. It is fairly common to hear one say, "I don't have privilege! I worked hard for everything I have!" In the following section, the authors demonstrate how the theoretical views of power discussed above can help individuals understand the concept of privilege and how it manifests in SEPP.

Although many scientists believe there is a single truth that diligent research will eventually reveal (i.e., ontological realism), other researchers assume that there are multiple realities and ways of knowing (i.e., ontological relativism). For example, there are multiple interpretations that are possible to describe a single phenomenon such as the varying theories for why mental illnesses occur. Nevertheless, just because there are multiple interpretations of an event or phenomenon does not mean that all interpretations are considered equally legitimate and true. For example, as described earlier, there are multiple realities about the existence and experiences of racism and sexism in sport. However, the idea that sport brings people together is generally taken for granted in society and considered as truth (Kavoura et al., 2017; Lee et al., 2018). The problem is that, within the dominant society, the most represented reality can appear to be *the* one-and-only reality. Moreover, members of society are socialized to fit these dominant ideas, which manifest as societal norms. For example, because boys are told to stop crying and be a man, children are socialized to uphold and normalize specific ideologies about masculinity. The process of normalizing acts as a way of disciplining the body and society (Foucault, 1995). This process is how discursive power subtly, but pervasively, works. When certain truths become so dominant and normative, it appears difficult, if not impossible, to change. Moreover, when one does not fit into societal norms, not fitting in seems like a personal problem rather than a problem created by sociocultural contexts. Thus, instead of challenging social norms constructed based on a one-sided perspective, critical theorists such as Foucault have observed that society tends to challenge and blame those on the margins for not fitting in. For example, people are made to feel bad or guilty if they do not fit normative body types (e.g., skinny, muscular), even though research suggests that body types are inevitably diverse and that there are numerous ways of being healthy, regardless of one's body size or weight (Bacon, 2010; Busanich & McGannon, 2010)

Adhering to the assumptions of the critical theorists described above allows one to understand privilege as simply meaning a person with privilege is more likely to fit into current societal practices. To have privilege (and power) means fitting the dominant societal norms and rarely having to feel questioned, challenged, othered, or exoticized. For example, individuals who are heterosexual rarely have to think about whether they can engage in public acts of affection with their partners, whether they can get married, or whether their religion will accept them, because our society operates under the assumption that people are heterosexual. When individuals fit the norm of heteronormativity, they have the privilege of never having to think about how their sexual orientation can affect their safety and overall well-being. Others who do not have the benefit of such privilege, such as traditionally marginalized populations, have notably different experiences. Owing to heterosexuality being the norm, members of the LGBTQ+ community who do not fit heteronormativity experience interpersonal discrimination such as microaggressions or are faced with discriminatory laws and policies, in society as well as in sport (Carney & Chawansky, 2016; Lenskyj, 2012).

McIntosh (1988) observed society members are "taught to see racism [and other forms of oppression] only in individual acts of meanness, not in invisible systems conferring dominance on my group" (p. 1). Nevertheless, by viewing privilege as synonymous with being the norm, one can see how privilege is subtle and pervasive as well as institutionalized. Privilege is a result of normalizing certain ways of knowing and being over others. McIntosh's (1988) listed examples of White privilege as, "I easily buy posters, post-cards, picture books, greeting cards, dolls toys and children's magazines featuring people of my race" (p. 3) or "I can choose blemish cover or bandages in 'flesh' colour and have them more or less match my skin" (p. 4). These exemplify how whiteness is normalized in society rather than serve as a criticism or dismissal of a White person's hard work or efforts. Privilege and marginalization exist even in the absence of any individual's ill intentions. Moreover, all society members experience privilege in some domains in their lives, while they may experience being outside the norm in other aspects of their lives.

Research on Privilege in SEPP

Research on privilege has been scant in SEPP. Butryn (2002, 2009) was one of the few scholars to critically examine how white male privilege manifests in the field of SEPP through reflections on his own racial identity and experiences. For example, Butryn (2009) reflected on his experiences of writing about social justice, but at times he avoided unpacking actual problematic comments or conversations in real-life situations. He further reflected on his ability to choose to engage in, and subsequently withdraw from, his social justice work. He wondered,

> If I cared so much about combating white privilege and oppressions, why did I shift much of my research to other, comparably frivolous areas? The privilege to fight the fight only when I want to? Or when someone offers a chance to submit to a special issue?
>
> (Butryn, 2009, p. 335)

He also discussed the *feel* of conferences and the topics of interest to sport psychology professionals versus sport sociology professionals. Butryn (2002) called for SEPP professionals to further unpack power relations and their own privileges, arguing that, "when whiteness is critically analyzed and decentered, or 'made strange,' it is stripped of its conferred power in a predominantly white society" (p. 318).

Although explicit discussions of privilege have been limited in SEPP, critical research has been increasing in the past decade through the advancement of CSP. Several CSP scholars have conducted research through a culturally reflexive lens under the assumption that culture and power relations underlie all aspects of social lives, identities, and knowledge production, and have helped demonstrate the pervasiveness of power and inequities within SEPP (see Blodgett, Schinke, McGannon, & Fisher, 2015; Busanich & McGannon, 2010; Ryba et al., 2010).

Examples of Privilege

In the USA, individuals can legally get fired for wearing dreadlocks (Finley, 2016). A Black U.S. high school wrestler was forced to cut his dreadlocks in 90 seconds or forfeit a match because the referee insisted that the wrestler's hair "was not in its natural state" and was against state rules (Keneally, 2018). Some individuals struggle to find hair products that fit their hair type in the shampoo aisles at grocery stores (McIntosh, 1988). Black people can be called unprofessional or too political simply by wearing their hair as it naturally grows (Bates, 2017). When gymnast Gabby Douglas competed in the Olympics and became the first U.S. gymnast to ever win gold medals in both individual and team competitions in the same Olympic Games, there were still numerous news articles about her hair rather than her athletic accomplishments (Buckner, 2016; Wu, 2016). With the number of stereotypes and subconscious biases that lead to life and death consequences, such as the incidents of police brutality in the USA (Friedersdorf, 2017), to never have to think about possible consequences of one's natural hair would be an example of unearned privilege.

Although not having the historical context or horrific consequences of institutional discrimination against people from traditionally marginalized groups, another example of privilege (i.e., not being the societal norm) could be found in the tensions between the hard sciences and applied sciences. Many SEPP professionals may have experienced being considered as less legitimate and less rigorous compared with those in traditional disciplines such as economics or even different branches of psychology such as developmental psychology or organizational psychology. SEPP professionals may often have to explain and even defend their discipline to others, even other academics in related fields. Many SEPP programmes are either housed in a kinesiology or a psychology department and may experience tension from the hard sciences such as exercise physiology or more traditional disciplines such as clinical psychology. To not feel questioned, exoticized, or othered as academics in the traditional or hard sciences could be considered a form of privilege.

Similar tensions can be seen between quantitative research and qualitative research. This division is why there are separate conferences and journals focusing solely on qualitative research in sport and exercise (http://qrse.org/). It would be problematic to think of the conferences and journals created specifically for qualitative research as being discriminatory or unfair towards quantitative research. Quantitative research has been the dominant or taken-for-granted practice in curricula, academic conferences, and scholarly journals (Krane, 1994; Ryba & Schinke, 2009). Finding a space where qualitative research is not treated as an inferior pursuit is necessary if the field wants to benefit from the richness of qualitative methodologies. Similarly, having Black History Month and safe spaces for traditionally marginalized communities on college campuses are important because minority cultures are rarely included in curricula, emphasized, valued, or respected in dominant spaces. As seen from these examples, privilege is much subtler and more omnipresent than commonly discussed. To fit societal norms and expectations with relative ease is an unearned form of privilege.

Practice and Application

A preface to this practice and application section is that there is no quick and easy fix to achieving equality and social justice. If power is deeply entrenched in all aspects of society, the work of uncovering issues of power and inequality is not only extensive, but also never-ending. There is no one powerful *other* to dethrone, because power is omnipresent and embedded in our everyday language, thoughts, and knowledge (Foucault, 1995). Thus, challenging existing power structures is an extensive and, possibly, never-ending task. With these thoughts in mind, the following practical suggestions are offered regarding how SEPP professionals might incorporate knowledge of power into their teaching, research, and applied practice of SEPP.

Teaching

If one adheres to Foucault's description of discursive power, neither knowledge nor power is inherently good or bad. Power, however, can be productive (Foucault, 1995). Given that power and knowledge are intimately tied (Foucault, 1995), what one teaches and how one teaches knowledge become important questions on which to reflect (Markula & Pringle, 2006). Therefore, SEPP professionals could adopt critical pedagogies as a way to engage in more reflexive and socially just pedagogy.

Critical pedagogy is based on the ideas of critical theory (Brookfield, 2005). With the assumption there is a division between those who have power and those who do not, critical pedagogy scholars believe it is the educator's role to develop critical consciousness within the oppressed to free them from oppression and create an equal and just society (Brookfield, 2005). Scholars such as Freire (2000) and hooks (1994) have written extensively about critical pedagogy. When engaging in critical pedagogy, here are some ideas to consider.

In *Teaching to Transgress*, hooks (1994) discussed the need for teachers to reflect on the process of critical and liberatory pedagogy. Freire (2000), as well as hooks (1994), believed education could lead to the practice of freedom. For example, hooks did not believe it was enough that teachers add critical readings to their syllabi, although that is a first step. Rather, hooks encouraged educators to interrogate the process of how we teach, as well as the product of what we teach. She stated, "[It is] important to acknowledge that professors may attempt to deconstruct traditional biases while sharing that information through body posture, tone, word choice, and so on that perpetuate those very hierarchies and biases they are critiquing" (p. 141). She proposed that liberatory pedagogy should include purposeful reflection and reimagining of the entire teaching process, including how bodies are positioned in the classroom. For example, hooks encouraged teachers to think about what it means to stand behind the podium versus stepping into the classroom towards the students. Critical and liberatory pedagogy requires an understanding that everything we do, including our bodily positionings in the classroom, constitute the learning process.

Unlike Freire and hooks who theorized power as hegemonic, Markula and Pringle (2006) theorized that power is discursive. They offered suggestions for incorporating this understanding of power into one's teaching. Given the goal of poststructuralist theorists is not to replace one idea with another, because knowledge always has power implications, teaching from a poststructuralist perspective requires us to constantly question what has become taken for granted: How do we know we know? Why do we do the things we do? What are the consequences of the dominant ways of knowing and being? The process may look similar to that of critical theorists in that they continuously question the content as well as the process of teaching. Nevertheless, the end goal would differ because the goal of poststructuralists would be to constantly negotiate power relations, rather than to eradicate power altogether.

Besides continuously challenging and reimagining learning, critical pedagogy would require teaching how one knows what one knows, instead of simply teaching knowledge as if it appeared out of nowhere (i.e., knowledge as objective). One way to teach how one knows what one knows, which is a discussion of epistemology, is to teach the philosophical assumptions of knowledge. For example, SEPP professionals can help students become more aware of different philosophical assumptions of knowledge and how they can relate to research and practice (e.g., ontology, epistemology). This process would help students understand how one comes to know what one knows, how one acquires knowledge, and how one presents knowledge.

A practical exercise that can be used in classes to facilitate reflections on power and privilege is the privilege walk (www.albany.edu/ssw/efc/pdf/Module%205_1_Privilege%20Walk%20Activity.pdf). The privilege walk has many versions, but it can help facilitate self-awareness about one's privilege and what one takes for granted or considers normal. Discussions of power can be incorporated into the privilege exercise. For example, one can explain that taking a step forward because individuals grew up in heterosexual two-parent households does not mean they are better than others, but that they were not afraid to discuss their parents with others because they were often the norm and encountered less stigma or questioning than those who lived in single-parent households, had two parents of the same gender, or were orphans. This exercise facilitates reflections on how discourses surrounding identities shape experiences and meaning-making of these experiences. The content of some of the privilege walk questions may need to be adapted depending on where and with whom teachers are running the activity. SEPP professionals could familiarize themselves with critical theories and critically interrogate the content and the process of their teaching in SEPP.

Applied Practice/Consulting

If discourse constitutes reality (Weedon, 1997), the importance of critically examining language is evident. Because dominant discourses shape what we consider true, it is important that SEPP professionals, especially as helping professionals, are purposeful with the use of language. Nobel Prize winner Toni Morrison explained, "[Oppressive] language does more than represent violence; it is violence; does more than represent the limits of knowledge; it limits knowledge" (www.nobelprize.org/nobel_prizes/literature/laureates/1993/morrison-lecture.html). Consistent with Foucauldian poststructuralist theory, examining everyday language such as microaggressions (Sue, 2010) becomes essential because language is neither innocent nor neutral. Normalized language such as microaggressions not only reflects dominant discourses but also (re)produces them, constituting who and what we consider *normal* in society (Lee et al., 2018). For example, if working with a men's sporting team holding an open social activity, ensure athletes are invited to bring their partners, rather than using the heteronormative language of inviting them to bring their wives or girlfriends.

Another consideration in practice is to develop cultural competence in one's applied work by gaining cultural awareness, knowledge, and skill (Ryba et al., 2013). However, when gaining cultural knowledge, it is important to reflect on how one uses this knowledge. For example, cultural knowledge can be used to either generalize or to stereotype. Galanti (2015) explained that the content of generalizations and stereotypes may be similar, but they differ in how the information is used. When generalizing, one uses cultural information as a point of departure. Cultural information is a mere possibility and requires one to further investigate as to whether the cultural information is applicable to the particular individual one is working with. When stereotyping, on the other hand, one uses cultural information as the final destination. There is no further inquiry into the individual differences within cultural groups. Thus, when working with clients, practitioners must always consider sociocultural contexts and gather cultural information that could apply to the client, while also resisting stereotyping. This practice is consistent with Ryba et al.'s (2013) call for SEPP professionals to consider difference as relational rather than static and inherent. SEPP professionals should continue to gain cultural knowledge, but always be cautious of its implications.

Finally, Knowles and Gilbourne (2010) encouraged SEPP professionals to engage in critical reflective practice. Critical reflective practice is a way to interrogate how the personal is political (Fisher et al., 2003) by contextualizing one's experiences and knowledge within broader social contexts and power structures. In critical reflective practice, there is an explicit commitment to challenging power structures and promoting social justice and change. Moreover, Knowles and Gilbourne (2010) recommended autoethnographic writing as a potential methodology that facilitates critical reflective practice. They proposed that author-centred thinking and writing, in the form of an autoethnography, can help contextualize one's knowledge. These suggestions are some of the things SEPP professionals can take into consideration when working to become aware of, and challenge, power in applied SEPP practice.

Research

The ISSP position stand on "Cultural Competence" (Ryba et al., 2013) outlined various ways researchers can be culturally sensitive and safe when designing research projects (and, as a reminder, all researchers are cultural beings, so all research projects are "sociocultural" projects). Similar to what was discussed above, becoming aware and knowledgeable about identities, critical theories, and how knowledge works to (re)produce power relations applies to the research process. Knowledge is never neutral or without consequence. It is crucial to regularly ask oneself how one knows what one knows, and why one does what one does in the research process.

There are also increasing discussions on decolonizing methodologies and how SEPP professionals, as culprits of colonization in academia, can challenge traditional power relations (Cook, 2015; Goodman & Gorski, 2016). SEPP professionals could continue to challenge the power dynamics between the researcher and researched and ensure that, as researchers, we are benefiting, and not exploiting, the researched. Several years ago, the American Psychological Association changed the standard terminology of the researched from "subjects" to "participants" (Roediger, 2004). Researchers should not be subjecting participants to their whims. Ideally, participants should be participating not only in the collection of data, but also in creating the research questions and methodologies. This involvement is particularly important when working with communities or populations that historically have been oppressed, underrepresented, or unempowered. Researchers should challenge the role of scientific knowledge and question who and what benefits from existing research paradigms and methods.

Given the understanding of discursive power that knowledge and power are intertwined, explicitly aligning theories and methodologies with underlying philosophical assumptions is important. Moreover, it is important to regularly reflect on one's role as a researcher and how one participates in normalizing or challenging existing power structures and to seek research practices that challenge existing power structures.

Conclusion

In this contribution, the authors reviewed three theoretical views of power. Based on theoretical views of power as insidious and embedded within knowledge and discourse, the authors outlined how the concept of privilege can be better understood. The authors also reviewed research that incorporated theoretical views of power and privilege in SEPP. Finally, practical suggestions were offered regarding how one can teach, research, and practise while taking power and privilege into consideration. Adhering to the call for cultural praxis, which blends theory, research, practice, and lived experience (Ryba & Wright, 2005), the authors outlined suggestions about how SEPP professionals can engage in cultural praxis. Teachers were encouraged to incorporate critical theories and questioning of what we take for granted in the content and teaching. Practitioners were cautioned about using information on culture as a starting point rather than an endpoint, to avoid stereotyping. Researchers were invited to make their assumptions explicit and consider methodologies that explicitly challenge existing power structures. Finally, SEPP professionals were suggested to regularly discuss identities and privilege in their work using exercises such as the privilege walk. SEPP professionals are invited to continuously reflect on how power is relevant to all aspects of their profession, as well as their personal lives.

References

Allen, B. J. (2011). *Difference matters: Communicating social identity* (2nd ed.). Long Grove, IL: Waveland Press.

Bacon, L. (2010). *Health at every size: The surprising truth about your weight.* Dallas, TX: BenBella Books.

Bates, K. G. (2017, February 6). New evidence shows there's still bias against Black natural hair. *North State Public Radio.* Retrieved from www.npr.org/sections/codeswitch/2017/02/06/512943035/new-evidence-shows-theres-still-bias-against-black-natural-hair

Blodgett, A. T., Schinke, R. J., McGannon, K. R., & Fisher, L. A. (2015). Cultural sport psychology research: Conceptions, evolutions, and forecasts. *International Review of Sport and Exercise Psychology, 8*(1), 24–43. doi:https://doi.org/10.1080/1750984X.2014.942345

Bridges, T., & Pascoe, C. J. (2014). Hybrid masculinities: New directions in the sociology of men and masculinities. *Sociology Compass, 8*(3), 246–258.

Brookfield, S. D. (2005). *The power of critical theory: Liberating adult learning and teaching.* San Francisco, CA: Jossey-Bass.

Buckner, C. (2016, August 15). On Gabby Douglas's hair, Black women, why we care and why we shouldn't. *The Washington Post.* Retrieved from www.washingtonpost.com/news/sports/wp/2016/08/15/on-gabby-douglass-hair-black-women-why-we-care-and-why-we-shouldnt/

Burdsey, D. (2011). That joke isn't funny anymore: Racial microaggressions, color-blind ideology and the mitigation of racism in English men's first-class cricket. *Sociology of Sport Journal, 28*(3), 261–283.

Busanich, R., & McGannon, K. R. (2010). Deconstructing disordered eating: A feminist psychological approach to the body, food, and exercise relationship in female athletes. *Quest, 62,* 385–405.

Butryn, T. M. (2002). Critically examining white racial identity and privilege in sport psychology consulting. *The Sport Psychologist, 16*(3), 316–336.

Butryn, T. M. (2009). (Re)examining whiteness in sport psychology through autonarrative excavation. *International Journal of Sport and Exercise Psychology, 7*(3), 323–341.

Campanelli, B. (2017, September 25). Campanelli '18: Professional athletes deserve a political voice. *The Brown Daily Herald.* Retrieved from www.browndailyherald.com/2017/09/25/campanelli-18-profes sional-athletes-deserve-political-voice/

Carney, A., & Chawansky, M. (2016). Taking sex off the sidelines: Challenging heteronormativity within "sport in development" research. *International Review for the Sociology of Sport, 51*(3), 284–298.

Carter, L., & Davila, C. (2017). Is it because I'm Black? Microaggressive experiences against Black professionals in sport and exercise psychology. *Professional Psychology: Research and Practice, 48*(5), 287–293. doi:https://doi.org/10.1037/pro0000145

Chavez, C. (2018, February 16). Fox news' Laura Ingraham: LeBron should "shut up and dribble" after criticism of President Trump. *Sports Illustrated.* Retrieved from www.si.com/nba/2018/02/16/fox-news-laura-ingraham-lebron-james-president-donald-trump-shut-dribble

Comeaux, E., & Martin, A. (2018). Exploring NCAA Division I athletic administrator perceptions of male and female athletic directors' achievements: A photo elicitation study. *Sociology of Sport Journal, 35,* 132–140.

Cook, K. (2015). Grappling with wicked problems: Exploring photovoice as a decolonizing methodology in science education. *Cultural Studies of Science Education, 10*(3), 581–592. doi:https://doi.org/10.1007/s11422-014-9613-0

Dortants, M., & Knoppers, A. (2013). Regulation of diversity through discipline: Practices of inclusion and exclusion in boxing. *International Review for the Sociology of Sport, 48*(5), 535–549.

Félix, D. S. (2017, September 24). What will taking the knee mean now? *The New Yorker*. Retrieved from www.newyorker.com/culture/annals-of-appearances/what-will-taking-the-knee-mean-now

Fink, J. S., LaVoi, N. M., & Newhall, K. E. (2016). Challenging the gender binary? Male basketball practice players' views of female athletes and women's sports. *Sport in Society, 19*(8-9), 1316–1331. doi:10.1080/17430437.2015.1096252

Finley, T. (2016, September 20). Appeals court rules employers can ban dreadlocks at work. *The Huffington Post*. Retrieved from www.huffingtonpost.com/entry/appeals-court-rules-dreadlocks-work_us_57e0252ae4b0071a6e08a7c3

Fisher, L. A., Butryn, T. M., & Roper, E. A. (2003). Diversifying (and politicizing) sport psychology through cultural studies: A promising perspective. *The Sport Psychologist, 17*(4), 391–405.

Foucault, M. (1995). *Discipline and punish: The birth of the prison* (2nd ed.). New York: Vintage Books.

Freire, P. (2000). *Pedagogy of the oppressed*. 30th anniversary ed.. New York: Continuum.

Friedersdorf, C. (2017, April 18). A new exhibit in the case for the Black Lives Matter movement. *The Atlantic*. Retrieved from www.theatlantic.com/politics/archive/2017/04/a-new-exhibit-in-the-case-for-black-lives-matter/523209/

Galanti, G. A. (2015). *Caring for patients from different cultures* (5th ed.). Philadelphia, PA: University of Pennsylvania Press.

Goodman, R. D., & Gorski, P. C. (Eds.). (2016). *Decolonizing "multicultural" counseling through social justice*. New York: Springer.

Gramsci, A. (1999). *Selections from the prison notebooks*. Retrieved from http://courses.justice.eku.edu/pls330_louis/docs/gramsci-prison-notebooks-vol1.pdf

Guzzini, S. (2013). *Power, realism and constructivism*. Abingdon: Routledge.

Hoffman, B. (2017, September 23). Trump's comments on N.F.L. and Stephen Curry draw intense reaction. *The New York Times*. Retrieved from www.nytimes.com/2017/09/23/sports/trump-nfl-nba.html

hooks, b. (1994). *Teaching to transgress: Education as the practice of freedom*. Abingdon: Routledge.

Johnson, L. D. (2018, November 26). Re: Clay Travis on sports and politics [Electronic mailing list message]. Retrieved from https://listserv.temple.edu/cgi-

Jones, B. (2017, March 27). Colin Kaepernick is called a distraction, but from what? *The Undefeated*. Retrieved from https://theundefeated.com/features/colin-kaepernick-is-called-a-distraction-but-from-what/

Kamphoff, C. S., Gill, D. L., Araki, K., & Hammond, C. C. (2010). A content analysis of cultural diversity in the Association for Applied Sport Psychology's conference programs. *Journal of Applied Sport Psychology, 22*(2), 231–245.

Kavoura, A., Kokkonen, M., Chroni, S., & Ryba, T. V. (2017). "Some women are born fighters": Discursive constructions of a fighter's identity by female Finnish judo athletes. *Sex Roles*, 1–14. doi:https://doi.org/10.1007/s11199-017-0869-1

Kavoura, A., Ryba, T. V., & Chroni, S. (2015). Negotiating female judoka identities in Greece: A Foucauldian discourse analysis. *Psychology of Sport and Exercise, 17*, 88–98. doi:https://doi.org/10.1016/j.psychsport.2014.09.011

Keneally, M. (2018, December 25). High school wrestler who was forced to cut his dreadlocks displayed "character," his parents say. *ABC News*. Retrieved from https://abcnews.go.com/US/high-school-wrestler-forced-cut-dreadlocks-displayed-character/story?id=60001058

Knowles, Z., & Gilbourne, D. (2010). Aspiration, inspiration and illustration: Initiating debate on reflective practice writing. *The Sport Psychologist, 24*(4), 504–520.

Krane, V. (1994). A feminist perspective on contemporary sport psychology research. *The Sport Psychologist, 8*, 393–410.

Krane, V. (2001a). One lesbian feminist epistemology: Integrating feminist standpoint, queer theory, and feminist cultural studies. *The Sport Psychologist, 15*(4), 401–411.

Krane, V. (2001b). We can be athletic and feminine, but do we want to? Challenging hegemonic femininity in women's sport. *Quest, 53*(1), 115–133.

Lee, S., Bernstein, M. B., Etzel, E. F., Gearity, B. T., & Kuklick, C. R. (2018). Student- athletes' experiences with racial microaggressions in sport: A Foucauldian discourse analysis. *The Qualitative Report, 23*(5), 1016–1043.

Lenskyj, H. J. (2012). Reflections on communication and sport: On heteronormativity and gender identities. *Communication & Sport, 1*(1/2), 138–150.

Lucas-Carr, C. B., & Krane, V. (2011). What is the T in LGBT? Supporting transgender athletes through sport psychology. *The Sport Psychologist, 25*(4), 532–548.

Markula, P., & Pringle, R. (2006). *Foucault, sport and exercise: Power, knowledge and transforming the self.* New York: Routledge.

Marx, K., & Engels, F. (1848). *Manifesto of the Communist Party.* Retrieved from www.marxists.org/archive/marx/works/download/pdf/Manifesto.pdf

McGannon, K. R., & Mauws, M. K. (2000). Discursive psychology: An alternative approach for studying adherence to exercise and physical activity. *Quest, 52*(2), 148–165.

McGannon, K. R., & Mauws, M. K. (2002). Exploring the exercise adherence problem: An integration of ethnomethodological and poststructuralist perspectives. *Sociology of Sport Journal, 19*(1), 67–89.

McGannon, K. R., McMahon, J., & Gonsalves, C. A. (2017). Mother runners in the blogosphere: A discursive psychological analysis of online recreational athlete identities. *Psychology of Sport and Exercise, 28,* 125–135.

McGannon, K. R., & Schinke, R. J. (2013). "My first choice is to work out at work; then I don't feel bad about my kids": A discursive psychological analysis of motherhood and physical activity participation. *Psychology of Sport and Exercise, 14*(2), 179–188.

McIntosh, P. (1988). *White privilege: Unpacking the invisible knapsack.* Retrieved from www.racialequitytools.org/resourcefiles/mcintosh.pdf

Messner, M. A. (1990). When bodies are weapons: Masculinity and violence in sport. *International Review for the Sociology of Sport, 25*(3), 203–220.

Molnar, G., & Kelly, J. (2013). *Sport, exercise and social theory: An introduction.* New York: Routledge.

Moore, J. (2018, April 13). At least the NFL isn't pretending it's not blackballing Colin Kaepernick. *The Guardian.* Retrieved from www.theguardian.com/sport/2018/apr/13/kaepernick-reid-blackballed-nfl-kneeling-anthem

Myers, K. (2017, January 19). Re: I want to sincerely apologize for my postings, which I realize were inappropriate and unrelated to the purpose of this user group [Electronic mailing list message]. Retrieved from https://listserv.temple.edu/cgi-bin/wa?A0=SPORTPSY

Ortner, S. B. (1998). Identities: The hidden life of class. *Journal of Anthropological Research, 54*(1), 1–17.

Pringle, R. (2005). Masculinities, sport, and power: A critical comparison of Gramscian and Foucauldian inspired theoretical tools. *Journal of Sport and Social Issues, 29*(3), 256–278. doi:https://doi.org/10.1177/0193723505276228

Roediger, H. L. (2004). Presidential column: What should they be called? *APS Observer, 17*(4). Retrieved from www.psychologicalscience.org/observer/what-should-they-be-called

Roper, E. A., Fisher, L. A., & Wrisberg, C. A. (2005). Professional women's career experiences in sport psychology: A feminist standpoint approach. *The Sport Psychologist, 19*(1), 32–50.

Ross, S. R., & Shinew, K. J. (2008). Perspectives of women college athletes on sport and gender. *Sex Roles, 58*(1-2), 40–57. doi:https://doi.org/10.1007/s11199-007-9275-4

Ryba, T., Schinke, R. J., & Tenenbaum, G. (Eds.). (2010). *The cultural turn in sport psychology.* Morgantown, WV: Fitness Info Tech.

Ryba, T. V. (2005). *Applied sport psychology: Unearthing and contextualizing a dual genealogy.* (Unpublished doctoral dissertation). Knowxville, TN: University of Tennessee.

Ryba, T. V., & Schinke, R. J. (2009). Methodology as a ritualized eurocentrism: Introduction to the special issue. *International Journal of Sport and Exercise Psychology, 7*(3), 263–274. doi:https://doi.org/10.1080/1612197X.2009.9671909

Ryba, T. V., Stambulova, N. B., Si, G., & Schinke, R. J. (2013). ISSP position stand: Culturally competent research and practice in sport and exercise psychology. *International Journal of Sport and Exercise Psychology, 11*(2), 123–142.

Ryba, T. V., & Wright, H. K. (2005). From mental game to cultural praxis: A cultural studies model's implications for the future of sport psychology. *Quest, 57,* 192–212. doi:https://doi.org/10.1080/00336297.2005.10491853

Ryba, T. V., & Wright, H. K. (2010). Sport psychology and the cultural turn: Notes toward cultural praxis. In T. V. Ryba, R. J. Schinke, & G. Tenenbaum (Eds.), *The cultural turn in sport psychology* (pp. 3–28). Morgantown, WV: Fitness Info Tech.

Schinke, R. J., Stambulova, N. R., Lidor, R., Papaioannou, A., & Ryba, T. V. (2016). ISSP position stand: Social missions through sport and exercise psychology. *International Journal of Sport and Exercise Psychology, 14,* 4–22. doi:https://doi.org/10.1080/1612197X.2014.999698

Stoddart, M. C. J. (2007). Ideology, hegemony, discourse: A critical review of theories of knowledge and power. *Social Thought & Research, 28,* 191–225. doi:https://doi.org/10.2307/23252126

Sue, D. W. (2004). Whiteness and ethnocentric monoculturalism: Making the "invisible" visible. *The American Psychologist, 59*(8), 761–769. doi:https://doi.org/10.1037/0003-066X.59.8.761

Sue, D. W. (2010). *Microaggressions in everyday life: Race, gender, and sexual orientation.* Hoboken, NJ: Wiley.

Watkins, E. (2017, October 9). Pence leaves Colts game after protest during anthem. *CNN.* Retrieved from www.cnn.com/2017/10/08/politics/vice-president-mike-pence-nfl-protest/index.html

Weedon, C. (1997). *Feminist practice and poststructuralist theory* (2nd ed.). Hoboken, NJ: Wiley-Blackwell.

Willig, C. (2013). Foucauldian discourse analysis. In C. Willig (Ed.), *Introducing qualitative research in psychology* (3rd ed., pp. 129–142). London: McGraw-Hill Education.

Wu, S. (2016, August 9). Negative tweets about Gabby Douglas's hair inspire social media responses. *Teen Vogue.* Retrieved from www.teenvogue.com/story/gabby-douglas-olympics-hair-negative-tweets-response

38
QUALITATIVE METHODS

Toni Louise Williams and Brett Smith

Introduction

The word *testing* is commonly associated with quantitative research rather than qualitative inquiry. Accordingly, this entry begins by considering what is meant by the use of testing when using qualitative methods. A brief overview of the approaches taken when designing a qualitative study are offered before exploring the possibilities of testing qualitative research, and what this might offer the field of sport and exercise psychology. Different ways qualitative methods might be used to test qualitative research are then highlighted and critically discussed. To close, some recommendations for testing qualitative research in sport and exercise psychology are proposed.

Testing in Qualitative Research

There are fundamental differences between quantitative and qualitative research that impact upon the type of contribution each method of inquiry makes to our understanding of the world (Martin, 2011). For Gubrium and Holstein (1997), these differences are reflected in the 'methods talk' between quantitative and qualitative researchers. For example, quantitative research, which treats social facts as things, attempts to measure these and explain their relationships through talk of structural variables and causal models, units of analysis and sampling frames, operationalization, and measurement (Sparkes & Smith, 2014). In contrast, for qualitative researchers, there is talk about meaning, and what things mean to the people being studied:

> This is decidedly not talk about predictive models. Lived experience is on stage here. Rich description is the name of the game. There's little mention of standardized measurement. Instead we hear the trials and tribulations of 'entrée and engagement', 'access and rapport'. In contrast to descriptions of social facts and variable relations from an 'objective' distance – held at arm's length so to speak – we hear the admonition to get close to people, be involved. 'You've got to get out there, into the nitty-gritty, real world. Get your hands dirty. See it up close, for yourself.'
>
> *(Gubrium & Holstein, 1997, p. 4)*

Recognizing these differences provides a starting point for conversations regarding what is meant by the use of testing using qualitative methods. Typically, quantitative research is more concerned with testing and measurement and describing and explaining relationships. This is owing to the underlying post-positivistic philosophical assumptions of most quantitative research, that is, there is an independent reality that can be subject to measurement and testing, and thereby can be found (Smith & McGannon, 2018; see also Tamminen & Poucher, Volume 1, Chapter 39, in this encyclopedia). Indeed, the sport and exercise psychology field is dominated by quantitative research and overly concerned with the measurement of behaviour (Meredith, Dicks, Noel, & Wagstaff, 2018). As Meredith et al. (2018) argued, 'a central aim of psychology research is to emphasize the development of understanding on the control of behaviour, enabling psychologists to communicate theory for the benefit of society, wherein science and society constitute a feedback loop' (p. 26). As such, practitioners are interested in how psychological constructs might affect behaviour in sport and exercise contexts to implement interventions to positively impact health, performance, and well-being.

In contrast, qualitative research is typically positioned within an interpretative paradigm. The philosophical assumptions underpinning interpretivism include ontological relativism (i.e., there are multiple, mind-dependent realities) and epistemological constructionism (i.e., knowledge is socially constructed; Smith & Deemer, 2000; Smith & McGannon, 2018). Thus, there is no one true reality that can be independently measured and tested from this philosophical position. As Denzin and Lincoln (2011) explained:

> Qualitative research is a situated activity which locates the observer in the world. Qualitative research consists of a set of interpretive, material practices that make the world visible. These practices transform the world. They turn the world into a series of representations, including fieldnotes, interviews, conversations, photographs, recordings and memos to the self. At this level, qualitative research involves an interpretive, naturalistic approach to the world. This means that qualitative researchers study things in their natural settings, attempting to make sense of or interpret phenomena in terms of the meanings people bring to them.
>
> (p. 3)

With this definition in mind, consideration is given to how sport and exercise psychology researchers may approach and design a qualitative study, before attention is turned to testing within qualitative research. That said, there are more common instances of what might be seen as testing within qualitative research. These include researchers applying and testing theory, as well as building a new theory or developing an existing theory using qualitative methodologies and methods (Cassidy, 2016; Tamminen & Holt, 2010). Furthermore, qualitative methods are tested for their application within the sport and exercise sciences such as visual methods (Phoenix, 2010), narrative inquiry and discursive psychology (McGannon & Smith, 2015), and integrated and longitudinal qualitative methods (Williams, 2018). However, testing is not a word often used within qualitative research. If it is used in relation to qualitative research, it means something very different to how it is used in quantitative research.

Approaching a Qualitative Study

The first stage in approaching a qualitative study involves developing research questions, aims and/or objectives, and a statement of purpose. Conducting a literature review is a good starting point to assist sport and exercise psychology researchers in formulating their research questions and statement of purpose. As Agee (2009) explained, 'good questions do not necessarily produce good research, but poorly conceived or constructed questions will likely create problems that affect all subsequent stages of the study' (p. 431). Therefore, generating and refining research questions are important processes that will shape all phases of a qualitative study. In qualitative studies, research questions are open-ended to provide detailed descriptions and explanations of phenomena. Good qualitative research questions tend to be process-orientated, asking how and why something happens, rather than just what happens (Sparkes & Smith, 2014). Furthermore, qualitative research questions may change during the process of inquiry as new questions emerge that were not thought of at the start of a study. Thus, 'it is helpful to think of research questions as navigational tools that can help a researcher map possible directions but also inquiry about the unexpected' (Agee, 2009, p. 432).

A further consideration when approaching a qualitative research study is the design in terms of methodology and methods. Qualitative researchers can situate their research within a variety of traditions and draw upon a myriad of empirical methods of data collection. Each tradition has a different function within qualitative research and should be chosen based upon the purpose of the study and research questions. The traditions include (but are not limited to) ethnography, narrative inquiry, phenomenology, grounded theory, case study, and critical or openly ideological research (see Sparkes & Smith, 2014). For example, ethnography loosely refers to any qualitative project that focuses on observation and interaction of others to provide an inductive, detailed, and in-depth description of cultural practices (Atkinson, 2016). Narrative inquiry explores the stories people tell to make sense of their lives and experiences and the dominant cultural narratives in which these stories circulate (Sparkes & Smith, 2014). Grounded theory involves the systematic process of collecting and analysing data to explore theoretical explanations for empirical findings or to construct theories that are grounded in data (Bryant & Charmaz, 2007), whereas critical or openly ideological research encapsulates a range of traditions (e.g., feminism, queer theory, critical race theory, critical disability studies, postcolonial studies) to help individuals become aware of contradictions and distortions in their belief systems and social practices in a way that encourages them to change those beliefs and systems (Sparkes & Smith, 2014). Although there are some similarities within each tradition, the differences play themselves out further in the ways that researchers go about collecting and analysing data.

The next consideration when approaching a qualitative research study is what kinds of data will be needed to answer the research questions in line with the chosen qualitative tradition. Qualitative researchers have a wide range of data sources and methods of data collection to draw upon to understand the phenomenon in question. For instance, more traditional methods include interviews, which are a social activity where people actively engage in embodied talk, jointly constructing knowledge about themselves and the social world as they interact with each other (Sparkes & Smith, 2014), and participant observation, which permits a much lengthier and more involved engagement in the field where the researcher spends time getting to know people, rather than just knowing about them (O'Reilly, 2012). However, there are a plethora of novel data collection techniques available to sport and exercise psychology researchers such as visual methods (e.g., photography, film, timelining, etc.) and digital, virtual, and online methods (e.g., blogs, social media, etc.), to name but a few (see Braun, Clarke, & Gray, 2017; Phoenix, 2010; Smith, Caddick, & Williams, 2015). Once data collection techniques have been decided upon, further thought should be given to sampling (i.e., which people, places, settings, events, and times are best for gaining data), ethics (i.e., procedural ethics and ethics in practice), and how data will be analysed (see Sparkes & Smith, 2014). Following the collection and analysis of data, qualitative researchers may wish to deliberate on testing their findings.

Reframing Testing in Qualitative Research

There are numerous ways to respond to testing within qualitative research. The first is to draw upon post-positivistic methods and apply these to qualitative research processes and practices. For example, inter-rater reliability is one post-positivistic approach drawn upon as a tool within qualitative inquiry (Culver, Gilbert, & Sparkes, 2012). Inter-rater reliability is an approach that aims to ensure 'reliable' results through employing intercoder reliability and intercoder agreement during the analysis of data (Campbell, Quincy, Osserman, & Pedersen, 2013). However, as various scholars have suggested, (e.g., Braun & Clarke, 2013; Campbell et al., 2013; Smith & McGannon, 2018), inter-rater reliability is ineffective in ensuring reliable qualitative research for numerous reasons. These include philosophical contradictions with the aims of inter-rater reliability (i.e., that agreements on coding can, and should, exist between researchers) and those of qualitative research (i.e., agreements are unlikely to occur owing to the background knowledge and experience of the researcher inescapably influencing the coding and construction of knowledge; Smith & McGannon, 2018). Thus, careful consideration needs be taken when applying post-positivistic methods to qualitative research – a point returned to below.

The second way to respond is to reject the notion of *testing* and the word *test* altogether owing to the historical and philosophical connections to post-positivism. But, in this entry, attention is drawn to a third approach in which the word testing is kept, but its meaning is changed to create a different way to look at testing in qualitative research. This third approach involves reframing testing as something positive to work with. What follows is a critical exploration of two ways to explore testing in qualitative sport and exercise psychology research. These are: (1) the use of member checking and member reflections to test the methodological rigour of qualitative research, and (2) testing the generalizability of qualitative research.

Member Checking and Member Reflections to Test Methodological Rigour

In sport and exercise psychology research, member checking is extensively drawn upon as a measure of quality control and as an indicator of rigour when it comes to testing and validating qualitative inquiry (Culver et al., 2012). The notion of rigour is often viewed as a necessary marker of quality in qualitative research, yet the term rigour has multiple meanings. These meanings include, but are not limited to, intellectual precision, robustness, appropriateness and cohesiveness of ontology, epistemology, methodology, methods and concepts in the research process, and output (Burke, 2016; Tracy, 2010). Member checking, otherwise termed respondent or participant validation, involves the participants of a project judging the rigour of the research findings in terms of validating – or testing – the credibility of qualitative data and results (Lincoln & Guba, 1985). This testing of the research is achieved by returning the data (e.g., interview transcripts) and/or results (e.g., themes and interpretations) to participants and asking them to comment on whether the data and results accurately reflect their experiences. If the accuracy of the data and/or results is confirmed by participants, the findings can be deemed credible and the research valid. Thus, member checks can be used to control or correct for subjective bias and test the 'truth' of any knowledge (Birt, Scott, Cavers, Campbell, & Walter, 2016; Lincoln & Guba, 1985). Despite claims of member checking as a demonstration of rigorous research, the widespread use of this method in sport and exercise psychology is troubling (Smith & McGannon, 2018).

Philosophical, Empirical, and Practical Problems with Member Checking

As Smith and McGannon (2018) highlighted, there are at least three major philosophical, empirical, and practical problems with the use of member checking to test the rigour of qualitative research. First, at a philosophical level, there are underpinning ontological and epistemological challenges and problems with member checking. Understanding the ontology (i.e., What is the nature of reality?) and epistemology (i.e., What is the relationship between the inquirer and the known? What types of knowledge might be legitimately known?) of any research is essential (Sparkes & Smith, 2014). This is because the philosophical roots of any method of inquiry challenge the position researchers take as to what should be studied, what counts as knowledge, and how the results are best interpreted (Lincoln, 2010). One problem with using member checking to validate research findings is that the use of this claim often aligns – either implicitly or explicitly – with epistemological foundationalism (Smith & McGannon, 2018). Epistemological foundationalism refers to the assumption that the method of member checking is neutral, objective, and, therefore, able to control for bias and distinguish between trustworthy and less trustworthy findings (Lincoln & Guba, 1985; Smith & McGannon, 2018). The issue with epistemological foundationalism is that methods are not neutral, objective, or unbiased, but, rather, dependent upon the researcher and participant who are conducting the member checks (Culver et al., 2012; Smith & Deemer, 2000). Furthermore, understanding and representing people's experience requires 'interpretive activity; this is always informed by our own assumptions, values and commitments' (Braun & Clarke, 2013, p. 285). Thus, member checks cannot produce objective, theory-free knowledge or provide an independent foundation to judge trustworthy and less trustworthy findings (Smith & McGannon, 2018).

Second, in a recent review of published literature, Thomas (2017) concluded that there was little evidence that member checking enhances the credibility or trustworthiness of qualitative research. For example, many papers that reported the use of member checks provided little information on the procedures used or how such checks had influenced the construction of findings. Third, the claim that member checks can test rigour falls further apart owing to the numerous practical problems faced by researchers (Smith & McGannon, 2018). One practical problem is the possibility that the participant and researcher may provide contradictory interpretations of the findings. However, it is very rare in the sport and exercise psychology literature for any papers to disclose disagreements between participants and researchers during the process of member checking. It is unlikely that there is 100% member agreement in all papers utilizing member checks. Thus, another practical problem is knowing with certainty that each participant has faithfully engaged in the process of member checking and not just agreed with the researcher's interpretation. This could happen if the participant does not comprehend the results, or sees the researcher as an 'expert' and, therefore, agrees with the findings despite having different viewpoints. In addition, the time that passed between data collection/analysis and seeking participant feedback is another practical problem impacting the effectiveness of member checking to test the accuracy of experience. Lastly, member checking is ineffective as a test of rigour if participants have a political or personal interest in the outcomes of the research that may lead to the censoring or rejection of findings.

The Potential of Member Reflections

In light of the issues with using member checks to test rigour, sport and exercise psychology researchers may consider dropping the use of member checking and instead draw upon *member reflections* (Smith & McGannon, 2018). Rather than testing results or distinguishing contradictory claims about knowledge, member reflections can be reframed as a practical opportunity to generate additional data and insight (Braun & Clarke, 2013; Tracy, 2010). For example, researchers might engage in member reflections with participants to explore similarities, differences, and gaps in the interpretation of findings (Schinke, McGannon, & Smith, 2013). As part of this co-participatory process and dialogue, researchers and participants can address questions such as what to do with disagreements over findings. Or, how can any differences be incorporated into the final report? There is no right answer to these questions, as each will be dependent upon the context, practice, and situational demand of each project (Schinke et al., 2013). However, the inclusion of complementary or contradictory results may help to facilitate a meticulous, robust, and intellectually enriched understanding of the phenomena researched (Smith & McGannon, 2018). That said, there are some ethical concerns with using member reflections. For instance, disappointment, hurt feelings, and embarrassment may be experienced by both participants and researchers following the sharing of findings (Sparkes & Smith, 2014). To address these concerns, researchers may wish to adopt a culturally responsive, relational reflexive ethical position whereby member reflections are used to promote dignity, mutual respect, and connectedness with participants (Smith & McGannon, 2018).

There are some recent noteworthy examples of the use of member reflections within the sport and exercise psychology literature. For instance, Howells and Lucassen (2018) utilized member reflections to enhance the rigour of their study exploring the concept of 'post-Olympic blues' with British athletes following the Rio 2016 Olympics. Member reflections were drawn upon to 'encourage participant engagement, deep reflection, and as a means to understand the participant-constructed realities' (p. 70). To achieve this, during a follow-up interview, both the participant and researcher reflected upon the first interview and their respective appraisals, having had time to reflect. Given the small number of Olympic athletes, member reflections were also sought on the initial report to assist in the anonymizing process and avoid breaching confidentiality via deductive disclosure (i.e., when traits and rich descriptions of people unintentionally reveal who they are; Sparkes & Smith, 2014). Similarly, Salim and Wadey (2018) sought member reflections to demonstrate the methodological rigour of the qualitative analysis in their mixed methods study examining the efficacy of emotional disclosure to promote sport-injury-related growth. This involved sharing and discussing the findings with participants to ensure the authors understood the participants' growth-related experiences from their perspective. Furthermore, member reflections allowed participants to reflect upon how their perception of the intervention to promote sport-injury-related-growth had changed over time. For example, participants expressed how difficult the intervention was in the interview, yet also expressed the therapeutic impact of the intervention upon reflection 6 months later.

Testing for Generalizability

Generalizability is a term often used to discuss how the results of reliable quantitative research can be applied to a wider population or different context. Yet, there is a lack of discussion and understanding on generalizability in relation to qualitative research. What is often seen in sport and exercise psychology literature are claims that a limitation and/or weakness of qualitative research is that the results cannot be generalized. However, as Smith (2018) highlighted, it is a common misconception that qualitative research cannot be tested for generalizability. This misconception regarding qualitative research comes from the understanding of generalizability from a statistical-probabilistic model. In quantitative research, this type of generalization is normally sought through statistical sampling procedures to provide confidence in the representativeness of sample and allow broader inferences to be made. The use of this type of generalizability aligns with the ontological and epistemological assumptions that inform much post-positivistic quantitative research. Yet, to apply statistical-probabilistic generalizability to qualitative research makes little sense. For instance, the ontological and epistemological assumptions that inform qualitative research are different from those that inform quantitative research (see above). Furthermore, statistical-probabilistic generalizability is not a meaningful goal for qualitative research. In qualitative research, the goal is to examine people's lives in rich detail, which is achieved through purposefully sampling a small number of people (Braun & Clarke, 2013; Sparkes & Smith, 2014). Therefore, small samples purposefully chosen to gain rich knowledge are a *strength* and not a weakness of qualitative research.

With these critiques in mind, it begs the question: Why should a qualitative researcher consider testing the generalizability of their research? One reason that generalization should be a legitimate concern for qualitative researchers is that much is at stake when generalization is ignored (Green & Thorogood, 2009; Hayhurst, 2016; Lewis, Richie, Ormston, & Morrell, 2014; Sparkes & Smith, 2014). For example, ignoring generalizability implies that qualitative researchers do not need to care about testing the generalizability of their results. But qualitative researchers should care, because, if only quantitative results are considered generalizable, this reinforces quantitative research as the most desirable form of knowledge and the only one that counts (Smith, 2018). Likewise, the belief that qualitative research is inherently not generalizable provides a rationale for journal editors, reviewers, policymakers, and sports coaching and sporting organizations to critique qualitative research on this basis (Greenhalgh et al., 2016; Shaw & Hoeber, 2016). Thus, for researchers, organizations, or government to use qualitative research and make fair and appropriate judgements about this work, generalizability needs to be engaged with. This is especially so given that qualitative research *can* produce work that can be generalized (Smith, 2018). Qualitative researchers need to look beyond statistical-probabilistic generalizability to consider what kind of relationship qualitative research findings might have to multiple and different types of generalization (Green & Thorogood, 2009; Smith, 2018).

Types of Generalizability in Qualitative Research

There are various types of generalization available for researchers to consider when testing the relationship of their qualitative research study findings to generalizability. One type to consider is naturalistic generalizability (Stake, 2005) – otherwise termed representational generalization (Lewis et al., 2014) – whereby the research findings resonate with the reader's personal engagement in life's affairs and experiences. For example, when a person with spinal cord injury encounters research on the barriers and facilitators to physical activity participation for disabled people, do the findings reverberate with their personal experiences of trying to become or continue being physically active? Do they feel the research was about them? Or are the data and results recognizable in terms of what they witnessed? If so, it might be suggested the research displays naturalistic generalizability (Smith, 2018). If the research does not 'ring true' to their experiences, or is not generalizable to them, it does not mean the research is 'invalid' or not useful. Rather, this provides an opportunity to explore different responses to the research (Smith & Sparkes, 2011). Enabling readers to reflect on the case under study requires thick description and involves 'recording the circumstances, meanings, intentions, strategies, motivations, and so on that characterize a particular episode. It is this interpretive characteristic of description rather than details per se that makes it thick' (Schwandt, 2015, p. 306). One illustration of thick description and claims of naturalistic generalization can be found in the research by Sparkes, Brighton, and Inckle (2018) in their ethnographic exploration of becoming a disabled sporting cyborg following spinal cord injury.

Another type of generalization researchers may wish to consider is *transferability* (Tracy, 2010), which is also referred to as inferential generalization (Lewis et al., 2014) or case-to-case generalization (Chenail, 2010). This is not to be confused with Lincoln and Guba's (1985) definition of transferability as the 'fittingness' between two cases. Rather, here, transferability is defined as occurring when a person or group in one setting considers adopting something from another setting that the research has identified (Smith, 2018). For example, a physical educator, sports community leader, or health policymaker reading a qualitative report on how to promote active lifestyles might want to know: 'Is this something I can apply to my physical education class, local community group, or country to encourage active lifestyles?' For Tracy (2010), to enable readers to transfer research findings to their own actions, research reports should include rich description and accessible and inviting writing. Moreover, creative analytical practices that include evocative storytelling may also invite generalization through transferability (Smith, 2018; Tracy, 2010). Transferability is further related to the term generativity. According to Barone and Eisner (2012), generativity may occur when research invites people into an experience and moves them to act upon what they have read or seen performed. Although they did not explicitly discuss transferability, the generative potential of research and transferability can be seen in Hurley, Swann, Allen, Okely, and Vella's (2017) exploration of the role of community sports clubs in adolescent mental health.

A further type of generalizability that may be of interest to qualitative researchers is analytical generalization (Chenail, 2010; Lewis et al., 2014), also known as vertical generalizability (Stephens, 1982) and idiographic generalizability (Sandelowski, 2004). Analytical generalization can occur through both concept and theoretical generalization (Smith, 2018). For instance, if a researcher generalizes a particular set of results to an established concept or theory, they are displaying concept generalizability or theoretical generalizability. Analytical generalization can also occur when a new concept or new theory is constructed that later makes sense in other research across different contexts and populations. Furthermore, if a researcher can produce new conceptual and theoretical understandings of a topic, or show the value of such concepts and theories in other research, then this is another form of analytical generalization. Thus, in analytical generalizations, it is the concepts and theories that are generalizable, rather than the specific context or populations. An illustration of naturalistic, concept, and theoretical generalization can be seen in the work of Wadey and Day (2018) in their longitudinal examination of leisure-time physical activity among people in England with an amputation.

Lastly, another type of generalizability of concern to qualitative researchers is intersectional generalizability (Fine, Tuck, & Zeller-Berkman, 2008). For Fine et al. (2008), intersectional generalizability is work that digs deep and respectfully within a community over time to record the particulars of historically oppressed and/or colonized peoples/communities and their social movements of resistance. This form of generalizability is also about producing 'work that tracks patterns across nations, communities, homes and bodied to theorize the arteries of oppression and colonialism' (Fine et al., 2008, p. 174). Intersectional generalizability connects with theoretical generalizability in that the research team can glean theoretical lessons about social oppression and forms of resistance moving from one context to another (Smith, 2018). It also relates to provocative generalizability by provoking researchers and audiences to rethink 'the possible' and asks researchers to 'move their findings toward that which is not yet imagined, not yet in practice, not yet in sight' (Fine et al., 2008, p. 169). Accordingly, intersectional generalizability connects with community-based research, feminism, and indigenous research (Smith, 2018). Yet, there are very few instances of intersectional generalizability discussed within the field of sport and exercise. One rare example can be found in Hayhurst's (2016) work in sport for development and peace as she calls for transnational, multi-sited, postcolonial feminist research. In addition to the four types of generalization offered here, there are other methods, such as meta-synthesis, that may be used to extend the generalizability of research findings (see Williams & Shaw, 2016; see also Curran & Williams, Volume 1, Chapter 21, in this encyclopedia).

Conclusion

In this entry, the considerations to be made in approaching a qualitative research study have been briefly described before different ways to reframe testing as a positive process to consider working with in qualitative sport and exercise psychology research were offered. These were the use of member reflections to test the methodological rigour of qualitative research and testing the generalizability of qualitative research findings. Despite the opportunities offered by testing qualitative research, there are some challenges to negotiate that could not be fully explored in this entry. For example, with regards to generalizability, how and where to make claims of generalizability, issues with providing 'evidence' of generalizations, and the shared responsibility of the researcher and reader in making generalizations were not addressed (Chenail, 2010; Lewis et al., 2014; Smith, 2018). Furthermore, the possibilities of testing qualitative research offered within this entry should not be considered inflexible or final – each can be adapted. These strategies are options or starting points for how researchers may consider testing the findings of their qualitative works. When scholars move into the terrain of testing, care needs to be taken not to offer rigid recipes, because qualitative research is a craft – it should be dynamic and imaginative (Braun & Clarke, 2013; Sparkes & Smith, 2014). That said, qualitative researchers must not pursue member reflections or seek to establish the generalizability of qualitative research for the sake of it. Rather, the aim of this entry is to stimulate critical thinking and future conversations regarding the use of testing within qualitative research in the field of sport and exercise psychology and beyond.

References

Agee, J. (2009). Developing qualitative research questions: A reflective process. *International Journal of Qualitative Studies in Education, 22,* 431–447.

Atkinson, M. (2016). Ethnography. In B. Smith & A. C. Sparkes (Eds.), *Routledge handbook of qualitative research in sport and exercise* (pp. 49–61). London: Routledge.

Barone, T., & Eisner, E. (2012). *Arts based research.* London: Sage.

Birt, L., Scott, S., Cavers, D., Campbell, C., & Walter, F. (2016). Member checking: A tool to enhance trustworthiness or merely a nod to validation? *Qualitative Health Research, 26,* 1802–1811.

Braun, V., & Clarke, V. (2013). *Successful qualitative research: A practical guide for beginners.* London: Sage.

Braun, V., Clarke, V., & Gray, D. (2017). *Collecting qualitative data: A practical guide to textual, media and virtual techniques.* Cambridge: Cambridge University Press.

Bryant, A., & Charmaz, K. (2007). *The Sage handbook of grounded theory.* Thousand Oaks. CA: Sage.

Burke, S. (2016). Rethinking 'validity' and 'trustworthiness' in qualitative inquiry: How might we judge the quality of qualitative research in sport and exercise sciences? In B. Smith & A. C. Sparkes (Eds.), *Routledge handbook of qualitative research in sport and exercise* (pp. 330–339). London: Routledge.

Campbell, J. L., Quincy, C., Osserman, J., & Pedersen, O. (2013). Coding in-depth semistructured interviews: Problems of unitization and intercoder reliability and agreement. *Sociological Methods and Research, 42,* 294–320.

Cassidy, T. (2016). The role of theory, interpretation and critical thought within qualitative sport and exercise research. In B. Smith & A. C. Sparkes (Eds.), *International handbook of qualitative methods in sport and exercise* (pp. 397–408). London: Routledge.

Chenail, R. C. (2010). Getting specific about qualitative research generalizability. *Journal of Ethnographic & Qualitative Research, 5,* 1–11.

Culver, D., Gilbert, W., & Sparkes, A. C. (2012). Qualitative research in sport psychology journals: The next decade 2000–2009 and beyond. *The Sport Psychologist, 26,* 261–281.

Denzin, N., & Lincoln, Y. (2011). Introduction: The discipline and practice of qualitative research. In N. K. Denzin & Y. S. Lincoln (Eds.), *Handbook of qualitative research* (pp. 1–17). London: Sage.

Fine, M., Tuck, E., & Zeller-Berkman, S. (2008). Do you believe in Geneva? Methods and ethics at the global–local nexus. In N. K. Denzin, Y. S. Lincoln, & L. T. Smith (Eds.), *Handbook of critical and indigenous methodologies* (pp. 157–177). London: Sage.

Green, J., & Thorogood, N. (2009). *Qualitative methods for health research* (2nd ed.). London: Sage.

Greenhalgh, T., Annandale, E., Ashcroft, R., Barlow, J., Black, N., Bleakley, A., … & Checkland, K. (2016). An open letter to *The BMJ* editors on qualitative research. *British Medical Journal, 352,* i563.

Gubrium, J., & Holstein, J. (1997). *The new language of qualitative method.* Oxford, UK: Oxford University Press.

Hayhurst, L. (2016). Sport for development and peace: A call for transnational, multi-sited, postcolonial feminist research. *Qualitative Research in Sport, Exercise and Health, 8,* 424–443.

Howells, K., & Lucassen, M. (2018). 'Post-Olympic blues' – The diminution of celebrity in Olympic athletes. *Psychology of Sport and Exercise, 37,* 67–78.

Hurley, D., Swann, C., Allen, M. S., Okely, A. D., & Vella, S. A. (2017). The role of community sports clubs in adolescent mental health: The perspectives of adolescent males' parents. *Qualitative Research in Sport, Exercise and Health, 9,* 372–388.

Lewis, J., Richie, J., Ormston, R., & Morrell, G. (2014). Generalizing from qualitative research. In J. Ritchie, J. Lewis, C. McNaughton Nicholls, & R. Ormston (Eds.), *Qualitative research practice* (2nd ed., pp. 347–366). London: Sage.

Lincoln, Y. (2010). 'What a long, strange trip it's been': Twenty-five years of qualitative and new paradigm research. *Qualitative Inquiry, 16,* 3–9.

Lincoln, Y. S., & Guba, E. G. (1985). *Naturalistic inquiry.* Beverly Hills, CA: Sage.

Martin, J. (2011). Qualitative research in sport and exercise psychology: Observations of a non-qualitative researcher. *Qualitative Research in Sport, Exercise and Health, 3,* 335–348.

McGannon, K. R., & Smith, B. (2015). Centralizing culture in cultural sport psychology research: The potential of narrative inquiry and discursive psychology. *Psychology of Sport and Exercise, 17,* 79–87.

Meredith, S. J., Dicks, M., Noel, B., & Wagstaff, C. R. D. (2018). A review of behavioural measures and research methodology in sport and exercise psychology. *International Review of Sport and Exercise Psychology, 11,* 25–46.

O'Reilly, K. (2012). *Ethnographic methods* (2nd ed.). Abingdon: Routledge.

Phoenix, C. (2010). Seeing the world of physical culture: The potential of visual methods for qualitative research in sport and exercise. *Qualitative Research in Sport and Exercise, 2,* 93–108.

Salim, J., & Wadey, R. (2018). Can emotional disclosure promote sport injury-related growth? *Journal of Applied Sport Psychology, 30,* 367–387.

Sandelowski, M. (2004). Using qualitative research. *Qualitative Health Research, 14,* 1366–1386.

Schinke, R. J., McGannon, K. R., & Smith, B. (2013). Expanding the sport and physical activity research landscape through community scholarship: Introduction. *Qualitative Research in Sport, Exercise and Health, 5,* 287–290.

Schwandt, T. (2015). *The Sage dictionary of qualitative research.* London: Sage.

Shaw, S., & Hoeber, L. (2016). Unclipping our wings: Ways forward in qualitative research in sport management. *Sport Management Review, 19,* 255–265.

Smith, B. (2018). Generalizability in qualitative research: Misunderstandings, opportunities and recommendations for the sport and exercise sciences. *Qualitative Research in Sport, Exercise and Health, 10,* 137–149.

Smith, B., Caddick, N., & Williams, T. L. (2015). Qualitative methods and conceptual advances in sport psychology. In S. D. Mellalieu & S. Hanton (Eds.), *Contemporary advances in sport psychology: A review* (pp. 202–225). London: Routledge.

Smith, B., & McGannon, K. R. (2018). Developing rigor in qualitative research: Problems and opportunities within sport and exercise psychology. *International Review of Sport and Exercise Psychology, 11,* 101–121.

Smith, B., & Sparkes, A. C. (2011). Multiple responses to a chaos narrative. *Health: an Interdisciplinary Journal for the Social Study of Health, Illness & Medicine, 15,* 38–53.

Smith, J., & Deemer, D. (2000). The problem of criteria in the age of relativism. In N. K. Denzin & Y. S. Lincoln (Eds.), *Handbook of qualitative research* (2nd ed., pp. 877–896). London: Sage.

Sparkes, A. C., Brighton, J., & Inckle, K. (2018). 'It's a part of me': An ethnographic exploration of becoming a disabled sporting cyborg following spinal cord injury. *Qualitative Research in Sport, Exercise and Health, 10,* 151–166.

Sparkes, A. C., & Smith, B. (2014). *Qualitative research methods in sport, exercise & health: From process to product.* London: Routledge.

Stake, R. (2005). Qualitative case studies. In N. K. Denzin & Y. S. Lincoln (Eds.), *Handbook of qualitative research* (3rd ed., pp. 443–466). London: Sage.

Stephens, M. (1982). A question of generalizability. *Theory and Research in Social Education, 9,* 75–89.

Tamminen, K. A., & Holt, N. L. (2010). A meta-study of qualitative research examining stressor appraisals and coping among adolescents in sport. *Journal of Sport Sciences, 28,* 1563–1580.

Thomas, D. R. (2017). Feedback from research participants: Are member checks useful in qualitative research? *Qualitative Research in Psychology, 14,* 23–41.

Tracy, S. J. (2010). Qualitative quality: Eight 'big-tent' criteria for excellent qualitative research. *Qualitative Inquiry, 16,* 837–851.

Wadey, R., & Day, M. (2018). A longitudinal examination of leisure time physical activity following amputation in England. *Psychology of Sport and Exercise, 37,* 251–261.

Williams, T. L. (2018). Exploring narratives of physical activity and disability over time: A novel integrated qualitative methods approach. *Psychology of Sport and Exercise, 37,* 224–234.

Williams, T. L., & Shaw, R. L. (2016). Synthesizing qualitative research. In B. Smith & A. C. Sparkes (Eds.), *International handbook of qualitative methods in sport and exercise* (pp. 274–287). London: Routledge.

39

RESEARCH PHILOSOPHIES

Katherine A. Tamminen and Zoë A. Poucher

Introduction

A research philosophy (also called a paradigm or philosophical position) is a set of basic beliefs that guide the design and execution of a research study, and different research philosophies offer different ways of understanding scientific research (Creswell, 2013; Daly, 2007; Guba & Lincoln, 1994). Research philosophies are fundamental to conducting and assessing research studies, and they are embedded within all forms of research. However, researchers are often taught the tools and strategies for conducting research studies (i.e., methods), without being taught how these methods reflect underlying assumptions about the nature of reality, truth, and knowledge. To help researchers understand the philosophical assumptions that are conveyed in their research, in this chapter, we present information regarding different research philosophies and how these inform different approaches for research and evaluation. We describe the basic differences between some of the major philosophical positions, and we suggest how research conducted from each of these philosophical positions might differ, and how each would produce different types of knowledge. Through this chapter, researchers should come to understand how their choice of research question(s) and methods are underpinned by important assumptions about the nature of reality, knowledge, and science, and how these assumptions are embedded in the language used to describe their research study.

Qualitative and Quantitative Research

Before discussing the underlying assumptions associated with various research philosophies, it is important to distinguish between the different types of research study that one may conduct. Researchers commonly make a distinction between studies that use quantitative and qualitative data to answer their research question. Quantitative research uses numerical data to capture information about a phenomenon, experience, or event – researchers use quantitative measures to count or measure an outcome, event, phenomenon, or psychological construct as precisely as possible. For example, researchers may want to know how frequently a person experiences concerns related to their body image during the week, and whether this is associated with their level of physical activity during the week. Thus, a researcher would use various instruments or questionnaires to try and capture information about the individual's physical activity and their body-related thoughts and feelings to examine the statistical associations between these variables.

Qualitative research uses textual, audio, or visual data to understand the way that people experience a phenomenon and to understand the meanings that people attribute to their experiences. Thus, researchers using qualitative approaches attempt to capture what people say and do, and to interpret patterns of meaning in the data (Denzin & Lincoln, 2012; Maykut & Morehouse, 1994). Characteristics of qualitative research include an exploratory and descriptive focus; an emergent design that can change during the course of a study as important leads are identified; a purposive sample of participants, contexts, or phenomena; qualitative data collected in natural settings (e.g., interviews, observations, photos, documents); ongoing, inductive, and deductive analysis of the data; a reflexive account of the researcher's position within the research process; and a rich description of the research outcomes (Creswell & Poth, 2018; Maykut & Morehouse, 1994). Thus, researchers aiming to understand a phenomenon or experience by focusing on people's words, actions, or documents (Maykut & Morehouse, 1994) may not be concerned with measuring or counting the number of times a person experiences body-related thoughts or feelings; rather, researchers adopting qualitative approaches may use interviews, observations, documents, and other sources of information to understand how individuals develop meanings about their bodies and what the experience of negative body-related thoughts and feelings is like for participants.

It is important to note that this is a very basic distinction between studies that use quantitative and qualitative approaches to collecting and analysing data, and there are many different variations in the ways that researchers might use these types of data, particularly within the broad range of approaches and perspectives under the umbrella of qualitative research. Moreover, these different research approaches will produce different types of knowledge (Burke Johnson, 2008). For example, a researcher conducting a qualitative study might conduct interviews with participants who identify as perfectionists about their daily habits and health behaviours, and then count the number of times that participants talk about 'diet' or 'exercise' in the interview. Conversely, another researcher may not be interested in the frequency of a participant saying the word 'diet' or 'exercise', but, rather, the researcher might conduct interviews to explore how young women internalize broader societal messages about perfectionism and how these internalized standards influence their self-image and health behaviours. As this example illustrates, even under the broad umbrella of 'qualitative research', there is a great deal of variation in the approaches that researchers may take in designing their study and in collecting and analysing data. These different research approaches are underpinned by different research philosophies and will produce different types of information and knowledge about the phenomena of interest.

An important point about research philosophies is that language matters – the language that a researcher uses in describing a study conveys important information about the philosophical assumptions that underpin their study and guide their research approach. For example, the way a researcher uses the terms 'validity', 'reliability', and 'generalizability' conveys their philosophical position. Furthermore, it is the researcher's responsibility to understand what they are communicating when they use particular words to describe their research methods and findings: 'It is important that those engaged in research realize that the language they choose represents and communicates a paradigm and worldview ... researchers are responsible for understanding the implications of language being used' (Jones, Torres, & Arminio, 2014, p. 4). Regardless of whether researchers are conducting quantitative or qualitative studies, it is important for researchers to understand the philosophical assumptions that underpin their research choices and approaches.

Research Philosophies

Research philosophies represent 'a worldview that defines, for its holder, the nature of the "world," the individual's place in it, and the range of possible relationships to that world and its parts' (Guba & Lincoln, 1994, p. 107). Different philosophical positions are informed by different underlying assumptions about reality (ontological assumptions) and knowledge (epistemological assumptions), which in turn influence the methods used to conduct a study. *Ontology* refers to the philosophical assumptions one holds about the nature of reality (Creswell, 2013; Guba & Lincoln, 1998; Jones et al., 2014). Ontological assumptions concern one's beliefs about what exists and how: Whether a phenomenon or construct exists independently, 'out there', to be discovered, measured, and evaluated by the researcher (Lawson, Latsis, & Martins, 2007), or if the nature of a phenomenon or experience is dependent upon those interpreting it. A basic differentiation between ontological positions is the distinction between *realism* (or critical realism, in contemporary science and research) and *relativism*. The belief that there exists an external reality that can be accurately apprehended, measured, and represented is commonly referred to as a realist ontological position. Conversely, the belief that one's perception of an experience and reality is dependent on those interpreting it is commonly referred to as a relativist view of reality.[1]

Epistemology refers to the assumptions one holds about the nature of knowledge and how knowledge is produced; it is used as a way of understanding and explaining how one knows what one knows (Crotty, 2003; Guba & Lincoln, 1998; Lincoln, Lynham, & Guba, 2011). In other words, a researcher's stated epistemology concerns the question, 'how do we, as inquirers, come to know the realities we are trying to apprehend?' (Daly, 2007, p. 23). A prominent epistemological distinction is between a dualist and objectivist position and a subjectivist and transactional position. A dualist/objectivist epistemological position refers to the belief that there can be a complete separation of the researcher and the researched, wherein the researcher has complete objectivity and no influence on the research whatsoever (Daly, 2007). This position assumes that the researcher can completely remove their subjectivity from their assessment of the phenomenon they are studying, producing knowledge and 'truth' that are not influenced by the researcher's biases. Conversely, a subjectivist and transactional position assumes that no knowledge is ever value- or theory-free, and that it is impossible to remove one's subjectivity and influence from the research process and the production of knowledge. This position assumes that all knowledge is created through transactions between the researcher and the participant, and that it is impossible for researchers to completely separate themselves from their previous experiences and their interpretations of those experiences (Lincoln et al., 2011).

Questions about ontology and epistemology are interconnected: Our ontological assumptions inform our epistemological assumptions, and these make up the different philosophical positions that underpin our methodological choices for research and evaluation studies. The remainder of this chapter is dedicated to explaining some different philosophical positions and their associated ontological and epistemological assumptions (see Table 11). It is important to note that this is not an exhaustive review of research paradigms, and that these are not categorical distinctions with hard boundaries; there is often movement between paradigms that share similar ontological and epistemological assumptions (Lather, 2006). Rather, we present a brief overview of the research philosophies that are most commonly

Table 11 Overview of research philosophies and associated ontologial and epistemological assumptions

Paradigm	Post-positivism	Constructivism	Constructionism	Post-structuralist /critical
Primary aim of research	Accumulate knowledge through falsification of theory	Understanding meanings people create for and attribute to their experiences	Similar to constructivism, but emphasis on examining the role of society, culture, and power relations that contribute to individuals' constructions of their experiences	Examines ideological forces (e.g., capitalism, race, gender, and class) and taken-for-granted conditions that influence people's actions and experiences; also examines how these contribute to advantage and disadvantage
Ontology (What is the nature of reality?)	Critical realist: assumes that one universal reality or 'truth' exists independent of the individual, but it may never be fully understood owing to unknown variables within nature and uncertainty in measurement	Relativist: assumes no single external reality independent of the individual; reality exists in the form of multiple individual mental constructions about the world, which are shaped through lived experiences	Relativist: assumes no single external reality independent of the individual; reality exists in the form of multiple individual mental constructions about the world, which are shaped through lived experiences*	Sceptical relativism: rejects notion of universal truths and knowledge; instead assumes that knowledge is temporary and malleable, representing a crystallization of (current) dominant cultural discourses
Epistemology (How is knowledge established?)	Modified dualist/ objectivism: interactions between the researcher and the researched should be minimized, and efforts should be made to try and control for the influence of the researcher in order to produce knowledge that is free of bias and as objective as possible	Subjectivist & transactional: knowledge is created through transactions between the researcher and the participant; researchers cannot enter a study as a 'blank slate' by separating themselves from their previous experiences and their interpretations of those experiences	Subjectivist & transactional: knowledge is created through transactions between the researcher and the participant; researchers cannot enter a study as a 'blank slate' by separating themselves from their previous experiences and their interpretations of those experiences*	Critical subjectivist: meaning and knowledge are co-created through social interactions that are context-specific, but sceptical about claims that any one interpretation about reality is 'correct'; instead assumes that claims of knowledge and truth are mediated by values and serve to serve to maintain current arrangement of power and authority among some groups.

(Continued)

Table 11 (Cont.)

Paradigm	Post-positivism	Constructivism	Constructionism	Post-structuralist /critical
Helpful references	Budd, 2008; Burr, 2003; Cook, 2008; Crotty, 1998; Crotty, 2003; Daly, 2007; Fox, 2008; Gastaldo, 2017;Guba & Lincoln, 2005; Jones et al., 2014; Lincoln et al., 2011; Phillips, 1990; Ward, Hoare, & Gott, 2015			

* Key characteristics of constructionism that distinguish it from constructivism are: (a) critical stance toward taken-for-granted knowledge; (b) focus on historical and cultural specificity of knowledge and understanding; (c) assumption that knowledge is sustained by social processes and ongoing patterns of interactions; and (d) belief in interconnectedness of knowledge, power relations, and social action (Burr, 2003)

referenced in research within sport and exercise psychology (Culver, Gilbert, & Sparkes, 2012). For more in-depth discussions of various philosophical positions, please see Burr (2003), Jones et al. (2014), Lincoln et al. (2011), and Sparkes and Smith (2014).

Post-positivism

Post-positivism is the predominant philosophical position in which most researchers in sport and exercise psychology situate their studies (Culver et al., 2012). The aim of post-positivist research is generally to accumulate knowledge through falsification of theory (Crotty, 1998). Falsification is proposed to be a fundamental feature of a scientific theory (Popper, 1963): A falsifiable theory is one that proposes claims or predictions that can be tested and potentially proven to be false or incorrect; if the theory's predictions are tested through scientific examination and they are incorrect, then the theory is falsified or disproven, and a new theory or explanation is needed to explain a phenomenon (Okasha, 2016).

Post-positivism was borne out of the philosophical position of positivism, which supported the idea of ontological realism. Ontologically, realism assumes that there is one single external reality that can be identified, measured, and studied. However, as science has progressed, this ontological assumption has transitioned into a modified position called critical realism (Lincoln et al., 2011). *Critical realism* assumes that, although there is one single universal reality or 'truth' that exists independent of the individual or researcher, it may not ever be apprehended fully owing to unknown variables within nature and uncertainty in measurement (Guba & Lincoln, 1998, 2005; Lincoln et al., 2011; Phillips, 1990). Thus, researchers operating within a post-positivist research philosophy adhere to a critical realist ontological position, which implies the existence of a single external reality that is independent of the individual and can be closely approximated, but never entirely understood (Crotty, 1998, 2003).

If the research philosophy underpinning a study adheres to a critical realist ontological position, where a single external reality is believed to exist, the epistemological position typically associated with this view of reality is a modified dualist/objectivist position (Guba & Lincoln, 2005; Lincoln et al., 2011). *Dualism* refers to the complete separation of the researcher and the researched, wherein the researcher has complete objectivity and no influence on the research whatsoever (Daly, 2007). Researchers operating within a post-positivist research philosophy understand that this complete separation of the researcher from the researched is ideal, but impossible, as there is always going to be some small influence of the researcher on the phenomenon they are studying. Thus, a modified dualist/objectivist epistemological position is assumed in contemporary post-positivist research. This modified dualism/objectivism implies that interactions between the researcher and the researched should be minimized, and efforts should be made to try and control for the influence of the researcher in order to produce knowledge that is free of bias and that is as objective as possible. In this way, the researcher aims to approximate the 'truth' or reality of a phenomenon or experience by removing or reducing the influence of the researcher in a study as much as possible (Crotty, 1998, 2003; Jones et al., 2014).

Post-positivist researchers may try to establish the quality of their research by using terms and techniques such as generalizability, validity, and inter-rater reliability (see Volume 1, Chapter 18, in this encyclopedia). Understanding the use of these techniques is important because they indicate what paradigmatic assumptions a researcher has made within their study. It is important to note that these terms and techniques are commonly used in all types of post-positivist research and are not limited to quantitative or qualitative research. For example, a researcher conducting a post-positivist quantitative study uses statistical methods to identify reliable patterns of associations between measured variables to produce findings that can generalize across contexts and people. Based on the assumption that there is one single universal reality, a large and diverse sample may allow the researcher to make conclusions about individuals who were not involved in the study based on the findings from those who were involved. A researcher conducting a qualitative study from a post-positivist philosophical position may aim to use inter-rater reliability (e.g., multiple researchers independently coding the data, and the consistency of the coding across researchers being compared) as a means of establishing the validity of their analysis. Thus, a qualitative researcher operating from this philosophical position may use this approach to try and ensure that the 'true' meanings within the data have been discovered, the influence of any single researcher is minimized, and individual biases are removed from the results. The assumption underlying the use of inter-rater reliability is that, by having multiple researchers analyse the data and comparing the consistency of their analysis, it would be possible to minimize the influence of their individual subjectivity, allowing for a more accurate understanding of the 'true' meaning in the participants' data.

To provide an example of post-positivist research approaches, consider the study of stressors and coping in sport. One example of a quantitative post-positivist study was conducted by Gaudreau, Nicholls, and Levy (2010) to examine differences in golfers' coping across six rounds of golf. The researchers used surveys after each round of golf to measure athletes' perceived stress, their use of different coping strategies, and their performance satisfaction, and the results demonstrated statistically significant associations between athletes' coping and their performance satisfaction after each round of golf. This study adheres to the foundational assumptions of post-positivist research owing to its use of quantitative measures, statistical tests of associations between variables, and statistical indicators of the reliability of the measures used (e.g., Cronbach's alpha).

Alternatively, a qualitative post-positivist examination of stressors and coping among adolescent athletes also contributes to our understanding of the types of stressor that athletes experience and the strategies used to cope with sport-related stressors. For example, Reeves, Nicholls, and McKenna (2009) interviewed 40 male soccer players regarding their experiences of sport-related stressors and coping strategies. The authors did not explicitly state the study was conducted from a post-positivist position; however, there are several indications of this philosophical position within the study. For example, in their data analysis, the authors coded data in the interviews that reflected different stressors and coping strategies. These data and codes were grouped into themes, the themes were then tabulated, and the authors reported the number of times participants described different stressors or used different coping strategies. The authors also compared the relative frequency with which older and younger athletes reported different stressors and coping strategies. In their analysis, the authors reported the degree of inter-rater reliability in their coding of the interviews, to provide an index of the level of agreement in their analysis. These approaches are consistent with a post-positivist philosophical position, and the results of the study contribute to understanding some of the differences between the stressors experienced by older and younger adolescent athletes and the strategies that these athletes used to cope with stressors.

Constructivism

Research conducted from a constructivist philosophical position focuses on understanding the meanings people create for themselves and attribute to their experiences (Crotty, 1998; Guba & Lincoln, 1994; Lincoln et al., 2011). In contrast to post-positivism, which assumes a critical realist ontology and a modified dualist/objectivist epistemology, *constructivism* assumes a relativist ontology and a subjectivist and transactional epistemology as its underlying assumptions (Guba & Lincoln, 1998). A relativist ontological position assumes that there is no single external reality that is independent of the individual; rather, reality is understood as existing in the form of multiple individual mental constructions of the world that are shaped through lived experiences (Lincoln et al., 2011). Relativism posits that reality is dependent upon the person interpreting it and the social context in which the individual resides; thus, different individuals may have different interpretations of reality. This does not mean that one person holds a more 'correct' view of reality, but, instead, this view implies that different people will make different interpretations of their experiences (Guba & Lincoln, 1994). Hence, the purpose of qualitative research conducted from a relativist ontological position is to try and understand these different interpretations that people make about their experiences, to try and understand why people see things they way they do.[2]

In order to understand the multiple views that people may have about their experiences and the different ways that people may interpret or attribute meanings to their experiences, researchers working within a constructivist philosophy assume a subjectivist and transactional epistemological position (Guba & Lincoln, 1998). This means that knowledge is created through transactions between the researcher and the participant (e.g., interviews, interactions), and researchers cannot enter a study as a 'blank slate' by separating themselves from their previous experiences and their interpretations of those experiences (Lincoln et al., 2011). Just as the participant's subjectivity contributes to their understanding of a phenomenon or experience, the researcher's own subjective understandings about a phenomenon or experience cannot be removed from the research process or findings. Thus, a subjective and transactional epistemology posits that we cannot remove ourselves from what we know (Guba & Lincoln, 1994), that 'the knower and the known are interdependent' (Maykut & Morehouse, 1994, p. 12), and that meaning and knowledge are created based on interdependent interactions between individuals.

The notion of a subjective and transactional epistemology underlies the concept of co-constructing knowledge or meaning within qualitative research (Davidsen, 2013; Josephs, 2000). From this perspective, participants are thought to develop interpretations and attribute meanings to their experiences within the context of their personal background and past experiences, and these are communicated to the researcher, who brings their own personal background and knowledge to the interaction. Both the participant and the researcher bring their own understandings about the meanings of events or experiences to their interactions; this merging of the researcher's and the participant's understandings is referred to as the co-construction of knowledge (a similar idea within phenomenological research is described as a 'fusion of horizons'; Davidsen, 2013; Gadamer, 1989). Thus, in an interview, the researcher forms interpretations and meanings about the participant's interpretations of an experience, phenomenon, or event (Josephs, 2000). The notion of co-constructing knowledge also extends to other forms of qualitative data. For example, when conducting fieldwork and observations of athletes' interactions in team sports, the researcher attends to actions that they deem important based on past knowledge and understandings of the sport and context. However, these actions are also carried out by athletes who act in particular ways based on their interpretations of behaviours that might be considered appropriate in a particular team setting. Thus, the researcher makes interpretations about athletes' behaviours, which the athletes enact based on their interpretations about the situation and 'how to act' in that moment.

An example of a qualitative study conducted from a constructivist philosophical position is one conducted by Caron, Bloom, Johnston, and Sabiston (2013) examining the lived experiences of National Hockey League players who had sustained multiple concussions. In their study, the primary researcher describes his background and experiences that influenced the study and interpretations during the analysis of the data, and profiles of each participant are provided, thereby acknowledging each person's role in the research process and the co-construction of knowledge with participants. In the presentation of results, the authors do not present the frequency of themes or numerical data about the number of times a particular theme was reported by participants; rather, the results present the core features of the athletes' lived experiences of multiple concussions (uncertainty, physical symptoms, isolation and withdrawal, emotional turmoil, social influences, and transition from professional sport). Reflecting a relativist ontological position, the authors also describe the similarities and differences across the participants' accounts of their experiences. Thus, the study was conducted and the results were presented in a way that reflects the subjectivist and transactional epistemological assumptions of constructivism, as well as the relativist ontological assumptions of this philosophical position.

Constructionism

Constructionism is a research philosophy that shares some similar philosophical assumptions as constructivism. Ontologically, constructionism assumes a relativist position and rejects the idea that knowledge is a direct representation of an external, singular reality, and it assumes that there are no 'objective' facts that exist independently of human thought and interaction. Epistemologically, constructionism adheres to a subjectivist and transactional position, much like a constructivist approach. Thus, researchers working from a constructionist philosophical position accept that knowledge of the world is constructed via social interactions and passed along within social contexts (Crotty, 2003), and that knowledge is neither timeless nor universal (Jones et al., 2014). Within this epistemological position, the researcher and the participant co-construct knowledge about phenomena or experiences, and 'objectivity is an impossibility ... the task of the researcher therefore becomes to acknowledge and even to work with their own intrinsic involvement in the research process and the part that this plays in the results that are produced' (Burr, 2003, p. 152). However, some key characteristics of social constructionism that distinguish it from constructivism are: (a) a critical stance toward taken-for-granted knowledge; (b) a focus on historical and cultural specificity of knowledge and understanding; (c) the assumption that knowledge is sustained by social processes and ongoing patterns of interactions; and (d) a belief in the interconnectedness of knowledge, power relations, and social action (Burr, 2003). Research conducted within a constructionist research philosophy focuses on understanding how individuals understand and attribute meanings to their experiences (similar to constructivism), but a constructionist philosophy places a specific emphasis on examining the role of society, culture, and power relations that contribute to individuals' constructions about their experiences. Constructionism also places a specific focus on language to understand 'the socially interactive basis through which common knowledge is constructed and reconstructed via discourse' (Ward et al., 2015, p. 454).

As an example of a research study conducted from a constructionist research philosophy, Oghene, McGannon, Schinke, Watson, and Quartiroli (2015) examined the media representations of two elite-level masters athletes with the purpose of developing and extending 'the understanding of the multiple meanings constructed by a cultural site (i.e. the media) around the ageing body, sport, and the potential implications of such meanings for sport participation' (Oghene et al., 2015, p. 742). The focus on how meaning is constructed by broader social processes is the key component that indicates this study's constructionist paradigm. On the other hand, if the stated aim of the study was to 'understand master's athletes' experiences with their ageing bodies', this might reflect a constructivist research philosophy. Although both aim to explore the same topic, the focus on the social construction of meaning compared with the focus on understanding individual experience is a key distinction between these two research questions. Thus, it is important to note how the words a researcher uses in describing the purpose of their research implicitly indicates the research philosophy underpinning their study.

Owing to its focus on examining the power relations in the way people experience and attribute meanings to their experiences, and the particular focus on language and discourse within social constructionism, there is heightened attention to the relationship between researchers and participants, and the words used to describe the research relationship. For example, describing individuals who participate in a research study as 'subjects' implies a power relationship that privileges the position of the researcher over their participants (Burr, 2003), whereas calling them 'participants as co-researchers' (Boylorn, 2008) acknowledges the belief that knowledge and reality are co-created between the researcher and the individual. In summary, constructionism places a particular emphasis on power relations as they contribute to individuals' experiences, with the view that 'all knowledge, and therefore all meaningful reality as such, is contingent upon human practices, being constructed in and out of interaction between human beings and their world, and developed and transmitted within an essentially social context' (Crotty, 1998, p. 42).

Critical Research: Post-structuralism and Critical Theory

Critical research includes a number of forms of inquiry such as critical ethnography, critical discourse analysis, critical race studies, feminist research, queer theory, and postcolonial studies, among others (Carspecken, 2008). These research approaches aim to examine the ways that 'social, cultural, political, and economic issues can be interpreted and represented to illustrate the processes of oppression and engage people in addressing them' (Cook, 2008, p. 148). Broadly speaking, critical research studies informed by *post-structuralism* and *critical theory* share some common assumptions, including the beliefs that many forms of oppression and inequality exist in society, that mainstream social practices perpetuate and reproduce inequalities, and that 'critical research should engage in social criticism to support efforts for change' (Cook, 2008, p. 148). Although these approaches are not commonly associated with conventional uses of the terms 'measurement' and 'evaluation', they broaden the scope of ways that researchers may seek to investigate and examine individuals' experiences. For example, researchers may seek to examine the experiences and expectations of what community means in queer sport spaces and, in doing so, propose a reconceptualization of the notion of community as a site of tension and change, rather than accepting the taken-for-granted idealized concept of community (Carter & Baliko, 2017).

Generally, research informed by critical theory and post-structuralism seeks to interrogate patterns of coordinated social action, the conditions that are responsible for these patterns of coordinated action, and the experiences that people have within these patterns of action (Carspecken, 2008). Researchers operating from this position adopt a critical attitude toward knowledge, power relations, and claims of truth and universality, and seek to consider the possibilities that exist beyond the taken-for-granted limits imposed within modern society (Calkivik, 2017). Post-structuralism is described as a distinct response to and a critique of structuralism, challenging frameworks that impose structures upon an entity of any kind (Dickerson, 2010; Hoffman, 1992). Critical theory is described as a perspective that has at its core the assessment and critique of the current state of affairs (Budd, 2008). Research informed by critical theory examines ideological forces such as capitalism and aspects of race, gender, and class that influence people's actions and experiences; and critical research examines how these ideological forces contribute to advantage and disadvantage – for example, by examining whose voices are heard versus those who are silenced (Budd, 2008).

A post-structuralist research philosophy assumes an ontological position of sceptical relativism (Gastaldo, 2017). This position rejects the notion of a belief in universal truths or knowledge, assuming instead that knowledge is temporary and malleable, representing a crystallization of (current) dominant cultural discourses (Daly, 2007; Gastaldo, 2017; Jones et al., 2014). A person's beliefs about reality are a consequence of their interaction with media, texts, and other people, within specific political and social structures; therefore, their resulting experiences and beliefs are socially produced by dominant discourses (Gastaldo, 2017). Thus, research adopting this ontological position emphasizes the ways the meanings individuals construct about their experiences are developed as a consequence of imbalances within a context that consists of power dynamics between individuals in society (Jones et al., 2014). A sceptical relativist position is also critical of the role that dominant power structures play in the production of cultural discourses and, therefore, also critical of the ways in which knowledge and 'truths' are produced and maintained (Gastaldo, 2017). Researchers assuming this position make an effort to adopt an attitude of scepticism, questioning dominant assumptions and ways of knowing, and they attempt to present alternative or competing forms of knowledge that reflect the beliefs of underrepresented groups or people (Daly, 2007).

Epistemologically, researchers informed by these perspectives may be said to adopt a critical subjectivist position (Cook, 2008). This position is similar to the subjectivist and transactional position described above, and it maintains that meaning and knowledge are co-created through social interactions that are context-specific (Fox, 2008). However, it is argued that a subjectivist and transactional epistemology that attempts to equally represent the multiple lived realities that individuals may experience may not be seen as sufficient for analysing the social production of oppression (Carspecken, 1996; Cook, 2008). Therefore, a critical subjectivist position is sceptical about claims that any one interpretation about reality is 'correct', assuming instead that claims to knowledge and truth are mediated by values and serve to maintain the current arrangement of power and authority among some groups (Gastaldo, 2017; Fox, 2008): 'The aim of poststructuralism has in general been to expose these power plays and claims to truth and thus to undermine them and offer alternative ways of thinking about the social world' (Fox, 2008, p. 663).

Owing to its sceptical relativist ontological assumptions (Gastaldo, 2017) and critical subjectivist epistemological assumptions (Ettlinger, 2014), research informed by post-structuralist philosophical commitments does not seek to identify the 'truth' in participants' accounts of their experiences, but rather it seeks to identify the meanings within participants' responses that are context-specific, and also to identify the discursive practices that contribute to the way those responses are constructed (Fawcett, 2008). The goal of much critical research informed by post-structuralism and critical theory is to interrogate and problematize knowledge and taken-for-granted conditions (Carspecken, 2008). Critical researchers may also seek to create social action to transform a system or the emancipation of a group based on engagement and collaboration between researchers and their subjects. Although critical research approaches are not normally associated with measurement and evaluation, critical research informed by post-structuralism and critical theory is useful for deconstructing taken-for-granted processes and conditions that influence individuals' actions and experiences, and for addressing issues of inequality and oppression.

An example of a qualitative study conducted from a post-structural philosophical position was conducted by Clark and Markula (2017), examining the experiences of adolescent ballet dancers within a recreational dance studio. Using participant observations and interviews to collect data, the researchers, guided by Foucault's (1979) theoretical framework of disciplinary techniques, explored how the dancers' experiences were influenced by time, space, bodily practices, and power relationships in the studio. The results illustrate how the dance studio space and the people who occupy it reinforced practices of disciplinary power that enabled and constrained the dancers' bodies and movements. The researchers also describe how disciplinary techniques to train the body to move in specific ways enabled the dancers to perform with precision and skill, which the dancers experienced as pleasure and satisfaction. However, the researchers' analysis and interpretations of the dancers' experiences interrogate the taken-for-granted conditions of power and discipline within the specific context of the dance studio. The results demonstrate how the effects of power and disciplinary techniques within the ballet studio were not uniformly oppressive or totalizing for the dancers' experiences; instead, the effects of power within the dance studio space were unpredictable and offered possibilities for dancers to create their own pleasurable experiences and relationships with others and their bodies. Thus, their research illustrates the foundational assumptions of a post-structural philosophical position by exploring the meanings individuals constructed about their experiences, while identifying and critiquing the dominant power structures that produced and shaped the way the dancers constructed their experiences in particular spaces.

Conclusion

All research studies are underpinned by different philosophical positions that carry particular assumptions about the nature of reality (ontology) and knowledge (epistemology), which inform the methodological choices within a study. In other words, what one assumes about reality (ontology) constrains what one may assume about knowledge (epistemology), which further constrains the methodologies that one selects to conduct research. To demonstrate how these ideas are interconnected, take an example where a researcher attempts to remove their influence on the phenomenon they are studying, to try and be as 'objective' as possible in a controlled study. Such an approach would imply that the researcher assumes an external phenomenon or experience can be accurately measured by removing as much bias or influence as possible from the study. Alternatively, a different researcher might understand that they can never remove themselves and their influence from the research they are conducting, implying a relativist ontology and a subjectivist epistemology. In this case, the researcher seeks to embrace the subjectivity they bring to a study and reflexively consider how their biases contribute to and influence the research process and the knowledge that is produced in their study. Therefore, the methodological approach that one chooses when undertaking a research study of any kind comes with underlying assumptions and connotations about the way the researcher views reality and knowledge.

We also wish to emphasize that, although a post-positivist research philosophy is often associated with the use of quantitative methods, and although constructivist, constructionist, and postmodern/post-structural perspectives are often associated with the use of qualitative methods, these paradigms and methods are not synonymous. For example, qualitative data may be collected and analysed from a post-positivist philosophical position, and this is frequently seen in research in sport and exercise psychology. Although it is somewhat less common, quantitative data may also be used within a study that is approached from a constructivist or constructionist position. Maynard (1993) noted:

> Many researchers who engage in quantitative research do not do so naively and are prepared significantly to qualify claims to 'truth', objectivity and value-neutrality … Attention has been drawn to the ways in which the polarisation of quantitative versus qualitative impoverishes research, and there have been calls for the use of multiple methods to be used in a complementary rather than a competitive way.
>
> *(p. 330)*

The use of any one particular method or research philosophy is not inherently better or worse than any other; however, researchers should strive for coherence between the philosophical assumptions that underpin a research project and the research question, methodology, and methods that are used within the study.

It is also important to note that the ontological and epistemological assumptions associated with various philosophical positions also inform the ways that different research studies may be evaluated. Because these different philosophies take different views about what reality is and how it can be apprehended, they each lead to the production of vastly different types of knowledge. Therefore, the quality of research studies conducted from these different philosophical positions cannot be judged according to a universal set of criteria. For example, the notions of rigour, generalizability, validity, and reliability cannot be applied uniformly to assess the quality of research studies across all these philosophical positions, as these terms invoke different assumptions about truth, external reality, and universality of experience. A full discussion of the evaluation of research quality within different philosophical positions is beyond the scope of this chapter; however, for an extended discussion of these ideas, please refer to Williams and Smith (Volume 1, Chapter 38, in this encyclopedia), Bochner (2018), Burke (2016), and Smith and McGannon (2017).

Each philosophical perspective offers researchers different assumptions, allowing them to address different research questions and accomplish different things with their research. For example, a researcher wishing to make generalizable conclusions about a phenomenon may adopt research methods underpinned by a post-positivist philosophical position. However, if a researcher is hoping to understand the experiences of a person or group of people, then assuming a constructivist position may be most valuable for their research purposes. A constructionist research philosophy may be most useful to a researcher who is interested in understanding the way that social discourses contribute to shaping the experiences of individuals and the meanings that individuals attribute to their experiences. Or, perhaps, a researcher hoping to instigate social change via their research may best be served by adopting a critical research approach underpinned by a post-structuralist philosophical position. Each of these approaches is underpinned by a different research philosophy that carries different ontological and epistemological assumptions, which inform the methods that are used within the study, ultimately contributing to the production of different types of knowledge and findings about the topic of interest.

Notes

1 The idea of reality 'existing out there' versus reality as a social construction is a complicated issue. Natural science disciplines such as physics, chemistry, biology, and physiology are founded on a realist perspective that focuses on objectively understanding how natural phenomena occur and the laws that govern their occurrence (Christians, 2005; Markula & Silk, 2011). We do not dispute the existence of the physical world that exists, and we do not dispute the realist ontological assumptions that underpin research conducted within the natural sciences. However, social science disciplines such as psychology, anthropology, and sociology focus on the study of human behaviours, cognitions, emotions, interactions, and culture, rather than the physical world and natural laws. Thus, researchers may approach enquiry in social science disciplines from a critical realist ontological perspective or from a relativist perspective. As noted by Simmons (1993), 'What is beyond our own skin actually exists. But this "environment" is largely what we make of it' (p. 3); similarly, Smith (2008) noted that interpretivist researchers 'have no problem with the idea that there is a reality "out there," … [but] there is no way to factor out or eliminate the influence of the particular interests and purposes of particular researchers.' For further reading, see Willis (2007) and Proctor (1998).
2 The term interpretivism is sometimes used interchangeably with the term constructivism (e.g., Avramidis & Smith, 1999). We tend to view all social research as interpretive (Bhattacharya, 2008; Smith, 2008); thus, the philosophical positions of constructivism, constructionism, and postmodern positions are all considered to be interpretive paradigms (Bhattacharya, 2008).

References

Avramidis, E., & Smith, B. (1999). An introduction to the major research paradigms and their methodological implications for special needs research. *Emotional and Behavioural Difficulties, 4*, 27–36. doi:10.1080/1363275990040306

Bhattacharya, H. (2008). Interpretive research. In L. M. Given (Ed.), *The Sage encyclopedia of qualitative research methods* (pp. 465–467). Thousand Oaks, CA: Sage.

Bochner, A. P. (2018). Unfurling rigor: On continuity and change in qualitative inquiry. *Qualitative Inquiry, 24*(6), 359–368. doi:1077800417727766

Boylorn, R. M. (2008). Participants as co-researchers. In L. M. Given (Ed.), *The Sage encyclopedia of qualitative research methods* (pp. 599–601). Thousand Oaks, CA: Sage.

Budd, J. M. (2008). Critical theory. In L. M. Given (Ed.), *The SAGE encyclopedia of qualitative research methods* (pp. 174–178). London: Sage.

Burke Johnson, R. (2008). Knowledge. In L. M. Given (Ed.), *The Sage encyclopedia of qualitative research methods* (pp. 479–483). Thousand Oaks, CA: Sage.

Burke, S. (2016). Rethinking 'validity' and 'trustworthiness' in qualitative inquiry: How might we judge the quality of qualitative research in sport and exercise sciences. In B. Smith & A. Sparkes (Eds.), *Routledge handbook of qualitative research in sport and exercise* (pp. 330–339). New York: Routledge.

Burr, V. (2003). *Social constructionism* (2nd ed.). London: Routledge.

Calkivik, A. (2017). Poststructuralism/postmodernism. *Oxford research encyclopedia of international studies.* doi:10.1093/acrefore/9780190846626.013.102

Caron, J. G., Bloom, G. A., Johnston, K. M., & Sabiston, C. M. (2013). Effects of multiple concussions on retired National Hockey League players. *Journal of Sport and Exercise Psychology, 35*, 168–179.

Carspecken, P. F. (1996). *Critical ethnography in educational research.* New York: Routledge.

Carspecken, P. F. (2008). Critical research. In L. M. Given (Ed.), *The Sage encyclopedia of qualitative research methods* (pp. 170–174). Thousand Oaks, CA: Sage.

Carter, C., & Baliko, K. (2017). 'These are not my people': Queer sport spaces and the complexities of community. *Leisure Studies, 36*(5), 696–707. doi:10.1080/02614367.2017.1315164

Christians, C. G. (2005). Ethics and politics in qualitative research. In N. K. Denzin & Y. S. Lincoln (Eds.), *The Sage handbook of qualitative research* (pp. 139–164). Thousand Oaks, CA: Sage.

Clark, M. I., & Markula, P. (2017). Foucault at the barre and other surprises: A case study of discipline and docility in the ballet studio. *Qualitative Research in Sport, Exercise and Health, 9*, 435–452. doi:10.1080/2159676X.2017.1309451

Cook, K. E. (2008). Critical ethnography. In L. M. Given (Ed.), *The Sage encyclopedia of qualitative research methods* (pp. 148–151). Thousand Oaks, CA: Sage.

Creswell, J. W. (2013). *Qualitative inquiry & research design: Choosing among five approaches* (3rd ed.). Thousand Oaks, CA: Sage.

Creswell, J. W., & Poth, C. N. (2018). *Qualitative inquiry and research design: Choosing among five approaches*. Thousand Oaks, CA: Sage.

Crotty, M. (1998). *The foundations of social research: Meaning and perspective making in the research process*. Thousand Oaks, CA: Sage.

Crotty, M. (2003). *The foundations of social research: Meaning and perspective making in the research process*. Thousand Oaks, CA: Sage.

Culver, D. M., Gilbert, W., & Sparkes, A. (2012). Qualitative research in sport psychology journals: The next decade 2000–2009 and beyond. *The Sport Psychologist, 26*, 261–281.

Daly, K. J. (2007). *Qualitative methods for family studies and human development*. Thousand Oaks, CA: Sage.

Davidsen, A. S. (2013). Phenomenological approaches in psychology and health sciences. *Qualitative Research in Psychology, 10*, 318–339. doi:10.1080/14780887.2011.608466

Denzin, N., & Lincoln, Y. (2012). *The Sage handbook of qualitative research* (5th ed.). Thousand Oaks, CA: Sage.

Dickerson, V. C. (2010). Positioning oneself within an epistemology: Refining our thinking about integrative approaches. *Family Process, 49*(3), 349–368.

Ettlinger, N. (2014). Delivering on poststructural ontologies: Epistemological challenges and strategies. *ACME: An International E-Journal for Critical Geographies, 13*(4), 589–598.

Fawcett, B. (2008). Poststructuralism. In L. M. Given (Ed.), *The Sage encyclopedia of qualitative research methods* (pp. 666–670). Thousand Oaks, CA: Sage.

Foucault, M. (1979). *Discipline and punish: The birth of the prison* [*Surveiller et punir*] (2nd ed.). New York: Vintage Books.

Fox, N. J. (2008) Post-positivism. In L. M. Given (Ed.), *The SAGE encyclopaedia of qualitative research methods* (pp. 659–664). London: Sage.

Gadamer, H. (1989). *Truth and method* (2nd ed.). London: Stagbooks.

Gastaldo, D. (2017). *Research paradigms*. Retrieved from www.ccqhr.utoronto.ca/sites/default/files/Research%20Paradigms_2011_DG.pdf

Gaudreau, P., Nicholls, A., & Levy, A. R. (2010). The ups and downs of coping and sport achievement: An episodic process analysis of within-person associations. *Journal of Sport and Exercise Psychology, 32*(3), 298–311.

Guba, E. G., & Lincoln, Y. S. (1994). Competing paradigms in qualitative research. In N. K. Denzin & Y. S. Lincoln (Eds.), *The Sage handbook of qualitative research* (pp. 105–117). Thousand Oaks, CA: Sage.

Guba, E. G., & Lincoln, Y. S. (1998). Competing paradigms in qualitative research. In N. K. Denzin & Y. S. Lincoln (Eds.), *The landscape of qualitative research: Theories and issues* (pp. 195–220). Thousand Oaks, CA: Sage.

Guba, E. G., & Lincoln, Y. S. (2005). Paradigmatic controversies, contradictions, and emerging confluences. In N. K. Denzin & Y. S. Lincoln (Eds.), *The Sage handbook of qualitative research* (pp. 191–215). Thousand Oaks, CA: Sage.

Hoffman, L. (1992). A reflexive stance for family therapy. In S. McNamee & K. J. Gergen (Eds.), *Therapy as social construction* (pp. 7–24). London: Sage.

Jones, S. R., Torres, V., & Arminio, J. (2014). *Negotiating the complexities of qualitative research in higher education: Fundamental elements and issues*. New York: Routledge.

Josephs, I. E. (2000). A psychological analysis of a psychological phenomenon: The dialogical construction of meaning. *Social Science Information, 39*, 115–129. doi:10.1177/053901800039001007

Lather, P. (2006). Paradigm proliferation as a good thing to think with: Teaching research in education as a wild profusion. *International Journal of Qualitative Studies in Education, 19*, 35–57. doi:10.1080/09518390500450144

Lawson, C., Latsis, J., & Martins, N. (2007). *Contributions to social ontology.* New York: Routledge.

Lincoln, Y. S., Lynham, S. A., & Guba, E. G. (2011). Paradigmatic controversies, contradictions, and emerging confluences, revisited. In N. K. Denzin & Y. S. Lincoln (Eds.), *The SAGE handbook of qualitative research* (pp. 97–128). Thousand Oaks, CA: Sage.

Markula, P., & Silk, M. L. (2011). *Qualitative research for physical culture.* London: Palgrave Macmillan.

Maykut, P., & Morehouse, R. (1994). *Beginning qualitative research: A philosophic and practical guide.* Washington, DC: The Falmer Press.

Maynard, M. (1993). Feminism and the possibilities of a postmodern research practice. *British Journal of Sociology of Education, 14*(13), 321–327.

Okasha, S. (2016). *Philosophy of science: A very short introduction.* Oxford, UK: Oxford University Press.

Oghene, O. P., McGannon, K. R., Schinke, R. J., Watson, S., & Quartiroli, A. (2015). Understanding the meanings created around the aging body and sports through media representations of elite masters athletes. *Qualitative Research in Sport, Exercise and Health, 7*(5), 739–758.

Phillips, D. C. (1990). Postpositivistic science: Myths and realities. In E. G. Guba (Ed.), *The paradigm dialog* (pp. 31–45). Thousand Oaks, CA: Sage.

Popper, K. (1963). *Conjectures and refutations.* London: Routledge & Keagan Paul.

Proctor, J. D. (1998). The social construction of nature: Relativist accusations, pragmatist and critical realist responses. *Annals of the Association of American Geographers, 88*(3), 352–376.

Reeves, C. W., Nicholls, A. R., & McKenna, J. (2009). Stressors and coping strategies among early and middle adolescent Premier League academy soccer players: Differences according to age. *Journal of Applied Sport Psychology, 21*(1), 31–48.

Simmons, I. G. (1993). *Interpreting nature: Cultural constructions of the environment.* London: Routledge.

Smith, B., & McGannon, K. R. (2017). Developing rigor in qualitative research: Problems and opportunities within sport and exercise psychology. *International Review of Sport and Exercise Psychology, 11*, 101–121. doi:10.1080/1750984X.2017.1317357

Smith, J. (2008). Interpretive inquiry. In L. M. Given (Ed.), *The Sage encyclopedia of qualitative research methods* (pp. 460–461). Thousand Oaks, CA: Sage.

Sparkes, A. C., & Smith, B. (2014). *Qualitative research methods in sport, exercise and health from process to product.* New York: Routledge.

Ward, K., Hoare, K. J., & Gott, M. (2015). Evolving from a positivist to constructionist epistemology while using grounded theory: Reflections of a novice researcher. *Journal of Research in Nursing, 20*, 449–462. doi:10.1177/1744987115597731

Willis, J. W. (2007). *Foundations of qualitative research: Interpretive and critical approaches.* Thousand Oaks, CA: Sage.

40
RESILIENCE IN TEAMS AND ORGANIZATIONS

Christopher R. D. Wagstaff, Kirsten J. Fasey, and Mustafa Sarkar

Introduction

Over the past couple of decades, our understanding of the pressures faced by those involved in sport has expanded rapidly, with a growing realization that sources of strain in sport are prevalent and pervasive and can originate from a variety of sources (see, e.g., Arnold & Fletcher, 2012; Gould, Finch, & Jackson, 1993; Mellalieu, Neil, Hanton, & Fletcher, 2009; Scanlan, Stein, & Ravizza, 1991; Thelwell, Weston, & Greenlees, 2007). These stressors may be associated with an athlete's competitive performance, organizational environment, or personal "non-sporting" life events (Fletcher, Hanton, & Mellalieu, 2006; see also Sarkar & Fletcher, 2014). In addition to the growing understanding of these demands, it is common for researchers, as well as coaches, performance directors, and sports organizations, to delineate between athletes, teams, and most recently organizations who thrive under pressure and achieve peak performance and well-being and those who yield to pressure and underperform or whose well-being suffers at the expense of their success. These differences are often attributed to the concept of resilience, with some researchers indicating that resilience is a prerequisite for sporting success (Holt & Dunn, 2004; Mills, Butt, Maynard, & Harwood, 2012; Van Yperen, 2009).

Resilience is best understood when it is considered in a context-specific domain (Luthar & Cicchetti, 2000), and it follows that one should not assume that models of resilience will necessarily be transferable to other domains within or outwith the sport context. Thankfully, a body of work has recently emerged exploring resilience specifically in athletes (Fletcher & Sarkar, 2012; Galli & Vealey, 2008; Machida, Irwin, & Feltz, 2013; Martin-Krumm, Sarrazin, Peterson, & Famose, 2003; Mummery, Schofield, & Perry, 2004; Schinke & Jerome, 2002; Seligman, Nolen-Hoeksema, Thornton, & Thornton, 1990), teams (Morgan, Fletcher, & Sarkar, 2013, 2015, 2019), and organizations. Several reviews of this emerging literature exist (e.g., Fasey, 2017; Fletcher & Sarkar, 2013; Galli & Gonzalez, 2015; Linnenluecke, 2017; Morgan, Fletcher, & Sarkar, 2017; Wagstaff, Sarkar, Davidson, & Fletcher, 2017). For instance, Fletcher and Sarkar (2013) provided a review and critiqued the various definitions, concepts, and theories of psychological resilience. Galli and Gonzalez (2015) critically reviewed recent conceptual developments in psychological resilience research in sport and highlighted potential areas of future research. More recently, Wagstaff, Gilmore, and Thelwell (2016) highlighted the salience, but relative dearth, of systematic examination of the influence of sociocultural factors and context in understanding resilience (cf. Galli & Vealey, 2008; Machida et al., 2013). Taking the last of these reviews, its central observation – the importance but limited presence of sociocultural perspectives on resilience – is somewhat surprising, given the growing recognition of the value of such perspectives in non-sport resilience literature (cf. Ungar, 2012). To elaborate, Ungar (2012), argued both "culture and context shape the environment in which processes associated with resilience occur, making some processes more crucial to adaptation and growth than others" (p. 387). Indeed, Wagstaff et al. concurred with this perspective adding, "sociocultural factors and organizational contexts hold significant implications for the definition and development of resilience" (p. 121). In this chapter, we critically review the concept of resilience in sport, with a specific emphasis on the sociocultural influences on, and the organizational dynamics surrounding, resilience. Before considering the emerging team and organizational resilience work, we provide a background to the conceptualization of psychological resilience and early research examining this construct in sport.

Defining Psychological Resilience

Researchers across various domains of psychology have provided numerous definitions that vary significantly, depending on the context of investigation and application, and the conceptualization of resilience as a trait or process (for a review, see Fletcher & Sarkar, 2013). Despite resilience being conceived in different ways, researchers generally agree that, for this construct to be demonstrated, both adversity and positive adaptation must be evident (Fletcher & Sarkar, 2013). In an attempt to draw on the extant consistencies within the conceptual literature, Fletcher and Sarkar defined psychological resilience as, "the role of mental processes and behavior in promoting personal assets and protecting an individual from the potential negative effect of stressors" (2012, p. 675, 2013, p. 16). The authors proposed this definition to extend previous conceptual work in the area by offering a specific focus on psychological resilience, encapsulating aspects of both trait and process conceptualizations, an emphasis on the neutral term "stressor" rather than the negative term "adversity", and a focus on promoting personal assets and protecting an individual from the potential negative effect of stressors rather than positive adaptation per se.

Despite the definitional advances noted above, Wagstaff et al. (2017) noted several additional conceptual considerations regarding the development of socioculturally and contextually sensitive perspectives on resilience. First, the assumption that resilience is a virtue across all contexts leads well-intentioned theory, research, and praxis astray and is implicated in resilience becoming a vice instead of a virtue in some circumstances. That is, the decontextualization of resilience as a stand-alone virtue by researchers who characterize it as an individual trait leaves the concept open to misunderstanding and misapplication. A second consideration in the context of the definition of resilience relates to the limited acknowledgement of sociological and cultural utility (Fletcher & Sarkar, 2013) in many extant definitions and conceptualizations of resilience. That is, although psychological resilience is, by definition, centrally focused on intra-individual processes, greater consideration and sensitivity to sociocultural and organizational influences are required to gain a more complete understanding of the phenomenon (Fletcher & Sarkar, 2013; Sarkar & Fletcher, 2014). Third, some researchers have problemized the use of the term "resilience", noting that the inherent and perpetual pursuit of resilient soldiers (see McGarry, Walklate, & Mythen, 2015) casts a dark shadow of hegemonic masculinity, gender-role conflicts, and stigma, resulting in demobilization and reintegration problems for some military veterans.

Psychological Resilience Research in Sport

Early studies examining resilience in sport performers largely centred on the role of resilience as a dependent variable in the stress–injury relationship or an individual's explanatory style. For instance, Smith, Smoll, and Ptacek (1990) examined the ways in which moderator variables interact with one another to increase vulnerability or resilience in the life stress–athletic injury relationship. Smith et al. interpreted their data to indicate that social support and psychological coping skills were statistically independent psychosocial resources and operated in a conjunctive manner to influence the relationship between life stress and subsequent athletic injury in adolescents. Adopting an explanatory-style perspective on resilience, Seligman et al. (1990) found university swimmers with an optimistic explanatory style to swim faster in trials following false-negative performance feedback compared with their own original time. This work was later extended by Martin-Krumm et al. (2003), who manipulated the beliefs of high school students by telling them that they had not performed well in a basketball task in comparison with others. In findings that were similar to those of Seligman et al. (1990), participants with an optimistic explanatory style performed better on the second trial than comparable participants with a pessimistic outlook. In Martin-Krumm et al.'s study, the relationship between explanatory style and participants' dribbling performance after perceived failure was also affected by their anxiety levels and success expectations. Here, an optimistic explanatory style correlated with expectations of successful performance prior to the second trial and lower state anxiety, which, in turn, were also linked to improved performance in the dribbling task.

Mummery et al. (2004) sought to improve the ecological validity of the then nascent findings by exploring resilience in swimmers who were competing in a real national competition. Swimmers were classified as resilient if they were able to improve their qualifying time after initially failing to do so during an earlier round. The results showed that athletes classified as resilient had higher perceptions of physical endurance, indicating a more optimistic outlook. Interestingly, the results also demonstrated that these swimmers had lower levels of social support than those who did not perform well following initial failure. The authors explained these results by stating that the swimmers who displayed resilience may have been able to act in a more independent manner in unfamiliar surroundings than their non-resilient counterparts, in particular, placing less emphasis on requiring social support to achieve sporting success. Yet, it is important to note that the swimmers may not have perceived the inability to match their qualifying time as a stressor. This is because it is common practice for swimmers to limit their performance in earlier heats to preserve energy for later, more challenging races where optimum performance is required. Based on these studies, Schinke and colleagues (e.g., Schinke & Jerome, 2002; Schinke, Peterson, & Couture, 2004) created the first sport resiliency training programme primarily focused on developing optimism skills and were deemed relatively successful by the authors in enhancing resilience in athletes and teams. Despite these positive outcomes, it is important to note that there are several limitations allied with the early interventions and the research on which it was based. For example, by focusing solely on optimism and its role in enabling athletes to overcome setbacks, these interventions elided other factors that play a role in athletes' resilience (see Galli & Gonzalez, 2015; Sarkar & Fletcher, 2014). In addition, the studies also exclusively explored the role of explanatory style in overcoming the stressor of failure. This approach restricts our practical understanding of how applicable an optimistic style is to athletes encountering other demands such as organizational stressors (Hanton, Wagstaff, & Fletcher, 2012). In addition, the research reviewed in this section generally establishes resilience based on the criteria of winning or increased performance, such as swimming faster. From a sociocultural perspective, such criteria have limitations as they do not acknowledge the individual goals of the performer or characterize what success is for stakeholders, teams, or organizations (cf. Ungar, 2008). Finally, by focusing on resilience from a trait perspective, the early studies reviewed in this section failed to capture the person–environment interactions characteristic of contemporary conceptualizations of resilience as a dynamic process (Fletcher & Sarkar, 2013; Windle, 2011).

The literature outlined above provided an important foundation for the work conducted over the last decade, during which time researchers have adopted a more holistic approach to the conceptualization of resilience and incorporated the use of qualitative designs. The first study to investigate resilience in this way was by Galli and Vealey (2008), who explored athletes' perceptions of resilience in relation to the most difficult adversity they had encountered. The authors used their findings to propose a framework highlighting that, following adversity, athletes experienced agitation (e.g., the use of a variety of coping strategies). In turn, this process resulted in positive outcomes, including increased learning, motivation, and perspective. Further, the authors also remarked that these positive outcomes were in part a result of pre-existing sociocultural influences and personal resources. In an attempt to build on Galli and Vealey's (2008) work, several groups of researchers (e.g., Fletcher & Sarkar, 2012; White, Bennie, & McKenna, 2015) have employed inductive qualitative designs to explore resilience in sport. For example, Fletcher and Sarkar (2012) developed a grounded theory of psychological resilience in Olympic champions. Their findings revealed that numerous psychological factors (relating to a positive personality, motivation, confidence, focus, and perceived social support) protected the world's best athletes from the potential negative effect of stressors by influencing their challenge appraisal and meta-cognitions. These constructive cognitive reactions promoted facilitative responses that led to the realization of optimal sport performance. In another qualitative study, to clarify how sport might cultivate resilience, White et al. (2015) explored gymnast and coach perceptions about the development of resilience through gymnastics participation. Data analysis revealed that aspects of the gymnastics environment created stress and exposed gymnasts to many challenges in training and competition. Further, features of the sport environment, such as interpersonal relationships and positive coach behaviours, supported gymnasts through these challenges and encouraged them to overcome failure, and gymnastics participation was perceived to develop resilience, life skills, self-efficacy, and self-esteem. In addition to these exploratory studies, researchers have recently turned their attention to psychometric issues and the use of questionnaires to examine resilience or moderate its relationship with dependent variables (e.g., Gucciardi, Jackson, Coulter, & Mallett, 2011; Sarkar & Fletcher, 2013) and considered the predictive role of resilience for well-being (e.g., see Lu et al., 2016; Vitali, Bortoli, Bertinato, Robazza, & Schena, 2015).

Social and Organizational Influences on Resilience

As alluded to earlier in this chapter, research examining resilience has been critiqued for being too focused on individual capacities (see Ungar, 2008). Although some scholars have pointed to the potential salience of sociocultural factors (e.g., Galli & Vealey, 2008), most of the resilience research conducted in sport has focused on athletes' psychological processes, hitherto eliding the sociocultural context within which this process occurs (Sarkar & Fletcher, 2014). It follows that research that aims to address this omission is essential to the development of effective resilience interventions. The argument for such research endeavours is further supported by the identification of social and cultural factors that influence resilience in non-sport domains (e.g., see Clauss-Ehlers, 2008) and an emerging recognition of social and cultural influences that exist within sport (see, e.g., Blodgett, Schinke, McGannon, & Fisher,

2014; Schinke & Hanrahan, 2009; Wagstaff & Burton-Wylie, 2018). Indeed, Blodgett et al. recently took stock of the growing body of conceptual research aligned with cultural sport psychology (CSP; see Schinke & Hanrahan, 2009) and organizational sport psychology (OSP; Fletcher & Wagstaff, 2009; Wagstaff, 2017, 2019a, 2019b) agendas. Indeed, cultural praxis is central to CSP and OSP as a means of overcoming the taken-for-granted way of "doing" sport psychology, steeped in a post-positivist, white, Euro-American, male, performance-based discourse, and is pivotal for the future advancement of a socioculturally and contextually sensitive approach to the study and development of resilience.

Cultural praxis in sport psychology grew out of early writings that drew on cultural studies highlighting how issues of power and privilege were being perpetuated in and through the practices of the domain. Through cultural praxis, researchers and practitioners strive to consider their own, as well as others', cultural identities. The intent is to draw attention to issues of sociocultural difference, power, ethics, and politics, which are often concealed, and facilitate a more contextualized understanding of marginalized identities and a plurality of differences (e.g., race, ethnicity, class, gender, sexuality, dis/ability, physicality, nationality). For example, athletes originate from a diverse range of family backgrounds, with varying cultural and religious beliefs, factors that have been found to influence the resilience process (cf. Clauss-Ehlers, 2008). Athletes also operate within organizational environments that have similar, yet idiosyncratic, economic, political, and sociocultural characteristics (Fletcher & Wagstaff, 2009). In light of these influences, it would appear that "off-the-shelf" resilience interventions are unlikely to be effective across all athletes, teams, and sport organizations, and there is a need to better incorporate lessons from sociocultural and organizational dynamics research.

Within the general psychology literature, Ungar and colleagues (Ungar, 2008, 2008, 2012; Theron, Cameron, Didkowsky, & Lau, 2011) have written widely about the need for a more culturally and contextually embedded understanding of resilience. In doing so, these authors have used the tenets of ecological theory to draw from research and clinical experience with children, youth, and families to argue that resilience is not a phenomenon solely related to the individual, but also exists as a facet of one's social and political setting, thus being *negotiated* by individuals and their community. Other scholars (e.g., Gilligan, 2004; Seccombe, 2002) prefer an approach to resilience development of "changing the odds" rather than resourcing individuals to "beat[ing] the odds". To illustrate, in his manual for child and youth care workers, Gilligan (2004) argued that "resilience … is now more usefully considered as a variable quality that derives from a process of repeated interactions between a person and favourable features of the surrounding context in a person's life" (p. 94). Hence, and in line with a more culturally and contextually embedded view of resilience, "the degree of resilience displayed by a person in a certain context may be said to be related to the extent to which that context has elements that nurture this resilience" (p. 94).

Ungar (2012) highlighted the influence of three main sociocultural influences relevant to resilience. The first centres on the observation that facilitative environments can be more powerful than individual-level variables in the resilience process (see Ungar, 2012). To illustrate, Chauhan, Reppucci, Burnette, and Reiner (2010) found that, when matching for individual factors such as delinquency and psychological risk factors, the recidivism rates among girls were shown to be correlated with sociocultural factors and racial background. In the context of sport, Galli and Vealey (2008) noted that the majority of African American athletes in their study believed that the notion of success and overcoming challenges was a central part of their culture and a key influence on their ability to deal with the adverse events they encountered. In practical terms, these studies underline the need for researchers not only to focus interventions on athletes' personal qualities, but also to utilize aspects of their sociocultural environment to facilitate the development of resilience.

Ungar's (2012) second observation concerns the access to, and meaningfulness of, the findings from non-diverse samples. Policymakers in sport need to develop organizations and services that facilitate the development of resilience while being considerate of different contexts and cultures. Beyond sport, resilience researchers in general psychology have acknowledged that minority groups (Ungar, 2008) and disadvantaged individuals (Hutcheon & Lashewicz, 2014) are frequently not included in discussions when services are designed to aid their resilience. Accordingly, the aforementioned researchers recognized that interventions that target these populations are often not specific to their backgrounds or properly suited to their specific needs. This omission can have dramatic (negative) effects, as highlighted by Hansson and colleagues (Hansson, Tuck, Lurie, & McKenzie, 2012), who found that adult immigrants who assimilate into a culture and lack specific cultural support report more mental health issues than those who do not. Hence, given the global nature of contemporary sport, it is vital that practitioners work with athletes to ensure that resources are tailored to the specific sociocultural context in which they originate or with which they identify. Only then are resilience interventions likely to be both effective and efficacious.

The last observation made by Ungar (2012) was that individuals' benefit more from protective factors developed to alleviate risks when the level of exposure to the risk is at its greatest. Indeed, it is generally accepted that individuals with the greatest perceived needs benefit from unique individual provision rather than general resilience programmes designed for wider populations and situations (cf. Robertson, Cooper, Sarkar, & Curran, 2015). In addition, the support required can be disproportionately larger for an athlete facing substantial demands. Away from sport, education studies have shown smaller class sizes and a caring teacher are more advantageous to pupils with the most complex educational needs and disrupted home lives (Shernoff & Schmidt, 2008). Despite the different domains, the overall picture is that a homogeneous approach to developing resilience is not appropriate, and it is possible that athletes who are most at risk will benefit the most from resilience intervention resources.

Team Resilience in Sport

Resilience researchers, in various domains of psychology, have recently devoted attention to the group level (e.g., Carmeli, Friedman, & Tishler, 2013; Chapman et al., in press; Gucciardi et al., 2018; Stephens, Heaphy, Carmeli, Spreitzer, & Dutton, 2013). For instance, there has been a recent growth in attention paid to team resilience as a dynamic, multilevel phenomenon that requires clarity on the individual- and team-level factors that foster its emergence within occupational and organizational settings (see Gucciardi et al., 2018). Further, according to Chapman et al., several key findings regarding the literature on team resilience in occupational and organizational domains are observable: (a) definitions vary in terms of content (e.g., input or process), breadth (e.g., unidimensional versus multidimensional), and quality (e.g., essential and necessary attributes of key components); (b) there exists a predominance of single-level conceptualizations of team resilience; and (c) there has been a reliance on cross-sectional research designs in empirical studies, which is incongruent with the dynamic nature of this concept. In concluding their review, Chapman et al. noted key recommendations from the findings of their scoping review, including: the need to advance the definitional quality of team resilience; the need to develop an overarching theoretical framework to integrate existing research with future work; and the use of methodological approaches that are commensurate with the multilevel, dynamic nature of team resilience.

Within the sport psychology literature, Morgan et al. (2013) conducted the first study of *team resilience* in sport. Employing focus groups with members of five elite sport teams, a definition of team resilience was developed, and the resilient characteristics of elite sport teams were identified. Specifically, team resilience was defined as a "dynamic, psychosocial process which protects a group of individuals from the potential negative effect of the stressors they collectively encounter. It comprises of processes whereby team members use their individual and collective resources to positively adapt when experiencing adversity" (p. 552). Team resilience was described as a dynamic phenomenon, with participants stating that it was "dependent upon what time of the season it is" or "whether there is an injury in the team". In terms of its protective function, the participants described team resilience as akin to "having a barrier around you" and "having a thick skin". Furthermore, the participants emphasized that team resilience involved a shared experience of stressors (e.g., team disruptions, low team morale), and this was revealed through comments such as "we have been through so many setbacks together". Four resilient characteristics of elite sport teams emerged from this study: group structure (i.e., conventions that shape group norms and values), mastery approaches (i.e., shared attitudes and behaviours that promote an emphasis on team improvement), social capital (i.e., the existence of high-quality interactions and caring relationships within the team), and collective efficacy (i.e., the team's shared beliefs in its ability to perform a task).

The recent developments in resilience research have advanced psychologists' knowledge of the nature, meaning, and scope of team resilience. In the sport psychology literature, Morgan et al.'s (2013) study provided greater definitional clarity on resilience at the team level (i.e., what team resilience is) and a framework to profile the resilient characteristics of elite sport teams (i.e., what resilient teams "look" like). Although such knowledge provided descriptive information about the factors that enable teams to withstand stressors, these characteristics do not explain how resilient teams function. Morgan et al. described team resilience as a "dynamic, psychosocial process" (p. 552), which points to operational aspects of this construct and how it changes over time. They went on to argue that "due to the contextual and temporal nature of team resilience, future studies should aim to identify the processes that underpin the resilience characteristics" (p. 558). In an attempt to address this gap in our knowledge, Morgan et al. (2015) subsequently explored the psychosocial processes underpinning team resilience in elite sport. Using narrative inquiry, Morgan et al. (2015) analysed the autobiographies of eight members of the 2003 England Rugby Union World Cup-winning team. Findings revealed five main psychosocial processes underpinning team resilience: transformational leadership, shared team leadership, team learning, social identity, and positive emotions. The results indicated that these processes enabled the England rugby team to effectively utilize their cognitive, affective, and relational resources to act as leverage points for team resilience when facing stressors. Further, the findings of this study revealed that team resilience was illuminated through a progressive narrative form. This was portrayed by team members evaluating stressors in a positive fashion and focusing on moving forward as a team despite setbacks.

Research investigating team resilience in elite sport has begun to describe what resilient teams "look like" (i.e., their characteristics) and how they function (i.e., their processes). However, less is known about the psychosocial enablers and cues that stimulate such mechanisms and the associated pathways to team resilience (Morgan et al., 2017; Wagstaff et al., 2017). In their discussion of future research directions, Morgan et al. (2015) proposed that "creative qualitative approaches such as ethnography offer intriguing possibilities to study 'first-hand' the underlying team resilience mechanisms ... and how they are developed" (p. 76). Thus, through prolonged fieldwork, Morgan et al. (2019) conducted a season-long (11-month) ethnography to explore the psychosocial enablers and strategies that promote the development of team resilience within a high-level sports team. The sample consisted of members of a leading English national league-winning semi-professional rugby union team (*n* = 27). Multiple data collection methods were employed (i.e., observation, interviewing, field notes, reflexive diary) as part of a holistic ethnographic approach. An iterative process of content data analysis was employed to identify key themes. Findings revealed five categories comprising multiple practical strategies, actions, and enablers for team resilience development: inspiring, motivating, and challenging team members to achieve performance excellence; developing a team regulatory system based on ownership and responsibility; cultivating a team identity and togetherness based on a selfless culture; exposing the team to challenging training and unexpected/difficult situations; and promoting enjoyment and keeping a positive outlook during stressors. The findings of this study provide sport psychologists, coaches, and those working in teams with multiple psychosocial enablers and strategies to develop team resilience.

Collectively, the emerging research exploring team resilience in sport has contributed to our understanding of what team resilience is, highlighted some of the processes by which resilient teams function, and identified evidence-based practical strategies to improve team resilience. Nevertheless, there remains much to be explored regarding the interplay of sociocultural and organizational dynamics and both individual and team resilience. Indeed, some of the themes to emerge from Morgan et al.'s (2013) study of team resilience (e.g., psychosocial conventions shaping group norms and roles, managing change, and social capital) intersect with those highlighted in research on organizational functioning in sport (cf. Wagstaff, Fletcher, & Hanton, 2012). Moreover, future research within sport psychology might carefully consider the observations of the work being conducted on team resilience in organizational and occupational domains, and seek, where appropriate, definitional, conceptual, and methodological alignment and integration (cf. Chapman et al., in press; Gucciardi et al., 2018).

Organizational Resilience

As alluded to earlier in this chapter, recent resilience research has shifted from individuals toward the study of groups and teams (see, e.g., Alliger, Cerasoli, Tannenbaum, & Vessey, 2015; Bennett, Aden, Broome, Mitchell, & Rigdon, 2010; Meneghel, Salanova, & Martínez, 2016; Morgan et al., 2013, 2015; Stephens et al., 2013). Over the past couple of decades, the concept of resilience has also been applied to organizations (e.g., Gittell, Cameron, Lim, & Rivas, 2006; Lengnick-Hall, Beck, & Lengnick-Hall, 2011; McManus, Seville, Vargo, & Brunsdon, 2008). This work has been shaped not only by the individual and team resilience literature, but also by dominant influences from ecological and engineering resilience and from disaster management and business continuity research (Annarelli & Nonino, 2016), where the focus is often on the resilience of a system, rather than a single individual or team (van der Vegt, Essens, Wahlström, & George, 2015). Within this context, *organizational resilience* is seen as an emergent property of a complex system, with multiple interacting parts that include the employees and teams working within that organization.

Organizational resilience has been defined as, "the maintenance of positive adjustment under challenging circumstances such that the organization emerges from those conditions strengthened and more resourceful" (Vogus & Sutcliffe, 2007, p. 3418) and "having the capacity to change before the case for change becomes desperately obvious" (Hamel &

Valikangas, 2003, p. 54). Nevertheless, definitions and operationalizations of the concept remain quite fragmented (Tarba, Cooper, Ahammad, Khan, & Rao-Nickolson, 2017), in part owing to the heterogeneity of research streams within this literature (Linnenluecke, 2017). Despite this fragmented and siloed work, reviews of the organizational resilience literature have recently emerged (e.g., Annarelli & Nonino, 2016; Fasey, 2017; Linnenluecke, 2017).

Linnenluecke's (2017) review charts the historical development of organizational resilience research streams, with the earliest work (e.g., Meyer, 1982) considering organizational resilience as a response to external threats. This history is intertwined with societal events: For instance, a number of industrial accidents in the 1980s, including Chernobyl, Exxon Valdez, and the Space Shuttle Challenger, prompted an inward-facing focus on resilience as reliability (e.g., Boin & van Eeten, 2013; Weick & Roberts, 1993). Additionally, organizational resilience work has also been linked to key external threats (e.g. Gittell et al., 2006; McManus et al., 2008), prompted by the 9/11 terror attacks and the 2008–09 global financial crisis. Moreover, organizational resilience research has increasingly been influenced by concerns regarding the generalizability of the "reliability" research conducted in larger organizations to smaller businesses (Sullivan-Taylor & Branicki, 2011). This research, influenced by the contemporaneous development of management literature on business continuity and crisis management, can be divided into three principle streams, namely those focusing on organizational resilience as a function of employee strengths (e.g., Coutu, 2002; Lengnick-Hall et al., 2011), organizational resilience as the adaptability of the wider system (e.g. Hamel & Valikangas, 2003; Vogus & Sutcliffe, 2007), and organizational resilience in relation to inter-organizational networks of supply chains (e.g., Sheffi & Rice Jr, 2005).

First was the seminal research by Meyer (1982), whose empirical study explored hospital responses to an unexpected doctors' strike, analysing financial records, occupancy figures, and payrolls across 19 hospitals, in addition to a more intensive study of three hospitals with maximally disparate strategies. Meyer suggested that organizational adaptations are divisible into three phases: anticipatory, responsive, and readjustment, and that organizations display two different forms of adaptability, either absorbing the impact of events or undergoing change and learning. Predictors of adaptation included entrepreneurial strategies and adaptive ideologies that enhance learning, whereas formalized and complex structures were found to retard learning.

Following Meyer's seminal work, a second phase of research emerged, focusing on minimizing internal threats by pursuing "reliability" over efficiency; it was influenced by the work conducted by a body of researchers at the University of California at Berkeley studying organizations managing hazardous essential technical systems, labelled "high reliability organizations" (e.g. Bourrier, 2011; Roberts, 1989). Against this backdrop, Weick and Roberts (1993) introduced the idea of the "collective mind" for high reliability, emphasizing the need for cooperation, ongoing interrelating and dense interactions, and the importance of social processes, where individualism was subsumed by the collective mind. The principles were later expanded in the book *Managing the Unexpected*, in which Weick and Sutcliffe (2001) promulgated five core principles: monitor small failures, do not oversimplify, be sensitive to the messy reality of what is happening, be committed to resilience, and defer to expertise.

A third phase of research outlined by Linnenluecke (2017) was dedicated to how organizations of varying sizes cope and respond in conditions of great environmental uncertainty, such as those experienced at the start of the 21st century. For some (e.g., Coutu, 2002; Lengnick-Hall et al., 2011), the focus was on human resources as the most important part of an organizational system, where employee characteristics were seen as a critical source of resilience capacity, and relationship networks determine the accessibility of these resources (van der Vegt et al., 2015). More recently, Lengnick-Hall et al. (2011) proposed that an organization's capacity for resilience is developed through strategically managing human resources to create competencies among core employees that, when aggregated at the organizational level, make it possible for organizations to achieve the ability to respond in a resilient manner when they experience severe shocks. Specifically, their proposition is based on three elements: cognitive factors (e.g., strong core values, sense of purpose, constructive sense-making), behavioural characteristics (e.g., learned resourcefulness, bricolage, behavioural preparedness), and contextual conditions (e.g., psychological safety, deep social capital, diffused power and accountability).

Alongside the work on human resources, an alternative stream of research in response to external threats considered organizational resilience as the adaptability of business models (Linnenluecke, 2017). Influential work by a body of New Zealand researchers has emanated from an early study by McManus et al. (2008), where organizational resilience was characterized as consisting of three main dimensions, namely situation awareness (viz. an organization's understanding and perception of its entire operating environment), management of keystone vulnerabilities (viz. those aspects of an organization, operational and managerial, that have the potential to have significant negative impacts in a crisis situation), and adaptive capacity (viz. the culture and dynamics of an organization that allow it to make decisions in a timely and appropriate manner, both in day-to-day business and also in crises). A resilience benchmarking tool was subsequently developed, divided into three main attribute categories of leadership and culture, networks and relationships, and change readiness (Lee, Vargo, & Seville, 2013; Whitman, Kachali, Roger, Vargo, & Seville, 2013).

More recently, researchers have started to consider the processes that support the development of organizational resilience. Burnard, Bhamra, and Tsinopoulos (2018) used case study data from three energy sector organizations to propose four ways to build resilience, depending on an organization's abilities in preparation (i.e., the degree to which an organization has a systematic approach to risk management) and adaptation (i.e., the degree to which an organization flexibly allocates resources). Burnard et al. also highlighted the iterative decision-making processes in which events are initially detected, and their likely impact is evaluated to determine whether an existing response should be implemented or a new response should be adjusted and adopted. This process-based approach is consistent with the view that organizational resilience is not a "one-size-fits-all" construct, and that organizations seeking to develop their resilience need to consider strategies that are relevant to their orientations towards preparation and adaptation.

In addition to the work of Linnenluecke (2017) charting the development of different research streams within the organizational resilience literature, a review by Fasey (2017) provided a synthesis of empirical research concerning how resilience functions within organizations. In doing so, the characteristics an organization *has* that might predict or enable organizational resilience were grouped into resources (viz. human, financial, physical, social, informational, and intangible resources), capabilities (namely the organization's capacity to deploy resources towards a desired goal), culture (as shared values, beliefs, expectations, and practices), and structure (how employees and teams are grouped, and how information is shared). Relevant characteristics from each grouping are discussed, and areas of disagreement or ambiguity are highlighted. The underlying mechanisms through which organizational resilience operates were found to comprise planning, adaptation, learning, relationship networks, and leadership. Finally, key contextual variables were identified, including the size of an organization and the sector in which it operates. Somewhat surprisingly, the sport sector has been relatively slow to undertake research in this domain, particularly given the volatile nature of sport, and the high levels of organizational change (Wagstaff et al., 2016). Parenthetically, empirical research (e.g., Stephenson, Vargo, & Seville, 2010) indicates that organizational resilience may be greater in the health and community domain than other sectors, thus indicating that sport might be a fruitful context to example organizational resilience. To the best of our knowledge, the only study of organizational resilience in sport was conducted by Wicker, Filo, and Cuskelly (2013), exploring the organizational resilience of community sport clubs in the aftermath of major cyclone and flood events. Using data from a survey of sport clubs (*n* = 200) in Queensland, Australia, the findings showed that clubs predominantly used human and financial resources in their recovery efforts, with organizational resilience having a significant positive effect on the extent of the club's perceived overall recovery, alongside the number of members and the use of government grants. Those clubs that typically used outdoor sport facilities exclusively (viz. equestrian, golf, and motor sports) recovered to a significantly lesser extent than clubs providing other sports. These data can be interpreted to indicate that it may be preferable for organizations to dedicate their efforts to sharing and mobilizing third-party physical resources where possible to reduce susceptibility to external turbulence (such as natural disasters or terrorism), rather than maintain spare capacity to buffer the impact of turbulent events (cf. Gittell et al., 2006). This may be particularly pertinent for sport organizations, given the prevalent use of public policy to attempt to maximize utilization of sport facilities (Iversen & Cuskelly, 2015), and the potential public perception of inefficiency associated with under-utilization of resources provided by public funds (Dalgaard-Nielsen, 2017).

Overall, organizational resilience not only influences the positive, optimal functioning of the organization itself, but also has the potential to significantly influence resilience in athletes and teams. The body of knowledge in this area remains at a nascent stage, and empirical examination of organizational resilience is rather scant both in general and sport psychology contexts, with researchers facing challenges concerning conceptualization and operationalization. In particular, more research is needed to understand the complex relationships between individual, team, and organizational resilience. Nevertheless, the landscape of elite sport presents an array of complex adaptive systems that offer rich opportunities to examine and influence resilience in individuals and organizations.

Conclusion

To conclude, we draw on the words of Mahoney and Bergman (2002), who stated that the specific sociocultural conditions in which an individual functions must be considered when examining competence, and that "failing to do so may lead to a view of positive adaptation as a static phenomenon with relevance to only a minority of persons in select circumstances" (p. 212). Given there is growing evidence pointing to the central role of resilience in sustained sporting success and highlighting this construct as a key area of development for athletes, teams, and organizations, it is reassuring that researchers and practitioners have begun to gain a better practical understanding of resilience at multiple levels of analysis and intervention, in line with the praxis of our profession.

References

Alliger, G. M., Cerasoli, C. P., Tannenbaum, S. I., & Vessey, W. B. (2015). Team resilience: How teams flourish under pressure. *Organizational Dynamics, 44*, 176–184.

Annarelli, A., & Nonino, F. (2016). Strategic and operational management of organizational resilience: Current state of research and future directions. *Omega, 62*, 1–18.

Arnold, R., & Fletcher, D. (2012). A research synthesis and taxonomic classification of the organizational stressors encountered by sport performers. *Journal of Sport and Exercise Psychology, 34,* 397–429.

Bennett, J. B., Aden, C. A., Broome, K., Mitchell, K., & Rigdon, W. D. (2010). Team resilience for young restaurant workers: Research-to-practice adaptation and assessment. *Journal of Occupational Health Psychology, 15,* 223–236.

Blodgett, A. T., Schinke, R. J., McGannon, K. R., & Fisher, L. A. (2014). Cultural sport psychology research: Conceptions, evolutions, and forecasts. *International Review of Sport and Exercise Psychology, 8,* 24–43.

Boin, A., & van Eeten, M. J. G. (2013). The resilient organization. *Public Management Review, 15*(3), 429–445.

Bourrier, M. (2011). The legacy of the high reliability organization project. *Journal of Contingencies and Crisis Management, 19,* 9–13.

Burnard, K., Bhamra, R., & Tsinopoulos, C. (2018). Building organizational resilience: Four configurations. *IEEE Transactions on Engineering Management, 65,* 351–362.

Carmeli, A., Friedman, Y., & Tishler, A. (2013). Cultivating a resilient top management team: The importance of relational connections and strategic decision comprehensiveness. *Safety Science, 51*(1), 148–159.

Chapman, M. T., Lines, R. L., Crane, M., Ducker, K. J., Ntoumanis, N., Peeling, P., ... Gucciardi, D. F. (in press). Team resilience: A scoping review of conceptual and empirical work. *Work & Stress.* Published online ahead of print.

Chauhan, P., Reppucci, N. D., Burnette, M., & Reiner, S. (2010). Race, neighborhood disadvantage, and antisocial behavior among female juvenile offenders. *American Journal of Community Psychology, 38* (4), 532–540.

Clauss-Ehlers, C. S. (2008). Sociocultural factors, resilience, and coping: Support for a culturally sensitive measure of resilience. *Journal of Applied Developmental Psychology, 29*(3), 197–212.

Coutu, D. L. (2002). How resilience works. *Harvard Business Review, 80,* 46–55.

Dalgaard-Nielsen, A. (2017). Organizational resilience in national security bureaucracies: Realistic and practicable? *Journal of Contingencies and Crisis Management, 25,* 341–349.

Fasey, K. (2017). *A systematic review of organizational resilience research* (Unpublished master's thesis). Loughborough: Loughborough University.

Fletcher, D., Hanton, S., & Mellalieu, S. D. (2006). An organizational stress review: Conceptual and theoretical issues in competitive sport. In S. Hanton & S. D. Mellalieu (Eds.), *Literature reviews in sport psychology* (pp. 321–374). Hauppauge, NY: Nova Science.

Fletcher, D., & Sarkar, M. (2012). A grounded theory of psychological resilience in Olympic champions. *Psychology of Sport and Exercise, 13*(5), 669–678.

Fletcher, D., & Sarkar, M. (2013). Psychological resilience: A review and critique of definitions, concepts, and theory. *European Psychologist, 18,* 12–23.

Fletcher, D., & Wagstaff, C. R. D. (2009). Organizational psychology in elite sport: Its emergence, application and future. *Psychology of Sport and Exercise, 10,* 427–434.

Galli, N., & Gonzalez, S. P. (2015). Psychological resilience in sport: A review of the literature and implications for research and practice. *International Journal of Sport and Exercise Psychology, 3,* 243–257.

Galli, N., & Vealey, R. S. (2008). "Bouncing back" from adversity: Athletes' experiences of resilience. *Sport Psychologist, 22,* 316–335.

Gilligan, R. (2004). Promoting resilience in child and family social work: Issues for social work practice, education and policy. *Social Work Education, 23,* 93–104.

Gittell, J. H., Cameron, K., Lim, S., & Rivas, V. (2006). Relationships, layoffs, and organizational resilience. *The Journal of Applied Behavioral Science, 42,* 300–329.

Gould, D., Finch, L. M., & Jackson, S. A. (1993). Coping strategies used by national champion figure skaters. *Research Quarterly for Exercise and Sport, 64,* 453–468.

Gucciardi, D. F., Crane, M., Ntoumanis, N., Parker, S. K., Thøgersen-Ntoumani, C., Ducker, K. J., ... Temby, P. (2018). The emergence of team resilience: A multilevel conceptual model of facilitating factors. *Journal of Occupational and Organizational Psychology, 91,* 729–768.

Gucciardi, D. F., Jackson, B., Coulter, T. J., & Mallett, C. J. (2011). The Connor–Davidson resilience scale (CD-RISC): Dimensionality and age-related measurement invariance with Australian cricketers. *Psychology of Sport and Exercise, 12,* 423–433.

Hamel, G., & Valikangas, L. (2003). The quest for resilience. *Harvard Business Review, 81*(9), 52–65.

Hansson, E. K., Tuck, A., Lurie, S., & McKenzie, K. (2012). Rates of mental illness and suicidality in immigrant, refugee, ethnocultural, and racialized groups in Canada: A review of the literature. *Canadian Journal of Psychiatry, 57*, 111–121.

Hanton, S., Wagstaff, C. R. D., & Fletcher, D. (2012). Cognitive appraisals of stressors encountered in sport organizations. *International Journal of Sport and Exercise Psychology, 10*, 276–289.

Holt, N. L., & Dunn, J. G. (2004). Toward a grounded theory of the psychosocial competencies and environmental conditions associated with soccer success. *Journal of Applied Sport Psychology, 16*, 199–219.

Hutcheon, E., & Lashewicz, B. (2014). Theorizing resilience: Critiquing and unbounding a marginalizing concept. *Disability and Society, 29*, 1383–1397.

Iversen, E. B., & Cuskelly, G. (2015). Effects of different policy approaches on sport facility utilisation strategies. *Sport Management Review, 18*, 529–541.

Lee, A. V., Vargo, J., & Seville, E. (2013). Developing a tool to measure and compare organizations' resilience. *Natural Hazards Review, 14*, 29–41.

Lengnick-Hall, C. A., Beck, T. E., & Lengnick-Hall, M. L. (2011). Developing a capacity for organizational resilience through strategic human resource management. *Human Resource Management Review, 21*, 243–255.

Linnenluecke, M. K. (2017). Resilience in business and management research: A review of influential publications and a research agenda. *International Journal of Management Reviews, 19*, 4–30.

Lu, F. J., Lee, W. P., Chang, Y. K., Chou, C. C., Hsu, Y. W., Lin, J. H., & Gill, D. L. (2016). Interaction of athletes' resilience and coaches' social support on the stress–burnout relationship: A conjunctive moderation perspective. *Psychology of Sport and Exercise, 22*, 202–209.

Luthar, S. S., & Cicchetti, D. (2000). The construct of resilience: Implications for interventions and social policies. *Development and Psychopathology, 12*, 857–885.

Machida, M., Irwin, B., & Feltz, D. (2013). Resilience in competitive athletes with spinal cord injury: The role of sport participation. *Qualitative Health Research, 23*, 1054–1065.

Mahoney, J. L., & Bergman, L. R. (2002). Conceptual and methodological considerations in a developmental approach to the study of positive adaptation. *Applied Developmental Psychology, 23*, 195–217.

Martin-Krumm, C. P., Sarrazin, P. G., Peterson, C., & Famose, J. (2003). Explanatory style and resilience after sports failure. *Personality and Individual Differences, 35*, 1685–1695.

McGarry, R., Walklate, S., & Mythen, G. (2015). A sociological analysis of military resilience: Opening up the debate. *Armed Forces and Society, 41*, 352–378.

McManus, S., Seville, E., Vargo, J., & Brunsdon, D. (2008). Facilitated process for improving organizational resilience. *Natural Hazards Review, 9*, 81–90.

Mellalieu, S. D., Neil, R., Hanton, S., & Fletcher, D. (2009). Competition stress in sport performers: Stressors experienced in the competition environment. *Journal of Sports Sciences, 27*, 729–744.

Meneghel, I., Salanova, M., & Martínez, I. M. (2016). Feeling good makes us stronger: How team resilience mediates the effect of positive emotions on team performance. *Journal of Happiness Studies, 17*, 239–255.

Meyer, A. D. (1982). Adapting to environmental jolts. *Administrative Science Quarterly, 27*, 515–537.

Mills, A., Butt, J., Maynard, I., & Harwood, C. (2012). Identifying factors perceived to influence the development of elite youth football academy players. *Journal of Sports Sciences, 30*, 1593–1604.

Morgan, P. B. C., Fletcher, D., & Sarkar, M. (2013). Defining and characterizing team resilience in elite sport. *Psychology of Sport and Exercise, 14*, 549–559.

Morgan, P. B. C., Fletcher, D., & Sarkar, M. (2015). Understanding team resilience in the world's best athletes: A case study of a Rugby Union World Cup winning team. *Psychology of Sport and Exercise, 16*, 91–100.

Morgan, P. B. C., Fletcher, D., & Sarkar, M. (2017). Recent developments in team resilience research in elite sport. *Current Opinion in Psychology, 16*, 159–164.

Morgan, P. B. C., Fletcher, D., & Sarkar, M. (2019). Developing team resilience: A season-long study of psychosocial enablers and strategies in a high-level sports team. *Psychology of Sport and Exercise, 49*, 101543.

Mummery, W. K., Schofield, G., & Perry, C. (2004). Bouncing back: The role of coping style, social support and self-concept in resilience of sport performance. *Athletic Insight: The Online Journal of Sport Psychology of Sport and Exercise, 6*(3), 1–18. Retrieved from www.athleticinsight.com

Roberts, K. H. (1989). New challenges in organizational research: High reliability organizations. *Industrial Crisis Quarterly, 3*, 111–125.

Robertson, I., Cooper, C. L., Sarkar, M., & Curran, T. (2015). Resilience training in the workplace from 2003–2014: A systematic review. *Journal of Occupational and Organizational Psychology, 88,* 533–562.

Sarkar, M., & Fletcher, D. (2013). How should we measure psychological resilience in sport performers? *Measurement in Physical Education and Exercise Science, 17,* 264–280.

Sarkar, M., & Fletcher, D. (2014). Psychological resilience in sport performers: A review of stressors and protective factors. *Journal of Sports Sciences, 32,* 1419–1434.

Scanlan, T. K., Stein, G. L., & Ravizza, K. (1991). An in-depth study of former elite figure skaters: III. Sources of stress. *Journal of Sport and Exercise Psychology, 13,* 103–120.

Schinke, R. J., & Hanrahan, S. J. (Eds.). (2009). *Cultural sport psychology.* Champaign, IL: Human Kinetics.

Schinke, R. J., & Jerome, W. C. (2002). Understanding and refining the resilience of elite athletes: An intervention strategy. *Athletic Insight, 4,* 1–13. Retrieved from www.athleticinsight.com

Schinke, R. J., Peterson, C., & Couture, R. (2004). A protocol for teaching resilience to high performance athletes. *Journal of Excellence, 9,* 9–18.

Seccombe, K. (2002). "Beating the odds" versus "changing the odds": Poverty, resilience, and family policy. *Journal of Marriage and Family, 64,* 384–394.

Seligman, M. E., Nolen-Hoeksema, S., Thornton, N., & Thornton, K. M. (1990). Explanatory style as a mechanism of disappointing athletic performance. *Psychological Science, 1,* 143–146.

Sheffi, Y., & Rice Jr, J. B. (2005). A supply chain view of the resilient enterprise. *MIT Sloan Management Review, 47,* 41–48.

Shernoff, D. J., & Schmidt, J. A. (2008). Further evidence of an engagement–achievement paradox among U.S. high school students. *Journal of Youth and Adolescence, 37,* 564–580.

Smith, R. E., Smoll, F. L., & Ptacek, J. T. (1990). Conjunctive moderator variables in vulnerability and resiliency research: Life stress, social support and coping skills, and adolescent sport injuries. *Journal of Personality and Social Psychology, 58,* 360–370.

Stephens, J. P., Heaphy, E. D., Carmeli, A., Spreitzer, G. M., & Dutton, J. E. (2013). Relationship quality and virtuousness: Emotional carrying capacity as a source of individual and team resilience. *Journal of Applied Behavioral Science, 49,* 13–41.

Stephenson, A., Vargo, J., & Seville, E. (2010). Measuring and comparing organizational resilience in Auckland. *Australian Journal of Emergency Management, 25,* 27–32.

Sullivan-Taylor, B., & Branicki, L. (2011). Creating resilient SMEs: Why one size might not fit all. *International Journal of Production Research, 49,* 5565–5579.

Tarba, S. Y., Cooper, S. C. L., Ahammad, M. F., Khan, Z., & Rao-Nickolson, R. (2017). Special issue – Call for papers: Resilience in organizations. *Applied Psychology, 66,* 196–201.

Thelwell, R. C., Weston, N. J. V., & Greenlees, I. A. (2007). Batting on a sticky wicket: Identifying sources of stress and associated coping strategies for professional cricket batsmen. *Psychology of Sport and Exercise, 8,* 219–232.

Theron, L., Cameron, C. A., Didkowsky, N., Lau, C., Liebenberg, L., & Ungar, M. (2011). A "day in the lives" of four resilient youths: Cultural roots of resilience. *Youth & Society, 43,* 799–818.

Ungar, M. (2008). Resilience across cultures. *British Journal of Social Work, 38,* 218–235.

Ungar, M. (2012). Researching and theorizing resilience across cultures and contexts. *Preventive Medicine, 55,* 387–389.

van der Vegt, G. S., Essens, P., Wahlström, M., & George, G. (2015). Managing risk and resilience. *Academy of Management Journal, 58,* 971–980.

Van Yperen, N. W. (2009). Why some make it and others do not: Identifying psychological factors that predict career success in professional adult soccer. *The Sport Psychologist, 23,* 317–329.

Vitali, F., Bortoli, L., Bertinato, L., Robazza, C., & Schena, F. (2015). Motivational climate, resilience, and burnout in youth sport. *Sport Sciences for Health, 11,* 103–108.

Vogus, T. J., & Sutcliffe, K. M. (2007). Organizational resilience: Towards a theory and research agenda, *IEEE systems, man, and cybernetics 2007 conference proceedings,* 3418–3422.

Wagstaff, C. R. D. (Ed.). (2017). *The organizational psychology of sport: Key issues and practical applications.* Abingdon: Routledge.

Wagstaff, C. R. D. (2019a). Taking stock of organizational psychology in sport: An introduction to the special issue. *Journal of Applied Sport Psychology, 31,* 1–6.

Wagstaff, C. R. D. (2019b). A commentary and reflections on the field of organizational sport psychology: Epilogue to the special issue. *Journal of Applied Sport Psychology, 31,* 134–146.

Wagstaff, C. R. D., & Burton-Wylie, S. (2018). Organisational culture in sport: A conceptual, methodological and definitional review. *Sport & Exercise Psychology Review, 14*, 32–52.

Wagstaff, C., Fletcher, D., & Hanton, S. (2012). Positive organizational psychology in sport: An ethnography of organizational functioning in a national sport organization. *Journal of Applied Sport Psychology, 24*, 26–47.

Wagstaff, C. R. D., Gilmore, S., & Thelwell, R. C. (2016). When the show must go on: Investigating repeated organizational change in elite sport. *Journal of Change Management, 16*, 38–54.

Wagstaff, C. R. D., Sarkar, M., Davidson, C. L., & Fletcher, D. (2017). Resilience in sport: A critical review of psychological processes, sociocultural influences, and organizational dynamics. In C. R. D. Wagstaff (Ed.), *The organizational psychology of sport: Key issues and practical applications* (pp. 120–150). Abingdon UK: Routledge.

Weick, K. E., & Roberts, K. H. (1993). Collective mind in organizations: Heedful interrelating on flight decks. *Administrative Science Quarterly, 38*, 357–381.

Weick, K. E., & Sutcliffe, K. M. (2001). *Managing the unexpected.* San Francisco, CA: Jossey-Bass.

White, R. L., Bennie, A., & McKenna, J. (2015). Resilience in youth sport: A qualitative investigation of gymnastics coach and athlete perceptions. *International Journal of Sports Science and Coaching, 10*, 379–394.

Whitman, Z., Kachali, H., Roger, D., Vargo, J., & Seville, E. (2013). Short-form version of the Benchmark Resilience Tool (BRT-53). *Measuring Business Excellence, 17*, 3–14.

Wicker, P., Filo, K., & Cuskelly, G. (2013). Organizational resilience of community sport clubs impacted by natural disasters. *Journal of Sport Management, 27*, 510–525.

Windle, G. (2011). What is resilience? A review and concept analysis. *Reviews in Clinical Gerontology, 21*, 152–169.

41

SELF-DETERMINATION THEORY

Nikita Bhavsar, Nikos Ntoumanis, Eleanor Quested,
Cecilie Thøgersen-Ntoumani, and Nikos Chatzisarantis

Introduction

Motivation has been a ubiquitous topic in sport and exercise psychology research (Biddle, 1999; Weiss & Gill, 2005). Numerous theories have lent themselves as frameworks to study motivation in this domain, including self-determination theory (SDT; Deci & Ryan, 1985a; Ryan & Deci, 2017), theory of planned behaviour (Ajzen, 1991), and achievement goals theory (Nicholls, 1989), to name a few. In a recent bibliometric review study (Lindahl, Stenling, Lindwall, & Colliander, 2015), SDT was found to be widely applied to the study of motivation in sport and exercise psychology. In this encyclopedia entry, we provide an overview of the basic concepts and the six mini-theories within the SDT framework. Empirical findings from both in and outside of the sport and exercise domain are also presented as illustrative examples of the applications of the tenets of the theory.

Self-Determination Theory

We begin by presenting two hypothetical cases to illustrate the relevance of SDT principles in sport and exercise. First, consider a young basketball coach who is unsure of how to best motivate his athletes. He has sought advice from the more experienced coaches in the club. Although most of them tell him that his athletes will be highly motivated to follow a coach who is in complete control of planning and every aspect of decision-making, he finds that his athletes are happier and more engaged in training if he lets them have a say in decisions that affect their training and games. What is the best advice for him? We will consider some possible answers to this question later on in the chapter.

Next, let us look at a 45-year-old woman who is struggling to stay regularly active. It seems that her motivation for exercise is based on trying to avoid feeling guilty for not exercising. She wants to comply with her doctor's warning that she must lose weight to prevent health problems in the future, but she finds exercise a 'chore' and the gym environment intimidating. What would be the best advice for her?

SDT can help shed light on questions such as these. SDT is an organismic dialectic approach to human behaviour and personality. It distinguishes between different types of motivation that may regulate behaviour and also considers the social and psychological determinants and consequences of engaging in activities for different reasons. It is organized under six mini-theories, each attending to distinct theoretical features, yet connected by an organismic and dialectic meta-theory and the unifying concept of the basic psychological needs (Standage, Curran, & Rouse, 2019). SDT has been extensively applied to sport and, more recently, to the exercise domain. In this entry, we use the term exercise in the same way it is used in the term 'sport and exercise psychology', that is, to refer to both planned and organized (e.g., group fitness classes) and less organized and incidental (e.g., walking) types of physical activity. This is done for simplicity purposes, and we acknowledge that others (e.g., Caspersen, Powell, & Christenson, 1985) use the term 'exercise' for structured types of physical activity only.

Cognitive Evaluation Theory

Cognitive evaluation theory (CET), SDT's first mini-theory, focuses on the nature of motivation and the factors that impact the degree to which an activity is engaged in for 'its own sake'. Intrinsic motivation describes full engagement in activities out of curiosity, interest, or a sense of volition, in the absence of any external rewards or constraints (Deci & Ryan, 2000). CET was developed and refined in the 1970s and 1980s, from the examination of the influence of extrinsic events such as rewards on individuals' intrinsic motivation (Deci, 1975). Early experiments were conducted during the dominant phase of operant theory (Skinner, 1971) in psychology (Ryan & Deci, 2017). The findings of these experiments were controversial, as they demonstrated that extrinsic rewards undermined intrinsic motivation (Deci, 1971). However, these were later supported by a meta-analysis of 128 experiments where it was shown that tangible rewards undermined intrinsic motivation for a behaviour if they were contingent on the behaviour, expected while doing it, and relatively salient (Deci, Koestner, & Ryan, 1999). Additionally, positive feedback was found to enhance intrinsic motivation (Deci, 1971; Vallerand & Reid, 1984). Ryan and Deci (2000) subsequently provided a summary of additional conditions that decreased intrinsic motivation (e.g., threats of punishment, deadlines, evaluations, and surveillance) and those that enhanced it (e.g., provision of choice and acknowledgment of perspective, informative feedback). More recently, researchers have begun to examine the neurological processes associated with the undermining effect of rewards on intrinsic motivation (see Lee & Reeve, 2013; Murayama, Matsumoto, Izuma, & Matsumoto, 2010).

Taken together, these findings suggested that two fundamental psychological needs lie at the heart of intrinsic motivation – the need to feel autonomy (i.e., volitional, sense of freedom, that one's actions are aligned with one's personal values and goals) and competence (that one is capable and can use or learn the skills needed to meet challenges; see section on 'Basic psychological needs theory' for further details). Intrinsic motivation will only be sustained when feelings of competence are tied in with feelings of autonomy (Ryan & Deci, 2000), making satisfaction of both the needs prerequisites for behaviour that is intrinsically motivated. Although viewed as an innate characteristic of individuals, the maintenance and enhancement of intrinsic motivation depend on social and environmental contextual factors (Ryan & Deci, 2000). The theory posits that environmental factors can undermine or facilitate intrinsic motivation by being controlling or informational. Rewards, for example, can be perceived as controlling if the athlete feels obligated to have to perform well, undermining their feelings of autonomy. Rewards can also be perceived as informational, as an athlete might consider them to be a sign of a job well done, facilitating their feelings of competence. As intrinsically motivated behaviours are those that are engaged in volitionally, salient perception of external rewards as controlling (e.g., paying someone to exercise who is already intrinsically motivated to exercise) gives rise to an external perceived locus of causality and results in diminished feelings of autonomy and, consequently, intrinsic motivation. Thus, something that was previously 'play' and engaged in for intrinsic pleasures becomes 'work', and is engaged in to obtain the reward. Contrastingly, salient perceptions of external events as being informational, such as acknowledgement of effort or recognition of hard work that has led to good performance (e.g., an unexpected reward for an athlete for their efforts that have led to black belt level in karate), enhance both autonomy and competence, thus endorsing an internal perceived locus of causality and aiding intrinsic motivation. Put differently, a key premise of CET is that what significant others (e.g., exercise instructors, coaches, and PE teachers) say and do, including when, how, and why they instruct, praise, give feedback, or administer rewards, is critical in determining whether intrinsic motivation is undermined or supported, via the impact on feelings of autonomy and competence.

CET-Based Research in Sport and Exercise

The sport landscape is well entrenched with features (e.g., competition, trophies, scholarships) that lend themselves to examination under the CET framework. Ryan and Deci (2017) have summarized findings on competition and intrinsic motivation in sport where they highlight the controlling and informational elements of direct competition. When athletes participate in competitions and win, they are provided with rich feedback about their competence. This is of informational functional significance and can result in increased intrinsic motivation among athletes. However, competition can also have a controlling functional significance in that it often entails pressures to win, either externally (e.g., coach or parental expectations) or internally (e.g., ego involvement). Such pressures counteract the positive effects of feedback associated with winning, resulting in diminished intrinsic motivation. Losses in competitions can diminish perceived competence and negatively impact intrinsic motivation even further. However, this can be remedied to some extent with the provision of positive feedback in terms of aspects of the activity that were done well, what has improved, and what has been learnt.

Ryan (1977, 1980) investigated the influence of receiving scholarships on intercollegiate sports participants' desires to engage in their sport after college. Athletes receiving scholarships reported less sport-related enjoyment and more extrinsic reasons for sport participation compared with athletes who did not receive scholarships (Ryan, 1977). Subsequently, in the 1980 study, Ryan found that athletes receiving scholarships in uncommon settings (e.g., male athletes in sports where scholarships were not as common, or female athletes in receipt of scholarships, which at that time was rare) may perceive them as informational and indicative of competence. Contrarily, in settings where scholarships were common, they are likely to be perceived as controlling and result in decreased intrinsic motivation. Medic, Mack, Wilson, and Starkes (2007) compared US collegiate scholarship athletes with similar Canadian non-scholarship athletes and found athletes on scholarship to be more extrinsically motivated relative to those not on scholarship, thus providing additional support for the undermining role of scholarships and extrinsic rewards. More recently, White and Sheldon (2014) examined records of the National Basketball Association and Major League Baseball to find that emphasizing monetary rewards in the contract year led to a decrease in intrinsic motivation after the contract award. This effect was evident from objective statistics such as points scored, defensive performance, and batting averages. Contrastingly, however, Amorose and Horn (2000) studied male and female athletes from

Division I sports in the US and found that scholarship athletes were more intrinsically motivated and had higher feelings of competence and lower levels of tension compared with non-scholarship athletes. Such contradictory findings highlight that it is the psychological meaning of receiving a scholarship as interpreted by the individual that influences the nature of the motivational impact; that is, external events (e.g., scholarships) can have a specific functional significance of being controlling or informational for the recipient. This is in relation to for whom, how, when, and why they are administered, and their impact on feelings of autonomy and competence, which in turn affect the recipient's intrinsic motivation. Ryan and Deci (2017) have pointed out that conditions that make scholarships informational or controlling warrant further examination.

Another aspect of importance alongside the perceived functional significance of external events is the manner in which social agents communicate (also known as interpersonal styles). Researchers have demonstrated through various cross-sectional studies that positive feedback/praise is associated with intrinsic motivation (e.g., Mouratidis, Vansteenkiste, Lens, & Sideridis, 2008), and negative and change-oriented feedback, when delivered in a manner that is autonomy-supportive, is related to feelings of higher levels of autonomy, competence, and intrinsic motivation (Carpentier & Mageau, 2013; Mouratidis, Lens, & Vansteenkiste, 2010). The role of interpersonal styles is examined in detail later on in this review in the 'Basic psychological needs theory' section.

The role of feedback and rewards has also been examined in the exercise domain. Whitehead and Corbin (1991) experimentally demonstrated positive feedback to enhance intrinsic motivation, and negative feedback to decrease intrinsic motivation in a physical task in youth fitness testing. Incentives have been found to be successful in the short term (i.e., less than six months; Mitchell et al., 2013). However, the effects do not sustain in the long term, as behaviours engaged in at baseline are often reinstated on the withdrawal of the incentive. This suggests that incentives may be useful in the initiation of behaviour, but not in its maintenance (Burns et al., 2012). Moller and colleagues (Moller, Buscemi, McFadden, Hedeker, & Spring, 2014; Moller, McFadden, Hedeker, & Spring, 2012) assessed data from a healthy-lifestyle intervention in which participants were offered performance-contingent financial payments for making changes to four health risk behaviours (low fruit and vegetable intake, high saturated fat intake, low physical activity, and high sedentary screen time) over a three-week period. The researchers looked at participants' self-reported value of these incentives, termed 'financial motivation'. The authors found support for the undermining effect of financial incentives in successful maintenance of the new behaviours, where financial motivation was found to be negatively associated with weight loss maintenance once the incentives were withdrawn. Subsequently, Moller et al. (2014) found participants who were low in financial motivation grew to enjoy fruits, vegetable, and physical activity more, and food high in saturated fats less, whereas for individuals with high financial motivation, the potential for such adaptive changes was undermined, evident from fewer changes in enjoyment.

Organismic Integration Theory

Organismic integration theory (OIT) is the second mini-theory proposed by SDT, which focuses on extrinsic motivation and its multifaceted structure (see Figure 15). Extrinsic motivation is defined as engaging in an activity in order to attain an outcome separable from the activity itself (Ryan & Deci, 2000). For example, athletes might be participating in youth sport in order to gain parental approval or to comply with parental pressure. With reference to exercise, individuals might be active because they want to improve their health or appearance, and not

Motivation	Amotivation	Extrinsic motivation				Intrinsic motivation
		Self-determination theory's taxonomy of motivation				
Regulatory style		External regulation	Introjection	Identification	Integration	Intrinsic motivation
Attributes	Lack of perceived competence or Lack of value	External rewards or punishments Compliance Reactance	Ego involvement Focus on approval from self and others	Internalization → Personal importance Conscious valuing of an activity Self-endorsement of goals	Congruence Synthesis and consistency of identifications	Interest Enjoyment Inherent satisfaction
Location on the autonomy continuum		Controlled motivation		Autonomous motivation		

Figure 15 SDT's motivation continuum, adapted with permission from the Centre for Self-Determination Theory (2018)

because they find exercise to be fun. As an example, someone might find running for 30 minutes on a treadmill 5 days a week to be a chore, but values the outcomes of this activity, and so engages in it willingly.

Some extrinsic motives are more adaptive than others (e.g., exercising to improve health vs. exercising owing to pressure from others). Hence, OIT distinguishes between different types of extrinsic motivation, which vary in their degree of self-determination. The least autonomous (most controlled) type of extrinsic motivation is external regulation. When people's behaviours are externally regulated, motives are controlled by external contingencies, such as to attain rewards or to avoid punishment (Deci & Ryan, 2000). An individual who only attends the gym because they are told to by their partner or doctor is externally regulated. Introjected regulation lies next on the continuum. Although more self-determined than external regulation, this is still a controlled regulation as it reflects motives driven by self-administered contingencies, such as contingent self-esteem and guilt or shame avoidance (Deci & Ryan, 2000). An individual who goes to the gym because they would experience guilt on missing a session is acting out of introjected regulation. Next on the continuum is identified regulation, a relatively autonomous form of motivation. This motive reflects behaviours resulting from consciously valuing the activity and its benefits (Deci & Ryan, 2000). Individuals demonstrating identified regulation identify with the activity as being instrumental to their goals (Ryan & Deci, 2000). Individuals who choose to exercise because they value the health benefits (improved posture, stamina, etc.) of exercise demonstrate identified regulation. Finally, the most self-determined form of extrinsic motivation is integrated regulation. This regulation is evident when a behaviour is well internalized and has been assimilated into one's core values and structure of the self (Deci & Ryan, 2000). The distinction between integrated regulation and intrinsic motivation is that integrated regulation is still extrinsically motivated, as the behaviour is performed in order to achieve outcomes that are personally important as opposed to out of enjoyment or interest.

For example, an individual who chooses to exercise and lives a fit and healthy lifestyle might perceive that these behaviours are part of their identity and aligned with their true self and values, and yet they might not necessarily enjoy exercising. All types of extrinsic motivation, no matter how controlled, involve some amount of intentional or motivated behaviour.

Amotivation is a state in which an individual is entirely lacking in intention to engage in an activity and may be the result of feeling incompetent at an activity, not expecting the behaviour to lead to an anticipated outcome, or finding no value in it (Ryan & Deci, 2000). Amotivation and extrinsic and intrinsic motivation represent the full spectrum of motivation according to SDT.

OIT posits that individuals have the propensity to assimilate external motives into their self-concept through the process of internalization (Reeve, 2012). Internalization is described as the process of taking values or beliefs from external sources and converting them into one's own (Ryan, Connell, & Deci, 1985). Motivation for a behaviour might initially be externally regulated, but, through the process of internalization, the behaviour might be performed later on for reasons of identified or integrated regulation.

Researchers examining OIT have used varied approaches to represent motivation when exploring motivation-related determinants and outcomes. Some researchers have explored the predictions of each of the motivational regulations independently; others have calculated individuals' relative autonomy index by calculating a weighted average of all motivational regulations to produce a single score representing the degree to which motivation is self-determined (see Grolnick & Ryan, 1987). Others (e.g., Brunet, Gunnell, Gaudreau, & Sabiston, 2015) have demonstrated that the continuum can be modelled by the two key factors of autonomous (an arithmetic average of intrinsic motivation and integrated and identified regulations) and controlled motivation (an arithmetic average of introjected and external regulations). A newer approach, which is person- as opposed to variable-based, has been latent profile analysis (Wang, Morin, Ryan, & Liu, 2016), which aims to identify more or less uniform subgroups of individuals, known as latent profiles, with differing configurations on indicators, such as types of motivation (Morin, Meyer, Creusier, & Biétry, 2016; Ryan & Deci, 2017).

OIT-Based Research in Sport and Exercise

Numerous researchers have examined the associations between motivational regulations and a variety of outcomes in sport (see Ntoumanis, 2012, for a sport-specific review). Overall, more autonomous regulation styles (relative to controlled motivation styles) have been found to be associated with more adaptive outcomes such as enhanced learning, self-esteem, and health (Mageau & Vallerand, 2003), sportspersonship (Ntoumanis & Standage, 2009), objective sport performance (Gillet, Berjot, & Gobance, 2009; Gillet, Vallerand, Amoura, & Baldes, 2010), adherence to injury prevention behaviours (Chan & Hagger, 2012), and well-being (Gagné, Ryan, & Bargmann, 2003). Contrastingly, controlled regulation styles have been associated with maladaptive outcomes, including burn-out (Jowett, Hill, Hall, & Curran, 2013), drop-out (Garcia-Calvo, Cervello, Jimenez, Iglesias, & Moreno-Murcia, 2010), and anti-social behaviours (Hodge & Lonsdale, 2011). Researchers have also recently started to examine the motivational regulations underpinning the behaviours of individuals in positions of authority. McLean and colleagues (2012) developed the Coach Motivation Questionnaire to assess six forms of coach motivation as outlined by OIT. Rocchi, Pelletier, and Couture (2013) demonstrated coach self-determined motivation to be associated with autonomy-supportive coaching behaviours.

Exercise-related outcomes have also received considerable attention in terms of research on motivational regulations (for exercise-specific reviews, see Standage & Ryan, 2012; Teixeira, Carraça, Markland, Silva, & Ryan, 2012). Overall, autonomous types of regulation have been shown to be positively associated with positive outcomes such as self-reported and objective exercise behaviours (Gillison, Standage, & Skevington, 2006; Standage, Sebire, & Loney, 2008), increased self-efficacy to overcome exercise-related barriers (Thogersen-Ntoumani & Ntoumanis, 2006), and exercise adherence (Russell & Bray, 2010). Controlled types of extrinsic motivation, in contrast, have been found to be associated with maladaptive outcomes, such as social physique anxiety (Thogersen-Ntoumani & Ntoumanis, 2006).

Causality Orientations Theory

Whereas CET and OIT describe different types of motive that regulate specific behaviours and how they are manifested, causality orientations theory (COT), SDT's third mini-theory, focuses on the generalized tendencies of individuals that predispose them to manifest a specific type of motivation in a particular situation or context. Causality orientations are typical ways of perceiving and organizing information of motivational significance (Ryan & Deci, 2017). The theory differentiates among autonomy orientation, control orientation, and impersonal orientation (Deci & Ryan, 1985a).

When autonomy-oriented, individuals have a tendency to act in line with their own interests, seek out interesting and challenging activities, and take responsibility for their own behaviour. High autonomy orientation is more likely to result in a high level of intrinsic motivation or identified and integrated styles of extrinsic motivation in specific situations. When control-oriented, individuals neglect their own interests and instead act in compliance with rewards, deadlines, and approvals from others. High controlled orientation is associated with being motivated by external and introjected regulations. Lastly, when impersonally oriented, individuals demonstrate an absence of initiative and intentionality, perceive behaviour as beyond their personal control, and experience anxiety and feelings of incompetence. Impersonal orientation often cultivates amotivation, and individuals high on impersonal orientation are characterized by passivity and no initiative and experience their own emotions as well as external influences to be overpowering (Ryan & Deci, 2017).

Ryan and Deci (2017) highlighted that, similar to the case with motivational regulations, individuals do not have just one of these types of causality orientation; instead, they possess each orientation to varying extents. Further, autonomous, controlled, and impersonal orientations are likely to develop based on the degree to which an individual is repeatedly exposed to autonomy-supportive, controlling, or amotivating contexts.

Outside the sport and exercise domain, autonomous orientation has been found to be associated with adaptive outcomes such as self-esteem (Deci & Ryan, 1985a), high autonomous motivation (Williams, Grow, Freedman, Ryan, & Deci, 1996), and task persistence (Koestner, Bernieri, & Zuckerman, 1992). Controlled and impersonal orientations, in contrast, have been associated with maladaptive outcomes such as self-derogation, hostility and guilt (Deci & Ryan, 1985a), and higher defensive functioning (Knee, Neighbors, & Vietor, 2001). Hagger and Chatzisarantis (2011) have shown autonomous orientation to moderate the undermining effect of tangible rewards on situational intrinsic motivation. Specifically, autonomous orientation shielded undergraduate psychology student participants against the undermining effect of rewards, evident from no significant decreases in their intrinsic motivation. Controlled orientation afforded no such buffer, resulting in significant reductions in participants' intrinsic motivation after the rewards were introduced.

COT-Based Research in Sport and Exercise

COT-based research in the sport and exercise domain has been scarce. The strengths of these orientations have been assessed in the exercise domain using Rose, Markland, and Parfitt's (2001) Exercise Orientations Scale. Autonomous orientations have been linked with more autonomous types of motivation, whereas controlled orientations have been found to be associated with more controlled regulations and self-consciousness among adult exercisers (Rose et al., 2001; Rose, Parfitt, & Williams, 2005).

Basic Psychological Needs Theory

Our descriptions of CET and OIT included brief references to the satisfaction of basic psychological needs as a key determinant of intrinsic motivation and internalization. Basic psychological needs theory (BPNT; Ryan & Deci, 2000) is SDT's fourth mini-theory and centres on the critical role of the fulfilment of three basic psychological needs for optimal functioning and well-being, and the role of the context in supporting and thwarting these.

Basic Psychological Needs

The first of the three basic psychological needs is the need for autonomy, or the need to self-regulate one's actions and experiences such that one's behaviours are in congruence with one's authentic interests and values (Ryan & Deci, 2017). The second need is that of competence, or the need to feel effective and capable of task mastery (Ryan & Deci, 2017). The third need is that of relatedness, or the need to be accepted by others as well as care for others and feel cared for by them (Deci & Ryan, 2014). The three needs are theorized to be fundamental to all humans and prevalent across cultures. Satisfaction of these needs is essential for individuals to thrive and flourish. Importantly, the needs are considered to be complementary and interrelated, and optimal growth and functioning require the satisfaction of most, if not all, of the needs (Ryan & Deci, 2017).

Need frustration, on the other hand, will likely result in ill-being and other negative consequences. Bartholomew, Ntoumanis, Ryan, and Thøgersen-Ntoumani (2011) were the first to empirically test need frustration. The authors originally termed 'need frustration' 'need thwarting' in order to be in line with the writings of Ryan and Deci (2000); however, the term 'need frustration' has been more prevalent in recent SDT theorizing (e.g., Ryan & Deci, 2017). Earlier research indirectly tested the harmful effects of need frustration (e.g., negative affect; Gaudreau, Amiot, & Vallerand, 2009) by examining negative associations between need satisfaction and maladaptive outcomes. However, the authors argued that low scores on measures of need satisfaction are not accurate representations of the intensity of need frustration experienced when such needs are actively undermined by the social environment. Bartholomew and colleagues thus developed and validated a new measure of need frustration in sport, the Psychological Need Thwarting Scale (Bartholomew, Ntoumanis, Ryan, & Thøgersen-Ntoumani, 2011) and further demonstrated that need frustration was a better predictor of maladaptive outcomes, such as disordered eating, relative to psychological need satisfaction (Bartholomew, Ntoumanis, Ryan, Bosch, & Thøgersen-Ntoumani, 2011; Costa, Ntoumanis, & Bartholomew, 2015).

BPNT-Based Research in Sport and Exercise

Through a plethora of studies, researchers have demonstrated positive associations between psychological need satisfaction in sport and various indices of well-being including subjective vitality (Adie, Duda, & Ntoumanis, 2008; Mack et al., 2011), positive affect (Mack et al., 2011; Quested et al., 2013), self-esteem (Amorose, Anderson-Butcher, & Cooper, 2009; Coatsworth & Conroy, 2009), positive developmental experiences (Taylor & Bruner, 2012), and engagement (Curran, Hill, Ntoumanis, Hall, & Jowett, 2016). Need frustration, on the other hand, has been shown to be positively correlated with disordered eating, exhaustion, and depression (Bartholomew, Ntoumanis, Ryan, Bosch, et al., 2011), as well as burnout (Belaguer et al., 2012).

Need satisfaction has been shown to have positive associations with self-determined motivational regulations (Edmunds, Ntoumanis, & Duda, 2006; Russell & Bray, 2009), physical self-worth and psychological well-being (Sebire, Standage, & Vansteenkiste, 2009), subjective vitality, and self-reported exercise behaviour (Vlachopoulos, Ntoumanis, & Smith, 2010) in the exercise domain. Need frustration, on the other hand has been shown to be associated with ill-being outcomes such as negative affect (Gunnell, Crocker, Wilson, Mack, & Zumbo, 2013).

The Role of the Social Context

According to the organismic dialectical view of SDT, the context surrounding an individual serves as an antecedent to their experiences of need satisfaction and frustration (see Figure 16). Researchers have thus examined how social agents, such as coaches and exercise instructors, can actively support or thwart the basic psychological needs of their athletes and

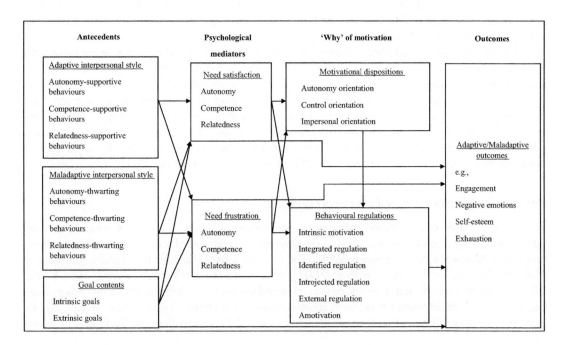

Figure 16 The SDT motivation sequence

exercisers. The initial distinction between autonomy-supportive versus controlling behaviours has been broadened to consider adaptive and maladaptive interpersonal styles such as need support and need thwarting (Hancox, Quested, Thøgersen-Ntoumani, & Ntoumanis, 2015; Ntoumanis, Quested, Reeve, & Cheon, 2018), which are exhibited through distinct sets of behaviours. For example, coaches can adopt adaptive interpersonal styles that support their athletes' needs for autonomy, competence, and relatedness. Autonomy-supportive coaching behaviours include offering athletes meaningful choices, demonstrating efforts to understand their perspective, providing rationales for requests or instructions, encouraging input in decision-making processes, and creating opportunities for self-initiated behaviour (Mageau & Vallerand, 2003; Ntoumanis & Mallett, 2014). Competence-supportive behaviours have been identified as those that guide athletes in feeling capable of dealing with challenging situations and/or experiencing meaningful success (Matosic, Ntoumanis, & Quested, 2016), by helping them to set realistic goals, and by providing constructive and thorough feedback (Ntoumanis & Mallett, 2014). Finally, relatedness-supportive behaviours include being empathetic, showing interest, and providing athletes with care and support (Pulido, Sánchez-Oliva, Leo, Sánchez-Cano, & García-Calvo, 2017; Rocchi, Pelletier, & Desmarais, 2017).

Coaches can also communicate using maladaptive styles that are thwarting of athletes' basic psychological needs. Coaches can be autonomy-thwarting (also referred to as 'controlling') by applying excessive personal control and coercion to have tasks performed in certain ways, by using intimidating language, using rewards to control athletes' behaviours, and by being conditionally accepting (Bartholomew, Ntoumanis, & Thøgersen-Ntoumani, 2010). More recently, researchers have also started exploring coach behaviours that thwart athletes' needs for competence and relatedness (e.g., Pulido et al., 2017; Rocchi et al., 2017). Competence-thwarting behaviours are demonstrated through showing doubt about athletes' capacities to improve in their sport, emphasizing their mistakes, and delivering critical and negative feedback in public (Pulido et al., 2017). Finally, relatedness-thwarting behaviours encompass showing hostility towards athletes (Smith et al., 2015) and excluding them from activities (Rocchi et al., 2017).

Whereas the two broad styles of need support and need thwarting have been previously viewed as bipolar (e.g., Deci, Schwartz, Sheinman, & Ryan, 1981), there is evidence to suggest that, although they are correlated, they are also distinct. Thus, any individual in a position of authority can adopt either style depending on circumstances, such as their perception of the quality of motivation of the people they interact with (e.g., Bartholomew et al., 2010). Aspects of the two styles can also be utilized concurrently. SDT-based interventions, hence, usually aim to promote a more need-supportive interpersonal style and, at the same time, lessen need-thwarting styles (Ntoumanis, Quested, et al., 2018).

Research on Interpersonal Styles in Sport and Exercise

Researchers have demonstrated positive associations between a coach's need-supportive interpersonal style and athletes' basic psychological need satisfaction and self-determined motivation (Amorose & Anderson-Butcher, 2007), well-being (Adie et al., 2008), persistence (Pelletier, Fortier, Vallerand, & Brière, 2001), and performance (Cheon, Reeve, Lee, & Lee, 2015). Perceptions of coaches adopting a need-thwarting interpersonal style have been associated with athlete need frustration (Bartholomew, Ntoumanis, Ryan, Bosch, et al., 2011), non-self-determined forms of motivation (Pelletier et al., 2001), and burn-out (DeFreese & Smith, 2014).

Need-supportive interpersonal styles have been found to be associated with identified regulation (Markland & Tobin, 2004), increased physical activity (Fortier et al., 2011), increased exercise class attendance, and increased positive affect (Edmunds, Ntoumanis, & Duda, 2008) in the exercise context. In a meta-analysis of both correlational and experimental studies grounded in SDT in the context of health, Ng and colleagues (2012) demonstrated the need-supportive interpersonal styles of leaders to be positively associated with recipients' reports of basic psychological need satisfaction and mental and physical health. Maladaptive interpersonal styles are not uncommon in exercise settings (Hancox, Ntoumanis, Thøgersen-Ntoumani, & Quested, 2015). Training instructors not only using more adaptive or need-supportive strategies, but also minimizing their use of maladaptive or need-thwarting instructional approaches have recently been shown to be effective in group exercise classes (Ntoumanis, Thøgersen-Ntoumani, Quested, & Hancox, 2017).

A question that follows from this line of research is what leads a coach or an exercise instructor to be more need-supportive or -thwarting in their interpersonal style? Matosic and colleagues (2016) synthesized SDT research from various life domains examining the antecedents of interpersonal communication style. Contextual factors (e.g., professional development opportunities and administrative pressure), perceptions of subordinates' behaviours and motivation (e.g., emotional and behavioural engagement and self-determined motivation), and personal factors (e.g., causality orientations and need satisfaction) were identified as potential antecedents of coach and instructor interpersonal styles.

Similar to the disentangling of need dissatisfaction from need frustration, such a distinction at the contextual level could also be assessed. Distinguishing coach/instructor interpersonal styles that are actively thwarting from those that are rather unsupportive of athletes' basic psychological needs presents a viable avenue for future research.

Goal Contents Theory

Goal contents theory (GCT) is the fifth mini-theory in the SDT framework. It explains how the content of a goal leads to distinct outcomes relevant to well-being and ill-being. There is a lot of focus on individuals' motives, or the reasons *why* they engage in certain behaviours in the SDT framework. GCT, however, examines the contents of individuals' goals, or the *what* of individuals' pursuits.

In their early work on goal content, Kasser and Ryan (1993, 1996) differentiated between the content of people's general life goals (also called 'aspirations') as being intrinsic and extrinsic. Intrinsic goals are those that are most closely associated with the pursuit of things of fundamental value (e.g., personal growth, close relationships, and physical health) and promote an inward orientation conducive to need satisfaction (Deci & Ryan, 2000). Extrinsic goals, in contrast, involve instrumental outcomes (such as money, image, and popularity) and foster an outward orientation, reducing need satisfaction and potentially hindering optimal development (Deci & Ryan, 2000). Evidence suggests that prioritizing intrinsic goals, compared with extrinsic goals, is associated with greater well-being (Vansteenkiste, Niemiec, & Soenens, 2010).

The association between intrinsic and extrinsic goal contents and psychological and physical outcomes is mediated by the experience of need satisfaction and frustration, respectively. When individuals' goal contents are predictive of their experience of basic psychological need satisfaction, they are likely to experience positive consequences from goal pursuit and attainment. However, if their goal content leads to low basic psychological need satisfaction, they are likely to experience negative consequences from the pursuit and attainment of such goals (Ryan, Sheldon, Kasser, & Deci, 1996).

Intrinsic and extrinsic goal contents should not be confused with autonomous and controlled motivation. Either type of goal may be influenced by autonomous or controlled reasons (Sheldon, Ryan, Deci, & Kasser, 2004). For example, an individual who exercises in order to better their health on being forced to do so by their doctor symbolizes a controlled regulation of an intrinsic goal. Likewise, an individual who exercises to look attractive as they value being thin exhibits an autonomous regulation of an extrinsic goal.

GCT-Based Research in Sport and Exercise

Goal contents have been investigated by numerous researchers in the exercise domain. Vansteenkiste and colleagues (2004) manipulated weight loss and attractiveness (extrinsic goals) and physical fitness and health (intrinsic goals) in their goal promotion study with high school students learning Tae-Bo. Results indicated that those assigned to the intrinsic goal group learned the activity of Tae-Bo better and were more persistent in engaging in it compared with those assigned to the extrinsic goal group. Ingledew and Markland (2008) examined the effectiveness of weight- and appearance-related goals versus health and fitness goals for engaging in exercise in a study with office workers and found fitness goals to be associated with increased identified regulation and increased participation. Furthermore, pursuing intrinsic rather than extrinsic exercise goals was found to be positively associated with psychological need satisfaction, physical self-worth, psychological well-being, and self-reported exercise behaviour, and negatively associated with exercise-based anxiety (Sebire et al., 2009). Sebire, Standage, and Vansteenkiste (2011) found evidence for a motivation sequence in a subsequent study, where intrinsic goal content was positively associated with autonomous motivation, which in turn positively predicted bouts of exercise behaviour. Gunnell and colleagues (2014) additionally demonstrated support for an SDT sequence whereby changes in relative intrinsic goals predicted changes in self-determined motivation, which then predicted changes in psychological need satisfaction, which in turn predicted psychological well-being and physical activity.

Research on goal contents and related outcomes in the sport domain has been hindered by the lack of a valid and reliable measure that is domain-specific. Given the abundance of extrinsic goals in sports such as prize money, medals, status, and fame, the development and validation of a sport-specific measure present another avenue for future research. Such a measure would help advance investigations based on the principles of GCT and explore topics such as the antecedents and consequences of pursuing intrinsic versus extrinsic goals in terms of the satisfaction and frustration of athletes' needs and outcomes related to their well-being and ill-being.

Relationships Motivation Theory

Relationships motivation theory (RMT; Deci & Ryan, 2014; Ryan & Deci, 2017) is the sixth and newest mini-theory to be added to the SDT framework. It examines the need for relatedness and its interactions with the other needs to determine the characteristics and consequences of close relationships. Although the satisfaction of the need for relatedness drives individuals to want to partake in close interpersonal relationships, it does not guarantee that these will be of high quality (Deci & Ryan, 2014). The highest-quality relationships will be encountered when, alongside satisfaction of the need for relatedness, the needs for autonomy and competence are also met. Within relationships, being in receipt of need support and providing the same is associated with well-being. In the case that one need is adversarial to the other, the theory posits that relationships will deteriorate in quality and result in diminished well-being of those involved.

RMT-Based Research

The tenets of RMT have been examined in a growing body of research outside the sport and exercise domain. Need satisfaction within relationships has been shown to be associated with higher relationship quality, greater psychological well-being, and an increased sense of attachment (LaGuardia, Ryan, Couchman, & Deci, 2000; Patrick, Knee, Canevello, & Lonsbary, 2007). Being autonomously engaged in relationships has been shown to be associated with experiencing greater relationship satisfaction and well-being in new as well as in close relationships (Gaine & LaGuardia, 2009; Niemiec & Deci, 2014; Weinstein, Hodgins, & Ryan, 2010). Examinations of mutuality of autonomy and autonomy support (e.g., Deci, LaGuardia, Moller, Scheiner, & Ryan, 2006) indicate that, when one person in a relationship feels autonomously motivated and provides autonomy support, their partner is likely to experience the same, and an enhanced degree of such mutuality is likely to result in improved relationship satisfaction (Ryan & Deci, 2017).

RMT has significant potential for application in sport and exercise settings, as these contexts offer numerous opportunities for people to build close interpersonal relationships. Relationships such as those between coaches and athletes, exercise instructors and clients, between peers, and between athletes and parents offer interesting research opportunities to widen the scope of RMT. Standage and colleagues (2019, 2014) have emphasized that these relationships entail varying degrees of complexity, mutuality, and authority. Such research could profit from the examination of interactions with multiple social agents (Standage & Emm, 2014) – for example, an athlete having to train with several coaches who adopt contrasting coaching styles.

Conclusion

Now that we have presented the meta- and mini-theories and sport- and exercise-relevant research grounded in SDT, let us reconsider the two scenarios we started out with. It becomes evident in the case of the basketball coach that the advice he received from the senior coaches involves exercising autonomy-thwarting – that is, controlling – behaviours with the athletes. We know from research on coach interpersonal styles that communicating with athletes in this manner fosters need frustration, which in turn is associated with maladaptive outcomes, and, thus, might not be the best way to motivate his players. However, his observation that his players are more engaged and happier when he includes them in decision-making seems promising. Theory and research on coach interpersonal styles tells us that this autonomy-supportive way of communicating leads to autonomy need satisfaction, more self-determined types of motivation, and greater well-being. It, thus, becomes apparent that his athletes would be better motivated if he continued to be supportive of their need for autonomy, but also their needs for competence and relatedness. Some tips for him would be to keep including his athletes in decision-making processes, try to understand their point of view before making suggestions, give constructive feedback, focus on skill improvement, show the athletes that he cares and that he likes them, and interact in a way that demonstrates warmth towards them.

In the case of the woman who is struggling to stay active on a regular basis, we now know that her reason for exercising is extrinsic. OIT explains that attending the gym so as to not feel guilty is reflective of introjected regulation. We also know that guilt might be motivating in getting an individual to exercise in the short run, but unfortunately does not have sustainable effects (Pelletier et al., 2001). The good news for her is that introjected regulation is Step 1 in the process of internalization, through which even unenjoyable and tedious behaviours such as exercise can be maintained, if she eventually internalizes to the extent of identified, integrated, and intrinsic motivation. Some advice for her, then, would be to seek out activities that she enjoys doing, so that she does not think of them as tedious. At the gym, she could benefit from working with an exercise instructor who is supportive of her needs and with whom she can set realistic intrinsic goals, which, once achieved, would build her levels of competence. She could also benefit from having an exercise buddy who she enjoys being around.

We draw this overview to a close by highlighting some critical considerations. Although SDT offers explanations for why individuals engage in behaviours and what the contents of these pursuits are, it does so in a somewhat restricted fashion. A holistic view of the underpinnings of human motivation is restricted by the fact that SDT does not consider other important predictors of behaviour, such as individuals' implicit attitudes, as well as the physical environment surrounding them (Ntoumanis, Thogersen-Ntoumani, Quested, & Chatzisarantis, 2018). Recently, however, researchers have endeavoured to bridge this gap between the tenets of SDT and the said automatic predictors (e.g., Hagger & Chatzisarantis, 2014), as well as the surrounding natural environment (Gay, Saunders, & Dowda, 2011).

References

Adie, J., Duda, J. L., & Ntoumanis, N. (2008). Autonomy support, basic need satisfaction and the optimal functioning of adult male and female sport participants: A test of basic needs theory. *Motivation and Emotion, 32,* 189–199.

Ajzen, I. (1991). The theory of planned behavior. *Organizational Behavior and Human Decision Processes, 50,* 179–211.

Amorose, A. J., & Anderson-Butcher, D. (2007). Autonomy-supportive coaching and self-determined motivation in high school and college athletes: A test of self-determination theory. *Psychology of Sport and Exercise, 8,* 654–670.

Amorose, A. J., & Horn, T. S. (2000). Intrinsic motivation: Relationships with collegiate athletes' gender, scholarship status, and perceptions of their coaches' behaviour. *Journal of Sport and Exercise Psychology, 22,* 63–84.

Amorose, J. A., Anderson-Butcher, D., & Cooper, J. (2009). Predicting changes in athletes' well-being from changes in need satisfaction over the course of a competitive season. *Research Quarterly for Exercise and Sport, 80,* 386–392.

Bartholomew, K. J., Ntoumanis, N., Ryan, R. M., Bosch, J. A., & Thøgersen-Ntoumani, C. (2011). Self-determination theory and diminished functioning: The role of interpersonal control and psychological need thwarting. *Personality and Social Psychology Bulletin, 37,* 1459–1473.

Bartholomew, K. J., Ntoumanis, N., Ryan, R. M., & Thøgersen-Ntoumani, C. (2011). Psychological need thwarting in the sport context: Assessing the darker side of athletic experience. *Journal of Sport and Exercise Psychology, 33,* 75–102.

Bartholomew, K. J., Ntoumanis, N., & Thøgersen-Ntoumani, C. (2010). The controlling interpersonal style in a coaching context: Development and initial validation of a psychometric scale. *Journal of Sport and Exercise Psychology, 32,* 193–216.

Belaguer, I., González, L., Fabra, P., Castillo, I., Mercé, J., & Duda, J. L. (2012). Coaches' interpersonal style, basic psychological needs and the well- and ill-being of young soccer players: A longitudinal analysis. *Journal of Sports Science, 30,* 1619–1629.

Biddle, S. J. H. (1999). Motivation and perceptions of control: Tracing its development and plotting its future in exercise and sport psychology. *Journal of Sport & Exercise Psychology, 21,* 1–23.

Brunet, J., Gunnell, K. E., Gaudreau, P., & Sabiston, C. M. (2015). An integrative analytical framework for understanding the effects of autonomous and controlled motivation. *Personality and Individual Differences, 84,* 2–15.

Burns, R. J., Donovan, A. S., Ackermann, R. T., Finch, E. A., Rothman, A. J., & Jeffery, R. W. (2012). A theoretically grounded systematic review of material incentives for weightloss: Implications for interventions. *Annals of Behavioral Medicine, 44,* 375–388.

Carpentier, J., & Mageau, G. (2013). When change oriented feedback enhances motivation, well-being and performance: A look at autonomy supportive feedback in sport. *Psychology of Sport and Exercise, 14,* 423–435.

Caspersen, C. J., Powell, E. C., & Christenson, G. M. (1985). Physical activity, exercise, and physical fitness: Definitions and distinctions for health-related research. *Public Health Reports, 100,* 126–131.

Center for Self-Determination Theory. (2018). SDT's motivation continuum. Retrieved from https://twitter.com/centerforSDT/status/989140986730373121

Chan, D. K. C., & Hagger, M. S. (2012). Self-determined forms of motivation predict sport injury prevention and rehabilitation intentions. *Journal of Science and Medicine in Sport, 15,* 398–406.

Cheon, S. H., Reeve, J., Lee, J., & Lee, Y. (2015). Giving and receiving autonomy support in a high-stakes sport context: A field-based experiment during the 2012 London Paralympic Games. *Psychology of Sport and Exercise, 19,* 1–11.

Coatsworth, J. D., & Conroy, D. E. (2009). The effects of autonomy-supportive coaching, need satisfaction, and self-perceptions on initiative and identity in youth swimmers. *Developmental Psychology, 45,* 320–328.

Costa, S., Ntoumanis, N., & Bartholomew, K. (2015). Predicting the brighter and darker sides of interpersonal relationships: Does psychological need thwarting matter?. *Motivation and Emotion, 39,* 11–24.

Curran, T., Hill, A. P., Ntoumanis, N., Hall, H. K., & Jowett, G. E. (2016). A three-wave longitudinal test of self-determination theory's mediation model of engagement and disaffection in youth sport. *Journal of Sport and Exercise Psychology, 38,* 15–29.

Deci, E. L. (1971). Effects of externally mediated rewards on intrinsic motivation. *Journal of Personality and Social Psychology, 18,* 105–115.

Deci, E. L. (1975). *Intrinsic motivation.* New York: Plenum.

Deci, E. L., Koestner, R., & Ryan, R. M. (1999). A meta-analytic review of experiments examining the effects of extrinsic rewards on intrinsic motivation. *Psychological Bulletin, 125,* 627–668.

Deci, E. L., LaGuardia, J. G., Moller, A. C., Scheiner, M. J., & Ryan, R. M. (2006). On the benefits of giving as well as receiving autonomy support: Mutuality in close friendships. *Personality and Social Psychology Bulletin, 32,* 313–327.

Deci, E. L., & Ryan, R. M. (1985a). The general causality orientations scale: Self-determination in personality. *Journal of Research in Personality, 19,* 109–134.

Deci, E. L., & Ryan, R. M. (1985b). *Intrinsic motivation and self-determination in human behavior.* New York: Plenum.

Deci, E. L., & Ryan, R. M. (2000). The 'what' and 'why' of goal pursuits: Human needs and the self-determination of behavior. *Psychological Inquiry, 11,* 227–268.

Deci, E. L., & Ryan, R. M. (2014). Autonomy and need satisfaction in close relationships: Relationships motivation theory. In N. Weinstein (Ed.), *Human motivation and interpersonal relationships* (pp. 53–73). New York: Springer.

Deci, E. L., Schwartz, A. J., Sheinman, L., & Ryan, R. M. (1981). An instrument to assess adults' orientations toward control versus autonomy with children: Reflections on intrinsic motivation and perceived competence. *Journal of Educational Psychology, 73,* 642–650.

DeFreese, J., & Smith, A. (2014). Athlete social support, negative social interactions, and psychological health across a competitive sport season. *Journal of Sport and Exercise Psychology, 36,* 619–630.

Edmunds, J., Ntoumanis, N., & Duda, J. (2006). A test of self-determination theory in exercise. *Journal of Applied Social Psychology, 36,* 2240–2265.

Edmunds, J., Ntoumanis, N., & Duda, J. (2008). Testing a self-determination theory based teaching style intervention in the exercise domain. *European Journal of Social Psychology, 38,* 375–388.

Fortier, M. S., Wiseman, E., Sweet, S. N., O'Sullivan, T. L., Blanchard, C. M., Sigal, R. J., & Hogg, W. (2011). A moderated mediation of motivation on physical activity in the context of the PAC randomized control trial. *Psychology of Sport and Exercise, 12,* 71–78.

Gagné, M., Ryan, R. M., & Bargmann, K. (2003). Autonomy support and need satisfaction in the motivation and well-being of gymnasts. *Journal of Applied Sport Psychology, 15,* 372–390.

Gaine, G. S., & LaGuardia, J. G. (2009). The unique contributions of motivations to maintain a relationships and motivations toward relational activities to relationship well-being. *Motivation and Emotion, 33,* 184–202.

Garcia-Calvo, T., Cervello, E., Jimenez, R., Iglesias, D., & Moreno-Murcia, J. A. (2010). Using self-determination theory to explain sport persistence and dropout in adolescent athletes. *Spanish Journal of Psychology, 13,* 677–684.

Gaudreau, P., Amiot, C. E., & Vallerand, R. J. (2009). Trajectories of affective states in adolescent hockey players: Turning point and motivational antecedents. *Developmental Psychology, 45,* 307–319.

Gay, J., Saunders, R., & Dowda, M. (2011). The relationship of physical activity and the built environment within the context of self-determination theory. *Annals of Behavioral Medicine, 42,* 188–196.

Gillet, N., Berjot, S., & Gobance, L. (2009). A motivational model of performance in the sport domain. *European Journal of Sport Science, 9,* 151–158.

Gillet, N., Vallerand, R. J., Amoura, S., & Baldes, B. (2010). Influence of coaches' autonomy support on athletes' motivation and sport performance: A test of the hierarchical model of intrinsic and extrinsic motivation. *Psychology of Sport and Exercise, 11,* 155–161.

Gillison, F. B., Standage, M., & Skevington, S. M. (2006). Relationships among adolescents' weight perceptions, exercise goals, exercise motivation, quality of life and leisure-time exercise behaviour: A self-determination theory approach. *Health Education Research, 21,* 836–847.

Grolnick, W. S., & Ryan, R. M. (1987). Autonomy in children's learning: An experimental and individual difference investigation. *Journal of Personality and Social Psychology, 52,* 890–898.

Gunnell, K. E., Crocker, P. R. E., Mack, D. E., Wilson, P. M., & Zumbo, B. D. (2014). Goal contents, motivation, psychological need satisfaction, well-being and physical activity over 6-months: A test of self-determination theory. *Psychology of Sport and Exercise, 15,* 19–29.

Gunnell, K. E., Crocker, P. R. E., Wilson, P. M., Mack, D. E., & Zumbo, B. D. (2013). Psychological need satisfaction and thwarting: A test of basic psychological needs theory in physical activity contexts. *Psychology of Sport and Exercise, 14,* 599–607.

Hagger, M. S., & Chatzisarantis, N. L. (2011). Causality orientations moderate the undermining effect of rewards on intrinsic motivation. *Journal of Experimental Social Psychology, 47,* 485–489.

Hagger, M. S., & Chatzisarantis, N. L. (2014). An integrated behaviour change model for physical activity. *Exercise and Sport Sciences Reviews, 2,* 62–69.

Hancox, J., Ntoumanis, N., Thøgersen-Ntoumani, C., & Quested, E. (2015). Self-Determination Theory. In J. Middelkamp (Ed.), *Essentials of motivation and behaviour change* (pp. 68–85). Brussels: EuropeActive.

Hancox, J., Quested, E., Thøgersen-Ntoumani, C., & Ntoumanis, N. (2015). An intervention to train group exercise class instructors to adopt a motivationally adaptive communication style: A quasi-experimental study protocol. *Health Psychology and Behavioral Medicine, 3,* 190–203.

Hodge, K., & Lonsdale, C. (2011). Prosocial and antisocial behavior in sport: The role of coaching style, autonomous vs. controlled motivation, and moral disengagement. *Journal of Sport and Exercise Psychology, 33,* 527–547.

Ingledew, D. K., & Markland, D. (2008). The role of motives in exercise participation. *Psychology and Health, 23,* 807–828.

Jowett, G. E., Hill, A. P., Hall, H. K., & Curran, T. (2013). Perfectionism and junior athlete burnout: The mediating role of autonomous and controlled motivation. *Sport, Exercise, and Performance Psychology, 2,* 48–61.

Kasser, T., & Ryan, R. M. (1993). A dark side of the American dream: Correlates of financial success as a central life aspiration. *Journal of Personality and Social Psychology, 65,* 410–422.

Kasser, T., & Ryan, R. M. (1996). Further examining the American dream: Differential correlates of intrinsic and extrinsic goals. *Personality and Social Psychology Bulletin, 22,* 280–287.

Knee, C. R., Neighbors, C., & Vietor, N. (2001). Self-determination theory as a framework for understanding road rage. *Journal of Applied Social Psychology, 31,* 889–904.

Koestner, R., Bernieri, F., & Zuckerman, M. (1992). Self-regulation and consistency between attitudes, traits, and behaviors. *Personality and Social Psychology Bulletin, 18,* 52–59.

LaGuardia, J. G., Ryan, R. M., Couchman, C. E., & Deci, E. L. (2000). Within-person variation in security of attachment: A self-determination theory perspective on attachment, need fulfillment, and well-being. *Journal of Personality and Social Psychology, 79,* 367–384.

Lee, W., & Reeve, J. (2013). Self-determined, but not non-self-determined, motivation predicts activations in the anterior insular cortex an fMRI study of personal agency. *Social Cognitive and Affective Neuroscience, 8,* 538–545.

Lindahl, J., Stenling, A., Lindwall, M., & Colliander, C. (2015). Trends and knowledge base in sport and exercise psychology research: A bibliometric review study. *International Review of Sport Exercise Psychology, 8,* 71–94.

Mack, D. E., Wilson, P. M., Oster, K. G., Kowalski, K. C., Crocker, P. R. E., & Sylvester, B. D. (2011). Well-being in volleyball players: Examining the contributions of independent and balanced psychological need satisfaction. *Psychology of Sport and Exercise, 12,* 533–539.

Mageau, G. A., & Vallerand, R. J. (2003). The coach–athlete relationship: A motivational model. *Journal of Sports Sciences, 21,* 883–904.

Markland, D., & Tobin, V. (2004). A modification of the behavioral regulation in exercise questionnaire to include an assessment of amotivation. *Journal of Sport and Exercise Psychology, 26,* 191–196.

Matosic, D., Ntoumanis, N., & Quested, E. (2016). Antecedents of need supportive and controlling interpersonal styles from a self-determination theory perspective: A review and implications for sport psychology research. In M. Raab, P. Wylleman, R. Seiler, A. M. Elbe, & A. Hatzigeorgiadis (Eds.), *New perspectives on sport and exercise psychology* (pp. 145–180). London: Elsevier.

McLean, K., Mallett, C., & Newcombe, P. (2012). Assessing coach motivation: The development of the Coach Motivation Questionnaire (CMQ). *Journal of Sport and Exercise Psychology, 34,* 184–207.

Medic, N., Mack, D. E., Wilson, P. M., & Starkes, J. L. (2007). The effects of athletic scholarship of motivation in sport. *Journal of Sport Behavior, 30,* 292–306.

Mitchell, M. S., Goodman, J. M., Alter, D. A., John, L. K., Oh, P. I., Pakosh, M. T., & Faulkner, G. E. (2013). Financial incentives for exercise adherence in adults: Systematic review and meta-analysis. *American Journal of Preventive Medicine, 45,* 658–667.

Moller, A. C., Buscemi, J., McFadden, H. G., Hedeker, D., & Spring, B. (2014). Financial motivation undermines potential enjoyment in an intensive diet and activity intervention. *Journal of Behavioral Medicine, 37,* 819–827.

Moller, A. C., McFadden, H. G., Hedeker, D., & Spring, B. (2012). Financial motivation undermines maintenance in an intensive diet and activity intervention. *Journal of Obesity.* doi:10.1155/2012/740519

Morin, A. J. S., Meyer, J. P., Creusier, J., & Biétry, F. (2016). Multiple-group analysis of similarity in latent profile solutions. *Organizational Research Methods, 19,* 231–254.

Mouratidis, M., Lens, W., & Vansteenkiste, M. (2010). How you provide corrective feedback makes a difference: The motivating role of communicating in an autonomy-supporting way. *Journal of Sport and Exercise Psychology, 32,* 619–637.

Mouratidis, M., Vansteenkiste, M., Lens, W., & Sideridis, G. (2008). The motivating role of positive feedback in sport and physical education: Evidence for a motivational model. *Journal of Sport and Exercise Psychology, 30,* 240–268.

Murayama, K., Matsumoto, M., Izuma, K., & Matsumoto, K. (2010). Neural basis of the undermining effect of extrinsic reward on intrinsic motivation. *Proceedings of the National Academy of Sciences of the United States of America, 107,* 20911–22091.

Ng, J. Y. Y., Ntoumanis, N., Thøgersen-Ntoumani, C., Deci, E. L., Ryan, R. M., Duda, J. L., & Williams, G. C. (2012). Self-determination theory applied to health contexts: A meta-analysis. *Perspectives on Psychological Science, 7,* 325–340.

Nicholls, J. (1989). *The competitive ethos and democratic education.* Cambridge, MA: Harvard University Press.

Niemiec, C. P., & Deci, E. L. (2014). *Contextual supports for autonomy and the development of high-quality relationships following mutual self-disclosure.* Unpublished manuscript. Rochester, NY: University of Rochester.

Ntoumanis, N. (2012). A self-determination theory perspective on motivation in sport and physical education: Current trends and possible future research directions. In G. C. Roberts & D. C. Treasure (Eds.), *Advances in motivation in sport and exercise* (Vol. 3, pp. 91–128). Champaign, IL: Human Kinetics.

Ntoumanis, N., & Mallett, C. (2014). Motivation in sport: A self-determination theory perspective. In A. Papaioannou & D. Hackfort (Eds.), *Routledge companion to sport and exercise psychology: Global perspectives and fundamental concepts* (pp. 67–82). Hove, UK: Taylor & Francis.

Ntoumanis, N., Quested, E., Reeve, J., & Cheon, S. H. (2018). Need supportive communication: Implications for motivation in sport, exercise, and physical activity. In B. Jackson, J. A. Dimmock, & J. Compton (Eds.), *Persuasion and communication in sport, exercise, and physical activity* (pp. 155–169). Abingdon: Routledge.

Ntoumanis, N., & Standage, M. (2009). Prosocial and antisocial behaviour in sport: A self-determination theory perspective. *Journal of Applied Sport Psychology, 21,* 365–380.

Ntoumanis, N., Thøgersen-Ntoumani, C., Quested, E., & Chatzisarantis, N. (2018). Theoretical approaches to physical activity promotion. In O. Braddick (Ed.), *Oxford research encyclopedia of psychology.* Oxford, UK: Oxford University Press. doi:10.1093/acrefore/9780190236557.013.212

Ntoumanis, N., Thøgersen-Ntoumani, C., Quested, E., & Hancox, J. C. (2017). The effects of training group exercise class instructors to adopt a motivationally adaptive communication style. *Scandinavian Journal of Medicine & Science in Sports, 27,* 1026–1034.

Patrick, H., Knee, C. R., Canevello, A., & Lonsbary, C. (2007). The role of need fulfilment in relationship functioning and well-being: A self-determination theory perspective. *Journal of Personality and Social Psychology, 92,* 434–457.

Pelletier, L. G., Fortier, M. S., Vallerand, R. J., & Brière, N. M. (2001). Associations among perceived autonomy support, forms of self-regulation, and persistence: A prospective study. *Motivation and Emotion, 25,* 279–306.

Pulido, J. J., Sánchez-Oliva, D., Leo, F. M., Sánchez-Cano, J., & García-Calvo, T. (2017). Development and validation of coaches' interpersonal style questionnaire. *Measurement in Physical Education and Exercise Science, 59,* 107–120.

Quested, E., Ntoumanis, N., Viladrich, C., Haug, E., Ommundsen, Y., Van Hoye, A., ... Duda, J. L. (2013). Intentions to drop-out of youth soccer: A test of the basic needs theory among European youth from five countries. *International Journal of Sport and Exercise Psychology, 11,* 395–407.

Reeve, J. (2012). A self-determination theory perspective on student engagement. In S. L. Christenson, A. L. Reschly, & C. Wylie (Eds.), *Handbook of research on student engagement* (pp. 149–172). New York: Springer.

Rocchi, M., Pelletier, L., & Desmarais, P. (2017). The validity of the Interpersonal Behaviors Questionnaire (IBQ) in sport. *Measurement in Physical Education and Exercise Science, 21,* 15–25.

Rocchi, M. A., Pelletier, L. G., & Couture, A. L. (2013). Determinants of coach motivation and autonomy supportive behaviours. *Psychology of Sport and Exercise, 14,* 852–859.

Rose, E. A., Markland, D., & Parfitt, G. (2001). The development and initial validation of the Exercise Causality Orientations Scale. *Journal of Sports Sciences, 19,* 445–462.

Rose, E. A., Parfitt, G., & Williams, S. (2005). Exercise causality orientations, behavioural regulation for exercise and stage of change for exercise: Exploring their relationships. *Psychology of Sport and Exercise, 6,* 399–414.

Russell, K. L., & Bray, S. R. (2009). Self-determined motivation predicts independent, home-based exercise following cardiac rehabilitation. *Rehabilitation Psychology, 54,* 150–156.

Russell, K. L., & Bray, S. R. (2010). Promoting self-determined motivation for exercise in cardiac rehabilitation: The role of autonomy support. *Rehabilitation Psychology, 55,* 74–80.

Ryan, E. D. (1977). Attribution, intrinsic motivation, and athletics. In L. I. Gedvilas & M. E. Kneer (Eds.), *National College Physical Education Association for Men/National Association for Physical Education of College Women. National Conference* (pp. 346–353). Chicago, IL: Office of Publications Services.

Ryan, E. D. (1980). Attribution, intrinsic motivation, and athletics: A replication and extension. In C. H. Nadeau, W. R. Halliwell, K. M. Newell, & G. C. Roberts (Eds.), *Psychology of motor behavior and sport* (pp. 19–26). Champaign, IL: Human Kinetics.

Ryan, R. M., Connell, J. P., & Deci, E. L. (1985). A motivational analysis of self-determination and self-regulation in education. In C. Ames & R. E. Ames (Eds.), *Research on motivation in education: The classroom milieu* (pp. 13–51). New York: Academic Press.

Ryan, R. M., & Deci, E. L. (2000). Self-determination theory and the facilitation of intrinsic motivation, social development, and well-being. *American Psychologist, 55,* 68–78.

Ryan, R. M., & Deci, E. L. (2017). *Self-determination theory. Basic psychological needs in motivation, development and wellness.* New York: Guilford Press.

Ryan, R. M., Sheldon, K. M., Kasser, T., & Deci, E. L. (1996). All goals are not created equal: An organismic perspective on the nature of goals and their regulation. In P. M. Gollwitzer & J. A. Bargh (Eds.), *The psychology of action: Linking cognition and motivation to behavior* (pp. 7–26). New York: Guilford Press.

Sebire, S. J., Standage, M., & Vansteenkiste, M. (2009). Exploring exercise goal content: Intrinsic vs. extrinsic exercise goals, exercise outcomes, and psychological need satisfaction. *Journal of Sport and Exercise Psychology, 31,* 189–210.

Sebire, S. J., Standage, M., & Vansteenkiste, M. (2011). Predicting objectively assessed physical activity from the content and regulation of exercise goals: Evidence for a mediational model. *Journal of Sport and Exercise Psychology, 33,* 175–197.

Sheldon, K. M., Ryan, R. M., Deci, E. L., & Kasser, T. (2004). The independent effects of goal contents and motives on well-being: It's both what you pursue and why you pursue it. *Personality and Social Psychology Bulletin, 30,* 475–486.

Skinner, B. F. (1971). *Beyond freedom and dignity.* New York: Knopf.

Smith, N., Tessier, D., Tzioumakis, Y., Quested, E., Appleton, P., Sarrazin, P., … Duda, J. L. (2015). Development and validation of the multidimensional motivational climate observation system. *Journal of Sport and Exercise Psychology, 37,* 4–22.

Standage, M., Curran, T., & Rouse, P. (2019). Self-determination based theories of sport, exercise, and physical activity motivation. In T. S. Horn & A. L. Smith (Eds.), *Advances in sport and exercise psychology* (4th ed., pp. 289–311). Champaign, IL: Human Kinetics.

Standage, M., & Emm, L. (2014). Relationships within physical activity settings. In N. Weinstein (Ed.), *Human motivation and interpersonal relationships: Theory, research, and applications* (pp. 239–262). Dordrecht: Springer.

Standage, M., & Ryan, R. M. (2012). Self-determination theory and exercise motivation: Facilitating self-regulatory processes to support and maintain health and well-being. In G. C. Roberts & D. C. Treasure (Eds.), *Advances in motivation in sport and exercise* (pp. 233–270). Champaign, IL: Human Kinetics.

Standage, M., Sebire, S. J., & Loney, T. (2008). Does exercise motivation predict engagement in objectively assessed bouts of moderate-intensity exercise behavior? A self-determination theory perspective. *Journal of Sport and Exercise Psychology, 30,* 337–352.

Taylor, I. M., & Bruner, M. W. (2012). The social environment and developmental experiences in elite youth soccer. *Psychology of Sport and Exercise, 13,* 390–396.

Teixeira, P. J., Carraça, E. V., Markland, D. A., Silva, M. N., & Ryan, R. M. (2012). Exercise, physical activity, and self-determination theory: A systematic review. *Journal of Behavioral Nutrition and Physical Activity, 9,* 78.

Thogersen-Ntoumani, C., & Ntoumanis, N. (2006). The role of self-determined motivation in the understanding of exercise-related behaviours, cognitions and physical self-evaluations. *Journal of Sports Sciences, 24,* 393–404.

Vallerand, R. J., & Reid, G. (1984). On the causal effects of perceived competence on intrinsic motivation: A test of cognitive evaluation theory. *Journal of Sport Psychology, 6,* 94–102.

Vansteenkiste, M., Niemiec, C. P., & Soenens, B. (2010). The development of the five mini-theories of self-determination theory: An historical overview, emerging trends, and future directions. In T. C. Urdan & S. A. Karabenick (Eds.), *Advances in motivation and achievement: The decade ahead* (pp. 105–165). London: Emerald.

Vansteenkiste, M., Simons, J., Lens, W., Sheldon, K. M., & Deci, E. L. (2004). Motivating learning, performance, and persistence: The synergistic effects of intrinsic goal contents and autonomy-supportive contexts. *Journal of Personality and Social Psychology, 87,* 246–260.

Vlachopoulos, S. P., Ntoumanis, N., & Smith, A. L. (2010). The basic psychological needs in exercise scale: Translation and evidence for cross-cultural validity. *International Journal of Sport and Exercise Psychology, 8,* 394–412.

Wang, C. K., Morin, A. J. S., Ryan, R. M., & Liu, W. C. (2016). Students' motivational profiles in the physical education context. *Journal of Sport and Exercise Psychology, 38,* 612–630.

Weinstein, N., Hodgins, H. S., & Ryan, R. M. (2010). Autonomy and control in dyads: Effects on interaction quality and joint creative performance. *Personality and Social Psychology Bulletin, 36,* 1603–1617.

Weiss, M., & Gill, D. (2005). What goes around comes around: Re-emerging themes in sport and exercise psychology. *Research Quarterly for Exercise and Sport, 76,* 71–87.

White, M., & Sheldon, K. (2014). The contract year syndrome in the NBA and MLB: A classic undermining pattern. *Motivation and Emotion, 38,* 196–205.

Whitehead, J. R., & Corbin, C. B. (1991). Effects of fitness test type, teacher, and gender exercise intrinsic motivation and physical self-worth. *Journal of School Health, 61,* 11–16.

Williams, G. C., Grow, V. M., Freedman, Z. R., Ryan, R. M., & Deci, E. L. (1996). Motivational predictors of weight loss and weight-loss maintenance. *Journal of Personality and Social Psychology, 70,* 115–126.

42
SELF-EFFICACY

Timothy J. H. Budden, Ben Jackson, and James A. Dimmock

Introduction

Grounded in social cognitive theory (SCT; Bandura, 1986), self-efficacy refers to one's 'beliefs in one's capability to organize and execute the courses of action required to produce given attainments' (Bandura, 1997, p. 3). The nature, causes, and consequences of self-efficacy perceptions have been widely studied within sport and exercise psychology; as such, the literature is replete with comprehensive reviews of both the construct and the broader theoretical framework within which it exists (Feltz, Short, & Sullivan, 2008). Accordingly, in this chapter, rather than providing another exhaustive overview of sport- and exercise-based self-efficacy research, we seek to (a) broadly consider the prevalence and significance of 'agentic' perceptions—such as self-efficacy—within motivation and behaviour change theories, (b) offer a relatively brief theoretical overview of the construct, and (c) highlight an important, broad issue that requires further research attention in this area.

Theoretical Overview

Defined broadly, perceptions of competence or agency (e.g., self-efficacy, perceived competence, perceived behavioural control) appear as important drivers of goal-directed action in several motivational and behavioural frameworks. In self-determination theory (Ryan & Deci, 2000), for example, it is outlined that high-quality (i.e., autonomous) motivation is supported, in part, by an individual's perceptions of competence (i.e., a sense of capability with regards to a focal activity). Individuals who consider themselves to be highly capable in a given athletic endeavour, therefore, are theorized to be more likely to be autonomously motivated for that endeavour. Within the theory of planned behaviour (Ajzen, 1991), meanwhile, perceived behavioural control is posited as a predictor of both intentions and behavioural engagement. Specifically, individuals who believe they possess a high degree of control over a behaviour are said to be more likely to intend to (and actually) engage in that behaviour. Similarly, in expectancy-value theoretical models (see Wigfield & Eccles, 2000), expectancies of success and ability beliefs predict achievement choices and, in turn, performance, effort, and persistence. Finally, within the health promotion literature, self-efficacy beliefs are proposed to contribute to behaviour change, planning, and/or maintenance in the transtheoretical model (Prochaska & Velicer, 1997), the health belief model (Rosenstock, Strecher, & Becker, 1988), the health action process approach framework (Schwarzer & Luszczynska, 2008), and the extended parallel process model (Witte, 1992). As is evident from the array of frameworks that incorporate self-efficacy (or related) perceptions as drivers of motivation and/or behaviour, the salience of individuals' competence beliefs is well recognized. It could be argued, however, that the most detailed account of these agentic perceptions is provided within Bandura's (1977, 1997) self-efficacy theory. In the following section, we provide a brief overview of the theoretical foundations of—and empirical support associated with—self-efficacy theory.

Self-Efficacy

In his seminal 1977 article, titled 'Self-efficacy: Toward a unifying theory of behavioral change', Bandura posited that perceptions of competence (i.e., self-efficacy) may be created, strengthened, and weakened through various cognitive and psychological processes (Bandura, 1977, 1997). In contrast with behaviourist principles, Bandura (1977) contended that it was in part through these situation-specific forms of self-confidence (or 'self-efficacy' beliefs) that humans have the capacity for 'proactive agency' in determining their own feelings, thoughts, and actions. In outlining this agentic principle, therefore, Bandura indicated that individuals possess the capacity to plan, monitor, regulate, and adapt their personal functioning.

Bandura also proposed that self-efficacy beliefs may vary along the dimensions of level, strength, and generality (see Bandura, 1997). Self-efficacy level refers to the varying degrees of task complexity with which one may be faced, ranging from the least demanding through to the most challenging pursuits or activities. The level at which an athlete is asked to rate his/her capabilities is substantially different, for example, when considering competing in a pre-season 'friendly' match compared with a play-off eliminator or grand final. Similarly, respondents would be rating their self-efficacy beliefs at different levels in an exercise context when asked to consider their ability to exercise for 5 minutes, 30 minutes, or 60 minutes per day. The strength of one's self-efficacy belief refers to the degree of certainty an individual has regarding his/her capacity to perform the required tasks/skills at a given level. It is postulated that efficacy strength can range from very low (or no) confidence through to absolute certainty in one's abilities. To illustrate, while holding constant the 'level' of one's self-efficacy appraisal, some respondents may be highly confident (a strong efficacy belief) in their ability to ride a bicycle a given distance five times per week (the efficacy 'level'), whereas others may have substantial self-doubts (a weak efficacy belief) regarding their ability to perform that same activity. Bandura argued that weak self-efficacy expectations can easily be disconfirmed by negative feedback through performance failures, whereas strong self-efficacy beliefs are characterized by resilience and resistance to negative feedback (Bandura, 1977, 1997). Finally, our self-efficacy beliefs may differ in the degree to which they generalize from one context to another. Tasks that are perceived to share similar behavioural (or other) requirements are likely to encourage efficacy generality, whereas tasks that do not—or are not perceived to—share such similarities may not encourage the transfer of efficacy beliefs from one context to another. As an example, one might expect a relatively high degree of efficacy transfer (or generality) between (similar) short-distance (e.g., 100 m, 200 m, 400 m) sprinting events, but one's confidence in one's sprinting ability is highly unlikely to transfer to shot put, discus, or javelin-throwing efficacy. Although a conceptually and practically important component of the construct, efficacy generality is perhaps the least widely assessed dimension in standard self-efficacy assessments (for exceptions, see Bong, 1997; Jackson & Dimmock, 2012).

Bandura (1997) positioned self-efficacy within a broader SCT (Bandura, 1986), the fundamental premise of which is that human functioning can be understood through the reciprocal relations that exist between salient personal, behavioural, and environmental factors. For instance, per an example provided by Feltz et al. (2008), environmental factors (e.g., feedback from an athlete's coach) may influence 'personal' factors (e.g., the athlete's self-efficacy), which, in turn, influence one or more 'behavioural' factors (e.g., the athlete's effort). In a reciprocal sense, the athlete's effort might subsequently elicit positive (or negative) feedback from the coach, serving to further modify his or her self-efficacy. Bandura also made an important conceptual distinction in SCT between self-efficacy beliefs and outcome expectations, which he defined as 'a person's estimate that a given behaviour will lead to certain outcomes' (Bandura, 1977, p. 193). Whereas self-efficacy beliefs reflect judgements of one's confidence in one's abilities, outcome expectations involve 'a judgement of the likely consequence such performances will produce' (Bandura, 1997, p. 21); typically, these outcome expectations are theorized to take the form of social (e.g., praise, reward), physical (e.g., weight), and/or self-evaluative (e.g., psychological state) considerations. Importantly, Bandura (1977, 1989) contended that individuals' outcome expectations may rely, at least in part, upon their efficacy judgements. For example, if a budding running enthusiast believes that she is not capable of completing an arduous training and dietary regime ahead of a marathon race (an efficacy belief), she is unlikely to picture pleasant outcomes associated with that course of action (an outcome expectation). At this point, having provided a brief account of the structure of self-efficacy, we turn our attention to overviewing the sources and consequences of self-efficacy perceptions.

Self-Efficacy: Sources and Consequences

Bandura (1977, 1997) presented four broad antecedents of self-efficacy beliefs: mastery experiences, vicarious modelling (or influences), verbal persuasion, and physiological and affective states. According to Bandura, the strongest antecedents of self-efficacy beliefs are mastery experiences in a given task, activity, or domain—that is, having experienced some personal-, normative-, or task-referenced 'success' in the endeavour in question. In addition, though, self-efficacy beliefs may also be bolstered by (a) observing similar models successfully performing, or coping with, task-related demands (vicarious modelling/influence); (b) having important others convey positive competence-based feedback about our capabilities (verbal persuasion); and (c) being in an optimal physiological (e.g., heartbeat, breathing rate) or affective (e.g., happy, calm) state. It is also worth noting that imaginal experiences (e.g., mental rehearsal, imagery techniques) have separately been described as an additional source of self-efficacy beliefs (Maddux, 1995).

An appreciation of the sources of self-efficacy beliefs provides valuable insight into the ways through which researchers and practitioners might intervene to bolster athletes' or exercisers' beliefs in their capabilities. The motive for developing such strategies, however, is grounded in the array of positive *outcomes* with which self-efficacy beliefs have often been shown to be associated. Sport and exercise psychologists have long investigated the differences between successful and unsuccessful athletes/exercisers, with a particular research emphasis devoted to understanding how self-efficacious athletes and exercisers differ from their counterparts who experience greater self-doubt. A central tenet within the self-efficacy theory is that strong self-efficacy beliefs play a significant role in driving adaptive motivational and behavioural outcomes (see Bandura, 1997). At a between-person level (i.e., across individuals), those with strong self-efficacy perceptions have been shown to report increased physical activity participation in a variety of healthy (e.g., Bauman et al., 2012; Chen, Sun, & Dai, 2017; Gillison et al., 2017; Wang, Fan, Zhao, Yang, & Fu, 2016) and specific populations, such as those living with multiple sclerosis (Casey et al., 2018) and those living with psychosis and diabetes (Gorczynski, Vancampfort, & Patel, 2018). Self-efficacy has also been shown to be associated with better performance in sport (Baretta, Greco, & Steca, 2017; Moritz, Feltz, Fahrbach, & Mack, 2000), increased motivation toward learning a behaviour (Colquitt, LePine, & Noe, 2000; Salas & Cannon-Bowers, 2001), greater effort (George, 1994; Hutchinson, Sherman, Martinovic, & Tenenbaum, 2008), increased use of sport-related mental skills (e.g., attentional control, self-talk, relaxation, imagery, goal-setting, and emotional control; Ortega & Wang, 2018), and more positive affective states in sport and exercise (George, 1994; Rudolph & Butki, 1998). Self-efficacious individuals have also been shown to demonstrate greater optimism (Kavussanu & McAuley, 1995), anticipate less negative outcomes (Cartoni, Minganti, & Zelli, 2005), set more challenging goals (Boyce & Bingham, 1997; Kane, Marks, Zaccaro, & Blair, 1996), react less negatively to adversity or failure (Brown, Malouff, & Schutte, 2005), overcome barriers to physical activity (Smith, Williams, O'donnell, & McKechnie, 2017), and display resilience in the face of negative feedback (Nease, Mudgett, & Quiñones, 1999). Finally, self-efficacy may also align with increased health-related quality of life in people with cardiovascular disease (Banik, Schwarzer, Knoll, Czekierda, & Luszczynska, 2018) and with mental and physical health in older adults (Mudrak, Stochl, Slepicka, & Elavsky, 2016).

In sum, perceptions of agency are recognized in many prominent motivational and behavioural theories, and, as Bandura prophesized in the title of his 1977 article, the construct has indeed provided a 'unifying' framework to drive research efforts in sport and exercise. As a result, well-established evidence exists regarding the development and implications associated with self-efficacy, particularly at the between-person level. The abundance of research attention directed to this construct over the last four decades, however, does not mean that self-efficacy research has become dormant today. In fact, there have been several interesting findings presented in recent years to challenge and/or advance what is known about the construct. Detailed overviews of many of these issues are provided in recent work (interested readers are encouraged to consult Bandura, 2012, 2015; Jackson, Beauchamp, & Dimmock, 2020), and it is neither necessary nor practical for us to restate those criticisms and challenges here. Instead, for the rest of this chapter, we direct our attention to highlighting one specific issue (or, more appropriately, group of related issues) that has been the subject of increasing debate in the self-efficacy literature in recent years—that is, the existence and implications of self-efficacy 'miscalibration'.

Self-Efficacy Miscalibration: Negative Effects Considered

There is strong empirical evidence to demonstrate that self-efficacy and performance are positively related at the between-person level (Feltz et al., 2008; Moritz et al., 2000; Yeo & Neal, 2006). That is not to say, however, that strong self-efficacy beliefs are universally considered adaptive (or useful) in nature. Bandura (1982), for example, acknowledged the potential pitfalls of strong self-efficacy beliefs long ago, noting that a degree of self-doubt may be valuable for stimulating effort and protecting against complacency when preparing for an event (e.g., sport competition). Bandura (1997) also highlighted a number of factors that might result in a 'disconnect' between self-efficacy beliefs and behaviour. These factors included faulty and/or deficient assessment of self-efficacy, ambiguity of task demands, and a mismatch between thought and action. Faulty (or deficient) self-efficacy assessment may arise when, for example, the timing of measurement is not optimized—a long period between self-efficacy and behaviour assessment may impair the utility of judgements about one's capabilities. Task ambiguity, meanwhile, affects the relevance of a self-efficacy judgement insofar as individuals are less accurate 'forecasters' of their capabilities in situations about which they do not have adequate knowledge (e.g., when asking someone to rate their confidence in a sporting endeavour of which they have little experience or knowledge).

According to Bandura (1997), in relation to the mismatching between thought and action, the most common disparity between self-efficacy and performance (or behaviour) occurs when self-efficacy judgements exceed performance; this process is typically the result of an exaggeration of one's abilities, which may be caused in part by insufficient knowledge of the demands of a task. Moore and Schatz (2017) refer to this notion of 'overconfidence' as instances whereby individuals report greater confidence than is justified, and identified three specific 'faces' of overconfidence. These aspects of overconfidence, according to Moore and Schatz, include overestimation (i.e., an exaggerated belief that one is better than one is), overplacement (i.e., an exaggerated belief that one is better than others), and over-precision (i.e., being too sure that one knows the truth). Moore and Schatz cautioned that the origins and potential adaptive and maladaptive outcomes of each of these types of overconfidence are disparate, and that treating them as homogeneous might lead to erroneous conclusions. Overconfidence, suggested Moore and Schatz, might be beneficial in certain instances; it could provide reassurance, attract favourable evaluations from others, and help individuals overcome aversion to risk. However, each of these various types of overconfidence might also engender a sense of complacency and, as a result, lead to poor outcomes (through insufficient preparation or motivation to improve, for example).

This theorizing lends broad support to a notion that has received increased attention in the self-efficacy literature in recent years—specifically, that there may be instances whereby, at a within-person level, self-efficacy and performance are inversely related to one another. In demonstrating these negative within-person effects, Vancouver and colleagues have now presented a compelling body of experimental (Vancouver, More, & Yoder, 2008; Vancouver, Thompson, Tischner, & Putka, 2002; Vancouver, Thompson, & Williams, 2001) and field-based (Vancouver & Kendall, 2006) evidence. Situated within control theory (Powers, 1973, 1991), Vancouver and colleagues have demonstrated that individuals who report strong self-efficacy beliefs after a first trial of (or series of early trials in) a task may subsequently perform worse than their peers who report weaker self-efficacy in the initial task. Control theory postulates that personal 'resources'—for example, effort and motivation—are catalysed as the discrepancy increases between one's desired state and one's current state. Accordingly, when individuals become 'overconfident', and thus overestimate their progress toward their goal, the discrepancy between the desired and current state is erroneously narrowed. This inaccurate perception leads to a reduction in resource allocation (e.g., reduced effort) toward attaining the desired goal and results in a somewhat paradoxical effect—that is, that self-efficacy may align positively with performance at the between-person level, but that the reverse may be true, in some cases at least, at the within-person level. Perceptions of strong self-efficacy may, therefore, drive a process of miscalibration, which Powers (1973, 1991) theorized may account for the negative within-person effects on performance (see also Yeo & Neal, 2006).

It is beyond the scope of this chapter to provide a detailed account of each of the aforementioned studies by Vancouver and colleagues. Instead, we will outline the results of the most recent publications on this topic by these authors (Halper & Vancouver, 2016; Halper,

Vancouver, & Bayes, 2018; Vancouver & Purl, 2017). Informed by control theory, Vancouver and Purl (2017) used a computational model to demonstrate the multiple processes that are assumed to underlie the differential (i.e., positive, negative, null) effects of self-efficacy on performance. The authors demonstrated, consistent with both SCT and control-theory postulates, that, when individuals' current performance level was known, self-efficacy had a positive effect on performance by encouraging task persistence. However, Vancouver and Purl's modelling also demonstrated a negative effect of self-efficacy on performance under ambiguous conditions. These findings corroborated other recent conclusions from research on the effects of self-efficacy on performance (e.g., (Beattie, Fakehy, & Woodman, 2014; Beck & Schmidt, 2012)—that individuals with relatively weak self-efficacy may, over time, allocate more resources and outperform those with relatively stronger self-efficacy beliefs.

Within the sport and exercise literature, negative within-person effects have been acknowledged (and studied) for some time (Gould, Petlichkoff, Simons, & Vevera, 1987; Hardy, Woodman, & Carrington, 2004). In recent years, Woodman and colleagues (Woodman, Akehurst, Hardy, & Beattie, 2010) suggested, based on findings demonstrated across two experimental skipping tasks, that 'a little self-doubt helps'; participants who were led to believe a second task would be more difficult than the first reported lower levels of task self-confidence (relative to a control group), but subsequently performed better on the second task than the control group. Accordingly, Woodman and colleagues hypothesized that an increase in current desired state discrepancy resulted in an increase in resource allocation in the second task in the experimental condition. These effects have similarly been demonstrated in golf putting tasks (Beattie et al., 2014) and racing car simulations (Beattie, Dempsey, Roberts, Woodman, & Cooke, 2017), suggesting that self-efficacy positively affects complex, dynamic task performance, but that this relationship disappears when tasks are relatively low in complexity.

As well as task complexity and ambiguity, there is evidence that feedback (and clarity of feedback) may also moderate the self-efficacy–performance relationship, as independently demonstrated by Halper and Vancouver (2016) and Beattie, Woodman, Fakehy, and Dempsey (2016). For example, using a hand-grip task, Vancouver and Halper experimentally manipulated performance feedback. In the absence of clear feedback, self-efficacy had a negative effect on hand-grip performance. The task involved performing alongside a confederate; when participants did not know of (i.e., had no or unclear feedback regarding) the confederate's performance and had low self-efficacy, they performed better when asked to hold a 50% maximum voluntary contraction (relative to their highly efficacious peers). When clarity was provided, and performance was unambiguously reported, however, self-efficacy had a positive effect on performance.

Halper et al. (2018) recently employed a mixed, between/within-subjects design to test whether self-efficacy mediates the relationship between training and performance on two tasks (i.e., hand-grip and mathematics task). In two studies, participants were allocated to either a high information veracity (i.e., participants were aware of capability/performance changes) or low information veracity (i.e., participants' capability/performance changes were kept hidden) condition. Participants in each study completed up to 9 (Study 1, hand-grip task) or 10 (Study 2, mathematics task) training sessions, each session separated by at least a day. The authors hypothesized that the positive effect of training should be higher in the high information veracity condition, as participants in this condition should exhibit a stronger positive effect of training on self-efficacy relative to participants in the low information veracity condition. In both studies, self-efficacy increased significantly in the high information veracity condition, whereas performance did not differ between conditions. As a result, the study suggests that self-efficacy does not mediate the effects of training on performance, contradicting a dominant notion within the literature on training (Colquitt et al., 2000; Salas & Cannon-Bowers, 2001). These results challenge the notion that a change in self-efficacy belief is required to result in changes in capability or performance. Although self-efficacy has been implicated in predicting behaviour and performance, particularly in between-person designs, the results of this study suggest that being aware (or unaware) of increases in performance may not affect actual performance increases over time.

The effects of self-efficacy on performance and behaviour are clearly complex. It is also important to note that the aforementioned findings have been criticized on numerous occasions (e.g., see Bandura, 2012, 2015; Bandura & Locke, 2003). As a result, the issue of negative within-person effects of self-efficacy has become a key part of an evolving debate in the sport and exercise (and wider) literature. First, Bandura and Locke (2003) outlined a number of 'methodological deficiencies' and conceptual considerations that suggest the early findings of negative self-efficacy effects may not contradict the principles of SCT, partly because they may not, in fact, test these principles. Bandura and Locke criticized the use of relatively trivial tasks (i.e., tasks that hold little or no real-world significance or relevance for participants) and contended that these tasks may not 'test' self-efficacy in the way that it truly operates in 'real-life' (i.e., personally meaningful) scenarios. Readers are encouraged to consult Gilson, Chow, and Feltz (2012) for empirical support.

Bandura and Locke also criticized the use of control theory, and the positioning of self-efficacy within that framework, on the basis that the 'agentic' principles of discrepancy production are not captured within control theory. Per SCT, individuals are capable of symbolically representing and imagining future states and, when they believe they are approaching a desired state, possess the capacity to revise goals; this process subsequently drives the generation of a 'new' gap between an individual's current and desired performance (i.e., discrepancy production). Further, Bandura has also acknowledged that self-efficacy may be negatively related (or, in fact, unrelated) to performance under certain, specific conditions, such as those characterized by task and feedback ambiguity, as noted above (e.g., (Bandura, 2012).

Self-Efficacy Miscalibration: The Dunning–Kruger Effect

In closing this chapter, we discuss another similar (but distinct) concept of miscalibration. The processes offered as explanations for the negative within-subjects effects discussed previously (e.g., resource allocation) may reflect 'miscalibration' in that they represent an inaccurate appraisal of situational demands and personal abilities required to meet those demands. Within the literature on self-confidence, specific attention has also been directed toward studying the most common types of (ability-related) miscalibration made by individuals. The conclusions drawn from this research are outlined in what has become known as the Dunning–Kruger effect (Dunning, 2011; Dunning, Johnson, Ehrlinger, & Kruger, 2003; Kruger & Dunning, 1999), and it is this effect to which we direct our attention for the remainder of the chapter.

The Dunning–Kruger effect captures the overly favourable views people tend to hold regarding their competencies in intellectual, social, and physical domains. Kruger and Dunning (1999) suggest that the 'least' competent (i.e., bottom quartile) individuals in any given domain tend to overestimate their capabilities because they lack 'metacognitive' skill (i.e., they lack the ability to distinguish accuracy from error) compared with both 'average' (second and third quartile) and 'above average' (i.e., top quartile) performers. In that sense, 'poor' (bottom quartile) performers are simply not aware of what (objectively speaking) constitutes 'good' performance. Interestingly, for those 'upper quartile' performers, who actually possess strong capabilities in the domain in question, the reverse effect may be apparent: Relatively highly competent individuals may be prone to underestimating their abilities (Kruger & Dunning, 1999). Kruger and Dunning (1999) ascribed this phenomenon to a potential 'false-consensus effect' (Ross, Greene, & House, 1977) in that highly competent individuals (erroneously) assume that their performance is reflected by their peers (i.e., that their performance is 'average' or 'normal'. This specific phenomenon presents a particularly interesting conundrum for sport coaches: How do they convince a highly competent athlete of their competence without encouraging complacency and restricting future motivation, effort, and performance?

Conclusion

The vast majority of recent findings relating to the negative within-subjects effects of self-efficacy on performance have been focused on people's task-related self-efficacy perceptions about their own capability and have often been conducted within laboratory settings (settings that, according to Bandura, may be arbitrary/artificial and may not test self-efficacy perceptions as they function in the 'real world'; Bandura, 2012, 2015). There are, however, many important efficacy perceptions beyond those that individuals hold about their own ability to complete a discrete task. These constructs include the confidence that individuals have in their own ability to regulate and manage their behaviour over time (self-regulatory efficacy; see Anderson, Winett, & Wojcik, 2007), their confidence in the ability of significant others to support their goal pursuit (proxy efficacy or other-efficacy; see Bray, Shields, Jackson, & Saville, 2014; Jackson, Bray, Beauchamp, & Howle, 2015), and their confidence in the capabilities of the interdependent groups or teams to which they belong (collective efficacy; see Myers, Feltz, & Short, 2004). It is important that researchers consider whether strong efficacy perceptions in each of these domains may display detrimental effects in certain situations. For example, it would be interesting to test whether negative outcomes may occur (in some instances) when individuals hold strong, positive beliefs about their coach's or exercise instructor's ability, or about their exercise/athletic partners' abilities (e.g., by being complacent, placing too much in the hands of the other person, or feeling anxious about 'living up to' their high standards). Support for such processes has been demonstrated by Jackson and colleagues (Jackson, Knapp, & Beauchamp, 2008), whereby some athletes in their interviews described how strong other-efficacy beliefs might engender a sense of complacency and/or anxiety in certain circumstances. In team settings, meanwhile, it would be interesting to extend existing within-person studies to consider within-team effects associated with collective efficacy beliefs. Is it possible, for instance, that strong collective efficacy beliefs (i.e., a high level of confidence in one's team's abilities) make individuals more prone to social loafing, and—should a 'collective miscalibration' process occur within a team—contribute over time to negative team performance outcomes, as has been demonstrated in individual tasks?

Self-efficacy research has a rich history in sport and exercise psychology—more than 40 years of research activity has provided us with a relatively detailed understanding of the nature, sources, and consequences of the construct. Nonetheless, despite this well-established literature, there remain pressing issues that require the continued attention of researchers and practitioners. We are yet to fully understand, for example, whether 'overconfidence' may be adaptive in certain contexts (e.g., as a means to overcome anxieties, to begin involvement in a task), and whether (and when) a degree of self-doubt may prove useful for goal pursuit and achievement. If researchers are able to more fully capture the nuances of self-efficacy, this detailed understanding would carry not only conceptual import, but also significant practical relevance for practitioners in sport and exercise (e.g., coaches, exercise instructors, physical education teachers).

References

Ajzen, I. (1991). The theory of planned behavior. *Organizational Behavior and Human Decision Processes, 50*, 179–211.

Anderson, E. S., Winett, R. A., & Wojcik, J. R. (2007). Self-regulation, self-efficacy, outcome expectations, and social support: Social cognitive theory and nutrition behavior. *Annals of Behavioral Medicine, 34*, 304–312.

Bandura, A. (1977). Self-efficacy: Toward a unifying theory of behavioral change. *Psychological Review, 84*, 191–215.

Bandura, A. (1982). Self-efficacy mechanism in human agency. *American Psychologist, 37*, 122–147.

Bandura, A. (1986). *Social foundations of thought and action*. Englewood Cliffs, NJ: Prentice Hall.

Bandura, A. (1989). Human agency in social cognitive theory. *American Psychologist, 44*(9), 1175–1184.

Bandura, A. (1997). *Self-efficacy: The exercise of control*. New York: W. H. Freeman.

Bandura, A. (2012). On the functional properties of perceived self-efficacy revisited. *Journal of Management, 38*, 9–44.

Bandura, A. (2015). On deconstructing commentaries regarding alternative theories of self-regulation. *Journal of Management, 41*, 1025–1044.

Bandura, A., & Locke, E. A. (2003). Negative self-efficacy and goal effects revisited. *Journal of Applied Psychology, 88*, 87–99.

Banik, A., Schwarzer, R., Knoll, N., Czekierda, K., & Luszczynska, A. (2018). Self-efficacy and quality of life among people with cardiovascular diseases: A meta-analysis. *Rehabilitation Psychology, 63*, 295–312.

Baretta, D., Greco, A., & Steca, P. (2017). Understanding performance in risky sport: The role of self-efficacy beliefs and sensation seeking in competitive freediving. *Personality and Individual Differences, 117*, 161–165.

Bauman, A. E., Reis, R. S., Sallis, J. F., Wells, J. C., Loos, R. J., & Martin, B. W. (2012). Correlates of physical activity: Why are some people physically active and others not? *The Lancet, 380*(9838), 258–271.

Beattie, S., Dempsey, C., Roberts, R., Woodman, T., & Cooke, A. (2017). The moderating role of narcissism on the reciprocal relationship between self-efficacy and performance. *Sport, Exercise, and Performance Psychology, 6*, 199–214.

Beattie, S., Fakehy, M., & Woodman, T. (2014). Examining the moderating effects of time on task and task complexity on the within person self-efficacy and performance relationship. *Psychology of Sport and Exercise, 15*, 605–610.

Beattie, S., Woodman, T., Fakehy, M., & Dempsey, C. (2016). The role of performance feedback on the self-efficacy–performance relationship. *Sport, Exercise, and Performance Psychology, 5*, 1–13.

Beck, J. W., & Schmidt, A. M. (2012). Taken out of context? Cross-level effects of between-person self-efficacy and difficulty on the within-person relationship of self-efficacy with resource allocation and performance. *Organizational Behavior and Human Decision Processes, 119*, 195–208.

Bong, M. (1997). Generality of academic self-efficacy judgments: Evidence of hierarchical relations. *Journal of Educational Psychology, 89*, 696–709.

Boyce, B. A., & Bingham, S. M. (1997). The effects of self-efficacy and goal setting on bowling performance. *Journal of Teaching in Physical Education, 16*, 312–323.

Bray, S. R., Shields, C. A., Jackson, B., & Saville, P. D. (2014). Proxy agency and other-efficacy in physical activity contexts. In M. R. Beauchamp & M. A. Eys (Eds.), *Group dynamics in exercise and sport psychology* (2 ed., pp. 121–139). New York: Routledge.

Brown, L. J., Malouff, J. M., & Schutte, N. S. (2005). The effectiveness of a self-efficacy intervention for helping adolescents cope with sport-competition loss. *Journal of Sport Behavior, 28*, 136–150.

Cartoni, A. C., Minganti, C., & Zelli, A. (2005). Gender, age, and professional-level differences in the psychological correlates of fear of injury in Italian gymnasts. *Journal of Sport Behavior, 28*, 3–15.

Casey, B., Uszynski, M., Hayes, S., Motl, R., Gallagher, S., & Coote, S. (2018). Do multiple sclerosis symptoms moderate the relationship between self-efficacy and physical activity in people with multiple sclerosis? *Rehabilitation Psychology, 63*, 104–110.

Chen, H., Sun, H., & Dai, J. (2017). Peer support and adolescents' physical activity: The mediating roles of self-efficacy and enjoyment. *Journal of Pediatric Psychology, 42,* 569–577.

Colquitt, J. A., LePine, J. A., & Noe, R. A. (2000). Toward an integrative theory of training motivation: A meta-analytic path analysis of 20 years of research. *Journal of Applied Psychology, 85,* 678–707.

Dunning, D. (2011). The Dunning–Kruger effect: On being ignorant of one's own ignorance. *Advances in Experimental Social Psychology, 44,* 247–296.

Dunning, D., Johnson, K., Ehrlinger, J., & Kruger, J. (2003). Why people fail to recognize their own incompetence. *Current Directions in Psychological Science, 12*(3), 83–87.

Feltz, D. L., Short, S. E., & Sullivan, P. J. (2008). *Self-efficacy in sport.* Champaign, IL: Human Kinetics.

George, T. R. (1994). Self-confidence and baseball performance: A causal examination of self-efficacy theory. *Journal of Sport and Exercise Psychology, 16,* 381–399.

Gillison, F., Standage, M., Cumming, S., Zakrzewski-Fruer, J., Rouse, P., & Katzmarzyk, P. T. (2017). Does parental support moderate the effect of children's motivation and self-efficacy on physical activity and sedentary behaviour? *Psychology of Sport and Exercise, 32,* 153–161.

Gilson, T. A., Chow, G. M., & Feltz, D. L. (2012). Self-efficacy and athletic squat performance: Positive or negative influences at the within- and between-levels of analysis. *Journal of Applied Social Psychology, 42,* 1467–1485.

Gorczynski, P., Vancampfort, D., & Patel, H. (2018). Evaluating correlations between physical activity, psychological mediators of physical activity, and negative symptoms in individuals living with psychosis and diabetes. *Psychiatric Rehabilitation Journal, 41,* 153–156.

Gould, D., Petlichkoff, L., Simons, J., & Vevera, M. (1987). Relationship between Competitive State Anxiety Inventory-2 subscale scores and pistol shooting performance. *Journal of Sport Psychology, 9,* 33–42.

Halper, L. R., & Vancouver, J. B. (2016). Self-efficacy's influence on persistence on a physical task: Moderating effect of performance feedback ambiguity. *Psychology of Sport and Exercise, 22,* 170–177.

Halper, L. R., Vancouver, J. B., & Bayes, K. A. (2018). Self-efficacy does not appear to mediate training's effect on performance based on the moderation-of-process design. *Human Performance, 31,* 216–237.

Hardy, L., Woodman, T., & Carrington, S. (2004). Is self-confidence a bias factor in higher-order catastrophe models? An exploratory analysis. *Journal of Sport and Exercise Psychology, 26,* 359–368.

Hutchinson, J. C., Sherman, T., Martinovic, N., & Tenenbaum, G. (2008). The effect of manipulated self-efficacy on perceived and sustained effort. *Journal of Applied Sport Psychology, 20,* 457–472.

Jackson, B., Beauchamp, M. R., & Dimmock, J. A. (2020). Efficacy beliefs in physical activity settings: Contemporary debate and unanswered questions. In G. Tenenbaum & R. C. Eklund (Eds.), *Handbook of sport psychology* (4th ed., pp. 57–80). Hoboken, NJ: Wiley.

Jackson, B., Bray, S. R., Beauchamp, M. R., & Howle, T. C. (2015). The tripartite efficacy framework in physical activity contexts. In S. D. Mellalieu & S. Hanton (Eds.) *Contemporary advances in sport psychology: A review* (pp. 120–147). New York: Routledge.

Jackson, B., & Dimmock, J. A. (2012). When working hard and working out go hand in hand: Generality between undergraduates' academic- and exercise-related self-regulatory efficacy beliefs. *Psychology of Sport and Exercise, 13,* 418–426.

Jackson, B., Knapp, P., & Beauchamp, M. R. (2008). Origins and consequences of tripartite efficacy beliefs within elite athlete dyads. *Journal of Sport and Exercise Psychology, 30,* 512–540.

Kane, T. D., Marks, M. A., Zaccaro, S. J., & Blair, V. (1996). Self-efficacy, personal goals, and wrestlers' self-regulation. *Journal of Sport and Exercise Psychology, 18,* 36–48.

Kavussanu, M., & McAuley, E. (1995). Exercise and optimism: Are highly active individuals more optimistic? *Journal of Sport and Exercise Psychology, 17,* 246–258.

Kruger, J., & Dunning, D. (1999). Unskilled and unaware of it: How difficulties in recognizing one's own incompetence lead to inflated self-assessments. *Journal of Personality and Social Psychology, 77,* 1121–1134.

Maddux, J. E. (1995). *Self-efficacy, adaptation, and adjustment: Theory, research, and application.* New York: Plenum Press.

Moritz, S. E., Feltz, D. L., Fahrbach, K. R., & Mack, D. E. (2000). The relation of self-efficacy measures to sport performance: A meta-analytic review. *Research Quarterly for Exercise and Sport, 71,* 280–294.

Moore, D. A., & Schatz, D. (2017). The three faces of overconfidence. *Social and Personality Psychology Compass, 11*(8), e12331.

Mudrak, J., Stochl, J., Slepicka, P., & Elavsky, S. (2016). Physical activity, self-efficacy, and quality of life in older Czech adults. *European Journal of Ageing, 13,* 5–14.

Myers, N. D., Feltz, D. L., & Short, S. E. (2004). Collective efficacy and team performance: A longitudinal study of collegiate football teams. *Group Dynamics: Theory, Research, and Practice, 8*, 126–138.

Nease, A. A., Mudgett, B. O., & Quiñones, M. A. (1999). Relationships among feedback sign, self-efficacy, and acceptance of performance feedback. *Journal of Applied Psychology, 84*, 806.

Ortega, E., & Wang, C. (2018). Pre-performance physiological state: Heart rate variability as a predictor of shooting performance. *Applied Psychophysiology and Biofeedback, 43*, 75–85.

Powers, W. T. (1973). *Behavior: The control of perception.* London: Wildwood House.

Powers, W. T. (1991). Commentary on Bandura's 'human agency'. *American Psychologist, 46*, 151–153.

Prochaska, J. O., & Velicer, W. F. (1997). The transtheoretical model of health behavior change. *American Journal of Health Promotion, 12*, 38–48.

Rosenstock, I. M., Strecher, V. J., & Becker, M. H. (1988). Social learning theory and the health belief model. *Health Education Quarterly, 15*, 175–183.

Ross, L., Greene, D., & House, P. (1977). The 'false consensus effect': An egocentric bias in social perception and attribution processes. *Journal of Experimental Social Psychology, 13*, 279–301.

Rudolph, D. L., & Butki, B. D. (1998). Self-efficacy and affective responses to short bouts of exercise. *Journal of Applied Sport Psychology, 10*, 268–280.

Ryan, R. M., & Deci, E. L. (2000). Self-determination theory and the facilitation of intrinsic motivation, social development, and well-being. *American Psychologist, 55*, 68–78.

Salas, E., & Cannon-Bowers, J. A. (2001). The science of training: A decade of progress. *Annual Review of Psychology, 52*, 471–499.

Schwarzer, R., & Luszczynska, A. (2008). How to overcome health-compromising behaviors: The health action process approach. *European Psychologist, 13*, 141–151.

Smith, G., Williams, L., O'donnell, C., & McKechnie, J. (2017). The influence of social-cognitive constructs and personality traits on physical activity in healthy adults. *International Journal of Sport and Exercise Psychology, 15*, 540–555.

Vancouver, J. B., & Kendall, L. N. (2006). When self-efficacy negatively relates to motivation and performance in a learning context. *Journal of Applied Psychology, 91*, 1146–1153.

Vancouver, J. B., More, K. M., & Yoder, R. J. (2008). Self-efficacy and resource allocation: Support for a nonmonotonic, discontinuous model. *Journal of Applied Psychology, 93*, 35–47.

Vancouver, J. B., & Purl, J. D. (2017). A computational model of self-efficacy's various effects on performance: Moving the debate forward. *Journal of Applied Psychology, 102*, 599–616.

Vancouver, J. B., Thompson, C. M., Tischner, E. C., & Putka, D. J. (2002). Two studies examining the negative effect of self-efficacy on performance. *Journal of Applied Psychology, 87*, 506–516.

Vancouver, J. B., Thompson, C. M., & Williams, A. A. (2001). The changing signs in the relationships among self-efficacy, personal goals, and performance. *Journal of Applied Psychology, 86*, 605–620.

Wang, S., Fan, J., Zhao, D., Yang, S., & Fu, Y. (2016). Predicting consumers' intention to adopt hybrid electric vehicles: Using an extended version of the theory of planned behavior model. *Transportation, 43*, 123–143.

Wigfield, A., & Eccles, J. S. (2000). Expectancy–value theory of achievement motivation. *Contemporary Educational Psychology, 25*, 68–81.

Witte, K. (1992). Putting the fear back into fear appeals: The extended parallel process model. *Communications Monographs, 59*, 329–349.

Woodman, T., Akehurst, S., Hardy, L., & Beattie, S. (2010). Self-confidence and performance: A little self-doubt helps. *Psychology of Sport and Exercise, 11*, 467–470.

Yeo, G. B., & Neal, A. (2006). An examination of the dynamic relationship between self-efficacy and performance across levels of analysis and levels of specificity. *Journal of Applied Psychology, 91*, 1088–1101.

43
SELF-IDENTITY
Discursive and Narrative Conceptions and Applications

Kerry R. McGannon and Brett Smith

Introduction

Within sport psychology, self-identity, or who we are, is an important concept used to make sense of sport participation and experiences (Fox, 1997; McGannon & Spence, 2010; Rees, Haslam, Coffee, & Lavalee, 2015). The reason for a focus on self-identity is because people think, feel, and behave in particular ways, within physical activity contexts, in light of 'who they are' (i.e., self-identity; McGannon & Mauws, 2000; Rees et al., 2015). Given that physical activity participation and performance are of interest in sport psychology, understanding how self-identity is formed, framed, and/or impacted in sport contexts has been centralized in sport psychology research and practice (McGannon & Spence, 2010; Ronkainen, Kavoura, & Ryba, 2015). The interest in self-identity within sport psychology can be traced to William James's (1890) cognitive conception of the self as a primary determinant of thoughts, feelings, and actions. Social psychologist Charles Cooley (1902) further conceptualized self and identity as a social phenomenon that is shaped and reflected back to us through interpersonal interactions.

Sport psychology research exploring identity first gained traction in the 1990s, with Brewer, Van Raalte, and Linder (1993) quantitatively studying 'athletic identity' as a cognitive structure and social role derived or formed from interacting with others in the sport context (e.g., coaches, parents, teammates). Additional work in the 1990s was quantitatively studied using a 'multidimensional' social cognitive conception of self-identity, which was formed and/or expressed within, and across, sport contexts (see Ronkainen et al., 2015, for an overview). Contemporary research in sport psychology continues to explore identity as a multidimensional social cognitive phenomenon impacted by social and/or group roles within sport (see Rees et al., 2015). In the late 1990s and early 2000s, feminist and cultural studies scholars within sport psychology also drew attention to aspects of identity privilege (e.g., white male heterosexual privilege; Butryn, 2002) and the marginalization and/or exclusion of identities in sport (e.g., non-white, lesbian, female; Gill, 2001; Krane, 2001). The critical feminist and cultural studies identity scholarship forms the foundation of additional contemporary work in sport psychology studying marginalized identities such as disability (Smith, Bundon, & Best, 2016), race and spirituality (Blodgett, Ge, Schinke, & McGannon, 2017), gay, lesbian, and transgender athletes (Krane, 2016), athlete mother identities (McGannon, McMahon, & Gonsalves, 2018), and indigenous athletes (Blodgett, Schinke, Smith, Peltier, Pheasant, 2011). These studies are not meant to be exhaustive; readers are referred to Ronkainen et al.'s

(2015) critical meta-study of 40 published qualitative studies on athlete identities for a more detailed overview of identity conception in sport psychology.

Although identity has been conceptualized and studied in multiple ways in sport psychology, within a dynamic sport landscape that includes athletes from multiple cultural backgrounds, researchers and practitioners have been urged to attend to the role of culture in the formation and expression of identity (Butryn, 2016; Ryba & Wright, 2005). These dialogues have been ongoing in sport psychology since the early 2000s and are sometimes referred to as part of the genre of cultural sport psychology (CSP; McGannon & Smith, 2015; Ryba, Schinke & Tennenbaum, 2010; Schinke & Hanrahan, 2009). Within CSP, culturally inclusive research and practice create space for socially constructed identities, which are fluid and made meaningful through particular language, social, and cultural practices, within the context of performance and power issues (McGannon & Smith, 2015; Ryba & Wright, 2005).

The foregoing is important to attend to because, as noted, sport has been shown to be an unequal playing field where some identities are privileged (e.g., white, male, heterosexual, certain masculinities) over others (e.g., non-white, female, non-heterosexual, certain femininities; Blodgett et al., 2017; Butryn, 2016; Krane, 2016; McGannon, Schinke, Ye & Blodgett, 2018; Schinke, Stambulova, Lidor, Papaioannou, & Ryba, 2016). Such privileging can result in the silencing and/ or marginalization of identities that do not align with narrow framings of what it means to be an 'athlete' and/or sport participant, compromising athletic potential, participation and growth opportunities, and well-being (Blodgett et al., 2011; Douglas, 2014; Gill, 2001; Krane, 2001). Moreover, within CSP writings, people's identities (e.g., physicality, sexuality, gender, race, and ethnicity) are conceptualized as social and cultural resources that people draw upon to construct 'who they are', with certain experiences and behaviours resulting (McGannon & Smith, 2015; Ronkainen, Kavoura & Ryba, 2016). Sport psychology research and practice grounded in a socially constructed conception of self-identity thus hold potential for learning more about identity and the intersection with culture (McGannon & Smith, 2015; Ronkainen et al., 2016). Such understanding also affords the creation of more inclusive sport contexts for people as cultural beings, whose identities are centralized (McGannon & Smith, 2015; Schinke et al., 2016; Smith et al., 2016), drawing from the legacy of feminist and cultural studies work in sport psychology (Butryn, 2002; Gill, 2001; Krane, 2001).

Within CSP, solutions and challenges that limit identity construction, expression, and acceptance have been put forward to create more inclusive sport participation contexts and enhance sport performance. In order to further illuminate this possibility in relation to centralizing identities, we first outline the meaning of a socially constructed self-identity, highlighting the concept's grounding in social constructionism. To explicate the features of this particular conception of self-identity, we also draw upon post-positivist conceptions of self-identity within sport psychology that have been used to understand sport participation. Next, two theoretical perspectives (i.e., discursive psychology and narrative inquiry) that fall under the 'umbrella' of social constructionism are outlined, with research examples in sport psychology to illustrate socially constructed aspects of self-identity. We conclude with convergences of discursive and narrative tenets and some applied recommendations to further highlight the value of a socially constructed self-identity conception to inform sport psychology practice.

Self-Identity: Social Constructionist Definition

The notion of self-identity as culturally constructed is grounded in *social constructionism* because of the reliance on a socially constructed view of meaning and practice that centralizes language, narrative, and discourses in the construction of 'who we are' (McGannon & Smith,

2015; McGannon & Spence, 2010; Smith et al., 2016). Social constructionists believe 'that all knowledge, and therefore all meaningful reality as such, is contingent upon human practices, being constructed in and out of interaction between human beings and their world, and developed and transmitted within an essentially social context' (Crotty, 1998, p. 42). As result of this view of language and experience as interdependent, identity is conceptualized as the product of individual, social, and cultural narratives and discourses that interact to create particular meanings and associated behaviours related to identities (McGannon & Smith, 2015; Smith et al., 2016).

From a social constructionist perspective, self-identity is, thus, viewed as a discursive and narrative accomplishment (McGannon & Spence, 2010; Ronkainen et al., 2016; Smith, 2010). By drawing upon certain cultural discourses and narratives, people acquire the resources with which to render their sense of self visible and 'real' (McGannon & Spence, 2010; Smith, 2010). We do not 'have a self-identity' somewhere within us directing thoughts, feelings, and behaviours; rather, we speak as if we do and, in so doing, we draw upon and use particular stories and discourses made available through social interactions and cultural institutions (e.g., the media, sport organizations and practices) to fashion and frame 'who we are' in multiple and fluid ways and have certain experiences (Douglas, 2014; McGannon & Smith, 2015; Smith, 2010; Smith & Sparkes, 2009). This social constructionist conception of self-identity is in contrast to social psychology's adherence to a view of the self-identity grounded in a post-positivist notion of a natural and obvious separation of self and society (Gergen, 1994; Harré & Gillett, 1994). Conceptions of self-identity within sport psychology that adhere to this post-positivist view of self-identity tend to view it as a structure or process residing within the mind, or as a social property of culture that becomes internalized into the mind (Cerulo, 1997). As a result, 'the self or its equivalent is treated as a *middle term*, an internal something that mediates between external input and behavior' (Tolmon, 1998, p. 7; emphasis added). Post-positivist perspectives on self-identity have been predominant within sport psychology and thus fruitful for learning more about sport experiences, performance, and participation (McGannon & Smith, 2015; Ronkainen et al., 2016).

Although it is beyond our scope to review work in sport psychology adhering to post-positivist views of self-identity, some examples include the use of social identity theory to study how aspects of the social realm (e.g., leaders, coaches, group/team dynamics) and society (e.g., sport roles within a team or organizational structure) offer distinct roles and/or pathways that are incorporated into one's self-identity. Within social identity theory, identity is ultimately conceptualized as a distinct cognitive mechanism within the person, influenced by social forces and/or group interactions that impact athlete 'self-regulation' and performance. From a post-positivist perspective, the features of self-identity are thus regarded as separate, predictable or identifiable from identity categories such as gender, sexuality, race, religion, ability, or age. These various identity categories are features of people that, in turn, impact who they are (i.e., self-identity), sense of belonging (e.g., group membership), and behaviour (McGannon & Smith, 2015; Ronkainen et al., 2016). Examples of this work include Krane and Barber's (2003) study of social identity theory components (e.g., social and self-categorization, social comparison) that were used to explore how attitudes and behaviours of lesbians and about lesbians in sport are impacted in inclusive and marginalized ways. A more extensive discussion of social identity theory in sport by Rees et al. (2015) explored sport groups as elements that are incorporated into a person's sense of self and, in turn, become determinants of sport-related behaviour (e.g., leadership, participation, peak performance). Additional work using social identity theory has explored team contexts as determining roles for female athletes that may lead to antisocial behaviour within sport when roles are not clarified for and/or identified by athletes (Benson, Bruner, & Eys, 2017).

Although a socially constructed view of self-identity holds promise for learning more about the sociocultural context of identity, in addition to post-positive views, this work is still developing in sport psychology (McGannon & Smith, 2015; Ronkainen et al., 2016). For those interested in carrying out research on self-identity grounded in social constructionism, it is essential that theoretical and methodological choices align with a focus on conceptualizing and studying identity as constructed by language, narrative, and discourse (McGannon & Smith, 2015). Such alignment relates to epistemological, theoretical, and methodological choices that impact the quality and rigor of research (Smith & McGannon, 2018; Smith & Sparkes, 2009). In this regard, discursive and narrative perspectives – specifically discursive psychology and narrative inquiry – are two useful theoretical starting points that align with a social constructionist conception of identity. Thus, these approaches are useful starting points for conceptualizing and studying socially constructed identities in sport psychology.

Researchers within sport psychology have engaged with the various theoretical tenets of discursive psychology and narrative inquiry in relation to self-identity we will put forward within this chapter. Although we draw and build upon that work, those interested in learning more may consult McGannon and Smith's (2015) discussion of discursive psychology and narrative inquiry as methodological tools to capture a socially constructed and nuanced analysis of culture, self-identity, and experience to expand critical forms of CSP research. Readers may also consult Ronkainen et al.'s (2016) meta-study and synthesis of 23 published qualitative research articles exploring social constructionist conceptions of identity in sport and recommendations, 18 using narrative approaches and 5 using discursive approaches. Other writings within the *International Handbook of Qualitative Research in Sport and Exercise* have further detailed elements of discursive perspectives (see McGannon, 2016) and narrative inquiry (see Papathomas, 2016), which we will draw upon. Those interested in learning more about the specific 'what's, why's and how's' of discursive and/or narrative approaches are encouraged to access these informative chapters.

Discursive Psychology: Theoretical Tenets and Research Examples

Numerous developments within psychology have contributed to discursive psychology (Potter & Wiggins, 2008), with origins often credited to Potter and Wetherell's (1987) form of discourse analysis and Edwards and Potter's (1992) work. These researchers have reworked the 'subject matter' of psychology (i.e., cognitions and mental states) by reconceptualizing psychological phenomena as 'worked up' and given meaning in everyday talk and discourse, rather than as categories or mechanisms within the mind (Harré & Gillett, 1994). As will be shown shortly when outlining research examples using discursive psychology in sport psychology, although there are different orientations for analysing discourse and texts, all discursive psychological investigations align with the assumption that discourse and language are constructed and constituted (McGannon, 2016). This point means that discourse is viewed as a primary medium of social action – we 'do things' with words (e.g., make sense of who we are, decide how we might or might not behave, interact with others in particular ways) – because words have associated meanings, actions, and consequences depending on the discourses available at institutional and cultural levels (Potter & Wiggins, 2008). For this reason, discursive psychological approaches in sport psychology studies are often referred to as focusing on 'language in use', and, with that, the interest is in the effects (e.g., psychological, behavioural, social) of speaking in various ways (Cosh, Crabb, & Tully, 2015; McGannon, 2016; Potter &

Wiggins, 2008). Discursive psychological approaches thus fall under the social constructionism umbrella because self-identity is theorized as the product of individual, social, and cultural discourses that interact to create particular meanings and associated actions related to identities (McGannon & Spence, 2010; Potter & Wiggins, 2008; Wetherell, 2008).

As the term is used here, 'discourse' is grounded in Foucault's (1978) post-structuralist concept of discourse to understand the relationship between socially constructed forms of truth and power and the implications for self-related knowledge and behavioural practices. For Foucault, language is always located in discourse, which refers to an interrelated 'system of statements that cohere around common meanings and values ... [that] are a product of social factors, of powers and practices *rather than an individual's set of ideas*' (Hollway, 1983, p. 231; emphasis added). Discourse is also a broad concept referring to different ways of constituting meaning specific to particular groups, cultures, and historical context (Wiggins, 2017). To make the connection between identity, language, discourse, and behaviour further apparent, it is also useful to highlight the concept of a 'subject position' (McGannon, 2016; Wetherell, 2008). Discourses – whether personal, social, or cultural – offer competing ways of giving meaning to the world. Known as 'subject positions' for individuals to take up (Davies & Harré, 1990; Wetherell, 1998), these positions are conditions of possibility for constituting subjectivity (i.e., identities, understandings, experiences) and vary in terms of the power and opportunity they afford people (Wetherell, 2008; Wiggins, 2017). Although people may be constituted in one position or another, individuals are not passive, as they can (re)negotiate subject positions by refusing the ones articulated and taking up alternatives within new and/or different discourses (Wetherell, 1998). The concept of a subject position offers an entry point for individual resistance and social change by increasing the availability of discursive resources, which are linked effects (i.e., psychological and behavioural possibilities; McGannon, McMahon, & Gonsalves, 2017; Wetherell, 2008).

Although the concept of a subject position offers the possibility for change of identity-related views and behaviour(s), discursive resources do not offer infinite possibilities owing to their connection to social networks and institutions (Cosh et al., 2015; McGannon & Schinke, 2013). The social network (e.g., peers, teammates, coaches, parents, partners, children) within which people are situated thus becomes important because identities are co-constructed through self-views, as well as others' views of us and themselves, as people draw upon discourses to make sense of themselves and each other (Gergen, 1994; McGannon & Schinke, 2013). If people within one's social network construct one's identity by drawing upon narrow or incompatible discourses, it can be difficult to construct a new identity (and, implicitly, have different psychological experiences and change behaviours; McGannon et al., 2017). Discursive resources are further limited because language practices are made within a web of discourses held in place by institutional rules and practices of which people may be unaware or to which they do not have access (McGannon, 2016; Wetherell, 2008). Important in this process is the role of ideology (i.e., expected behaviours based on cultural values and norms), which may perpetuate some discourses as factual and the way 'things were meant to be'. When certain discourses and social and institutional practices are more prevalent, expansion of discursive resources becomes difficult (McGannon & Schinke, 2013). In turn, some identities are subverted or marginalized because discursive resources are not made available, and, thus, discursive practices have ideological effects that (re)produce unequal power relations.

Research Examples

In studying the role of discourse in identity construction, sport psychology researchers might use different forms of discursive psychological analysis to understand and 'capture' a socially constructed, nuanced analysis of culture, identity, and experience (see McGannon, 2016; McGannon & Smith, 2015; Ronkainen et al., 2016). For those using discursive psychological approaches, the interest is in the identification of taken-for-granted discourses at individual and institutional levels (e.g., sport organizations, various forms of media) used to construct discursive identities and the implications for social and behavioural practices. In terms of the sort of 'data' collected to study identity-related talk or representations in discourse and the effects (e.g., psychological, social, ideological, power), 'any written (e.g., newspapers, magazines, drama, text messages, internet websites, blogs, emails), visual (e.g., film, photographs, television broadcasts, visual art), audible (e.g., lyrics, conversations) or combination of these texts can be chosen as sources of analysis' (Markula & Silk, 2011, p. 113).

Since McGannon and Mauws (2000) first introduced discursive psychology to expand understandings of exercise participation beyond mainstream theoretical approaches (e.g., social cognitive), a number of studies have used discursive psychology within sport and exercise psychology (see Cosh & Tully, 2014; Locke, 2008; McGannon & Schinke, 2013). Here, we focus only on studies using discursive psychology to investigate identity in sport contexts, and these are more limited in number compared with discursive psychological studies on additional topics within sport and exercise psychology (McGannon & Smith, 2015; Ronkainen et al., 2016).

Kavoura, Ryba, and Chroni (2015) used Foucauldian discourse analysis to identify the discourses through which female Greek judokas (i.e., judo athletes) made sense of experiences and the implications for subjectivity/identity through sport participants' negotiation of sociocultural beliefs and gender stereotypes circulated within sport and Greek culture. From the analysis, four taken-for-granted concepts were identified – biology, gender, femininity, and judo/sport – which were used to centralize the discursive resources through which judokas constructed identities/subject positions and sport experiences. Athletes were shown to have some agency in negotiating multiple identities in discourse when associated meanings were favourable for women doing sport in ways that did not overly compromise femininity, which allowed women partly to resist gender stereotypes in sport through the construction of athletic identities. However, when women drew primarily upon discourses that positioned women as weaker, or when femininity was constructed in a narrow manner within women's sport discourse, gender stereotypes that oppress women in sport (e.g., women cannot be too strong and aggressive, women need to consider roles within the home/family first, over and above sport pursuits) structured women's experiences as 'lesser athletes' and/or limited sport development and engagement.

Outside the above study where sport participants were interviewed, most of the work using discursive psychology to study self-identity in sport psychology has focused on the media as a cultural site in which to learn more about the cultural, institutional context in relation to self-identity (Cosh, Crabb, & LeCouteur, 2013; McGannon & McMahon, 2016). The study of media representations is influenced by sport studies research, which has shown the media to be a source of cultural representation via circulation of certain meanings of athletes' identities (see Millington & Wilson, 2016) and how athletes view themselves as they navigate identity constructions and associated meanings within media discourses.

Examples of discursive psychological work focusing on the media come from three studies in sport psychology by Suzanne Cosh and colleagues (Cosh et al., 2015, 2013; Cosh, LeCouteur, Crabb, & Kettler, 2013). Within this work, discursive psychology has been used to study the media's construction of athlete identity within the context of nuanced discourses in relation to athletic career transitions (e.g., retirement, deselection from sport). All three studies highlighted the advantage of studying media discourses within the context of athlete retirement, showing that the media portrayed causes and solutions to career transition difficulties as located within individuals (i.e., athletes were held responsible for transition issues with solutions directed at 'fixing' athletes) because they were portrayed as having flawed, singular identities as athletes (Douglas, 2014). Such portrayals downplayed and/or negated the role that the social and cultural realms of sport play in the construction of limited identities and solutions. These discursive constructions of athletic identities were also shown to have wider implications for decisions to compete in sport, allowing researchers to highlight the nuanced ways in which alternative reasons for (returning to) competing were presented as inappropriate and, thus, compromising athlete well-being. Nuanced and taken-for-granted discourses such as these offer entry points of education, awareness, and resistance in terms of problematizing their impact on identity construction, opening the possibility for resistance of such identity meanings (Cosh et al., 2015).

A recent study in sport psychology focusing on digital media/online identities of competitive recreational athlete mothers looked at competitive recreational athlete mother runners' identity construction within discourses in an online running community with more than 75,000 subscribers (McGannon et al., 2017). Within this study, two primary discourses were identified: 'discourse of transformation and empowerment' and a 'discourse of disruption and resolution', which constructed identities/subject positions of 'role mother/advocate' and 'resilient mother runner'. These discursively constructed online identities can be used to provide a window into the emancipative and constraining potential of cultural discourses and implications of these for women's motivation to compete with or without stress. The meaning of sport was linked to possibilities for athlete mothers to overcome difficulties (e.g., motivation, good mother ideals) through identity construction, but also highlighted difficulties athlete mothers have negotiating good motherhood pressures. Again, we see from this discursive psychological study that discourses, and the subject positions offered within them, can serve as entry points for understanding socially constructed identities and their link to resistance, change, and well-being issues in people's lives (McGannon & Smith, 2015).

Narrative Inquiry: Theoretical Tenets and Research Examples

Although there are various approaches to narrative within the social sciences (Schiff, 2013), narrative inquiry can be described as a psychosocial approach distinguished from other qualitative approaches (e.g., ethnography or phenomenology) by its focus on stories (Smith & Sparkes, 2009). The basic tenets of narrative inquiry are as follows. First, within narrative inquiry, the focus is on stories because it is argued that people are, either naturally or culturally, storytellers. Second, within narrative inquiry, human beings are conceptualized as meaning makers who, in order to interpret, direct, and intelligibly communicate life, configure and constitute their experiences and sense of who they are (i.e., identity) using narratives that their social and cultural world have passed down. As Gabriel (2000) argued, stories are given a central role because they are 'the great factories of meaning, creating it, transforming it, testing it, sustaining it, fashioning it, and refashioning it' (p. 4). Third, in narrative inquiry, narratives are considered the resources from which people construct meaning, experience, and personal stories, and understand the particular stories they hear. To unpack what this means, a subtle distinction between the notions of 'story' and 'narrative' is necessary. A story is a specific tale that people tell about themselves or others. In contrast, a narrative is a resource that culture and social relations make available to us, and, in turn, we use narratives to help construct meaning, experience, and our stories. Thus, people tell stories, not narratives.

Narratives are the crucial resources that provide people with a template – a scaffolding of sorts – with which to build and structure meaning, experience, and their own identity-related stories, as well understand the stories they hear or see in action (Smith, 2016).

Although a consistent difference in usage is difficult to sustain because the words 'story' and 'narrative' overlap so frequently, the following distinction and implications are important. The distinction makes the points that a narrative is not in itself a story, and stories can be collected into types of narrative (Frank, 2010). The implications of the foregoing distinctions are also important in that, in narrative inquiry, people may tell stories that are very personal and that communicate meaning and experience. However, these stories do not spring from their mind, nor are they made up by themselves, even if they are coming from the individual. Instead, personal identity-related stories are constructed from the narratives that surround them. Thus, people's stories and their understanding of stories they hear are not pristine reflections of the experiences they depict. Nor are they transparent windows into psychological phenomena or derived from their private internal workings of the mind. (Smith, 2010). Rather, when a person tells a story, they draw on the menu of narrative resources that culture and social relations make available. In that regard, the stories people tell are constructed from the resources that emerge from outside them, and these stories need to be considered analytically as culturally and relationally constructed, as partly manifested in types of narrative that surround them within culture and relationships, rather than inside their minds (McGannon & Smith, 2015; Papathomas, 2016; Smith, 2016).

Another tenet of narrative inquiry is that, as alluded to in the points above, narratives can be used to socially constitute and construct identity. Narratives are, thus, not only resources for telling personal stories, making meaning, and constituting experience, but also are used as the crucial equipment to create and communicate identities. We actualize our identities by drawing on narratives that circulate in culture and through the activity of narrating with ourselves and others (Smith et al., 2016). Such identity work is, thus, manifested within culture and social relationships, not solely within the individual's interiority and mind, as with mainstream sport psychology approaches, including the social identity approaches outlined earlier (see McGannon & Smith, 2015; Smith, 2010). Rather than producing an individualized conception of identity, within narrative inquiry, identities are viewed as socially constructed and made intelligible in and through the narratives that circulate in culture and relationships with others (Gergen, 1994). In that way, narrative inquiry, like discursive approaches, can be used to challenge the dominant ideology of autonomous, bounded beings who have an identity inside them. It flips the switch, as it were, from seeing individuals as simply forging identities and relationships to viewing (multiple) narratives and the stories told in relationships as forging individuals and identities. In light of this focus on the social and cultural construction of self-identity and destabilizing social cognitive and/or cognitive conceptions of self-identity, narrative inquiry can be thought of as also falling under the social constructionist umbrella (McGannon & Smith, 2015; Papathomas, 2016).

Similar to a discursive psychological focus on 'language in use', narrative inquiry is used to view narratives as performative and generative in that they have the capacity to do things; narratives act on, with, for, and in humans, shaping behaviour and identities and affecting emotions and actions (Frank, 2010; Smith, 2013a, 2013b). In such ways, the psychological meaning and function of narratives go deep (Mayer, 2014). Narratives imbue our experience with meaning and, indeed, as noted earlier, are thus inseparable from who we are (i.e., our identities). Events become meaningful to the extent that they can be fitted into or evoke some larger narrative about ourselves and/or our social and cultural world. Stories create and recreate our identities, and, as a result, our sense of self-identity depends on our ability to cast ourselves as the main actor in our own autobiographical narrative. It is impossible to say and make sense of 'who we are' without telling an intelligible story in relation to someone. Finally, stories have been argued to be what :

> motivate our actions. When we act we are often to a great extent enacting, we are acting out the story as the script demands, acting in ways that are meaningful in the context of some story and that are true to our character's identity.
>
> (Mayer, 2014, p. 7)

Research Examples

Narrative researchers traditionally have adopted either a 'story analyst' or 'storyteller' approach to narrative inquiry (Bochner & Riggs, 2014; Smith & Sparkes, 2009). The former means that the researcher places narratives under analysis and communicates results in the form of a realist tale to produce an analytical account of narratives. The research conducted, then, is *on* narratives, whereby narratives are the object of study and placed under scrutiny in analysis. An example of narrative inquiry in which researchers operate as a story analyst can be found in the work of Carless and Douglas (2013), who explored the processes and consequences of identity development among young elite athletes and how sport culture influences identity creation. Drawing on the life stories of elite male athletes, and analysing these stories through the lens of narrative theory, they offered insights into various strands of sport psychology literature. For instance, responding to calls for a cultural sport psychology, their study revealed how taken-for-granted aspects of elite sport culture (e.g., emphasis on performance, singular athletic identity, winning) shape psychological processes of identity development in ways that do not always lead to well-being and adjustment for athletes. This research by Carless and Douglas further highlighted how the origins of a potentially problematic athletic identity are seeded in early sport experiences that draw upon the foregoing cultural sport narratives in limited ways, shedding light on how certain meanings and experiences of athletic identity can be resisted or developed.

Another example of researchers operating as a story analyst can be found in the research by Smith et al. (2016) on para-sport. Drawing on qualitative data collected from 36 elite disabled athletes, their narrative research found that all participants in the study adopted an athletic identity and an athletic activist identity. A small group of people interviewed and observed also adopted a political activist identity. Smith et al. (2016) highlighted several reasons why athletes adopted or eschewed activist identities and how these were embodied and culturally framed. For example, it was argued that embodied feelings were important for motivating the development of identities for disabled athletes. The use of emotional regulation in constraining and enabling the development of activist identities was moreover noted. It was proposed, however, that emotions and feelings should not be subordinated to cognition or the mind. Emotion and feeling are, instead, often somewhat ineffable and emergent from and immanent within the flows of language, narratives within culture, and social relationships. Finally, Smith et al. suggested several performative dimensions of these identities by arguing that activist identities can do certain things, including challenging the social oppression that many disabled people face. Further examples of narrative approaches in sport psychology can be found in the meta-study on identity by Ronkainen et al. (2016).

Another way of doing narrative inquiry is to operate as a storyteller. Here, the analysis *is* the story, and the story is communicated in the form of a *creative analytical practice* to produce a tale *as* a story. To say that 'analysis is the story' is to emphasize that, rather than putting a story under analysis and doing research on narratives, the story in its own right is analytical and theoretical; it does the job of analysis as analysis happens within a story (Bochner & Riggs, 2014). Given this notion, storytellers do not transform the story into another language, but use the stories they gathered to do the work of analysis and theorizing. In so doing, storytellers recast data to produce a story, and the story is a theory. To help do this, rather than tell a story and represent results through a realist tale, they use a creative analytical practice (CAP). CAP is an umbrella term for research that is cast into evocative and highly accessible forms, such as autoethnography and creative non-fiction (McMahon, 2016). An example of researchers operating as storytellers to study identity within sport psychology can be found in the work of Irish, Cavallerio, and McDonald (2017). Using a narrative approach, these authors studied the ways in which a deaf athlete's experiences of participation in sport can affect psychological and social well-being, positive identity creation, and how social and interpersonal relationships play a role in shaping these experiences. As they adopted the position of the storyteller, data were represented through an evocative autoethnography, with the aim to self-reflexively describe emotional experiences and identity construction to increase awareness and encourage reflection in the reader in terms of what it can mean to be a deaf athlete.

McMahon, McGannon, and Zehntner (2017) further provide an example of sport researchers operating as storytellers. Specifically, using analytic autoethnography (i.e., a personal, evocative story of first author McMahon was created), they examined and showed the sociocultural issues in the development and persistence of stigmatization in elite swimming and a masters swimming context. Through this self-related story, they further highlighted how social agents contributed to both 'enacted' and 'felt' competitive performance stigma and the consequences/effects on identities (e.g., withdrawal from sport, feelings of shame) for this swimmer (i.e., McMahon). Their analysis further highlighted the role of particular cultural insiders (e.g., coaches, team managers, and other swimmers) in the reproduction of competitive performance stigma through acts of labelling, discrimination, and social isolation and through the creation of this autoethnographic tale. For McMahon et al., these acts positioned the female swimmer as an 'outsider' because of her competitive performance, which in turn led to identity dilemmas and her to withdrawing from sporting contexts (see also McMahon, Zehntner, & McGannon, 2017).

Conclusion

We have written previously about the convergences of discursive psychology and narrative inquiry within sport psychology in relation to their use as research tools in advancing CSP research (see McGannon & Smith, 2015). Within this section, we offer some modest thoughts concerning how the central tenets of discursive psychology and narrative inquiry might be used in applied practice. Before outlining these suggestions, we note some points of convergence between narrative inquiry and discursive psychology. The first of these convergences is that, despite the different research foci and points of analysis – stories in narrative inquiry and micro-talk, conversation and texts in discursive psychology – both perspectives converge on a conception of identity as socially and culturally constructed in and through 'language in use'. Following from this point, socially constructed identities are multiple and fluid, as people move within and between social and cultural contexts that may afford or limit identities, experiences, and behaviours, depending on the narrative resources (in the case of narrative inquiry) or discursive resources (in the case of discursive psychology). If people have limited narrative or discursive resources at their disposal with which to make sense of who they are and experience and act within sport contexts, they can have their identities marginalized and silenced, becoming disadvantaged in terms of health, well-being, and opportunities to better their lives (McGannon & Schinke, 2013; Smith, 2013a, 2013b). Given these convergences, stories, micro-talk, and various forms of 'language in use' continue to serve as concrete entry points of personal awareness and practical change. This focus would mean that practitioners would seek to listen to and/or collect stories and everyday forms of identity talk, to illuminate understanding of identities and experiences, with the goal of centralizing marginalized identities.

Where would such stories, micro-level identity talk, come from? How would practitioners use stories? Because discursive psychology and narrative inquiry converge on stories/talk/ conversations as the product of social and cultural narratives/discourses, the answers to such questions again lie in the elicitation of stories and exploring taken-for-granted identity talk. For example, at the personal level, practitioners may ask sport participants to communicate personal stories in relation to an issue or experience, and then reflect on the story in terms of experiences, behaviours, and their lives. Practitioners might facilitate this process by asking questions such as, 'Who were the key people in the story? What sort of things were said and unsaid? What experiences resulted?' Practitioners might also focus on the taken-for-granted ways of speaking about various identities that circulate socially (e.g., team/group, exchanges with coaches and staff) to further make sense of what the team's identity is, how it is relational, and where one's personal stories fit (or do not fit), with different effects resulting. Practitioners could take a broader focus to look at cultural narratives and discourses in terms of stories circulated in the media about athlete identities. These stories could then be discussed with athletes about what aligns with experiences, along with counter/resistance stories that might facilitate different or positive experiences and performance outcomes.

Another useful starting point for application via the use of discourse and narrative as tools would be for practitioners to write their own stories in relation to sport and the various identities/subject positions (e.g., sport psychologist, coach, former athlete). This use of storytelling and/or, more critically, articulating one's own identity talk and conversations would be an autoethnographic, self-reflexive story that may open up one's understanding about the privilege one has within sport (Butryn, 2002) and/or the vulnerability or marginalization one experienced or enabled in sport contexts (McMahon, 2016; McMahon, McGannon, et al., 2017). This self-reflexive work could be also be used in a co-participatory manner, whereby practitioners acknowledge how their own taken-for-granted assumptions may have unintentionally marginalized participants' identities or impacted the communities whose needs they sought to best serve (see Blodgett et al., 2011).

Another application could be to use media representations and discourses/narratives as a concrete entry point for educating practitioners and athletes about the circulation and power of stories, through showing them forms of 'identity talk' within various media forms (e.g., narrative or documentary film, Facebook, Twitter, news). Through one-on-one or group discussions, meanings could be highlighted, along with exploration of whether or not these align with athlete experiences, and the implications for mental health and performance. In turn, critical awareness can again be raised as to how concrete forms of talk (rather than mental states within the person), as shown within media forms, offer entry points for social action by consultants and athletes, expanding narrative resources at individual and social levels. In the case of certain identities, athletes might be shown textual and image representations of different marginalized aspects of identities (e.g., sexuality, race, and ethnicity) and asked, 'How do media narratives and representations ring true or differ for you?' and 'How do these similarities and differences impact your life?' From here, conversations can again be started about the role of others (e.g., teammates, significant others, coaches) in reinforcing, or countering, identity-related views as tied to particular stories and forms of talk. In turn, co-constructed solutions can be developed that may enhance access to additional narrative/discursive resources to offer identity-related stories that encourage well-being. Consultants could also use 'naturalistic' forms of digital media identity talk to learn more about how athletes view themselves through online forums, Instagram, or blog postings that are anonymized around certain topics. Tools such as these may further open up conditions of possibility via the creation of additional narrative and discursive resources in a virtual community. Finally, self-related stories, group stories, and sport culture/subculture stories, including those circulated in media forms, could also be used by athletes to resist or counter narratives/discourses that are less productive for identity-related views, psychological well-being, and performance. In this regard, athletes might take an active role through controlling stories produced, to give voice to aspects of who they are in ways that are less marginalizing or resist problematic portrayals.

References

Benson, A. J., Bruner, M. W., & Eys, M. (2017). A social identity approach to understanding the conditions associated with antisocial behaviors among teammates in female teams. *Sport, Exercise, and Performance Psychology, 6,* 129–142.

Blodgett, A., Schinke, R., Smith, B., Peltier, D., & Pheasant, C. (2011). Exploring vignettes as a narrative strategy for co-producing the research voices of Aboriginal community members. *Qualitative Inquiry, 17,* 522–533.

Blodgett, A. T., Ge, Y., Schinke, R. J., & McGannon, K. R. (2017). Intersecting identities of female boxers: Stories of cultural difference and marginalization in sport. *Psychology of Sport and Exercise, 32,* 83–92.

Bochner, A., & Riggs, N. (2014). Practicing narrative inquiry. In P. Levy (Ed.), *Oxford handbook of qualitative research* (pp. 195–222). Oxford, UK: Oxford University Press.

Brewer, B. W., Van Raalte, J. L., & Linder, D. E. (1993). Athletic identity: Hercules' muscles or Achilles heel? *International Journal of Sport Psychology, 24,* 237–254.

Butryn, T. M. (2002). Critically examining White racial identity and privilege in sport psychology. *The Sport Psychologist, 16,* 316–336.

Butryn, T. M. (2016). Whiteness in sport psychology. In R. J. Schinke, K. R. McGannon, & B. Smith (Eds.), *Routledge international handbook of sport psychology* (pp. 228–237). New York: Routledge.

Carless, D., & Douglas, K. (2013). 'In the boat' but 'selling myself short': Stories, narratives and identity development in elite sport. *The Sport Psychologist, 27,* 27–39.

Cerulo, K. A. (1997). Identity construction: New issues, new directions. *Annual Review of Sociology, 23,* 385–409.

Cooley, C. H. (1902). *Human nature and the social order.* New York: Scribner's.

Cosh, S., Crabb, S., & LeCouteur, A. (2013). Elite athletes and retirement: Identity, choice and agency. *Australian Journal of Psychology, 66,* 89–97.

Cosh, S., Crabb, S., & Tully, P. J. (2015). A champion out of the pool? A discursive exploration of two Australian Olympic swimmers' transition from elite sport to retirement. *Psychology of Sport and Exercise, 19,* 33–41.

Cosh, S., LeCouteur, A., Crabb, S., & Kettler, L. (2013). Career transitions and identity: A discursive psychological approach to exploring athlete identity in retirement and the transition back into elite sport. *Qualitative Research in Sport, Exercise and Health, 5,* 21–42.

Cosh, S., & Tully, P. J. (2014). 'All I have to do is pass': A discursive analysis of student athletes' talk about prioritising sport to the detriment of education to overcome stressors encountered in combining elite sport and tertiary education. *Psychology of Sport and Exercise, 15,* 180–189.

Crotty, M. (1998). *The foundations of social research: Meaning and perspective in the research process.* London: Sage.

Davies, B., & Harré, R. (1990). Positioning: The discursive production of selves. *Journal for the Theory of Social Behaviour, 20,* 43–63. doi:10.1111/j.1468-5914.1990.tb00174

Douglas, K. (2014). Challenging interpretive privilege in elite and professional sport: One [athlete's] story, revised, reshaped and reclaimed. *Qualitative Research in Sport, Exercise and Health, 6*, 220–243.

Edwards, D., & Potter, J. (1992). *Discursive psychology*. London: Sage.

Foucault, M. (1978). *The history of sexuality, volume 1: An introduction*. London: Penguin.

Fox, K. R. (1997). *The physical self: From motivation to well-being*. Champaign, IL: Human Kinetics.

Frank, A. W. (2010). *Letting stories breathe*. Chicago, IL: University of Chicago Press.

Gabriel, Y. (2000). *Storytelling in organization: Facts, fiction and fantasies*. Oxford, UK: Oxford University Press.

Gergen, K. J. (1994). *Realities and relationships: Soundings in social construction*. Cambridge, MA: Harvard University Press.

Gill, D. (2001). In search of feminist sport psychology: Then, now, and always. *The Sport Psychologist, 15*, 363–449.

Harré, R., & Gillett, G. (1994). *The discursive mind*. Thousand Oaks, CA: Sage.

Hollway, W. (1983). Heterosexual sex: Power and desire for the other. In S. Cartledge & J. Ryan (Eds.), *Sex and love: New thoughts on old contradictions* (pp. 124–140). London: Women's Press.

Irish, T., Cavallerio, F., & McDonald, K. (2017). 'Sport saved my life' but 'I am tired of being an alien!': Stories from the life of a deaf athlete. *Psychology of Sport and Exercise*. doi: 10.1016/j.psychsport.2017.10.007

James, W. (1890). *Principles of psychology*. New York: Holt.

Kavoura, A., Ryba, T. V., & Chroni, S. (2015). Negotiating female judoka identities in Greece: A Foucaulidan discourse analysis. *Psychology of Sport and Exericse, 17*, 88–98.

Krane, V. (2001). One lesbian feminist epistemology: Integrating feminist standpoint, queer theory and cultural studies. *The Sport Psychologist, 15*, 401–411.

Krane, V. (2016). Inclusion to exclusion: Sport for LGBT athletes. In R. J. Schinke, K. R. McGannon, & B. Smith (Eds.), *Routledge international handbook of sport psychology* (pp. 238–247). London: Routledge.

Krane, V., & Barber, H. (2003). Lesbian experiences in sport: A social identity perspective. *Quest, 55*, 328–346.

Locke, A. (2008). Managing agency for athletic performance. *A Discursive Approach to the Zone Qualitative Research in Psychology, 5*, 103–126.

Markula, P., & Silk, M. (2011). *Qualitative research for physical culture*. New York: Palgrave MacMillan.

Mayer, F. W. (2014). *Narrative politics*. Oxford, UK: Oxford University Press.

McGannon, K. R. (2016). Critical discourse analysis in sport and exercise: What, why and how. In B. Smith & A. E. Sparkes (Eds.), *Routledge international handbook of qualitative research in sport and exercise* (pp. 230–242). London: Routledge.

McGannon, K. R., & Mauws, M. K. (2000). Discursive psychology: An alternative approach for studying adherence to exercise and physical activity. *Quest, 52*, 148–165.

McGannon, K. R., & McMahon, J. (2016). Media representations and athlete identities: Examining benefits for sport psychology. *Qualitative Methods in Psychology Bulletin, 21*, 43–54.

McGannon, K. R., McMahon, J., & Gonsalves, C. A. (2017). Mother runners in the blogosphere: A discursive psychological analysis of online recreational athlete identities. *Psychology of Sport and Exercise, 28*, 125–135.

McGannon, K. R., McMahon, J., & Gonsalves, C. A. (2018). Juggling motherhood and sport: A qualitative study of the negotiation of competitive recreational athlete mother identities. *Psychology of Sport and Exercise, 36*, 41–49.

McGannon, K. R., & Schinke, R. J. (2013). 'My first choice is to work out at work; then I don't feel bad about my kids': A discursive psychological analysis of motherhood and physical activity participation. *Psychology of Sport and Exercise, 14*, 179–188.

McGannon, K. R., Schinke, R. J., Ge, Y., & Blodgett, A. T. (2018). Negotiating gender and sexuality: A qualitative analysis of elite women boxer intersecting identities and sport psychology implications. *Journal of Applied Sport Psychology*. doi:10.1080/10413200.2017.1421593

McGannon, K. R., & Smith, B. (2015). Centralizing culture in cultural sport psychology research: The potential of narrative inquiry and discursive psychology. *Psychology of Sport and Exercise, 17*, 79–87.

McGannon, K. R., & Spence, J. C. (2010). Speaking of the self and physical activity participation: What discursive psychology can tell us about an old problem. *Qualitative Research in Sport and Exercise, 2*, 17–38.

McMahon, J., McGannon, K. R., & Zehntner, C. (2017). I am fast but I do not fit: An autoethnography of a swimmer's experiences of 'competitive performance' stigma in two sporting contexts. *Sport, Education and Society*. doi:10.1080/13573322.2017.1348941

McMahon, J., Zehntner, C., & McGannon, K. R. (2017). Fleshy, female and forty: A docudrama of a former elite swimmer who re-immersed herself into the elite swimming culture. *Qualitative Research in Sport, Exercise and Health, 5*, 546–553.

McMahon, J. A. (2016). Creative analytical practices. In B. Smith & A. C. Sparkes (Eds.), *Routledge handbook of qualitative research in sport and exercise* (pp. 302–315). London: Routledge.

Millington, B., & Wilson, B. (2016). Media research: From text to context. In B. Smith & A. Sparkes (Eds.), *Routledge international handbook of qualitative research in sport and exercise* (pp. 152–242). London: Routledge.

Papathomas, A. (2016). Narrative inquiry: From cardinal to marginal … and back?. In B. Smith & A. E. Sparkes (Eds.), *Routledge international handbook of qualitative research in sport and exercise* (pp. 37–48). London: Routledge.

Potter, J., & Wetherell, M. (1987). *Discourse and social psychology: Beyond attitudes and behavior.* London: Sage.

Potter, J., & Wiggins, S. (2008). Discursive psychology. In C. Willig & W. Stainton-Rogers (Eds.), *Handbook of qualitative research in psychology* (pp. 73–90). London: Sage.

Rees, T., Haslam, S. A., Coffee, P., & Lavalee, D. (2015). A social identity approach to sport psychology: Principles, practice and prospects. *Sports Medicine, 45*, 1083–1096.

Ronkainen, N. J., Kavoura, A., & Ryba, T. V. (2015). A meta-study of athletic identity research in sport psychology: Current status and future directions. *International Review of Sport and Exercise Psychology, 9*, 45–64.

Ronkainen, N. J., Kavoura, A., & Ryba, T. V. (2016). Narrative and discursive perspectives on athlete identity: Past, present and, future. *Psychology of Sport and Exercise, 27*, 128–137.

Ryba, T. V., Schinke, R. J., & Tenenbaum, G. (Eds.). (2010). *The cultural turn in sport and exercise psychology.* Morgantown, WV: Fitness Information Technology.

Ryba, T. V., & Wright, H. K. (2005). From mental game to cultural praxis: A cultural studies model's implications for the future of sport psychology. *Quest, 57*, 192–219.

Schiff, B. (2013). Fractured narratives: Psychology's fragmented narrative psychology. In M. Hyvärinen, M. Hatavara, & L. C. Hydén (Eds.), *The travelling concept of narrative* (pp. 245–264). Amsterdam: John Benjamins.

Schinke, R. J., & Hanrahan, S. J. (Eds.). (2009). *Cultural sport psychology.* Champaign, IL: Human Kinetics.

Schinke, R. J., Stambulova, N. B., Lidor, R., Papaioannou, A., & Ryba, T. V. (2016). ISSP position stand: Social missions through sport and exercise psychology. *International Journal of Sport and Exercise Psychology, 14*, 4–22.

Smith, B. (2010). Narrative inquiry: Ongoing conversations and questions for sport and exercise psychology research. *International Review of Sport and Exercise Psychology, 3*, 87–107.

Smith, B. (2013a). Sporting spinal cord injuries, social relations, and rehabilitation narratives: An ethnographic creative non-fiction of becoming disabled through sport. *Sociology of Sport Journal, 30*, 132–152.

Smith, B. (2013b). Disability, sport, and men's narratives of health: A qualitative study. *Health Psychology, 32*, 110–119.

Smith, B. (2016). Narrative analysis. In E. Lyons & A. Coyle (Eds.), *Analysing qualitative data in psychology* (2nd ed., pp. 202–221). London: Sage.

Smith, B., Bundon, A., & Best, M. (2016). Disability sport and activist identities: A qualitative study of narratives of activism among elite athletes with impairment. *Psychology of Sport and Exercise, 26*, 139–148.

Smith, B., & McGannon, K. R. (2018). Developing rigor in qualitative research: Problems and opportunities within sport and exercise psychology. *International Review of Sport and Exercise Psychology, 11*, 101–121.

Smith, B., & Sparkes, A. C. (2009). Narrative analysis and sport and exercise psychology: Understanding lives in diverse ways. *Psychology of Sport and Exercise, 10*, 279–288.

Tolmon, C. W. (1998). Sumus ergo sum: The ontology of self and how Descartes got it wrong. In W. E. Smythe (Ed.), *Toward a psychology of persons* (pp. 3–24). Mahwah, NJ: Lawrence Erlbaum.

Wetherell, M. (1998). Positioning and interpretive repertoires: Conversation analysis and post- structuralism in dialogue. *Discourse and Society, 9*, 387–412.

Wetherell, M. (2008). Subjectivity or psycho-discursive practices? Investigating complex, intersectional identities. *Subjectivity, 22*, 73–81.

Wiggins, S. (2017). *Discursive psychology: Theory, method and applications.* London: Sage.

44
SPIRITUALITY IN SPORT

Thierry R. F. Middleton, Robert J. Schinke, Brennan Petersen,
and Cole Giffin

Introduction

Human beings have always felt the urge to search for a deeper meaning to life, a meaning that transcends the mundane of everydayness (Jirásek, 2015). Historically, researchers have equated this search for inner spirituality with one's religiousness (Zinnbauer et al., 1997). There is a significant amount of literature where authors have examined the relationship between religion and sport, a relationship perhaps best encapsulated by Pierre de Coubertin's writings on the connection between religion and the modern Olympic games (de Coubertin, 1935/2000; Jirásek, 2015). However, with the rise of secularism in North America, there is a need to differentiate between *religiosity* and spirituality and how each of these terms is connected to sport (Hyman & Handal, 2006; Zinnbauer et al., 1997). Our aim within this contribution is to provide an overview of how researchers in sport psychology have explored the concept of spirituality, and to a lesser extent religiosity, within and outside the context of sport. The contribution begins by providing working definitions for spirituality and religion. The authors provide these with the acknowledgement that, depending on whom one asks, the definition may change (see Hyman & Handal, 2006; Zinnbauer et al., 1997); however, it is believed that it is important that the reader understands how they may relate to one another and how they may be differentiated. The authors then unpack how researchers have explored the connection between spirituality and sport performance. Next, building on the broadening scope of sport psychology research, the authors explore how helping athletes develop an understanding of their spirituality can aid in ensuring their mental well-being. Finally, pathways are provided for how sport psychology consultants (SPCs) may integrate an appreciation for athletes' spirituality into their practice, as well as future research directions.

Spirituality and Religiosity

The constant construction of the relationship between spirituality and religion has resulted in both terms often being used interchangeably and without clear definitions for differentiating between the two (Hyman & Handal, 2006; Jirásek, 2015; Zinnbauer et al., 1997). However, researchers continue to develop working definitions for both concepts. Generally, in these definitions, there is acknowledgement that there is a degree of overlap between religion and spirituality, while it is noted that there is no hierarchy between the concepts and that neither concept is larger than, or encompasses, the other (Hyman & Handal, 2006; Zinnbauer et al., 1997). Religion, as conceptualized here, is the recognition of a higher being that is absolutely different to the world in which people live (Jirásek, 2015). Reverence of this higher being is often conducted in a group setting through rituals and practices that are tied to the formal structure of a religious body (e.g., Christianity, Islam, Judaism; Hyman & Handal, 2006; Jirásek, 2015). One's connection to a formal religion impacts one's cultural and personal values and priorities (including those associated with sport) and influences how one constructs one's *identity* in relation to those around oneself (Zinnbauer et al., 1997). Contrastingly, spirituality is a deeper connection to oneself and how one is connected to the community around oneself in the search for the meaning of life (Jirásek, 2015). This sense of personal meaning is internal, subjective, derived from one's sense of higher ideals and deeper ideas, and connected to one's relationship with what one holds sacred (Hyman & Handal, 2006; Jirásek, 2015).

The definitions provided here are not carved in stone; in fact, it would be difficult to provide a definition for both spirituality and religion that every person could agree on. As Jirásek (2015) wrote: "spirituality cannot be captured by a strict definition sensu stricto, and every attempt to capture the notion might remain a mere approximation, estimate, or metaphor" (p. 292). Most people would also agree that the two terms are not mutually exclusive, though to what extent each differs from the other also depends on who one asks. Hyman and Handal (2006) provided an example of the different views individuals hold in relation to religion and spirituality in their work with Catholic, Protestant, Muslim, and Jewish religious leaders. An agreement that all religious leaders had was that the two concepts had some overlap. Jewish and Christian leaders varied in their views on the relationship between spirituality and religion; however, perhaps related to the cultural dimensions of spirituality and religion, the Imams (i.e., Muslim religious leaders) all said that the terms were one and the same. With sport psychology research being dominated by scholars from increasingly secular societies (i.e., generally Europe and North America; see Blodgett, Schinke, McGannon, & Fisher, 2015; Ryba & Wright, 2005), exploring the cultural basis for the distinction between spirituality and religion within sport psychology has lagged behind and resulted in the domination of a Euro-American world-view that a difference must exist. The authors recognize that the authors also are culturally Euro-American and that, by writing this chapter, they further ingrain the narrative that there is a difference between spirituality and religion. The authors, therefore, urge readers to refer to our understanding of these conceptualizations as provided above when reading the following sections, but remain open-minded to differing ways in which these concepts may be understood by those they work with.

Spirituality and Sport Performance

Scientific approaches to research, which have dominated the field of sport psychology, emphasize a statistical, impersonal approach to developing quantifiable explanations for how best to improve performance (Martens, 1979). The principal focus on performance-oriented outcomes has left little room for explorations into athletes' spiritual beliefs (Watson & Nesti, 2005). However, following Martens' (1979) urging for researchers to begin treating the athletes they consult as human beings who are capable of interacting with those around them, the scope of research has begun to expand. Nesti (2011) made the case for spirituality as an area of research for sport psychology scholars owing to frequent references to spirit in sport.

He pointed out that the term spirit is frequently mentioned by coaches, athletes, and spectators as being imperative to ensuring sporting success (e.g., team spirit used to describe cohesiveness). For many athletes, feeling a sense of spirituality in performance relates to the transcendence of their physical, emotions, and mental states into one during their pursuit of a goal that is bigger than them and leads to optimal or peak performances (Watson & Nesti, 2005).

The pursuit of this transcendent state in relation to achieving optimal performance is often done through mental skills training (Watson & Nesti, 2005) and the use of pre-performance routines (Cotterill, 2010). Although the spiritual elements of these mental skills and routines often go unnoticed, many of the techniques may have religious and non-religious spiritual elements. One example is provided by Gallwey (2015), who incorporated techniques drawn from Zen Buddhism within his humanistic psychological approach. Using these mindfulness techniques, he was able to teach athletes how to focus on the present moment and overcome mental obstacles (e.g., worry, fear of failure) associated with poor performance. Growing in popularity within sport psychology, mindfulness is the practice of becoming aware of one's moment-by-moment experience arising from purposeful attention paid to one's inner state (Kabat-Zinn, 2003). An approach related more to a formal religion, and one seen practised by athletes worldwide, is the use of prayer. Perhaps the most obvious examples of athletes using prayer prior to, and within, competition are Christian athletes who can be seen making the sign of the cross and lifting up prayers to God as they enter the field of play (Moraes & Salmela, 2009). However, Muslim athletes are also inclined to use prayer prior to sport (Shahrokhi, 2013). Although prayer may be tied to religious beliefs, for some it is undertaken as a spiritual obligation (Hochstetler, 2009). The use of prayer before and during sport performance can facilitate optimal performance through helping athletes develop an appropriate level of pre-competition awareness and, in turn, alleviate performance-related stress (Czech, Wrisberg, Fisher, Thompson, & Hayes, 2004). These findings are not surprising as they reflect the age-old use of prayer in most monotheistic religions (i.e., Judaism, Christianity, Islam) to gain strength and comfort during times of adversity (Watson & Nesti, 2005).

The use of religious rituals, such as prayer, in sport has been one area that has received attention from researchers (Watson & Czech, 2005). Whether religious or not, routines and rituals are often engaged in by athletes with the aim of entering an optimal zone of attentional, emotional, and confident motivational states prior to performance (Cotterill, 2010). For example, a professional boxer might make the sign of the cross in his/her corner before the first bell and the beginning of combat. Athletes who have been able to achieve these optimal states often perform exceptionally and have sometimes referred to the experiences and feelings during these performances as transcendent; their descriptions of these feelings also share a number of similarities with feelings of spirituality. For most athletes, entering a transcendent state has been referred to as experiencing "flow" (e.g., Csikszentmihalyi, 1975), achieving peak performance (e.g., Ravizza, 2002), and/or feeling a state of Zen (Cooper, 1998; Scott-Hamilton, Schutte, & Brown, 2016). Although each conceptualization may differ slightly, consider the following descriptions of each state: Csikszentmihalyi (1975) used semi-structured interviews to examine the experience of flow in 30 rock climbers of various skills and abilities. Participants described their experience of flow states as "transcendent, religious, visionary, or ecstatic" (Csikszentmihalyi, 1975, p. 88), and one rock climber described that the flow state was similar to a "Zen feeling, like meditation or concentration. One thing you're after is a pointless mind ... somehow the right thing is done without even thinking about it" (p. 87). Hill (2001), exploring peak performance, wrote that these experiences were filled with "joyness [and] transcendence" (p. 129). Further, although these performances are often associated with optimal athletic performance (Nesti, 2007), the transcendent experience results "in personal integration, growth, and expansion of personal identity" (Hill, 2001, p. 129). Comparably, a Zen-like state has been described as an increased feeling of effortlessness, increased mastery, feeling of awe and perfection, acute intuition, profound joy, increased flow experiences, and feelings of transcendence (Cooper, 1998; Scott-Hamilton et al., 2016).These descriptions are similar to several aspects of a spiritual experience in sport Robinson (2007) described, including: "a sense of holism with mind, feelings, and body stretched together ... a sense of transcendence, being taken beyond the self ... a sense of transformation and development" (p. 8). Watson (2007) suggested that it is legitimate to group concepts such as flow, peak experiences, feelings of Zen, and spiritual experiences into a broad category called altered states of consciousness (ASCs). ASCs have been defined as "an introspective awareness of a different mode of experiencing the world" (Hood, Spilka, Hunbergerm, & Gorsuch, 1996, p. 198).

Although ASCs have been studied in numerous sport contexts, extreme sports have become a focal point for many researchers. The risk and adversity that athletes face in sports such as skydiving (see Lipscombe, 1999), ultra-marathon running (see Acevedo, Dzewaltowski, Gill, & Noble, 1992), high-altitude mountaineering (Fave, Bassi, & Massimini, 2003), and surfing (Anderson, 2013) have been suggested as catalysts for inducing ASCs. One reason for this is the ability of these sports to provide challenges that force athletes to access inner resources in order to succeed, subsequently pushing athletes beyond their previously conceived limitations (Nakamura & Csikszentmihalyi, 2014; Watson, 2007). These sports have also been characterized by the development of a relational sense with the surrounding context (which may include other individuals). Ravizza (2002) expounded on the feeling of connection to a greater whole during moments of peak performance, and that this often led to athletes becoming totally immersed in their actions. Anderson (2013), working with surfers, termed this a relational sensibility – an emotion that surfers felt was co-constituted with every aspect of the environment around them and left them with a sense of awe. The coming together of these components results in feelings of unbridled joy and exuberance. For most athletes, participating in these challenging and sometimes dangerous activities can become a transformative experience as they revel in the awe of having accomplished an incredible feat and feeling connected to something that is bigger than them (Robinson, 2007; Watson & Nesti, 2005).

Spirituality and Well-Being

Beyond considering spiritual experiences within competition, working with athletes to develop an understanding of their spiritual identity can help bring about a deeper understanding of who they are and how they are connected with the human and natural world around them (Jirásek, 2015; Watson & Nesti, 2005). Some sport psychology researchers have begun to explore the benefits of enhancing athletes' well-being through developing their sense of spirituality (for examples, see Danish, Fazio, Nellen, & Owens, 2002; Sarkar, Hill, & Parker, 2014; Watson & Nesti, 2005). Consider the following quote from Greg Oden, a former number one overall draft pick in the NBA who struggled with alcoholism when his career was cut short owing to injury:

> Eventually, you realize that basketball got you this far, but being a good person will get you even further. I had so much self-made pressure, not realizing all I had to do was be happy with myself. Now I'm in a different space where I realize I have nothing

to prove to anybody as long as I'm a good person for my wife and daughter and family; that's what it's all about.

(Kravitz, 2019)

Although Oden said little about performance, he noted that his development of a deeper understanding of how to care for oneself and for others, while recovering from a condition in which he felt inauthentic to himself, was more important and resulted in feeling at one with his life purpose and meaning (Jirásek, 2015).

Jirásek (2015) advocated for spirituality to become an important aspect of an athlete that professionals must consider and respect when helping to foster a greater sense of well-being. A spiritual identity is not uncommon within athletes, and researchers have contended that engaging with athletes in a more holistic manner, including this spiritual aspect, will benefit the athletes' overall well-being by helping them see themselves as more than athletes (Gamble, Hill, & Parker, 2013; Watson & Nesti, 2005). Additionally, Nesti (2011) indicated that athletes identified their spirituality as an integral part of who they are, and that a significant amount of time during consultations with athletes is spent speaking about human nature, virtues, and meaning, rather than focusing solely on athletics and performance. Acceptance of this aspect demonstrates that athletes see themselves as embodying more than just an athletic identity, which can be beneficial for psychological well-being and prevent several issues athletes often face during transition periods (Douglas & Carless, 2009). Furthermore, Nesti (2011) highlighted the importance of consultants adopting a person-centred approach to engaging with these athletes as a result of athletes' understanding of their multiple identities. That is, focusing on athletes as people first and athletes second can assist athletes in remaining balanced during the ups and downs of their career, especially in work with professional athletes (Nesti, 2011).

Building on the benefits of athletes' development of their spiritual identity, researchers have found that active engagement in spiritual and religious activities may lead to athletes who are healthier, develop more positive routines, and benefit from higher levels of positive social support than others (Czech & Bullet, 2007). Additionally, a positive relationship between spirituality and the ability to cope with adversity outside sport has been seen (Czech & Bullet, 2007; Ridnour & Hammermeister, 2008) and may potentially replace more destructive coping strategies commonly seen in other athletes, such as substance use and risky sexual behaviour, which may negatively impact athletes' psychological well-being (Hagan, Schack, & Schinke, 2019; Plante, 2008). Exemplified by Greg Oden's quote above (Kravitz, 2019), even during athletes' tough times, spirituality can help them to find purpose or meaning within the hardships they face, helping them overcome the obstacles and carry on (Emmons, 2003).

Integrating Spirituality Considerations into One's Sport Psychology Practice

Integrating spirituality into sport psychology practice is ripe with potential difficulties. Crust (2006) posited that spirituality and sport psychology may be diametrically opposed, as sport psychology aims to promote internal control and self-actualization, whereas spirituality can be associated with the belief that your destiny is determined by a higher power or God; this may be especially relevant for athletes whose spirituality is rooted in religious beliefs. He further felt that the integration of spirituality into sport psychology practice could, thus, be seen as a step backward in the development of the discipline. Furthermore, spiritual and/or religious beliefs could at times restrict the use of some commonly used sport psychology tools. As examples, some Muslims see music, commonly used in pre-performance rituals or motivational tools, as forbidden (Galloway, 2009), and Balague (1999) indicates that self-talk, when used to reinforce the athlete's confidence through statements about their incredible ability, may clash with the humility practised in some religions. Correspondingly, some religious figures have posited that an increasing pursuit of sport excellence may be detrimental to athletes' spirituality and get in the way of their religious behaviours (e.g., prayer; Galloway, 2009). However, there are some researchers who have demonstrated that there are ways of embracing an athlete's spirituality that can be beneficial in sport psychology practice and can aid athletes in coping with adversity and/or improving mental skills training (Egli, Fisher, & Gentner, 2014; Watson & Nesti, 2005).

One of the main complications SPCs may face when integrating spirituality is the aforementioned difficulty in separating the concepts of spirituality and religion. To begin, owing to the deeply subjective nature of how one understands spirituality, SPCs should develop and be cognizant of their own understanding of spirituality, while remaining open-minded to alternate understandings. For example, SPCs whose spirituality is grounded in their religious beliefs may view spirituality in stark contrast to an athlete who does not follow, or follows a different, formal religion. This may be a step that SPCs have to take on themselves as, in addition to the personal nature of each person's understanding of spirituality, many SPCs have indicated that they felt that their sport psychology training and graduate courses did not prepare them for discussing and/or including spirituality within the scope of their work (Egli et al., 2014). Furthermore, SPCs are encouraged to acknowledge their own position relative to their athlete through reflexive introspection and engaging in daily journaling and critical conversations with colleagues and/or a mentor. Developing one's ability to become a reflexive practitioner is one step towards developing into a culturally competent researcher/practitioner (see Schinke, McGannon, Parham, & Lane, 2012). This entails both understanding one's own background and beliefs and an athlete's background and beliefs and considering the role that these positions play within the relationship (Kontos & Breland-Noble, 2002).

Another step towards developing a deeper and more diverse cultural competence is through gaining formal knowledge of cultures and cultural differences (Schinke & Moore, 2011). Galloway (2009), early in his work with Muslim athletes in Kuwait, recognized that a cultural outsider may never fully understand the dominant Islamic traditions present in the community he had chosen to work in. Seeking to acquaint himself with the cultural and religious norms of the community, he sought out religious leaders and scholars. He found that, through discussions with these community leaders he was able to gain enough knowledge to help him avoid making offensive cultural and/or religious mistakes in his practice. He subsequently advised SPCs working in culturally dissimilar settings to use this approach when first becoming immersed in a new culture. This may be especially relevant when working in cultural settings where sport psychology is viewed in a negative light, with athletes preferring to seek advice from leaders within their religious communities (Ikulayo & Semidara, 2009). Coming to understand why athletes see sport psychology as a negative may help SPCs to develop different pathways to contribute to their success and well-being. Additionally, taking these steps will aid SPCs in coming to understand how they can work in tandem with spiritual and religious leaders to provide proper care for the athletes they work with.

Having developed one's personal understanding of spirituality, it is similarly important to recognize the individuality of each athlete and how the intersection of their various identities may cause them to differ from other members of their community (Sarkar et al., 2014). For example, although many Brazilian athletes may be devout Catholics, in times of stress they may rely on alternative spiritual elements and/or rituals, some of which may be connected to indigenous beliefs (Moraes & Salmela, 2009). To this end, engaging the athlete in a discussion about how they define their religious and spiritual beliefs is another necessary step for SPCs exploring spirituality within their practice. Importantly, athletes may not be interested in seeking out the most recent scientific operational definitions or taking these to define their own understanding. For some, their understanding may be dictated by their religious beliefs or backgrounds. That being said, attempting to incorporate spirituality prior to exploring the athlete's understanding of spirituality can potentially result in a grievous misunderstanding, especially when the practitioner's and athlete's understandings differ. This can lead to the failure of the intervention or consultation, while also damaging the trust and relationship the SPC has built with the athlete, through a lack of understanding of the athlete's core values (Balague, 1999). Consequently, understanding an athlete's spiritual (and religious) beliefs is an important first step in attempting to incorporate spirituality into sport psychology practice. One method of fostering a positive relationship and understanding is put forth by Egli and colleagues (2014), who found that SPCs benefited from letting athletes lead the discussion when sharing their spiritual beliefs so as not to impose their own beliefs from the outset. This way, the SPCs were able to use the athlete's own language, while also learning more about their beliefs and building rapport.

Despite the contention that spirituality and sport psychology do not mix, examples from other researchers have demonstrated how an athlete's spiritual nature could be used to enhance mental skills training or performance. Some common sport psychology tools, such as meditation, may even stem from spiritual practices and can be used to promote relaxation in athletes. For athletes who equate spirituality and religion, using religious verses, prayers, or songs can be implemented as self-affirming statements, motivational cues, or as part of a pre-performance routine (Egli et al., 2014; Hagan et al., 2019). Through these tools, SPCs can help athletes reach the optimal pre-performance states and subsequent experiences of transcendent or peak performance. Additionally, as discussed previously and highlighted by Greg Oden's quote above (Kravitz, 2019), spirituality has also been used as a coping mechanism for athletes and can help athletes reframe injuries as a time for reflection and an opportunity to learn how to persevere through adversity (Egli et al., 2014; Hagan et al., 2019; Hoffman, 1992; Ridnour & Hammermeister, 2008). Though Crust (2006) discussed both sides of the argument, that those who believe in psychology or spirituality will prefer to talk about psychological or spiritual issues, respectively, it is worth questioning if a difference exists, as long as the athlete continues to improve in a way that is meaningful and comfortable to them. Although there is still a common belief that SPCs may be able to suspend their beliefs when working with athletes, by becoming a reflexive practitioner, recognizing their own individuality and the individuality of the athlete(s) they work with, SPCs may earn the respect of spiritual and religious athletes (Sarkar et al., 2014).

Future Directions

There remains much to be explored regarding the relationship between spirituality, enhancing athletes' well-being, and subsequently improving sport performance. SPCs and researchers have been urged to consider the subjective individuality of each athlete, and this push has intensified with the increase in culturally informed scholarship that has developed into an area of research now termed cultural sport psychology (see Schinke, Blodgett, Ryba, Kao, & Middleton, 2019). However, despite one focal area of this research being the intersectionality of athlete identity (see Schinke et al., 2019), the inclusion of spirituality is still rarely present. This may be a result of spirituality often being cast as a "taboo" subject that is rarely discussed within graduate sport psychology programmes (Egli et al., 2014). One reason for this may be the "invisible nature" of spirituality. Within secular societies, the realm of what is considered "real" is dominated by what is visible, and, even when invisible identities such as spirituality (another example being sexuality) are discussed, it is often the visible markers, such as religious rituals, that are focused on (Alcoff, 2006). Perhaps owing to the invisible nature of spirituality, many certified mental performance consultants feel that spiritual matters fall outside the sphere of sport psychology work and would only be introduced if athlete-initiated (Egli et al., 2014). To further our understanding and bring about new ways of thinking about the relationship between spirituality and sport and what spirituality means to athletes, the use of qualitative methodologies (and methods) is promoted. Moving towards qualitative approaches will result in a deeper understanding of the subjective nature of ASCs, furthering our understanding of why they occur and how they impact well-being and performance (Watson & Nesti, 2005).

One line of research that may be enhanced by different ways of thinking about sport psychology practice, brought about by qualitative methodologies, may be the development of different strategies that can be used to better integrate spirituality into applied practice, with the aim of enhancing the mental health of the athletes sport psychology professionals work with. Although a strong sense of spirituality has been equated with a stronger ability to cope with adversity (e.g., Czech & Bullet, 2003; Ridnour & Hammermeister, 2008), there remains a lack of understanding of how spirituality impacts rates of mental ill-health among athletes. With the recent focus on athlete mental health in sport psychology (see Schinke, Stambulova, Si, & Moore, 2018), this seems an avenue that is ripe for exploration. This may involve exploring how athletes' spiritual (and religious) beliefs may be healthy and/or unhealthy, how dominant narratives in the sporting context may constrain an athlete's ability to express their spiritual beliefs, and to what extent collaboration with religious and spiritual leaders is necessary and beneficial (Sarkar et al., 2014).

Finally, further exploration into the role that formal religious beliefs and/or spiritual beliefs can play in helping athletes broaden the scope of their identities is an area of research that requires more attention. Correspondingly, understanding the cultural basis for athletes' religious and spiritual beliefs (and how these relate to each other) has rarely been explored. The taboo nature of spirituality within the dominant Euro-American approach in sport psychology has limited the extent to which spirituality has entered into the realm of sport psychology research and practice (Crust, 2006; Egli et al., 2014). At the very least, it is being proposed that sport psychologists bringing focus to this area of research, so that the concept of spirituality may begin to enter their discussions. This may provide a further impetus for SPCs to develop a more person-centred approach that helps athletes seeking to incorporate their spirituality into their performance enhancement strategies to feel comfortable in doing so, while also exploring its connection with their identity as both an athlete and a non-athlete.

Conclusion

The aim of this contribution was to provide readers with an overview of how spirituality has been explored and considered within sport psychology research and practice. Although we acknowledged that the constant construction of how spirituality and religiosity are conceptualized complicates how these are approached within sport, it is hoped that the following points have come across clearly: First, participating and competing in sport can bring about an altered state of consciousness in which one feels a sense of transcendence. The feelings associated with this state are subjective in nature and may be referred to as flow, peak performance, Zen, and/or feeling a greater sense of spirituality. Second, these experiences may be developed through rituals and routines that may or may not have religious affiliations. Third, although discussing spirituality with athletes may be uncomfortable for SPCs, the aim should be to develop a more person-centred approach that helps athletes to feel comfortable in examining and developing their identities, including their spiritual identities. A deeper sense of spirituality can aid athletes in times of adversity and transition and result in healthier athletes who feel a sense of purpose in their lives beyond the realm of sport. Fourth, integrating the ability to help athletes with their spiritual development requires an SPC to continuously be reflexive in how they engage with the athletes they work with, by critically reflecting on the services they provide and the way in which they are provided. SPCs are urged to move beyond viewing spirituality as a taboo subject and embrace the opportunity to empower athletes to develop their spiritual identity. Finally, there remains much to be explored and understood regarding spirituality and athletes' performance and well-being. It is advocated that researchers employ a diverse range of qualitative methodologies in their work with athletes with the aim of bringing about new and different ways of thinking about spirituality in sport.

References

Acevedo, E. O., Dzewaltowski, D. A., Gill, D. L., & Noble, J. M. (1992). Cognitive orientations of ultramarathoners. *The Sport Psychologist, 6*, 242–252.

Alcoff, L. M. (2006). *Visible identities: Race, gender, and the self.* Oxford, UK: Oxford University Press.

Anderson, J. (2013). Cathedrals of the surf zone: Regulating access to a space of spirituality. *Social and Cultural Geography, 14*, 954–972.

Balague, G. (1999). Understanding identity, value, and meaning when working with elite athletes. *The Sport Psychologist, 13*, 89–98.

Blodgett, A. T., Schinke, R. J., McGannon, K. R., & Fisher, L. A. (2015). Cultural sport psychology research: Conceptions, evolutions, and forecasts. *International Review of Sport and Exercise Psychology, 8*, 24–43.

Cooper, A. (1998). *Playing in the zone: Exploring the spiritual dimensions of sports* (1st ed.). Boston, MA: Shambhala.

Cotterill, S. (2010). Pre-performance routines in sport: Current understandings and future directions. *International Review of Sport and Exercise Psychology, 3*, 132–153.

Crust, L. (2006). Challenging the 'myth' of a spiritual dimension in sport. *Athletic Insight, 8*(2), 17–31.

Csikszentmihalyi, M. (1975). *Beyond boredom and anxiety.* San Francisco, CA: Jossey-Bass.

Czech, D. R., Wrisberg, C., Fisher, L., Thompson, C., & Hayes, G. (2004). The experience of Christian prayer in sport – An existential phenomenological investigation. *Journal of Psychology and Christianity, 23*, 3–11.

Czech, D. R., & Bullet, E. (2007). An explanatory description of Christian athletes' perceptions of prayer in sport: A mixed methodological study. *International Journal of Sports Science & Coaching, 2*, 49–56.

Danish, S., Fazio, R., Nellen, V., & Owens, S. (2002). Teaching life skills through sport: Commentary-based programs to enhance adolescent development. In B. Van Raalte & B. Brewer (Eds.), *Exploring sport and exercise psychology* (pp. 269–288). Washington, DC: American Psychological Association.

de Coubertin, P. (1935/2000). The philosophic foundation of modern Olympism. In N. Müller (Ed.), *Pierre de Coubertin 1863–1937 Olympism: Selected writings* (pp. 580–583). Lausanne, Switzerland: International Olympic Committee.

Douglas, K., & Carless, D. (2009). Abandoning the performance narrative: Two women's stories of transition from professional sport. *Journal of Applied Sport Psychology, 21*, 213–230.

Egli, T. J., Fisher, L. A., & Gentner, N. (2014). AASP-certified consultants' experiences of spirituality within sport psychology consultation. *The Sport Psychologist, 28*, 394–405.

Emmons, R. A. (2003). Personal goals, life meaning, and virtue: Wellsprings of a positive life. In C. L. M. Keyes & J. Haidt (Eds.), *Flourishing: Positive psychology and the life well-lived* (pp. 105–128). Washington, DC: American Psychological Association.

Fave, A. D., Bassi, M., & Massimini, F. (2003). Quality of experience and risk perception in high-altitude rock climbing. *Journal of Applied Sport Psychology, 15*, 82–98.

Galloway, S. (2009). A Canadian sport psychologist in Kuwait. In R. J. Schinke & S. J. Hanrahan (Eds.), *Cultural sport psychology* (pp. 155–167). Champaign, IL: Human Kinetics.

Gallwey, W. T. (2015). *The inner game of tennis: The ultimate guide to the mental side of peak performance*. London: Pan Macmillan.

Gamble, R., Hill, D. M., & Parker, A. (2013). Revs and psychos: Role, impact and interaction of sport chaplains and sport psychologists within English premiership soccer. *Journal of Applied Sport Psychology, 25*, 249–264.

Hagan, J. E., Jr., Schack, T., & Schinke, R. (2019). Sport psychology practice in Africa: Do culture-specific religion and spirituality matter? *Advances in Social Sciences Research Journal, 6*(3), 183–197.

Hill, K. L. (2001). *Frameworks for sport psychologists: Enhancing sport performance*. Champaign, IL: Human Kinetics.

Hochstetler, D. R. (2009). Striving towards maturity: On the relationship between prayer and sport. *Christian Education Journal, 6*, 325–336.

Hoffman, S. J. (1992). Religion in sport. In S. J. Hoffman (Ed.), *Sport and religion* (pp. 127–141). Champaign, IL: Human Kinetics.

Hood, R. W., Spilka, B., Hunsberger, B., & Gorsuch, R. (1996). *The psychology of religion* (2nd ed.). New York: Guilford Press.

Hyman, C., & Handal, P. J. (2006). Definitions and evaluation of religion and spirituality items by religious professionals: A pilot study. *Journal of Religion and Health, 45*, 264–282.

Ikulayo, P. B., & Semidara, J. A. (2009). Working with Nigerian athletes. In R. J. Schinke & S. J. Hanrahan (Eds.), *Cultural sport psychology* (pp. 169–177). Champaign, IL: Human Kinetics.

Jirásek, I. (2015). Religion, spirituality, and sport: From *religio athletae* toward *spiritus athletae*. *Quest, 67*, 290–299.

Kabat-Zinn, J. (2003). Mindfulness-based interventions in context: Past, present, and future. *Clinical Psychology: Science and Practice, 10*, 144–156.

Kontos, A. P., & Breland-Noble, A. M. (2002). Racial/ethnic diversity in applied sport psychology: A multicultural introduction to working with athletes of color. *The Sport Psychologist, 16*, 296–315.

Kravitz, B. (2019, July 3). Kravitz: It isn't all about basketball now for Greg Oden who is happy, healthy and sober. *The Athletic*. Retrieved from https://theathletic.com/1057877/2019/07/03/kravitz-it-isnt-all-about-basketball-now-for-greg-oden-who-is-happy-healthy-and-sober/

Lipscombe, N. (1999). The relevance of the peak experience to continued skydiving participation: A qualitative approach to assessing motivations. *Leisure Studies, 18*, 267–288.

Martens, R. (1979). About smocks and jocks. *Journal of Sport Psychology, 1*, 94–99.

Moraes, L. C., & Salmela, J. H. (2009). Working with Brazilian athletes. In R. J. Schinke & S. J. Hanrahan (Eds.), *Cultural sport psychology* (pp. 117–124). Champaign, IL: Human Kinetics.

Nakamura, J., & Csikszentmihalyi, M. (2014). The concept of flow. In M. Csikszentmihalyi (Ed.), *Flow and the foundations of positive psychology* (pp. 239–263). Chicago, IL: Springer.

Nesti, M. (2007). Persons and players: A psychological perspective. In J. Parry, S. Robinson, N. Watson, & M. Nesti (Eds.), *Sport and spirituality: An introduction* (pp. 135–150). New York: Routledge.

Nesti, M. S. (2011). Sporting recommendations for spiritual encounters: Delivering sport psychology inside the English Premier League. *Physical Culture and Sport Studies and Research, 52*, 14–21.

Plante, T. G. (2008). What do the spiritual and religious traditions offer the practicing psychologist? *Pastoral Psychology, 56*, 429–444.

Ravizza, K. H. (2002). A philosophical construct: A framework for performance enhancement. *International Journal of Sport Psychology, 33*, 4–18.

Ridnour, H., & Hammermeister, J. (2008). Spiritual well-being and its influence on athletic coping profiles. *Journal of Sport Behavior, 31*, 81–92.

Robinson, S. (2007). Spirituality: A story so far. In J. Parry, S. Robinson, N. J. Watson, & M. Nesti (Eds.), *Sport and spirituality: An introduction* (pp. 7–21). New York: Routledge.

Ryba, T. V., & Wright, H. K. (2005). From mental game to cultural praxis: A cultural studies model's implications for the future of sport psychology. *Quest, 57*, 192–212.

Sarkar, M., Hill, D. M., & Parker, A. (2014). Working with religious and spiritual athletes: Ethical considerations for sport psychologists. *Psychology of Sport and Exercise, 15*, 580–587.

Schinke, R. J., Blodgett, A. T., Ryba, T. V., Kao, S. F., & Middleton, T. R. F. (2019). Cultural sport psychology as a pathway to advances in identity and settlement research to practice. *Psychology of Sport and Exercise, 42*, 58–65.

Schinke, R. J., McGannon, K. R., Parham, W. D., & Lane, A. M. (2012). Toward cultural praxis and cultural sensitivity: Strategies for self-reflexive sport psychology practice. *Quest, 64,* 34–46.

Schinke, R. J., & Moore, Z. E. (2011). Culturally informed sport psychology: Introduction to the special issue. *Journal of Clinical Sport Psychology, 5,* 283–294.

Schinke, R. J., Stambulova, N. B., Si, G., & Moore, Z. (2018). International Society of Sport Psychology position stand: Athletes' mental health, performance, and development. *International Journal of Sport and Exercise Psychology, 16,* 622–639.

Scott-Hamilton, J., Schutte, N. S., & Brown, R. F. (2016). Effects of a mindfulness intervention on sports-anxiety, pessimism, and flow in competitive cyclists. *Applied Psychology: Health and Well-Being, 8,* 85–103.

Shahrokhi, H. A. (2013). *Talking to God and talking to self among Muslim athletes* (master's thesis). Retrieved from http://ir.lib.uth.gr/bitstream/handle/11615/44196/12262.pdf?sequence=1

Watson, N. J. (2007). Nature and transcendence: The mystical and sublime in extreme sports. In J. Parry, S. Robinson, N. J. Watson, & M. Nesti (Eds.), *Sport and spirituality: An introduction* (pp. 95–115). New York: Routledge.

Watson, N. J., & Czech, D. R. (2005). The use of prayer in sport: Implications for sport psychology consulting. *Athletic Insight, 7,* 26–35.

Watson, N. J., & Nesti, M. (2005). The role of spirituality in sport psychology consulting: An analysis and integrative review of literature. *Journal of Applied Sport Psychology, 17,* 228–239.

Zinnbauer, B. J., Pargament, K. I., Cole, D., Rye, M. S., Butter, E. M., Belavich, T. G., ... Kadar, J. L. (1997). Religion and spirituality: Unfuzzying the fuzzy. *Journal for the Scientific Study of Religion, 36,* 549–564.

45

STRESS AND WELL-BEING OF THOSE OPERATING IN GROUPS

Lee Baldock, Brendan Cropley, Stephen D. Mellalieu, and Rich Neil

Introduction

The influence of stress on the performance and well-being of sports performers has been a focal point of considerable academic attention (e.g., Hanton & Mellalieu, 2014; Neil, McFarlane, & Smith, 2016), with performers' potential to experience stress in their sport environments widely acknowledged (Hanton, Mellalieu, & Williams, 2015). Recently, the stress experiences of other key stakeholders in sport organizations (e.g., coaches, sport science staff) have also been a focus of researchers (e.g., Kerai, Wadey, & Salim, 2019; Olusoga, Butt, Hays, & Maynard, 2009). This research has recognized the potential demands (e.g., long working hours, internal/external expectations) associated with the roles these key stakeholders undertake to help athletes achieve optimal levels of performance (Wagstaff, 2019a, 2019b; Wagstaff, Gilmore, & Thelwell, 2015). The demands these key stakeholders encounter are accentuated by the notion that, alongside athletes, they themselves do not operate in isolation, but function within highly complex social groups and organizational environments in sport that may also have an influence on their own performance and well-being (Fletcher & Arnold, 2016). Yet, although athletes and other key stakeholders usually operate as part of groups in sport organizations, "groups and organisations don't behave, people do" (Wagstaff, 2019b, p. 1). It is through this perspective that stress and well-being in sport have been explored, with a focus on the individuals operating as parts of groups in sport organizations, rather than the impact of an individual's stress and well-being on others operating in the same group. This chapter will, therefore, critique the research on individuals' stress and well-being, but, where possible, attempt to highlight the potential implications that the stress and well-being of individuals can have on others within groups in sport organizations.

Although the developments of the literature on stress in sport have led to an increased consideration of the stress experiences of athletes and other key stakeholders operating in sport organizations (as opposed to solely athletes), the consequences of these experiences have generally been explored solely from a performance perspective. There appears to be a consensus, however, concerning the potential implications that stress has upon the well-being of those operating in sport (Neil, McFarlane, et al., 2016). To date, research into these concepts has been largely dichotomized, with the direct link between them receiving scant empirical consideration. Specifically, the impact of stress on well-being has tended to mainly be considered in relation to ill-being outcomes (e.g., burnout), and the potential impact of individual key stakeholder stress upon the well-being of themselves and their colleagues who operate within their group has largely been neglected. To address the recent advances in the study of stress in sport, and the limited attention paid to the impact of stress on the well-being of athletes and other key stakeholders in sport, this chapter seeks to: (a) provide an overview of the contemporary conceptualizations of stress and well-being in sport; (b) discuss the main developments in stress and well-being research in sport; and (c) offer considerations as to how researchers can seek a more comprehensive understanding of how stress may impact upon the well-being of those operating as part of groups within sport organizations.

Conceptualizing Stress in Sport

Early research exploring stress in sport focused solely on athlete experiences and was informed by different conceptualizations of the construct (Neil, Fletcher, Hanton, & Mellalieu, 2007). This resulted in stress-related terminology being operationalized differently across different studies, which can lead to confusion when one is attempting to collectively interpret findings. For example, stress has been described as an environmental stimulus, a response to a stimulus, and as an interaction between an athlete and the environment, sometimes interchangeably (Fletcher & Scott, 2010). Fletcher, Hanton, and Mellalieu (2006) highlighted the particular issue around this inconsistent utilization of the term stress, suggesting that the findings of such research were limited owing to a failure to distinguish between the causes and consequences of stress and the oversimplification of a complex process caused by failure to consider the cognitive-evaluative underpinnings of the stress experience. Based on these limitations, Fletcher et al. proposed a framework of stress to guide future research, which was informed by Lazarus and Folkman's (1984) transactional theory of stress and Lazarus's (1991) cognitive-motivational-relational theory of stress and emotion (CMRT).

Through their transactional theory, Lazarus and Folkman (1984) defined stress as, "An ongoing process that involves individuals transacting with their environments, making appraisals of the situations they find themselves in, and endeavouring to cope with any issues that may arise" (Fletcher et al., 2006, p. 329). According to transactional theory, individuals experience stressors (e.g., environmental demands, such as pressure to perform), to which they attribute relational meaning. Relational meaning is construed from the individual's relationship with the demand and the environment in which it is experienced, and it is represented by an ongoing process of cognitive evaluation (otherwise known as appraisal). According to Lazarus and Folkman, there are interconnected stages of appraisals: primary appraisal and secondary appraisal. Primary appraisal occurs when a stressor is considered to have the potential to harm the well-being of an individual. Here, it is proposed that stressors are viewed as a threat (i.e., one perceives the stressor as potentially damaging to one's goal, values, or beliefs), a challenge (i.e., one perceives the stressor as a positive obstacle towards their goal, values, or beliefs), or a harm/loss (i.e., a perception that damage to one's goal, values, or beliefs has occurred). Secondary appraisal refers to whether the individual believes that they possess the resources required to effectively cope with the stressor they encounter (Lazarus & Folkman, 1984). It is from this process of appraisal that an individual will then respond emotionally and, potentially, behaviourally, while selecting the *coping* strategies (where possible) to be employed to deal with the stressor encountered. If there is a perceived imbalance between the stressors experienced and an individual's appraisal of their available coping resources to manage the stressors (e.g., social support), the transaction results in strain, manifesting as negative emotional and, if the emotional experience is not controlled, negative behavioural responses. Whether an individual experiences further strain from this point is determined by how successful the coping strategy employed is within the context in which the stressor has occurred (Lazarus & Folkman, 1984).

Building on this body of work, Lazarus (1991) proposed the CMRT to better illuminate the synthesis of appraisal and emotion. Within this perspective, Lazarus suggested that, in environments that are stressful, the duration, intensity, and quality of an elicited emotion are dependent on the expectancies manifested by individuals in relation to the significance and potential outcome of an encounter for their well-being (i.e., stressor; Lazarus, 1999). As in the transactional theory of stress, these expectancies are suggested to be manifested by an individual's cognitive-evaluative reactions (appraisals) to stressors. However, Lazarus proposed that, within the primary appraisal, individuals may also view the transaction as a benefit (i.e., transaction has been beneficial to one's goals, values, or beliefs). Lazarus also stated that this primary appraisal is determined by three appraisal judgements: goal relevance, goal congruence, and the type of ego involvement of the individual (for a review, see Lazarus, 1999). In relation to an individual's perceived ability to cope, secondary appraisal is suggested to be comprised of cognitive-evaluative thoughts related to three areas: blame or credit, coping potential, and future expectations (Lazarus, 1999). It is such cognitive-evaluative thoughts that are posited to influence an individual's emotional responses, which, in the sporting context, can affect actual performance (Lazarus, 2000).

An Overview of Stress Research in Sport

In attempts to better understand the stress experiences of sport performers, many researchers adopting either the transactional theory of stress or CMRT have focused on exploring the main components underpinning the stress process in isolation (e.g., stressors, appraisal, responses, coping, or outcomes; e.g., Fletcher & Hanton, 2003; Thatcher & Day, 2008) and the relationships between these components to develop a more holistic understanding of the mechanisms underpinning the stress–emotion process (e.g., Neil, Bowles, Fleming, & Hanton, 2016; Neil, Hanton, Mellalieu, & Fletcher, 2011). This section will explore some of the key developments of this research by summarizing the main findings and discussing the potential impact of stress on the performance and well-being of different key stakeholders (e.g., athletes, coaches, support staff) operating as part of groups in sport organizations.

Early research exploring the transactional process of stress in sport focused specifically on athletes, who reported experiencing a wide range of potential stressors (e.g., performing poorly in practice, weak teammates) in relation to their sporting engagement (see Mellalieu, Neil, Hanton, & Fletcher, 2009). Subsequent research explored the origins of these stressors and, as a result, categorized demands as emanating from either competitive (i.e., demands primarily and directly associated with competitive performance – e.g., the standard of the opponent) or organizational (i.e., demands associated primarily and directly with the sports organization – e.g., travel) sources (e.g., Fletcher & Hanton, 2003; Woodman & Hardy, 2001). In exploring the prevalence of these different sources of stressors, the athletes in Hanton, Fletcher, and Coughlan's (2005) study recalled more stressors originating from organizational sources than competitive. Further, Hanton et al. found that, although their participants experienced the same competitive stressors, the participating athletes highlighted experiencing a number of different organizational stressors unique to their sport. These findings regarding the prevalence and uniqueness of organizational stressors have subsequently led researchers to explore organizational stress and its impact on sport performance and well-being outcomes, with the findings of this body of work discussed throughout this chapter.

Researchers also began to examine the stress experiences of those potentially termed as the "team behind the team", with coaches receiving significant consideration over the last decade (for a review, see Norris, Didymus, & Kaiseler, 2017). Following the approach of the athlete-stress literature, researchers initially explored the nature and sources of stressors experienced by coaches (e.g., Olusoga et al., 2009; Thelwell, Weston, Greenlees, & Hutchings, 2008) and found that coaches also reported experiencing a range of performance (related to themselves and their athletes) and organizational (e.g., environment, leadership, personal, and team) stressors in their roles. The stressors experienced by other key stakeholders in sport organizations have also been considered, with physiotherapists (e.g., Kerai et al., 2019) and sport psychologists (e.g., Fletcher, Rumbold, Tester, & Coombes, 2011) reporting experiencing a variety of performance and organizational stressors. Consequently, the range of stressors reported by key stakeholders in sport illuminates the potentially demanding environment within which they operate.

Beyond the identification of stressors, researchers have explored the coping strategies utilized by a range of elite and non-elite athletes (e.g., Didymus & Fletcher, 2014; Thelwell, Weston, & Greenlees, 2007) and coaches (e.g., Olusoga, Butt, Maynard, & Hays, 2010; Thelwell, Weston, & Greenlees, 2010). Thelwell et al. (2007) highlighted that elite athletes utilized numerous coping strategies to manage stressors both during (e.g., reappraising, blocking distraction, venting) and after (e.g., social support, self-reflection) performance, and emphasized that athletes experience stressors that are unique to their individual sports. Similar findings were also identified for coaches, with Thelwell et al. (2010) reporting that elite coaches utilized a range of *coping strategies* in their roles (e.g., reflection, venting, communicating with other coaches) to cope with performance and organizational stressors. Although research examining the coping strategies of other key stakeholders in sport is scant, sport psychologists have reported a greater prevalence towards the use of problem-focused coping strategies (Cropley et al., 2016). Despite this research providing insight into the strategies that key stakeholders adopt to cope with the stressors they experience, a lack of understanding exists around what is effective in manipulating their stress–emotion experiences positively for the benefit of performance and well-being.

When examining the coping strategies that performers adopt, many researchers have categorized them according to their function (for a review, see Nicholls & Polman, 2007). Some of the more prevalent strategies and categories reported include: cognitive (e.g., blocking distractions); behavioural (e.g., removing oneself from situation); problem-focused (e.g., increased effort); emotion-focused (e.g., venting); and avoidance-focused (e.g., behavioural disengagement; for reviews, see Nicholls & Polman, 2007; Norris, Didymus, & Kaiseler, 2017) strategies. In attempts to better understand the function of coping strategies beyond the aforementioned categorizations, Didymus and colleagues (e.g., Didymus, 2016; Didymus & Fletcher, 2014) identified that coping is an adaptive process (i.e., constantly changing in response to perceived environmental cues and available personal resources) and categorized coping strategies into coping families according to their adaptive function (e.g., dyadic coping, information-seeking, self-reliance). The adaptive nature of this conceptualization links to the dynamic process perspective of stress and emotion proposed in CMRT, as it aligns with the view that coping efforts may change as an individual appraises and responds to stressors over time.

Research has also examined athletes' appraisals of stressors. Findings from this work have indicated that athletes from a range of sports and levels (e.g., elite to non-elite) report threat, harm/loss, and challenge appraisals, with a range of situational properties of stressors (e.g., novelty, unpredictability, ambiguity) being reported as key determinants in the type of appraisal elicited (e.g., Dugdale, Eklund, & Gordon, 2002; Thatcher & Day, 2008). Focusing on athlete appraisals of organizational stressors, Hanton, Wagstaff, and Fletcher (2012) reported that athletes appraised the organizational stressors they experienced solely as threat or harm. Hanton et al.'s participants also reported a lack of perceived control over the organizational stressors they experienced and few coping resources to manage them. Collectively, these findings highlight the unpredictable nature of stressors, with those emanating from organizational sources being appraised as threatening owing to them being perceived as uncontrollable. Supplemented by a lack of resources to manage these demands, the implications for performance behaviour and well-being are potentially harmful.

To better represent the dynamic nature of the stress and emotion process, and to examine the impact of this process on performance behaviour, researchers began to move away from examining components of this process in isolation and adopt a more holistic approach to their inquiry (e.g., Neil et al., 2011; Neil, Bowles, et al., 2016; Miles, Neil, & Barker, 2016). Neil et al. (2011) considered the stressors, appraisals, emotional responses, and the role of further appraisals in the behavioural responses of elite and non-elite athletes. Neil et al. reported that, despite athletes initially negatively appraising the stressors they were experiencing, which was accompanied by negative emotional responses, many athletes reported a further level of appraisal represented by whether they perceived the initial appraisals and emotional responses to be facilitative or debilitative for performance. This further appraisal determined their subsequent performance behaviour. For example, when negative emotions were experienced and perceived as debilitative for performance, some athletes reported engaging in a range of negative behavioural responses (e.g., focusing on extraneous factors). In contrast, when the emotional response was interpreted as facilitative, this experience was associated with a range of positive behavioural responses (e.g., increases in motivation, effort, and focus). The studies of Neil, Bowles, et al. (2016) and Miles et al. (2016) supported and built upon these findings when examining temporally the stress and emotion experiences of non-elite and elite cricketers across different performances and prior to, and during, competition, respectively. Their collective findings highlighted that the participants experienced a range of reoccurring stressors at different times across competitions. Their findings also supported the fundamental tenets of CMRT, in that their participants' emotional and behavioural responses to stressors were suggested to be mediated by a continuous and ongoing process of appraisal over time, which was determined by the stressor's perceived impact on the participants' goal attainment. The participants also reported that these appraisals were influenced by their previous performances, levels of confidence, and their perceptions of control over stressors, which highlighted the adaptive nature of how appraisals of similar stressors may change over time.

For other key stakeholders in sport organizations, the scant existing literature considering the appraisal of stressors is limited to coaches. For example, Didymus (2016) examined the stressors, their situational properties, subsequent appraisals, and coping of elite coaches and found that the participants appraised the variety of stressors they experienced mainly as a threat or challenge and, to a lesser extent, as harm/loss or beneficial. These findings supported the tense-based conceptions of primary appraisal outlined in CMRT. Specifically, participants' threat and challenge appraisals arose only when they perceived future harm or benefit to occur from stressors, whereas harm/loss and benefit appraisals were reported only if the participants perceived that such impact had already occurred. Although the responses of coaches to stressors were not examined by Didymus, Olusoga et al. (2010) had highlighted previously that elite coaches reported psychological (e.g., negative cognitions and emotions), behavioural (e.g., negative body language), and physical (e.g., increased heart rate, shaking) responses to the stressors they experienced. Perhaps more importantly, the coaches in Olusoga et al.'s research reported that these responses influenced their performance behaviour (mainly negatively), and such responses could be projected on to their athletes. These findings have since led to studies identifying athlete and coach perspectives on coaches' responses to stressors (see Thelwell, Wagstaff, Chapman, & Kenttä, 2017; Thelwell, Wagstaff, Rayner, Chapman, & Barker, 2017). Collectively, the findings of these studies suggest that athletes are able to detect when coaches are experiencing stress via verbal and behavioural cues, and that the impact of coach stress on coach performance is mainly negative owing to the associated negative perceptions of competence, self-awareness, and coaching quality.

The study of other key stakeholders' responses to stress is limited and has also tended to be explored in relation to the impact on their performance. For example, Cropley et al. (2016) examined the responses of sport psychology practitioners when effectively and ineffectively coping with stressors. Cropley et al. found that effective coping led to positive beliefs (e.g., optimism, confidence), and ineffective coping led to negative beliefs (e.g., incompetence, distraction), which ultimately impacted on their performance. Given that coping ineffectively has been suggested to lead to responses (e.g., emotions) in coaches that may be detected by athletes and influence performance, this may also be the case for other individuals who operate within sport groups. Although limited in sport, research has found that emotions and affective states can be transferred from one individual to others in groups via emotional contagion and, subsequently, influence group behaviour (e.g., Barsade, 2002). Given that athletes and key stakeholders usually operate alongside each other as part of groups in sport, a range of potential consequences for the performance and well-being of group members may also exist should any athlete and/or stakeholder ineffectively cope with the stressors they experience. With this in mind, importance has been placed on key stakeholders in sport regulating their emotions and aligning them with the expectations of the organizations within which they operate (Wagstaff, Fletcher, & Hanton, 2012). In line with the tenets of emotional labour theory (see Hochschild, 1983), researchers have explored the potential outcomes for sport science support staff when adopting the emotional regulation strategy of emotional suppression (e.g., Hings, Wagstaff, Anderson, Gilmore, & Thelwell, 2018; Larner, Wagstaff, Thelwell, & Corbett, 2017). This limited body of research has found that, although suppressing emotional responses may lead to better professional outcomes (e.g., buy-in, better relationships), it may come at personal psychological cost and lead to outcomes associated with burnout (e.g., emotional exhaustion). Consequently, the responses of athletes and key stakeholders to the stressors they experience and their management of them may have performance and well-being implications not just for themselves, but also for other individuals they operate alongside in sport groups.

As highlighted throughout, the investigation of stress in sport has generally tended to refer to key stakeholders' acute responses to stressors and their impact on performance. Largely neglected, however, are the implications of the stress and emotional experience upon their well-being. Attention has, however, been afforded to ill-being indicators, such as *burnout*, which is considered to be a chronic, debilitating form of strain traditionally characterized by symptoms of emotional exhaustion, depersonalization, and a lack of personal accomplishment (Maslach, 1982). Burnout has been associated with a range of negative consequences for athletes and coaches (e.g., decreased motivation, job dissatisfaction and withdrawal, and decreased performance and well-being; Goodger, Gorely, Lavallee, & Harwood, 2007). Nevertheless, although we can assume that burnout may be an indicator of low well-being, the direct relationship between stress and well-being has received scant consideration in sport. This warrants attention, as the components of the stress–emotion process (e.g., appraisal, emotion, coping) may help explain well-being changes and provide a better understanding of how to enhance the well-being and performance of key stakeholders in sport groups.

Conceptualizing Well-Being

Although research has explored well-being in a range of populations for some time, only over the last decade has well-being been afforded consistent research attention in the sporting context (McNeil, Durand-Bush, & Lemyre, 2018). This attention seems to have mirrored the recent increase in wider public and government interest in well-being, with the majority of researchers in sport only previously paying lip-service to well-being when exploring related concepts (e.g., burnout; see Carson, Walsh, Main, & Kremer, 2018). When examining well-being, researchers have adopted different conceptualizations of well-being that have led several authors from different fields (and now sport) to take issue with the lack of consensus as to how well-being should be defined (e.g., Didymus, Rumbold, & Staff, 2019; Neil, McFarlane et al., 2016). Most researchers tend to agree that well-being is a global, subjective, multidimensional construct linked to happiness and is important for health, productivity, and job performance (e.g., Diener, 2009). Nevertheless, the issue remains of the lack of consensus as to which components actually constitute well-being, leading to a variety of approaches adopted by researchers to understand well-being.

Traditionally, research has adopted one of two distinct approaches to explore well-being: the hedonic or the eudaemonic approach (Ryan & Deci, 2001). The hedonic approach conceptualizes well-being as a subjective construct, comprised of life satisfaction, positive affect, and an absence of negative affect (Diener, Suh, Lucas, & Smith, 1999). Often referred to as subjective well-being, this conceptualization accentuates how outcomes of happiness, pleasure, and positive emotions best reflect well-being and includes cognitive (measured through life satisfaction) and affective (measured through both positive and negative affect) components (Neil, McFarlane, et al., 2016). Through subjective well-being, the hedonic conceptualization has received significant research attention in a range of fields (including sport), with its being consistently associated with positive mental and physical health outcomes and relationships and increased life expectancy (for a review, see Diener, 2009). However, advocates of the eudaemonic approach have raised issues about the concept of subjective well-being for its failure to account for the importance of positive human functioning on well-being, highlighting that life has to be meaningful and not solely pleasant (Ryan & Deci, 2001).

The eudaemonic approach proposes that well-being is determined by the realization of human potential, symbolized by personal growth and linked to individuals living and functioning in a way that is congruent with their core values (Ryan & Deci, 2001). Moreover, Ryff (1989) postulated that there are six defining components of eudaemonic well-being (often referred to as psychological well-being): self-acceptance, personal growth, purpose in life, positive relations with others, environmental mastery, and autonomy. With this in mind, Ryff and Singer (2008) suggested that, in order to experience self-realization, purposeful and goal-directed action towards satisfying these components is essential. Eudaemonic well-being, often examined via measures of vitality, has generally received less research attention than the hedonic approach despite being linked with positive health outcomes (i.e., reduced risk of disease, lower mortality; Neil, McFarlane, et al., 2016). That said, there are suggestions that, although contrasting approaches are proposed, well-being might be most aptly conceptualized in sport as a construct consisting of aspects of both eudaemonic and hedonic principles, as they refer to the process and outcome of well-being, respectively (cf. Lundqvist, 2011).

A plethora of research studies exists that explore well-being in sport, mainly through the hedonic and/or eudaemonic lenses (Neil, McFarlane, et al., 2016). Of these studies, the majority have explored well-being from an outcome perspective and through the premise that motivation plays a key role in predicting well-being (e.g., Stenling & Tafvelin, 2014). One theory of motivation consistently researched in relation to well-being is self-determination theory (SDT; Deci & Ryan, 1985). SDT proposes that there are three basic psychological human needs (autonomy, competence, and relatedness) that need fulfilling for an individual to experience psychological growth and well-being. There is obvious overlap with Ryff's defining components of eudaemonic well-being, such as autonomy, environmental mastery (competence), and positive relations (relatedness). However, Ryan and Deci (2001) also suggested that satisfying these needs can influence hedonic well-being through fostering life satisfaction and positive mood. Consequently, many studies have examined how a range of *environmental factors* (e.g., motivational climate) influence psychological need satisfaction and impact upon the well-being of athletes and coaches (e.g., Alcaraz, Torregrosa, & Viladrich, 2015; Cronin & Allen, 2018), or, alternatively, studies have considered the impact of *individual factors* (i.e., perceptions of stress) and their relationship with well-being (e.g., Bentzen, Lemyre, & Kenttä, 2016; Houltberg, Wang, Qi, & Nelson, 2018).

An Overview of Well-Being Research in Sport

A number of reviews of the extant literature on well-being in sport have been published. These have encapsulated: (a) a full review of the literature existing between 2003 and 2011 (see Lundqvist, 2011); (b) a review of well-being specific to sport organizations (see Neil, McFarlane, et al., 2016); and (c) a review of factors linked specifically to coach well-being (see Didymus et al., 2019). This section will provide an overview of some of the main research developments pertaining to the well-being of key stakeholders operating in sport groups.

Environmental Factors

Many of the recent research developments in well-being in sport have examined the influence of factors pertaining to the performance environment (mainly the coaching climate and the coach–athlete relationship) on athlete and coach well-being. Regarding the coaching climate, coaches' transformational leadership (e.g., Stenling & Tafvelin, 2014), coach autonomy support (e.g., Stenling, Lindwall, & Hassmen, 2015), coach-created perceived task-involving climates (e.g., Alvarez, Balguer, Castillo, & Duda, 2012), and life-skill-fostering coaching climates (e.g., Cronin & Allen, 2018) have all been found to be positively related to the well-being of athletes, mainly via the satisfaction of athletes' basic psychological needs. Linked to these findings, studies have also found that performance climates that satisfied the psychological needs of coaches (e.g., through job security and opportunities for professional development) led to increased coach psychological well-being, and that this increase positively predicted their perceived autonomy support to their athletes (e.g., Alcaraz et al., 2015; Stebbings, Taylor, Spray, & Ntoumanis, 2012). Moreover, Solstad, Ivarsson, Haug, and Ommundsen (2018) found that youth coaches providing higher levels of empowering coaching to their athletes over time reported higher levels of well-being in themselves. Collectively, these findings indicate that sport organizations should consider the working environments of coaches and the coaching education their coaches receive, as the environments they operate in and largely create can influence their own well-being and performance and, indirectly, the well-being and performance of their athletes.

The potential impact on well-being of the relationship between athletes, coaches, and others in the performance environment has also been considered. For example, athletes with an avoidance attachment style, who perceived that the coach–athlete relationship satisfied their basic psychological needs, reported increased hedonic and eudaemonic well-being (Felton & Jowett, 2013). Further, low and high levels of interpersonal conflict with coaches have been associated with athletes reporting positive and negative affect, respectively (Davis & Jowett, 2014). Further, Felton and Jowett (2017) examined athlete attachment with coaches and parents and found that increases in athletes' levels of anxious attachment led to reduced vitality and self-esteem and increased negative affect. Finally, Wayment and Walters (2017) examined the relationship between athletic connectedness, goal orientation, and well-being in college athletes. They found that having a social, emotional, and psychological connection to teammates had a significant and positive impact on athlete well-being, and that the sense of connectedness may be impacted positively and negatively by task- and ego-related motivation, respectively.

Individual Factors

Some of the recent developments in the well-being in sport literature have seen researchers examine a range of individual factors and their influence on the well-being of athletes and coaches. Indeed, self-compassion (Ferguson, Kowalski, Mack, & Sabiston, 2014), emotional intelligence (DeFreese & Barczak, 2017), and high trait self-esteem and low trait perfectionism (Lundqvist & Raglin, 2015) have all been found to positively relate to athlete well-being, with some of the relationships suggested to be determined by athletes being increasingly positive, persevering in their sport, and taking responsibility for their thoughts, emotions, and actions. Further, Houltberg et al. (2018) recently examined the impact that the narrative identities of athletes have on their well-being. Houltberg et al. found that a performance-based narrative (e.g., high perfectionism, fear of failure, contingent self-worth) was linked with symptoms associated with low levels of well-being (e.g., low levels of life satisfaction), whereas a purpose-based narrative identity (e.g., high purpose, global self-worth, positive view of self after sport) was associated with high levels of well-being. These findings may have potential implications for athletes and other key stakeholders in sport groups, given their often-joint pursuit of achieving athletic excellence.

The different types and motives of the goals set by athletes have also been explored in relation to well-being outcomes. For example, autonomous goals have been found to lead to increased effort, goal attainment, and, subsequently, positive affect (Smith, Ntoumanis, Duda, & Vansteenkiste, 2011), and more adaptive autonomous motives led to athletes exhibiting higher levels of vitality (Healey, Ntoumanis, Veldhuijzen van Zanten, & Paine, 2014). The ability of athletes to adapt and adjust to goals has also been examined, with Nicholls, Levy, Carson, Thompson, and Perry (2016) reporting that responses to unattainable goals via goal re-engagement positively predicted well-being, whereas goal disengagement negatively predicted well-being.

Researchers have also explored the individual factors associated with the well-being of coaches. For example, Bentzen et al. (2016) examined how changes in motivation and burnout impacted upon the well-being of high-performance coaches and found that high-performance coaches' levels of burnout and well-being across a competitive season increased and decreased, respectively. This was reportedly due to perceived environmental and subsequent negative psychological need satisfaction changes. Further, McNeil et al. (2018) explored how self-regulation capacity and perceptions of stress were linked with previously determined burnout and well-being profiles in high-performance coaches: thriving (low burnout, high well-being), depleted (relatively high burnout and relatively low well-being), and at-risk (relatively high burnout and relatively high well-being). Those "thriving" reported higher levels of self-regulation and lower perceived stress than those in the other profiles. These findings indirectly indicate the potential relationship between the ability to cope with stress and its impact on well-being.

Despite consistent reference to concepts linked to stress throughout the extant well-being literature, only recently has a study examined the direct relationship between stress components and well-being indicators in sport. Arnold, Fletcher, and Daniels (2017) quantitatively explored the effects of organizational stressors and the coping styles of athletes on positive and negative affect and performance satisfaction. Findings indicated that, for the organizational stressor categories of goals and development (e.g., coach feedback) and team and culture (e.g., attitudes and behaviour of the team), a positive relationship existed between the frequency and intensity of stressors experienced and increases in negative affect (an indicator of lower subjective well-being). Arnold et al. also found no significant relationship between the experience of organizational stressors and positive affect or performance satisfaction (both indicators of higher subjective well-being in sports performers). Although such findings are embryonic, they suggest that organizational stressors may lead to more negative well-being outcomes for sports performers. Further, the relationships between specific coping categories and the well-being of athletes were also explored, with positive relationships reported between problem-focused coping and positive affect, and emotion-focused coping and negative affect. Arnold et al. suggested that these relationships might be explained by athletes' perceptions of control over stressors and their ability/inability to take direct action to overcome them.

Despite being progressive and advancing our understanding, the study by Arnold et al. (2017) only identifies the relationship between certain stress components and hedonic well-being indicators. To explore further the direct relationship between the more holistic stress and emotion process and well-being, a broader representation of stress and emotion (including appraisals and emotional/behavioural responses) and the inclusion of eudaemonic well-being components may warrant consideration. Indeed, it is reasonable to assume that the experiences of stress and emotion throughout a day would affect the hedonic well-being of an individual, but this would likely be dependent on how well the individual managed the experiences and how impactful the experiences were on them – that is, whether the individual felt that: (a) they had control over the experiences; (b) they had mastered them; (c) they grew as a result of experiencing them; (d) they had a purpose due to experiencing them and/or coping effectively with them; (e) they had support to manage them; or (f) they had an increased acceptance of self owing to navigating them effectively. Consequently, for athletes and other key stakeholders operating in groups in sport organizations, managing their own stressful experiences and creating supportive group environments to help others cope and grow may have significant implications for their own stress and well-being experiences, as well as those of others.

Conclusion

Stress has been afforded significant research attention with athletes and now, more recently, with other key stakeholders in sport organizations (e.g., coaches, sport science staff). The findings of this research have highlighted the potential implications of these individuals' stress experiences for the performance and well-being of themselves and those they may operate alongside within groups. Nevertheless, research that examines well-being in sport is limited to athletes' and coaches' experiences, has been explored mainly from an outcome perspective, and has largely focused on how differing levels of satisfaction of basic psychological needs may lead to changes in well-being. These insights are helpful as they provide an understanding that athlete and coach perceptions of the climates they operate in and create influence well-being changes. Research is, however, yet to provide detailed conceptual underpinning for why these changes in well-being occur. Indeed, preliminary findings with athletes and coaches have highlighted the direct relationship between key aspects of the stress process (e.g., stressors, coping) and hedonic well-being predictors (e.g., negative and positive affect, levels of satisfaction) and indirectly proposed that perceptions of stress and regulation of thoughts, emotions, and behaviours are linked with well-being outcomes. However, such findings lack consistent empirical support, are limited to only some of the individual components of the stress–emotion process, and largely neglect their relationship with the *process* of well-being (e.g., the six components of eudaemonic well-being). Consequently, we echo the postulations of Didymus et al. (2019), who suggested that adopting theoretical frameworks such as Lazarus's (1991) CMRT to further explore the cognitive and affective elements associated with managing demanding sport environments may provide a more comprehensive understanding of the underlying mechanisms behind changes in well-being for athletes and other key stakeholders operating in sport groups. Given what we have covered in this chapter, we offer some considerations for future research in the area of stress and well-being in sport:

- Despite researchers adopting CMRT to examine stress in athletes and other key stake-holders in sport, limited research exists that explores all of the key components of the stress and emotion process. Research doing so may provide us with a more comprehensive understanding of this process and its implications for performance and well-being;
- The majority of research examining stress in sport has focused on the experiences of athletes and coaches. Given that other key stakeholders exist in sport groups and may have significant influence on the performance environment, researchers should continue to provide further insight into their stress experiences;
- A lack of detailed conceptual underpinning exists that explains why well-being levels may fluctuate over time. Researchers may advance our understanding of well-being in sport by examining the direct link between the stress and emotion process and the components constituting both hedonic and eudaemonic well-being in athletes and key stakeholders operating in sport groups;
- Little research has explored the impact of the stress and emotion experiences of athletes and key stakeholders in sport on those they operate alongside. Research attending to this area may provide us with a better understanding of the wider implications of stress on group performance and well-being.

References

Alcaraz, S., Torregrosa, M., & Viladrich, C. (2015). How coaches' motivations mediate between basic psychological needs and wellbeing/ill-being. *Research Quarterly for Exercise & Sport, 86*, 292–302.

Alvarez, M., Balaguer, I., Castillo, I., & Duda, J. (2012). The coach-created motivational climate, young athletes' well-being, and intentions to continue participation. *Journal of Clinical Sport Psychology, 6*, 166–179.

Arnold, R., Fletcher, D., & Daniels, K. (2017). Organisational stressors, coping, and outcomes in competitive sport. *Journal of Sports Sciences, 35*, 694–703.

Barsade, S. G. (2002). The ripple effect: Emotional contagion and its influence on group behavior. *Administrative Science Quarterly, 47,* 644–675.

Bentzen, M., Lemyre, P., & Kenttä, G. (2016). Changes in motivation and burnout indices in high-performance coaches over the course of a competitive season. *Journal of Applied Sport Psychology, 28,* 28–48.

Carson, F., Walsh, J., Main, L., & Kremer, P. (2018). High performance coaches' mental health and well-being: Applying the areas of work life model. *International Sport Coaching Journal, 5,* 293–300.

Cronin, L., & Allen, J. (2018). Examining the relationships among the coaching climate, life skills development and well-being in sport. *International Journal of Sports Science & Coaching, 13,* 815–827.

Cropley, B., Baldock, L., Mellalieu, S. D., Neil, R., Wagstaff, C. R. D., & Wadey, R. (2016). Coping with the demands of professional practice: Sport psychology consultants' perspectives. *The Sport Psychologist, 30*(3), 290–302.

Davis, L., & Jowett, S. (2014). Coach–athlete attachment and the quality of the coach–athlete relationship: Implications for athlete's well-being. *Journal of Sports Sciences, 32,* 1454–1464.

Deci, E., & Ryan, R. (1985). *Intrinsic motivation and self-determination in human behavior.* New York: Plenum.

DeFreese, J., & Barczak, N. (2017). A pilot study of trait emotional intelligence as a moderator of the associations among social perceptions, athlete burnout, and well-being in collegiate athletes. *Athletic Training and Sports Health Care, 9,* 246–253.

Didymus, F. (2016). Olympic and international level sports coaches' experiences of stressors, appraisals, and coping. *Qualitative Research in Sport, Exercise and Health, 9,* 214–232.

Didymus, F., & Fletcher, D. (2014). Swimmers' experiences of organizational stress: Exploring the role of cognitive appraisal and coping behaviors. *Journal of Clinical Sport Psychology, 8,* 159–183.

Didymus, F., Rumbold, J., & Staff, H. (2019). Promoting and protecting coach psychological well-being and performance. In R. Thelwell & M. Dicks (Eds.), *Professional advances in sports coaching: Research and practice* (pp. 261–276). Abingdon: Routledge.

Diener, E. (2009). Subjective well-being. In E. Diener (Ed.), *Social indicators of research series. The science of well-being* (pp. 11–58). New York: Springer.

Diener, E., Suh, E., Lucas, R., & Smith, H. (1999). Subjective well-being: Three decades of progress. *Psychological Bulletin, 125,* 276–302.

Dugdale, J. R., Eklund, R. C., & Gordon, S. (2002). Expected and unexpected stressors in major international competition: Appraisal, coping, and performance. *The Sport Psychologist, 16,* 20–33.

Felton, L., & Jowett, S. (2013). Attachment and well-being: The mediating effects of psychological needs satisfaction within the coach-athlete and parent-athlete relational contexts. *Psychology of Sport and Exercise, 14,* 57–65.

Felton, L., & Jowett, S. (2017). A self-determination theory perspective on attachment, need satisfaction, and well-being in a sample of athletes: A longitudinal study. *Journal of Clinical Sport Psychology, 11,* 304–323.

Ferguson, L., Kowalski, K., Mack, D., & Sabiston, C. (2014). Exploring self-compassion and eudaimonic well-being in young women athletes. *Journal of Sport & Exercise Psychology, 36,* 203–216.

Fletcher, D., & Arnold, R. (2016). Stress in sport: The role of the organizational environment. In C. R. D. Wagstaff (Ed.), *An organizational psychology of sport: Key issues and practical applications* (pp. 83–100). Abingdon: Routledge.

Fletcher, D., & Hanton, S. (2003). Sources of organizational stress in elite sports performers. *The Sport Psychologist, 17,* 175–195.

Fletcher, D., Hanton, S., & Mellalieu, S. (2006). An organizational stress review: Conceptual and theoretical issues in competitive sport. In S. Hanton & S. D. Mellalieu (Eds.), *Literature reviews in sport psychology* (pp. 321–374). New York: Nova Science.

Fletcher, D., Rumbold, J., Tester, R., & Coombes, M. (2011). Sport psychologists' experiences of organizational stressors. *The Sport Psychologist, 25,* 363–381.

Fletcher, D., & Scott, M. (2010). Psychological stress in sports coaches: A review of concepts, research, and practice. *Journal of Sports Sciences, 28,* 127–137.

Goodger, K., Gorely, T., Harwood, C., & Lavallee, D. (2007). Burnout in sport: A systematic review. *The Sport Psychologist, 21,* 127–151.

Hanton, S., Fletcher, D., & Coughlan, G. (2005). Stress in elite sport performers: A comparative study of competitive and organizational stressors. *Journal of Sports Sciences, 23,* 1129–1141.

Hanton, S., & Mellalieu, S. D. (2014). Coping with stress and anxiety. In A. D. Papaioannou & D. Hackfort (Eds.), *Routledge companion to sport and exercise psychology* (pp. 428–443). London: Routledge.

Hanton, S., Mellalieu, S. D., & Williams, J. (2015). Understanding and managing stress in sport. In J. Williams & V. Krane (Eds.), *Applied sport psychology: Personal growth to peak performance* (7th ed., pp. 207–239). New York: McGraw Hill.

Hanton, S., Wagstaff, C. R. D., & Fletcher, D. (2012). Cognitive appraisals of stressors encountered in sport organizations. *International Journal of Sport and Exercise Psychology, 10*, 276–289.

Healey, L., Ntoumanis, N., Veldhuijzen van Zanten, J., & Paine, N. (2014). Goal striving and well-being in sport: The role of contextual and personal motivation. *Journal of Sport & Exercise Psychology, 36*, 446–459.

Hings, R., Wagstaff, C. R. D., Anderson, V., Gilmore, S., & Thelwell, R. (2018). Professional challenges in elite sports medicine and science: Composite vignettes of practitioner emotional labor. *Psychology of Sport and Exercise, 35*, 66–73.

Hochschild, A. (1983). *The managed heart.* Berkeley, CA: University of California Press.

Houltberg, B., Wang, K., Qi, W., & Nelson, C. (2018). Self-narrative profiles of elite athletes and comparisons on psychological well-being. *Research Quarterly for Exercise and Sport, 89*, 354–360.

Kerai, S., Wadey, R., & Salim, J. (2019). Stressors experienced in elite sport by physiotherapists. *Sport, Exercise, and Performance Psychology.* Advance online publication. doi:10.1037/spy0000154.

Larner, R. J., Wagstaff, C. R. D., Thelwell, R. C., & Corbett, J. (2017). A multistudy examination of organizational stressors, emotional labor, burnout, and turnover in sport organizations. *Scandinavian Journal of Medicine and Science in Sports, 27*, 2103–2115.

Lazarus, R. (1991). Cognition and motivation in emotion. *American Psychologist, 46*, 352–367.

Lazarus, R. (1999). *Stress and emotion: A new synthesis.* New York: Springer.

Lazarus, R. (2000). How emotions influence performance in competitive sports. *The Sport Psychologist, 14*, 229–252.

Lazarus, R., & Folkman, S. (1984). *Stress, appraisal, and coping.* New York: Springer.

Lundqvist, C. (2011). Well-being in competitive sports – The feel-good factor? A review of conceptual considerations of well-being. *International Review of Sport & Exercise Psychology, 4*, 109–127.

Lundqvist, C., & Raglin, J. (2015). The relationship of basic need satisfaction, motivational climate and personality to well-being and stress patterns among elite athletes: An exploratory study. *Motivation and Emotion, 39*, 237–246.

Maslach, C. (1982). *The cost of caring.* Englewood Cliffs, NJ: Prentice Hall.

McNeil, K., Durand-Bush, N., & Lemyre, P. (2018). Thriving, depleted, and at-risk Canadian coaches: Profiles of psychological functioning linked to self-regulation and stress. *International Sport Coaching Journal, 5*, 145–155.

Mellalieu, S. D., Neil, R., Hanton, S., & Fletcher, D. (2009). Competition stress in sport performers: Stressors experienced in the competition environment. *Journal of Sports Sciences, 29*, 729–744.

Miles, A. J., Neil, R., & Barker, J. B. (2016). Preparing to take the field: A qualitative exploration of stress, emotion, and coping in cricket. *The Sport Psychologist, 30*, 101–112.

Neil, R., Bowles, H., Hanton, S., & Fleming, S. (2016). The experience of competition stress and emotion within cricket. *The Sport Psychologist, 30*, 76–88.

Neil, R., Fletcher, D., Hanton, S., & Mellalieu, S. D. (2007). (Re)conceptualizing competition stress in sport performers. *Sport & Exercise Psychology Review, 3*, 23–29.

Neil, R., Hanton, S. D., Mellalieu, S., & Fletcher, D. (2011). Competition stress and emotions in sport performers: The role of further appraisals. *Psychology of Sport and Exercise, 12*, 460–470.

Neil, R., McFarlane, H., & Smith, A. (2016). Positive wellbeing in sport organizations. In C. R. D. Wagstaff (Ed.), *The organizational psychology of sport: Key issues and practical applications* (pp. 101–119). London: Routledge.

Nicholls, A., Levy, A., Carson, F., Thompson, M., & Perry, J. (2016). The applicability of self-regulation theories in sport: Goal adjustment capacities, stress appraisals, coping, and well-being among athletes. *Psychology of Sport & Exercise, 27*, 47–55.

Nicholls, A., & Polman, R. (2007). Coping in sport: A systematic review. *Journal of Sports Sciences, 25*, 11–31.

Norris, L., Didymus, F., & Kaiseler, M. (2017). Stressors, coping, and well-being among sports coaches: A systematic review. *Psychology of Sport & Exercise, 33*, 93–112.

Olusoga, P., Butt, J., Hays, K., & Maynard, I. (2009). Stress in elite sports coaching: Identifying stressors. *Journal of Applied Sport Psychology, 21*, 442–459.

Olusoga, P., Butt, J., Maynard, I., & Hays, K. (2010). Stress and coping: A study of world class coaches. *Journal of Applied Sport Psychology, 22*, 274–293.

Ryan, R., & Deci, E. (2001). On happiness and human potentials: A review of research on hedonic and eudaimonic well-being. *Annual Review of Psychology, 52*, 141–166.

Ryff, C. (1989). Happiness is everything, or is it? Explorations on the meaning of psychological well-being. *Journal of Personality and Social Psychology, 57*, 1069–1081.

Ryff, C., & Singer, B. (2008). Know thyself and become what you are: A eudaimonic approach to psychological well-being. *Journal of Happiness Studies, 9*, 13–39.

Smith, A., Ntoumanis, N., Duda, J., & Vansteenkiste, M. (2011). Goal striving, coping, and well-being: A prospective investigation of the self-concordance model in sport. *Journal of Sport & Exercise Psychology, 33*, 124–145.

Solstad, B., Ivarsson, A., Haug, E., & Ommundsen, Y. (2018). Youth sport coaches' well-being across the season: The psychological costs and benefits of giving empowering and disempowering sports coaching to athletes. *International Sport Coaching Journal, 5*, 124–135.

Stebbings, J., Taylor, I., Spray, C., & Ntoumanis, N. (2012). Antecedents of perceived coach interpersonal behaviors: The coaching environment and coach psychological well and ill-being. *Journal of Sport & Exercise Psychology, 34*, 481–502.

Stenling, A., Lindwall, M., & Hassmen, P. (2015). Changes in perceived autonomy support, need satisfaction, motivation, and well-being in young elite athletes. *Sport, Exercise, and Performance Psychology, 4*, 50–61.

Stenling, A., & Tafvelin, S. (2014). Transformational leadership and well-being in sports: The mediating role of need satisfaction. *Journal of Applied Sport Psychology, 26*, 182–196.

Thatcher, J., & Day, M. C. (2008). Re-appraising stress appraisals: The underlying properties of stress in sport. *Psychology of Sport & Exercise, 9*, 318–335.

Thelwell, R., Wagstaff, C. R. D., Chapman, M., & Kenttä, G. (2017). Examining coaches' perceptions of how their stress influences the coach–Athlete relationship. *Journal of Sports Sciences, 35*, 1928–1939.

Thelwell, R., Wagstaff, C. R. D., Rayner, A., Chapman, M., & Barker, J. (2017). Exploring athletes' perceptions of coach stress in elite sport environments. *Journal of Sports Sciences, 35*, 44–55.

Thelwell, R., Weston, N., & Greenlees, I. (2007). Batting on a sticky wicket: Identifying sources of stress and associated coping strategies for professional cricket batsmen. *Psychology of Sport and Exercise, 8*, 219–232.

Thelwell, R., Weston, N., & Greenlees, I. (2010). Coping with stressors in elite sport: A coach perspective. *European Journal of Sport Science, 10*, 243–253.

Thelwell, R., Weston, N., Greenlees, I., & Hutchings, N. (2008). Stressors in elite sport: A coach perspective. *Journal of Sports Sciences, 26*, 905–918.

Wagstaff, C. R. D. (2019a). A commentary and reflections on the field of organizational sport psychology. *Journal of Applied Sport Psychology, 31*, 134–146.

Wagstaff, C. R. D. (2019b). Taking stock of organizational psychology in sport. *Journal of Applied Sport Psychology, 31*, 1–6.

Wagstaff, C. R. D., Fletcher, D., & Hanton, S. (2012). Positive organizational psychology in sport. *International Review of Sport and Exercise Psychology, 5*, 87–103.

Wagstaff, C. R. D., Gilmore, S., & Thelwell, R. (2015). Sport medicine and sport science practitioners' experiences of organizational change. *Scandinavian Journal of Medicine and Science in Sport, 25*, 85–98.

Wayment, H., & Walters, A. (2017). Goal orientation and well-being in college athletes: The importance of athletic social connectedness. *Journal of Sports Sciences, 35*, 2114–2120.

Woodman, T., & Hardy, L. (2001). A case study of organizational stress in elite sport. *Journal of Applied Sport Psychology, 13*, 207–238.

46

TRAUMA

The Invisible Tattoos

William D. Parham

Introduction

Illuminated in the following narrative are specific and myriad ways trauma manifests in the lives of athletes, both domestic and global. The compelling and complex confluence of variables that frame individual experiences of trauma are best understood when viewed through multiple contextual lenses, including environmental, familial, relational, cultural, social, political, and other dimensions of individual identity and lived experiences. The profound and often unfathomed impact that traumatic experiences can have on the lives of individuals, across the developmental continuum, will be highlighted. This narrative also doubles as an invitation for coaches, certified athletic trainers, strength and conditioning personnel and others in an athlete's circle of influence to learn how to spot trauma-impacted warning signs in athletes with whom they work. Ways of responding appropriately and with care and sensitivity to athletes whose lives have been impacted by trauma will be emphasized. Lastly, implications for creating an expanded research agenda relative to re-examining experiences of trauma within athletic communities will be suggested.

Historical Backdrop

Academic and applied approaches and practices relative to trauma and mental well-being enjoy histories that date back to the late 19th century (Ringel, 2012). A French physician, Jean Martin Charcot, studied hysteria in women and hypothesized a link between trauma and the expression of emotional pain and suffering through hysteria. Charcot's work influenced many, including his student Pierre Janet and Sigmund Freud and Josef Breuer. Pierre Janet asserted the belief that hypnosis, as an intervention, fostered a decrease in patient symptoms of trauma. Freud and Breuer argued that sexual abuse of women contributed to an altered state of consciousness labelled subsequently as dissociation. Fast forward, and the establishment of the first suicide hotline in San Francisco, California, in early 1900, the profession of psychiatry's observation of soldiers returning from World War I with "shell shock" (known today as post-traumatic stress disorder), Lindemann's (1944) scholarship centring on survivors of a Boston nightclub fire that produced his stage-based articulation of survivors' grief and the component parts of crisis intervention, Krystal's (1968) work with concentration camp survivors and their management of traumatic experiences, and Lifton's (1973) work on veterans returning from the

Vietnam War all represent examples of scholarship and applied practices that collectively and sequentially advanced the academic discourse and clinical interventions relative to trauma (Ringel & Brandell, 2012).

Defining Terms

Definitions of trauma (e.g., National Institute of Mental Health (NIMH), Centers for Disease Control and Prevention (CDC), Substance Abuse and Mental Health Services Administration (SAMHSA)) vary depending on many factors, including, but not limited to, government agencies as authors, the academic discipline (e.g., psychology, sociology, anthropology, medicine) framing the theories, conceptual premises, key principles, and research agendas of scholars pursuing this area of inquiry (Levers, 2012). With the foregoing as backdrop, scholars across disciplines pursuing trauma as an area of investigative inquiry agree, nonetheless, with the observation that, whether it is experienced individually, relationally, within a community, regionally, or globally, trauma is a very personal and complex human experience.

Additionally, scholars agree that trauma is a situation-resultant, deeply personal, uniquely nuanced, intricately emotional, and violent proprioceptive interruption of a person's physical, psychological, and existential being. Trauma represents experiences that cannot be unseen, unfelt, or unremembered. Further, traumatic experiences often exhaust the intrapersonal resources and self-protective boundaries used as tailored safeguards when responding to life's ups and downs. This poignant, keenly distressing, stark, surreal, and instantly dramatic shift in personal reality and safety represents the ink that etches an invisible tattoo of remembrance that consequentially influences the degree to which survivors decide to embrace relational, familial, educational, economic, and other life challenges.

Caution and Contexts

Trauma undeniably and indelibly impacts the "whole person" – body, mind, emotions, and spirit – and represents equal opportunity experiences relative to its sequel repercussions across dimensions of age, gender, culture, race, ethnicity, sexual identity, disability, religion, and social class (Brown, 2008). A compelling and complex confluence of variables frame individual experiences of trauma and, collectively, can be best understood when viewed through multiple contextual lenses, including environmental, familial, relational, cultural, social, political, and other dimensions of individual identity and lived experiences. Bronfenbrenner and Ceci's bioecological model (1994) is offered as a way of framing big-picture understanding and appreciation of events such as trauma and its potential wide and adverse impact on individuals and the communities where they reside. In brief, the bioecological model invites consideration that human development is influenced by a complex interaction between individuals and their environments. Further, environmental variables including, but not limited to, parents, family, community, school systems, spiritual practices, and the media in all its manifestations impact the course and trajectory of development. The complex interaction between athletes and the environments and people who surround them, including other athletes, coaches, administrators, certified athletic trainers, strength and conditioning staff, boosters, and devoted fans, is important in this regard.

Conceptual Templates

Familiarity with models of human growth and development become critical prerequisites for coaches, certified athletic trainers, strength and conditioning personnel, and others in the athlete's circle of influence relative to understanding and appreciating traumatic experiences. Researchers who explore and examine the treasures and the trials experienced inevitably across the developmental spectrum remind us of the critical importance of the formative nature of early childhood (Miller, 2016). There is a shared understanding among lifespan development scholars that infancy, toddler, pre-school, and early childhood, collectively, set the stage for how adolescents, adults, and the elderly subsequently approach, manage, and reconcile stage-relevant challenges. During early and formative years, critical competencies including, but not limited to cognitive, social-emotional, and physical, are learned, developed, and synthesized. Equally important during these formative years are the development, honing, and sharpening of insights, perspectives, and interpretive abilities used synergistically and in self-protective ways to navigate life's journey. Exposure to trauma during the formative years contributes to neurodevelopment disruption; impairment of social, emotional, and cognitive abilities; adoption of health-risk behaviours; development of disease, substance abuse, disabilities, and social problems; and premature death (Felitti et al., 1998).

Neurocognitive development scholars (Stien & Kendall, 2003), for example, advance positions that early life stressors can produce adaptive neurochemical and neurobiological changes that persist across time. Related, these scholars also suggest that traumatic responses impact a non-exhaustive list of physiological responses including, mood, gastrointestinal and temperature regulation, nervousness, sleep disturbances, hypervigilance, and thought processing.

Early conversations and discourse within a developmental framework relative to trauma used Sigmund Freud's assertions and propositions, though subsequently questioned, as conceptual templates for understanding personal responses to traumatic events (Levers, 2012). Freud's articulations of "repression", the process of pushing traumatic responses into forgetfulness, and "disassociation", compartmentalizing traumatic memories, are particularly relevant (Bellig, 1999). Josef Breuer, along with Sigmund Freud, advanced the concept of hysteria as relevant to understanding responses to traumatic events. Freud also advanced theories of seduction and fantasy (Oedipal and Electra complexes) as frames for particularly understanding sexual trauma. Freudian formulations gave rise to the notions of "triggers" (e.g., auditory, visual, tactile, olfactory, and relational), stimuli that emotionally unearth buried memories that are sometimes thought to have been forgotten but, surprisingly, are very much alive.

Other models and theories of human growth and development, including, Jean Piaget's theory about infant development, attachment theory advanced by John Bowlby, Erik Erikson's eight-stage task resolution model, Vygotsky's theory of social development, and social learning theory promoted by Bandura, collectively represent additional appropriate conceptual premises within which to situate, understand, and appreciate the day-to-day realities and lived experiences of persons experiencing trauma (Miller, 2016). Collectively, these developmental theories represent contextual frames for understanding age-expected and -appropriate responses of athletes who are survivors of trauma while developing and honing sport-related activity.

Responding to Trauma

Responding to athlete survivors of trauma with compassion, sensitivity, and humility also demands of coaches, certified athletic trainers, strength and conditioning personnel, and others in the athlete's circle of influence that they develop conversant knowledge about theories and models of trauma. These equally important foci help to sculpt an awareness of the nuanced details that define individual and subjective, as well as shared, experiences of trauma and its aftermath. In this regard, for example, are the seminal works of Judith L. Herman (1997), who characterizes trauma experiences as terror and shattered trust. Christine Courtois and Julian Ford (2013) advanced the conversation about complex trauma particularly in situations of incest and domestic violence. Peter Levine (2010) asserted that trauma is physiological, and healing from traumatic experiences is facilitated by self-regulating bodily sensation. In short, abundant scholarship focusing on trauma exists and provides both foundational insights into the life-altering nature of early-age as well as later-age trauma experiences and evidence-based, age-appropriate interventions goal-directed to managing the emotional aftermath and paving the way for healing.

Though a unified theory of trauma remains elusive, common agreement exists relative to acknowledging that varying degrees of emotional, physical, and sometimes existential suffering represent by-products of individual and subjective experiences of trauma. Bigger-picture perspectives of trauma, as well as appreciation for the multiple and intersecting contextual parameters characteristic of each traumatic experience, are best captured when culture, gender, race, ethnicity, social class, disability, sexual identity, and other dimensions of personal identity are factored into the must-know-to-be-effective equation of support (Brown, 2008).

Worthy of consideration is the observation that trauma comes in many forms, and evidence of its aftermath lingers in the long term, sometimes lifelong. Trauma can spawn from person-made situations including, but not limited to, community, school, domestic, transportation (automobile, aeroplane), technological (cyber-attacks), industrial, and medical (traumatic brain injury, spinal cord injury) violence. Trauma also is set in motion by nature-made events including geophysical (earthquakes, landslides), hydrological (avalanches, floods), climatological (extreme temperature, wildfires), biological (diseases, epidemics) and meteorological (storms, cyclones).

Responding to athletes with compassion, sensitivity, and humility as persons, before performers, invites those in the athlete's circle of influence (e.g., coaches, certified athletic trainers, nutritionists, strength and conditioning personnel) to anticipate that athletes with whom they are working and who, on the surface, appear to be doing well, may actually be survivors, directly or indirectly, of any one or a combination of the aforementioned trauma-resultant situations. For example, it is not uncommon to learn that athletes have committed to their sports and to perfecting their craft partly because of their emotional need to escape early-age horrors and fear of domestic violence, family systems with alcohol and substance abuse, or community or school violence that they either witnessed or experienced directly (Collins & MacNamara, 2012; Hardy & Warr, 2017; Howells & Fletcher, 2015; Savage, Collins, & Cruickshank, 2016; Schinnerer, 2018). Using their time, focus, and abilities to pay attention to details as a way of coping emotionally with the difficult-to-forget images of abuse, neglect, or other traumas, including life-changing injuries, are not uncommon stories to hear from athletes whose personal and sport performances look good. Offered for consideration is the observation that traumatic events are often secondary to the life-altering adjustments that need to be made by the athlete and those in their inner circle they hold closely.

International athletes who have been exposed to situations such as war, political unrest, epidemics, or refugee exodus from their homeland, though these experiences are not often or easily talked about, nonetheless may be at risk for compromised play and performing at levels lower than expected by others as well as themselves. Data regarding female and male sexual assault (Black et al., 2011) suggest that 1 in 5 women and 1 in 71 men will be raped at some point in their lives, and that 91% of victims/survivors of rape and sexual assault are women, and 9% are men. These data are alarming, the tip of the proverbial iceberg, and invite serious reflection on and receptive delicacy with respect to relational dynamics that develop and persist between athletes and their service providers.

It is important to note that an athlete's apparent survival and successful integration of their past into current personal and athletic successes should not be interpreted as meaning that their invisible tattoo of trauma is now erased and no longer able to be triggered. Nothing could be further from the truth. It is simply lying dormant, ripe for activation by any number of known, as well as off-the-radar, experiences.

The CDC/Kaiser ACE Study

The CDC/Kaiser Permanente Adverse Childhood Experiences (ACE) study (Felitti et al., 1998) is apropos to these latter observations. It is, arguably, the largest-scale study (approximately 17,500 subjects) relative to understanding the short- and longer-term consequences of experiencing early-age trauma. The CDC/Kaiser Permanente ACE study has provided a sneak peek into the lives of a diverse cross-section of men and women who, on the surface, appear to be doing well and managing life on their own terms.

The study invites consideration that abuse (e.g., emotional, physical, and sexual), household challenges (e.g., mother treated violently, substance abuse, parental separation, family member went to prison), and neglect (e.g., emotional and physical) portray the profiles of two-thirds of the study participants who report at least one adverse childhood experience. Additionally, approximately 20% of the study participants reported three or more adverse childhood experiences. Further, the study strongly suggested that cumulative adverse childhood experiences and childhood stress are strongly related to consequential adverse health and well-being outcomes throughout every stage of development. The high burden of exposure to life adversities, including racism, adds to the impact of trauma (Liu et al., 2015).

When applied to the system of athletics, whether club, high school, collegiate, professional, or elite, the CDC/Kaiser Permanente ACE study offers opportunities to see, understand, and appreciate athletes in a broader, whole-person framework. The ACE study has clear implications for athletes. The applicability of this study for coaches, certified athletic trainers, nutritionists, sport medicine physicians, sport psychology professionals, athletic department and team executive leadership, and team owners is equally clear and represents the proverbial elephant in the room, clouding the wider contextual lens of insight relative to seeing, understanding, and appreciating a whole-person portrait of each of these persons behind their respective performances.

Salt in the Wounds: Collusion as an Element of Trauma

The world of athletics becomes vulnerable to collusion when held loosely accountable for its actions, motivated to find and manipulate systemic loopholes, and fuelled by high-octane win-at-all-cost ambitions. Broadly defined, collusion is a relational experience of betrayal characterized by secret pacts goal-directed to cheating, lying, deceiving, and taking advantage of more vulnerable "prey" using perceived or real power to humiliate and intimidate. Collusion is progressive and corrosive, can be short- or longer-term, and results often in the victim/survivor feeling confused, in disbelief, unsafe, afraid to come forward to report the ruthless transgressions, and traumatized. Multiple aggressions, transgressions, sexual abuse, and systemic betrayal of hundreds of minors over decades were seen in arguably the largest sexual abuse scandal in sports. The highly publicized behind-the-scenes stories of USA Gymnastics brought a stark reality to a dark side of athletic competition

(Gervis & Dunn, 2004; Stirling & Kerr, 2009, 2013, 2014). The betrayal of trust, promised safety and protection, and reverence for human life, by multiple persons associated with the organization represents the salt in the wounds of more than 350 survivors who were simultaneously being sexually abused under the guise of recognized medical practice by a licensed physician now serving prison time. This two-fisted punch has likely set in motion a long-term, multipart, complex journey of healing for the gymnasts who were directly assaulted, the larger domestic and global gymnastics community, and the support systems (e.g., family, friends) who embrace the survivors.

At one time, Penn State University was, arguably, one of the more storied collegiate football teams in America prior to its fall from grace. Jerry Sandusky and the systemic collusion that allowed his sexual abuse of minors to continue for several year jettisoned Penn State into a time of needed reflection and wholesale change in the business of football. The lives of the survivors of Penn State's systemic collusion in sex abuse of minors are forever altered, necessitating ongoing support toward their journey of healing.

Stories of coach–athlete abuse (emotional and sexual) in youth, collegiate, and professional sports are not uncommon (Gervis, Rhind, & Luzar, 2016; Kerr, Stirling, & Bandealy, 2016; Stirling, 2013). The totality of stories told and the lives adversely impacted across generations by coach–athlete abuse dynamics position the variety of athlete services providers to become familiar with trauma literature paying special attention to identifying signs and symptoms of trauma, trauma assessment, treatment options, and the importance of service-provider self-reflection. Contextualizing the study of trauma using culture, race, ethnicity, gender, age, sexual orientation, religion, and other dimensions of identity as templates for understanding trauma survivors and their emotional journeys to healing is strongly encouraged.

Facilitating Outcomes

When coaches, certified athletic trainers, and other support personnel are responding to athletes managing the considerable, sometimes crushing, and usually overpowering, aftermath of traumatic experiences, best-practice responses are to refer them to professionals trained to respond to trauma and the often co-occurring concerns and issues that frame the athlete's distress. Best-practice habits for professionals, using strength-based approaches, invite focus on conducting a thorough assessment in accordance with professional standards using multiple assessment tools. Relative to trauma, it is also important to consider: (a) identifying, understanding, and appreciating athletes' past trauma; (b) teasing out variables that are fuelling the distress caused by current traumatic stimuli; and (c) helping athletes prepare for the future, in part, by helping them to recall their successes in overcoming past challenges, despite having felt overwhelmed and out of balance emotionally during parts of their journey to recovery. An assessment of an athlete's overall functioning across life domains juxtaposed to the athlete's experiences of trauma is standard practice. A cautionary tale echoed by Figley (1995) and others warns of compassion fatigue, or secondary traumatic stress, defined as a gradual decrease in compassion for serving following immersion into the lives of others, helping them cope with traumatic experiences. Symptoms may include sleeplessness, heightened anxiety, hopelessness, and decreases in pleasurable activities (Figley, 1995). This self-protective response often seen in first responders serves as a reminder of the importance of ongoing healer self-care.

Several contemporary interventions show promise in the treatment of trauma. Mindfulness and meditation-based therapies, rooted in Eastern philosophical and applied practices, are finding increased acceptance in athletics and the health care industry. Mindfulness-based stress reduction (Kabat-Zinn, 2018) and mindfulness-based cognitive approaches (Segal, Williams, &

Teasedale, 2001) represent examples of interventions thought to be successful when responding to trauma.

Though differences exist among the different approaches, all mindfulness and meditation-based interventions share common process and outcome goals. Relative to process, key similarities include invitations to: (a) focus on internal experiences non-judgementally while becoming aware of in-the-moment feelings, thoughts, and bodily sensations and allowing them to exist; (b) integrate awareness and practice of emotional self-regulation; and (c) know that current thoughts, feelings, and behaviours are transitory mental states that come and go during the meditation exercise. Outcome goals include: (a) symptom reduction; (b) heightened awareness of moment-to-moment thoughts, feelings, and behaviours; (c) developing comfort with self-reflective contemplative exercises with the intention to integrate said practices into daily routines; and (d) acknowledging intra-personal strengths as innate resources accessible when needed to manage post-trauma cognitive, affective, and behavioural reactions.

Interventions targeting very specific post-trauma challenges also merit attention. In this regard, Linehan's dialectical behaviour therapy (1993) for the treatment of borderline personality disorders, Shapiro's eye movement desensitization and reprocessing (EDMR; 2017) for the treatment of PTSD, and the work of Cohen, Mannarino, and Deblinger (2016) relative to treating children and adolescent post-trauma are offered for consideration. Using early-age trauma experiences as motivational triggers for future success represents conversations (Collins & MacNamara, 2012; Hardy & Warr, 2017; Howells & Fletcher, 2015; Savage et al., 2016) that merit ongoing focused attention.

Athletes are not immune to mental-health and wellness challenges. Given gender, celebrity, and other identity-anchored contexts that influence athletes to remain silent about their personal and emotional struggles, athletes, arguably, are more vulnerable to the unpropitious and emotionally injurious consequences of keeping quiet about their possibly truer lived experiences. Efforts by coaches, certified athletic trainers, athletic administrators, family, agents, and others in the athlete's circle of influence to understand and appreciate the athlete as a person before the performer represent healthy approaches to discovering what might be hiding in plain sight.

An additional strategy is to invoke the work of scholars (Tedischi, Calhoun, & Groleau, 2015) who offer a proverbial silver lining for every dark cloud in their work on post-traumatic growth. Offered for consideration is the notion that persons who have experienced trauma are positioned to also experience a positive change in their perception of self, appreciation for life, strengthened or renewed spiritual commitment, and increased hope in forthcoming possibilities and options.

Scholarship addressing hope and forgiveness (Snyder, 1994, 2000) offers yet another opportunity to think through approaches to responding to athletes as survivors of trauma. Snyder (2000, 1994) suggests that three variables help develop and hone the cognitive skill of hopeful thinking. These variables are: (a) goal-directed aspirations, (b) identifying pathways for achieving identified goals, and (c) personal beliefs – also known as agency – in one's ability to ignite and sustain forward movement toward identified goals. Echoed in the memoir of Viktor Frankl (2006) is a similar observation and conclusion that, while persons cannot necessarily avoid trauma in their lives, they can choose how best to respond to it, discover meaning in the experiences, and move forward buoyed by resilience and a revived and reignited sense of hope.

Conclusion

Experiences of trauma are a part of everyday life, domestically and globally. The emotional aftermath of traumatic experiences is felt both immediately and long term and, consequentially, influences how athletes think, feel, behave, and navigate the world around them. The kinds, types, and timing of situations, juxtaposed to the psychological vulnerabilities of athletes at the exact moment when unpredicted or predicted situations emerge, influence which emotions surface and how athletes respond to them. At one end of the emotional spectrum, athletes responding to trauma-triggering situations may experience anger, confusion, depression, disbelief, disequilibrium, grief, hopelessness, pain, and sadness. At the other end of the emotional spectrum, athletes are likely to experience emotions that fuel hope, resilience, fortitude, clarity of purpose, excitement about yet-to-be-discovered opportunities, and a drive to find the treasures hidden in every trial (Howells & Fletcher, 2015; Savage et al., 2016).

Athletes are not immune to experiencing trauma at any age. Early-age experiences of trauma are especially important, as the formative years from 1 to 10 set the stage for lifelong decision-making across every area (e.g., school, athletics, relational experiences, health status) that frames an athlete's identity. With that being said, athletes remaining silent about their traumatic experiences is as common as their finding both healthy and unhealthy self-protective ways of managing the ongoing emotional overload with which they feel silently burdened. Persons in an athlete's circle of influence incur responsibilities to learn about trauma and the contextual parameters that frame an athlete's individual journey to emotional reconciliation with life-altering challenges. To reiterate a point made earlier in this narrative, athlete service providers (e.g. coaches, certified athletic trainers, nutritionists, strength and conditioning personnel) are strongly encouraged to refer athlete survivors of abuse to professionals who are trained to respond to trauma and co-occurring life challenges. Other persons in the athlete's circle of influence (e.g., family, friends, relatives) are encouraged to honour the same practice. Apropos to these latter recommendations, athlete service providers, as well as family, friends, and relatives, are reminded to keep a pulse on their early-age, present, and likely future challenges, concern, and issues. Lack of attention to personal struggles renders persons vulnerable to unforeseen environmental triggers that, consequentially, could result in their managing additional worries.

Many athletes, and persons in the athlete's circle of influence, do not grapple or labour with mental-health and wellness problems or traumatic pasts in need of emotional détente. These groups manage life's dynamic change and growth process by making intentional decisions in three areas. First, they invest in developing and maintaining healthy practices relative to managing familial, social, occupational, financial, intellectual, emotional, and spiritual domains. Second, challenges that inevitably emerge are responded to with measured concern, big-picture perspectives, strategic planning for short- and longer-term success, and a sense of agency or personal belief in their abilities to bring about change (Bandura, 2006). Third, persons succeeding in managing life's dynamic change and growth process make decisions to not take themselves too seriously (Economakis, 2013).

The body–mind connection relative to experiences of trauma remains an ongoing topic of medical, psychological, sociological, anthropological, and other academic discipline-specific exploration. Much has been learned about trauma, physiologically, emotionally, with regards to its aftermath, and in identifying effective strategies for responding to life-changing experiences. Further, athletes continue to be beneficiaries of knowledge accumulated to date in each of the aforementioned areas. More exploration, however, needs to occur with the goal of further unpacking the infused and interactional complexities of personal and environmental variables and the part each plays in triggering, maintaining, and reconciling trauma experiences. The potential rewards for advancing the scientific study of all aspects of trauma including prevention, treatment, and rehabilitation, all viewed within identity-anchored contexts and the socio-political zeitgeist, are enormous and worth pursuing.

References

Bandura, A. (2006). Toward a psychology of human agency. *Perspective on Psychological Science, 1*(2), 164–181.

Bellig, M. (1999). *Freudian repression: Conversation creating the unconscious.* New York: Cambridge University Press.

Black, M. C., Basile, K. C., Breiding, M. J., Smith, S. G., Walters, M. L., Merrick, M. T., ... Stevens, M. R. (2011). *The National Intimate Partner and Sexual Violence Survey (NISVS): 2010 summary report.* Atlanta, GA: National Center for Injury Prevention and Control, Centers for Disease Control and Prevention.

Bronfenbrenner, U., & Ceci, S. J. (1994). Nature–nurture reconceptualized in developmental perspective: A bioecological model. *Psychological Review, 101,* 568–586.

Brown, L. S. (2008). *Cultural competence in trauma therapy: Beyond the flashback.* Washington, DC: American Psychological Association.

Cohen, J. A., Mannarino, A. P., & Deblinger, E. (2016). *Treating trauma and traumatic grief in children and adolescents* (2nd ed.). New York: Guilford Press.

Collins, D., & MacNamara, A. (2012). The rocky road to the top: Why talent needs trauma. *Sports Medicine, 42,* 907–914.

Courtois, C. A., & Ford, J. D. (2013). *Treatment of complex trauma: A sequenced, relationship-based approach.* New York: Guilford Press.

Economakis, F. (2013). *Harden up: How to be resilient, stop taking tings personally, and get what you want in life.* New York: New Holland.

Felitti, V. J., Anda, R. F., Nordenberg, D., Williamson, D. F., Spitz, A. M., Edwards, V., ... Marks, J. S. (1998). Relationship of childhood abuse and household dysfunction to many of the leading causes of death in adults. *American Journal of Preventive Medicine, 14,* 245–258.

Figley, C. R. (1995). *Compassion fatigue: Coping with secondary traumatic stress disorder in those who treat the traumatized.* New York: Routledge.

Frankl, V. (2006). *Man's search for meaning.* New York: Beacon Press.

Gervis, M., & Dunn, N. (2004). The emotional abuse of elite child athletes by their coaches. *Child Abuse Review, 13*(3), 215–223.

Gervis, M., Rhind, D., & Luzar, A. (2016). Perceptions of emotional abuse in the coach–athlete relationship in youth sport: The influence of competitive level and outcome. *International Journal of Sports Science & Coaching, 11*(6), 772–779.

Hardy, L., & Warr, C. (2017). Great British medalists: Psychosocial biographies of super-elite and elite athletes from Olympic sports. *Progress in Brain Research, 232,* 1–119.

Herman, J. L. (1997). *Trauma and recovery.* New York: Basic Books.

Howells, K., & Fletcher, D. (2015). Sink or swim: Adversity- and growth-related experiences in Olympic swimming champions. *Psychology of Sport and Exercise, 16,* 37–48.

Kabat-Zinn, J. (2018). *Meditation is not what you think: Mindfulness and why it is so important.* New York: Hachette.

Kerr, G., Stirling, A., & Bandealy, A. (2016). Film depictions of emotionally-abusive coach–athlete interactions. *Sport Coach Review, 5,* 87–101.

Krystal, H. (1968). Studies of concentration camp survivors. In H. Krystal (Ed.), *Massive psychic trauma* (pp. 23–46). New York: International Universities Press.

Levers, L. L. (2012). *Trauma counseling: Theories and interventions.* New York: Springer.

Levine, P. A. (2010). *In an unspoken voice: How the body releases trauma and restores goodness.* Berkeley, CA: North Atlantic Books.

Lifton, R. J. (1973). *Home from the war: Vietnam veterans: neither victims nor executioners.* New York: Simon & Schuster.

Lindemann, E. (1944). Symptomatology and management of acute grief. *American Journal of Psychiatry, 101*(2), 141–148.

Linehan, M. M. (1993). *Cognitive-behavior therapy for borderline personality disorder.* New York: Guilford Press.

Liu, H., Prause, N., Wyatt, G. E., Williams, J. K., Chin, D., Davis, T., ... Myers, H. F. (2015). Development of a composite trauma exposure risk index. *Psychological Assessment, 27,* 965–974.

Miller, P. H. (2016). *Theories of developmental psychology* (6th ed.). New York: Worth.

Ringel, S. (2012). Overview. In S. Ringle and J. Brandell (Eds.), *Trauma: Contemporary directions in theory, practice, and research* (pp. 1–12). Thousand Oaks, CA: Sage.

Ringel, S., & Brandell, J. (2012). *Trauma: Contemporary directions in theory, practice, and research*. Thousand Oaks, CA: Sage.

Savage, J., Collins, D., & Cruickshank, A. (2016). Exploring traumas in the development of talent: What are they, what do they do, and what do they require? *Journal of Applied Sport Psychology, 29,* 101–117.

Schinnerer, J. (2018). The consequences of verbally abusive athletic coaches. *Psych Central*. Retrieved on April 15, 2019, from https://psyccentral.com/lib/the-consequences-of-verbally-abusive-coaches/

Segal, Z. V., Williams, J. M. G., & Teasedale, J. D. (2001). *Mindfulness-based cognitive therapy for depression*. New York: Guilford Press.

Shapiro, F. (2017). *Eye movement desensitization and reprocessing (EDMR) therapy: Basic principles, protocols and procedures* (3rd ed.). New York: Guilford Press.

Snyder, C. R. (1994). *The pycology of hope: You can get there from here*. New York: Free Press.

Snyder, C. R. (2000). Hypothesis: There is hope. In C. R. Snyder (Ed.), *Handbook of hope: Theory, measures, and applications* (pp. 3–21). San Diego, CA: Academic Press.

Stien, P., & Kendall, J. C. (2003). *Psychological trauma and the developing brain: Neurologically-based interventions for troubled children*. London: Routledge.

Stirling, A. E. (2013). Understanding the use of emotionally abusive coaching practices. *International Journal of Sports Science & Coaching, 8*(4), 625–639.

Stirling, A. E., & Kerr, G. A. (2009). Abused athlete's perceptions of the coach–athlete relationship. *Sport in Society, 12,* 227–239.

Stirling, A. E., & Kerr, G. A. (2013). The perceived effects of elite athletes' experiences of emotional abuse in the coach–athlete relationship. *International Journey of Sport and Exercise Psychology, 11,* 87–110.

Stirling, A. E., & Kerr, G. A. (2014). Initiating and sustaining emotional abuse in coach–athlete relationships: An ecological transactional model of vulnerability. *Journal of Aggression, Maltreatment and Trauma, 23,* 116–135.

Tedischi, R. G., Calhoun, L. G., & Groleau, J. M. (2015). Clinical applications of post-traumatic growth. In S. Joseph (Ed.), *Positive psychology in practice: Promoting human flourishing in work, health, education and everyday life* (pp. 503–518). Hoboken, NJ: Wiley.

47
VALIDITY AND RELIABILITY

Katie E. Gunnell

Introduction

In sport and exercise psychology, measurement scales typically consist of multiple items that are often combined into some composite score with the intention of quantifying some theoretical variable that is not directly observable (DeVellis, 2017). For example, a researcher interested in performance anxiety might develop multiple items that reflect different dimensions of the theoretical variable such that they can quantify levels of performance anxiety in participants. In order to understand relationships between variables or predict outcomes, sport and exercise psychology researchers must have confidence that they have selected a measurement scale that produces accurate and stable scores. Measurement, therefore, lies at the heart of every statement made from research in sport and exercise psychology. If a measure does not produce scores that are valid and reliable, the researcher and knowledge user will have very little confidence in any finding. Good measurement scales are a necessary prerequisite for valid research (DeVellis, 2017).

How, then, does one go about statistically testing the validity and reliability of scores from measurement scales? The purpose of this chapter is to introduce readers to common methods that can be used to assess different sources of reliability and validity evidence. The Standards for Educational and Psychological Testing (the Standards; American Education Research Association [AERA], American Psychological Association [APA], & National Council on Measurement in Education [NCME], 2014) is used as a guiding psychometric framework. Emphasis is placed on quantitative techniques and methods that are commonly used in sport and exercise psychology. A brief overview of select methods along with their strengths and limitations will be presented. Finally, examples from sport and exercise psychology wherein researchers used the techniques will be provided.

Methods to Assess Reliability

The consistency of scores across time on a measurement scale is called reliability/precision (AERA, APA, & NCME, 2014). Having consistent scores or high reliability/precision is important for measurement, but how high do the scores need to be? In general, higher reliability/precision is needed for salient measurement where the outcome of measurement could affect decisions that are not easily reversed. For example, if a measure were used to evaluate if an athlete is permitted to return to sport after a concussion, one would want a high degree of reliability/precision to ensure the health and safety of the athlete. Conversely, if a measure were used in conjunction with other measures, and information can be corrected or reversed, modest reliability/precision may be sufficient (AERA, APA, & NCME, 2014).

There are three broad approaches to understanding reliability from a statistical point of view (see Table 12). The first approach is based within classical test theory and produces reliability coefficients that are typically based on the correlation between scores from items on the measurement scale (e.g., test-retest coefficients, alternate-form coefficient, internal-consistency coefficients). Another approach is based on generalizability theory (G-theory), wherein the researcher decomposes the components of variance associated with sources of error, typically through analysis of variance methods. Unlike classical test theory, which assumes one distribution for errors, G-theory is used to understand multiple sources of error such as items, occasions, or raters. Finally, a further approach concerns test information and includes item response theory (IRT) models wherein the researcher summarizes if a measure discriminates between people with various levels of ability on the construct being measured. An information function within IRT provides an indication of precision for which a participant's ability is measured (Vaughn, Lee, & Kamata, 2012). In sport and exercise psychology, reliability coefficients from a classical test theory perspective dominate the literature, although examples of G-theory (Rees, Freeman, Bell, & Bunney, 2012) and IRT analyses are available (Fletcher, 1999; Prapavessis, Maddison, & Fletcher, 2005). Given the prominence of the reliability coefficients based on classical test theory, a few reliability coefficients are summarized below.

Internal Consistency

Estimates of internal consistency such as coefficient alpha are used to examine the homogeneity of relationships between scores on individual items within a unidimensional measurement scale (DeVellis, 2017). Coefficient alpha (often labelled 'Cronbach's alpha') is a commonly used index of score reliability in sport and exercise psychology (Wilson, Mack, & Sylvester, 2011). Despite its popularity, many critiques have been written about coefficient alpha (Cortina, 1993; McNeish, in press; Sijtsma, 2009). Alpha represents a lower-bound

Table 12 Approaches to examining score reliability in sport and exercise psychology

Approaches to examining reliability	Example methods	Example application in sport and exercise psychology
Classical test theory	Internal consistency, Omega, composite reliability, coefficient H	Myers, Chase, Pierce, & Martin, 2011 (coefficient H) Sylvester et al., 2014 (composite reliability)
Generalizability theory (G-theory)	Analysis of variance	Rees et al., 2012
Item response theory (IRT)	1-parameter, 2-parameter, 3-parameter models	Prapavessis et al., 2005

Note: Example methods listed are not inclusive of all possible techniques for examining each approach to score reliability estimate of score reliability, suggesting that in many cases it underestimates reliability (Sijtsma, 2009). On the one hand, this might not seem problematic, as it may encourage researchers to create stronger instruments. On the other hand, it could be problematic when researchers alter their measurement scale (e.g., drop items) to enhance alpha (Sijtsma, 2009), thereby reducing generalizability across studies that use complete versions of the measurement scale. An additional problem with coefficient alpha is that researchers inappropriately use it to make claims about measurement dimensionality (Sijtsma, 2009). Using an estimate of score reliability to make inferences about dimensionality could compromise assessments of validity. Another limitation of coefficient alpha is that it is a function of the number of measurement scale items (Cortina, 1993) – as the number of items increases, so too does alpha. Therefore, caution is warranted when interpreting measurement scales with few items or many items. Other limitations of coefficient alpha are that it assumes tau equivalence (i.e., that each item contributes equally to the total score), assumes the data are continuous (although there are estimates of internal consistency for ordinal measures; see Gadermann, Guhn, & Zumbo, 2012), and assumes that the data are normally distributed (McNeish, in press).

Researchers interested in a pilot review on the application of coefficient alpha in exercise psychology are encouraged to consult Wilson and colleagues (2011). In this review, Wilson and colleagues (2011) highlight issues with reporting coefficient alpha such as relying on mythical cut scores (e.g., alpha > .70 demarcates 'good reliability'), inferring that, if another study found evidence of score reliability, it will be present in your own study without verifying, and inappropriate language when describing score reliability.

Omega and Composite Reliability

As an alternative to coefficient alpha, some researchers have begun to calculate omega or composite reliability. Both are related to coefficient alpha in that they examine the ratio of variability explained by the items to the total variance in the subscale, but are different because they assume a congeneric model (McNeish, in press). A congeneric model assumes that the items do not contribute equally to the total score (e.g., results of a factor analysis would yield different factor loadings; McNeish, in press). Composite reliability can be used when the total scale score is created via unit weighting. Unit weighting occurs when a researcher creates the total scores simply by adding up the item raw scores and each item is given equal weight (Geldhof, Preacher, & Zyphur, 2014). Readers are referred to McNeish (in press) for an overview of the various types of omega and their formulas and syntax for R software.

Coefficient H

Coefficient H was designed to overcome some of the shortcomings associated with composite reliability (Hancock & Mueller, 2001). Coefficient H is appropriate when factor analysis is used, and a scale score is created through optimal weighting. Optimally weighted scales are those whose items contribute different amounts of information to the total scale scores (McNeish, in press). There are several key advantages to coefficient H over composite reliability. First, the factor loadings can be positive or negative (Hancock & Mueller, 2001). Second, items with weak factor loadings do not negatively affect coefficient H, because error variances are not included in the formula. In other words, a weak item will not penalize score reliability, because the total score is created through optimal weighting (McNeish, in press). Finally, coefficient H will never be smaller than the best indicator (Hancock & Mueller, 2001).

Table 13 Approaches to examining score validity in sport and exercise psychology

Source of validity evidence	Example methods	Example application in sport and exercise psychology
Content	Using qualitative (e.g., focus groups) or quantitative (e.g., Likert rating scales) methods to critique wording and format of items, themes, clarity of items, representation of content, theoretical alignment	Dunn et al., 1999
Internal structure	Factor analytic techniques such as confirmatory factor analysis, exploratory factor analysis, exploratory structural equation modelling	Wilson, Rogers, Rodgers, & Wild, 2006
Relations with other variables	Correlation, analysis of variance, regression, structural equation modelling	Williams et al., 2012
Response processes	Think-aloud protocols, reaction time, eye tracking, implicit measures	Sylvester et al., 2014
Consequences	Examining the unintended and/or intended consequences of making inferences from a measurement scale	–

Note: Example methods listed are not inclusive of all possible techniques for examining score validity

Methods to Assess Validity

According to the Standards (AERA, APA, & NCME, 2014), there are five sources of validity evidence: content, internal structure, relations with other variables, response processes, and consequences (see Table 13). Validity evidence based on content is used to examine the relationship between the construct being assessed and the content of the items used to assess it (AERA, APA, & NCME, 2014). In other words, content validity examines if the set of items developed or assembled in a measurement scale reflect the content domain based on its conceptual definition and do not capture other potentially related yet external constructs (DeVellis, 2017). To assess validity evidence based on content, researchers might employ quantitative and qualitative procedures to examine item wording and format, themes, and questions (AERA, APA, & NCME, 2014). For example, a researcher may develop a large pool of items that represent the construct they are trying to measure based on a conceptual definition. They may then use interviews or focus groups with experts and/or the target population to determine if the items have good content representation and clarity, or if there are any aspects of the conceptual definition missing (DeVellis, 2017). In a quantitative analysis, they may seek feedback from a panel of experts using Likert-type scales to rate items based on clarity, construct relevance, theoretical alignment, and so on. Examples of methods used to assess validity evidence based on content in sport and exercise psychology can be seen in Dunn, Bouffard, and Rogers (1999).

Validity evidence based on internal structure allows researchers to ascertain if items align with the construct in the way the scores are proposed to be used (AERA, APA, & NCME, 2014). In other words, if five items were developed to measure one construct, those five items should conform to that one construct. To assess the internal structure of scale scores, researchers commonly employ factor analytic techniques. Both confirmatory (CFA) and exploratory factor analysis (EFA) can be used for this purpose, and researchers have recently begun using a hybrid of the two techniques through exploratory structural equation modelling (ESEM). A more thorough discussion of these techniques is presented below.

As discussed elsewhere in this volume (see Pila, Epp, & Kowalski, Volume 1, Chapter 18, in this encyclopedia), validity evidence based on relations to other variables is used to examine the relationship between the construct of interest and external variables that it should (or should not) be related to (AERA, APA, & NCME, 2014). This source of evidence provides information about the degree to which the relationships between the construct and external variable(s) are consistent with the proposed score use (AERA, APA, & NCME, 2014). To examine relations with other variables, researchers can use a host of statistical techniques including (but not limited to) correlation, analysis of variance, regression, and structural equation modelling (SEM). A researcher will often use these statistical techniques to investigate relations with other variables to examine evidence based on convergent or discriminant evidence, criterion evidence, known group difference, or predictive evidence. For example, convergent evidence might be tested by examining the correlation between perceived competence satisfaction and intrinsic motivation. Based on theory (Deci & Ryan, 2002), the researcher would expect to find a positive correlation between these two constructs, and the correlational analysis could provide such evidence.

Validity evidence based on response processes is used to test assumptions about the cognitive processes participants undergo when completing measurement scales (AERA, APA, & NCME, 2014). Response process validity evidence provides researchers with knowledge about the fit of the construct and the process actually engaged in by the participants when responding to measurement scales (AERA, APA, & NCME, 2014). Beauchamp and McEwan (2017) recently outlined the importance of examining validity evidence based on response processes, highlighting an emerging debate within health psychology about whether or not participants who respond to self-efficacy questionnaires are unintentionally responding about their capability and intention, thereby confounding two distinct constructs. To examine response processes, a researcher might employ techniques to determine how and why participants are responding to items such as through a think-aloud protocol (e.g., Sylvester et al., 2014) or tracking eye movements, reaction time (AERA, APA, & NCME, 2014), and implicit and behaviour measures (Beauchamp & McEwan, 2017). Finally, validity evidence based on consequences allows researchers to examine if the interpretation of the scores has been used as intended and to examine the soundness of those interpretations (AERA, APA, & NCME, 2014). To examine consequences, researchers might conduct an investigation into the intended and unintended consequences of interpreting scores from the measurement scale and their implications for people, intervention, or policy.

A review of a prominent journal in sport and exercise psychology revealed that the most commonly tested sources of validity evidence in validation research was internal structure and relations with other variables (Gunnell et al., 2014). More specifically, factor analytic techniques and examining convergence and discriminant evidence were frequently used methods to assess score validity (Gunnell et al., 2014). Given the prominence of these two sources of validity evidence in sport and exercise psychology, the following sections will outline statistical methods for each. Emphasis is placed on factor analytic techniques given their flexibility and applicability to examining multiple strands of validity evidence. At this juncture, however, it is important to remind readers that running factor analytic models is not validity in and of itself (Marsh, 1998), and that the validity of measurement scale scores should be ascertained through multiple integrative sources of evidence (AERA, APA, & NCME, 2014).

Exploratory Factor Analysis

After developing measurement scale items and examining validity evidence based on content, researchers are typically interested in testing the dimensionality of responses to their measures. That is, they are interested in testing whether or not the scores from the items they have selected conform to the number of subscales (or factors) originally hypothesized. EFA is a technique that is used to examine multiple items to determine the smallest number of factors that are interpretable and theoretically aligned (Brown, 2015). A factor (or latent variable) is an unobserved variable that causes covariation between observed measures (e.g., indicators or items; Brown, 2015). Therefore, EFA is predicated on the notion that the correlations between items can be accounted for by the factor(s). In other words, the relationships between items are caused by the latent factor, and, once it is accounted for, the item residuals should not be related. EFA is considered an exploratory technique because the researcher does not pre-specify the pattern of the relationships between observed items and latent factors (Brown, 2015). That is, all items are allowed to load freely on all factors. EFA is commonly estimated with maximum likelihood procedures and can be estimated in numerous statistical software packages such as SPSS. EFA and principal components analysis are not identical and should not be conflated as such. With EFA, the goal is to account for the correlations between items, whereas, with principal components analysis, the goal is to account for the variance in the items (Brown, 2015).

Often, researchers will have a large number of items and use EFA to reduce the number of items for their measure. When the researcher is making decisions about the number of factors to retain, strong theoretical and substantive reasoning should be used. Researchers should consider whether the factor or factors align with theoretical concepts and whether or not the factors are interpretable. Further, researchers should ensure that each factor has a sufficient number of items such that the factor is well defined (Brown, 2015). Undetermined or unstable factors might result from having only two or three items (Brown, 2015).

A strength of EFA is that it allows researchers to test measurement models when substantive theory provides little a priori information or when post hoc modifications may be needed (Myers, 2013). Examples of EFA in sport and exercise psychology can be seen in Williams and Cumming (2011) and Wilson et al. (2006). There are, however, limitations of EFA that may have led sport and exercise psychology researchers to favor CFA (Myers, 2013). For example, in some software programs, EFA does not produce standard errors for parameters, a priori knowledge about the measurement model or pattern of relationships among items, and factors cannot be taken into account, and more advanced procedures cannot be used (e.g., multi-group analysis, structural equation modelling; Myers, 2013).

Confirmatory Factor Analysis

With EFA, the researcher does not specify the pattern of factor loadings, which means that items can load on to their intended factor and freely cross-load on to other factors. In contrast, in CFA, the researcher explicitly specifies the measurement model. The researcher has a priori hypotheses about the number of factors and the pattern of the factor loadings. Similar to EFA, however, with CFA, the goal is to account for the covariation between items. Because CFA requires a strong theoretical background, a priori hypotheses about the number of factors, and pattern of factor loadings, it is typically used to evaluate measurement scale scores' internal structure in later phases of measurement development (Brown, 2015).

Commonly, researchers begin to examine validity evidence of factor structure using EFA and, once sufficient justification exists for the dimensionality of their measure, they collect new data and proceed to CFA (e.g., Williams & Cumming, 2011; Wilson et al., 2006). Because researchers specify the measurement model a priori, CFA has several advantages over EFA. First, CFA is more parsimonious than EFA. Second, it provides researchers with additional statistical criteria to examine the fit of the measurement model through indexes such as the comparative fit index or root mean square error of approximation (see Hu & Bentler, 1999;

Marsh, Hau, & Wen, 2004). Third, researchers can specify the error theory and pattern of relationships between factors. That is, they can allow for select correlated errors between items that might have theoretical or substantive importance, as in the case of method effects or temporal relations (Brown, 2015; Cole, Ciesla, & Steiger, 2007). Furthermore, because the amount of error in each item is estimated, researchers can examine error-free correlations or regressions between factors (Brown, 2015).

A fourth strength of CFA is that researchers can examine convergent and discriminant evidence using multi-trait–multi-method procedures (Campbell & Fiske, 1959). In multi-trait–multi-method models, researchers use multiple measures of the same constructs (e.g., two different measures of motivation) and multiple methods to assess the construct (e.g., self-report and parent report). For more information on specifying multi-trait–multi-method models in a latent variable framework, see Marsh and Grayson (1995), and, for an example in sport and exercise psychology, see Williams and colleagues (2012).

A fifth strength is that CFA allows researchers to examine multidimensionality. Typically, it is assumed that items and factors are unidimensional; however, it is possible that items and factors are multidimensional. For example, in a bifactor model specification, researchers can directly examine if the items have variance attributable to (a) specific factors (e.g., subscales of quality of life) and (b) a global factor (e.g., global quality of life). In this specification, it is assumed that all items have (a) error and (b) variance attributable to the global factor, and only specific items have variance attributable to specific factors (Reise, Moore, & Haviland, 2010). An example of a bifactor model from sport and exercise psychology can be seen in Brunet, Gunnell, Teixeira, Sabiston, and Bélanger (2016). Another method of testing multidimensionality using CFA is to examine higher-order models. In this model, the researcher assumes lower-order factors (e.g., subscales of quality of life) are subsumed under a high-order factor (e.g., overall quality of life). The key difference between a bifactor model and a higher-order model is that, with the bifactor model, both specific and global factors are assumed to cause the items, whereas, with the higher-order model, the higher-order factors cause the lower-order factors, which in turn cause the items (Chen, West, & Sousa, 2006; DeVellis, 2017; Reise et al., 2010).

Finally, CFA can be used to examine if scores from a measurement scale retain their meaning across different conditions (Kline, 2011). For example, researchers can use measurement invariance procedures to test if scores are equivalent across different groups of people (e.g., males and females, young and old), different contexts (physical education classes and sport), or time (e.g., Time 1 and Time 2). To examine these differences in groups, contexts, and time, researchers use measurement invariance testing (sometimes called multi-group analysis), which is a procedure that involves comparing nested models with increasing equality constraints on different model parameters (Cheung & Rensvold, 2002; Meredith, 1993; Wu, Li, & Zumbo, 2007). The parameters typically constrained are the item factor loadings, intercepts, and errors. Each level of invariance established provides greater confidence that the measurement model is the same across groups, contexts, and time, and that scores between these conditions can be meaningfully compared. In this way, measurement invariance helps researchers establish the generalizability of the measurement scale scores (Brown, 2015). Lastly, measurement invariance allows researchers to compare means across groups (as is done with a *t*-test or analysis of variance), with confidence that the scores are measuring the same factors on the same metric across the conditions tested for invariance.

When conducting CFA, researchers typically use maximum likelihood or robust maximum likelihood procedures for continuous data. Other estimation procedures such as weighted least squares means and variance adjusted are available when the data are ordered categorically. When using maximum likelihood, most researchers assume their data are continuous and rely on the covariance matrices from their data; however, when the data are ordered categorically, polychoric correlations matrices and robust estimation procedures should be used (Flora & Curran, 2004).

A limitation of CFA is that it is prone to misspecification. For example, when latent variables are specified to load on to only one item, even though there might be non-zero cross-loadings, it can upwardly bias the correlations between factors, which, in turn, can bias the paths in the non-measurement portion of the model (Asparouhov & Muthén, 2009; Myers, 2013). Other limitations include the need for substantive theoretical knowledge to specify the measurement model (Myers, 2013), relying too heavily on fit criteria to make model specifications, and specifying too many factors that might not be meaningful (DeVellis, 2017).

Exploratory Structural Equations Modelling

Although researchers strive to be precise when creating measurement scale items, the items rarely conform perfectly to the a priori structure (Gucciardi & Zyphur, 2016). Therefore, use of highly restrictive techniques such as CFA to examine dimensionality might be too restrictive (Marsh, Morin, Parker, & Kaur, 2014). ESEM is a technique that combines EFA, CFA, and SEM techniques and can take an exploratory or confirmatory approach (Myers, Ntoumanis, Gunnell, Gucciardi, & Lee, 2018). Whereas EFA allows all factors to load freely on all items, CFA does not permit cross-loadings on non-target factors. In CFA, restricting these cross-loadings to zero results in inflated correlations between subscales (Marsh et al., 2009). In other words, in a measurement scale that has multiple factors (or subscales) that are theoretically related, when items are restricted to only load on one factor and not load (i.e., are constrained to zero) on the other factors, it could artificially inflate the correlations between the factors. ESEM allows researchers to specify primary (or target) loadings and cross-loadings. Further, researchers can use prior knowledge and allow some factors to be specified as they would in CFA (i.e., with primary factor loadings and zero cross-loadings) and others to be specified as they would in EFA (i.e., with primary loadings and non-zero cross-loadings; Brown, 2015). Researchers have shown that, when ESEM is used, correlations between subscales are not inflated because it allows for small non-trivial cross-loadings (Asparouhov & Muthén, 2009; Marsh et al., 2014).

The advantages of ESEM are that it can be used to estimate more complex models such as bifactor models, account for covariates, test relationships between latent variables (e.g., correlations, direct and indirect effects), examine measurement invariance, and estimate latent growth models (among other models; Brown, 2015; Marsh et al., 2014). Furthermore, similar to CFA, ESEM allows researchers to investigate goodness of fit statistics to evaluate their models. Limitations of ESEM include the inability to use summary data (i.e., raw data are required) and limitations in modelling (e.g., exploratory factors cannot be regressed on other exploratory factors in the same block; Brown, 2015). Numerous examples of ESEM are evident in the sport and exercise psychology literature, used to examine score validity of instruments (see Crocker, Pedrosa, Mosewich, & Sabiston, 2018; Stenling, Ivarsson, Hassmén, & Lindwall, 2015; Stenling, Ivarsson, Lindwall, & Gucciardi, 2018).

Structural Equation Modelling and Other Statistical Techniques

Once a researcher has established a good measurement model and examined the internal structure of scores, they may then be interested in determining the pattern of relationships between the factors to examine validity evidence based on relations to other variables. This can be accomplished through the structural component of an SEM. Notably, in SEM, a researcher will typically add regression paths between factors. Most researchers will evaluate the measurement portion of the model first (i.e., using CFA or ESEM). This model typically includes all the items and their respective factors, which are all correlated. The purpose of this measurement model is to ensure that any sources of misfit within a structural model are not caused by measurement issues and establish that parameters are interpretable and within range (Brown, 2015). Next, the researcher will extend the measurement model to estimate a structural model, wherein they will specify how the factors are related to each other (e.g., correlated, direct effects, indirect effects).

SEM is advantageous over regression-based models based on ordinary least squares because SEM can account for measurement error, whereas regression models do not. This is an unrealistic assumption in sport and exercise psychology, and the consequences of this assumption could distort conclusions, because the degree to which measurement error attenuates correlations or regression paths is unknown (Brown, 2015). With SEM, error is removed from the factor (i.e., the latent variable) in the measurement model portion, and, therefore, correlations and regression coefficients derived from SEM between latent factors are thought to be closer to the true population value (Brown, 2015). Another advantage of SEM is that it allows researchers to use both latent factors (based on the measurement portion of the model) and composite variables based on observed scores. SEM is flexible when estimating complex models. In SEM, researchers can specify multiple mediators, moderators, exogenous variables (similar independent variables in regression), and endogenous variables (similar to dependent variables in regression). Given its flexibility and advantageous ability to remove measurement error, SEM has become a popular technique within sport and exercise psychology to examine validity evidence based on relationships with other variables (e.g., examining nomological networks). An example from sport and exercise psychology can be seen in Lonsdale, Hodge, and Rose (2008).

Other techniques used by sport and exercise psychology researchers to examine validity evidence include IRT, cross-lagged models, latent growth models (also called latent curve models), and Bayesian statistics. IRT can be used to examine reliability, as outlined above, as well as factor structure. IRT examines the relationships between the characteristics of items and individuals and the probability of the person endorsing a particular response (Brown, 2015). Recall that, with CFA, the purpose is to account for the covariation between items. With IRT, the purpose is to account for participants' responses to items (Brown, 2015). Therefore, the IRT model can be used to understand how the level of the latent trait and item properties relate to the person's response (Brown, 2015). IRT models can be estimated with different numbers of parameters, ranging from a one-parameter logistic model (also called the Rasch model) that includes item difficulty or a two-parameter logistic model that includes item discrimination to a three-parameter logistic model that includes a guessing parameter (or false positive). IRT is less frequently used in sport and exercise psychology, but there are examples in the literature (see Emm-Collison, Standage, & Gillison, 2016; Fletcher, 1999; Prapavessis et al., 2005).

Cross-lagged models and latent growth models are commonly used to assess predictive validity evidence when researchers have measured variables over time. Cross-lagged models carry the assumption that the best predictor of future behaviours is past behaviour (Stenling, Ivarsson, & Lindwall, 2016). Cross-lagged analyses are best suited for examining between-person changes and when the objective is to examine remaining variability rather than directly examine the autoregressive effects (Stenling et al., 2016). Taylor (2017) used a cross-lagged analysis within a sport and exercise psychology framework. Latent growth modelling is a statistical technique that can be used to examine between-person and within-person changes in a construct over time (Bollen & Curran, 2006). It can be used to examine an intercept (i.e., starting point) and rate of change (e.g., linear or quadratic change over time), both of which can vary across people. Lindwall, Asci, and Crocker (2014) used latent growth modelling within a sport and exercise psychology framework.

Finally, Bayesian statistical procedures are being used more frequently in sport and exercise psychology. Bayesian statistics allow researchers to incorporate prior knowledge from past research or theory into their models, such as through model parameters (Gucciardi & Zyphur, 2016; Myers, Ntoumanis, Gunnell, Gucciardi, & Lee, 2017). In Bayesian statistics, the researcher is interested in the probability that their hypothesis is true based on their data, whereas, with frequentist statistics (i.e., statistics that rely on the p-value), researchers are interested in the probability of obtaining the same score or some more extreme score, assuming the null hypothesis is true (Gucciardi & Zyphur, 2016). The interpretation of the data is different in Bayesian statistics compared with frequentist statistics, and readers are encouraged to consult resources that outline Bayesian statistics more thoroughly (Gucciardi & Zyphur, 2016). Most of the models described above, such as factor analysis (Gucciardi, Zhang, Ponnusamy, Si, & Stenling, 2016), SEM, latent curve model (Stenling, Ivarsson, Hassmén, & Lindwall, 2017), and other models such as multilevel models (Tamminen, Gaudreau, McEwen, & Crocker, 2016), can be estimated within a Bayesian framework rather than a frequentist framework.

Conclusion

Foundational to any claim made in sport and exercise psychology is the assurance that the measurement scales used for such a claim produce valid and reliable scores. There are numerous methods that can be used to examine score reliability and validity of measurement scales in sport and exercise psychology. Score reliability is commonly assessed with coefficient alpha, although researchers are embracing newer statistical techniques, including composite reliability, omega, and coefficient H. Score validity is commonly assessed with factor analytic techniques, with a shift towards exploratory structural equation modelling. Researchers are encouraged to employ advanced methods for their data to ensure their inferences are based on sound measurement.

References

AERA, APA, & NCME. (2014). *The standards for educational and psychological testing*. Washington, DC: American Educational Research Association.

Asparouhov, T., & Muthén, B. (2009). Exploratory structural equation modeling. *Structural Equation Modeling: A Multidisciplinary Journal, 16,* 397–438.

Beauchamp, M. R., & McEwan, D. (2017). Response processes and measurement validity in health psychology. In B. D. Zumbo & A. M. Hubley (Eds.), *Understanding and investigating response processes in validation research* (pp. 13–30). Cham, Switzerland: Springer International.

Bollen, K. A., & Curran, P. J. (2006). *Latent curve models: A structural equation perspective*. Hoboken, NJ: John Wiley.

Brown, T. A. (2015). *Confirmatory factor analysis for applied research* (2nd ed.). New York: Guilford Press.

Brunet, J., Gunnell, K. E., Teixeira, P., Sabiston, C. M., & Bélanger, M. (2016). Should we be looking at the forest or the trees? Overall psychological need satisfaction and individual needs as predictors of physical activity. *Journal of Sport and Exercise Psychology, 38,* 317–330.

Campbell, D. T., & Fiske, D. W. (1959). Convergent and discriminant validation by the multitrait–multimethod matrix. *Psychological Bulletin, 56,* 81–105.

Chen, F. F., West, S. G., & Sousa, K. H. (2006). A comparison of bifactor and second-order models of quality of life. *Multivariate Behavioral Research, 41,* 189–225.

Cheung, G. W., & Rensvold, R. B. (2002). Evaluating goodness-of-fit indexes for testing measurement invariance. *Structural Equation Modeling: A Multidisciplinary Journal, 9,* 233–255.

Cole, D. A., Ciesla, J. A., & Steiger, J. H. (2007). The insidious effects of failing to include design-driven correlated residuals in latent-variable covariance structure analysis. *Psychological Methods, 12,* 381–398.

Cortina, J. M. (1993). What is coefficient alpha? An examination of theory and applications. *Journal of Applied Psychology, 78,* 98–104.

Crocker, P. R. E., Pedrosa, I., Mosewich, A. D., & Sabiston, C. M. (2018). Examining gender invariance of the sport-multidimensional perfectionism scale-2 in intercollegiate athletes. *Psychology of Sport and Exercise, 34,* 57–60.

Deci, E. L., & Ryan, R. M. (2002). *Handbook of self-determination research.* Rochester, NY: University of Rochester Press.

DeVellis, R. F. (2017). *Scale development: Theory and applications.* L. Bickman & D. J. Rog Eds. (4th ed.) Thousand Oaks, CA: Sage.

Dunn, J. G. H., Bouffard, M., & Rogers, W. T. (1999). Assessing item content-relevance in sport psychology scale-construction research: Issues and recommendations. *Measurement in Physical Education and Exercise Science, 3,* 15–36.

Emm-Collison, L. G., Standage, M., & Gillison, F. B. (2016). Development and validation of the adolescent psychological need support in exercise questionnaire. *Journal of Sport and Exercise Psychology, 38,* 505–520.

Fletcher, R. (1999). Incorporating recent advances in measurement in sport and exercise psychology. *Journal of Sport and Exercise Psychology, 21,* 24–38.

Flora, D. B., & Curran, P. J. (2004). An empirical evaluation of alternative methods of estimation for confirmatory factor analysis with ordinal data. *Psychological Methods, 9,* 466–491.

Gadermann, A. M., Guhn, M., & Zumbo, B. D. (2012). Estimating ordinal reliability for Likert-type and ordinal item response data&58; A conceptual, empirical, and practical guide [text]. Retrieved June 26, 2018, from www.ingentaconnect.com/content/doaj/15317714/2012/00000017/00000003/art00001

Geldhof, G. J., Preacher, K. J., & Zyphur, M. J. (2014). Reliability estimation in a multilevel confirmatory factor analysis framework. *Psychological Methods, 19,* 72–91.

Gucciardi, D. F., Zhang, C.-Q., Ponnusamy, V., Si, G., & Stenling, A. (2016). Cross-cultural invariance of the mental toughness inventory among Australian, Chinese, and Malaysian athletes: A Bayesian estimation approach. *Journal of Sport and Exercise Psychology, 38,* 187–202.

Gucciardi, D. F., & Zyphur, M. J. (2016). Exploratory structural equation modeling and Bayesian estimation. In N. Ntoumanis & N. D. Myers (Eds.), *An introduction to intermediate and advanced statistical analyses for sport and exercise scientist* (pp. 155–182). Chichester: John Wiley.

Gunnell, K. E., Schellenberg, B. J. I., Wilson, P. M., Crocker, P. R. E., Mack, D. E., & Zumbo, B. D. (2014). A review of validity evidence presented in the journal of sport and exercise psychology (2002–2012): Misconceptions and recommendations for validation research. In D. Zumbo & E. K. H. Chan (Eds.) *Validity and validation in social, behavioral, and health sciences* (pp. 137–156). Cham: Springer.

Hancock, G. R., & Mueller, R. O. (2001). Rethinking construct reliability within latent variable systems. In R. Cudeck, S. duToit, & D. Sörbom (Eds.), *Structural equation modeling: Present and futured - A Festschrift in honor of Karl Jöreskog* (pp. 195–216). Lincolnwood, IL: Scientific Software International.

Hu, L., & Bentler, P. M. (1999). Cutoff criteria for fit indexes in covariance structure analysis: Conventional criteria versus new alternatives. *Structural Equation Modeling: A Multidisciplinary Journal, 6,* 1–55.

Kline, R. (2011). *Principles and practice of structural equation modeling* (3rd ed.). New York: New York: Guilford Press.

Lindwall, M., Asci, H., & Crocker, P. (2014). The physical self in motion: Within-person change and associations of change in self-esteem, physical self-concept, and physical activity in adolescent girls. *Journal of Sport and Exercise Psychology, 36,* 551–563.

Lonsdale, C., Hodge, K., & Rose, E. A. (2008). The Behavioral Regulation in Sport Questionnaire (BRSQ): Instrument development and initial validity evidence. *Journal of Sport and Exercise Psychology, 30,* 323–355.

Marsh, H. W. (1998). Foreword. In J. L. Duda (Ed.), *Advances in sport and exercise psychology measurement* (pp. xv–xix). Morgantown, WV: Fitness Information Technology.

Marsh, H. W., & Grayson, D. (1995). Latent variable models of multitrait-multimethod data. In R. H. Hoyle (Ed.), *Structural equation modeling: Concepts, issues, and applications* (pp. 177–198). Thousand Oaks, CA: Sage.

Marsh, H. W., Hau, K.-T., & Wen, Z. (2004). In search of golden rules: Comment on hypothesis-testing approaches to setting cutoff values for fit indexes and dangers in overgeneralizing Hu and Bentler's (1999) findings. *Structural Equation Modeling: A Multidisciplinary Journal, 11,* 320–341.

Marsh, H. W., Morin, A. J. S., Parker, P. D., & Kaur, G. (2014). Exploratory structural equation modeling: An integration of the best features of exploratory and confirmatory factor analysis. *Annual Review of Clinical Psychology, 10*, 85–110.

Marsh, H. W., Muthén, B., Asparouhov, T., Lüdtke, O., Robitzsch, A., Morin, A. J., & Trautwein, U. (2009). Exploratory structural equation modeling, integrating CFA and EFA: Application to students' evaluations of university teaching. *Structural equation modeling: A multidisciplinary Journal, 16*(3), 439–476.

McNeish, D. (in press). Thanks coefficient alpha, we'll take it from here. *Psychological Methods.* doi:doi. org/10.1037/met0000144

Meredith, W. (1993). Measurement invariance, factor analysis and factorial invariance. *Psychometrika, 58*, 525–543.

Myers, N. D. (2013). Coaching competency and (exploratory) structural equation modeling: A substantive-methodological synergy. *Psychology of Sport and Exercise, 14*, 709–718.

Myers, N. D., Chase, M. A., Pierce, S. W., & Martin, E. (2011). Coaching efficacy and exploratory structural equation modeling: A substantive-methodological synergy. *Journal of Sport and Exercise Psychology, 33*, 779–806.

Myers, N. D., Ntoumanis, N., Gunnell, K. E., Gucciardi, D. F., & Lee, S. (2017). A review of some emergent quantitative analyses in sport and exercise psychology. *International Review of Sport and Exercise Psychology, 0*(0), 1–31. doi:10.1080/1750984X.2017.1317356

Myers, N. D., Ntoumanis, N., Gunnell, K. E., Gucciardi, D. F., & Lee, S. (2018). A review of some emergent quantitative analyses in sport and exercise psychology. *International Review of Sport and Exercise Psychology, 11*(1), 70–100.

Prapavessis, H., Maddison, R., & Fletcher, R. (2005). Further examination of the factor integrity of the sport anxiety scale. *Journal of Sport and Exercise Psychology, 27*, 253–260.

Rees, T., Freeman, P., Bell, S., & Bunney, R. (2012). Three generalizability studies of the components of perceived coach support. *Journal of Sport and Exercise Psychology, 34*, 238–251.

Reise, S. P., Moore, T. M., & Haviland, M. G. (2010). Bifactor models and rotations: Exploring the extent to which multidimensional data yield univocal scale scores. *Journal of Personality Assessment, 92*, 544–559.

Sijtsma, K. (2009). On the use, the misuse, and the very limited usefulness of Cronbach's alpha. *Psychometrika, 74*(1), 107. doi:10.1007/s11336-008-9101-0

Stenling, A., Ivarsson, A., Hassmén, P., & Lindwall, M. (2015). Using bifactor exploratory structural equation modeling to examine global and specific factors in measures of sports coaches' interpersonal styles. *Frontiers in Psychology, 6.* doi:10.3389/fpsyg.2015.01303

Stenling, A., Ivarsson, A., Hassmén, P., & Lindwall, M. (2017). Longitudinal associations between athletes' controlled motivation, ill-being, and perceptions of controlling coach behaviors: A Bayesian latent growth curve approach. *Psychology of Sport and Exercise, 30*, 205–214.

Stenling, A., Ivarsson, A., & Lindwall, M. (2016). Cross-lagged structural equation modeling and latent growth modeling. In N. Ntoumanis & N. D. Myers (Eds.), *An introduction to intermediate and advanced statistical analyses for sport and exercise scientists* (pp. 131–154). Chichester: John Wiley.

Stenling, A., Ivarsson, A., Lindwall, M., & Gucciardi, D. F. (2018). Exploring longitudinal measurement invariance and the continuum hypothesis in the Swedish version of the Behavioral Regulation in Sport Questionnaire (BRSQ): An exploratory structural equation modeling approach. *Psychology of Sport and Exercise, 36*, 187–196.

Sylvester, B. D., Standage, M., Dowd, A. J., Martin, L. J., Sweet, S. N., & Beauchamp, M. R. (2014). Perceived variety, psychological needs satisfaction and exercise-related well-being. *Psychology & Health, 29*, 1044–1061.

Tamminen, K. A., Gaudreau, P., McEwen, C. E., & Crocker, P. R. E. (2016). Interpersonal emotion regulation among adolescent athletes: A Bayesian multilevel model predicting sport enjoyment and commitment. *Journal of Sport and Exercise Psychology, 38*, 541–555.

Taylor, I. M. (2017). Reciprocal effects of motivation in physical education and self-reported physical activity. *Psychology of Sport and Exercise, 31*, 131–138.

Vaughn, B. K., Lee, H., & Kamata, A. (2012). Reliability. In G. Tenenbaum, R. C. Eklund, & A. Kamata (Eds.), *Measurement in sport and exercise psychology* (pp. 25–33). Champaign, IL: Human Kinetics.

Williams, S. E., & Cumming, J. (2011). Measuring athlete imagery ability: The sport imagery ability questionnaire. *Journal of Sport and Exercise Psychology, 33*, 416–440.

Williams, S. E., Cumming, J., Ntoumanis, N., Nordin-Bates, S. M., Ramsey, R., & Hall, C. (2012). Further validation and development of the movement imagery questionnaire. *Journal of Sport and Exercise Psychology, 34*, 621–646.

Wilson, P. M., Mack, D. E., & Sylvester, B. D. (2011). When a little myth goes a long way: The use (or misuse) of cut-points, interpretations, and discourse with coefficient-alpha in exercise psychology. In A. M. Columbus (Ed.), *Advances in psychology research* (Vol. 77, pp. 263–280). Hauppauge, NY: Nova Science.

Wilson, P. M., Rogers, W. T., Rodgers, W. M., & Wild, T. C. (2006). The psychological need satisfaction in exercise scale. *Journal of Sport and Exercise Psychology, 28*, 231–251.

Wu, A. D., Li, Z., & Zumbo, B. D. (2007). Decoding the meaning of factorial invariance and updating the practice of multi-group confirmatory factor analysis: A demonstration with TIMSS data. *Practical Assessment Research and Evaluation, 12*(3), 1–26.

INDEX